Fodor's

GERMANY

WELCOME TO GERMANY

From half-timbered medieval towns to cosmopolitan cities, Germany offers a thoroughly engaging mix of tradition and modernity. You can explore Bavaria's magnificent baroque palaces one day, and immerse yourself in Hamburg's cool, redeveloped HafenCity the next. In hip Berlin, historic sites such as the Brandenburg Gate and contemporary art galleries create exciting contrasts. Throughout the country, discovering world-class museums and cutting-edge design is as quintessentially German as grabbing a stein of beer at a centuries-old *biergarten*.

TOP REASONS TO GO

★ **Castles:** Majestic palaces such as Neuschwanstein seem straight out of a fairy tale.

★ **Fun Cities:** You can party all night in Berlin or soak up culture in Munich.

★ **Music:** From Bach to Beethoven to Wagner, Germany is the birthplace of the classics.

★ **Beer and Wine:** The home of Oktoberfest also surprises with top-notch regional wines.

★ **Markets:** Locally made crafts shine, especially during the Christmas season.

★ **Great Drives:** Scenic roads wind through the Alps and past vineyards and villages.

Fodor's GERMANY

Publisher: Amanda D'Acierno, *Senior Vice President*

Editorial: Arabella Bowen, *Editor in Chief*; Linda Cabasin, *Editorial Director*

Design: Fabrizio La Rocca, *Vice President, Creative Director*; Tina Malaney, *Associate Art Director*; Chie Ushio, *Senior Designer*; Ann McBride, *Production Designer*

Photography: Melanie Marin, *Associate Director of Photography*; Jessica Parkhill and Jennifer Romains, *Researchers*

Maps: Rebecca Baer, *Senior Map Editor*; Mark Stroud (Moon Street Cartography) and David Lindroth *Cartographers*

Production: Linda Schmidt, *Managing Editor*; Evangelos Vasilakis, *Associate Managing Editor*; Angela L. McLean, *Senior Production Manager*

Sales: Jacqueline Lebow, *Sales Director*

Marketing & Publicity: Heather Dalton, *Marketing Director*; Katherine Fleming, *Senior Publicist*

Business & Operations: Susan Livingston, *Vice President, Strategic Business Planning*; Sue Daulton, *Vice President, Operations*

Fodors.com: Megan Bell, *Executive Director, Revenue & Business Development*; Yasmin Marinaro, *Senior Director, Marketing & Partnerships*

Writers: Leonie Adeane, Dan Allen, Kimberly Bradley, Lee A. Evans, Liz Humphreys, Evelyn Kanter, Jeff Kavanagh, Ben Knight, Sally McGrane, Catherine C. Moser, Giulia Pines, Katherine Sacks, Paul Wheatley

Editorial Contributors: Alexis Kelly, Andrea Lehman, Penny Phenix

Editors: Salwa Jabado, *lead editor*; Caroline Trefler, *Berlin editor*; John Rambow, Amanda Sadlowski

Production Editor: Jennifer DePrima

Fodor's is a registered trademark of Random House LLC. All rights reserved. Published in the United States by Fodor's Travel, a division of Random House LLC, New York, a Penguin Random House Company, and in Canada by Random House of Canada Limited, Toronto. No maps, illustrations, or other portions of this book may be reproduced in any form without written permission from the publisher.

27th Edition

ISBN 978-0-8041-4197-0

ISSN 1525-5034

All details in this book are based on information supplied to us at press time. Always confirm information when it matters, especially if you're making a detour to visit a specific place. Fodor's expressly disclaims any liability, loss, or risk, personal or otherwise, that is incurred as a consequence of the use of any of the contents of this book.

SPECIAL SALES

This book is available at special discounts for bulk purchases for sales promotions or premiums. For more information, e-mail specialmarkets@randomhouse.com

PRINTED IN COLOMBIA

10 9 8 7 6 5 4 3 2 1

CONTENTS

Contents

MAPS

ABOUT
THIS GUIDE

Fodor's Recommendations

Everything in this guide is worth doing—we don't cover what isn't—but exceptional sights, hotels, and restaurants are recognized with additional accolades. **Fodor's**Choice★ indicates our top recommendations; and **Best Bets** call attention to notable hotels and restaurants in various categories. Care to nominate a new place? Visit Fodors.com/contact-us.

Trip Costs

We list prices wherever possible to help you budget well. Hotel and restaurant price categories from $ to $$$$ are noted alongside each recommendation. For hotels, we include the lowest cost of a standard double room in high season. For restaurants, we cite the average price of a main course at dinner or, if dinner isn't served, at lunch. For attractions, we always list adult admission fees; discounts are usually available for children, students, and senior citizens.

Hotels

Our local writers vet every hotel to recommend the best overnights in each price category, from budget to expensive. Unless otherwise specified, you can expect private bath, phone, and TV in your room. For expanded hotel reviews, facilities, and deals visit Fodors.com.

Restaurants

Unless we state otherwise, restaurants are open for lunch and dinner daily. We mention dress code only when there's a specific requirement and reservations only when they're essential or not accepted. To make restaurant reservations, visit Fodors.com.

Credit Cards

The hotels and restaurants in this guide typically accept credit cards. If not, we'll say so.

Top Picks	Hotels & Restaurants
★ **Fodor's**Choice	🏨 Hotel
Listings	⤴ Number of rooms
✉ Address	🍽 Meal plans
✉ Branch address	✕ Restaurant
☎ Telephone	⚭ Reservations
🖷 Fax	👗 Dress code
⊕ Website	▭ No credit cards
✉ E-mail	$ Price
🖃 Admission fee	
☉ Open/closed times	**Other**
Ⓜ Subway	⇨ See also
✛ Directions or Map coordinates	☞ Take note
	🏌 Golf facilities

1

EXPERIENCE GERMANY

GERMANY TODAY

About the size of Montana but home to Western Europe's largest population, Germany is in many ways a land of contradictions. The land of "Dichter und Denker" ("poets and thinkers") is also one of the world's leading export countries, specializing in mechanical equipment, vehicles, chemicals, and household goods. It's a country that is both deeply conservative, valuing tradition, hard work, precision, and fiscal responsibility, and one of the world's most liberal countries, with a generous social welfare state, a strongly held commitment to environmentalism, and a postwar determination to combat xenophobia. But Germany, which reunited 22 years ago after 45 years of division, is also a country in transition. As the horrors of World War II, though not forgotten, recede, the country that is Europe's most important economic powerhouse has once again taken a leading economic and political role in Europe, setting, for example, the EU's austerity-oriented policies in an attempt to counteract Europe's current economic downturn.

Integration

During the "Wirtschaftswunder," the postwar economic boom of the 1950s and 1960s, West Germany invited "guest workers" from Italy, Greece, and above all Turkey to help in the rebuilding of the country. Because the Germans assumed these guest workers would return home, they provided little in the way of cultural integration policies. But the guest workers, usually manual workers from the countryside with little formal education, often did not return to the economically depressed regions they had come from. Instead, they brought wives and family members to join them and settled in Germany, often forming parallel societies cut off from mainstream German life. Today, Germany's largest immigrant group is Turkish. In fact, Berlin is the largest Turkish city after Istanbul. Though these Turkish communities are now an indelible part of the German society—one blond-hair, blue-eyed German soldier deployed to Afghanistan famously said that the thing he missed most about home was the *döner kebab,* the ubiquitous Turkish-German fast-food dish—thus far, the country has fumbled somewhat when it comes to successful integration. Efforts, however, are currently underway to redress the situation. Unlike the United States, Germany is historically a land of emigrants, not immigrants, but Germany's demographics are undergoing a radical shift: one in three children in Germany today is foreign-born or has a parent who is a foreign-born; in bigger cities, as many as two-thirds of school-age children don't speak German at home.

Worldwide Recession

Germany, the world's fourth-largest economy, was the world's largest exporter until 2009, when China overtook it. The worldwide recession hit Germany squarely, though thanks to a strong social network, the unemployed and underemployed did not suffer on the level we are used to in the United States. In Germany, losing your job does not mean you lose your health insurance, and the unemployed receive financial help from the state to meet housing payments and other basic expenses. More recently, Germany has been a bastion of economic strength during the euro zone crisis, maintaining a solid economy while countries like Greece, Spain, and Portugal have entered into economic tailspins. By far the most important economy in the European Union, Germany, with its traditional, don't-spend-more-than-you-earn culture, has a strong voice in setting the EU's economic agenda and has traditionally acted as a kind of rich uncle that other countries turn to when they need an economic bailout. But Germany's push for austerity measures hasn't always been met with enthusiasm: on an official visit to Greece, Angela Merkel was met by protesters dressed in Nazi uniforms.

Engineer This!

Germany has a well-deserved reputation as a land of engineers. The global leader in numerous high-tech fields, German companies are hugely successful on the world's export markets, thanks to lots of innovation, sophisticated technology and quality manufacturing. German cars, machinery, and electrical and electronic equipment are all big sellers. But recent years have seen series of bloopers. Three major building projects in Germany—the Elbphilharmonie concert hall in Hamburg; Stuttgart 21, a new train station in Stuttgart; and the new airport in Berlin—have run way over budget and dragged on for years. Of the three, the airport is the most egregious: Originally planned to open in 2010, Berlin Brandenburg Airport has suffered delays due to poor construction planning, management, and execution (in 2012, the airport canceled its grand opening only days before flights were scheduled to begin). No one knows when it will open, and numerous politicians have expressed concern that failures like these will tarnish Germany's reputation as a country of can-do engineers.

Privacy, Please!

The Germans are not big fans of Facebook. With good reason: With recent experiences of life in a police state under both the Nazi regime and the East German regime, they don't like the idea of anyone collecting personal information about them. Germany has some of the most extensive data privacy laws in the world, with everything from credit card numbers to medical histories strictly protected.

To the Left, to the Left

By American standards, German politics are distinctly left-leaning. One thing that's important to know is that the Germans don't have a two-party system; rather they have several important parties, and these must form alliances after elections to pass initiatives. Thus, there's an emphasis on cooperation and deal-making, sometimes (but not always) making for odd bedfellows. A "Red-Green" (or "stoplight") coalition between the Green Party and the socialist SPD held power from 1998 to 2002; since then, there has been a steady move to the center-right in Germany, with recent reforms curtailing some social welfare benefits and ecological reforms. In 2005, Germany elected the first female chancellor, center-right Christian Democratic party member Angela Merkel. A politician from the former East Germany who speaks Russian, Merkel has enjoyed much popularity.

Renew, Recycle, Reuse

The Green Party, founded in 1980, is an established and important player in the German government. Thanks to aggressive government legislation initiated by the Greens in the past decades, Germany today is a leader in green energy technology and use—in 2012, 25% of the electricity used in Germany came from renewable sources.

WHAT'S WHERE

The following numbers refer to chapters.

2 Munich. Beautiful Munich boasts wonderful opera, theater, museums, and churches—and the city's chic residents dress their best to visit them. This city also has lovely outdoor spaces, from parks, beer gardens, and cafés, to the famous Oktoberfest grounds.

3 The Bavarian Alps. Majestic peaks, lush green pastures, and frescoed houses brightened by flowers make for one of Germany's most photogenic regions. Quaint villages like Mittenwald, Garmisch-Partenkirchen, Oberammergau, and Berchtesgaden have preserved their charming historic architecture. Nature is the prime attraction here, with the country's finest hiking and skiing.

4 The Romantic Road. The Romantische Strasse is more than 355 km (220 miles) of soaring castles, medieval villages, *fachwerk* (half-timber) houses, and imposing churches, all set against a pastoral backdrop. Winding its way from Würzburg to Füssen, it features such top destinations as Rothenburg-ob-der-Tauber and Schloss Neuschwanstein, King Ludwig II's fantastical castle.

5 Franconia and the German Danube. Thanks to the centuries-old success of craftsmanship and trade, Franconia is a proud, independent-minded region in northern Bavaria. Franconia is home to historic Nürnberg, the well-preserved medieval jewel-box town of Bamberg, and Bayreuth, where Wagner lived and composed.

6 The Bodensee. The sunniest region in the country, the Bodensee (Lake Constance) itself is the highlight. The region is surrounded by beautiful mountains, and the dense natural surroundings offer an enchanting contrast to the picture-perfect towns and manicured gardens.

7 The Black Forest. Synonymous with cuckoo clocks and primeval woodland that is great for hiking, the Black Forest includes the historic university town of Freiburg—one of the most colorful and hip student cities in Germany—and proud and elegant Baden-Baden, with its long tradition of spas and casinos.

8 Heidelberg and the Neckar Valley. This medieval town is quintessential Germany, full of cobblestone alleys, half-timber houses, vineyards, castles, wine pubs, and Germany's oldest university.

Oldenburg
Bremen
Osnabrück
Hannover
Braunschweig
Hildesheim
Bielefeld
Magdeburg
Potsdam
BERLIN
Cottbus
Oder
Weser
HARZ MTS
Göttingen
Kassel
Halle
Leipzig
Elbe
Dresden
Siegen
Weimar
Erfurt
Jena
Gera
Zwickau
Chemnitz
Liberec
Fulda
PRAGUE
CZECH
REPUBLIC
Wiesbaden
Frankfurt
Mainz
Darmstadt
Würzburg
Bamberg
Bayreuth
Plzen
Mannheim
Heidelberg
Nürnberg
Rhine
Rothenburg-
ob-der-Tauber
8
Heilbronn
Karlsruhe
Regensburg
Danube
Deggendorf
5
Baden-
Baden
Stuttgart
4
Ingolstadt
7
Ulm
Augsburg
BAVARIA
Passau
Munich
2
Inn
Memmingen
Salzburg
6
Konstanz
Oberammergau
3
Bad Reichenhall
Berchtesgaden
Friedrichshafen
Füssen
Bodensee
Garmisch-
Partenkirchen
BAVARIAN ALPS
Zürich
SWITZERLAND
ALPS
LIECHT
VADUZ
Innsbruck
AUSTRIA
BLACK FOREST

0   50 mi

0   50 km

WHAT'S WHERE

9 Frankfurt. Nicknamed "Mainhattan" because it is the only German city with appreciable skyscrapers, Frankfurt is Germany's financial center and transportation hub.

10 The Pfalz and Rhine Terrace. Wine reigns supreme here. Bacchanalian festivals pepper the calendar between May and October, and wineries welcome drop-ins for tastings year-round. Three great cathedrals are found in Worms, Speyer, and Mainz.

11 The Rhineland. The region along the mighty Rhine River is one of the most dynamic in all of Europe. Fascinating cities such as Köln (Cologne), steeped in Roman and medieval history, offer stunning symbols of Gothic architecture, such as the Kölner Dom. Visit during Karneval for boisterous celebrations.

12 The Fairy-Tale Road. The Märchenstrasse, stretching 600 km (370 miles) between Hanau and Bremen, is definitely the Brothers Grimm country. They nourished their dark and magical imaginations as children in Steinau an der Strasse, a beautiful medieval town in this region of misty woodlands and ancient castles.

13 Hamburg. Hamburg, with its long tradition as a powerful and wealthy Hanseatic port city, is quintessentially elegant. World-class museums of modern art; the wild red-light district along the Reeperbahn; and HafenCity, a new supermodern, environmentally, and architecturally avant-garde quarter currently under construction, make Hamburg well worth a visit.

14 Schleswig-Holstein and the Baltic Coast. Off the beaten path, this region is scattered with medieval towns, fishing villages, unspoiled beaches, and summer resorts like Sylt, where Germany's jet set go to get away.

15 Berlin. No trip to Germany is complete without a visit its capital, Europe's hippest urban destination. Cheap rents drew artists from all over the world to this gritty, creative, and broke city. Cutting-edge art exhibits, stage dramas, musicals, and bands compete for your attention with two cities' worth of world-class museums, three opera houses, eight state theaters, and two zoos.

16 Saxony, Saxony-Anhalt, and Thuringia. The southeast is a secret treasure trove of German high culture. Friendly, vibrant cities like Dresden, Leipzig, Weimar, and Eisenach are linked to Schiller, Goethe, Bach, Luther, and the like.

GERMANY PLANNER

When to Go

A year-round destination, Germany is particularly wonderful May through September for the long mild days that stretch sightseeing hours and are perfect for relaxing in beer gardens.

In the north, January can be dark, cold, and moody, with wind that cuts to the bone. Southern Germany, on the other hand, is a great winter destination, with world-class skiing, spas, and wellness options.

Getting Here

Most flights into Germany arrive at Frankfurt's Flughafen Frankfurt Main (FRA) or Munich's Flughafen München (MUC). Eventually, the Berlin Brandenburg Willy Brandt Airport (BER) will open (in the meantime, Berlin has two smaller airports, Tegel in the north, and Schönefeld in the south). Flying time to Frankfurt is 1½ hours from London, 7½ hours from New York, 10 hours from Chicago, and 12 hours from Los Angeles. Some international carriers serve Köln (Cologne), Hamburg, and Berlin. Germany has a fantastic train system, and is well connected to all overland European destinations. Hamburg, followed by Bremen, is Germany's most important harbor, and cruise ships and ferries connect the German north coast to England, Scandinavia, Russia, and the Baltics.

Getting Around

Once in Germany you can travel by train, car, bus, or air. Travel by train is the most relaxing and often fastest way to go. The Deutsche Bahn (German Railways) serves most destinations with great frequency, speed, and comfort. Train stations are in the city center, and served by extensive intercity public transportation networks. Domestic air travel can be cheaper than the train, especially between bigger cities. Air Berlin and Germanwings offer low fares on inter-German routes.

All major car-rental companies are represented in Germany. Gasoline is expensive (about €5.96 per gallon), and parking in major cities can be difficult. Germany has one of the world's best maintained and most extensive highway systems, and a car gives you the flexibility to explore on your own, particularly in less densely populated areas. Most cars in Germany have manual transmission. If you are going to drive, be sure to familiarize yourself with the rules of the road in Germany. And, while it is true that some stretches of the autobahn have no speed limit, you'll need to be sure you know where that does and does not apply as you drive.

Dining: The Basics

A *Tageskarte* lists the menu of the day. Seasonal menus, or *Saisonkarten,* feature seasonal dishes, like white asparagus or red cabbage.

In most restaurants it is not customary to wait to be seated. Simply walk in and take any unreserved space.

German restaurants do not automatically serve water. If you order water, you will be served mineral water and be expected to pay for it. The concept of free refills or the bottomless cup of coffee is also completely foreign.

While German restaurants will occasionally accept credit cards, most expect you to pay cash (even for large and expensive meals). If you are having something small, like coffee and cake, you will definitely need to pay in cash.

Tipping: When you get the check for something small, like a cup of coffee, round up to the next even euro. For larger amounts, tip 10%. Also, instead of leaving the tip on the table, add it to the total amount when you pay. For example, if the bill is €14, and you want to tip €2, when the waitress comes to collect the bill, tell her the total amount (cost plus tip) you want to pay ("€16, please").

German waitstaff are more than happy to split the check so that everyone can pay individually. Remember to pay the waiter directly; do not place the money on the table and leave.

Money

Most Germans still make most of—if not all—their purchases the old-fashioned way: with cash. The use of credit cards in Germany is among the lowest in Europe. That said, you should be able to pay your hotel bill, train tickets, or car rental with a credit card.

But if you're picking up a snack at a bakery, a little souvenir, or having a cup of coffee, you'll need cash. The same goes for buying tickets on public transportation or paying for a taxi.

Exchange services and banks are plentiful in cities and towns. However keep in mind that you'll generally get the best exchange rate at a *Geldautomat* (ATM), not to mention the convenience of 24-hour access. Before starting your trip, check on the fees your bank charges for international ATM transactions. You may find that these are less than the commissions charged at currency exchange booths and banks.

Social Mores

When addressing someone always use the formal *Sie* until you are begged by them to switch to the informal *du*. When in doubt, shake hands; both as a greeting and at parting.

It's polite to ask if someone speaks English (*Sprechen Sie Englisch?*) before addressing them in English.

Germans have done a lot of soul searching as a nation as to their role in and responsibility for the atrocities of World War II. They tend to be very well informed about world affairs—and often know more about the minute workings of the American political process than Americans do. Discussions about history and politics will almost always make for an interesting evening.

Dress and Undress

Casual clothes and jeans can be worn just about anywhere (even to the opera). If you want to be on the safe side, make sure they're clean and neat. Don't be surprised to find nude sunbathers, even in the most public parks. It's also normal to see children running around without clothes on in parks, at swimming pools, or at the beach. Plus, if there's no changing room at the beach, don't worry: Germans change right out in public.

GERMANY TOP ATTRACTIONS

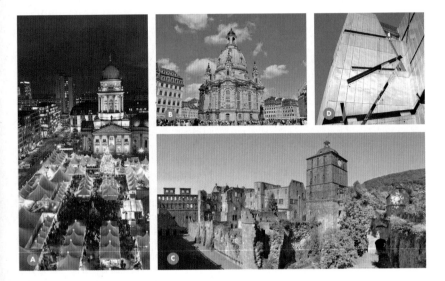

Berlin, Capital City

(A) Berlin was the capital of Prussia, the German Empire, the Weimar Republic, and the Third Reich before being divided after World War II. The must-visit Reichstag (parliament building) was reconstructed with a special glass dome after reunification. From the dome, you can see directly down into the parliament chambers below—a symbol of government transparency. The iconic East German TV tower, a symbol of political power, also makes a great stop. The Checkpoint Charlie museum details accounts of people escaping the GDR. The Topography of Terror exhibit hall, another must-see, is a rich source of information on the Nazi regime.

Frauenkirche, Dresden

(B) Dresden's Church of Our Lady is a masterpiece of baroque architecture. Completed in 1743, the magnificent domed church was destroyed as a result of Allied bombing in February 1945. In 2005, the church was rebuilt from the original rubble, thanks entirely to private donations.

Heidelberg Castle

(C) Heidelberg's immense ruined fortress is a prime example of Gothic and Renaissance styles. It inspired the 19th-century Romantic writers, especially the poet Goethe, who admired its decay amidst the beauty of the Neckar Valley.

Jüdisches Museum, Berlin

(D) Under the Nazis, at least 6 million Jews, along with homosexuals, the disabled, Gypsies, and political and religious dissidents, were rounded up and sent to slave labor and death camps. Berlin's Jewish Museum, a riveting, angular building designed by Daniel Libeskind, documents Jewish life in Germany and confronts the scars of World War II.

Kölner Dom

(E) Köln's breathtaking cathedral, one of Germany's best-known monuments, is the first thing that greets you when you step out of the train station. The Gothic marvel took more than 600 years to build.

Munich's Oktoberfest

(F) For 12 days at the end of September and into early October, Munich hosts the world's largest beer bonanza.

Neuschwanstein Castle

(G) Walt Disney modeled the castle in *Sleeping Beauty* and later the Disneyland castle itself on Neuschwanstein. "Mad" King Ludwig II's creation is best admired from the heights of the Marienbrücke, a delicate-looking bridge over a deep, narrow gorge.

The Berlin Wall

(H) When the wall fell in 1989 Berliners couldn't wait to get rid of it. As a result, there is very little of it left. The longest is "The East Side Gallery," a mile-long stretch where international artists converged in 1990 to paint murals in a tribute to peace. The excellent Berlin Wall Memorial, located along another remaining stretch, has a museum and open-air exhibition dedicated to the years of division. Cobblestones mark the streets where the wall once ran throughout the city.

The Lorelei Rock

The beautiful Lorelei rock soars above the Rhine river at this UNESCO World Heritage site in the Rhineland.

Weimar: Goethe, Schiller, Bauhaus

(I) Weimar was once home to such German luminaries as Goethe and Schiller, whose homes are now museums. The Bauhaus movement, which gave rise to much of modern architecture and design, was also born here—as you'll learn on a visit to the Bauhaus Museum Weimar.

TOP EXPERIENCES

Imbibe in a Beer Garden

As soon as the sun comes out, beer gardens sprout all over Germany. With as much sunshine per year as Anchorage, Alaska, the Germans know a good thing when they see it, and are quick to set up tables and chairs under the open skies as soon as temperatures allow. Bavaria is the "home" of the beer garden, but you can sample local variations of beer and bratwurst outdoors wherever you happen to be. If the sun's out and you don't see a beer garden, take a beer to the park: Germany has no open-container laws.

Hike a Mountain

The Germans are a fiercely outdoor folk, and if you are anywhere near the mountains (or a hill, or even a relatively flat open space), you'll likely see plenty of people out walking. Pack a bag lunch and some extra bandages and join the crowd—it's a great way to get a feel for the real Germany.

Eat White Asparagus

If you visit between April and June, you're in luck: it's asparagus season. Not just any asparagus, either. Germans are crazy for their very own white asparagus, which is only available during this season. Thicker and larger than green asparagus, the white stuff has to be peeled of its hard sheath (done before cooking). Enjoy it with a slice of ham and potatoes with butter or hollandaise sauce.

Go to a Museum

No matter where you are in Germany, chances are you're close to a museum. Every big city has major, world-class art museums. Technical museums, like Munich's Deutsches Museum, are also impressive and informative. *Freiluft*, or open-air museums, offer collections of buildings from previous epochs that visitors can walk through to get a sense of daily life in the past. Even sparsely populated areas have their own quirky museums that depict the history of everything from marzipan to beds.

Take a Bike Tour through the City

Whether you're discovering Munich, Dresden, Cologne, Hamburg, Berlin, or one of Germany's many smaller cities, a bike tour is the way to do it. Tour companies offer guided tours (and bikes and helmets, though Germans often don't wear them), or you can rent a bike and set out on your own. Wind your way through Munich's English Garden or along Hamburg's harbor and you'll find that you see much more than you would from a tour bus.

Eat a German Breakfast

The German breakfast is a major affair, involving several types of bread rolls, a salami and dry sausage spread, hard cheeses, butter, chocolate spread, honey, jam, sliced tomatoes, sliced cucumber, liver pate, other meats, hard-boiled eggs eaten in the shell, and coffee. Show up hungry.

Visit the Baker

Germany has an incredible *Brotkultur*, or bread culture. Bread is a historically important part of the German diet, and there are many, many types of bread to sample. Breads vary greatly from region to region, but they are without exception delicious. Go to a good artisanal bakery and you will be astounded by what you find.

Take a Curative Bath

With more than 300 *Kurorte* (health spas) and *Heilbäder* (spas with healing waters), Germany has a long tradition of spa destinations. Located by the sea, near mineral-rich mud sources, near salt deposits, or natural springs, these spas date back to the time of the Kaisers. Visit, and you'll be treated to salt baths, mud baths, saunas, thermal hot springs, and mineral-rich air, depending on the special attributes of the region you're visiting.

Cruise along the Rhine

No trip to Germany is complete without a boat tour of the Rhine. Board in Rudesheim and follow the river to Bingen (or do the reverse). Along the way, you'll see an unparalleled number of castles rising up from the banks along the river. Keep a look out for the rock of the Loreley, the beautiful river maiden of legend who lures sailors to their deaths with her song.

Visit a Christmas Market

Just about every city, town, and village has a Christmas market (and larger cities have more than one—in Berlin, for example, there are as many as 60 small markets each year). The most famous are the markets in Dresden and Nuremburg, both of which have long traditions. Christmas markets, which are held outdoors, open the last week of November and run through Christmas. Bundle up and head to one with money in your pocket to buy handmade gifts like the famous wooden figures carved in the Erzgebirge region as you sip traditional, hot-spiced *Glühwein* wine to stay warm.

Find a Volksfest

Nearly every city, town, and village hosts an annual *Volksfest,* or folk festival. These can be very traditional and lots of fun. A cross between a carnival and county fair, these are great places to sample local food specialties, have a home-brewed beer, and generally join in the fun.

Take a Spin in a Fine German Automobile

Germany is the spiritual home of precision auto engineering, and Germans love their cars. You can rent a Porsche, Mercedes, or BMW for a day to see what it's like to drive like the Germans. Take your car-for-a-day to the Nürburgring, a world-famous racetrack built in the 1920s. There, you can get a day pass to drive your car around the track. Visit the on-site auto museum afterward. Both BMW and Mercedes-Benz have recently opened fantastic new museums, as well.

Swim in a Lake

Germany is dotted with lakes, and when the weather is warm, locals strip down and go swimming. Don't worry if you don't have your suit with you: it's usually fine (even normal) to skinny-dip.

Rent a Paddleboat

If swimming's not your thing, most lakes have paddleboat rentals in summer. While away the afternoon in the company of the ducks. This is what summer is all about.

Go to a Soccer Game

Soccer is the national sport and it provokes even the most stoic German man's passion (some women follow eagerly, as well). Even if you aren't a soccer fan, going to a live game is exciting. There's a palpable energy and it's easy to follow the action. You can catch a soccer game just about anywhere, anytime except for June and July, and over the Christmas break.

Go Sledding

In winter, children and adults alike head for the nearest incline, sleds in hand. If you don't have a sled, just stand back and enjoy the spectacle. The children's old-fashioned wooden sleds are truly charming.

QUINTESSENTIAL GERMANY

Culture Vultures

With more theaters, concert halls, and opera houses per capita than any other country in the world, high culture is an important part of German life. Before the formation of the German state, regional courts competed to see who had the best artists, actors, musicians, and stages, resulting in the development of a network of strong cultural centers that exists to this day. For Germans, high culture is not just for the elite, and they consider it so important to provide their communities with a rich cultural life that they use their tax money to do it. One of the results, aside from a flourishing, world-class cultural scene, is that tickets to these publicly funded operas, classical music concerts, ballet, and plays are quite inexpensive, with tickets readily available in the €10 to €40 range. Drop in on a performance or concert—it's one of the best travel bargains around.

Another Beer, Bitte

The German *Kneipekultur,* or pub culture, is an important and long-standing tradition. *Stammgäste,* or regulars, stop by their local pub as often as every evening to drink beer and catch up. In summer, *Kneipe* life moves outdoors to beer gardens. Some, such as the famous Chinese Pavilion in Munich's English Garden, are institutions, and might seat hundreds. Others are more casual, consisting of a café's graveled back garden under soaring chestnut trees. Most beer gardens offer some sort of food: self-serve areas might sell pastas or lamb in addition to grilled sausages and pretzels. Although beer gardens are found all over Germany, the smoky beer-hall experience—with dirndls and oompah bands—is traditionally Bavarian. You'll discover how different the combinations of three key ingredients—malt, hops, and water—can taste.

If you want to get a sense of contemporary German culture and indulge in some of its pleasures, start by familiarizing yourself with the rituals of daily life.

Easy Being Green

Germany has one of the world's most environmentally conscious societies. Conserving resources, whether electricity or food, is second nature for this country where postwar deprivation has not yet faded from memory. Recycling is practically a national sport, with separate garbage bins for regular trash, clear glass, green glass, plastics and cans, and organic garbage. Keep your eyes out for the giant brown, green, and yellow pods on the streets—these are used for neighborhood recycling in cities. Particularly in cities, there are well-defined bike lanes and many people ride their bikes to work (even in high heels or business suits) much of the year. Drivers know to look for them, and as a visitor you'll need to be careful not to walk in the bike lanes, or you'll hear a bell chiming to let you know a biker is nearby. Great public transportation is also part of this environmental commitment.

Kaffe und Kuchen

The tradition of afternoon coffee and cake, usually around 3 pm, is a serious matter. If you can, finagle an invitation to someone's house to get the real experience, which might involve a simple homemade *Quarkkuchen* (cheese cake), or a spread of several decadent creamy cakes, topped with apples, rhubarb, strawberries, or cherries and lots of whipped cream. Otherwise, find an old-fashioned *Konditorei*, or pastry shop and choose from their amazing selection. Germans bake more than a thousand different kinds of cakes, with infinite regional variations. Among the most famous is the *Schwarzwälder Kirschtorte* (Black Forest cake), a chocolate layer cake soaked in *Kirsch* schnapps, with cherries, whipped cream, and chocolate shavings. Another favorite is the *Bienenstich* (bee sting), a layered sponge cake filled with cream and topped with a layer of crunchy honey-caramelized almonds.

IF YOU LIKE

Being Outdoors

The Germans have a long-standing love affair with Mother Nature. The woods, as well as the mountains, rivers, and oceans, surface repeatedly in the works of the renowned German poets and thinkers. That nature is the key to the mysteries of the soul can be seen in works as different as those of naturalist Romantic painter Caspar David Friedrich and the 20th-century philosopher Martin Heidegger. Today, Germany has designated large tracts of land as national recreation areas, and cities boast extensive urban parks and gardens.

A particularly lovely mountain landscape of twisting gorges and sheer cliffs can be found about 30 km (19 miles) south of Dresden, in the **Sächsische Schweiz** park. Rock climbers fascinate those driving up the steep switchbacks to reach bald mesas. At a much higher altitude are the Bavarian Alps, where the Winter Olympics town **Garmisch-Partenkirchen** offers cable cars to ascend Germany's highest mountain. This is one of the country's best spots for skiing in winter and hiking in summer.

Lakes such as **Chiemsee** and **Bodensee** dot the area between the Alps and Munich and many hikers and bikers enjoy circling them. Boat rentals are possible, but you'll often need a German-recognized license. On the island of **Rügen,** the turn-of-the-20th-century resort town **Binz** fronts the gentle (and cold) waters of the Baltic Sea. Even on windy days you can warm up on the beach in a sheltered beach chair for two. Among the Baltic Coast's most dramatic features are Rügen's white chalk cliffs in **Jasmund National Park,** where you can hike, bike, or sign up for nature seminars and tours.

Medieval Towns

The trail of walled towns and half-timber houses known as the **Romantic Road** is a route long marketed by German tourism, and therefore the road more traveled. The towns, particularly Rothenburg-ob-der-Tauber, are lovely, but if you'd prefer fewer tour groups spilling into your photographs, venture into the **Harz Mountains** in the center of Germany.

Goslar, the unofficial capital of the Harz region, is one of Germany's oldest cities, and is renowned for its Romanesque Kaiserpfalz, an imperial palace. Goslar has been declared a UNESCO World Heritage site, as has the town of **Quedlinburg,** 48 km (30 miles) to the southeast. With 1,600 half-timber houses, Quedlinburg has more of these historic, typically northern German buildings than any other town in the country.

A mighty fortress south of the Harz Mountains is the **Wartburg,** in the ancient, half-timber town of **Eisenach.** Frederick the Wise protected Martin Luther from papal proscription within these stout walls in the 16th century.

Options for exploring closer to Munich include **Regensburg** and **Nürnberg.** The former is a beautiful medieval city, relatively unknown even to Germans, and has a soaring French Gothic cathedral that can hold 6,000 people. Nürnberg dates to 1050, and is among the most historic cities in the country. Not only emperors but artists convened here, including the Renaissance genius Albrecht Dürer. If you're in Hessen, the birthplace of the brothers Grimm, you can follow the **Fairy-Tale Route.** Stop off for a day natural saltwater swimming in the idyllic medieval town of **Bad Sooden-Allendorf.**

The Arts

With as many as 600 galleries, world-class private collections, and ateliers in every *Hinterhof* (back courtyard), **Berlin** is one of Europe's contemporary art capitals. For not-so-modern art, Berlin's **Museumsinsel** (Museum Island), a UNESCO World Heritage site, is the absolute must-see. A complex of five state museums packed onto one tiny island, these include the **Altes Museum,** with a permanent collection of classical antiquities; the **Alte Nationalgalerie,** with 18th- to early-20th-century paintings and sculptures from the likes of Cézanne, Rodin, Degas, and Germany's own Max Liebermann; the **Bode-Museum,** containing German and Italian sculptures, Byzantine art, and coins; and the **Pergamonmuseum,** whose highlight is the world-famous Pergamon Altar, a Greek temple dating from 180 BC.

Leipzig is a "new" star in the European art world. The **Museum der Bildenden Künste** (Museum of Fine Arts) is the city's leading gallery, followed closely by the **Grassimuseum** complex. The **Spinnerei** (a former cotton mill) has become Leipzig's prime location for contemporary art, and houses more than 80 artists and galleries, especially those of the New Leipzig School.

Fans of old master painters must haunt the halls of the **Zwinger** in Dresden, where most works were collected in the first half of the 18th century, and the **Alte Pinakothek** in Munich, which has one of the world's largest collections of Rubens.

Castles and Palaces

Watching over nearly any town whose name ends in "-burg" is a medieval fortress or Renaissance palace, often now serving the populace as a museum, restaurant, or hotel.

The **Wartburg** in Eisenach is considered "the mother of all castles" and broods over the foothills of the Thuringian Forest. Abundant vineyards surround **Schloss Neuenburg,** which dominates the landscape around the sleepy village of Freyburg (Unstrut). The castle ruins overlooking the Rhine River are the result of ceaseless fighting with the French, but even their remains were picturesque enough to inspire 19th-century Romantics. **Burg Rheinstein** is rich with Gobelin tapestries, stained glass, and frescoes.

Schloss Heidelberg mesmerizes with its Gothic turrets, Renaissance walls, and abandoned gardens. Other fortresses lord over the **Burgenstrasse** (Castle Road) in the neighboring **Neckar Valley.** You can stay the night (or just enjoy an excellent meal) at the castles of **Hirschhorn** or **Burg Hornberg,** or at any of a number of other castle-hotels in the area.

The medieval **Burg Eltz** in the Mosel Valley looms imposingly, and with its high turrets looks like it's straight out of a Grimm fairy tale. The castle has been perfectly preserved and has been owned by the same family for almost a thousand years.

Louis XIV's Versailles inspired Germany's greatest castle-builder, King Ludwig II, to construct the opulent **Schloss Herrenchiemsee.** One of Ludwig's palaces in turn inspired a latter-day visionary—his **Schloss Neuschwanstein** is the model for Walt Disney's Sleeping Beauty Castle. **Schloss Linderhof,** also in the Bavarian Alps, was Ludwig's favorite retreat.

FLAVORS OF GERMANY

Traditional German cuisine fell out of fashion several decades ago, and was replaced by Italian and Mediterranean food, Asian food, and Middle Eastern food. But there's a growing movement to go back to those roots, and even high-class German chefs are rediscovering old classics, from sauerkraut to *Sauerbraten* (traditional German pot roast). Traditional fruits and vegetables, from parsnips and pumpkins to black salsify, sunchoke, cabbage, yellow carrots, and little-known strawberry and apple varietals, are all making a comeback. That said, "German food" is a bit of a misnomer, as traditional cooking varies greatly from region to region. Look for the "typical" dish, wherever you are, to get the best sense of German cooking in that region.

Generally speaking, regions in the south, like Baden-Württemberg and Bavaria, have held onto their culinary traditions more than regions in the North. But with a little effort, you can find good German food just about anywhere you go.

Bavaria: White Sausage and Beer (for Breakfast)

In Bavaria, a traditional farmer's *Zweites Frühstück* (second breakfast) found at any beer hall consists of fat white sausages, called *Weisswurst* made of veal and eaten with sweet mustard, pretzels, and, yes, a big glass of *Helles* or *Weissbier* (light or wheat beer). Other Bavarian specialties include *Leberkäse* (literally, "liver cheese"), a meat loaf of pork and beef that can be eaten sliced on bread and tastes a lot better than it sounds. *Knödelgerichte*, or noodle dishes are also popular.

Swabia: The Sausage Salad

Swabia (the area surrounding Stuttgart) is generally thought to have some of the best traditional food in Germany, having held on to its culinary heritage better than other areas. *Schwäbische Wurstsalat* (Swabian sausage salad), a salad of sliced sausage dressed with onions, vinegar, and oil, is a typical dish, as is *Kässpätzle* (Swabian pasta with cheese), a noodlelike dish made from flour, egg, and water topped with cheese. *Linsen mit Spätzle* (lentils and spätzle) could be considered the Swabian national dish: it consists of egg noodles topped with lentils and, often, a sausage.

Franconia: Nürnberger Bratwürste

Perhaps the most beloved of all *bratwürste* (sausages) in a country that loves sausages is the small, thin sausage from the city of Nürnberg. Grilled over a beech-wood fire, this sausage is served 6 or 12 at a time with horseradish and sauerkraut or potato salad. Fresh marjoram and ground caraway seeds give the pork-based sausage its distinctive flavor.

Hessen: Apfelwein in Frankfurt

Apfelwein (hard apple cider) is a specialty in and around Frankfurt. Look for an *Apfelweinkneipe* (cider bar), where you can spend a pleasant evening sipping this tasty alcoholic drink. Order *Handkäse*, traditional Hessian curdled milk cheese, to go with it. If you order *Handkäse mit Musik* (Handkäse with music), you'll get it with onions. Another winner is *Frankfurter Rippchen*, spareribs served with sauerkraut.

Rhineland: Horse Meat and Kölsch

In Köln, influenced by nearby Belgium and Holland, there's a traditional taste for horse meat, which they use in their local version of the pot roast, *Rheinische Sauerbraten*. Wash this down with the local beer, *Kölsch*. Or try the *Kölsche Kaviar*—blood sausage with onions.

Northwest Germany: Herring with That?

States on the north coast, like Bremen, Hamburg, Westphalia, and Schleswig-Holstein, all have cuisines that are oriented toward the sea. Cod, crab, herring, and flatfish are all common traditional foods. *Labskaus*, a meat stew, is also a traditional northern German dish that might be served with a fried egg, pickle, and red beets. Potatoes, cabbage, and rutabagas are all important vegetables, and are served stewed or pickled. *Rote Grütze*, a traditional dessert, is a berry pudding often served with whipped cream.

Northeast Germany: Currywurst and More

Berlin is known for its *Eisbein* (pork knuckle), *Kasseler* (smoked pork chop), *Bockwurst* (large sausage), and *Boulette* (a kind of hamburger made of beef and pork), though its most famous dish might be its *Currywurst*, a Berlin-born dish that consists of sausage cut in pieces and covered in ketchup with curry. Idyllic Spreewald is famous for its pickles.

The East: Da, Soljanka

In former GDR states like Saxony, Saxony-Anhalt, and Thuringia, the Soviet influence can be felt in the popularity of traditionally Russian dishes like *Soljanka* (meat soup). *Rotkäppchen* sparkling wines come from Saxony-Anhalt, Germany's northernmost wine-making region (named for the company's bottles with red tops, Rotkäppchen is also the German name for Little Red Riding Hood). Another local treat is *Baumkuchen*, or tree cake, so named because it is formed by adding layer upon layer of batter on a spit and rotating this around a heat source, such that when you cut into it, it looks like the rings of a tree.

The Döner: It's for Dinner

Although not a traditional German dish, the Turkish döner kebab is ubiquitous in Germany and it would be hard to spend much time here without trying one. Made from some combination of lamb, chicken, pork, or beef roasted on a spit then sliced into pita pockets with cabbage, lettuce, and yogurt sauce, döners are one of the most popular fast foods around. A spicy, inexpensive alternative to German fare, they're good for a meal or a pick-me-up.

Seasonal Favorites

Germans are still very much attuned to seasonal fruits and vegetables. Traditional German produce like white asparagus, strawberries, plums, cherries, blueberries, and apples are available in supermarkets, farmers' markets, and sidewalk sellers in abundance, and are eagerly snapped up by locals. When in season, these are delicious items to add to your diet and a healthy way to keep your blood sugar up as you set off to explore Germany.

BEERS OF GERMANY

Beer, or "liquid bread" as it was described by medieval monks who wanted to avoid God's anger, is not just a vital element of German cuisine, but of German culture. The stats say Germans are second only to the Czechs when it comes to per capita beer consumption, though they have been losing their thirst recently—from a peak of 145 liters (38.3 gallons) per head in 1980, each German now only manages 102 liters (26.9 gallons) every year. And yet the range of beers has never been wider.

Reinheitsgebot (Purity Law)

There are precisely 1,327 breweries in Germany, offering more than 5,000 types of beer. Thanks to Germany's legendary "Beer Purity Law," or *Reinheitsgebot*, which allows only three ingredients (water, malt, and hops), they are pretty much all terrific. The water used in German beer also has to meet certain standards—a recent discussion about introducing fracking in certain parts Germany was roundly criticized by the German Beer Association because the water in the area would become too dirty to be made into beer.

Germany's Major Beer Varieties

Pils: One effect of the Beer Purity Law was that Germany became dominated by one kind of beer: *Pils*. Invented in Bohemia (now the Czech Republic) in 1842, and aided by Bavarian refrigeration techniques, Pils was the first beer to be chilled and stored thus allowing bottom fermentation, better clarity, and a longer shelf-life. Today, the majority of German beers are brewed in the Pils, or Pilsner, style. German Pils tends to have a drier, bitterer taste than what you might be used to, but a trip to Germany is hardly complete without the grand tour along

these lines: Augustiner in Bavaria, Bitburger in the Rhineland, Flensburger in the North.

Helles: *Hell* is German for "light," but when it comes to beer, that refers to the color rather than the alcohol content. *Helles* is a crisp and clear Bavarian pale lager with between 4.5% and 6% alcohol. It was developed in the mid-19th century by a German brewer named Gabriel Sedlmayr, who adopted and adapted some British techniques to create the new beer for his famous Spaten Brewery in Bavaria. Another brewer, Josef Groll, used the same methods to produce one of the first German Pils, Pilsner Urquell. Spaten is still one the best brands for a good Helles, as are Löwenbräu, Weihenstephaner, and Hacker-Pschorr—all classic Bavarian beers.

Dunkelbier: At the other end of the beer rainbow from Helles is dark beer, or *Dunkelbier*. The dark, reddish color is a consequence of the darker malt that is used in the brewing. Despite suspicions aroused by the stronger, maltier taste, Dunkelbier actually contains no more alcohol than Helles. Dunkelbier was common in rural Bavaria in the early 19th century. All the major Bavarian breweries produce a Dunkelbier to complement their Helles.

Bock: Dunkelbier should not be confused with *Bock*, which also has a dark color and a malty taste but is a little stronger. It was first created in the middle ages in the northern German town of Einbeck, before it was later adopted by the Bavarian breweries, which had come to regard themselves as the natural home of German beer. In fact, the name Bock comes from the Bavarian interpretation of the word "Einbeck." Bock often has a sweeter flavor, and is traditionally drunk on public holidays. There are also sub-categories, like *Eisbock* and *Doppelbock*, which have been refined to make an even stronger beverage.

Kölsch: If you're looking for lighter refreshment, then *Kölsch* is ideal. The traditional beer of Cologne, Kölsch is a mild, carbonated beer that goes down easily. It is usually served in a small, straight glass, called a *Stange*, which is much easier to wrangle than the immense Bavarian *Mass* (liter) glasses. If you're part of a big party, you're likely to get Kölsch served in a *Kranz*, or wreath—a circular wooden rack that holds up to 18 *Stangen*. Kölsch is very specific to Cologne and its immediate environs, so there's little point in asking for it anywhere else. Consequently, the major Kölsch brands are all relatively small; they include Reissdorf, Gaffel, and Früh.

Hefeweizen: Also known as *Weissbier* or *Weizenbier*, *Hefeweizen* is essentially wheat beer, and it was originally brewed in southern Bavaria. It has a very distinctive taste and cloudy color. It's much stronger than standard Pils or Helles, with an alcohol content of more than 8%. On the other hand, that content is slightly compensated for by the fact that wheat beer can be very filling. For a twist, try the clear variety called *Kristallweizen*, which tastes crisper, and is often served with half a slice of lemon. Hefeweizen is available throughout Germany, and the major Bavarian breweries all brew it as part of their range.

Top Brews by Region

Bavaria: Helles, Dunkelbier, Hefeweizen.

The six most famous brands, and the only ones allowed to be sold at the Oktoberfest are: Löwenbräu, Augustiner, Paulaner, Hacker-Pschorr, Spaten-Franziskanerbräu and Hofbräu. Tegernseer Hell is also very good.

Rhineland: Kölsch, Pils.

Apart from Kölsch, which is impossible to avoid, look out for Krombacher and Bitburger.

Eastern Germany: Pils.

Radeberger and Hasseröder, are two of the few beers in the region to have survived the fall of communism in the former East Germany.

Berlin: Pils.

The most famous brands are Berliner Kindl, Schultheiss, and Berliner Pilsner, which are all worth trying.

Hamburg: Pils.

Astra—with its anchor-heart logo—is a cult Pils that is very much identified with Germany's biggest port city.

Northern Germany: Pils, Bock.

The best brands include Flensburger, Jever, and, of course, Beck's, which comes from the northern city of Bremen.

WINES OF GERMANY

Germany produces some of the finest white wines in the world. Although more and more quality red wine is being produced, the majority of German wines are white due to the northern continental climate. Nearly all wine production in Germany takes place by the River Rhine in the southwest. As a result, a single trip to this lovely and relatively compact wine region can give you a good overview of German wines.

German Wines: Then and Now
A BRIEF HISTORY
The Romans first introduced viticulture to the southernmost area of what is present-day Germany about 2,000 years ago. By the time of Charlemagne, wine making centered on monasteries. A 19th-century grape blight necessitated a complete reconstitution of German grape stock, grafted with pest-resistant American vines, and formed the basis for today's German wines. With cold winters, a relatively northern climate, and less sun than other wine regions, the Germans have developed a reputation for technical and innovative panache. The result has traditionally been top-quality sweet Rieslings, though Germany has been making excellent dry and off-dry white wines and Rieslings in the past 30 years.

TODAY'S WINE SCENE
For years, German wines were known by their lowest common denominator, the cheap, sweet wine that was exported en masse to the United States, England, and other markets. However, more recently there has been a push to introduce the world to the best of German wines. Exports to the United States, Germany's largest export market, have grown steadily, followed by England, The Netherlands, Sweden, and Russia. Eighty-three percent of its exports are white wines. The export of *Liebfraumilch*, the sugary, low-quality stuff that gave German wine a bad name, has been steadily declining, and now 66% of exports are so-called *Qualitätswein*, or quality wines. Only 15% of exports are destined to be wine-in-a-box. This is a more accurate representation of German wine as it exists in Germany.

Germany's Dominant Varietals
WHITES
Müller-Thurgau: Created in the 1880s, this grape is a cross between a Riesling and a Madeleine Royale. Ripening early, it's prone to rot and, as the grape used in most Liebfraumilch, has a less than golden reputation.

Riesling: The most widely planted (and widely famous) of German grapes, the Riesling ripens late. A hardy grape, it's ideal for late-harvest wines. High levels of acidity help wines age well. When young, grapes have a crisp, floral character.

Silvaner: This grape is dying out in most places, with the exception of Franconia, where it is traditionally grown. With low acidity and neutral fruit, it can be crossed with other grapes to produce sweet wines like Kerner, Grauburgunder (pinot gris), Weissburgunder (pinot blanc), Bacchus, and others.

REDS
Dornfelder: A relatively young varietal. Dornfelder produces wines with a deep color, which distinguishes them from other German reds, which tend to be pale, light, and off-dry.

Spätburgunder (pinot noir): This grape is responsible for Germany's full-bodied, fruity wines, and is grown in more southerly vineyards.

Terminology

German wine is a complex topic, even though the wine region is relatively small. Wines are ranked according to the ripeness of the grapes when picked, and instead of harvesting a vineyard all at once, German vineyards are harvested up to five times. The finest wines result from the latest harvests of the season, due to increased sugar content. Under the category of "table wine" fall *Deutscher Tafelwein* (German table wine) and *Landwein* (like the French Vin de Pays). Quality wines are ranked according to when they are harvested. *Kabinett* wines are delicate, light, and fruity. *Spätlese* ("late-harvest" wine) has more-concentrated flavors, sweetness, and body. *Auslese* wines are made from extra-ripe grapes, and are even richer, even sweeter, and even riper. *Beerenauslese* are rare and expensive, made from grapes whose flavor and acid has been enhanced by noble rot. *Eiswein* ("ice" wine) is made of grapes that have been left on the vine to freeze and may be harvested as late as January. They produce a sugary syrup that creates an intense, fruity wine. Finally, *Trockenbeerenauslese* ("dry ice" wine) is made in tiny amounts using grapes that have frozen and shriveled into raisins. These can rank amongst the world's most expensive wines. Other terms to keep in mind include *Trocken* (dry) and *Halbtrocken* (half-dry, or "off-dry").

Wine Regions

Mosel: The Mosel's steep, mineral-rich hillsides produce excellent Rieslings. With flowery rather than fruity top-quality wines, the Mosel is a must-stop for any wine lover. The terraced hillsides rising up along the banks of the River Mosel are as pleasing to the eye as the light-bodied Rieslings are to the palate.

Nahe: Agreeable and uncomplicated: this describes the wines made from Müller-Thurgau and Silvaner grapes of the Nahe region. The earth here is rich not just in grapes, but also in semiprecious stones and minerals, and you might just detect a hint of pineapple in your wine's bouquet.

Rheinhessen: The largest wine-making region of Germany, Rheinhessen's once grand reputation was tarnished in the mid-20th century, when large, substandard vineyards were cultivated and low-quality wine produced. Nonetheless, there's plenty of the very good stuff to be found, still. Stick to the red sandy slopes over the river for the most full-bodied of Germany's Rieslings.

Rheingau: The dark, slatey soil of the Rheingau is particularly suited to the German Riesling, which is the major wine produced in this lovely hill country along the River Rhine. Spicy wines come from the hillsides, while the valley yields wines with body, richness, and concentration.

Pfalz: The second-largest wine region in Germany, the Pfalz stretches north from the French border. Mild winters and warm summers make for some of Germany's best pinot noirs and most opulent Rieslings. Wine is served here in a special dimpled glass called the *Dubbeglas*.

Baden: Farther to the south, Baden's warmer climate helps produce ripe, full-bodied wines that may not be well known but certainly taste delicious. The best ones, both red and white, come from Kaiserstuhl-Tuniberg, between Freiburg and the Rhine. But be forewarned: The best things in life do tend to cost a little extra.

GREAT ITINERARIES

GRAND TOUR OF GERMANY

Coming to Germany for the first time? Consider a journey of the best the country has to offer: stunning landscapes, charming medieval towns, and cosmopolitan capital cities. Make the most of your time by taking the train between stops. You'll eliminate the hassles of parking and the high cost of gasoline. Best of all, you'll take in the views—in complete relaxation—as they roll by your window.

Days 1 and 2: Munich

Kick off your circle tour of quintessential Germany in Bavaria's capital city. Get your bearings by standing in the center of Munich's Marienplatz, and watch the charming, twirling figures of the Glockenspiel in the tower of the *Rathaus* (town hall). Visit the world-class art museums, then wander through the *Englischer Garten* (English Garden) to the beer garden for a cool beer and pretzel. ⇨ *See Chapter 2, Munich.*

Day 3: Garmisch-Partenkirchen

Take a day trip to visit Germany's highest mountain peak (9,731 feet), the Zugspitze. You'll take in astounding views of the mountains and breathe the bracing Alpine air. Have lunch at one of two restaurants on the peak, then bask in the sun like the Germans on the expansive terrace. If you're feeling sporty, hundreds of kilometers of trails offer some of Germany's best hiking across blooming mountain meadows and along steep mountain gorges. Otherwise take the cable car up and down and savor the dramatic vistas. ⇨ *See Chapter 3, The Bavarian Alps.*

Days 4 and 5: Freiburg

In the late morning, arrive in Freiburg, one of Germany's most beautiful historic cities. Damaged during the war, it's been meticulously rebuilt to preserve its delightful medieval character. Residents love to boast that Freiburg is the country's sunniest city, which is true according to meteorological reports. Freiburg's cathedral is a masterpiece of Gothic architecture, built over three centuries. Explore on foot, or by bike, and look out for the *Bächle*, or little brooks, that run for kilometers through Freiburg. ⇨ *See Chapter 7, The Black Forest.*

Day 6: The Black Forest

Freiburg puts you at the perfect point from which to explore the spruce-covered low-lying mountains of the Black Forest. Set out for Titisee, a placid glacial lake, visiting dramatic gorges along the way. Or, head toward the northern Black Forest to visit tony Baden-Baden. Then spend the afternoon relaxing in the curative waters at one of the famous spas. ⇨ *See Chapter 7, The Black Forest.*

Day 7: Würzburg

This gorgeous city sits on the Main River, and as you look out onto the hills that surround the city, you'll see that lush vineyards encircle the valley. Würzburg's two must-see attractions are the massive *Festung Marienburg* (Marienburg Fortress) and the Residenz an awe-inspiring baroque palace. The palace is considered to be one of Europe's most luxurious. The best way to sample the local wine is to go straight to the source: the vineyards. In the afternoon, follow the Stein-Wein-Pfad, a pathway that takes you straight to the local vintners, and try their wines while also drinking in incredible views of the city below. ⇨ *See Chapter 4, The Romantic Road.*

Day 8: Bamberg

In the morning, arrive in Bamberg, which is on UNESCO's World Heritage Site list. The town is remarkable for not having sustained damage during World War II, and for looking much as it has for hundreds of years. Narrow cobblestone streets lead you to Bamberg's heart, a small island ringed by the Regnitz River. Bamberg has almost a dozen breweries—try the *Rauchbier*, a dark beer with a smoky flavor. ⇨ *See Chapter 5, Franconia and the German Danube.*

Days 9 and 10: Hamburg

Hamburg is one of Germany's wealthiest cities. It's also an important port, and served as a leader of the medieval Hanseatic League. If you're in Hamburg on Sunday, visit the open-air *Fischmarkt* (fish market) early in the morning. Then, take a cruise through the city's canals to see the historic warehouse district. Exploring the harbor you'll see the enormous ocean liners that stop in Hamburg before crossing the Atlantic. The city offers exclusive shopping along the Junfernstieg, a lakeside promenade. ⇨ *See Chapter 13, Hamburg.*

Days 11 and 12: Berlin and Potsdam

Berlin is Germany's dynamic capital, a sprawling and green city. No matter where you go, it's hard to escape Berlin's recent history as a divided city. You're brought face-to-face with the legacy of World War II, and contrast of East and West. Walk from the Brandenburg Gate to the famous Museum Island and visit the Pergamon Alter. In the afternoon, visit KaDeWe, Europe's largest department store, and walk along the *Kurfürstendamm*, the posh shopping boulevard. Spend the next morning in Potsdam, touring the opulent palaces and manicured gardens. Return to the city to explore its neighborhoods, like Turkish Kreuzberg or hip Prenzlauer Berg. ⇨ *See Chapter 15, Berlin.*

GERMAN ABCS: ARCHITECTURE, BEER, CASTLES AND CAPITALS

Day 1: Arrival Munich

Though it is a wealthy city with Wittelsbach palaces, great art collections, and a technology museum holding trains, planes, and even an imitation coal mine, what really distinguishes Munich from other state capitals are its beer halls, beer gardens, and proud identity: even designer-conscious Müncheners wear traditional dirndls and hunter-green jackets for special occasions. Stroll the streets of the Altstadt (Old City), visit the Frauenkirche, choose a museum (the best ones will occupy you for at least three hours), and save the Hofbräuhaus or any other teeming brew house for last. Munich might be touristy, but hordes of German tourists love it as well. ⇨ *See Chapter 2, Munich.*

Day 2: Neuschwanstein

From Munich it's an easy day trip to Germany's fairy-tale castle in Schwangau. Though the 19th-century castle's fantastic silhouette has made it famous, this creation of King Ludwig II is more opera set than piece of history—the interior was never even completed. A tour reveals why the romantic king earned the nickname "Mad" King Ludwig. Across the narrow wooded valley from Schloss Neuschwanstein is the ancient castle of the Bavarian Wittelsbach dynasty, Schloss Hohenschwangau, also open for tours. ⇨ *See Chapter 4, The Romantic Road.*

Day 3: Munich to Dresden

That Saxony's capital, Dresden, is the pinnacle of European baroque is obvious in its courtyards, newly rebuilt Frauenkirche, and terrace over the Elbe River. The city was largely shaped by Augustus the Strong, who in 1730 kindly invited the public to view the works crafted from precious stones in his Green Vault. Many of Dresden's art treasures lie within the Zwinger, a baroque showpiece. Spend the evening at the neo-Renaissance Semper Opera, where Wagner premiered his works, and drink Radeberger Pilsner at intermission. It's the country's oldest pilsner. ⇨ *See Chapter 16, Saxony, Saxony-Anhalt, and Thuringia.*

Day 4: Dresden and Berlin

Spend the morning touring some of Dresden's rich museums before boarding a train to Berlin. Germany's capital is not only unique for its division between 1949 and 1989, but is unlike any other German city in its physical expanse and diversity. Attractions that don't close until 10 pm or later are Sir Norman Foster's glass dome on the Reichstag, the TV tower at Alexanderplatz, and the Checkpoint Charlie Museum. ⇨ *See Chapters 15 and 16, Berlin and Saxony, Saxony-Anhalt, and Thuringia.*

Days 5 and 6: Berlin

Begin your first Berlin morning on a walk with one of the city's excellent tour companies. They'll connect the broadly spaced dots for you and make the events of Berlin's turbulent 20th century clear. Berlin is a fascinating city in and of itself, so you don't have to feel guilty if you don't get to many museums. Since the mid-1990s, world-renowned architects have changed the city's face. You'll find the best nightlife in hip neighborhoods like Kreuzberg,

Friedrichshain, or Mitte. Berlin is a surprisingly inexpensive city, so you can treat yourself to more here than in Munich. ⇨ *See Chapter 15, Berlin.*

Day 7: Munich

On your last day, have breakfast with the morning shoppers at the open-air Viktualienmarkt. Try to find *Weisswurst,* a mild, boiled sausage normally eaten before noon with sweet mustard, a pretzel—and beer! ⇨ *See Chapter 2, Munich.*

CASTLES IN WINE COUNTRY

Day 1: Arrival Koblenz

Start your tour in Koblenz, at the confluence of the Rhine and Mosel rivers. Once you have arrived in the historic downtown area, head straight for the charming little Hotel Zum weissen Schwanen, a half-timber inn and mill since 1693. Explore the city on the west bank of the Rhine River and then head to Europe's biggest fortress, the impressive Festung Ehrenbreitstein on the opposite riverbank. ⇨ *See Chapter 11, The Rhineland.*

Day 2: Koblenz and Surrounding Castles

Get up early and drive along the most spectacular and historic section of "Vater Rhein." Stay on the left riverbank and you'll pass many mysterious landmarks on the way, including Burg Stolzenfels, and later the Loreley rock, a 430-foot slate cliff named after a legendary, beautiful, blonde nymph. Stay the night at St. Goar or St. Goarshausen, both lovely river villages. ⇨ *See Chapter 11, The Rhineland.*

Day 3: Eltville and the Eberbach Monastery

The former Cistercian monastery Kloster Eberbach, in Eltville, is one of Europe's best-preserved medieval cloisters. Parts of the film *The Name of the Rose*, based on Umberto Eco's novel and starring Sean Connery, were filmed here. If you're interested in wine, spend the night at the historic wine estate Schloss Reinhartshausen. This is a great opportunity to sample the fantastic wines of the region. ⇨ *See Chapter 11, The Rhineland.*

Day 4: Heidelberg

On Day 4, start driving early so you can spend a full day in Heidelberg (the drive from Eltville takes about an hour). No other city symbolizes German spirit and history better than this meticulously restored, historic town. Do not miss the impressive Schloss, one of Europe's greatest Gothic-Renaissance fortresses. Most of the many pubs and restaurants here are touristy, overpriced, and of poor quality—so don't waste your time at them. Instead, head for the Romantik Hotel zum Ritter St. Georg, a charming 16th-century inn with a great traditional German restaurant. ⇨ *See Chapter 8, Heidelberg and the Neckar Valley.*

Days 5 and 6: The Burgenstrasse and the Neckar Valley

Superb food and wine can be enjoyed in the quaint little villages in the Neckar Valley just east of Heidelberg—the predominant grapes here are Riesling (white) and Spätburgunder (red). Try to sample wines from small, private wineries—they tend to have higher-quality vintages. Sightseeing is equally stunning, with a string of castles and ruins along the famous Burgenstrasse (Castle Road). Since you have two days for this area, take your time and follow B-37 to Eberbach and its romantic Zwingenberg castle, tucked away in the deep forest just outside the village. In the afternoon, continue on to Burg Hornberg at Neckarzimmern, the home to the legendary German knight Götz von Berlichingen. Stay the night here, in the former castle stables.

The next morning, continue farther to Bad Wimpfen, the most charming valley town at the confluence of the Neckar and Jagst rivers. Spend half a day in the historic city center and tour the Staufer Pfalz (royal palace). Soaring high above the city, the palace was built in 1182, and emperor Barbarossa liked to stay here. ⇨ *See Chapter 8, Heidelberg and the Neckar Valley.*

Day 7: German Wine Route

Devote your last day to the German Wine Route, which winds its way through one of the most pleasant German landscapes, the gentle slopes and vineyards of the Pfalz. The starting point for the route is Bad Dürkheim, a spa town proud to have the world's largest wine cask, holding 1.7 million liters (450,000 gallons). You can enjoy wine with some lunch in the many Weinstuben here or wait until you reach Neustadt farther south, Germany's largest wine-making community. Thirty of the vintages grown here can be sampled (and purchased) at the downtown Haus des Weines. If time permits, try to visit one of the three major castles along the route in the afternoon: Burg Trifels near Annweiler is a magnificent Hohenzollern residence, perched dramatically on three sandstone cliffs, the very image of a medieval castle in wine country. ⇨ *See Chapter 10, The Pfalz and the Rhine Terrace.*

Travel Times By Train

LODGING PRIMER

When it comes to hotels, Germans do it right. Whether budget and spare, or luxurious and opulent, German lodgings tend to be wonderfully spic and span. You'll find top-quality accommodations throughout Germany to rest your travel-weary bones at the end of the day. From a chic, big-city design hotel to a cozy village Gasthof to life on the farm at a Bauernhof, there's a broad spectrum of choices wherever your journey takes you.

Hotels

German hotels adhere to a high standard, and you'll find that even the most basic offerings are scrupulously clean and comfortable. Of course, as the number of stars goes up, so do the amenities, and you can count on the largest and best city hotels to offer concierge services and fine dining. If you prefer something more intimate, *Gasthöfe* (country inns that also serve food) offer a great value. You can also opt to stay at a winery's *Winzerhof* or at an historic castle (*Schloss*). Families can consider a *Familienhotel*, which cater to children with special menus, activities, pools, and play areas. Depending on the hotel, rates are calculated by room or by person. Prices are generally higher in summer, so consider visiting during the off-season. Most resorts offer between-season (*Zwischensaison*) and off-season (*Nebensaison*) rates, and tourist offices can provide lists of hotels that offer low-price weekly packages (*Pauschalangebote*). It's wise to avoid cities during major trade fairs as rates skyrocket. Consider staying in nearby towns and commuting in.

Bed-and-Breakfasts

If you're looking for a more personal—and less expensive—alternative to a hotel, B&Bs are a good choice. Often called *Pensions,* they offer simple rooms and friendly, helpful staff. Keep in mind that not all rooms will have a private bathroom, but your stay will, of course, include breakfast. Another option is a *Fremdenzimmer,* meaning simply "rooms," normally in private houses. These are found most often in resort towns. And although it's not nearly as private as staying in a hotel or inn, it will give you a peek at how the locals live. For a taste of rural life, try an *Urlaub auf dem Bauernhof,* a farm that rents rooms.

Apartment and House Rentals

To really get a sense of how the natives live, rent a house or apartment. Known as *Ferienwohnung* or *Ferienappartements,* it's a popular option in Germany. In a city, you'll feel the pulse of a neighborhood, or in the country you might step out onto your balcony to take in a mountain view. When traveling with family or a group, a private home may be a better deal than booking multiple hotel rooms. Not to mention that you're likely to end up with more space.

Wellness Hotels

Germany has a long-established tradition of spa towns (Kurorte). Officially recognized for having special mineral waters, particularly fresh sea air, or other health-enhancing natural resources, these spa towns are found throughout the country, and often have lovely hotels for visitors who want to relax and improve their health. Look for sauna and massage on offer, here.

⇨ *For resources and booking information, see Travel Smart Germany.*

TRACING YOUR GERMAN ROOTS

More than 51 million Americans claim German ancestry, and many of these Americans have a strong desire to trace their long-lost roots. The first significant waves of immigration from Germany came after the failed democratic revolutions of 1848, a time period coupled with potato blight in parts of Germany. The numbers of German immigrants did not let up until the early 20th century. Of course, Jewish Germans fleeing fascism also left much of what had been their cultural heritage (as well as material possessions), behind. If you've ever been curious about wandering your family's ancestral village, standing in the church where your great-grandmother was baptized, or meeting the cousins who share your name, it's easier than ever to make it happen.

Before You Go

The more you can learn about your ancestors before you go, the more fruitful your search will be. The first place to seek information is directly from members of your family. Even relatives who don't know any family history may have documents stored away that can help with your sleuthing—old letters, wills, diaries, photo albums, birth and death certificates, and Bibles or other religious books can be great sources of information. The first crucial facts you'll need are the name of your ancestor; his or her date of birth, marriage, or death; town or city of origin in Germany; date of emigration; ship on which he or she emigrated; and where in America he or she settled.

If family resources aren't leading you anywhere, try turning to the **Mormon Church.** The Mormon Church has made it its mission to collect mountains of genealogical information, much of which it makes available free of charge at ⊕ *www.*

familysearch.org. The **National Archives** (⊕ *www.nara.gov*) keeps census records, and anyone can, for a fee, get information from the censuses of 1940 and earlier.

The spelling of your family name may not be consistent through time. Over the course of history varying rates of literacy in Germany meant that the spelling of names evolved through recent centuries. And on arrival in the States many names changed again to make them more familiar to American ears.

Once you've established some basic facts about your ancestor it's possible to start searching some German resources. Because Germany as we know it today didn't unify until 1871, records are scattered. Lists of German ship passengers—many of which are now available online—are a good next step since they often included a person's "last residence." So if you can target your ancestor's hometown, you'll open the door to a potential trove of records. Many parish registers go back to the 15th century and document births, baptisms, marriages, deaths, and burials.

Check out the links at the **German National Tourist Office's** websites ⊕ *germanoriginality.com, www.germany. travel,* and if you're tracking down living cousins, try the German phonebook at ⊕ *DasTelefonbuch.de.*

On the Ground in Germany

Once you arrive, you can use the computerized facilities of Bremerhaven's **German Emigration Center** (⊕ *www.dah-bremerhaven.de*) or enlist the help of an assistant to search the passenger lists of the HAPAG shipping line, at Hamburg's **Family Research Center** (⊕ *www. BallinStadt.de*).

WORLD WAR II SITES

Germany's darkest days began with Adolf Hitler's rise to power in 1933. Hitler led Germany into war in 1939 and perpetrated the darkest crimes against humanity, murdering 6 million Jews in the Holocaust. To gain perspective on the extent of the horror, it's possible to visit sites around Germany that document the atrocities.

Upon his election, Hitler set about turning **Obersalzburg** into the southern headquarters for the Nazi party and as a mountain retreat for its elite. Located in the Bavarian Alps, the enormous compound included luxurious homes for party officials. Today you can walk through the extensive bunker system while learning about the Nazi's takeover of the area. Not far from Obersalzburg you'll find the **Kehlsteinhaus,** Hitler's private home. Designed as a 50th birthday gift for Hitler by the Nazi party, the house is also known as *Adlerhorst* (Eagle's Nest). It's perched on a cliff, seemingly at the top of the world. The house's precarious location probably saved it from British bombing raids. ⇨ *See Chapter 3, The Bavarian Alps.*

The Nazis organized nationwide book-burnings, one of which took place in Berlin on **Bebelplatz.** On an evening in May 1933, Nazis and Hitler Youth gathered here to burn 20,000 books considered offensive to the party. Today there is a ghostly memorial of empty library shelves sunken in the center of the square. ⇨ *See Chapter 15, Berlin.*

Masters of propaganda, the Nazis staged colossal rallies intended to impress the German people. Hitler considered Nürnberg so quintessentially German he developed an enormous complex here, the **Nazi Party Rally Grounds,** to host massive parades, military exercises, and major assemblies of the Nazi party. The Congress Hall, meant to outshine Rome's Colosseum, is the largest remaining building from the Nazi era. It houses a **Documentation Center** that explores the Nazi's tyranny. At the **Nürnberg Trials Memorial** you'll see where the war crimes trials took place between November 1945 and October 1946. In this courthouse Nazi officials stood before an international military tribunal to answer for their crimes. The Allied victors chose Nürnberg on purpose—it's the place Germany's first anti-Semitic laws passed, decreeing the boycott of Jewish businesses. ⇨ *See Chapter 5, Franconia and the German Danube.*

The **KZ-Gedenkstätte Dachau** is a memorial and site of the former notorious death camp. Hitler created Dachau soon after taking power, and it became the model for all other camps. Tens of thousands of prisoners died here. Today you'll see a few remaining cell blocks and the crematorium, along with moving shrines and memorials to the dead. ⇨ *See Chapter 2, Munich.*

Bergen-Belsen, another infamous concentration camp, is where Anne Frank perished along with more than 80,000 others. The starving and sick prisoners lived in abject squalor, deliberately neglected by their captors. A meadow is all that remains of the camp, but it is still a chilling place to visit. The documentation center shows wrenching photos of unburied bodies and emaciated prisoners. ⇨ *See Chapter 12, The Fairy-Tale Road.*

In fact, nearly anywhere you are in Germany, you should be able to visit a concentration camp: Others include **Buchenwald, Oranienburg, Sachsenhausen,** and **Dora-Mittelbau.**

MUNICH

WELCOME TO MUNICH

TOP REASONS TO GO

★ **Deutsches Museum:**
The museum has an impressive collection of science and technology exhibits, and its location on the Isar River is perfect for a relaxing afternoon stroll.

★ **Englischer Garten:**
With expansive greens, beautiful lakes, and beer gardens, the English Garden is a great place for a bike ride or a long walk.

★ **Gärtnerplatz:**
Gärtnerplatz and the adjoining Glockenbachviertel are the hip hoods of the moment, with trendy bars, restaurants, cafés, and shops.

★ **Views from the Frauenkirche:** This 14th-century church tower gives you a panorama of downtown Munich that can't be beat. There are 86 steps in a circular shaft to get to the elevator, but the view is worth it.

★ **Viktualienmarkt:**
Experience farmers'-market-style shopping, where there's fresh produce, finger food, and a beer garden; it's not to be missed.

1 The City Center.
Marienplatz, the Rathaus, and the surrounding streets are a hub for locals and tourists alike. Here you'll find the soaring towers of the Frauenkirche, Munich's landmark church. East of Marienplatz, down toward the Isar River, is the maze of the Old Town's smaller streets.

2 Royal Munich. The Residenz, or royal palace, is the focus here. Bordering the Residenz to the north is the Hofgarten, or Court Garden. Farther northeast is the Englischer Garten, great for sunbathing or something sportier.

3 Schwabing and Maxvorstadt. On one side of Maxvorstadt is Ludwigstrasse, a wide avenue flanked by

GETTING ORIENTED

In the relaxed and sunnier southern part of Germany, Munich (München) is the proud capital of the state of Bavaria. Even Germans come here to vacation, mixing the city's pleasures with the nearby natural surroundings—on clear days, from downtown the Alps appear to be much closer than around 40 miles away. The city bills itself *"Die Weltstadt mit Herz"* ("The Cosmopolitan City with Heart"), but in rare bouts of self-deprecatory humor, friendly Bavarians will remind you that it isn't much more than a country town with 1.4 million people. Münchners will also tell visitors that the city is special because of its *Gemütlichkeit*—loosely translated as "conviviality." This can be overdone, but with open-air markets, numerous parks, the lovely Isar River, and loads of beer halls, Munich has a certain charm that few cities can match.

impressive buildings, running from the Feldherrnhalle and Odeonsplatz to the Victory Arch. A block farther west are Maxvorstadt's smaller streets, lined with shops and restaurants frequented by students. The big museums lie another two blocks west. Schwabing starts north of the Victory Arch, where Ludwigstrasse becomes Leopoldstrasse.

4 Outside the Center. Ludwigvorstadt is southwest of the City Center and includes the Oktoberfest grounds. The western part of the city is dominated by Nymphenburg Castle and its glorious grounds. Across the Isar is fashionable Lehel, and Au-Haidhausen areas.

VIKTUALIENMARKT
MUNICH'S FARMERS' MARKET

It's not just the fascinating array of fruit, vegetables, olives, breads, cheeses, meats, pickles, and honey that make *Viktualienmarkt* (victuals market) so attractive. The towering maypole, small *Wirtshäuser* (pub-restaurants), and beer gardens also set the scene for a fascinating trek through Munich's most famous market.

Vegetables, fruits, and prepared foods are available at Munich's biggest farmers' market.

The Viktualienmarkt's history can be traced to the early 19th century, when King Max I Joseph decreed that Marienplatz was too small to house the major city market. In 1807, a bigger version was created a few hundred meters to the south, where it stands today. You are just as likely to find a Münchner buying something here as you are a visitor. Indeed, a number of City Center restaurants proudly proclaim that they get their ingredients "fresh from the market." This is the place to pick up a *Brotzeit*: bread, olives, cheeses, gherkins, and whatever else strikes your fancy, then retreat to a favorite Biergarten to enjoy the bounty.

—Paul Wheatley

MARKET ETIQUETTE

All stalls are open weekdays 10–6 and Saturday 10–3, though some stalls open earlier or close later. It's not kosher to touch the fresh produce but it is to ask to taste a few different olives or cheeses before buying. The quality of the various produce is invariably good; competition is fierce, so it has to be. Therefore, buy the best of what you fancy from a number of stalls, not just one or two.

VIKTUALIENMARKT BEST BUYS

BEER AND PREPARED FOOD

If it's just a beer you're after, there are a number of beer stalls not far from the towering maypole. **Biergarten am Viktualienmarkt** is the main location, but there are also small *Imbissstände* (snack bars) where you can pick up roast pork and beer. **Kleiner Ochsenbrater** sells delicious organic roast dishes. **Poseidon** and the nearby **Fisch Witte** rustle up a fine selection of fish dishes, including very good soups and stews. **Luigino's Bio Feinkost**, an organic deli that also has fine cheeses and wines, is the spot for a quick grilled sandwich. And the modest-looking **Münchner Suppenküche** dishes out delightful helpings of soup, including oxtail, chicken, and spicy lentil.

FRUITS AND VEGETABLES

The mainstay of the market is fruit and vegetables, and there are a number of top-quality stalls to choose from. The centrally located **Fruitique** has some of the freshest, most attractive-looking, and ripest produce on display. For something a little more exotic, try out **Exoten Müller,** which specializes in unusual fruits and vegetables from around the world.

HONIGHÄUSEL AM MÜNCHNER VIKTUALIENMARKT

Honighäusel means "small honey house" and is an apt description of this petite honey wonderland. Much of

the produce comes from Bavaria, but there's also a selection of honeys from farther afield: Italy, France, even New Zealand. This is also the place to buy honey marmalades and soaps, and beeswax candles. For a chilly evening, pick up a bottle of Bavarian honey schnapps.

LUDWIG FREISINGER'S "SAURE ECKE"

This is the place to create the perfect *Biergarten Brotzeit* (beer garden snack). Ask for a mixture of green and black olives with different fillings. You can also pick up the traditional biergarten cheese spread, *Obatzter,* which is made of Camembert and other white cheeses, butter, paprika, and onions. There's a huge selection of peppers filled with cheese, plus feta salad, hummus, and the enormous *Essiggurke* (gherkins). The best are crunchy when you bite into them but tender inside, with a light tanginess. A *Fladenbrot,* a circular, flat white bread, is enough for two people, and the perfect accompaniment.

SCHENK'S

There are numerous stalls at the market that serve mouthwatering, freshly pressed fruit drinks, so no matter where you buy, you won't be disappointed. Schenk's is a favorite because the drinks are top-notch and the staff are engaging, speak English, and take the time to explain the ingredients in each drink.

MUNICH'S BEER GARDENS

With a bit of sunshine, a handful of picnic tables, and a few of the finest beers around, you have yourself a *Biergarten* (beer garden). There are beer gardens throughout Germany, and many imitations across the world but the most traditional, and the best, are still found in and around Munich. The elixir that transforms the traditional Munich beer garden into something special is the unbeatable atmosphere.

(above and lower right) It's easy to make friends in the convivial atmosphere of a beer garden. (upper right) The Englischer Garten's Chinese Tower is one of the most famous beer gardens in Munich.

Beer gardens formed out of necessity. Brewers in the 18th and 19th centuries struggled to keep beer cool to prevent it from spoiling in warm weather. As early as 1724, Munich brewers dug cellars and began to store beer next to the shady shores of the Isar River. Local residents promptly took along their beer glasses for a cool drink and before long the odd table and bench appeared, and the beer garden tradition was born.

—Paul Wheatley

BIERGARTEN ETIQUETTE

Often, a beer garden is separated between where guests can bring food and where they must buy it. Simply ask to avoid confusion, or look for tablecloths—generally these are table-service only. The basis of a beer garden Brotzeit is delicious black bread, Obatzter, sausage, gherkin, and radish. As tradition dictates, remember to also order *Ein Mass Bier bitte!* (A liter of beer please!)

MUNICH'S BEST BEER GARDENS

AUGUSTINER KELLER BIERGARTEN

This is perhaps the most popular beer garden in Munich and certainly one of the largest. It is part of the **Augustiner Keller** restaurant, a few hundred meters from Hackerbrücke S-bahn station, or 5–6 minutes from the Hauptbahnhof. The main garden is separated half between where you can bring your own food and half where you buy food from the beer garden. The leaves from countless horse chestnut trees provide a canopy covering, which adds to the dreamy atmosphere.

HOFBRÄUKELLER AM WIENER PLATZ

Some of the best beer gardens are found away from the City Center. This one is a 15-minute walk (or take Tram No. 18 or 19 from the Hauptbahnhof) over the Isar River, past the Maximilianeum, to Wiener Platz, a delightful square well worth visiting. The beer garden attracts Münchners, as well as groups of British, Australian, and American expats. The staple beer garden chicken, fries, roast pork, and spare ribs are better here than most.

KÖNIGLICHER HIRSCHGARTEN

With seating for 8,000, this is the biggest and most family-friendly beer garden in Munich. In a former royal hunting area outside the City Center, it takes a little time and effort to reach.

Your best bet is to rent a bike and cycle there. The rewards are clear: surrounded by trees and green parkland, the tables and benches seem to go on forever. The food and beer is good and there is even a small deer sanctuary, lending the "Deer Park" its name.

PARK CAFÉ

This is where trendsetters head for a more modern and sunny—there isn't much shade here—take on the traditional beer garden. Set in Munich's old botanical garden, five minutes from the Hauptbanhof, this medium-size beer garden regularly has DJs and other musical events in the evenings. It also has a good selection of cakes and a hip indoor bar.

SEEHAUS IM ENGLISCHEN GARTEN

Within Munich's very own oasis, the **Englischer Garten**, it was an inspired decision to build this beer garden next to a boating lake. A leisurely stroll through the garden to the Seehaus takes about an hour, but go early because it's popular after 11:30. Lots of people visit the Englischer Garten to play soccer and other sports, and if you want to join in you might want to pass on the roast dinner and instead snack on a *Brezn* (pretzel), Obatzter, and salad.

Updated by
Paul Wheatley

Known today as the city of laptops and lederhosen, modern Munich is a cosmopolitan playground that nevertheless represents what the rest of the world incorrectly sees as "typically German": world-famous Oktoberfest, traditional *lederhosen* (leather pants), busty Bavarian waitresses in *dirndls* (traditional dresses), beer steins, and sausages.

Munich's cleanliness, safety, and Mediterranean pace give it a slightly rustic feel. The broad sidewalks, fashionable boutiques and eateries, views of the Alps, a sizable river running through town, and a huge green park make Munich one of Germany's most visited cities. When the first rays of spring sun begin warming the air, follow the locals to their beloved beer gardens, shaded by massive chestnut trees.

The number of electronics and computer firms—Siemens, Microsoft, and SAP, for starters—makes Munich a sort of mini–Silicon Valley of Germany, but for all its business drive, this is still a city with roots in the 12th century, when it began as a market town on the "salt road" between mighty Salzburg and Augsburg.

That Munich was the birthplace of the Nazi movement is a difficult truth that those living here continue to grapple with. To distance the city from its Nazi past, city leaders looked to Munich's long pre-Nazi history to highlight what they decreed was the real Munich: a city of great architecture, high art, and fine music. Many of the Altstadt's architectural gems were rebuilt postwar, including the lavish Cuvilliés-Theater, the Altes Rathaus, and the Frauenkirche.

The city's appreciation of the arts began under the kings and dukes of the Wittelsbach Dynasty, which ruled Bavaria for eight centuries, until 1918. The Wittelsbach legacy is alive and well in many of the city's museums and exhibition centers, the Opera House, the philharmonic, and, of course, the Residenz, the city's royal palace. Any walk in the City Center will take you past ravishing baroque decoration and grand 19th-century neoclassical architecture.

PLANNING

WHEN TO GO

Munich is a year-round city, but it's nicer to walk through the Englischer Garten and have your beer under a shady chestnut tree when the weather's fine in summer. If fate takes you to Munich through its long, cold winter, though, there are world-class museums and good restaurants to keep you entertained. Theater and opera fans will especially enjoy the winter season, when the tour buses and the camera-toting crowds are gone. A few postsummer sunny days are usual, but the Oktoberfest is also an indication that fall is here, and the short march to winter has arrived.

FESTIVALS

Munich comes alive during Fasching, the German Mardi Gras, in the pre-Easter season. The festival of festivals, Oktoberfest, takes place from the end of September to early October.

Long Night of Music. In late May the Long Night of Music is devoted to live performances through the night by untold numbers of groups, from heavy-metal bands to medieval choirs, at more than 100 locations throughout the city. One ticket covers everything, including transportation on special buses between locations. ☎ *089/3061–0041* ⊕ *www.muenchner.de/musiknacht* 🎫 *€15.*

GETTING HERE AND AROUND

AIR TRAVEL

Munich's International Airport is 28 km (17 miles) northeast of the City Center and has excellent air service from all corners of the world. An excellent train service links the airport with downtown. The S-1 and S-8 lines operate from a terminal directly beneath the airport's arrival and departure halls. S-bahn trains leave at 20-minute intervals on both lines, and the journey takes around 40 minutes. The easiest way is to buy a *Tageskarte* (day card) for the Gesamtnetz, costing €10.80, which allows you to travel anywhere on the system for the rest of the day until 6 am the next morning. The similarly priced bus service is slower than the S-bahn link and not recommended. A taxi from the airport costs around €56. During rush hours (7 am–10 am and 4 pm–7 pm), allow up to an hour of driving time. If you're driving from the airport to the city yourself, take the A-9 and follow the signs for "München Stadtmitte" (downtown). If you're driving from the City Center, head north through Schwabing, join the A-9 autobahn at the Frankfurter Ring intersection, and follow the signs for the "Flughafen" (airport).

Airport Information Flughafen München ☎ *089/97500* ⊕ *www.munich-airport.de.*

BUS TRAVEL

With its futuristic architecture, Munich's 2009-finished Central Bus Terminal (ZOB) means that many excursions and longer trips are now centralized five minutes from the main train station. As well as numerous shops and banks, travel firms offer bus tickets and destination advice at the ZOB.

Touring Eurolines buses arrive at and depart from the ZOB. Check their excellent website for trips to Neuschwanstein and the Romantic Road.

Bus Information Central Bus Station Munich (*ZOB*). ✉ *Hackerbrücke, Ludwigvorstadt* ✛ *ZOB is about 800 m from the main train station along Arnulfstrasse; if traveling by S-bahn, it's adjacent to Hackerbrücke S-bahn station* ☎ *089/4520–9890* ⊕ *www.muenchen-zob.de.* **Touring Eurolines** ✉ *DTG-Ticket-Center München, Hackerbrücke 4, ZOB, Ludwigvorstadt* ☎ *089/8898–9513* ⊕ *www.eurolines.de.*

CAR TRAVEL

If you're driving to Munich from the north (Nürnberg or Frankfurt), leave the autobahn at the Schwabing exit. From Stuttgart and the west, the autobahn ends at Obermenzing, one of Munich's most westerly suburbs. The autobahns from Salzburg and the east, Garmisch and the south, and Lindau and the southwest all join the Mittlerer Ring (city beltway). When leaving any autobahn, follow the signs reading "Stadtmitte" for downtown Munich.

PUBLIC TRANSIT

Munich has one of the most efficient and comprehensive public-transportation systems in Europe, consisting of the U-bahn (subway), the S-bahn (suburban railway), the Strassenbahn (streetcar, also called "Tram"), and buses. Marienplatz forms the heart of the U-bahn and S-bahn network, which operates regularly from around 5 am to 1 am (intermittently otherwise, so check times if you're expecting a long night or early start). The main service counter under Marienplatz sells tickets and gives out information, also in English. The website ⊕ *www.muenchen.de* has an excellent and extensive transportation section, also in English.

A basic *Einzelfahrkarte* (one-way ticket) costs €1.30 for a journey of up to four stops, €2.60 for a longer ride in the inner zone. If you're taking a number of trips around the city, save money by buying a *Streifenkarte,* or multiple 10-strip ticket for €12.50. On a journey of up to four stops validate one ticket, for the inner zone, two. If you plan to do several trips during one day, buy a *Tageskarte* (day card) for €11.20, which allows you to travel anywhere until 6 am the next morning. For a family of up to five (two adults and three children under age 15) the Tageskarte costs €20.40. A three-day card costs €14.30 for a single and €24.60 for the partner version. All tickets must be validated at one of the blue time-stamping machines at the station, or on buses and trams as soon as you board (wait till you've found a seat, and if an inspector's around you'll get a fine). Spot checks for validated tickets are common, and you'll be fined €40 if you're caught without a valid ticket. All tickets are sold at the blue dispensers at U- and S-bahn stations and at some bus and streetcar stops. Bus drivers have only single tickets (the most expensive kind). ■TIP→ Holders of a EurailPass, a Youth Pass, or an Inter-Rail card can travel free on all suburban railway trains (S-bahn). Be forewarned: If caught on anything but the S-bahn without a normal public transport ticket, you will be fined €40, with no exceptions.

Public Transportation Information Munich Transport Company (*MVG*). ☎ *089/4142–4344* ⊕ *www.mvg-mobil.de.*

TAXI TRAVEL

Munich's cream-color taxis are numerous. Hail them in the street or phone for one (there's an extra charge of €1.20 if you call). Rates start at €3.10. Expect to pay €8–€10 for a short trip within the city. There's a €0.60 charge for each piece of non–hand luggage.

Taxi Information Taxi München ☎ *089/21610, 089/19410* ⊕ *www.taxi-muenchen.com.*

TRAIN TRAVEL

All long-distance rail services arrive at and depart from the Hauptbahnhof; trains to and from some destinations in Bavaria use the adjoining Starnberger Bahnhof, which is under the same roof. The high-speed InterCity Express (ICE) trains connect Munich, Augsburg, Frankfurt, and Hamburg on one line, Munich, Nürnberg, Würzburg, and Hamburg on another. Regensburg can be reached from Munich on Regio trains. You can purchase tickets by credit card at vending machines. For travel information at the main train station, go to one of the Deutsche Bahn (German Rail) counters at the center of the main arrival and departures hall with German- and English-speaking personnel or contact ⊕ *www.bahn.de*. With more complex questions, go to the EurAide office, which also serves English-speaking train travelers.

Train Information Deutsche Bahn ☎ *0800/150–7090* ⊕ *www.bahn.de.* EurAide ⊕ *www.euraide.com.*

TOURS

The tourist office offers individual guided tours in English for fees ranging between €115 and €290. Bookings must be made at least 10 days in advance. ⇨ *See Sports and the Outdoors for information on bike tours.*

A novel way of seeing the city is to hop on one of the bike-rickshaws. The bike-powered two-seater cabs operate from Marienplatz and cost around €35 an hour; you can also let a driver take you on one of various city tours, from €35 for 30 minutes.

BUS TOURS

The best way to get a feel of Munich is to board one of the double-decker sightseeing buses with big signs that read "Stadtrundfahrten" (city sightseeing). They leave from across the main railway station. There are the blue ones run by Autobus Oberbayern and, 80 meters to the left, yellow and red ones run by Yellow Cab Muenchen. Tours cost €15 per person (cheaper if booked online) and offer hop-on, hop-off service throughout the City Center with commentary via headphones available in eight languages. There are numerous stops and the full tour takes about an hour. Both bus lines run about every 20 to 30 minutes,

Munich Public Transit System

2

between 9 am and 5 pm. The only difference is that the blue line has—in addition to the headphones for other languages—a live host who offers running commentary in English and German, so seamlessly that after five minutes you're sure you speak both languages. On the bus ask for a brochure with many other suggestions for bus trips.

WALKING TOURS

Radius Tours & Bikes has theme walks of Munich highlights, Third Reich Munich, and the Dachau concentration camp. Third Reich tours depart from the Radius offices, in the Hauptbahnhof, just across from Platform 32, daily at 3 pm between early April and mid-October (Friday to Tuesday at 11:30 am the rest of the year). The Dachau tour is daily at 9:15 and 12:15 from early April to mid-October and daily at 10 for the rest of the year. Advance booking is not necessary for individuals.

Gray Line Sightseeing Munich ⊠ *Hauptbahnhof, Bahnhofpl. 7, Ludwigvorstadt* ✛ *Wait outside Karstadt department store* ☎ *089/5490–7560* ⊕ *www.sightseeing-munich.com.*

Tour Information Munich Tourist Office ☎ *089/2339–6500* ⊕ *www.muenchen.de/tam.* **Radius Tours & Bike Rental** ⊠ *Hauptbahnhof, Arnulfstr. 3, Ludwigvorstadt* ✛ *The office is at the Hauptbahnhof, near Track 32* ☎ *089/54348–77740* ⊕ *www.radiustours.com.* **City Sightseeing Tours Munich** ⊠ *Bahnhofplatz, Elisenhof, Maxvorstadt* ✛ *Wait outside Elisenhof* ⊕ *www.citysightseeing-muenchen.de.*

VISITOR INFORMATION

The Munich Tourist office has two locations. The Hauptbahnhof (main train station) tourist office is open Monday through Saturday 9–8 and Sunday 10–6. The Tourist office in the Rathaus (town hall) is open weekdays 9–7, Saturday 9–6, and Sunday 10–4.

For information on the Bavarian mountain region south of Munich, contact the Tourismusverband München-Oberbayern.

As well as tourist offices, a great way to start your Munich visit is to go to infopoint, in the Alterhof's Kaiserburg, an information center for castles across Bavaria. Here, in a superbly atmospheric vaulted cellar, there are two films (ask for English versions), which combined make a great introduction to any Munich visit. One film is about the city's history, the other about the Alterhof. From Marienplatz, walk 170 meters down the attractive Burgstrasse, through the Alterhof tower. On the right is infopoint. Around 100 meters farther, you'll pass the Münzhof entrance, and another 50 meters is the Residenz Theater, next to the Residenz. Along with the films, this walk is an incredible 350-meter introduction to 1,000 years of Munich history.

Visitor Information Munich Tourist Office—Hauptbahnhof ⊠ *Hauptbahnhof, Bahnhofpl. 2, Ludwigvorstadt* ☎ *089/23396500* ⊕ *www.muenchen.de/tam.* **Munich Tourist Office—Rathaus** ⊠ *Tourist Office at Rathaus, Marienplatz 2, City Center* ☎ *089/2339–6500.* **Tourismusverband München-Oberbayern** (*Upper Bavarian Regional Tourist Office*). ⊕ *www.oberbayern.de.*

PLANNING YOUR TIME

Set aside at least a whole day for the Old Town, hitting Marienplatz when the glockenspiel plays at 11 am or noon before a crowd of spectators. There's a reason why Munich's Kaufingerstrasse has Germany's most expensive shop rents. Munich is Germany's most affluent city and Münchners like to spend. The pedestrian zone can get maddeningly full between noon and 2, when everyone in town seems to be taking a quick shopping break, though it's hardly any better up until around 5. If you've already seen the glockenspiel, try to avoid the area at that time. Avoid the museum crowds in Maxvorstadt by visiting as early in the day as possible. All Munich seems to discover an interest in art on Sunday, when most municipal and state-funded museums are €1; you might want to take this day off from culture and have a late breakfast or brunch at the Elisabethmarkt or around the Gärtnerplatz-Glockenbach areas. Some beer gardens and taverns have Sunday-morning jazz concerts. Many Schwabing bars have happy hours between 6 and 8—a relaxing way to end your day.

EXPLORING MUNICH

Munich is a wealthy city—and it shows. At times this affluence may come across as conservatism. But what makes Munich so unique is that it's a new city superimposed on the old. Hip neighborhoods are riddled with traditional locales, and flashy materialism thrives together with a love of the outdoors.

CITY CENTER

Munich's Old Town (Altstadt) has been rebuilt so often over the centuries that it no longer has the homogeneous look of so many other German towns. World War II leveled a good portion of the center, but an amazing job has been done to restore a bit of the fairy-tale feel that once prevailed here.

TOP ATTRACTIONS

FAMILY

Fodor's Choice

★

Deutsches Museum (*German Museum*). Aircraft, vehicles, cutting-edge technology, historic machinery, and even a mine fill a monumental building on an island in the Isar River, which comprises one of the best science and technology museums in the world. The collection is spread out over 47,000 square meters, six floors of exhibits, and about 50 exhibition areas. The Centre for New Technologies includes interactive exhibitions, such as nanotechnology, biotechnology, and robotics. It could change the way you think about science forever. Children have their own area, the Kinderreich, where they can learn about modern technology and science through numerous interactive displays (parents must accompany their children). One of the most technically advanced planetariums in Europe has four shows daily. The Internet café on the third floor is open daily 9–3, other cafés until 4. ■ TIP➔ To arrange for a two-hour tour in English, call at least six weeks in advance. The **Verkehrszentrum** (Center for Transportation), on the former trade fair grounds at the Theresienhöhe, has been completely renovated and

The Aeronautics Hall of the Deutsches Museum displays aircraft from the early days of flight to jets and helicopters.

houses an amazing collection of the museum's transportation exhibits. ✉ *Museumsinsel 1, Ludwigvorstadt* ☎ *089/21791* ⊕ *www.deutsches-museum.de* 🖃 *Museum €8.50* ⊘ *Daily 9–5* Ⓜ *Isartor (S-bahn)*.

Frauenkirche (*Church of Our Lady*). Munich's *Dom* (cathedral) is a distinctive late-Gothic brick structure with two huge towers. Each is 99 meters high, an important figure today because, in a nonbinding referendum, Münchners narrowly voted to restrict all new buildings to below this height within the city's middle ring road. The main body of the cathedral was completed in 20 years (1468–88)—a record time in those days—and the distinctive onion dome–like cupolas were added by 1525. Shortly after the original work was completed in 1688, Jörg von Halspach, the Frauenkirche's architect, died, but he became celebrated for the unique achievement of seeing through a project on such a scale from start to finish. The twin towers are easily the most recognized feature of the city skyline and a Munich trademark. In 1944–45, the building suffered severe damage during Allied bombing raids, and was restored between 1947 and 1957. Inside, the church combines most of von Halspach's plans, with a stark, clean modernity and simplicity of line, emphasized by slender, white octagonal pillars that sweep up through the nave to the tracery ceiling. As you enter the church, look on the stone floor for the dark imprint of a large foot—the *Teufelstritt* (Devil's Footprint). According to lore, the devil challenged von Halspach to build a church without windows. The architect accepted the challenge. When he completed the job, he led the devil to a spot in the bright church from which the 66-foot-high windows could not be seen. The devil triumphantly stomped his foot and left the Teufelstritt, only to be enraged when he ventured further inside and realized that windows had been included. The cathedral houses an elaborate 15th-century black-marble tomb guarded by four 16th-century armored knights. It's the final resting place of Duke Ludwig IV (1302–47), who became Holy Roman Emperor Ludwig the Bavarian in 1328. One of the Frauenkirche's great treasures is the collection of numerous wooden busts of the apostles, saints, and prophets above the choir, carved by the 15th-century Munich sculptor Erasmus Grasser. The observation platform high up in the south tower offers a splendid view of the city and the Alps. But beware, you must climb 86 steps to reach the tower elevator. ✉ *Frauenpl. 2, City Center* ☏ *089/290–0820* ✉ *Cathedral free, tower €3* ⊗ *Tower closed until at least 2015 for renovation* Ⓜ *Marienplatz (U-bahn and S-bahn).*

Marienplatz. Bordered by the Neues Rathaus, shops, and cafés, this square is named after the gilded statue of the Virgin Mary that has watched over it for more than three centuries. It was erected in 1638 at the behest of Elector Maximilian I as an act of thanksgiving for the city's survival of the Thirty Years War, the cataclysmic, partly religious struggle that devastated vast regions of Germany. When the statue was taken down from its marble column for cleaning in 1960, workmen found a small casket in the base containing a splinter of wood said to be from the cross of Christ. ■**TIP**➔ On the fifth floor of a building facing the Neues Rathaus is Café Glockenspiel. It overlooks the entire square and provides a perfect view of the glockenspiel from the front and **St. Peter's Church** from the back terrace. Entrance is around the back. ✉ *Bounded by Kaufingerstr., Rosenstr., Weinstr., and Dienerstr., City Center* Ⓜ *Marienplatz (U-bahn and S-bahn).*

Michaelskirche (*St. Michael's Church*). A curious story explains why this hugely impressive Renaissance church, adjoining a former extensive Jesuit college, has no tower. Seven years after the start of construction, in 1583, the main tower collapsed. Its patron, pious Duke Wilhelm V, regarded the disaster as a heavenly sign that the church wasn't big enough, so he ordered a change in the plans—this time without a tower. Completed in 1597, the barrel vaulting of St. Michael's is second in size only to that of St. Peter's in Rome. The duke is buried in the crypt, along with 40 other Wittelsbach family members, including the eccentric King Ludwig II. A severe neoclassical monument in the north transept contains the tomb of Napoleon's stepson, Eugène de Beauharnais, who married a daughter of King Maximilian I and died in Munich in 1824. Once again a Jesuit church, it is the venue for free performances of church music. A poster to the right of the front portal gives the dates. ✉ *Neuhauserstr. 6, City Center* ☏ *089/231–7060* ✉ *€2 crypt* ⊗ *Mon. and Fri. 10–7, Tues.–Thurs. and Sat. 8–7, Sun. 7–10:15; closed during services* Ⓜ *Karlsplatz (U-bahn and S-bahn).*

Neues Rathaus (*New Town Hall*). Munich's present neo-Gothic town hall was built in three sections and two phases between 1867 and 1908. It was a nessesary enlargement on the nearby Old Town Hall, but city fathers also saw it as presenting Munich as a modern city, independent from the waning powers of the Bavarian Wittelsbach royal house. Architectural historians are divided over its merits, although its dramatic scale and lavish detailing are impressive. Perhaps the most serious criticism is that the Dutch and Flemish styles of the building seem out of place amid the baroque and rococo styles of parts of the Altstadt. The main tower's 1908-finished **glockenspiel** (a chiming clock with mechanical figures), the largest in Germany, plays daily at 11 am, noon, and 9 pm, with an additional performance at 5 pm March through October. As chimes peal out over the square, the clock's doors flip open and brightly colored dancers and jousting knights act out two events from Munich's past: a tournament held in Marienplatz in 1568 and the *Schäfflertanz* (Dance of the Coopers), which commemorated the end of the plague of 1515–17. ■ TIP➜ You, too, can travel up there, by elevator, to an observation point near the top of one of the towers. On a clear day the view across the city and the Alps behind is spectacular. ✉ *Neues Rathaus, Marienpl. 8, City Center* 🏛 *Tower €2.50* 🕐 *Nov.–Apr., weekdays 10–5; May–Oct., Mon.–Sun. 10–7* Ⓜ *Marienplatz (U-bahn and S-bahn).*

Peterskirche (*St. Peter's Church*). The Altstadt's oldest parish church (called locally "Alter Peter," or "Old Peter") traces its origins to the 12th century, and has been restored in various architectural styles, including Gothic, baroque, and rococo. The rich baroque interior has a magnificent high altar and aisle pillars decorated with exquisite 18th-century figures of the apostles. In clear weather it's well worth the long climb up the approximately 300-foot-high tower, with a panoramic view of the Alps. ✉ *Rindermarkt 1, City Center* ☎ *089/260–4828* 🏛 *Tower €1.50* 🕐 *Summer, weekdays 9–6:30, weekends 10–6:30; winter, weekdays 9–5:30, weekends 10–5:30* Ⓜ *Marienplatz (U-bahn and S-bahn).*

Viktualienmarkt (*Victuals Market*). The city's open-air market really is the beating heart of downtown Munich. It has just about every fresh fruit or vegetable you can imagine, as well as German and international specialties. All kinds of people come here for a quick bite, from well-heeled businesspeople and casual tourists to mortar- and paint-covered workers. It's also the realm of the garrulous, sturdy market women who run the stalls with dictatorial authority. ■ TIP➜ Whether here, or at a bakery, do *not* try to select your pickings by hand. Ask, and let it be served to you. Try Poseidon's for quality fish treats, Mercado Latino on the south side of the market for an empanada and fine wines from South America, or Freisinger for Bavarian and Mediterranean delights. There's also a great beer garden (open pretty much whenever the sun is shining), where you can enjoy your snacks with cold local beer. A sign above the counter tells you what's on tap. The choice rotates throughout the year among the six major Munich breweries, which are displayed on the maypole. These are also the only six breweries officially allowed to serve their wares at the Oktoberfest. ✉ *15 Viktualienmarkt, City Center* 🕐 *Weekdays 10–6; Sat. 10–3* Ⓜ *Marienplatz (U-bahn and S-bahn).*

WORTH NOTING

Alter Hof (*Münchner Kaiserburg*). The Alter Hof was the original medieval residence of the Wittelsbachs, the ruling dynasty of Bavaria, established in 1180. The palace now serves various functions. Its **infopoint** serves as a tourist information center for Bavaria's many castles. Beneath this, in the atmospheric late-Gothic vaulted hall of the **Münchner Kaiserburg,** there is a multimedia presentation about the palace's history.

The west wing was previously home to the refined restaurant **Vinorant Alter Hof**; it's now closed, but rumor has it that another restaurant will take its place in 2014. ⊠ *Alter Hof 1, City Center* ☎ *089/2101–4050* ⊕ *www.alter-hof-muenchen.de* ☉ *Infopoint: Mon.–Sat. 10–6* Ⓜ *Marienplatz (U-bahn and S-bahn).*

FAMILY   **Altes Rathaus** (*Old Town Hall*). Much of the work on Munich's first town hall was done in the 15th century, though it had various alterations through the centuries. Its great hall—destroyed in 1943–45 but now fully restored—was the work of great architect Jörg von Halspach. Postwar the tower was rebuilt as it looked in the 15th century and now it's used for official receptions and is not usually open to the public. The tower provides a fairy-tale-like setting for the **Spielzeugmuseum** (Toy Museum), accessible via a winding staircase. Its toys, dolls, and teddy bears are on display, with a collection of Barbies from the United States. ⊠ *Marienpl. 15, City Center* ☎ *089/294–001 for Spielzeugmuseum* 🏛 *Museum €4 adults* ☉ *Daily 10–5:30* Ⓜ *Marienplatz (U-bahn and S-bahn).*

Asamkirche (*St.-Johann-Nepomuk-Kirche*). Perhaps Munich's most ostentatious church, it has a suitably extraordinary entrance, framed by raw rock foundations. The insignificant door, crammed between its craggy shoulders, gives little idea of the opulence and lavish detailing within the small 18th-century church (there are only 12 rows of pews). Above the doorway St. Nepomuk, the 14th-century Bohemian monk and patron saint of Bavaria, who drowned in the Danube, is being led by angels from a rocky riverbank to heaven. The church's official name is Church of St. Johann Nepomuk, but it's known as the Asamkirche for its architects, the brothers Cosmas Damian and Egid Quirin Asam. The interior of the church is a prime example of true southern German late-baroque architecture. Frescoes by Cosmas Damian Asam and rosy marble cover the walls. The sheer wealth of statues and gilding is stunning—there's even a gilt skeleton at the sanctuary's portal. ⊠ *Sendlinger Str. 32, City Center* ☉ *Daily 9–5:30* Ⓜ *Sendlingertor (U-bahn).*

Deutsches Jagd- und Fischereimuseum (*German Museum of Hunting and Fishing*). This quirky museum is in the enormous former St. Augustus Church, and it contains the world's largest collection of fishhooks, some 500 stuffed animals (including a 6½-foot-tall North American grizzly bear), a 12,000-year-old skeleton of a deer found in Ireland, and a valuable collection of hunting weapons. You'll even find the mythical *Wolpertinger,* the Bavarian equivalent of the jackalope. The museum also sells fine hunting equipment, from knives and rifles to sturdy clothing. ⊠ *Neuhauserstr. 2, City Center* ☎ *089/220–522* ⊕ *www.jagd-fischerei-museum.de* 🏛 *€3.50* ☉ *Fri.–Wed. 9:30–5, Thurs. 9:30–9* Ⓜ *Karlsplatz (U-bahn and S-bahn).*

Hauptbahnhof (*Central Station*). The train station isn't a cultural site, but it's a particularly handy starting point for exploring. The city tourist office here has maps and helpful information on events around town. On the underground level are all sorts of shops that remain open even on Sunday and holidays. There are also a number of places to get a late-night snack in and around the station. ⊠ *Bahnhofpl., Hauptbahnhof* ☎ *089/1308–10555* ⊕ *www.hauptbahnhof-muenchen.de* Ⓜ *Hauptbahnhof (U-bahn and S-bahn).*

Jewish Center Munich (*Jüdisches Zentrum*). The striking new Jewish Center at St.-Jakobs-Platz has transformed a formerly sleepy area into an elegant, busy modern square. The buildings signify the return of the Jewish community to Munich's city center, six decades after the end of the Third Reich. The center includes a museum focusing on Jewish history in Munich (plus kosher café), and the impressive Ohel Jakob Synagogue (⊕ *www.juedisches-museum-muenchen.de*), with its rough slabs topped by a latticelike cover, manifesting a thought-provoking sense of permanence. The third building is a community center, which includes the kosher Einstein restaurant (⊕ *www.einstein-restaurant.de*). Guided tours of the synagogue are in great demand, so to see it, arrange a time weeks in advance (☎ *089/202400–100*). ✉ *St.-Jakobspl. 16, City Center* ☎ *089/233–989–96096* ⊕ *www.ikg-m.de* 🖭 *Museum €6; synagogue tour €5* ⊗ *Museum Tues.–Sun. 10–6; synagogue by appointment* Ⓜ *Marienplatz (U-bahn and S-bahn).*

Karlsplatz. In 1728 Eustachius Föderl opened an inn and beer garden here, which, according to one theory, is why it became known as Stachus. The beer garden is long gone, but the name has remained—locals still refer to this busy intersection as Stachus. One of Munich's most popular fountains is here—it acts as a magnet on hot summer days, when city shoppers and office workers seek a place to relax. ▥**TIP**➜ **In winter it makes way for an ice-skating rink.** It's a bustling meeting point, more so since the complete renovation and extension of the underground shopping center in 2010–11. ✉ *Karlspl.* ⊕ *www.stachus-passagen.com* Ⓜ *Karlsplatz (U-bahn and S-bahn).*

Münchner Stadtmuseum (*City Museum*). On St.-Jakobs-Platz, this museum is as eclectic inside as the architecture is outside. The buildings, facing St.-Jakobs-Platz, originally date to the 15th century, though were destroyed by Allied bombs in 1944–45 and subsequently rebuilt. Recent extensive renovation has revitalized the City Museum, exemplified by its fabulous **Typical Munich!** exhibition, charting a riotous history few other city's can match: royal capital, brewery center, capital of art and classical music, and now wealthy, high-tech and cultural center par excellence. There is also a separate, permanent exhibtion dealing with the city's Nazi past. The museum is home to a film museum showing rarely screened movies, a puppet theater, while there are numerous photo and other temporary exhibitions. Checkout the museum shop, servus.heimat, with the great and good of Munich kitsch, and some pretty good Munich souvenirs. ▥**TIP**➜ **Even the threat of sunshine makes it difficult to get a table outside the lively museum café on St.-Jakobs-Platz. Try the inner courtyard, which still catches the sun but can be less packed.** ✉ *St.-Jakobs-Pl. 1, City Center* ☎ *089/2332–2370* ⊕ *www.stadtmuseum-online.de* 🖭 *€4 (€6 special exhibitions), €1 Sun.* ⊗ *Tues.–Sun. 10–6* Ⓜ *Marienplatz (U-bahn and S-bahn).*

Münzhof (*Mint*). Originally built between 1563 and 1567, the ground floor was home to Duke Albrecht V's stables, the second to living quarters for the servants, and the third for the ducal collection of high art and curiosities (6,000 pieces by 1600). Between 1809 and 1983 it was home to the Bavarian mint, and a neoclassical facade, with allegories to copper, silver, and gold, was added in 1808–09. Today, with its slightly

KEY

⌐⌐ *Pedestrian Shopping Zone*

🛈 *Tourist information*

Ⓤ *U-Bahn*

SCHWABING

University

Ⓤ Universität

Englischer Garten

Haus der Kunst

Hofgarten

Residenz

ROYAL MUNICH

Nationaltheater

St. Anna Pl.

Deutsches Museum

HAIDHAUSEN

garish green exterior on three sides, it can appear to be little more than the slightly undistinguished home to the Bavarian Land Bureau for the Conservation of Historic Monuments. But step inside the inner arcade to see a jewel of German Renaissance architecture. ⊠ *Hofgraben 4, City Center* ✛ *Entrance via Pfisterstr.* ▨ *Free* ⊙ *Mon.–Thurs. 8–4, Fri. 8–2* Ⓜ *Marienplatz (U-bahn and S-bahn).*

ROYAL MUNICH

From the modest palace of the Alter Hof, the Wittelsbachs expanded their quarters northward, away from the jumble of narrow streets in the old quarter. Three splendid avenues radiated outward from their new palace and garden grounds, and fine homes arose along them. One of them—Prinzregentenstrasse—marks the southern edge of Munich's huge public park, the Englischer Garten, a present from the royal family to the locals. Lehel, an upmarket residential neighborhood that straddles Prinzregentenstrasse, plays host to one of Munich's most famous museums, the Haus der Kunst, as well as to some lesser-known but architecturally stunning museums.

TOP ATTRACTIONS

Englischer Garten (*English Garden*). Bigger than New York's Central Park and London's Hyde Park, this seemingly endless green space blends into the open countryside at the north of the city. It was a former favorite royal hunting ground until partly opened to the public by Benjamin Thompson, later Count Rumford, a great American-British reformer and scientist. Born in Massachusetts, he left after siding with the British during the Revolutionary War. Thompson's Munich garden plans were expanded on and the park became a gift from Elector Karl Theodor to the people of Munich. Today's park covers more than 1,000 acres and has 78 km (48 miles) of paths, 8.5 km (5.2 miles) of streams, and more than 100 foot- and other bridges. The open, informal landscaping—reminiscent of the rolling parklands with which English aristocrats of the 18th century liked to surround their country homes—gave the park its name. It has a boating lake, four beer gardens, and a series of curious decorative and monumental constructions, including the Monopteros, a Greek temple designed by Leo von Klenze for King Ludwig I, and built in 1837 on an artificial hill in the southern section of the park. There are great sunset views of Munich from the Monopteros hill. In the center of the park's most popular beer garden is a Chinese pagoda, erected in 1790. It was destroyed during the war and then reconstructed. ■TIP➜ The Chinese Tower beer garden is hugely popular, but the park has prettier places for sipping a beer: the Aumeister, for example, along the northern perimeter, is in an early-19th-century hunting lodge. At the Seehaus, on the shore of the Kleinhesseloher *See* (lake), choose between a smart restaurant or a cozy *Bierstube* (beer tavern) in addition to the beer garden right on the lake.

The Englischer Garten is a paradise for joggers, cyclists, musicians, soccer players, sunbathers, and, in winter, cross-country skiers. The park has semi-official areas for nude sunbathing—the Germans have a positively pagan attitude toward the sun—so in some areas don't be surprised to see naked bodies bordering the flower beds and paths. ⊠ *Main entrances at various points on Prinzregentenstr. and Königin-str., City Center/Schwabing.*

Feldherrnhalle (*Field Marshals' Hall*). Erected in 1841–44, this open pavilion, fronted with three huge arches, was modeled on the 14th-century Loggia dei Lanzi in Florence. It opens the grand Ludwigstrasse (closed by the Siegestor) on Odeonsplatz, and was built to honor Bavarian military leaders and the Bavarian army. Two huge Bavarian lions are flanked by the larger-than-life statues of Count Johann Tserclaes Tilly, who led Catholic forces in the Thirty Years' War, and Prince Karl Philipp Wrede, hero of the 19th-century Napoleonic Wars.

There's an astonishing photograph of a 25-year-old Adolf Hitler standing in front of the Feldherrnhalle on August 2, 1914, amid a huge crowd gathered to celebrate the beginning of World War I. The imposing structure was turned into a militaristic shrine in the 1930s and '40s by the Nazis, to whom it was significant because it marked the site of Hitler's abortive coup, or *Putsch*, in 1923 (today, there's a plaque on the ground, 20 meters from the lion on the left, commemorating the four policemen who were killed in the putsch attempt). During the Third Reich, all who passed it had to give the Nazi salute. Viscardigasse, a tiny alley behind the Feldherrnhalle, linking Residenzstrasse and Theatinerstrasse, and now lined with exclusive boutiques, was used by those who wanted to dodge the routine. Its nickname was *Drückebergergassl*, or Dodgers' Alley. ⊠ *South end of Odeonspl., Residenzstr. 1, City Center* Ⓜ *Odeonsplatz (U-bahn).*

Haus der Kunst (*House of Art*). This colonnaded, classical-style building is one of Munich's most significant examples of Hitler-era architecture, and was officially opened as Haus der Deustchen Kunst (House of German Art) by the Führer himself. During the Third Reich it showed only work deemed to reflect the Nazi aesthetic. One of its most successful postwar exhibitions was devoted to works banned by the Nazis. It now hosts cutting-edge exhibitions on art, photography, and sculpture, as well as theatrical and musical happenings. After the departure to London's prestigious Tate Modern in October 2011 of the gallery's hugely successful director Chris Derkon, Nigerian-born (formerly U.S.-based) Okwui Enwezor has made a good start. The survival-of-the-chicest disco, P1, is in the building's west wing. ⊠ *Prinzregentenstr. 1, Lehel* ☎ *089/2112–7113* ⊕ *www.hausderkunst.de* 🎟 *Varies €5–€15* ✆ *Mon.–Sun. 10–8, Thurs. 10–10* Ⓜ *Odeonsplatz (U-bahn).*

Hofbräuhaus. Duke Wilhelm V founded Munich's most famous brewery in 1589; it's been at its present location since 1808. As beer and restaurants became major players in the city's economy, it needed to be completely rebuilt and modernized in 1897. The last major work was its reconstruction in 1950 after its destruction in the war. Hofbräu means "court brewery," and the golden beer is poured in pitcher-size liter mugs. If the cavernous ground-floor hall is too noisy for you, there is a quieter restaurant upstairs. In this legendary establishment Americans, Australians, and Italians often far outnumber locals, who regard it as too much of a tourist trap. The brass band that performs here most days adds modern pop and American folk music to the traditional German numbers. ⊠ *Platzl 9, City Center* ☎ *089/2913–6100* ☉ *Daily 9–11:30* Ⓜ *Marienplatz (U-bahn and S-bahn).*

Hofgarten (*Court Garden*). The formal court garden was once part of the royal palace grounds, dating back to at least the early 15th century. It's now bordered on two sides by arcades designed in the 19th century by court architect Leo von Klenze. On the east side of the garden is the state chancellery (office of the Bavarian Minister President), built in 1990–93 around the ruins of the 19th-century Army Museum and incorporating the remains of a Renaissance arcade. Bombed during World War II air raids, the museum stood untouched for almost 40 years as a reminder of the war. Critics were horrified that a former army museum building could be used to represent modern, democratic Bavaria, not to mention about the immense cost. In front of the chancellery stands one of Europe's most unusual—some say most effective—war memorials. Instead of looking up at a monument, you are led down to a **sunken crypt** covered by a massive granite block. In the crypt lies a German soldier from World War I. The crypt is a stark contrast to the **memorial** that stands unobtrusively in front of the northern wing of the chancellery: a simple cube of black marble bearing facsimiles of handwritten wartime manifestos by anti-Nazi leaders, including the youthful members of the White Rose resistance movement. ▥**TIP**➔ **As you enter the garden from Odeonsplatz, take a look at the frescoes (drawn by art students 1826–29 and of varying degrees of quality) in the passage of the Hofgartentor with depictions from Bavarian history.** ⊠ *Hofgartenstr., north of Residenz, City Center* Ⓜ *Odeonsplatz (U-bahn).*

Residenz (*Royal Palace*). One of Germany's true treasures, Munich's royal Residenz (Residence) began in 1363 as the modest **Neuveste** (New Fortress) on the northeastern city boundary. By the time the Bavarian monarchy fell, in 1918, the palace could compare favorably with the best in Europe. The Wittelsbach dukes moved here when the tenements of an expanding Munich encroached on their Alter Hof. In succeeding centuries the royal residence developed according to the importance, requirements, and whims of its occupants. It came to include, for example, the Königsbau (on Max-Joseph-Platz); the Festsaal (Banquet Hall); the newly renovated Cuvilliés-Theater (Altes Residenztheater); the Allerheiligen-Hofkirche (All Saints' Church); and the adjoining Nationaltheater (Bavarian State Opera).

Fire was one of the biggest fears for all citizens for centuries: in 1674, fire destroyed large parts of the palace on Residenzstr., while most of the Neuevest complex burned to the ground in 1750, including the theater. This meant a new court theater was needed, and the result was the incomparable rococo Cuvilliés-Theater.

With the Residenz's central location, it was pretty much inevitable that the Allied bombing of 1944–45 would cause immense damage, and susbequent reconstruction took decades. For tourists today, however, it really is a treasure chamber of delight. To wander around the Residenz can last anywhere from 3 hours to all day. The 16th-century, 70-meter-long arched **Antiquarium,** built for Duke Albrecht

V's collection of antiques and library, is recognized as one of the most impressive Renaissance creations outside Italy (today it's used chiefly for state receptions). There are a number of halls and courtyards that show concerts, from the postwar **Neuer Herkulessaal** to the outdoor **Brunnenhof.** And particular favorites for visitors are the re-creation of many private royal chambers and apartments. The accumulated Wittelsbach treasures are on view in several museums that comprise the Residenz. ■■■TIP➜ **All the different rooms, halls, galleries, chapels, and museums within the Residenzmuseum, as well as the Cuvilliés-Theater and Treasury, can be visited with a combination ticket that costs €13.** ⊠ *Max-Joseph-Pl. 3, City Center* ☎ *089/290–671* ⊕ *www.residenz-muenchen.de* ⊙ *Museum and Treasury mid-Apr. –mid-Oct., daily 9–6; mid-Oct.–mid-Mar., daily 10–5* Ⓜ *Odeonsplatz (U-bahn).*

Schatzkammer (*Treasury*). The Schatzkammer comprises many hundreds of masterworks, including a host of treasures from the Wittelsbach royal crown jewels. A highlight is the crown belonging to Bavaria's first king, Maximilian I, created in Paris in 1806–07. The Schatzkammer collection has a staggering centerpiece—a renowned 50-cm-high Renaissance statue of St. George studded with diamonds, pearls, and rubies. ⊠ *1a Residenzstr.* ▧ *€7, combined ticket with Residenzmuseum €11* ⊙ *Mid-Apr.–mid-Oct., daily 9–6; mid-Oct.–mid-Mar., daily 10–5.*

Residenzmuseum (*Museum*). The Residenzmuseum comprises everything in the Residenz apart from the Schatzkammer and the Cuvilliés-Theater. Paintings, tapestries, furniture, and porcelain are housed in various rooms and halls. Look out for the **Grüne Galerie (Green Gallery),** named after its green silk decoration, and the great and the good of the Wittelsbach royal family in the Ahnengalerie (Ancestral Gallery). Entrance on Max-Jospeh-Platz. ⊠ *Max-Koseph-Pl., Altstadt-Lehel* ▧ *€7* ⊙ *Mid-Apr.–mid-Oct., daily 9–6; mid-Oct.–mid-Mar., daily 10–5.*

Staatliche Münzsammlung(*State Coin Collection*). More than 300,000 coins, bank notes, medals and stones, some 5,000 years old, star in the Staatliche Münzsammlung. ⊠ *1 Residenzstr.* ✛ *Entrance via Residenzstr.* ☎ *089/227–221* ▧ *€2.50, €1 Sun.* ⊙ *Tues.–Sun. 10–5.*

Staatliche Sammlung Ägyptischer Kunst(*State Collection of Egyptian Art*). Various Bavarian rulers were fascinated with the ancient world and in the 19th century accumulated huge quantities of significant Egyptian treasures, part of which make up the Staatliche Sammlung Ägyptischer Kunst. In 2013 the collection moved from the Residenz to an impressive new building in Munich's superb Kunstareal (Art Quarter). ⊠ *Arcisstr. 16, Maxvorstadt* ☎ *089/2892–7630* ⊕ *www.aegyptisches-museum-muenchen.de* ▧ *€7, Sun. €1* ⊙ *Wed.–Sun. 10–6, Tues. 10–8* Ⓜ *Königsplatz (U-bahn).*

Cuvilliés-Theater (*Bavarian State Opera*). This stunning example of a rococo theater was originally built by court architet François Cuvilliés between 1751 and 1753 and it soon became the most famous in Germany. In 1781 it premiered Mozart's *Idomeneo*, commissioned by the Elector of Bavaria, Karl Theodor. The lavish rococo style went out of fashion with the emergence of the less ostentatious, more elegant period of 18th classicism. But in 1884 it became the first theater in Germany to be fitted out with electric lighting and in 1896 the first to have a revolving stage. As with so much of the Altstadt, it was destroyed during Allied bombing raids, although some of the original rococo decoration had been removed. In its place the New Residenztheater (now the Bavarian State Drama Theatre Company) was built (1948–51). In 1956–58, using some of the original rococo furnishings, Cuvilliés's lavish theater was rebuilt in its present location, at a corner of the Residenz's Apothekenhof (courtyard). After extensive restoration work, it reopened in 2008 with a performance of *Idomeneo*. It's home to the hugely respected Bavarian State Opera, led by American conductor Kent Nagano. ✉ *Max-Joseph-Pl. 2* ✛ *Enter via Residenzstr. 1* ⊕ *www.bayerische.staatsoper.de for opera tickets* 🎟 *€3 to view the theater* ⏲ *Closed during rehearsals.*

Theatinerkirche (St. Kajetan) (*Theatine Church*). This glorious baroque church owes its Italian appearance to its founder, Princess Henriette Adelaide of Savoy, who commissioned it in gratitude for the birth of her son and heir, Max Emanuel, in 1662. A native of Turin, the princess distrusted Bavarian architects and builders and thus summoned Agostino Barelli, a master builder from Bologna, to construct her church. It is modeled on Rome's Sant'Andrea della Valle. Barelli worked on the building for 12 years, but he was dismissed for being too quarrelsome. It was another 100 years before the building was finished in a style similar to today's. Its striking yellow facade stands out, and its two lofty towers, topped by delightful cupolas, frame the entrance, with the central dome at the back. The superb stuccowork on the inside has a remarkably light feeling owing to its brilliant white color. ■ TIP➔ The expansive Odeonsplatz in front of the Feldherrnhalle and Theatinerkirche is often used for outdoor stage events. ✉ *Theatinerstr. 22, City Center* ☎ *089/210–6960* Ⓜ *Odeonsplatz (U-bahn).*

Tambosi. Open since 1775, Tambosi is Munich's longest-running café. As well as an impressive provenance, its location is superb, partly sitting in full view of Theatinerkirche on Odeonsplatz and partly in the Hofgarten. Watch the hustle and bustle of Munich's street life from an outdoor table in the city side, or retreat through a gate in the Hofgarten's western wall to the café's tree-shaded beer garden. If the weather is cool or rainy, find a corner in the cozy, eclectically furnished interior. ✉ *Odeonspl. 18, City Center* ☎ *089/298–322* ⊕ *www.tambosi.de.*

WORTH NOTING

Archäologische Staatssammlung (*Bavarian State Archaeological Collection*). This is Bavaria's fascinating record of its prehistoric, Roman, and Celtic past. The perfectly preserved body of a ritually sacrificed young girl, recovered from a Bavarian peat moor, is among the more spine-chilling exhibits. Head down to the basement to see the fine Roman mosaic floor. ✉ *Lerchenfeldstr. 2, Lehel* ☎ *089/211–2402* ⊕ *www.archaeologie-bayern.de* 🎟 *€1* ⏲ *Tues.–Sun. 9:30–5* Ⓜ *Lehel (U-bahn), Nationalmuseum (Tram).*

Bayerisches Nationalmuseum (*Bavarian National Museum*). Although the museum places emphasis on Bavarian cultural history, it has art and artifacts of international importance and regular exhibitions that attract worldwide attention. The museum is a journey through time, principally from the early Middle Ages to the 20th century, with medieval and Renaissance wood carvings, works by the great Renaissance sculptor Tilman Riemenschneider, tapestries, arms and armor, a unique collection of Christmas crèches (the *Krippenschau*), Bavarian and German folk art and a significant Jugendstil collection. ⊠ *Prinzregentenstr. 3, Lehel* ☎ *089/211–2401* ⊕ *www.bayerisches-nationalmuseum.de* ☜ *€7 combined ticket for museum and Bollert collection, €1 Sun.* ⊙ *Tues., Wed., Fri.–Sun. 10–5, Thurs. 10–8* Ⓜ *Lehel (U-bahn).*

DenkStätte Weisse Rose (*Memorial to the White Rose Resistance Group*). Siblings Hans and Sophie Scholl, fellow students Alexander Schmorell and Christian Probst, and Kurt Huber, professor of philosophy, were the key members of the Munich-based resistance movement against the Nazis in 1942–43 known as the Weisse Rose (White Rose). All were executed by guillotine. A small exhibition about their work is in the inner quad of the university, where the Scholls were caught distributing leaflets and denounced by the janitor. ⊠ *Ludwig-Maximilians-Universität, Geschwister-Scholl-Pl. 1, Maxvorstadt* ☎ *089/2180–3053* ☜ *Free* ⊙ *Nov.–Mar., weekdays 10–4; Apr.–Oct., Sat. 11:30–2:30* Ⓜ *Universität (U-bahn).*

Kunsthalle der Hypo-Kulturstiftung (*Hall of the Hypobank's Cultural Foundation*). Chagall, Giacometti, Picasso, and Gauguin are among the artists featured in the past at this highly regarded exhibition hall in the middle of the commercial pedestrian zone, within the upscale **Fünf Höfe shopping mall**, designed by the Swiss architect team Herzog and de Meuron, who also designed London's Tate Modern. Exhibitions at the Kunsthalle rarely disappoint, making it one Germany's most interesting exhibition venues. It often works in cooperation with international institutes of the highest repute, such as in its 2010 version of London's Victorian & Albert Museum Maharja exhibition. The accompanying Cafe Kunsthalle is a destination for exhibition visitors and general public alike. The very good main menu changes weekly, though it's worth a visit just for the cakes. ⊠ *Theatinerstr. 8, City Center* ☎ *089/224–412* ⊕ *www.hypo-kunsthalle.de* ☜ *Varies but usually around €10* ⊙ *Daily 10–8; Cafe Kunsthalle weekdays 8:30–8, Sat. 9–8, Sun. 10–8* Ⓜ *Odeonsplatz (U-bahn).*

Ludwigskirche (*Ludwig's Church*). Planted halfway along the stark, neoclassical Ludwigstrasse is this superb twin-towered Byzantine- and Italian-influenced church, built between 1829 and 1838 at the behest of King Ludwig I to provide his newly completed suburb with a parish church. From across the other side of the road, look up to see the splendidly colored, 2009-finished mosaic on the church's roof. Inside, see one of the great modern frescoes, the *Last Judgment* by Peter von Cornelius, in the choir. At 60 feet by 37 feet, it's also one of the world's largest. ⊠ *Ludwigstr. 20, Maxvorstadt* ☎ *089/287–7990* ⊙ *Daily 7–7* Ⓜ *Universität (U-bahn).*

2

Maximilianstrasse. Munich's most expensive and exclusive shopping street was named after King Maximilian II, who wanted to break away from the Greek-influenced classical architecture favored by his father, Ludwig I. He thus created this broad boulevard lined with majestic buildings culminating on a rise above the river Isar at the stately **Maximilianeum.** Finished in 1874, this building was conceived as an elite education foundation for the most talented young people across Bavaria, regardless of status or wealth. It is still home to an education foundation, but its principle role is as the grand, if slightly confined, home to the Bavarian state parliament. ■ TIP➔ Rather than take the tram to see the Maximilianeum, the whole walk along Maximilianstrasse (from Max-Joesph-Platz) is rewarding. You'll pass various boutiques, plus the five-star Hotel Vier Jahreszeiten, the Upper Bavarian Parliament, the Museum für Völkerkunde (State Museum of Ethnology) and cross the picturesque river Isar. Five minutes past the Maximilianeum, on the charming Wiener Platz, is the Hofbräukeller and its excellent beer garden. ✉ *Maximilianstrasse* Ⓜ *Maximilianeum (Tram).*

Museum Villa Stuck. This dramatic neoclassical villa is the former home of one of Germany's leading avant-garde artists from the turn of the 20th century, Franz von Stuck (1863–1928). His work, at times haunting, frequently erotic, and occasionally humorous, covers the walls of the ground-floor rooms. Stuck was prominent in the Munich art Secession (1892), though the museum is today famous for its fabulous Jugendstil (art nouveau) collections. The museum also features the artist's former quarters as well as special exhibits. ✉ *Prinzregentstr. 60, Haidhausen* ☎ *089/455–5510* ⊕ *www.villastuck.de* 💶*€9* ⊙ *Tues.–Sun. 11–6 (1st Fri. of month till 10)* Ⓜ *Prinzregentenplatz (U-bahn).*

Nationaltheater (*National Theater*). Bavaria's original National Theater at Max-Joseph-Platz didn't last long. Though opened in 1818, in 1823, before it was completely finished, it burned to the ground. It had been rebuilt by 1825 with its eight-column portico, and went on to premiere Richard Wagner's world-famous *Tristan und Isolde* (1865), *Meistersinger von Nürnberg* (1868), *Rheingold* (1869), and *Walküre* (1870). Allied bombs destroyed much of the interior in 1943, and its facade and elements of its interior were rebuilt as it was prewar. It finally reopened in 1963. Today, it is one of Europe's largest opera houses and contains some of the world's most advanced stage technologies. Moreover, as the principle home to the Bavarian State Opera, it is considered one of the world's outstanding opera houses. ⇨ *See also Cuvilliès-Theatre and Prinzregententheater, which are also home to the Bavarian State Opera.* ✉ *Max-Joseph-Pl. 2, City Center* ☎ *089/218–501 for tickets* ⊕ *www.bayerische.staatsoper.de* Ⓜ *Odeonsplatz (U-bahn).*

Sammlung Schack (*Schack-Galerie*). Around 180 German 19th-century paintings from the Romantic era up to the periods of Realism and Symbolism make up the collections of the Sammlung Schack, originally the private collection of Count Adolf Friedrich von Schack. ■ TIP➔ A day ticket to the state museums of the three Pinakotheks, Brandhorst, and Sammlung Schack costs €12. ✉ *Prinzregentstr. 9, Lehel* ☎ *089/2380–5224* ⊕ *www.sammlungschack.de* 💶*€4, €1 Sun.* ⊙ *Wed.–Sun. 10–6 (1st and 3rd Wed. of the month till 8)* Ⓜ *Lehel (U-bahn).*

Siegestor (*Victory Arch*). Built to bookend the Feldherrnhalle and mark the end of Ludwigstrasse, Siegestor nowadays also marks the beginning of Leopoldstrasse. Unsurprisingly, it has Italian origins and was modeled on the Arch of Constantine in Rome, and was built (1849) to honor the achievements of the Bavarian army during the Wars of Liberation (1813–15) against Napoléon. It received heavy bomb damage in 1944, and at the end of the war Munich authorities decided it should be torn down for safety reasons. Major Eugene Keller, the head of the U.S. military government in the postwar city intervened and saved it. Its postwar inscription on the side facing the inner city is best translated as: "dedicated to victory, destroyed by war, a monument to peace." ⊠ *Intersection of Leopoldstr. and Shackstr., Maxvorstadt* Ⓜ *Universität (U-bahn).*

Staatliches Museum für Völkerkunde (*State Museum of Ethnology*). Arts and crafts from around the world are displayed in this extensive museum. There are also regular special exhibits. ⊠ *Maximilianstr. 42, Altstadt-Lehel* ☎ *089/2101–36100* ⊕ *www.voelkerkundemuseum-muenchen.de* ☜ *€5, €1 Sun.* ☉ *Tues.–Sun. 9:30–5:30* Ⓜ *Lehel (U-bahn), Maxmonument (Tram).*

SCHWABING AND MAXVORSTADT

Some of the finest museums in Europe are in lower Schwabing and Maxvorstadt, particularly the *Kunstareal* (Art Quarter), crossing Barer Strasse and Theresienstrasse. Schwabing, the former artists' neighborhood, is no longer quite the bohemian area where such diverse residents as Lenin and Kandinsky were once neighbors, but the cultural foundations of Maxvorstadt are immutable. Where the two areas meet, in the streets behind the university, life hums with a creative vibrancy probably only matched in the Gärtnerplatz-Glockenbach areas. The difficult part is having time to see it all.

Head east or west of Leopoldstrasse to explore the side streets: around Wedekindplatz near Münchner Freiheit, a few hundred yards from the Englischer Garten, or enjoy the shops and cafés in the student quarter to the west of Leopoldstrasse. On Sunday, €1 gets you admission to all three of the fantastic Pinakothek museums and Museum Brandhorst. As for snacks along the way as you explore, Elisabethmarkt is the place to pick up a quick bite to eat or to relax with a beer in the small beer garden.

TOP ATTRACTIONS

Fodor'sChoice
★

Alte Pinakothek. With numerous Old Master paintings from the Netherlands, Italy, France, and Germany, the long redbrick Alte Pinakothek holds one of the most significant art collections in the world. It was originally constructed by Leo von Klenze between 1826 and 1836 to exhibit the collection of 14th- to 18th-century works (started by Duke Wilhelm IV in the 16th century). Wittelsbach rulers through the centuries were avid collectors and today the collection comprises about 700 pieces. Among the European masterpieces on view are paintings by Dürer, Titian, Rembrandt, da Vinci, Rubens (the museum has one of the world's largest Rubens collections), and two celebrated Murillos. Most of the picture captions are in German only, so it is best to rent an English audio guide, although the audio tour does not cover every painting. Nevertheless, this museum is not to be missed. Along with the Pinakothek der Moderne, Neue Pinakothek, and Museum Brandhorst, the Alter Pinakothek forms a central part of Munich's world-class Kunstareal. Museums and collections here are of the highest quality, and are a few hundred meters apart. ■ TIP➡ **To save money, get a Tageskarte, which provides entry to all these museums (plus the Schack Gallery, in Lehel) for just €12.** ✉ *Barerstr. 27 (entrance facing Theresienstr.), Maxvorstadt* ☎ *089/2380–5216* ⊕ *www. pinakothek.de* ✎ *€9, €1 Sun.* ☉ *Wed.–Sun. 10–6, Tues. 10–8* Ⓜ *Königsplatz (U-bahn).*

Königsplatz. Bavaria's greatest monarch, Ludwig I, was responsible for Munich in the 19th century becoming known as Athens on the Isar, and the impressive buildings designed by Leo von Klenze that line this elegant and expansive square bear testement to his obsession with antiquity. The two templelike structures facing one another are now the **Antikensammlungen** (an acclaimed collection of Greek and Roman antiquities) and the **Glyptothek** (a fine collection of Greek and Roman statues) museums. During the Third Reich, this was a favorite parade ground for the Nazis, and it was paved over for that purpose in the 1930s. Although today a busy road passes through it, Munich authorities ensured the square returned to the more dignified appearance intended by Ludwig I. Today, the broad green lawns in front of the museums attract students and tourists in the warmer months, who gather for concerts, films, and other events. ■ TIP➡ **The area around here, focused on Briennerstrasse, became the national center of the Nazi Party in the 1930s and '40s, with various buildings taken over or built by Nazi authorities.** Nazi headquarters—the Brown House—was between Königsplatz and the obelisk at Karolinenplatz. Destroyed in the war, the new Munich Documentation Centre for the History of National Socialism is due to open here in 2014. On Arcisstrasse 12 is the Nazi-era building (now a music school) where in 1938 Britain's Prime Minister, Neville Chamberlain, infamously thought he had negotiated "peace in our time" with Hitler. ✉ *1 Königspl., Maxvorstadt* ☎ *089/5998–8830 for Antikensammlungen, 089/286–100 for Glyptothek* ✎ *Both €3.50; combination card €5.50* ☉ *Antikensammlungen: Thurs.–Tue. 10–5, Wed. 10–8. Glyptothek: Fri.–Wed. 10–5; Thurs. 10–8* Ⓜ *Königsplatz (U-bahn).*

Museum Brandhorst. This multicolor abstract box is filled with videos, painting, sculptures, and installations by artists such as Andy Warhol, Damien Hirst, Gerhard Richter, and Joseph Beuys, and is a real treat for contemporary art fans. The location in the middle of the historic Kunstareal art district, although shocking to some less progressive art aficionados, highlighted that the city has broken out of the shackles of its postwar conservatism. ■ TIP➡ **Königsplatz U-Bahn is a simple way to get to the Kunstareal, though it involves a pleasant 15-minute walk. Tram No. 27 takes you directly from Karlsplatz to the Pinakothek stop, in the heart of the Kunstareal.** ✉ *Theresienstr. 35a, Maxvorstadt* ☎ *089/2380–52286* ⊕ *www.museum-brandhorst.de* ✎ *€7, €1 Sun.* ☉ *Tues., Wed., and Fri.–Sun. 10–6, Thurs. 10–8* Ⓜ *Königsplatz (U-bahn), Pinakotheken (Tram).*

The Glyptothek museum on Königsplatz houses Greek and Roman statues.

Fodor's Choice ★

Neue Pinakothek. Another museum packed with masters, the fabulous Neue Pinakothek reopened in 1981 to house the royal collection of modern art left homeless and scattered after its original building was destroyed in the war. The exterior of the modern building mimics an older one with Italianate influences. The interior offers a magnificent environment for picture gazing, partly owing to the natural light flooding in from skylights. French impressionists—Monet, Degas, Manet—are all well represented, while the comprehensive collection also includes great Romantic landscape painters Turner and Caspar David Friedrich, and other artists of the caliber of Van Gogh, Cezanne, and Monet. This is another must-see. ⊠ *Barerstr. 29, Maxvorstadt* ☎ *089/2380–5195* ⊕ *www.neue-pinakothek.de* ✉*€7, €1 Sun.* ⊗ *Wed. 10–8, Thurs.–Mon. 10–6* Ⓜ *Königsplatz (U-bahn), Pinakotheken (Tram).*

Pinakothek der Moderne. Opened to much fanfare in 2002, this fascinating, light-filled building is home to four outstanding museums under one cupola-topped roof: art, graphic art, architecture, and design. The striking 12,000-meter-square glass-and-concrete complex by Stefan Braunfels has permanent and temporary exhibitions throughout the year in each of the four categories. The design museum is particularly popular, showing permanent exhibitions in vehicle design, computer culture, and design ideas. ⊠ *Barerstr. 40, Maxvorstadt* ☎ *089/2380–5360* ⊕ *www.pinakothek.de* ✉*€10, €1 Sun.* ⊗ *Tues., Wed., Fri.–Sun. 10–6, Thurs. 10–8* Ⓜ *Königsplatz (U-bahn), Pinakotheken (Tram).*

QUICK
BITES

Brasserie Tresznjewski. A good spot, especially if you're visiting the neighboring Pinakothek museums, the ever-popular Brasserie Tresznjewski serves an eclectic menu, well into the wee hours. ⊠ *Theresienstr. 72, corner of Barerstr., Maxvorstadt* ☎ *089/282–349* ⊕ *www.tresznjewski.com* ⊗ *Sun.–Thurs. 8–1, Fri. and Sat. 8–2.*

Städtische Galerie im Lenbachhaus. Art aficionados were waiting in anticipation for the reopening of this exquisite late-19th-century Florentine-style villa, the former home and studio of the artist Franz von Lenbach (1836–1904). In the middle of the 19th century, Munich was one of the most important art centres in Europe, and in the 1880s, Lenbach was one of the most famous artists in Germany. He painted Germany's Chancellor Bismarck around 80 times. Nowadays, Lenbachhaus is home to the stunning assemblage of art from the early-20th-century Blaue Reiter (Blue Rider) group: Kandinsky, Klee, Jawlensky, Macke, Marc, and Münter. Indeed, only New York's Guggenheim comes close to holding as many works from a group that was at the forefront in the development of abstract art. There are also vivid pieces from the New Objectivity movement, and a variety of local Munich artists are represented here. Renowned British architecture firm Foster+Partners was commissioned with the renovation work, and crucially to design a new building on the grounds. Now with the addition of a significant Joseph Beuys collection, its new gallery and renovated exhibition spaces were met with great acclaim on the museum's unveiling in spring 2013. ▥ TIP➜ The adjoining Kunstbau (art building) within the Königsplatz U-Bahn station hosts changing exhibitions of modern art. ⊠ *Luisenstr. 33, Maxvorstadt* ☎ *089/2333–2000* ⊕ *www.lenbachhaus.de* 🎫 *€10* ⊗ *Tues. 10–9, Wed.–Sun. 10–8* Ⓜ *Königsplatz (U-bahn).*

WORTH NOTING

Dreifaltigkeitskirche (*Church of the Holy Trinity*). Take a quick look at this characteristic church built to commemorate Bavaria's part in the Spanish War of Succession. A further motivation for its construction was a prophecy from the devout Maria Anna Lindmayr that if the city survived the war intact and a church was not erected in thanks the city was doomed. The city was saved and a church was built between 1711 and 1718. It has a striking baroque exterior, and its interior is brought to life by frescoes by Cosmas Damian Asam depicting various heroic scenes. Remarkably, it is the only church in the city's Altstadt spared destruction in the war. ⊠ *Pacellistr. 6, City Center* ☎ *089/290–0820* ⊗ *Daily 7–7, except during services* Ⓜ *Karlsplatz (U-bahn and S-bahn).*

Elisabethmarkt (*Elisabeth Market*). Founded in 1903, Schwabing's permanent outdoor market is smaller than the more famous Viktualienmarkt, but hardly less colorful. It has a pocket-size beer garden, where a jazz band performs Saturday in summer. ⊠ *Elisabethpl., Arcisstr. and Elisabethstr., Schwabing* ⊗ *Weekdays 10–6, Sat. 10–3* Ⓜ *Josephsplatz (U-bahn), Elisabethplatz (Tram).*

Continued on page 84

CELEBRATING
OKTOBERFEST By Ben Knight

Oktoberfests are found around the world, but the original Munich Oktoberfest has never been equaled. Six million participants over 17 days make this one of Europe's largest and best-attended festivals. It's a glorious celebration of beer, Bavarian culture, beer, folk traditions, and still more beer. So tap a barrel, grab a *Mass*, and join the party with the immortal cry: *O'zapft is!* ("It's tapped!").

You could be forgiven for reducing the world's most famous beer festival to a string of clichés—drunken revelers, deafening brass bands, and red-faced men in leather shorts and feathered hunting hats singing uproariously. But Oktoberfest appeals to a broad range of people—it can be a great day out for families, a fun night for couples, or the scene of a spectacular party for larger groups—and provides enough entertainment to exhaust kids of all ages. Party aside, Oktoberfest is a cultural institution that the people of Munich are extremely proud of. The costumes, parades, and traditions play an important role in Oktoberfest and are an integral part of local identity.

OKTOBERFEST BY THE NUMBERS
More than 7 million liters (1.85 million gallons) of beer are put away, along with 650,000 sausages, 530,000 roast chickens, and around 120 oxen on the 103-acre Theresienwiese every year.

Left, Theresienwiese fairground. Top, Festival procession band.

OKTOBERFEST 101

HISTORY

The original Oktoberfest was a royal wedding party conceived in 1810 by Major Andreas Michael Dall'Armi, an officer in the Bavarian national guard. The major suggested a horse race to celebrate the wedding of Crown Prince Ludwig I (the future king) and Princess Therese of Saxony-Hildburghausen. The sports event proved popular, and was repeated every year, but in the long–term it did not prove as popular as the barrels of beer and wagons of roasted meat that came from the countryside to feed the onlookers. Out of these catering departments, the Oktoberfest was born.

The Oktoberfest grounds were named *Theresienwiese* after Princess Therese (literally "Therese meadow"), which gave rise to the popular nickname *Wiesn* now used to denote the grounds and sometimes the festival itself.

Above, Opening ceremony.
Opposite. Top, Münchner Kindl. Below, Bavarian couple dancing at Oktoberfest. Far right, Bratwurst sausage with beer and mustard.

TOP EVENTS

Three not-to-miss Oktoberfest events are worth planning your trip around. First, there's the **ceremonial arrival of the brewers and landlords,** which starts at about 10:50 am on the first day of the festival. Setting off from Josephspitalstrasse approximately a mile east of the Theresienwiese, the brewers and beer-tent landlords arrive at the Oktoberfest grounds on horse-drawn carriages festooned with flowers.

This is followed at noon by the **tapping of the first barrel,** performed by the mayor of Munich with a cry of "*O'zapft is!*" in the Schottenhamel tent.

The next day, the first Sunday of the festival, sees the **Costume and Rifleman's Procession** (*Trachten- und Schützenzug*). This is Europe's biggest folk parade, consisting of some 9,000 people promenading through Munich on horse-drawn wagons, in marching bands, or in formation, all in their full folk regalia. It begins between 9 and 10 am at the Maximilianeum and follows a four-mile route to the Oktoberfest grounds.

COSTUMES

Walking to the Theresienwiese, you'll see more and more people wearing the traditional Oktoberfest costumes—*dirndls* (traditional dresses with a fitted bodice, blouse, skirt, and apron) for the ladies, and *lederhosen* (leather breeches) and leather waistcoats for the gentlemen. As a first-time visitor, you might be surprised by how many people of all ages actually wear the traditional Bavarian garb, also known as *Trachten*. Plenty of visitors wear it too; you can buy your Trachten from **Angermaier, Moser,** or more cheaply at department stores like **C&A** and **Galeria Kaufhof. Kostümverleih Breuer** (⊕ *www.kostuemverleih.com*) is a good place to rent, but call ahead to check availability.

NOSTALGIA ZONE

The introduction of a "nostalgia area" in 2010, to mark the 200th anniversary of the first Oktoberfest, showed how well-loved the old sights and sounds remain. It recreated the Oktoberfests of simpler eras, complete with horse-racing, wooden fairground rides, and beer brewed using traditional recipes. It has now become a regular feature of the fest, known as the **Oide Wiesn** (Old Wiesn).

FOOD

The full range of hearty and surprisingly excellent Bavarian cuisine is available by table service in the tents. Tents that specialize in food, rather than beer (although they sell beer too), include sausage-centered **Zur Bratwurst;** fish emporium **Fischer-Vroni; Able's Kalbs-Kuchl,** where you can try veal in myriad forms, among them the famous *Wiener Schnitzel;* and the **Ochsenbraterei,** which features ox meat.

The wide avenues between the tents are lined with stalls selling roast chicken, sugared almonds, *Lebkuchen* (decorated Bavarian gingerbread), and plenty of other baked or deep-fried treats for those who don't get a seat in a tent.

A main course in a tent can easily cost €15–20, while half a chicken from a stall can cost €8–10. Purchases are made in cash only, but there are ATMs near the main entrance, at the Theresienwiese U-bahn station, and throughout the Oktoberfest grounds.

GUIDE TO MAJOR BEER TENTS

The spectacular vista inside a beer tent is really what a trip to Oktoberfest is all about. There is something awe-inspiring about the sight of up to 10,000 people raising immense glasses of beer above their heads while a band leads a robust sing-along. This is a setting where the often reserved Germans let their inhibitions go, and since most of the seats are at long, communal tables, it's easy to make new friends. Below are descriptions of five of the 14 major tents. There are also 21 smaller beer tents. Altogether the tents, both large and small, provide some 114,000 seats.

SCHOTTENHAMEL
Scene: This is arguably the center of the Oktoberfest, because the mayor of Munich officially opens the festival here by tapping the first barrel. There's room for 10,000 people and it's considered the central party tent, where the young, single people of Munich gather.

Pros: Extremely lively, uninhibited atmosphere.
Cons: The emphasis is on drinking and dancing. This is not the place for a quiet, cozy chat.
Beer: Spaten-Franziskaner-Bräu has a fresh, malty taste with a clear amber color.

HIPPODROM
Scene: The ornate, Ringling Brothers–style red-and-gold facade suits the Hippodrom, which often plays host to the Oktoberfest's media circus. This is the unofficial red carpet area for celebrity guests. In the past few years, these have included Kim Kardashian, Salma Hayek, and *True Blood* star Alexander Skarsgaard. German glitterati like Boris Becker are also regulars.

Pros: The very popular champagne bar is a great place to chat with the beautiful people.
Cons: With room for only 4,200 people, this is one of the smallest of the big beer tents, making it fairly hard to get a seat. Still, it's worth wandering around.
Beer: Spaten-Franziskaner-Bräu

Above, Revelers in the Hacker-Festzelt tent. Opposite Top left, Hofbräu-Festzelt tent. Opposite below, Circus-like exterior of the Hippodrom.

ABOUT THE BEER

Only the six Munich brewer-ies (Spaten-Franziskaner-Bräu, Augustiner, Paulaner, Hacker-Pschorr, Hofbräu, and Löwen-bräu) are allowed to sell beer at Oktoberfest. Each brews a special beer for the Oktoberfest with a higher alcohol percent-age (6%, as opposed to 5%), and runs a major beer tent. Beer costs between €9.40 and €9.85 per *Mass* (liter).

HOFBRÄU-FESTZELT

Scene: This is the official Oktober-fest presence of the Hofbräuhaus, the immense beer hall in central Munich that has become one of the city's main tourist attractions. The proprietors take special pride in their international guests, and the tent has become an Oktoberfest launchpad for many U.S. and Australian revelers, with close to 10,000 seats.

Pros: This is the only main tent with a dance floor in front of the band. So you're spared precariously getting your groove on atop a wooden bench.

Cons: Since it's connected to the Hof-bräuhaus, it can feel pretty touristy.

Beer: Hofbräu München has a sweet, yeasty flavor with a good frothy head.

LÖWENBRÄU-FESTZELT

Scene: The traditional home tent of Munich's soccer club TSV 1860 München, this 8,500-seat tent is the closest the Oktoberfest comes to a real, working-class Munich feel. Patrons are regaled at the entrance by a giant, beer-swilling plastic lion, who occasionally roars the name of his favorite beer—Löwenbräu—at new arrivals.

Pros: This tent has an unpretentious, what-you-see-is-what-you-get atmosphere.

Cons: Although the food here is good, it is pretty basic fare.

Beer: Löwenbräu is a strong beer with a slightly spicy flavor.

HACKER-FESTZELT

Scene: This tent is often nicknamed the "Bavarian heaven," mainly because of the painted clouds and other sky-related decor that hang from the ceiling (installed by Oscar-winning designer Rolf Zehetbauer). It has also become a favorite tent for native Bavarians.

Pros: This tent offers unique features including a rotating bandstand and a partially retractable roof for sunny days.

Cons: Because it's generally considered the most attractive of the tents, it fills up particularly quickly—so get a seat early.

Beer: Copper-colored Hacker-Pschorr has a bready taste and is one of the best of the Oktoberfest beers.

PLANNING FOR OKTOBERFEST

ADVANCE PLANNING Oktoberfest is one of Germany's biggest tourist events—it's estimated to contribute over one billion euros to Munich's economy—so you should plan everything at least six months in advance.

WHERE TO STAY Booking in advance is advisable for hotels, although you're unlikely to get a cheap deal anywhere in the immediate vicinity of Oktoberfest. For cheaper city-center options, especially if you're part of a bigger group, check out **Jaeger's Hotel** (⊕ *www.jaegershotel.de*) or **Easy Palace** (⊕ *www.easypalace.de*). Otherwise book a hotel in Munich's outskirts and take public transit in.

RESERVATIONS The tents are free to enter, but if you want to sit and carouse into the evening, you need to reserve a seat at least six months in advance and up to ten months. Reservations are free, but the beer tents require you to buy food and drink vouchers with the reservation. Two liters of beer and half a chicken per seat is the usual standard minimum, and will cost a minimum of €30 per person, though could cost more depending on the tent and the time of day (evenings and weekends are more expensive). The vouchers can either be sent to you by mail (for a small fee), or picked up from special offices in Munich up to two weeks in advance. Reservations are only available through the individual beer tents, not through the Oktoberfest organizers. You can find the websites of the tents, plus addresses of the ticket offices on ⊕ *www.oktoberfest.de*.

WITHOUT RESERVATIONS There is only table service at the major tents, so in order to get served you must have a seat. If you don't have a reservation, come as early as you can; by mid-morning at the latest. One section of the central area of each tent (known as the *Mittelschiff*, or "mid-ship") is always reservation-free and you can snag a seat if you get there early. You can also sit in a reserved seat until its owner arrives.

HOURS Oktoberfest takes place the third weekend in September through the first weekend in October. It is open from 10 am to 11:30 pm every day, although the

Above, interior of Hippodrom tent. Opposite, chain carousel at Oktoberfest fairground.

tents open at 9 am on weekends and public holidays. Last call is 10:30 pm.

RESTROOMS You can use the restrooms in any tent even if you're not drinking there. They are generally clean, well lit, and easy to find.

FAMILY DAYS Tuesdays are designated family days when there are discounts on all the fairground rides and food for kids. Rides range from old-fashioned carousels to vertiginous modern roller-coasters and cost between €3 and €8. There are also haunted houses, halls of mirrors, a flea circus, and many carnival games. Children are allowed in the beer tents, but kids under 6 years old must exit the tents after 8 pm.

PUBLIC TRANSIT The **Theresienwiese U-Bahn** (subway) stop is right outside Oktoberfest. However, this stop gets extremely crowded, particularly at closing time, so consider walking to either the nearby **Goetheplatz** or **Poccistrasse** stations. The **Hauptbahnhof**, where virtually all public transit lines converge, is just a 10- to 15-minute walk away.

TAXIS There is one taxi stand at the southern end of the Oktoberfest area, and taxis are easy to flag down in the city. Fares start at €1.70 per km (roughly $2.50 per 0.6 mile), although the per-km price drops the farther the distance traveled.

SAFETY Oktoberfest is generally very safe. There are plenty of security personnel in the tents and at the doors, and fights are rare. There is an information center, first aid, and police station behind the Schottenhamel tent. Sexual assault is not unknown at the Oktoberfest, but facilities have been revamped to increase safety, and a security point for women is located below the Bavaria statue in the service center next to the police and Red Cross. See ⊕ *www.sicherewiesn.de* for more safety information for women.

FOR MORE INFORMATION The official Oktoberfest website is ⊕ *www.oktoberfest.de*, which includes a useful English guide. The official "Oktoberfest.de" iPhone app offers news on upcoming events and a location feature in case you get lost.

OUTSIDE THE CENTER

TOP ATTRACTIONS

Oktoberfest Grounds at Theresienwiese. The site of Munich's famous **Oktoberfest** and the winter version of the city's **Tollwood music, art, and food festival** (it's at the Olympic area in summer) is a 10-minute walk from the Hauptbahnhof, or one stop on the subway (U-4 or U-5). The enormous exhibition ground is named after Princess Therese von Sachsen-Hildburghausen, who celebrated her marriage to future King Ludwig I here in 1810 with thousands of Münchners. The event was such a success that it became an annual celebration that has now grown into a 16-day international beer and fair-ride bonanza attracting more than 6 million people each year (it is the *Oktober*fest because it always ends on the first Sunday in October). ⊠ *Theresienwiese, Ludwigvorstadt-Isarvorstadt* Ⓜ *Theresienwiese (U-bahn).*

Bavaria Statue. Overlooking the Theresienwiese, home of the Oktoberfest, is a 19th-century hall of fame (Ruhmeshalle) featuring busts of famous Bavarian scientists, artists, engineers, generals, and philosophers, and a monumental bronze statue of the maiden Bavaria. Unsurprisingly, it was commissioned by the art- and architecture-obsessed King Ludwig I, though not finished before his abdication in 1848. The Bavaria is more than 60 feet high and at the time was the largest bronze figure since antiquity. The statue is hollow, and an initial 48 steps take you up to its base. Once inside, there are 66 steps to her knee, and a further 52 all the way into the braided head, the reward being a view of Munich through Bavaria's eyes. ⊠ *Theresienhöhe 16* 🖃 *€3.50* ☯ *Apr.–Oct. 15, daily 9–6 (till 8 during Oktoberfest).*

FAMILY **Olympiapark** (*Olympic Park*). Built for the 1972 Olympic Games on the staggering quantities of rubble delivered from the war-time destruction of Munich, the Olympiapark was—and still is—considered an architectural and landscape wonder. The jewel in the crown is the **Olympic Stadium,** former home of Bayern Munich soccer team. With its truly avant-garde sweeping canopy roof, winding its way across various parts of the complex, it was an inspired design for the big events of the 1972 Olympic Games. Tragically, a bigger event relegated what was heading to be the most successful Games to date to the sidelines. It was from the adjacent accommodation area that a terrorist attack on the Israeli team began, eventually leaving 17 people dead.

Unlike many former Olympic sites around the world, today the area is heavily used and is home to numerous events, such as the **summer Tollwood** festival, concerts, sporting events, and it is a haven for joggers and people just wishing to relax. Tours of the park are conducted on a Disneyland-style train throughout the day. For the more adventurous, how about climbing the roof of the Olympic Stadium and rappelling down? For the best view of the whole city and the Alps, take the elevator up the 955-foot **Olympiaturm** (Olympic Tower) or try out the revolving Michelin-starred **Restaurant 181** on the same level. ⊠ *Spiridon-Louis-Ring, Milbertshofen* ☎ *089/3509–48181 for restaurant* ⊕ *www.olympiapark-muenchen.de* 🖃 *Stadium tour €7.50; tower €5.50* ☯ *Tour schedules vary; call ahead for departure times* Ⓜ *Olympiazentrum (U-bahn).*

Schloss Nymphenburg. This glorious baroque and rococo palace, the largest of its kind in Germany, draws around 500,000 visitors a year; only the Deustches Museum is more popular in Munich. The palace grew in size and scope over more than 200 years, beginning as a summer residence built on land given by Prince Ferdinand Maria to his beloved wife, Henriette Adelaide, on the occasion of the birth of their son and heir, Max Emanuel, in 1663. The princess hired the Italian architect Agostino Barelli to build both the Theatinerkirche and the palace, which was completed in 1675 by his successor, Enrico Zuccalli. It represents a tremendous high point of Italian cultural influence, in what is undoubtedly Germany's most Italian city. Within the original building, now the central axis of the palace complex, is the magnificent **Steinerner Saal** (Great Hall). It extends over two floors and is richly decorated with stucco and grandiose frescoes by masters such as Francois Cuvilliés the Elder and Johann Baptist Zimmermann. In summer, chamber-music concerts are given here. One of the surrounding royal chambers houses Ludwig I's famous **Schönheitsgalerie** (Gallery of Beauties). The walls are hung from floor to ceiling with portraits of women who caught the roving eye of Ludwig, among them a shoemaker's daughter and Lady Jane Ellenborough, the scandal-thriving English aristocrat. Lady Jane's affair with Ludwig, however, was a minor dalliance compared with the adventures in Munich of the most famous female on the walls here. Lola Montez was born in Ireland and passed herself off as a Spanish dancer during a tour of Europe's major cities, during which time she became the mistress of Franz Liszt and later Alexandre Dumas. Montez arrived in Munich in 1846 and so enchanted King Ludwig I that she became his closest advisor, much to the chagrin of his ministers and many Münchners. With revolution in the air across France and the German lands in 1848, Bavaria's greatest monarch abdicated rather than be told whom he could and could not appoint as his advisor. And Lola? She left Munich and left the king for adventures in the U.S., where she eventually died.

The palace is in a park laid out in formal French style, with low hedges and gravel walks extending into woodland. Among the ancient tree stands are three fascinating pavilions. The **Amalienburg** hunting lodge is a rococo gem built by François Cuvilliés. The detailed stucco work of the little Amalienburg creates an atmosphere of courtly high life, making clear that the pleasures of the chase did not always take place outdoors. Of the lodges, only Amalienburg is open in winter. In the lavishly appointed kennels you'll see that even the dogs lived in luxury. The **Pagodenburg** was built for slightly informal royal tea parties. Its elegant French exterior disguises an Asian-influenced interior, in which exotic teas from India and China were served. Swimming parties were held in the **Badenburg,** Europe's first post-Roman heated pool. Take Tram No. 17 or Bus No. 51 from the city center to the Schloss Nymphenburg stop. ⊠ *Schloss Nymphenburg, Nymphenburg* ☎ *089/179–080* ⊕ *www. schloss-nymphenburg.de* ⊠ *Schloss Nymphenburg complex (combined ticket includes Marstallmuseum and Museum Nymphenburger Porzellan): Apr.–mid-Oct. €11.50; mid-Oct.–Mar. €8.50* ☽ *Apr.–mid-Oct., daily 9–6; mid-Oct.–Mar., daily 10–4.*

Wander the extensive grounds of Schloss Nymphenburg.

Marstallmuseum & Porzellan Manufaktur Nymphenburg (*Museum of Royal Carriages & Porcelain Manufacturer Nymphenburg*). Nymphenburg contains so much of interest that a day hardly provides enough time. Don't leave without visiting the former royal stables, now the Marstallmuseum. It houses a fleet of vehicles, including an elaborately decorated sleigh in which King Ludwig II once glided through the Bavarian twilight, flaming torches lighting the way. Also exhibited in the Marstallmuseum are examples of the world-renowned Nymphenburg porcelain, which has been produced on the palace grounds since 1761. ■ TIP→ Nymphenburg porcelain has dedicated stores at Odeonsplatz and in the luxurious Bayerischer Hof hotel (Promenadeplatz), but it is also available at numerous other retailers around the city. ⊠ *208 Schloss Nymphenburg, Nymphenburg* ☎ *089/179–080 Schloss Nymphenburg* 🔼 *€4.50* ⊙ *Apr.–mid-Oct., daily 9–6; mid-Oct.–Mar., daily 10–4.*

Museum Mensch und Natur (*Museum of Man and Nature*). This popular museum in the north wing of Schloss Nymphenburg has nothing to do with the Wittelsbachs but is one of the palace's major attractions. The Museum Mensch und Natur concentrates on three areas of interest: the variety of life on Earth, the history of humankind, and our place in the environment. Main exhibits include a huge representation of the human brain and a chunk of Alpine crystal weighing half a ton. ⊠ *Schloss Nymphenburg, Nymphenburg* ☎ *089/179–5890* ⊕ *www.musmn.de* 🔼 *€3, Sun. €1* ⊙ *Tues., Wed., Fri. 9–5, Thurs. 9–8, weekends 10–6.*

WORTH NOTING

FAMILY **Bavaria Filmstadt.** For real movie buffs, Munich has its own Hollywood-like neighborhood, the Geiselgasteig, in the affluent Grünwald district, on the southern outskirts of the city. A number of notable films, such as *Das Boot* (*The Boat*) and *Die Unendliche Geschichte* (*The Neverending Story*), were made here. It was also here that in 1925 British filmmaker Alfred Hitchcock shot his first film, *The Pleasure Garden*. There are a number of tours and shows, and extra events for kids. ⊠ *Bavaria Filmpl. 7, Geiselgasteig* ☎ *089/6499–2000* ⊕ *www.filmstadt.de* 🎫 *Tour €12.50* ⊙ *Daily 9–6; English tour daily at 1.*

BMW Museum. Munich is the home of the famous BMW car company. The circular tower of its museum is one of the defining images of Munich's modern cityscape. It contains not only a dazzling collection of BMWs old and new but also items and exhibitions relating to the company's social history and its technical developments. It's a great place to stop in if you're at the Olympiapark already. ⊠ *Am Olympiapark 2, Milbertshofen* ☎ *089/1250–16001 for tours* ⊕ *www.bmw-welt.com* 🎫 *BMW Museum €9, €12 tour; BMW Welt free* ⊙ *BMW Museum, Tues.–Sun. 10–6; BMW Welt, daily 7:30 am–11 pm* Ⓜ *Olympiazentrum (U-bahn).*

BMW Welt. Opened in 2007, the cutting-edge design of BMW Welt, with its sweeping, futuristic facade, is just one structure helping to overcome the conservative image Munich has had in the realm of architecture since 1945. Even if you have just a passing interest in cars and engines, this is the place to see. This is also where around 15,000 of the firm's cars are handed over to customers every year. It is already one of the most popular must-sees in the city, averaging 2 million visitors a year since opening. As well as tours of the building, there are readings, concerts, and exhibitions. Tours can only be booked via telephone or email.

The adjacent **BMW factory** can be toured on weekdays. Registration for plant tours (which last a maximum of 2½ hours) is only possible in advance via phone. The tours start (from 4 o'clock) and finish at the information counter at BMW Welt. Due to plant reconstruction, the tour does not include the car assembly area, which also means there is no wheelchair access at present. ▥**TIP➜ Reserve at least two weeks in advance for all tours.** ⊠ *BMW Welt, Am Olympiapark 1, Milbertshofen* ☎ *01802/118–822 for tours* ✐ *infowelt@bmw-welt.com for tours* ⊕ *www.bmw-plant-munich.com* 🎫 *BMW Welt tour €7; factory tour €8* ⊙ *Mon.–Sat. 9–6, Sun. 10–6* Ⓜ *Olympiazentrum (U-bahn).*

Botanischer Garten (*Botanical Garden*). On the northern edge of Schloss Nymphenburg, this collection of 14,000 plants, including orchids, cacti, cycads, Alpine flowers, and rhododendrons, makes up one of the most extensive botanical gardens in Europe. Take Tram No. 17 from the city center. ⊠ *Menzingerstr. 65, Nymphenburg* ☎ *089/1786–1350* ⊕ *www.botmuc.de* 🎫 *€4* ⊙ *Garden: Nov.–Jan. daily 9–4:30; Feb., Mar., and Oct., daily 9–5; Apr. and Sept., daily 9–6; May–Aug., daily 9–7. Hothouses close 30 mins early.*

Deutsches Museum Flugwerft Schleissheim. Connoisseurs of airplanes and flying machines will appreciate this magnificent offshoot of the Deutsches Museum, some 20 km (12 mi) north of the city center. It's an ideal complement to a visit to Schloss Schleissheim. ■ **TIP➔ A combination ticket with the Deutsches Museum costs €15.** ✉ *Effnerstr. 18, Oberschleissheim* ☎ *089/315-7140* ⊕ *www.deutsches-museum.de/flugwerft* 🎫 *€6, combined ticket with Deutsches Museum and Verkehrszentrum (Travel Museum) €15* ⊗ *Daily 9–5* Ⓜ *Oberschleissheim (S-bahn).*

Neues Schloss Schleissheim (*Schleissheim Palace*). Duke Wilhelm V found the perfect peaceful retreat outside Munich, and in 1598 built what is now known as the **Altes Schloss Schleissheim** (Schleissheim Old Palace). In 1685 Elector Max Emanuel added **Lustheim,** which houses one of Germany's most impressive collections of Meissen porcelain, and at the beginning of the 18th century the **Neues Schloss Schleissheim** (Schleissheim New Palace). Take the S-bahn Line No. 1 to Oberschleissheim station and then walk about 15 minutes or take Bus No. 292 (no weekend service). ✉ *Maximilianshof 1, Oberschleissheim* ☎ *089/315-8720* ⊕ *www.schloesser-schleissheim.de* 🎫 *Combined ticket for 3 palaces €8* ⊗ *Apr.–Sept., Tues.–Sun. 9–6; Oct.–Mar., Tues.–Sun. 10–4.*

FAMILY   **Tierpark Hellabrunn.** On the Isar, just upstream from the city, this attractive zoo has many parklike enclosures but a minimum of cages. This zoo is slightly different from most others in that it's a self-styled nature reserve, and it follows a concept called Geo-Zoo, which means care has been taken to group animals according to their natural and geographical habitats. Critics of the concept of zoos won't agree, but supporters appreciate the extra attention to detail. As well as the usual tours, there are also nighttime guided tours with special night-vision equipment (call ahead of time). The huge zoo area also includes restaurants and children's areas, and some of the older buildings are in typical Jugendstil (art nouveau) style. From Marieneplatz, take U-bahn Line No. 3 to Thalkirchen, at the southern edge of the city. ✉ *Tierparkstr. 30, Thalkirchen* ☎ *089/625-080* ⊕ *www.tierpark-hellabrunn.de* 🎫 *€12* ⊗ *Late Mar.–late Oct., daily 9–6; late Oct.–Mar., daily 9–5* Ⓜ *Thalkirchen (U-bahn).*

WHERE TO EAT

Munich claims to be Germany's gourmet capital. It certainly has an inordinate number of fine restaurants, but you won't have trouble finding a vast range of options in both price and style.

Typical, more substantial dishes in Munich include *Tellerfleisch,* boiled beef with freshly grated horseradish and boiled potatoes on the side, served on wooden plates. Among roasts, *Sauerbraten* (beef) and *Schweinebraten* (roast pork) are accompanied by dumplings and sauerkraut. *Hax'n* (ham hocks) are roasted until they're crisp on the outside and juicy on the inside. They are served with sauerkraut and potato puree. Game in season (venison or boar, for instance) and duck are served with potato dumplings and red cabbage. As for fish, the region has not only excellent trout, served either smoked as an hors d'oeuvre or fried or boiled as an entrée, but also the perchlike *Rencke* from Lake Starnberg.

You'll also find soups, salads, casseroles, hearty stews, and a variety of baked goods—including pretzels. For dessert, indulge in a bowl of Bavarian cream, apple strudel, or *Dampfnudel,* a fluffy leavened-dough dumpling usually served with vanilla sauce.

The generic term for a snack is *Imbiss,* and thanks to growing internationalism you'll find a huge variety, from the generic *Wiener* (hot dogs) to the Turkish *döner kebab* sandwich (pressed and roasted lamb, beef, or chicken). Almost all butcher shops and bakeries offer some sort of Brotzeit, which can range from a modest sandwich to a steaming plate of goulash with potatoes and salad.

Some edibles come with social etiquette attached. The *Weisswurst,* a tender minced-veal sausage—made fresh daily, steamed, and served with sweet mustard and a crisp roll or a pretzel—is a Munich institution and, theoretically, should be eaten before noon with a *Weissbier* (wheat beer), supposedly to counteract the effects of a hangover. Some people use a knife and fork to remove the inside from the skin, while others might indulge in *auszuzeln,* sucking the sausage out of the Weisswurst.

Another favorite Bavarian specialty is *Leberkäs*—literally "liver cheese," though neither liver nor cheese is among its ingredients. Rather, it's a sort of meat loaf baked to a crust each morning and served in pink slabs throughout the day. A *Leberkäs Semmel*—a wedge of the meat loaf between two halves of a bread roll slathered with a slightly spicy mustard—is the favorite Munich on-the-go snack.

Prices in the reviews are the average cost of a main course at dinner, or if dinner is not served, at lunch. Use the coordinate (✛ B3) at the end of each listing to locate a site on the corresponding map.

CITY CENTER

$ | GERMAN ⨯ **Andechser am Dom.** At this Munich mainstay for both locals and visitors, the vaulted, frescoed ceiling and the old stone floor recall the nearby Andechs monastery. As with many smaller Bavarian *Wirtshäuser* (pub-restaurant), it's invariably pretty full, so be prepared to find seats on a table already half full, though this is part of the lively charm of the place. The boldly Bavarian food—blood sausage with potatoes or roast duck—and fine selection of delectable Andechs beers will quickly put you at ease. The covered terrace, steps from the Frauenkirche, is a favorite meeting place, rain or shine, for shoppers, local businesspeople, and even the occasional VIP. ⑤ *Average main: €9* ⊠ *Weinstr. 7a, City Center* ☎ *089/298–481* ⊕ *www.andechser-am-dom.de* Ⓜ *Marienplatz (U-bahn and S-bahn)* ✛ *D4.*

$ | GERMAN ⨯ **Bier- und Oktoberfest Museum.** In one of the oldest buildings in Munich, dating to the 14th century, the museum takes an imaginative look at the history of this popular elixir, the monasteries that produced it, the purity laws that govern it, and Munich's own long tradition with it. The rustic Museumsstüberl restaurant, consisting of a few heavy wooden tables, accompanies the museum. It serves traditional *Brotzeit* (breads, cheeses, and cold meats) during the day and hot Bavarian dishes from 6 pm. ▉ TIP➔ You can visit the Museumsstüberl restaurant

BEST BETS FOR MUNICH DINING

Fodor's Choice ★

Limoni, $$$, p. 99
Mark's, $$$$, p. 95
Restaurant Dallmayr, $$$$, p. 96
Tantris, $$$$, p. 99

Best By Price

$

Andechser am Dom, p. 89
Bier- und Oktoberfest Museum, p. 89
Bratwurstherzl, p. 91
Due passi, p. 91
L'Atelier Art & Vin, p. 95

$$

Buffet Kull, p. 91

Café Dukatz, p. 91

$$$

Brasserie OskarMaria, p. 90
Limoni, p. 99

$$$$

Mark's, p. 95
Restaurant Dallmayr, p. 96
Tantris, p. 99

Best By Cuisine

BAVARIAN

Alter Simpl, $, p. 98
Gasthaus Isarthor, $, p. 98
Wirtshaus in der Au, $, p. 100

EUROPEAN

Mark's, $$$$, p. 95
Restaurant Dallmayr, $$$$, p. 96

FRENCH

Café Dukatz, $$, p. 91
Brasserie OskarMaria, $$, p. 90
L'Atelier Art & Vin, $, p. 95

GERMAN

Halali, $$$, p. 91
Weinhaus Neuner, $$$$, p. 97

ITALIAN

Due passi, $, p. 91
Limoni, $$$, p. 99

without paying the museum's admission fee and try beer from one of Munich's oldest breweries, the Augustiner Bräu. $ *Average main: €8* ✉ *Sterneckerstr. 2, City Center* ☎ *089/2424–3941* ⊕ *www.bier-und-oktoberfestmuseum.de* 🖾 *Museum €4* ☉ *Museum, Tue.–Sat. 1–6; restaurant, Mon. 6 pm–midnight, Tue.–Sat. 1 pm–midnight* Ⓜ *Isartor (U-bahn and S-bahn)* ✛ *F5.*

$$ ✕ **Brasserie OskarMaria.** After New York, Munich has more publishing
FRENCH houses than any other city in the world. Literaturhaus is a converted Renaissance-style schoolhouse that, as the name suggests, is now a "literature" center, for authors, publishers, and book fans. The front side of the building is a stylish brasserie, named after Munich writer Oskar Maria Graf, an exile after the Nazis took power in Germany in 1933, and who eventually settled in New York. The brasserie's vaulted high ceiling and plate-glass windows create a light and spacious atmosphere. The range of dishes here is pretty eclectic, from beetroot with garden vegetables and goat's cheese to lobster risotto. It has a sprawling terrace, and it's one of the city's best outdoor eating locations, whether for a main meal or cappaccino and *Kuchen* (cake). ■ TIP→ About 100 meters away, on Jungfernturmstrasse, is one of the oldest remaining remnants of the city wall. $ *Average main: €18* ✉ *Salvatorpl. 1, City Center* ☎ *089/2919–6029* ⊕ *www.oskarmaria.com* Ⓜ *Odeonsplatz (U-bahn)* ✛ *D4.*

$
GERMAN
✕ **Bratwurstherzl.** Tucked into a quaint little square off the Viktualien-markt, this delightful Bratwurst joint cooks up specialty sausages right in the main room over an open grill. For those looking for a bit less meat, there is also a hearty farmer's salad with veal strips and tasty oys-ter mushrooms. They have outdoor seating, perfect for people-watching when the weather is good. ⑤ *Average main: €8* ✉ *Dreifaltigkeitspl. 1, City Center* ☏ *089/295–113* ⊕ *www.bratwurstherzl.de* ☉ *Closed Sun. and public holidays* Ⓜ *Marienplatz (U-bahn and S-bahn)* ✛ *E5.*

$$
EUROPEAN
✕ **Buffet Kull.** This simple yet comfortable international bistro delivers a high-quality dining experience accompanied by a good variety of wines and friendly service. Dishes range from bouillabaisse (halibut with king prawns and calamari) to the excellent New York steak. The daily spe-cials are creative, portions are generous, and the prices are good value for the quality. Reservations are recommended (dinner service starts at 6). ⑤ *Average main: €18* ✉ *Marienstr. 4, City Center* ☏ *089/221–509* ⊕ *www.buffet-kull.de* Ⓜ *Marienplatz (U-bahn and S-bahn)* ✛ *F5.*

$
ITALIAN
✕ **Due passi.** So small it's easy to miss, this former dairy shop, now an Italian specialty shop, offers Italian meals for a quick lunch. There's a small but fine selection of fresh antipasti and pasta. You can eat at the high wooden tables and counters or have your food to go. Menus change daily. ⑤ *Average main: €7* ✉ *Ledererstr. 11, City Cen-ter* ☏ *089/224–271* ⊕ *www.duepassi.de* ▬ *No credit cards* ☉ *Closed weekends* Ⓜ *Marienplatz (U-bahn and S-bahn)* ✛ *F5.*

$$
FRENCH
✕ **Café Dukatz.** This café has been a popular, relatively upmarket eatery on the Munich scene for years. Even with the closure of their city-center restaurant, it has been a busy time for owners as they now have two cafés—one in Maxvorstadt on Klenzestrasse 69 and another in Lehel at St.-Anna-Strasse 11. They specialize in French-style pâtisseries, with daily home-baked delights and fine coffees expected of such a renowned name. ⑤ *Average main: €16* ✉ *Klenzestr. 69, Maxvorstadt* ☏ *089/7104–07373 for Klenzestr., 089/2303–2444 for St.-Anna-Pl.* ⊕ *www.dukatz. de* Ⓜ *Frauenhoferstrasse (U-bahn)* ✛ *D6 and G4.*

$
ECLECTIC
✕ **Faun.** Not quite city center, but still central to the action, the beloved Faun is on Hans-Sachs-Strasse, one of the city's most interesting streets, with great restaurants and boutique shops—even a century-old cinema. It's a happy combination of Munich tavern and international bistro, with great outdoor seating on a small square where five streets meet and five trees are planted. The Thai curries are wonderful, and their juicy Schweinebraten will satisfy any meat cravings. The dishes on the daily changing menu are tasty, filling, and easy on your wallet. The beer served is Augustiner, so you can't go wrong there. Build up your appetite by browsing your way through the neighborhood shops and boutiques, or walk off your meal along the river back toward Isartor and the city center. ⑤ *Average main: €9* ✉ *Hans-Sachs-Str. 17, Ludwigvorstadt* ☏ *089/263–798* ⊕ *www.faun.mycosmos.biz* ▬ *No credit cards* ✛ *D6.*

$$$
GERMAN
✕ **Halali.** With nearly 100 years of history to its credit, polished wood paneling, and antlers on the walls, the Halali is an old-style Munich restaurant that is *the* place to try traditional dishes of venison, pheasant, partridge, and other game in a quiet and elegant atmosphere. Save room for the crème brûlée with potted nectarine-and-mocha-bean ice cream.

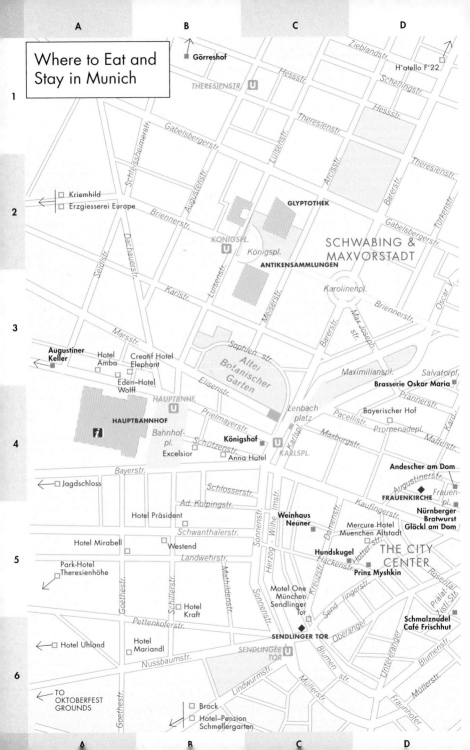

Where to Eat and Stay in Munich

A   **B**   **C**   **D**

■ Görreshof

THERESIENSTR. Ⓤ

Zieblandstr.

H'otello F'22

Schellingstr.

Hessstr.

Hessstr.

Theresienstr.

Gabelsbergerstr.

Luisenstr.

Theresienstr.

Arcisstr.

Barerstr.

Türkenstr.

Theresienstr.

□ Kriemhild
□ Erzgiesserei Europe

Briennerstr.

Augustenstr.

GLYPTOTHEK

Gabelsbergerstr.

Barerstr.

Oscar v.

Schleissheimerstr.

Dachauerstr.

KÖNIGSPL.
Ⓤ

Königspl.

ANTIKENSAMMLUNGEN

SCHWABING & MAXVORSTADT

Karolinenpl.

Max Joseph str.

Briennerstr.

Seidlstr.

Karlstr.

Luisenstr.

Meiserstr.

Barerstr.

Marsstr.

Augustiner Keller ■

Hotel Amba □

Creatif Hotel Elephant □

Sophien str.

Alter Botanischer Garten

Maximilianspl.

Salvatorpl.

Brasserie Oskar Maria ■

Eden–Hotel Wolff □

Elisenstr.

HAUPTBAHNHOF

Prielmayerstr.

Lenbach platz

Pacellistr.

Prannerstr.

Bayerischer Hof □

Promenadepl.

Maffeistr.

HAUPTBAHNHOF

ℹ

Bahnhof-pl.

Schützenstr.

Königshof
Ⓤ

Karlspl.

Maxburgstr.

Kard.

Excelsior □

Anna Hotel □

KARLSPL.

Andescher am Dom ■

←□ Jagdschloss

Bayerstr.

Schlosserstr.

Augustinerstr.

FRAUENKIRCHE ◆

Frauen-pl.

Ad. Kolpingstr.

Kaufingerstr.

Nürnberger Bratwurst Glöckl am Dom

Hotel Präsident □

Schwanthalerstr.

Weinhaus Neuner

Damenstr.

Mercure Hotel Muenchen Altstadt

Sonnenstr.

Herzog - Wilhe lmstr.

Hundskugel

Hotter str.

THE CITY CENTER

Hotel Mirabell □

□ Westend

Landwehrstr.

Hackenstr.

Kreuzstr.

Prinz Myshkin ■

Rosental

Park-Hotel Theresienhöhe □

Goethestr.

Schillerstr.

Matthildenstr.

Motel One München Sendlinger Tor □

Send lingerstr.

Oberanger

Schmalznudel Café Frischhut ■

Pralat

21st Str.

Pettenkoferstr.

□ Hotel Kraft

Sonnenstr.

SENDLINGER TOR ◆

Unteranger

Blumenstr.

←□ Hotel Uhland

Hotel Mariandl □

Nussbaumstr.

SENDLINGER TOR Ⓤ

Blumen str.

Müllerstr.

Fraunhofer

Müllerstr.

← TO OKTOBERFEST GROUNDS

Goethestr.

Lindwurmstr.

□ Brack

□ Hotel-Pension Schmellergarten

A   **B**   **C**   **D**

Ⓢ *Average main: €25* ✉ *Schönfeldstr. 22, City Center* ☎ *089/285–909* ⊕ *www.restaurant-halali.de* ⌆ *Reservations essential* 🎩 *Jacket and tie* ⊗ *Closed Sun. and public holidays. No lunch Sat.* Ⓜ *Odeonsplatz (U-bahn and S-bahn)* ✛ *F2.*

$ ✕ **Hofbräuhaus.** The Hofbräuhaus is simply the most famous beer hall
GERMAN not just in Munich but in the world. Regulars aside, many Bavarians
see it as the biggest tourist trap ever created, and few ever go more
than once, but they are still proud that it attracts so many visitors.
Yes, it's a little kitschy, but the pounding oompah band draws the curious, and the singing and shouting drinkers contribute to the festive
atmosphere. This, then, is no place for the fainthearted, and a trip to
Munich would be incomplete without at least having a look. Upstairs
is a quieter restaurant, where the food is fine, although there are better
places for Bavarian cuisine. In March, May, and September ask for one
of the special, extra-strong seasonal beers (Starkbier, Maibock, Märzen)
which complement the traditional Bavarian fare. Ⓢ *Average main: €10*
✉ *Platzl 9, City Center* ☎ *089/2901–36100* ⊕ *www.hofbraeuhaus.de*
⌆ *Reservations not accepted* Ⓜ *Marienplatz (U-bahn and S-bahn)* ✛ *F5.*

$$$ ✕ **Hotel Lux Restaurant.** The chef here learned his trade at Munich's much-
ECLECTIC vaunted Königshof. Much of the meat here is organic; ask the ever-charm-
ing staff for information. The creamy asparagus risotto is a real treat for
lunch, while the duck with ratatouille and potato-celery gratin is a high-
light of the evening menu. Though the restaurant is small, it deliberately
has a front-room feel, with red velvetlike upholstery complementing the
wooden ceiling and walls that survived the recent renovation. The small
bar is also terrific. Hotel Lux is also a hotel with 17 rooms (€149), free
Wi-Fi, and simply furnished rooms—except for the top floor Ponyhof
room, designed by Hans Langner, who is famous for his bird depictions.
This extraordinary blue, bird-filled room is not to everyone's taste, but
good fun for a night or two. Ⓢ *Average main: €24* ✉ *Lerdererstr. 13, City
Center* ☎ *089/4520–7300* ⊕ *www.hotel-lux-muenchen.de* ✛ *F5.*

$ ✕ **Jodlerwirt.** This cozy Alpine lodge–style restaurant in a small street
GERMAN behind the Rathaus is a treat for those craving an Old World tavern,
complete with live accordion playing. As its name suggests, yodelers
perform most nights, telling jokes and poking fun at their adoring
guests in unintelligible Bavarian slang. The food is traditional, including
Käsespätzle (a hearty German version of macaroni and cheese), goulash,
and meal-size salads. The tasty beer is from the Ayinger brewery. The
place is small and fills up fast. Ⓢ *Average main: €12* ✉ *Altenhofstr. 4,
City Center* ☎ *089/221–249* ⊕ *www.jodlerwirt-muenchen.net* ⊟ *No
credit cards* ⊗ *Closed Sun. and Mon. No lunch* Ⓜ *Marienplatz (U-bahn
and S-bahn)* ✛ *E5.*

$$$$ ✕ **Königshof.** Don't be fooled as you cross the threshold of the dour and
ECLECTIC unremarkable-looking postwar Hotel Königshof. The contrast with the
opulent interior is remarkable. From a window table in this elegant and
luxurious restaurant in one of Munich's grand hotels, you can watch
the hustle and bustle of Munich's busiest square, Karlsplatz, below.
You'll forget the outside world, however, when you taste the outstand-
ing French- and Japanese-influenced dishes created by Michelin-starred
chef Martin Fauster, former sous-chef at Tantris. Ingredients are fresh

2

and menus change often, but you might see lobster with fennel and candied ginger, or venison with goose liver and celery, and for dessert, flambéed peach with champagne ice cream. Service is expert and personal; let the sommelier help you choose from the fantastic wine selection. $ *Average main: €45* ⊠ *Karlspl. 25, City Center* ☎ *089/551–360* ⊕ *www.koenigshof-hotel.de* ⟳ *Reservations essential* 🏛 *Jacket and tie* ⊘ *Closed 1st wk in Aug.–1st wk in Sept.; closed Sun. and Mon., Jan.– Sept.* Ⓜ *Karlsplatz (U-bahn and S-bahn)* ✣ *C4.*

$

FRENCH

✕ **L'Atelier Art & Vin.** Take a seat by the wall of windows, or at the long blond-wood bar, in this airy, casual brasserie, which specializes in French food and wine. On nice days, tables are also set outside on the sidewalk of the pleasant, relatively quiet street. The light, crisp quiches, in particular, are a delight, and the wine list is a curated list of French wines. The Bier & Oktoberfest Museum is a few doors away, highlighting the wonderful contrasts that are so typical of this city. $ *Average main: €12* ⊠ *Westenriederstr. 43, City Center* ☎ *089/2126–6782* ⊕ *www.atelier-artetvin.de* ▭ *No credit cards* ⊘ *Closed Sun. and public holidays* Ⓜ *Marienplatz (U-bahn and S-bahn)* ✣ *F5.*

$$$$

EUROPEAN

Fodor's Choice

★

✕ **Mark's.** A wonderful culinary experience is reached on three literal levels at Mark's in the Hotel Mandarin Oriental, itself synonymous with excellence and luxury. You can enjoy lunch either in the hotel lobby or—weather permitting—eight floors up on the magnificent roof terrace, which has 360-degree views of the city. And at dinnertime, Mark's is set on the balcony of the luxurious lobby, with a wide white marble staircase leading up to it. The 2011 appointed head chef, Simon Larese, creates decadent dishes, for example a starter of langoustine with grilled watermelon, charentais melon, and coriander pistou. Equally impressive is the pan-fried Pommerian beef tenderloin calf's-head carpaccio with braised oxtail praline and foie gras–sautéed baby vegetables. Desserts are impressive: try the beetroot meringue with mascarpone lemon cream and "fromage blanc" sherbet. $ *Average main: €40* ⊠ *Neuturmstr. 1, City Center* ☎ *089/290–980* ⊕ *www.mandarinoriental.com* ✣ *E5.*

$

ITALIAN

✕ **Nero Pizza & Lounge.** The pizzas and pastas are great at this independent restaurant: try the Diavola, with spicy Neopolitan salami. On a side street between Gärtnerplatz and Isartor, Nero has high ceilings and large windows that give it an open, spacious feel; you can sit upstairs in the lounge for a cozier experience. $ *Average main: €13* ⊠ *Rumfordstr. 34, City Center* ☎ *089/2101–9060* ⊕ *www.nero-muenchen.de* Ⓜ *Isartor (S-bahn)* ✣ *F6.*

$

GERMAN

✕ **Nürnberger Bratwurst Glöckl am Dom.** One of Munich's most popular beer taverns is dedicated to the delicious *Nürnberger Bratwürste* (finger-size sausages), a specialty from the rival Bavarian city of Nüremberg. They're served by a busy team of friendly waitresses dressed in Bavarian dirndls who flit between the crowded tables with remarkable agility. There are other options available as well. In warmer months, tables are placed outside, partly under a large awning, beneath the towering Frauenkirche. In winter the mellow dark-panel dining rooms provide relief from the cold. ▮▮**TIP**➔ For a quick, cheaper beer go to the side door where, just inside, there is a little window serving fresh Augustiner from a wooden barrel. You can stand around with the regulars or enjoy the small courtyard if the weather is nice. ⑤ *Average main: €10* ✉ *Frauenpl. 9, City Center* ☎ *089/291–9450* ⊕ *www.bratwurst-gloeckl. de* Ⓜ *Marienplatz (U-bahn and S-bahn)* ✛ *D5.*

$ ✕ **Pfälzer Residenz Weinstube.** A huge stone-vaulted room, a few smaller
GERMAN rooms on the side, wooden tables, flickering candles, dirndl-clad waitresses, and a long list of wines add up to a storybook image of a timeless Germany. The wines are mostly from the Pfalz (Palatinate), as are many of the specialties on the limited menu. Beer drinkers, take note—it is not served here. ⑤ *Average main: €8* ✉ *Residenzstr. 1, City Center* ☎ *089/225–628* ⊕ *www.bayernpfalz.de* Ⓜ *Odeonsplatz (U-bahn)* ✛ *E4.*

$$ ✕ **Prinz Myshkin.** Traditional Bavarian dishes can sometimes be heavy
VEGETARIAN affairs, and after a meal or three they can become a bit much. This restaurant is one of the finest in the city, and it's vegetarian to boot, with a selection of vegan dishes. The delightful holiday from meat here provides an eclectic choice of skillfully prepared antipasti, quiche, pizza, gnocchi, tofu, crepes, stir-fried dishes, plus excellent wines. The airy room has a high, vaulted ceiling, and there's always some art exhibited to feed the eye and mind. ⑤ *Average main: €18* ✉ *Hackenstr. 2, City Center* ☎ *089/265–596* ⊕ *www.prinzmyshkin.com* Ⓜ *Marienplatz (U-bahn and S-bahn)* ✛ *D5.*

$$$$ ✕ **Restaurant Dallmayr.** Enter one of Munich's premier delicatessens,
EUROPEAN where rows of specialties tempt your nose. If you can tear yourself
Fodor's Choice away from the mesmerizing displays of foods, take a carpeted flight of
★ stairs either to the much-vaunted **Restaurant Dallmayr** or the adjoining elegant-yet-casual **Café-Bistro.** Whether your choice is restaurant or café, this place is a sheer delight, showcasing delicacies from the delicatessen, while the service is friendly and attentive. Few are surprised that Diethard Urbansky, head chef at Restaurant Dallmayr, has won Michelin stars from 2009 onward. Menus change often, but a typical starter might be red king prawns with vegetables and yogurt. For mains, try the Nebraska beef with goose liver, tarragon, and pineapple. ⑤ *Average main: €48* ✉ *Dienerstr. 14–15, City Center* ☎ *089/213–50* ⊕ *www. dallmayr.de* ⊘ *Restaurant closed Sun. and Mon.* ✛ *E4.*

$ ✕ **Schmalznudel Café Frischhut.** From the deep Bavarian accent to the
GERMAN food on offer, this is as Bavarian as one could get, though it serves neither typical great slabs of meat nor Knödel. The fryers are turned on each day and by mid-day lines of people are waiting for helpings of freshly cooked *Schmalznudel*, a selection of doughnut-type creations, from apple to sugar-coated to plain. It's really no more than a narrow-passage, kind-of café, located on a busy street between the Stadtmuseum and Viktualienmarkt, and easily missed by those not in the know. Regulars are equally happy whether they manage to find a seat inside or at the handful of tables outside. And there's always the option to take away and eat as you wind your way through the ever-colourful market. ⑤ *Average main: €2* ✉ *Prälat-Zistl-Str. 8, City Center* ▭ *No credit cards* ⊘ *Closed Sun.* ✛ *D5.*

$$$ ✕ **Spatenhaus an der Oper.** The best seats are the window tables on the
GERMAN second floor. The quiet dining room walls and ceiling are paneled with old hand-painted wood and have a wonderful view of the square and the opera house. Make a reservation if you want to come after a

performance. The outdoor tables are a favorite for people-watching. There are few better places for roasted fillet of brook trout, lamb with ratatouille, or duck with apple and red cabbage. And they do the best Wiener Schnitzel in the city. Leave room for one of the wonderful desserts featuring fresh fruit. ⑤ *Average main: €26* ⊠ *Residenzstr. 12, City Center* ☎ *089/290–7060* ⊕ *www.kuffler-gastronomie.de* Ⓜ *Odeonsplatz (U-bahn)* ✛ *E4.*

$$$$ ⨯ **Weinhaus Neuner.** Munich's oldest wine tavern serves good food as

GERMAN well as superior wines in its two nooks: the wood-panel restaurant and the Weinstube. The choice of food is remarkable, from roast duck to fish to traditional Bavarian. ⑤ *Average main: €26* ⊠ *Herzogspitalstr.8, City Center* ☎ *089/260–3954* ⊕ *www.weinhaus-neuner.de* ⦷ *Closed Sun. and holidays* Ⓜ *Marienplatz (U-bahn and S-bahn)* ✛ *C5.*

$ ⨯ **Weisses Bräuhaus.** If you've developed a taste for Weissbier, this insti-

GERMAN tution in downtown Munich is the place to indulge. The tasty brew from Schneider, a Bavarian brewery in existence since 1872, is served with hearty Bavarian dishes, mostly variations of pork and dumplings or cabbage. The restaurant itself was beautifully restored in 1993 to something approaching how it would have looked when first opened in the 1870s. The waitresses here are famous in Munich for being a little more straight talking than visitors might be used to in restaurants back home. But if you're good-natured, the whole thing can be quite funny. There is the possibility to sit outside, though it is quite a busy street. Credit cards are accepted for totals over 20 euros, but with the good beer and food, this shouldn't be difficult to reach. ⑤ *Average main: €11* ⊠ *Tal 7, City Center* ☎ *089/290–1380* ⊕ *www.weisses-brauhaus. de* Ⓜ *Marienplatz (U-bahn and S-bahn)* ✛ *E5.*

$$ ⨯ **Zum Dürnbräu.** In existence in one form or another since 1487, this

GERMAN is easily one of the oldest establishments serving food in Munich, and there's little surprise that the food is resolutely traditional: lots of roast meat, potato and bread dumplings, fish, and equally hearty desserts. As the "Bräu" in the name suggests, this was also a brewery centuries ago. The front Biergarten is small so get there early in good weather. Inside, the central 21-foot table is a favorite spot and fills up first. It's popular and attracts everyone from business people to students. ⑤ *Average main: €16* ⊠ *Dürnbräugasse 2, City Center* ☎ *089/222–195* ⊕ *www. zumduernbraeu.de* Ⓜ *Marienplatz (U-bahn and S-bahn)* ✛ *F5.*

ROYAL MUNICH

$$$ ⨯ **Gandl.** This Italian specialty shop, where you can buy various sta-

ITALIAN ples from vinegar to coffee, doubles as a comfortable, relaxed restaurant. Their extensive Saturday buffet breakfast is popular in the neighborhood. Seating can become a little crowded inside, but the excellent service will make up for it and you'll feel right at home. For lunch it's just the place for a quick pastry or excellent antipasto misto before proceeding with the day's adventures. Dinner is more relaxed, with Mediterranean-influenced cuisine. ⑤ *Average main: €21* ⊠ *St.-Anna-Pl. 1, Lehel* ☎ *089/2916–2525* ⊕ *www.gandl.de* ⦷ *Closed Sun.* Ⓜ *Lehel (U-bahn)* ✛ *G4.*

$ ✕**Gasthaus Isarthor.** This old-fashioned *Wirtshaus* is one of the few
GERMAN places that serve Augustiner beer exclusively from wooden kegs, freshly
tapped on a daily basis. Beer simply doesn't get any better than this.
The traditional Bavarian fare is good, and the mid-day menu changes
daily. All kinds are drawn to the simple wooden tables of this unspectacular establishment. Antlers and a wild boar look down on actors,
government officials, apprentice craftspersons, journalists, and retirees,
all sitting side by side. $ *Average main: €10* ⊠ *Kanalstr. 2, Altstadt-
Lehel* ☎ *089/227–753* ⊕ *www.gasthaus-isarthor.de* ⊟ *No credit cards*
Ⓜ *Isartor (S-bahn)* ✛ *F5.*

SCHWABING AND MAXVORSTADT

$ ✕**Alter Simpl.** Named after Germany's most famous satirical magazine,
GERMAN *Simplicissimus,* this pub-restaurant has been a Munich institution since
1903, when it was a meeting and discussion center for leading writers,
comedians, and artists. Today the pictures of those days hang on the dark
wood-panel walls. It's quite small inside and far from salubrious, but the
beer's good and the equally good food is served until 2 am (beer until
3 am). The menu includes filling options like roast pork, Munich schnitzel, and a bacon-cheeseburger with french fries. Students are at home here
and will welcome anyone at their table when the others are all taken.
$ *Average main: €11* ⊠ *Türkenstr. 57, Maxvorstadt* ☎ *089/272–3083*
⊕ *www.altersimpl.com* ⊟ *No credit cards* Ⓜ *Universität (U-bahn)* ✛ *E1.*

$ ✕**Cohen's.** There is little overly fancy at Cohen's. There doesn't need to
ISRAELI be. Reviving the old Jewish central European tradition of good, healthy
cooking combined with hospitality and good cheer seems to be the
underlying principle. Dig into a few hearty latkes, a steaming plate of
Chulend stew, or standard gefilte fish doused with excellent Golan wine
from Israel. The kitchen is open from noon to 3 and 6 to 10:30, later
when patrons and staff are in the mood to chatter until the wee hours.
■ TIP➔ **Klezmer singers perform on some Friday evenings.** $ *Average
main: €15* ⊠ *Theresienstr. 31, Maxvorstadt* ☎ *089/280–9545* ⊕ *www.
cohens.de* ⊗ *Closed Sun.* Ⓜ *Theresienstrasse (U-bahn)* ✛ *E2.*

$ ✕**Görrreshof.** In 1893 Augustiner, the oldest brewery in Munich, built
GERMAN this sturdy Wirtshaus to sustain travelers on the 12-km trek from Munich
to the castles at Schleissheim. This pub-restaurant has been renovated
over the years and is today as much a forum for good eating and drinking as it was more than 100 years ago. You'll get hearty food in a dining
room festooned with antlers. If you want to relax further, retire to the
small *Bibliothek* (library), or head outside to sit on the covered terrace.
$ *Average main: €14* ⊠ *Görresstr. 38, Maxvorstadt* ☎ *089/2020–9550*
⊕ *www.goerreshof.de* Ⓜ *Josephsplatz (U-bahn)* ✛ *B1.*

$ ✕**Kaisergarten.** Locals get together for a beer or two and some traditional
GERMAN Bavarian food at this understated neighborhood standby. Beef served
several ways is the specialty, but the kitchen also does a good job with
fish, fresh from a Bavarian stream. Outside, the small Biergarten under
chestnut trees faces the church in the middle of Kaiserplatz (Emperor's
Square); inside, racks of wine provide atmosphere and a good alternative
to beer. $ *Average main: €15* ⊠ *Kaiserstr. 34, Schwabing* ☎ *089/3402–
0203* ⊕ *www.kaisergarten.com* Ⓜ *Münchner Freiheit (U-bahn)* ✛ *E1.*

2

$$$
ITALIAN
Fodor'sChoice
★

✕ **Limoni.** It's not just Munich's neoclassical architecture that underpins its playful, centuries-old moniker as Italy's most northern city. There are a number of fine Italian restaurants around the city, but this is certainly one of the best. You'll pay more for meat and fish dishes, but there are also lovely pasta dishes that are a little more budget friendly. There is a Bavarian professionalism combined with Italian grace and elegance in how the delicacies are served: pea and ginger cream soup, fusilli and veal ragout, artichokes and grated horseradish to name just a few, and then the fantastic chocolate cake with mascarpone cream. ∎ TIP➜ Be sure to reserve your table in good weather so you can sit on the charming patio in the back; note that warm food is only served from 6:30 pm to 11 pm. Ⓢ *Average main: €24* ✉ *Amalienstr. 38, Maxvorstadt* ☎ *089/2880–6029* ⊕ *www.limoni-ristorante.com* ☾ *Closed Sun. and holidays* Ⓜ *Universität (U-bahn)* ✛ *E2.*

$
GERMAN

✕ **Max-Emanuel-Brauerei.** This historic old brewery tavern, first opened in 1880, is a great value, with great-value Bavarian dishes. The best part about this place, however, is the cozy, secluded little beer garden with huge chestnut trees, tucked in the back amid the apartment blocks. Ⓢ *Average main: €11* ✉ *Adalbertstr. 33, Schwabing* ☎ *089/271–5158* ⊕ *www.max-emanuel-brauerei.de* Ⓜ *Universität (U-bahn)* ✛ *E1.*

$$$$
EUROPEAN
Fodor'sChoice
★

✕ **Tantris.** Despite the slightly dramatic exterior, which is adorned by three concrete animals, few restaurants in Germany can match the Michelin-starred Tantris. Select the menu of the day and accept the suggestions of the sommelier or choose from the à la carte options and you'll be in for a treat, for example: variation of char with marinated white asparagus and orange hollandaise, followed by roast lamb filets with spinach, beans and fennel-curry puree, superbly complemented by stuffed semolina dumpling with raspberries and curd cheese ice cream. It surprises few that head chef Hans Haas has kept his restaurant at the top of the critics' charts in Munich for so long. ∎ TIP➜ Look out for the Tantris Standl, a small outlet at the city-centre Schrannenhalle, selling spirits, wines, coffees, chutneys, and sweets. Ⓢ *Average main: €100* ✉ *Johann-Fichte-Str. 7, Schwabing* ☎ *089/361–9590* ⊕ *www.tantris. de* ⌂ *Reservations essential* ⌂ *Jacket and tie* ☾ *Closed Sun., Mon., and bank holidays* Ⓜ *Münchener Freiheit (U-bahn)* ✛ *F1.*

$
GERMAN

✕ **Vorstadt Café.** Young professionals mix with students at this lively restaurant on the corner of Adalbert and Türkenstrasse. The 13 different breakfasts are a big draw: the Vorstadt Classic includes ham and eggs, rolls and several kinds of bread, with a plate of salami and home made jam; the Veggie has scrambled eggs with tomatoes, cheese and spinach, and muesli with fresh fruit, and cheese with nuts. Their daily lunch specials, served quickly, are good value. The atmosphere at dinner is relaxed, complete with candlelight. Reservations are advised at weekends. Ⓢ *Average main: €13* ✉ *Türkenstr. 83, Maxvorstadt* ☎ *089/272–0699* ⊕ *www.vorstadtcafe.de* ▭ *No credit cards* Ⓜ *Universität (U-bahn)* ✛ *E1.*

LEOPOLDVORSTADT

$ ✕ **Augustiner Keller.** This flagship beer restaurant of one of Munich's
GERMAN   oldest breweries originated about 1812. It is also the location of the
unbeatable Augustiner beer garden, which should be at the top of any
visitor's beer-garden list. The menu offers Bavarian specialties, including
half a duck with a good slab of roast suckling pig, dumpling, and blue
cabbage. If you're up for it, end your meal with a *Dampfnudel* (yeast
dumpling served with custard), though you probably won't feel hungry
again for quite a while. $ *Average main: €14* ✉ *Arnulfstr. 52, Max-
vorstadt* ☎ *089/594–393* ⊕ *www.augustinerkeller.de* Ⓜ *Hauptbahnhof
(U-bahn and S-bahn)* ✛ *A3.*

HAIDHAUSEN

$$$ ✕ **Vinaiolo.** Munich is sometimes referred to as Italy's northernmost
ITALIAN   city, and this bright, busy place is the proof. In the setting of an old
apothecary, diners can enjoy specialties from Venice and other north-
ern Italian regions, such as spaghetti with sardines or roast goat, pre-
pared to perfection by chef Marco Pizzolato. Service is good-humored
and conscientious and the menu changes regularly. $ *Average main:
€22* ✉ *Steinstr. 42, Haidhausen* ☎ *089/4895–0356* ⊕ *www.vinaiolo.de*
Ⓜ *Rosenheimer Platz (S-bahn)* ✛ *H6.*

$ ✕ **Wirtshaus in der Au.** *Wirtshaus* is a word that describes a kind of bar-
GERMAN   restaurant serving traditional Bavaria food and beer. This has been serving
since 1901 and it's one of the best. A stone's throw from the Deutsches
Museum, it has a great vaulted room and collections of beer steins, provid-
ing one of the best atmospheres around. It has a combination of fantastic
service and outstanding local dishes, and it serves everything from *Hofente*
(roast duck) to *Schweinsbraten* (roast pork). But the real specialty, and for
which it is renowned, is *Knödel* (dumplings), which, in addition to tradi-
tional *Semmel* (bread) and *Kartoffel* (potato) varieties, come in spinach,
cheese, and even red-beet flavors. Weather permitting, you can sit in the
small beer garden under, of course, chestnut trees. A day in the Deutsches
Museum followed by an evening here, and Munich doesn't get much bet-
ter. $ *Average main: €11* ✉ *Lilienstr. 51, Haidhausen* ☎ *089/4809–0589*
⊕ *www.wirtshausinderau.de* Ⓜ *Isartor (S-bahn and Tram)* ✛ *H6.*

WHERE TO STAY

Though Munich has a vast number of hotels in all price ranges, booking
one can be a challenge, as this is a trade-show city as well as a prime
tourist destination. If you're visiting during any of the major trade fairs
such as the ISPO (sports, fashion) in January or the IHM (crafts) in
mid-March, or during Oktoberfest at the end of September, try to make
reservations at least a few months in advance. It is acceptable practice
in Europe to request to see a room before committing to it, so feel free
to ask the concierge.

Some of the large, upscale hotels that cater to expense-account business
travelers have attractive weekend discount rates—sometimes as much
as 50% below normal prices. Conversely, most hotels raise their regular

rates by at least 30% during big trade fairs and Oktoberfest. Online booking sites like Hotel Reservation Service (⊕ *www.hrs.com*) often have prices well below the hotel's published prices (i.e., price ranges in this book) in slow periods and on short notice. Look for the names we suggest here and search online for potential deals.

■**TIP**➜ Munich's tourist information office has two outlets that can help you with hotel bookings if you haven't reserved in advance. One is at the central station and the other is on Marienplatz, in the Rathaus. Your best bet is to visit in person.

A technical note: A few years ago, some hotels in Munich chose to farm out their wireless Internet services to third parties—meaning that you could get online with their Wi-Fi hotspot, but you had to log in with a credit card and pay with a separate service provider. Thankfully, this is changing, and most of the newer hotels, plus some forward-thinking older establishments, offer Wi-Fi for free throughout.

Prices in the reviews are the lowest cost of a standard double room in high season. For expanded reviews, facilities, and current deals, visit Fodors.com. Use the coordinate (✛ B3) at the end of each listing to locate a site on the corresponding map.

CITY CENTER

$$$
HOTEL

▦ **Anna Hotel.** Modern, slightly minimalist decor and features are the characteristic of this design hotel. **Pros:** terrific location; fabulous views from the top floor; beds are huge; free Wi-Fi throughout. **Cons:** bar and restaurant get hectic from passersby on the busy street; no single rooms. ⑤ *Rooms from: €220* ✉ *Schützenstr. 1, City Center* ☎ *089/599–940* ⊕ *www.annahotel.de* ↜ *73 rooms* ⑩ *Breakfast* ✛ *B4.*

$$$$
HOTEL
Fodor's Choice
★

▦ **Bayerischer Hof.** There's the Michelin-starred restaurant, the swanky suites, the rooftop Blue Spa and Lounge with panoramic city views, fitness studio, pool, private cinema, and to top it all suites in Palais Montgelas, the adjoining early 19th-century palace. **Pros:** superb public rooms with valuable oil paintings; the roof garden restaurant has an impressive view of the Frauenkirche two blocks away; Atelier restaurant has again been awarded a Michelin star. **Cons:** expensive; Wi-Fi is extra. ⑤ *Rooms from: €360* ✉ *Promenadepl. 2–6, City Center* ☎ *089/21200* ⊕ *www. bayerischerhof.de* ↜ *340 rooms, 65 suites* ⑩ *Breakfast* Ⓜ *Karlsplatz (U-bahn and S-bahn), Marienplatz (U-bahn and S-bahn)* ✛ *D4.*

$$
HOTEL

▦ **Cortiina.** One of Munich's design hotels, Cortiina follows the minimalist gospel. **Pros:** welcoming modern reception and bar; nice, comfortable rooms; personalized service. **Cons:** Hotel's Bar Central is over the road. ⑤ *Rooms from: €169* ✉ *Ledererstr. 8, City Center* ☎ *089/242– 2490* ⊕ *www.cortiina.com* ↜ *75 rooms* ⑩ *Breakfast* Ⓜ *Marienplatz (U-bahn and S-bahn)* ✛ *E5.*

$
HOTEL

▦ **Hotel am Markt.** You can literally stumble out the door of this hotel onto the Viktualienmarkt. **Pros:** excellent location; friendly and helpful staff; free Wi-Fi; decent restaurant. **Cons:** rooms are simple; some spots could use fresh paint; no credit cards. ⑤ *Rooms from: €77* ✉ *Heiliggeiststr. 6, City Center* ☎ *089/225–014* ⊕ *www.hotel-am-markt.eu* ↜ *22 rooms* ⑩ *Breakfast* Ⓜ *Marienplatz (U-bahn and S-bahn)* ✛ *E5.*

BEST BETS FOR MUNICH LODGING

Fodor's Choice★	$$$	BEST LOBBY
Admiral, $$$, p. 106	Platzl Hotel, p. 103	Hotel Vier Jahreszeiten München Kempinski, $$$$, p. 102
Bayerischer Hof, $$$$, p. 101	$$$$	
Hotel Uhland, $, p. 107	Bayerischer Hof, p. 101	BEST LOCATION
The Louis Hotel, $$$, p. 102	Hotel Vier Jahreszeiten München Kempinski, p. 102	Eden-Hotel Wolff, $$$, p. 105
Hotel Pension am Siegestor, $, p. 105		Hotel Amba, $$, p. 105
Best by Price	**Best by Experience**	BEST FOR OKTOBERFEST
$	BEST HOTEL BARS	Brack, $, p. 106
Hotel Am Markt, p. 101	Admiral, $$$, p. 106	Hotel Uhland, $, p. 107
Hotel Uhland, p. 107	Bayerischer Hof, $$$$, p. 101	BEST VIEWS
Hotel Pension am Siegestor, p. 105	BEST FOR JOGGERS	Anna Hotel, $$$, p. 101
$$	Biederstein, $$, p. 104	
Cortiina, p. 101	Gästehaus am Englischen Garten, $, p. 104	

$ **Hotel Kraft.** Conveniently located between the city center and the
HOTEL Oktoberfest grounds, the lobby of this basic hotel is inviting with wood
paneled walls and comfortable armchairs. **Pros:** privately owned; hotel
and rooms well cared for; quiet neighborhood. **Cons:** quiet neighborhood, so no nightlife. $ *Rooms from: €100* ⊠ *Schillerstr. 49, Lud-*
wigvorstadt ☏ *089/550–5940* ⊕ *www.hotel-kraft.com* ⤳ *33 rooms*
Breakfast Ⓜ *Marienplatz (U-bahn and S-bahn)* ✛ *B5.*

$$$$ **Hotel Vier Jahreszeiten Kempinski München.** It likes to call its lobby the
HOTEL "most beautiful living room in Munich," and just as the world's wealthy
and titled have felt for more than 150 years, you'll feel at home enjoying
a drink and a bite in this "lived-in" spacious and luxurious room with
glass dome and with dark-wood paneling. **Pros:** great location; occasional special packages that are a good value; Wi-Fi free. **Cons:** everything
is expensive. $ *Rooms from: €260* ⊠ *Maximilianstr. 17, City Center*
☏ *089/2125–2799* ⊕ *www.Kempinski-Vierjahreszeiten.de* ⤳ *230 rooms,*
67 suites *Breakfast* Ⓜ *Tram 19 Kammerspiele (Tram)* ✛ *F4.*

$$$ **The Louis Hotel.** No other hotel in Munich manages to combine the
HOTEL subdued elegance of a design hotel, first-rate service, and perhaps the
Fodor's Choice best city center location, overlooking Viktualienmarkt, as this hotel.
★ **Pros:** brilliant location; attentive service; modern designs; very good
restaurant. **Cons:** some rooms pricey; the bustle of the Viktualien-
markt is not for everyone; parking costs €24 a day. $ *Rooms from:*

€189 ✉ *Viktualienmarkt 6, City Center* ☎ *089/4111–9080* ⊕ *www. louis-hotel.com* ↝ *72 rooms* ⊙❘ *Breakfast* Ⓜ *Marienplatz (U-bahn and S-bahn)* ⊹ *E5.*

$$ ⛣ **Mercure Hotel Muenchen Altstadt.** This straightforward, comfortable
HOTEL hotel is a decent deal for its great location; there are a number of Mercure hotels in Munich, but this location, between Marienplatz and Sendlingertor, is in the city center. **Pros:** central location; moderate price; free mineral water; free Wi-Fi. **Cons:** public parking garage is a bit of a hike. $ *Rooms from: €168* ✉ *Hotterstr. 4, City Center* ☎ *089/232– 590* ⊕ *www.mercure-muenchen-altstadt.de* ↝ *75 rooms* ⊙❘ *Breakfast* Ⓜ *Marienplatz (U-bahn and S-bahn)* ⊹ *D5.*

$ ⛣ **Motel One München-Sendlinger Tor.** With well-thought-out designs and
HOTEL free Wi-Fi, the Motel One chain jumped ahead of the game with its simple but classy concept. **Pros:** great prices and location; decent designs; amiable, attentive service; kids ages 1–6 get a free breakfast. **Cons:** staying in one is like staying in all of them; no restaurant or room service; breakfast, parking, and pets cost extra. $ *Rooms from: €84* ✉ *Herzog-Wilhelm-Str. 28, City Center* ☎ *089/5177–7250* ⊕ *www.motel-one.com/de* ↝ *241 rooms* ⊙❘ *Breakfast* Ⓜ *Karlsplatz (U-bahn and S-bahn)* ⊹ *C6.*

$$$ ⛣ **Platzl Hotel.** The privately owned Platzl has won awards and wide
HOTEL recognition for its ecologically aware management, which uses heat recyclers in the kitchen, environmentally friendly detergents, recyclable materials, waste separation, and other eco-friendly practices. **Pros:** good restaurant; progressive environmental credentials; around the corner from the Hofbräuhaus; free Wi-Fi throughout. **Cons:** rooms facing the Hofbräuhaus get more noise; some rooms are on the small side. $ *Rooms from: €212* ✉ *Sparkassenstr. 10, City Center* ☎ *089/2370– 3722* ⊕ *www.platzl.de* ↝ *167 rooms* ⊙❘ *Breakfast* Ⓜ *Marienplatz (U-bahn and S-bahn)* ⊹ *E5.*

$$$ ⛣ **Torbräu.** The welcoming Torbräu has been looking after guests in one
HOTEL form or another since 1490, making it the oldest hotel in Munich, and it has been run by the same family for more than a century. **Pros:** nice rooms; central location; good restaurant; very attentive service. **Cons:** underground parking difficult; front rooms a little noisy. $ *Rooms from: €205* ✉ *Tal 41, City Center* ☎ *089/242–340* ⊕ *www.torbraeu. de* ↝ *90 rooms* ⊙❘ *Breakfast* Ⓜ *Isartor (S-bahn)* ⊹ *F5.*

ROYAL MUNICH

$$ ⛣ **Adria.** This modern hotel is near a number of great museums and the
HOTEL English Garden. **Pros:** good location; nice lobby. **Cons:** no bar or restaurant; Wi-Fi costs extra. $ *Rooms from: €124* ✉ *Liebigstr. 8a, Lehel* ☎ *089/242–1170* ⊕ *www.adria-muenchen.de* ↝ *45 rooms* ⊙❘ *Breakfast* Ⓜ *Lehel (U-bahn)* ⊹ *G4.*

$$ ⛣ **Hotel Concorde.** The privately owned Concorde is in the middle of
HOTEL Munich and yet peaceful owing to its location on a narrow side street. **Pros:** quiet; functional; good location. **Cons:** no restaurant or bar; Wi-Fi costs extra. $ *Rooms from: €136* ✉ *Herrnstr. 38–40, Lehel* ☎ *089/224– 515* ⊕ *www.concorde-muenchen.de* ↝ *72 rooms* ⊙❘ *Breakfast* Ⓜ *Isartor (S-bahn)* ⊹ *F5.*

$$ ⊞ **Hotel Opera.** In the quiet residential district of Lehel, Hotel Opera
HOTEL offers rooms decorated in an elegant style—lots of Empire, some art
deco; some rooms even have glassed-in balconies. **Pros:** free Wi-Fi
throughout; elegant; pleasant courtyard; quiet location; special service.
Cons: not enough parking close to the hotel; no restaurant. ⑤ *Rooms
from: €175* ✉ *St.-Anna-Str. 10, Lehel* ☎ *089/2104–9410* ⊕ *www.hotel-
opera.de* ↩ *25 rooms* ⑪ *Breakfast* Ⓜ *Lehel (U-bahn)* ✛ *G4.*

SCHWABING AND MAXVORSTADT

$$ ⊞ **Biederstein.** A modern, block of a building, but covered with gera-
HOTEL niums in summer, the Biederstein seems to want to fit into its old
Schwabing surroundings at the edge of the English Garden. **Pros:**
wonderfully quiet location; all rooms have balconies; exemplary service; U-bahn is four blocks away. **Cons:** not the most handsome building; no restaurant. ⑤ *Rooms from: €129* ✉ *Keferstr. 18, Schwabing*
☎ *089/3302–9390* ⊕ *www.hotel-biederstein.de* ↩ *34 rooms, 7 suites*
⑪ *Breakfast* Ⓜ *Münchner Freiheit (U-bahn)* ✛ *G1.*

$$ ⊞ **Carlton Astoria.** Its downtown location, near the Pinakotheken (art
HOTEL museums) and the university, means you can reach many places on
foot. **Pros:** centrally located; fairly priced; free Wi-Fi. **Cons:** rooms on
main street can be noisy; parking is a short walk away. ⑤ *Rooms from:*
€150 ✉ *Fürstenstr. 12, Maxvorstadt* ☎ *089/383–9630* ⊕ *www.carlton-
astoria.de* ↩ *48 rooms* ⑪ *Breakfast* Ⓜ *Universität (U-bahn), Odeon-
splatz (U-bahn)* ✛ *E2.*

$$ ⊞ **Cosmopolitan.** The entrance to this inviting hotel is on the lively
HOTEL Hohenzollernstrasse, but once you pass through what looks like a
garage opening, you'll find yourself in a quiet courtyard. **Pros:** right
in the middle of Schwabing, Münchner Freiheit a city block away;
quiet courtyard rooms. **Cons:** no restaurant; streetside rooms are noisy.
⑤ *Rooms from: €135* ✉ *Hohenzollernstr. 5, Schwabing* ☎ *089/383–
810* ⊕ *www.cosmopolitanhotel.de* ↩ *71 rooms, 8 suites* ⑪ *Breakfast*
Ⓜ *Münchner Freiheit (U-bahn)* ✛ *F1.*

$ ⊞ **Gästehaus am Englischen Garten.** Reserve well in advance for a room at
HOTEL this popular converted water mill, more than 300 years old, adjoining
the English Garden. **Pros:** quiet location; ideal for walking or cycling;
wonderfully cozy rooms. **Cons:** no elevator; no restaurant; you have
to go to their partner hotel, around the corner, for free Internet access.
⑤ *Rooms from: €83* ✉ *Liebergesellstr. 8, Schwabing* ☎ *089/383–9410*
⊕ *www.hotelenglischergarten.de* ↩ *12 rooms, 6 with bath or shower;*
13 apartments ⑪ *Breakfast* Ⓜ *Münchner Freiheit (U-bahn)* ✛ *G1.*

$$ ⊞ **H'otello F'22.** This is a high-caliber example of the design- and style-
HOTEL driven nature of the new Munich hotel scene—the style is minimalist, but
with a roomy feel. **Pros:** great location; well-thought-out design; some
rooms have balconies; free Wi-Fi. **Cons:** no restaurant. ⑤ *Rooms from:*
€126 ✉ *Fallmerayerstr. 22, Schwabing* ☎ *089/4583–1200* ⊕ *www.hotello.
de* ↩ *74 rooms* ⑪ *Breakfast* Ⓜ *Hohenzollernplatz (U-bahn)* ✛ *E1.*

$$ ⊞ **H'otello H'09.** The second in the H'otello chain to open in Munich,
HOTEL this high-design hotel is a five-minute walk to the Englischer Garten; the
style is minimalist but still luxurious with king-size beds and a breakfast buffet. **Pros:** free Wi-Fi; great location; well-thought-out design;

uncomplicated rooms. **Cons:** no restaurant. $ *Rooms from: €126* ⊠ *Hohenzollernstr. 9, Schwabing* ☏ *089/4583–1200* ⊕ *www.hotello. de* ⤳ *71 rooms* ⫶❍⫶ *Breakfast* Ⓜ *Giselastrasse (U-bahn)* ✛ *F1.*

$

B&B/INN

Fodor'sChoice

★

⬚ **Hotel Pension Am Siegestor.** Modest but appealing, the pension—which takes up three floors of a fin de siècle mansion between the Siegestor monument, on Leopoldstrasse, and the university—is a great deal in Germany's most expensive city. **Pros:** a delightful and homey place to stay; very good value stay for the price; not far to walk to the English Garden. **Cons:** if elevators make you nervous, don't use this old one; no restaurant or bar. $ *Rooms from: €74* ⊠ *Akademiestr. 5, Maxvorstadt* ☏ *089/399–550* ⊕ *www.siegestor.com* ⤳ *20 rooms* ▬ *No credit cards* ⫶❍⫶ *Breakfast* Ⓜ *Universität (U-bahn)* ✛ *F1.*

HAUPTBAHNHOF

$$

HOTEL

⬚ **Creatif Hotel Elephant.** Tucked away on a quiet street near the train station, this hotel appeals to a wide range of travelers, from businesspeople to tourists on a budget. **Pros:** close to main station. **Cons:** no restaurant; modest furnishings; Wi-Fi costs extra. $ *Rooms from: €102* ⊠ *Lämmerstr. 6, Maxvorstadt* ☏ *089/555–785* ⊕ *www.creatifelephanthotel. com* ⤳ *40 rooms* Ⓜ *Hauptbahnhof (U-bahn and S-bahn)* ✛ *A3.*

$$$

HOTEL

⬚ **Eden-Hotel Wolff.** Beyond a light-filled lobby, a spacious bar with dark-wood paneling beckons, contributing to the old-fashioned elegance of this downtown favorite. **Pros:** all rooms have a/c; breakfast is included. **Cons:** a little too close to the hustle and bustle of the main station; Wi-Fi costs extra. $ *Rooms from: €188* ⊠ *Arnulfstr. 4, Hauptbahnhof* ☏ *089/551–150* ⊕ *www.ehw.de* ⤳ *210 rooms, 2 suites* ⫶❍⫶ *Breakfast* Ⓜ *Hauptbahnhof (U-bahn and S-bahn)* ✛ *A3.*

$$$

HOTEL

⬚ **Hotel Excelsior.** Just a short walk along an underpass from the Hauptbahnhof station, the Excelsior welcomes you with smiles after the hustle and bustle of the busy train station. **Pros:** welcoming reception; spacious rooms; excellent breakfast; free Wi-Fi throughout. **Cons:** Schützenstrasse can get very busy. $ *Rooms from: €220* ⊠ *Schützenstr. 11, Hauptbahnhof* ☏ *089/551–370* ⊕ *www.excelsior-hotel.de* ⤳ *118 rooms, 9 suites* ⊗ *No lunch Sun. in restaurant* ⫶❍⫶ *Breakfast* Ⓜ *Hauptbahnhof (U-bahn)* ✛ *B4.*

$$

HOTEL

⬚ **Hotel Amba.** Right across the street from the main train station, Amba provides clean, bright rooms, good service, no expensive frills, and everything you need to plug and play. **Pros:** convenient to train station and sights. **Cons:** no restaurant; rooms that face the main street and the station are noisy; there's a cost for Wi-Fi. $ *Rooms from: €101* ⊠ *Arnulfstr. 20, Hauptbahnhof* ☏ *089/545–140* ⊕ *www.hotel-amba.de* ⤳ *86 rooms* ⫶❍⫶ *Breakfast* Ⓜ *Hauptbahnhof (U-bahn and S-bahn)* ✛ *B3.*

$$

HOTEL

⬚ **Hotel Mirabell.** This family-run hotel is used to American tourists who appreciate the friendly service, central location (between the main railway station and the Oktoberfest fairgrounds), and reasonable room rates. **Pros:** Wi-Fi free throughout; family-run; personalized service. **Cons:** no restaurant; this area of the Hauptbahnhof is not the most salubrious. $ *Rooms from: €115* ⊠ *Landwehrstr. 42, entrance on Goethestr., Hauptbahnhof* ☏ *089/549–1740* ⊕ *www.hotelmirabell. de* ⤳ *65 rooms, 3 apartments* ⫶❍⫶ *Breakfast* Ⓜ *Hauptbahnhof (U-bahn and S-bahn)* ✛ *A5.*

$ [⊞] **Hotel Präsident.** The location—just a block from the main train sta-
HOTEL tion—is the biggest draw of this hotel; the second draw is the price.
Pros: central location; filling breakfast. **Cons:** rooms toward the street
are noisy; streets around the hotel are not the most salubrious; parking 100 yards away costs €5. ⑤ *Rooms from: €97* ⊠ *Schwanthalerstr.
20, Ludwigvorstadt* ☎ *089/549–0060* ⊕ *www.hotel-praesident.de* ⟿ *42
rooms* ¶◯| *Breakfast* Ⓜ *Hauptbahnhof (U-bahn and S-bahn)* ✣ *B5.*

ISARVORSTADT

$$$ [⊞] **Admiral.** The small, privately owned, tradition-rich Admiral enjoys
HOTEL a quiet side-street location and its own garden, close to the river Isar,
Fodor's Choice minutes from the Deutsches Museum. **Pros:** attention to detail; quiet;
★ excellent service. **Cons:** no restaurant. ⑤ *Rooms from: €199* ⊠ *Kohlstr.
9, Isarvorstadt* ☎ *089/216–350* ⊕ *www.hotel-admiral.de* ⟿ *33 rooms*
¶◯| *Breakfast* Ⓜ *Isartor (S-bahn)* ✣ *F6.*

$ [⊞] **Pension Seibel.** If you're looking for an affordable little "pension" a
HOTEL stone's throw from the Viktualienmarkt, this is the place. **Pros:** great
location at a great price; pets are welcome. **Cons:** tiny breakfast room;
no elevator; Wi-Fi and pets cost extra. ⑤ *Rooms from: €79* ⊠ *Reichen-
bachstr. 8, Isarvorstadt* ☎ *089/231–9180* ⊕ *www.seibel-hotels-munich.
de* ⟿ *15 rooms* ¶◯| *Breakfast* Ⓜ *Marienplatz (U-bahn and S-bahn)* ✣ *E6.*

LUDWIGVORSTADT

$ [⊞] **Brack.** A nice, light-filled lobby makes a first good impression,
HOTEL but Oktoberfest revelers value Brack's proximity to the beer-festival
grounds, and its location—on a busy, tree-lined thoroughfare just south
of the city center—is handy for city attractions. **Pros:** good location
for accessing Oktoberfest and city; late breakfast; free use of bikes.
Cons: noisy front rooms. ⑤ *Rooms from: €99* ⊠ *Lindwurmstr. 153,
Ludwigvorstadt* ☎ *089/747–2550* ⊕ *www.hotel-brack.de* ⟿ *50 rooms*
¶◯| *Breakfast* Ⓜ *Poccistrasse (U-bahn)* ✣ *B6.*

$$ [⊞] **Hotel am Viktualienmarkt.** This highly recommendable middle-market
HOTEL design-led hotel is perfectly located a few hundred meters from Viktu-
alienmarkt and the Gärtnerplatz quarter. **Pros:** refreshing atmosphere;
service attentive but not overbearing; great location; lovely courtyard
for breakfast; competitive prices. **Cons:** no a/c; no restaurant; parking around the corner. ⑤ *Rooms from: €120* ⊠ *Utzschneiderstr. 14,
Ludwigvorstadt* ☎ *089/231–1090* ⊕ *www.hotel-am-viktualienmarkt.de*
⟿ *26 rooms* ¶◯| *Breakfast* Ⓜ *Marienplatz (U-bahn and S-bahn)* ✣ *E6.*

$ [⊞] **Hotel Mariandl.** The American armed forces commandeered this turn-
HOTEL of-the-20th-century neo-Gothic mansion in May 1945 and established
Munich's first postwar nightclub, the Femina, on the ground floor.
Pros: hotel and café are charmingly worn and a bit bohemian. **Cons:**
no elevator. ⑤ *Rooms from: €70* ⊠ *Goethestr. 51, Ludwigvorstadt*
☎ *089/552–9100* ⊕ *www.hotelmariandl.com* ⟿ *28 rooms* ¶◯| *Break-
fast* Ⓜ *Hauptbahnhof (U-bahn and S-bahn)* ✣ *A6.*

$ [⊞] **Hotel-Pension Schmellergarten.** Popular with young budget travel-
B&B/INN ers, this genuine family business tries to make everyone feel at home.
Pros: good location; good price; free Wi-Fi. **Cons:** no elevator; no

hotel services. $ *Rooms from: €64* ✉ *Schmellerstr. 20, Ludwigvorstadt* ☎ *089/773–157* ⊕ *www.schmellergarten.de* ⌁ *14 rooms* ❖ *Breakfast* Ⓜ *Poccistrasse (U-bahn)* ✛ *B6.*

$ 🛏 **Hotel Uhland.** This stately villa is a landmark building and is addition-

HOTEL ally special in that the owner and host was born here and will make you

Fodor'sChoice feel at home, too. **Pros:** a real family atmosphere; care is given to details;

★ free Wi-Fi. **Cons:** no restaurant or bar. $ *Rooms from: €95* ✉ *Uhland-str. 1, Ludwigvorstadt* ☎ *089/543–350* ⊕ *www.hotel-uhland.de* ⌁ *27 rooms* ❖ *Breakfast* Ⓜ *Theresienwiese (U-bahn)* ✛ *A6.*

THERESIENHÖHE

$ 🛏 **Park-Hotel Theresienhöhe.** The Park-Hotel claims that none of its rooms

HOTEL is less than 400 square feet and its suites are larger than many luxury apartments, and some of them come with small kitchens. **Pros:** spacious rooms; good quiet location. **Cons:** no restaurant; modern but not great charm; Wi-Fi costs extra. $ *Rooms from: €89* ✉ *Parkstr. 31a, There-sienhöhe* ☎ *089/519–950* ⊕ *www.parkhoteltheresienhoehe.de* ⌁ *40 rooms* ❖ *Breakfast* Ⓜ *Theresienwiese (U-bahn)* ✛ *A5.*

$ 🛏 **Hotel Westend.** Visitors have praised the friendly welcome and ser-

HOTEL vice they receive at this well-maintained and affordable lodging above the Oktoberfest grounds. **Pros:** good location; good prices; free Wi-Fi. **Cons:** no restaurant; rooms are simple; it's best to confirm your res-ervation. $ *Rooms from: €49* ✉ *Schwanthalerstr. 121, Theresienhöhe* ☎ *089/540–9860* ⊕ *www.kurpfalz-hotel.de* ⌁ *44 rooms* ❖ *Breakfast* Ⓜ *Hackerbrücke (S-bahn)* ✛ *B5.*

NYMPHENBURG

$ 🛏 **Erzgiesserei Europe.** Rooms in this modern hotel are bright, decorated

HOTEL in soft pastels with good reproductions on the walls. **Pros:** relatively quiet location; nice courtyard; air-conditioning in all rooms. **Cons:** charm of a business hotel; Wi-Fi costs extra. $ *Rooms from: €90* ✉ *Erzgiessereistr. 15, Nymphenburg* ☎ *089/126–820* ⊕ *www.topinternational.com* ⌁ *106 rooms, 1 suite* ❖ *Breakfast* Ⓜ *Stiglmaierplatz (U-bahn)* ✛ *A2.*

$ 🛏 **Kriemhild.** This welcoming, family-run pension is in a quiet western

HOTEL suburb. **Pros:** quiet location; family run; free Wi-Fi. **Cons:** far from

FAMILY the city sights. $ *Rooms from: €88* ✉ *Guntherstr. 16, Nymphenburg* ☎ *089/171–1170* ⊕ *www.kriemhild.de* ⌁ *18 rooms, 3 suites* ❖ *Break-fast* Ⓜ *Kriemhildstrasse (Tram)* ✛ *A2.*

BOGENHAUSEN

$ 🛏 **Westin Grand München.** The building itself, with 22 floors, may raise

HOTEL a few eyebrows as it stands on a slight elevation and is not the shapeli-est of the Munich skyline. **Pros:** luxurious lobby and restaurant; rooms facing west toward the city have a fabulous view. **Cons:** it's not pos-sible to reserve west-facing rooms; hotel is difficult to reach via pub-lic transportation; at €27, breakfast is expensive; high-speed Wi-Fi cost is expensive. $ *Rooms from: €100* ✉ *Arabellastr. 6, Bogenhau-sen* ☎ *089/92640* ⊕ *www.westin.com/munich* ⌁ *627 rooms, 28 suites* ❖ *Breakfast* Ⓜ *Arabellapark (U-bahn)* ✛ *F1.*

OUTSIDE THE CENTER

$$ **⬚ Jagdschloss.** This century-old hunting lodge in Munich's leafy Ober-
HOTEL menzing suburb is a delightful hotel. **Pros:** peaceful location; beer gar-
den; easy parking. **Cons:** away from the city center; convenient only
with a car; no elevator. ⑤ *Rooms from: €105* ⊠ *Alte Allee 21, München-
Obermenzing* ☎ *089/820–820* ⊕ *www.jagd-schloss.com* ⟿ *35 rooms,
1 suite* ⑩ *Breakfast* ✦ *A4.*

NIGHTLIFE AND THE ARTS

THE ARTS

Bavaria's capital has an enviable reputation as an artistic hot spot.
Details of concerts and theater performances are listed in *in münchen*
and *Monatsprogramm*, booklets available at most hotel reception desks,
newsstands, and tourist offices. *Prinz* magazine lists almost everything
happening in the city, as do a host of other city magazines, while the
superb and official city website (⊕ *www.muenchen.de*) has listings.
Otherwise, just keep your eye open for advertising pillars and posters.

Box Office of the Bavarian State Theaters. Tickets for performances at the
Bavarian State Theater, Nationaltheater, Staatstheater am Gärtnerplatz,
plus many other locations, are sold at the central box office. It's open
Monday to Saturday 10–7. ⊠ *Marstallpl. 5, City Center* ☎ *089/2185–
1920* ⊕ *www.staatstheater-tickets.bayern.de.*

München Ticket. This ticket agency has a German-language website where
tickets for most Munich venues can be booked. ☎ *089/5481–8181*
⊕ *www.muenchenticket.de.*

Zentraler Kartenverkauf. Two Zentraler Kartenverkauf ticket kiosks are in
the underground concourse at Marienplatz, and one at Stachus. ⊠ *City
Center* ☎ *089/292–540 for Marienplatz, 089/5450–6060 for Stachus*
⊕ *www.zkv-muenchen.de.*

CONCERTS

Munich and music go together. The city has two world-renowned
orchestras. The Philharmonic has been directed by Lorin Maazel, for-
merly of the New York Philharmonic, since the 2012/2013 season;
the Bavarian State Opera Company is managed by Japanese-American
director Kent Nagano (he leaves in 2015 for the equivalent position in
Hamburg). The leading choral ensembles are the Munich Bach Choir,
the Munich Motettenchor, and Musica Viva, the last specializing in
contemporary music. The choirs perform mostly in city churches.

Bayerischer Rundfunk Ticket. The Bavarian Radio Symphony Orchestra
sometimes performs at the Bayerischer Rundfunk and other city venues,
such as Gasteig. The box office is open weekdays 9–5:30. ⊠ *Arnulfstr.
42, Ludwigvorstadt* ☎ *089/5900–10880* ⊕ *info.br-klassikticket.de.*

Gasteig Culture Center. This world-class concert hall is in the Gasteig
Culture Center, a hugely expensive, not particularly beautiful brick
complex standing high above the Isar River, east of downtown. Its

Philharmonic Hall is the permanent home of the Munich Philharmonic Orchestra and the largest concert hall in Munich. Gasteig also hosts the occasional English-language work. It hosts the annual book fair and numerous other events and celebrations. ■ TIP→ The sizeable open kitchen Gast (⊕ *www.gast-muenchen.de*), part of the Gasteig complex, is a good option for a range of quick foods, from Thai curries to pizzas. ⊠ *Rosenheimerstr. 5, Haidhausen* ☎ *089/480–980* ⊕ *www.gasteig.de* Ⓜ *Rosenheimerplatz (S-bahn)*.

Herkulessaal in der Residenz. This highly regarded orchestral and recital venue is in the former throne room of King Ludwig I. ⊠ *Residenzstr. 1, City Center* ☎ *0180/5481–8181 via München Ticket* ⊕ *www.muenchenticket.de*.

Hochschule für Musik. Free concerts featuring conservatory students are given at the Hochschule für Musik. ⊠ *Arcisstr. 12, Maxvorstadt* ☎ *089/28903* ⊕ *www.musikhochschule-muenchen.de*.

Nationaltheater (*Bayerische Staatsoper*). The Bavarian State Orchestra is based at the Nationaltheater. ⊠ *Max-Joseph-Pl. 2, City Center* ☎ *089/218–501* ⊕ *www.staatsorchester.de*.

Olympiahalle. One of Munich's major pop-rock concert venue is the Olympiahalle, and the official ticket seller is München Ticket. ⊠ *Spiridon-Louis-Ring 21 Olympiazentrum stop, Milbertshofen* ⊕ *www.olympiapark-muenchen.de; www.muenchenticket.de for tickets*.

Staatstheater am Gärtnerplatz. Under renovation until 2015, the romantic art nouveau Staatstheater am Gärtnerplatz has a variety of performances including operas, ballet, and musicals. Tickets from the theater weekdays 10–6, Saturday 10–1 or Zentraler Kartenvorverkauf in Marienplatz, and Stachus. ⊠ *Gärtnerpl. 3, Isarvorstadt* ☎ *089/2185–1960* ⊕ *www.staatstheater-am-gaertnerplatz.de*.

OPERA, BALLET, AND MUSICALS

Nationaltheater. Munich's Bavarian State Opera Company and its ballet ensemble perform at the Nationaltheater. ⊠ *Max-Joseph-Pl. 2, City Center* ☎ *089/218–501*.

THEATER

Munich has scores of theaters and variety-show venues, although most productions will be largely impenetrable if your German is shaky. Listed here are all the better-known theaters, as well as some of the smaller and more progressive spots. Note that most theaters are closed during July and August.

Cuvilliés-Theater. This is an incredible venue, and though not used too frequently, it is particularly famous for its Mozart productions. ⊠ *Max-Joseph-Pl., entrance on Residenzstr., City Center* ☎ *089/2185–1940* ⊕ *www.residenztheater.de; www.staatstheater-tickets.bayern.de for tickets*.

Amerika Haus (*America House*). Amerika Haus is the venue for the very active American Drama Group Europe, which presents regular English-language productions and talks. ⊠ *Karolinenpl. 3, Maxvorstadt* ☎ *089/552–5370* ⊕ *www.amerikahaus.de*.

Bayerisches Staatsschauspiel (*Bavarian State Theater*). Bayerisches Staatsschauspiel is Munich's leading ensemble for classic playwrights such as Goethe, Schiller, Lessing, Shakespeare, and Chekhov. Its main home is the Residenz Theater, but it also plays at the Cuvilliés-Theater and at Marstall. ⌂ *Max-Joseph-Pl. 1, City Center* ☏ *089/2185–1940* ⊕ *www.bayerischesstaatsschauspiel.de; www.staatstheater-tickets. bayern.de for tickets.*

Deutsches Theater. After years of renovation work, the Deutsches Theater has reopened and is again the premier spot for musicals, revues, balls, and big-band shows. ⌂ *Schwanthalerstr. 9–11, Ludwigvorstadt* ☏ *089/5523–4444 for tickets* ⊕ *www.deutsches-theater.de.*

Münchner Kammerspiele. A city-funded rival to the nearby state-backed Bayerisches Staatsschauspiel, Münchner Kammerspiele-Schauspielhaus presents the classics as well as new works by contemporary playwrights. ⌂ *Maximilianstr. 26–28, City Center* ☏ *089/2339–6600* ⊕ *www. muenchner-kammerspiele.de.*

NIGHTLIFE

Munich has a lively night scene ranging from beer halls to bars to chic clubs. The fun areas for a night out are the City Center, Isarvorstadt (Gärtnerplatz and Glockenbachviertel are arguably the best in the city), and Schwabing around Schellingstrasse and Münchner Freiheit. Regardless of their size or style, many bars, especially around Gärtnerplatz, have DJs spinning either mellow background sounds or funky beats.

However many fingers you want to hold up, just remember the easy-to-pronounce *Bier* (beer) *bit-te* (please) when ordering a beer. The tricky part is, Germans don't just produce *one* beverage called beer; they brew more than 5,000 varieties. Germany has about 1,300 breweries, 40% of the world's total.

In Munich you'll find the most famous breweries, the largest beer halls and beer gardens, the biggest and most indulgent beer festival, and the widest selection of brews. Even the beer glasses are bigger: a *Mass* is a 1-liter (almost 2-pint) serving; a *Halbe* is half a liter and the standard size. The Hofbräuhaus is Munich's best-known beer hall, but you'll find locals in one of the English Garden's four beer gardens or in a *Wirtshaus* (tavern).

In summer, last call at the beer gardens is around 11 pm. Most of the traditional places stay open until 1 am or so and are great for a few hours of wining and dining before heading out on the town. Most bars stay open until at least 3 am on weekends; some don't close until 5 or 6 am.

Munich has hundreds of beer gardens, ranging from huge establishments that seat several hundred to small terraces tucked behind neighborhood pubs; the rest of the beer gardens are a bit farther afield and can be reached handily by bike or S- and U-bahn. Beer gardens are such an integral part of Munich life that a council proposal to cut down their hours provoked a storm of protest in 1995, culminating in one of the largest demonstrations in the city's history. They open whenever the thermometer creeps above 10°C (50°F) and the sun filters through the chestnut trees that are a necessary part of the scenery.

Everybody in Munich has at least one favorite beer garden, so you're usually in good hands if you ask someone to point you in the right direction. You do not need to reserve. No need to phone either: if the weather says yes, then go. Some—but not all—allow you to bring your own food, but if you do, don't defile this hallowed territory with something so foreign as pizza or a burger. Note that Munich has very strict noise laws, so beer gardens tend to close around 11.

There are a few dance clubs in town worth mentioning, but be warned: the larger the venue, the more difficult the entry. In general, big nightclubs are giving way to smaller, more laid-back lounge types of places scattered all over town. If you're really hankering for a big club, go to Optimolwerke in the Ostbahnhof section. Otherwise, enjoy the handful of places around the City Center.

Munich also has a decent jazz scene, and some beer gardens have even taken to replacing their brass oompah bands with funky combos. Jazz musicians sometimes accompany Sunday brunch, too.

CITY CENTER

BARS

Atomic Café. Near the Hofbräuhaus, this club/lounge has excellent DJs nightly, playing everything from '60s Brit pop to '60s/'70s funk and soul. Atomic also has great live acts on a regular basis. ⊠ *Neuturmstr. 5, City Center* ☎ *089/228–3053* ⊕ *www.atomic.de.*

Bar Centrale. Around the corner from the Hofbräuhaus, Bar Centrale is very Italian—the waiters don't seem to speak any other language. The coffee is excellent; small fine meals are served as well. They have a retro-looking back room with leather sofas. ⊠ *Ledererstr. 23, City Center* ☎ *089/223–762* ⊕ *www.bar-centrale.com.*

Eisbach. This bar occupies a corner of the Max Planck Institute building opposite the Bavarian Parliament. It is among Munich's biggest and is overlooked by a mezzanine restaurant area where you can choose from a limited but ambitious menu. Outdoor tables nestle in the expansive shade of huge parasols. The nearby Eisbach brook, which gives the bar its name, tinkles away, lending a relaxed air. ⊠ *Marstallpl. 3, City Center* ☎ *089/2280–1680* ⊕ *www.eisbach.eu.*

Hotel Vier Jahreszeiten Kempinski. The hotel offers piano music until 9 pm, and then dancing to recorded music or a small combo. ⊠ *Maximilianstr. 17, City Center* ☎ *089/2125–2799* ⊕ *www.kempinski.com/de/munich.*

Kilian's Irish Pub and Ned Kelly's Australian Bar. Just behind the Frauenkirche, Kilian's Irish Pub and Ned Kelly's Australian Bar offer an escape from the German tavern scene. Naturally, they have Guinness and Foster's, but they also serve Munich's lager, Augustiner, and regularly televise international soccer, rugby, and sports in general. ⊠ *Frauenpl. 11, City Center* ☎ *089/2421–9899 for both bars* ⊕ *www.kiliansirishpub. com; www.nedkellysbar.com.*

Night Club Bar. The Bayerischer Hof's Night Club Bar has live music, most famously international stars from the jazz scene, but also reggae to hip-hop and everything in between. ⊠ *Promenadepl. 2–6, City Center* ☎ *089/212–0994 for table reservation* ⊕ *www.bayerischerhof.de/en/bars.*

Schumann's. At Schumann's, Munich's most famous bar, the bartenders are busy shaking cocktails after the curtain comes down at the nearby opera house. ⊠ *Odeonspl. 6–7, City Center* ☎ *089/229–060* ⊕ *www. schumanns.de.*

Trader Vic's. Exotic cocktails are the specialty at Trader Vic's, a smart cellar bar in the Hotel Bayerischer Hof that's as popular among out-of-town visitors as it is locals. It's open till 3 in the morning. ⊠ *Promenadenpl. 2–6, City Center* ☎ *089/212–0995* ⊕ *www.bayerischerhof. de/en/bars.*

Pusser's Bar Munich. At the American-inspired, nautical-style Pusser's Bar Munich, great cocktails and Irish-German black-and-tans (Guinness and strong German beer) are made to the sounds of live jazz. Try the "Pain Killer," a specialty of the house. ⊠ *Falkenturmstr. 9, City Center* ☎ *089/220–500* ⊕ *www.pussersbar.de.*

BEER GARDENS

Biergarten am Viktualienmarkt. The only true beer garden in the city center, and therefore the easiest to find, is the one at the Viktualienmarkt. The beer on tap rotates every six weeks among the six Munich breweries to keep everyone happy throughout the year. ⊠ *Viktualienmarkt* ☎ *089/2916–5993* ⊕ *www.biergarten-viktualienmarkt.com.*

Park Café. This is one of Munich's hippest cafés, restaurants, nightclubs, and beer gardens. It often draws a younger crowd, attracted by a thriving music scene in the café itself, which ranges from DJs to live bands, and the occasional celebrity spotting. There's a great atmosphere to go with the good food and drinks, even better when the sun is shining and the beer garden is open. ⊠ *Sophienstr. 7, City Center* ☎ *089/5161–7980* ⊕ *www.parkcafe089.de.*

ROYAL MUNICH

BEER GARDENS

Biergarten am Chinesischen Turm. The famous Biergarten is at the five-story Chinese Tower in the Englischer Garten. Enjoy your beer to the strains of oompah music played by traditionally dressed musicians. ⊠ *Englischer Garten 3* ☎ *089/383–8730* ⊕ *www.chinaturm.de.*

Hirschau. The Hirschau, pleasantly located in the Englischer Garten, has room for 2,500 guests, and it's about 10 minutes north of the Kleinhesselohersee. ⊠ *Gysslingstrasse 15, Englischer Garten* ☎ *089/3609–0490* ⊕ *www.hirschau-muenchen.de.*

Seehaus im Englischen Garten. The Seehaus is on the banks of the artificial lake Kleinhesseloher See, where all of Munich converge on hot summer days. Take Bus No. 44 and exit at Osterwaldstrasse or U-bahn No. 3/6 and stroll through the park. ⊠ *Kleinhesselohe 3* ☎ *089/381–6130* ⊕ *www.kuffler-gastronomie.de/de/muenchen/seehaus.*

DANCE CLUBS

P1. Bordering the Englischer Garten, in a wing of Haus der Kunst, P1 is definitely one of the most popular clubs in town for the see-and-be-seen crowd. It is chockablock with the rich and the wannabe rich and can be fun if you're in the mood. The bouncers can be choosy about whom they let in, so you'll need to dress in style. It also includes the

2013-opened Studio Schwarz, a so-called "performative, excessive, alternative and experimental club area." ⊠ *Prinzregentenstr. 1, on west side of Haus der Kunst, Altstadt-Lehel* ☎ *089/211–1140* ⊕ *www. p1-club.de.*

SCHWABING

BARS

Alter Simpl. Media types drink Weissbier, Helles, as well as Guinness and Kilkenny, at the square bar at Alter Simpl. More than 100 years old, this establishment serves German food until 2 am (weekends till 3 am). ⊠ *Türkenstr. 57, Maxvorstadt* ☎ *089/272–3083* ⊕ *www.eggerlokale.de.*

Schall und Rauch. Up on Schellingstrasse, this legendary student hangout, whose name literally means "Noise and Smoke," has great music and food. ⊠ *Schellingstr. 22, Schwabing* ☎ *089/2880–9577.*

Schelling Salon. Another absolute cornerstone in the neighborhood is the Schelling Salon. On the corner of Barerstrasse, this sizeable bar has several pool tables and even a secret ping-pong room in the basement with an intercom for placing beer orders. The food's not bad and pretty inexpensive. It's closed Tuesday and Wednesday. ⊠ *Schellingstr. 54, Schwabing* ☎ *089/272–0788* ⊕ *www.schelling-salon.de.*

Türkenhof. Across the street is the Türkenhof, another solid local joint that serves Augustiner and good food. ⊠ *Türkenstr. 78, Schwabing* ☎ *089/280–0235* ⊕ *www.augustiner-braeu.de.*

JAZZ

Alfonso's Live Music Club. At tiny Alfonso's the nightly live music redefines the concept of intimacy. ⊠ *Franzstr. 5, Schwabing* ☎ *089/338–835* ⊕ *www.alfonsos.de.*

HAUPTBAHNHOF

BEER GARDENS

Augustiner Keller Biergarten. The Augustiner Keller is one of the more authentic of the beer gardens, with excellent food, beautiful chestnut shade trees, a mixed local crowd, and Munich Augustiner beer. It's a few minutes from the Hauptbahnhof and Hackerbrucke. ⊠ *Arnulfstr. 52, Ludwigvorstadt* ☎ *089/594–393* ⊕ *www.augustinerkeller.de.*

ISARVORSTADT

BARS

Around Gärtnerplatz and Glockenbachviertel are a number of cool bars and clubs for a somewhat younger, hipper crowd.

Café am Hochhaus. If you're looking for a bit more action, check out the Café am Hochhaus. The glass-fronted former coffee shop is now a scene bar with funky DJs playing music to shake a leg to (if it's not too crowded). ⊠ *Blumenstr. 29, City Center* ☎ *089/8905–8152* ⊕ *www. cafeamhochhaus.de.*

Cafe Trachtenvogl. Take a seat on Grandma's retro couches at Cafe Trachtenvogl. The cafe serves all sorts of tasty treats from good sandwiches to hearty Bavarian meals, which you can top off with a Tegernseer beer—a Munich favorite. ⊠ *Reichenbachstr. 47, Ludwigvorstadt* ☎ *089/201–5160* ⊕ *www.trachtenvogl.de.*

Holy Home. For a New York City, corner-bar type experience, check out Holy Home. A hip local crowd frequents this smoky hole-in-the-wall that books great low-key DJs. ✉ *Reichenbachstr. 21, Ludwigvorstadt* ☎ *089/201–4546.*

GAY AND LESBIAN BARS
Munich's well-established gay scene stretches between Sendlingertor-platz and Isartorplatz in the Glockenbach neighborhood. For an overview, check ⊕ *www.munich-cruising.de.*

Ochsengarten. This is Munich's bar for lovers of leather and rubber. ✉ *Müllerstr. 47, Isarvorstadt* ☎ *089/266–446* ⊕ *www.ochsengarten.de.*

Paradiso Tanzbar. Formerly Old Mrs. Henderson, this is still one of the most lively clubs on the scene, combining dance, champagne, and open to all kinds of music. ✉ *Rumfordstr. 2, Isarvorstadt* ☎ *089/263–469* ⊕ *www.paradiso-tanzbar.de.*

JAZZ
Jazzbar Vogler. The Vogler is a nice bar with jam sessions on Monday nights and regular jazz concerts. ✉ *Rumfordstr. 17, City Center/Isarvorstadt* ☎ *089/294–662* ⊕ *www.jazzbar-vogler.com.*

NYMPHENBURG
BEER GARDENS
Königlicher Hirschgarten. Out in the district of Nymphenburg is the huge Königlicher Hirschgarten, a great family-oriented beer garden. To get there, rent bikes and make a day of it in the park and beer garden, or take Bus No. 51 or 151 to Hirschgarten, then walk for 10 to 15 minutes. Bike or bus, use a map, it'll be worth it. ✉ *Hirschgarten 1, Nymphenburg* ☎ *089/1799–9119* ⊕ *www.hirschgarten.de.*

Taxisgarten. The crowd at the Taxisgarten in the Gern district (U-bahn Gern, Line No. 1 toward Olympia Einkaufszentrum) is more white-collar and tame, but the food is excellent, and while parents refresh themselves, children exhaust themselves on the playground. ✉ *Taxisstr. 12, Neuhausen-Nymphenburg* ☎ *089/156–827* ⊕ *www.taxisgarten.de.*

DANCE CLUBS
Backstage. The Backstage is mostly a live-music venue for alternative music of all kinds, but there's also a chilled-out club and a beer garden. Purchase tickets at various websites, including **München Ticket** (*www.muenchenticket.de*). ✉ *Reitknechtstr. 6, Neuhausen-Nymphenburg* ☎ *0180/5481–8181 for tickets, 089/126–6100 for club* ⊕ *www.backstage.eu* Ⓜ *Hirschgarten (S-bahn).*

JAZZ
The Big Easy. This classy restaurant features jazz-accompanied Sunday brunch for €16.50–€18.50, not including drinks. It's pricey, but good. ✉ *Frundsbergstr. 46, Nymphenburg* ☎ *089/1589–0253* ⊕ *www.thebigeasy.de.*

LUDWIGVORSTADT

JAZZ

Mr. B's. The tiny Mr. B's is a treat. It's run by New Yorker Alex Best, who also mixes great cocktails and, unlike so many other barkeeps, usually wears a welcoming smile. ⊠ *Herzog-Heinrich-Str. 38, Ludwigvorstadt* ☎ *089/534–901* ⊕ *www.misterbs.eu.*

HAIDHAUSEN

BEER GARDENS

Hofbräukeller am Wiener Platz. This is of the city's middle-size beer gardens but undoubtedly one of the best. Situated off Wiener Platz makes it attractive enough, plus the food's good, and it serves the same beer as the Hofbräuhaus. Inside, the restaurant is well worth a look. Take Tram No. 19 to Wiener-Platz, or U-bahn Line No. 4 or 5 to Max-Weber-Platz. ⊠ *Innere Wiener Str. 19, Haidhausen* ☎ *089/459–9250* ⊕ *www.hofbraeukeller.de.*

DANCE CLUBS

Optimolwerke. A former factory premises hosts the city's largest late-night party scene: the Optimolwerke has no fewer than eight clubs (the number changes) including a Brazil bar; self-styled "party bar" Die Burg; and Theaterfabrik, venue for concerts and more partys. ⊠ *Friedenstr. 10, Haidhausen* ☎ *089/450–6920* ⊕ *www.optimolwerke.de* Ⓜ *Ostbahnhof (S-bahn).*

Muffathalle. One of the best live venues in the city, this club puts on up-and-coming bands as well as ones on their second or third or more appearances after making it big. Many leading acts from the U.K. and U.S. scenes have played here. The café-bar here has different DJs nearly every night of the week, and the modest beer garden serves organic food. Muffathalle is five minutes from Rosenheimer Platz S-bahn station. ⊠ *Muffatwerk, Zellstr. 4, behind Müllersches Volksbad near river, Haidhausen* ☎ *089/4587–5010* ⊕ *www.muffatwerk.de.*

JAZZ

Unterfahrt. The Unterfahrt is the place for the serious jazzologist, though hip-hop is making heavy inroads into the scene. ⊠ *Einsteinstr. 42, Haidhausen* ☎ *089/448–2794* ⊕ *www.unterfahrt.de.*

SPORTS AND THE OUTDOORS

Olympiapark. The Olympiapark, built for the 1972 Olympics, is one of the largest sports and recreation centers in Europe. The Olympic-size pool is open for swimming. ⊠ *Spiridon-Louis-Ring 21, Milbertshofen* ☎ *089/30670* ⊕ *www.olympiapark.de* Ⓜ *Olympiazentrum (U-bahn).*

Sporthaus Schuster. The focus here is on adventure sports, so if it's climbing, trekking, biking, or walking you're into, this huge store, meters off Marienplatz, is the place. ⊠ *Rosenstr. 1–5, City Center* ☎ *089/237–070* ⊕ *www.sport-schuster.de.*

SportScheck. For general information about sports in and around Munich, contact the sports emporium SportScheck. Recently moved to Neuhauser Strasse, this big store not only sells every kind of equipment but is very handy with advice. ⊠ *Neuhauser Str. 19–21, City Center* ☎ *089/2166–1219* ⊕ *www.sportscheck.com.*

BICYCLING

A bike is hands-down the best way to experience this flat, pedal-friendly city. There are loads of bike lanes and paths that wind through its parks and along the Isar River. The rental shop will give you maps and tips, or you can get a map at any city tourist office.

Weather permitting, here is a route to try: Go through Isartor to the river and head north to the Englischer Garten. Ride around the park and have lunch at a beer garden. Exit the park and go across Leopoldstrasse into Schwabing, making your way back down toward the museum quarter via the adorable Elisabethmarkt. Check out one or two of the galleries then head back to town passing Königsplatz.

You can also take your bike on the S-bahns (except during rush hours from 6 am to 9 am and from 4 pm to 6 pm), which take you out to the many lakes and attractions outside town. Bicycles on public transportation cost either one strip on a multiple ticket or €2.50 for a day ticket.

RENTALS **Mike's Bike Tours.** Mike's Bike Tours also rents bikes, which is around the corner from the rear entrance of the Hofbräuhaus. Day rental is €15 for the first day, €70 for a week. Return time is 8 pm May through August, earlier in other seasons. ⊠ *Bräuhausstr. 10, City Center* ☎ *089/2554–3987* ⊕ *www.mikesbiketours.com.*

Radius Tours and Bikes. Based at the central station, Radius Tours and Bikes rents bikes. A three- to eight-gear bike costs €14.50 a day. A 24–27-gear bike costs €22. Hourly rates are €3 and €5, respectively. E-Bikes (regular bikes that also use electricity) are also available, from €29 a day. ⊠ *Opposite platform 32, Hauptbahnhof* ☎ *089/54348–77730* ⊕ *www.radiustours.com.*

TOURS **Mike's Bike Tours.** The oldest bike tour operation in Munich, Mike's tours last 4–7 hours, typically with an hour break at a beer garden, and cover upward of 6 km (4 miles). Tours start daily at the Altes Rathaus at the end of Marienplatz. A standard tour costs €25 (bike included) and starts at 11:30 and 4:30 (April 15–August 31) and 12:30 (September 1–November 10); November 11–March by appointment. Reserve to be sure, though you'll probably get a bike if you just show up. Bus Bavaria, part of the same company, also offers day trips by bus to Neuschwanstein castle, which costs €49. ⊠ *Bräuhausstr. 10, City Center* ☎ *089/2554–3987* ⊕ *www.mikesbiketours.com.*

ICE-SKATING

Global warming permitting, there's outdoor skating on the lake in the Englischer Garten and on the Nymphenburger Canal in winter. Watch out for signs reading "gefahr" (danger), warning you of thin ice.

Karlsplatz. In winter the fountain on Karlsplatz is turned into a public rink with music and an outdoor bar.

JOGGING

Englischer Garten. The best place to jog is the Englischer Garten, which is 11 km (7 miles) around and has dirt and asphalt paths throughout.

Isar River. The banks of the Isar River are a favorite route for local runners.

Olympiapark. The 500-acre park of Schloss Nymphenburg is also ideal for running, as is the Olympiapark, if you're in the area. ⊠ *Tram No. 12 to Romanpl.*

SHOPPING

2

Munich has three of Germany's most exclusive shopping streets as well as flea markets to rival those of any other European city. In between are department stores, where acute German-style competition assures reasonable prices and often produces outstanding bargains. Artisans bring their wares of beauty and originality to the Christmas markets. Collect their business cards—in summer you're sure to want to order another of those little gold baubles that were on sale in December.

Munich has an immense central shopping area, a 2-km (1-mile) *Fussgängerzone* (pedestrian zone) stretching from the train station to Marienplatz and then north to Odeonsplatz. The two main streets here are Neuhauser Strasse and Kaufingerstrasse, the sites of most major department stores. For upscale shopping, Maximilianstrasse, Residenzstrasse, and Theatinerstrasse are unbeatable. Schwabing, north of the university, has more offbeat shopping streets—Schellingstrasse and Hohenzollernstrasse are two to try. ▉TIP➜ **The neighborhood around Gärtnerplatz also has lots of new boutiques.**

A few small shops around Viktualienmarkt sell Bavarian antiques, though their numbers are dwindling under the pressure of high rents. Antique shoppers should also try the area north of the university—Türkenstrasse, Theresienstrasse, and Barerstrasse are all filled with antiques stores.

Strictly for window-shopping—unless you're looking for something really rare and special and money's no object—are the exclusive shops lining Prannerstrasse, at the rear of the Hotel Bayerischer Hof. Interesting and inexpensive antiques and assorted junk from all over Europe are laid out at the weekend flea market at the Olympiapark (not far from the Olympic Stadium), which has around 460 sellers.

If you want to deck yourself out in lederhosen or a dirndl, or acquire a green loden coat and little pointed hat with feathers, you have a wide choice in the Bavarian capital. ▉TIP➜ **There are a couple of other shops along Tal Street that have new and used lederhosen and dirndls at good prices in case you want to spontaneously get into the spirit of the 'Fest.**

Munich is also a city of beer, and items related to its consumption are obvious choices for souvenirs and gifts. Munich is also the home of the famous Nymphenburg Porcelain factory. Between Karlsplatz and the Viktualienmarkt there are loads of shops for memorabilia and trinkets.

CITY CENTER

ANTIQUES

Antike Uhren Eder. In Antike Uhren Eder, the silence is broken only by the ticking of dozens of highly valuable German antique clocks and by discreet negotiation over the high prices. ⊠ *Prannerstr. 4, opposite back of Hotel Bayerischer Hof, City Center* ☎ *089/220–305* ⊕ *www. uhreneder.ch.*

Roman Odesser. Antique German silver is the specialty at Roman Odesser. ⊠ *Westenriederstr. 21, City Center* ☎ *089/226–388.*

BOOKS

Hugendubel. There is a good selection of novels in English on the fifth floor of Hugendubel. ⊠ *Marienpl. 22, City Center* ☎ *089/3075–7575* ⊕ *www.hugendubel.de* ⊠ *Karlspl. 11–12, City Center.*

CERAMICS AND GLASS

Kunstring. For Dresden and Meissen porcelain wares, go to Kunstring near Odeonsplatz. ⊠ *Briennerstr. 4, City Center* ⊕ *www.meissen.com/ de/geschaefte/de/kunstring.*

Porzellan Nymphenburg. This opulent space resembles a drawing room in the Munich palace of the same name. It has delicate, expensive porcelain safely locked away in bowfront cabinets. ⊠ *Odeonspl. 1, City Center* ☎ *089/282–428* ⊕ *www.nymphenburg.com/de/nymphenburg.*

  Schloss Nymphenburg. You can buy directly from the factory called Porzellanmanufaktur Nymphenburg on the grounds of Schloss Nymphenburg. ⊠ *Nördliches Schlossrondell 8, Nymphenburg* ⊹ *Take Tram No. 17 from Karlsplatz Stachus to Schloss Nymphenburg* ☎ *089/179– 1970* ⊙ *Weekdays 10–5, Sat. 11–4.*

CLOTHING

C&A. For a more affordable option on loden (water-resistant woolen material used for traditional coats and hats) and general fashion, try the department store C&A in the pedestrian zone. ⊠ *Kaufingerstr. 13, City Center* ☎ *089/231–930.*

Lederhosen Wagner. The tiny Lederhosen Wagner, right up against the Heiliggeist Church, carries lederhosen, woolen sweaters called *Walk* (not loden), and children's clothing. ⊠ *Tal 2, City Center* ☎ *089/225–697.*

Loden-Frey. Much of the fine loden clothing on sale at Loden-Frey is made at the company's own factory, on the edge of the Englischer Garten. ⊠ *Maffeistr. 7, City Center* ☎ *089/210–390.*

CRAFTS

Bayerischer Kunstgewerbe–Verein. Bavarian craftspeople have a showplace of their own, the Bayerischer Kunstgewerbe–Verein; here you'll find every kind of handicraft, from glass and pottery to textiles. ⊠ *Pacellistr. 6–8, City Center* ☎ *089/290–1470.*

Max Krug. If you've been to the Black Forest and forgot to acquire a clock, or if you need a good Bavarian souvenir, try Max Krug in the pedestrian zone. ⊠ *Neuhauser Strasse 2, City Center* ☎ *089/224–501* ⊕ *www.max-krug.com.*

FOOD AND BEER

Chocolate & More. Opened in 2001, this tiny shop, located in the Viktualienmarkt, specializes in all things chocolate. ⊠ *Westenrieder Str. 15, City Center* ☏ *089/2554–4905* ⊕ *www.chocolate-and-more-munich.de.*

Dallmayr. Dallmayr is the city's most elegant and famous gourmet food store, with delights that range from exotic fruits and English jams to a multitude of fish and meats, all served by efficient Munich matrons in smart blue-and-white linen costumes. The store's famous specialty is coffee, with more than 50 varieties to blend as you wish. It even has its own chocolate factory. This is the place to prepare a high-class–if pricey–picnic. ⊠ *Dienerstr. 14–15, City Center* ☏ *089/21350* ⊕ *www. dallmayr.com.*

GIFT AND SOUVENIRS

Sebastian Wesely. Located on this street since 1923, Sebastian Wesely is the place to come for beer-related vessels and schnapps glasses (*Stampferl*), walking sticks, scarves, and napkins with the famous Bavarian blue-and-white lozenges. ⊠ *Rindermarkt 1, at Peterspl., City Center* ☏ *089/264–519* ⊕ *www.wesely.de.*

MARKETS

Christkindlmarkt. From the end of November until December 24, the open-air stalls of the *Christkindlmarkt* (Christmas market) are a great place to find gifts and warm up with mulled wine. Two other perennial Christmas-market favorites are those in Schwabing (Münchner-Freiheit Square) and at the Chinese Tower, in the middle of the Englischer Garten. ⊠ *Marienpl., City Center.*

Viktualienmarkt. Munich's Viktualienmarkt is *the* place to shop and to eat. Just south of Marienplatz, it's home to an array of colorful stands that sell everything from cheese to sausages, flowers to wine. A visit here is more than just an opportunity to find picnic makings; it provides an opening into Müncheners' robust—though friendly—nature, especially at the Viktualienmarkt's Bavarian Biergärten (beer garden). ⊠ *Viktualienmarkt, City Center* ☉ *Weekdays 10–6, Sat. 10–3.*

SHOPPING MALLS AND DEPARTMENT STORES

Breiter. For a classic selection of German clothing, including some with a folk touch, and a specialism in hats, try Munich's traditional family-run Breiter. ⊠ *Kaufingerstrasse 23–26, City Center* ☏ *089/599–8840* ⊕ *www.hutbreiter.de.*

Fünf Höfe. For a more upscale shopping experience, visit the many stores, boutiques, galleries, and cafés of the Fünf Höfe, a modern arcade carved into the block of houses between Theatinerstrasse and Kardinal-Faulhaber-Strasse. The architecture of the passages and courtyards is cool and elegant, in sharp contrast to the facades of the buildings. There's a decent Thai restaurant in there as well. ⊠ *Between Theatinerstr. and Kardinal-Faulhaber-Str., City Center* ⊕ *www.fuenfhoefe.de.*

Galeria Kaufhof. Shop here for mid-price goods. ▥ TIP➜ The end-of-season sales are bargains. ⊠ *Kaufingerstr. 1–5, Marienplatz, City Center* ☏ *089/231–851.*

Hirmer. With a markedly friendly and knowledgeable staff, Hirmer has Munich's most comprehensive collection of German-made men's clothes. International brands are also here, such as Polo, Diesel, and Levi's. ✉ *Kaufingerstr. 28, City Center* ☎ *0800/063–8190* ⊕ *www.hirmer.de.*

Karstadt. Karstadt commands an entire city block between the train station and Karlsplatz. It is the largest and one of the best department stores in the city. On the fourth floor is a cafeteria with a great selection of excellent and inexpensive dishes. ✉ *Bahnhofpl. 7, City Center* ☎ *089/55120* ⊕ *www.karstadt.de.*

Kaufinger Tor. Kaufinger Tor has several floors of boutiques and cafés packed neatly together under a high glass roof. ✉ *Kaufingerstr. 117, City Center* ⊕ *www.kaufingertor.de.*

Ludwig Beck. Ludwig Beck is considered a step above other department stores by Müncheners. It's packed from top to bottom with highly original wares and satisfies even the pickiest of shoppers. ✉ *Marienpl. 11, City Center* ☎ *089/236–910* ⊕ *www.kaufhaus.ludwigbeck.de.*

Pool. Pool is a hip shop on the upscale Maximilianstrasse, with fashion, music, and accessories for house and home. It's a shopping experience for the senses. ✉ *Maximilianstr. 11, City Center* ☎ *089/266–035* ⊕ *www.verypoolish.com.*

TEXTILES

Johanna Daimer Filze aller Art. In an arcade of the Neues Rathaus is tiny Johanna Daimer Filze aller Art, a shop founded in 1883 that sells every kind and color of felt imaginable. ✉ *Dienerstr., im Rathaus, City Center* ☎ *089/776–984* ⊕ *www.daimer-filze.com.*

TOYS

Spielwaren Obletters. Spielwaren Obletters has two extensive floors of toys, with the usual favorites plus many handmade playthings of great charm and quality. ✉ *Karlspl. 11–12, City Center* ☎ *089/5508–9510.*

SCHWABING AND MAXVORSTADT

ANTIQUES

Die Puppenstube. For Munich's largest selection of dolls and marionettes, head to Die Puppenstube. ✉ *Luisenstr. 68, Maxvorstadt* ☎ *089/272–3267.*

BOOKS

Lehmkuhl. Lehmkuhl is Munich's oldest and one of its finest bookshops; it also sells beautiful cards. ✉ *Leopoldstr. 45, Schwabing* ☎ *089/380–1500* ⊕ *www.lehmkuhl.net* Ⓜ *Münchner Freiheit (U-Bahn).*

FOOD AND BEER

Ludwig Mory. This shop has everything relating to beer, from mugs of all shapes and sizes and in all sorts of materials to warmers for those who don't like their beer too cold. ✉ *Amalienstr. 16, Maxvorstadt* ☎ *089/224–542.*

MARKETS

Elisabethplatz. If you're in the Schwabing area, the daily market at Elisabethplatz is worth a visit—it's much smaller than the Victualienmarkt but the range and quality of produce are comparable. Whereas at the Viktualienmarkt you have visitors from many lands pushing past the stands, here life is more peaceful and local. There is a beer garden here as well. ⊠ *Elisabethpl., Schwabing* ⊘ *Daily 8–6.*

SHOPPING MALLS AND DEPARTMENT STORES

Oberpollinger. The more-than-100-year-old Oberpollinger—one of Germany's finest upscale department stores—was renovated in 2008. It's seven floors are packed with pricey, glamorous fashion, furniture, and beauty items. The large, open-plan self-service restaurant on the top floor is well worth a visit, and isn't expensive. ⊠ *Neuhauserstr. 18, City Center* ☎ *089/290–230* ⊕ *www.oberpollinger.de.*

HAUPTBAHNHOF

BOOKS

Internationale Presse. Locations in the main train station, Ostbahnhof, and Stachus have magazines and novels. ⊠ *Opposite Track 23, Hauptbahnhof* ☎ *089/5511–7170* ⊕ *www.einkaufsbahnhof.de.*

ISARVORSTADT

FOOD AND BEER

Götterspeise. Across the street from the restaurant Faun in Glockenbachviertel, the name of this delectable chocolate shop means "ambrosia," a fitting name for their gifts, delights, and hot drinks. ⊠ *Jahnstr. 30, Ludwigvorstadt* ☎ *089/2388–7374* ⊕ *www.goetterspeise-muenchen.de.*

SHOPPING MALLS AND DEPARTMENT STORES

Slips. A beautiful shop on Gärtnerplatz, Slips has a wide range of dresses, jeans, shoes, and accessories. Prices are a bit outrageous, but it's a successful store, so they must be doing something right. ⊠ *Gärtnerplatz. 2, Isarvorstadt* ☎ *089/202–2500* ⊕ *www.slipsfashion.com.*

SIDE TRIPS FROM MUNICH

Munich's excellent suburban railway network, the S-bahn, brings several quaint towns and attractive rural areas within easy reach for a day's excursion. Dachau attracts overseas visitors, mostly because of its concentration-camp memorial site, but it's a picturesque and historic town in its own right.

■ TIP➜ Keep in mind that there are quite a few options for day trips to the famous castles built by King Ludwig, which are only a couple of hours away. Mike's Bike Tours organizes trips, or ask at your hotel for bus-tour excursions. A train out to Füssen and Schloss Neuschwanstein takes two hours. ⇨ *For more information on this fairy-tale castle and others, see Chapter 4, The Romantic Road.*

Shops line Marienplatz in Munich's city center.

AMMERSEE

40 km (25 miles) southwest of Munich.

Ammersee, or the Peasants' Lake, is the country cousin of the better-known, more cosmopolitan Starnbergersee (the Princes' Lake), and, accordingly, many Bavarians (and tourists, too) like it all the more. Munich cosmopolites of centuries past thought it too distant for an excursion, not to mention too rustic, so the shores remained relatively free of villas and parks. Though some upscale holiday homes claim some stretches of the eastern shore, Ammersee still offers more open areas for bathing and boating than the larger lake to the east. Bicyclists circle the 19-km-long (12-mile-long) lake (it's nearly 6 km [4 miles] across at its widest point) on a path that rarely loses sight of the water. Hikers can spread out the tour for two or three days, staying overnight in any of the comfortable inns along the way. Dinghy sailors and wind-surfers zip across in minutes with the help of the Alpine winds that swoop down from the mountains. A ferry cruises the lake at regular intervals in summer, stopping at several piers. Board it at Herrsching.

Herrsching has a delightful promenade, part of which winds through the resort's park. The 100-year-old villa that sits so comfortably there seems as if it had been built by Ludwig II; such is the romantic and fanciful mixture of medieval turrets and Renaissance-style facades. It was actually built for the artist Ludwig Scheuermann in the late 19th century, and became a favorite meeting place for Munich and Bavarian artists. It's now a municipal cultural center and the setting for chamber-music concerts on some summer weekends.

GETTING HERE AND AROUND

Take A-96, follow the signs to Lindau, and 20 km (12 miles) west of Munich take the exit for Herrsching, the lake's principal town.

Herrsching is also the end of S-bahn Line No. 8, a 53-minute ride from Munich's Marienplatz. From the Herrsching train station, Bus No. 952 runs north along the lake, and Bus No. 951 runs south and continues on to Starnberg in a 40-minute journey.

Getting around by boat is the best way to visit. Each town on the lake has an *Anlegestelle* (pier).

ESSENTIALS

Tour Information Starnberg Five-Lake-Region Tourist-Information ⌧ *Wittelsbacherstr. 2c, Starnberg* ☏ *08151/90600* ⊕ *en.sta5.de* ☉ *May–Oct., weekdays 9–1 and 2–6, Sat. 9–1; Nov.–Apr., weekdays 10–5.*

EXPLORING

Andechs Monastery. The Benedictine monastery Andechs, one of southern Bavaria's most famous pilgrimage sites, lies 5 km (3 miles) south of Herrsching. You can reach it on Bus No. 951 from the S-bahn station (the bus also connects Ammersee and Starnbergersee). This extraordinary ensemble, surmounted by an octagonal tower and onion dome with a pointed helmet, has a busy history going back more than 1,000 years. The church, originally built in the 15th century, was entirely redone in baroque style in the early 18th century. The **Heilige Kapelle** contains the remains of the old treasure of the Benedictines in Andechs, including Charlemagne's "Victory Cross" and a monstrance containing the three sacred hosts brought back from the crusades by the original rulers of the area, the Counts of Diessen-Andechs. One of the attached chapels contains the remains of composer Carl Orff, and one of the buildings on the grounds has been refurbished as a concert stage for the performance of his works.

Admittedly, however, the crowds of pilgrims are drawn not just by the beauty of the hilltop monastery but primarily by the beer brewed here (600,000 liters [159,000 gallons] annually) and the stunning views. The monastery makes its own cheese as well, and serves hearty Bavarian food, an excellent accompaniment to the rich, almost black beer. You can enjoy both at large wooden tables in the monastery tavern or on the terrace outside. ⌧ *Bergstr. 2, 5 km (3 miles) south of Herrsching* ☏ *08152/3760* ⊕ *www.andechs.de* ☉ *Church daily 9–7; restaurant daily 10–8.*

WHERE TO STAY

$$ **Ammersee Hotel.** This very comfortable, modern resort hotel is located
HOTEL on the lake. **Pros:** prime location (request a room with balcony); good restaurant. **Cons:** rooms facing the street are noisy; limited balcony rooms. ⓢ *Rooms from: €120* ⌧ *Summerstr. 32* ☏ *08152/96870, 08152/399–440 for restaurant* ⊕ *www.ammersee-hotel.de* ⤳ *40 rooms* ⦿ *Breakfast.*

DACHAU

20 km (12 miles) northwest of Munich.

Dachau predates Munich, with records going back to the time of Charlemagne. It's a handsome town, too, built on a hilltop with views of Munich and the Alps, which was why it became such a favorite for numerous artists. A guided tour of the town, including the castle and church, leaves from the Rathaus on Saturday at 11, from May through mid-October. Dachau is infamous worldwide as the site of the "model" Nazi concentration camp, which was built just outside it. Dachau preserves the memory of the camp and the horrors perpetrated there with deep contrition while trying, with commendable discretion, to signal that the town has other points of interest.

GETTING HERE AND AROUND

Take the B-12 country road or the Stuttgart autobahn to the Dachau exit from Munich. Dachau is also on S-bahn Line No. 2, a 25-minute ride from Munich's Marienplatz.

ESSENTIALS

Visitor Information Tourist-Information Dachau ⊠ *Konrad-Adenauer-Str. 1* ☎ *08131/75286* ⊕ *www.dachau.de.*

EXPLORING

Bezirksmuseum. To get a sense of the town's history, visit the Bezirksmuseum, the district museum, which displays historical artifacts, furniture, and traditional costumes from Dachau and its surroundings. ⊠ *Augsburgerstr. 3* ☎ *08131/56750* ⊕ *www.dachauer-galerien-museen. de* ☑ *€5* ☉ *Tues.–Fri. 11–5, weekends 1–5.*

Dachau Concentration Camp Memorial Site (*Dachau Concentration Camp Memorial*). The site of the infamous camp, now the KZ-Gedenkstätte Dachau, is just outside town. Photographs, contemporary documents, the few cell blocks, and the grim crematorium create a somber and moving picture of the camp, where more than 41,000 of the 200,000-plus prisoners lost their lives. A documentary film in English is shown daily at 11:30 and 3:30. The former camp has become more than just a grisly memorial: it's now a place where people of all nations meet to reflect upon the past and on the present. Several religious shrines and memorials have been built to honor the dead, who came from Germany and nations around the world. By public transport take S-bahn Line No. 2 from Marienplatz or Hauptbahnhof in the direction of Petershausen, and get off at Dachau. From there, take the clearly marked bus from right outside the Dachau S-bahn station (No. 726 towards Saubachsiedlung, it leaves about every 20 minutes). If you are driving from Munich, take the autobahn toward Stuttgart, get off at Dachau, and follow the signs. ⊠ *Alte Römerstrasse 75* ☎ *08131/669– 970* ⊕ *www.kz-gedenkstaette-dachau.de* ☑ *Free* ☉ *Tues.–Sun. 9–5. Tours in English Tues.–Sun. at 11 and 1.*

Gemäldegalerie. An artists' colony formed here during the 19th century, and the tradition lives on. Picturesque houses line Hermann-Stockmann-Strasse and part of Münchner Strasse, and many of them are still the homes of successful artists. The Gemäldegalerie displays the works of many of the town's 19th-century artists. ✉ *Konrad-Adenauer-Str. 3* ☎ *08131/56750* ⊕ *www.dachauer-galerien-museen. de* 🎫 *€5* 🕐 *Tues.–Fri. 11–5, weekends 1–5.*

Schloss Dachau. This hilltop castle, dominates the town. What you'll see is the one remaining wing of a palace built by the Munich architect Josef Effner for the Wittelsbach ruler Max Emanuel in 1715. During the Napoleonic Wars the palace served as a field hospital and then was partially destroyed. King Max Joseph lacked the money to rebuild it, so all that's left is a handsome cream-and-white building, with an elegant pillared and lantern-hung café on the ground floor and a former ballroom above. About once a month the grand Renaissance hall, with a richly decorated and carved ceiling, covered with painted panels depicting figures from ancient mythology, is used for chamber concerts. The east terrace affords panoramic views of Munich and, on fine days, the distant Alps. There's also a 250-year-old *Schlossbrauerei* (castle brewery), which hosts the town's beer and music festival each year in the first two weeks of August. The Schloss restaurant serves good Bavarian food with regional ingredients, as well as great homemade cakes. ✉ *Schlossstr. 2* ☎ *08131/279–9278 for restaurant, 08131/87923 for castle* ⊕ *www.schloss-dachau.com* 🎫 *€2* 🕐 *Apr.–Sept., Tues.–Sun. 9–6; Oct.–Mar., Tues.–Sun. 10–4.*

St. Jakob. Dachau's parish church was built in the early 17th century in late-Renaissance style on the foundations of a 13th-century Gothic structure. Baroque features and a characteristic onion dome were added in the late 17th century. On the south wall you can admire a very fine sundial from 1699. ✉ *Pfarrstr. 7* ☎ *08131/36380* ⊕ *www.pv-dachau-st-jakob.de* 🕐 *Daily 7–7.*

WHERE TO STAY

$ 🏨 **Hotel Fischer.** You can see this hotel across the square from the S-bahn
HOTEL station. **Pros:** free Wi-Fi; prime location; good restaurant. **Cons:** on nice evenings, noise from the patio may filter up to your room. 💲 *Rooms from: €84* ✉ *Bahnhofstr. 4, City Center* ☎ *08131/612–200* ⊕ *www. hotelfischer-dachau.de* 🛏 *28 rooms* 🍽 *Breakfast.*

THE BAVARIAN ALPS

WELCOME TO THE BAVARIAN ALPS

TOP REASONS TO GO

★ **Herrenchiemsee:** Take the old steam-driven ferry to the island in Chiemsee to visit the last and most glorious castle of "Mad" King Ludwig II.

★ **Great nature:** From the crystalline Königsee lake and grandiose Karwendel Mountains, to Garmisch's powdery snow, and the magical forests, it's everything a nature lover needs.

★ **Meditating in Ettal monastery:** If it isn't the sheer complexity of the baroque ornamentation and the riot of frescoes, then it might be the fluid sound of the ancient organ that puts you in a deep, relaxing trance. A great brewery and distillery round out the deeply religious experience.

★ **Rejuvenation in Reichenhall:** The new Rupertus spa in Bad Reichenhall has the applications you need to turn back your body's clock, from saltwater baths to mudpacks.

★ **Confronting History in Berchtesgaden:** Explore the darkest chapter of German history at Obersalzberg, Hitler's mountain retreat.

1 **Werdenfelser Land and Wetterstein Mountains.** Like a village lost in time, Mittenwald and Oberammergau are both famous for their half-timber houses covered in *Lüftlmalerei* frescoes. The entire region sits serenely in the shadow of Germany's highest point: the Zugspitze. The Wetterstein Mountains offer fantastic skiing and hiking.

2 **Chiemgau.** Bavaria's Lake District is almost undiscovered by Westerners but has long been a secret destination for Germans. Several fine, hidden lakes dot the area. The Chiemsee dominates the Chiemgau, with one of the most impressive German palaces and great water sports. Residents, or Chiemgauer, especially in Bad Tölz, often

GETTING ORIENTED

3

Ask a Bavarian about the "Bavarian Alps" and he'll probably shake his head in confusion. To Bavarians "the Alps" consist of several adjoining mountain ranges spanning the Ammergau, Wetterstein, and Karwendel Alps in the West to the Chiemgauer and Berchtesgadener Alpen in the East. Each region has its die-hard fans. The constants, however, are the incredible scenery, clean air, and a sense of Bavarian *Gemütlichkeit* (coziness) omnipresent in every *Hütte* (cottage), *Gasthof* (guesthouse), and beer garden. The area is an outdoor recreation paradise, and almost completely lacks the high-culture institutions that dominate German urban life.

wear traditional *Trachten*, elaborate lederhosen and dirndl dresses, as an expression of their proud cultural heritage.

3 Berchtesgadener Land. The Berchtesgadener Land is not the highest point in the country, but is certainly one of the most ruggedly beautiful regions. Hundreds of miles of hiking trails with serene Alpine cottages and

the odd cow make the area a hiking and mountaineering paradise. Berchtesgaden and Bad Reichenhall are famous for the salt trade, and the salt mines provide the visitor with a unique and entertaining insight into the history and wealth of the region. The Königsee is the most photographed place in the country, and for good reason.

OUTDOORS IN THE BAVARIAN ALPS

Bursting up from the lowlands of southern Germany like a row of enormous, craggy teeth, the Bavarian Alps form both an awe-inspiring border with Austria and a superb natural playground for outdoor enthusiasts.

(above) Mountain bikers in the Bavarian foothills (upper right) Bavarian Alps (lower right) Backcountry skiers

Visible from Munich on a clear day, this thin strip of the Alps stretches over 300 km (186 miles) from Lake Constance in the west to Berchtesgaden in the east, and acts as a threshold to the towering mountain ranges that lie farther south. Lower in altitude than their Austrian, Swiss, and French cousins, the Bavarian Alps have the advantage of shorter distances between their summits and the valleys below, forming an ideal environment for casual walkers and serious mountaineers alike.

In spring and summer cowbells tinkle and wild flowers blanket meadows beside trails that course up and down the mountainsides. In winter snow engulfs the region, turning trails into paths for cross-country skiers and the mountainsides into pistes for snowboarders and downhill skiers to carve their way down.

—Jeff Kavanagh

LEDERHOSEN

Along with sausages and enormous mugs of frothy beer, lederhosen form the holy trinity of what many foreigners believe to be stereotypically "German." The reality, however, is that the embroidered leather breeches are traditionally worn in the south of the country, particularly in Alpine areas, where the durability and protection of leather have their advantages. Nowadays they are worn at special events.

BEST WAYS TO EXPLORE

BY FOOT

It's not without good reason that wanderlust is a German word. The desire to travel and explore has been strong for hundreds of years in Germany, especially in places like the Alps where strenuous strolls are rewarded with breathtaking vistas. There are more than 7,000 km (4,350 miles) of walking trails in the Allgäu region alone to wander, conveniently divided into valley walks, mid-altitude trails, and summit hikes reflecting the varying altitude and difficulty. Hikes can be undertaken as day trips or as weeks-long endeavors, and there are campsites, mountain huts, farmhouses, and hotels to overnight in along the way, as well as a decent infrastructure of buses, trains, and cable cars to get you to your starting point. The Bavaria Tourism Office (⊕ *www.bavaria.by*) has more information on hiking trails.

BY BIKE

You don't actually need to venture onto their slopes to appreciate the Alps' beauty, and cycling through the foothills at their base affords stunning views of the mountains combined with the luxury of refreshing stop-offs in beer gardens and dips in beautiful lakes like the Tegernsee. There's plenty of accommodation tailored to cyclists throughout the region and local trains are normally equipped with a cycle carriage or two to transport you to more remote locations. The Alps also have thousands of miles of mountain-bike-friendly trails and a number of special bike parks serviced by cable cars.

BY SKIS

Neither as high nor famous as their neighbors, the Bavarian Alps are frequently overlooked as a winter sport destination. Resorts on the German side of the border may have shorter seasons than places like Zermatt and Chamonix, but they're also generally cheaper in terms of food and accommodation, and many, including Zugspitze, are easily accessed from Munich for day trips.

BEST PHOTO OPS

No matter where you are around the Alps you'll be inundated with sights worth snapping. Here are a few:

■ More Disney than Disney, **Neuschwanstein Castle** sits theatrically on the side of a mountain, its grand towers set against a background of tree- and snow-covered peaks.

■ The panoramic view from close to 10,000 feet at the peak of Germany's highest mountain, the **Zugspitze** takes in 400 peaks in four countries.

■ Reputedly the cleanest lake in Germany, **Königsee** is also endowed with steep rock formations that soar thousands of meters up above the lake, beautifully framing its crystalline waters.

■ If sitting outside **Tegernsee's** lovely Benedictine monastery with a liter of the local beer in one hand and a bratwurst in the other isn't the shot you're after, you can wander down to the lake for spectacular vistas of its glittering surface and the Alps beyond.

Updated by
Paul Wheatley

Fir-clad mountains, rocky peaks, lederhosen, and geranium-covered houses: the Bavarian Alps come closest to what many of us envision as "Germany." Quaint towns full of frescoed half-timber houses covered in snow pop up among the mountain peaks and shimmering hidden lakes, as do the creations of "Mad" King Ludwig II. The entire area has sporting opportunities galore, regardless of the season.

Upper Bavaria (Oberbayern) fans south from Munich to the Austrian border, and as you follow this direction, you'll soon find yourself on a gently rolling plain leading to lakes surrounded by ancient forests. In time the plain merges into foothills, which suddenly give way to jagged Alpine peaks. In places such as Königsee, near Berchtesgaden, snow-capped mountains rise straight up from the gemlike lakes.

Continuing south, you'll encounter cheerful villages with richly painted houses, churches, and monasteries filled with the especially sensuous Bavarian baroque and rococo styles, and several spas where you can "take the waters" and tune up your system. Sports possibilities are legion: downhill and cross-country skiing, snowboarding, and ice-skating in winter; tennis, swimming, sailing, golf, and, above all (sometimes literally), hiking, paragliding, and ballooning in summer.

PLANNING

WHEN TO GO

This mountainous region is a year-round holiday destination. Snow is promised by most resorts from December through March, although there's year-round skiing on the glacier slopes at the top of the Zugspitze. Spring and autumn are ideal times for leisurely hikes on the many mountain trails. November is a between-seasons time, when many hotels and restaurants close down or attend to renovations. Note, too, that many locals take a vacation after January 6, and businesses may be closed for anywhere up to a month. The area is extremely popular with European visitors, who flood the Alps in July and August.

GETTING HERE AND AROUND

AIR TRAVEL

Munich, 95 km (59 miles) northwest of Garmisch-Partenkirchen, is the gateway to the Bavarian Alps. If you're staying in Berchtesgaden, consider the closer airport in Salzburg, Austria—it has fewer international flights, but it is a budget-airline and charter hub.

Airport Information Salzburg Airport (*SZG*). ⊠ *Salzburg, Austria* ☎ *0662/8580–0* ⊕ *www.salzburg-airport.com.*

CAR TRAVEL

The Bavarian Alps are well connected to Munich by train, and an extensive network of buses links even the most remote villages. Since bus schedules can be unreliable and are timed for commuters, the best way to visit the area is by car. Three autobahns reach into the Bavarian Alps: A-7 comes in from the northwest (Frankfurt, Stuttgart, Ulm) and ends near Füssen in the western Bavarian Alps; A-95 runs from Munich to Garmisch-Partenkirchen; take A-8 from Munich for Tegernsee, Chiemsee, and Berchtesgaden. ⚠ **The A-8 is statistically the most dangerous autobahn in the country, partially due to it simultaneously being the most heavily traveled highway and the road most in need of repair.** The driving style is fast, and tailgating is common, though it is illegal. The "guideline speed" (Richtgeschwindigkeit) on the A-8 is 110 kph (68 mph); if an accident occurs at higher speeds, your insurance will not necessarily cover it. It is a good idea to pick a town like Garmisch-Partenkirchen, Bad Tölz, or Berchtesgaden as a base and explore the area from there. The Bavarian Alps are furnished with cable cars, steam trains, and cog railroads that whisk you to the tops of Alpine peaks allowing you to see the spectacular views without hours of mountain climbing.

TRAIN TRAVEL

Most Alpine resorts are connected with Munich by regular express and slower service trains. Due to the rugged terrain, train travel in the region can be challenging, but with some careful planning—see ⊕ *www.bahn.de* for schedules and to buy tickets—you can visit this region without a car.

RESTAURANTS

Restaurants in Bavaria run the gamut from the casual and *gemütlich* (cozy) Gasthof to formal gourmet offerings. More-upscale establishments try to maintain a feeling of casual familiarity, but you will probably feel more comfortable at the truly upscale restaurants if you dress up a bit. Note that many restaurants take a break between 2:30 and 6 pm. If you want to eat during these hours, look for the magic words *Durchgehend warme Küche,* indicating warm food is served throughout the day, possibly snacks during the off-hours. Many restaurants in the region still don't accept credit cards.

Prices in the reviews are the average cost of a main course at dinner, or if dinner is not served, at lunch.

The Zugspitze is the highest mountain in Germany and is reachable from Garmisch-Partenkirchen.

HOTELS

With few exceptions, a hotel or *Gasthof* in the Bavarian Alps and lower Alpine regions has high standards and is traditional in style, with balconies, pine woodwork, and gently angled roofs on which the snow sits and insulates. Many in the larger resort towns offer special packages online. Private homes all through the region offer Germany's own version of bed-and-breakfasts, indicated by signs reading "Zimmer frei" ("Rooms available"). Their rates may be less than €25 per person. As a general rule, the farther from the popular and sophisticated Alpine resorts you go, the lower the rates. Note, too, that many places offer a small discount if you stay more than one night. By the same token, some places frown on staying only one night, especially during the high seasons, in summer, at Christmas, and on winter weekends. In spas and many mountain resorts a "spa tax," or *Kurtaxe*, is added to the hotel bill. It amounts to no more than €3 per person per day and allows free use of spa facilities, entry to local attractions and concerts, and use of local transportation at times. Breakfast is included, unless indicated otherwise.

Prices in the reviews are the lowest cost of a standard double room in high season. For expanded reviews, facilities, and current deals, visit Fodors.com.

PLANNING YOUR TIME

The Alps are spread along Germany's southern border, but are fairly compact and easy to explore. Choose a central base and fan out from there. Garmisch-Partenkirchen and Berchtesgaden are the largest towns with the most convenient transportation connections.

Although the area is a popular tourist destination, the smaller communities like Mittenwald and Ettal are quieter and make for pleasant overnight stays. For an unforgettable experience, try spending the night in an Alpine hut, feasting on a simple but hearty meal and sleeping in the cool night air.

DISCOUNTS AND DEALS

One of the best deals in the area is the German Railroad's Bayern Ticket. The Bayern Ticket allows between one and five people to travel on any regional train—and almost all buses in the Alps. Prices range between €22 for a single traveler to €38 for five people. Ticket holders receive discounts on a large number of attractions in the area, including the Zugspitzbahn, a cog railroad and cable car that takes you up to the top of the Zugspitze. The ZugspitzCard (three days €49) offers discounts in almost every city near the Zugspitze. Visitors to spas or spa towns receive a Kurkarte, an ID that proves payment of the spa tax. The document allows discounts and often free access to sights in the town or area. If you've paid the tax, be sure to show the card everywhere you go.

VISITOR INFORMATION

Tourismusverband München Oberbayern ✉ *Radolfzeller Str. 15, Munich* ☎ *089/829–2180* ⊕ *www.oberbayern-tourismus.de.*

WERDENFELSER LAND AND WETTERSTEIN MOUNTAINS

With Germany's highest peak and picture-perfect Bavarian villages, the Werdenfelser Land offers a splendid mix of natural beauty combined with Bavarian art and culture. The region spreads out around the base of the Zugspitze, where the views from the top reach from Garmisch-Partenkirchen to the frescoed houses of Oberammergau, and to the serene Cloister Ettal.

GARMISCH-PARTENKIRCHEN

90 km (55 miles) southwest of Munich.

Garmisch, as it's more commonly known, is a bustling, year-round resort and spa town and is the undisputed capital of Alpine Bavaria. Once two separate communities, Garmisch and Partenkirchen fused in 1936 to accommodate the Winter Olympics. Today, with a population of 28,000, the area is the center of the Werdenfelser Land and large enough to offer every facility expected from a major Alpine resort. Garmisch is a spread-out mess of wide car-friendly streets, hordes of tourists, and little charm. The narrow streets and quaint architecture of smaller Partenkirchen make it a slightly better choice. In both parts of town pastel frescoes of biblical and bucolic scenes decorate facades.

Maibaum: Bavaria's Maypole

The center of every town in Bavaria is the *Maibaum* or Maypole. The blue-and-white-striped pole is decorated with the symbol of every trade and guild represented in the town, and is designed to help visitors determine what services are available there. The effort and skill required to build one is a source of community pride.

The tradition dates back to the 16th century, and is governed by a strict set of rules. Great care is taken in selecting and cutting the tree, which must be at least 98 feet tall. Once completed, it cannot be erected before May 1. In the meantime, tradition and honor dictate that men from surrounding towns attempt to steal the pole and ransom it for beer and food, so it must be guarded 24 hours a day. Once the pole goes up, with quite a bit of leveraging and manual labor, it cannot be stolen and may only stand for three years.

Winter sports rank high on the agenda here. There are more than 99 km (62 miles) of downhill ski runs, 40 ski lifts and cable cars, and 180 km (112 miles) of *Loipen* (cross-country ski trails). One of the principal stops on the international winter-sports circuit, the area hosts a week of races every January. You can usually count on good skiing from December through April (and into May on the Zugspitze).

GETTING HERE AND AROUND

Garmisch-Partenkirchen is the cultural and transportation hub of the Werdenfelser Land. The autobahn A-95 links Garmisch directly to Munich. Regional German Rail trains head directly to Munich (90 minutes), Innsbruck (80 minutes), and Mittenwald (20 minutes). German Rail operates buses that connect Garmisch with Oberammergau, Ettal, and the Wieskirche. Garmisch is a walkable city, and you probably won't need to use its frequent city-bus services.

Partenkirchen was founded by the Romans, and you can still follow the Via Claudia they built between Partenkirchen and neighboring Mittenwald, which was part of a major route between Rome and Germany well into the 17th century.

Bus tours to King Ludwig II's castles at Neuschwanstein and Linderhof and to the Ettal Monastery, near Oberammergau, are offered by DER travel agencies. Local agencies in Garmisch also run tours to Neuschwanstein, Linderhof, and Ettal, and into the neighboring Austrian Tyrol.

The Garmisch mountain railway company, the Bayerische Zugspitzbahn, offers special excursions to the top of the Zugspitze, Germany's highest mountain, by cog rail and cable car.

ESSENTIALS

Bus Tours Biersack ⊠ *Omnibusse und Reisebüro, Chamonixstr. 4* ☎ *08821/4920* ⊕ *www.bus-biersack.com.* **DER Travel Office** ⊠ *Bahnhofstr. 33* ☎ *08821/55125* ⊕ *www.der.com.* **Weiss-Blau-Reisen** ⊠ *Promenadestr. 5* ☎ *08821/3805* ⊕ *www.weiss-blau-reisen.de.*

Werdenfelser Land and
Wetterstein Mountains

Railway Tour Bayerische Zugspitzbahn ☎ 08821/7970 ⊕ www.zugspitze.de.

Visitor Information Garmisch-Partenkirchen ✉ Richard-Strauss-Pl. 2
☎ 08821/180–700 ⊕ www.gapa.de ⊙ Mid-Oct.–mid-Dec. and mid-Mar.–mid-May,
weekdays 9–5, Sat. 9–3; mid-Dec.–mid-Mar. and mid-May–mid-Oct., weekdays
9–6, Sun. 10–noon.

EXPLORING

Richard Strauss Institut. On the eastern edge of Garmisch, at the end
of Zöppritzstrasse, stands the home of composer Richard Strauss,
who lived here until his death in 1949. It's not open to visitors but
across town the Richard Strauss Institut is the center of activity during the *Richard-Strauss-Tage*, an annual music festival held in mid-
June that features concerts and lectures on the town's most famous
son. Other concerts are given year-round and there is also a Strauss
exhibition (€3.50). ✉ *Schnitzschulstr. 19, Garmisch* ⊕ *www.richard-
strauss-institut.de.*

St. Martin Church. Garmisch-Partenkirchen isn't all sports and cars, however. In Garmisch, some beautiful examples of Upper Bavarian houses
line Frühlingstrasse, and a pedestrian zone begins at Richard-Strauss-
Platz. Off Marienplatz, at one end of the car-free zone, is the 18th-
century parish church. It contains some significant stuccowork by the

Wessobrunn artist Jospeh Schmutzer and rococo work by Matthäus Günther. ⊠ *Marienplatz, Garmisch* ⊕ *www.erzbistum-muenchen.de/ Pfarrei/Page007033.aspx.*

St. Martin Church. Across the Loisach River, on Pfarrerhausweg, stands another St. Martin church, dating from 1280, whose Gothic wall paintings include a larger-than-life-size figure of St. Christopher. ⊠ *Pfarrerhausweg 4* ⊕ *www.erzbistum-muenchen.de/Pfarrei/ Page002550.aspx.*

Werdenfelser Museum. Objects and exhibitions on the region's history can be found in this excellent museum, which is itself housed in a building dating back to around 1200. The museum is spread over 19 rooms and five floors, and explores every aspect of life in the Werdenfelser region, which was an independent state for more than 700 years (until 1802). ⊠ *Ludwigstr. 47, Partenkirchen* ☎ *08821/751–710* ⊕ *www.werdenfelsmuseum.de* 🎫 *€2.50* ⊘ *Tues.–Sun. 10–5.*

Fodor'sChoice
★
Zugspitze. The highest mountain (9,717 feet) in Germany, this is the number one attraction in Garmisch. There are two ways up the mountain: a leisurely 75-minute ride on a cog railway from the train station in the town center, combined with a cable-car ride up the last stretch; or a 10-minute hoist by cable car, which begins its giddy ascent from the Eibsee, 10 km (6 miles) outside town on the road to Austria. There are two restaurants with sunny terraces at the summit and another at the top of the cog railway. ■TIP➔ A round-trip combination ticket allows you to mix your modes of travel up and down the mountain. Prices are lower in winter than in summer, even though winter rates include use of all the ski lifts on the mountain. You can rent skis at the top. ■TIP➔ Ascending the Zugspitze from the Austrian side is cheaper and more scenic. The *Tiroler Zugspitzbahn* departs three times per hour from near the village of Ehrwald. The round-trip ticket costs €37.50 and buses connect the gondolas to the Ehrwald train station. There are also a number of other peaks in the area with gondolas, but the views from the Zugspitze are the best. A four-seat cable car goes to the top of one of the lesser peaks: the **Wank** or the **Alpspitze,** many thousand feet lower than the Zugspitze. You can tackle both mountains on foot, provided you're properly shod and physically fit. ⊠ *Cog railway leaves from Olympiastr. 27 (approximately 100 m from the Garmisch train station)* ☎ *08821/7970* ⊕ *www.zugspitze.de* 🎫 *Summer: funicular or cable car €50 round-trip; winter: funicular or cable car €41.50 round-trip; parking €3* ⊘ *Daily (depends on weather and season) 7:39–5:15.*

WHERE TO EAT

$
GERMAN
✕ See-Hotel Riessersee. On the shore of a small, blue-green, tranquil lake—a leisurely 3-km (2-mile) walk from town—this café-restaurant is an ideal spot for lunch or afternoon tea (on summer weekends there's live zither music from 3 to 5). House specialties are fresh trout and seasonal local game (which fetches the higher prices on the menu). Ⓢ*Average main: €13* ⊠ *Riess 5* ☎ *08821/758–123* ⊕ *www.riessersee. de* ⊘ *Closed Mon. and Dec. 1–15.*

EATING WELL IN THE BAVARIAN ALPS

Bavarian cooking originally fed a farming people, who spent their days out of doors doing heavy manual labor. *Semmelknödel* (dumplings of old bread), pork dishes, sauerkraut, bread, and hearty soups were felt necessary to sustain a person facing the elements. The natural surroundings provided further sustenance, in the form of fresh trout from brooks, *Renke* (pike-perch) from the lakes, venison, and mushrooms. This substantial fare was often washed down with beer, which was nourishment in itself, especially during the Lenten season, when the dark and powerful "Doppelbock" was on the market. Today this regimen will suit sporty types who have spent a day hiking in the mountains, skiing in the bracing air, or swimming or windsurfing in chilly lakes.

Bavaria is not immune to eclectic culinary trends, however: minimalist Asian daubs here, a touch of French sophistication and Italian elegance there, a little Tex-Mex to brighten a winter evening, even some sprinklings of curry. Menus often include large sections devoted to salads, and there are tasty vegetarian dishes even in the most traditional regions. Schnapps, which customarily ended meals, has gone from being a step above moonshine to a true delicacy extracted from local fruit by virtuoso distillers. Yes, Bavarian cooking—hearty, homey, and down-to-earth—is actually becoming lighter.

One area remains an exception: desserts. The selection of sinfully creamy cakes in the *Konditorei* (cake shop), often enjoyed with whipped-cream-topped hot chocolate, continues to grow. These are irresistible, of course, especially when homemade. A heavenly experience might be a large portion of warm *Apfelstrudel* (apple-and-nut-filled pastry) fresh from the oven in some remote mountain refuge.

WHERE TO STAY

For information about accommodation packages with ski passes, call the Zugspitze or get in touch with the tourist office in Garmisch (☎ 08821/180–700 ⊕ www.zugspitze.de).

$$
B&B/INN
⚅ **Edelweiss.** Like its namesake, the "nobly white" Alpine flower of *The Sound of Music* fame, this small downtown hotel has plenty of mountain charm. **Pros:** small; comfortable; homey; great for families with children. **Cons:** small hotel; lacking in many services. ⑤ *Rooms from: €112* ✉ *Martinswinkelstr. 15–17* ☎ *08821/2454* ⊕ *www.hoteledelweiss. de* ⇱ *31 rooms* ⑩ *Breakfast.*

$
B&B/INN
⚅ **Gasthof Fraundorfer.** You can ride to dreamland in this beautiful old Bavarian Gasthof—some of the bed frames are carved like antique automobiles and sleighs. **Pros:** free Wi-Fi; great location and dining experience. **Cons:** noise a problem for the rooms in the back of hotel. ⑤ *Rooms from: €86* ✉ *Ludwigstr. 24* ☎ *08821/9270* ⊕ *www.gasthof-fraundorfer.de* ⇱ *20 rooms, 7 suites* ⑩ *Breakfast.*

$
HOTEL
⚅ **Hotel-Gasthof Drei Mohren.** All the simple, homey comforts you'd expect can be found in this 150-year-old Bavarian inn tucked into Partenkirchen village. **Pros:** perfect setting in a quaint corner of the town center; free Wi-Fi. **Cons:** restaurant noise on the first floor; some double rooms too

small. $ *Rooms from: €90* ✉ *Ludwigstr. 65* ☎ *08821/9130* ⊕ *www.dreimohren.de* ⌁ *29 rooms, 1 apartment* ⦿ *Breakfast.*

$
RESORT
📶 **Hotel Waxenstein.** It's worth the 7-km (4½-mile) drive eastward to Grainau just to spend a night or a few at the delightful Waxenstein. **Pros:** great service; beautiful views of the Zugspitze from the north-facing rooms. **Cons:** only accessible by car; rooms somewhat small; no views of the Zugspitze from the south-facing rooms. $ *Rooms from: €98* ✉ *Höhenrainweg 3* ☎ *08821/9840* ⊕ *www.waxenstein.de* ⌁ *35 rooms, 6 suites* ⦿ *Breakfast.*

$$
HOTEL
📶 **Reindl's Partenkirchner Hof.** Karl Reindl ranked among the world's top hoteliers, and his daughter Marianne Holzinger has maintained high standards since taking over this hotel. **Pros:** ample-size rooms; great views. **Cons:** front rooms are on a busy street. $ *Rooms from: €130* ✉ *Bahnhofstr. 15* ☎ *08821/943–870* ⊕ *www.reindls.de* ⌁ *35 rooms, 17 suites* ⦿ *Breakfast.*

NIGHTLIFE AND THE ARTS

In season there's a busy après-ski scene. Many hotels have dance floors, and some have basement discos that pound away until the early hours. Bavarian folk dancing and zither music are regular features of nightlife.

Bayernhalle. In summer there's entertainment, such as traditional Bavarian singing and dancing, every Saturday evening at the Bayernhalle. ✉ *Brauhausstr. 19* ☎ *08821/4877* ⊕ *www.vtv-garmisch.de/bayernhalle.*

Garmisch-Partenkirchen-Ticket. Concerts are presented from Saturday to Thursday, mid-May through September, in the park bandstand in Garmisch, and on Friday in the Partenkirchen park. Tickets are available at Garmisch-Partenkirchen-Ticket. ✉ *Richard-Strauss-Pl. 1* ☎ *08821/730–1995* ⊕ *www.ticketshop-gap.de* ☉ *Mon.–Sat. 9:30–1 and 2–6, Sat. 9–noon.*

Gasthof Fraundorfer. Wednesday through Monday the cozy tavern-restaurant Gasthof Fraundorfer hosts yodeling and folk dancing. ✉ *Ludwigstr. 24* ☎ *08821/9270* ⊕ *www.gasthof-fraundorfer.de.*

Spielbank Garmisch. The casino is open Sunday through Thursday 3 pm–2 am and Friday and Saturday 3 pm–3 am, with more than 150 slot machines and roulette, blackjack, and poker tables. ✉ *Am Kurpark 10* ☎ *08821/95990* ⊕ *www.spielbanken-bayern.de.*

SPORTS AND THE OUTDOORS

HIKING AND WALKING

There are innumerable spectacular walks on 300 km (186 miles) of marked trails through the lower slopes' pinewoods and upland meadows. If you have the time and good walking shoes, try one of the two trails that lead to striking gorges (called Klammen).

3

Deutscher Alpenverein (*German Alpine Association*). Call here for details on hiking and on staying in the mountain huts. ✉ *Von-Kahr-Str. 2–4, Munich* ☎ *089/140–030* ⊕ *www.alpenverein.de.*

Höllentalklamm. The Höllentalklamm route starts in the town and ends at the mountaintop (you'll want to turn back before reaching the summit unless you have mountaineering experience). You can park in the villages of Hammersbach and Grainau, and start your tour. ☎ *08821/8895* ⊕ *www.hoellentalklamm-info.de* ☉ *May–Oct. (depending on weather).*

Partnachklamm. The Partnachklamm route is quite challenging, and takes you through a spectacular, tunneled water gorge (entrance fee), past a pretty little mountain lake, and far up the Zugspitze; to do all of it, you'll have to stay overnight in one of the huts along the way. Ride part of the way up in the **Eckbauer cable car,** which sets out from the Skistadion off Mittenwalderstrasse. The older, more scenic **Graseckbahn** takes you right over the dramatic gorges. Day cards for the cable car cost €23 (cheaper depending on how far you want to ride and time of year). There's a handy inn at the top, where you can gather strength for the hour-long walk back down to the Graseckbahn station. ✉ *Olympia-Skistadion* ⊕ *www.eckbauerbahn.de.*

Lohnkutschevereinigung. Horse-drawn carriages also cover the first section of the route in summer; in winter you can skim along it in a sleigh. The carriages wait near the Skistadion. Or you can call the local coaching society, the Lohnkutschevereinigung, for information. ✉ *Olympia Skistadion* ☎ *0172/860–4105* ⊕ *www.kutschenfahrten-garmisch.de*

SKIING AND SNOWBOARDING

Garmisch-Partenkirchen was the site of the 1936 Winter Olympics, and remains Germany's premier winter-sports resort. The upper slopes of the Zugspitze and surrounding mountains challenge the best ski buffs and snowboarders, and there are also plenty of runs for intermediate skiers and families. The area is divided into two basic regions. The **Riffelriss** with the **Zugspitzplatt** is Germany's highest skiing area, with snow pretty much guaranteed from November to May. Access is via the **Zugspitzbahn** funicular. Cost for a day pass is €41.50; for a 2½-day pass €93 (valid from noon on the first day). The **Garmisch-Classic** has numerous lifts in the **Alpspitz, Kreuzeck,** and **Hausberg** regions. Day passes cost €38.50, and a 2½-day pass €93. The town has a number of ski schools and tour organizers.

Alpine Auskunftstelle. The best place for information for all your snow-sports needs is the Alpine office at the Garmisch tourist-information office. ⊠ *Richard-Strauss-Pl. 2, Garmisch* ☎ *08821/180–700* ⊕ *www. gapa.de* ☉ *Mid-Oct.–mid-Dec. and mid-Mar.–mid-May, weekdays 9–5, Sat. 9–3; mid-Dec.–mid-Mar. and mid-May–mid-Oct., weekdays 9–6, Sun. 10–noon.*

Erste Skilanglaufschule Garmisch-Partenkirchen. Cross-country skiers should check with the Erste Skilanglaufschule Garmisch-Partenkirchen at the eastern entrance of the Olympic stadium in Garmisch. ⊠ *Olympia-Skistadion* ☎ *08821/1516* ⊕ *www.ski-langlauf-schule.de.*

Skischule Alpin. Skiers looking for instruction can try the Skischule Alpin. ⊠ *Reintalstr. 8, Garmisch* ☎ *08821/945–676* ⊕ *www.alpin-skischule.de.*

ETTAL

16 km (10 miles) north of Garmisch-Partenkirchen, 85 km (53 miles) south of Munich.

The village of Ettal is presided over by the massive bulk of Kloster Ettal, a great monastery and centuries-old distillery.

GETTING HERE AND AROUND

Ettal is easily reached by bus and car from Garmisch and Oberammergau. Consider staying in Oberammergau and renting a bike. The 4-km (2½-mile) ride along the river is clearly marked, relatively easy, and a great way to meet locals.

ESSENTIALS

Visitor Information Tourist Information Ettal ⊠ *Ammergauer Str. 8* ☎ *08822/923–634* ⊕ *www.ammergauer-alpen.de/ettal.*

EXPLORING

Fodor'sChoice ★ **Kloster Ettal.** The great monastery was founded in 1330 by Holy Roman Emperor Ludwig the Bavarian for a group of knights and a community of Benedictine monks. This is the largest Benedictine monastery in Germany; approximately 55 monks live here. The abbey was replaced with new buildings in the 18th century and now serves as a school. The original 10-sided church was brilliantly redecorated in 1744–53, becoming one of the foremost examples of Bavarian rococo. The church's chief treasure is its enormous dome fresco (83 feet wide), painted by Jacob Zeiller circa 1751–52. The mass of swirling clouds and the pink-and-blue vision of heaven are typical of the rococo fondness for elaborate ceiling painting.

Today, the Kloster owns most of the surrounding land and directly operates the Hotel Ludwig der Bayer, the Kloster-Laden, and the Kloster-markt. All of the Kloster's activities, from beer production to running the hotel serve one singular purpose: to fund the famous college-prep and boarding schools which are tuition-free.

Ettaler liqueurs, made from a centuries-old recipe, are still distilled at the monastery. The monks make seven different liqueurs, some with more than 70 mountain herbs. Originally the liqueurs were made as medicines, and they have legendary health-giving properties. The ad tells it best: "Two monks know how it's made, 2 million Germans

The dome fresco at Kloster Ettal (Ettal Monastery) was painted by Jacob Zeiller and is an excellent example of Bavarian rococo.

know how it tastes." ▥ TIP➜ You can visit the distillery right next to the church and buy bottles of the libation from the gift shop and bookstore. The honey-saffron schnapps is the best.

It's possible to tour the distillery (€6) and the brewery (€9). ✉ *Kaiser-Ludwig-Pl. 1* ☏ *08822/740 for guided tour of church, 08822/746–228 for distillery, 08822/746–450 for brewery* ⊕ *www.abtei.kloster-ettal. de* 🎫 *Free* ☉ *Church: winter, daily 8–6; summer, daily 8–7:45. Distillery tours: call ahead. Brewery tours: Tues. and Thurs. at 1:30, register before 11 on day of tour.*

Schaukäserei. Besides its spirit and spirits, Ettal has made another local industry into an attraction: namely cheese, yogurt, and other milk derivatives. You can see cheese, butter, cream, and other dairy products in the making at this public cheese-making plant. There is even a little buffet for a cheesy break. ✉ *Mandlweg 1* ☏ *08822/923–926* ⊕ *www. milch-und-kas.de* 🎫 *Free, €3.50 with tour and interpreter* ☉ *June–Oct., daily 10–5; Nov.–May, Tues.–Sun. 10–5.*

WHERE TO EAT AND STAY

$
GERMAN
✕ **Edelweiss.** This friendly café and restaurant next to the monastery is an ideal spot for a light lunch or coffee and homemade cakes. ⑤ *Average main: €9* ✉ *Kaiser-Ludwig-Pl. 3* ☏ *08822/92920* ⊕ *www.restaurant-edelweiss-ettal.de* ▭ *No credit cards.*

$
RESORT
🏨 **Hotel Ludwig der Bayer.** Backed by mountains, this fine old hotel is run by the Benedictine order. **Pros:** good value; close to Kloster; indoor pool. **Cons:** no Wi-Fi, just cable. ⑤ *Rooms from: €99* ✉ *Kaiser-Ludwig-Pl. 10* ☏ *08822/9150* ⊕ *www.ludwig-der-bayer.de* ⤦ *70 rooms, 30 apartments* ❙◯❙ *Breakfast.*

SCHLOSS LINDERHOF

Schloss Linderhof. ⇨ *See "The Fairy-Tale Castles of King Ludwig II" in Chapter 4.*

OBERAMMERGAU

20 km (12 miles) northwest of Garmisch-Partenkirchen, 4 km (2½ miles) northwest of Ettal, 90 km (56 miles) south of Munich.

Its location alone, in an Alpine valley beneath a sentinel-like peak, makes this small town a major attraction (allow a half hour for the drive from Garmisch). Its main streets are lined with painted houses (such as the 1784 Pilatushaus on Ludwig-Thoma-Strasse), and in summer the village bursts with color. Many of these lovely houses are occupied by families whose men are highly skilled in the art of wood carving, a craft that has flourished here since the early 12th century. Oberammergau is completely overrun by tourists during the day, but at night you'll feel like you have a charming Bavarian village all to yourself.

GETTING HERE AND AROUND

The B-23 links Oberammergau to Garmsich-Partenkirchen and to the A-23 to Munich. Frequent bus services connect to Garmisch, Ettal, the Wieskirche, and Füssen. No long-distance trains serve Oberammergau, but a short ride on the Regional-Bahn to Murnau will connect you to the long-distance train network.

ESSENTIALS

Visitor Information Tourist Information Oberammergau ⊠ *Eugen-Papst-Str. 9a* ☎ *08822/922–740* ⊕ *www.oberammergau.de.*

EXPLORING

Oberammergau Museum. Here you'll find historic examples of the wood craftsman's art and an outstanding collection of Christmas crèches, which date from the mid-18th century. Numerous exhibits also document the wax and wax-embossing art, which also flourishes in Oberammergau. A notable piece is that of a German soldier carved by Georg Kornheuer on the Eastern Front in 1943: the artist was later killed in 1944. ⊠ *Dorfstr. 8* ☎ *08822/94136* 💶 *€6, includes Pilatushaus* ⊗ *Mar. 23–Nov. 3 and Nov. 30–Jan. 5, Tues.–Sun. 10–5.*

Pilatushaus. You'll find many wood-carvers at work in town, and shop windows are crammed with their creations. From June through October a workshop is open free to the public here at Pilatushaus; working potters and painters can also be seen. Pilatushaus was completed in 1775, and the frescoes—considered among the most beautiful in town—were done by Franz Seraph Zwinck, one of the greatest Lüftlmalerei painters. The house is named for the fresco over the front door depicting Christ before Pilate. A collection of reverse glass paintings depicting religious and secular scenes has been moved here from the Heimatmuseum. Contact the tourist office to sign up for a weeklong course in wood carving (classes are in German), which costs about €450 to €600, depending on whether you stay in a Gasthof or a hotel. ⊠ *Ludwig-Thoma-Str. 10* ☎ *08822/949–511 for tourist office* ⊕ *www.oberammergaumuseum.de* 💶 *€6* ⊗ *Mar. 23–Nov. 11, Tue.–Sun. 10–5; Nov. 30–Dec. 23, Tue.–Sun. 10–1.*

St. Peter and St. Paul Church. The 18th-century church is regarded as the finest work of rococo architect Josef Schmutzer, and it has striking frescoes by Matthäus Günther and Franz Seraph Zwinck (in the organ loft). Schmutzer's son, Franz Xaver Schmutzer, also did a lot of the stuccowork. ⊠ *Pfarrpl. 1* ☉ *Daily 9 am–dusk.*

WHERE TO EAT

$ ✕ **Ammergauer Stub'n.** A homey
GERMAN   restaurant at Hotel Wittelsbach with pink tablecloths and a lot of wood, the Ammergauer Stub'n has a comprehensive menu that serves both Bavarian specialties and international dishes. You can expect nice roasts and some Swabian dishes, such as *Maultaschen,* a large, meat-filled ravioli. ⑤ *Average main: €13* ⊠ *Wittelsbach Hotel, Dorfstr. 21* ☎ *08822/92800* ⊕ *www.hotelwittelsbach.de* ☉ *Closed late Oct.–late Nov. No lunch.*

$ ✕ **Gasthaus zum Stern.** This is a traditional place (around 500 years
GERMAN   old), with coffered ceilings, thick walls, an old Kachelofen (enclosed, tiled, wood-burning stove) that heats the dining room beyond endurance on cold winter days, and smiling waitresses in dirndls. The food is hearty, traditional Bavarian. For a quieter dinner or lunch, reserve a space in the Bäckerstube (Baker's Parlor). ⑤ *Average main: €13* ⊠ *Dorfstr. 33* ☎ *08822/867* ⊕ *www.gasthaus-stern-oberammergau.de* ☉ *Closed Wed.*

$ ✕ **Hotel Alte Post.** You can enjoy carefully prepared local cuisine, includ-
GERMAN   ing several venison and boar dishes, at the original pine tables in this 350-year-old inn. There's a special children's menu, and, in summer, meals are also served in the beer garden. The front terrace of this delightful old building is a great place to watch traffic, both pedestrian and automotive. A part of the café has been reserved for web surfing. ⑤ *Average main: €12* ⊠ *Dorfstr. 19* ☎ *08822/9100* ⊕ *www.altepost.com* ☉ *Closed Nov.–mid-Dec.*

WHERE TO STAY

$ ⌂ **Gasthof zur Rose.** Everything is pretty rustic in this spacious remod-
B&B/INN   eled barn, but the welcome and hospitality are genuine and gracious, even for Bavarian standards. **Pros:** quiet; affordable; right off the city center; friendly service. **Cons:** rustic and worn; few amenities. ⑤ *Rooms from: €80* ⊠ *Dedlerstr. 9* ☎ *08822/4706* ⊕ *www.rose-oberammergau.de* ⇲ *19 rooms* ⊟ *No credit cards* ☉ *Restaurant closed Mon.* ⦿ *Breakfast.*

$
HOTEL
⊞ **Hotel Landhaus Feldmeier.** This quiet family-run hotel, idyllically set just outside the village, has mostly spacious rooms with modern pinewood furniture. **Pros:** small and distinguished; quiet; Internet access in the rooms. **Cons:** outside the city center. $ *Rooms from: €98* ⊠ *Ettalerstr. 29* ☎ *08822/3011* ⊕ *www.hotel-feldmeier.de* ⊅ *27 rooms, 4 apartments* ⊗ *Closed mid-Nov.–mid-Dec.* ⦿⦗ *Breakfast.*

$
HOTEL
⊞ **Hotel Turmwirt.** Rich wood paneling reaches from floor to ceiling in this transformed 18th-century inn, set in the shadow of Oberammergau's mountain, the Kofel. **Pros:** great for families with children. **Cons:** service can be brusque; nearby church bells ring every 15 minutes. $ *Rooms from: €99* ⊠ *Ettalerstr. 2* ☎ *08822/92600* ⊕ *www.turmwirt.de* ⊅ *22 rooms, 1 suite* ⊗ *Closed 1 wk in early Dec.* ⦿⦗ *Breakfast.*

THE ARTS

Though the Passion Play theater was traditionally not used for anything other than the Passion Play (next performance, 2020), Oberammergauers decided that using it for opera or other theatrical events during the 10-year pause between the religious performances might be a good idea. The first performances of Verdi's *Nabucco* and Mozart's *Magic Flute* in 2002 established a new tradition. Other passion plays are also performed here. Ticket prices are between around €19 and €50.

Oberammergau Passionsspielhaus. This immense theater is where the Passion Play is performed. Visitors are given a glimpse of the costumes, the sceneries, the stage, and even the auditorium. ▮▮**TIP**➔ The Combi-ticket for the Oberammergau Museum, Pilatushaus, and the Passionsmuseum costs €6. ⊠ *Passionstheater, Passionswiese, Theaterstr. 16* ☎ *08822/945–8888 for tickets for performances, 08822/94136 for tickets for guided tour* ⊕ *www.oberammergaumuseum.de; www.passionstheater.de* 🎫 *€6* ⊗ *Mar. 23–Nov. 3 and Dec. 23–Jan. 6, Tues.–Sun. 10–5; Nov. 30–Dec. 23, Tues.–Sun. 10–1.*

Passion Play. Oberammergau is best known for its Passion Play, first presented in 1634 as an offering of thanks after the Black Death stopped just short of the village. In faithful accordance with a solemn vow, it will next be performed in the year 2020, as it has every 10 years since 1680. Its 16 acts, which take 5½ hours, depict the final days of Christ, from the Last Supper through the Crucifixion and Resurrection. It's presented daily on a partly open-air stage against a mountain backdrop from late May to late September. The entire village is swept up in the production, with some 1,500 residents directly involved in its preparation and presentation. Men grow beards in the hope of capturing a key role; young women have been known to put off their weddings—the role of Mary went only to unmarried girls until 1990, when, amid much local controversy, a 31-year-old mother of two was given the part. ⊠ *Passionstheater, Theaterstr. 16* ⊕ *www.passionstheater.de.*

SPORTS AND THE OUTDOORS

BICYCLING

It's easy to bike to Schloss Linderhof (14 km) and to Ettal (4 km) along the scenic paths along the river, where there are several good places to go swimming and have a picnic. The trail to Ettal branches off in the direction of Linderhof (marked as Graswang) where it becomes part of an old forestry road. Take the branch of the Ettal path that goes via the Ettaler-Mühle (Ettal Mill); it's quieter, the river is filled with trout, and the people you meet along the way give a friendly *Grüss Gott!* (Greet God!). The path opens up at a local-heavy restaurant with fantastic views of the Kloster.

Sport-Zentrale Papistock. This outfit rents bikes for €10 per day. They are located across the street from the train station, directly at the trailhead to Ettal and Linderhof. ✉ *Bahnhofstr. 6a* ☎ *08822/4178* ⊕ *www. sportzentrale-papistock.de* ⊘ *Closed Sun.*

MITTENWALD

20 km (12 miles) southeast of Garmisch, 105 km (66 miles) south of Munich.

Many regard Mittenwald as the most beautiful town in the Bavarian Alps. It has somehow avoided the architectural sins found in other Alpine villages by maintaining a balance between conservation and the needs of tourism. Its medieval prosperity is reflected on its main street, **Obermarkt,** which has splendid houses with ornately carved gables and brilliantly painted facades. Goethe called it "a picture book come alive," and it still is. The town has even re-created the stream that once flowed through the market square. In the Middle Ages, Mittenwald was the staging point for goods shipped from the wealthy city-state of Venice by way of the Brenner Pass and Innsbruck. From Mittenwald, goods were transferred to rafts, which carried them down the Isar River to Munich. By the mid-17th century the international trade routes shifted to a different pass, and the fortunes of Mittenwald evaporated.

In 1684 Matthias Klotz, a farmer's son turned master violin maker, returned from a 20-year stay in Cremona, Italy. There, along with Antonio Stradivari, he studied under Nicolo Amati, who developed the modern violin. Klotz taught the art of violin making to his brothers and friends and before long, half the men in the village were crafting the instruments, using woods from neighboring forests. Mittenwald became known as the Village of a Thousand Violins and the locally crafted instruments are still treasured around the world. In the right weather— sunny, dry—you may even catch the odd sight of laundry lines hung with new violins out to receive their natural dark hue. The violin has made Mittenwald a small cultural oasis in the middle of the Alps. Not only is there an annual violin- (and viola-, cello-, and bow-) building contest each year in June, with concerts and lectures, but also an organ festival in the church of St. Peter and St. Paul held from the end of July to the end of September. The town also boasts a violin-making school.

GETTING HERE AND AROUND

The B-11 connects Mittenwald with Garmisch. Mittenwald is last stop on the Munich-Garmisch train line.

ESSENTIALS

Visitor Information Tourist Information Mittenwald ✉ *Dammkarstr. 3* ☎ *08823/33981* ⊕ *www.alpenwelt-karwendel.de/mittenwald.*

EXPLORING

The Geigenbaumuseum. The local museum describes in fascinating detail the history of violin making in Mittenwald. Ask the museum curator to direct you to the nearest of several violin makers—they'll be happy to demonstrate the skills handed down to them. ⊠ *Ballenhausg. 3* ☎ *08823/2511* ⊕ *www.geigenbaumuseum-mittenwald.de* ⌐€*4.50* ⊙ *Early Feb–mid-Mar., mid-May–mid-Oct., and early Dec.–early Jan., Tues.–Sun. 10–5; early Jan.–late Jan., mid-Mar.–mid-May, and mid-Oct.–early Nov., Tues.–Sun. 11–4.*

St. Peter and St. Paul Church. On the back of the altar in this 18th-century church (as in Oberammergau, built by Josef Schmutzer and decorated by Matthäus Günther), you'll find Matthias Klotz's name, carved there by the violin maker himself. ▉**TIP→** Note that on some of the ceiling frescoes, the angels are playing violins, violas da gamba, and lutes. In front of the church, Klotz is memorialized as an artist at work in vivid bronze sculpted by Ferdinand von Miller (1813–79), creator of the mighty Bavaria Monument in Munich. The church, with its elaborate and joyful stuccowork coiling and curling its way around the interior, is one of the most important rococo structures in Bavaria. Note its Gothic choir loft, added in the 18th century. The bold frescoes on its exterior are characteristic of Lüftlmalerei, where images, usually religious motifs, were painted on the wet stucco exteriors of houses and churches. On nearby streets you can see other fine examples on the facades of three famous houses: the Goethehaus, the Pilgerhaus, and the Pichlerhaus. Among the artists working here was the great Franz Seraph Zwinck. ⊠ *Ballenhausg., next to Geigenbaumuseum.*

WHERE TO EAT

$$
EUROPEAN
✕**Arnspitze.** Get a table at the large picture window and soak in the views of the towering Karwendel mountain range as you ponder a menu that combines the best traditional ingredients with international touches. Chef and owner Herbert Wipfelder looks beyond the edge of his plate all the way to Asia, if need be, to find inspiration. The fish pot-au-feu has a Mediterranean flair; the jugged hare in red wine is truly Bavarian. The restaurant also offers accommodations in a separate house. $ *Average main: €20* ⊠ *Innsbrucker Str. 68* ☎ *08823/2425* ⊕ *www.arnspitze-mittenwald.de* ⊙ *Closed Nov.–mid-Dec., and Tues. and Wed.*

WHERE TO STAY

$
HOTEL
Alpenrose. Once part of a monastery and later given one of the town's most beautiful painted baroque facades, the Alpenrose is one of the area's handsomest hotels. **Pros:** great German decor; friendly staff. **Cons:** some rooms are cramped; accommodations can get warm in summer. $ *Rooms from: €76* ⊠ *Obermarkt 1* ☎ *08823/92700* ⊕ *www.hotel-alpenrose-mittenwald.de* ⌐ *16 rooms, 2 apartments* ⌐○⌐ *Breakfast.*

$
HOTEL
Bichlerhof. Carved oak furniture gives the rooms of this Alpine-style hotel a solid German feel. **Pros:** amazing views; well-kept spa area. **Cons:** disorganized reservation system; built to look traditionally Bavarian, but is actually only 30 years old. $ *Rooms from: €74* ⊠ *Adolf-Baader-Str. 5* ☎ *08823/9190* ⊕ *www.bichlerhof-mittenwald.de* ⌐ *30 rooms* ⌐○⌐ *Breakfast.*

$ 🛏 **Gasthof Stern.** This white house with brilliant blue shutters is right
B&B/INN   in the middle of Mittenwald. **Pros:** friendly service; clean, basic hotel with a great beer garden. **Cons:** needs a renovation; upper rooms warm in summer; credit cards not accepted. ⑤ *Rooms from: €70* ✉ *Fritz-Plössl-Pl. 2* ☎ *08823/8358* ⊕ *www.stern-mittenwald.de* ⤴ *5 rooms* ▭ *No credit cards* ⊘| *Breakfast.*

$ 🛏 **Post.** The hotel retains much of its historic charm—stagecoaches car-
HOTEL   rying travelers and mail across the Alps stopped here as far back as the 17th century—though the elegant rooms come in various styles, from modern to art nouveau to Bavarian rustic. **Pros:** art-nouveau rooms in the back. **Cons:** no elevator; street noise in the evening. ⑤ *Rooms from: €99* ✉ *Obermarkt 9* ☎ *08823/938–2333* ⊕ *www.posthotel-mittenwald. de* ⤴ *74 rooms, 7 suites* ⊘| *Breakfast.*

SPORTS AND THE OUTDOORS

Mittenwald lies literally in the shadow of the mighty **Karwendel** Alpine range, which rises to a height of nearly 8,000 feet. There are a number of small lakes in the hills surrounding Mittenwald. You can either walk to the closer ones or rent bikes and adventure farther afield. The information center across the street from the train station has maps, and they can help you select a route.

The **Dammkar** run is nearly 8 km (5 miles) long and offers some of the best free-riding skiing, telemarking, and snowboarding in the German Alps.

Erste Schischule Mittenwald. Skiers, cross-country and downhill, and snow-boarders can find all they need, including equipment and instruction, at the Erste Schischule Mittenwald. ✉ *Bahnhofspl. 14* ☎ *08823/3582* ⊕ *www.skischule-mittenwald.de.*

Karwendelbahn cable car. The cable car carries hikers and skiers to a height of 7,180 feet, the beginning of numerous trails down, or farther up into the Karwendel range. ✉ *Karwendelbahn, Alpenkorpsstr. 1* ☎ *08823/937–6760* ⊕ *www.karwendelbahn.de* ⛰ *€15 one-way, €24 round-trip* ⊘ *May–Oct., daily 8:30–5; Nov.–Apr. 9–4.*

SHOPPING

It's not the kind of gift every visitor wants to take home, but if you'd like a violin, a cello, or even a double bass, the Alpine resort of Mittenwald can oblige. There are more than 30 craftspeople whose work is coveted by musicians throughout the world.

Anton Maller. If you're buying or even just feeling curious, call on Anton Maller. He's been making violins and other stringed instruments for more than 25 years. ✉ *Obermarkt 2* ☎ *08823/5865* ⊕ *www.violin-maller.de.*

Gabriele Schneider's SchokoLaden. Find out where all the milk from the local cows goes with a visit to Gabriele Schneider's SchokoLaden, a homemade-chocolate shop. ✉ *Obermarkt 42* ☎ *08823/938–939* ⊕ *www.schokoladen-mittenwald.de.*

Trachten Werner. For traditional Bavarian costumes—dirndls, embroidered shirts and blouses, and lederhosen—try Trachten Werner. ✉ *Obermarkt 39* ☎ *08823/8282* ⊕ *www.trachten-werner.de* ⊘ *Closed Mon.–Thurs.*

CHIEMGAU

With its rolling hills and serene lakes in the shadow of the Alpine peaks, the Chiemgau is a natural paradise and a good transition to the Alps. The main attraction is, without a doubt, the Chiemsee with the amazing palace on the Herreninsel, the biggest of the islands on the lake. The area is dotted with clear blue lakes and, although tourism is fairly well established, you'll feel that you have much of the area all to yourself. Beer lovers flock to the Tegernsee and relax afterward in the iodine spa in Bad Tölz.

BAD TÖLZ

14 km (8 miles) north of Sylvenstein Lake, 48 km (30 miles) south of Munich.

Bad Tölz's new town, dating from the mid-19th century, sprang up with the discovery of iodine-laden springs, which allowed the locals to call their town *Bad* (bath or spa) Tölz. You can take the waters, either by drinking a cupful from the local springs or going all the way with a full course of health treatments at a specially equipped hotel. ■TIP→ If you can, visit on a Friday morning, when a farmers' market stretches along the main street to the Isar River and on the Jungmayr-Fritzplatz.

This town clings to its ancient customs more tightly than any other Bavarian community. It is not uncommon to see people wearing traditional clothing as their daily dress. If you're in Bad Tölz on November 6, you'll witness one of the most colorful traditions of the Bavarian Alpine area: the Leonhardiritt equestrian procession, which marks the anniversary of the death in 559 of St. Leonhard of Noblac, the patron saint of animals, specifically horses. The procession ends north of town at an 18th-century chapel on the Kalvarienberg, above the Isar River.

> **SPAS**
>
> *Bad* is the German word for bath or spa. You can take the waters at several towns in the Bavarian Alps region, from the Bad Tölz *Jodquellen*, iodine springs, to the Bad Reichenhall saline spring. Most Alpine towns have some sort of wellness offering. Ask at information centers for details.

GETTING HERE AND AROUND

Bad Tölz is on the B-472, which connects to the A-8 to Munich. Hourly trains link Bad Tölz with Munich. Bad Tölz is easily walkable and has frequent city-bus services.

ESSENTIALS

Visitor Information Bad Tölz Tourist-Information ✉ *Max-Höfler-Pl. 1* ☎ *08041/78670* ⊕ *www.bad-toelz.de.*

EXPLORING

The Alpamare. Bad Tölz's very attractive spa complex pumps spa water into its pools, one of which is disguised as a South Sea beach complete with surf. Its five waterslides include a 1,082-foot-long adventure run. Another—the Alpa-Canyon—has 90-degree drops, and only the hardiest swimmers are advised to try it. A nightmarish dark tunnel is aptly named the Thriller. There is a complex price structure, depending on time spent in the spa and other wellness activities for the various individual attractions, or combo tickets for more than one. ✉ *Ludwigstr. 14* ☎ *08041/509–999* ⊕ *www.alpamare.de* 💲 *€29 4-hr ticket, €27 till 11 am, €23 after 5 pm* ⊙ *Daily 9:30 am–10 pm.*

The Stadtmuseum. Located in the Altes Rathaus (Old Town Hall), you'll find many fine examples of *Bauernmöbel* (farmhouse furniture), as well as a fascinating exhibit on the history of the town and its environs. ✉ *Marktstr. 48* ☎ *08041/793–5156* ⊕ *www.bad-toelz.de* 💲 *€4* ⊙ *Late Nov.–late Dec., Tues.–Sun. 10–5; Jan.–late Nov., Tues.–Sun. 10–4.*

WHERE TO STAY

$$$
RESORT
🏨 **Hotel Jodquellenhof-Alpamare.** The *Jodquellen* are the iodine springs that have made Bad Tölz wealthy. **Pros:** elegant hotel; free access to the spa. **Cons:** busy during local school holidays. 💲 *Rooms from: €199* ✉ *Ludwigstr. 13–15* ☎ *08041/5090* ⊕ *www.jodquellenhof.com* 🛏 *71 rooms* ⍟ *Breakfast.*

$
HOTEL
🏨 **Hotel Kolbergarten.** Located right near the Old Town and surrounded by a quiet garden with old trees, this hotel offers comfortable rooms, each carefully done in a particular style such as baroque or Biedermeier. **Pros:** large clean rooms; staff is great with children. **Cons:** often

The brine pool at Alpamare spa has green water due to the mineral iodine; it is meant to stimulate circulation.

fully booked. $⑤ Rooms from: €98 ⊠ Fröhlichg. 5 ☎ 08041/78920 ⊕ www.hotel-kolbergarten.de ⤳ 12 rooms, 2 suites ⦿ Breakfast.

NIGHTLIFE AND THE ARTS

Boys' choir. Bad Tölz is world renowned for its outstanding boys' choir. When not on tour, the choir gives regular concerts in the Kurhaus. Check the Bad Tölz website for details. ⊠ *Kurhaus Bad Tölz, Ludwigstr. 25 ⊕ www.bad-toelz.de.*

TanzBar KULT. TanzBar KULT has a rather wide range of themes, and it features live music in the terrific setting of an old brewery, with barrel vaults and painted brick walls. ⊠ *Wachterstr. 19 ☎ 08041/799–3699 ⊕ www.kult-toelz.de.*

SPORTS AND THE OUTDOORS

FAMILY **Blomberg.** Bad Tölz's local mountain, the Blomberg, 3 km (2 miles) west of town, has moderately difficult ski runs and can also be tackled on a toboggan in winter and on a luge in summer. The winter run of 5 km (3 miles) is the longest in Bavaria. The concrete summer luge-run snakes 3,938 feet down the mountain and is great fun; you'll want the three-ride ticket. A ski-lift ride to the start of the run and toboggan or roller luge are included in the price. ☎ *08041/3726 ⊕ www.blombergbahn.de ⊗ Winter tobogganing from Nov. (weather permitting), daily 9–4; summer tobogganing, daily 10–4; check website for skiing.*

SHOPPING

Bad Tölz is famous for its painted furniture, particularly farmhouse cupboards and chests. Several local shops specialize in this type of *Bauernmöbel* (farmhouse furniture, usually hand carved from pine) and will usually handle export formalities. Ask at your hotel or tourist-information center for a recommendation on where to shop.

Antiquitäten Schwarzwälder. For traditional Bauernmöbel furniture, try Antiquitäten Schwarzwälder. ⊠ *Badstr. 2* ☎ *08041/41222* ⊕ *www. antiquitaeten-schwarzwaelder.de.*

TEGERNSEE

16 km (10 miles) east of Bad Tölz, 50 km (31 miles) south of Munich.

The beautiful shores of the Tegernsee are among the most expensive property in all of Germany. The interest in the region shown by King Maximilian I of Bavaria at the beginning of the 19th century attracted VIPs and artists, which led to a boom that has never really faded. Most accommodations and restaurants, however, still have reasonable prices, and there are plenty of activities for everyone. Tegernsee's wooded shores, rising gently to scalable mountain peaks of no more than 6,300 feet, invite hikers, walkers, and picnicking families. The lake itself draws swimmers and yachters. In fall the russet-clad trees provide a colorful contrast to the snowcapped mountains. Beer lovers are drawn to Tegernsee by one of the best breweries in Europe. There are three main towns on the lake: Tegernsee, Rottach-Egern, and Bad Wiessee.

GETTING HERE AND AROUND

The best way to reach all three towns is to take the BOB train from Munich to Tegernsee (hourly) and then take a boat ride on one of the eight boats that circle the lake year-round. The boats dock near the Tegernsee train station and make frequent stops, including stops at the Benedictine monastery in Tegernsee, in Rottach-Egern, and in Bad Wiessee. The monastery is a pleasant half-mile walk from the train station. Buses connect Tegernsee to Bad Tölz.

ESSENTIALS

Visitor Information Rottach-Egern/Tegernsee Tourist Information ⊠ *Hauptstr. 2* ☎ *08022/180–140* ⊕ *www.tegernsee.de.*

EXPLORING

Benedictine monastery. On the eastern shore of the lake, the laid-back town of Tegernsee is home to this large Benedictine monastary. Founded in the 8th century, this was one of the most productive cultural centers in southern Germany; the Minnesänger (wandering lyrical poets) Walther von der Vogelweide (1170–1230) was a welcome guest. Not so welcome were Magyar invaders, who laid waste to the monastery in the 10th century. During the Middle Ages the monastery made a lively business producing stained-glass windows, thanks to a nearby quartz quarry, and in the 16th century it became a major center of printing. The late-Gothic **church** was refurbished in Italian baroque style in the 18th century. The frescoes are by Hans Georg Asam, whose work also

Horses pull a sleigh through the snow in Rottach-Egern, one of the three main towns on Lake Tegernsee.

graces the Benediktbeuren monastery in Bavaria. Secularization sealed the monastery's fate at the beginning of the 19th century: almost half the buildings were torn down. Maximilian I bought the surviving ones and had Leo von Klenze redo them for use as a summer retreat.

Today there is a high school on the property, and students write their exams beneath inspiring baroque frescoes in what had been the monastery. The **Herzogliches Bräustüberl,** a brewery and beer hall, is also on site. ▧ **TIP→ Try a Mass (a liter-size mug) of their legendary Tergernseer Helles or Spezial beer.** ⊠ *Schlosspl.*

The Grosses Paraplui. Maximilian showed off this corner of his kingdom to Czar Alexander I of Russia and Emperor Franz I of Austria during their journey to the Congress of Verona in October 1821. You can follow their steps through the woods to the Grosses Paraplui, one of the loveliest lookout points in Bavaria. A plaque marks the spot where they admired the open expanse of the Tegernsee and the mountains beyond. The path starts opposite Schlossplatz in Tegernsee town and is well marked. ⊠ *Schlosspl.*

The Olaf Gulbransson Museum. This museum is devoted to the Norwegian painter Olaf Gulbrannson, who went to Munich in 1902 and worked as a caricaturist for the satirical magazine *Simplicissimus*. His poignant caricatures and numerous works of satire depict noisy politicians and snooty social upper-crusters as well as other subjects. The museum is housed in a discreet modern building set back from the main lakeside road of Tegernsee. ⊠ *Im Kurgarten 5* ☎ *08022/3338* ⊕ *www.olaf-gulbransson-museum.de* ⊠ *€6* ⊙ *Tues.–Sun. 10–5.*

WHERE TO EAT

$$
GERMAN

✕ **Boutique Hotel Relais-Chalet Wilhelmy.** Although everything is modern, this inn in Bad Wiessee takes you back to a less-frantic era. Classical music accompanies unpretentious yet tasty meals. Try the fish specialties or the light guinea fowl with herb rice and enjoy tea and cake in the little garden. $ *Average main: €16* ⊠ *Freihausstr. 15, Bad Wiessee* ☎ *08022/98680.*

$$$$
EUROPEAN

✕ **Freihaus Brenner.** Proprietor Josef Brenner has brought a taste of nouvelle cuisine to the Tegernsee. His attractive restaurant commands fine views from high above Bad Wiessee. Try any of his suggested dishes, ranging from roast pheasant in wine sauce to fresh lake fish. There are flexible portion sizes for smaller appetites. $ *Average main: €30* ⊠ *Freihaus 4, Bad Wiessee* ☎ *08022/86560* ⊕ *www.freihaus-brenner.de.*

$
GERMAN

✕ **Herzogliches Bräustüberl.** Once part of Tegernsee's Benedictine monastery, then a royal retreat, the Bräustüberl is now an immensely popular beer hall and brewery. The tasty Bavarian snacks (sausages, pretzels, all the way up to steak tartare), all under €10, can't be beat. Next to here, more-substantial fare can be had in the adjoining **Schlossbrennerei** ($ ⊕ *www.tegernseer-schlossrestaurant.de*). In summer, quaff your beer beneath the huge chestnut trees and admire the delightful view of the lake and mountains. $ *Average main: €10* ⊠ *Schlosspl. 1* ☎ *08022/4141 for Bräustüberl, 08022/4560 for Schlossbrennerei* ⊕ *www.braustuberl. de* ♿ *Reservations not accepted* ▭ *No credit cards* ☉ *Closed Mon.*

WHERE TO STAY

$$
HOTEL

🏨 **Das Tegernsee Hotel & Spa.** The elegant, turreted Hotel Tegernsee and its two spacious annexes sit high above the Tegernsee, backed by the wooded slopes of Neureuth Mountain. **Pros:** hotel in almost mint condition due to renovations completed in 2009; historical elegance; Czar Nicholas I was a frequent guest; great views. **Cons:** a little away from the hub of the town. $ *Rooms from: €159* ⊠ *Neureuthstr. 23* ☎ *08022/1820* ⊕ *www.dastegernsee.de* ↵ *63 rooms, 10 suites* �‖ *Breakfast.*

$
HOTEL

🏨 **Seehotel Zur Post.** The lake views from most rooms are somewhat compromised by the main road outside, but a central location, a winter garden, a terrace, and a little beer garden are pluses. **Pros:** great views; friendly service; excellent breakfast. **Cons:** the property is a little old fashioned and could do with an update. $ *Rooms from: €55* ⊠ *Seestr. 3* ☎ *08022/66550* ⊕ *www.seehotel-zur-post.de* ↵ *43 rooms* �‖ *Breakfast.*

NIGHTLIFE AND THE ARTS

Every resort has its **spa orchestra**—in summer they play daily in the music-box-style bandstands that dot the lakeside promenades. A strong Tegernsee tradition is the summer-long program of **festivals,** some set deep in the forest. Tegernsee's lake festival in August, when sailing clubs deck their boats with garlands and lanterns, is an unforgettable experience.

Casino. Bad Wiessee's casino lies near the entrance of town coming from Gmund. The main playing rooms are open daily from 3 pm, and it is the biggest and liveliest venue in town for the after-dark scene. ⊠ *Spielbank Bad Wiessee, Winner 1, Bad Wiessee* ☎ *08022/98350* ⊕ *www. spielbanken-bayern.de/wDeutsch/wiessee/.*

SPORTS AND THE OUTDOORS

Tourist Information Tegernsee. Contact the tourist office in the town of Tegernsee for hiking maps. ✉ *Hauptstr. 2, Bad Wiessee* ☎ *08022/180–140* ⊕ *www.tegernsee.de.*

Wallberg. For the best vista in the area, climb the Wallberg, the 5,700-foot mountain at the south end of the Tegernsee. It's a hard four-hour hike or a short 15-minute cable-car ride up (€10 one-way, €18 round-trip). At the summit are a restaurant and sun terrace and several trailheads; in winter the skiing is excellent. ✉ *Wallbergbahn, Wallbergstr. 28, Rottach-Egern* ⊕ *www.wallbergbahn.de.*

GOLF

Tegernseer Golf-Club e.V. Besides swimming, hiking, and skiing, the Tegernsee area has become a fine place for golfing. The Tegernseer Golf-club e. V. has an 18-hole course overlooking the lake with a clubhouse and excellent restaurant. It also has fine apartments for rent. ✉ *Rohbognerhof, Bad Wiessee* ☎ *08022/271–130* ⊕ *www.tegernseer-golf-club.de.*

CHIEMSEE

80 km (50 miles) southeast of Munich, 120 km (75 miles) northeast of Garmisch-Partenkirchen.

Chiemsee is north of the Deutsche Alpenstrasse, but it demands a detour, if only to visit King Ludwig's huge palace on one of its idyllic islands. It's the largest Bavarian lake, and although it's surrounded by reedy flatlands, the nearby mountains provide a majestic backdrop. The town of **Prien** is the lake's principal resort. ■ TIP→ The tourist offices of Prien and Aschau offer a €26 transportation package covering a boat trip, a round-trip rail ticket between the two resorts, and a round-trip ride by cable car to the top of Kampen Mountain, above Aschau.

GETTING HERE AND AROUND

Prien is the best jumping-off point for exploring the Chiemsee. Frequent trains connect Prien with Munich and Salzburg. The regional trains are met by a narrow-gauge steam train for the short trip to Prien-Stock, the boat dock. The only way to reach the Herreninsel and the Fraueninsel is by boat.

ESSENTIALS

Visitor Information Chiemsee Infocenter ✉ *Felden 10, Bernau am Chiemsee* ☎ *08051/96555–0* ⊕ *www.chiemsee-alpenland.de.*

EXPLORING

Fraueninsel. Boats going between Stock and Herrenchiemsee Island also call at this small retreat known as Ladies' Island. The **Benedictine convent** there, founded 1,200 years ago, now serves as a school. One of its earliest abbesses, Irmengard, daughter of King Ludwig der Deutsche, died here in the 9th century. Her grave in the convent chapel was discovered in 1961, the same year that early frescoes there were brought to light. The chapel is open daily from dawn to dusk. Otherwise, the island has just a few private houses, a couple of shops, and a hotel. ■ TIP→ The Benedictine Sisters make delicious fruit liqueurs and marzipan. ✉ *Fraueninsel, Chiemsee* ⊕ *www.frauenwoerth.de.*

Schloss Herrenchiemsee, King Ludwig II's last building project, lies in the middle of Lake Chiemsee on the Herreninsel.

Fodor'sChoice ★ **Schloss Herrenchiemsee.** ⇨ *See "The Fairy-Tale Castles of King Ludwig II" in Chapter 4.*

WHERE TO STAY

$ HOTEL **⚑ Hotel Luitpold am See.** Boats to the Chiemsee islands tie up right outside your window at this handsome old Prien hotel, which organizes shipboard disco evenings as part of its entertainment program. **Pros:** directly on the lake (though the sister property is 328 feet away); "limousine service" offers pick-up from Munich airport for €100. **Cons:** near a busy boat dock. ⑤ *Rooms from: €82* ⊠ *Seestr. 110, Prien am Chiemsee* ☎ *08051/609–100* ⊕ *www.luitpold-am-see.de* ⤴ *54 rooms* ⦿*Breakfast.*

$$ HOTEL **⚑ Inselhotel zur Linde.** Catch a boat to this enchanting inn on the car-free Fraueninsel for dinner: but remember, if you miss the last connection to the mainland (at 9 pm), you'll have to stay the night. **Pros:** set in lush gardens; nice beer garden. **Cons:** the Fraueninsel isn't exactly famous for its nightlife. ⑤ *Rooms from: €126* ⊠ *Fraueninsel, Chiemsee* ☎ *08054/90366* ⊕ *www.linde-frauenchiemsee.de* ⤴ *14 rooms* ⦿ *Closed mid-Jan.–mid-Mar.* ⦿*Breakfast.*

SPORTS AND THE OUTDOORS

Chiemsee Golf-Club Prien e.V. The gentle hills of the region are ideal for golf. Chiemsee Golf-Club Prien e.V., in Prien, has a year-round 9-hole course. ⊠ *Bauernberg 5* ☎ *08051/62215* ⊕ *www.cgc-prien.de.*

SportLukas. Equipment can be provided for any kind of sport imaginable, from skiing to kayaking, climbing to curling, and it organizes tours. ⊠ *Hauptstr. 3, Schleching* ☎ *08649/243* ⊕ *www.sportlukas.de.*

Surfschule Chiemsee. For those wanting to learn windsurfing or to extend their skills, the Surfschule Chiemsee provides lessons and offers a package deal including board, stand up paddling, and bike rentals. ✉ *Surfschule Bernau am Chiemsee, Rasthausstr. 11, Bernau* ☎ *08051/8877* ⊕ *www.surfschule-chiemsee.de.*

BERCHTESGADENER LAND

Berchtesgadener Land is the Alps at their most dramatic and most notorious. Although some points are higher, the steep cliffs, hidden mountain lakes, and protected biospheres make the area uniquely beautiful. The salt trade brought medieval Berchtesgaden and Bad Reichenhall incredible wealth, which is still apparent in the large collection of antique houses and quaint streets. Bad Reichenhall is an impressive center of German spa culture. Berchtesgaden's image is a bit tarnished by its most infamous historical resident, Adolf Hitler. Berchtesgaden National Park is a hiker's dream, and the resounding echo of the trumpet on the Königssee shouldn't be missed.

BAD REICHENHALL

60 km (30 miles) east of Prien, 20 km (12 miles) west of Salzburg.

Bad Reichenhall is remarkably well located, near the mountains for hiking and skiing, and near Salzburg in Austria for a lively cultural scene. The town shares a remote corner of Bavaria with another prominent resort, Berchtesgaden. Although the latter is more famous, Bad Reichenhall is older, with saline springs that made the town rich. Salt is so much a part of the town that you can practically taste it in the air. Europe's largest source of brine was first tapped here in pre-Christian times; salt mining during the Middle Ages supported the economies of cities as far away as Munich and Passau. The town prospered from a spa in the early 20th century. Lately, it has successfully recycled itself from a somewhat sleepy and stodgy "cure town" to a modern, attractive center of wellness.

GETTING HERE AND AROUND

Bad Reichenhall is well connected to Berchtesgaden and Salzburg Hauptbahnhof once every hour. The hourly trains to Munich require a change in Freilassing. To reach the Bürgerbräu and the Predigtstuhl cable car, take Bus No. 180 and Bus No. 841 to Königssee.

ESSENTIALS

Visitor Information Tourist-Info Bad Reichenhall ✉ *Wittelsbacherstr. 15* ☎ *08651/6060* ⊕ *www.bad-reichenhall.de.*

EXPLORING

The Alte Saline und Quellenhaus. In the early 19th century King Ludwig I built this elaborate saltworks and spa house, in vaulted, pseudomedieval style. The pump installations, which still run, are astonishing examples of 19th-century engineering. A "saline" **chapel** is part of the spa's facilities, and was built in exotic Byzantine style. An interesting museum in the same complex looks at the history of the salt trade.

⊠ *Alte Saline 9* ☏ *08651/700–2146* ⊕ *www.alte-saline-bad-reichenhall. de* ▣ *€7.50, combined ticket with Berchtesgaden's salt mine €19* ☉ *May–Oct., daily 10–11:30 and 2–4; Nov.–Apr., Tues., Fri., and 1st Sun. in the month 2–4.*

Predigtstuhl. The pride and joy of the Reichenhallers is the steep, craggy mountain appropriately named the Preacher's Pulpit, which stands at 5,164 feet, southeast of town. A ride to the top offers a splendid view of the area. You can hike, ski in winter, or just enjoy a bite to eat and drink at the **Almütte Schlegemuldel** ($), 15 minutes from the cable car station. The cable-car ride costs €11 one-way, €18 round-trip. Departures begin at 9:30 am and continue (as needed) until the last person is off the mountain. The hotel is closed in winter. ⊠ *Südtiroler Pl. 1* ☏ *08651/2127* ⊕ *www. predigtstuhl-bahn.de.*

Rupertus Therme. Part of Bad Reichenhall's revival included building this new spa facility, the brand-new "spa and fitness resort." Pools, saunas, and steam rooms are rounded off with a host of special applications using salt, essential oils, mud packs, and massages. The therme can be popular, especially in winter, so online reservations are a good idea ⊠ *Friedrich-Ebert-Allee 21* ☏ *08651/76220 for reservation hotline* ⊕ *www.rupertustherme.de* ▣ *€21 all day ticket; €18 4 hrs* ☉ *Daily 9 am–10 pm.*

St. Zeno. This ancient church is dedicated to the patron saint of those imperiled by floods and the dangers of the deep, an ironic note in a town that flourishes on the riches of its underground springs. This 12th-century basilica, the largest in Bavaria, was remodeled in the 16th and 17th centuries, but some of the original Romanesque cloisters remain, although these can be seen only during services and from 11 to noon on Sunday and holidays. ⊠ *Salzburger Str. 30* ⊕ *www.kath-stadtkirche-badreichenhall.de.*

Wandelhalle. Hotels here base spa treatments on the health-giving properties of the saline springs and the black mud from the area's water-logged moors. The waters can also be taken in this elegant, pillared pavilion of the attractive spa gardens throughout the year. Breathing salt-laden air is a remedy for various lung conditions. All you need to do is walk along the 540-foot Gradierhaus, a massive wood-and-concrete construction that produces a fine salty mist by trickling brine down a 40-foot wall of dense blackthorn bundles. ⊠ *Königlichen Kurgarten* ☏ *08651/6060 Touristinformation Wandelhalle im Kurgarten* ☉ *Nov.–May.*

BOATING AND SAILING

All the Bavarian Alpine lakes have sailing schools that rent sailboards as well as various other types of boats. At Tegernsee you can hire motorboats at the pier in front of the Schloss Cafe, in the Tegernsee town center. Chiemsee, with its wide stretch of water whipped by Alpine winds, is a favorite for both sailing enthusiasts and windsurfers. There are boatyards all around the lake and the very good windsurfing school, Surf-schule Chiemsee, at Bernau.

Berchtesgadener
Land

WHERE TO EAT

$ ✕ **Brauereigasthof Bürgerbräu.** Each dining area in this old brewery inn
GERMAN reflects the social class that once met here: politicos, peasants, burghers,
and salt miners. Reichenhallers from all walks of life still meet here to
enjoy good conversation, hearty local beer, and excellent food. Rooms
at the inn are simple, but airy and modern, and centrally located. $ *Average main: €11* ✉ *Waagg. 1–2* ☎ *08651/6089* ⊕ *www.brauereigasthof-
buergerbraeu.de.*

$ ✕ **Gasthaus Obermühle.** Tucked away off the main road leading from
GERMAN Bad Reichenhall to the autobahn, this 16th-century mill is a well-kept
secret. Fish is the specialty here, though meats (the game in season is
noteworthy) are also on the menu. The terrace is an inviting place for
a few helpings of excellent homemade pastries. $ *Average main: €12*
✉ *Tumpenstr. 11* ☎ *08651/2193* ▭ *No credit cards* ☾ *Closed Mon.
and Tues.*

WHERE TO STAY

$$ 🏨 **Parkhotel Luisenbad.** If you fancy spoiling yourself in a typical Ger-
HOTEL man fin de siècle spa hotel, consider staying here. **Pros:** quiet; centrally
located. **Cons:** Slightly old-fashioned for some tastes. $ *Rooms from:*
€118 ✉ *Ludwigstr. 33* ☎ *08651/6040* ⊕ *www.parkhotel-luisenbad-bad-
reichenhall-berchtesgaden.de* ⤳ *70 rooms, 8 suites* 🍽 *Breakfast.*

$ 🖼 **Pension Hubertus.** This delightfully traditional family-run lodging
B&B/INN stands on the shore of the tiny Thumsee, 5 km (3 miles) from the town
center. **Pros:** incredible views; private guests-only sunbathing area. **Cons:**
far from city center; no elevator. ⑤ *Rooms from: €66* ⊠ *Thumsee 5*
☎ *08651/2252* ⊕ *www.hubertus-thumsee.de* ⤳ *18 rooms* ❍❘ *Breakfast.*

NIGHTLIFE AND THE ARTS

Casino. As a spa town and winter resort, Bad Reichenhall is a natural
for night haunts. The big draw is the elegant casino, open daily starting
at noon. ⊠ *Wittelsbacherstr. 17* ☎ *08651/95800* ⊕ *www.spielbanken-
bayern.de/w Deutsch/reichenhall* 🔒 *Jacket and tie.*

Orchesterbüro. Bad Reichenhall is proud of its long musical tradition
and of its orchestra, founded more than a century ago. It performs on
numerous occasions throughout the year in the chandelier-hung Kur-
gastzentrum Theater or, when weather permits, in the open-air pavilion,
and at a special Mozart Week in March. Call the Orchesterbüro for
program details. ⊠ *Salzburger Str. 7* ☎ *08651/762–8080* ⊕ *www.bad-
reichenhaller-philharmonie.de.*

Tanzcafe am Kurgarten. For some traditional ballroom dancing to live
music in the evenings, head for the Tanzcafe am Kurgarten. Occasionally they also show soccer games. ⊠ *Salzburger Str. 7* ☎ *08651/1691*
⊕ *www.kurcafe-bgl.de.*

SPORTS AND THE OUTDOORS

Though Berchtesgaden definitely has the pull for skiers, Bad Reichenhall
is proud of its Predigtstuhl, which towers over the town to the south.
Besides fresh air and great views, it offers some skiing, lots of hiking,
biking, and even rock climbing. The tourist information office on Wit-
telsbacherstrasse, a couple of hundred yards from the train station, has
all the necessary information regarding the numerous sporting activities
possible in Bad Reichenhall and its surrounding area.

SHOPPING

Josef Mack Company. Using flowers and herbs grown in the Bavarian
Alps, the Josef Mack Company has made medicinal herbal preparations
since 1856. ⊠ *Ludwigstr. 36* ☎ *08651/78280* ⊕ *www.macknatur.de.*

Paul Reber. Your sweet tooth will be fully satisfied at the confection emporium of Paul Reber, makers of the famous chocolate, nougat, and marzipan *Mozartkugel* and many other caloric depth-charges. ⊠ *Ludwigstr.
10–12* ☎ *08651/60030* ⊕ *www.reber-spezialitaeten.de/home.html.*

BERCHTESGADEN

*18 km (11 miles) south of Bad Reichenhall, 20 km (12 miles) south
of Salzburg.*

Berchtesgaden's reputation is unjustly rooted in its brief association
with Adolf Hitler, who dreamed of his "1,000-year Reich" from the
mountaintop where millions of tourists before and after him drank
in only the superb beauty of the Alpine panorama. The historic old
market town and mountain resort has great charm. In winter it's a
fine place for skiing and snowboarding; in summer it becomes one

of the region's most popular (and crowded) resorts. An ornate palace and working salt mine make up some of the diversions in this heavenly setting.

Salt was once the basis of Berchtesgaden's wealth. In the 12th century Emperor Barbarossa gave mining rights to a Benedictine abbey that had been founded here a century earlier. The abbey was secularized early in the 19th century, when it was taken over by the Wittelsbach rulers. Salt is still important today because of all the local wellness centers. The entire area has been declared a *Kurgebiet* ("health resort region"), and was put on the UNESCO biosphere list.

> ## WHITE GOLD
>
> Salt, or white gold as it was known in medieval times, has played a key role in the history of both Bad Reichenhall and Berchtesgaden. Organized salt production in the region began around 450 BC, and even included a 30-km (20-mile) wooden pipeline for salt built in the early 1600s. It wasn't until the early 19th century, however, that the town began utilizing its position and geological advantages to attract tourists. The production of salt continues to this day, as does the flow of travelers on the search for the healing saline pools.

GETTING HERE AND AROUND

The easiest way to reach Berchtesgaden is with the hourly train connection, or with the bus from Salzburg Hauptbahnhof. To get to Berchtesgaden from Munich requires a change in Freilassing or Salzburg. Salzburg's newly renovated main train station connects regularly to Berchtesgaden (choose the train without a Freilassing change). Frequent local bus service makes it easy to explore the town and to reach Berchtesgaden National Park and the Königssee. Local bus services, except from Documentation center to the Eagle's Nest, are included when you pay the Kurtaxe. The Schwaiger bus company runs tours of the area and across the Austrian border as far as Salzburg. An American couple runs Berchtesgaden Mini-bus Tours out of the local tourist office, opposite the railroad station.

ESSENTIALS

Visitor and Tour Information Berchtesgaden Land Tourismus ✉ *Bahnhofpl. 4* ☎ *08652/656–5050* ⊕ *www.berchtesgadener-land.com.* **Eagle's Nest Historical Tours** ✉ *Königseer Str. 2* ☎ *08652/64971* ⊕ *www.eagles-nest-tours.com.* **Schwaiger** ☎ *08652/2525* ⊕ *www.bus-schwaiger.de/en.*

EXPLORING

The Heimatmuseum. This museum located in the Schloss Adelsheim displays examples of wood carving and other local crafts. Wood carving in Berchtesgaden dates to long before Oberammergau established itself as the premier wood-carving center of the Alps. ✉ *Schroffenbergallee 6* ☎ *08652/4410* ⊕ *www.heimatmuseum-berchtesgaden.de* 💶 *€2.50* ⊙ *Dec.–Oct., Tues.–Sun. 10–5.*

Königliches Schloss Berchtesgaden Museum. The last royal resident of the Berchtesgaden abbey, Crown Prince Rupprecht (who died here in 1955), furnished it with rare family treasures that now form the basis of this permanent collection. Fine Renaissance rooms exhibit the prince's sacred art, which is particularly rich in wood sculptures by such great late-Gothic artists as Tilman Riemenschneider and Veit Stoss. You can also visit the abbey's original, cavernous 13th-century dormitory and cool cloisters. ✉ *Schlosspl. 2* ☎ *08652/947–980* ⊕ *www.haus-bayern. com* 🖅 *€9.50 with tour* ⊙ *Mid-May–mid-Oct., Sun.–Fri. 10–noon and 2–4; mid-Oct.–mid-May, Sun.–Fri. 11–2.*

The Obersalzberg. The site of Hitler's luxurious mountain retreat is part of the north slope of the Hoher Goll, high above Berchtesgaden. It was a remote mountain community of farmers and foresters before Hitler's deputy, Martin Bormann, selected the site for a complex of Alpine homes for top Nazi leaders. Hitler's chalet, the Berghof, and all the others were destroyed in 1945, with the exception of a hotel that had been taken over by the Nazis, the Hotel zum Türken. The round trip from Berchtesgaden's post office by bus and elevator costs €16.10 per person. The bus runs mid-May through September, daily from 9 to 4:50. By car you can travel only as far as the Obersalzberg bus station. The full round trip takes one hour. ■ TIP→ To get the most out of your visit to the Kehlsteinhaus, consider taking one of the informative tours offered by David Harper. Reserve in advance online or by phone at ☎ *08652/64971.* Tours meet across from the train station and cost €50. ✉ *Königseer Str. 2* ⊕ *www.eagles-nest-tours.com.*

Bunkers. Beneath the hotel is a section of the labyrinth of tunnels built as a last retreat for Hitler and his cronies; the macabre, murky bunkers can be visited. ✉ *Hintereck 2* ☎ *08652/2428* ⊕ *www.hotel-zum-tuerken.de/hotel.html* 🖅 *€3* ⊙ *Apr.–Oct., daily 10–5; Nov.–Mar., by appointment.*

Dokumentation Obersalzberg. Nearby, the Dokumentation Obersalzberg documents the notorious history of the Third Reich, and a special focus on Obersalzberg, with some surprisingly rare archive material. ✉ *Salzbergstr. 41* ☎ *08652/947–960* ⊕ *www.obersalzberg.de* 🖅 *€3* ⊙ *Apr.–Oct., daily 9–5; Nov.–Mar., Tues.–Sun. 10–3.*

Kehlsteinhaus. Beyond Obersalzberg, the hairpin bends of Germany's highest road come to the base of the 6,000-foot peak on which sits the Kehlsteinhaus, also known as the Adlerhorst (Eagle's Nest), Hitler's personal retreat and his official guesthouse. It was Martin Bormann's gift to the führer on Hitler's 50th birthday. The road leading to it, built in 1937–39, climbs more than 2,000 dizzying feet in less than 6 km (4 miles). A tunnel in the mountain will bring you to an elevator that whisks you up to what appears to be the top of the world (you can walk up in about half an hour). There are refreshment rooms and a restaurant. ✉ *Kehlstein Busabfahrt, Hintereck* ☎ *08652/2969* ⊕ *www.kehlsteinhaus.de.*

The Salzbergwerk. This salt mine is one of the chief attractions of the region. In the days when the mine was owned by Berchtesgaden's princely rulers, only select guests were allowed to see how the source of the city's wealth was extracted from the earth. Today, during a 90-minute tour, you can sit astride a miniature train that transports you nearly 1 km (½ mile) into the mountain to an enormous chamber where the salt is mined. Included in the tour are rides down the wooden chutes used by miners to get from one level to another and

Rupertus Therme, in Bad Reichenhall offers spa treatments such as the full-body salt scrub.

a boat ride on an underground saline lake the size of a football field. Although the tours take about an hour, plan an extra 45–60 minutes for purchasing the tickets and changing into and out of miners clothing. You may wish to partake in the special four-hour **brine dinners** down in the mines (€90). These are very popular, so be sure to book early. ⊠ *2 km (1 mile) from center of Berchtesgaden on B–305 Salzburg Rd., Bergwerkstr. 83* ☏ *08652/600220* ⊕ *www.salzzeitreise.de* ⊠ *€15.50, combined ticket with Bad Reichenhall's saline museum €18.50* ⊙ *May–Oct., daily 9–5; Nov.–Apr., Mon.–Sat. 11–3.*

Watzmann Therme. Here you'll find fragrant steam rooms, saunas with infrared cabins for sore muscles, an elegant pool, whirlpools, and more. If you happen to be staying a few days, you might catch a tai chi course, enjoy a bio-release facial massage, or partake in an evening of relaxing underwater exercises. ⊠ *Bergwerkstr. 54* ☏ *08652/94640* ⊕ *www.watzmann-therme.de* ⊠ *2 hrs €10.50, 4 hrs €13.90, day pass including sauna €15.50* ⊙ *Sun.–Wed. 10–10; Fri. and Sat. 10 am–midnight.*

WHERE TO STAY

$ **Alpenhotel Denninglehen.** The house was built in 1981 in Alpine style,
HOTEL with lots of wood paneling, heavy beams, and wide balconies with cascades of geraniums in summer. **Pros:** heated pool with views of the Alps; great hotel for kids. **Cons:** narrow and steep access road difficult to find. ⑤ *Rooms from: €74* ⊠ *Am Priesterstein 7, Berchtesgaden-Oberau* ☏ *08652/97890* ⊕ *www.denninglehen.de* ⤴ *23 rooms* ⊙ *Restaurant closed Tues. evening* ⑂ *Breakfast.*

$ ⌂ **Hotel Grünberger.** Only a few strides from the train station in the
HOTEL town center, the Grünberger overlooks the River Ache—it even has
a private terrace beside the river you can relax on. **Pros:** quaintly
situated on the river; close to the train station. **Cons:** quite far from
skiing and outdoor activities. $ *Rooms from: €90* ⊠ *Hansererweg
1* ☎ *08652/976–590* ⊕ *www.hotel-gruenberger.de* ⤶ *65 rooms*
⊙ *Closed Nov.–mid-Dec.* ❡ *Breakfast.*

$ ⌂ **Hotel Wittelsbach.** This is one of the oldest (built in 1892) and most
HOTEL traditional lodgings in the area, so it is wise to reserve well ahead
of time. **Pros:** nice, comfortable rooms; exceptional staff; daily pam-
phlets show local events and weather. **Cons:** horrible parking; streetside rooms can get noisy. $ *Rooms from: €94* ⊠ *Maximilianstr. 16*
☎ *08652/96380* ⊕ *www.hotel-wittelsbach.com* ⤶ *26 rooms, 3 apartments* ❡ *Breakfast.*

$ ⌂ **Hotel zum Türken.** The view alone is worth the 10-minute journey
HOTEL from Berchtesgaden to this hotel. **Pros:** great location; sense of history; Frau Schafenberg can cook! **Cons:** not all rooms have attached
bathrooms. $ *Rooms from: €90* ⊠ *Hintereck 2, Obersalzberg-
Berchtesgaden* ☎ *08652/2428* ⊕ *www.hotel-zum-tuerken.de* ⤶ *17
rooms, 12 with bath or shower* ⊙ *Closed Nov.–Dec. 20* ❡ *Breakfast.*

$ ⌂ **Stoll's Hotel Alpina.** Set above the Königsee in the delightful little
HOTEL village of Schönau, the Alpina offers rural solitude and easy access
to Berchtesgaden. **Pros:** bedrooms are large and comfortable; good
for families with children; great view of the Adlershorst. **Cons:** service can be brusque. $ *Rooms from: €90* ⊠ *Ulmenweg 14, Schönau*
☎ *08652/65090* ⊕ *www.stolls-hotel-alpina.de* ⤶ *52 rooms, 8 apartments* ⊙ *Closed early Nov.–mid-Dec.* ❡ *Breakfast.*

SPORTS AND THE OUTDOORS

Buried as it is in the Alps, Berchtesgaden is a place for the active. The
Rossfeld ski area is one of the favorites, thanks to almost guaranteed
natural snow. The piste down to Oberau is nearly 6 km (4 miles) long
(with bus service at the end to take you back to Berchtesgaden). There
is a separate snowboarding piste as well. Berchtesgaden also has many
cross-country trails and telemark opportunities. The other popular area
is on the slopes of the Götschenkopf, which is used for World Cup races.
Snow is usually artificial, but the floodlit slopes at night and a lively
après-ski scene make up for the lesser quality.

In summer, hikers, power-walkers, and paragliders take over the region.
The Obersalzberg even has a summer luge track. Avid hikers should ask
for a map featuring the refuges (Berghütten) in the mountains, where
one can spend the night either in a separate room or a bunk. Simple,
solid meals are offered. In some of the smaller refuges you will have
to bring your own food. For more information, check out ⊕ *www.
berchtesgaden.de.* And though the Königsee is beautiful to look at, only
cold-water swimmers will appreciate its frigid waters.

Consider walking along the pleasant mountain path from the Eagle's
Nest back to Berchtesgaden.

The gemlike Königsee Lake is the most photographed panorama in Germany.

Berchtesgaden Golf Club. Germany's highest course, the Berchtesgaden Golf Club, is on a 3,300-foot plateau of the Obersalzberg. Only fit players should attempt the demanding 9-hole course. Ten Berchtesgaden hotels offer their guests a 30% reduction on the €40 (€50 for weekends) green fee—contact the tourist office or the club for details. ✉ *Salzbergstr. 33* ☎ *08652/2100* ⊕ *www.golfclub-berchtesgaden.de.*

Erste Bergschule Berchtesgadenerland. Whatever your mountain-related needs, whether it's climbing and hiking in summer or cross-country tours in winter, you'll find it at the Erste Bergschule Berchtesgadenerland. ✉ *Silbergstr. 25, Bischofswiesen* ☎ *08652/5371* ⊕ *www. berchtesgaden-bergschule.de.*

SHOPPING

Berchtesgadener Handwerkskunst. This shop offers handicrafts—such as wooden boxes, woven tablecloths, wood carvings, and Christmas-tree decorations—from Berchtesgaden, the surrounding region, and other parts of Bavaria. ✉ *Schlosspl. 1½* ☎ *08652/979–790* ⊕ *www. berchtesgadener-handwerkskunst.de.*

BERCHTESGADEN NATIONAL PARK

5 km (3 miles) south of Berchtesgaden.

The park covers 210 square km (81 square miles), around two-thirds of the park's border is shared with Austria, and is characterized by mountain vistas and the beautiful Königsee. In 2012 alone, the region had 3.4 million overnight stays, which is a true testament to the area's popularity.

GETTING HERE AND AROUND

Berchtesgaden National Park is around 150 kilometers (93 miles) southeast of Munich by car. Many people find the train connection, with a change at Freilassing, and a 30-minute bus journey (total time is around two hours 50 minutes), a more rewarding, if adventurous journey.

EXPLORING

Berchtesgaden National Park. The deep, mysterious, and fabled Königsee is the most photographed panorama in Germany. Together with its much smaller sister, the Obersee, it's nestled within the Berchtesgaden National Park, 210 square km (82 square miles) of wild mountain country where flora and fauna have been left to develop as nature intended. No roads penetrate the area, and even the mountain paths are difficult to follow. The park administration organizes guided tours of the area from June through September. ⊠ *Nationalparkhaus, Franziskanerpl. 7* ☎ *08652/64343* ⊕ *www.nationalpark-berchtesgaden.de.*

Königsee. One less strenuous way into the Berchtesgaden National Park is by boat. A fleet of 21 excursion boats, electrically driven so that no noise disturbs the peace, operates on the Königsee (King Lake). Only the skipper of the boat is allowed to shatter the silence—his trumpet fanfare demonstrates a remarkable echo as notes reverberate between the almost vertical cliffs that plunge into the dark green water. A cross on a rocky promontory marks the spot where a boatload of pilgrims hit the cliffs and sank more than 100 years ago. The voyagers were on their way to the tiny, twin-tower baroque chapel of St. Bartholomä, built in the 17th century on a peninsula where an early-Gothic church once stood. The princely rulers of Berchtesgaden built a hunting lodge at the side of the chapel; a tavern and restaurant now occupy its rooms.

Smaller than the Königsee but equally beautiful, the **Obersee** can be reached by a 15-minute walk from the second stop (Salet) on the boat tour. The lake's backdrop of jagged mountains and precipitous cliffs is broken by a waterfall, the Rothbachfall, which plunges more than 1,000 feet to the valley floor.

Boat service. Boat service on the Königsee runs year-round, except when the lake freezes. A round-trip to St. Bartholomä and Salet, the landing stage for the Obersee, lasts almost two hours, without stops, and costs €16.30. A round trip to St. Bartholomä lasts a little over an hour and costs €13.30. In summer the Berchtesgaden tourist office organizes evening cruises on the Königsee, which include a concert in St. Bartholomä Church and a four-course dinner in the neighboring hunting lodge. ⊠ *Seestr. 29, Schönau* ☎ *08652/96360* ⊕ *www. bayerische-seenschifffahrt.de.*

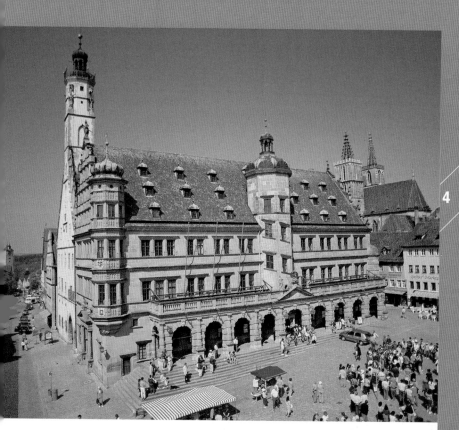

THE ROMANTIC ROAD

WELCOME TO THE ROMANTIC ROAD

TOP REASONS TO GO

★ **Neuschwanstein:** Emerald lakes, the pastoral countryside, and the rugged peaks of the Alps surround what's become the most famous storybook castle in the world.

★ **Rothenburg-ob-der-Tauber:** The Middle Ages never looked so good as in this quaint walled village. If you stay overnight, you can patrol the city walls with the night watchman after the tour buses have left town.

★ **Wieskirche:** Join the local Bavarians who flock to this pilgrimage church, a rococo gem in pristine Alpine fields.

★ **Ulm's Münster:** Work off all that hearty Swabian cuisine with a climb up the 768 steps of this church's tower, the highest of its kind in the world.

★ **Würzburg's Residenz:** Explore the gilt and crystal splendor of this lavish palace, once the home of prince-bishops.

1 Toward the Alps.
In this region, vineyards
are replaced by Alpine
meadows, and beer beats
out wine in the small inns
of towns like Landsberg and
Schongau. The marvelous
Wieskirche (Church of the
Meadow) is here, just a
bit off the Romantic Road,
and mountains give way
to the baroque and the
genuinely medieval as the
Neuschwanstein and Hohen-
schwangau castles come
into view.

2 Central Romantic
Road. After crossing the
Danube from the south, the
route takes you through the
affluent city of Augsburg
and its countryside, before
continuing on through
the lovely Tauber valley.
Vineyards slope down to
the hills to the small valleys as make your way
to charming old towns
such as Dinkelsbühl and
Rothenburg-ob-der-Tauber.

3 Northern Roman-
tic Road. Wine lovers
should plan an extra day
for the Frankish capital of
Würzburg, where they can
sample delicious local wines
at reasonable prices. Bad
Mergentheim is also well
worth a look.

GETTING ORIENTED

To a large degree, the
Romantic Road is Germany
in a nutshell. The route runs
from Füssen, on the moun-
tainous Austrian border,
and near Neuschwanstein,
"Mad" King Ludwig II's
fantastical castle, through
the handsome Renaissance
city of Augsburg. From
there it continues on to
the northwest, to the
best-preserved medieval
town on the continent,
Rothenburg-ob-der-Tauber,
finishing up in Würzburg,
in central Germany and
an hour from Frankfurt.

4

Updated by Catherine Moser Horlacher

Of all the tourist routes that crisscross Germany, none rivals the Romantische Strasse, or Romantic Road. The scenery is more pastoral than spectacular, but the route is memorable for the medieval towns, villages, castles, and churches that anchor its 355-km (220-miles) length. Many of these are tucked away beyond low hills, their spires and towers just visible through the greenery.

The Romantic Road concept developed as this corner of West Germany, occupied by the American forces, sought to rebuild its tourist industry after World War II. A public-relations wizard coined the catchy title for a historic passage through Bavaria and Baden-Württemberg that could be advertised as a unit. In 1950 the Romantic Road was born. The name itself isn't meant to attract lovebirds, but rather uses the word *romantic* as meaning wonderful, fabulous, and imaginative. And, of course, the Romantic Road started as a road on which the Romans traveled 2,000 years ago.

Along the way, the road crosses centuries-old battlefields. The most cataclysmic conflict, the Thirty Years' War, destroyed the region's economic base in the 17th century. The depletion of resources prevented improvements that would have modernized the area—thereby assuring that these towns would become the quaint tourist destinations they are today.

PLANNING

WHEN TO GO

Late summer and early autumn are the best times to travel the Romantic Road, when the grapes ripen on the vines around Würzburg and the geraniums run riot on the medieval walls of towns such as Rothenburg and Dinkelsbühl. You'll also miss the high-season summer crush of tourists. Otherwise, consider visiting the region in the depths of December, when Christmas markets pack the ancient squares of the Romantic Road towns and snow gives the turreted Schloss Neuschwanstein a final magic touch.

PLANNING YOUR TIME

The two bigger cities on the Romantic Road, Augsburg and Würzburg, can handle large influxes of visitors at any time. But when it comes the two most popular places, Rothenburg-ob-der-Tauber and Neuschwanstein, it pays to stay overnight. You can follow the night watchman in Rothenburg as he makes his rounds, and then tour the town in the early morning. Have a late but leisurely breakfast as you watch the bus-tour groups push through the streets around 11. The crowds at Neuschwanstein mean it's even more important to get an early start. Reserve your tickets ahead of time, too.

GETTING HERE AND AROUND

AIR TRAVEL

The major international airports serving the Romantic Road are Frankfurt and Munich. Regional airports include Nürnberg and Augsburg.

Airport Contacts Nürnberg Airport ⊠ *Flughafenstr.* ☎ *0911/93700* ⊕ *www.airport-nuernberg.de.*

BUS TRAVEL

Daily bus service covers the northern stretch of the Romantic Road, between Frankfurt and Munich, from April through October. A second bus covers the section of the route between Dinkelsbühl and Füssen. All buses stop at the major sights along the road. Deutsche Touring also operates six more-extensive tours along the Romantic Road; make a reservation ahead of time for these.

Bus Contact Deutsche Touring ⊠ *Am Römerhof 17, Frankfurt am Main* ☎ *069/790–3501* ⊕ *www.touring.de.*

CAR TRAVEL

The Romantic Road is most easily traveled by car. If you're coming up from the south and using Munich as a gateway, Augsburg is 70 km (43 miles) from Munich via A-8. The roads are busy, and most have only two lanes, so figure on covering no more than 70 km (43 miles) each hour, particularly in summer. From there, you will continue north and end in Würzburg, the northernmost city on the route, which is 124 km (77 miles) from Frankfurt. If you're traveling from the north, begin in Würzburg and follow country highway B-27 south to meet roads B-290, B-19, B-292, and B-25 along the Wörnitz River. It's on the Frankfurt–Nürnberg autobahn, A-3, and is 115 km (71 miles) from Frankfurt. For route maps, with roads and sights highlighted, contact the Romantische Strasse Touristik-Arbeitsgemeinschaft (Romantic Road Central Tourist-Information) based in Dinkelsbühl.

TRAIN TRAVEL

Infrequent trains link most major towns of the Romantic Road, but both Würzburg and Augsburg are on the InterCity and high-speed InterCity Express routes, and have fast, frequent service to and from Munich, Stuttgart, and Frankfurt.

BIKE TOURS

From April through September, Velotours offers a five-day bike trip from Würzburg to Rothenburg for €365 per person, and a five-day trip from Rothenburg to Donauwörth for €365 per person. These two trips can be combined for an eight-day tour for €583. The tour operator Alpenland-Touristik offers several guided six- to eight-day bike tours that start from Landsberg am Lech into the Alpine foothills.

Bike Tour Contacts Alpenlandtouristik ☎ *08191/308–620*
⊕ *www.alpenlandtouristik.de.* **Velotours** ✉ *Bücklestr. 13, Konstanz*
☎ *07531/98280* ⊕ *www.velotours.de.*

RESTAURANTS

During peak season, restaurants along the Romantic Road tend to be crowded, especially in the larger towns. ■ TIP→ You may want to plan your mealtimes around visits to smaller villages, where there are fewer people and the restaurants are often more low-key. The food will be more basic Franconian or Swabian, but it will also be generally less expensive than in the well-known towns, and it might also be locally sourced. You may find that some of the small, family-run restaurants close around 2 pm, or whenever the last lunch guests have left, and then open again at 5 or 5:30 pm. Some serve cold cuts or coffee and cake during that time, but no hot food.

Prices in the reviews are the average cost of a main course at dinner, or if dinner is not served, at lunch.

HOTELS

With a few exceptions, Romantic Road hotels are quiet and rustic, and you'll find high standards of comfort and cleanliness. If you plan to stay in one of the bigger hotels in the off-season, ask about discounted weekend rates. Make reservations as far in advance as possible if you plan to visit in summer. Hotels in Würzburg, Rothenburg, and Füssen are often full year-round. Augsburg hotels are in great demand during trade fairs in nearby Munich. Tourist-information offices can usually help with accommodations, especially if you arrive early in the day.

Prices in the reviews are the lowest cost of a standard double room in high season. For expanded reviews, facilities, and current deals, visit Fodors.com.

VISITOR INFORMATION

Contacts Romantische Strasse Touristik-Arbeitsgemeinschaft (*Romantic Road Central Tourist-Information*). ✉ *Segringerstr. 19, Dinkelsbühl* ☎ *09851/551–387* ⊕ *www.romantischestrasse.de.*

TOWARD THE ALPS

An hour west of Munich, the Romantic Road climbs gradually into the foothills of the Bavarian Alps, which burst into view between Landsberg and Schongau. The route's most southern tip can be found at the northern wall of the Alps at Füssen, on the Austrian border. Landsberg was founded by the Bavarian ruler Heinrich der Löwe (Henry the Lion) in the 12th century, and the town grew wealthy from the salt trade. Solid old houses are packed within its turreted walls; the early-18th-century Rathaus is one of the finest in the region.

Schongau has virtually intact wall fortifications, complete with towers and gates. In medieval and Renaissance times the town was an important trading post on the route from Italy to Augsburg. The steeply gabled 16th-century Ballenhaus was a warehouse before it was elevated to the rank of Rathaus. A popular Märchenwald ("fairy-tale forest") lies 1½ km (1 mile) outside Schongau, suitably set in a clearing in the woods. It comes complete with mechanical models of fairy-tale scenes, deer enclosures, and an old-time miniature railway.

HOHENSCHWANGAU AND NEUSCHWANSTEIN

103 km (64 miles) south of Augsburg, 121 km (75 miles) southwest of Munich.

These two famous castles belonging to the Wittelbachs are 1 km (½ mile) across a valley from each other, near the town of Schwangau. Bavaria's King Ludwig II (1845–86) spent much of his youth at Schloss Hohenschwangau (Hohenschwangau Castle). It's said that its neo-Gothic atmosphere provided the primary influences that shaped his wildly romantic Schloss Neuschwanstein (Neuschwanstein Castle), the fairy-tale castle he built after he became king. It has long been one of Germany's most recognized sights.

GETTING HERE AND AROUND

From Schwangau (5 km [3 miles] north of Füssen, 103 km [64 miles] south of Augsburg, 121 km [75 miles] southwest of Munich), follow the road signs marked "Königschlösser" (King's Castles). After 3 km (2 miles) you come to Hohenschwangau, a small village consisting of a few houses, some good hotels, and five big parking lots (parking €5). You have to park in one of them and then walk to the ticket center serving both castles. If you are staying in Füssen, take the bus to Hohenschwangau. The clearly marked bus leaves from the train station in Füssen every hour from morning to night, and the cost is €1.60 per person one-way. Tickets are for timed entry, and the average wait to enter Neuschwanstein is one hour. With a deposit or credit-card number you can book your tickets up to two days in advance for either castle through the ticket center. You can change entrance times or cancel up to two hours before the confirmed entrance time. The main street of the small village Hohenschwangau is lined with many restaurants

TIMING

The best time to see either castle without waiting a long time is a weekday between January and April. The prettiest time, however, is in fall. ■TIP➜ Bear in mind that more than 1 million people pass through one or both castles every year. If you visit in summer, get there early and reserve ahead if possible.

ESSENTIALS

Ticket Center ✉ *Alpseestr. 12, Hohenschwangau* ☏ *08362/930–830* ⊕ *www.hohenschwangau.de.*

EXPLORING

Museum of the Bavarian Kings. Once the Alpenrose hotel, this grand building opened in 2012 as a museum chronicling the history of the Wittelsbach kings and queens, from the 11th century to the present day. Focusing primarily on King Maximilian II and his son Ludwig, it tells the story behind their neighboring castles. The influence of the Wittelsbach family in the region, from the development of Munich, their founding of the first Oktoberfest, and the family's role as resistors of the Nazi regime and their eventual imprisonment during World War II, are detailed. The interactive exhibits couple state-of-the-art technology with the gold and gilt belongings of the royal family. ■TIP➜ The café overlooking the lake is the good spot to relax and take in the views after a day of castles. ✉ *Alpseestr. 27, Hohenschwangau* ☏ *08362/926–4640* ⊕ *www.museumderbayerischenkoenige.de* 🎫 *€9.50, combinaiton ticket with both castles and museum €29.50* ⏱ *Apr.–Sept., daily 9–7; Oct.– Mar., daily 10–6.*

Schloss Hohenschwangau. Built by the knights of Schwangau in the 12th century, this castle was remodeled later by King Ludwig II's father, the Bavarian crown prince and future king Maximilian, between 1832 and 1836. Unlike Ludwig's more famous castle across the valley, Neuschwanstein, the mustard-yellow Schloss Hohenschwangau actually feels like a noble home, where comforts would be valued as much as outward splendor. Ludwig spent his childhood summers surrounded by the castle's murals, depicting ancient Germanic legends. It was here that the young prince met the composer Richard Wagner. Their friendship shaped and deepened the future king's interest in theater, music, and German mythology—the mythology Wagner drew upon for his *Ring* cycle of operas.

After obtaining your ticket at the ticket center in the village, you can take a 25-minute walk up either of two clearly marked paths to the castle, or board one of the horse-drawn carriages that leave from the ticket center (uphill €4, downhill €2) or the Hotel Müller (uphill €6, downhill €3). ✉ *Alpseestr. 12, Hohenschwangau* ☎ *08362/930–830* ⊕ *www.hohenschwangau.de* ▨ *€12, including guided tour; combined ticket for Hohenschwangau and Neuschwanstein €23* ⊘ *Late Mar.– mid-Oct., daily 8–5:30; mid-Oct.–mid-Mar., daily 9–3:30.*

Fodor's Choice   **Schloss Neuschwanstein.**
★   ⇨ *See "The Fairy-Tale Palaces of King Ludwig II" in this chapter.*

WHERE TO EAT AND STAY

$$$ ✗ **Alpenrose am See.** There is no spot more idyllic in Hohenschwangau to
EUROPEAN   enjoy excellent food and stunning views over the Alpsee and mountains beyond. The café, which is next to the Museum of Bavarian Kings, is a good way spot to escape the crowded streets in the center of town. Enjoy lunch or afternoon coffee and cake on the terrace. The continental European dishes include several game and pork dishes, as well as several vegetarian dishes. The romantic five-course "Rosendinner" is served in a private room off the terrace that's filled with roses. $ *Average main: €22* ✉ *Alpseestr. 27, Hohenschwangau* ☎ *08362/926–4660* ⊕ *www.alpenrose-am-see.de.*

$$ ☷ **Hotel Müller.** With a convenient location between the two Schwangau
HOTEL   castles, the Müller fits beautifully into the stunning landscape, its creamy Bavarian baroque facade a contrast to the mountain forest. **Pros:** view of the castles; personalized service; variety of rooms. **Cons:** crowds during the day; expensive in season. $ *Rooms from: €150* ✉ *Alpseestr. 16, Hohenschwangau* ☎ *08362/81990* ⊕ *www.hotel-mueller.de* ↪ *39 rooms, 4 suites* ⊘ *Closed Nov. and early Jan.–late Mar.* ⦿*Breakfast.*

FÜSSEN

5 km (3 miles) southwest of Schwangau, 129 km (80 miles) south of Munich.

The red roofs and turrets of this small town fit in well with the famous castles nearby. The town is easily toured on foot; its tidy, meandering streets and small squares are filled with cafés, restaurants, and shops. Füssen is at the foot of the mountains that separate Bavaria from the Austrian Tyrol; the Lech River, which accompanies much of this section of the Romantic Road, embraces the town as it rushes northward.

ESSENTIALS

Visitor Information **Füssen Tourismus und Marketing** ✉ *Kaiser-Maximilian-Pl. 1* ☎ *08362/93850* ⊕ *www.tourismus-fuessen.de.*

Continued on page 186

FAIRY-TALE CASTLES OF KING LUDWIG II

By Catherine Moser

King Ludwig II's image permeates Bavarian culture—the picture of the raven-haired king with soulful eyes adorns everything from beer steins to the local autobahn. The fairy-tale palaces he built have drawn millions of visitors, but who was Ludwig II? Adopting the words of his favorite poet, Friedrich Schiller, he wrote: "I wish to remain an eternal enigma to myself and to others." A tour of his castles reveals a glimpse of the man behind the story of the "Dreamer King."

Born on August 25, 1845, in Nymphenburg Palace, Ludwig II became king at 18 after his father's, King Maximilian II's, sudden death in 1864. He would become the most famous king in the 900-year Wittelsbach dynasty, known not for his rule—he had little power, as Bavaria was governed by a constitutional monarchy—but for his eccentricities.

Ludwig attended Richard Wagner's *Lohengrin* at age 15. Identifying with the Swan Knight, he yearned for the heroic medieval world Wagner portrayed. As king, Ludwig became Wagner's greatest patron and funded the creation of his opera festival in Bayreuth. Wagner was so influential, and Ludwig's love for him so unabashed, that concerned Munich officials sent the composer away in 1865.

Seeking solace in the isolated, idealized world of his own creation, Ludwig embarked on three palace-building projects beginning in 1868. By 1885, he had amassed a personal debt of 14 million marks, putting a massive strain on the Wittelsbach fortune. A commission of doctors, enthralled with the emerging studies of psychology, was assembled to analyze the behavior of the recluse king. Led by Dr. von Gudden, the commission diagnosed the king with paranoia and declared him insane without ever examining Ludwig himself. Ludwig was arrested in the early-morning hours of June 12, 1886, and taken from Schloss Neuschwanstein to Castle Berg on the shores of Lake Starnberg. Just before midnight the following day, the bodies of Ludwig and Dr. von Gudden were found floating in the lake. Theories abound to this day about their deaths, but the truth of Ludwig's demise is unknown.

Opposite, Schloss Neuschwanstein. Above left, King Ludwig II. Above right, Golden angel fountain, Schloss Linderhof.

SCHLOSS LINDERHOF

Set in sylvan seclusion in Graswang Valley, high in the Alps, lies the royal palace of Linderhof. Built on the site of his father's hunting lodge, this was the first of Ludwig's building projects and the only one completed during his lifetime. Begun in 1868, the small villa based on the Petit Trianon of Versailles took six years to complete.

ENTRANCE HALL

Two lifesize Sèvres **peacocks** were placed outside the entry doors to signify when Ludwig was in residence. Upon entering the castle, there is a large bronze **statue of King Louis XIV**, Ludwig's idol. On the ceiling above the statue is a gold sun, symbolizing the "Sun King" of France, inscribed with his motto: *Nec Pluribus Impar* ("I stand above others").

Above, Schloss Linderhof. Opposite (top) Venus grotto, (bottom) Hall of Mirrors.

THRONE ROOM AND BEDCHAMBER

With paintings of Louis XIV and XV watching over him, Ludwig spent hours meticulously overseeing the architectural plans of his other projects from the green and gold **throne room**. The **bedchamber**, with its three-dimensional golden tapestries set against his favorite color, royal blue, look out to a waterfall cascading down the hill to the **Neptune fountain**, with its 100-foot water jet.

DINING ROOM

Ludwig would eat alone in the adjoining **dining room**. His extreme sweet tooth had wreaked havoc on his mouth so that by the time he was 30, most of his teeth were missing and dining was a messy affair. For his privacy, the dining table could be lowered down through the floor by cables and pulleys to the kitchen below. It would then reappear with Ludwig's meal so that he never had to dine with servants in the room.

HALL OF MIRRORS

The reclusive king spent his time reading and literally reflecting in the **hall of mirrors,** with its optical illusion infinitely reflecting his image and vast collection of vases lining the walls.

LINDERHOF'S GROUNDS

In the **Venus grotto,** Ludwig spent many evenings being paddled around in a scallop-shaped boat imagining he was in the world of Wagner's *Tannhäuser.* Ludwig would gather his equerries for decadent evenings spent in the **Moorish kiosk,** which was purchased wholesale from the 1867 Paris Universal Exposition, imagining himself as an Arabian knight lounging on his magnificent **peacock throne.** Deeper into the park is the **Hunding's hut,** a medieval-style lodge based on the set designs for the opening act of Wagner's *Die Walküre.* Ludwig took moonlit rides in winter to the original Hut, set deeply in the Alpine forest, in his gilt **gala sleigh.**

GETTING HERE AND AROUND

✉ Linderhof 12, Ettal-Linderhof

☎ 08822/92030 or -21

⊕ www.schlosslinderhof.de

💶 €8.50, €7.50 winter

🕐 Open April–Oct. 15, daily 9–6; Oct. 16–March, daily 10–4; park buildings (grotto, Moorish kiosk, etc.) closed in winter

Car Travel: Take the A–95 motorway and the B–2 to Oberau. Follow the signs in Oberau to the B–23 (Ettaler Strasse). Outside Ettal turn left onto ST–2060. In Linderhof turn right to reach the palace.

Train Travel: Take the regional Deutsche Bahn train from Munich Hauptbahnhof to Oberammergau. Buy the Bayern Ticket, which allows for a full day of travel, including bus fare, for €25 for up to five people. From there, take bus 9622 to Linderhof.

Bus Tours: There are several tours combining both Linderhof and Neuschwanstein castles, but none that go just to Linderhof. **Gray Line Tours** (☎ *8954/907–560* ⊕ *www.grayline.com*) offers a day trip, including Linderhof, Neuschwanstein, and a short stop to shop in Oberammergau. It leaves daily at 8:30 am from the Karstadt Department store in front of the Munich Hauptbahnhof. Tickets are €72 for adults and €35 for children, not including admission.

SCHLOSS NEUSCHWANSTEIN

Neuschwanstein, the most famous of the three castles, was King Ludwig's crowning achievement. The castle soars from its mountainside like a stage creation—it should hardly come as a surprise that Walt Disney took it as the model for his castle in the movie *Sleeping Beauty* and later for the Disneyland castle itself.

Prince Ludwig spent idyllic childhood summers at **Hohenschwangau**, the neighboring medieval-style palace. The young prince was undoubtedly influenced by the vast murals of the legends of *Lohengrin* and romantic vision of these ancient times. Perhaps he envisioning his own, mightier palace when looking north to the mountains and the old ruins of a fortress of the Knights

of Schwangau. Upon commencing construction in 1868, Ludwig wrote to Wagner, "The Gods will come to live with us on the lofty heights, breathing the air of heaven."

THRONE ROOM
Wagner's *Tannhäuser* inspired the Byzantine-style **throne room**, drawn from plans for the original stage set for the opera; however, the actual throne was never constructed. The massive chandelier is styled after a Byzantine crown and surrounded by images of angels, apostles, and six kings of history who were canonized as saints. Look closely at the image of St. George, the patron saint of the Wittelsbachs, slaying a dragon in front of another medieval castle. That castle, Falkenstein, was set to be the next, even grander castle of Ludwig II. The elaborate mosaic floor contains two million stones.

Above, Schloss Neuschwanstein. Opposite (top) Singers' Hall, (bottom) Ludwig II's bedchamber.

BEDCHAMBER

The king spent his last days as ruler huddled in his late-Gothic-style **bedchamber** modeled after the nuptial chamber of *Lohengrin*. It took fourteen craftsman more than four years to carve this room alone. The symbol of the swan occurs throughout Neuschwanstein, appearing here in the fixtures of the sink.

GROTTO

Reminiscent of the larger one at Linderhof, but stranger for its placement inside the palace, the **grotto** overlooking the Schwangau Valley once had a running waterfall lit by tinted lights.

SINGERS' HALL

Ludwig's favorite room, the **Singers' Hall**, was modeled after the stage design for the Forest of the Holy Grail from *Parsifal* and designed for the best acoustics. On moonless nights, the king would hike out to the Marienbrücke, over the rocky gorge, to watch the candlelit splendor of this hall. Ludwig never saw a performance here, but concerts are now held every September.

GETTING HERE AND AROUND

✉ Alpseestrasse 12, Hohenschwangau

☎ 8362/930–830

⊕ www.neuschwanstein.de

🎫 €12 tickets are for a set tour time, reserve ahead online. English tours every 15 minutes.

🕗 Open April–Sept. daily 8–5; Oct.–March daily 9–3

Car Travel: Take the A–7 (direction Ulm-Kempten-Füssen) to the end. From Füssen, take B–17 to Schwangau, then follow signs to Hohenschwangau.

Train Travel: Take the regional Deutsche Bahn train from Munich Hauptbahnhof to Füssen (buy the Bayern Ticket). From Füssen, take either bus 73 toward Steingaden/Garmisch-Partenkirchen or bus 78 toward Schwangau until the Hohenschwangau/Alpseestrasse stop.

Getting to the Castle: Allow 30–40 minutes for the uphill walk from the ticket center to the castle. In summer, you can take a bus (€1.80 uphill, €1 downhill) or horse-drawn carriage (€6 uphill, €3 downhill) up to the castle.

Bus Tours: Bus Bavaria (☎ 89255/43987 or -988 ⊕ mikesbiketours.com) leaves from central Munich daily from mid-April through mid-October. Tours cost €39–€49, not including admission.

SCHLOSS HERRENCHIEMSEE

The third and what would be the last of King Ludwig II's building projects, Herrenchiemsee, modeled after Louis XIV's Versailles, stands as a monument to the institution of the monarchy and the Bourbon kings he idolized. Ludwig never intended to use this palace as a place to live but rather a place to visit to transport himself to the days when the Sun King ruled the glorious court of Versailles. Ludwig stayed at this palace only once, for a brief ten-day visit in September 1885.

CONSTRUCTION OF HERRENCHIEMSEE

Ludwig purchased the Herreninsel, the biggest of the three islands on Lake Chiemsee in 1873. Work soon began on gardens to rival the ones at Versailles.

Above, Schloss Herrenchiemsee. Opposite (top) Hall of Mirrors, (bottom) fountain.

By the time the foundation stone of the palace was laid in 1878, the soaring fountains were already in use. Although 300 local craftsmen worked day and night to replicate the Sun King's palace, only 20 of the planned 70 rooms saw completion during the following eight years of construction. They abound with marble, gilt, and paintings of the Bourbon court, the French style replicated by skilled Bavarian artists.

PARADE BEDCHAMBER

The sumptuous red brocade bedspread and wall hangings in the **parade bedchamber**, which is twice the size of the original in Versailles, took 30 women seven years to embroider. Red silk curtains can be pulled over the bay windows to give the room a glow of regal red, the symbolic color of the Bourbon court. Ludwig never slept in this room; it was created in memory of Louis XIV. Instead, Ludwig slept in the **king's bed-**

chamber, softly lit by blue candlelight from the large blue orb over his bed.

HALL OF MIRRORS

In the **hall of mirrors**, longer than the original in Versailles, Ludwig held private concerts during his short stay here. A team of 35 servants took a half-hour to light the 2,000 candles of the chandeliers and candelabra lining the golden room.

LUDWIG II MUSEUM

Ludwig gave strict orders that no image of the Wittelsbach rulers or of himself should be found in his French palace. Today, however, this is the only one of his three palaces to have a museum devoted to the king. You can see his christening gown, uniforms, architectural plans for future building projects, and even sample his favorite cologne in the castle's **Ludwig II Museum.**

GETTING HERE AND AROUND

✉ Herrenchiemsee
📠 8051/68870
🌐 www.herrenchiemsee.de
💶 €8
🕐 Open April–Oct. 15, daily 9-6; Oct. 16–March, daily 9:40-4:15

Boat Travel: Herrenchiemsee lies on the island of Herreninsel in Lake Chiemsee. **Chiemsee Schifffahrt's** (✉ *Seestrasse 108, Prien am Chiemsee* 📠 *8051/6090* 🌐 *www.chiemsee-schifffahrt.de*) ferries leave regularly from Prien/Stock daily from 7 am–6:30 pm. Tickets cost €6.90.

Car Travel: Take the A-8 motorway (Salzburg-Munich), leaving at the Bernau exit to continue to Prien am Chiemsee. At the roundabout outside Prien follow the signs to Chiemsee or Königsschloss.

Train Travel: Take the regional Deutsche Bahn train to Prien am Chiemsee, about an hour's ride from Munich (buy the Bayern Ticket). From the station, take the quaint **Chiemsee Bahn**, which winds through the town to the boats. It runs from April–October. Train and boat combination tickets cost €9.

Bus Tours: Gray Line Tours (📠 *8954/907-560* 🌐 *www.grayline.com*) offers a day trip, including the boat trip out to the castle (but not admission) and a visit to the Fraueninsel on Chiemsee for €47.

EXPLORING

Hohes Schloss (*High Castle*). One of the best-preserved late-Gothic castles in Germany, Hohes Schloss was built on the site of the Roman fortress that once guarded this Alpine section of the Via Claudia, the trade route from Rome to the Danube. Evidence of Roman occupation of the area has been uncovered at the foot of the nearby Tegelberg Mountain, and the **excavations** next to the Tegelberg cable-car station are open for visits daily. The Hohes Schloss was the seat of Bavarian rulers before Emperor Heinrich VII mortgaged it and the rest of the town to the bishop of Augsburg for 400 pieces of silver. The mortgage was never redeemed, and Füssen remained the property of the Augsburg episcopate until secularization in the early 19th century. The bishops of Augsburg used the castle as their summer Alpine residence. It has a spectacular 16th-century **Rittersaal** (Knights' Hall) with a carved ceiling, and a princes' chamber with a Gothic tile stove. ✉ *Magnuspl. 10* ☎ *08362/903–146* 🖃 *€6* 🕘 *Apr.–Oct., Tues.–Sun. 11–5; Nov.–Mar., Fri.–Sun. 1–4.*

Rathaus *(Town Hall).* The summer presence of the bishops of Augsburg ensured that Füssen would gain an impressive number of baroque and rococo churches. Füssen's Rathaus was once a Benedictine abbey, built in the 9th century at the site of the grave of St. Magnus, who spent most of his life ministering in the area. A Romanesque crypt beneath the baroque abbey church has a partially preserved 10th-century fresco, the oldest in Bavaria. In summer, chamber concerts are held in the high-ceiling baroque splendor of the former abbey's **Fürstensaal** (Princes' Hall). Program details are available from the tourist office. ✉ *Lechalde 3* ⊕ *www.stadt-fuessen.de.*

Reichenstrasse. Füssen's main shopping street Reichenstrasse was once part of the Roman Via Claudia. This cobblestone walkway is lined with high-gabled medieval houses and backed by the bulwarks of the castle and the easternmost buttresses of the Allgäu Alps.

WHERE TO EAT AND STAY

$ — GERMAN   ✕ **Markthalle.** At this farmers' market you can grab a quick bite and drink at reasonable prices. Try the fish soup. The building started in 1483 as the *Kornhaus* (grain storage) and then became the *Feuerhaus* (fire station). It's open weekdays from 10 to 6 and on Saturday from 10 to 2. 🖃 *Average main: €8* ✉ *Schranneg. 12* ▬ *No credit cards* 🕘 *Closed Sun.*

$ — HOTEL   🛏 **Altstadthotel Zum Hechten.** Directly below the castle, this is one of the town's oldest inns; its updated, airy rooms are tidy and comfortable, and geraniums flower most of the year from its balconies. **Pros:** in the center of town; parking available; good value restaurant. **Cons:** difficult stairs to climb; some rooms are noisy. 🖃 *Rooms from: €97* ✉ *Ritterstr. 6* ☎ *08362/91600* ⊕ *www.hotel-hechten.com* ⤴ *35 rooms* 🍽 *Breakfast.*

$$ — HOTEL   🛏 **Hotel Hirsch.** A mother-and-daughter team provides friendly service at this traditional Füssen hotel. **Pros:** in the center of town; eclectic rooms; good restaurant. **Cons:** front rooms noisy; modern lobby. 🖃 *Rooms from: €135* ✉ *Kaiser-Maximilian-Pl. 7* ☎ *08362/93980* ⊕ *www. hotelhirsch.de* ⤴ *53 rooms* 🕘 *Closed Dec. 23–Jan. 7* 🍽 *Breakfast.*

Northern and Central Romantic Road

$$$
B&B/INN
FAMILY
Fodor's Choice
★

Schlossanger Alp. One hundred years of family tradition embrace guests of this superb hotel, which combines the surroundings of a grand alpine hotel with the intimacy of a bed-and-breakfast. **Pros:** great food; attentive service; great for families. **Cons:** you'll need GPS to find it; a half-hour drive from Neuschwanstein; expensive. ⑤ *Rooms from: €210 ⊠ Am Schlossanger 1, Pfronten ☎ 08363/914–550 ⊕ www. schlossanger.de ⤳ 35 rooms* ⦿ *Breakfast.*

OFF THE
BEATEN
PATH

Wieskirche. This church—a glorious example of German rococo architecture—stands in an Alpine meadow just off the Romantic Road. Its yellow-and-white walls and steep red roof are set off by the dark backdrop of the Trauchgauer Mountains. The architect Dominicus Zimmermann, former mayor of Landsberg and creator of much of that town's rococo architecture, built the church in 1745 on the spot where six years earlier a local woman saw tears running down the face of a picture of Christ. Although the church was dedicated as the Pilgrimage Church of the Scourged Christ, it's now known simply as the Wieskirche (Church of the Meadow). ■**TIP→** Visit it on a bright day if you can, when light streaming through its high windows displays the full glory of the glittering interior. A complex oval plan is animated by brilliantly colored stuccowork, statues, and gilt. A luminous ceiling fresco completes the decoration. Concerts are presented in the church from the end of June through the beginning of August. To get here from the village of Steingaden (22 km [14 miles] north of Füssen on the B-17), turn east and follow the signs to Wieskirche. ⊠ *Wies 12, Steingaden* ☎ *8862/932–930* ⊕ *www.wieskirche.de* ✉ *Free* ☉ *Summer, daily 8–8; winter, daily 8–6.*

CENTRAL ROMANTIC ROAD

Picturesque Rothenburg-ob-der-Tauber is the highlight of this region, though certainly not the road less traveled. For a more intimate experience check out the medieval towns of Dinkelsbühl or Nördlingen, or go off the beaten track and off the Romantic Road to see the tower at Ulm's famous *Münster* (church).

AUGSBURG

70 km (43 miles) west of Munich.

Augsburg is Bavaria's third-largest city, after Munich and Nürnberg. It dates to 15 BC, when a son of Augustus set up a military camp here on the banks of the Lech River. The settlement that grew up around it was known as Augusta, which is what Italians call it to this day. The fashionable **Maximilianstrasse** lies on the Via Claudia Augusta, the same route that led from Italy to the silver-rich Augsburg and onward to the north. City rights were granted Augsburg in 1156, and 200 years later the Fugger family were first noted in municipal records. This family of bankers would become to Augsburg what the Medici were to Florence. Their wealth surpassed that of their Italian counterparts, though, such that they loaned funds to them from time to time. Some present-day members of the family run local charitable foundations.

GETTING HERE AND AROUND

Augsburg is on a main line of the high-speed ICE trains, which run hourly and take 45 minutes the get here from Munich. The center of town and its main attractions can be visited on foot. To continue on the Romantic Road, take a regional train from the main train station to Ulm, Donauwörth, or Nördlingen.

Walking tours (€8) set out from the tourist office on the Rathaus square daily at 2. The tours, which are available in German and English, include entrance to the Fuggerei and the Goldener Saal of the Rathaus.

TIMING

It's easy to see the sights here, because signs on almost every street corner point the way to the main ones. See the tourist board's website for some additional walking-tour maps. You'll need a complete day to see Augsburg if you linger in any of the museums.

ESSENTIALS

Visitor Information Augsburg Tourist-Information ⊠ *Rathauspl. 1* ☎ *0821/324–9410* ⊕ *www.augsburg.de.*

EATING WELL ON THE ROMANTIC ROAD

To sample the authentic food of this area, venture off the beaten track of the official Romantic Road into any small town with a nice-looking Gasthof or Wirtshaus. Order *Sauerbraten* (roast beef marinated in a tangy sauce) with *Spätzle* (small boiled ribbons of rolled dough), or try *Maultaschen* (oversize Swabian ravioli stuffed with meat and herbs), another typical regional dish.

Franconia (the *Franken* region, which has its "capital" in Würzburg) is the sixth-largest wine-producing area of Germany. Franconian wines—half of which are made from the Müller-Thurgau grape hybrid, made from crossing Riesling with another white-wine grape—are served in distinctive green, flagon-shape wine bottles. Riesling and red wines account for only about 5% of the total production of Franconian wine.

Before you travel north on the Romantic Road, be sure to enjoy the beer country in the south. There is a wide range of Franconian and Bavarian brews available, from *Rauchbier* (literally, "smoked beer") to the lighter Pilsners of Augsburg. If this is your first time in Germany, beware of the potency of German beer—some can be quite strong. (In the past few years more and more breweries offer excellent alcohol-free versions of their products.) The smallest beers are served at 0.3 liters (slightly under 12 ounces). Restaurants typically serve 0.5 liters at a time; in most beer tents and beer gardens the typical service is a full 1-liter stein.

EXPLORING
TOP ATTRACTIONS

Dom St. Maria (*Cathedral of St. Mary*). Augsburg's cathedral, which was built in the 9th century, stands out because of its square Gothic towers, the product of a 14th-century update. A 10th-century Romanesque crypt also remains from the cathedral's early years. The 11th-century windows on the south side of the nave, depicting the prophets Jonah, Daniel, Hosea, Moses, and David, form the oldest cycle of stained glass in central Europe. Five important paintings by Hans Holbein the Elder adorn the altar.

A short walk from the cathedral will take you to the quiet courtyards and small raised garden of the former episcopal residence, a series of 18th-century baroque and rococo buildings that now serve as the Swabian regional government offices. ⊠ *Dompl., Johannisg. 8* ⊕ *www. bistum-augsburg.de* ⊙ *Daily 9–dusk.*

Diözesanmuseum St. Afra. The cathedral's treasures are on display at this museum, which is directly behind the Dom. ⊠ *Kornhausg. 3–5* ⊕ *www.bistum-augsburg.de/museum* ⌂ *€4* ⊙ *Tues.–Sat. 10–5, Sun. noon–6.*

Fuggerei. This neat little settlement is the world's oldest social housing project. It was established by the Fugger family in 1516 to accommodate the city's deserving poor. The 67 homes with 140 apartments still serve the same purpose and house about 150 people today. It's financed almost exclusively from the assets of the foundation, because the annual rent of "one Rhenish guilder" (€1) hasn't changed, either. Residents must be Augsburg citizens, Catholic, and destitute through no fault of their own—and they must pray three times daily for their original benefactors, the Fugger family. The most famous resident was Mozart's great-grandfather. ✉ *Main entrance on Jakoberstr., Fuggerei 56* ☎ *0821/3198–8114* ⊕ *www.fugger.de* 🔳 *€4* ⊙ *Apr.–Oct., daily 8–8; Nov.–Mar., daily 9–6.*

Maximilian-Museum. Augsburg's main museum houses a permanent exhibition of Augsburg arts and crafts in a 16th-century merchant's mansion. ✉ *Fuggerpl. 1, Philippine-Welser-Str. 24* ☎ *0821/324–4102* ⊕ *www. kunstsammlungen-museen.augsburg.de* 🔳 *€7* ⊙ *Tues.–Sun. 10–5.*

Perlachturm (*Perlach Tower*). This 258-foot-high plastered brick bell tower has foundations dating to the 12th century. Although it's a long climb to the top of the tower, the view over Augsburg and the countryside is worth it. ✉ *Rathauspl.* 🔳 *€1.50* ⊙ *May–Nov., daily 10–6.*

Rathaus. Augsburg's town hall was Germany's largest when it was built in the early 17th century; it's now regarded as the finest secular Renaissance structure north of the Alps. Its **Goldener Saal** (Golden Hall) was given its name because of its rich decoration—eight pounds of gold are spread over its wall frescoes, carved pillars, and coffered ceiling. ✉ *Rathauspl. 2* ⊕ *www.augsburg.de* 🔳 *€2.50* ⊙ *Daily 10–6 (closed for official functions).*

Sts. Ulrich and Afra. Standing at the highest point of the city, this Catholic basilica with an attached Protestant chapel symbolizes the Peace of Augsburg, the treaty that ended the religious struggle between the two groups. Built on the site of a Roman cemetery where St. Afra was martyred in AD 304, the original structure was begun in the late-Gothic style in 1467. St. Afra is buried in the crypt, near the tomb of St. Ulrich, a 10th-century bishop who helped stop a Hungarian army at the gates of Augsburg in the Battle of the Lech River. The remains of a third patron of the church, St. Simpert, are preserved in one of the church's most elaborate side chapels. From the steps of the magnificent altar, look back along the high nave to the finely carved baroque wrought iron and wood railing that borders the entrance. As you leave, look into the separate but adjacent church of St. Ulrich, the Baroque preaching hall that was added for the Protestant community in 1710, after the Reformation. ✉ *Ulrichspl. 19* ⊕ *www. ulrichsbasilika.de* ⊙ *Daily 9–dusk.*

Schaezlerpalais. This elegant 18th-century city palace was built by the von Liebenhofens, a family of wealthy bankers. Schaezler was the name of a baron who married into the family. Today the palace rooms contain the **Deutsche Barockgalerie** (German Baroque Gallery), a major art collection that features works of the 17th and 18th centuries. The palace adjoins the former church of a Dominican monastery. A steel door behind the banquet hall leads into another world of high-vaulted ceilings, where the **Staatsgalerie Altdeutsche Meister,** a Bavarian state collection, highlights old-master paintings, among them a Dürer portrait of one of the Fuggers. ✉ *Maximilianstr. 46* ☎ *0821/324–4102* 🔳 *€7* ⊙ *Tues.–Sun. 10–5.*

KEY

🗊 *Tourist information*

WORTH NOTING

Brechthaus. This modest artisan's house was the birthplace of the renowned playwright Bertolt Brecht (1898–1956), author of *Mother Courage* and *The Threepenny Opera*. It's now a museum documenting his life and work. ⊠ *Auf dem Rain 7* ☎ *0821/324–2779* 💷 *€2* 🕙 *Tues.– Sun. 10–5.*

Fuggerhäuser. The 16th-century house and business quarters of the Fugger family now has restaurant in its cellar and offices on the upper floors. In the ground-floor entrance are busts of two of Augsburg's most industrious Fuggers, Raymund and Anton. Beyond a modern glass door is the *Damenhof* (Ladies' Courtyard), originally reserved for the Fugger women. Only the three courtyards here are open to the public. ⊠ *Maximilianstr. 36–38* 🕙 *Courtyards: summer, daily 11–3 and 6–midnight.*

Holbein Haus. The rebuilt 16th-century home of painter Hans Holbein the Elder, one of Augsburg's most famous residents, and birthplace of his son the Younger, is now a city art gallery with changing modern art exhibitions. ⊠ *Vorderer Lech 20* ⊕ *www.kunstverein-augsburg.de* 💷 *Admission varies* 🕙 *May–Oct., Tues., Wed., and Fri.–Sun. 10–5, Thurs. 10–8; Nov.–Apr., Tues., Wed., and Fri.–Sun. 10–4, Thurs. 10–8.*

Maximilianstrasse. Most of the city's sights are on Augsburg's main shopping street or a short walk away. It was once a medieval wine market along the Roman road. Two monumental and elaborate fountains punctuate the long street. At the north end is the **Merkur,** designed in 1599 by the Dutch master Adrian de Vries (after a Florentine sculpture by Giovanni da Bologna), which shows winged Mercury in his classic pose. Farther up Maximilianstrasse is another de Vries fountain: a bronze **Hercules** struggling to subdue the many-headed Hydra.

TOURING TIPS

Scenic spot: There's an excellent view over the center of the city (and beyond, to the Alps and Munich) from the spot where Maximilianstrasse joins Rathausplatz (Town Hall Square).

Snacks: Recuperate from the climb at the cafés and restaurants on Rathausplatz and Maximilianstrasse.

Mozart-Haus (*Mozart House*). Leopold Mozart, the father of Wolfgang Amadeus Mozart, was born in this bourgeois 17th-century residence; he was an accomplished composer and musician in his own right. The house now serves as a Mozart memorial and museum, with some fascinating contemporary documents on the Mozart family. Many descendants still live in the area today. ⊠ *Frauentorstr. 30* ☎ *0821/518–588* ⊕ *www.mozartgesellschaft.de* ⊠ *€3.50* ⊗ *Tues.–Sun. 10–5.*

Rotes Tor (*Red Gate*). The city's most important medieval gate once straddled the main trading road to Italy. It's the backdrop to an openair opera and operetta festival in June and July. ⊠ *Rote-Torwall-Str.*

St. Anna-Kirche (*St. Anna's Church*). This site was formerly part of a Carmelite monastery, where Martin Luther stayed in 1518 during his meetings with Cardinal Cajetanus, the papal legate sent from Rome to persuade the reformer to renounce his heretical views. Luther refused, and the place where he publicly declared his rejection of papal pressure is marked with a plaque on Maximilianstrasse. ■ TIP→ You can wander through the quiet cloisters, dating from the 14th century, and view the chapel used by the Fugger family until the Reformation. ⊠ *Anna-Str., west of Rathauspl.* ⊗ *Mon. noon–5, Tues.–Sat. 10–12:30 and 3–5, Sun. 10–12:30 (for services) and 3–4.*

WHERE TO EAT

$$$
EUROPEAN
Fodor's Choice
★

╳ **Die Ecke.** In season, the venison dishes are among Bavaria's best at this imaginative restaurant, on an *Ecke* (corner) of the small square right behind Augsburg's town hall. The fish, in particular the *Zander* (green pike) or the trout (sautéed in butter with herbs and lemon), is magnificent, and complemented nicely by the Riesling Gimmeldinger Meersspinne, the house wine for 40 years. In summer ask for a table on the patio. ⑤ *Average main: €21* ⊠ *Elias-Holl-Pl. 2* ☎ *0821/510–600* ⊕ *www.restaurant-die-ecke.de* ⊜ *Reservations essential.*

$
GERMAN

╳ **Ratskeller Augsburg.** Underneath the impressive Ratshaus lies this vaulted redbrick destination for Bavarian food and drink, especially at the end of a long day. It's surprisingly airy here, despite being underground. The friendly staff serve up traditional fare with plenty of

Climb the 258 steps of the Perlachturm (Perlach Tower) beside the Rathaus for a spectacular vantage point over Augsburg.

choices, and it stays open late (till 1 am most nights, and 2 am on Friday and Saturday), when most other local restaurants have closed. There's an expansive cocktail menu, and you can make the most of it during the daily happy hour. $ *Average main: €13* ✉ *Ratshauspl. 2* ☎ *0821/319–88238* ⊕ *www.ratskeller-augsburg.de.*

WHERE TO STAY

$ **Dom Hotel.** Just around the corner from Augsburg's cathedral, this snug
HOTEL establishment has personality to spare. **Pros:** family-run; attention paid to details; nice view from upper rooms, complimentary parking. **Cons:** stairs to entrance and some rooms; no restaurant or bar. $ *Rooms from: €85* ✉ *Frauentorstr. 8* ☎ *0821/343–930* ⊕ *www.domhotel-augsburg.de* ⤶ *44 rooms, 8 suites* ☉ *Closed late Dec.–mid-Jan.* ⦿*Breakfast.*

$$ **Romantikhotel Augsburger Hof.** A preservation order protects the beau-
HOTEL tiful Renaissance facade of this old Augsburg mansion, but the hotel itself is full of modern comfort. **Pros:** welcoming lobby; rooms with a personal touch; good food and handy location. **Cons:** noisy front rooms; must book far in advance. $ *Rooms from: €110* ✉ *Auf dem Kreuz 2* ☎ *0821/343–050* ⊕ *www.augsburger-hof.de* ⤶ *36 rooms* ⦿*Breakfast.*

$$ **Steigenberger Drei Mohren Hotel.** Kings and princes, Napoléon, and the
HOTEL Duke of Wellington have all slept here, and these days all the rooms have been modernized without losing their traditional luxury. **Pros:** spacious lobby with inviting bar; very good restaurants; cheaper weekend rates. **Cons:** some rooms on top floor are small, with only one window. $ *Rooms from: €130* ✉ *Maximilianstr. 40* ☎ *0821/50360* ⊕ *www.augsburg.steigenberger.de* ⤶ *131 rooms* ⦿*Breakfast.*

THE ARTS

Augsburg has chamber and symphony orchestras, as well as ballet and opera companies. The city stages a Mozart Festival of international stature in September.

FAMILY **Augsburger Puppenkiste** (*Puppet theater*). This children's puppet theater has been an institution in Germany since its inception in 1948. It's still loved by kids and parents alike. ☒ *Spitalg. 15, next to Rotes Tor* ☏ *0821/450–3450* ⊕ *www.augsburger-puppenkiste.de.*

Freilichtbühne. One of Germany's most beautiful open-air theaters, Augsburg's Freilichtbühne is the setting for a number of operas, operettas and musicals from mid-June through July. ☒ *Am Roten Tor* ☏ *0821/324–4900 for tourist office* ⊕ *www.theater.augsburg.de.*

ULM

85 km (49 miles) west of Augsburg.

Ulm isn't considered part of the Romantic Road, but it's definitely worth visiting, if only for one reason: its mighty Münster, which has the world's tallest church tower (536 feet). Ulm grew as a medieval trading city thanks to its location on the Danube River. Today the proximity of the Old Town to the river adds to Ulm's charm. In the Fishermen's and Tanners' quarters the cobblestone alleys and stone-and-wood bridges over the Blau (a small Danube tributary) are especially picturesque. And down by the banks of the Danube, you'll find long sections of the old city wall and fortifications intact.

GETTING HERE AND AROUND

To get to Ulm from Augsburg, take Highway A-8 west or take a 40-minute ride on one of the ICE (InterCity Express) trains that run to Ulm every hour.

The tourist office's 90-minute tours include a visit to the Münster, the Old Town Hall, the Fischerviertel (Fishermen's Quarter), and the Danube riverbank. The departure point is the tourist office (Stadthaus) on Münsterplatz. The cost is €8, and tours take place throughout the day.

ESSENTIALS

Visitor Information Ulm Tourist-Information ☒ *Münsterpl. 50* ☏ *0731/161–2830* ⊕ *www.tourismus.ulm.de.*

EXPLORING

Marktplatz. The central Marktplatz is bordered by medieval houses with stepped gables. Every Wednesday and Saturday farmers from the surrounding area arrive by 6 am to erect their stands and unload their produce. Potatoes, vegetables, apples, pears, berries, honey, fresh eggs, poultry, homemade bread, and many other edible things are carefully displayed. ■ TIP➜ Get here early; the market packs up around noon.

Münster. Ulm's Münster is the largest evangelical church in Germany, but its true claim to fame is its church tower, the world's highest. It stands over the huddled medieval gables of Old Ulm, visible long before you hit the ugly suburbs encroaching on the Swabian countryside. The single, filigree tower challenges the physically fit to plod

536 feet up the 768 steps of a giddily twisting spiral stone staircase to a spectacular observation point below the spire. On clear days the steeple will reward you with views of the Swiss and Bavarian Alps, 160 km (100 miles) to the south. The Münster was begun in the late-Gothic age (1377) and took five centuries to build, with completion in the neo-Gothic years of the late 19th century. It contains some notable treasures, including late-Gothic choir stalls and a Renaissance altar. Ulm itself was heavily bombed during World War II, but Allied forces avoided the tower, using it instead as a navigational aid. ■ TIP➜ The mighty organ can be heard in special recitals every Sunday at noon from Easter until November. ⊠ *Münsterpl. 21* ⊕ *www.ulmer-muenster. de* ▭ *Tower €4* ☉ *Church daily 9–6:45, tower daily 9–3:45.*

Museum der Brotkultur (*German Bread Museum*). German bread is world renowned, so it's not surprising that a national museum is devoted to it. It's by no means as crusty or dry as you might fear, with some amusing exhibits showing how bread has been baked over the centuries. The museum is in a former salt warehouse, just north of the Münster. ⊠ *Salzstadelg. 10* ▭ *0731/69955* ⊕ *www.museum-brotkultur.de* ▭ *€4* ☉ *Daily 10–5.*

WHERE TO EAT AND STAY

$ | GERMAN | ✕ **Zunfthaus der Schiffleute.** The sturdy half-timber *Zunfthaus* (Guildhall) has stood for more than 500 years, first as a fishermen's pub and now as a charming tavern-restaurant that was renovated in 2013. Ulm's fishermen had their guild headquarters here, and when the nearby Danube flooded, the fish swam right up to the door. Today they land on the menu, which also includes dry-aged steak as well as "Swabian oysters" (actually snails, drenched in garlic butter). The local beer makes an excellent accompaniment. Ⓢ *Average main: €15* ⊠ *Fischerg. 31* ▭ *0731/64411* ⊕ *www.zunfthaus-ulm.de.*

$$ | GERMAN | Fodor's Choice | ★ | ✕ **Zur Forelle.** For more than 350 years Forelle ("Trout") has stood over the small, clear River Blau, which flows through a large trout basin right under the restaurant. In addition to the trout, there are five other fish dishes available, as well as excellent venison in season. ■ TIP➜ On a nice summer evening, try to get a table on the small terrace. You sit over the small river, with a weeping willow on one side, half-timber houses around you, and the towering cathedral in the background. Ⓢ *Average main: €19* ⊠ *Fischerg. 25* ▭ *0731/63924* ⊕ *www.zurforelle.com.*

$ | HOTEL | ▦ **Hotel am Rathaus/Reblaus.** Some of the rooms have vintage furniture at this family-owned hotel, which is also furnished with antique paintings, furniture, and dolls. **Pros:** center of the city; artistic touches; good value. **Cons:** no elevator; not enough parking; no breakfast in annex. Ⓢ *Rooms from: €98* ⊠ *Kroneng. 8–10* ▭ *0731/968–490* ⊕ *www.rathausulm.de* ⊅ *34 rooms* ☉ *Closed Christmas–early Jan.* ⦿*Breakfast.*

NÖRDLINGEN

28 km (17 miles) southeast of Donauwörth, 72 km (44 miles) northwest of Augsburg.

In Nördlingen a medieval watchman's cry still rings out every night across the ancient walls and turrets. As in Rothenburg, its sister city, the medieval walls are completely intact, but the riot of architecture here, from the medieval to the Renaissance and the baroque, doesn't come with the same masses of tourists. The ground plan of the town is two concentric circles. The inner circle of streets, whose central point is St. Georg, marks the earliest medieval boundary. A few hundred yards beyond it is the outer boundary, a wall built to accommodate expansion. Fortified with 11 towers and punctuated by five massive gates, it's one of the best-preserved town walls in Germany. And if the Old Town looks a little familiar, it might be because the closing aerial shots in the 1971 film *Willy Wonka and the Chocolate Factory* were filmed over its red roofs.

Nördlingen was established along the same Roman road that goes through Augsburg, but its "foundation" goes much farther back—the town is built in the center of a huge, basinlike depression, the Ries, which was at first believed to be the remains of an extinct volcano. In 1960 it was proven by two Americans that the 24-km-wide (15-mile-wide) crater was caused by an asteroid at least 1 km (½ mile) in diameter that hit the spot some 15 million years ago. The compressed rock, or *Suevit,* formed by the explosive impact of the meteorite was used to construct many of the town's buildings, including St. Georg's tower.

ESSENTIALS

Visitor Information Nördlingen Tourist-Information ✉ *Marktpl. 2* ☎ *09081/84116* ⊕ *www.noerdlingen.de.*

EXPLORING

St. Georg. Watchmen still sound out the traditional *"So G'sell so"* ("All's well") message from the 300-foot tower of the central parish church of St. Georg at half-hour intervals between 10 pm and midnight. The tradition goes back to an incident during the Thirty Years' War, when an enemy attempted to slip into the town and was detected by a resident. You can climb the 365 steps up the tower—known locally as the Daniel—for an unsurpassed view of the town and countryside, including, on clear days, 99 villages. ✉ *Marktpl.* 🗼 *Tower €3* ۞ *Church: Apr.–Oct., weekdays 9:30–12:30 and 2–5, weekends 9:30–5; Nov.–Mar., Tues.–Sat. 10:30–12:30. Tower: Jan. Feb., and Nov., daily 10–4; Mar. Apr., and Oct., daily 10–5; May Jun., and Sep., daily 9–6; Jul. and Aug., daily 9–7; Dec. 9–5.*

WHERE TO STAY

$
FAMILY
HOTEL
🏨 **Hotel Goldene Rose.** This small, modern hotel just inside the town wall is ideal for those wishing to explore Nördlingen on foot. **Pros:** family-friendly; parking in courtyard. **Cons:** front rooms noisy; restaurant closed Sunday. $ *Rooms from: €65* ✉ *Baldingerstr. 42* ☎ *09081/86019* ⊕ *www.goldene-rose-noerdlingen.de* ⮑ *17 rooms, 1 apartment* 🍽 *Breakfast.*

SPORTS AND THE OUTDOORS

Nördlingen Ries. Ever cycled around a huge meteor crater? You can do just that in the Nördlingen Ries, the depression left by an asteroid that hit the area 14.5 million years ago. This impact crater is a designated national geopark and the best-preserved impact crater in all of Europe.

Nördlingen tourist office. The tourist office has a list of 10 recommended bike routes, including one 47-km (29-mile) trail around the northern part of the meteor crater. ⊠ *Marktpl. 2* ☎ *09081/84116* ⊕ *www.noerdlingen.de* .

EN ROUTE

Donauwörth. At the old walled town of Donauwörth, 28 km (17 miles) southeast of Nördlingen, the Wörnitz River meets the Danube. If you're driving, pull off into the clearly marked lot on B-25, just north of town. Below you sprawls a striking natural relief map of Donauwörth and its two rivers. ⊕ *www.donauwoerth.de.*

DINKELSBÜHL

32 km (20 miles) north of Nördlingen.

Within the walls of Dinkelsbühl, a beautifully preserved medieval town, the rush of traffic seems a lifetime away. Although there is less to see here than in Rothenburg, the town is a pleasant break from the crowds, and you can relax among the locals at one of the Gasthauses in the town's central Marktplatz. You can patrol the illuminated Old Town with the night watchman at 9 pm free of charge, starting from the Münster St. Georg.

ESSENTIALS

Visitor Information Dinkelsbühl Tourist-Information ⊠ *Marktpl., Altrathauspl. 14* ☎ *09851/902–440* ⊕ *www.dinkelsbuehl.de* ☉ *May–Oct., weekdays 9–6, weekends 10–5; Nov.–Apr., daily 10–5.* **Romantische Strasse Touristik-Arbeitsgemeinschaft** (*Romantic Road Central Tourist-Information*). ⊠ *Segringerstr. 19* ☎ *09851/551–387* ⊕ *www.romantischestrasse.de.*

EXPLORING

Münster St. Georg (*Church of St. George*). Dinkelsbühl's main church is the standout sight in town. At 235 feet long it's large enough to be a cathedral, and it's among the best examples in Bavaria of the late-Gothic style. Note the complex fan vaulting that spreads sinuously across the ceiling. If you can face the climb, head up the 200-foot tower for amazing views over the jumble of rooftops. ⊠ *Marktpl., Kirchhöflein 6* ☎ *09851/2245* ⊕ *www.st-georg-dinkelsbuehl.de* ◱ *Tower €1.50* ☉ *Church: summer, daily 9–noon and 2–7; winter, daily 9–noon and 2–5. Tower: May–Sept., Fri.–Sun. 2–5.*

WHERE TO STAY

$ **Goldene Rose.** Since 1450 the inhabitants of Dinkelsbühl and their
B&B/INN   guests—among them Queen Victoria in 1891—have enjoyed a good night's sleep, great food, and refreshing drinks in this half-timber house. **Pros:** family-friendly; good food; parking lot. **Cons:** some rooms need renovating; front rooms are noisy. ⑤ *Rooms from: €78* ⊠ *Marktpl. 4* ☎ *09851/57750* ⊕ *www.hotel-goldene-rose.com* ⤢ *34 rooms* ⑩ *Breakfast.*

$$ **HOTEL** 🏨 **Hotel Deutsches Haus.** As you step into this medieval inn with a facade of half-timber gables and flower boxes, an old sturdy bar gives you a chance to register while sitting down and enjoying a drink. **Pros:** modern touches like free Wi-Fi. **Cons:** some rooms noisy; pricey; steps to climb. [$] *Rooms from: €129* ⊠ *Weinmarkt 3* ☎ *09851/6058* ⊕ *www.deutsches-haus-dkb.de* ⤴ *16 rooms, 2 suites* ❑ *Breakfast.*

$ **B&B/INN** 🏨 **Hotel Kunst Stuben.** A husband and wife team welcomes guests at this charming B and B, which is filled with handmade furniture, four-poster beds, and the owners' artwork on the walls. **Pros:** unique, local atmosphere; parking available. **Cons:** older building, with creaky floorboards; must check in before 6 pm. [$] *Rooms from: €80* ⊠ *Segringer Str. 52* ☎ *09851/6750* ⊕ *www. kunst-stuben.de* ⤴ *9 rooms* ❑ *Breakfast.*

LOCAL LEGEND

When Dinkelsbühl was under siege by Swedish forces and in imminent danger of destruction, a young girl led the children of the town to the enemy commander and implored him in their name for mercy. The commander of the Swedish army is said to have been so moved by the plea that he spared the town. The story is retold every year during the Kinderzech Festival, a children's pageant that's held during a 10-day festival in July.

ROTHENBURG-OB-DER-TAUBER

50 km (31 miles) north of Dinkelsbühl, 90 km (56 miles) west of Nürnberg.

Fodor's Choice ★ Rothenburg-ob-der-Tauber (literally, the "red castle on the Tauber") is the kind of medieval town that even Walt Disney might have thought too picturesque to be true, with half-timber architecture galore and a wealth of fountains and flowers against a backdrop of towers and turrets. Truth be told, it's partly a tourist trap these days, but it's genuine all the same. As late as the 17th century, it was a small but thriving market town that had grown up around the ruins of two 12th-century churches destroyed by an earthquake. Then it was laid low economically by the havoc of the Thirty Years' War, and with its economic base devastated, the town remained a backwater until modern tourism rediscovered it.

GETTING HERE AND AROUND

The easiest way to get here is by car. There are large parking lots just outside the town wall. You can also come by the Romantic Road bus from Augsburg via Donauwörth, Nördlingen, and Dinkelsbühl, with an optional layover on the way. By local train it takes about 2½ hours from Augsburg, with two train changes.

All attractions within the walled town can easily be reached on foot. The costumed night watchman conducts a nightly tour of the town, leading the way with a lantern. From Easter to December a one-hour tour in English begins at 8 pm and costs €6 (a 90-minute daytime tour begins at 2 pm). All tours start at the Marktplatz. Private group tours with the night watchman can be arranged through ⊕ *www.nightwatchman.de.*

FESTIVALS

Der Meistertrunk Festspiel (*The Meister Drink Historical Fest*). For four days over Whitsun (Pentecost) weekend (in early summer) every year, the town celebrates the famous wager said to have saved the town from destruction in the Thirty Years' War. A play of the events takes place every day, and handicraft and artisan markets, along with food stands, fill the town squares. ⊕ *www.meistertrunk.de.*

TIMING

Sights are dotted around town, and the streets don't lend themselves to a particular route. Be aware that crowds will affect the pace at which you can tour the town. Early morning is the only time to appreciate the place in relative calm. The best times to see the mechanical figures on the Rathaus wall are in the evening, at 8, 9, or 10.

ESSENTIALS

Visitor Information Rothenburg-ob-der-Tauber Tourist-Information
✉ *Rathaus, Marktpl. 2* ☎ *09861/404–800* ⊕ *www.tourismus.rothenburg.de.*

EXPLORING

TOP ATTRACTIONS

Meistertrunkuhr. Tales of the *Meistertrunk* (Master Drink) and a mighty civil servant are still told in Rothenburg. The story originates from 1631, when the Protestant town was captured by Catholic forces during the Thirty Years' War. During the victory celebrations, the conquering general was embarrassed to find himself unable to drink a great tankard of wine in one go, as his manhood demanded. He volunteered to spare the town further destruction if any of the city councilors could drain the mighty six-pint draft. The mayor took up the challenge and succeeded, and Rothenburg was preserved. The tankard itself is on display at the Reichsstadtmuseum. On the north side of the main square is a fine clock, placed there 50 years after the mayor's feat. A mechanical figure acts out the epic Master Drink daily on the hour from 11 to 3 and in the evening at 8, 9, and 10. The feat is also celebrated at two annual pageants, when townsfolk parade through the streets in 17th-century garb. ✉ *Marktpl. 1.*

Stadtmauer (*City Wall*). Rothenburg's city walls are more than 2 km (1 mile) long and provide an excellent way of circumnavigating the town from above. Let your imagination take you back 500 years as you explore the low, covered sentries' walkway, which are punctuated by cannons, turrets, and areas where the town guards met. Stairs every 200 or 300 yards provide ready access. There are superb views of the tangle of pointed and tiled red roofs and of the rolling country beyond.

WORTH NOTING

Rathaus. The Rathaus's tower gives you a good view of town. Half of the town hall is Gothic, begun in 1240; the other half is neoclassical, started in 1572, and renovated after its original facade was destroyed by a fire 500 years ago. ✉ *Rathauspl., Marktpl. 1* ⊕ *www.rothenburg. de* 🎫 *Tower €2* ☉ *Jan.–Mar. and Nov., weekends noon–3; Apr.–Oct., daily 9:30–5; daily 10:30–6.*

Rothenburg-ob-der-Tauber

KEY

— City Wall

🛈 Tourist information

0   300 meters

0   300 yards

4

Historiengewölbe (*Historic Vaults*). Below the Rathaus building are the historic vaults and dungeons, which house a museum that brings the Thirty Years' War to life. ✉ *Rathaus Building* 🎫*€2* 🕐 *Mid-Mar.–Apr., daily 10–4; May–Oct., daily 9:30–5:30; Dec., weekdays 1–4, weekends 10–4.* 🕐 *Closed Nov., Jan., and Feb.*

Reichsstadtmuseum (*Imperial City Museum*). This city museum is two attractions in one. Its artifacts illustrate Rothenburg and its history. Among them is the great tankard, or *Pokal*, of the Meistertrunk. The setting of the museum is the other attraction; it's in a former Dominican convent, the oldest parts of which date from the 13th century. Tour the building to see the cloisters, the kitchens, and the dormitory; then see the collections. ✉ *Klosterhof 5* ☎ *09861/939–043* ⊕ *www. reichsstadtmuseum.rothenburg.de* 🎫*€4* 🕐 *Apr.–Oct., daily 10–5; Nov.–Mar., daily 1–4.*

St. Wolfgang. Local shepherds gathered for prayer and protection at this spot for for years before building this historic parish church. Despite its Gothic origins and a baroque interior, St. Wolfgang's is most notable for the way it blends into the forbidding city wall. ✉ *Klingeng.* 🎫*€2* 🕐 *Apr.–Sept., Wed.–Mon. 11–1 and 2–5; Oct., Wed.–Mon. 11–4.*

Stadtpfarrkirche St. Jakob (*Parish Church of St. Jacob*). The towers of this pilgrimage church dominate the skyline; much of its art and artifacts have been donated by local townspeople over the centuries. The church has notable Riemenschneider sculptures, including the famous *Heiliges Blut* (Holy Blood) altar. Above the altar is a crystal capsule said to contain drops of Christ's blood. There are three 14th- and 15th-century stained-glass windows in the choir, and the Herlin-Altar is famous for its 15th-century painted panels. ⊠ *Klosterg. 15* ☎ *09861/700–620* ⬚ *€2* ⊙ *Jan.–Mar. and Nov., daily 10–noon and 2–4; Apr.–Oct., daily 9–5; Dec. daily 10–4:45. English tours Sat. at 3:30.*

WHERE TO EAT

$ ✕ **Restaurant-Burgerkeller.** An especially good choice for a blustery fall or
GERMAN   winter day, this restaurant in an Old Town cellar has in a rustic, family-friendly atmosphere. For a sampling of all the traditional pork dishes, tuck into the *Bauernschmaus*, smoked and roasted pork and sausages with a potato dumpling and gravy. $ *Average main: €15* ⊠ *Herrng. 24* ☎ *09861/2126.*

$ ✕ **Restaurant-Zur Höll.** This restaurant "To Hell" is a great place to head
GERMAN   for a snack after a night watchman's tour. The basic but delicious main menu is complemented throughout the year by seasonal and local dishes and ingredients, such as *Pfefferlinge* (chanterelles, served in soups, salads, and sauces); you'll probably also want to try the house beer. In the busier months, reserve a table ahead of time to guarantee a spot for later in the evenings. $ *Average main: €12* ⊠ *Burgg. 8* ☎ *098/614–229* ⊕ *www.hoell.rothenburg.de* ⊙ *Closed Mon.*

WHERE TO STAY

$$ ⊡ **Burg-Hotel.** At this exquisite little hotel most rooms have a view of
B&B/INN   the romantic Tauber Valley, and they also have plush furnishings, with
Fodor's Choice   antiques or fine reproductions. **Pros:** no crowds; terrific view from most
★   rooms; nice touches throughout; parking and bike rentals available for small fee. **Cons:** no restaurant; too quiet for kids. $ *Rooms from: €165* ⊠ *Klosterg. 1–3* ☎ *09861/94890* ⊕ *www.burghotel.eu* ⬚ *30 rooms, 2 apartments* ⦿ *Breakfast.*

$ ⊡ **Gasthof Klingentor.** This sturdy former staging post run by the wel-
B&B/INN   coming Wagenländer Family is outside the city walls but still within a 10-minute walk of Rothenburg's historic center. **Pros:** good value; friendly restaurant liked by locals and guests. **Cons:** front rooms noisy; no elevator. $ *Rooms from: €70* ⊠ *Mergentheimerstr. 14* ☎ *09861/3468* ⊕ *www.hotel-klingentor.de* ⬚ *20 rooms, 16 with bath* ⦿ *Breakfast.*

$$ ⊡ **Hotel Eisenhut.** It's fitting that the prettiest small town in Germany
HOTEL   should have one of the prettiest small hotels in its center. **Pros:** elegant lobby; exceptional service; good food. **Cons:** expensive; nothing for kids. $ *Rooms from: €150* ⊠ *Herrng. 3–5/7* ☎ *09861/7050* ⊕ *www. eisenhut.com* ⬚ *78 rooms, 2 suites* ⦿ *No meals.*

$ ⊡ **Hotel-Gasthof Post.** This small family-run hotel, two minutes on foot
B&B/INN   from the eastern city gate, must be one of the friendliest in town. **Pros:** good value; friendly-family. **Cons:** front rooms noisy; no elevator, some bathrooms need renovating. $ *Rooms from: €70* ⊠ *Ansbacher-str. 27* ☎ *09861/938–880* ⊕ *www.post-rothenburg.com* ⬚ *23 rooms* ⦿ *Breakfast.*

With its half-timber houses, fountains, statues, and flowers, Rothenburg-ob-der-Tauber makes for great photo ops.

$ 🏨 **Hotel Reichs-Küchenmeister.** Master chefs in the service of the Holy
B&B/INN   Roman Emperor were the inspiration for the name of this historic hotel-
restaurant, one of the oldest trader's houses in Rothenburg. **Pros:** central; excellent restaurant. **Cons:** small reception area. ⑤ *Rooms from:*
€100 ⊠ *Kirchpl. 8* ☎ *09861/9700* ⊕ *www.reichskuechenmeister.com*
↪ *45 rooms, 2 suites, 5 apartments* ⑩ *Breakfast.*

$$ 🏨 **Hotel-Restaurant Burg Colmberg.** East of Rothenburg, this thousand
B&B/INN   year old castle-turned-hotel maintains a high standard of comfort
FAMILY   within its original medieval walls. **Pros:** romantic; you're staying in a
real castle. **Cons:** remote location; quite a few stairs to climb. ⑤ *Rooms*
from: €110 ⊠ *An der Burgenstr., 18 km (11 miles) east of Rothenburg,*
Colmberg ☎ *09803/91920* ⊕ *www.burg-colmberg.de* ↪ *24 rooms, 2*
suites ⊙ *Closed Feb.* ⑩ *Breakfast.*

$$ 🏨 **Romantik-Hotel Markusturm.** The Markusturm began as a 13th-century
B&B/INN   customs house, an integral part of the city defense wall, and has since
developed over the centuries into an inn and staging post and finally
into a luxurious small hotel. **Pros:** tasteful decor; elegant atmosphere;
responsive owner. **Cons:** no bar; steps to climb. ⑤ *Rooms from: €145*
⊠ *Röderg. 1* ☎ *09861/94280* ⊕ *www.markusturm.de* ↪ *23 rooms, 2*
suites ⑩ *Breakfast.*

SHOPPING

Anneliese Friese. You'll find cuckoo clocks, beer tankards, porcelain,
glassware, and much more at this old and atmospheric shop run by
the delightful Anneliese herself. ⊠ *Grüner Markt 7–8, near Rathaus*
☎ *09861/7166.*

Haus der 1000 Geschenke. If you are looking for Hummel figurines, you've found the right place. ⊠ *Obere Schmiedeg. 13* ☏ *09861/4801.*

Käthe Wohlfahrt. The Christmas Village part of this store is a wonderland of mostly German-made toys and decorations, particularly traditional ornaments. Go to Christmas museum within the store for a full history of the traditions over the centuries. ⊠ *Herrng. 1* ☏ *09861/4090* ⊕ *www. wohlfahrt.com* ☉ *Mon.–Sat. 9–6:30, Sun. 10–6.*

FAMILY **Teddyland.** Germany's largest teddy-bear population, numbering more than 5,000, is housed here. ■TIP➔ Children adore the place, but be prepared: these toys don't come cheap. ⊠ *Herrng. 10* ☏ *09861/8904* ⊕ *www.teddyland.de* ☉ *Mon.–Sat., 9–6; Sun., Apr.–Dec. 10–6.*

EN
ROUTE

Schloss Schillingsfürst. This baroque castle of the Princes of Hohenlohe-Schillingsfürst is 20 km (12 miles) south of Rothenburg-ob-der-Tauber. Standing on an outcrop, it can be seen from miles away. You can watch eagles and falcons shoot down from the sky to catch their prey during one of the Bavarian falconry demonstrations held in the courtyard here, at 11 and 3 from March to October. ⊠ *Am Wall 14, Schillingsfürst* ☏ *09868/812* ⊕ *www.schloss-schillingsfuerst. de* ⊑ *€4.50, €8 with falconry demonstration* ☉ *Tues.–Sun. 10:30–5; tours at 10, noon, 2, and 4.*

NORTHERN ROMANTIC ROAD

After heading through the plains of Swabia in the south, your tour of the Romantic Road skirts the wild, open countryside of the Spessart uplands. It's worth spending a night in Würzburg, but Bad Mergentheim can be a quick stop.

BAD MERGENTHEIM

24 km (15 miles) west of Creglingen.

Between 1525 and 1809, Bad Mergentheim was the home of the Teutonic Knights, one of the most successful medieval orders of chivalry. In 1809, Napoléon expelled them as he marched toward his ill-fated Russian campaign. The expulsion seemed to sound the death knell of the little town, but in 1826 a shepherd discovered mineral springs on the north bank of the river. They proved to be the strongest sodium sulfate and bitter spa waters in Europe, with supposedly health-giving properties that ensured the town's future prosperity.

ESSENTIALS

Visitor Information Bad Mergentheim Tourist-Information ⊠ *Marktplatz 1* ☏ *07931/57135* ⊕ *www.bad-mergentheim.de.*

EXPLORING

Deutschordensschloss. The Deutschordensschloss, the Teutonic Knights' former castle, at the eastern end of the town, has a museum that follows the history of the order. The castle also hosts classical concerts, lectures, and events for families and children. ⊠ *Schloss 16* ☏ *07931/52212* ⊕ *www.deutschordensmuseum.de* ⊑ *€6, tours €2* ☉ *Apr.–Oct., Tues.–Sun. 10:30–5; Nov.–Mar., Tues.–Sun. 2–5.*

FAMILY **Wildpark Bad Mergentheim.** You can help feed the animals twice a day, at 9:45 and 1:30, at this wildlife park that's a few miles outside of Bad Mergentheim. It has the continent's largest selection of European species, including wolves and bears. ⊠ *Wildpark 1 ✛ Off B-290, 1 km (½ mile) south of town ☎ 07931/41344 ⊕ www.wildtierpark.de ⌦ €9 ⊗ Mid-Mar.–Oct., daily 9–6; last entrance at 4:30.*

WHERE TO STAY

$$ 🛏 **Hotel Victoria.** An elegant lounge, complete with library and open
HOTEL fireplace, greets you as you enter this hotel, which makes it a sophisticated alternative to the many small guesthouses in the area. **Pros:** good food with excellent service; spacious rooms. **Cons:** some rooms are not well ventilated; reception understaffed. ⑤ *Rooms from: €110* ⊠ *Poststr. 2–4 ☎ 07931/5930 ⊕ www.victoria-hotel.de ⌦ 40 rooms, 6 junior suites, 1 suite ⊗ Zirbelstube closed Jan., Aug., and Sun. and Mon. ⦿ Breakfast.*

EN ROUTE **Schloss Weikersheim.** It's slightly surprising to find a stately castle, Schloss Weikersheim, inside a village as sleepy as Weikersheim, some 10 km (6 miles) east of Bad Mergentheim on the Romantic Road. The perfectly preserved palatial residence and its surroundings embody the Renaissance ideals in their designs. You can stroll through the vast gardens and enjoy the view of the Tauber River. Inside, the **Rittersaal** (Knights' Hall) contains life-size stucco wall sculptures of animals, reflecting the counts' love of hunting. In the cellars you can drink a glass of wine drawn from the huge casks that seem to prop up the building. ⊠ *Marktpl. 11* ⊕ *www.schloss-weikersheim.de ⌦ €6, gardens only €3 ⊗ Apr.–Oct., daily 9–6; Nov.–Mar., daily 10–noon and 1–5.*

WÜRZBURG

200 km (124 miles) north of Ulm, 115 km (71 miles) east of Frankfurt.

The baroque city of Würzburg, the pearl of the Romantic Road, shows what happens when great genius teams up with great wealth. Beginning in the 10th century, Würzburg was ruled by powerful (and rich) prince-bishops, who created the city with all the remarkable attributes you see today.

The city is at the junction of two age-old trade routes, in a calm valley backed by vineyard-covered hills. Festung Marienberg, a fortified castle on the steep hill across the Main River, overlooks the town. Constructed between 1200 and 1600, the fortress was the residence of the prince-bishops for 450 years.

Present-day Würzburg is by no means completely original. On March 16, 1945, seven weeks before Germany capitulated, Würzburg was all but obliterated by Allied saturation bombing. The 20-minute raid destroyed 87% of the city and killed at least 4,000 people. Reconstruction has returned most of the city's famous sights to their former splendor. Except for some buildings with modern shops, it remains a largely authentic restoration.

GETTING HERE AND AROUND

Würzburg is on a main line of the superfast InterCity Express (ICE) trains, two hours from Munich and a bit more than an hour from Frankfurt. Most attractions in the old part of town are easily reached on foot. There's a bus to take you to Marienberg Castle, up on the hill across the river. A car is the best means of transport if you want to continue your journey, but you can also use regional trains and buses.

One-hour guided strolls (in English) through the Old Town start at the Haus zum Falken tourist office and take place from mid-June to mid-September, daily at 6:30 pm. Tickets (€5) can be purchased from the guide. If you'd rather guide yourself, pick up a map from the same tourist office and follow the extremely helpful directions that are marked throughout the city by distinctive signposts.

The Würzburger Schiffstouristik Kurth & Schiebe operates excursions. A wine tasting (€8) is offered as you glide past the vineyards.

FESTIVALS

Würzburg's cultural year starts with the International Film Weekend in January and ends with a Johann Sebastian Bach Festival in November. The annual jazz festival is also in November.

Barbarossa Spectaculum. Every other August, in even-numbered years, the Marienberg Fortress comes back to its full medieval glory with a fest of the court of Barbarossa. A Middle Ages market, acrobats, pyrotechnic shows, and court jesters are all on hand. Each day culminates with the Drachenzepter Ritterturnier, in which knights battle to win the Dragon Scepter in a fiery jousting tournament. ⊠ *Festung Marienberg, Oberer Burgweg* ☎ *0931/372–398* ⊕ *www.barbarossa-spectaculum.de* ⌧ *€6 entrance, €15 entrance and evening show.*

Frühjahrs-Volksfest (*Spring Fair*). During this spring festival, the biggest in the region, more than 50 carnival rides, roller coasters, games, and (of course) a huge beer tent await. The fest takes place every year in the three weeks preceding Easter. ⊠ *Talavera* ☎ *0931/373–692* ⊕ *www. wuerzburg.de.*

Mozartfest. The city of Würzburg hosts its annual Mozart Festival between May and July. Most concerts are held in the magnificent setting of the Residenz and feature world-class performers interpreting Mozart's works. Be sure to reserve tickets early. ⊠ *Rückermainstr. 2* ☎ *0931/372–336* ⊕ *www.mozartfest-wuerzburg.de.*

Weinparade am Marktplatz. It is no surprise that a region known for its wine and love of good party has so many wine fests. This one, held for a week in early September, is the largest and the best. More than 100 wineries gather on the Marktplatz and are joined by some of the finest restaurants in the city. ⊠ *Marktpl.* ☎ *0931/35170* ⊕ *www. weinparade.de.*

TIMING

You need two days to do full justice to Würzburg. The Residenz alone demands several hours of attention. If time is short, head for the Residenz as the doors open in the morning, before the first crowds assemble, and aim to complete your tour by lunchtime. Then continue to the nearby Juliusspital Weinstuben or one of the many traditional taverns in the area for lunch. In the afternoon, explore central Würzburg. The next morning cross the Main River to visit the Festung Marienberg.

ESSENTIALS

Visitor Information Stadt Würzburg Tourist Information ✉ Rückermainstra. 2 ☎ 0931/372–398 ⊕ www.wuerzburg.de. **Würzburger Schiffstouristik Kurth & Schiebe** ✉ St.-Norbert-Str. 1, Zell ☎ 0931/58573 ⊕ www.schiffstouristik.de.

EXPLORING

TOP ATTRACTIONS

Alte Mainbrücke (*Old Main Bridge*). A stone bridge—Germany's first—built in 1120 once stood on this site, over the Main River. That ancient structure was restored beginning in 1476. Twin rows of graceful statues of saints now line the bridge. They were placed here in 1730, at the height of Würzburg's baroque period, and were largely destroyed in 1945, but have been lovingly restored since then. Note the *Patronna Franconiae* (commonly known as the Weeping Madonna). There's a beautiful view of the Marienberg Fortress from the bridge.

Dom St. Kilian (*St. Kilian Basilica*). Construction on Würzburg's Romanesque cathedral, the fourth-largest of its kind in Germany, began in 1045. Centuries of design are contained under one roof; the side wings were designed in a late Gothic style in the 16th century, followed by extensive baroque stucco work 200 years later. The majority of the building collapsed in the winter, after bombs fell on the city near the end of World War II. Reconstruction, completed in 1967, brought a combination of modern design influences alongside a faithful restoration of the past thousand years of the church's history. Visit the side chapel designed by the baroque architect Balthasar Neumann, and a series of tombs of the bishops of Würzburg, designed by Tilman Riemenschneider. ⊠ *Domerpfarrg. 10* ☎ *0931/3866–2800* ⊕ *www.dom-wuerzburg.de* ⊗ *Daily 10–5.*

Festung Marienberg (*Marienberg Fortress*). This complex was the original home of the prince-bishops, beginning in the 13th century. The oldest buildings, including the **Marienkirche** (Church of the Virgin Mary) on the hilltop, date from around 700, although excavations have disclosed evidence that there was a settlement here in the Iron Age, 3,000 years ago. In addition to the rough-hewn medieval fortifications, there are a number of Renaissance and baroque apartments. Tours in English, held at 3 pm, meet at the Pferdeschwemme. ■ TIP➔ To reach the Marienberg, make the fairly steep climb on foot through vineyards or take Bus No. 9, starting at the Residenz, with several stops in the city. It runs about every 40 minutes from April to October. From April through October, tours around the fortress itself are offered for €2 per person, starting from the Scherenberg Tor. ⊠ *Oberer Burgweg* ⊕ *www.schloesser.bayern.de* ⊠ *Tours €3.50* ⊗ *Mid-Mar.–Oct., Tues.–Sun. 10–5.*

Mainfränkisches Museum (*Main-Franconian Museum*). A highlight of any visit to Festung Marienberg is likely to be this remarkable collection of art treasures. Be sure to visit the gallery devoted to Würzburg-born sculptor Tilman Riemenschneider (1460–1531). Also on view are paintings by Tiepolo and Cranach the Elder, as well as exhibits of porcelain, firearms, antique toys, and ancient Greek and Roman art. Other exhibits include enormous old winepresses and exhibits about the history of Franconian wine making. ⊠ *Festung Marienberg, Oberer Burgweg* ☎ *0931/205–940* ⊕ *www.mainfraenkisches-museum.de* ⊠ *€8* ⊗ *Mid-May–Oct., Tues.–Sun. 9–6; Nov.–May, Tues.–Sun. 10–4.*

Fürstenbaumuseum (*Princes' Quarters Museum*). The Marienberg collections are so vast that they spill over into another outstanding museum that's also part of the fortress. This one, the Fürstenbaumuseum, traces 1,200 years of Würzburg's history. The holdings include breathtaking exhibits of local goldsmiths' art. ⊠ *Festung Marienberg, Oberer Burgweg* ⊕ *www.schloesser.bayern.de* ⊠ *Combined ticket for Mainfränkisches and Fürstenbau museums €8* ⊗ *Mid-Mar.–Oct., Tues.–Sun. 9–6.*

Juliusspital. Founded in 1576 by Prince-Bishop Julius Echter as a foundation for the poor, the elderly, and the sick, this enormous edifice now houses a hospital and the second largest wine estate in Germany. Wander through the hospital park and grounds, then do a wine tasting, which includes six half-glasses of wine from the vineyards. All profits from the Vinothek and the neighboring restaurant are used to fund the foundation. ⊠ *Juliuspromenade 19* ☎ *0931/393–1401* ⊕ *www.juliusspital.de* ⊠ *Tour €22* ⊗ *Vinothek weekdays 9:30–6, Sat. 9–4.*

The baroque Würzburg Residenz is a UNESCO World Heritage Site.

Fodor'sChoice
★

Residenz (*Residence*). Würzburg's prince-bishops lived in this glorious baroque palace after moving down from the hilltop Festung Marienberg. Construction started in 1719 under the brilliant direction of Balthasar Neumann. Most of the interior decoration was entrusted to the Italian stuccoist Antonio Bossi and the Venetian painter Giovanni Battista Tiepolo. It's the spirit of the pleasure-loving prince-bishop Johann Philipp Franz von Schönborn, however, that infuses the Residenz. Now considered one of Europe's most sumptuous palaces, this dazzling structure is a 10-minute walk from the railway station, along pedestrian-only Kaiserstrasse and then Theaterstrasse.

Tours start in the **Vestibule,** which was built to accommodate carriages drawn by six horses. The king's guests were swept directly up the **Treppenhaus,** the largest baroque staircase in the country. Halfway up, the stairway splits and peels away 180 degrees to the left and to the right. Soaring above on the vaulting is Tiepolo's giant fresco *The Four Continents*, a gorgeous exercise in blue and pink that's larger than the Sistine Chapel's. Each quarter of the massive ceiling depicts the European outlook on the world in 1750—the savage Americas; Africa's and its many unusual creatures; cultured Asia, where learning and knowledge originated; and finally the perfection of Europe, with Würzburg as the center of the universe. Take a careful look at the Asian elephant's trunk and find the ostrich in Africa. Tiepolo had never seen these creatures but painted on reports of them; he could only assume that the fast largest bird in the world would have large muscular legs. He immortalized himself and Balthasar Neumann as two of the figures—they're not too difficult to spot.

Next, make your way to the **Weissersaal** (White Room) and then beyond to the grandest of the state rooms, the **Kaisersaal** (Throne Room). Tiepolo's frescoes show the 12th-century visit of Emperor Frederick Barbarossa, when he came to Würzburg to claim his bride. If you take part in the guided tour, you'll also see private chambers of the various former residents (guided tours in English are given daily at 11 and 3). The **Spiegelkabinett** (Mirror Cabinet) was completely destroyed by Allied bombing but then reconstructed using the techniques of the original rococo artisans.

Finally, visit the formal **Hofgarten** (Court Gardens), to see its stately gushing fountains and trim ankle-high shrubs that outline geometric flowerbeds and gravel walks.

■ **TIP**→ On weekends, the Hofkeller wine cellar, below the Residenz, runs tours that include tasting seven wines. Ask at the ticket counter. ✉ *Residenzpl. 2* ☎ *0931/355–170* ⊕ *www.residenz-wuerzburg.de* ⌨ *€7.50, including guided tour* ⊗ *Apr.–Oct., daily 9–6; Nov.–Mar., daily 10–4:30.*

WORTH NOTING

Alte Universität (*Old University*). Founded by Prince-bishop Julius Echter and built in 1582, this rambling institution is one of Würzburg's most interesting Renaissance structures. You may want to take some time to wander its grounds and soak in the student culture of one of Germany's best universities. ✉ *Sanderring 2* ⊕ *www.uni-wuerzburg.de.*

Alter Kranen. Near the Main River and north of the Old Main Bridge, the "Old Crane" was erected in 1772–73 by Balthasar Neumann's son, Franz Ignaz Michael. It was used to unload boats; beside it is the old customs building, which now has some lovely outdoor cafes overlooking the river. ✉ *Kranenkai 1.*

Augustinerkirche (*Church of St. Augustine*). This baroque church, a work by Balthasar Neumann, was built onto a 13th-century Dominican chapel. Neumann retained the soaring, graceful choir and commissioned Antonio Bossi to add colorful stuccowork to the rest of the church. ✉ *Dominikanerpl. 2* ☎ *0931/30970* ⊕ *www.augustinerkirche-wuerzburg.de* ⊗ *Daily 7–7.*

Bürgerspital (*Almshouse*). Wealthy businessmen founded this refuge for the city's poor and needy in 1319. The buildings also house a winery, which produces highly respected wines (sales are used to support the facility). The arcade courtyard is baroque in style and features its own glockenspiel. The winery offers tours of the facilities with wine tastings on the first Friday of each month; there's also a wine festival in mid-June. ✉ *Theaterstr. 19* ☎ *0931/3503–441* ⊕ *www.buergerspital.de* ⌨ *Tour €7* ⊗ *Store: Mon.–Thurs. 8–5, Fri. 8–3.*

Haus zum Falken. The city's most splendid baroque mansion, once a humble inn, now houses the city tourist office. Its colorful rococo facade was added in 1751. ✉ *Falkenhaus, Am Marktpl. 9* ☎ *0931/372–398* ⊕ *www.wuerzburg.de* ⊗ *Jan.–Mar., weekdays 10–4, Sat. 10–2; Apr., Nov., and Dec., weekdays 10–6, Sat. 10–2; May–Oct., weekdays 10–6, weekends 10–2.*

Marienkapelle (*St. Mary's Chapel*). This tranquil Gothic church (1377–1480) that stands modestly away at one end of Würzburg's market square is almost lost among the other old facades; keep an eye out for its red bell tower. The architect Balthasar Neumann lies buried here. ⊠ *Marktpl.* ☎ *0931/3861–1150* ⊕ *www.wuerzburger-markt.de* ☉ *Daily 9–6.*

Neumünster (*New Cathedral*). Next to the Dom St. Kilian, this 11th-century Romanesque basilica was completed in 1716. The original church was built above the grave of the early Irish martyr St. Kilian, who brought Christianity to Würzburg and, with two companions, was put to death here in 689. Their missionary zeal bore fruit, however—17 years after their death a church was consecrated in their memory. By 742 Würzburg had become a diocese, and over the following centuries 39 flourishing churches were established throughout the city. ⊠ *Domerpfarrg. 10* ☎ *0931/3866–2800* ⊕ *www.neumuenster-wuerzburg.de* ☉ *Daily 8–5.*

Stift Haug. Franconia's first baroque church, designed by the Italian architect Antonio Petrini, was built between 1670 and 1691. Its elegant twin spires and central cupola make an impressive exterior. The altarpiece is a 1583 Crucifixion scene by Tintoretto. ⊠ *Haugerpfarrg. 14* ☎ *0931/54102* ⊕ *stift-haug.de* ☉ *Daily 8–7.*

WHERE TO EAT

$ ✕ **Alte Mainmühle.** Sample Frankish bratwurst cooked over a wood-fire
GERMAN grill and other regional dishes in this converted mill alongside the Main River. The menu also includes local fish and a variety of vegetarian options. In good weather, you can sit outside on the terrace for the best views of the Alte Mainbrücke and the Festung Marienberg. The small bar at the entrance of this easygoing restaurant serves local wine streetside, so you can get a glass of crisp Silvaner and watch the sun set over the city and surrounding vineyards. ⑤ *Average main: €13* ⊠ *Mainkai 1* ☎ *0931/16777* ⊕ *www.alte-mainmuehle.de.*

$ ✕ **Backöfele.** More than 400 years of tradition are embedded in this
GERMAN old tavern. Hidden away behind huge wooden doors on a backstreet, the Backöfele's cavelike interior is a popular meeting and eating place. The surprisingly varied menu includes local favorites such as suckling pig and marinated pot roast, as well as good fish entrées and classic desserts, all at reasonable prices. ⑤ *Average main: €13* ⊠ *Ursulinerg. 2* ☎ *0931/59059* ⊕ *www.backoefele.de.*

$$ ✕ **Juliusspital Weinstuben.** Giving a gastropub's twist to traditional
GERMAN Franconian fare, this restaurant is also a draw for its local wines. The 400-year-old Juliusspital foundation still funds the neighboring hospital, school, and local nature preserves with profits from its vineyards and this bustling spot. Sample local game and fish specialties, you can also buy a bottle of wine to take home directly from the wait staff. ■TIP➔ In summer you can enjoy your food and drinks on a quiet terrace in the courtyard. ⑤ *Average main: €17* ⊠ *Juliuspromenade 19, Ecke Barbarossapl.* ☎ *0931/54080* ⊕ *www.juliusspital-weinstuben.de.*

$ ✕ **Ratskeller.** Practically every German city has a restaurant in its city
GERMAN hall, but Würzburg's stands out. The daily menu offers excellent regional food, such as *Fränkischer Sauerbraten,* along with plenty of fish and vegetarian offerings. The smaller dishes offered throughout the day are a good excuse to take a break while touring. Beer is available,

but local wine is what the regulars drink. As for the Gothic town hall itself, it's been the center of municipal government since 1316. ⑤ *Average main: €14 ⊠ Beim Grafeneckart, Langg. 1 ☎ 0931/13021 ⊕ www. wuerzburger-ratskeller.de.*

WHERE TO STAY

$$ 🖥 **Hotel Greifensteiner Hof.** The modern Greifensteiner offers comfort-
HOTEL   able, individually furnished rooms in a quiet corner of the city, just off the market square. **Pros:** center of town; excellent restaurants; nice bar packed with locals. **Cons:** no spectacular views or grand lobby. ⑤ *Rooms from: €130 ⊠ Dettelbacherg. 2 ☎ 0931/35170 ⊕ www. greifensteiner-hof.de ⤳ 49 rooms ⑩ Breakfast.*

$$ 🖥 **Hotel Rebstock zu Würzburg.** This hotel's rococo facade has welcomed
HOTEL   guests for centuries; the rooms are all individually decorated and fur-nished in an English country-house style. **Pros:** historical building with modern amenities and quick access to the town's sights. **Cons:** some-times fills up with conferences and large groups. ⑤ *Rooms from: €140 ⊠ Neubaustr. 7 ☎ 0931/30930 ⊕ www.rebstock.com ⤳ 63 rooms, 9 suites ⑩ Breakfast.*

$$ 🖥 **Hotel Walfisch.** Guest rooms are furnished in solid Franconian style,
B&B/INN   with farmhouse cupboards, bright fabrics, and heavy drapes. **Pros:** nice view from front rooms; good restaurant. **Cons:** difficult park-ing; small improvements needed. ⑤ *Rooms from: €130 ⊠ Am Plei-denturm 5 ☎ 0931/35200 ⊕ www.hotel-walfisch.com ⤳ 40 rooms ⑩ Breakfast.*

$$$ 🖥 **Schloss Steinburg.** Set atop vineyards and overlooking the towers of
HOTEL   Würzburg, the Schloss Steinburg offers regal manor rooms as well as crisp and calm modern lodgings. **Pros:** beautiful views; nice variety of rooms; pool open year-round. **Cons:** outside the city center; expensive. ⑤ *Rooms from: €210 ⊠ Mittlerer Steinburgweg 100 ☎ 0931/970–20 ⊕ www.steinburg.com ⤳ 69 rooms ⑩ Breakfast.*

SPORTS AND THE OUTDOORS

Stein-Wein-Pfad. Wine lovers and hikers should visit the Stein-Wein-Pfad, a signposted trail through the vineyards that rise up from the north-west edge of Würzburg. The starting point is the Weingut am Stein (Ludwig Knoll vineyard), 10 minutes on foot from the main railway station. A two-hour round trip affords stunning views of the city as well as the chance to try the excellent local wines directly at the source. ▓TIP➜ From May through mid-October, you can join a guided tour of the wineries every other Saturday for €7. This includes a glass of wine. ⊠ *Mittlerer Steinbergweg 5 ⊕ www.wuerzburger-steinweinpfad.de.*

SHOPPING

Würzburg is the true wine center of the Romantic Road. Visit any of the vineyards that rise from the Main River and choose a *Bocksbeutel,* the distinctive green, flagon-shape wine bottle of Franconia. One fanciful claim is that the shape came about because wine-guzzling monks found it the easiest to hide under their robes.

FRANCONIA AND THE GERMAN DANUBE

WELCOME TO FRANCONIA AND THE GERMAN DANUBE

TOP REASONS TO GO

★ **Bamberg's Altstadt:** This one isn't just for the tourists. Bamberg may be a UNESCO World Heritage Site, but it's also a vibrant town living very much in the present.

★ **Vierzehnheiligen:** Just north of Bamberg, this church's swirling rococo decoration earned it the nickname "God's Ballroom."

★ **Nürnberg's Kaiserburg:** Holy Roman emperors once resided in the vast complex of this imperial castle, which has fabulous views over the entire city.

★ **Steinerne Brücke in Regensburg:** This 12th-century Stone Bridge was considered an amazing feat of engineering in its time.

★ **An organ concert in Passau:** You can listen to the mighty sound the 17,774 pipes of Dom St. Stephan's organ create at weekday concerts.

1 **Northern Franconia.** As one of the few towns not destroyed by World War II, Bamberg lives and breathes German history. Wagner fans flock to Bayreuth in July and August for the classical music festival. The beer produced in Kulmbach is famous all over the country.

2 **Nürnberg (Nuremberg).** It may not be as well-known as Munich, Heidelberg, or Berlin, but when you visit Nürnberg you feel the wealth, power, and sway this city has had through the centuries. Standing on the ramparts of the Kaiserburg (Imperial Castle) and looking down on the city, you'll begin to understand why emperors made Nürnberg their home.

3 **The German Danube.** Regensburg and Passau are two relatively forgotten cities tucked away in the southeast corner of Germany in an area bordered by Austria and the Czech Republic. Passau is one of the oldest cities on German soil, built by the Celts and then ruled by the Romans 2,000 years ago. Regensburg is a bit younger; about a thousand years ago it was one of the largest and most affluent cities in Germany.

GETTING ORIENTED

Franconia's northern border is marked by the Main River, which is seen as the dividing line between northern and southern Germany. Its southern border is the Danube, where Lower Bavaria (Niederbayern) begins. Despite its size, Franconia is a homogeneous region of rolling agricultural landscapes and thick forests climbing the mountains of the Fichtelgebirge. Nürnberg is a major destination in the area and makes a good base for exploration. The towns of Bayreuth, Coburg, and Bamberg are an easy day trip from one another. The Danube River defines the region as it passes through the Bavarian Forest on its way from Germany to Austria. West of Regensburg, river cruises and cyclists follow its path.

5

CZECH REPUBLIC

B22

Roding   Cham

Patersdorf

B8
Straubing   **3**   B85   Deggendorf

Rottenmann

Pilsting   A3   Preying

A92   B8   Danube

Landau an der Isar   Passau

B20

AUSTRIA

CRUISING THE DANUBE

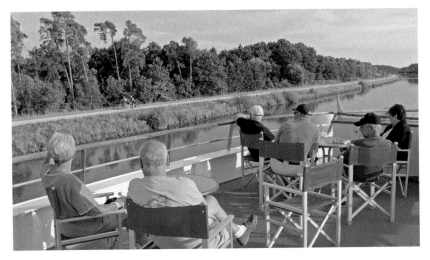

Rising from the depths of the Black Forest and emptying into the Black Sea, the Danube is the queen of rivers; cloaked in myth and legend, it cuts through the heart and soul of Europe.

(above and lower right) Cruise ship passengers relax on the Danube. (upper right) Enjoy views of Passau from various river cruises.

The name Dānuvius, borrowed from the Celts, means swift or rapid, but along the Danube, there is no hurry. Boats go with the flow and a river journey is a relaxed affair with plenty of time to drink in the history.

Whether you choose a one-hour, one-week, or the complete Danube experience, cruising Europe's historical waterway is a never-to-be-forgotten experience. Of the Danube's 1,770-mile length, almost 1,500 miles is navigable and the river flows through some of Europe's most important cities. You can head to major boating hubs, like Passau, Vienna, and Budapest or through historical stretches from Ulm to Regensburg. The Main-Donau Canal connects Nürnberg.

—Lee A. Evans

WHEN TO GO

Between May and July the Danube is busy with passenger and commercial traffic; this is the best time of year for a cruise. Fall is also good, when the changing leaves bathe the river in a sea of color. The Danube rarely freezes in the winter and several companies offer Christmas market tours from Nürnberg to Regensburg, Passau, and Vienna. Spring is the least optimal time to go as the river often floods.

A DAY ON THE DANUBE

On the map, the sheer length of the Danube is daunting at best. A great option is to choose an idyllic daylong boat excursion.

One of the best day cruises leaves from **Regensburg** and reaches the imposing temple **Walhalla**, a copy of the Parthenon erected by Ludwig I. **Personenschifffahrt Klinger** boats depart from the Steinerne Brücke daily at 10:30 and 2. Each departure gives you about an hour to explore the temple and the whole trip lasts three hours.

Donauschiffahrt Wurm + Köck offers a variety of Danube day trips. Their most popular is a daily excursion from **Passau** to the Austrian city of **Linz**, which departs at 9 am. If you don't have all day, they also offer a three-river tour that explores Passau at the convergence of the Ilz, Inn, and Danube that lasts about 45 minutes.

CRUISING ALL OF THE DANUBE

Although Passau is the natural gateway to the cruising destinations of Eastern Europe on the Danube, it is by no means the only starting point. You can board a deluxe river cruise ship in Nürnberg, landlocked but for the very small Pegnitz River, then cruise "overland" through Franconia on the Main-Danube canal across the Continental Divide until you join the Danube at Kelheim, a few miles west of Regensburg. After Passau you enter Austria, where you come to the city that most people automatically associate with the "Blue Danube," **Vienna**. The next border crossing brings you into Slovakia and to your second capital, **Bratislava**. **Budapest**, Hungary is next, and capital number four is **Belgrade**, Serbia. Some of the Danube cruises begin in Amsterdam, making them five-capital cruises.

Amadeus Cruises (☎ *888/829–1394* ⊕ *www.amadeuscruises.com*) offers half a dozen cruises through Franconia and the German Danube, including a Christmastime cruise, which stops at the fascinating Christmas markets between Nürnberg and Budapest. The reverse direction is also available.

Viking River Cruises (☎ *800/304–9616* ⊕ *www.vikingrivercruises.com*) has a Grand European Tour from Amsterdam to Budapest. The two-week Eastern European Odyssey starts in Nürnberg and ends at Bucharest. The reverse direction is also available on both cruises.

The British **Blue Water Holidays** (☎ *01756/706–500* ⊕ *www.cruising-holidays.co.uk*) has nine cruises starting on the Rhine, some from Basel in Switzerland, which follow the Main-Danube Canal to the Danube and four cruises from Nürnberg or Passau to Vienna or Budapest.

5

GERMANY'S CHRISTMAS MARKETS

Few places in the world do Christmas as well as Germany, and the country's Christmas markets, sparkling with white fairy lights and rich with the smells of gingerbread and mulled wine, are marvelous traditional expressions of yuletide cheer.

(above and lower right) You can purchase handmade ornaments at the atmospheric Nürnberg Christkindlesmarkt. (upper right) The Spandau Christmas market is one of 60 in Berlin.

Following a centuries-old tradition, more than 2,000 *Weihnachtsmärtke* spring up outside town halls and in village squares across the country each year, their stalls brimming with ornate tree decorations and handmade pralines. Elegant rather than kitsch, the markets last the duration of Advent—the four weeks leading up to Christmas Eve—and draw festive crowds to their bustling lanes, where charcoal grills sizzle with sausages and cinnamon and spices waft from warm ovens. Among the handcrafted angels and fairies, kids munch on candy apples and ride old-fashioned carousels while their parents shop for stocking stuffers and toast the season with steaming mugs of *Glühwein* and hot chocolate.

—Jeff Kavanagh

GLÜHWEIN

The name for mulled wine, Glühwein, literally means "glowing wine" and a few cups of it will definitely add some color to your cheeks. Usually made with red wine, it can be fortified with a *Schuss* or shot of schnapps, often rum or amaretto. *Feuerzangenbowle*, a supercharged version, is made by dripping burning, rum-soaked sugar into the wine. The nonalcoholic version is called *Kinderpunsch*, or children's punch.

Dating from the late Middle Ages, Christmas markets began as a way to provide people with supplies, food, and clothing for the winter; families came for the sugary treats and Christmas shopping. Now a bit more touristy, a visit to a traditional Christmas Market is still a truly a quintessential German experience. Starting on the first Sunday of Advent, the pace of life slows down when the cheerful twinkling lights are lit and the smells of hot wine linger in the air, promising respite during the drab winter.

The most famous markets are in Nürnberg and Dresden; each drawing more than 2 million visitors every year. While these provide the essential market experience, it's well worth visiting a market in a smaller town to soak in some local flavor. Bautzen hosts Germany's oldest Christmas market, while Erfurt's market, set on the Cathedral Square, is the most picturesque. No matter which you choose, keep in mind that the best time to visit is during the week when the crowds are the smallest; try to go in the early evening, when locals visit the markets with their friends and family. You'll experience a carnival-like atmosphere and won't be able to resist trying a mulled wine before heading home.

Despite the market theme, the real reason to visit is to endlessly snack on greasy, sweet, and warm market food.

Each market has its own specialties—gingerbread in Nürnberg and stollen in Dresden—but the thread through all is candied almonds, warm chestnuts, and roasted, local sausages. Be sure to pair your snacks with a cup of hot-spiced-wine, which is served in small mugs that make great souvenirs. The wine varies from region to region and special hot white wine is a trendy alternative. Other drinks include a warm egg-punch, hot chocolate, and warm berry juices for children.

TIPS FOR VISITING

Always ask for local goods. Craftspeople, especially from the Ore Mountains in Saxony, produce some of the finest smoking-man incense burners, nativity scenes, candle pyramids, glass balls, and advent stars in the world.

Think about how you're getting your purchases home. Although some larger vendors will ship your purchases for you, it's wise to plan some extra baggage space and purchase some bubble wrap.

Dress warmly and wear comfortable shoes. All markets are outside and even the smallest require walking.

Bring some small bills and coins. This will make food and wine transactions faster and more efficient. All plastic dishes and cups require a deposit, which is politely refunded to you when you return the items.

Updated by Lee A. Evans

All that is left of the huge, ancient kingdom of the Franks is the region known today as Franken (Franconia), stretching from the Bohemian Forest on the Czech border to the outskirts of Frankfurt. The Franks were not only tough warriors but also hard workers, sharp tradespeople, and burghers with a good political nose. The word *frank* means bold, wild, and courageous in the old Frankish tongue. It was only in the early 19th century, following Napoléon's conquest of what is now southern Germany, that the area was incorporated into northern Bavaria.

Although more closely related to Thuringia, this historic homeland of the Franks, one of the oldest Germanic peoples, is now begrudgingly part of Bavaria. Franconian towns such as Bayreuth, Coburg, and Bamberg are practically places of cultural pilgrimage. Rebuilt Nürnberg (Nuremberg in English) is the epitome of German medieval beauty, though its name recalls both the Third Reich's huge rallies at the Zeppelin Field and its henchmen's trials held in the city between 1945 and 1950.

Franconia is hardly an overrun tourist destination, yet its long and rich history, its landscapes and leisure activities (including skiing, golfing, hiking, and cycling), and its gastronomic specialties place it high on the enjoyment scale. Franconia is especially famous for its wine and for the fact that it's home to more than half of Germany's breweries.

PLANNING

WHEN TO GO

Summer is the best time to explore Franconia, though spring and fall are also fine when the weather cooperates. Avoid the cold and wet months from November to March; many hotels and restaurants close, and no matter how pretty, many towns do seem quite dreary. If you're in Nürnberg in December, you're in time for one of Germany's largest and loveliest Christmas markets. Unless you plan on attending the Wagner Festival in Bayreuth, it's best to avoid this city in July and August.

GETTING HERE AND AROUND

AIR TRAVEL

The major international airport serving Franconia and the German Danube is Munich. Nürnberg's airport is served mainly by regional carriers.

Airport Information Airport Nürnberg ✉ *Flughafenstr. 100, Nürnberg* ☎ *0911/93700* ⊕ *www.airport-nuernberg.de.*

CAR TRAVEL

Franconia is served by five main autobahns: A-7 from Hamburg, A-3 from Köln and Frankfurt, A-81 from Stuttgart, A-6 from Heilbronn, and A-9 from Munich. Nürnberg is 167 km (104 miles) north of Munich and 222 km (138 miles) southeast of Frankfurt. Regensburg and Passau are reached by way of the A-3 from Nürnberg.

TRAIN TRAVEL

Franconia boasts one of southern Germany's most extensive train networks and almost every town is connected by train. Nürnberg is a stop on the high-speed InterCity Express (ICE) north–south routes, and there are hourly trains from Munich direct to Nürnberg. Regular InterCity services connect Nürnberg and Regensburg with Frankfurt and other major German cities. Trains run hourly from Frankfurt to Munich, with a stop at Nürnberg. The trip takes about three hours to Munich, two hours to Nürnberg. There are hourly trains from Munich to Regensburg.

Some InterCity Express trains stop in Bamberg, which is most speedily reached from Munich. Local trains from Nürnberg connect with Bayreuth and areas of southern Franconia. Regensburg and Passau are on the ICE line from Nürnberg to Vienna.

RESTAURANTS

Many restaurants in the rural parts of this region serve hot meals only between 11:30 am and 2 pm, and 6 pm and 9 pm. ■TIP➔ "Durchgehend warme Küche" means that hot meals are also served between lunch and dinner.

Prices in the reviews are the average cost of a main course at dinner, or if dinner is not served, at lunch.

HOTELS

Make reservations well in advance for hotels in all the larger towns and cities if you plan to visit anytime between June and September. During the Nürnberg Toy Fair at the beginning of February, rooms are at a premium. If you're visiting Bayreuth during the annual Wagner Festival in July and August, consider making reservations up to a year in advance. Remember, too, that during the festival prices can be double the normal rates.

Prices in the reviews are the lowest cost of a standard double room in high season. For expanded reviews, facilities, and current deals, visit Fodors.com.

PLANNING YOUR TIME

Nürnberg warrants at least a day of your time. It's best to base yourself in one city and take day trips to others. Bamberg is the most central of the northern Franconia cities and makes a good base. It is also a good idea to leave your car at your hotel and make the trip downstream to Regensburg or Passau by boat, returning by train.

VISITOR INFORMATION

Franconia Tourist Board ⊠ *Tourismusverband Franken e.V., Wilhelminenstr. 6, Nürnberg* ☎ *0911/941–510* ⊕ *www.frankentourismus.de.*

NORTHERN FRANCONIA

Three major German cultural centers lie within easy reach of one another: Coburg, a town with blood links to royal dynasties throughout Europe; Bamberg, with its own claim to German royal history and an Old Town area designated a UNESCO World Heritage Site; and Bayreuth, where composer Richard Wagner finally settled, making it a place of musical pilgrimage for Wagner fans from all over the world.

COBURG

105 km (65 miles) north of Nürnberg.

Coburg is a surprisingly little-known treasure that was founded in the 11th century and remained in the possession of the dukes of Saxe-Coburg-Gotha until 1918; the current duke still lives here. The remarkable Saxe-Coburg dynasty established itself as something of a royal stud farm, providing a seemingly inexhaustible supply of blue-blood marriage partners to ruling houses the length and breadth of Europe. The most famous of these royal mates was Prince Albert (1819–61), who married the English Queen Victoria, after which she gained special renown in Coburg. Their numerous children, married off to other kings, queens, and emperors, helped to spread the tried-and-tested Saxe-Coburg influence even farther afield. Despite all the history that sweats from each sandstone ashlar, Coburg is a modern and bustling town.

ESSENTIALS

Visitor Information Coburg ⊠ *Tourismus Coburg, Herrng. 4* ☎ *09561/898–000* ⊕ *www.coburg-tourist.de.*

FESTIVALS

Brazilian Samba Festival. This three-day bacchanal is held in mid-July. Check the Coburg tourist office's Web site for more information about the event. ⊕ *wwww.coburg-tourist.de.*

EXPLORING

Marktplatz (*Market Square*). Coburg's Marktplatz has a statue of Prince Albert, Victoria's high-minded consort, surrounded by gracious Renaissance and baroque buildings. The **Stadhaus,** former seat of the local dukes, begun in 1500, is the most imposing structure here. A forest of ornate gables and spires projects from its well-proportioned facade. Opposite is the **Rathaus** (Town Hall). ■**TIP→ Look on the building's tympanum for the statue of the Bratwurstmännla (it's actually St. Mauritius in armor); the staff he carries is said to be the official length against which the town's famous bratwursts are measured.** These tasty sausages, roasted on pinecone fires, are available on the market square. ⊠ *Marktplatz.*

Schloss Callenberg. Perched on a hill 5 km (3 miles) west of Coburg is Schloss Callenberg, until 1231 the main castle of the Knights of Callenberg. In the 16th century it was taken over by the Coburgs. From 1842 on it served as the summer residence of the hereditary Coburg prince and later Duke Ernst II. It holds a number of important collections, including that of the Windsor gallery; arts and crafts from Holland, Germany, and Italy from the Renaissance to the 19th century; precious baroque, Empire, and Biedermeier furniture; table and standing clocks from three centuries; a selection of weapons; and various handicrafts. The best way to reach the castle is by car via Baiersdorf. City Bus No. 5 from Coburg's Marktplatz stops at the castle only on Sunday; on other days you need to get off at the Beirsdorf stop and walk 25 minutes. ⊠ *Callenberger Str. 1* ☎ *09561/55150* ⊕ *www.schloss-callenberg. de* 🖭 *€5* ☾ *Tues.–Sun. 11–5.*

Schloss Ehrenburg. Prince Albert spent much of his childhood in Schloss Ehrenburg, the ducal palace. Built in the mid-16th century, it has been greatly altered over the years, principally following a fire in the early 19th century. Duke Ernst I invited Karl Friedrich Schinkel from Berlin to redo the palace in the then-popular neo-Gothic style. Some of the original Renaissance features were kept. The rooms of the castle are quite special, especially those upstairs, where the ceilings are heavily decorated with stucco and the floors have wonderful patterns of various woods. The Hall of Giants is named for the larger-than-life caryatids that support the ceiling; the favorite sight downstairs is Queen Victoria's flush toilet, which was the first one installed in Germany. Here, too, the ceiling is worth noting for its playful, gentle stuccowork. The baroque chapel attached to Ehrenburg is often used for weddings. ⊠ *Schlosspl. 1* ☎ *09561/80880* ⊕ *www.sgvcoburg.de* 🎫*€4.50* ⊙ *Tours Tues.–Sun. 10–3 on the hr.*

QUICK BITES | **Burgschänke.** Relax and soak up centuries of history while sampling a traditional Coburg beer at this tavern. The basic menu has traditional dishes. ⊠ *Veste Coburg* ☎ *09561/80980* ⊙ *Closed Mon. and Jan.–mid-Feb.*

Veste Coburg. This fortress, one of the largest and most impressive in the country, is Coburg's main attraction. The brooding bulk of the castle guards the town from a 1,484-foot hill. Construction began around 1055, but with progressive rebuilding and remodeling today's predominantly late-Gothic/early-Renaissance edifice bears little resemblance to the original crude fortress. One part of the castle harbors the **Kunstsammlungen,** a grand set of collections including art, with works by Dürer, Cranach, and Hans Holbein, among others; sculpture from the school of the great Tilman Riemenschneider (1460–1531); furniture and textiles; magnificent weapons, armor, and tournament garb spanning four centuries (in the so-called **Herzoginbau,** or Duchess's Building); carriages and ornate sleighs; and more. The room where Martin Luther lived for six months in 1530 while he observed the goings-on of the Augsburg Diet has an especially dignified atmosphere. The **Jagdintarsien-Zimmer** (Hunting Marquetry Room), an elaborately decorated room that dates back to the early 17th century, has some of the finest woodwork in southern Germany. Finally, there's the **Carl-Eduard-Bau** (Carl-Eduard Building), which contains a valuable antique glass collection, mostly from the baroque age. Inquire at the ticket office for tours and reduced family tickets. ⊠ *Veste Coburg* ☎ *09561/8790* ⊕ *www.kunstsammlungen-coburg.de* 🎫*€6, combination ticket with with Schloss Ehrenburg €12* ⊙ *Museums Apr.–Oct., daily 10–5; Nov.–Mar., Tues.–Sun. 1–4.*

WHERE TO EAT AND STAY

$ **✕ Ratskeller.** The basic local specialties taste better here beneath the old
GERMAN vaults and within earshot of the Coburg marketplace. Try the *Tafelspitz* (boiled beef with creamed horseradish), along with a glass of crisp Franconian white wine. The prices become a little higher in the evening, when the menu adds a few more dishes. ⑤ *Average main: €12* ⊠ *Markt 1* ☎ *09561/92400* ⊕ *www.ratskeller-coburg.de* 🚭 *No credit cards.*

$ ⊡ **Goldene Rose.** One of the region's oldest, this agreeable inn is located
HOTEL about 5 km (3 miles) southeast of Coburg. **Pros:** friendly; family run;
very good value; large parking lot behind the hotel. **Cons:** in a small
village; front rooms noisy. ⑤ *Rooms from: €49* ⊠ *Coburgerstr. 31, Grub
am Forst* ☎ *09560/92250* ⊕ *www.goldene-rose.de* ⤴ *14 rooms* ⊘ *Restaurant closed Mon.* ⑩ *Breakfast.*

$ ⊡ **Romantic Hotel Goldene Traube.** Rooms are individually decorated in
HOTEL this fine historical hotel (1756), and for dining you can choose between
the elegant restaurant Esszimmer or the more casual Meer und Mehr
(Sea and More), which serves fine seafood and regional specialties.
Pros: welcoming spacious lobby; two good restaurants; center of town;
nice small wineshop. **Cons:** traffic noise in front rooms; stairs up to the
lobby. ⑤ *Rooms from: €105* ⊠ *Am Viktoriabrunnen 2* ☎ *09561/8760*
⊕ *www.goldenetraube.com* ⤴ *72 rooms, 1 suite* ⑩ *Breakfast.*

$ ⊡ **Arcadia Hotel Coburg.** You can expect modern, clean, well-designed
HOTEL rooms that are airy and functional here. **Pros:** modern three-star business hotel; easy access; free parking and garage. **Cons:** modern three-
star business hotel; edge of town; surrounded by garages and shopping
outlets; breakfast costs €15 extra. ⑤ *Rooms from: €66* ⊠ *Ketschen-
dorfer Str. 86* ☎ *09561/8210* ⊕ *www.arcadia-hotel.de* ⤴ *123 rooms*
⑩ *Breakfast.*

SHOPPING

■ TIP→ Coburg is full of culinary delights; its Schmätzen (gingerbread)
and Elizenkuchen (almond cake) are famous. You'll find home-baked
versions in any of the many excellent **patisseries** or at a Grossman store
(there are three in Coburg).

Hummel Museum. Rödental, northeast of Coburg, is the home of the
world-famous M. I. Hummel figurines, made by the Göbel porcelain
manufacturer. There's a Hummel Museum devoted to them, and 18th-
and 19th-century porcelain from other manufacturers. Besides the
museum's store, there are several retail outlets in the village. ⊠ *Coburgerstr. 7, Rödental* ☎ *09563/92303* ⊕ *www.goebel.de* ⊘ *Weekdays
9–5, Sat. 9–noon.*

KULMBACH

19 km (12 miles) southeast of Kronach.

A quarter of Kulmbachers earn their living directly or indirectly from
beer. Kulmbach celebrates its brewing traditions every year in a nine-
day festival that starts on the last Saturday in July. The main festival
site, a mammoth tent, is called the *Festspulhaus*—literally, "festival
swill house"—a none-too-subtle dig at nearby Bayreuth and its tony
Festspielhaus, where Wagner's operas are performed. If you're here in
winter, be sure to try the seasonal *Eisbock*, a special dark beer that is
frozen as part of the brewing process; making it stronger.

ESSENTIALS

Visitor Information Kulmbach Tourismusservice ⊠ *Stadthalle, Sutte 2*
☎ *09221/958–820* ⊕ *www.kulmbach.de.*

EXPLORING

Kulmbacher Brewery. This brewery, which merged four Kulmbach breweries into one, produces, among others, the *Doppelbock Kulminator 28*, which takes nine months to brew and has an alcohol content of 12%. ⊠ *Lichtenfelserstr. 9* ☎ *09221/7050* ⊕ *www.kulmbacher.de.*

Bayerisches Brauereimuseum Kulmbach (*Bavarian Brewery Museum*). The Kulmbacher Brewery runs this museum jointly with the nearby Mönchshof-Bräu brewery and inn. ▪TIP→ The price of admission includes a "taste" from the museum's own brewery. ⊠ *Hoferstr. 20* ☎ *09221/80514* ⊕ *www.kulmbacher-moenchshof.de* ⊠ *€4.50* ⊙ *Tues.–Sun. 10–5*

KULMBACH BREWS

In a country where brewing and beer drinking, despite a steady decline, still breaks all records, Kulmbach produces more beer per capita than anywhere else: 9,000 pints for each man, woman, and child. The locals claim it's the sparkling-clear spring water from the nearby Fichtelgebirge hills that makes their beer so special.

FAMILY **Neuenmarkt.** In this "railway village" near Kulmbach, more than 25 beautifully preserved gleaming locomotives huff and puff in a living railroad museum. Every now and then a nostalgic train will take you to the Brewery Museum in Kulmbach, or you can enjoy a round-trip to Marktschorgast; both trips take you up the very steep "schiefe Ebene" stretch (literally, "slanting level"). The museum also has model trains set up in incredibly detailed replicas of landscapes. ⊠ *Birkenstr. 5, Neuenmarkt* ☎ *09227/5700* ⊕ *www.dampflokmuseum.de* ⊠ *€7* ⊙ *Tues.–Sun. 10–5.*

FAMILY **Plassenburg.** The most impressive Renaissance fortress in the country, it stands on a rise overlooking Kulmbach, a 20-minute hike from the Old Town. The first building here, begun in the mid-12th century, was torched by marauding Bavarians who were eager to put a stop to the ambitions of Duke Albrecht Alcibiades—a man who spent several years murdering, plundering, and pillaging his way through Franconia. His successors built today's castle, starting in about 1560. Externally, there's little to suggest the graceful Renaissance interior, but as you enter the main courtyard the scene changes abruptly. The tiered space of the courtyard is covered with precisely carved figures, medallions, and other intricate ornaments, the whole comprising one of the most remarkable and delicate architectural ensembles in Europe. Inside, the **Deutsches Zinnfigurenmuseum** (Tin Figures Museum), with more than 300,000 miniature statuettes and tin soldiers, holds the largest collection of its kind in the world. The figures are arranged in scenes from all periods of history. During the day you cannot drive up to the castle. There's a shuttle bus that leaves from the main square every half hour from 9 to 6; cost is €2.20. ⊠ *Plassenburg* ☎ *09221/947–505* ⊠ *€4.50* ⊙ *Apr.–Oct., daily 9–6; Nov.–Mar., daily 10–4.*

WHERE TO STAY

$ **Hotel Kronprinz.** This old hotel tucked away in the middle of Kulm-
HOTEL bach's Old Town, right in the shadow of Plassenburg Castle, covers all basic needs, with the help of an extraordinary breakfast buffet. **Pros:**

center of town; excellent cakes in café; 3 nice rooms in annex. **Cons:** plain rooms above café; no elevator. ⑤ *Rooms from: €85* ⊠ *Fischerg. 4–6* ☏ *09221/92180* ⊕ *www.hotel-kulmbach.eu* ⤳ *22 rooms* ⊘ *Closed Dec. 24–29* ⑩ *Breakfast.*

BAYREUTH

24 km (15 miles) south of Kulmbach, 80 km (50 miles) northeast of Nürnberg.

The small town of Bayreuth, pronounced "bye-*roit,*" owes its fame to the music giant Richard Wagner (1813–83). The 19th-century composer, musical revolutionary, ultranationalist, and Nazi poster-child finally settled here after a lifetime of rootless shifting through Europe. Here he built his great theater, the Festspielhaus, as a suitable setting for his grand operas on Germanic mythological themes. The annual Wagner Festival dates to 1876, and brings droves of Wagner fans who push prices sky-high, fill hotels to bursting, and earn themselves much-sought-after social kudos in the process. The festival is held from late July until late August, so unless you plan to visit the town specifically for it, this is the time to stay away.

GETTING HERE AND AROUND

To reach Bayreuth, take the Bayreuth exit off the Nürnberg–Berlin autobahn. It's 1½ hours north of Nürnberg. The train trip is an hour from Nürnberg. In town you can reach most points on foot.

ESSENTIALS

Visitor Information Bayreuth Kongress- und Tourismuszentrale ⊠ *Luitpoldpl. 9* ☏ *0921/88588* ⊕ *www.bayreuth.de.*

EXPLORING

Altes Schloss Eremitage. This palace, 5 km (3 miles) north of Bayreuth on B-85, makes an appealing departure from the sonorous and austere Wagnerian mood of much of the town. It's an early 18th-century palace, built as a summer retreat and remodeled in 1740 by the Margravine Wilhelmine. Although her taste is not much in evidence in the drab exterior, the interior, alive with light and color, displays her guiding hand in every elegant line. The extraordinary **Japanischer Saal** (Japanese Room), filled with Asian treasures and chinoiserie furniture, is the finest room. The park and gardens, partly formal, partly natural, are enjoyable for idle strolling. Fountain displays take place at the two fake grottoes at the top of the hour 10–5 daily. ⊠ *Eremitagestr. 4* ☏ *0921/759–6937* 🎟 *Schloss €4.50, park free* ⊘ *Schloss Apr.–Sept., daily 9–6.*

Brauerei und Büttnerei-Museum (*Brewery and Coopers Museum*). Near the center of town, in the 1887 Maisel Brewery building, this museum reveals the tradition of the brewing trade over the past two centuries with a focus on the Maisel's trade, of course. The brewery operated here until 1981, when its much bigger home was completed next door. ■ **TIP**➔ After the 90-minute tour you can quaff a cool, freshly tapped traditional Bavarian *Weissbier* (wheat beer) in the museum's pub. The pub is also one of a handfull of places to try Maisel's Dampfbier; a delicious steam-brewed ale. ⊠ *Kulmbacherstr. 40* ☏ *0921/401–234* ⊕ *www.maisel.com* 🎟 *€5* ⊘ *Tour daily at 2 pm; individual tours by appointment.*

Markgräfliches Opernhaus (*Margravial Opera House*). In 1745 Margravine Wilhelmine commissioned the Italian architects Guiseppe and Carlo Bibiena to build this rococo jewel, sumptuously decorated in red, gold, and blue. Apollo and the nine Muses cavort across the baroque frescoed ceiling. It was this delicate 500-seat theater that originally drew Wagner to Bayreuth; he felt that it might prove a suitable setting for his own operas. It's a wonderful setting for the concerts and operas of Bayreuth's "other" musical festivals, which the theater hosts throughout the year. You can still visit the Theater despite the ongoing reconstruction. ✉ *Opernstr.* ☎ *0921/759–6922* 💶 *€2.50* ◷ *Apr.–Sept., daily 9–6; Oct.–Mar., daily 10–4. Closed during performances and on rehearsal days.*

Neues Schloss (*New Palace*). This glamorous 18th-century palace was built by the Margravine Wilhelmine, sister of Frederick the Great of Prussia and a woman of enormous energy and decided tastes. Though Wagner is the man most closely associated with Bayreuth, his choice of this setting is largely due to the work of this woman, who lived 100 years before him. Wilhelmine devoured books, wrote plays and operas (which she directed and, of course, acted in), and had buildings constructed, transforming much of the town and bringing it near bankruptcy. Her distinctive touch is evident at the palace, built when a mysterious fire conveniently destroyed parts of the original one. Anyone with a taste for the wilder flights of rococo decoration will love it. Some rooms have been given over to one of Europe's finest collections of faience. ✉ *Ludwigstr. 21* ☎ *0921/759–6921* 💶 *€12* ◷ *Apr.–Sept., daily 9–6; Oct.–Mar., Tues.–Sun. 10–4.*

WAGNER IN BAYREUTH

Festspielhaus (*Festival Theater*). This high temple of the Wagner cult—where performances take place only during the annual Wagner Festival—is surprisingly plain. The spartan look is explained partly by Wagner's desire to achieve perfect acoustics. The wood seats have no upholstering, for example, and the walls are bare. The stage is enormous, capable of holding the huge casts required for Wagner's largest operas. The festival is still meticulously controlled by Wagner's family. ✉ *Festspielhügel 1* ☎ *0921/78780* ⊕ *www.bayreuther-festspiele.de* 💶 *€5* ◷ *Tours Dec.–Oct., Tues.–Sun. at 10, 2, and 3. Closed during rehearsals and on performance days during festival.*

Richard-Wagner-Museum. "Wahnfried," built by Wagner in 1874 and the only house he ever owned, is now the Richard-Wagner-Museum. It's a simple, austere neoclassical building whose name, "peace from madness," was well earned. Wagner lived here with his wife Cosima, daughter of pianist Franz Liszt, and they were both laid to rest here. King Ludwig II of Bavaria, the young and impressionable "Fairy-Tale King" who gave Wagner so much financial support, is remembered in a bust before the entrance. The exhibits, arranged along a well-marked tour through the house, require a great deal of German-language reading, but it's a must for Wagner fans. The original scores of such masterpieces as *Parsifal, Tristan und Isolde, Lohengrin, Der Fliegende Holländer,* and *Götterdämmerung* are on display. You can also see designs for productions of his operas, as well as his piano and

The torch-bearing figure of Apollo on his chariot adorns the Sonnentempel (Sun Temple) of Bayreuth's Neues Schloss.

huge library. A multimedia display lets you watch and listen to various productions of his operas. The little house where Franz Liszt lived and died is right next door and can be visited with your Richard-Wagner-Museum ticket, but be sure to express your interest in advance. It, too, is heavy on the paper, but the last rooms—with pictures, photos, and silhouettes of the master, his students, acolytes, and friends—are well worth the detour. ■ TIP→ **The museum will be closed until 2015, but true loyalists will still want to come to see the outside of the house.** ✉ *Richard-Wagner-Str. 48* ☎ *0921/757–2816* ⊕ *www.wagnermuseum. de* ☽ *Closed until 2015.*

WHERE TO EAT

$ ✕ **Oskar.** A huge glass ceiling gives the large dining room a light atmo-
GERMAN sphere even in winter. In summer, try for a table in the beer garden to enjoy fine Franconian specialties and Continental dishes. The kitchen uses the freshest produce. The room fills up at night and during Sunday brunch, especially if a jazz band is playing in one of the alcoves. ⑤ *Average main: €13* ✉ *Maximilianstr. 33* ☎ *0921/516–0553* ⊕ *www. oskar-bayreuth.de* ▭ *No credit cards.*

$ ✕ **Wolffenzacher.** This self-described "Franconian nostalgic inn" harks
GERMAN back to the days when the local *Wirtshaus* (inn-pub) was the meeting place for everyone from the mayor's scribes to the local carpenters. Beer and hearty traditional food are shared at wooden tables either in the rustic interior or out in the shady beer garden, weather permitting. The hearty Franconian specialties are counterbalanced by a few lighter Mediterranean dishes. ⑤ *Average main: €11* ✉ *Sternenpl. 5* ☎ *0921/64552* ⊕ *www.wolffenzacher.de.*

WAGNER: GERMANY'S TOP ROMANTIC

UNDERSTANDING WAGNER

Born in 1813, Richard Wagner has become modern Germany's most iconic composer. His music, which is best understood in its simple message of national glory and destiny, contributed greatly to the feeling of pan-Germanism that united Germany under the Prussian crown in 1871. However, his overtly nationalistic themes and blatant anti-Semitism also makes his music a bit controversial as it's also connected to the Nazi movement and Adolf Hitler; Hitler adored Wagner and saw him as the embodiment of his own vision for the German people. Wagner's focus on the cult of the leader and the glories of victory are prevalent in his works *Lohengrin* and *Parsifal*. Some of his most famous compositions are the four opera cycle *The Ring of the Nibelung* (aka *Ring Cycle*), *Parsifal*, and *Lohengrin*.

WAGNER TODAY

In 1871 Wagner moved to the city of Bayreuth and began construction of the Festspielhaus, an opera house that would only perform Wagner's operas. The performance space opened its doors in 1876 with a production of *Das Rheingold* and the first full performance of the four-part *Ring Cycle*. The Festspielhaus continues to showcase Wagner's works during the annual Bayreuther Festspiel, a pilgrimage site for die-hard Wagner fans. The waiting list for tickets is years long; it's almost impossible for mere mortals to gain entrance to the holy temple. However, almost all German opera and symphony companies perform Wagner's works throughout the year. The best places to see Wagner's longer works are at Berlin's State Opera; the National Theater in Weimar; the Gewandhaus Orchestra and Opera in Leipzig; and Munich's Bavarian State Opera.

WHERE TO STAY

$$
HOTEL
Fodor's Choice
★

Goldener Anker. No question about it, Bayreuth's grande dame is *the* place to stay; the hotel is right next to the Markgräfliches Opernhaus and has been entertaining composers, singers, conductors, and instrumentalists for hundreds of years. **Pros:** authentic historic setting with all modern amenities; exemplary service; excellent restaurant. **Cons:** no elevator; some rooms are on the small side; restaurant closed Monday and Tuesday. $ *Rooms from: €138* ⊠ *Opernstr. 6* ☎ *0921/65051* ⊕ *www.anker-bayreuth.de* ⇱ *38 rooms, 2 suites* ⊗ *Restaurant closed Mon. and Tues., except during the festival* ⑩ *Breakfast.*

$$
HOTEL

Hotel Lohmühle. The old part of this hotel is in Bayreuth's only half-timber house, a former sawmill by a stream. **Pros:** nice setting with reasonable prices; good food. **Cons:** stairs between hotel and restaurant; front rooms let in traffic noise. $ *Rooms from: €166* ⊠ *Badstr. 37* ☎ *0921/53060* ⊕ *www.hotel-lohmuehle.de* ⇱ *42 rooms* ⊗ *No dinner Sun.* ⑩ *Breakfast.*

NIGHTLIFE AND THE ARTS

Markgräfliches Opernhaus. If you don't get Wagner Festival tickets, console yourself with visits to the exquisite 18th-century Markgräfliches Opernhaus. In May the Fränkische Festwochen (Franconian Festival Weeks) take the stage with works of Wagner, of course, but also Paganini and Mozart. ⊠ *Opernstr.* ☎ *0921/759–6922.*

Wagner Festival. Opera lovers swear that there are few more intense operatic experiences than the annual Wagner Festival in Bayreuth, held July and August. You'll do best if you plan your visit several years in advance. ■ TIP➔ **It is nearly impossible to find a hotel room during the festival: try finding a room in Kronach instead of Bayreuth.**

Bayreuther Festspiele Kartenbüro. For tickets to the Wagner Festival, write to the Bayreuther Festspiele Kartenbüro by the middle of October the year before, at the latest. Be warned: The waiting list is years long, and they only offer tickets by mail or online and will ignore any other inquiries. ☎ *0921/78780* ⊕ *www.bayreuther-festspiele.de*

SHOPPING

Hofgarten Passage. Off Richard-Wagner-Strasse, you'll find one of the fanciest shopping arcades in the region; it's full of smart boutiques selling everything from German high fashion to simple local craftwork. ⊠ *Richard-Wagner-Str. 22.*

BAMBERG

Fodor's Choice ★

65 km (40 miles) west of Bayreuth, 80 km (50 miles) north of Nürnberg.

Few towns in Germany survived the war with as little damage as Bamberg, which is on the Regnitz River. ■ TIP➔ **This former residence of one of Germany's most powerful imperial dynasties is on UNESCO's World Heritage Site list.** Bamberg, originally nothing more than a fortress in the hands of the Babenberg dynasty (later contracted to Bamberg), rose to prominence in the 11th century thanks to the political and economic drive of its most famous offspring, Holy Roman Emperor Heinrich II. He transformed the imperial residence into a flourishing Episcopal city. His cathedral, consecrated in 1237, still dominates the city center. For a short period Heinrich II proclaimed Bamberg the capital of the Holy Roman Empire of the German Nation. Moreover, Bamberg earned fame as the second city to introduce book printing, in 1460.

GETTING HERE AND AROUND

Traveling to Bamberg by train will take about 45 minutes from Nürnberg; from Munich it takes about two hours. Bamberg is a worthwhile five-hour train trip from Berlin. Bamberg's train station is a 30-minute walk from the Altstadt (Old Town). On the A-73 autobahn, Bamberg is two hours from Munich. Everything in town can be reached on foot.

TOURS

In Bamberg, Personenschiffahrt Kropf boats leave daily from March through October beginning at 11 am for short cruises on the Regnitz River and the Main-Donau Canal; the cost is €7.

The Bamberg Tourist Information center offers an audio tour in English for €8.50 for four hours. It also offers brewery and beer-tasting tours of the nine Bamberg breweries.

ESSENTIALS

Boat Tours Personenschiffahrt Kropf ✉ *Kapuzinerstr. 5* ☎ *0951/26679*
⊕ *www.personenschiffahrt-bamberg.de.*

Visitor Information Bamberg Tourismus und Congresservice
✉ *Geyerswörthstr. 5* ☎ *0951/297–6200* ⊕ *www.bamberg.info.*

EXPLORING

Altes Rathaus (*Old Town Hall*). At Bamberg's historic core, the Altes
Rathaus, is tucked snugly on a small island in the Regnitz. To the
west of the river is the so-called Bishops' Town; to the east, Burghers'
Town. The citizens of Bamberg built this rickety, extravagantly decorated building on an artificial island when the Bishop of Bamberg
refused to give the city the land for a town hall. The excellent collection
of porcelain is a sampling of 18th-century styles, from almost sober
Meissens with bucolic Watteau scenes to simple but rare Haguenau
pieces from Alsace and faience from Strasbourg. ✉ *Obere Brücke 1*
☎ *0951/871–871* 🎟 *€4* ◷ *Tues.–Sun. 9:30–4:30.*

QUICK
BITES
Rathaus-Schänke. Before heading up the hill to the main sights in the
Bishops' Town, take a break with coffee, cake, small meals, or cocktails in
the half-timber Rathaus-Schänke. It overlooks the river on the Burghers'
Town side of the Town Hall. ✉ *Obere Brücke 3* ☎ *0951/208–0890*
⊕ *www.rathausschaenke-bamberg.com.*

Diözesanmuseum (*Cathedral Museum*). Directly adjacent to the Bamberg Dom, this museum contains one of many nails and splinters of
wood reputed to be from the cross of Jesus. The "star-spangled" cloak
stitched with gold that was given to Emperor Heinrich II by an Italian
prince is among the finest items displayed. More macabre exhibits in
this rich ecclesiastical collection are the elaborately mounted skulls of
Heinrich and Kunigunde. The building itself was designed by Balthasar
Neumann (1687–1753), the architect of Vierzehnheiligen, and constructed between 1730 and 1733. ✉ *Dompl. 5* ☎ *0951/502–325* 🎟 *€4*
◷ *Tues.–Sun. 10–5; tour in English by appointment.*

Dom (*Cathedral*). Bamberg's great cathedral is a unique building that
tells not only the town's story but that of Germany as well. The first
building here was begun by Heinrich II in 1003, and it was in this partially completed cathedral that he was crowned Holy Roman Emperor
in 1012. In 1237 it was destroyed by fire, and replaced by present
late-Romanesque/early-Gothic building. The dominant features are
the massive towers at each corner. Heading into the dark interior,
you'll find a striking collection of monuments and art treasures. The
most famous piece is the **Bamberger Reiter** (Bamberg Horseman), an
equestrian statue carved—no one knows by whom—around 1230 and
thought to be an allegory of chivalrous virtue or a representation of
King Stephen of Hungary. Compare it with the mass of carved figures
huddled in the tympana above the church portals. In the center of the
nave you'll find another masterpiece, the massive tomb of Heinrich
and his wife, Kunigunde. It's the work of Tilman Riemenschneider.
Pope Clement II is also buried in the cathedral, in an imposing tomb

EATING WELL IN FRANCONIA

Franconia is known for its good and filling food and for its simple and atmospheric *Gasthäuser*. Pork is a staple, served either as *Schweins-braten* (a plain roast) or with *Knödel* (dumplings made from either bread or potatoes). The specialties in Nürnberg, Coburg, and Regensburg are the *Bratwürste*—short, spiced sausages. The Nürnberg variety is known all over Germany; they are even on the menu on the ICE trains. You can have them grilled or heated in a stock of onions and wine (*saurer Zipfel*). Bratwürste are traditionally served in denominations of 3, 6, or 8 with sauerkraut and potato salad or dark bread.

On the sweet side, try the *Dampf-nudel*, a kind of sweet yeast-dough dumpling that is tasty and filling. *Nürnberger Lebkuchen*, a sort of gingerbread eaten at Christmastime, is loved all over Germany. A true purist swears by Elisen Lebkuchen, which are made with no flour. Both Lebkuchen and Bratwürste are protected under German law and are only "legal" when made in or around Nürnberg.

Not to be missed are Franconia's liquid refreshments from both the grape and the grain. Franconian wines, usually white and sold in distinctive flat bottles called *Bocksbeutel*, are renowned for their special bouquet. (Silvaner is the traditional grape.) The region has the largest concentration of local breweries in the world (Bamberg alone has 9, Bayreuth 7), producing a wide range of brews, the most distinctive of which is the dark, smoky *Rauchbier* and the even darker and stronger *Schwärzla*. Then, of course, there is Kulmbach, with the *Doppelbock Kulminator 28*, which takes nine months to brew and has an alcohol content of 12%.

beneath the high altar; he's the only pope buried north of the Alps. ✉ *Dompl.* ☎ *0951/502–330* 🕙 *Nov.–Mar., daily 10–5; Apr.–Oct., daily 10–6. Closed during services.*

Kloster St. Michael (*Monastery of St. Michael*). Once a Benedictine monastery, this structure has been gazing over Bamberg since 1015. After being overwhelmed by so much baroque elsewhere, entering this haven of simplicity can be a relief. The entire choir is intricately carved, but the ceiling is gently decorated with very exact depictions of 578 flowers and healing herbs. The tomb of St. Otto is in a little chapel off the transept, and the stained-glass windows hold symbols of death and transfiguration. The monastery is now used as a home for the aged. One tract, however, was taken over by the **Franconian Brewery Museum,** which exhibits everything that has to do with beer, from the making of malt to recipes. ✉ *Michelsberg 10f* ☎ *0951/53016* 🔖 *Museum €4* 🕙 *Apr.–Oct., Wed.–Sun. 1–5.*

Neue Residenz (*New Residence*). This glittering baroque palace was once the home of the prince-electors. Their plan to extend the immense palace even further is evident at the corner on Obere Karolinenstrasse, where the ashlar bonding was left open to accept another wing. The most memorable room in the palace is the **Kaisersaal** (Throne Room), complete with impressive ceiling frescoes and elaborate stucco. The rose garden behind the Neue Residenz provides an aromatic and romantic spot for a stroll with a view of Bamberg's roof landscape. You have to take a tour to see the Residenz itself, but you can visit the library free of charge at any time during its open hours. ⊠ *Neue Residenz, Dompl. 8* ☎ *0951/955–030* 🖾 *€4.50* ⊘ *Neue Residenz by tour only, Apr.–Sept., daily 9–6; Oct.–Mar., daily 10–4.*

Staatsbibliothek (*State Library*). The Neue Residenz is also home to the Staatsbibliothek. Among the thousands of books and illuminated manuscripts here are the original prayer books belonging to Heinrich II and his wife, a 5th century codex of the Roman historian Livy, and manuscripts by the 16th-century painters Dürer and Cranach. ⊠ *Dompl. 8* ☎ *0951/955–030* ⊕ *www.staatsbibliothek-bamberg.de* 🖾 *Free* ⊘ *Weekdays 9–5, Sat. 9–noon.*

Obere Pfarre (*Upper Parish*). Bamberg's wealthy burghers built no fewer than 50 churches. The Church of Our Lady, known simply as the Obere Pfarre, dates back to around 1325, and is unusual because the exterior is entirely Gothic, while the interior is heavily baroque. The grand choir, which lacks any windows, was added much later. An odd square-ish box tops the church tower; this watchman's post was placed there to keep the tower smaller than the neighboring cathedral, thus avoiding a medieval scandal. Note the slanted floor, which allowed crowds of pilgrims to see the object of their veneration, a 14th-century Madonna. Don't miss the *Ascension of Mary* by Tintoretto at the rear of the church. Around Christmas, the Obere Pfarre is the site of the city's greatest Nativity scene. Avoid the church during services, unless you're worshipping. ⊠ *Untere Seelg.* ⊘ *Daily 7–7.*

NEAR BAMBERG

Kloster Banz (*Banz Abbey*). This abbey, which some call the "holy mountain of Bavaria," proudly crowns the west bank of the Main north of Bamberg. There had been a monastery here since 1069, but the present buildings—now a political-seminar center and think tank—date from the end of the 17th century. The highlight of the complex is the **Klosterkirche** (Abbey Church), the work of architect Leonard Dientzenhofer and his brother, the stuccoist Johann Dientzenhofer (1663–1726). Balthasar Neumann later contributed a good deal of work. Concerts are occasionally held in the church, including some by members of the renowned Bamberger Symphoniker. To get to Banz from Vierzehnheiligen, drive south to Unnersdorf, where you can cross the river. ⊠ *Kloster-Banz-Str. 1, Bad Staffelstein* ☎ *09573/7311* ⊘ *May–Oct., daily 9–5; Nov.–Apr., daily 9–noon. Call to request a tour.*

Fodor's Choice ★ **Vierzehnheiligen.** In Bad Staffelstein, on the east side of the Main north of Bamberg, is a tall, elegant yellow-sandstone edifice whose interior represents one of the great examples of rococo decoration. The church was built by Balthasar Neumann (architect of the Residenz at Würzburg) between 1743 and 1772 to commemorate a vision of Christ and 14 saints—*vierzehn Heiligen*—that appeared to a shepherd in 1445. The interior, known as "God's Ballroom," is supported by 14 columns. In the middle of the church is the Gnadenaltar (Mercy Altar) featuring the 14 saints. Thanks to clever play with light, light colors, and fanciful gold-and-blue trimmings, the interior seems to be in perpetual motion. Guided tours of the church are given on request; a donation is expected. On Saturday afternoon and all day Sunday the road leading to the church is closed and you have to walk the last half mile. ⊠ *Vierzehnheiligen 2, 36 km (22 miles) north of Bamberg via Hwy. 173, Bad Staffelstein* ☎ *09571/95080* ⊕ *www.vierzehnheiligen.de* ☉ *Mar.–Oct., daily 7–6; Nov.–Feb., daily 8–5.*

WHERE TO EAT

$
GERMAN ✕ **Bischofsmühle.** It doesn't always have to be beer in Bamberg. The old mill, its grinding wheel providing a sonorous backdrop for patrons, specializes in wines from Franconia and elsewhere. The menu offers Franconian specialties such as the French-derived *Böfflamott,* or beef a la mode. ⑤ *Average main: €11* ⊠ *Geyerswörthstr. 4* ☎ *0951/27570* ⊕ *www.bischofsmuehle-mueller.de* ⊟ *No credit cards* ☉ *Closed Wed.*

$
GERMAN ✕ **Klosterbräu.** This massive old stone-and-half-timber house has been standing since 1533, making it Bamberg's oldest brewpub. Regulars nurse a dark, smoky beer called *Schwärzla* near the big stove—though the best beer is the Klosterbraun. If you like the brew, you can buy a 5-liter bottle (called a *Siphon*) as well as other bottled beers and the requisite beer steins at the counter. The cuisine is basic, robust, filling, and tasty, with such items as a bowl of beans with a slab of smoked pork, or marinated pork kidneys with boiled potatoes. ⑤ *Average main: €8* ⊠ *Obere Mühlbrücke* ☎ *0951/52265* ⊕ *www.klosterbraeu. de* ⊟ *No credit cards.*

$
GERMAN ✕ **Schlenkerla.** Set in the middle of the old town, this tavern has been serving beer inside an ancient half-timbered house since 1405. The fare, atmosphere, and partons are the definition of traditional Bamberg. Be sure to try the *Bamberger Zwiebel,* a local onion stuffed with pork. The real reason to come here is to try the *Aecht Schenkerla Rauchbier,* a beer brewed with smoked malt. This *Rauchbier* (smoked beer) is served from huge wooden barrels and tastes like liquid ham—it's an aquired taste, but one worth sampling. ⑤ *Average main: €10* ⊠ *Dominikanerstr. 6* ☎ *951/56050* ⊕ *www.schlenkerla.de.*

WHERE TO STAY

$$
B&B/INN
Fodor's Choice
★ 🏨 **Hotel-Restaurant St. Nepomuk.** This half-timber house seems to float over the river Regnitz; many of the comfortable rooms have quite a view of the water and the Old Town Hall on its island. **Pros:** nice view; an elegant dining room with excellent food. **Cons:** hotel on a pedestrian-only street; in need of some renovation; public garage 200 meters away. ⑤ *Rooms from: €130* ⊠ *Obere Mühlbrücke 9* ☎ *0951/98420* ⊕ *www. hotel-nepomuk.de* ⤴ *47 rooms* ❖ *Breakfast.*

$$
HOTEL 🏨 **Romantik Hotel Weinhaus Messerschmitt.** This comfortable hotel has spacious and luxurious rooms, some with exposed beams and many of them lighted by chandeliers. **Pros:** elegant dining room with good food; variety of rooms to choose from. **Cons:** older property; front rooms are noisy; expensive. ⑤ *Rooms from: €145* ⊠ *Langestr. 41* ☎ *0951/297–800* ⊕ *www.hotel-messerschmitt.de* ⤴ *67 rooms* ❖ *Breakfast.*

5

Bamberg's Altes Rathaus is perched precariously on an artificial island in the middle of the Regnitz River.

THE ARTS

Capella Antiqua Bambergensis. The city's first-class choir, Capella Antiqua Bambergensis, concentrates on ancient music. They play at several venues in town. ⊕ *www.capella-antiqua.de*.

Dom. Throughout summer organ concerts are given Saturday at noon in the Dom. Call for program details and tickets to all cultural events. ⊠ *Dompl.* ☎ *0951/297–6200*.

Hoffmann Theater. Opera and operettas are performed here from September through July. ⊠ *E.-T.-A.-Hoffmann-Pl. 1* ☎ *0951/873–030*.

Sinfonie an der Regnitz. This fine riverside concert hall, is home to Bamberg's own world-class resident symphony orchestra, the *Bamberger Symphoniker*. ⊠ *Muss-Str. 1* ☎ *0951/964–7200*.

SHOPPING

■ TIP→ If you happen to be traveling around Christmastime, make sure you keep an eye out for crèches, a Bamberg specialty. Check the tourism website (⊕ *www.bamberg.info*) for the locations of nativity scenes and descriptions.

Café am Dom. For an edible souvenir, take home handmade chocolates like the only-in-Bamberg Rauchbier truffles made with Schlenkerla smoked beer. This café also has a roomy seating area to take a load off while you nibble a delicious pastry. ⊠ *Ringleinsg. 2* ☎ *0951/519–290*.

Magnus Klee. This shop sells nativity scenes, called *Krippen* in German, of all different shapes and sizes, including wood-carved and with fabric clothes. ⊠ *Obstmarkt 2* ☎ *0951/26037*.

Vinothek im Sand. Head to this wine store for Franconian wine as well as a sampling of Bamberg's specialty beers. ⊠ *Obere Sandstr. 8* ☏ *0151/5473–8779.*

EN ROUTE

From Bamberg you can take either the fast autobahn (A-73) south to Nürnberg or the parallel country road (B-4) that follows the Main-Donau Canal (running parallel to the Regnitz River at this point) and joins A-73 just under 25 km (15 miles) later at Forchheim-Nord.

Levi-Strauss Museum. Eighteen kilometers (11 miles) south of Bamberg in the village of Buttenheim is a little blue-and-white half-timber house where Löb Strauss was born—in great poverty—in 1829. Take the audio tour of the Levi-Strauss Museum and learn how Löb emigrated to the United States, changed his name to Levi, and became the first name in denim. The stonewashed color of the house's beams, by the way, is the original 17th-century color. ⊠ *Marktstr. 33, Buttenheim* ☏ *09545/442–602* ⊕ *www.levi-strauss-museum.de* ≤ *€2.60* ⊙ *Tues. and Thurs. 2–6, weekends 11–5 and by appointment.*

NÜRNBERG (NUREMBERG)

With a recorded history stretching back to 1050, the main city in Bavarian is among the most historic of all of Germany; the core of the Old Town, through which the Pegnitz River flows, is still surrounded by its original medieval walls. Nürnberg has always taken a leading role in German affairs. It was here, for example, that the Holy Roman emperors traditionally held the first Diet, or convention of the estates, of their incumbency. And it was here, too, that Hitler staged the most grandiose Nazi rallies; later, this was the site of the Allies' war trials, where top-ranking Nazis were charged with—and almost without exception convicted of—crimes against humanity. The rebuilding of Nürnberg after the war was virtually a miracle, considering the 90% destruction of the Old Town. As a major intersection on the medieval trade routes, Nürnberg became a wealthy town where the arts and sciences flowered. Albrecht Dürer (1471–1528), the first indisputable genius of the Renaissance in Germany, was born here. He married in 1509 and bought a house in the city where he lived and worked for the rest of his life. Other leading Nürnberg artists of the Renaissance include painter Michael Wolgemut (a teacher of Dürer), stonecutter Adam Kraft, and the brass founder Peter Vischer. The tradition of the Meistersinger also flourished here in the 16th century, thanks to the high standard set by the local cobbler Hans Sachs (1494–1576). The Meistersinger were poets and musicians who turned songwriting into a special craft, with a wealth of rules and regulations. They were celebrated three centuries later by Wagner in his *Meistersinger von Nürnberg.*

The Thirty Years' War and the shift to sea routes for transportation led to the city's long decline, which ended only in the early 19th century when the first railroad opened in Nürnberg. Among a great host of inventions associated with the city, the most significant are the pocket watch, gun casting, the clarinet, and the geographic globe. Among Nürnberg's famous products are *Lebkuchen* (gingerbread of sorts) and Faber-Castell pencils.

GETTING HERE AND AROUND

Nürnberg is centrally located and well connected, an hour north of Munich and two hours east of Frankfurt by train. Five autobahns meet here: A-3 Düsseldorf–Passau, A-6 Mannheim–Nürnberg, A-9 Potzdam–München, A-73 Coburg–Feucht, and B-8 (four lane near Nürnberg) Würzburg–Regensburg. Most places in the Old Town may be reached on foot.

English-language bus tours of the city are conducted April–October and in December, daily at 9:30, starting at the Mauthalle, Hallplatz 2. The 2½-hour tour costs €15. For more information, call ☎ *0911/202–290.* An English-language tour on foot through the Old Town is conducted daily May–October at 1; it departs from the tourist-information office on the Hauptmarkt. The tour costs €9 (plus entrance to the Kaiserburg €2). City tours are also conducted in brightly painted trolley buses April–October, daily at one-hour intervals beginning at 10 at the Schöner Brunnen. The cost is €6. For more information call the Nürnberg tourist office.

TIMING

You'll need a full day to walk around Nürnberg's Old Town, two if you wish to take more time at its fascinating museums and churches. Most of the major sights are within a few minutes' walk of each other. The Kaiserburg is a must-visit on any trip to Nürnberg. Plan at least half a day for the Germanisches National-almuseum, which is just inside the city walls near the main station. Add another half a day to visit the Nazi Party Rally Grounds.

FESTIVALS

By far the most famous local festival is the **Christkindlesmarkt** (Christmas Market), an enormous pre-Christmas fair that runs from the Friday before Advent to Christmas Eve. One of the highlights is the candle procession, held every second Thursday of the market season, during which thousands of children parade through the city streets.

Christkindlesmarkt. Perhaps the most famous Christmas Market in Germany, the Nürnberg Christkindlesmarkt sits on the town's cobblestoned main square beneath the wonderful Frauenkirche. Renowned for its food, particularly Nürnberger Bratwurstchen, tasty little pork and marjoram sausages, and Lebkuchen, gingerbread made with cinnamon and honey, the market is also famed for its little figures made out of prunes called Nürnberger Zwetschgenmännla or "Nürnberg Prune People." ⊠ *Hauptmarkt* ⊕ *www.christkindlesmarkt.de* ⊙ *Nov. 25–Dec. 24, Mon.–Thurs. 9:30–8, Fri. and Sat. 9:30–10, Sun. 10:30–8, Christmas Eve 9:30–2.*

Kaiserburg. From May through July classical music concerts are given in the Rittersaal of the Kaiserburg. ☎ *0911/244–6590.*

Sommer in Nürnberg. Nürnberg has an annual summer festival, Sommer in Nürnberg, from May through July, with more than 200 events. Its international organ festival in June and July is regarded as Europe's finest.

ESSENTIALS

Visitor Information Nürnberg Congress- und Tourismus-Zentrale
⊠ *Frauentorgraben 3* ☎ *0911/23360* ⊕ *www.nuernberg.de.*

NÜRNBERG'S OLD TOWN

Walls, finished in 1452, surround Nürnberg's Old Town. Year-round floodlighting adds to the brooding romance of their moats, sturdy gateways, and watchtowers.

TOP ATTRACTIONS

Albrecht-Dürer-Haus (*Albrecht Dürer House*). The great painter Albrecht Dürer lived here from 1509 until his death in 1528. This beautifully preserved late-medieval house is typical of the prosperous merchants' homes that once filled Nürnberg. Dürer, who enriched German art with Italianate elements, was more than a painter. He raised the woodcut, a notoriously difficult medium, to new heights of technical sophistication, combining great skill with a haunting, immensely detailed drawing

APFELWEIBLA

As you peruse the shops in Bamberg's Altstadt, you may notice an applelike face that adorns jewelry and housewares, the *Apfelweibla*. A replica of the Apfelweibla, a whimsical doorknob depicting an elderly woman's face, can be found at Eisgrube 14. The original doorknob is on display at the Museum of History at Domplatz. The doorknob inspired E. T. A. Hoffmann's novella *The Golden Pot.* It's said that rubbing the Apfelweibla will bring you good luck.

5

style and complex, allegorical subject matter, while earning a good living at the same time. A number of original prints adorn the walls, and printing techniques using the old press are demonstrated in the studio. An excellent opportunity to find out about life in the house of Dürer is the Saturday 2 pm tour with a guide role-playing Agnes Dürer, the artist's wife. ⊠ *Albrecht-Dürer-Str. 39* ☏ *0911/231–2568* ⊠ *€5, with tour €7.50* ⊗ *Tues., Wed., and Fri.–Sun. 10–5; Thurs. 10–8; guided tour in English Sat. at 2.*

> ### UNDERGROUND NUREMBERG
>
> Beer aficionados can get a deeper look at Nürnberg's brewing history with a tour into the cellars where beer was made and stored since the 1300s. The tour, offered by Underground Nuremberg, costs €7, which includes a beer tasting, but is only offered in German. English-language group tours are available by appointment, see ⊕ *www. felsengaenge-nuernberg.de.*

Fodor's Choice ★ **Germanisches Nationalmuseum** (*German National Museum*). You could spend days visiting this vast museum, which showcases the country's cultural and scientific achievements, ethnic background, and history. It's the largest of its kind in Germany, and perhaps the best arranged. The museum is in a former Carthusian monastery, complete with cloisters and monastic outbuildings. The extensions, however, are modern. The exhibition begins outside, with the tall, sleek pillars of the Strasse der Menschenrechte (Street of Human Rights), designed by Israeli artist Dani Karavan. Thirty columns are inscribed with the articles from the Universal Declaration of Human Rights. One highlight is the superb collection of Renaissance German paintings (with Dürer, Cranach, and Altdorfer well represented). Others may prefer the exquisite medieval ecclesiastical exhibits—manuscripts, altarpieces, statuary, stained glass, jewel-encrusted reliquaries—the collections of arms and armor, the scientific instruments, or the toys. ⊠ *Kartäuserg 1* ☏ *0911/13310* ⊕ *www.gnm. de* ⊠ *€8* ⊗ *Tues. and Thurs.–Sun. 10–6, Wed. 10–9.*

Fodor's Choice ★ **Kaiserburg** (*Imperial Castle*). The city's main attraction is a grand yet playful collection of buildings standing just inside the city walls; it was once the residence of the Holy Roman Emperor. The complex comprises three separate groups. The oldest, dating from around 1050, is the **Burggrafenburg** (Castellan's Castle), with a craggy old pentagonal tower and the bailiff's house. It stands in the center of the complex. To the east is the **Kaiserstallung** (Imperial Stables), built in the 15th century as a granary and now serving as a youth hostel. The real interest of this vast complex of ancient buildings, however, centers on the westernmost part of the fortress, which begins at the **Sinwell Turm** (Sinwell Tower). The **Kaiserburg Museum** is here, a subsidiary of the Germanisches Nationalmuseum that displays ancient armors and has exhibits relating to horsemanship in the imperial era and to the history of the fortress. This section of the castle also has a wonderful Romanesque **Doppelkappelle** (Double Chapel). The upper part—richer, larger, and more ornate than the lower chapel—was where the emperor and his family worshipped. Also visit the **Rittersaal** (Knights' Hall) and the **Kaisersaal** (Throne Room). Their heavy oak beams, painted ceilings,

Outside the Germanisches Nationalmuseum is the "Way of Human Rights," an outdoor sculpture consisting of 30 columns inscribed with the articles from the Universal Declaration of Human Rights.

and sparse interiors have changed little since they were built in the 15th century. ⊠ *Burgstr.* ☎ *0911/2446–59115* ⊕ *www.kaiserburg-nuernberg. de* 🎫*€7* ☉ *Apr.–Sept., daily 9–6; Oct.–Mar., daily 10–4.*

Neues Museum (*New Museum*). Anything but medieval, this museum is devoted to international design since 1945. The collection, supplemented by changing exhibitions, is in a slick, modern edifice that achieves the perfect synthesis between old and new. It's mostly built of traditional pink-sandstone ashlars, while the facade is a flowing, transparent composition of glass. The interior is a work of art in itself—cool stone, with a ramp that slowly spirals up to the gallery. Extraordinary things await, including a Joseph Beuys installation (*Ausfegen,* or *Sweep-out*) and *Avalanche* by François Morellet, a striking collection of violet, argon-gas-filled fluorescent tubes. The café-restaurant adjoining the museum contains modern art, silver-wrapped candies, and video projections. ⊠ *Luitpoldstr. 5* ☎ *0911/ 240–200* ⊕ *www.nmn.de* 🎫*€4* ☉ *Tues.–Fri. 10–8, weekends 10–6.*

WORTH NOTING

Altes Rathaus (*Old Town Hall*). This ancient building on Rathausplatz abuts the rear of St. Sebaldus Kirche; it was erected in 1332, destroyed in World War II, and subsequently reconstructed. Its intact medieval dungeons, consisting of 12 small rooms and one large torture chamber called the **Lochgefängnis** (or the Hole), provide insight into the gruesome applications of medieval law. **Gänsemännchenbrunnen** (Gooseman's Fountain) faces the Altes Rathaus. This lovely Renaissance bronze fountain, cast in 1550, is a work of rare elegance and great technical sophistication. ⊠ *Rathauspl. 2* ☎ *0911/231–2690* 🎫*€3.50, minimum of 5 people for tours* ☉ *Tues.–Sun. 10–4.*

Frauenkirche (*Church of Our Lady*). The fine late-Gothic Frauenkirche was built in 1350, with the approval of Holy Roman Emperor Charles IV, on the site of a synagogue that was burned down during the1349 pogrom. The modern tabernacle beneath the main altar was designed to look like a Torah scroll as a memorial to that despicable act. The church's main attraction is the **Männleinlaufen**, a clock dating from 1509, which is set in its facade. It's one of those colorful mechanical marvels at which Germans have long excelled. ▮▮TIP➔ Every day at noon the seven electors of the Holy Roman Empire glide out of the clock to bow to Emperor Charles IV before sliding back under cover. It's worth scheduling your morning to catch the display. ⊠ *Hauptmarkt* ⊘ *Mon.–Sat. 9–6, Sun. 12:30–6.*

TOURING TIPS

Information: The tourist office at the Hauptbahnhof, the main train station, has maps and brochures.

Scenic spots: The ramparts of the Kaiserburg offer a spectacular view over this medieval gem of a town.

Scenic spots: Where the Königstrasse crosses the Pegnitz River is one of the most photogenic points of the city.

Snacks: Look to the restaurants and bars around the Hauptmarkt for refreshment.

Hauptmarkt (*Main Market*). Nürnberg's central market square was once the city's Jewish Quarter. When the people of Nürnberg petitioned their emperor, Charles IV, for a big central market, the emperor was in desperate need of money and, above all, political support. The Jewish Quarter was the preferred site, but as the official protector of the Jewish people, the emperor could not just openly take away their property. Instead, in 1349 he instigated a pogrom that left the Jewish Quarter in flames and more than 500 dead. He then razed the ruins and resettled the remaining Jews.

Towering over the northwestern corner of the Hauptmarkt, **Schöner Brunnen** (Beautiful Fountain) looks as though it should be on the summit of some lofty cathedral. Carved around the year 1400, the elegant 60-foot-high Gothic fountain is adorned with 40 figures arranged in tiers—prophets, saints, local noblemen, sundry electors of the Holy Roman Empire, and one or two strays such as Julius Caesar and Alexander the Great. ▮▮TIP➔ A gold ring is set into the railing surrounding the fountain, reportedly placed there by an apprentice carver. Touching it is said to bring good luck. A market still operates in the Hauptmarkt. Its colorful stands are piled high with produce, fruit, bread, homemade cheeses and sausages, sweets, and anything else you might need for a snack or picnic. It's here that the Christkindlesmarkt is held. ⊠ *Hauptmarkt.*

Jüdisches Museum Franken. The everyday life of the Jewish community in Franconia and Fürth is examined in this Jewish museum: books, seder plates, old statutes, and children's toys are among the exhibits. Among the most famous members of the Fürth community was Henry Kissinger, born here in 1923. Changing exhibitions relate to contemporary Jewish life in Germany, and in the basement is the *Mikwe*, the ritual bath, which was used by the family who lived here centuries ago. In the museum you will also find a good Jewish bookshop as well as a nice small café. A subsidiary to the museum, which houses special exhibitions, is in the former synagogue in nearby Schnaittach. To get to the museum from Nürnberg, you can take the U1 U-bahn to the Rathaus stop. ⊠ *Königstr. 89, 10 km (6 miles) west of Nürnberg, Fürth* ☎ *0911/770–577* ⊠ *€3* ☾ *Wed.–Sun. 10–5, Tues. 10–8.*

Museum für Kommunikation (*Communication Museum*). Two museums have been amalgamated under a single roof here: the German Railway Museum and the Museum of Communication—in short, museums about how people stay connected. The first train to run in Germany did so on December 7, 1835, from Nürnberg to nearby Fürth. A model of the epochal train is here, along with a series of original 19th- and early-20th-century trains and stagecoaches. Philatelists will want to check out some of the 40,000-odd stamps in the extensive exhibits on the German postal system. You can also find out about the history of sending messages—from old coaches to optical fiber networks. ⊠ *Lessingstr. 6* ☎ *0911/219–2428* ⊕ *www.mfk-nuernberg.de* ⊠ *€5* ☾ *Tues.–Sun. 10–5.*

St. Lorenz Kirche (*St. Laurence Church*). In a city with several striking churches, St. Lorenz is considered by many to be the most beautiful. Construction began around 1250 and was completed in about 1477; it later became a Lutheran church. Two towers flank the main entrance, which is covered with a forest of carvings. In the lofty interior, note the works by sculptors Adam Kraft and Veit Stoss: Kraft's great stone tabernacle, to the left of the altar, and Stoss's *Annunciation,* at the east end of the nave, are their finest works. There are many other carvings throughout the building, testimony to the artistic wealth of late-medieval Nürnberg. ⊠ *Lorenzer Pl.* ☾ *Mon.–Sat. 9–5, Sun. noon–4.*

St. Sebaldus Kirche (*St. Sebaldus Church*). Although St. Sebaldus lacks the quantity of art treasures found in its rival St. Lorenz, its nave and choir are among the purest examples of Gothic ecclesiastical architecture in Germany: elegant, tall, and airy. Veit Stoss carved the crucifixion group at the east end of the nave, while the elaborate bronze shrine containing the remains of St. Sebaldus himself was cast by Peter Vischer and his five sons around 1520. Not to be missed is the **Sebaldus Chörlein,** an ornate Gothic oriel that was added to the Sebaldus parish house in 1361 (the original is in the Germanisches Nationalmuseum). ⊠ *Albrecht-Dürer-Pl. 1* ☎ *0911/214–2500* ☾ *Daily 10–5.*

FAMILY **Spielzeugmuseum** (*Toy Museum*). Young and old are captivated by this playful museum, which has a few exhibits dating from the Renaissance; most, however, are from the 19th century. Simple dolls vie with mechanical toys of extraordinary complexity, such as a wooden Ferris wheel from the Ore Mountains adorned with little colored lights. The top floor displays Barbies and intricate Lego constructions. ⊠ *Karlstr. 13–15* ☎ *0911/231–3164* ⊠ *€5* ☾ *Tues.–Sun. 10–5.*

Climb to the top of Nürnberg's Kaiserburg (Imperial Castle) for wonderful views of the city.

Stadtmuseum (*City Museum*). This city history museum is in the Fembo-haus, a dignified patrician dwelling completed in 1598. It's one of the finest Renaissance mansions in Nürnberg. Each room explores another aspect of Nürnberg history, from crafts to gastronomy. The 50-minute multivision show provides a comprehensive look at the city's long history. ⊠ *Burgstr. 15* ☏ *0911/231–2595* 🎫 *€5* ⊘ *Tues.–Sun. 10–5.*

NÜRNBERG'S NAZI SIGHTS

Documentation Centre Nazi Party Rally Grounds. On the eastern outskirts of the city, the **Ausstellung Faszination und Gewalt** (Fascination and Terror Exhibition) documents the political, social, and architectural history of the Nazi Party. The sobering museum helps illuminate the whys and hows of Hitler's rise to power during the unstable period after World War I and the end of the democratic Weimar Republic. This is one of the few museums that documents how the Third Reich's propaganda machine influenced the masses. The 19-room exhibition is within a horseshoe-shape Congressional Hall that was intended to harbor a crowd of 50,000; the Nazis never completed it. The Nazis did make famous use of the nearby Zeppelin Field, the enormous parade ground where Hitler addressed his largest Nazi rallies. Today it sometimes shakes to the amplified beat of pop concerts. ▦ **TIP→ To get to the Documentation Center, take Tram No. 9 from the city center to the Doku-Zentrum stop.** ⊠ *Bayernstr. 110* ☏ *0911/231–5666* ⊕ *www.museen.nuernberg.de* 🎫 *€5* ⊘ *Museum daily 9–6, weekends 10–6.*

Nürnberg Trials Memorial. Nazi leaders and German organizations were put on trial here in 1945 and 1946 during the first international war-crimes trials, conducted by the victorious Allied forces of World War II. The trials were held in the Landgericht (Regional Court) in court-room No. 600 and resulted in 11 death sentences, among other convic-tions. The guided tours are in German, but English-language material is available. ▉TIP➔ Take the U1 subway line to Bärenschanze. ⊠ *Bä-renschanzstr. 72* ☎ *0911/231–8411* ⊕ *www.memorium-nuremberg.de* 🎫 *€5* ⊘ *Wed.–Mon. 10–6.*

WHERE TO EAT

$$$$
GERMAN
Fodor'sChoice
★

✕**Essigbrätlein.** The oldest restaurant in Nürnberg is also the top restau-rant in the city and among the best in Germany. Built in 1550, it was originally used as a meeting place for wine merchants. Today its tiny but elegant period interior caters to the distinguishing gourmet with a taste for special spice mixes (owner Andrée Köthe's hobby). The menu changes daily, but the four-course menu can't be beat. Don't be put off if the restaurant looks closed, just ring the bell and a friendly receptionist will help you. ⑤ *Average main: €28* ⊠ *Weinmarkt 3* ☎ *0911/225–131* ⌖ *Reservations essential* ⊘ *Closed Sun., Mon., and late Aug.*

$
GERMAN

✕**Hausbrauerei Altstadthof.** For traditional regional food, such as Nürn-berg bratwurst, head to this atmospheric brewery. You can see the copper kettles where the brewery's organic *Rotbier* (red beer) is made. For a bit of shopping after lunch, the brewery store sells a multitude of beer-related products such as beer vinegar, brandy, and soap. Located above a network of deep, dark cellars where beer was once brewed and stored, this brewery is the meeting point for cellar tours (⊕ *www.historische-felsengaenge.de*), which are offered in English on Sunday at 11:30 am and cost €5.50. ⑤ *Average main: €15* ⊠ *Bergstr. 19–21* ☎ *911/244–9859.*

$
GERMAN

✕**Heilig-Geist-Spital.** Heavy wood furnishings and a choice of more than 100 wines make this huge, 650-year-old wine tavern—built as the refec-tory of the city hospital—a popular spot. Try for a table in one of the alcoves, where you can see the river below you as you eat your seasonal fresh fish. The menu also includes grilled pork chops, panfried pota-toes, and other Franconian dishes. ⑤ *Average main: €13* ⊠ *Spitalg. 16* ☎ *0911/221–761* ⊕ *www.heilig-geist-spital.de.*

$
GERMAN
FAMILY

✕**Historische Bratwurst-Küche Zum Gulden Stern.** The city council meets here to decide the official size and weight of the Nürnberg Bratwürste, so this should be your first stop to try the ubiquitous Nürnberg delicacy. The sausages have to be small enough to fit through a medieval keyhole, which in earlier days enabled pub owners to sell them after hours. It's a fitting venue for such a decision, given that this house, built in 1375, holds the oldest bratwurst restaurant in the world. The famous Nürn-berg bratwursts are always freshly roasted on a beech-wood fire; the boiled variation is prepared in a tasty stock of Franconian wine and onions. ⑤ *Average main: €9* ⊠ *Zirkelschmiedg. 26* ☎ *0911/205–9288* ⊕ *www.bratwurstkueche.de.*

5

WHERE TO STAY

$ 🏨 **Agneshof.** This comfortable hotel is north of the Old Town between
HOTEL   the fortress and St. Sebaldus Church. **Pros:** many rooms have great views
of the castle; warm yet professional welcome; lobby and rooms modern
yet tasteful. **Cons:** deluxe rooms overpriced; parking and hotel access
difficult; no restaurant. ⑤ *Rooms from: €77 ⊠ Agnesg. 10 ☎ 0911/214–
440 ⊕ www.agneshof-nuernberg.de ⬎ 72 rooms ⃝ Breakfast.*

$ 🏨 **Burghotel Stammhaus.** At this quaint hotel the accommodations are
HOTEL   small but cozy and the service is familial and friendly. **Pros:** great location in the city center; comfortable; pool; good value. **Cons:** small
rooms; tiny lobby; parking not easy; service sometimes too casual.
⑤ *Rooms from: €59 ⊠ Schildg. 14 ☎ 0911/203–040 ⊕ www.invite-
hotels.de ⬎ 22 rooms ⃝ Breakfast.*

$$ 🏨 **Hotel Drei Raben.** Legends and tales of Nürnberg form the leitmo-
HOTEL   tif running through the designer rooms at this hotel. **Pros:** free drink
at the reception desk; designer rooms; valet parking; Wi-Fi. **Cons:**
neon-lighted bar isn't relaxing; no restaurant. ⑤ *Rooms from: €150
⊠ Königstr. 63 ☎ 0911/274–380 ⊕ www.hotel-drei-raben.de ⬎ 25
rooms ⃝ Breakfast.*

$$ 🏨 **Hotel-Weinhaus Steichele.** An 18th-century bakery has been skill-
HOTEL   fully converted into this hotel, which has been managed by the same
family for four generations. **Pros:** comfortable; good location; good
restaurants. **Cons:** small rooms and lobby; some rooms show their
age. ⑤ *Rooms from: €109 ⊠ Knorrstr. 2–8 ☎ 0911/202–280 ⊕ www.
steichele.de ⬎ 56 rooms ⃝ Breakfast.*

$$ 🏨 **Le Meridien Grand Hotel.** Across the square from the central railway
HOTEL   station is this stately building with the calling card "Grand Hotel" arch-
ing over its entranceway. **Pros:** luxury property; impressive lobby; excel-
lent food; valet parking. **Cons:** expensive, with additional fees for every
possible contingency; Germanic efficiency at reception desk; difficult to
reach the hotel with big bags from the main station as you have to go
through an underpass with stairs. ⑤ *Rooms from: €140 ⊠ Bahnhofstr.
1 ☎ 0911/23220 ⊕ www.nuremberg.lemeridien.com ⬎ 186 rooms, 5
suites ⃝ Multiple meal plans.*

SHOPPING

Handwerkerhof. Step into this "medieval mall," in the tower at the Old
Town gate (Am Königstor) opposite the main railway station, and you'll
think you're back in the Middle Ages. Craftspeople are busy at work
turning out the kind of handiwork that has been produced in Nürnberg
for centuries: pewter, glassware, basketwork, wood carvings, and, of
course, toys. The Lebkuchen specialist **Lebkuchen-Schmidt** has a shop
here as well. ⊠ *Am Königstor ⊙ Mid-Mar.–Dec. 24, weekdays 10–6:30,
Sat. 10–4; Dec. 1–24 also open Sun. 10–6:30.*

THE GERMAN DANUBE

For many people, the sound of the Danube River (Donau in German) is the melody of *The Blue Danube,* the waltz written by Austrian Johann Strauss. The famous 2,988-km-long (1,800-mile-long) river, which is actually a pale green, originates in Germany's Black Forest and flows through 10 countries. In Germany it's mostly a rather unremarkable stream as it passes through cities such as Ulm on its southeasterly route. However, that changes at Kelheim, just west of Regensburg, where the Main-Donau Canal (completed in 1992) brings big river barges all the way from the North Sea. The river becomes sizable in Regensburg, where the ancient Steinerne Brücke (Stone Bridge) needs 15 spans of 30 to 48 feet each to bridge the water. Here everything from small pleasure boats to cruise liners joins the commercial traffic. In the university town of Passau, two more rivers join the waters of the Danube before Europe's longest river continues into Austria.

5

REGENSBURG

85 km (52 miles) southeast of Nürnberg, 120 km (74 miles) northwest of Munich.

Few visitors to Bavaria venture this far off the well-trodden tourist trails, and even Germans are surprised when they discover medieval Regensburg. ▦TIP➜ The town escaped World War II with no major damage, and it is one of the best-preserved medieval cities in Germany.

Regensburg's story begins with the Celts around 500 BC. In AD 179, as an original marble inscription in the Historisches Museum proclaims, it became a Roman military post called Castra Regina. The Porta Praetoria, or gateway, built by the Romans, remains in the Old Town, and whenever you see huge ashlars incorporated into buildings, you are looking at bits of the old Roman settlement. When Bavarian tribes migrated to the area in the 6th century, they occupied what remained of the Roman town and, apparently on the basis of its Latin name, called it Regensburg. Anglo-Saxon missionaries led by St. Boniface in 739 made the town a bishopric before heading down the Danube to convert the heathen in even more far-flung lands. Charlemagne, first of the Holy Roman emperors, arrived at the end of the 8th century and incorporated Regensburg into his burgeoning domain. Regensburg benefited from the fact that the Danube wasn't navigable to the west, and thus it was able to control trade as goods traveled between Germany and Central Europe.

By the Middle Ages Regensburg had become a political, economic, and intellectual center. For many centuries it was the most important city in southeast Germany, serving as the seat of the Perpetual Imperial Diet from 1663 until 1806, when Napoléon ordered the dismantling of the Holy Roman Empire.

Today the ancient and hallowed walls of Regensburg continue to buzz with life. Students from the university fill the restaurants and pubs, and locals tend to their daily shopping and run errands in the inner city, where small shops and stores have managed to keep international consumer chains out.

GETTING HERE AND AROUND

Regensburg is at the intersection of the autobahns 3 and 93. It is an hour away from Nürnberg and two hours from Munich by train. Regensburg is compact; its Old Town center is about 1 square mile. All of its attractions lie on the south side of the Danube, so you won't have to cross it more than once—and then only to admire the city from the north bank.

English-language guided walking tours are conducted May through September and during the Christmas markets, Wednesday and Saturday at 1:30. They cost €6 and begin at the tourist office.

In Regensburg all boats depart from the Steinerne Brücke. The most popular excursions are boat trips to Ludwig I's imposing Greek-style Doric temple of Walhalla. There are daily sailings to Walhalla from Easter through October. The round trip costs €10.50 and takes three hours. Don't bother with the trip upriver from Regensburg to Kelheim.

TIMING

Although the Old Town is quite small, you can easily spend half a day strolling through its narrow streets. Any serious tour of Regensburg includes an unusually large number of places of worship. If your spirits wilt at the thought of inspecting them all, you should at least see the Dom, famous for its Domspatzen (boys' choir—the literal translation is "cathedral sparrows"). You'll need about another two hours or more to explore Schloss Emmeram and St. Emmeram church.

ESSENTIALS

Boat Tours Personenschifffahrt Klinger ⊠ *Thundorfstr. 1* ☎ *0941/55359* ⊕ *www.schifffahrtklinger.de.*

Visitor Information Regensburg Tourismus ⊠ *Altes Rathaus, Rathauspl. 4* ☎ *0941/507–4410* ⊕ *www.regensburg.de.*

EXPLORING

TOP ATTRACTIONS

Altes Rathaus (*Old Town Hall*). The picture-book complex of medieval half-timber buildings, with windows large and small and flowers in tubs, is one of the best-preserved town halls in the country, as well as one of the most historically important. It was here, in the imposing Gothic **Reichssaal** (Imperial Hall), that the Perpetual Imperial Diet met from 1663 to 1806. This parliament of sorts consisted of the emperor, the electors (seven or eight), the princes (about 50), and the burghers, who assembled to discuss and determine the affairs of the far-reaching German lands of the Holy Roman Empire. The hall is sumptuously appointed with tapestries, flags, and heraldic designs. Note the wood ceiling, built in 1408, and the different elevations for the various estates. The Reichssaal is occasionally used for concerts. The neighboring **Ratssaal** (Council Room) is where the electors met for their consultations. The cellar holds the city's torture chamber; the **Fragstatt** (Questioning Room); and the execution room, called the **Armesünderstübchen** (Poor Sinners' Room). Any prisoner who withstood three degrees of questioning without confessing was considered innocent and released—which tells you something about medieval notions of justice. ⊠ *Rathauspl.* ☎ *0941/507–4411* 🖾 *€8* ⊗ *Guided tours in English Apr.–Oct., daily at 3.*

5

QUICK
BITES

Prinzess Confiserie Café. Just across the square from the Altes Rathaus is the Prinzess Confiserie Café, Germany's oldest coffeehouse, which first opened its doors in 1686. The homemade chocolates are highly recommended, as are the rich cakes. ⊠ *Rathauspl. 2* ☎ *0941/595–310.*

Brückturm Museum (*Bridge Tower Museum*). With its tiny windows, weathered tiles, and pink plaster, this 17th-century tower stands at the south end of the Steinerne Brücke. The tower displays a host of items relating to the construction and history of the old bridge. It also offers a gorgeous view of the Regensburg roof landscape. The brooding building with a massive roof to the left of the Brückturm is an old salt warehouse. ⊠ *Steinerne Brücke, Weisse-Lamm-G. 1* ☎ *0941/507–5888* 🖾 *€2* ⊘ *Apr.–Oct., daily 10–5; call ahead for tours in English.*

Dom St. Peter (*St. Peter's Cathedral*). Regensburg's transcendent cathedral, modeled on the airy, powerful lines of French Gothic architecture, is something of a rarity this far south in Germany. Begun in the 13th century, it stands on the site of a much earlier Carolingian church. Remarkably, the cathedral can hold 6,000 people, three times the population of Regensburg when building began. Construction dragged on for almost 600 years, until Ludwig I of Bavaria, then ruler of Regensburg, finally had the towers built. These had to be replaced in the mid-1950s. Behind the Dom is a little workshop where a team of 15 stonecutters is busy full-time in summer re-cutting and restoring parts of the cathedral.

Before heading into the Dom, take time to admire the intricate and frothy carvings of its facade. Inside, the glowing 14th-century stained glass in the choir and the exquisitely detailed statues of the archangel Gabriel and the Virgin in the crossing (the intersection of the nave and the transepts) are among the church's outstanding features.

Be sure to visit the **Kreuzgang** (Cloisters), reached via the garden. There you'll find a small octagonal chapel, the Allerheiligenkapelle (All Saints' Chapel), a Romanesque building that is all sturdy grace and massive walls, a work by Italian masons from the mid-12th century. You can barely make out the faded remains of stylized 11th-century frescoes on its ancient walls. The equally ancient shell of St. Stephan's Church, the cloisters, the chapel, and the Alter Dom (Old Cathedral), are included in the Cathedral tour. ⊠ *Dompl. 50* ☏ *0941/586–5500* ⚑ *Tour €3, in German only (call ahead for tours in English)* ⊘ *Cathedral tour daily at 2.*

Domschatzmuseum (*Cathedral Museum*). This museum contains valuable treasures going back to the 11th century. Some of the vestments and the monstrances, which are fine examples of eight centuries' worth of the goldsmith's trade, are still used during special services. The entrance is in the nave. ⊠ *Dompl.* ☏ *0941/597–2530* ⚑ *€2* ⊘ *Apr.–Oct., Tues.–Sat. 10–5, Sun. noon–5; Dec.–Mar., Fri. and Sat. 10–4, Sun. noon–4.*

Historisches Museum (*Historical Museum*). The municipal museum vividly relates the cultural history of Regensburg. It's one of the highlights of the city, both for its unusual and beautiful setting—a former Gothic monastery—and for its wide-ranging collections, from Roman artifacts to Renaissance tapestries and remains from Regensburg's 16th-century Jewish ghetto. The most significant exhibits are the paintings by Albrecht Altdorfer (1480–1538), a native of Regensburg and, along with Cranach, Grünewald, and Dürer, one of the leading painters of the German Renaissance. ⊠ *Dachaupl. 2–4* ☏ *0941/507–2448* ⊕ *www. museen-regensburg.de* ⚑ *€5* ⊘ *Tues.–Sun. noon–4.*

Schloss Emmeram (*Emmeram Palace*). Formerly a Benedictine monastery, this is the ancestral home of the princely Thurn und Taxis family, which made its fame and fortune after being granted the right to carry official and private mail throughout the empire and Spain by Emperor Maximilian I (1493–1519) and by Philip I, the king of Spain, who ruled during the same period. Their business extended over the centuries into the Low Countries (Holland, Belgium, and Luxembourg), Hungary, and Italy. The horn that still symbolizes the post office in several European countries comes from the Thurn und Taxis coat of arms. In its heyday Schloss Emmeram was heavily featured in the gossip columns thanks to the wild parties and somewhat extravagant lifestyle of the young dowager Princess Gloria von Thurn und Taxis. After the death of her husband, Prince Johannes, in 1990, she had to

Regensburg's Dom St. Peter is an excellent example of the French Gothic style.

auction off belongings in order to pay inheritance taxes. Ultimately a deal was cut, allowing her to keep many of the palace's treasures as long they were put on display.

The **Thurn und Taxis Palace,** with its splendid ballroom and throne room, allows you to witness the setting of courtly life in the 19th century. A visit usually includes the fine **Kreuzgang** of the former Benedictine abbey of St. Emmeram. ▥TIP➔ The palace can only be visited by taking the guided tour. The items in the **Thurn und Taxis Museum,** which is part of the Bavarian National Museum in Munich, have been carefully selected for their fine craftsmanship—be it dueling pistols, a plain marshal's staff, a boudoir, or a snuffbox. The palace's **Marstallmuseum** (former royal stables) holds the family's coaches and carriages as well as related items. ⊠ *Emmeramspl. 5* ☎ *0941/504–8133* ⊕ *www.thurnundtaxis.de* ⊠ *Museum €4.50, palace and cloisters €13.50* ☉ *Museum: Apr.–Oct., daily 1–5. Tours of palace and cloisters: premium tour (90 mins), daily at 10:30, 12:30, 2:30, and 4:30; compact tour (60 mins), daily at 11:30 and 2:30.*

Fodor's Choice **Steinerne Brücke** (*Stone Bridge*). This impressive old bridge resting on ★ massive pontoons is Regensburg's most celebrated sight. It was completed in 1146 and was rightfully considered a miraculous piece of engineering at the time. As the only crossing point over the Danube for miles, it effectively cemented Regensburg's control over trade. The significance of the little statue on the bridge is a mystery, but the figure seems to be a witness to the legendary rivalry between the master builders of the bridge and those of the Dom. ⊠ *Steinerne Brücke.*

WORTH NOTING

Alte Kapelle (*Old Chapel*). Erected by the Calolingian order in the 9th century, the Old Chapel's dowdy exterior hides joyous rococo treasures within—extravagant concoctions of sinuous gilt stucco, rich marble, and giddy frescoes, the whole illuminated by light pouring in from the upper windows. ⊠ *Alter Kornmarkt 8* ☉ *Daily 9–dusk.*

Karmelitenkirche (*Church of the Carmelites*). This lovely church, in the baroque style from crypt to cupola, stands next to the Alte Kapelle. It has a finely decorated facade designed by the 17th-century Italian master Carlo Lurago. ⊠ *Alter Kornmarkt.*

Neupfarrplatz. This oversize square was once the heart of the Jewish ghetto. Hard economic times and superstition led to their eviction by decree in 1519. While the synagogue was being torn down, one worker survived a very bad fall. A church was promptly built to celebrate the miracle, and before long a pilgrimage began. The **Neupfarrkirche** (New Parish Church) was built as well to accommodate the flow of pilgrims. During the Reformation, the Parish Church was given to the Protestants, hence its bare-bones interior. In the late 1990s, excavation work (for the power company) on the square uncovered well-kept cellars and, to the west of the church, the old synagogue, including the foundations of its Romanesque predecessor. Archaeologists salvaged the few items they could from the old stones (including a stash of 684 gold coins) and, not knowing what to do with the sea of foundations, ultimately carefully reburied them. Recovered items were carefully restored and are on exhibit in the Historisches Museum. Only one small underground area to the south of the church, the **Document,** accommodates viewing of the foundations. In a former cellar, surrounded by the original walls, visitors can watch a short video reconstructing life in the old Jewish ghetto. Over the old synagogue, the Israeli artist Dani Karavan designed a stylized plaza where people can sit and meet. Call the educational institution VHS for a tour of the Document (reservations are requested). For spontaneous visits, tickets are available at Tabak Götz on the western side of the square, at Neupfarrplatz 3. ⊠ *Neupfarrpl.* ☎ *0941/507–2433 for tours led by VHS* ⊕ *www.vhs-regensburg.de* ✉ *Document €5* ☉ *Church daily 9–dusk, document tour Thurs.–Sat. at 2:30.*

NEED A BREAK?

Dampfnudel Uli. A Dampfnudel is a steamed, often sweet but sometimes savory, yeast-dough dumpling that is tasty and filling. The best in Bavaria can be had at this small establishment in a former chapel. The decoration is incredibly eclectic, from Bavarian crafts to an autographed portrait of Ronald Reagan. ⊠ *Watmarkt 4* ☎ *0941/53297* ☉ *Tues.–Fri. 10–6, Sat. 10–4.*

Niedermünster. This 12th-century building with a baroque interior was originally the church of a community of nuns, all of them from noble families. ⊠ *Alter Kornmarkt 5.*

Porta Praetoria. The rough-hewn former gate to the old Roman camp, built in AD 179, is one of the most interesting relics of Roman Regensburg. Look through the grille on its east side to see a section of the original Roman road, about 10 feet below today's street level. ⊠ *North side of Alter Kornmarkt, Unter den Schwibbögen.*

The Golden Gate Bridge may be better known today, but the 12th-century Steinerne Brücke (Stone Bridge) was its match in terms of engineering ingenuity and importance in its day.

St. Emmeram. The family church of the Thurn und Taxis family stands across from their ancestral palace, the Schloss Emmeram. The foundations of the church date to the 7th and 8th centuries. A richly decorated baroque interior was added in 1730 by the Asam brothers. St. Emmeram contains the graves of the 7th-century martyred Regensburg bishop Emmeram and the 10th-century saint Wolfgang. ⊠ *Emmeramspl. 3* ☎ *0941/51030* ⊘ *Mon.–Thurs. and Sat. 10–4:30, Fri. 1–4:30, Sun. noon–4:30.*

St. Kassian. Regensburg's oldest church was founded in the 8th century. Don't be fooled by its plain exterior; inside, it's filled with ornate rococo decoration. ⊠ *St.-Kassianpl. 1* ⊘ *Daily 9–5:30.*

NEAR REGENSBURG

Weltenburg Abbey (*Abbey Church of Sts. George and Martin*). Roughly 25 km [15 miles] southwest of Regensburg you'll find the great Weltenburg Benedictine Abbey perched on the bank of the Danube River. The most dramatic approach to the abbey is by boat from Kelheim, 10 km (6 miles) downstream. On the stunning ride the boat winds between towering limestone cliffs that rise straight up from the tree-lined riverbanks. The abbey, constructed between 1716 and 1718, is commonly regarded as the masterpiece of the brothers Cosmas Damian and Egid Quirin Asam, two leading baroque architects and decorators of Bavaria. Their extraordinary composition of painted figures whirling on the ceiling, lavish and brilliantly polished marble, highly wrought statuary, and stucco figures dancing in rhythmic arabesques across the curving walls is the epitome of Bavarian baroque. Note especially the bronze equestrian statue of St. George above the high altar, reaching down imperiously with his flamelike, twisted gilt sword to dispatch the winged dragon at his feet. In Kelheim there are two boat companies that offer trips to Kloster Weltenburg every 30 minutes in summer. You cannot miss the landing stages and the huge parking lot. ▥**TIP→ No Bavarian monastary is complete without a brewery, and Kloster Weltenburg's is well worth visiting.** ⊠ *Asamstr. 32, Kelheim* ☉ *Daily 9–dusk.*

Walhalla. Walhalla (11 km [7 miles] east of Regensburg) is an excursion you won't want to miss, especially if you have an interest in the wilder expressions of growing 19th-century German nationalism. Walhalla— a name resonant with Nordic mythology—was where the god Odin received the souls of dead heroes. Ludwig I erected this monumental temple in 1840 to honor important Germans from ages past. In keeping with the neoclassic style of the time, the Greek-style Doric temple is actually a copy of the Parthenon in Athens. The expanses of costly marble are evidence of both the financial resources and the craftsmanship at Ludwig's command. Walhalla may be kitschy, but the fantastic view it affords over the Danube and the wide countryside is definitely worth a look.

A boat ride from the Steinerne Brücke in Regensburg is the best way to go. On the return trip, you can steer the huge boat about half a mile, and, for €5 extra, you can earn an "Honorary Danube Boat Captain" certificate. Kids and grown-ups love it (⇨ *See Getting Here and Around, above*). To get to the temple from the river, you'll have to climb 358 marble steps.

To drive to it, take the Danube Valley country road (unnumbered) east from Regensburg 8 km (5 miles) to Donaustauf. The Walhalla temple is 1 km (½ mile) outside the village and well signposted. ⊠ *Walhalla-Str. 48, Donaustauf* ⊕ *www.walhalla-regensburg.de.*

WHERE TO EAT

$ ✕ **Café Felix.** A modern bilevel café and bar, Felix offers everything from
CAFÉ   sandwiches to steaks, and buzzes with activity from breakfast until the early hours. Light from an arty chandelier and torchlike fixtures bounces off the many large framed mirrors. The crowd tends to be young. ⑤ *Average main: €9* ⊠ *Fröhliche-Türkenstr. 6* ☎ *0941/59059* ⊕ *www.cafefelix.de* ⊟ *No credit cards.*

$ ✕ **Historische Wurstküche.** At the world's oldest, and possibly smallest,
GERMAN   bratwurst grill, succulent Regensburger sausages—the best in town— are prepared right before your eyes on an open beech-wood charcoal grill. If you want to eat them inside in the tiny dining room, you'll have to squeeze past the cook to get there. On the walls—outside and in—are plaques recording the levels the river reached in over a century of floods that temporarily interrupted service. ⑤ *Average main: €7* ⊠ *Thundorferstr. 3, just by stone bridge* ☎ *0941/466–210* ⊟ *No credit cards.*

$ ✕ **Leerer Beutel.** The "Empty Sack" serves excellent international cui-
ECLECTIC   sine—from antipasti to solid pork roast—is served in a pleasant vaulted room supported by massive rough-hewn beams. The restaurant is in a huge warehouse that's also a venue for concerts, exhibitions, and film screenings, making it a good place to start or end an evening. ⑤ *Average main: €13* ⊠ *Bertoldstr. 9* ☎ *0941/58997.*

WHERE TO STAY

$ **Am Peterstor.** The clean and basic rooms of this popular hotel in
HOTEL the heart of the Old Town are a solid value. **Pros:** low prices; good
location. **Cons:** spartan rooms; no restaurant or bar; no phones in
rooms; breakfast extra. $ *Rooms from: €48* ⊠ *Fröhliche-Türken-Str. 12*
☎ *0941/54545* ⊕ *www.hotel-am-peterstor.de* ⤴ *36 rooms* ⏀ *No meals.*

$ **Hotel Münchner Hof.** This little hotel provides top service at a good
HOTEL price with Regensburg at your feet. **Pros:** some rooms with historic
touch; center of town; nice little lobby. **Cons:** entrance on narrow street;
difficult parking. $ *Rooms from: €98* ⊠ *Tändlerg. 9* ☎ *0941/58440*
⊕ *www.muenchner-hof.de* ⤴ *53 rooms* ⏀ *Multiple meal plans.*

$ **Hôtel Orphée.** It's difficult to choose from among the very spacious
HOTEL rooms at the three different properties of this establishment—the
Fodor's Choice Grand Hotel Orphée; the Petit Hotel Orphée on the next street; and
★ the Country Manor Orphée on the other side of the river about 2 km
(1 mile) away. **Pros:** very tastefully renovated; excellent restaurant; center of town. **Cons:** difficult parking; front rooms are noisy. $ *Rooms
from: €100* ⊠ *Grand Hôtel Orphee, Untere Bachg. 8* ☎ *0941/596–020*
⊕ *www.hotel-orphee.de* ⤴ *56 rooms* ⏀ *Multiple meal plans.*

$$ **Hotel-Restaurant Bischofshof am Dom.** This is one of Germany's most
HOTEL historic hostelries, a former bishop's palace where you can sleep in
an apartment that includes part of a Roman gateway. **Pros:** historic
building; nonsmoking rooms only; nice courtyard beer garden. **Cons:**
nonsmoking rooms only; restaurant not up to hotel's standards.
$ *Rooms from: €147* ⊠ *Krauterermarkt 3* ☎ *0941/58460* ⊕ *www.*
hotel-bischofshof.de ⤴ *55 rooms, 4 suites* ⏀ *Multiple meal plans.*

$ **Kaiserhof am Dom.** Renaissance windows punctuate the green facade
HOTEL of this historic city mansion, but the rooms are 20th-century mod-
ern. **Pros:** front rooms have a terrific view; historic breakfast room.
Cons: front rooms are noisy; no restaurant or bar. $ *Rooms from: €95*
⊠ *Kramg. 10–12* ☎ *0941/585–350* ⊕ *www.kaiserhof-am-dom.de* ⤴ *30*
rooms ⊙ *Closed Dec. 21–Jan. 8* ⏀ *Breakfast.*

SHOPPING

The winding alleyways of the Altstadt are packed with boutiques, ate-
liers, jewelers, and other small shops offering a vast array of arts and
crafts. You may also want to visit the Neupfarrplatz market (Monday
through Saturday 9–4), where you can buy regional specialties such
as *Radi* (juicy radish roots), which locals wash down with a glass of
wheat beer.

NIGHTLIFE AND THE ARTS

Regensburg offers a range of musical experiences, though none so mov-
ing as a choral performance at the cathedral. ■**TIP**➜ **Listening to the
Regensburger Domspatzen, the boys' choir at the cathedral, can be a
remarkable experience, and it's worth scheduling your visit to the city
to hear them. The best sung Mass is held on Sunday at 9 am.** If you're
around in summer, look out for the Citizens Festival (Bürgerfest) and
the Bavarian Jazz Festival (Bayerisches Jazzfest ⊕ *www.bayernjazz.de*)
in July, both in the Old Town.

The kind of friendly, mixed nightlife that has become hard to find in some cities is alive and well in this small university city in the many *Kneipen,* combination bars and restaurants, such as the Leerer Beutel.

PASSAU

137 km (86 miles) southeast of Regensburg, 179 km (111 miles) northeast of Munich.

Flanking the borders of Austria and the Czech Republic, Passau dates back more than 2,500 years. Originally settled by the Celts, then by the Romans, Passau later passed into the possession of prince-bishops whose domains stretched into present-day Hungary. At its height, the Passau episcopate was the largest in the entire Holy Roman Empire.

Passau's location is truly unique. Nowhere else in the world do three rivers—the Ilz from the north, the Danube from the west, and the Inn from the south—meet. Wedged between the Inn and the Danube, the Old Town is a maze of narrow cobblestone streets lined with beautifully preserved burgher and patrician houses and riddled with churches. Many streets have been closed to traffic making the Old Town a fun and mysterious place to explore.

GETTING HERE AND AROUND

Passau is on the A-3 autobahn from Regensburg to Vienna. It's an hour from Regensburg and about four hours from Vienna by train.

TOURS

The Passau tourist office leads tours May through October at 10:30 and 2:30 on weekdays and at 2:30 on Sunday; November through April the tours are held weekdays at noon. Tours start at the entrance to the cathedral. A one-hour tour costs €4.

In Passau cruises on the three rivers begin and end at the Danube jetties on Fritz-Schäffer Promenade. Donauschifffahrt Wurm + Köck runs eight ships.

TIMING

Passau can be toured leisurely in the course of one day. Try to visit the Dom at noon to hear a recital on the world's largest organ. Early morning is the best time to catch the light falling from the east on the Old Town walls and the confluence of the three rivers.

FESTIVALS

Christkindlmarkt. Passau's Christmas fair is the biggest and most spectacular of the Bavarian Forest. It's held in front of Dom St. Stephan from late November until just before Christmas. ⊠ *Dompl.*

Europäische Wochen (*European Weeks*). Passau is the cultural center of Lower Bavaria. Its Europäische Wochen festival—featuring everything from opera to pantomime—is a major event on the European music calendar. The festival runs from June to July and is held in venues all over the city. For program details and tickets for the Europäische Wochen, register on the website. ⊠ *Dr.-Hans-Kapfinger-Str. 22* ⊕ *www.ew-passau.de.*

ESSENTIALS

Boat Tours Donauschifffahrt Wurm + Köck ☎ *0851/929–292* ⊕ *www.donauschiffahrt.de.*

Visitor Information Tourist-Information Passau ⊠ *Rathauspl. 3* ☎ *0851/955–980* ⊕ *www.passau.de.*

EXPLORING

TOP ATTRACTIONS

Fodor'sChoice
★

Dom St. Stephan (*St. Stephan's Cathedral*). The cathedral rises majestically on the highest point of the earliest-settled part of the city. A baptismal church stood here in the 6th century. Two hundred years later, when Passau became a bishop's seat, the first basilica was built. It was dedicated to St. Stephan and became the original mother church of St. Stephan's Cathedral in Vienna. A fire reduced the medieval basilica to ruins in 1662; it was then rebuilt by Italian master architect Carlo Lurago. What you see today is the largest baroque basilica north of the Alps, complete with an octagonal dome and flanking towers. Little in its marble- and stucco-encrusted interior reminds you of Germany, and much proclaims the exuberance of Rome. Beneath the dome is the largest church organ assembly in the world. Built between 1924 and 1928 and enlarged in 1979–80, it claims no fewer than 17,774 pipes and 233 stops. The church also houses the most powerful bell chimes in southern Germany. ⊠ *Dompl.* ☎ *0851/3930* 🖼 *Concerts midday €4, evening €8* ⊘ *Daily 6:30–10:45 and 11:30–6. Tours: May–Oct., weekdays at 12:30; Nov.–Apr., weekdays at noon.*

Domplatz (*Cathedral Square*). This large square in front of the Dom is bordered by sturdy 17th- and 18th-century buildings, including the **Alte Residenz**, the former bishop's palace and now a courthouse. The neoclassical statue at the center is Bavarian king Maximilian I, who watches over the Christmas Market in December. ✉ *Dompl.*

Domschatz- und Diözesanmuseum (*Cathedral Treasury and Diocesan Museum*). The cathedral museum houses one of Bavaria's largest collections of religious treasures, the legacy of Passau's rich episcopal history. The museum is part of the **Neue Residenz**, which has a stately baroque entrance opening onto a magnificent staircase—a scintillating study in marble, fresco, and stucco. ✉ *Residenzpl.* 💳 *€1.50* 🕐 *May–Oct., Mon.–Sat. 10–4.*

Veste Oberhaus (*Upper House Stronghold*). The powerful fortress and summer castle commissioned by Bishop Ulrich II in 1219 looks over Passau from an impregnable site on the other side of the river, opposite the Rathaus. Today the Veste Oberhaus is Passau's most important museum, containing exhibits that illustrate the city's 2,000-year history. ▮TIP➔ From the terrace of its café-restaurant (open Easter–October), there's a magnificent view of Passau and the convergence of the three rivers. ✉ *Oberhaus 125* ☎ *0851/493–3512* 💳 *Museum €5* 🕐 *May–Oct., weekdays 9–5, weekends 10–6* 🚌 *Bus (€5) from Rathauspl. to museum Apr.–Nov., daily every ½ hr 10:30–5.*

WORTH NOTING

Glasmuseum (*Glass Museum*). The world's most comprehensive collection of European glass is housed in the lovely Hotel Wilder Mann. The history of Central Europe's glassmaking is captured in 30,000 items, from baroque to art deco, spread over 35 rooms. ✉ *Höllg. 1* ☎ *0851/35071* 💳 *€7* 🕐 *Daily 1–6.*

Rathaus. Passau's 14th-century town hall sits like a Venetian merchant's house on a small square fronting the Danube. It was the home of a wealthy German merchant before being declared the seat of city government after a 1298 uprising. Two assembly rooms have wall paintings depicting scenes from local history and legend, including the (fictional) arrival in the city of Siegfried's fair Kriemhild, from the Nibelungen fable. ▮TIP➔ The Rathaus tower has Bavaria's largest glockenspiel, which plays daily at 10:30, 2, and 7:25, with an additional performance at 3:30 on Saturday. ✉ *Rathauspl.* ☎ *0851/3960* 💳 *€1.50* 🕐 *Apr.–Oct. and late Dec.–early Jan., daily 10–4.*

Römermuseum Kastell Boiotro (*Roman Museum*). While excavating a 17th-century pilgrimage church, archaeologists uncovered a stout Roman fortress with five defense towers and walls more than 12 feet thick. The Roman citadel Boiotro was discovered on a hill known as the Mariahilfberg on the south bank of the river Inn, with its Roman well still plentiful and fresh. Pottery, lead figures, and other artifacts from the area are housed in this museum at the edge of the site. ✉ *Ledererg. 43* ☎ *0851/34769* 💳 *€4* 🕐 *Mar.–Nov., Tues.–Sun. 10–4.*

WHERE TO EAT

$$
EUROPEAN
✕ **Gasthaus zur blauen Donau.** Passau's esteemed chef Richard Kerscher turned this old house with thick walls and recessed windows into a simple but stylish restaurant. The first-floor dining room has a commanding view of the Danube. His delicacies are all based on traditional German recipes. ⑤ *Average main: €17* ✉ *Höllg. 14* ☎ *0851/490–8660* 🚫 *No credit cards.*

$
GERMAN
✕ **Hacklberger Bräustüberl.** Shaded by magnificent old trees, locals sit in this famous brewery's enormous beer garden (seating more than 1,000), sipping a Hacklberger and tucking into a plate of sausages. In winter they simply move to the wood-panel interior, where beer has been on tap from the brewery next door since 1618. ⑤ *Average main: €11* ✉ *Bräuhauspl. 7* ☎ *0851/58382* ⊕ *www.hacklbergers.de.*

$
GERMAN
✕ **Heilig-Geist-Stiftsschenke.** For atmospheric dining this 14th-century monastery-turned-wine-cellar is a must. In summer eat beneath chestnut trees; in winter seek out the warmth of the vaulted, dark-paneled dining rooms. The wines—made in Austria from grapes from the Spitalkirche Heiliger Geist vineyards—are excellent and suit all seasons. The fish comes from the Stift's own ponds. ⑤ *Average main: €14* ✉ *Heilig-Geist-G. 4* ☎ *0851/2607* ⊕ *www.stiftskeller-passau.de* ⊗ *Closed Wed. and last 3 wks in Jan.*

$
GERMAN
✕ **Peschel Terrasse.** The beer you sip on the high, sunny terrace overlooking the Danube is brought fresh from Peschl's own brewery below, which, along with this traditional Bavarian restaurant, has been in the same family since 1855. ⑤ *Average main: €11* ✉ *Rosstränke 4* ☎ *0851/2489* ⊕ *www.peschl-terrasse.de.*

WHERE TO STAY

$$
HOTEL
🏨 **Hotel König.** Though built in 1984, the König blends successfully with the graceful Italian-style buildings alongside the elegant Danube waterfront. **Pros:** some rooms with an impressive view of the Danube; spacious rooms. **Cons:** no restaurant; uninspired bathrooms; some small rooms. ⑤ *Rooms from: €119* ✉ *Untere Donaulände 1* ☎ *0851/3850* ⊕ *www.hotel-koenig.de* 🛏 *61 rooms* ⑩ *Breakfast.*

$
HOTEL
🏨 **Hotel Weisser Hase.** The "White Rabbit" began accommodating travelers in the early 16th century but is thoroughly modernized. **Pros:** good, central location; friendly staff; great breakfast. **Cons:** street noise in the early morning; no a/c. ⑤ *Rooms from: €89* ✉ *Heiliggeistgasse 1* ☎ *0851/92110* ⊕ *www.weisser-hase.de* 🛏 *108 rooms, 1 suite* ⊗ *Closed Jan.–mid-Feb.* ⑩ *Multiple meal plans.*

$$
HOTEL
🏨 **Hotel Wilder Mann.** Passau's most historic hotel dates from the 11th century and is near the ancient town hall on the waterfront market square. **Pros:** luxurious suites; center of town; some rooms with nice view of the river; others are a good value. **Cons:** some rooms in need of updating; some face bell tower; no restaurant or bar. ⑤ *Rooms from: €120* ✉ *Am Rathauspl. 1* ☎ *0851/35071* ⊕ *www.wilder-mann.com* 🛏 *49 rooms, 5 suites* ⑩ *Breakfast.*

$
HOTEL
🏨 **Schloss Ort.** This 13th-century castle's large rooms have views of the Inn River, which flows beneath the hotel's stout walls. **Pros:** great views; nice garden; good restaurant. **Cons:** old linens; thin walls; not in the center of town. ⑤ *Rooms from: €68* ✉ *Ort 11* ☎ *0851/34072* ⊕ *www.schlosshotel-passau.de* 🛏 *18 rooms* ⑩ *Breakfast.*

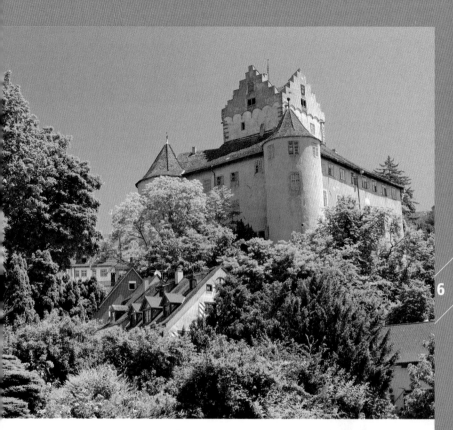

THE BODENSEE

WELCOME TO THE BODENSEE

TOP REASONS TO GO

★ **Zeppelin Museum, Friedrichshafen:** Step inside the gracious passenger rooms of the airship, and you may question whether the air transport of today, though undeniably bigger and faster, is a real improvement.

★ **Altes Schloss in Meersburg:** Explore the oldest continuously inhabited castle in Germany, from the sinister dungeons to the imposing knights' hall.

★ **Schloss Salem, near Überlingen:** The castle itself has plenty to see, with furnished rooms, stables, gardens, and museums.

★ **Wallfahrtskirche Birnau, near Überlingen:** A vineyard slopes down from this pilgrimage church to Schloss Maurach on the lakeshore. The scene inside the church is a riot of color and embellishment.

★ **Mainau Island:** More than a million tulips and narcissi grace the flower island in spring—later they're followed by rhododendrons and azaleas, roses, and dahlias.

1 The Northern Shore. A dozen charming little villages and towns line the northern shore of the lake. In good weather there's a wonderful view across the water to the Swiss mountains.

2 The Upper Swabian Baroque Road. Nearly every village has its own baroque treasure, from the small village church to the mighty Basilica Weingarten. The more miles between you and the Bodensee, the easier it is on your wallet, which may be reason enough to venture to this region.

3 Around the Bodanrück Peninsula. Konstanz is the biggest city on the international lakeshore, situated on the Bodanrück Peninsula and separated from the northern shore by a few miles of water. Konstanz survived WWII unscathed by leaving its lights burning every night, so the Allied bomber

GETTING ORIENTED

The Bodensee (Lake Constance) is off the beaten path for visitors from overseas and from other parts of Europe. If you venture here, you can be pretty sure you won't meet anyone else from back home. Even the Swiss and the Austrians, who own part of the shore of the Bodensee, tend to vacation elsewhere. For Germans, however, it's a favorite summer vacation spot, so it's wise to reserve rooms in advance.

6

pilots could not distinguish it from the neighboring Swiss city of Kreuzlingen. The small towns of the "Untersee" (Lower Lake), as this part of the Bodensee is called, have a more rural atmosphere than those of the northern shore.

BIKING THE BODENSEE

The best way to experience the Bodensee area is by bike. In as little as three days, you can cross the borders of three nations. The largely flat landscape makes this cycle tour suitable for all ages and fitness levels.

(above and upper right) Cyclists on the banks of the Bodensee (lower right) You can take in the sights from the seat of your bike.

You could start and finish anywhere, but this three-day tour circumnavigates the entire lake. Book a room in Meersburg or Konstanz for the first night; in Arbon, Switzerland, for the second; and in Lindau for the third. Store your baggage, bringing with you only what you can comfortably carry on your back or in panniers (don't forget your bathing suit). A sign displaying a bicyclist with a blue back wheel will be your guide through all three countries. Much of the route follows dedicated bike paths—some lakeside, some farther away. However, you'll occasionally find yourself riding along the road, so a helmet is recommended, although it's not required by law. At some points, you might like to disregard this official route in favor of a more scenic path. Follow your instincts—even without the signs or a map, the water is an easy point of reference.

—Leonie Adeane

BIKING ESSENTIALS

You can rent a bike as a guest at many hotels, at some tourist offices, from bike shops, and from bicycle tour operators. Biking maps are available from newspaper stands, bookshops, and tourist offices, and you can leave your baggage in the long-term storage available at the train stations in Konstanz, Überlingen, Friedrichshafen, and Lindau. You can cut across the lake on a ferry at numerous points.

Departing Lindau, head west along the lake toward Wasserburg, 5 km (3 miles) away. Continue on through meadows, marshland, and orchards, passing charming villages like Nonnenhorn and Langenargen—9 km (5½ miles) from Wasserburg. Friedrichshafen is another 10 km (6 miles) from Langenargen. Pay a visit to the Zeppelin Museum. After Friedrichshafen the path runs along the main road; follow the sign to Immenstaad (10 km [6 miles]) to get away from the traffic. Pass through the village and continue to Hagnau. After another 5 km (3 miles), stay overnight in lovely Meersburg, rising early to catch the ferry to Konstanz.

When you come off the ferry, head to the flower island of Mainau to enjoy the blooms. Continue onward to Konstanz, pass the ferry dock again, and keep as close as you can to the water, which will bring you into Konstanz through the scenic "back entrance." Cross the bridge over the Rhine. Take in the old town, and the buzzing small harbor. When you set off again, you'll be in the Swiss city of Kreuzlingen in a few minutes. Head east out of the city. After 32 km (20 miles) of rolling Swiss countryside, you'll arrive in Arbon for your second overnight.

Leave Arbon early in the morning, passing Rorschach (after 7 km [4½ miles]) and Rheineck on the Austrian border (another 9 km [5½ miles]). After the border, keep as close to the lake as possible, and you'll pass through protected marshlands and lush meadows. Twenty kilometers (12 miles) beyond the border is Bregenz, Austria. Ascend the Pfänder cablecar 3,870 feet for a marvelous view. If you're too tired to bike the 9 km (5½ miles) back to Lindau, you can board a train or ferry with your bicycle in Bregenz.

REFUELING

Copious amounts of fresh lake air and pedaling are bound to trigger your appetite. If the weather is ripe for a picnic, be on the lookout for supermarket chains such as Rewe, Edeka, and Lidl, where you can fill your picnic basket. For *Brot* (bread), a fresh *Brezel* (pretzel) or *Kaffee und Kuchen* (coffee and cake), seek out a local *Bäckerei* (bakery) or *Stehcafé* (standing café). Don't be shy about venturing into the village *Metzgerei* (butcher), either. Most of them offer delicious *Leberkässemmel* or *Fleischkäsweckle* (its respective names in Bavaria and Baden Württemburg)—a slice of warm sausage-meat loaf in a bread roll. Or, try some sliced *Fleischwurst* (bologna sausage) in various flavors, or tangy *Fleischsalat* (sliced sausage-meat salad and pickles with salad dressing)—both best eaten on bread fresh from the bakery.

6

Updated by
Leonie Adeane

Lapping the shores of Germany, Switzerland, and Austria, the Bodensee (Lake Constance), at 65 km (40 miles) long and 15 km (9 miles) wide, is the largest lake in the German-speaking world.

Though called a lake, it's actually a vast swelling of the Rhine, gouged out by a massive glacier in the Ice Age and flooded by the river as the ice receded. The Rhine flows into its southeast corner, where Switzerland and Austria meet, and flows out at its west end. On the German side, the Bodensee is bordered almost entirely by the state of Baden-Württemberg (a small portion of the eastern tip, from Lindau to Nonnenhorn, belongs to Bavaria).

A natural summer playground, the Bodensee is ringed with little towns and busy resorts. It's one of the warmest areas of the country, not just because of its southern latitude but also owing to the warming influence of the water, which gathers heat in summer and releases it in winter. The lake itself practically never freezes over—it has done so only once in the past two centuries. The climate is excellent for growing fruit, and along the roads you'll find stands and shops selling apples, peaches, strawberries, jams, juices, wines, and schnapps, much of it homemade.

PLANNING

WHEN TO GO

The Bodensee's temperate climate makes for pleasant weather from April to October. In spring, orchard blossoms explode everywhere, and on Mainau, the "island of flowers," more than a million tulips, hyacinths, and narcissi burst into bloom. Holiday crowds come in summer, and autumn can be warm and mellow. Some hotels and restaurants as well as many tourist attractions close for winter.

GETTING HERE AND AROUND

AIR TRAVEL

The closest major international airport is in Zürich, Switzerland, 60 km (37 miles) from Konstanz, connected by the autobahn. There are also direct trains from the Zürich airport to Konstanz. There are several domestic and international (primarily of United Kingdom and European origin) flights to the regional airport at Friedrichshafen—these are mostly operated by budget airlines.

Airport Contacts Flughafen Friedrichshafen (FDH) ✉ *Am Flugpl. 64, Friedrichshafen* ☎ *07541/284–01* ⊕ *www.fly-away.de.* **Zürich Airport (ZRH)** ✉ *Flughafenstr., Kloten, Switzerland* ☎ *410/4381–62211* ⊕ *www.zurich-airport.com.*

BOAT AND FERRY TRAVEL

■ TIP→ Note that the English pronunciation of "ferry" sounds a lot like the German word "fähre," which means car ferry. "Schiffe" is the term used for passenger ferries. Car and passenger ferries have different docking points in the various towns. The car ferries run all year; in summer you may have to wait in line. The passenger routes, especially the small ones, often do not run from November to March. Sailing on a car ferry as a passenger can be cheaper than taking a passenger ferry—and most car ferries are reasonably comfortable. Bicycles can be taken on both types of ferry.

The Weisse Flotte line of boats, which is run by the BSB, or Bodensee-Schiffsbetriebe, links most of the larger towns and resorts. One of the nicest trips is from Konstanz to Meersburg and then on to the island of Mainau. Excursions around the lake last from one hour to a full day. Many cross to Austria and Switzerland; some head west along the Rhine to Schaffhausen and the Rheinfall, the largest waterfall in Europe. Information on lake excursions is available from all local tourist offices and travel agencies.

Boat and Ferry Contacts Bodensee-Schiffsbetriebe. Ticket offices for this ferry line are in Konstanz, Überlingen, Meersburg, Friedrichshafen and Lindau. ✉ *Hafenstr. 6, Konstanz* ☎ *07531/364–0389* ⊕ *www.bsb.de.*

BUS TRAVEL

Buses serve most smaller communities that have no train links, but service is infrequent. Along the shore there are buses that run regularly throughout the day from Überlingen to Friedrichshafen, stopping in towns such as Meersburg, Hagnau, and Immenstaad.

CAR TRAVEL

The A-96 autobahn provides the most direct route between Munich and Lindau. For a more scenic, slower route, take B-12 via Landsberg and Kempten. For another scenic and slower route from Frankfurt, take B-311 at Ulm and follow the Oberschwäbische Barockstrasse (Upper Swabian Baroque Road) to Friedrichshafen. From Stuttgart, follow the A-81 autobahn south. At Exit 40 take B-33 to Konstanz, or the A-98 autobahn and B-31 for the northern shore. Lindau is also a terminus of the picturesque Deutsche Alpenstrasse (German Alpine Road), running east–west from Salzburg to Lindau.

Lakeside roads, particularly those on the northern shore, boast wonderful vistas but experience occasional heavy traffic in summer, and on weekends and holidays year-round. Stick to the speed limits in spite of tailgaters—speed traps are frequent, especially in built-up areas. Formalities at border-crossing points are few. However, in addition to your passport you'll need insurance and registration papers for your car. For rental cars, check with the rental company to make sure you are allowed to take the car into other countries. Crossing into Switzerland, you're required to have an autobahn tax sticker (CHF40, but purchasable in euros) if you plan to drive on the Swiss autobahn. These are available from border customs offices, and from petrol stations and post offices in Switzerland. This sticker is not necessary if you plan to stick to nonautobahn roads. Car ferries link Romanshorn, in Switzerland, with Friedrichshafen, as well as Konstanz with Meersburg. Taking either ferry saves substantial mileage. The fare depends on the size of the car.

TRAIN TRAVEL

From Frankfurt to Friedrichshafen and Lindau, take the ICE (InterCity Express) to Ulm and then transfer (total time 4½ hours). A combination of ICE and regional train gets you to Konstanz from Frankfurt in 4½ hours, passing through the beautiful scenery of the Black Forest. From Stuttgart to Konstanz, take the IC (InterCity) to Singen, and transfer to an RE or IRE (Regional/Inter Regio Express) for the brief last leg to Konstanz (total time 2½ hours). From Munich to Lindau, the EC (Europe Express) train or the ALX (Alex) train take 2½ hours. From Zürich to Konstanz, the trip lasts 1½ hours. Local trains encircle the Bodensee, stopping at most towns and villages.

TOURS

Most of the larger tourist centers have city tours with English-speaking guides. The Bodensee is a great destination for bike travelers, with hundreds of miles of well-signposted paths that keep riders safe from cars. You can go on your own or enjoy the comfort of a customized tour with accommodations and baggage transport (and a rental bike, if need be). Wine-tasting tours are available in Überlingen, Konstanz, and Meersburg. Call the local tourist offices for information. Zeppelin tours operated by the DZR (Deutsche Zeppelin Reederei) are not cheap (sightseeing trips cost €200–€745), but they do offer a special experience and a reminder of the grand old days of flight. The zeppelins depart from the airport in Friedrichshafen.

Tour Contacts Radweg-Reisen GmbH ✉ *Fritz-Arnold-Str. 16a, Konstanz* ☎ *07531/819–930* ⊕ *www.radweg-reisen.com.* **Deutsche Zeppelin Reederei** ✉ *Allmannsweilerstr. 132, Friedrichshafen* ☎ *07541/59000* ⊕ *www.zeppelinflug. de.* **Velotours Touristik GmbH** ✉ *Bücklestr. 13, Konstanz* ☎ *07531/98280* ⊕ *www.velotours.de.*

RESTAURANTS

In this area, international dishes are not only on the menu but also on the map—you have to drive only a few miles to try the Swiss or Austrian dish you're craving in its own land. *Seeweine* (lake wines) from vineyards in the area include Müller-Thurgau, Spätburgunder, Ruländer, and Kerner.

Prices in the reviews are the average cost of a main course at dinner, or if dinner is not served, at lunch.

HOTELS

Accommodations in the towns and resorts around the lake include venerable wedding-cake-style, fin de siècle palaces as well as more modest *Gasthöfe*. If you're visiting in July and August, make reservations in advance. For lower rates in a more rural atmosphere, consider staying a few miles away from the lake.

Prices in the reviews are the lowest cost of a standard double room in high season. For expanded reviews, facilities, and current deals, visit Fodors.com.

PLANNING YOUR TIME

Choosing a place to stay is a question of finance and interest. The closer you stay to the water, the more expensive and lively it becomes. Many visitors pass by on their way from one country to another, so during the middle of the day, key hubs like Konstanz, Mainau, Meersburg, and Lindau tend to be crowded. Try to visit these places either in the morning or in the late afternoon, and make your day trips to the lesser-known destinations: the baroque churches in upper Swabia, the Swiss towns along the southern shore, or the nearby mountains.

VISITOR INFORMATION

Visitor Information Internationale Bodensee Tourismus ✉ *Hafenstr. 6, Konstanz* ☎ *07531/9094–90* ⊕ *www.bodensee.eu.*

6

THE NORTHERN SHORE

There's a feeling here, in the midst of a peaceful Alpine landscape, that the Bodensee is part of Germany and yet separated from it—which is literally the case for Lindau, which sits in the lake tethered to land by a causeway. Überlingen, a beautiful resort at the northwestern finger of the lake, attracts many vacationers and spa goers. Clear days reveal the snowcapped mountains of Switzerland to the south and the peaks of the Austrian Vorarlberg to the east.

LINDAU

180 km (112 miles) southwest of Munich.

By far the best way to get to know this charming old island town is on foot. Lose yourself in the maze of small streets and passageways flanked by centuries-old houses. Wander down to the harbor for magnificent views, with the Austrian shoreline and mountains close by to the east. Just 13 km (8 miles) away, they are nearer than the Swiss mountains visible to the southwest.

Lindau was made a Free Imperial City within the Holy Roman Empire in 1275. It had developed as a fishing settlement and then spent hundreds of years as a trading center along the route between the rich lands of Swabia and Italy. The Lindauer Bote, an important stagecoach service between Germany and Italy in the 18th and 19th centuries, was based here; Goethe traveled via this service on his first visit to Italy in 1788. The stagecoach was revived a few years ago, carrying passengers on a 13-day journey to Italy. This service only runs occasionally—ask at the Lindau tourist office.

As the German empire crumbled toward the end of the 18th century, battered by Napoléon's revolutionary armies, Lindau fell victim to competing political groups. It was ruled by the Austrian Empire before passing into Bavarian control in 1805. Lindau's harbor was rebuilt in 1856.

GETTING HERE AND AROUND

Lindau is halfway between Munich and Zurich, and about two hours from both on the EC (European Express) train. From Frankfurt it takes about four hours—change from the ICE (InterCity Express) train in Ulm to the IRE (InterRegio Express) train. You can also reach Lindau by boat: it takes about 20 minutes from Bregenz across the bay. Once in Lindau, you can reach everything on foot. Its *Altstadt* (old town) is a maze of ancient streets with half-timber and gable houses making up most of the island. The center and main street is the pedestrian-only Maximilianstrasse.

ESSENTIALS

Visitor Information Lindau Tourist-Information ⊠ *Alfred-Nobel-Pl. 1*
☎ *08382/260–030* ⊕ *www.lindau-tourismus.de.*

EXPLORING

TOP ATTRACTIONS

Altes Rathaus (*Old Town Hall*). The Old Town Hall is the finest of Lindau's handsome historic buildings. It was constructed between 1422 and 1436 in the midst of a vineyard and given a Renaissance face-lift 150 years later, though the original stepped gables remain. Emperor Maximilian I held an imperial diet (deliberation) here in 1496; a fresco on the south facade depicts the scene. The building now houses offices and is closed to the public. ⊠ *Bismarckpl. 4* ⊕ *www.lindau-tourismus.de.*

Bavarian Lion (*Der Bayerische Löwe*). A proud symbol of Bavaria, Der Bayerische Löwe (the Bavarian Lion) is Lindau's most striking landmark. Carved from Bavarian marble and standing 20 feet high, the lion stares out across the lake from a massive plinth. ⊠ *Lindau Harbor entrance, Römerschanze* ⊕ *www.lindau-tourismus.de.*

Mangenturm (*Mangturm*). At the harbor's inner edge, across the water from the Neuer Leuchtturm, stands this 13th century former lighthouse, one of the lake's oldest. Although the structure is old, its vibrantly colored rooftop is not—after a lightning strike in the 1970s, the roof tiles were replaced, giving the tower the bright top it now bears. ⊠ *Hafenpl. 4.*

Neuer Leuchtturm (*New Lighthouse; Neuer Lindauer Leuchtturm*). Germany's southernmost lighthouse stands sentinel, with the Bavarian Lion across the inner harbor's passageway. ⊠ *Schützingerweg 2.*

WORTH NOTING

Barfüsserkirche—Stadttheatre Lindau and Lindauer Marionettenoper (*Church of the Barefoot Pilgrims*). This church, built from 1241 to 1270, is now Lindau's principal theater, and it also hosts the Lindauer Marionettenoper (Puppet Theater). Tickets for shows—starring humans or puppets—are available at the adjacent box office. ⊠ *Barfüsserpl. 1a* ☎ *08382/944–650* ⊕ *www.kultur-lindau.de* ☉ *Mon.–Thurs. 10–1:30 and 3–6.*

Haus zum Cavazzen (*Stadtmuseum Lindau*). Dating to 1728, this house belonged to a wealthy merchant and is now considered one of the most beautiful in the Bodensee region, owing to its rich decor of frescoes. Today it serves as a local history museum, with collections of glass and pewter items, paintings, and furniture from the past five centuries, alongside touring exhibitions. ⊠ *Marktpl. 6* ☎ *08382/944073* ⊕ *www.kultur-lindau.de/museum* 🖭 *€3* ⊘ *Apr.–Oct., daily 10–6.*

Marktplatz. Lindau's market square is lined by a series of sturdy and attractive old buildings. The Gothic **Stephanskirche** (St. Stephen's Church) is simple and sparsely decorated, as befits a Lutheran place of worship. It dates to the late 12th century but went through numerous transformations. One of its special features is the green-hue stucco ornamentation on the ceiling, which immediately attracts the eye toward the heavens. In contrast, the Catholic **Münster Unserer Lieben Frau** (St. Mary's Church), which stands right next to the Stephanskirche, is exuberantly baroque. ⊠ *Marktpl.*

Peterskirche (*St. Peter's Church*). This solid 10th-century Romanesque building may be the oldest church in the Bodensee region. On the inside of the northern wall, frescoes by Hans Holbein the Elder (1465–1524) depict scenes from the life of St. Peter, the patron saint of fishermen. Peterskirche houses a memorial to fallen German soldiers from World Wars I and II, and a memorial plaque for victims of Auschwitz. Attached to the church is the 16th-century bell foundry, now a pottery works. Also of note is the adjacent fairy-tale-like **Diebsturm.** Look closely and you might see Rapunzel's golden hair hanging from this 13th-century tower, awaiting a princely rescuer. Follow the old city wall behind the tower and church to the adjoining Unterer Schrannenplatz, where the bell-makers used to live. A 1989 fountain depicts five of the *Narren* (Fools) that make up the VIPs of *Fastnacht*, the annual Alemannic Carnival celebrations. ⊠ *Oberer Schrannenpl.*

WHERE TO EAT

$$
GERMAN

✕ **Gasthaus zum Sünfzen.** This ancient inn was serving warm meals to the patricians, officials, merchants, and other good burghers of Lindau back in the 14th century. The current chef insists on using fresh ingredients preferably from the region, such as fish from the lake in season, venison from the mountains, and apples—pressed to juice or distilled to schnapps—from his own orchard. Try the herb-flavored *Maultaschen* (large ravioli), the excellent *Felchen* (whitefish) fillet in wine sauce, or the peppery Schübling sausage. ⑤ *Average main: €19* ⊠ *Maximilianstr. 1* ☎ *08382/5865* ⊕ *www.suenfzen.de* ⊘ *Closed Thurs. mid-Jan.–mid-Mar.*

BREGENZ, AUSTRIA

Bregenz is a mere 13 km (8 miles) from Lindau, on the other side of the bay. It's a 20-minute boat ride to get there, which makes for a great side trip. Wander around the lakeshore and the lovely, romantic remains of the once-fortified medieval town. An enormous floating stage is the site for performances of grand opera and orchestral works under the stars. Ascend Pfänder Mountain, in Bregenz's backyard, via the *Pfänderbahn* cable tramway for views that stretch as far as the Black Forest and the Swiss Alps.

6

WHERE TO STAY

$$$ ⚏ **Hotel Bayerischer Hof.** This is *the* address in town, a stately hotel
HOTEL directly on the edge of the lake, its terrace lush with semitropical,
long-flowering plants, trees, and shrubs. **Pros:** pretty lake view from
many rooms; elegant dining room with good food, nearly all rooms
have a/c. **Cons:** not all rooms have a lake view; no free parking; on
weekends in summer parking is difficult; expensive. ⑤ *Rooms from:*
€194 ✉ *Seepromenade* ☎ *08382/9150* ⊕ *www.bayerischerhof-lindau.*
de ⤳ *91 rooms, 6 suites* ¶◎¶ *Breakfast.*

$$ ⚏ **Hotel Garni Brugger.** This small, family-run hotel stands on the site
HOTEL occupied by the city wall in the Middle Ages. **Pros:** center of town;
FAMILY family-run atmosphere; good value for families. **Cons:** caters to
families; no elevator. ⑤ *Rooms from: €116* ✉ *Bei der Heidenmauer*
11 ☎ *08382/93410* ⊕ *www.hotel-garni-brugger.de* ⤳ *23 rooms*
¶◎¶ *Breakfast.*

$$ ⚏ **Insel-Hotel.** In fine weather, you can enjoy breakfast al fresco as you
HOTEL watch the town come alive at this friendly central hotel on the pedes-
trian-only Maximilianstrasse. **Pros:** center of town; family run. **Cons:**
some rooms need some new furnishings and paint; parking is difficult.
⑤ *Rooms from: €123* ✉ *Maximilianstr. 42* ☎ *08382/5017* ⊕ *www.insel-*
hotel-lindau.de ⤳ *26 rooms* ¶◎¶ *Breakfast.*

NIGHTLIFE AND THE ARTS

Bregenzer Festspiele (*Bregenz Music Festival*). A dramatic floating stage
supports orchestras and opera stars during the famous Bregenzer Fest-
spiele from mid-July to the end of August. Make reservations well in
advance. The Austrian town of Bregenz is 13 km (8 miles) from Lin-
dau, on the other side of the bay. ✉ *Platz Der Wiener Symphoniker 1,*
Bregenz, Austria ☎ *0043/5574–4076* ⊕ *www.bregenzerfestspiele.com.*

Spielbank Lindau Casino. You can play roulette, blackjack, poker, and
slot machines at the town's modern and elegant casino. The dress code
requires that men wear a blazer or sports jacket. ✉ *Chelles-Allee 1*
☎ *08382/27740* ⊕ *www.spielbanken-bayern.de* ☽ *Sun.–Thu. noon–2*
am, Fri.–Sat. noon–3 am.

SPORTS AND THE OUTDOORS

Bodensee Yachtschule. This sailing school in Lindau charters yachts and
offers sailing courses for all ages, from beginner to advanced levels.
✉ *Christoph Eychmüller Schiffswerfte 2* ☎ *08382/944–588* ⊕ *www.*
bodensee-yachtschule.de.

Surfschule Kreitmeir. You can rent boards and take windsurfing and stand-
up paddleboarding lessons at Surfschule Kreitmeir. ✉ *Strandbad Eich-*
wald, Eichwaldstr. 20 ☎ *08382/279–9459* ⊕ *www.surfschule-lindau.de.*

SHOPPING

Biedermann en Vogue. This high-end boutique carries various luxury
fashion brands, as well as custom-made clothing, cashmere sweaters,
and Italian shoes. ✉ *Maximilianstr. 2* ☎ *08382/944–913.*

Böhm. A destination for interior decorators, Böhm consists of three old
houses full of lamps, mirrors, precious porcelain, and elegant furniture.
✉ *Maximilianstr. 21* ☎ *08382/94880* ⊕ *www.boehm-dieeinrichtungen.de.*

EATING WELL BY THE BODENSEE

On a nice day you could sit on the terrace of a Bodensee restaurant forever, looking across the sparkling waters to the imposing heights of the Alps in the distance. The fish on your plate, possibly caught that very morning in the lake, is another reason to linger. Fish predominates on the menus of the region; 35 varieties swim in the lake, with *Felchen* (whitefish) the most highly prized. Felchen belongs to the salmon family and is best eaten *blau* ("blue"—poached in a mixture of water and vinegar with spices, called *Essigsud*) or *Müllerin* (baked in almonds). A white *Seewein* (lake wine) from one of the vineyards around the lake provides the perfect pairing. Sample a German and a Swiss version. Both use the same kind of grape, from vineyards are only a few miles apart, but they produce wines with very different tastes. The Swiss like their wines very dry, whereas the Germans prefer them slightly sweeter.

One of the best-known Swabian dishes is *Maultaschen,* a kind of ravioli, usually served floating in a broth strewn with chives. Another specialty is *Pfannkuchen* (pancakes), generally filled with meat, or chopped into fine strips and scattered in a clear consommé known as *Flädlesuppe.* Hearty *Zwiebelrostbraten* (beef steak with lots of fried onions) is often served with a side of *Spätzle* (hand-cut or pressed, golden soft-textured egg noodles) and accompanied by a good strong Swabian beer.

EN ROUTE

Wasserburg. Six kilometers (4 miles) west of Lindau lies Wasserburg, whose name means "water castle," a description of what this enchanting island town once was—a fortress. It has some of the most photographed sights of the Bodensee: the yellow, stair-gabled presbytery; the fishermen's St. Georg Kirche, with its onion dome; and the little Malhaus museum, with the castle, Schloss Wasserburg, in the background. ⊕ *www.wasserburg-bodensee.de.*

Schloss Montfort (*Montfort Castle*). Another 8 km (5 miles) west of Wasserburg is the small, pretty town of Langenargen, famous for the region's most unusual castle, Schloss Montfort. Named for the original owners, the counts of Montfort-Werdenberg, this structure was a conventional medieval fortification until the 19th century, when it was rebuilt in pseudo-Moorish style by its new owner, King Wilhelm I of Württemberg. If you can, see it from a passenger ship on the lake; the castle is especially memorable in the early morning or late afternoon. The tower is open to visitors, and the castle houses a café-restaurant, which is open for dinner from Tuesday to Sunday, March through October. The café is also open for Sunday brunch year-round. ✉ *Untere Seestr. 3, Langenargen* ☎ *07543/912–712* ⊕ *www.vemax-gastro.de* ⬚ *Tower €2* ☉ *Tower mid-Mar.–Oct., 10–noon and 1–5.*

FRIEDRICHSHAFEN

24 km (15 miles) west of Lindau.

Named for its founder, King Friedrich I of Württemberg, Friedrichshafen is a relatively young town (dating to 1811). In an area otherwise given over to resort towns and agriculture, Friedrichshafen played a central role in Germany's aeronautics tradition, which saw the development of the zeppelin airship before World War I and the Dornier seaplanes in the 1920s and '30s. The zeppelins were once launched from a floating hangar on the lake, and the Dornier water planes were tested here. The World War II raids on its factories virtually wiped the city off the map. The current layout of the streets is the same, but the buildings are all new and not necessarily pretty. The atmosphere, however, is good and lively, and occasionally you'll find a plaque with a picture of the old building that stood at the respective spot. The factories are back, too. Friedrichshafen is home to such international firms as EADS (airplanes, rockets, and helicopters) and ZF (gear wheels).

GETTING HERE AND AROUND

It takes about two hours from Ulm on the IRE (InterRegio Express) train, then a bus or BOB (Bodensee Oberschwaben Bahn). Most trains stop at Friedrichshafen airport. The car ferry takes you on a 40-minute run across the lake to Romanshorn in Switzerland, where you have direct express trains to the airport and Zürich. In town you can reach most places on foot.

ESSENTIALS

Airplane Tours Konair. Konair provide scenic flights, flight lessons, and an air-taxi service around the Bodensee region. ⊠ *Riedstr. 82, Konstanz* ☎ *07531/361–6905* ⊕ *www.konair.de.*

Visitor Information Friedrichshafen Tourist-Information ⊠ *Bahnhofpl. 2* ☎ *07541/30010* ⊕ *www.friedrichshafen.info.*

EXPLORING

Deutsche Zeppelin Reederei GmbH. For an unforgettable experience, take a scenic zeppelin flight out of Friedrichshafen airport. The flying season runs from March to November, and prices start at €200 for half an hour. For those who prefer to stay grounded, you can also tour the *Zeppelin NT* (New Technology) in its hangar. ⊠ *Allmannsweilerstr. 132* ☎ *07541/59000* ⊕ *www.zeppelinflug.de.*

Zeppelin Museum. Graf Zeppelin (Ferdinand Graf von Zeppelin) was born across the lake in Konstanz, but Friedrichshafen was where, on July 2, 1900, his first "airship"—the LZ 1—was launched. The story is told in the Zeppelin Museum, which holds the world's most significant collection of artifacts pertaining to airship history. In a wing of the restored Bauhaus **Friedrichshafen Hafenbahnhof** (harbor railway station), the main attraction is the reconstruction of a 108-foot-long section of the legendary *Hindenburg*, the LZ 129 that exploded at its berth in Lakehurst, New Jersey, on May 6, 1937. (The airships were filled with hydrogen, because in 1933 the United States had passed an act banning helium sales to foreign governments due to its military utility and scarcity at that time.) Climb aboard the airship via a retractable

The Zeppelin Museum houses a collection of fascinating artifacts from the days of the airship. You can also tour a reproduction of the *Hindenburg*.

stairway and stroll past the authentically furnished passenger room, the original lounges, and the dining room. The illusion of traveling in a zeppelin is followed by exhibits on the history and technology of airship aviation: propellers, engines, dining-room menus, and films of the airships traveling or at war. Car fans will appreciate the great Maybach standing on the ground floor; passengers once enjoyed being transported to the zeppelins in it. The museum's restaurant, a good place to take a break, is open for lunch and dinner. ⊠ *Seestr. 22* ☎ *07541/38010* ⊕ *www.zeppelin-museum.de* 🖻 *€8* ⊙ *May–Oct., daily 9–5 (last entry at 4:30); Nov.–Apr., Tues.–Sun. 10–5.*

Schloss Hofen (*Hofen Castle*). A short walk from town along the lakeside promenade is a small palace that served as the summer residence of Württemberg kings until 1918. The palace was formerly a priory—its foundations date from the 11th century. Today it is the private home of Duke Friedrich von Württemberg and isn't open to the public. You can visit the adjoining priory **church,** a splendid example of regional baroque architecture. The swirling white stucco of the interior was executed by the Schmuzer family from Wessobrunn whose master craftsman, Franz Schmuzer, also created the priory church's magnificent marble altar. ⊙ *Easter–Oct., daily 9–6; Nov.–Easter, Sun. 9–6.*

WHERE TO EAT

$$
ECLECTIC

✕ **Lukullum.** This lively, novel restaurant is divided into seven *Stuben* (rooms), all themed: sit in a wine barrel, dine in Tirol, relax under the image of an airship in the Zeppelin Bräustüble—or enjoy the beer garden in summer. Dishes are good and basic, with some international touches. Friendly service keeps up with the pace of the socializing at this friendly dining spot. $ *Average main: €16* ✉ *Friedrichstr. 21* ☎ *07541/6818* ⊕ *www.lukullum.de* ⊗ *Closed Mon. No lunch Tues.–Fri.*

$ ✕ **Zeppelin-Museumrestaurant.** A
GERMAN grand view of the harbor and the lake is only one of the attractions of this art deco-styled restaurant in the Zeppelin Museum. Soak up the retro airship travel theme as you enjoy cakes and drinks, a wide range of Swabian specialties, and several Italian dishes. $ *Average main: €14* ✉ *Seestr. 22* ☎ *07541/953–0088* ⊕ *www. zeppelinmuseum-restaurant.de.*

WHERE TO STAY

$$ 🏨 **Buchhorner Hof.** This traditional
HOTEL family-run hotel near the train station is decorated with hunting trophies, leather armchairs, and Turkish rugs; bedrooms are large and comfortable. **Pros:** business floor; cozy and big lobby; excellent restaurant; many rooms have nice views. **Cons:** many rooms look onto a busy main street; parking is difficult. $ *Rooms from: €100* ✉ *Friedrichstr. 33* ☎ *07541/2050* ⊕ *www.buchhorn.de* ↗ *92 rooms, 4 suites, 2 apartments* ⦿*Breakfast.*

$$ 🏨 **Flair Hotel Gerbe.** A former farm and tannery that's about 5 km (3
HOTEL miles) from the city center, is now a pleasant, spacious hotel; its rooms (many with balconies) overlook the gardens, the countryside, and—on a clear day—the Swiss mountains. **Pros:** spacious rooms with good views; ample parking. **Cons:** 5 km (3 miles) from center of town; some rooms have street noise. $ *Rooms from: €120* ✉ *Hirschlatterstr. 14, Ailingen* ☎ *07541/5090* ⊕ *www.hotel-gerbe.de* ↗ *59 rooms* ⦿*Breakfast.*

$$ 🏨 **Ringhotel Krone.** This large Bavarian-themed hotel in the Schnetzen-
HOTEL hausen district's semirural surroundings, 6 km (4 miles) from the center of town, has a lot to offer active guests, including tennis, minigolf, bicycles to rent, a gym, saunas, and an indoor pool. **Pros:** great variety of rooms; good food; lots of parking. **Cons:** not near the center of town; a few rooms have street noise. $ *Rooms from: €152* ✉ *Untere Mühlbachstr. 1, Schnetzenhausen* ☎ *07541/4080* ⊕ *www.ringhotel-krone.de* ↗ *135 rooms* ⦿*Breakfast.*

NIGHTLIFE AND THE ARTS

Cafebar Belushi. College students and a mostly young crowd raise their glasses and voices above the din at Cafebar Belushi. ✉ *Montfortstr. 3* ☎ *07541/32531* ⊕ *www.cafe-bar-belushi.de* ⊗ *Closed Sun.*

Graf-Zeppelin-Haus. This modern convention center on the lakeside promenade also functions as a cultural center, where musicals, light opera, and classical as well as pop-rock concerts take place several times a week. The Graf-Zeppelin-Haus has a good modern restaurant with a big terrace overlooking the harbor. ✉ *Olgastr. 20* ☎ *07541/2880* ⊕ *www.gzh.de.*

SWISS STOPS

There are two towns on the Swiss shores of the Bodensee that are convenient for quick trips from Germany. Ferries travel between Friedrichshafen in Germany and **Romanshorn**, a yachting and sportfishing center, in Switzerland. You can catch trains in Romanshorn to eastern Switzerland and to Zürich. **Kreuzlingen** is the small Swiss city across the border from Konstanz. There's little to see here, but you can catch a train to Zürich.

Upper Swabia and
The Northern Shore

SHOPPING

Marktkörble Ebe. This century-old gift shop sells tableware and kitchenware, handmade candles, toys, stationary, and postcards, alongside some clothing and accessories. ✉ *Buchhornpl. 5* ☎ *07541/388–430* ⊕ *www.marktkoerble.de.*

Weber & Weiss. Look for the zeppelin airship–shape chocolates and candies at this excellent candy store. ✉ *Charlottenstr. 11* ☎ *07541/21771* ⊕ *www.weber-weiss.de.*

MEERSBURG

18 km (11 miles) west of Friedrichshafen.

Meersburg is one of the most romantic old towns on the German shore of the lake. Seen from the water on a summer afternoon with the sun slanting low, the steeply terraced town looks like a stage set, with its bold castles, severe patrician dwellings, and a gaggle of half-timber houses arranged around narrow streets. It's no wonder that cars have been banned from the center: the crowds of people who come to visit the sights on weekends fill up the streets. The town is divided into the Unterstadt (Lower Town) and Oberstadt (Upper Town), connected by several steep streets and stairs.

The Altes Schloss in Meersburg, a true medieval castle, has a museum with armor and jousting equipment.

ESSENTIALS

Visitor Information Tourism Meersburg ✉ *Kirchstr. 4* ☎ *07532/440–400* 🌐 *www.meersburg.de.*

EXPLORING

Altes Schloss (*Old Castle; Burg Meersburg*). Majestically guarding the town is the Altes Schloss, the original Meersburg ("sea castle"). It's Germany's oldest inhabited castle, founded in 628 by Dagobert, king of the Franks. The massive central tower, with walls 10 feet thick, is named after him. The bishops of Konstanz used it as a summer residence until 1526, at which point they moved in permanently. They remained until the mid-18th century, when they built themselves what they felt to be a more suitable residence—the baroque Neues Schloss. Plans to tear down the Altes Schloss in the early 19th century were shelved when it was taken over by Baron Joseph von Lassberg, a man much intrigued by the castle's medieval romance. He turned it into a home for like-minded poets and artists, among them the Grimm brothers and his sister-in-law, the poet Annette von Droste-Hülshoff (1797–1848). The Altes Schloss is still private property, but much of it can be visited, including the richly furnished rooms where Droste-Hülshoff lived and the chamber where she died, as well as the imposing knights' hall, the minstrels' gallery, and the sinister dungeons. The **Altes Schloss Museum** (Old Castle Museum) contains a fascinating collection of weapons and armor, including a rare set of medieval jousting equipment. ✉ *Schlosspl. 10* ☎ *07532/80000* 🌐 *www.burg-meersburg.de* 💶 *€8.50* 🕐 *Mar.–Oct., daily 9–6:30; Nov.–Feb., daily 10–6.*

Droste Museum (*Fürstenhäusle*). An idyllic retreat almost hidden among the vineyards, the Fürstenhäusle was built in 1640 by a local vintner and later used as a holiday house by the poet Annette von Droste-Hülshoff. It's now the Droste Museum, containing many of her personal possessions and giving a vivid sense of Meersburg in her time. ✉ *Stettenerstr. 11, east of Obertor, the town's north gate* ☎ *07532/6088* ⊕ *www.fuerstenhaeusle.de* 💶 *€5* ⊗ *Apr.–Oct., Tues.– Sat. 10–12:30 and 2–6, Sun. 2–6.*

WORD OF MOUTH

"Meersburg is a wonderful small hillside town full of half-timbered buildings that spills down to a lakeside promenade, in the area of Germany with the mildest climate. You won't find that description for too many other German towns."
—Aramis

Neues Schloss. The spacious and elegant "New Castle" is directly across from its predecessor. Designed by Christoph Gessinger at the beginning of the 18th century, it took nearly 50 years to complete. The grand double staircase, with its intricate grillwork and heroic statues, was the work of Balthasar Neumann. The interior's other standout is the glittering **Spiegelsaal** (Hall of Mirrors). ✉ *Schlosspl. 12* ☎ *07532/440–4900* ⊕ *www.neues-schloss-meersburg.de* 💶 *€5* ⊗ *Apr.–Oct., daily 9–6:30; Nov.–Mar., weekends and holidays 11–4.*

Stadtmuseum. Right next to the local tourist office stands the City Museum, in a former Dominican priory. You can see an overview of the town's history that celebrates some of its famous residents, such as Franz Anton Mesmer, who developed the theory of "animal magnetism." (His name gave rise to the verb "mesmerize.") ✉ *Kirchstr. 4* ☎ *07532/440–4801* ⊕ *www.meersburg.de/158* 💶 *€2* ⊗ *Apr.–Oct., Wed., Thurs., and Sat. 2–6.*

Weinbau Museum (*Vineyard Museum*). Sunbathed, south-facing Meersburg and the neighboring towns have been the center of the Bodensee wine trade for centuries. You can pay your respects to the noble profession in the Weinbau Museum. A barrel capable of holding 50,000 liters (over 13,000 gallons) and an immense winepress dating from 1607 are highlights of the collection. ✉ *Vorburgg. 11* ☎ *07532/440– 400* ⊕ *www.meersburg.de/160* 💶 *€2* ⊗ *Apr.–Oct., Tues., Fri., and Sun. 2–6.*

WHERE TO EAT

$$
GERMAN
✕ **Winzerstube zum Becher.** Fresh fish from the lake is a specialty at this traditional restaurant, which has been in the Benz family for three generations. You can pair the day's catch with white wine from their own vineyard. A popular entrée is *badische Ente* (duck with bacon and apples in a wine-kirsch sauce). The restaurant is near the New Castle, and reservations are recommended. 💲 *Average main: €20* ✉ *Höllg. 4* ☎ *07532/9009* ⊕ *www.winzerstube-zum-becher.de* ⊗ *Closed Mon. and for 1 wk in Jan.*

WHERE TO STAY

$
HOTEL
🖼 **Gästehaus am Hafen.** This family-run, half-timber pension is in the middle of the Old Town, near the harbor. **Pros:** close to the harbor; in the center of the Lower Town; good value. **Cons:** small rooms; no credit cards; parking is five minutes away on foot. $ *Rooms from: €54* ✉ *Spitalg. 3–4* ☎ *07532/7069* ⊕ *www.amhafen.eu* ↪ *7 rooms* ▭ *No credit cards* ⊙ *Closed Nov.–Mar.* ⦿ *Breakfast.*

$
HOTEL
🖼 **Hotel Weinstube Löwen.** Rooms at this local landmark—a centuries-old, ivy-clad tavern on Meersburg's market square—have their own corner sitting areas, some with genuine Biedermeier furniture. **Pros:** center of town; pleasant rooms; good food in a cozy restaurant. **Cons:** lots of daytime noise from tourists; no elevator. $ *Rooms from: €90* ✉ *Marktpl. 2* ☎ *07532/43040* ⊕ *www.hotel-loewen-meersburg.de* ↪ *20 rooms* ⦿ *Breakfast.*

$$$
HOTEL
🖼 **Romantik Hotel Residenz am See.** This tastefully modern hotel overlooking the lake features two restaurants, including the Michelin-starred Casala, and Residenz Restaurant, which specializes in regional fare. **Pros:** good food; pleasant rooms with lake view; quiet rooms toward the vineyards. **Cons:** not in center of town. $ *Rooms from: €180* ✉ *Uferpromenade 11* ☎ *07532/80040* ⊕ *www.hotel-residenz-meersburg.com* ↪ *25 rooms* ⦿ *Multiple meal plans.*

$
HOTEL
🖼 **See Hotel Off.** Nearly all rooms at this bright, airy and crisply renovated hotel just a few steps from the shore offer balconies with views across the lake or vineyards. **Pros:** close to the lake; individually decorated rooms; away from center of town. **Cons:** not in center of town. $ *Rooms from: €100* ✉ *Uferpromenade 51* ☎ *07532/44740* ⊕ *www.seehotel-off.de* ↪ *13 rooms, 7 junior suites* ⊙ *Closed Jan.* ⦿ *Breakfast.*

$
HOTEL
🖼 **Zum Bären.** Individually furnished rooms lend character to this historic hotel, whose ivy-covered facade, with its characteristic steeple, hasn't changed much over the centuries. **Pros:** center of town; historic building; good value. **Cons:** no elevator; some rooms are small; no credit cards. $ *Rooms from: €86* ✉ *Marktpl. 11* ☎ *07532/43220* ⊕ *www.baeren-meersburg.de* ↪ *20 rooms* ▭ *No credit cards* ⊙ *Closed mid-Nov.–mid-Mar.* ⦿ *Breakfast.*

SPORTS AND THE OUTDOORS

FAMILY **Meersburg Therme** (*Meersburg Spa*). This lakeside pool complex east of the harbor has three outdoor pools, an indoor "adventure" pool, an indoor-outdoor thermal bath (34°C [93.2°F]), a sauna, and a beach-volleyball court. ✉ *Uferpromenade 12* ☎ *07532/440–2850* ⊕ *www.meersburg-therme.de* 🌊 *Bathing and sauna €16.50 (3 hrs), €18.50 (full day)* ⊙ *Mon.–Thurs. 10–10, Fri.–Sat. 10 am–11 am, Sun. 9 am–10 pm.*

SHOPPING

FAMILY **Omas Kaufhaus.** If you can't find something at this incredible gift shop (with toys, enamelware, books, dolls, model cars, and much more), then you should at least see the exhibition of toy trains and tin boats on the first floor. The boats are displayed in a long canal filled with real water. ✉ *Steigstr. 2* ☎ *07532/433–9611* 🎫 *Exhibition €2* ⊙ *Daily 10–6:30.*

Pfahlbauten. As you proceed northwest along the lake's shore, a settlement of "pile dwelling"—a reconstructed village of Stone Age and Bronze Age houses built on stilts—sticks out of the lake. This is how the original lake dwellers lived, surviving off the fish that swam outside their humble huts. Real dwellers in authentic garb give you an accurate picture of prehistoric lifestyles. The on-site **Pfahlbaumuseum** (Open-Air Museum and Research Institute) contains actual finds excavated in the area. Admission includes a 45-minute tour. ⊠ *Strandpromenade 6, Unteruhldingen* ☎ *07556/928–900* ⊕ *www.pfahlbauten.de* 🎫 *€8* ⏰ *Apr.–Sept., daily 9–7; Oct., daily 9–5; Nov.–Mar., hrs vary.*

ÜBERLINGEN

13 km (8 miles) west of Meersburg, 24 km (15 miles) west of Friedrichshafen.

This Bodensee resort has an attractive waterfront and an almost Mediterranean feel. It's midway along the north shore of the Überlingersee, a narrow finger of the Bodensee that points to the northwest. Überlingen is ancient—it's first mentioned in records dating back to 770. In the 14th century it earned the title of Free Imperial City and was known for its wines. No fewer than seven of its original city gates and towers remain from those grand days, as well as substantial portions of the old city walls. What was once the moat is now a grassy walkway, with the walls of the Old Town towering on one side and the Stadtpark stretching away on the other. The **Stadtgarten** (city garden), which opened in 1875, cultivates exotic plants and has a famous collection of cacti, a fuchsia garden, and a small deer corral. The heart of the city is the Münsterplatz.

ESSENTIALS

Visitor Information Überlingen Tourist-Information ⊠ *Landungspl. 5* ☎ *07551/947–1522* ⊕ *www.ueberlingen-bodensee.de.*

EXPLORING

Altes Rathaus (*Old Town Hall*). Inside the late-Gothic Altes Rathaus is a high point of Gothic decoration, the **Rathaussaal,** or council chamber, which is still in use today. Its most striking feature amid the riot of carving is the series of figures, created between 1492 and 1494, representing the states of the Holy Roman Empire. To visit the interior, you'll need to take the short, guided tour. Tours are free; simply show up shortly before the set start time. ⊠ *Münsterstr. 15* ⊕ *www.ueberlingen-bodensee.de* 🎫 *Free* ⏰ *Tours Wed. and Thurs. 11.*

Münster St. Nikolaus (*Church of St. Nicholas*). The huge Münster St. Nikolaus was built between 1512 and 1563 on the site of at least two previous churches. The interior is all Gothic solemnity and massiveness, with a lofty stone-vaulted ceiling and high, pointed arches lining the nave. The single most remarkable feature is not Gothic at all but opulently Renaissance—the massive high altar, carved by Jörg Zürn from lime wood that almost looks like ivory. The focus of the altar is that of the Nativity. ⊠ *Münsterpl.*

FAMILY
Fodor's Choice
★

Schloss Salem (*Salem Castle*). This huge castle in the tiny inland village of Salem, 10 km (6 miles) north of Überlingen, began its existence as a convent and large church. After many architectural permutations, it was transformed into a palace for the Baden princes, though traces of its religious past can still be seen. You can view the royally furnished rooms of the abbots and princes, a library, stables, and the church. The castle also houses an interesting array of museums, workshops, and activities, including a museum of firefighting, a potter, a musical instrument builder, a goldsmith shop, a glassblowing shop, pony farms, a golf driving range, and a fantasy garden for children. There is a great path that leads from the southwestern part of the grounds through woods and meadows to the pilgrimage church of Birnau. The route was created by the monks centuries ago and is still called the Prälatenweg (path of the prelates) today. It's an 8-km (5-mile) walk (no cars permitted). ⊠ *Salem* 🕾 *07553/916–5336* ⊕ *www.salem.de* ⊠ €7 ☉ *Apr.–Oct., Mon.–Sat. 9:30–6, Sun. 10:30–6; Nov.–Mar., guided tours only, Sun. at 3.*

Städtisches Museum (*City Museum*). This museum is housed in the Reichlin-von-Meldegg house, built in 1462, one of the earliest Renaissance dwellings in Germany. It displays exhibits tracing Bodensee history and Germany's largest collection of antique dollhouses. ⊠ *Krummebergstr. 30* 🕾 *07551/991–079* ⊕ *www.museum-ueberlingen.de* ⊠ €5 ☉ *Apr.–Oct., Tues.–Sat. 9–12:30 and 2–5, Sun. 10–3.*

Wallfahrtskirche Birnau (*Pilgrimage Church; Basilika Birnau*). Just northwest of Unteruhldingen, the Wallfahrtskirche Birnau stands among vineyards overlooking the lake. The church was built by the master architect Peter Thumb between 1746 and 1750. Its exterior consists of pink-and-white plaster and a tapering clock-tower spire above the main entrance. The interior is overwhelmingly rich, full of movement, light, and color. It's hard to single out highlights from such a profusion of ornament, but look for the *Honigschlecker* ("honey sucker"), a gold-and-white cherub beside the altar, dedicated to St. Bernard of Clairvaux, "whose words are sweet as honey" (it's the last altar on the right as you face the high altar). The cherub is sucking honey from his finger, which he's just pulled out of a beehive. The fanciful spirit of this play on words is continued in the small squares of glass set into the pink screen that rises high above the main altar; the gilt dripping from the walls; the swaying, swooning statues; and the swooping figures on the ceiling. ⊠ *Birnau-Maurach 5, Uhldingen-Mühlhofen* 🕾 *07556/92030* ⊕ *www.birnau.de* ☉ *May–Sept., daily 7:30–7; Oct.– Apr., daily 7:30–5:30.*

■ OFF THE
BEATEN
PATH

Affenberg (*Monkey Mountain*). On the road between Überlingen and Salem, the Affenberg (Monkey Mountain) is a 50-plus-acre park that serves as home to more than 200 free-roaming Barbary apes, as well as deer, aquatic birds, gray herons, ducks, coots, and—during nesting time—a colony of white storks. ⊠ *Mendlishauser Hof, on rd. between Überlingen and Salem* 🕾 *07553/381* ⊕ *www.affenberg-salem.de* ⊠ €8 ☉ *Mid-Mar.–Nov., daily 9–6; last entry at 5:30.*

Near Überlingen, Schloss Salem was constructed as a convent and then transformed into a palace. Leading from the palace grounds is a 5-mile path to Wallfahrtskirche Birnau (Pilgrimage Church).

WHERE TO STAY

$
HOTEL
FAMILY
Landgasthof zum Adler. This unpretentious, rustic country inn in a village a few miles north of Überlingen has a blue-and-white half-timber facade, scrubbed wooden floors, maple-wood tables, and thick down comforters on the beds. **Pros:** good food in old wooden restaurant; modern rooms in annex; family friendly. **Cons:** rooms on the street side can be noisy; a bit far from Überlingen; family-oriented. $ *Rooms from: €78 ⊠ Hauptstr. 44, Lippertsreute ☎ 07553/82550 ⊕ www.adler-lippertsreute.de ⤳ 16 rooms* ⦿*Breakfast.*

$$
HOTEL
Romantik Hotel Johanniter Kreuz. Parts of this half-timber hotel in a small village north Überlingen date from the 17th century, setting a romantic tone that's further enhanced by the huge fireplace in the center of the restaurant. **Pros:** choice of very different rooms; spacious; modern, and yet welcoming lobby; family run; cozy restaurant; golf course close by. **Cons:** 3 km (2 miles) from center of town; long corridors from historic part of hotel to reach elevator in new part of the hotel. $ *Rooms from: €130 ⊠ Johanniterweg 11, Andelshofen ☎ 07551/937–060 ⊕ www.johanniter-kreuz.de ⤳ 29 rooms* ⦿*Breakfast.*

$$
HOTEL
Schäpfle. The charm of this ivy-covered hotel in the center of town has been preserved and supplemented through time—in the hallways you'll find quaint furniture and even an old Singer sewing machine painted with flowers. **Pros:** center of town; local atmosphere in restaurant; annex with lake view. **Cons:** parking nearby, but for a fee; no credit cards. $ *Rooms from: €105 ⊠ Jakob-Kessenringstr. 12 and 14 ☎ 07551/83070 ⊕ www.schaepfle.de ⤳ 32 rooms in 2 houses* ▬ *No credit cards* ⦿*Breakfast.*

SHOPPING

The beauty and charm of Überlingen is one reason so many artists work and live here; there are more than 20 workshops and artists' shops where you can browse and buy at reasonable prices. ■ TIP→ Ask at the tourist office for the brochure listing all the galleries.

Holzer Goldschmiede. You'll find this master goldsmith's studio near the city's Franziskanertor. ✉ *Turmg. 8, Am Franziskanertor* ☎ *07551/61525* ⊕ *www.goldschmiede-holzer.de.*

THE UPPER SWABIAN BAROQUE ROAD

From Friedrichshafen, B-30 leads north along the valley of the little River Schussen and links up with one of Germany's less-known but most attractive scenic routes. The Oberschwäbische Barockstrasse (Upper Swabian Baroque Road) follows a rich series of baroque churches and abbeys, including Germany's largest baroque church, the basilica in Weingarten.

RAVENSBURG

20 km (12 miles) north of Friedrichshafen.

The Free Imperial City of Ravensburg once competed with Augsburg and Nürnberg for economic supremacy in southern Germany. The Thirty Years' War put an end to the city's hopes by reducing it to little more than a medieval backwater. The city's loss proved fortuitous only in that many of its original features have remained much as they were built (in the 19th century, medieval towns usually tore down their medieval walls and towers, which were considered ungainly and constraining). Fourteen of Ravensburg's town gates and towers survive, and the Altstadt is among the best preserved in Germany.

GETTING HERE AND AROUND

Consider taking an official tour of the city, which grants you access to some of the towers for a splendid view of Ravensburg and the surrounding countryside. Tours are available at the tourist office.

ESSENTIALS

Visitor Information Ravensburg Tourist-Information ✉ *Kirchstr. 16* ☎ *0751/82800* ⊕ *www.ravensburg.de.*

EXPLORING
TOP ATTRACTIONS

Defensive Towers. Ravensburg is home to a remarkable collection of well-preserved medieval towers and city gates. Highlights include the **Grüner Turm** (Green Tower), so called for its green tiles, many of which are 14th-century originals. Another stout defense tower is the massive **Obertor** (Upper Tower), the oldest gate in the city walls. The curiously named **Mehlsack** (Flour Sack) tower—so called because of its rounded shape and whitewash exterior—stands 170 feet high and sits upon the highest point of the city. From April to October, visitors can climb to the top of the Mehlsack or the equally tall **Blaserturm** (Trumpeter's Tower) for rooftop views over the city. ☎ *0751/82800* ⊕ *www. ravensburg.de* ✂ *Towers €1.50* ⊗ *Mehlsack: Apr. and Oct., weekends*

10–3; May–Sept., daily 10–3. Blaserturm: Apr.–July, Sept., and Oct., weekdays 2–5, Sat. 10–3; Aug., weekdays 10–5, Sat. 10–3.

Marienplatz. Many of Ravensburg's monuments that most recall the town's wealthy past are concentrated on this central square. To the west is the 14th-century **Kornhaus** (Granary); once the corn exchange for all of Upper Swabia, it now houses the public library. The late-Gothic **Rathaus** is a staid, red building with a Renaissance bay window and imposing late-Gothic rooms inside. Next to it stands the 15th-century **Waaghaus** (Weighing House), the town's weigh station and central warehouse. Its tower, the **Blaserturm** (Trumpeter's Tower), which served as the watchman's abode, was rebuilt in 1556 after a fire and now bears a pretty Renaissance helmet. Finally there's the colorfully frescoed **Lederhaus,** once the headquarters of the city's leather workers, and now home to a café. ■ TIP➔ On Saturday morning the square comes alive with a large market.

WORTH NOTING

Evangelische Stadtkirche (*Protestant Church*). That ecclesiastical and commercial life were never entirely separate in medieval towns is evident in this church, once part of a 14th-century monastery. The stairs on the west side of the church's chancel lead to the meeting room of the Ravensburger Gesellschaft (Ravensburg Society), an organization of linen merchants established in 1400. After the Reformation, Catholics and Protestants shared the church, but in 1810 the Protestants were given the entire building. The neo-Gothic stained-glass windows on the west side, depicting important figures of the Reformation such as Martin Luther and Ulrich Zwingli, were sponsored by wealthy burghers. ✉ *Marienpl. 5* ⊕ *www.ravensburg-evangelisch.de.*

Humpis-Quartier Museum. Glass walkways, stairways, and a central courtyard connect the well-preserved medieval residences at this museum, where visitors can take a close look into the lives of Ravensburgers in the middle ages. The residences once belonged to the Humpis family, who were traders in the 15th century. ✉ *Marktstr. 45* ☎ *0751/82820* ⊕ *www.museum-humpis-quartier.de* 🎫 *€4* ⊙ *Tues., Wed., and Fri.–Sun. 11–6, Thurs. 11–8.*

Kirche St. Peter und Paul (*St. Petrus und Paulus*). Just to the southwest of Ravensburg in the village of Weissenau stands this old church, which was part of a 12th-century Premonstratensian monastery and now has a high baroque facade. The interior is a stupendous baroque masterpiece, with ceiling paintings by Joseph Hafner that create the illusion of cupolas, and vivacious stuccowork by Johannes Schmuzer, one of the famous stucco artists from Wessobrunn. ✉ *Abteistr. 2–3, Weissenau* ☎ *0751/61590* ⊕ *www.pfarrgemeinde-weissenau.de* ⊙ *Daily 9–6.*

Liebfrauenkirche (*Church of Our Lady*). Ravensburg's true parish church, the Gothic 14th-century Liebfrauenkirche, is elegantly simple on the outside but almost entirely rebuilt inside, having reopened in early 2011 following major renovations. Among the finest treasures within are the 15th-century stained-glass windows in the choir and the heavily gilt altar. In a side altar is a copy of a carved Madonna, the *Schutzmantelfrau;* the late-14th-century original is in Berlin's Dahlem Museum. ✉ *Kirchstr. 18* ⊕ *www.kath-rv.de* ⊙ *Daily 7–7.*

DID YOU KNOW?

The Weingarten Basilica's altar is said to hold a vial of Christ's blood. On the day after Ascension Thursday, a huge procession of pilgrims makes its way to the basilica.

FAMILY **Museum Ravensburger.** Ravensburg is a familiar name to all jigsaw-puzzle fans, because the Ravensburg publishing house produces the world's largest selection of puzzles, in addition to many other children's games. Here you can explore the history of the company, founded in 1883 by Otto Robert Maier. Be sure to try out new and classic games via the interactive game stations throughout the museum. ⊠ *Marktstr. 26* ☎ *07542/400–110* ⊕ *www.museum-ravensburger.de* 🎫*€5.50* ⊘ *Apr.– Sept., Tues.–Sun. 10–6; Oct.–Mar., Tues.–Sun. 11–6.*

WHERE TO EAT AND STAY

$ ✕ **Firenze Caffé e Gelateria.** This bustling multilevel café opens early and
ITALIAN closes late and offers a mind-boggling array of ice-cream dishes and other sweet and savory fare. For a quick and inexpensive meal, consider the tasty breakfasts, sandwiches, and German- and Italian-influenced items on offer. 💲*Average main: €10* ⊠ *Marienpl. 47* ☎ *0751/24665* ⊟ *No credit cards.*

$$ ✕ **Rebleutehaus.** Follow a small alley off the Marienplatz to this warm,
GERMAN relaxed restaurant set in an old guildhall with a beautiful *Tonnendecke*
Fodor's Choice (barrel ceiling). The restaurant shares a kitchen with the Restaurant
★ Waldhorn; the quality is the same, but the prices at Rebleutehaus are easier on the wallet. Try fish from the Bodensee in season. Reservations are a good idea for dinner. 💲*Average main: €20* ⊠ *Schulg. 15* ☎ *0751/36120* ⊕ *www.waldhorn.de* ⊘ *Closed Sun.*

$ 🏨 **Gasthof Ochsen.** At this typical, family-owned Swabian inn, the per-
HOTEL sonable Kimpfler family extends a warm welcome. **Pros:** warm atmosphere and good Swabian food in the cozy restaurant; many rooms newly refurbished. **Cons:** parking not on site. 💲*Rooms from: €89* ⊠ *Burgstr. 1* ☎ *0751/25480* ⊕ *www.ochsen-rv.de* ⇄ *26 rooms* ⊘ *Restaurant closed to public Sun.* ⦿ *Breakfast.*

WEINGARTEN

5 km (3 miles) north of Ravensburg.

Weingarten is famous throughout Germany for its huge and hugely impressive basilica, which you can see up on a hill from miles away, long before you get to the town. The city has grown during the last century as several small and midsize industries settled here. It's now an interesting mixture, its historic old town surrounded by a small, prosperous industrial city.

ESSENTIALS

Visitor Information Weingarten Amt für Kultur- und Tourismus ⊠ *Münsterpl. 1* ☎ *0751/405–232* ⊕ *www.weingarten-online.de.*

EXPLORING

Alemannenmuseum. If you want to learn about early Germans—residents from the 6th, 7th, and 8th centuries whose graves are just outside town—visit the Alemannenmuseum in the Kornhaus, which was once a granary. Archaeologists discovered the hundreds of Alemannic graves in the 1950s. ⊠ *Karlstr. 28* ☎ *0751/49343 for general info, 0751/405–255 for tours* ⊕ *www.weingarten-online.de* 🎫*€2* ⊘ *Wed.–Sun. 2–5.*

Weingarten Basilica (*St. Martin Basilica*). At 220 feet high and more than 300 feet long, Weingarten Basilica is the largest baroque church in Germany. It was built as the church of one of the oldest and most venerable convents in the country, founded in 1056 by the wife of Guelph IV. The Guelph dynasty ruled large areas of Upper Swabia, and generations of family members lie buried in the church. The majestic edifice was renowned because of its little vial said to contain drops of Christ's blood. First mentioned by Charlemagne, the vial passed to the convent in 1094, entrusted to its safekeeping by the Guelph queen Juditha, sister-in-law of William the Conqueror. Weingarten then became one of Germany's foremost pilgrimage sites. ■TIP➜ **To this day, on the day after Ascension Thursday, the anniversary of the day the vial of Christ's blood was entrusted to the convent, a huge procession of pilgrims wends its way to the basilica. It's well worth seeing the procession, which is headed by nearly 3,000 horsemen (many local farmers breed horses just for this occasion).** The basilica was decorated by leading early-18th-century German and Austrian artists: stuccowork by Franz Schmuzer, ceiling frescoes by Cosmas Damian Asam, and a Donato Frisoni altar—one of the most breathtakingly ornate in Europe, with nearly 80-foot-high towers on either side. The organ, installed by Josef Gabler between 1737 and 1750, is among the largest in the country. ⊠ *Kirchpl. 6* ⊕ *www.st-martin-weingarten.de* ⊗ *Nov.–Mar., daily 8–5; Apr.–Oct., daily 8–7.*

<table>
<tr><td>

OFF THE BEATEN PATH

</td><td>

Hopfenmuseum Tettnang (*Tettnang Hops Museum*). This museum, dedicated to brewing, is in the tiny village of Siggenweiler, 3 km (2 miles) northwest of Tettnang—the second-largest hops-growing area in Germany. Tettnang exports most of its so-called "green gold" to the United States. In the museum there is a small pub where you can buy a pretzel and of course a beer made with Tettnang hops. ⊠ *Hopfengut 20, Siggenweiler* ☎ *07542/952–206* ⊕ *www.hopfenmuseum-tettnang.de* ☞ *€5* ⊗ *Apr.–Oct., Tues.–Sun. 10:30–6.*

</td></tr>
</table>

AROUND THE BODANRÜCK PENINSULA

The immense Bodensee owes its name to a small, insignificant town, Bodman, on the Bodanrück Peninsula, at the northwestern edge of the lake. ■TIP➜ **The peninsula's most popular destinations, Konstanz and Mainau, are reachable by ferry from Meersburg—by far the most romantic way to get to the area.** The other option is to take the road (B-31, then B-34, and finally B-33) that skirts the western arm of the Bodensee and ends its German journey at Konstanz.

KONSTANZ

A ½-hr ferry ride from Meersburg.

The university town of Konstanz is the largest on the Bodensee; it straddles the Rhine as it flows out of the lake, placing itself both on the Bodanrück Peninsula and the Switzerland side of the lake, where it adjoins the Swiss town of Kreuzlingen. Konstanz is among the best-preserved medieval towns in Germany; during the war the Allies were

Around the Bodanrück Peninsula

unwilling to risk inadvertently bombing neutral Switzerland. On the peninsula side of the town, east of the main bridge connecting Konstanz's two halves, runs **Seestrasse,** a stately promenade of neoclassical mansions with views of the Bodensee. The Old Town center is a labyrinth of narrow streets lined with restored half-timber houses and dignified merchant dwellings. This is where you'll find restaurants, hotels, pubs, and much of the nightlife.

It's claimed that Konstanz was founded in the 3rd century by Emperor Constantine Chlorus, father of Constantine the Great. The story is probably untrue, though it's certain there was a Roman garrison here. In the late 6th century Konstanz was made a bishopric; in 1192 it became a Free Imperial City. What put it on the map was the Council of Constance, held between 1414 and 1418 to settle the Great Schism (1378–1417), the rift in the church caused by two separate lines of popes, one ruling from Rome, the other from Avignon. The Council resolved the problem in 1417 by electing Martin V as the true, and only, pope. The church had also agreed to restore the Holy Roman emperor's (Sigismund's) role in electing the pope, but only if Sigismund silenced the rebel theologian Jan Hus, of Bohemia. Even though Sigismund had allowed Hus safe passage to Konstanz for the Council, he won the church's favor by having Hus burned at the stake in July 1415. In a satiric short story, the French author Honoré de Balzac created the character of Imperia, a courtesan of great beauty and cleverness, who raised the blood pressure of both religious and secular VIPs during the council. No one visiting the harbor today can miss the 28-foot statue of **Imperia** standing out on the breakwater. Dressed in a revealing and alluring style, in her hands she holds two dejected figures: the emperor and the pope. This hallmark of Konstanz, created by Peter Lenk, caused controversy when it was unveiled in April 1993.

Most people enjoy Konstanz for its worldly pleasures—the elegant Altstadt, trips on the lake, walks along the promenade, elegant shops, the restaurants, the views. The heart of the city is the **Marktstätte** (Marketplace), near the harbor, with the simple bulk of the Konzilgebäude looming behind it. Erected in 1388 as a warehouse, the **Konzilgebäude** (Council Hall) is now a concert hall. Beside the Konzilgebäude are states of Jan Hus and native son Count Ferdinand von Zeppelin (1838–1917). The Dominican monastery where Hus was held before his execution is still here, doing duty as a luxurious hotel, the Steigenberger Insel-Hotel.

GETTING HERE AND AROUND

Konstanz is in many ways the center of the lake area. You can reach Zürich airport by direct train in about an hour, and Frankfurt in 4½ hours. Swiss autobahn access to Zürich is about 10 minutes away, and you can reach the autobahn access to Stuttgart in about the same time. To reach the island of Mainau, you can take a bus, but a much more pleasant way to get there is by boat, via Meersburg. You can take another boat downriver to Schaffhausen in Switzerland, or east to the northern shore towns as well as Bregenz in Austria. The Old Town is manageable on foot.

ESSENTIALS

Visitor Information Tourist-Information Konstanz ⊠ *Bahnhofpl. 43* ☏ *07531/133–030* ⊕ *www.konstanz-tourismus.de.*

EXPLORING

Altes Rathaus (*Old Town Hall*). This old town hall was built during the Renaissance and painted with vivid frescoes—swags of flowers and fruits, shields, and sturdy knights wielding immense swords. Walk into the courtyard to admire its Renaissance restraint. ⊠ *Kanzleistr. 13.*

Münster. Konstanz's cathedral, the Münster, was the center of one of Germany's largest bishoprics until 1827, when the seat was moved to Freiburg. Construction on the cathedral continued from the 10th through the 19th century, resulting in an interesting coexistence of architectural styles: the twin-tower facade is sturdily Romanesque; the elegant and airy chapels along the aisles are full-blown 15th-century Gothic; the complex nave vaulting is Renaissance; and the choir is severely neoclassical. The Mauritius Chapel behind the altar is a 13th-century Gothic structure, 12 feet high, with some of its original vivid coloring and gilding. It's studded with statues of the Apostles and figures depicting the childhood of Jesus. ▪TIP➡ Climb the Münsterturm (Münster Tower) for views over the city and lake. ⊠ *Münsterpl. 4* 🖼*€2* ⊗ *Daily 8–6. Tower: Mon.–Sat. 10–5:30, Sun. 12:30–6.*

Niederburg. The Niederburg, the oldest part of Konstanz, is a tangle of twisting streets leading to the Rhine. From the river take a look at two of the city's old towers: the **Rheintorturm** (Rhine Tower), the one nearer the lake, and the aptly named **Pulverturm** (Powder Tower), the former city arsenal.

Rosgartenmuseum (*Rose Garden Museum*). Within the medieval guildhall of the city's butchers, this museum has a rich collection of art and artifacts from the Bodensee region. Highlights include exhibits of the life and work of the people around the Bodensee, from the Bronze Age through the Middle Ages and beyond. There's also a collection of sculpture and altar paintings from the Middle Ages. ⊠ *Rosgartenstr. 3–5* ☏ *07531/900–246* ⊕ *www.rosgartenmuseum-konstanz.de* 🖼*€3* ⊗ *Tues.–Fri. 10–6, weekends 10–5.*

For views of the Bodensee from Konstanz, head to the Seestrasse promenade.

FAMILY **Sealife.** This huge aquarium has gathered all the fish species that inhabit the Rhine and the Bodensee, from the river's beginnings in the Swiss Alps to its end in Rotterdam and the North Sea. Also check out the **Bodensee Naturmuseum** at the side entrance, which gives a comprehensive overview of the geological history of the Bodensee and its fauna and flora right down to the microscopic creatures of the region. You can buy tickets in advance online for a significantly cheaper price. ✉ *Hafenstr. 9* ☎ *07531/128–270* ⊕ *www.sealife.de* 🎟 *€16.50* 🕙 *Sept.–June, daily 10–5, July and Aug., daily 10–6.*

WHERE TO EAT

$ ✕ **Brauhaus Joh. Albrecht.** This small brewery with shiny copper cauldrons, part of a chain of five throughout Germany, serves simple
GERMAN dishes as well as regional specialties and vegetarian food on large wooden tables. Tuesday is schnitzel day, with half a dozen varieties on the menu, all of them filling—and all costing €9.99. $ *Average main: €13* ✉ *Konradig. 2* ☎ *07531/25045* ⊕ *konstanz.brauhaus-joh-albrecht.de.*

$ ✕ **Hafenhalle.** Enjoy eclectic cooking—including Italian, Bavarian, and
GERMAN Swabian fare—at this warm-weather spot on the harbor. Sit outside on the terrace and watch the busy harbor traffic, or enjoy the beer garden with sandbox for children and big TV screen for watching sports. The restaurant frequently presents sporting, culinary, and live-music events. $ *Average main: €15* ✉ *Hafenstr. 10* ☎ *07531/21126* ⊕ *www.hafenhalle.com* 🕙 *Closed Jan. and Feb.*

WHERE TO STAY

$ · HOTEL **ABC Hotel.** This hotel offers large, comfortable, individually furnished rooms, all with kitchen facilities; book the unusual Turmsuite (Tower Suite) for an especially memorable stay among exposed beams and steeply sloping walls, and with private access to the top of the tower. **Pros:** warm welcome; large airy rooms; quiet location; enough parking space; free Wi-Fi. **Cons:** not in the center of town; no elevator. $ *Rooms from: €99* ⊠ *Steinstr. 19* ☎ *07531/8900* ⊕ *www.abc-hotel.de* ⤴ *37 rooms* ⏤⎮ *Breakfast.*

$ · HOTEL **Barbarossa.** This historic hotel in the heart of Old Town has been modernized inside, but such original elements as wooden support beams lend a romantic, authentic feel. **Pros:** historic building; cozy restaurant with good food; free hotel-wide Wi-Fi. **Cons:** some rooms simply furnished; parking available but a third of a mile walk away. $ *Rooms from: €97* ⊠ *Obermarkt 8* ☎ *07531/128–990* ⊕ *www.hotelbarbarossa. de* ⤴ *50 rooms* ⏤⎮ *Breakfast.*

$$ · HOTEL **Stadthotel.** It's a five-minute walk to the lake from this friendly hotel, where rooms are modern, airy, and decorated in bright colors. **Pros:** center of town; quiet location with little traffic. **Cons:** no restaurant; parking garage five minutes away on foot. $ *Rooms from: €110* ⊠ *Bruderturmg. 2* ☎ *07531/90460* ⊕ *www.stadthotel-konstanz.com* ⤴ *24 rooms* ⏤⎮ *Breakfast.*

$$$ · HOTEL · Fodor's Choice ★ **Steigenberger Insel-Hotel.** With its original cloisters intact, this former 16th-century monastery is now the most luxurious lodging in town. **Pros:** wonderful lake views; luxurious; good restaurants. **Cons:** a few rooms look out on railroad tracks; some others need refurnishing; expensive. $ *Rooms from: €188* ⊠ *Auf der Insel 1* ☎ *07531/1250* ⊕ *www. konstanz.steigenberger.com* ⤴ *100 rooms, 2 suites* ⏤⎮ *Breakfast.*

NIGHTLIFE AND THE ARTS

Casino. Try your luck on the machines and tables of the casino in Konstanz. You must be over 21 to enter the casino. ⊠ *Seestr. 21* ☎ *07531/ 81570* ⊕ *www.casino-konstanz.de* ⤳ *€3* ⏱ *Sun.–Thurs. 2 pm–2 am, Fri.–Sat. 2 pm–3 am.*

K9 (*Kommunales Kunst- und Kulturzentrum K9*). This cultural center draws all ages with its music and dance club, theater, comedy, and cabaret. It's in the former Church of St. Paul. ⊠ *Hieronymusg. 3* ☎ *07531/16713* ⊕ *www.k9-kulturzentrum.de.*

Kulturladen (*Kula*). Concerts and variously themed DJ nights are held at Kulturladen. ⊠ *Joseph Belli Weg 5* ☎ *07531/52954* ⊕ *www. kulturladen.de.*

Rock am See. This annual late-summer rock music festival has been drawing rock fans to the Bodensee since 1985. Held at Bodensee-Stadion in Konstanz, the festival features both German and international acts. ⊠ *Bodensee-Stadion, Eichhornstr. 89* ☎ *07531/908844 for ticket service* ⊕ *www.rock-am-see.de.*

Seekuh. This cozy and crowded Italian restaurant and bar features the occasional live jazz night and also screens live football games from time to time. ⊠ *Konzilstr. 1* ☎ *07531/27232* ⊕ *www.seekuh.de.*

Seenachtfest (*Lake Night Festival*). In August, Konstanz shares this one-day city festival with neighboring Kreuzlingen in Switzerland, with street events, music, clowns, and magicians, and ending with fireworks over the lake. ⊠ *Lakefront* ⊕ *www.seenachtfest.de.*

Stadttheater (*Theater Konstanz*). The Stadttheater, Germany's oldest active theater, has staged plays since 1609 and has its own repertory company. ⊠ *Konzilstr. 11* ☎ *07531/900–150 for tickets* ⊕ *www.theaterkonstanz.de.*

SPORTS AND THE OUTDOORS

BICYCLING

Bike rentals generally cost €12 per day.

Velotours Touristik GmbH. You can book bicycle tours and rent bikes at Velotours Touristik GmbH. ⊠ *Bücklestr. 13* ☎ *07531/98280* ⊕ *www.velotours.de.*

Kultur-Rädle. This friendly store rents bikes at the main train station. A two-day rental costs 20 euros. ⊠ *Bahnhofpl. 29* ☎ *07531/27310* ⊕ *www.kultur-raedle.de.*

BOATING

Wilde Flotte — Segel & Wassersportschule Konstanz Wallhausen (*Wild Fleet*). This sailing school offers boat charters—both skippered and solo—as well as lessons in sailing, wakeboarding and waterskiing. ⊠ *Uferstr. 16, Wallhausen* ☎ *07533/997–8802* ⊕ *www.wilde-flotte.de.*

Yachtcharter Konstanz. Sail and motor yachts are available at Yachtcharter Konstanz. ⊠ *Hafenstr. 7b* ☎ *07531/363–3970* ⊕ *www.yachtcharter-konstanz.de.*

SHOPPING

It's worthwhile to roam the streets of the old part of town, where there are several gold- and silversmiths and jewelers.

Modehaus Fischer. This elegant fashion store has enough style for a city ten times the size of Konstanz. Much of its business comes from wealthy Swiss who visit Konstanz for what they consider bargain prices. Modehaus Fischer deals in well-known international fashion stock, including handbags and exquisite shoes. The store is actually spread over three branches a few blocks apart—two for women, and one for men at Obermarkt. ⊠ *Rosgartenstr. 36, Hussenstr. 29, and Obermarkt. 1* ☎ *07531/22990* ⊕ *www.modefischer.de.*

MAINAU

Fodor'sChoice ★

7 km (4½ miles) north of Konstanz by road; by ferry, ½–1 hr from Konstanz (depending on route), or 20 mins from Meersburg.

One of the most unusual sights in Germany, Mainau is a tiny island given over to the cultivation of rare plants and splashy displays of more than a million tulips, hyacinths, and narcissi. Rhododendrons and roses bloom from May to July; dahlias dominate the late summer. A greenhouse nurtures palms and tropical plants.

The island was originally the property of the Teutonic Knights, who settled here during the 13th century. In the 19th century Mainau passed to Grand Duke Friedrich I of Baden, a man with a passion for botany.

Mainau Island, on the Bodensee, is covered with flowering gardens.

He laid out most of the gardens and introduced many of the island's more exotic specimens. His daughter Victoria, later queen of Sweden, gave the island to her son, Prince Wilhelm, and it has remained Swedish ever since. Today it's owned by the family of Prince Wilhelm's son, Count Lennart Bernadotte. In the former main reception hall in the castle are changing art exhibitions.

GETTING HERE AND AROUND

Ferries to the island from Meersburg and Konstanz depart from April to October approximately every 1½ hours between 9 and 5. You must purchase a ticket to enter the island, which is open year-round from dawn until dusk. There's a small bridge to the island. At night you can drive across it to the restaurants.

ESSENTIALS

Visitor Information Insel Mainau ⊠ *Mainaustr. 1, Konstanz* ☎ *07531/3030* ⊕ *www.mainau.de* ✉ *Late Mar.–late Oct., dawn–5 pm €17.50, 5 pm–dusk, €8.75; late Oct.–late Mar., €8.75 anytime* ☉ *Daily dawn–dusk.*

EXPLORING

Das Schmetterlinghaus. Beyond the flora, the island of Mainau's other colorful extravagance is Das Schmetterlinghaus, Germany's largest butterfly conservatory. On a circular walk through a semitropical landscape with water cascading through rare vegetation, you'll see hundreds of butterflies flying, feeding, and mating. The exhibition in the foyer explains the butterflies' life cycle, habitats, and ecological connections. Like the park, this oasis is open year-round. ⊠ *Insel Mainau, Mainaustr. 1, Konstanz* ⊕ *www.mainau.de/schmetterlingshaus.html* ☉ *Daily 10–7.*

Gärtnerturm. In the island's information center in the Gärtnerturm (Gardener's Tower) in the middle of the island, several films on Mainau and the Bodensee are shown.

WHERE TO EAT

There are nine restaurants and cafés on the island, but nowhere to stay overnight.

$$
SCANDINAVIAN
✗ **Schwedenschenke.** The lunchtime crowd gets what it needs here—fast and good service. At dinnertime candlelight adds some extra style. The resident Bernadotte family is Swedish, and so are the specialties of the chef. Have your hotel reserve a table for you. ■ TIP➔ After 6 pm your reservation will be checked at the gate, and you can drive onto the island without having to pay admission. $ *Average main: €18* ⊠ *Insel Mainau* ☎ *07531/303–156* ⊕ *www.mainau.de/schwedenschenke.html* ⊗ *Closed Jan.–mid-Mar. No dinner Nov. or Dec.*

REICHENAU

10 km (6 miles) northwest of Konstanz, 50 mins by ferry from Konstanz.

Reichenau is an island rich in vegetation, but unlike Mainau, it features vegetables, not flowers. In fact, 15% of its area (the island is 5 km [3 miles] long and 1½ km [1 mile] wide) is covered by greenhouses and crops of one kind or another. It also has three of Europe's most beautiful Romanesque churches, a legacy of Reichenau's past as a monastic center in the early Middle Ages. The churches are in each of the island's villages—**Oberzell, Mittelzell,** and **Niederzell,** which are separated by only 1 km (½ mile). Along the shore are pleasant pathways for walking or biking.

ESSENTIALS

Visitor Information Reichenau Tourist-Information ⊠ *Pirminstr. 145* ☎ *07534/92070* ⊕ *www.reichenau.de.*

EXPLORING

Münster of St. Maria and St. Markus. Begun in 816, the Münster of St. Maria and St. Markus, the monastery's church, is the largest and most important of Reichenau's island's of Romanesque churches. Perhaps its most striking architectural feature is the roof, whose beams and ties are open for all to see. The monastery was founded in 725 by St. Pirmin and became one of the most important cultural centers of the Carolingian Empire. It reached its zenith around 1000, when 700 monks lived here. It was then probably the most important center of book illumination in Germany. The building is simple but by no means crude. Visit the **Schatzkammer** (Treasury) to see some of its more important holdings. They include a 5th-century ivory goblet with two carefully incised scenes of Christ's miracles, and some priceless stained glass that is almost 1,000 years old. ⊠ *Münsterpl. 3, Mittelzell* ☎ *07534/92070* ⊗ *Schatzkammer: Mon.–Sat. 10–noon and 3–5.*

Museum Reichenau. This museum of local history, in the Old Town Hall of Mittelzell, lends interesting insights into life on the island over the centuries. ⊠ *Ergat 1–3, Mittelzell* ☎ *07534/999–321* ⊕ *www.museumreichenau.de* ⊡ *€3* ⊗ *Apr.–July, Sept., and Oct., daily 10:30–4:30; July and Aug., daily 10:30–5:30; Nov.–Mar., weekends and holidays 2–5.*

6

Stiftskirche St. Georg (*Collegiate Church of St. George*). The Stiftskirche St. Georg, in Oberzell, was built around 900; now cabbages grow in ranks up to its rough plaster walls. Small round-head windows, a simple square tower, and massive buttresses signal the church's Romanesque origin from the outside. The interior is covered with frescoes painted by the monks in around 1000. They depict the eight miracles of Christ. ⊠ *Seestr. 4, Oberzell* ⊕ *www.reichenau.de.*

Stiftskirche St. Peter und Paul (*St. Peter and Paul Parish Church*). This Stiftskirche, at Niederzell, was revamped around 1750. The faded Romanesque frescoes in the apse contrast with bold rococo paintings on the ceiling and flowery stucco. ⊠ *Cnr. Eginostr. and Fischerg., Niederzell* ⊕ *www.reichenau.de.*

WHERE TO EAT AND STAY

$
GERMAN

✗ **Kiosk am Yachthafen.** This small restaurant is an ideal lunch, drink, or snack stop. In good weather, you can sit outside and watch the boats come and go. It's also a perfect place to try the Bodensee specialty *Zanderknusperle* (crispy battered pike-perch bites). ⑤ *Average main: €10* ⊠ *Yacht Harbor, Hermannus-Contractus-Str. 30* ☎ *07534/999–655* ⊕ *www.sbrestaurant-reichenau.de* ⊟ *No credit cards* ⊘ *Closed Nov.–Mar.*

$
HOTEL

☷ **Strandhotel Löchnerhaus.** Standing commandingly on the water's edge fronted by its own boat pier, the Strandhotel (Beach Hotel) Löchnerhaus exudes a retro Riviera feel. **Pros:** nice location; views over the lake into Switzerland; quiet. **Cons:** closed in winter; some rooms expensive. ⑤ *Rooms from: €90* ⊠ *An der Schiffslände 12* ☎ *07534/8030* ⊕ *www.loechnerhaus.de* ↴ *41 rooms* ⊘ *Closed Nov.–Feb.* ⦿| *Breakfast.*

THE BLACK
FOREST

WELCOME TO
THE BLACK FOREST

TOP REASONS TO GO

★ **Extraordinary regional specialties:** Dig into Black Forest cake, Schwarzwald ham (only authentic if smoked over pinecones), and the incredible brews from the Alpirsbach Brewery.

★ **Freiburg Münster:** One of the most beautiful gothic churches in Germany, the Cathedral of Freiburg survived the war unscathed. The view from the bell tower is stunning.

★ **Going cuckoo:** Look for a cuckoo clock from Triberg (or a nice watch from Pforzheim).

★ **Healing waters:** More than 30 spas with a wide range of treatments await to make visitors feel whole again, but nothing beats the 3½-hour session at the Friedrichsbad in Baden-Baden.

★ **Libations at Kaiserstuhl:** Enjoy a local wine in the wine-maker's yard or cellar with Black Forest ham and dark bread. It's especially nice when the grapes are being harvested.

1 The Northern Black Forest. The gem of the northern Black Forest is the genteel spa town of Baden-Baden, full of quiet charm and dripping with elegance.

2 The Central Black Forest. The central Black Forest typifies the region as a whole. Alpirsbach's half-timber houses, Triberg's cuckoo clocks, and the nation's highest waterfalls all nestle among a series of steep-sided valleys.

3 The Southern Black Forest. In the south, Freiburg is one of the country's most historic cities, and even the hordes of summer visitors can't quell the natural beauty of the Titisee Lake.

GETTING ORIENTED

The southwest corner of Germany divides itself neatly into two distinct geographical regions. The western half borders France and lies in the wide flat plains of the Rhine Valley, where all the larger cities are located. To the east tower the rugged hills of the Black Forest itself, crisscrossed by winding mountain roads and dotted with picturesque villages.

7

SPAS

The restorative powers of a good soak in a hot pool or sweating it out in a 190-degree sauna are the cornerstones of the German notion of physical and mental wellness and relaxation. The concept of *Erholiung* (regeneration) is taken seriously.

(above and lower right) Relax in the warm thermal pools of the Black Forest's spas. (upper right) Waterfall at the Caracalla Therme in Baden-Baden

Endowed with mountain air, salty coastlines, and natural thermal springs, Germany has long enjoyed a spa tradition. Seeking relief from the pains of battle, the Romans erected baths here almost 2,000 years ago, and the 19th century saw spa towns across the country flourish as Europe's upper classes began to appreciate the soothing effects of fresh air and mineral waters. These days there are hundreds of facilities throughout the country ranging from huge, sophisticated resorts offering precious stone massages and chocolate baths to smaller "wellness" hotels with not much more than a sauna and a relaxation room. There are also plenty of public spas, where a day's bathing won't set you back much more than the price of a movie ticket.

—Jeff Kavanagh

DRINKING IT IN

Taking the waters in a spa town often involves imbibing some as well. Bad Mergentheim and Baden-Baden are renowned for their drinking-water springs and the healing properties of the mineral waters that spill from them. Used for everything from the stimulation of the pancreas to curing a sore throat, they are drunk by thousands of visitors every year.

SPA ETIQUETTE

NUDITY

Sitting naked in a dimly lit, scorching-hot room or floating au naturel in a thermal pool among a group of strangers may not be everyone's idea of relaxation. Most Germans have been taken in by the *Frei Körper Kultur* (Free Body Culture) that stresses a connection to nature through public nudity. Saunas and steam rooms are almost always "textile-free" areas, as are some hot pools. They're also all mainly mixed sex. The theory is that the body needs to be unencumbered to enjoy the full curative effects of the heat and water. You'll also be expected to strip down if you've booked a massage, although a towel will be provided to preserve some modesty. If you're not sure what to take off and what to leave on, don't be afraid to ask.

BATHROBES, TOWELS, AND SANDALS

More upmarket wellness locations will provide you with all three, while public spas will expect you to at least bring your own towel. Bathrobes and sandals should be worn in relaxation areas and left outside saunas and steam baths, and towels laid beneath you in the sauna to absorb excess sweat. Most facilities provide these items for purchase or will loan them to you for a small fee.

SHOWERING

A quick shower before first jumping in a pool or entering a sauna is expected, and required between transferring yourself from a sweaty sauna to a plunge pool. A refreshing rinse between each sauna session is part of the procedure, not just for hygiene but also for its therapeutic effects.

TALKING

Given that spas are designed to be oases of wellness and relaxation, loud conversation in "adult" areas of the facility, particularly in saunas, steam rooms, and relaxation areas, may be met with sighs of disapproval or even a telling-off.

SPA GLOSSARY

Algae and mud therapy: Applied as packs or full-body bath treatments to nourish the skin and draw out toxins.

Aromatherapy baths: Oils such as bergamot, cypress, and sandalwood are added to hot baths in order to lift the spirits and reduce anxiety.

Ayurveda: Refers to Indian techniques including massage, oils, herbs, and diet to encourage perfect body balance.

Jet massage: Involves standing upright and being sprayed with high-pressure water jets that follow the direction of your blood flow, thereby stimulating circulation.

Liquid sound therapy: A relaxation technique that entails lying in body temperature saltwater and listening to classical or electronic music being played through the water while a kaleidoscope of colors illuminates your surroundings.

Reflexology: Massage on the pressure points of feet, hands, and ears.

Thalasso therapy: A spa treatment employing sea air, water, and mud to heal the body.

7

Updated by
Lee A. Evans

The name conjures up images of a wild, isolated place where time passes slowly. The dense woodland of the Black Forest—*Schwarzwald* in German—stretches away to the horizon, but this southwest corner of Baden-Württemberg (in the larger region known as Swabia) is neither inaccessible nor dull.

The Black Forest is known the world over for cuckoo clocks; the women's native costume with huge red or black hat pom-poms; and the wild, almost pagan way the Carnival season is celebrated. Swabians are the butt of endless jokes about their frugality and supposedly simplistic nature. The first travelers checked in here 19 centuries ago, when the Roman emperor Caracalla and his army rested and soothed their battle wounds in the natural-spring waters at what later became Baden-Baden.

Europe's upper-crust society discovered Baden-Baden when it convened nearby for the Congress of Rastatt from 1797 to 1799, which attempted to end the wars of the French Revolution. In the 19th century kings, queens, emperors, princes, princesses, members of Napoléon's family, and the Russian nobility, along with actors, writers, and composers, flocked to the little spa town. Turgenev, Dostoyevsky, and Tolstoy were among the Russian contingent. Victor Hugo was a frequent visitor. Brahms composed lilting melodies in this calm setting. Queen Victoria spent her vacations here. Mark Twain put the Black Forest on the map for Americans by stating, "Here [. . .] you lose track of time in ten minutes and the world in twenty," in his 1880 book *A Tramp Abroad*. Today it's a favorite getaway for movie stars and millionaires. The spa is the great social equalizer where you can "take the waters," just as the Romans first did 2,000 years ago. The Black Forest sporting scene caters particularly to the German enthusiasm for hiking. The Schwarzwald-Verein, an outdoor association in the region, maintains no fewer than 30,000 km (18,000 miles) of hiking trails. In winter the terrain is ideally suited for cross-country skiing.

PLANNING

WHEN TO GO

The Black Forest is one of the most heavily visited mountain regions in Europe, so make reservations well in advance for the better-known spas and hotels. In summer the area around Titisee is particularly crowded. In early fall and late spring, the Black Forest is less crowded (except during the Easter holidays) but just as beautiful. Some spa hotels close for winter.

GETTING HERE AND AROUND

AIR TRAVEL

The closest major international airports in Germany are Stuttgart and Frankfurt. Strasbourg, in neighboring French Alsace, and the Swiss border city of Basel, the latter just 70 km (43 miles) from Freiburg, are also reasonably close. An up-and-coming airport is the Baden-Airpark, now known more commonly as Karlsruhe-Baden, near Baden-Baden. It is used by European budget carriers including Ryanair (⊕ *www.ryanair. com*) and Air Berlin (⊕ *www.airberlin.com*), serving short-haul international destinations such as London, Dublin, and Barcelona.

Airport Information Aeroport International de Strasbourg ☎ *00333/8864– 6767* ⊕ *www.strasbourg.aeroport.fr.* **EuroAirport Basel-Mulhouse-Freiburg** ☎ *0389/9031–11 in France* ⊕ *www.euroairport.com.* **Flughafen Frankfurt Main** ☎ *01805/372–4636* ⊕ *www.frankfurt-airport.de.* **Flughafen Stuttgart** ☎ *01805/948–444* ⊕ *www.flughafen-stuttgart.de.* **Karlsruhe-Baden** ☎ *07229/662–000* ⊕ *www.badenairpark.de.*

BUS TRAVEL

The bus system is partially owned by and coordinated with the German Railways, so it's easy to reach every corner of the Black Forest by bus and train. Bus stations are usually at or near the train station. For more information, contact the Regionalbusverkehr Südwest (Regional Bus Lines) in Karlsruhe.

Bus Information Regionalbusverkehr Südwest (*Regional Bus Lines*). ✉ *Karlsruhe* ☎ *0721/84060* ⊕ *www.suedwestbus.de.*

CAR TRAVEL

The main autobahns are the A-5 (Frankfurt–Karlsruhe–Basel), which runs through the Rhine Valley along the western length of the Black Forest; A-81 (Stuttgart–Bodensee) in the east; and A-8 (Karlsruhe–Stuttgart) in the north. Good two-lane highways crisscross the entire region. B-3 runs parallel to A-5 and follows the Baden Wine Road. Traffic jams on weekends and holidays are not uncommon. Taking the side roads might not save time, but they are a lot more interesting. The Schwarzwald-Hochstrasse is one of the area's most scenic (but also most trafficked) routes, running from Freudenstadt to Baden-Baden. The region's tourist office has mapped out thematic driving routes: the Valley Road, the Spa Road, the Baden Wine Road, the Asparagus Road, and the Clock Road. Most points along these routes can also be reached by train or bus.

Freiburg, the region's major city, is 275 km (170 miles) south of Frankfurt and 410 km (254 miles) west of Munich.

TRAIN TRAVEL

Karlsruhe, Baden-Baden, and Freiburg are served by fast ICE trains zipping between Frankfurt-am-Main and Basel in Switzerland. Regional express trains also link these hubs with many other places locally, including Freudenstadt, Titisee, and, in particular, the spectacular climb from Baden-Baden to Triberg, one of the highest railways in Germany.

Local lines connect most of the smaller towns. Two east–west routes—the Schwarzwaldbahn (Black Forest Railway) and the Höllental Railway—are among the most spectacular in the country. Many small towns participate in the KONUS program that allows you to travel for free on many Black Forest train lines while staying in the region. Details are available from Deutsche Bahn.

Train Information Deutsche Bahn ☏ *11861* ⊕ *www.bahn.de.*

RESTAURANTS

Restaurants in the Black Forest range from award-winning dining rooms to simple country inns. Old *Kachelöfen* (tile stoves) are still in use in many area restaurants; try to sit near one if it's cold outside.

Prices in the reviews are the average cost of a main course at dinner, or if dinner is not served, at lunch.

HOTELS

Accommodations in the Black Forest are varied and plentiful, from simple rooms in farmhouses to five-star luxury. Some properties have been passed down in the same family for generations. *Gasthöfe* offer low prices and local color. Keep in mind that most hotels in the region do not offer air-conditioning.

Prices in the reviews are the lowest cost of a standard double room in high season. For expanded reviews, facilities, and current deals, visit Fodors.com.

PLANNING YOUR TIME

The lively, student-driven city of Freiburg, Germany's "greenest" town, is the obvious base from which to explore the Black Forest. Don't miss "taking the water" at a spa in Baden-Baden, a charming place with all facilities on tap. Bear in mind that driving times and distances push the farthest points in the Black Forest out of reach of easy day trips from these cities. The winding, often steep Black Forest highways can make for slow driving, so you may want to consider adding overnight stays at other locations. Freudenstadt's vast market square lends it a uniquely pleasant atmosphere, and Triberg's mountain location is popular, but it remains picturesque. If there is one place in the region to go out of your way to get a beer, head to Alpirsbach.

VISITOR INFORMATION

Schwarzwald Tourismus GmbH ✉ *Ludwigstr. 23, Freiburg* ☏ *0761/896–460* ⊕ *www.schwarzwald-tourismus.info.*

THE NORTHERN BLACK FOREST

This region is densely wooded, and dotted with little lakes such as the Mummelsee and the Wildsee. The Black Forest Spa Route (270 km [167 miles]) links many of the spas in the region, from Baden-Baden (the best known) to Bad Wildbad. Other regional treasures are the lovely Nagold River; ancient towns such as Hirsau; and the magnificent abbey at Maulbronn, near Pforzheim.

PFORZHEIM

35 km (22 miles) southeast of Karlsruhe, just off the A-8 autobahn, the main Munich–Karlsruhe route.

Although Pforzheim is not exactly the attractive place the Romans found at the junction of three rivers—the Nagold, the Enz, and the Würm—it is the "gateway to the Black Forest." Allied bombs almost completely destroyed the city center, and postwar reconstruction is hardly inspired. Pforzheim still owes its prosperity to its role in Europe's jewelry trade and its wristwatch industry. To get a sense of the "Gold City," explore the jewelry shops on streets around Leopoldplatz and the pedestrian area.

ESSENTIALS

Visitor Information Pforzheim Tourist-Information ✉ *Marktpl. 1* ☎ *07231/393–700* ⊕ *www.pforzheim.de.*

EXPLORING

Kloster Maulbronn (*Maulbronn Monastery*). Kloster Maulbronn, in the little town of Maulbronn, 18 km (11 miles) northeast of Pforzheim, is the best-preserved medieval monastery north of the Alps, with an entire complex of 30 buildings on UNESCO's World Heritage list. The name Maulbronn (Mule Fountain) derives from a legend. Monks seeking a suitably watered site for their monastery considered it a sign from God when one of their mules discovered and drank at a spring. The Kloster is also known for inventing the Maultasche, a kind of large ravioli. The monks thought that by coloring the meat filling green by adding parsley and wrapping it inside a pasta pocket, they could hide it from God on fasting days. Today the Maultasche is the cornerstone of Swabian cuisine. ▇ TIP➔ **An audio guide in English is available.** ✉ *Klosterhof 31, off B-35, Maulbron* ☎ *07043/926–610* ⊕ *www.kloster-maulbronn.de* 🎫 *€6* 🕘 *Mar.–Oct., daily 9–5:30; Nov.–Feb., Tues.–Sun. 9:30–5; guided tour daily at 11:15 and 3.*

St. Michael. The restored church of St. Michael, near the train station, is the final resting place of Baden royalty. The original mixture of 13th- and 15th-century styles has been faithfully reproduced; compare the airy Gothic choir with the church's sturdy Romanesque entrance. ✉ *Schlossberg 10* 🕘 *Oct.–Apr., weekdays 3–6; May–Sept., Mon. and Wed.–Fri. 3–6.*

Schmuckmuseum (*Jewelry Museum*). The Reuchlinhaus, the city cultural center, houses the Schmuckmuseum. Its collection of jewelry from five millennia is one of the finest in the world. The museum nearly doubled in size in 2006, adding pocket watches and ethnographic jewelry to its collection, plus a shop, a café, and a gem gallery where young designers exhibit and sell their work. Guided tours in English are available on request. ⊠ *Jahnstr. 42* ☏ *07231/392–126* ⊕ *www.schmuckmuseum-pforzheim.de* ⌑*€3* ⊙ *Tues.–Sun. 10–5.*

Technisches Museum (*Technical Museum*). Pforzheim has long been known as a center of the German clock-making industry. In the Technisches Museum, one of the country's leading museums devoted to the craft, you can see makers of watches and clocks at work; there's also a reconstructed 18th-century clock factory. ⊠ *Bleichstr. 81* ☏ *07231/392–869* ⊕ *www.technisches-museum.de* ⌑*Free* ⊙ *Wed. 9–noon and 3–6, 2nd and 4th Sun. of month 10–5.*

WHERE TO EAT

$$

MODERN FRENCH

✕ **Chez Gilbert.** The Alsatian owners of this cozy restaurant serve classic French-inspired cuisine, using the freshest local seasonal ingredients. The menu and wine lists are relatively small, but from the moment that you're greeted by Frau Nosser until the time you leave, you'll be convinced that everything was planned just for you. The best bet is one of Chef Gilbert Noesser's seasonal four-course menus for €57. If you must dine a la carte, try the duck with raspberries or the foie gras with peaches. ⑤ *Average main: €19* ⊠ *Altstädter Kirchenweg 3* ☏ *07231/441–159* ⊕ *www.chez-gilbert.de* ⊙ *Closed 2 wks in Aug. No lunch Sat.; no dinner Sun.*

EN
ROUTE

Weil der Stadt. Weil der Stadt, a former imperial city, is in the hills 17 km (10 miles) southeast of Pforzheim. This small, sleepy town of turrets and gables has only its well-preserved city walls and fortifications to remind you of its onetime importance. ⊠ *Paul-Reusch-Str. 27, Weil der Stadt* ⊕ *www.weil-der-stadt.de.*

Kepler Museum. The astronomer Johannes Kepler, born here in 1571, was the first man to track and accurately explain the orbits of the planets, although most experts agree that Kepler stole his calculations from, and then quite possibly murdered, Tycho de Brahe. And, appropriately, the town now has a planetarium to graphically show you what he learned. The little half-timber house in which he was born is now the Kepler Museum in the town center. It's devoted to his writings and discoveries. ⊠ *Keplerg. 2, Weil der Stadt* ☏ *07033/6586* ⊕ *www.kepler-museum.de* ⌑*€2* ⊙ *Thurs. and Fri. 10–noon and 2–4, Sat. 11–noon and 2–4, Sun. 11–noon and 2–5*

CALW

24 km (14 miles) south of Pforzheim on B-463.

Calw, one of the Black Forest's prettiest towns, is the birthplace of Nobel Prize–winning novelist Hermann Hesse (1877–1962). The town's market square, with its two sparkling fountains surrounded by 18th-century half-timber houses whose sharp gables pierce the sky, is an ideal spot for relaxing, picnicking, or people-watching, especially during market time.

ESSENTIALS

Visitor Information Stadtinformation Calw ⊠ *Marktbrücke 1* ☏ *07051/167–399* ⊕ *www.calw.de.*

The Northern Black Forest

EXPLORING

Hermann Hesse Museum. The museum recounts the life of the Nobel Prize–winning writer, Hermann Hesse, author of *Steppenwolf* and *The Glass Bead Game,* who rebelled against his middle-class German upbringing to become a pacifist and the darling of the Beat Generation. The museum tells the story of his life in personal belongings, photographs, manuscripts, and other documents. ■ **TIP→ An audioguide in English available** ⊠ *Marktpl. 30* 🕾 *07051/7522* 🖃 *€5* 🕙 *Apr.–Oct., Tues.–Sun. 11–5; Nov.–Mar., Tues.–Sun. 2–5.*

Hirsau. Three km (2 miles) north of Calw, Hirsau has ruins of a 9th-century monastery, now the setting for the Klostersummer (open-air theater performances) in July and August. Buy advance tickets at the Calw tourist office. ⊠ *Wildbader Straße 2, Calw-Hirsau.*

WHERE TO STAY

$$ 🏨 **Hotel Kloster Hirsau.** This hotel, a model of comfort and gracious hospitality, is in Hirsau, 3 km (2 miles) from Calw. **Pros:** quiet location; homey atmosphere. **Cons:** located a bit far out of town. 💲 *Rooms from: €107* ⊠ *Wildbaderstr. 2, Calw-Hirsau* 🕾 *07051/96740* ⊕ *www. hotel-kloster-hirsau.de* 🛏 *42 rooms* ⧖ *Breakfast.*

HOTEL

$ ⛉ **Ratsstube.** Most of the original features, including 16th-century beams
HOTEL   and brickwork, are preserved at this historic house in the center of
Calw, next to Hesse's birthplace. **Pros:** great location overlooks historical market square; beautiful old half-timber building. **Cons:** parking
around the corner; some rooms quite small; historic building means no
elevator. $ *Rooms from: €70* ⊠ *Marktpl. 12* ☎ *07051/92050* ⊕ *www.*
hotel-ratsstube-calw.de ⤴ *13 rooms* ⦿ *Breakfast.*

FREUDENSTADT

65 km (35 miles) south of Calw, 22 km (14 miles) southwest of Altensteig.

At an altitude of 2,415 feet, Freudenstadt claims to be the sunniest German resort town. The French Army flattened the town in April 1945,
but it has since been painstakingly rebuilt. Refugees and silver miners
founded the "city of joy" in 1599 after escaping religious persecution in
the Austrian province of Carinthia. The expansive central square, more
than 650 feet long and edged with arcaded shops, is Germany's largest
marketplace. The square still awaits the palace that was supposed to
be built here for the city's founder, Prince Frederick I of Württemberg,
who died before work could begin. It is difficult to admire its vastness,
since a busy, four-lane street cuts it nearly in half. ▪**TIP**➜ When the
fountains all spout on this square, it can be quite a sight, and a refreshing one as well.

GETTING HERE AND AROUND
Freudenstadt is served by regular trains from both Karlsruhe and Stuttgart. The huge main square makes the city feel larger than it actually
is. The central zone can easily be covered on foot.

ESSENTIALS
Visitor Information Freudenstadt ⊠ *Marktpl. 64* ☎ *07441/8640*
⊕ *www.freudenstadt.de.*

EXPLORING
Stadtkirche. Don't miss Freudenstadt's Protestant Stadtkirche, just off the
Market Square. Its lofty L-shaped nave is a rare architectural liberty from
the early 17th century. It was constructed in this way so the sexes would
be separated and unable to see each other during services. ⊠ *Marktpl. 36.*

WHERE TO EAT
$ ✗ **Ratskeller.** Though there's a cellar, this restaurant with pine furnish-
GERMAN   ings is more a modern bistro than traditional Ratskeller. Meatless Black
Forest dishes, served in frying pans, are huge and filling. Also offered
are such Swabian dishes as *Zwiebelrostbraten* (steak and fried onions),
served with sauerkraut, and pork fillet with wild-mushroom sauce. A
special menu for senior citizens has smaller portions. $ *Average main:*
€13 ⊠ *Marktpl. 8* ☎ *07441/952–805.*

$ ✗ **Turmbräu Freudenstädter.** Lots of wood paneling, exposed beams, and
GERMAN   a sprinkling of old sleds and hay wagons give this place, right on the
main square, its rustic atmosphere. So do the large brass kettle and the
symphony of pipes that produce the establishment's own beer. The restaurant serves hearty solid local fare, including the Alsatian flatbread
Flammkuchen, and a kebab of various types of meat marinated in wheat

beer. Fondue is offered on Wednesday. Part of the restaurant turns into a disco on weekends. ⑤ *Average main: €9* ⊠ *Brauhaus am Markt, Marktpl. 64* ☎ *07441/905–121* ⊕ *www.turmbraeu.de.*

$$$
GERMAN
✕ **Warteck.** The leaded windows with stained glass, vases of flowers, and beautifully upholstered banquettes create a bright setting in the two dining rooms. Chef Werner Glässel uses only organic products and spotlights individual ingredients. The variety of seasonal menus (€40) are always a good choice. Top off the meal with one of the many varieties of schnapps. ⑤ *Average main: €25* ⊠ *Stuttgarterstr. 14* ☎ *07441/91920* ⊕ *www.warteck-freudenstadt.de* ☉ *Closed Tues.*

> ## BIKING AND HIKING
>
> Bicycles can be rented in nearly all towns and many villages, as well as at the Deutsche Bahn train stations. Several regional tourist offices sponsor tours on which the biker's luggage is transported separately from one overnight stop to the next. Six- to 10-day tours are available at reasonable rates, including bed-and-breakfast and bike rental. This region is also ideal for hikers. Similar to the bike tours, *Wandern ohne Gepäck* (hike without luggage) tours are available from tourist offices.

WHERE TO STAY

$
HOTEL
🏨 **Bären.** The Montigels have owned this sturdy old hotel and restaurant, just two minutes from the marketplace, since 1878. **Pros:** great central location; friendly atmosphere. **Cons:** some rooms on the small side. ⑤ *Rooms from: €85* ⊠ *Langestr. 33* ☎ *07441/2729* ⊕ *www.hotel-baeren-freudenstadt.de* ⇆ *33 rooms* ☉ *Restaurant closed Fri. No lunch Mon.–Sat.* ⏀ *Breakfast.*

$
HOTEL
🏨 **Hotel Adler.** This simple hotel sits between the main square and the train station. **Pros:** friendly; informal; centrally located. **Cons:** some rooms small; furnishings from 1970s quite modest. ⑤ *Rooms from: €82* ⊠ *Forststr. 15–17* ☎ *07441/91520* ⊕ *www.adler-fds.de* ⇆ *16 rooms* ☉ *Restaurant closed Wed.* ⏀ *Breakfast.*

$
HOTEL
🏨 **Hotel Schwanen.** This bright, white building just a few steps from the main square has a guest room with a water bed for those with allergies. **Pros:** great location; excellent-value restaurant. **Cons:** no elevator in historic building. ⑤ *Rooms from: €94* ⊠ *Forststr. 6* ☎ *07441/91550* ⊕ *www.schwanen-freudenstadt.de* ⇆ *17 rooms, 1 apartment* ⏀ *Breakfast.*

SHOPPING

Germans prize Black Forest ham (*Schwarzwaldschinken*) as an aromatic souvenir. You can buy one at any butcher shop in the region, but it's more fun to visit a *Schinkenräucherei* (smokehouse), where the ham is actually cured in a stone chamber. ■TIP➔ By law the ham must be smoked over pinecones.

Hermann Wein. Hermann Wein, in the village of Musbach, near Freudenstadt, has one of the leading smokehouses in the area. If you have a group of people, call ahead to find out if the staff can show you around. ■TIP➔ If you are looking for Black Forest Ham, this is the place to go. ⊠ *Dornstetterstr. 29, Musbach* ☎ *07443/2450* ⊕ *www.schinken-wein.de.*

7

Baden-Baden's Festspielhaus (Festival Hall) hosts concerts, operas, and ballets throughout the year; outside is a sculpture by Henry Moore.

BAIERSBRONN

7 km (4½ miles) northwest of Freudenstadt.

The mountain resort of Baiersbronn has an incredible collection of hotels and bed-and-breakfasts providing rest and relaxation in beautiful surroundings. Most people come here to walk, ski, golf, and ride horseback. ■ TIP→ You may want to walk through the streets to preview the many restaurants.

ESSENTIALS

Visitor Information Baiersbronn Touristik ✉ *Rosenpl. 3* ☎ *07442/84140* ⊕ *www.baiersbronn.de.*

EXPLORING

Hauffs Märchenmuseum (*Fairy-Tale Museum*). Near the town hall and church in the upper part of town is the little Hauffs Märchenmuseum, devoted to the crafts and life around Baiersbronn and the fairy-tale author Wilhelm Hauff (1802–27). ✉ *Alte Reichenbacherstr. 1* ☎ *07442/84100* 🎫 *€1.50* ⊘ *Wed. and weekends 2–5.*

WHERE TO STAY

$$$ **Hotel-Café Sackmann.** This imposing cluster of white houses, set in the
HOTEL narrow Murg Valley north of Baiersbronn, has broad appeal—fami-
FAMILY lies can nest here thanks to children's programs; wellness-seekers can take advantage of the spa facilities on the roof; and sightseers can use this as a base for exploring much of the Black Forest. **Pros:** good for families; beautiful location. **Cons:** far from the sights. ⑤ *Rooms from:*

€160 ✉ Murgtalstr. 602, Schwarzenberg-Baiersbronn ☎ 07447/2980 ⊕ www.hotel-sackmann.de ⤵ 65 rooms ⦿ Breakfast.

$$
HOTEL
🏨 **Hotel Lamm.** The steep-roof exterior of this 200-year-old typical Black Forest building presents a clear picture of the heavy oak fittings and fine antiques inside. **Pros:** beautiful traditional building; friendly staff. **Cons:** can feel remote in winter. $ *Rooms from: €120 ✉ Ellbacherstr. 4, Mitteltal-Baiersbronn ☎ 07442/4980 ⊕ www.lamm-mitteltal.de ⤵ 33 rooms, 13 apartments ⦿ Breakfast.*

$$$$
HOTEL
Fodor'sChoice
★
🏨 **Traube Tonbach.** Dating from 1778, this luxurious hotel is true to the original, yet the rooms, each of which presents a sweeping view of the Black Forest, meet contemporary standards; there are four fine restaurants on-site to choose from as well. **Pros:** beautiful countryside setting; friendly and efficient staff; good choice of dining. **Cons:** expensive; credit cards only accepted in the restaurants, not in the hotel. $ *Rooms from: €269 ✉ Tonbachstr. 237 ☎ 07442/4920 ⊕ www.traube-tonbach. de ⤵ 135 rooms, 23 apartments, 12 suites ⦿ Breakfast.*

BADEN-BADEN

51 km (32 miles) north of Freudenstadt, 24 km (15 miles) north of Mummelsee.

Fodor'sChoice
★
Baden-Baden, the most famous and fashionable spa town rests in a wooded valley north of the Mummelsee on B-500. The town sits atop an extensive underground hot springs that gave the city its name. Roman legions of the emperor Caracalla discovered the springs and named the area Aquae Aureliae. The upper classes of the 19th century, seeking leisurely pursuits, rediscovered the bubbling waters, establishing Baden-Baden as the unofficial summer residence of many European royal families. The town's fortunes also rose and fell with gaming: gambling began in the mid-18th century but was banned by the Kaiser between 1872 and 1933. Palatial homes and stately villas grace the tree-lined avenues, and the spa tradition continues at the ornate casino and two thermal baths, one historic and luxurious, the other modern and well used by families. Since Baden-Baden is only two hours from Frankfurt Airport by train, the spa makes a nice last stop on the way home.

Though some Germans come here for two- to three-week doctor-prescribed treatments (German health insurance pays for a weeklong Kur [cure] once every five years), the spa concept also embraces facilities for those just looking for pampering. Shops line several pedestrian streets that eventually climb up toward the old marketplace. Two theaters present frequent ballet performances, plays, and concerts (by the excellent Southwest German Radio Symphony Orchestra).

GETTING HERE AND AROUND
High-speed ICE trains stop at Baden-Baden en route between Frankfurt and Basel. However, the station is some 4 km (2½ miles) northwest of the center. To get downtown, take one of the many buses that leave from outside the station. Once in the center, Baden-Baden is manageable on foot, but there is a range of alternatives available if you get tired, including a tourist train and horse-drawn carriages.

ESSENTIALS

Visitor Information Baden-Baden Kur- und Tourismus GmbH ✉ *Solmsstr. 1* ☏ *07221/275–266* ⊕ *www.baden-baden.de.*

EXPLORING

TOP ATTRACTIONS

Casino. Baden-Baden is quite proud of its casino, Germany's oldest, opened in 1855 after Parisian interior decorators and artists polished the last chandelier. Its concession to the times is that you may wear your jeans amid all the frescoes, stucco, and porcelain (but why would you?). Gentlemen must wear a jacket and tie with their jeans, but whatever you do, leave your sneakers at the hotel. If you don't have a jacket and tie, one will be provided for a minimal charge. In 1853 a Parisian, Jacques Bénazet, persuaded the sleepy little Black Forest spa to build gambling rooms to enliven its evenings. The result was a series of richly decorated gaming rooms in which even an emperor could feel at home—and did. Kaiser Wilhelm I was a regular visitor, as was his chancellor, Bismarck. The Russian novelist Dostoyevsky, the Aga Khan, and Marlene Dietrich all patronized the place. The minimum stake is €2; maximum, €7,000. Passports are necessary as proof of identity. Guided tours (25 minutes) are offered in English, on request. ✉ *Kaiserallee 1* ☏ *07221/30240* ⊕ *www.casino-baden-baden.de* 🎫 *€5, tour €5* ⊙ *Sun.–Thurs. 2 pm–2 am, Fri. and Sat. 2 pm–3 am. Tours: Apr.–Sept., daily 9:30–11:30 am; Oct.–Mar., daily 10–11:30 am.*

Russian church. The sandstone church is located on the corner of Robert Kochstrasse and Lichtentalerstrasse. The Russian diaspora community in Baden-Baden consecrated it in 1882; it's identifiable by its golden onion dome. ✉ *Lichtentalerstr. 76* 🎫 *€2* ⊙ *Feb.–Nov., daily 10–6.*

WORTH NOTING

Abtei Lichtenthal. The Lichtentaler Allee ends at Abtei Lichtenthal, a medieval Cistercian abbey surrounded by stout defensive walls. The small royal chapel next to the church was built in 1288 and was used from the late 14th century onward as a final resting place for the Baden dynasty princes. Call ahead if your group wants a tour in English. ✉ *Hauptstr. 40* ☏ *07221/504–910* ⊕ *www.abtei-lichtenthal.de* 🎫 *Tours €5* ⊙ *Tours Wed. and weekends at 3.*

Lichtentaler Allee. Bordering the slender Oos River, which runs through town, the Lichtentaler Allee is a groomed park with two museums and an extensive rose garden, the **Gönneranlage,** which contains more than 300 types of roses. ✉ *Lichtentaler Allee 64.*

EATING WELL IN THE BLACK FOREST

Don't pass up the chance to try *Schwarzwälder Schinken* (pine-cone-smoked ham) and *Schwarzwälder Kirschtorte* (kirsch-soaked layers of chocolate cake with sour cherry and whipped-cream filling). *Kirschwasser,* locally called *Chriesewässerle* (from the French *cerise,* meaning "cherry"), is cherry brandy, the most famous of the region's excellent schnapps varieties. If traveling from May to June, keep an eye out for the "king of vegetables," white asparagus. Most restaurants develop special menus that feature this locally grown delicacy.

Museum Frieder Burda. The Museum Frieder Burda occupies a modern structure by acclaimed New York architect Richard Meier. Construction of this institution contributed greatly to pulling Baden-Baden out of its slumber. The private collection focuses on classic modern and contemporary art. Highlights are works of Picasso, German expressionists, the New York School, and American abstract expressionists. ✉ *Lichtentaler Allee 8b* ☎ *07221/398–980* ⊕ *www.museum-frieder-burda.de* 🎫 *€12* ⊙ *Tues.–Sun. 11–6.*

Gut Nägelsförst Vineyard. The region's wines, especially the dry Baden whites and delicate reds, are highly valued in Germany. ■ TIP➔ Buy them directly from any vintner on the Baden Wine Road. At Yburg, outside Baden-Baden, the 400-year-old Gut Nägelsförst vineyard has a shop where you can buy the product and sample what you buy (weekdays 9–6, Saturday 10–4). ✉ *Nägelsförst 1* ☎ *07221/398–980.*

SPAS

The history of "taking the waters" in Baden-Baden dates back to AD 75, when the Roman army established the city of Aquæ Aureliæ. The legions under Emperor Caracalla soon discovered that the regions' salty underground hot springs were just the thing for aching joints.

In a modern sense, bathing became popular within the upper-class elite when Friedrich I banned gambling in 1872. Everyone from Queen Victoria to Karl Marx dangled their feet in the pool and sang the curative praises of the salty warm water bubbling from the ground.

Caracalla Therme. If you are a bit modest and prefer to wear a swimsuit in the water, walk across the square to the more modern Caracalla Therme, named in honor of the Roman emperor who brought bathing to Baden-Baden. The indoor-outdoor pool area has three separate baths, with temperatures between 18°C and 38°C (64°F–100°F). Supplement the soaking experience with whirlpools, Jacuzzis, and waterfalls. Children under 7 are not allowed in the spa and children under 14 must be accompanied by an adult. ✉ *Römerpl. 1* ☎ *07221/275–940* ⊕ *www. carasana.de* 🎫 *€18 for 3 hrs* ⊙ *Daily 8 am–10 pm.*

Friedrichsbad. In a city with many spa options, the Friedrichsbad, also known as the Roman-Irish Baths, is the most noble and elegant choice. If you choose to take the waters, the Friedrichbad's ornate copper and terra-cotta temple is the best place to do it, though keep in mind that you'll have to bathe in the buff, as swimsuits aren't allowed. The spa treatment offers everything from a soap and brush massage to thermal steam baths. ■ TIP➔ Spend at least a half hour in the relaxation area afterward to ease the transition back into the real world. Note children under 14 are not allowed. ✉ *Römerpl. 1* ☎ *07221/275–920* ⊕ *www.carasana.de* 🎫 *€55 for 4 hrs all-inclusive, €23 with no massage.* ⊙ *Daily 9 am–10 pm. Tues., Wed., Fri., and Sun. mixed bathing. Mon., Thurs., and Sat. gender-separate bathing.*

Römische Badruinen. The remains of the original Roman settlement can be seen at the Römische Badruinen. The remains of the Roman bathhouse are explained with a computer animation that virtually reconstructs the entire area. ✉ *Römerpl. 1, D–76530* 🎫 *€2.50* ⊙ *Mar.–Nov., daily 11–1 and 2–5.*

WHERE TO EAT

$$$$ ✕ **Der Kleine Prinz.** This gourmet hotel restaurant *(➾ See hotel review*
FRENCH *below)* is a local favorite in Baden-Baden. The cheery fireplace, lighted in winter, and candlelit dining provide an elegant atmosphere that complements the finest French-inspired dishes. The extensive wine list includes some excellent local offerings. As in the hotel, all the decor—designed by the owner's wife—right down to the dinner plates, reflect the children's tale from which the restaurant takes its name. $ *Average main: €27* ☒ *Lichtentalerstr. 36* ☎ *07221/346–600* ⊕ *www.derkleineprinz.de* ⚝ *Reservations essential.*

$$$$ ✕ **Le Jardin de France.** This clean, crisp little French restaurant, whose
FRENCH owners are actually French, emphasizes elegant, imaginative dining in a modern setting. The restaurant sits in a quiet courtyard away from the main street, offering the possibility of alfresco dining in summer. The milk-fed suckling pig and Russian cuisine are well worth the visit. It also runs a school for budding chefs. $ *Average main: €40* ☒ *Lichtentalerstr. 13* ☎ *07221/300–7860* ⊕ *www.lejardindefrance.de* ⊗ *Closed Sun. and Mon.*

$ ✕ **Weinstube im Baldreit.** This lively little wine bar enchants you with its
WINE BAR lovely terraces and courtyard. It's nestled in the middle of the Old Town, making the garden and terrace the perfect place to meet friends over a dry Riesling. Enjoy some of the best *Maultaschen* (ravioli) and solid Black Forest cuisine in the huge barrel-vaulted cellar near the fireplace. $ *Average main: €11* ☒ *Küferstr. 3* ☎ *07221/23136* ⊗ *Closed Sun. No lunch weekdays Nov.–Mar.*

WHERE TO STAY

$ ☖ **Am Markt.** This 250-plus-year-old building houses a modest inn run
HOTEL for more than 50 years by the Bogner family. **Pros:** quiet location; some rooms have great views. **Cons:** a stiff climb up from the main sights. $ *Rooms from: €86* ☒ *Marktpl. 17–18* ☎ *07221/27040* ⊕ *www.hotel-am-markt-baden.de* ☞ *25 rooms, 17 with bath* ⍾ *Breakfast.*

$$$$ ☖ **Brenner's Park Hotel & Spa.** With some justification, this stately hotel set
HOTEL in a private park claims to be one of the best in the world. **Pros:** elegant rooms; good location; quiet. **Cons:** professional staff sometimes lack personal touch. $ *Rooms from: €375* ☒ *Schillerstr. 6* ☎ *07221/9000* ☞ *70 rooms, 30 suites* ⍾ *Multiple meal plans.*

$$$ ☖ **Der Kleine Prinz.** Owner Norbert Rademacher, a veteran of New York's
HOTEL Waldorf-Astoria, and his interior-designer wife Edeltraud have skillfully
Fodor's Choice combined two elegant city mansions into a unique, antiques-filled lodg-
★ ing. **Pros:** friendly and welcoming; some rooms have wood-burning fireplaces; most bathrooms have whirlpool tubs. **Cons:** rooms in one of the hotel's two buildings are only accessible via stairs. $ *Rooms from: €199* ☒ *Lichtentalerstr. 36* ☎ *07221/346–600* ⊕ *www.derkleineprinz. de* ☞ *26 rooms, 15 suites* ⍾ *Breakfast.*

$ ☖ **Deutscher Kaiser.** This centrally located hotel provides homey and indi-
HOTEL vidually styled rooms at prices that are easy on the wallet. **Pros:** some rooms have balconies; central location. **Cons:** some rooms quite small; down side street so views not great. $ *Rooms from: €89* ☒ *Merkurstr. 9* ☎ *07221/2700* ⊕ *www.deutscher-kaiser-baden-baden.de* ☞ *28 rooms* ⍾ *Breakfast.*

WORD OF MOUTH

"On a recent trip to Germany, friends told us about the [Friedrichsbad] spa at Baden-Baden. You go through 17 different stations involving water, heat, and cold. Men on one side and women on another. In the middle, men and women meet in the thermal therapy pool. On certain days, men and women share all the facilities, on others the sexes are separated. On holidays, it is coed. Why must you know this? Because the spa is not a clothing-optional zone. Clothing is not allowed. . . . Nudity here is no big thing. In the summer people in the parks of Munich sunbathe topless and no one bats an eye. Going to a spa is just part of life here and it's considered therapeutic. . . . You change into your birthday suit, and take from your locker a sheet, which turns out is your towel. At each station, there are instructions on the wall, in English, telling you how long to stay in that particular room. After a good dousing, you go to the 'warm air bath.' It's then you discover that the sheet is not for covering you up, but to lay upon on the very hot wood tables in the sauna where the temperature is a balmy 129 degrees.

Next, it's the 'hot air bath' and you ask yourself, what did I just have. Then you find out what hot is. 154 degrees for 5 minutes, I think. . . . Next you get to shower again before heading to the steam baths, 113 and 118 degrees, after which you start to cool down in the thermal whirlpool and therapy pools. The latter is under a huge domed room done in the Roman style. Next it's another shower before the cold water immersion bath at 64 degrees, which after what you just experienced feels like 30 degrees. Next you get a warm towel to dry off before going to the cream service room, where if you choose, you can rub various lotions on your body. Hey, I paid for it, I'm doing it. Lastly the relaxation room for 30 minutes. Here you lay on a table and the attendant wraps you in a warm sheet and blanket. The whole thing takes about 2.5 hours and you never have felt so relaxed and clean. . . . Was it worth it? You bet. Did I feel uncomfortable? Only for the first 5 minutes when I didn't know what to do with the sheet. Would I do it again? Why not?"

—dgassa

$$$ **Hotel Belle Epoque.** The sister hotel to Der Kleine Prinz is in a building with large rooms, soaring ceilings, spacious beds, genuine antiques from Louis XV to art deco, and luxurious baths—in some cases cleverly built to comply with strict monument-protection laws. **Pros:** beautiful gardens; room price includes afternoon tea; personal and friendly service. **Cons:** only the newer wing has an elevator. *$ Rooms from: €230 ✉ Maria-Viktoriastr. 2c ☎ 07221/300–660 ⊕ www.hotel-belle-epoque. de ➘ 20 rooms ¶◎¶ Breakfast.*

$$$$ **Schlosshotel Bühlerhöhe.** This "castle-hotel" stands majestically on its own extensive grounds 10 km (6 miles) from Baden-Baden, with spectacular views over the heights of the Black Forest. **Pros:** quiet location; great for hikers. **Cons:** a long way from downtown. *$ Rooms from: €180 ✉ Schwarzwaldhochstr. 1, Bühl ☎ 07226/550 ⊕ www. buehlerhoehe.de ➘ 77 rooms, 13 suites ¶◎¶ Multiple meal plans.*

NIGHTLIFE AND THE ARTS

Nightlife revolves around Baden-Baden's elegant **casino.**

Festspielhaus. This state-of-the-art concert hall is actually a renovated old train station. ⊠ *Beim Alten Bahnhof 2* ☎ *07221/301–3101* ⊕ *www.festspielhaus.de.*

Kurhaus. The Kurhaus adjoining the casino is an intimate concert venue that hosts classical music concerts year-round. ⊠ *Kaiserallee 1* ☎ *07221/353–202* ⊕ *www.kurhaus-baden-baden.de.*

Living Room. The Hotel Merkur has a small nightclub called the Living Room that serves a slightly older crowd. ⊠ *Merkurstr. 8* ☎ *07221/303–366.*

Oleander Bar. For a subdued evening in a quiet horse-racing-themed lounge, stop by the Oleander Bar and enjoy cocktails among a diverse adult crowd. ⊠ *Schillerstr. 6* ☎ *07221/9000.*

Theater Baden-Baden. Baden-Baden has one of Germany's most beautiful performance halls, Theater Baden-Baden, a late-baroque jewel built in 1860–62 in the style of the Paris Opéra. It opened with the world premiere of Berlioz's opera *Beatrice et Benedict.* Today the theater presents a regular series of dramas, operas, and ballets. ⊠ *Goethepl. 1* ☎ *07221/932–700* ⊕ *www.theater.baden-baden.de.*

Trinkhalle. Baden-Baden attracts an older crowd, but the deep leather seats of the Trinkhalle make a hip lounge for those under 40. At night this daytime bistro also takes over the portion of the hall where the tourist office has a counter, transforming it into a dance floor. ⊠ *Kaiserallee 3.*

SPORTS AND THE OUTDOORS
HORSEBACK RIDING

Iffezheim. The racetrack at nearby Iffezheim harks back to the days when Baden-Baden was a magnet for royalty and aristocrats. Its tradition originated in 1858; now annual international meets take place in late May, late August, early September, and October. ⊠ *Rennbahnstr. 16, Iffezheim* ☎ *07229/1870.*

Reitzentrum Balg. Those wishing to ride can rent horses and get instruction at the Reitzentrum Balg. ⊠ *Buchenweg 42* ☎ *07221/55920.*

KARLSRUHE

10 km (6 miles) north of Ettlingen.

Karlsruhe, founded at the beginning of the 18th century, is a young upstart, but what it lacks in years it makes up for in industrial and administrative importance, sitting as it does astride a vital autobahn and rail crossroads. It's best known as the seat of Germany's Supreme Court, and has a high concentration of legal practitioners.

GETTING HERE AND AROUND

The Autobahn A-5 connects Freiburg, Baden-Baden, and Karlsruhe. Karlsruhe's train station is an easy 15-minute walk from the city center and trains run frequently throughout the region; south to baden Baden (15 minutes) and Freiburg (1 hour), and east to Pforzheim (25 minutes) and Frankfurt (1 hour).

At the Zentrum für Kunst und Medientechnologie (Center for Art and Media Technology), known simply as the ZKM, you can view contemporary art or interact with media.

ESSENTIALS

Visitor Information Karlsruhe Tourist-Information ✉ *Bahnhofpl. 6* ☎ *0721/3720–5383* ⊕ *www.karlsruhe.de.*

EXPLORING

Badisches Landesmuseum (*Baden State Museum*). The Badisches Landesmuseum, in the palace, has a large number of Greek and Roman antiquities and trophies that Ludwig the Turk brought back from campaigns in Turkey in the 17th century. Most of the other exhibits are devoted to local history. ✉ *Schloss, Schlossbezirk 10* ☎ *0721/926–6514* ⊕ *www. landesmuseum.de* 🎟 *€4* ☉ *Tues.–Thurs. 10–5, Fri.–Sun. 10–6.*

Schloss. The town quite literally grew up around the former Schloss of the Margrave Karl Wilhelm, which was begun in 1715. Thirty-two avenues radiate from the palace, 23 leading into the extensive grounds, and the remaining 9 forming the grid of the Old Town. ✉ *Schlossbezirk 10.*

Staatliche Kunsthalle (*State Art Gallery*). One of the most important collections of paintings in the Black Forest region hangs in the Staatliche Kunsthalle. Look for masterpieces by Grünewald, Holbein, Rembrandt, and Monet, and also for work by the Black Forest painter Hans Thoma. In the **Kunsthalle Orangerie,** next door, is work by such modern artists as Braque and Beckmann. ✉ *Hans-Thoma-Str. 2–6* ☎ *0721/926–3359* ⊕ *www.kunsthalle-karlsruhe.de* 🎟 *Both museums €8* ☉ *Tues.–Fri. 10–5, weekends 10–6.*

FAMILY **Zentrum für Kunst und Medientechnologie** (*Center for Art and Media Technology*). In a former munitions factory, the vast Zentrum für Kunst und Medientechnologie, or simply ZKM, is an all-day adventure consisting

The Central and Southern Black Forest

FRANCE

of two separate museums. At the **Medienmuseum** (Media Museum) you can watch movies, listen to music, try out video games, flirt with a virtual partner, or sit on a real bicycle and pedal through a virtual New York City. ▓ TIP→ Take Tram No. 6 to ZKM to get here. ✉ *Lorenzstr. 19* ☎ *0721/81000* ⊕ *www.zkm.de* 🖃 *Either museum €6, combined ticket €10, free after 2 on Fri.* ☉ *Wed.–Fri. 10–6, weekends 11–6.*

Museum für Neue Kunst (*Museum of Modern Art*). There is a top-notch collection of media art in all genres from the end of the 20th century. ✉ *Lorenzstr. 19* ☎ *0721/81000* ⊕ *www.mnk.zkm.de* 🖃 *€4*

WHERE TO EAT AND STAY

$$$
GERMAN

✕ **Buchmanns.** Elke and Günter Buchmann run a "linen tablecloth and real silver" establishment, with a beer garden and a bar. The various suggested courses are grouped on the fancy handwritten menu, along with the fancy price of each dish. You can just order one of the courses, but be prepared for a disapproving look. The proprietors are Austrian, and the specialties of their homeland, such as *Tafelspitz* (boiled beef with horseradish applesauce) and *Kaiserschmarrn* (torn-up fluffy egg pancakes with apples, raisins, cinnamon, and jam), are recommended, but the Wiener schnitzel is divine. If you have trouble with the extensive wine list, the waitstaff is ready and willing to help. ⑤ *Average main: €22* ✉ *Mathystr. 22* ☎ *0721/820–3730* ☉ *Closed Sun. No lunch Sat.*

$$ ⊡ **Schlosshotel.** A few steps from the main station, this hotel looks,
HOTEL   and sometimes behaves, like a palace. **Pros:** elegant hotel; friendly service; advanced onilne booking saves can save up to €50. **Cons:** on a noisy street; modern rooms don't live up to the historic feel of the hotel. ⑤ *Rooms from: €140* ⊠ *Bahnhofpl. 2* ☎ *0721/38320* ⊕ *www. schlosshotel-karlsruhe.de* ↴ *93 rooms, 3 suites* ⊙ *Multiple meal plans.*

THE ARTS

Badisches Staatstheater. One of the best opera houses in the region is Karlsruhe's Badisches Staatstheater. ⊠ *Baumeisterstr. 11* ☎ *0721/35570* ⊕ *www.staatstheater.karlsruhe.de.*

THE CENTRAL BLACK FOREST

The Central Black Forest takes in the Simonswald, Elz, and Glotter valleys as well as Triberg and Furtwangen, with their clock museums. The area around the Triberg Falls—the highest falls in Germany—is also renowned for pom-pom hats, thatch-roof farmhouses, and mountain railways. The Schwarzwaldbahn (Black Forest Railway; Offenburg–Villingen line), which passes through Triberg, is one of the most scenic in all of Europe.

ALPIRSBACH

16 km (10 miles) south of Freudenstadt.

The hamlet of Alpirsbach was founded in 1035 and developed around the Benedictine monastery Kloster Alpirsbach. Although the wages of the reformation forced the abbey to close its doors in 1535, the tradition of brewing is still going strong. Locals claim that it's the pristine artesian water that makes the beer from the Alpirsbacher Klosterbräu (brewery) so incredible. The village maintains a preserved historic core with a fine collection of half-timber houses that only add to the charm.

GETTING HERE AND AROUND

Alpirsbach is on the direct train line between Freudenstadt and Offenburg. Alpirsbach is a great day trip by train from Freiburg (two hours with a change in Offenburg)

ESSENTIALS

Visitor Information Alpirsbach Tourist-Information ⊠ *Hauptstr. 20* ☎ *07444/951–6281* ⊕ *www.alpirsbach.de.*

EXPLORING

Brauerei (*Brewery*). The Brauerei was once part of the monastery, and has brewed beer since the Middle Ages. The unusually soft water gives the beer a flavor that is widely acclaimed. There are guided tours of the brewery museum daily at 2:30. If there's one place in Germany to go out of your way for a beer, Alpirsbach is it. ⊠ *Marktpl. 1* ☎ *07444/67149* ⊕ *www.alpirsbacher-brauwelt.de* ⊡ *Tour €6.90* ⊙ *Mar.–Oct., weekdays 9:30–4:30, weekends 11–3; Nov.–Feb., daily 11–3.*

CLOSE UP

Cuckoo for Cuckoo Clocks

"In Switzerland they had brotherly love—they had 500 years of democracy and peace, and what did that produce? The cuckoo clock."

So says Harry Lime, played by Orson Welles in the classic 1949 film *The Third Man*. He misspoke in two ways. First, the Swiss are an industrious, technologically advanced people. And second, they didn't invent the cuckoo clock. That was the work of the Germans living in the adjacent Black Forest.

The first Kuckucksuhr was designed and built in 1750 by Franz Anton Ketterer in Schönwald near Triberg. He cleverly produced the cuckoo sound with a pair of wooden whistles, each attached to a bellows activated by the clock's mechanism.

The making of carved wooden clocks developed rapidly in the Black Forest. The people on the farms needed ways to profitably occupy their time during the long snowbound winters, and the carving of clocks was the answer. Wood was abundant, and the early clocks were entirely of wood, even the works.

Come spring one of the sons would don a traditional smock and hat, mount the family's winter output on a big rack, hoist it to his back, and set off into the world to sell the clocks. In 1808 there were 688 clock makers and 582 clock peddlers in the districts of Triberg and Neustadt. The *Uhrenträger* (clock carrier) is an important part of the Black Forest tradition. Guides often wear the traditional costume.

The traditional cuckoo clock is made with brown stained wood with a gabled roof and some sort of woodland motif carved into it, such as a deer's head or a cluster of leaves. The works are usually activated by cast-iron weights, in the form of pinecones, on chains.

Today's clocks can be much more elaborate. Dancing couples in traditional dress automatically move to the sound of a music box, a mill wheel turns on the hour, a farmer chops wood on the hour, the Uhrenträger even makes his rounds. The cuckoo itself moves its wings and beak and rocks back and forth when calling.

The day is long past when the clocks were made entirely of wood. The works are of metal and therefore more reliable and accurate. Other parts of the clock, such as the whistles, the face, and the hands, are usually of plastic now, but hand-carved wood is still the rule for the case. The industry is still centered in Triberg. There are two museums in the area with sections dedicated to it, and clocks are sold everywhere, even in kiosks.

WHERE TO EAT

$ ✕ **Zwickel & Kaps.** The name is a highly sophisticated brewing term, describing the means by which the brewmaster samples the fermenting product. Sit down at one of the simple beech-wood tables and order a satisfying Swabian lentil stew with dumplings and sausages, or something more Mediterranean, such as salmon with pesto. All the pasta, bread, and sauces are home-made. $ *Average main: €11* ⊠ *Marktstr. 3* ☎ *07444/51727* ⊘ *Closed Mon.*

GERMAN

GUTACH

17 km (11 miles) north of Triberg.

Gutach lies in Gutachtal, a valley famous for the traditional costumes, complete with pom-pom hats, worn by women on feast days and holidays. Married women wear black pom-poms, unmarried women red ones. The village is one of the few places in the Black Forest where you can still see thatch roofs. However, escalating costs caused by a decline in skilled thatchers, and soaring fire-insurance premiums, make for fewer thatch roofs than there were 20 years ago.

GETTING HERE AND AROUND

Gutach is a 20-minute train ride from Freiburg. Trains leave once per hour.

EXPLORING

Schwarzwälder Freilichtmuseum Vogtsbauernhof (*Black Forest Open-Air Museum*). Near Gutach is one of the most appealing museums in the Black Forest, the Schwarzwälder Freilichtmuseum Vogtsbauernhof. Farmhouses and other rural buildings from all parts of the region have been transported here from their original locations and reassembled, complete with traditional furniture, to create a living museum of Black Forest building types through the centuries. Demonstrations ranging from traditional dances to woodworking capture life as it was in centuries past. ✉ *B-33, Vogtsbauernhof* ☎ *07831/93560* ⊕ *www.vogtsbauernhof.org* 💶 *€8* ⏱ *Apr.–Oct., daily 9–5 (Aug. until 6).*

OFF THE BEATEN PATH

Schwarzwalder Trachtenmuseum. Regional traditional costumes can be seen at this museum in a former monastery in the village of Haslach, 10 km (6 miles) northwest of Gutach. The village is quaint, with a fine collection of half-timber houses. Pom-pom-topped straw hats, bejeweled headdresses, embroidered velvet vests, and *Fasnet* (Carnival) regalia of all parts of the forest are on display. ✉ *Klosterstr. 1* ☎ *07832/706–172* 💶 *€2* ⏱ *Apr.–mid-Oct., Tues.–Sat. 9–5, Sun. 10–5; mid-Oct.–Dec., Feb.–Mar., Tues.–Fri. 9–noon and 1–5; Jan. by appointment.*

TRIBERG

16 km (10 miles) south of Gutach.

The cuckoo clock, that symbol of the Black Forest, is at home in the Triberg area. It was invented here, it's made and sold here, it's featured in two museums, and there are two house-size cuckoo clocks here.

GETTING HERE AND AROUND

Triberg is accessible via one of the prettiest train rides in Germany, with direct services to Lake Constance and Karlsruhe. The train station is at the lower end of the long main street, and the waterfalls are a stiff uphill walk away. You can take a bus up the hill from the train station to the entrance to the waterfalls, relieving most of the uphill struggle.

ESSENTIALS

Visitor Information Triberg Tourist-Information ✉ *Wahlfahrtstr. 4* ☎ *07722/866–490* ⊕ *www.triberg.de.*

EXPLORING

Eble Uhren-Park. You can buy a cuckoo clock, or just about any other timepiece or souvenir, at the huge Eble Uhren-Park, about 3 km (2 miles) from the town center in the district of Schonachbach. It's also the location of one of the house-size cuckoo clocks. You can enter it for €2 and examine the works. ✉ *Schonachbach 27, on B-33 between Triberg and Hornberg,* ☎ *07722/96220* ⊕ *www.eble-uhren-park.de* ⊙ *Apr.–Oct., Mon.–Sat. 9–6, Sun. 10–6; Nov.–Mar., Mon.–Sat. 9–6, Sun. 11–4:30.*

Haus der 1000 Uhren (*House of 1,000 Clocks*). The Haus der 1000 Uhren has a shop right at the waterfall. The main store, just off B-33 toward Offenburg in the suburb of Gremmelsbach, boasts another of the town's giant cuckoo clocks. Both stores offer a rich variety of clocks, some costing as much as €3,000. ✉ *Hauptstr. 79–81* ☎ *07722/96300* ⊕ *www.houseof1000clocks.de* ⊙ *Mon.–Sat. 11–5, Sun. 11–4.*

Hubert Herr. Hubert Herr is the only factory that continues to make nearly all of its own components for its cuckoo clocks. The present proprietors are the fifth generation from Andreas and Christian Herr, who began making the clocks more than 150 years ago. The company produces a great variety of clocks, including one that, at 5¼ inches high, is claimed to be "the world's smallest." ✉ *Hauptstr. 8* ☎ *07722/4268* ⊕ *www.hubertherr.de* ⊙ *Weekdays 9–noon and 1:30–4.*

Schwarzwaldbahn (*Black Forest Railway*). The Hornberg–Triberg–St. Georgen segment of the Schwarzwaldbahn is one of Germany's most scenic train rides. The 149-km (93-mile) Schwarzwaldbahn, built from 1866 to 1873, runs from Offenburg to Lake Constance via Triberg. It has no fewer than 39 tunnels, and at one point climbs almost 2,000 feet in just 11 km (6½ miles). It's now part of the German Railway, and you can make inquiries at any station. ☎ *11861* ⊕ *www.bahn.de.*

Schwarzwaldmuseum (*Black Forest Museum*). Triberg's famous Schwarzwaldmuseum is a treasure trove of the region's traditional arts: wood carving, costumes, and handicrafts. The Schwarzwaldbahn is described, with historical displays and a working model. The Black Forest was also a center of mechanical music, and, among many other things, the museum has an "Orchestrion"—a cabinet full of mechanical instruments playing like an orchestra. ✉ *Wallfahrtstr. 4* ☎ *07722/4434* ⊕ *www.schwarzwaldmuseum.de* 🎟 *€5* ⊙ *Daily 10–5.*

Triberg Waterfalls. At the head of the Gutach Valley, the Gutach River plunges more than 500 feet over seven huge granite cascades at Triberg's waterfall, Germany's highest. The pleasant 45-minute walk from the center of town is well signposted. A longer walk goes by a small pilgrimage church and the old Mesnerhäuschen, the sacristan's house. ✉ *Friedrichstr.* 🎟 *Waterfall €3.50.*

WHERE TO STAY

$
HOTEL
☷ **Hotel-Restaurant-Pfaff.** Rooms at this restaurant-hotel are very comfortable; some have balconies overlooking the famous waterfall. **Pros:** friendly service; close to waterfall. **Cons:** some rooms quite small; no elevator. ⑤ *Rooms from: €76* ⊠ *Hauptstr. 85* ☎ *07722/4479* ⊕ *www.hotel-pfaff.com* ⇱ *10 rooms* ⦿ *Breakfast.*

$$
HOTEL
☷ **Parkhotel Wehrle.** This large mansion, which dominates the town center, has a wisteria-covered facade, steep eaves, and individually furnished, wood-accented rooms. **Pros:** elegant rooms; friendly service. **Cons:** main street outside can be noisy. ⑤ *Rooms from: €149* ⊠ *Gartenstr. 24* ☎ *07722/86020* ⊕ *www.parkhotel-wehrle.de* ⇱ *50 rooms, 1 suite* ⦿ *Breakfast.*

OFF THE
BEATEN
PATH
Stadtmuseum. Rottweil, 26 km (16 miles) east of Triberg, has the best of the Black Forest's Fasnet celebrations. Outside the Black Forest, the celebrations are good-natured and sophisticated, but here and in adjacent areas of Switzerland they're pagan and fierce. In the days just before Ash Wednesday, usually in February, witches and devils roam the streets wearing ugly wooden masks and making fantastic gyrations as they crack whips and ring bells. If you can't make it to Rottweil during the Carnival season, you can still catch the spirit of Fasnet. There's an exhibit on it at the Stadtmuseum, and tours are organized to the shops where they carve the masks and make the costumes and bells. The name "*Rottweil*" may be more familiar as the name for a breed of dog. The area used to be a center of beef production, and locals bred the Rottweiler to herd the cattle. ⊠ *Hauptstr. 20, Rottweil* ☎ *0741/494–330* ▦ *€2* ◷ *Tues.–Sun. noon–4* ◷ *Closed Mon.*

EN
ROUTE
Uhren Museum (*Clock Museum*). In the center of Furtwangen, 16 km (10 miles) south of Triberg, drop in on the Uhren Museum, the largest such museum in Germany. It charts the development of Black Forest clocks and exhibits all types of timepieces, from cuckoo clocks, church clock mechanisms, kinetic wristwatches, and old decorative desktop clocks to punch clocks and digital blinking objects. The most elaborate piece is the "art clock" by local artisan August Noll, built from 1880 to 1885 and featuring the time in Calcutta, New York, Melbourne, and London, among other places. It emits the sound of a crowing rooster in the morning, and other chimes mark yearly events. ⊠ *Robert-Gerwig-Pl. 1* ☎ *07723/920–2800* ⊕ *www.deutsches-uhrenmuseum.de* ▦ *€4* ◷ *Apr.–Oct., daily 9–6; Nov.–Mar., daily 10–5.*

THE SOUTHERN BLACK FOREST

In the south you'll find the most spectacular mountain scenery in the area, culminating in the Feldberg—at 4,899 feet the highest mountain in the Black Forest. The region also has two large lakes, the Titisee and the Schluchsee. Freiburg is a romantic university city with vineyards and a superb Gothic cathedral.

TITISEE

37 km (23 miles) south of Furtwangen.

Beautiful Titisee, carved by a glacier in the last ice age, is the most scenic lake in the Black Forest. The heavily wooded landscape is ideal for long bike tours, which can be organized through the Titisee tourist office. The lake measures 2½ km (1½ miles) long and is invariably crowded in summer. Stop by one of the many lakeside cafés to enjoy some of the region's best Black Forest cherry cake with an unparalleled waterside view. ■ TIP➜ Boats and Windsurfers can be rented at several points along the shore.

ESSENTIALS
Visitor Information Titisee-Neustadt Tourist-Information ⊠ *Strandbadstr. 4, Titisee-Neustadt* ☎ *07651/98040* ⊕ *www.titisee.de.*

WHERE TO STAY

$ **Gasthaus Sonnenmatte.** There are countless hotels and restaurants
HOTEL   clustered around the lakeshore, but for a quieter time and to escape the crowds in summer, it's worth heading farther from the lake. **Pros:** quiet rural location; friendly service; away from the Titisee crowds. **Cons:** away from the Titisee views; some rooms quite small. [$] *Rooms from: €49* ⊠ *Spriegelsbach 5, Titisee-Neustadt* ☎ *07651/8277* ⊕ *www.sonnenmatte.de* ↴ *30 rooms* ⦿| *Breakfast.*

EN   To get to Freiburg, the largest city in the southern Black Forest, you
ROUTE   have to brave the curves of the winding road through the **Höllental** (Hell Valley). In 1770 Empress Maria Theresa's 15-year-old daughter—the future queen Marie Antoinette—made her way along what was then a coach road on her way from Vienna to Paris. She traveled with an entourage of 250 officials and servants in some 50 horse-drawn carriages. The first stop at the end of the valley is a little village called **Himmelreich,** or Kingdom of Heaven. Railroad engineers are said to have given the village its name in the 19th century, grateful as they were to finally have laid a line through Hell Valley. At the entrance to Höllental is a deep gorge, the **Ravennaschlucht.** It's worth scrambling through to reach the tiny 12th-century chapel of **St. Oswald,** the oldest parish church in the Black Forest (there are parking spots off the road). Look for a bronze statue of a deer high on a roadside cliff, 5 km (3 miles) farther on. It commemorates the legend of a deer that amazed hunters by leaping the deep gorge at this point. Another 16 km (10 miles) will bring you to Freiburg.

FREIBURG

25 km (15½ miles) northwest of Hinterzarten.

Duke Berthold III founded Freiburg im Breisgau in the 12th century as a free trading city. World War II left extensive damage, but skillful restoration helped re-create the original and compelling medieval atmosphere of one of the loveliest historic towns in Germany. The 16th-century geographer Martin Waldseemüller was born here; in 1507 he was the first to put the name *"America"* on a map.

For an intimate view of Freiburg, wander through the car-free streets around the Münster or follow the main shopping artery of Kaiser-Joseph-Strasse. After you pass the city gate (Martinstor), follow Gerberau off to the left. You'll come to quaint shops along the banks of one of the city's larger canals, which continues past the former Augustinian cloister to the equally picturesque area around the *Insel* (island). This canal is a larger version of the *Bächle* (brooklets) running through many streets in Freiburg's Old Town. The Bächle, so narrow you can step across them, were created in the 13th century to bring freshwater into the town. Legend has it that if you accidentally step into one of them—and it does happen to travelers looking at the sights—you will marry a person from Freiburg. The tourist office sponsors English walking tours daily at 10:30, with additional tours on Friday and Saturday at 10. The two-hour tour costs €8.

GETTING HERE AND AROUND

Freiburg is on the main railway line between Frankfurt and Basel, and regular ICE (InterCity Express) trains stop here. The railway station is a short walk from the city center. Although Freiburg is a bustling metropolis, the city center is compact. In fact, the bulk of the Old Town is closed to traffic, so walking is by far the most practical and pleasurable option. The Old Town is ringed with parking garages for those who arrive by car.

ESSENTIALS

Visitor Information Freiburg Tourist-Information ✉ *Rathauspl. 2–4*
☎ *0761/388–1880* ⊕ *www.freiburg.de.*

EXPLORING

Augustinermuseum. A visit to Freiburg's cathedral is not really complete without also exploring the Augustinermuseum, in the former Augustinian cloister. Original sculpture from the cathedral is on display, as well as gold and silver reliquaries. The collection of stained-glass windows, dating from the Middle Ages to today, is one of the most important in Germany. ✉ *Augustinerpl.* ☎ *0761/201–2531* ⊕ *www.museen.freiburg. de* ✉ *€6* ⊙ *Tues.–Sun. 10–5.*

Fodor'sChoice
★

Münster unserer Lieben Frau (*Cathedral of Our Dear Lady*). The Münster unserer Lieben Frau, Freiburg's most famous landmark, towers over the medieval streets. The cathedral took three centuries to build, from around 1200 to 1515. You can easily trace the progress of generations of builders through the changing architectural styles, from the fat columns and solid, rounded arches of the Romanesque period to the lofty Gothic windows and airy interior of the choir. The delicately perforated 380-foot spire has been called the finest in Europe. ■TIP→ If you can summon the energy, climb the tower. In addition to a magnificent view, you'll get a closer look at the 16 bells, including the 1258 "Hosanna," one of Germany's oldest functioning bells. ⊠ *Münsterpl. 1* ☎ *0761/388–101* 🗐 *Bell tower €1.50* ⊗ *Mon.– Sat. 9:30–5, Sun. 1–5.*

Münsterplatz. The square around Freiburg's cathedral once served as a cemetery; today it holds a market Monday to Saturday. You can stock up on local specialties, from wood-oven-baked bread to hams, wines, vinegars, fruits, and *Kirschwasser* (cherry brandy). The southern side, in front of the Renaissance **Kaufhaus** (Market House), is traditionally used by merchants. On the northern side of the square are farmers with their produce. This is where you can sample some local sausages served with a white roll and heaps of onions. The square is also lined with traditional taverns.

Museum für Stadtgeschichte (*Museum of City History*). The former home of painter, sculptor, and architect Johann Christian Wentzinger (1710–97) houses the Museum für Stadtgeschichte. It contains fascinating exhibits on the history of the city, including the poignant remains of a typewriter recovered from a bombed-out bank. The ceiling fresco in the stairway, painted by Wentzinger himself, is the museum's pride and joy. ⊠ *Münsterpl. 30* ☎ *0761/201–2515* ⊕ *www.museen.freiburg.de* 🗐 *€3* ⊗ *Tues.–Sun. 10–5.*

Rathaus. Freiburg's famous Town Hall is actually two 16th-century patrician houses joined together. Among its attractive Renaissance features is an oriel, or bay window, clinging to a corner and bearing a bas-relief of the romantic medieval legend of the Maiden and the Unicorn. ⊠ *Rathauspl. 2–4* ⊗ *Mon.–Thurs. 8–5:30, Fri. 8–4.*

WHERE TO EAT

$
GERMAN

✕ **Der Goldene Engel.** Oak beams festooned with plaster casts of cherubs, and angelic paintings on the walls, combine to create a charmingly kitschy atmosphere in "the golden angel." Local dishes are the specialty here, and the Flammkuchen in particular are a good choice. Try the Schwarzwälder Kirchsteak, a wonderful pork-chop with cherries. ⑤ *Average main: €14* ⊠ *Münsterpl. 14* ☎ *0761/37933* ⊕ *www. goldenerengel-freiburg.de.*

$$
GERMAN

✕ **Kühler Krug.** Fresh fish and wild game are the specialties at this elegant yet homey restaurant around 2 km (1½ miles) south of the Old Town. Interesting dishes include rabbit in hazelnut sauce with baby vegetables, as well as salmon in saffron foam with a Riesling risotto. ⑤ *Average main: €16* ⊠ *Torpl. 1* ☎ *0761/29103* ⊗ *Closed Wed.*

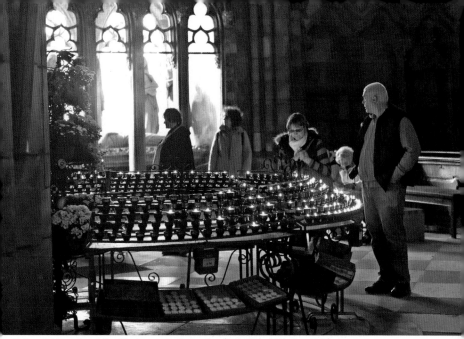

Visitors light candles at the Münster unserer Lieben Frau (Cathedral of Our Dear Lady).

WHERE TO STAY

$$
HOTEL

🏨 **Best Western Premier Hotel Victoria.** Despite its traditional appearance and comfort, this is a very eco-friendly hotel. **Pros:** eco-friendly; free city bus tickets available to guests. **Cons:** outside the medieval center. 💲 *Rooms from: €137* ✉ *Eisenbahnstr. 54* ☎ *0761/207–340* ⊕ *www.victoria.bestwestern.de* 🛏 *63 rooms* �‖ *Breakfast.*

$$$
HOTEL
Fodor'sChoice
★

🏨 **Colombi.** Freiburg's most luxurious hotel is one of the few where the owners are there to make sure your stay is perfect. **Pros:** friendly service; quiet location; comfortable rooms. **Cons:** business hotel; often fully booked by conference visitors. 💲 *Rooms from: €220* ✉ *Rotteck-ring 16* ☎ *0761/21060* ⊕ *www.colombi.de* 🛏 *111 rooms, 5 suites* �‖ *Multiple meal plans.*

$
HOTEL

🏨 **Hotel Schwarzwälder Hof.** Located in a downtown pedestrian zone, part of this hotel occupies a former mint, complete with graceful cast-iron railings on the spiral staircase. **Pros:** good central location; clean rooms. **Cons:** parking in public garage around the corner; can be noisy; thin walls. 💲 *Rooms from: €95* ✉ *Herrenstr. 43* ☎ *0761/38030* ⊕ *www.shof.de* 🛏 *42 rooms, 3 suites* �‖ *Breakfast.*

$$
HOTEL

🏨 **Oberkirchs Weinstube.** Across from the cathedral, this wine cellar, res-taurant, and hotel is a bastion of tradition and *Gemütlichkeit* (com-fort and conviviality). **Pros:** great central location; personal charm. **Cons:** difficult parking access. 💲 *Rooms from: €139* ✉ *Münsterpl. 22* ☎ *0761/202–6868* ⊕ *www.hotel-oberkirch.de* 🛏 *26 rooms* ☉ *Restau-rant closed Sun. and 2 wks in Jan.* �‖ *Breakfast.*

$$
HOTEL

🏨 **Park Hotel Post Meier.** This century-old building near the train sta-tion has a copper dome and stone balconies overlooking a park. **Pros:** friendly; some rooms have park views. **Cons:** outside the medieval center. $\boxed{\$}$ *Rooms from: €129* ✉ *Eisenbahnstr. 35–37* ☎ *0761/385–480* ⊕ *www.park-hotel-post.de* ⇗ *43 rooms, 2 apartments* ⦿ *Breakfast.*

$$
HOTEL

🛏 **Rappen.** This hotel's brightly painted rooms are on the sunny side of the cobblestone cathedral square and marketplace. **Pros:** central location; friendly service; clean rooms. **Cons:** difficult to access by car-located in pedestrian zone. $\boxed{\$}$ *Rooms from: €129* ✉ *Münsterpl. 13* ☎ *0761/31353* ⊕ *www.rappen-freiburg.de* ⇗ *24 rooms* ⦿ *Breakfast.*

$$
HOTEL

🛏 **Zum Roten Bären.** Like several other hotels, the "Red Bear" claims to be the "oldest in Germany," but this one has authenticated documentation going back 700 years to prove its heritage. **Pros:** dripping with history; great location. **Cons:** some rooms quite small. $\boxed{\$}$ *Rooms from: €158* ✉ *Oberlinden 12* ☎ *0761/387–870* ⊕ *www.roter-baeren.de* ⇗ *22 rooms, 3 suites* ⦿ *Restaurant closed Sun.* ⦿ *Breakfast.*

NIGHTLIFE AND THE ARTS

Nightlife in Freiburg takes place in the city's *Kneipen* (pubs), wine bars, and wine cellars, which are plentiful on the streets around the cathedral. For student pubs, wander around Stühlinger, the neighborhood immediately south of the train station.

Cocktailbar Hemingway. Plenty of people take their nightcap in the Best Western Premier Hotel Victoria at the Cocktailbar Hemingway, which stays open until 2 am on weekends. ✉ *Eisenbahnstr. 54* ☎ *0761/207–340.*

Jazzhaus. Jazzhaus sometimes has live music and draws big acts and serious up-and-coming artists to its brick cellar. ✉ *Schnewlinstr. 1* ☎ *0761/34973* ⊕ *www.jazzhaus.de.*

Kagan. A very mixed crowd meets daily and nightly at Kagan on the 18th floor of the skyscraper over the train station, with an incomparable view of the Old Town. The club is open Wednesday through Saturday from 10 pm until the wee hours. The café is open Tuesday through Sunday. ✉ *Bismarckallee 9* ☎ *0761/767–2766* 💳 *€6.*

STAUFEN

20 km (12 miles) south of Freiburg via B-31.

Once you've braved Hell Valley to get to Freiburg, visit the nearby town of Staufen, where Dr. Faustus is reputed to have made his pact with the devil. The Faustus legend is remembered today chiefly because of Goethe's *Faust* (published in two parts, 1808–32). In this account, Faust sells his soul to the devil in return for eternal youth and knowledge. The historical Faustus was actually an alchemist whose pact was not with the devil but with a local baron who convinced him that he could make his fortune by converting base metal into gold. The explosion leading to his death at Gasthaus zum Löwen produced so much noise and sulfurous stink that the townspeople were convinced the devil had carried him off.

GETTING HERE AND AROUND

To reach Staufen, take the twice-hourly train from Freiburg and change at Bad Krozingen. The train station is a 15-minute walk northwest of the town center. The B-31 highway connects Staufen with Freiburg and the A-5 motorway.

For a break from cathedrals and historic sites, take the kids to Europa Park in Rust.

EXPLORING

Gasthaus zum Löwen. You can visit the ancient Gasthaus zum Löwen, where Faust lived, allegedly in room No. 5, and died. Guests can stay overnight in the room, which has been decked out in period furniture and had all-modern conveniences removed (including the telephone) to enhance the effect. The inn is right on the central square of Staufen, a town with a visible inclination toward modern art in ancient settings. ✉ *Rathausg. 8* ☎ *07633/908–9390* ⊕ *www.fauststube-im-loewen.de.*

WHERE TO STAY

$
HOTEL
🛏 **Landgasthaus zur Linde.** Guests have been welcomed here for more than 350 years, but the comforts inside the inn's old walls are contemporary. **Pros:** friendly; quiet; good restaurant. **Cons:** remote; no elevator. $ *Rooms from: €95* ✉ *Krumlinden 13, 14 km (9 miles) southeast of Staufen, Münstertal* ☎ *07636/447* ⊕ *www.landgasthaus.de* ⌁ *11 rooms, 3 suites* ☉ *Restaurant closed Mon.* ⧗ *Breakfast.*

KAISERSTUHL

20 km (12 miles) northwest of Freiburg on B-31.

One of the unusual sights of the Black Forest is the Kaiserstuhl (Emperor's Chair), a volcanic outcrop clothed in vineyards that produce some of Baden's best wines—reds from the Spätburgunder grape and whites that have an uncanny depth. A third of Baden's wines are produced in this single area, which has the warmest climate in Germany. ▥ **TIP→** The especially dry and warm microclimate has given rise to tropical vegetation, including sequoias and a wide variety of orchids.

EXPLORING

Weinbaumuseum (*Wine Museum*). The fine little Weinbaumuseum is in a renovated barn in the village center. A small vineyard out front displays the various types of grapes used to make wine in the Kaiserstuhl region. ✉ *Schlossbergstr., Vogtsburg im Kaiserstuhl* ☎ *07662/81263* 💷 *€2* ☉ *Apr.–Oct., Tues.–Fri. 2–5, weekends 11–5.*

WHERE TO STAY

$$
B&B/INN

Hotel Zur Krone. You could spend an entire afternoon and evening here even if you don't stay overnight in the comfortable guest rooms. **Pros:** friendly; quiet. **Cons:** can feel remote. $ *Rooms from: €120* ✉ *Schlossbergstr. 15, Vogtsburg-Achkarren* ☎ *07662/93130* ⊕ *www. Hotel-Krone-Achkarren.de* 🛏 *23 rooms* ☉ *Restaurant closed Wed., and Thurs. in winter* ❍|*Breakfast.*

$
B&B/INN

Posthotel Kreuz-Post. Set right in the middle of the Kaiserstuhl vineyards, this somewhat plain but contemporarily furnished establishment has been in the hands of the Gehr family since its construction in 1809. **Pros:** quiet; in the middle of nowhere. **Cons:** quiet; in the middle of nowhere. $ *Rooms from: €95* ✉ *Landstr. 1, Vogtsburg-Burkheim* ☎ *07662/90910* ⊕ *www.kreuz-post.de* 🛏 *35 rooms* ❍|*Breakfast.*

RUST

35 km (22 miles) north of Freiburg.

The town of Rust, on the Rhine almost halfway from Freiburg to Strasbourg, boasts a castle dating from 1577 and painstakingly restored half-timber houses. But its big claim to fame is Germany's biggest amusement park, with its own autobahn exit.

EXPLORING

FAMILY

Fodor's Choice

★

Europa Park. On an area of 160 acres, Europa Park draws more than 3 million visitors a year with its variety of shows, rides, dining, and shops. Among many other things, it has the "Eurosat" to take you on a virtual journey past clusters of meteors and falling stars; the "Silver Star," Europe's highest roller coaster; a Spanish jousting tournament; and even a "4-D" movie in which you might get damp in the rain or be rocked by an earthquake. ✉ *Europa-Park-Str. 2* ☎ *01805/776–688* ⊕ *www.europapark.de* 💷 *€39* ☉ *Apr.–Oct., daily 9–6.*

WHERE TO STAY

$$
HOTEL

Hotel am Park. This handy hotel, with a waterfall and a statue of a "friendly dragon" in the lobby, is just across the road from the entrance to Europa Park. **Pros:** friendly; great for kids; convenient for Europa Park. **Cons:** proximity to Europa Park means it can get noisy. $ *Rooms from: €110* ✉ *Austr. 1* ☎ *07822/444–900* ⊕ *www.hotels-in-rust.de* 🛏 *47 rooms* ❍|*Breakfast.*

8

HEIDELBERG AND
THE NECKAR VALLEY

WELCOME TO HEIDELBERG AND THE NECKAR VALLEY

TOP REASONS TO GO

★ **Heidelberg Castle:**
The architectural highlight of the region's most beautiful castle is the Renaissance courtyard—harmonious, graceful, and ornate.

★ **Heidelberg's Alte Brücke:** Walk under the twin towers that were part of medieval Heidelberg's fortifications, and look back for a picture postcard view of the city and the castle.

★ **Burg Hornberg:** With its oldest parts dating from the 12th century, this is one of the best of more than a dozen castles between Heidelberg and Stuttgart.

★ **Stuttgart's museums:** Top art collections in the Staatsgalerie and the Kunstmuseum contrast with the Mercedes and Porsche museums, where the history of the *auto mobil* is illustrated by historic classic cars and sleek racing cars.

★ **Tübingen Altstadt:** With its half-timber houses, winding alleyways, and hilltop setting overlooking the Neckar, Tübingen is the quintessential German experience.

1 Heidelberg. The natural beauty of Heidelberg is created by the embrace of mountains, forests, vineyards, and the Neckar River, all crowned by the famous ruined castle. The Neckar and the Rhine meet at nearby Mannheim, the biggest train hub for the superfast ICE (InterCity Express) trains of Germany, a major industrial center, and the second-largest river port in Europe.

2 The Burgenstrasse (Castle Road). If you or your kids like castles, this is the place to go. The crowded Heidelberg Castle is a must-see, but the real fun starts when you venture up the Neckar River. There seems to be a castle on every hilltop in the valley, including Burg Hohenzollern, home to the most powerful family in German history.

3 Swabian Cities. Stuttgart, the state capital, has elegant streets, shops, hotels, and museums, as well as some of Germany's top industries, among them Mercedes, Porsche, and Bosch. Ludwigsburg, with its huge baroque castles and baroque flower gardens, is worth a visit. The most charmingly "Swabian" of all these cities is the old half-timber university town of Tübingen.

GETTING ORIENTED

Although not as well known as the Rhine, the Neckar River has a wonderful charm of its own. After Heidelberg, it winds through a small valley guarded by castles. It then flows on, bordered by vineyards on its northern slopes, passing the interesting and industrious city of Stuttgart, before it climbs toward the Swabian Hills. You follow the Neckar until the old half-timber university town of Tübingen. The river continues toward the eastern slopes of the Black Forest, where it originates less than 80 km (50 miles) from the source of the Danube.

8

Updated by
Evelyn Kanter

Heidelberg remains one of the best-known and most visited cities in Germany, identifiable by its graceful baroque towers and the majestic ruins of its red sandstone castle. From this grand city, the narrow and quiet Neckar Valley makes its way east, then turns to the south, taking you past villages filled with half-timber houses and often guarded by their own castle—sometimes in ruins but often revived as a museum or hotel. This part of Germany is aptly named the *Burgenstrasse* (Castle Road).

The valley widens into one of the most industrious areas of Germany, with Stuttgart at its center. In this wealthy city, world-class art museums like the Staatsgalerie or the Kunstmuseum in the center of town contrast with the new and striking Mercedes and Porsche museums in the suburbs, adjoining their sprawling manufacturing facilities.

A bit farther south, the rolling Swabian Hills cradle the university town of Tübingen, a center of learning in a beautiful historic setting on the banks of the Neckar River. Overlooking the town is—of course—a mighty castle.

PLANNING

WHEN TO GO

If you plan to visit Heidelberg in summer, make reservations well in advance and expect to pay top rates. To get away from the crowds, consider staying out of town and driving or taking the bus or train into the city. Hotels and restaurants are much cheaper just a little upriver. A visit in late fall, when the vines turn a faded gold, or early spring, with the first green shoots of the year, can be captivating. In the depths of winter, river mists creep through the narrow streets of Heidelberg's Old Town and awaken the ghosts of a romantic past.

GETTING HERE AND AROUND

AIR TRAVEL

From the Frankfurt and Stuttgart airports, there's fast and easy access, by car and train, to all major centers along the Neckar.

BUS AND SHUTTLE TRAVEL

From Frankfurt Airport to Heildelberg, hop aboard the Lufthansa Airport Bus, which takes about an hour and is not restricted to Lufthansa passengers. Buses depart 11 times a day between 7 am and 10:30 pm from Arrivals Hall B of Terminal 1. Airport-bound buses leave the Crowne Plaza Heidelberg between 5:30 am and 8 pm. One-way tickets are €24 per person, or €22 with a Lufthansa flight ticket. With advance reservations you can also get to downtown Heidelberg via the shuttle service TLS. The trip costs €34 per person.

Bus Information Lufthansa Airport Bus ☎ 06152/976–9099 ⊕ *www.transcontinental-group.com/en/frankfurt-airport-shuttles.* **TLS** ☎ *06221/770–077* ⊕ *www.tls-heidelberg.de.*

CAR TRAVEL

Heidelberg is a 15-minute drive (10 km [6 miles]) on A-656 from Mannheim, a major junction of the autobahn system. The Burgenstrasse (Route B-37) follows the north bank of the Neckar River from Heidelberg to Mosbach, from which it continues south to Heilbronn as B-27, the road parallel to and predating the autobahn (A-81). B-27 still leads to Stuttgart and Tübingen.

TRAIN TRAVEL

Heidelberg is 17 minutes from Mannheim, by S-bahn regional train, or 11 minutes on hourly InterCity Express (ICE) trains. These sleek, super-high-speed trains reach 280 kph (174 mph), so travel time between Frankfurt Airport and Mannheim is a half hour. From Heidelberg to Stuttgart, direct InterCity (IC) trains take 40 minutes. Local services link many of the smaller towns.

RESTAURANTS

Mittagessen (lunch) in this region is generally served from noon until 2 or 2:30, *Abendessen* (dinner) from 6 until 9:30 or 10. *Durchgehend warme Küche* means that hot meals are also served between lunch and dinner. While credit cards are widely accepted, many small family owned restaurants, cafés, and pubs will accept only cash or debit cards issued by a German bank. Casual attire is typically acceptable at restaurants here, and reservations are generally not needed.

Prices in the reviews are the average cost of a main course at dinner, or if dinner is not served, at lunch.

HOTELS

This area is full of castle-hotels and charming country inns that range in comfort from upscale rustic to luxurious. For a riverside view, ask for a *Zimmer* (room) or *Tisch* (table) *mit Neckarblick* (with a view of the Neckar). The Neckar Valley offers idyllic alternatives to the cost and crowds of Heidelberg. Driving or riding the train from Neckargemünd, for example, takes 20 minutes.

Prices in the reviews are the lowest cost of a standard double room in high season. For expanded reviews, facilities, and current deals, visit Fodors.com.

PLANNING YOUR TIME

To fully appreciate Heidelberg, try to be up and about before the tour buses arrive. After the day-trippers have gone and many shops have closed, the good restaurants and the nightspots open up. Visit the castles on the Burgenstrasse at your leisure, perhaps even staying overnight. Leaving the valley toward the south, you'll drive into wine country. Even if you are not a car enthusiast, the museums of Mercedes and Porsche in Stuttgart are well worth a visit. Try to get to Tübingenduring the week to avoid the crowds of Swabians coming in for their *Kaffee und Kuchen* (coffee and cake). During the week, try to get a room and spend a leisurely evening in this charming half-timber university town.

VISITOR INFORMATION

Die Burgenstrasse ✉ *Allee 28, Heilbronn* ☎ *07131/564–028* ⊕ *www.burgenstrasse.de.*

State Tourist Board Baden-Württemberg ✉ *Esslingerstr. 8, Stuttgart* ☎ *0711/238–580* ⊕ *www.tourismus-bw.de.*

HEIDELBERG

57 km (35 miles) northeast of Karlsruhe.

If any city in Germany encapsulates the spirit of the country, it is Heidelberg. Scores of poets and composers—virtually the entire 19th-century German Romantic movement—have sung its praises. Goethe and Mark Twain both fell in love here: the German writer with a beautiful young woman, the American author with the city itself. Sigmund Romberg set his operetta *The Student Prince* in the city; Carl Maria von Weber wrote his lushly Romantic opera *Der Freischütz* here. Composer Robert Schumann was a student at the university. The campaign these artists waged on behalf of the town has been astoundingly successful. Heidelberg's fame is out of all proportion to its size (population 140,000); more than 3½ million visitors crowd its streets every year.

Heidelberg was the political center of the Lower Palatinate. At the end of the Thirty Years' War (1618–48), the elector Carl Ludwig married his daughter to the brother of Louis XIV in the hope of bringing peace to the Rhineland. But when the elector's son died without an heir, Louis XIV used the marriage alliance as an excuse to claim Heidelberg, and in 1689 the town was sacked and laid to waste. Four years later he sacked the town again. From its ashes arose what you see today: a baroque town built on Gothic foundations, with narrow, twisting streets and alleyways.

Above all, Heidelberg is a university town, with students making up some 20% of its population. And a youthful spirit is felt in the lively restaurants and pubs of the Altstadt (Old Town). In 1930 the university was expanded, and its buildings now dot the entire landscape of

Heidelberg and neighboring suburbs. Modern Heidelberg changed as U.S. Army barracks and industrial development stretched into the suburbs, but the old heart of the city remains intact, exuding the spirit of romantic Germany.

GETTING HERE AND AROUND

Heidelberg is 15 minutes from Mannheim, where four ICE trains and five Autobahn routes meet. Everything in town may be reached on foot, but wear sturdy, comfortable shoes, since much of the Old City is uneven cobblestones. A funicular takes you up to the castle and Heidelberg's Königstuhl Mountain, and a streetcar runs from the city center to the main train station.

TOURING TIPS

Information: Tourist offices in front of the main train station and in the Rathaus have maps and brochures, as well as discount cards.

Scenic spot: From the Old Bridge over the Neckar you'll have an excellent view toward Heidelberg's Altstadt (Old Town) and its famous castle.

Scenic spot: Looking down from the ramparts of Heidelberg's Castle you can see the Neckar flowing toward the Rhine.

From April through October there are daily walking tours of Heidelberg in German (Friday and Saturday also in English) at 10:30 am; from November through March, tours are in German only, Friday at 2:30 and Saturday at 10:30; the cost is €7. They depart from the main entrance to the Rathaus (Town Hall). Bilingual bus tours run April through October on Thursday and Friday at 1:30 and on Saturday at 1:30 and 3. From November through March, bus tours are on Saturday at 1:30. They cost €17 and depart from Universitätsplatz.

DISCOUNTS AND DEALS

The two-day HeidelbergCARD, which costs €14.50 per person or €31.50 for a family of up to five people, includes free or reduced admission to most tourist attractions as well as free use of all public transportation—including the Bergbahn (funicular) to the castle—and other extras such as free entrance to the castle courtyard, free guided walking tours, discounts on bus tours, and a city guidebook. It can be purchased at the tourist-information office at the main train station or the Rathaus, and at many local hotels.

TIMING

Walking the length of Heidelberg's Hauptstrasse (main street) will take an hour—longer if you are easily sidetracked by the shopping opportunities. Strolling through the Old Town and across the bridge to look at the castle will add at least another half hour, not counting the time you spend visiting the sites.

ESSENTIALS

Visitor Information Heidelberg Tourist-Information ✉ *Im Rathaus, Marktpl.* ☎ *06221/58444* ✉ *Am Hauptbahnhof, Willy-Brandt-Pl. 1* ☎ *06221/19433* ⊕ *www.heidelberg-marketing.de.*

EXPLORING

TOP ATTRACTIONS

Alte Brücke (*Old Bridge*). Framed by two *Spitzhelm* towers (so called for their resemblance to old German helmets), this bridge was part of Heidelberg's medieval fortifications. In the west tower are three dank dungeons that once held common criminals. Above the portcullis you'll see a memorial plaque that pays warm tribute to the Austrian forces that helped Heidelberg beat back a French attempt to capture the bridge in 1799. The bridge itself is one of many to be built on this spot; ice floes and floods destroyed its predecessors. The elector Carl Theodor, who built it in 1786–88, must have been confident this one would last: he had a statue of himself erected on it, upon a plinth decorated with river gods and goddesses (symbolic of the Neckar, Rhine, Danube, and Mosel rivers). As you enter the bridge from the Old Town, you'll also notice a statue of an animal that appears somewhat catlike. It's actually a monkey holding a mirror. Legend has it the statue was erected to symbolize the need for both city-dwellers and those who lived on the other side of the bridge to take a look over their shoulders as they cross—that neither group was more elite than the other. The pedestrian-only bridge is at the end of Steingasse, not far from the Marktplatz. ⊠ *End of Steing.*

Alte Universität (*Old University*). The three-story baroque structure was built between 1712 and 1735 at the behest of the elector Johann Wilhelm, although Heidelberg's Ruprecht Karl University was originally founded in 1386. Today it houses the **University Museum**, with exhibits that chronicle the history of Germany's oldest university. The present-day Universitätsplatz (University Square) was built over the remains of an Augustinian monastery that was destroyed by the French in 1693. ⊠ *Grabeng. 1–3* ☎ *06221/542–152* 🎫 *€3* ☉ *Apr.– Sept., Tues.–Sun. 10–6; Oct., Tues.–Sun. 10–4; Nov.–Mar., Tues.– Sat. 10–4.*

Heiliggeistkirche (*Church of the Holy Ghost*). The foundation stone of this Gothic church was laid in 1398, but it was not actually finished until 1544. The gargoyles looking down on the south side (where Hauptstrasse crosses Marktplatz) are remarkable for their sheer ugliness. The church fell victim to plundering by the Catholic League during the Thirty Years' War, when the church's greatest treasure—the Bibliotheca Palatina, at the time the largest library in Germany—was loaded onto 500 carts and trundled off to the Vatican. Few volumes found their way back. At the end of the 17th century, French troops plundered the church again, destroying the tombs; only the 15th-century tomb of Elector Ruprecht III and his wife, Elisabeth von Hohenzollern, remain. Today, the huge church is shared by Heidelberg's Protestant and Catholic populations. ⊠ *Marktpl.* ☎ *06221/21117* ⊕ *www.heiliggeistkirche. de* ☉ *Late Mar.–Oct., Mon.–Sat. 11–5, Sun. 12:30–5; Nov.–mid-Mar., Fri. and Sat. 11–3, Sun. 12:30–3.*

Königstuhl (*King's Throne*). The second-highest hill in the Odenwald range—1,800 feet above Heidelberg—is only a hop, skip, and funicular ride from Heidelberg. On a clear day you can see as far as the Black Forest to the south and west to the Vosges Mountains of France. The hill is at the center of a close-knit network of hiking trails. Signs and colored arrows from the top lead hikers through the woods of the Odenwald.

Königstuhl Bergbahn (*funicular*). Hoisting visitors to the summit of the Königstuhl in 17 minutes, the funicular stops on the way at the ruined Heidelberg Schloss and Molkenkur. A modern funicular usually leaves every 10 minutes, and a historical train comes every 20 minutes. ⊠ *Kornmarkt* ⊕ *www.bergbahn-heidelberg.de* 🚡 *Königstuhl €12 (round-trip), Schloss €6.50 (round-trip; additional charge to visit Schloss)* ⏲ *Mid-Apr.–mid-Oct., daily 9–8:25; mid-Oct.–mid-Apr., daily 9–5:45.*

Kurpfälzisches Museum (*Palatinate Museum*). It's a pleasure just to wander around this baroque palace—built as a residence for a university professor in 1712—which is more or less unavoidable, since the museum's layout is so confusing. Among the exhibits are two standouts. One is a replica of the jaw of Heidelberg Man, a key link in the evolutionary chain thought to date from a half million years ago (the original was unearthed near the city in 1907). The larger attraction is the *Windsheimer Zwölfbotenaltar* (*Twelve Apostles Altarpiece*), one of the largest and finest works of early Renaissance sculptor Tilman Riemenschneider.

Its exquisite detailing and technical sophistication are evident in the simple faith that radiates from the faces of the Apostles. The top floor of the museum showcases 19th-century German paintings and drawings, many depicting Heidelberg. ■TIP➡ The restaurant in the museum's quiet courtyard is a good place for a break. ⊠ *Hauptstr. 97* ☎ *06221/583–4020* ⊕ *www.museum-heidelberg.de* ⊠ *€3* ⊙ *Tues.–Sun. 10–6.*

Marktplatz (*Market Square*). Heidelberg's main square, with the Rathaus (town hall) on one side and the Heiliggeistkirche on the other,

has been its focal point since the Middle Ages. Public courts of justice were held here in earlier centuries, and people accused of witchcraft and heresy were burned at the stake. The baroque fountain in the middle, the *Herkulesbrunnen* (Hercules Fountain), is the work of 18th-century artist H. Charrasky. Until 1740 a rotating, hanging cage stood next to it. For minor crimes, people were imprisoned in it and exposed to the abuse of their fellow citizens. ■TIP➡ Today the Marktplatz hosts outdoor markets every Wednesday and Saturday.

Molkenkur. The next stop after the castle on the Königstuhl funicular, Molkenkur was the site of Heidelberg's second castle. Lightning struck it in 1537, and it was never rebuilt. Today it's occupied by a small restaurant—which bears the creative name Molkenkur Restaurant—with magnificent views of the Odenwald and the Rhine plain. ⊠ *Molkenkurweg, off Klingenteichstr.*

Philosophenweg (*Philosophers' Path*). You can reach this trail high above the river in one of two ways—either from Neuenheim or by taking the Schlangenweg (Snake Path). Both are steep climbs, but you'll be rewarded with spectacular views of the Old Town and castle. From Neuenheim, turn right after crossing the bridge and follow signs to a small alleyway.

Rathaus (*Town Hall*). Work began on the town hall in 1701, a few years after the French destroyed the city. The massive coat of arms above the balcony is the work of Heinrich Charrasky, who also created the statue of Hercules atop the fountain in the middle of the square. ⊠ *Marktpl.*

Schlangenweg (*Snake Path*). This walkway starts just above the Alte Brücke opposite the Old Town and cuts steeply through terraced vineyards until it reaches the woods, where it crosses the Philosophenweg (Philosophers' Path). ⊠ *Off Ziegelhäuser Landstr.*

Fodor'sChoice
★ **Schloss** (*Castle*). What's most striking is the architectural variety of this great complex. The oldest parts still standing date from the 15th century, though most of the castle was built during the Renaissance in the baroque styles of the 16th and 17th centuries, when the castle was

the seat of the Palatinate electors. There's an "English wing," built in 1612 by the elector Friedrich V for his teenage Scottish bride, Elizabeth Stuart; its plain, square-window facade is positively foreign compared to the castle's more opulent styles. (The enamored Friedrich also had a charming garden laid out for his young bride; its imposing arched entryway, the Elisabethentor, was put up overnight as a surprise for her 19th birthday.) The architectural highlight remains the Renaissance courtyard—harmonious, graceful, and ornate.

Even if you have to wait, make a point of seeing the *Grosses Fass* (Great Cask) in the cellar, possibly the world's largest wine barrel, made from 130 oak trees and capable of holding 58,500 gallons. It was used to hold wines paid as taxes by wine producers in the Palatinate. In summer there are fireworks displays (on the first Saturday in June and September and the second Saturday in July). In July and August the castle hosts a theater festival. Performances of *The Student Prince* often figure prominently. ■ TIP➜ Take the Königstuhl Bergbahn, or funicular (€6.50 round-trip), faster and less tiring than hiking to the castle on the Burgweg. Audioguides are available in seven languages. ⊠ *Schloss-hof* ☎ *06221/538–431* ⊕ *www.heidelberg-schloss.de* ☞ *€6 (funicular round-trip an additional €6.50); audioguide €4* ☼ *Daily, 8–5; tours in English daily 11:15–3:15, when demand is sufficient.*

Deutsches Apotheken–Museum (*German Apothecary Museum*). The castle includes the Deutsches Apotheken–Museum. This museum, on the lower floor of the Ottheinrichsbau (Otto Heinrich Building), is filled with ancient flagons and receptacles (each with a carefully painted enamel label), beautifully made scales, little drawers, shelves, dried beetles and toads, and marvelous reconstructions of six apothecary shops from the 17th through the 20th centuries. The museum also offers young visitors the chance to smell various herbs and mix their own teas. ☎ *06221/25880* ⊕ *www.deutsches-apotheken-museum.de* ☼ *Apr.–Oct., daily 10–6, Nov.–Mar., daily 10–5:30*

WORTH NOTING

Neue Universität (*New University*). The plain building on the south side of Universitätsplatz was erected between 1930 and 1932 through funds raised by the U.S. ambassador to Germany, J. G. Schurman, who had been a student at the university. The only decoration on the building's three wings is a statue of Athena, the Greek goddess of wisdom, above the entrance. The inner courtyard contains a medieval tower from 1380, the **Hexenturm** (Witches' Tower). Suspected witches were locked up there in the Middle Ages. It later became a memorial to former students killed in World War I. ⊠ *Grabeng.*

OFF THE BEATEN PATH

Neuenheim. To escape the crowds of central Heidelberg, walk across the Theodor Heuss Bridge to the suburb of Neuenheim. At the turn of the 20th century this old fishing village developed into a residential area full of posh art nouveau villas. North of the *Brückenkopf* (bridgehead) you'll find antiques and designer shops, boutiques, and cafés on Brückenstrasse, Bergstrasse (one block east), and Ladenburger Strasse (parallel to the river). To savor the neighborhood spirit, visit the charming farmers' market on Wednesday or Saturday morning at the corner of Ladenburger and Luther streets.

Heidelberg's Alte Brücke (Old Bridge), now a pedestrian walkway with picture-postcard views, was part of the city's medieval fortifications and is a top site.

Peterskirche (*St. Peter's Church*). Many famous Heidelberg citizens' tombstones, some more than 500 years old, line the outer walls of the city's oldest parish church (1485–1500). ✉ *Plöck 70* ☯ *Apr.–Oct., weekdays.*

Studentenkarzer (*Student Prison*). Between 1778 and 1914, university officials used this as a lock-up for students, mostly incarcerated for minor offenses. They could be held for up to 14 days and were left to subsist on bread and water for the first 3 days; thereafter, they were allowed to attend lectures, receive guests, and have food brought in from the outside. ▪ TIP→ There's bravado, even poetic flair, to be deciphered from two centuries of graffiti that cover the walls and ceilings of the narrow cells. ✉ *Augustinerg. 2* ☎ *06221/543–554* ✉ *€2.50; free with Heidelberg Card* ☯ *Apr.–Oct., Tues.–Sun., 10–6; Nov.–Mar., Tues.–Sat., 10–4.*

Synagogueplatz. The site of the former Heidelberg Synagogue, built in 1877 and burned down in 1938, is now a memorial to the local Jewish population lost in World War II, their names listed on a bronze plaque on an adjoining building. On this residential corner, 12 stone blocks represent the synagogue's pews and the 12 tribes of Israel. ✉ *Corner of Lauerstrafle and Grosse Mantelg., Alte Stadt* ⊕ *www.tourism-heidelberg.com.*

Universitätsbibliothek (*University Library*). The 3½ million volumes here include the 14th-century *Manesse Codex*, a unique collection of medieval songs and poetry once performed in the courts of Germany by the *Minnesänger* (troubadors). The original is too fragile to be exhibited, so a copy is on display. ✉ *Plöck 107–109* ☎ *06221/542–380* ⊕ *www. ub.uni-heidelberg.de* ✉ *Free* ☯ *Weekdays 9–7, Sat. 9–1.*

WHERE TO EAT

$ ✕**Café Knösel.** Heidelberg's oldest (1863) coffeehouse has always been a
CAFÉ popular meeting place for students and professors, and offers traditional
Schwabian food, pastries and ambiance. A historic change is that café
no longer is producing café founder Fridolin Knösel's *Heidelberger Stu-
dentenkuss.* This iconic "student kiss" is a chocolate wrapped in paper
showing two sets of touching lips—an acceptable way for 19th-century
students to "exchange kisses" in public. They are now being sold exclusively in Knösel Chocolatier, a small, charming shop, owned by the
Knösel family, just down the street. ⑤ *Average main: €5* ✉ *Haspelg. 20*
☏ *06221/727–2754* ⊕ *www.cafek-hd.de.*

$$$$ ✕**Scharff's Schlossweinstube.** Elegant, romantic and expensive, this
GERMAN baroque dining room inside the famous Heidelberg castle specializes
in *Ente von Heidelberg* (roast duck), but there's always something
new on the seasonal menu. Whatever you order, pair it with a bottle
from the extensive selection of international wines. Less pricey is the
adjacent Bistro Backhaus, which has rustic furnishings and a nearly
50-foot-high *Backkamin* (baking oven). Light fare as well as coffee and cake are served indoors and on the shaded terrace. You can
sample rare wines (Eiswein, Beerenauslese) by the glass in the shared
wine cellar, or pick up a bottle with a designer label depicting Heidelberg. Reservations are essential for terrace seating in summer. ⑤ *Average main: €100* ✉ *Schlosshof, on castle grounds* ☏ *06221/872–7010*
⊕ *www.heidelberger-schloss-gastronomie.de* ⊗ *Closed late Dec.–Jan.
and Wed. No lunch.*

$ ✕**Schnitzelbank.** Little more than a hole in the wall, this former cooper's
GERMAN workshop has been transformed into a candlelit pub. No matter when
Fodor's Choice you go, it seems to be filled with people seated around the wooden
★ tables. The menu features specialties from Baden and the Pfalz, such as
Schäufele (pickled and slightly smoked pork shoulder); or a hearty plat-
ter of bratwurst, *Leberknödel* (liver dumplings), and slices of *Saumagen*
(a spicy meat-and-potato mixture encased in a sow's stomach). ⑤ *Average main: €11* ✉ *Bauamtsg. 7* ☏ *06221/21189* ⊕ *www.schnitzelbank-
heidelberg.de* ⊗ *No lunch weekdays.*

$$$ ✕**Simplicissimus.** Olive oil and herbs of Provence accentuate many of
MEDITERRANEAN the chef's culinary delights. Saddle of lamb and sautéed liver in honey-
pepper sauce are specialties, as are season specialties with asparagus
and mushrooms. The *Dessertteller,* a sweet sampler, is a crowning fin-
ish to any meal. The wine list focuses on old-world estates, particularly
clarets. The elegant art-nouveau interior is done in shades of red with
dark-wood accents, and a quiet courtyard offers alfresco dining in sum-
mer. ⑤ *Average main: €25* ✉ *Ingrimstr. 16* ☏ *06221/183–336* ⊕ *www.
restaurant-simplicissimus.de* ⊗ *Closed Mon. No lunch.*

$ ✕**Trattoria Toscana.** Traditional Italian fare is on offer here, including
ITALIAN antipasti platters, pasta dishes, pizzas, and special daily offerings, all
served in generous portions. The restaurant is in a central location in the
main square, and in warm weather you can opt for a table outside on
the cobblestones—perfect for people-watching with your meal. ⑤ *Aver-
age main: €11* ✉ *Marktpl. 1* ☏ *06221/28619.*

EATING WELL IN THE NECKAR VALLEY

Fish and *Wild* (game) from the streams and woods lining the Neckar Valley, as well as seasonal favorites—*Spargel* (asparagus), *Pilze* (mushrooms), *Morcheln* (morels), *Pfifferlinge* (chanterelles), and *Steinpilze* (porcini)—are regulars on menus. Pfälzer specialties are also common, but the penchant for potatoes yields to *Knödel* (dumplings) and pasta farther south. The latter includes the Swabian and Baden staples *Maultaschen* ("pockets" of pasta stuffed with meat or spinach) and *Spätzle* (roundish egg noodles), as well as *Schupfnudeln* (finger-size noodles of potato dough), also called *Buwespitzle*. Look for *Linsen* (lentils) and sauerkraut in soups or as sides. *Schwäbischer Rostbraten* (beefsteak topped with fried onions) and *Schäufele* (pickled and slightly smoked pork shoulder) are popular meat dishes, along with a variety of *Würste*.

Considerable quantities of red wine are produced along the Neckar Valley. Crisp, light Trollinger is often served in the traditional *Viertele*, a round, quarter-liter (8-ounce) glass with a handle. Deeper-color, more-substantial reds include Spätburgunder (pinot noir) and its mutation Schwarzriesling (pinot meunier), Lemberger, and Dornfelder. Riesling, Kerner, and Müller-Thurgau (synonymous with Rivaner), as well as Grauburgunder (pinot gris) and Weissburgunder (pinot blanc), are the typical white wines. A birch broom or wreath over the doorway of a vintner's home signifies a *Besenwirtschaft* ("broomstick inn"), a rustic pub where you can enjoy wines with snacks and simple fare. Many vintners offer economical B&Bs. These places are ideal spots to try out your newly learned German phrases; you'll be surprised how well you speak German after the third glass of German wine.

$
GERMAN
Fodor's Choice
★

✕ **Zum Roten Ochsen.** Many of the rough-hewn oak tables here have initials carved into them, a legacy of the thousands who have visited Heidelberg's most famous old tavern. Mark Twain, Marilyn Monroe, and John Wayne may have left their mark—they all ate here, and Twain's photo is on one of the memorabilia-covered walls. Wash down simple fare, such as goulash soup and bratwurst, or heartier dishes like *Tellerfleisch* (boiled beef) or Swabian *Maultaschen* (meat filled raviolis) with regional German wines or local Heidelberg beer. The "Red Ox" has been run by the Spengel family for more than 170 years. Come early to get a good seat, and stay late for the piano player and *Gemütlichkeit* (easy-going friendliness). $ *Average main: €12* ✉ *Hauptstr. 217* ☎ *06221/20977* ⊕ *www.roterochsen.de* ⊗ *Closed Sun. and mid-Dec.–mid-Jan. No lunch Nov.–Mar.*

$
GERMAN

✕ **Zum Weissen Schwanen.** Founded in 1398 and in this location on Heidelberg's Hauptstrasse (main street) since 1778—so you know they are doing something right—the White Swan specializes in regional fare. The menu includes several versions of Maultaschen and local mushrooms feature in season. Unlike most German restaurants and pubs, which serve one local brew, there are a dozen on tap here; the most popular are Klosterhof and Heidelberger. $ *Average main: €15* ✉ *Hauptstr. 143* ☎ *06221/659–692* ⊕ *zumweissenschwanen.trineca.de.*

$$$ ✕ **Zur Herrenmühle.** A 17th-century grain mill has been transformed into
EUROPEAN this romantic restaurant in the heart of Altstadt (Old Town). The old
beams add to the warm atmosphere. In summer, try to arrive early to get
a table in the idyllic courtyard. Fish, lamb, and homemade pasta are spe-
cialties. Or, opt for the three- or four-course prix-fixe menu ⑤ *Average
main: €21* ⊠ *Near Karlstor, Hauptstr. 239* ☎ *06221/602–909* ⊕ *www.
herrenmuehle-heidelberg.de* ⊗ *Closed Sun. No lunch.*

WHERE TO STAY

$$ 🏨 **Bergheim 41.** Sleek and trendy, this new hotel (it opened in 2013) in
HOTEL the "new" part of Heidelberg, is built into one side of the Alten Hal-
lenbad, the covered former city pool that is now a popular upscale
international food court. **Pros:** roof garden and some rooms have view
of the Schloss. **Cons:** no parking; 15 minutes from Old Town; on a busy
street (although windows are soundproofed); no restaurant. ⑤ *Rooms
from: €110* ⊠ *Bergheim 41* ☎ *06221/750–040* ⊕ *www.bergheim41.de*
↪ *32 rooms, 4 suites* ⦿ *Breakfast.*

$$ 🏨 **Crowne Plaza Heidelberg.** This grand hotel has a spacious lobby, styl-
HOTEL ish furnishings, soaring ceilings, and an enviable location—it's a five-
minute walk from Old Town. **Pros:** parking garage; pool; direct shuttle
from Frankfurt airport (80 km [50 miles] away). **Cons:** chain hotel feel.
⑤ *Rooms from: €140* ⊠ *Kurfürsten-Anlage 1* ☎ *06221/9170* ⊕ *www.
crowneplaza.com* ↪ *232 rooms, 4 suites* ⦿ *Breakfast.*

$$ 🏨 **Der Europäische Hof–Hotel Europa.** On secluded grounds next to the
HOTEL Old Town, this most luxurious of Heidelberg hotels has been welcom-
Fodor'sChoice ing guests since 1865. **Pros:** indoor pool; castle views from the two-
★ story fitness and spa center. **Cons:** restaurant closed in July and August.
⑤ *Rooms from: €170* ⊠ *Friedrich-Ebert-Anlage 1* ☎ *06221/5150*
⊕ *www.europaeischerhof.com* ↪ *100 rooms, 14 suites, 3 apartments,
1 penthouse* ⦿ *Breakfast.*

$$ 🏨 **Gasthaus Backmulde.** This traditional Gasthaus in the heart of Hei-
B&B/INN delberg has very nice modern rooms at—for Heidelberg—affordable
prices. **Pros:** quiet rooms; nice restaurant. **Cons:** difficult parking; some
rooms have shared baths; restaurant closed Sunday and for lunch on
Monday. ⑤ *Rooms from: €120* ⊠ *Schiffg. 11* ☎ *06221/53660* ⊕ *www.
gasthaus-backmulde.de* ↪ *25 rooms* ⦿ *Breakfast.*

$$ 🏨 **Holländer Hof.** Opposite the Alte Brücke, and with views across the busy
HOTEL Neckar River to the forested hillside beyond, this ornate 19th-century
building is in a good Old Town location. **Pros:** nice view of river and
beyond; comfortable accommodations; some rooms are handicap accessible. **Cons:** noisy at times; no restaurant or bar (although both are in adjoining building). ⑤ *Rooms from: €108* ⊠ *Neckarstaden 66* ☎ *06221/60500*
⊕ *www.hollaender-hof.de* ↪ *38 rooms, 1 suite* ⦿ *Breakfast.*

$$$ 🏨 **Hotel Die Hirschgasse.** A stunning castle view, fine restaurants, a literary
HOTEL connection, and a touch of romance distinguish this historic inn (1472)
Fodor'sChoice across the river from the Old Town, opposite Karlstor. **Pros:** terrific view;
★ very good food in both restaurants; close to "museum row." **Cons:** limited
parking; 15-minute walk to Old Town. ⑤ *Rooms from: €205* ⊠ *Hirsch.
3* ☎ *06221/4540* ⊕ *www.hirschgasse.de* ↪ *20 suites* ⊗ *Le Gourmet closed
Sun. and Mon., 2 wks in early Jan., and 2 wks in early Aug.; Mensurstube
closed Sun. No lunch at either restaurant* ⦿ *Multiple meal plans.*

8

$$ ⊞ **KulturBrauerei Heidelberg.** Rooms with warm, sunny colors and mod-
HOTEL ern style are brilliantly incorporated into this old brewery in the heart of
Old Town. **Pros:** stylish rooms; lively restaurant; Wi-Fi in most rooms;
beer garden. **Cons:** noisy in summer; difficult parking; rooms above
Zum Seppl restaurant are accessed by steep, narrow stairs and dark
hallways, and you have to walk a block to get breakfast. ⑤ *Rooms
from: €140* ⊠ *Leyerg. 6* ☎ *06221/502–980* ⊕ *www.heidelberger-
kulturbrauerei.de* ↩ *41 rooms, 2 suites* ⦿ *Breakfast.*

$$ ⊞ **NH Heidelberg.** The glass-covered entrance hall of this primarily busi-
HOTEL ness hotel is spacious—not surprising, as it was the courtyard of a
former brewery. **Pros:** good food; reasonably priced; free Wi-fi. **Cons:**
lacks charm; located about 1 km (½ mile) from the Old Town; parking
expensive. ⑤ *Rooms from: €120* ⊠ *Bergheimerstr. 91* ☎ *06221/13270*
⊕ *www.nh-hotels.com* ↩ *156 rooms, 18 suites* ⦿ *Breakfast.*

$$ ⊞ **Hotel zum Ritter.** If this is your first visit to Germany, try to stay here—it's
HOTEL the only Renaissance building in Heidelberg (1592), built as the private
Fodor's Choice home of a wealthy merchant, and has an unbeatable location opposite the
★ market square in the heart of Old Town. **Pros:** charm and elegance; nice
views; spacious rooms. **Cons:** off-site parking, rooms facing the square
can be noisy. ⑤ *Rooms from: €118* ⊠ *Hauptstr. 178* ☎ *06221/1350*
⊕ *www.ritter-heidelberg.de* ↩ *36 rooms, 1 suite* ⦿ *No meals.*

$$ ⊞ **Weisser Bock.** Exposed beams, stucco ceilings, warm wood furnish-
HOTEL ings, and individually decorated, comfortable rooms are all part of this
hotel's charm. **Pros:** nicely decorated rooms; exceptional food; this is
a smoke-free facility. **Cons:** parking difficult to find. ⑤ *Rooms from:
€115* ⊠ *Grosse Mantelg. 24* ☎ *06221/90000* ⊕ *www.weisserbock.de*
↩ *21 rooms, 2 suites* ⦿ *Multiple meal plans.*

NIGHTLIFE AND THE ARTS

Information on all upcoming events can be found in the monthly *Heidelberg aktuell,* free and available from the tourist office or on the
Internet (⊕ *www.heidelberg-aktuell.de*).

heidelbergTicket. Theater tickets may be purchased here. ⊠ *Theaterstr. 4*
☎ *06221/582–0000* ⊕ *www.theaterheidelberg.de.*

THE ARTS

Heidelberg has a thriving theater and concert scene.

Kulturhaus Karlstorbahnhof. This 19th-century train station has been repur-
posed as a theater and concert venue. ⊠ *Am Karlstor 1* ☎ *06221/978–
911* ⊕ *www.karlstorbahnhof.de.*

Schlossfestspiele. Theatrical and musical performances are held at the
Heidelberg castle during this annual festival from late June through July.
☎ *06221/582–0000 for tickets* ⊕ *www.schlossfestspiele-heidelberg.de.*

Theater & Orchester Heidelberg. This is the best-known theater company
in town, with a variety of theater, opera and concert performances. The
historic theater reopened in 2013 after a renovation and the addition
of a modern second stage in the new adjoining building. ⊠ *Theaterstr.
10* ☎ *06221/582–0000* ⊕ *www.theaterheidelberg.de.*

Zimmertheater. Avant-garde theater productions are staged here.
⊠ *Hauptstr. 118* ☎ *06221/21069* ⊕ *www.zimmertheaterhd.de.*

NIGHTLIFE

Heidelberg nightlife is concentrated in the area around the Heiliggeistkirche (Church of the Holy Ghost), in the Old Town. Don't miss a visit to one of the old student taverns that have been in business for generations.

Fodor'sChoice ★ **Zum Roten Ochsen.** Mark Twain rubbed elbows with students here during his 1878 stay in Heidelberg—look for his photo on one of the memorabilia-covered walls. Zum Roten Oschen (⇨ *See Where to Eat*) is popular with students and local residents for its hearty meals at reasonable prices and friendly atmosphere, and has been operated by the same family for more than 170 years. A pianist plays German and international favorites, starting at 9 pm. ✉ *Hauptstr. 217* ☎ *06221/20977* ⊕ *www.roterochsen.de.*

Zum Seppl. When this traditional restaurant (⇨ *See Where to Eat*) and bar opened at the end of the 17th century, it even had its own brewery on the premises (it's now a block away and called KulturBrauerei Heidelberg). The Seppl crowd is a mix of Heidelberg students, local residents and visitors, all attracted by the traditional old-world charm and ample servings of traditional German specialties. Every inch of wall space is covered with historic photos, menus, and other memorabilia. ✉ *Hauptstr. 213* ☎ *06221/23085* ⊕ *www.heidelberger-kulturbrauerei. de/en/scheffels-wirtshaus-zum-seppl.*

Today's students, however, are more likely to hang out in one of the dozen or more cafés and bars on **Untere Strasse**, which runs parallel to and between Hauptstrasse and the Neckar River, starting from the market square.

Billy Blues (im Ziegler). This restaurant, bar, and disco, popular with university students, has live music on Thursday and a Salsa party on Wednesday. ✉ *Bergheimer Str. 1b* ☎ *06221/25333* ⊕ *www.billyblues.de.*

Destille. The club plays rock music until 2 am on weekdays and 3 am on weekends, and the young crowd that packs the place is always having a good time. A tree in the middle of this club is decorated according to season. ✉ *Untere Str. 16* ☎ *06221/22808* ⊕ *www.destilleonline.de.*

Nachtschicht. In the Landfried complex near the main train station, this is Heidelberg's biggest disco, pulsing with 15,000 LEDs that change colors and pattern with the music. Nachtschicht (night story) is open until 4 am Thursday through Saturday. ✉ *Bergheimer Str. 147* ☎ *06221/438–550* ⊕ *www.nachtschicht.com.*

8

Print Media Lounge. Facing the main train station, this is a chic, modern place where you can dine all day or dance till the wee hours. It's open Monday–Saturday, with DJs Friday and Saturday and live bands on Monday. ⊠ *Kurfürsten–Anlage 60* ☎ *06221/653–949* ⊕ *www. printmedialounge.de* ⊗ *Closed Sun. No lunch Sat.*

Schwimmbad Musikclub. Near the zoo, this is a fixture of Heidelberg's club scene. It occupies what was once a swimming pool, hence the name. It's open Thursday to Saturday with two floors plus an open air disco when weather permits. ⊠ *Tiergartenstr. 13* ☎ *06221/470–201* ⊕ *www. schwimmbad-club.de.*

Vetters Alt-Heidelberger Brauhaus. It's worth elbowing your way into this bar for the brewed-on-the-premises beer. As with most German brew-pubs, there's a full menu, too, including a long list of wurst dishes. ⊠ *Steing. 9* ☎ *06221/165–850* ⊕ *www.brauhaus-vetter.de.*

SPORTS AND THE OUTDOORS

The riverside path is an ideal route for walking, jogging, and bicycling, since it's traffic-free and offers excellent views of the area. If you access the paved pathway in the center of town, you can follow it for many kilometers in either direction.

SHOPPING

Heidelberg's **Hauptstrasse,** or Main Street, is a pedestrian zone lined with shops, sights, and restaurants that stretches more than 1 km (½ mile) through the heart of town. But don't spend your money before exploring the shops on such side streets as **Plöck, Ingrimstrasse,** and **Untere Strasse,** where there are candy stores, bookstores, and antiques shops on the ground floors of baroque buildings. If your budget allows, the city can be a good place to find reasonably priced German antiques, and the Neckar Valley region produces fine glass and crystal.

Aurum & Argentum. The finely executed, modern gold and silver pieces here are impeccably crafted. Prices start at €150. ⊠ *Brückenstr. 22* ☎ *06221/473–453* ⊗ *Tues.–Fri. 2:30–6:30, Sat. 10–2.*

Farmers' markets. Heidelberg has open-air farmers' markets on Wednesday and Saturday mornings on Marktplatz and Tuesday and Friday mornings, as well as Thursday afternoons, on Friedrich-Ebert-Platz.

Heidelberger Zuckerladen. The old glass display cases and shelves here are full of lollipops and "penny" candy. If you're looking for an unusual gift or special sweet treat, the shop fashions colorful, unique items out of sugary ingredients such as marshmallow and sweetened gum. ▮▮TIP➔ Avoid early afternoon, when the tiny shop is crowded with schoolchildren. ⊠ *Plöck 52* ☎ *06221/24365* ⊕ *www.zuckerladen.de* ⊗ *Weekdays noon–7, Sat. 11:15–3.*

OFF THE BEATEN PATH

A rare pleasure awaits you if you are in **Schwetzingen** in April, May, or June. This is Germany's asparagus center, and nearly every local restaurant has a *Spargelkarte,* a special menu featuring fresh white asparagus dishes such as *Spargel mit Schinken* (asparagus with ham). The town also has a beautiful castle you can visit before or after a meal.

The Burgenstrasse (Castle Road)

Schloss Schwetzingen. This formal 18th-century palace was constructed as a summer residence by the Palatinate electors. It is a noble rose-color building, imposing and harmonious; a highlight is the rococo theater in one wing. The extensive park blends formal French and informal English styles, with neatly bordered gravel walks trailing off into the dark woodland. Fun touches include an exotic mosque, complete with minarets and a shimmering pool (although they got a little confused and gave the building a very baroque portal), and the "classical ruin" that was de rigueur in this period. The palace interior can only be visited by tour. ✉ *Schloss Mittelbau, Schwetzingen* ☎ *06202/128–828* ⊕ *www.schloss-schwetzingen.de* 🎫 *€9 Apr.–Oct., €7 Nov.–Mar. (includes palace tour and gardens). Gardens only: €5 Apr.–Oct., €3 Nov.–Mar.* ◷ *Apr.–Oct., daily 9–8; Nov.–Mar., daily 9–5, last admission 30 mins before closing. Palace tours (in German): Apr.–Oct., weekdays hrly 11–4, weekends and holidays hrly 11–5; Nov.–Mar., Fri. at 2, weekends and holidays at 11, 1:30, and 3. Palace tours (in English) weekends at 2, or by appointment.*

THE BURGENSTRASSE (CASTLE ROAD)

The Neckar Valley narrows upstream from Heidelberg, presenting a landscape of orchards, vineyards, and wooded hills crowned with castles rising above the gently flowing stream. It's one of the most impressive stretches of the Burgenstrasse. Along the B-37 are small valleys—locals call them *Klingen*—that cut north into the Odenwald and are off-the-beaten-track territory. One of the most atmospheric is the Wolfsschlucht, which starts below the castle at Zwingenberg. The dank, shadowy little gorge inspired Carl Maria von Weber's opera *Der Freischütz* (*The Marksman*).

NECKARGEMÜND

11 km (7 miles) from Heidelberg.

Coming from the hustle and bustle of Heidelberg, you'll find the hamlet of Neckargemünd is a quiet place where you can relax by the Neckar River and watch the ships go by. The town also makes a good base from which to visit Heidelberg. Leave the car here and enjoy the 10-minute ride by bus or train.

GETTING HERE AND AROUND

The S1, S2, S5, and S51 commuter trains from Heidelberg run every few minutes and will get you here in less than 10 minutes. By car, it will take 25 minutes via the B-37. Once here, the Altstadt (Old Town) and Neckar River views are walkable, but you'll need a car or take a taxi to visit the Schloss Zwingennberg, about a half-hour distant via the S1 (toward Osterburken) or the B-37 and B-45.

WHERE TO STAY

$
B&B/INN
🏨 **Art Hotel.** In a historic building in the heart of the Altstadt (Old Town), this stylish hotel has spacious rooms and suites, including three- and four-bed junior suites that are perfect for families. **Pros:** good for families; reasonable rates. **Cons:** on a busy street; no elevator. $ *Rooms from: €92* ✉ *Hauptstr. 40* 📞 *06223/862–768* ⊕ *www.art-hotel-neckar. de* ➐ *7 rooms, 6 suites* ⦿| *Breakfast.*

$
B&B/INN
🏨 **Gasthaus Reber.** If you're looking for a clean, simple and inexpensive room, this small inn is an ideal candidate, and it's conveniently located opposite the railway station for trips to or from Heidelberg. **Pros:** unbeatable rates; close to public transportation. **Cons:** on busy street; not all rooms have an en suite bathroom. $ *Rooms from: €70* ✉ *Bahnhofstr. 52* 📞 *06223/8779* ⊕ *www.gasthaus-reber.de* ➐ *10* ⊘ *Restaurant closed Wed. No lunch weekdays* ⦿| *Breakfast.*

EN ROUTE
Mosbach. The little town of Mosbach, 78 km (48 miles) southeast of Heidelberg, is one of the most charming towns on the Neckar. Its main street is pure half-timber, and its ancient market square contains one of Germany's most exquisite half-timber buildings—the early 17th-century Palm'sches Haus (Palm House), its upper stories laced with intricate timbering. The Rathaus, built 50 years earlier, is a modest affair by comparison. ✉ *Mosbach.*

You can tour Burg Hornberg or spend the night at this spectacular castle.

Schloss Zwingenberg. Many people say this castle on a crag above the village of Zwingenberg, about 53 km (33 miles) from Heidelberg, is the most romantic of all the castles along the Neckar (except for Heidelberg, of course). It is the residence of Ludwig, Prince of Baden and his family, so castle tours are by advance arrangement only, and can include the family vineyards. The woodland trails around the castle, including to a deep gorge, are open daily. ⊠ *Schlossstr., Zwingenberg* ☎ *6263/411–010* ⊕ *www.schloss-zwingenberg.de.*

Schlossfestspiele Zwingenberg. The annual castle festival, which features theater and concert performances, takes place within the ancient walls of the Zwingenberg in August. ⊠ *Schloss Zwingenberg* ☎ *06263/771* ⊕ *www.schlossfestspiele-zwingenberg.de*

NECKARZIMMERN

83 km (52 miles) from Heidelberg.

The main attraction here is the Burg Hornberg castle high above the town, but visitors will find the village itself to be a charming respite, with a traditional town square surrounded by historic buildings, and pleasant riverfront walks.

GETTING HERE AND AROUND
By road from Heidelberg, take the E-5 Autobahn south (toward Bruschal) then the E-6 east to Sinsheim, where you connect with local road 292 northeast past Mossbach to Neckarzimmern, then follow signs. If you have time en route, stop off at the Sinsheim Auto & Technik Museum for displays including Formula 1 racecars and a Concorde supersonic jet.

EXPLORING

Fodor'sChoice **Burg Hornberg.** The largest and oldest castle in the Neckar Valley, the
★ circular bulk of Burg Hornberg rises above the town of Neckarzimmern. The road to the castle leads through vineyards that have been providing dry white wines for centuries. These days, the castle is part hotel (23 rooms, 1 suite) and part museum. In the 16th century it was home to the larger-than-life Götz von Berlichingen (1480–1562). When the knight lost his right arm in battle, he had a blacksmith fashion an iron replacement. Original designs for this fearsome artificial limb are on view in the castle, as is his suit of armor. For most Germans, this larger-than-life knight is best remembered for a remark that was faithfully reproduced in Goethe's play *Götz von Berlichingen*. Responding to an official reprimand, von Berlichingen told his critic, more or less, to "kiss my ass" (the original German is substantially more earthy). To this day the polite version of this insult is known as a *Götz von Berlichingen*. Inquire at the hotel reception about visiting the castle, or just enjoy the walking trails and views from the top of the hilltop. ⊠ *Hornbergerweg* ⊕ *www.burg-hornberg.de.*

WHERE TO STAY

$$ 🍴 **Burg Hornberg Hotel.** Your host at this hotel with comfortable, modern
HOTEL rooms is the present baron of the Burg Hornberg castle. **Pros:** historic
Fodor'sChoice setting; nice restaurant; on-site wine shop. **Cons:** no elevator; restaurant
★ can be crowded in season on weekends; not enough parking. $ *Rooms from: €140* ⊠ *Marucs Freiherr von Gemmingen* ☎ *06261/92460* ⊕ *www.castle-hotel-hornberg.com* 🛏 *23 rooms, 1 suite* ⊙ *Closed late Dec.–late Jan.* 🍴 *Breakfast.*

Burg Guttenberg. One of the best-preserved Neckar castles is the 15th-
📍EN century Burg Guttenberg. Within its stone walls are a museum and a
ROUTE restaurant (closed January, February, and Monday) with views of the river valley. The castle also is home to Europe's leading center for the study and protection of birds of prey, the German Raptor Research Center, with 100 falcons and other birds of prey. There are demonstration flights from the castle walls from April through October, daily at 11 and 3. ⊠ *Burgstr., 6 km (4 miles) west of Gundelsheim, Neckarmühlbach* ☎ *06266/388* ⊕ *www.burg-guttenberg.de* 🎟 *Castle €4, castle and flight demonstration €11* ⊙ *Apr.–Oct., daily 10–6; Mar., weekends 10–5.*

BAD WIMPFEN

Fodor'sChoice *8 km (5 miles) south of Neckarzimmern.*
★
At the confluence of the Neckar and Jagst rivers, Bad Wimpfen is one of the most stunning towns of the Neckar Valley. The Romans built a fortress and a bridge here, on the riverbank site of an ancient Celtic settlement, in the 1st century AD. A millennium later, the Staufen emperor Barbarossa chose this town as the site of his largest *Pfalz* (residence). The ruins of this palace still overshadow the town and are well worth a stroll.

GETTING HERE AND AROUND

There's a direct regional commuter train from Heidelberg that will get you to Bad Wimpfen in 45 minutes, and from Neckarzimmern there's an hourly service that takes 30 minutes. By road, take the B-27 east from Neckarzimmern to the L-1100. The old city is good for walking, but wear comfortable shoes for the uneven cobblestones.

TOURS

Medieval Bad Wimpfen offers a town walk year-round, Sunday at 2 (€2), departing from the visitor center inside the old train station. Private group tours may also be arranged for other days by calling the visitor center in advance.

DISCOUNTS AND DEALS

On arrival, ask your hotel for a free *Bad Wimpfen à la card* for reduced or free admission to historic sights and museums.

FESTIVALS

Zunftmarkt. On the last weekend in August, the Old Town's medieval past comes alive during the Zunftmarkt, a historical market dedicated to the *Zünfte* (guilds). "Artisans" in period costumes demonstrate the old trades and open the festivities with a colorful parade on horseback. ⊕ *www.zunftmarkt.de.*

ESSENTIALS

Visitor Information Bad Wimpfen–Gundelsheim Tourist-Information ✉ *Carl-Ulrich-Str. 1* ☎ *07063/97200* ⊕ *www.badwimpfen.de.*

EXPLORING

Ritterstiftskirche St. Peter. Wimpfen im Tal (Wimpfen in the Valley), the oldest part of town, is home to the Benedictine monastery of Gruessau and its church, Ritterstiftskirche St. Peter, which dates from the 10th and 13th centuries. The cloisters are delightful, an example of German Gothic at its most uncluttered. ✉ *Lindenpl.*

Stadtkirche (*city church*). The 13th-century stained glass, wall paintings, medieval altars, and the stone pietà in the Gothic Stadtkirche are worth seeing, as are the Crucifixion sculptures (1515) by the Rhenish master Hans Backoffen on Kirchplatz, behind the church. ✉ *Kirchsteige 8* ⊕ *www.kirche-badwimpfen.de.*

Steinhaus. Germany's largest Romanesque living quarters and once the imperial women's apartments, this is now a history museum with relics from the Neolithic and Roman ages along with the history of the Palatinate, including medieval art and ceramics. Next to the Steinhaus are the remains of the northern facade of the palace, an arcade of superbly carved Romanesque pillars that flanked the imperial hall in its heyday. The imperial chapel, next to the Red Tower, holds a collection of religious art. ✉ *Burgviertel 25* ☎ *07063/97200* 💳 *€2.50* ⊙ *Apr. 15–Oct. 15, Tues.–Sat. 10–noon and 2–4:30.*

WHERE TO EAT AND STAY

$

GERMAN

✗**Weinstube Feyerabend.** There are three adjoining eateries here: the Weinstube for a glass of good Swabian wine with a snack, the Restaurant for a full meal at lunch or dinner, or let yourself be tempted by the good-looking cakes from their own bakery in the Konditorei

Café. ⑤ *Average main: €12* ✉ *Hauptstr. 74* ☎ *07063/950–566* ⊕ *www. friedrich-feyerabend.de* ⊘ *Closed Mon.*

$

HOTEL

⌂ **Hotel Neckarblick.** You get a good *Neckarblick* (Neckar view) from the terrace, the dining room, and most guest rooms of this pleasant lodging. **Pros:** terrific view; personal touch. **Cons:** no restaurant or bar; not enough parking. ⑤ *Rooms from: €89* ✉ *Erich-Sailer-Str. 48* ☎ *07063/961–620* ⊕ *www.neckarblick.de* ⤴ *14 rooms* ⦿| *Breakfast.*

OFF THE
BEATEN
PATH

Deutsches Zweirad–Museum (*German Motorcycle Museum*). Although its name is the German Motorcycle Museum, there are historic cars here, too. Displays include the the 1885 Daimler machine that started us on the road to motorized mobility, the world's first mass-produced motorcycles (Hildebrand and Wolfmüller), and exhibits on racing. Also here is the NSU Museum, for an early motorbike manufacturer acquired by the precedessor of the company now called Audi, which has an auto production facility in Neckarsulm. The collections are arranged over five floors in a handsome 400-year-old castle that belonged to the Teutonic Knights until 1806. ■ TIP→ The Audi factory offers tours. ✉ *Urbanstr. 11, Neckarsulm* ☎ *07132/35271* ⊕ *www.zweirad-museum.de* ⧉ *€4.50* ⊘ *Tues.–Sun. 9–5.*

SWABIAN CITIES

Ludwigsburg, Stuttgart, and Tübingen are all part of the ancient province of Swabia, a region strongly influenced by Protestantism and Calvinism. The inhabitants speak the Swabian dialect of German. Ludwigsburg is known for its two splendid castles. Stuttgart, the capital of the state of Baden-Württemberg, is one of Germany's leading industrial cities, home to both Mercedes and Porsche, and is cradled by hills on three sides, with the fourth side opening up toward its river harbor. The medieval town of Tübingen clings to steep slopes and hilltops above the Neckar.

LUDWIGSBURG

15 km (9 miles) north of Stuttgart.

Although its residents would never call it a suburb of Stuttgart, its proximity to the modern industrial and commercial center of Baden-Wurttenberg has made it one. Ludwigsburg's attraction is its fabulous Baroque castle, with more than 450 rooms spread over 18 buildings, surrounded by the beautiful Schlosspark (gardens). A music festival, held each summer since 1932, features performances both outdoors and in the original palace theater.

GETTING HERE AND AROUND

There is regular commuter rail service from Stuttgart's Hauptbahnhof (main train station). Take the S4 or S5 for the journey of around 45 minutes. The castle is close enough to the station to walk, or you can take a taxi.

Fodor'sChoice

★

Residenzschloss Ludwigsburg. One of Europe's largest palaces to survive in its original condition, Residenzschloss Ludwigsburg certainly merits a visit for its sumptuous interiors and exquisite gardens. The main palace is also home to the **Keramikmuseum,** a collection of historical treasures from the porcelain factories in Meissen, Nymphenburg, Berlin, Vienna, and Ludwigsburg, as well as an exhibit of contemporary ceramics. The **Barockgalerie** is a collection of German and Italian baroque paintings from the 17th and 18th centuries. The **Modemuseum** showcases three centuries of fashion, particularly royal clothing of the 18th century. In another part of the palace you'll find the **Porzellan-Manufaktur Ludwigsburg** (⊕ *www.ludwigsburger-porzellan.de*); you can tour the porcelain factory where each piece is handmade and handpainted. The castle is surrounded by the fragrant, colorful 74-acre park **Blühendes Barock** (Blooming Baroque), filled with thousands and thousands of tulips, huge masses of rhododendrons, and fragrant roses. A Märchengarten (fairy-tale garden) delights visitors of all ages. In the midst of it all, you can take a break in the cafeteria in the Rose Garden. ■**TIP→ Guided tours in English are at 1:30 on weekdays, with addiitional tours on weekends at 11 and 3.** ⊠ *Schloss Str. 30* ☎ *07141/182–004* ⊕ *www.schloesser-und-gaerten. de* ⊠ *Palace €7, park €8, museums with audioguide €3.50, museum tour with audio €6.50, guide combination ticket €16* ⊗ *Park daily 7:30 am–8:30 pm, palace and museums daily 10–5.*

STUTTGART

50 km (31 miles) south of Heilbronn.

Stuttgart is a city of contradictions. It has been called, among other things, "Germany's biggest small town" and "the city where work is a pleasure." For centuries Stuttgart, whose name derives from *Stutengarten*, or "stud farm," remained a pastoral backwater along the Neckar. Then the Industrial Revolution propelled the city into the machine age. Leveled in World War II, Stuttgart has regained its position as one of Germany's top industrial centers.

This is Germany's can-do city, whose natives have turned out Mercedes-Benz and Porsche cars, Bosch electrical equipment, and a host of other products exported worldwide. Yet Stuttgart is also a city of culture and the arts, with world-class museums, opera, and ballet. Moreover, it's the domain of fine local wines; the vineyards actually approach the city center in a rim of green hills. Forests, vineyards, meadows, and orchards compose more than half the city, which is enclosed on three sides by woods. Each year in October, Stuttgart is home to Germany's second largest Oktoberfest (after Munich), called the Canstatter Volksfest.

An ideal introduction to the contrasts of Stuttgart is a guided city bus tour. Included is a visit to the needle-nose TV tower, high on a mountaintop above the city, affording stupendous views. Built in 1956, it was the first of its kind in the world. The tourist office also offers superb walking tours. On your own, the best place to begin exploring Stuttgart is the Hauptbahnhof (main train station); from there walk down the pedestrian street Königstrasse to Schillerplatz, a small, charming square named after the 18th-century poet and playwright Friedrich Schiller, who was born in nearby Marbach. The square is surrounded by historic buildings, many of which were rebuilt after the war.

GETTING HERE AND AROUND

Stuttgart is the major hub for the rail system in southwestern Germany, and two autobahns cross here. It's about 2½ hours away from Munich and a bit more than an hour from Frankfurt. The downtown museums and the main shopping streets are doable on foot. For the outlying attractions and to get to the airport, there is a very efficient S-bahn and subway system.

TOURS

The tourist office is the meeting point for city walking tours in German (year-round, Saturday at 10) for €8. There are daily bilingual walks April–October at 11 am for €18. Bilingual bus tours costing €8 depart from the bus stop around the corner from the tourist office, in front of Hotel am Schlossgarten (April–October, daily at 1:30; November–March, Friday–Sunday at 1:30). All tours last from 1½ to 2½ hours. Stuttgart Tourist-Information offers altogether 12 different special-interest tours. Call for details.

DISCOUNTS AND DEALS

The three-day **StuttCard** (€9.70) offers discounts to museums and attractions, with or without a free public transit pass. (€22 includes a transit card valid in the whole city or €18 for a transit card for the city center). All the cards are available from the Stuttgart tourist office opposite the main train station.

ESSENTIALS

Visitor Information Stuttgart Touristik-Information i-Punkt ⊠ *Königstr. 1A* ☎ *0711/222–8246* ⊕ *www.stuttgart-tourist.de.*

EXPLORING

TOP ATTRACTIONS

Kunstmuseum Stuttgart (*Stuttgart Art Museum*). This sleek structure encased in a glass facade is a work of art in its own right. The museum contains artwork of the 19th and 20th centuries and the world's largest Otto Dix collection, including the *Grossstadt* (*Metropolis*) triptych, which captures the essence of 1920s Germany. ▓ TIP➡ The bistro-café on the rooftop terrace affords great views; the lobby houses another café and the museum shop. ⊠ *Kleiner Schlosspl.1* ☎ *0711/216–2188* ⊕ *www.kunstmuseum-stuttgart.de* ⌨ *€6; special exhibitions €8–€11; guided tours €2.50* ⊗ *Tues.–Sun. 10–6 (Fri. until 9).*

FAMILY

Fodor'sChoice

★

Mercedes-Benz Museum. The stunning futuristic architecture of this museum is an enticement to enter, but the stunning historic and futuristic vehicles inside are the main attraction. Visitors are whisked to the top floor to start this historical timeline tour of motorized mobility in the 1880s, with the first vehicles by Gottlieb Daimler and Carl Benz. Other museum levels focus on a particular decade or category of vehicle, such as trucks and buses, race cars, concept cars, and future technology, including fuel cells. Historic photos and other artifacts line the walls of the circular walkway that links the levels. A restaurant on the lower level serves mostly German cuisine with a modern twist, and stays open after the museum has closed, and there's a huge gift shop with all kinds of Mercedes-Benz branded items. In the adjoining new car showroom you can muse over appealing models that are sold in Europe but not in North America. ▓ TIP➡ Guided tours of the factory are also available. ⊠ *Mercedesstr. 100, Stuttgart-Untertürkheim* ☎ *0711/173–0000* ⊕ *www.mercedes-benz-classic.com* ⌨ *€8 (€4 after 4:30), guided tour €4; factory tour €4* ⊗ *Tues.–Sun. 9–6 (last admission at 5).*

FAMILY

Fodor'sChoice

★

Porsche Museum. In the center of the Porsche factory complex in the northern suburb of Zuffenhausen, the architecturally dramatic building expands outward and upward from its base. Inside is a vast collection of around 100 legendary and historic Porsche cars including racing cars, nearly 1,000 racing trophies and design and engineering awards, and several vehicles designed by Ferdinand Porsche that eventually became the VW Beetle. It is astounding how some 1930s models still look contemporary today. The museum includes a coffee shop, snack bar, and the sophisticated Christophorus restaurant, regarded as the best American-style steakhouse in Stuttgart, open for lunch and dinner beyond museum hours. The gift shop sells some Porsche logo clothing, but mostly miniature collectibles. ▓ TIP➡ Stand under the special "cones" on the upper level to hear the different engine sounds of various Porsche models. ⊠ *Porschepl. 1, Stuttgart-Zuffenhausen* ☎ *0711/911–20911* ⊕ *www. porsche.com/museum* ⌨ *€8* ⊗ *Tues.–Sun. 9–6.*

8

Schlossplatz (*Palace Square*). A huge area enclosed by royal palaces and planted gardens, the square has elegant arcades branching off to other stately plazas. The magnificent baroque **Neues Schloss** (New Palace), now occupied by Baden-Württemberg state government offices, dominates the square. Schlossplatz is the extension of the Kaiserstrasse pedestrian shopping street. ⊠ *Corner of Koenigstr. and Planie, Mitte.*

Fodor's Choice
★
Staatsgalerie (*State Gallery*). This not-to-be-missed museum displays one of the finest art collections in Germany. The old part of the complex, dating from 1843, has paintings from the Middle Ages through the 19th century, including works by Cranach, Holbein, Hals, Memling, Rubens, Rembrandt, Cézanne, Courbet, and Manet. Connected to the original building is the **Neue Staatsgalerie** (New State Gallery), designed by British architect James Stirling in 1984 as a melding of classical and modern, sometimes jarring, elements (such as chartreuse window mullions). Considered one of the most successful postmodern buildings, it houses works by such 20th-century artists as Braque, Chagall, de Chirico, Dalì, Kandinsky, Klee, Mondrian, and Picasso. ⊠ *Konrad-Adenauer-Str. 30–32, Mitte* ☎ *0711/470–400, 0711/470–40249 for info-line* ⊕ *www.staatsgalerie.de* 🎫 *Permanent collection €7 (free Wed. and Sat.), special exhibitions €8–€12, guided tours €5* ☉ *Tues. and Thurs. 10–8, Wed. and Fri.–Sun. 10–6.*

WORTH NOTING

FAMILY
Fodor's Choice
★
Altes Schloss (*Old Castle*). Across the street from the Neues Schloss stands this former residence of the counts and dukes of Württemberg, which was originally built as a moated castle around 1320. Wings were added in the mid-15th century, creating a Renaissance palace. The palace now houses the **Landesmuseum Württemberg** (Württemberg State Museum), with imaginative exhibits tracing the area's development from the Stone Age to modern times. There's also a separate floor as a dedicated children's museum. ■ TIP➔ The second floor, which reopened in 2012 after an extensive renovation, includes jaw-dropping family jewels of the fabulously rich and powerful Württemberg royals. ⊠ *Schillerpl. 6, Mitte* ☎ *0711/279–3498* ⊕ *www.landesmuseum-stuttgart.de* 🎫 *€12* ☉ *Tues.–Sun. 10–5.*

Haus der Geschichte Baden-Württemberg (*Museum of the History of Baden-Württemberg*). Adjoining the Staatsgalerie (State Gallery), this museum chronicles the history of Baden-Württemberg state during the 19th and 20th centuries. Multimedia presentations enable you to interact with the thousands of objects on display. ⊠ *Konrad-Adenauer-Str. 16, Mitte* ☎ *0711/212–3989* ⊕ *www.hdgbw.de* 🎫 *€4* ☉ *Tues., Wed., Fri.–Sun. 10–6, Thurs. 10–9.*

Schlossgarten (*Palace Garden*). This huge city park borders the Schlossplatz and extends northeast across Schillerstrasse all the way to Bad Cannstatt on the Neckar River. The park is graced by an exhibition hall, planetarium, lakes, sculptures, and the hot-spring mineral baths Leuze and Berg. ⊠ *Off Cannstattstr.*

Stiftskirche (*Collegiate Church of the Holy Cross*). Just off Schillerplatz, this is Stuttgart's most familiar sight, with its two oddly matched towers. Built in the 12th century, it was later rebuilt in a

The fountain in Schlossplatz (Palace Square) is a great place for people-watching, or to contemplate the surrounding architecture.

late-Gothic style. The choir has a famous series of Renaissance figures of the counts of Württemberg sculpted by Simon Schlör (1576–1608). ⊠ *Stiftstr. 12, Mitte.*

FAMILY **Wilhelma Zoologische-Botanische Garten** (*Wilhelma Zoological and Botanical Garden*). Adjacent to Rosenstein Park, this wildlife park and zoological garden, with more than 9,000 animals in more than 1,000 species and around 7,000 species of plants and flowers, was originally intended as a garden for King Wilhelm I. The Moorish style buildings led it to be called the "Alhambra on the Neckar." There are two restaurants on site and a less formal bistro/cafe with outdoor seating in warm weather. ■**TIP➜ A modern Ape House opened in 2013, with gorillas and bonobos.** ⊠ *Neckartalstr., Wilhelma* ☎ *0711/54020* ⊕ *www.wilhelma. de* ⬜ *€14; €10 Nov.–Feb. and after 4 pm Mar.–Oct.* ☉ *May–Aug., daily 8:15–6; Sept.–Apr., daily 8:15–4.*

WHERE TO EAT

$$$$ ✕**Wielandshöhe.** One of Germany's top chefs, Vincent Klink, and EUROPEAN his wife Elisabeth, are very down-to-earth, cordial hosts. Her floral arrangements add a baroque touch to the otherwise quiet interior, designed to focus on the artfully presented cuisine. To the extent possible, all ingredients are grown locally. House specialties, such as saddle of lamb with a potato gratin and green beans or the Breton lobster with basil potato salad, are recommended. The wine list is exemplary. ⑤ *Average main: €40* ⊠ *Alte Weinsteige 71, Degerloch* ☎ *0711/640–8848* ⊕ *www.wielandshoehe.de* ⬚ *Reservations essential* ☉ *Closed Sun. and Mon.*

WHERE TO STAY

$$$$
HOTEL
📷 **Am Schlossgarten.** Stuttgart's top accommodations are in a modern structure set in spacious gardens, a stone's throw from many of the top sights and opposite the main station. **Pros:** views of the park; welcoming lobby. **Cons:** not all rooms face the park; rates are on the high end; driving here is not straightforward; parking limited and expensive. ⑤ *Rooms from: €300* ✉ *Schillerstr. 23, Mitte* ☎ *0711/20260* ⊕ *www.hotelschlossgarten.com* ⤵ *106 rooms, 10 suites* ⊙ *Zirbelstube closed 1st 2 wks in Jan., 3 wks in Aug., Sun. and Mon. Schlossgarten closed Fri. and Sat. Vinothek closed Sun. and Mon.* ⦿| *Breakfast.*

$$$$
B&B/INN
📷 **Der Zauberlehrling.** The "Sorcerer's Apprentice" is aptly named, as Karen and Axel Heldmann have conjured up a lovely luxury hotel with each room's style based on a theme (Asian, Mediterranean, country manor). **Pros:** fabulous rooms with lots of surprises; enjoyable restaurant. **Cons:** minuscule lobby; no elevator. ⑤ *Rooms from: €290* ✉ *Rosenstr. 38, Bohnenviertel* ☎ *0711/237–7770* ⊕ *www.zauberlehrling.de* ⤵ *17 rooms* ⦿| *Breakfast.*

$$
HOTEL
📷 **Hotel Wartburg.** This comfortable hotel is on a quiet side-street a five-minute walk from the Konigstrasse pedestrian mile and the museums around Schlossplatz. **Pros:** free parking; free Internet. **Cons:** rooms facing street can be noisy. ⑤ *Rooms from: €110* ✉ *Langestr. 49* ☎ *0711/20450* ⊕ *www.hotel-wartburg-stuttgart.de* ⤵ *74 rooms* ⦿| *Breakfast.*

$$$
HOTEL
📷 **Mövenpick Hotel Stuttgart Airport.** Across the street from Stuttgart Airport, the doors of this hotel open into a completely soundproof glass palace. **Pros:** spacious; modern yet welcoming. **Cons:** swells with business travelers; not convenient to downtown museums, theater or shopping. ⑤ *Rooms from: €200* ✉ *Flughafenstr. 50, Flughafen* ☎ *0711/553–440* ⊕ *www.moevenpick-stuttgart-airport.com* ⤵ *326 rooms, 12 junior suites* ⦿| *No meals.*

$$
RESORT
Fodor'sChoice
★
📷 **Wald Hotel.** On the edge of a forest (wald) with miles of hiking and biking trails, yet just a 10-minute streetcar ride from downtown, this modern resort hotel offers lots of amenities and peaceful nights. **Pros:** free Wi-Fi; ample free parking; spacious modern bathrooms. **Cons:** walk from streetcar station after dark is not well lit. ⑤ *Rooms from: €120* ✉ *Guts-Muths-Weg 18, Degerloch* ☎ *0711/185–720, 0711/185–72120 for reservations* ⊕ *www.waldhotel-stuttgart.de* ⤵ *94 rooms, 2 suites* ⦿| *Multiple meal plans.*

NIGHTLIFE AND THE ARTS

i-Punkt tourist office. Across the street from the main train station, this is the place to check out a current calendar of events and buy tickets. ✉ *Königstr. 1A, Mitte* ☎ *0711/22280 for tickets (weekdays 8:30–6)* ⊕ *www.stuttgart-tourist.de* ⊙ *Weekdays 9–8, Sat. 9–6, Sun. 1–6 (10–6 May–Oct.).*

THE ARTS

SI-Centrum. Built to showcase big-budget musicals, including American imports such as *42nd Street*, this entertainment complex contains theaters, hotels, bars, restaurants, a casino, a wellness center, movie theaters, and shops. A calendar of events can be found on its website. ✉ *Plieninger Str. 100, Stuttgart-Möhringen* ☎ *0711/721–1111* ⊕ *www.si-centrum.de.*

The postmodern Neue Staatsgalerie (New State Gallery) is where you'll find 20th-century masterpieces by artists including Picasso and Chagall.

Staatstheater. Stuttgart's internationally renowned ballet company performs at this elegant historic theater. The ballet season—including works choreographed by Stuttgart Ballet's John Cranko—runs from September through July and alternates with the highly respected State Opera. The box office is open weekdays 10–8, Saturday 10–2. ⊠ *Oberer Schlossgarten 6, Mitte* ☎ *0711/20320* ⊕ *www.staatstheater. stuttgart.de.*

NIGHTLIFE

There's no shortage of rustic beer gardens, wine pubs, or sophisticated cocktail bars in and around Stuttgart. Night owls should head for the **Schwabenzentrum** on Eberhardstrasse; the **Bohnenviertel**, or "Bean Quarter" (Charlotten-, Olga-, and Pfarrstrasse); the "party mile" along **Theodor-Heuss-Strasse; Calwer Strasse;** and **Wilhelmsplatz.**

Café Stella. If you enjoy live music, visit this trendy restaurant and bar, perfect for an evening of dinner and drinks. The entertainment focus is on singer-songwriters, but includes jazz, comedy, and literary events, with swing dance every Sunday. ⊠ *Hauptstätterstr. 57, Mitte* ☎ *0711/640–2583* ⊕ *www.cafe-stella.de.*

SPORTS AND THE OUTDOORS

BOAT TRIPS

Neckar-Käpt'n. From the pier opposite the entrance to the zoo, Neckar-Käpt'n offers a wide range of boat trips, as far north as scenic Besigheim. ⊠ *Off Neckartalstr., Am Leuzebad* ☎ *0711/5499–7060* ⊕ *www.neckar-kaeptn.de.*

HIKING

Stuttgart has a 53-km (33-mile) network of marked hiking trails in the nearby hills; follow the signs with the city's emblem: a horse set in a yellow ring.

SWIMMING AND SPAS

Mineralbad Berg. Take the waters in the indoor and outdoor pools and sauna here; there are also therapeutic water treatments. ✉ *Am Schwanenpl. 9, Bad Canstatt* ☎ *0711/216–7090.*

Mineralbad Cannstatt. Bad Cannstatt's mineral springs are more than 2,000 years old and, with a daily output of about 5.8 million gallons, the second most productive in Europe (after Budapest). There are indoor and outdoor mineral pools, hot tubs, a sauna, a steam room, and spa facilities. ✉ *Sulzerrainstr. 2, Canstatt* ☎ *0711/216–9240.*

Mineralbad Leuze. On the banks of the Neckar near the König-Karl Bridge is the Mineralbad Leuze, with eight pools indoors and out and an open-air mineral-water sauna. ✉ *Am Leuzebad 2–6, Bad Canstatt* ☎ *0711/216–4210.*

SHOPPING

Stuttgart is a shopper's paradise, from the department stores on the Königstrasse to the boutiques in the Old Town's elegant passages and the factory outlet stores.

Bohnenviertel (*Bean Quarter*). Some of Stuttgart's more unique shops are found in this older quarter. A stroll through the neighborhood's smaller streets reveals many tucked-away shops specializing in fashion, jewelry, artwork, and gifts.

Breuninger. This leading regional department-store chain has glass elevators that rise and fall under the dome of the central arcade, whisking you to multiple floors of designer boutiques. ✉ *Marktstr. 1–3, Mitte* ☎ *0711/2110.*

Calwer Passage. This glitzy chrome-and-glass arcade is lined with boutique shops selling everything from local women's fashion (Beate Mössinger) to furniture. The adjoining Calwer Strasse is a pedestrian zone of restaurants and more shops. ✉ *Off Calwerstr.*

Markthalle. The beautiful art nouveau Markthalle on Dorotheenstrasse is one of Germany's finest market halls, with a curved glass ceiling for natural light to show off a mouthwatering selection of exotic fresh fruits, spices, meats, cheeses, chocolates, and flowers (closed Sunday). ■TIP→ Check out the recently renovated fountain, which spouts water from the original well. ✉ *Dorotheenstr. 4* ⊕ *www.markthalle-stuttgart.de.*

TOURING TIPS

Information: The tourist office at the Neckarbrücke has maps, brochures, and information on hotels.

Scenic spot: From the ramparts of the HohenTübingen Castle you have an excellent view over the Old Town.

Scenic spot: Walking along Kirchgasse, which opens up into the Marktplatz, you find yourself surrounded by the imposing houses that belonged to the leading families of the town.

BEBENHAUSEN

6 km (4 miles) north of Tübingen.

Between Stuttgart and Tübingen lies this small hamlet consisting of a few houses, a monastery, and the Waldhorn, an excellent and well-known restaurant. The monastery was founded in the 12th century by the count of Tübingen. Today it belongs to the state.

GETTING HERE AND AROUND

To get here by public transportation, take the train from Stuttgart to Tübingen (45 minutes) then a bus to Bebenhausen (15 minutes). Trains and bus connections are several times an hour on weekdays, less on weekends. If you're driving, take the B-27 and B-464 south from Stuttgart.

Fodor's Choice ★ **Zisterzienzerkloster** (*Cistercian Monastery*). This is a rare example of a well-preserved medieval monastery from the late 12th century. Following the secularization of 1806, the abbot's abode was rebuilt as a hunting castle for King Frederick of Württemberg. Expansion and restoration continued as long as the palace and monastery continued to be a royal residence. Visits to the palace are with guided tours only. ✉ *Im Schloss* ☎ *07071/602–802* ✉ *Monastery €4, palace €4.50* ☉ *Nov.–Mar., Tues.–Sun. 10–noon and 1–5; Apr.–Oct. daily 9–5.*

WHERE TO EAT

$$$$
EUROPEAN
Fodor's Choice ★ ✕ **Waldhorn.** Old favorites such as the *Vorspeisenvariation* (a medley of appetizers), local fish and goose keep people coming back to this historic eatery. The wine list features a well-chosen selection of top Baden and Württemberg wines. Garden tables have a castle view. A meal here is a perfect start or finale to the concerts held on the monastery-castle grounds in the summer. $ *Average main: €30* ✉ *Schönbuchstr. 49* ☎ *07071/61270* ⊕ *www.waldhorn-bebenhausen.de* ✍ *Reservations essential* ☉ *Closed Mon. and Tues.*

TÜBINGEN

40 km (25 miles) south of Stuttgart.

With its half-timber houses, winding alleyways, and hilltop setting overlooking the Neckar, Tübingen provides the quintessential German experience. The medieval flavor is quite authentic, as the town was untouched by wartime bombings. Dating to the 11th century, Tübingen flourished as a trade center; its weights and measures and currency were the standard through much of the area. The town declined in importance after the 14th century, when it was taken over by the counts of Württemberg. Between the 14th and the 19th century, its size hardly changed as it became a university and residential town, its castle the only symbol of ruling power.

Yet Tübingen hasn't been sheltered from the world. It resonates with a youthful air. Even more than Heidelberg, Tübingen is virtually synonymous with its university, a leading center of learning since it was founded in 1477. The best way to see and appreciate Tübingen is simply to stroll around, soaking up its age-old atmosphere of quiet erudition.

8

GETTING HERE AND AROUND

By regional train or by car on the autobahn, Tübingen is an hour south of Stuttgart on B-27. Trains run several times an hour on weekdays, less often on weekends. In the Old Town you reach everything on foot.

TOURS

The Tübingen tourist office runs guided city tours year-round at 2:30. From March through October there are also tours that take place daily and cost €9. From November through February, tours are on weekends only. Tours start at the Rathaus on the market square.

DISCOUNTS AND DEALS

Overnight guests receive a free Tourist-Regio-Card from their hotel (ask for it) for reduced admission fees to museums, concerts, theaters, and sports facilities.

TIMING

A leisurely walk around the old part of town will take you about two hours, if you include the castle on the hill and Platanenallee looking at the Old Town from the other side of the river.

ESSENTIALS

Visitor Information Verkehrsverein Tübingen ✉ *An der Neckarbrücke* ☎ *07071/91360* ⊕ *www.tuebingen-info.de.*

EXPLORING

TOP ATTRACTIONS

Marktplatz (*Market Square*). Houses of prominent burghers of centuries gone by surround this square. At the open-air market on Monday, Wednesday, and Friday you can buy flowers, bread, pastries, poultry, sausage, and cheese.

Rathaus (*Town Hall*). Begun in 1433, this building slowly expanded over the next 150 years. Its ornate Renaissance facade is bright with colorful murals and a marvelous astronomical clock dating from 1511. The halls and reception rooms are adorned with half-timber and paintings from the late 19th century. ✉ *Marktpl.*

Stiftskirche (*Collegiate Church*). The late-Gothic church has been well preserved; its original features include the stained-glass windows, the choir stalls, the ornate baptismal font, and the elaborate stone pulpit. The windows are famous for their colors and were much admired by Goethe. The dukes of Württemberg, from the 15th through the 17th century, are interred in the choir. ✉ *Holzmarkt.* ⊙ *Daily 9–4.*

WORTH NOTING

Alte Aula (*Old Auditorium*). Erected in 1547, the half-timber university building was significantly altered in 1777, when it acquired an Italian roof, a symmetrical facade, and a balcony decorated with two crossed scepters, symbolizing the town's center of learning. In earlier times grain was stored under the roof as part of the professors' salaries. ✉ *Münzg.*

Hölderlinturm (*Hölderlin's Tower*). Friedrich Hölderlin, a visionary poet who succumbed to madness in his early thirties, lived here until his death in 1843, in the care of the master cabinetmaker Zimmer and his daughter. There's a small literary museum and art gallery inside, and a schedule of events includes concerts and poetry readings. ✉ *Bursag. 6* ☎ *07071/22040* ⊕ *www.hoelderlin-gesellschaft.de* ☐ *€2.50* ⊙ *Tues.– Fri. 10–noon and 3–5.*

Kornhaus (*Grain House*). During the Middle Ages, townspeople stored and sold grain on the first floor of this structure built in 1453; social events took place on the second floor. It now houses the City Museum. ✉ *Kornhausstr. 10* ☎ *07071/204–1711* ☐ *€2.50* ⊙ *Tues.–Sun. 11–5.*

OFF THE
BEATEN
PATH

Kunsthalle (*Art Gallery*). An art gallery north of the Neckar, the Kunsthalle has become a leading local exhibition venue and generates a special kind of "art tourism," making it difficult to find lodging if a popular exhibition is shown. ✉ *Philosophenweg 76* ☎ *07071/96910* ⊕ *www. kunsthalle-tuebingen.de* ☐ *€7* ⊙ *Tues. 11–7, Wed.–Sun. 11–6.*

Schloss HohenTübingen. The original castle of the counts of Tübingen (1078) was significantly enlarged and altered by Duke Ulrich during the 16th century. Particularly noteworthy is the elaborate Renaissance portal patterned after a Roman triumphal arch. The coat of arms of the duchy of Württemberg depicted in the center is framed by the emblems of various orders, including the Order of the Garter. Today the castle's main attraction is its magnificent view over the river and town. It's a 90-minute walk from Schlossbergstrasse, over the Spitzberg, or via the Kapitänsweg that ends north of the castle. ✉ *Burgsteige 11.*

Studentenkarzer (*Student Prison*). The oldest surviving university prison in Germany consists of just two small rooms. For more than three centuries (1515–1845) students were locked up here for such offenses as swearing, failing to attend sermons, wearing clothing considered lewd, or playing dice. The figures on the walls are not graffiti but scenes from biblical history that were supposed to contribute to the moral improvement of the incarcerated students. You can enter the prison on a guided tour organized by the Tübingen tourist board. ✉ *Münzg. 20* ☎ *07071/91360* ☐ *€1* ⊙ *Tour weekends at 2.*

WHERE TO EAT AND STAY

$$

GERMAN

Fodor's Choice

★

✕ **Forelle.** Beautiful ceilings painted with vine motifs, exposed beams, wooden wainscoting and an old tile stove make for a *gemütlich* (cozy) atmosphere. This small restaurant fills up fast, not least because of the Swabian cooking, including the region's signature Maultaschen. The chef makes sure the ingredients are from the region, including the inn's namesake, trout, often served in French-style amandine. Save room for dessert, especially the housemade *Schwäbische Apfelküchle* (Schwabian applecake) with vanilla sauce. ⑤ *Average main: €17* ✉ *Kronenstr. 8* ☎ *07071/24094* ⊕ *www.weinstube-forelle.de.*

$

GERMAN

Fodor's Choice

★

✕ **Wurstküche.** For more than 200 years, all sorts of people have come here: students, because many of the dishes are filling yet inexpensive; locals, because the food is the typical Swabian fare their mothers made; and out-of-town visitors, who love the old-fashioned atmosphere. In summer you may get a seat at one of the tables on the sidewalk in front of the restaurant. Try the Alb-Leisa ond Schbatza, or sausages with spätzle and lentils. ⑤ *Average main: €13* ✉ *Am Lustnauer Tor 8* ☎ *07071/92750* ⊕ *www.wurstkueche.com.*

8

$$ ⊡ **Hotel Am Schloss.** There are lovely views of the Old Town from the
HOTEL rooms in this charming small hotel, and it's close to the castle that
towers over the town. **Pros:** very nice views; valet parking. **Cons:**
no elevator, difficult parking. ⑤ *Rooms from: €118* ⊠ *Burgsteige 18*
☎ *07071/92940* ⊕ *www.hotelamschloss.de* ↪ *37 rooms* ⦿*Breakfast.*

$$ ⊡ **Hotel Hospiz.** This modern, family-run hotel provides friendly service,
HOTEL comfortable rooms, and a convenient Altstadt location near the castle.
Pros: some old beams; convenient location. **Cons:** many stairs in spite
of elevator; rooms simply furnished; no bar or restaurant. ⑤ *Rooms
from: €110* ⊠ *Neckarhalde 2* ☎ *07071/9240* ⊕ *www.hotel-hospiz.de*
↪ *45 rooms* ⦿*Breakfast.*

NIGHTLIFE AND THE ARTS

Die Kelter. You'll find jazz, light fare, and a wine shop here. ⊠ *Schmied-
torstr. 17* ☎ *07071/254–690* ⊕ *www.diekelter.de* ⊗ *Closed Mon.*

Jazzkeller. Like dozens of other Old Town student pubs, Jazzkeller
attracts a lively crowd after 9. ⊠ *Haagg. 15/2* ☎ *07071/550–906*
⊕ *www.jazz-keller.eu* ⊗ *Closed Sun. and Mon.*

Tangente-Jour. This cafe morphs into a bistro and cocktail lounge after
dark, so you can find action from breakfast until past midnight, next
to the Stiftskirche. ⊠ *Münzg. 17* ☎ *07071/24572* ⊕ *www.tangente-
marktschenke.de.*

SPORTS AND THE OUTDOORS

The Tübingen tourist office has maps with hiking routes around the
town, including historical and geological *Lehrpfade,* or educational
walks. A classic Tübingen walk goes from the castle down to the little chapel called the **Wurmlinger Kapelle,** taking about two hours. On
the way you can stop off at the restaurant Schwärzlocher Hof (closed
Monday and Tuesday) for a glass of *Most* (apple wine), bread, and
sausages—all are homemade.

OFF THE   **Burg Hohenzollern.** The majestic silhouette of this massive castle is vis-
BEATEN   ible from miles away. The Hohenzollern House of Prussia was the most
PATH   powerful family in German history. It lost its throne when Kaiser William II abdicated after Germany's defeat in World War I. The Swabian
branch of the family owns one third of the castle, the Prussian branch
two thirds. Today's neo-Gothic structure, perched high on a conical
wooded hill, is a successor of a castle dating from the 11th century.
On the fascinating castle tour you'll see the Prussian royal crown and
beautiful period rooms, all opulent from floor to ceiling, with such
playful details as door handles carved to resemble peacocks and dogs.
The restaurant on the castle grounds, Burgschänke (closed January,
and Monday in February and March) serves regional food. From the
castle parking lot (€2) it's a 20-minute walk to the entrance, or in summer take the shuttle bus (€3 round-trip, €1.85 one-way). ⊠ *25 km (15
miles) south of Tübingen on B-27, Hechingen* ☎ *07471/2428* ⊕ *www.
burg-hohenzollern.com* ⊡*€10* ⊗ *Castle and shuttle bus, mid-Mar.–
Oct., daily 9–5:30; Nov.–mid-Mar., daily 10–4:30.*

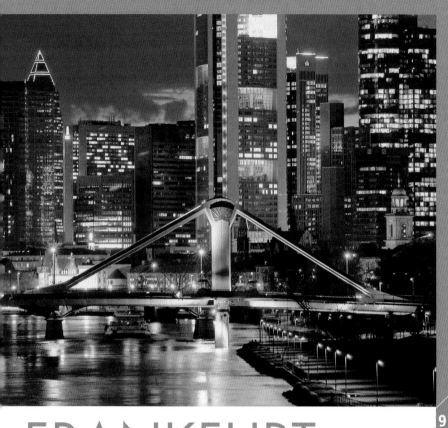

FRANKFURT

WELCOME TO FRANKFURT

TOP REASONS TO GO

★ **Sachsenhausen:** Frankfurt's "South Bank"—with upscale restaurants, fast-food joints, bars with live music, and traditional Apfelwein pubs—is one big outdoor party in summer.

★ **Paleontology paradise:** Beyond a huge dinosaur skeleton, the Senckenberg Natural History Museum has exhibits of many other extinct animals and plants, plus dioramas of animals in their habitats.

★ **Enjoy the outdoors:** The parks and riverbanks are popular with locals and tourists for strolls, sunbathing, and picnics.

★ **Get some wheels:** Hop on and tour the city sites from a bike; you'll be in good company alongside locals.

★ **Exotic experience:** Head to the Frankfurt Zoo's "exotarium," where coral, fish, snakes, alligators, amphibians, insects, and spiders are on display.

1 Altstadt and City Center. Frankfurt downtown includes the Altstadt (Old City), parts of which have been carefully restored after wartime destruction; the Zeil, allegedly Germany's number-one "shop 'til you drop" mile; the Fressgass ("Pig-Out Alley"); and the bank district.

2 Ostend. This area near the East Harbor is where you'll find lots of corporations and banks, although there are also some sights, including the zoo, as well as restaurants, cafés, and clubs catering to those working in the neighboring skyscrapers.

3 Messe and Westend. The Westend is a mix of the villas of the prewar rich and a skyscraper extension of the business district. It's a popular place for the city's elite to live. Messe is the area around Frankfurt's huge and busy convention center (*Messe*), but unless you are attending the huge book fair here or Europe's largest auto show and need a nearby beer or meal to refuel, there's not much reason to go.

4 Nordend and Bornheim. These residential areas are a great place to get away from the crowds and enjoy small neighborhood restaurants and shops.

KEY

S S-Bahn

i Tourist information

U U-Bahn

GETTING ORIENTED

Legend has it that the Frankish Emperor Charlemagne was chasing a deer on the Main's south bank when the animal plunged into the river and, to the emperor's amazement, crossed it with its head always above water. A stone ridge had made the river shallow at that point. That supposedly was the origin of Frankfurt (literally "Frankish Ford") as an important river crossing. Commerce flourished from then on: to this day Frankfurt is an important center of business and finance.

9

5 **Sachsenhausen.** Just across the river from downtown, Sachsenhausen is distinguished by the *Apfelwein* (Apple Wine) district and the *Museumufer* (Museum Riverbank). The Apple Wine district, now with every sort of restaurant and tavern, is one big party, especially in summer, when the tables spill out onto traffic-free streets. The Museum Riverbank has seven museums within as many blocks along the riverfront street Schaumainkai.

GERMAN SAUSAGES

(above) Landjäger sausage
(lower right) Thüringer
Rostbratwurst (upper right)
Frankfurter

The one thing you're guaranteed to find wherever your travels in Germany take you: sausages. Encased meats are a serious business here, and you could spend a lifetime working your way through 1,500 varieties of German sausages, also known as *Wurst*.

The tradition of making sausages goes back centuries, both as a method to preserve food long before refrigeration and as the best way to use every last piece of precious meat. Sausage recipes go back for generations, and like most German cooking, sausage types vary from region to region. There's also an abundance of ways to serve a sausage—grilled sausages are served up in a small roll, essentially just a sausage "holder"; Weisswursts come to the table after a gentle bath in warm water; cured sausages often are served sliced, while other cooked sausages are dished up with sauerkraut. Germans don't mess around when it comes to their love for sausage, eating about 62 pounds of sausage per person each year.

—Tania Ralli

WEISSWURST ETIQUETTE

Weisswurst is a delicate white sausage made with veal, bacon, lemon, and parsley. It's traditional in the southern state of Bavaria, where they are sticklers about the way of eating them. The casing is never eaten; instead, you *zuzeln* (suck) out the meat. Make a slit at the top, dunk it in sweet mustard, and suck out the insides. It's all right to slit and peel it as well.

FRANKFURTER

In Germany a frankfurter isn't something that must be doused in condiments to make it palatable, like a subpar ballpark frank—instead you'll immediately notice the crisp snap of the frankfurter's skin and a delicious smoky taste. Frankfurters are long and narrow by design, to absorb as much flavor as possible during cold smoking. When served on a plate for lunch or dinner, they're normally served in a pair, and you should eat them dipped in mustard, with your fingers. Frankfurters and other würste also are served inside a small roll, called a *Brotchen.* The only condiment used is mustard, never sauerkraut or other toppings.

THÜRINGER ROSTBRATWURST

This bratwurst dates back to 1613 and it's clear why it has stood the test of time: it's one of Germany's most delicious sausages. The *Rostbratwurst* is a mix of lean pork belly, veal, and beef, seasoned with herbs and spices. Most families closely guard their recipes, but often use garlic, caraway, or nutmeg. You'll smell the scent of grilled *Thüringer* wafting through the streets because they're popular at street markets and festivals.

LANDJÄGER

This small, narrow, and dense rectangular sausage is sold in pairs. It's cured by air-drying, so it resembles a dry salami

in color and texture *Landjäger* are made of beef, sometimes with pork, and red wine and spices. Historically, fieldworkers and wine grape harvesters liked to eat these salty sausages. Landjäger keep well, so they're a great snack to tuck in your backpack when you head out for a day of hiking in the mountains.

BLUTWURST

Sometimes called *Rotwurst* (red sausage), *Blutwurst* is a combination of ground pork, spices, and—the key ingredient—blood, fresh from the slaughter. After it's been cooked and smoked, the blood congeals, and the sausage takes on a dark hue and looks almost black. Depending on the region, it can be studded with bacon, pickled ox tongue, or potatoes. For most of its history Blutwurst has been considered a luxury item.

BOCKWURST

This sausage got its name when hungry students ordered it with a round of *Bockbier,* a style of beer, in Berlin in 1889. The sausage came from a nearby Jewish butcher, who made it with veal and beef. *Bockwurst* is a thick sausage seasoned with salt, white pepper, and paprika, in a natural casing. It's usually boiled and served hot, but it can also be grilled. It's one of Germany's most popular sausages, so you'll find it on menus all over the country.

9

Updated by
Evelyn Kanter

Although many consider Frankfurt more or less a gateway to their Europe travels, the city's rich culture and history, dining, and amusement options might just surprise you.

Standing in the center of the Römerberg (medieval town square), you'll see the city's striking contrasts at once. Re-creations of neo-Gothic houses and government buildings enfold the square, while just beyond them modern skyscrapers pierce the sky. The city cheekily nicknamed itself "Mainhattan," using the name of the Main River that flows through it to suggest that other famous metropolis across the Atlantic. Although only fifth in size among German cities, with a population of nearly 700,000, Frankfurt is Germany's financial powerhouse. The German Central Bank (*Bundesbank*) is here, as is the European Central Bank (ECB), which manages the Euro. Some 300 credit institutions (more than half of them foreign banks) have offices in Frankfurt, including the headquarters of five of Germany's largest banks. You can see how the city acquired its other nickname, "Bankfurt am Main." It's no wonder that Frankfurt is Europe's financial center. The city's stock exchange, one of the most important in the world, was established in 1585, and the Rothschild family opened their first bank here in 1798.

The long history of trade might help explain the temperament of many Frankfurters—competitive but open-minded. It's also one of the reasons Frankfurt has become Germany's most international city. Close to a quarter of its residents are foreign, with a growing number from Eastern Europe and the Middle East.

Because of its commercialism, Frankfurt has a reputation for being cold and boring, but people who know the city think this characterization is unfair. The district of Sachsenhausen is as *gemütlich* (fun, friendly, and cozy) as you will find anywhere. The city has world-class ballet, opera, theater, and art exhibitions; an important piece of Germany's publishing industry (and the world's largest annual book fair); a large university (43,000 students); and two of the three most important daily newspapers in Germany. Despite the skyscrapers, especially in the *Hauptbahnhof* (main train station) area and adjoining Westend district, there's much here to remind you of the Old World, along with much that explains the success of postwar Germany.

PLANNING

WHEN TO GO

The weather in Frankfurt is moderate throughout the year, though often damp and drizzly. Summers are mild, with the occasional hot day, and it rarely gets very cold in winter and hardly ever snows. Because Frankfurt is one of the biggest trade fair cities in all of Europe, high season at all hotels is considered to be during trade shows throughout the year. Be sure to check dates to avoid paying premium price for a room or even finding yourself without a place to stay.

GETTING HERE AND AROUND

AIR TRAVEL

There are two airports with the name "Frankfurt": Flughafen Frankfurt Main (FRA), which receives direct flights from many U.S. cities and from all major cities in Europe, Africa, Asia, and the Mideast; and Frankfurt-Hahn (HHN), a former U.S. air base a full 112 km (70 miles) west of Frankfurt that handles some bargain flights, mainly to and from secondary European airports.

Airport Contacts Flughafen Frankfurt Main (FRA). ✉ 200 Flughafen Frankfurt am Main ☎ 0800/2345679 ⊕ www.frankfurt-airport.de. **Frankfurt-Hahn** (HHN). ✉ 1 Saonestr., Hahn-Flughafen ☎ 06543/509–113 ⊕ www.hahn-airport.de.

AIRPORT TRANSFERS

Flughafen Frankfurt Main is 10 km (6 miles) southwest of downtown via the A-5 autobahn, and has its own railway station for high-speed InterCity (IC) and InterCity Express (ICE) trains. Getting into Frankfurt from the airport is easy, via S-bahn line nos. 8 and 9 that run between the airport and downtown. Most travelers get off at the Hauptbahnhof (main train station, or HBF) or at Hauptwache, in the heart of Frankfurt. Trains run at least every 15 minutes, and the trip takes about 15 minutes. The one-way fare is €4.25. A taxi from the airport into the City Center normally takes around 25 minutes (double that during rush hours). The fare is around €35. If you are driving a rental car from the airport, take the main road out of the airport and follow the signs reading "Stadtmitte" (downtown).

Bohr Busreisen offers a regular bus service to and from Frankfurt-Hahn Airport. It leaves every hour to every 1½ hours, 3 am to 8 pm, from the south side of the Frankfurt Hauptbahnhof, with a stop 15 minutes later at the Terminal 1 bus station at Flughafen Frankfurt Main. The trip to Frankfurt-Hahn takes an hour and 45 minutes, and costs €14.

BUS AND SUBWAY TRAVEL

Frankfurt's smooth-running, well-integrated public transportation system (called RMV) consists of the U-bahn (subway), S-bahn (suburban railway), Strassenbahn (streetcars), and buses. Buses are the public-transit option between 1 am and 4 am.

Fares for the entire system, which includes an extensive surrounding area, are uniform, though they are based on a complex zone system. Within the time that your ticket is valid (one hour for most inner-city destinations), you can transfer from one part of the system to another.

9

Tickets may be purchased from automatic vending machines, which are at all U-bahn and S-bahn stations. Weekly and monthly tickets are sold at central ticket offices and newsstands. A basic one-way ticket for a ride in the inner zone costs €2.60 during the peak hours of 6 am–9 am and 4 pm–6:30 pm weekdays (€2.30 the rest of the time). There's also a reduced *Kurzstrecke* ("short stretch") fare of €1.60 the whole day. A day ticket for unlimited travel in the inner zones costs €6.60. If you're caught without a ticket, there's a fine of €40.

Some 200 European cities have bus links with Frankfurt, largely through Deutsche Touring. Buses arrive at and depart from the south side of the Hauptbahnhof and terminal 1 at the Frankfurt Main airport.

Bus Contacts Bohr Busreisen ☏ *0654/350190* ⊕ *www.omnibusse.bohr.de.*
Deutsche Touring ✉ *Mannheimerstr. 15, City Center* ☏ *069/46092780*
⊕ *www.touring.de.* **Verkehrsgesellschaft Frankfurt am Main** (*Municipal Transit Authority*). ☏ *069/19449* ⊕ *www.vgf-ffm.de.*

CAR TRAVEL

Frankfurt is the meeting point of a number of major autobahns. The most important are A-3, running south from Köln and then on east to Würzburg and Nürnberg, and A-5, running south from Giessen and then on toward Heidelberg and Basel.

In Frankfurt, hidden cameras are used to catch speeders, so be sure to stick to the speed limit. Tow trucks cruise the streets in search of illegal parkers. There are many reasonably priced parking garages around the downtown area and a well-developed "park-and-ride" system with the suburban train lines. The transit map shows nearly a hundred outlying stations with a blue "P" symbol beside them, meaning there is convenient parking there.

TAXI TRAVEL

Cabs are not always easy to hail from the sidewalk; some stop, but others will pick up only from the city's numerous taxi stands or outside hotels or the train station. You can always order a cab. Fares start at €2.80 (€3.30 in the evening) and increase by a per-kilometer (½ mile) charge of €1.75 (€1.60 after 10 km). Frankfurt also has Velotaxis, covered tricycles seating two passengers and a driver that are useful for sightseeing or getting to places on the traffic-free downtown streets. They charge €2.50 per kilometer.

Taxi Contacts Taxis ☏ *069/230001.* **Velotaxi** ☏ *0700/8356–8294.*

TRAIN TRAVEL

EuroCity, InterCity (IC), and InterCity Express (ICE) trains connect Frankfurt with all German cities and many major European ones. The InterCity Express line links Frankfurt with Berlin, Hamburg, Munich, and a number of other major hubs. All long-distance trains arrive at and depart from the Hauptbahnhof, and many also stop at the long-distance train station at the main airport. The red-light district southwest of the main station should be avoided.

Train Contact Deutsche Bahn (*German Railways*). ☏ *01805/996633*
⊕ *www.bahn.de.*

DID YOU KNOW?

The Main River is lined with paths on both sides that are popular places for recreation and relaxing. The paths even allow biking.

VISITOR INFORMATION

Tourismus und Congress GmbH Frankfurt–Main has its main office at Römerberg 27, in Old Town. It's open weekdays 9:30–5:30 and weekends 9–6.

The airport's information office is on the first floor of Arrivals Hall B and open daily 7 am–10:30 pm. Another information office in the main hall of the railroad station is open weekdays 8 am–9 pm, weekends 9–6. Both can help you find accommodations.

Visitor Information Tourismus und Congress GmbH Frankfurt/Main
✉ *Römerberg 27, City Center* ☎ *069/2123–8800* ⊕ *www.frankfurt-tourismus.de.*

DISCOUNTS AND DEALS

The Frankfurt tourist office offers a one- or two-day ticket—the Frankfurt Card (€9.20 for one day, €13.50 for two days)—allowing unlimited travel on public transportation in the inner zone, and to the airport. It also includes a 50% reduction on admission to 24 museums, the zoo, and the Palmengarten, and price reductions at some restaurants and stores.

TOURS

APPLE WINE EXPRESS TOUR

The one-hour Apple Wine Express (Ebbelwei Express) tour in a vintage streetcar is offered hourly weekends and some holidays. It gives you a quick look at the city's neighborhoods, a bit of Frankfurt history, and a chance to sample Apfelwein (a bottle, along with pretzels, is included in the €7 fare).

Contacts Ebbelwei Express ☎ *069/213–22425* ⊕ *www.ebbelwei-express.com.*

BOAT TRIPS

Day trips on the Main River and Rhine excursions run from April through October and leave from the Frankfurt Mainkai am Eiserner Steg, just south of the Römer complex. ■TIP➜ The boats are available for private parties, too.

Contact Frankfurt Personenschiffahrt Primus-Linie ✉ *Mainkai 36, Altstadt* ☎ *069/1338370* ⊕ *www.primus-linie.de.*

BUS TOURS

Two-hour city bus tours with English-speaking guides are available from the Frankfurt Tourist Office throughout the year.

WALKING TOURS

The tourist office's walking tours cover a variety of topics, including Goethe, Jewish history, apple wine, architecture, and banking. Tours can also be tailored to your interests. For an English-speaking guide, a group tour cost starts at €110 for up to two hours (prices vary depending on the type of tour).

Tour Contact Tourismus und Congress GmbH Frankfurt/Main ☎ *069/2123–8800* ⊕ *www.frankfurt-tourismus.de.*

EXPLORING FRANKFURT

ALTSTADT

TOP ATTRACTIONS

Alte Oper (*Old Opera House*). Kaiser Wilhelm I traveled from Berlin for the gala opening of this opera house in 1880. Gutted in World War II, the house remained a hollow shell for 40 years while controversy raged over its reconstruction. The exterior and lobby are faithful to the original, though the remainder of the building is more like a modern multipurpose hall. Although classical music performances are held here, most operas these days are staged at the Frankfurt Opera. ⊠ *Opernpl. 1, Altstadt* ☎ *069/13400* ⊕ *www.alteoper.de* Ⓜ *Alte Oper (U-bahn).*

Fressgass. Grosse Bockenheimer Strasse is the proper name of this pedestrian street, but it's nicknamed "Pig-Out Alley" because of its amazing choice of delicatessens, wine merchants, cafés, and restaurants, offering everything from crumbly cheeses and smoked fish to vintage wines and chocolate creams. ■ TIP→ Check the side streets for additional cafes and restaurants. ⊠ *Grosse Bockenheimerstr., Altstadt* ⊕ *www.frankfurt-fressgass.de* Ⓜ *Hauptwache (U-bahn and S-bahn), Alte Oper (U-bahn).*

Goethehaus und Goethemuseum (*Goethe's Residence and Museum*). The house where Germany's most famous poet was born is furnished with many original pieces that belonged to his family, including manuscripts in his own hand. The original house, which was destroyed by Allied bombing, has been carefully rebuilt and restored in every detail. Johann Wolfgang von Goethe (1749–1832) studied law and became a member of the bar in Frankfurt. He was quickly drawn to writing, however, and in this house he eventually wrote the first version of his masterpiece, *Faust*. The adjoining museum contains works of art that inspired Goethe (he was an amateur painter) and works associated with his literary contemporaries. ⊠ *Grosser Hirschgraben 23–25, Altstadt* ☎ *069/138–800* ⊕ *www.goethehaus-frankfurt. de* ⊡ *€7* ⊗ *Mon.–Sat. 10–6, Sun. 10–5:30* Ⓜ *Hauptwache or Willy-Brandt-Platz (U-bahn and S-bahn).*

FAMILY **Historisches Museum** (*Historical Museum*). This fascinating museum encompasses 2,000 years of all aspects of Frankfurt's history. It contains a scale model of historic Frankfurt, with every street, house, and church, plus photos of the devastation of World War II. Parts of the building date from the 1300s. A new wing is scheduled to open by early 2015. ⊠ *Fahrtor 2 (Römerberg), Altstadt* ☎ *069/2123–5599* ⊕ *www. historisches-museum.frankfurt.de* ⊡ *€6* ⊗ *Tues. and Thurs.–Sun. 10–6, Wed. 10–9* Ⓜ *Römer (U-bahn).*

Kaiserdom. Because the Holy Roman emperors were chosen and crowned here from the 16th to the 18th century, the church is known as the Kaiserdom (Imperial Cathedral), even though it isn't the seat of a bishop. Officially the Church of St. Bartholomew, but called simply "The Dom" by locals, it was built largely between the 13th and 15th century and

9

survived World War II with the majority of its treasures intact. The most impressive exterior feature is the tall, red sandstone tower (almost 300 feet high), which was added between 1415 and 1514. Climb it for a good view. The **Dommuseum** (Cathedral Museum) occupies the former Gothic cloister. ✉ *Dompl. 1, Altstadt* ☎ *069/1337–6184* ⊕ *www.dom-frankfurt.de* 🖾 *Dommuseum €3* ☉ *Church Mon.–Thurs. and Sat. 9– noon and 2:30–6, Fri. and Sun. 2:30–6. Dommuseum Tues.–Fri. 10–5, weekends 11–5* Ⓜ *Römer (U-bahn).*

Museum für Moderne Kunst (*Museum of Modern Art*). Austrian architect Hans Hollein (born in 1934) designed this distinctive triangular building, shaped like a wedge of cake. The collection features works by artists such as Andy Warhol and Joseph Beuys. ✉ *Domstr. 10, Altstadt* ☎ *069/21230447* ⊕ *www.mmk-frankfurt.de* 🖾 *€10* ☉ *Tues. and Thurs.–Sun. 10–6, Wed. 10–8* Ⓜ *Römer (U-bahn).*

Paulskirche (*St. Paul's Church*). The first all-German parliament was held here in 1848. The parliament lasted only a year, having achieved little more than offering the Prussian king the crown of Germany. Today the church, which has been extensively restored, remains a symbol of German democracy and is used mainly for ceremonies. The most striking feature of the interior is a giant, completely circular mural showing an "endless" procession of the people's representatives into the Paulskirche. The work of Johannes Grützke, completed in 1991, it also shows such symbols as a mother and child, a smith to represent the common people, and a rejected crown. The plenary chamber upstairs is flanked by the flags of Germany, the 16 states, and the city of Frankfurt. ✉ *Paulspl. 11, Altstadt* ☎ *069/212–38934* ☉ *Daily 10–5* Ⓜ *Römer (U-bahn).*

Römerberg. This square north of the Main River, restored after wartime bomb damage, is the historical focal point of the city. The Römer, the Nikolaikirche, and the half-timber Ostzeile houses are all clustered around this huge plaza. The 16th-century Fountain of Justitia (Justice), which flows with wine on special occasions, stands in the center of the Römerberg. The square is also the site of many public festivals throughout the year, including the Christmas market in December. Kleine Krame is a pedestrian street just north of the square that's lined with snack shops and cafes. ✉ *Between Braubachstr. and Main R., Altstadt* Ⓜ *Römer (U-bahn).*

Zeil. The heart of Frankfurt's shopping district is this bustling pedestrian street running east from Hauptwache Square. It's lined with department stores, a few smaller boutiques, drugstores, cell-phone franchises, electronics shops, restaurants, and more. ■ TIP→ Stop in at the outdoor farmers' market every Thursday and Saturday for a freshly grilled bratwurst and a beer. ✉ *Hauptwache Sq., Altstadt* Ⓜ *Hauptwache, Konstablerwache (U-bahn and S-bahn).*

WORTH NOTING

Alte Nikolaikirche (*Old St. Nicholas Church*). This small red sandstone church was built in the late 13th century as the court chapel for emperors of the Holy Roman Empire. Try to time your visit to coincide with the chimes of the carillon, which rings three times a day, at 9:05 in

Goethe's House and Museum is filled with the manuscripts and paintings of Germany's best-loved poet.

the morning, and at 12:05 and 5:05 in the afternoon. ✉ *South side of Römerberg, Altstadt* ☎ *069/284–235* ⊗ *Oct.–Mar., daily 10–6; Apr.–Sept., daily 10–8* Ⓜ *Römer (U-bahn).*

Eiserner Steg (*Iron Bridge*). A pedestrian walkway and the first suspension bridge in Europe, the Eiserner Steg connects the city center with Sachsenhausen and offers great views of the Frankfurt skyline. Excursions by boat and an old steam train leave from here. ✉ *Mainkai, Altstadt.*

Hauptwache. The attractive baroque building with a steeply sloping roof is the actual Hauptwache (Main Guardhouse), from which the square takes its name. The 1729 building, which had been tastelessly added to over the years, was partly demolished to permit excavation for a vast underground shopping mall. The building was then restored to its original appearance and is now considered the heart of the Frankfurt pedestrian shopping area. ■ TIP➜ The outdoor patio of the building's restaurant-café is a popular "people-watching" spot on the Zeil. ✉ *An der Hauptwache 15, Altstadt* Ⓜ *Hauptwache (U-bahn and S-bahn).*

Archaologisches Museum. The soaring vaulted ceilings make the Gothic Karmeliterkirche (Carmelite Church) an ideal setting for huge Roman columns and other local and regional artifacts, including Stone Age and Neolithic tools and ancient papyrus documents. Modern wings display Greek, Roman and Persian pottery, carvings and more. Adjacent buildings house the city's Institut für Stadtgeschichte (Institute of History). The basement, titled "Die Schmiere" (The Grease), is a satirical theater. ✉ *Karmeliterg. 1, Altstadt* ☎ *069/2123–5896* ⊕ *www.archaeologisches-museum.frankfurt.de* 🎫 *Museum €7, free last Sat. of month* ⊗ *Tues.–Sun. 10–5, Wed. 10–8* Ⓜ *Willy-Brandt-Platz (U-bahn).*

Römer (*City Hall*). Three individual patrician buildings make up the Römer, Frankfurt's town hall. The mercantile-minded Frankfurt burghers used the complex not only for political and ceremonial purposes but also for trade fairs and other commercial ventures. Its gabled facade with an ornate balcony is widely known as the city's official emblem.

The most important events to take place in the Römer were the festivities celebrating the coronations of the Holy Roman emperors. The first was in 1562 in the glittering **Kaisersaal** (Imperial Hall), which was last used in 1792 to celebrate the election of the emperor Francis II, who would later be forced by Napoléon to abdicate. Unless official business is being conducted you can see the impressive, full-length 19th-century portraits of the 52 emperors of the Holy Roman Empire, which line the walls of the reconstructed banquet hall. ⊠ *West side of Römerberg, Römerberg 27, Altstadt* ☎ *069/2123–4814* 💳 *€3* ⊙ *Daily 10–1 and 2–5; often closed for events, so check hrs before going* Ⓜ *Römer (U-bahn).*

Schirn Kunsthalle (*Schirn Art Gallery*). One of Frankfurt's most modern museums is devoted exclusively to changing exhibits of modern art and photography. The gallery, right beside the Kaiserdom, has a restaurant. ⊠ *Römerberg, Altstadt* ☎ *069/299–8820* ⊕ *www.schirn.de* 💳 *Admission varies from €7 to €9 depending on exhibit.* ⊙ *Tues. and Fri.–Sun. 10–7, Wed. and Thurs. 10–10* Ⓜ *Römer (U-bahn).*

CITY CENTER

Frankfurt was rebuilt after World War II with little attention paid to the past. Nevertheless, important historical monuments can still be found among the modern architecture. The city is very walkable; its growth hasn't encroached on its parks, gardens, pedestrian arcades, or outdoor cafés. The riverbank paths make for great strolls or bike rides.

TOP ATTRACTIONS

OFF THE BEATEN PATH

Alter Jüdischer Friedhof (*Old Jewish Cemetery*). Containing hundreds of moss-covered gravestones, this cemetery was in use between the 13th and mid-19th centuries, and is one of the few reminders of prewar Jewish life in Frankfurt. It suffered minimal vandalization in the Nazi era, even though its adjoining grand Börneplatz Synagogue was destroyed on Kristallnacht, in 1938. That space is now part of Museum Judengasse; ask the admissions desk for the key to open the vandal-proof steel gates to the cemetery. Mayer Amschel Rothschild, founder of the banking family, who died in 1812, is buried here, along with some family members (the Rothschild mansion is now the main Jewish Museum). The wall around the cemetery is dotted with more than 1,000 small memorial plaques, each with the name of a Jewish Frankfurter and the concentration camp where they died. There is a newer Jewish cemetery at Eckenheimer Landstrasse 238 (about 2½ km [1½ miles] north). ⊠ *Battonnstr. 2, City Center* ☎ *069/212–40000* ⊕ *juedischesmuseum.de/museumjudengasse* 💳 *Free* ⊙ *Sun.–Fri. 8:30–4:30* Ⓜ *Bornerplatz (S-bahn).*

Jüdisches Museum (*Jewish Museum*). The story of Frankfurt's Jewish community is told in the former Rothschild Palais, which overlooks the river Main. Prior to the Holocaust, Frankfurt's Jewish quarter was the second largest in Germany (after Berlin), and the silver and gold household items on display are a testament to its prosperity. The museum contains a library of 5,000 books, a large photographic collection, and a documentation center. ■ **TIP→** Be sure to check out the wall of ceremonial menorahs. ⊠ *Untermainkai 14/15, City Center* ☎ *069/2123–5000* ⊕ *www.juedischesmuseum.de* ⊠€6 ⊗ *Tues. and Thurs.–Sun. 10–5, Wed. 10–8* Ⓜ *Willy-Brandt-Platz (U-bahn).*

Museum Judengasse. This branch of the Jewish museum is built on the site of the Börneplatz Synagogue, destroyed in 1938, and the foundations of mostly 18th-century buildings that were once part of the Jewish quarter. ⊠ *Kurt-Schumacher-Str. 10, City Center* ☎ *069/297–7419* ⊠€3 ⊗ *Tues. and Thurs.–Sun. 10–5, Wed. 10–8* Ⓜ *Bornerplatz (U-bahn).*

WORTH NOTING

Börse (*Stock Exchange*). This is the center of Germany's stock and money market. The Börse was founded in 1585, but the present domed building dates from the 1870s. These days computerized networks and telephone systems have removed much of the drama from the dealers' floor, but it's still fun to visit the visitor gallery and watch the hectic activity. You must reserve your visit 24 hours in advance. ⊠ *Börsenpl. 4, City Center* ☎ *069/2110* ⊕ *www.boerse-frankfurt.de* ⊠ *Free* ⊗ *Visitor gallery weekdays 10–8* Ⓜ *Hauptwache (U-bahn and S-bahn).*

Eschenheimer Turm (*Eschenheim Tower*). Built in the early 15th century, this tower, a block north of the Hauptwache, remains the finest example of the city's original 42 towers. It now contains a restaurant-bar. ⊠ *Eschenheimer Tor, City Center* Ⓜ *Eschenheimer Tor (U-bahn).*

OSTEND

Named for its location around the city's East Harbor, the business-oriented Ostend is sprouting new restaurants and cafés, attracting by the 2014 opening of the new European Central Bank headquarters building.

FAMILY **Zoologischer Garten** (*Zoological Garden*). Founded in 1858, this is one of the most important and attractive zoos in Europe. Its remarkable collection includes some 4,500 animals of 500 different species, an exotarium (an aquarium plus reptiles), a large ape house, and an aviary, one of the largest in Europe. Nocturnal creatures move about in a special section. ⊠ *Bernhard-Grzimek-Allee 1, Ostend* ☎ *069/2123–3735* ⊕ *www.zoo-frankfurt.de* ⊠€10, family ticket €25 ⊗ *Nov.–Mar., daily 9–5; Apr.–Oct., daily 9–7* Ⓜ *Zoo (U-bahn).*

MESSE AND WESTEND

The city's huge, sprawling convention center (Messe) is one of the busiest in Europe, and the area around it isn't especially interesting. Westend, on the other hand, is a charming residential neighborhood dotted with some good restaurants.

FAMILY **Naturkundemuseum Senckenberg** (*Natural History Museum*). The important collection of fossils, animals, plants, and geological exhibits here is upstaged by the permanent dinosaur exhibit: it's the most extensive of its kind in all of Germany. The diplodocus dinosaur here, imported

KEY

S *S-Bahn*

i *Tourist information*

U *U-Bahn*

from New York, is the only complete specimen of its kind in Europe. ▓TIP➜ Many of the exhibits of prehistoric animals here, including a series of dioramas, have been designed with children in mind. ✉ *Senckenberganlage 25, Westend* ☎ *069/75420* ⊕ *www.senckenberg.de* ⌨ *€8* ⊙ *Mon., Tues., Thurs., and Fri. 9–5, Wed. 9–8, weekends 9–6* Ⓜ *Bockenheimer Warte (U-bahn).*

FAMILY　**Palmengarten und Botanischer Garten** (*Tropical Garden and Botanical Gardens*). The splendid cluster of tropical and semitropical greenhouses here contains cacti, orchids, palms, and other plants. The surrounding park, which can be surveyed from a miniature train, has many recreational facilities, including a small lake where you can rent rowboats, a play area for children, and a wading pool. ▓TIP➜ The Palmengarten offers free tours on a variety of topics on Sunday. In summer there's also an extensive concert program that takes place in an outdoor pavilion. ✉ *Siesmayerstr. 63, Westend* ☎ *069/2123–3939* ⊕ *palmengarten.frankfurt.de* ⌨ *€7* ⊙ *Feb.–Oct., daily 9–6; Nov.–Jan., daily 9–4* Ⓜ *Westend (U-bahn).*

FAMILY　**Struwwelpeter Museum** (*Slovenly Peter Museum*). This charming little museum honors the Frankfurt physician who created the sardonic children's classic *Struwwelpeter*, or Slovenly Peter. Heinrich Hoffmann wrote the poems and drew the rather amateurish pictures in 1844, to warn children of the dire consequences of being naughty. The book has seen several English translations, including one by Mark Twain, which can be purchased at the museum. The kid-friendly museum has a puppet theater and game room, and is popular for birthday parties. ✉ *Schubertstr. 20, Westend* ☎ *069/747–969* ⊕ *www.struwwelpeter-museum.de* ⌨ *€5* ⊙ *Tues.–Sat. 10–5, Sun. 2–5* Ⓜ *Westend (U-bahn).*

NORDEND AND BORNHEIM

Nordend was the center of antigovernment student demonstrations in the 1960s and 1970s—it still retains a little shabby, bohemian flavor. For its part, Bornheim holds on to some of the liveliness it had as the city's red-light district a century ago. Both have some pleasant, small shops and restaurants.

SACHSENHAUSEN

The old quarter of Sachsenhausen, on the south bank of the Main River, has been sensitively preserved, and its cobblestone streets, half-timber houses, and beer gardens make it a popular area to stroll. Sachsenhausen's two big attractions are the **Museumufer** (Museum Riverbank), which has nine museums almost next door to one another and offers beautiful views of the Frankfurt skyline, as well as the famous Apfelwein taverns around the Rittergasse pedestrian area. You can eat well—and quite reasonably—in these small traditional establishments.

TOP ATTRACTIONS

FAMILY　**Deutsches Filmmuseum** (*German Film Museum*). Germany's first museum of cinematography, set in a historical villa on "museum row" on the Sachsenhausen side of the river Main, offers visitors a glimpse at the

Climb to the top of Kaiserdom, officially called the Church St. Bartholomew, for a fantastic view of the city.

history of film, with artifacts that include "magic lanterns" from the 1880s, costume drawings from Hollywood and German films, and multiple screens playing film clips. Interactive exhibits show how films are photographed, given sound, and edited, and let visitors play with lighting and animation. A theater in the basement screens every imaginable type of film, from historical to avant-garde. ☒ *Schaumainkai 41, Sachsenhausen* ☏ *069/9612–20220* ⊕ *www.deutschesfilmmuseum. de* 💳 *€5* ☉ *Tues., Thurs., and Fri. 10–6, Sun. and Wed. 10–7, Sat. 2–7* Ⓜ *Schweizer Platz (U-bahn)*.

Ikonen-Museum. This is one of very few museums in the world to exhibit a wide spectrum of the Christian Orthodox world of images. The art and ritual of icons from the 15th to the 20th century are on display here in a collection that totals more than 1,000 artifacts. Admission is free on the last Saturday of the month. ☒ *Brückenstr. 3–7, Sachsenhausen* ☏ *069/21236262* ⊕ *www.ikonenmseum.de* 💳 *€4* ☉ *Tues.–Sun. 10–5, Wed. 10–8*.

Museum Giersch. This museum, set in a beautiful neoclassical villa along the strip of museums in Sachsenhausen, focuses on paintings from the 19th century and early 20th century. The artists are drawn mainly from the Rhine-Main region. ☒ *Schaumainkai 83, Sachsenhausen* ☏ *069/631–48724* ⊕ *www.museum-giersch.de* 💳 *€5* ☉ *Tues.–Thurs. noon–7, Fri.–Sun. 10–6*.

Museum für Kommunikation (*Museum for Communication*). This is the place for talking on picture telephones and learning about the newest advances in communication technology. Exhibitions on historic methods include mail coaches, a vast collection of stamps from many countries and eras, and ancient dial telephones, with their clunky switching equipment. ✉ *Schau-mainkai 53, Sachsenhausen* ☏ *069/60600* ⊕ *www.museumsstiftung.de* 🎫 *€2.50* ⊙ *Tues.–Fri. 9–6, weekends 11–7* Ⓜ *Schweizer Platz (U-bahn).*

Städelsches Kunstinstitut und Städtische Galerie (*Städel Art Institute and Municipal Gallery*). One of Germany's most important art collections is housed at this museum, with a vast collection of paintings by Dürer, Vermeer, Rembrandt, Rubens, Monet, Renoir, and other masters. An annex features a large collection of works from contemporary artists, including a huge portrait of Goethe by Andy Warhol. ▮TIP→ The section on German Expressionism is particularly strong, with representative works by the Frankfurt artist Max Beckmann and Ernst Ludwig Kirchner. ✉ *Schaumainkai 63, Sachsenhausen* ☏ *069/605–0980* ⊕ *www. staedelmuseum.de* 🎫 *€14* ⊙ *Tues. and Fri.–Sun. 10–6, Wed. and Thurs. 10–9* Ⓜ *Schweizer Platz (U-bahn).*

WORTH NOTING

Deutsches Architekturmuseum. The German Architecture Museum is housed in a late 19th-century villa, which was converted in the early 1980s by the Köln-based architect Oswald Mathias Ungers. He created five levels, including a simple basement space with a visible load-bearing structure, a walled complex on the ground floor, and a house-within-a-house on the third floor. The museum features a wealth of documents on the history of architecture and hosts debates on its future. Each year, several major and numerous smaller exhibitions highlight issues in architectural history and current topics in architecture and urban design, including sustainability. A permanent exhibit features the most comprehensive collection of model panoramas in the history of German architecture. ✉ *Schaumainkai 43, Sachsenhausen* ☏ *069/2123–8844* ⊕ *www.dam-online.de* 🎫 *€9* ⊙ *Tues. and Thurs.–Sat. 11–6, Sun., 11–7, Wed. 11–8* Ⓜ *Schweizer Platz (U-bahn).*

Museum für Angewandte Kunst (*Museum of Applied Arts*). More than 30,000 decorative objects are exhibited in this modern white building set back in grassy grounds along "museum row" in Saschenhausen. Chairs and furnishings and medieval craftwork are some of the thematic sections you'll find on the same floor. The exhibits are mainly from Europe and Asia. ✉ *Schaumainkai 17, Sachsenhausen* ☏ *069/2123–4037* ⊕ *www.museumfuerangewandtekunst.frankfurt.de* 🎫 *€10, free last Sat. of month* ⊙ *Tues. and Thurs.–Sun. 10–5, Wed. 10–9* Ⓜ *Schweizer Platz (U-bahn).*

Städtische Galerie Liebieghaus (*Liebieg Municipal Museum of Sculpture*). The sculpture collection in this museum, from 5,000 years of civilizations and epochs, is considered one of the most important in Europe. Antiquity, the Middle Ages, the Renaissance, classicism, and the baroque are all represented. Some pieces are exhibited in the lovely gardens surrounding the house. ▮TIP→ Don't miss out on the freshly baked German cakes in the museum café. ✉ *Schaumainkai 71, Sach-senhausen* ☏ *069/650–0490* ⊕ *www.liebieghaus.de* 🎫 *€9* ⊙ *Tues. and Fri.–Sun. 10–6, Wed. and Thurs. 10–9* Ⓜ *Schweizer Platz (U-bahn).*

Sachsenhausen comes alive at night with a lively restaurant and bar scene.

WHERE TO EAT

Many international cuisines are represented in the financial hub of Europe. For vegetarians there's usually at least one meatless dish on a German menu, and substantial salads are popular, too (though often served with bacon). The city's most famous contribution to the world's diet is the *Frankfurter Würstchen*—a thin smoked pork sausage—better known to Americans as the hot dog. *Grüne Sosse* is a thin cream sauce of herbs served with potatoes and hard-boiled eggs. The oddly named *Handkäs mit Musik* (literally, "hand cheese with music") consists of slices of cheese covered with raw onions, oil, and vinegar, served with bread and butter (an acquired taste for many). There is the *Rippchen* or cured pork chop, served on a mound of sauerkraut, and the *Schlachtplatte*, an assortment of sausages and smoked meats. All these things are served with Frankfurt's distinctive drink, Apfelwein.

Smoking is prohibited inside Frankfurt's bars and restaurants, but allowed in most beer gardens.

Prices in the reviews are the average cost of a main course at dinner, or if dinner is not served, at lunch. Use the coordinate (✛ C3) at the end of each listing to locate a site on the corresponding map.

ALTSTADT

$
VEGETARIAN
✕ **Langosch am Main.** This eclectic vegetarian and vegan spot, one of the few in Frankfurt, serves breakfast, lunch, dinner, and late-night snacks made only with organic ingredients. There's also wine and beer (also organic) and homemade drinks such as lemonade garnished with sprigs

BEST BETS FOR FRANKFURT DINING

With hundreds of restaurants to choose from, how will you decide where to eat? Fodor's writers and editors have selected their favorite restaurants by price, cuisine, and experience in the Best Bets lists here. In the first column, Fodor's Choice properties represent the "best of the best" in every price category. You can also search by neighborhood for excellent eats—just peruse our reviews on the following pages.

Fodor's Choice ★

Adolf Wagner, $, p. 397

Doepfner's im Maingau, $$$, p. 397

Erno's Bistro, $$$$, p. 395

M Steakhouse, $$$$, p. 395

Vinum Weinkeller, $, p. 394

Weisse Lilie, $, p. 397

Zum Gemalten Haus, $, p. 399

By Price

$

Adolf Wagner, p. 397

Omonia, p. 395

Pizza Pasta Factory, p. 398

Souper, p. 391

$$

Gerbermühle, p. 399

Holbeins, p. 397

$$$

Frankfurter Botschaft, p. 391

$$$$

Erno's Bistro, p. 395

M Steakhouse, p. 395

Surf'n Turf, p. 396

Weidemann, p. 399

Zenzakan, p. 396

By Cuisine

CAFÉ

Café Laumer, $, p. 395

Café Siesmayer, $, p. 395

Metropol, $, p. 391

ECLECTIC

Grössenwahn, $, p. 397

FRENCH

Erno's Bistro, $$$$, p. 395

GERMAN

Adolf Wagner, $, p. 397

Steinernes Haus, $, p. 391

Zwölf Apostel, $, p. 394

ITALIAN

Pizza Pasta Factory, $, p. 398

SEAFOOD

La Boveda, $$, p. 395

Lobster, $$, p. 398

SPANISH

La Boveda, $$, p. 395

Weisse Lilie, $, p. 397

By Experience

APFELWEIN

Adolf Wagner, $, p. 397

Zum Gemalten Haus, $, p. 399

BEST BEER GARDEN

Gerbermühle, $$, p. 399

Weidemann, $$$$, p. 399

BRUNCH

El Pacifico, $, p. 396

Frankfurter Botschaft, $$$, p. 391

BUSINESS DINING

Embassy, $, p. 391

Erno's Bistro, $$$$, p. 395

Surf'n Turf, $$$$, p. 396

COCKTAILS

Zenzakan, $$$$, p. 396

GREAT VIEW

Frankfurter Botschaft, $$$, p. 391

QUIET LOCATION

Erno's Bistro, $$$$, p. 395

Weidemann, $$$$, p. 399

of fresh mint and rosemary. Homemade desserts are made with honey instead of refined sugar. Centrally located a few blocks from the Dom, the café has low lighting and rough-hewn wood tables; the rock 'n' roll and Motown tunes are played here at a volume low enough not to discourage quiet conversation. ⑤ *Average main: €10* ✉ *Fahrg. 3, Altstadt* ☎ *069/9203–9510* Ⓜ *Römer (U-bahn)* ✛ *F4.*

$

CAFÉ

✕ **Metropol.** Breakfast is the main attraction at this café near the Römerberg and Dom. The dining room is large, and in the warmer months there are also tables on a garden patio. In addition to the daily selection of tantalizing cakes and pastries, the menu features salads, pastas, and a few traditional German dishes. The kitchen serves until 11 pm. ⑤ *Average main: €11* ✉ *Weckmarkt 13–15, Altstadt* ☎ *069/288–287* ⊕ *www.metropolcafe. de* ▭ *No credit cards* ⊘ *Closed Mon.* Ⓜ *Römer (U-bahn)* ✛ *F4.*

$

FAST FOOD

✕ **Souper.** Hearty soups seem to be the favorite light lunch in Frankfurt these days. The best selection can be found in this place near the Hauptwache, although the bowls seem a little small for the price. The daily selection may include such creations as Thai-style coconut chicken or lentil with sausage. Eat at the counter or take your soup and sandwich to go. ⑤ *Average main: €5* ✉ *Weissadlerg. 3, Altstadt* ☎ *069/2972–4545* ⊕ *www.souper.de* ▭ *No credit cards* ⊘ *Closed Sun. No dinner* Ⓜ *Hauptwache (U-bahn and S-bahn)* ✛ *E4.*

$

GERMAN

✕ **Steinernes Haus.** At this friendly spot, diners share long wooden tables beneath traditional clothing that's been mounted on the walls. The house specialty is a raw steak brought to the table with a heated rock tablet (*Stein* is the German word for stone) for cooking it on. The beef broth is the perfect antidote to cold weather. The menu has other old German standards along with daily specials. Note that if you don't specify a *Kleines*, or small glass of beer, you'll automatically get a liter. ⑤ *Average main: €14* ✉ *Braubachstr. 35, Altstadt* ☎ *069/283–491* ⊕ *www. steinernes-haus.de* 🍴 *Reservations essential* Ⓜ *Römer (U-bahn)* ✛ *E4.*

CITY CENTER

$

ECLECTIC

✕ **Embassy.** Embassy's location near many of the city's largest banks makes it a natural for business lunches, but it's also a popular spot for socializing. This modern restaurant, bar, and lounge attracts many young professionals for dinner and drinks. The moderately priced menu of contemporary dishes includes pizzas, pastas, salads, steaks, duck, and a long list of appetizers. ⑤ *Average main: €15* ✉ *Zimmerweg 1 (corner of Mainzer Landstr.), City Center* ☎ *069/7409–0844* ⊕ *www.embassy-frankfurt.de* ⊘ *Closed weekends* Ⓜ *Taunusanlage (S-bahn)* ✛ *C3.*

$$$

ECLECTIC

✕ **Frankfurter Botschaft.** Frankfurt's Westhafen (West Harbor), once busy and commercial, has been transformed into an upscale neighborhood of apartments, a yacht club, and waterfront restaurants. One of the chicest is Frankfurter Botschaft, with a glass facade and a big terrace overlooking the Main River. Frankfurt's elite descend here for business lunches, a cocktail on the terrace at sunset, or the Sunday brunch. There is also a sandy beach area with folding chairs and umbrellas. The international food is mainly organic, and even the dinnerware is of a prizewinning design. ⑤ *Average main: €24* ✉ *Westhafenpl. 6–8, City Center* ☎ *069/2400–4899* ⊕ *www.frankfurter-botschaft.de* ⊘ *Closed Sun.* Ⓜ *Hauptbahnhof* ✛ *B6.*

9

Where to Eat and Stay in Frankfurt

Don't leave Frankfurt without sampling a tall glass of Apfelwein.

$$

MIDDLE EASTERN

✕ **L'Emir.** The atmosphere is right out of *One Thousand and One Nights* at this restaurant near the train station, with belly dancers performing every Friday and Saturday night urging patrons to join in. Those who are so inclined can retire to the lounge and smoke flavored tobacco from a water pipe. The exotic menu is largely vegetarian and heavy on garlic, olive oil, and lemon juice. The falafel is made from crushed beans and chickpeas, leeks, onions, parsley, coriander, peppermint, and more than 15 spices. ⑤ *Average main: €17* ✉ *Ramada Hotel, Weserstr. 17, City Center* ☎ *069/2400–8686* ⊕ *www.lemir.de* ⌲ *Reservations essential* Ⓜ *Hauptbahnhof* ✛ *C4.*

$

GERMAN

Fodor's Choice

★

✕ **Vinum Weinkeller.** Housed in a former wine cellar that dates from 1893 in one of the alleys off Fressgasse, Vinum specializes in regional wines, by the glass or bottle, and the burnished brickwork and low lighting adds to the charm. The wine-themed decor includes such items as glass bowls filled with wine corks. Menu choices focus on wine-friendly dishes, including cheese platters, as well as German specialties more often associated with beer, such as wursts and sauerbraten with dumplings and red cabbage. ⑤ *Average main: €15* ✉ *Kleine Hochstr. 9, Center City* ☎ *069/293–037* ⊕ *www.vinum-frankfurt.de* ⊘ *Closed Sun., Oct.–Apr. No lunch* ✛ *D3.*

$

GERMAN

✕ **Zwölf Apostel.** There are few inner-city restaurants that brew their own beer, and the Twelve Apostles is one of the pleasant exceptions. Enjoy homemade pilsners in the dimly lighted, cavernous cellar, and sample traditional international and Croatian dishes. Servings are large, prices are reasonable, and you can have a small portion at half price. ⑤ *Average main: €11* ✉ *Rosenbergerstr. 1, City Center* ☎ *069/288–668* ⊕ *www.12aposteln-frankfurt.de* Ⓜ *Konstablerwache (U-bahn and S-bahn)* ✛ *F2.*

MESSE AND WESTEND

$

CAFÉ

✕ **Café Laumer.** The ambience of an old-time Viennese café pervades this popular spot, where there's a lovely garden in summer—as well as some of the city's best freshly baked cakes year-round. It owes its literary underpinnings to Theodor Adorno, a philosopher and sociologist of the Frankfurt School who dined here frequently. The café closes at 7. ⓈAverage main: €8 ⊠ Bockenheimer Landstr. 67, Westend ☎ 069/727–912 ⊕ www.cafe-laumer.de ⊗ No dinner Ⓜ Westend (U-bahn) ♦ C2.

$

GERMAN

✕ **Café Siesmayer.** This sleek establishment is at the Palmengarten, accessible either from the botanical garden or from the street. It has a terrace where you can enjoy your coffee and cake with a splendid garden view. It's also popular for breakfast, with a full range of main courses. Note that it closes at 7. Ⓢ Average main: €14 ⊠ Siesmayerstr. 59, Westend ☎ 069/9002–9200 ⊕ www.palmengarten-gastronomie.de ⊗ No dinner Ⓜ Westend (U-bahn) ♦ B1.

$$$$

FRENCH

Fodor's Choice

★

✕ **Erno's Bistro.** This tiny, unpretentious place in a quiet Westend neighborhood seems an unlikely candidate for the best restaurant in Germany. Yet that's what one French critic called it. The bistro's specialty, fish, is often flown in from France, as are the wines. It's closed weekends, during the Christmas and Easter seasons, and during much of summer—in other words, when its patrons, well-heeled business executives, are unlikely to be in town. Ⓢ Average main: €40 ⊠ Liebigstr. 15, Westend ☎ 069/721–997 ⊕ www.ernosbistro.de ⌂ Reservations essential ⌂ Jacket required ⊗ Closed weekends and for 6 wks during Hesse's summer school vacation Ⓜ Westend (U-bahn) ♦ C2.

$$

SPANISH

✕ **La Boveda.** This quaint, somewhat expensive restaurant is inside the dimly lit basement of a Westend residential building. (Appropriate, as the name means "wine cellar.") In addition to the smaller plates of tapas, the menu features a long list of entrées. Especially interesting are the creative seafood combinations. And true to its name, La Boveda offers an extensive wine menu. Reservations are recommended on weekends. Ⓢ Average main: €18 ⊠ Feldbergstr. 10, Westend ☎ 069/723–220 ⊕ www.la-boveda.de ⊗ No lunch weekends Ⓜ Westend (U-bahn) ♦ C1.

$$$$

STEAKHOUSE

Fodor's Choice

★

✕ **M Steakhouse.** Many say the M Steakhouse serves the best steak in Germany. A set of steps leads down into the restaurant's beautifully lit outdoor patio, which is the perfect setting for a private romantic dinner. The main dining room inside is warm, welcoming, and offers an intimate setting for an unforgettable meal. The restaurant doesn't serve any seafood main courses, but why should it? The beef, imported from the U.S., doesn't disappoint. Prices are in line with the quality of meat, and the sides complement the dishes perfectly. ▮TIP➜ Be sure to make reservations, and ask for a table on the patio in nice weather. Ⓢ Average main: €30 ⊠ Feuerbachstr. 11a, Westend ☎ 069/7103–4050 ⌂ Reservations essential ⊗ Closed Sun. No lunch Sat. ♦ C3

$

GREEK

✕ **Omonia.** This cozy cellar serves the city's best Greek cuisine. If you have a big appetite, try the Omonia platter, with lamb cooked several ways and accompanied by Greek-style pasta. Vegetarians go for the *mestos sestos*, a plate of lightly breaded grilled vegetables served in a rich tomato-and-feta sauce. This family-owned place is popular, so make a reservation for one of the few tables. Ⓢ Average main: €13 ⊠ Vogtstr. 43, Westend

9

CLOSE UP

Apfelwein

Apfelwein, the local hard cider and the quintessential Frankfurt drink, is more sour than the sweet versions you may be used to. To produce Apfelwein, the juice of pressed apples is fermented for approximately eight weeks. Its alcohol content of 5%–7% makes it comparable to beer. Straight up, it is light and slightly fizzy. You can also try it carbonated with seltzer (*Sauergespritzer*), or sweetened with lemonade (*Süssgespritzer*).

Apfelwein is drunk from a lattice-patterned glass called a *Gerippte*.

When among friends, it is poured from blue stoneware pitchers called *Bembels*, which range in size from big (a liter) to enormous (4 liters and up).

Popular throughout the state of Hesse, locals drink Apfelwein with pride. The largest concentration of Frankfurt's Apfelwein establishments is in the old neighborhood of Sachsenhausen. Look for establishments with a pine wreath hanging over the door; this signifies that Apfelwein is sold.

☎ *069/593–314* ⊕ *www.restaurant-omonia.de* ⌖ *Reservations essential* �Ⓝ *No lunch weekends* Ⓜ *Holzhausenstrasse (U-bahn)* ✛ *D1.*

$$$$
STEAKHOUSE

✗ **Surf'n Turf.** This staple among businesspeople and steak connoisseurs alike is in a residential area near the Grüneburgpark. The restaurant feels intimate and warm, with dark leather, wood paneling, and small tables scattered throughout the main dining room. The beef is imported from Nebraska, and each cut of meat is presented to guests before taking their orders. The waitstaff is knowledgeable, helpful, and friendly, making this as great a place for a romantic dinner for two as for a casual business lunch. Highlights on the menu include the beer carpaccio with truffles and the yellowfin tuna tartare. Ⓢ *Average main: €30* ⊠ *Grüneburgweg 95, Westend* ☎ *069/722–122* ⊕ *www.mook-group.de/surfnturf* ⌖ *Reservations essential* Ⓝ *Closed Sun. No lunch Sat.* ✛ *C1.*

$$$$
JAPANESE

✗ **Zenzakan.** Hailed as a sort of pan-Asian supper club, this large restaurant with Buddha heads and other Asian decor has a bar scene that's just as good a reason to visit as its exceptional food, especially its sushi. Beef lovers also will find plenty to choose from, including sliced hanger steak with Japanese BBQ sauce. The equally innovative cocktails at the bar include a lemograss martini and the Balsamic Touch. Ⓢ *Average main: €30* ⊠ *Taunusanlage 15, Westend* ☎ *069/9708–6908* ⊕ *www.mook-group.de/zenzakan* ⌖ *Reservations essential* Ⓝ *Closed Sun. No lunch* ✛ *C3.*

NORDEND AND BORNHEIM

$
MEXICAN

✗ **El Pacifico.** Some of Frankfurt's best Mexican cuisine is found in this festive little place. Warm and colorful, this restaurant serves a variety of fruity margaritas and is well known for its hearty chicken-wing appetizer. The dimly lighted dining room is fairly small; reservations are recommended on weekends, including for its good Sunday brunch. Ⓢ *Average main: €14* ⊠ *Sandweg 79, Bornheim* ☎ *069/446–988* ⊕ *www.elpacifico-ffm.de* Ⓝ *No lunch* Ⓜ *Merianplatz (U-bahn)* ✛ *H2.*

$ ✕**Grössenwahn.** The Nordend is noted for its trendy establishments,
CONTEMPORARY and this corner restaurant, which is often crowded, is one of the best. The name translates as "megalomania," which says it all. The menu is creative, with German, Greek, Italian, and French elements. Reservations are a good idea. $ *Average main: €14* ✉ *Lenaustr. 97, Nordend* ☎ *069/599–356* ⊕ *www.cafe-groessenwahn.de* ☾ *No lunch* Ⓜ *Glauburgstrasse (U-bahn)* ✛ *F1.*

$ ✕**Weisse Lilie.** Come to this Bornheim favorite for the delicious selection
SPANISH of tapas, paella, and other Spanish specialties and reasonably priced
Fodor's Choice red wines. The dark interior has wooden tables brightened by fresh-
★ cut flowers and candles, making it a good spot for an intimate dinner. In summer you can dine outside, German style, at long tables. $ *Average main: €10* ✉ *Berger str. 275, Bornheim* ☎ *069/453–860* ⊕ *www. weisse-lilie.com* ⌔ *Reservations essential* ☾ *No lunch* Ⓜ *Bornheim Mitte (U-bahn)* ✛ *H1.*

SACHSENHAUSEN

$ ✕**Adolf Wagner.** With sepia-tone murals of merrymaking, this Apfelwein
GERMAN classic succeeds in being touristy and traditional all at once, and it's
Fodor's Choice a genuine favorite of local residents. The kitchen produces the same
★ hearty German dishes as other apple-cider taverns, only better. Try the schnitzel or the *Tafelspitz mit Frankfurter Grüner Sosse* (stewed beef with a sauce of green herbs), or come on Friday for fresh fish. Cider is served in large quantity in the noisy, crowded dining room. ⚠ **Warning: it serves no beer!** $ *Average main: €12* ✉ *Schweizerstr. 71, Sachsenhausen* ☎ *069/612–565* ⊕ *www.apfelwein-wagner.com* Ⓜ *Schweizer Platz (U-bahn)* ✛ *E6.*

$$$ ✕**Doepfner's im Maingau.** Chef Jörg Döpfner greets you himself and lights
GERMAN your candle at this excellent restaurant. A polished clientele is drawn
Fodor's Choice by the linen tablecloths, subdued lighting, and such nearly forgotten
★ practices as carving the meat at your table. The menu includes asparagus salad with homemade wild-boar ham, braised veal cheek with wild-garlic risotto, and some vegetarian dishes. The place also has a cellar full of rare German wines. $ *Average main: €22* ✉ *Schifferstr. 38–40, Sachsenhausen* ☎ *069/610–752* ⊕ *maingau.de/de/restaurant* ☾ *Closed Mon. No lunch Sat.; no dinner Sun.* Ⓜ *Schweizer Platz (U-bahn)* ✛ *F5.*

$ ✕**Exenberger.** In many ways this place is typical of Old Sachsenhausen:
FAST FOOD apple wine and sauerkraut are served, there's no menu, and old sayings are written on the walls. But the interior is modern and the Frankfurt specialties are a cut above the rest. As proprietor Kay Exenberger puts it, "We're nearly as fast as a fast-food restaurant, but as gemütlich as an apple-wine locale must be." You order your food at the counter or by calling ahead, and everything can be wrapped up to go. It's so popular that reservations are a good idea even at lunch. Many rave about the chocolate pudding with vanilla sauce. $ *Average main: €7* ✉ *Bruchstr. 14, Sachsenhausen* ☎ *069/6339–0790* ⊕ *www.exenberger-frankfurt.de* ▬ *No credit cards* ☾ *Closed Sun.* Ⓜ *Südbahnhof (U-bahn and S-bahn)* ✛ *F5.*

$$ ✕**Holbeins.** Portions are not large at this restaurant in the Städel museum,
ECLECTIC but selections on the international menu are creative. Choose from a variety of pastas, fish, steak, even sushi and a few traditional German

9

CLOSE UP

Riesling: Try It Dry

Germany's mild, wet climate and a wine-making tradition that dates back 2,000 years combine to produce some of the world's finest white wines.

The king of German varietals is Riesling. Grown on the banks of Germany's many rivers, most notably the Rhine, the grape produces wines of stunning variety and quality. Rieslings are noted for their strong acidity, sometimes-flowery aroma, and often mineral-tasting notes—stemming from the grape's susceptibility to influences from the soil. Riesling made its name throughout the world through sweet (*lieblich*) wines, but many Germans prefer them dry (*trocken*). Importers, especially in the United States, don't bring over many dry German Rieslings, so take the opportunity to sample some while in Frankfurt.

SIP IT HERE

The **Bockenheimer Weinkontor** (⌧ *Schlossstr. 92* ☎ *069/702–031* ⊕ *www.bockenheimer-weinkontor.de* Ⓜ *Bockenheimer Warte [U-bahn]*) is nearby the Messegelände (Exhibition Center), in the Bockenheim area. Through a courtyard and down a set of stairs, the cozy bar offers 15–20 reasonably priced local wines by the glass. The trellis-covered back garden is a treat.

For prestige wines, head to **Piccolo** (⌧ *Bornheimer Landstr. 56* ☎ *069/9441–1277* ⊕ *www.weinbar-piccolo.de* Ⓜ *Merianplatz [U-bahn]*), where the bilingual staff make solid recommendations. Try a glass from the Markus Molitor or Alexander Freimuth wineries. Along with wine, they serve a range of snacks and main courses. The space is small, so make reservations if you plan to dine here.

dishes. Holbein's changes from a casual bistro at lunch to an elegant restaurant open until midnight. ⑤ *Average main: €20* ⌧ *Holbeinstr. 1, Sachsenhausen* ☎ *069/6605–6666* ⊕ *www.holbeins.de* ⌔ *Reservations essential* ⊘ *No lunch Mon.* Ⓜ *Schweizer Platz (U-bahn)* ✛ *D5*.

$$ ✕ **Lobster.** This small restaurant is a favorite of locals and visitors alike.
SEAFOOD   The menu, dramatically different from those of its neighbors, includes mostly seafood. Oddly, lobster's not on the menu, but it does occasionally come up as a special. The fish and shellfish here are prepared in a variety of styles, but the strongest influence is French. For dessert, try the vanilla ice cream with warm raspberry sauce. Reservations are strongly recommended on weekends. ⑤ *Average main: €17* ⌧ *Wallstr. 21, Sachsenhausen* ☎ *069/612–920* ⊕ *www.lobster-weinbistrot.de* ⊘ *Closed Sun. No lunch* Ⓜ *Schweizer Platz (U-bahn)* ✛ *F5*.

$ ✕ **Pizza Pasta Factory.** This restaurant started off with a proven theory: if
ITALIAN   you offer your food cheaply enough, you can make up the difference by selling a lot of it. So between 11:30 am and 4 pm and after 10 pm, this place sells its pizzas and pastas (except lasagna) for only €3.80. There are 37 possible toppings, including some unlikely ones like pineapple, corn, and eggs. ⑤ *Average main: €5* ⌧ *Martin Luther Str. 33, Sachsenhausen* ☎ *069/6199–5004* ⊕ *www.pizzapastafactory.de* ⚏ *No credit cards* Ⓜ *Lokalbahnhof (S-bahn)* ✛ *F5*.

$ ✕ **Zum Gemalten Haus.** There aren't many classic Apfelwein locales left,
GERMAN but this is one of them. It's just as it has been since the end of the
Fodor'sChoice 19th century: walls covered with giant paintings darkened with age,
★ giant stoneware pitchers called *Bembels,* glasses that are ribbed to give
greasy hands traction, long tables that can seat 12 people, schmaltzy
music, hearty food, and, as is traditional, no beer. Try this one if
you want to truly capture the spirit of Old Sachsenhausen. $ *Aver-
age main: €7* ⊠ *Schweizerstr. 67, Sachsenhausen* ☎ *069/614–559*
⊕ *www.zumgemaltenhaus.de* ⊗ *Closed. Mon. and mid-July–early Aug.*
Ⓜ *Schweizer Platz (U-bahn)* ✛ *E6.*

OUTER FRANKFURT

$ ✕ **Arche Nova.** This sunny establishment is a feature of Frankfurt's Öko-
VEGETARIAN haus, which was built according to environmental principles (solar panels, catching rainwater, etc.). It's mainly vegetarian, with such dishes as a
vegetable platter with feta cheese or curry soup with grated coconut and
banana. Much of what's served, including some of the beer, is organic.
$ *Average main: €12* ⊠ *Kasselerstr. 1a, Bockenheim* ☎ *069/707–5859*
⊕ *www.arche-nova.de* ⊗ *No dinner Sun.* Ⓜ *Westbahnhof (S-bahn)* ✛ *A2.*

$$ ✕ **Gerbermühle.** So beautiful that it inspired works by Goethe, a frequent
GERMAN visitor, this 14th-century building is now a restaurant once again, and the
century-long-plus tradition of hiking or biking to the chestnut-tree-shaded,
riverside beer garden has returned. The garden is as nice as ever, and there's
an indoor restaurant, guest rooms, an attractive bar with the original stone
walls, burnished leather chairs, and even a bust of Goethe. An hour east-
ward down the Main's south bank, the place is so remote it is difficult to
reach with public transportation. $ *Average main: €20* ⊠ *Gerbermühlestr.
105, Oberrad* ☎ *069/6897–7790* ⊕ *www.gerbermuehle.de* ✛ *H5.*

$$$$ ✕ **Weidemann.** This half-timber farmhouse dating from the 19th century
MEDITERRANEAN is in a quiet neighborhood across the river from downtown. It's little
wonder that business executives and gourmets have discovered this
inviting place with a chestnut-tree-shaded beer garden and a glassed-in
winter garden. Customers are cordially greeted by proprietor Angelo
Vega, a Spaniard who has set out to prove to Germans that there's a
lot more to his country's cuisine than tapas and gazpacho. He has won
a steady clientele with imaginative versions of Spanish, French, Ital-
ian, and other Mediterranean dishes. $ *Average main: €28* ⊠ *Kelster-
bacher Str. 66, Niederrad* ☎ *069/675–996* ⊕ *www.weidemann-online.
de* ⊗ *Closed Sun.* Ⓜ *Odenwaldstr. (streetcar)* ✛ *C6.*

$ ✕ **Zum Rad.** Named for the huge *Rad* (wagon wheel) that serves as
GERMAN a centerpiece, this is one of the few Apfelwein taverns in Frankfurt
that makes its own apple wine, which it's been doing since 1806. It's
located in the villagelike district of Seckbach, on the northeastern edge
of the city. Outside tables are shaded by chestnut trees in an extensive
courtyard. The typically Hessian cuisine, with giant portions, includes
such dishes as *Ochsenbrust* (brisket of beef) with the ubiquitous herb
sauce. Take the U-4 subway to Seckbacher Landstrasse, then Bus No. 43
to Draisbornstrasse. $ *Average main: €10* ⊠ *Leonhardsg. 2, Seckbach*
☎ *069/479–128* ⊕ *www.zum-rad.de* ▭ *No credit cards* ⊗ *Closed Tues.
No dinner Sun. and holidays* ✛ *F1.*

9

WHERE TO STAY

Businesspeople descend on Frankfurt year-round, so most hotels in the city are frequently booked up well in advance and are expensive (though many offer significant reductions on weekends). Many hotels add as much as a 50% surcharge during trade fairs (*Messen*), of which there are about 30 a year. The majority of the larger hotels are close to the main train station, fairgrounds, and business district (Bankenviertel). The area around the station has a reputation as a red-light district, but is well policed. More atmosphere is found at smaller hotels and pensions in the suburbs; the efficient public transportation network makes them easy to reach.

Prices in the reviews are the lowest cost of a standard double room in high season. For expanded reviews, facilities, and current deals, visit Fodors.com.

Use the coordinate (✢ C3) at the end of each listing to locate a site on the corresponding map.

CITY CENTER

$$
HOTEL

⚐ **Bristol.** You'll notice that great attention is paid to making you comfortable at the Bristol, one of the nicest hotels in the neighborhood around the main train station. **Pros:** lobby bar is open 24 hours; beautiful garden patio. **Cons:** unappealing neighborhood; small rooms. ⑤ *Rooms from: €160* ✉ *Ludwigstr. 15, City Center* ☎ *069/242–390* ⊕ *www.bristol-hotel.de* 🛏 *145 rooms* � *Breakfast* Ⓜ *Hauptbahnhof (U-bahn and S-bahn)* ✢ *B4.*

$$$$
HOTEL
FAMILY
Fodor's Choice
★

⚐ **Hilton Frankfurt.** This international chain's downtown Frankfurt outpost has all the perks the business traveler wants, from secretarial services to video conferencing facilities and a hip lobby bar, Gekkos, which is definitely worth a visit. **Pros:** child-friendly facilities; indoor pool, and a large terrace overlooking a park. **Cons:** expensive; small bathrooms. ⑤ *Rooms from: €260* ✉ *Hochstr. 4, City Center* ☎ *069/133–8000* ⊕ *www.frankfurt.hilton.com* 🛏 *342 rooms* � *No meals* Ⓜ *Eschenheimer Tor (U-bahn)* ✢ *D2.*

$$
HOTEL

⚐ **Hotel Nizza.** This beautiful Victorian building close to the main train station is filled with antiques and hand-painted murals by the owner, and features a lovely roof garden with a view of the skyline. **Pros:** antique furnishings; roof garden with shrubbery and a view of the skyline; very comfortable. **Cons:** the hotel is in the Bahnhof district, which can be a bit seedy at night. ⑤ *Rooms from: €110* ✉ *Elbestr. 10, City Center* ☎ *069/242–5380* ⊕ *www.hotelnizza.de* 🛏 *26 rooms* � *Breakfast* Ⓜ *Willy-Brandt-Platz (U-bahn and S-bahn) or Hauptbahnhof (U-bahn and S-bahn)* ✢ *C4.*

$
HOTEL
Fodor's Choice
★

⚐ **Ibis Frankfurt Centrum.** The Ibis is a reliable budget hotel chain, and this location offers simple, straightforward rooms on a quiet street near the river. **Pros:** short walk from the station and museums; 24-hour bar. **Cons:** far from stores and theaters. ⑤ *Rooms from: €99* ✉ *Speicherstr. 4, City Center* ☎ *069/273–030* ⊕ *www.ibishotel.com* 🛏 *233 rooms* � *No meals* Ⓜ *Hauptbahnhof (U-bahn and S-bahn)* ✢ *B6.*

In summer, riverside bars and DJs spinning music are all part of the local scene.

$ **Leonardo.** Across the street from the main train station, this modern, sparkling hotel has its own underground garage. **Pros:** underground garage; quiet summer garden. **Cons:** on a busy street; in the red-light district. **$** *Rooms from: €59* ⊠ *Münchenerstr. 59, City Center* ☎ *069/242–320* ⊕ *www.leonardo-hotels.com* ⥂ *106 rooms* ⓘ *Breakfast* Ⓜ *Hauptbahnhof (U-bahn and S-bahn)* ✛ *C5.*

$ **Manhattan.** Get to all parts of town quickly from this centrally located hotel. **Pros:** opposite the main train station; free Wi-Fi. **Cons:** no restaurant; in the red-light district. **$** *Rooms from: €100* ⊠ *Düsseldorferstr. 10, City Center* ☎ *069/269–5970* ⊕ *www.manhattan-hotel.com* ⥂ *60 rooms* ⓘ *Breakfast* Ⓜ *Hauptbahnhof (U-bahn and S-bahn)* ✛ *B4.*

$ **Pension Aller.** Quiet, solid comforts come with a modest price and a friendly welcome at this pension near the river. **Pros:** economical; near the station. **Cons:** need to reserve well in advance. **$** *Rooms from: €49* ⊠ *Gutleutstr. 94, City Center* ☎ *069/252–596* ⊕ *www.pension-aller.de* ⥂ *10 rooms* ⓘ *Breakfast* Ⓜ *Hauptbahnhof (U-bahn and S-bahn)* ✛ *B5.*

$$$$ **Steigenberger Hotel Frankfurter Hof.** The neo-Gothic Frankfurter Hof is the first choice of visiting heads of state and business moguls, who keep coming back because of its service and luxurious rooms. **Pros:** old-fashioned elegance; burnished wood floors; fresh flowers; thick carpeting. **Cons:** expensive rates. **$** *Rooms from: €249* ⊠ *Am Kaiserplatz, City Center* ☎ *069/21502* ⊕ *www.frankfurter-hof.steigenberger.de* ⥂ *280 rooms, 41 suites* ⓘ *No meals* Ⓜ *Willy-Brandt-Platz (U-bahn)* ✛ *D4.*

HOTEL

HOTEL

B&B/INN

HOTEL
Fodor's Choice
★

BEST BETS FOR FRANKFURT LODGING

Fodor's offers a selective listing of quality lodging experiences in every price range, from the city's best budget beds to its most sophisticated luxury hotels. Here, we've compiled our top recommendations by price and experience. The very best properties—in other words, those that provide a particularly remarkable experience in their price range—are designated in the listings with the Fodor's Choice logo.

Fodor's Choice ★

Hilton Frankfurt, $$$$, p. 400
Ibis Frankfurt Centrum, $, p. 400
InterCity Hotel, $, p. 403
Roomers Hotel, $$$, p. 403
Steigenberger Hotel Frankfurter Hof, $$$$, p. 401

By Price

$

Ibis Frankfurt Centrum, p. 400
Pension Aller, p. 401

$$

Hotel Nizza, p. 400
Maritim, p. 403
Palmenhof, p. 403

$$$

Roomers Hotel, p. 403
Westin Grand, p. 403

$$$$

Hilton Frankfurt, p. 400
Steigenberger Hotel Frankfurter Hof, p. 401

By Experience

BEST ALL-NIGHT BARS

Bristol, $$, p. 400
Ibis Frankfurt Centrum, $, p. 400
Roomers Hotel, $$$, p. 403

BEST ANTIQUE FURNISHINGS

Hessischer Hof, $$$$, p. 403
Hotel Nizza, $$, p. 400

BEST FOR BUSINESS TRAVEL

Hilton Frankfurt, $$$$, p. 400
InterCity Hotel, $, p. 403

Roomers Hotel, $$$, p. 403
Wyndham Grand, $$, p. 403

BEST HOTEL BARS

Hessischer Hof, $$$$, p. 403
Steigenberger Bad Homburg, $$$, p. 414

BEST INTERIOR DESIGN

Hessischer Hof, $$$$, p. 403
Hotel Nizza, $$, p. 400
Roomers Hotel, $$$, p. 403

BEST NEAR SACHSENHAUSEN

Maingau, $, p. 404

BEST NEAR TRAIN STATION

Bristol, $$, p. 400
InterCity Hotel, $, p. 403

BEST OLD-WORLD ELEGANCE

Palmenhof, $$, p. 403
Steigenberger Hotel Frankfurter Hof, $$$$, p. 401

BEST BEDS

Villa Orange, $$, p. 404
Westin Grand, $$$, p. 403

BEST PARKING

Leonardo, $, p. 401
Maritim, $$, p. 403

BEST VIEW

Maritim, $$, p. 403

QUIETEST LOCATION

Ibis Frankfurt Centrum, $, p. 400
Villa Orange, $$, p. 404

BEST NEAR AIRPORT

Sheraton Frankfurt, $$$$, p. 404
Steigenberger Airport Hotel, $$$, p. 404

BEST NEAR FAIRGROUNDS

Hessischer Hof, $$$$, p. 403
Maritim, $$, p. 403

BEST NO-SMOKING HOTELS

Villa Orange, $$, p. 404

$$$
HOTEL
Westin Grand. Those who like downtown Frankfurt will appreciate the Westin's location, just steps from the famous Zeil shopping street, plus all the features of a high-end chain hotel, including a fitness room, spa, pool, and sauna. **Pros:** every luxury; handy to downtown. **Cons:** on a noisy street. $ *Rooms from: €199* ⊠ *Konrad Adenauer Str. 7, City Center* ☎ *069/29810* ⊕ *www.westingrandfrankfurt.com* ⌁ *371 rooms* ⃓⃝⃓ *No meals* Ⓜ *Konstablerwache (U-bahn and S-bahn)* ✛ *F3.*

$$
HOTEL
Wyndham Grand. Opened in late 2013, this newest addition to the "Mainhattan" skyline caters to business guests with free Wi-Fi, air-conditioning (unusual in German hotels), and great city views from floor-to-ceiling windows. **Pros:** central location; modern decor. **Cons:** expensive; busy lobby. $ *Rooms from: €150* ⊠ *Wilhelm-Leuschner-Str. 32/34, City Center* ☎ *69/9074–5335* ⊕ *www.wyndhamgrandfrankfurt. com* ⌁ *285 rooms, 8 suites* ⃓⃝⃓ *No meals* ✛ *C5.*

MESSE AND WESTEND

$$$$
HOTEL
Hessischer Hof. This is the choice of many businesspeople, not just for its location across from the convention center but also for the air of class that pervades its handsome interior. **Pros:** close to the convention center and public transportation; site of Jimmy's, one of the town's cult bars. **Cons:** far from the stores and theaters; lobby can be crowded; very expensive. $ *Rooms from: €350* ⊠ *Friedrich-Ebert-Anlage 40, Messe* ☎ *069/75400* ⊕ *www.hessischer-hof.de* ⌁ *110 rooms, 7 suites* ⃓⃝⃓ *No meals* Ⓜ *Messe (S-bahn)* ✛ *B3.*

$
HOTEL
Fodor's Choice
★
InterCity Hotel. If there ever was a hotel at the vortex of arrivals and departures, it's this centrally located one in an elegant Old World building across the street from the main train station. **Pros:** free passes for local transportation; discount rates for seniors. **Cons:** overlooks a cargo facility. $ *Rooms from: €90* ⊠ *Poststr. 8, Bahnhof* ☎ *069/273–910* ⊕ *www.intercityhotel.com* ⌁ *384 rooms, 2 suites* ⃓⃝⃓ *Breakfast* Ⓜ *Hauptbahnhof (U-bahn and S-bahn)* ✛ *B4.*

$$
HOTEL
Maritim. It's so close to the Messegelände (Exhibition Center) that you can reach the exhibition halls, as this top-notch business hotel puts it, "with dry feet." **Pros:** direct access to the convention center. **Cons:** fairly expensive; hectic during fairs. $ *Rooms from: €145* ⊠ *Theodor-Heuss-Allee 3, Messe* ☎ *069/75780* ⊕ *www.maritim.de* ⌁ *519 rooms, 24 suites* ⃓⃝⃓ *No meals* Ⓜ *Messe (S-bahn)* ✛ *A3.*

$$
HOTEL
Palmenhof. This luxuriously modern hotel, held in the same family for three generations, occupies a renovated art nouveau building dating from 1890. **Pros:** near the Palmengarten; less expensive than similar hotels. **Cons:** no restaurant; top floor can get very hot. $ *Rooms from: €165* ⊠ *Bockenheimer Landstr. 89–91, Westend* ☎ *069/753–0060* ⊕ *www.palmenhof.com* ⌁ *45 rooms, 37 apartments, 1 suite* ⃓⃝⃓ *Breakfast* Ⓜ *Westend (U-bahn)* ✛ *B2.*

$$$
HOTEL
Fodor's Choice
★
Roomers Hotel. This lively boutique hotel features modern and sleek designs everywhere you look. **Pros:** great-looking rooms. **Cons:** expensive; probably not the best choice for families. $ *Rooms from: €220* ⊠ *Gutleutstr. 85, Gutleutviertel* ☎ *069/271342–0* ⊕ *www.roomers.eu* ⌁ *116 rooms* ⃓⃝⃓ *No meals* ✛ *C5.*

9

NORDEND AND BORNHEIM

$$ 　⊡ **Villa Orange.** The moderately priced rooms at this bright, charm-
HOTEL　ing hotel include canopy beds and spacious bathrooms. **Pros:** centrally
located; on a quiet residential street; all rooms are smoke-free; free
Wi-Fi. **Cons:** hard beds. Ⓢ *Rooms from: €155* ✉ *Hebelstr. 1, Nordend*
☏ *069/405–840* ⊕ *www.villa-orange.de* ⤵ *38 rooms* ⦿| *Breakfast*
Ⓜ *Musterschule (U-bahn)* ✛ *F1.*

SACHSENHAUSEN

$ 　⊡ **Maingau.** This pleasant hotel in the middle of the lively Sachsenhau-
HOTEL　sen quarter has rooms that are modest but comfortable; the nightly rate
includes a substantial breakfast buffet. **Pros:** handy to nightlife; fantastic
restaurant. **Cons:** on a busy street. Ⓢ *Rooms from: €95* ✉ *Schiffer-
str. 38–40, Sachsenhausen* ☏ *069/609–140* ⊕ *www.maingau.de* ⤵ *78
rooms* ⦿| *Breakfast* Ⓜ *Schweizer Platz (U-bahn)* ✛ *F5.*

OUTER FRANKFURT

$$ 　⊡ **Falk Hotel.** In the heart of Bockenheim and near numerous cafés, bars,
HOTEL　and shops, this hotel is a good deal. **Pros:** fairly low rates. **Cons:** well
outside the city center; small rooms; no restaurant. Ⓢ *Rooms from:
€115* ✉ *Falkstr. 38A, Bockenheim* ☏ *069/7191–8870* ⊕ *www.hotel-
falk.de* ⤵ *29 rooms* ⦿| *Breakfast* Ⓜ *Leipzigerstrasse (U-bahn)* ✛ *A1.*

$$$$ ⊡ **Sheraton Frankfurt.** This huge hotel is connected to one of Frankfurt
HOTEL　Airport's terminals. **Pros:** handy to the airport and the autobahn. **Cons:**
far from the city center; long walk to the elevator; expensive. Ⓢ *Rooms
from: €559* ✉ *Hugo-Eckener-Ring 15, Flughafen Terminal 1, Airport*
☏ *069/69770* ⊕ *www.sheraton.com/frankfurt* ⤵ *1,008 rooms, 28 suites*
⦿| *Breakfast* Ⓜ *Flughafen (S-bahn)* ✛ *A6.*

$$$ 　⊡ **Steigenberger Airport Hotel.** The sylvan beauty of this skyscraper hotel
HOTEL　is surprising, considering that it's a half-mile from the airport and con-
nected to it by a steady stream of shuttle buses. **Pros:** near the airport;
forest location. **Cons:** restaurants are expensive; far from downtown.
Ⓢ *Rooms from: €200* ✉ *Unterschweinstiege 16, Airport* ☏ *069/69750*
⊕ *www.steigenberger.com/en/Frankfurt_Airport* ⤵ *550 rooms, 20
suites* ⦿| *No meals* Ⓜ *Flughafen (S-bahn)* ✛ *A6.*

NIGHTLIFE AND THE ARTS

THE ARTS

The Städtische Bühnen—municipal theaters, including the city's opera
company—are the prime venues for Frankfurt's cultural events. The
city has what is probably the most lavish theater in the country, the
Alte Oper, a magnificently ornate 19th-century opera house that's now
a multipurpose hall for pop and classical concerts, and dances. (These
days operas are presented at the Städtische Bühnen.)

Best Tickets. Theater tickets can be purchased from Best Tickets downtown in the Zeilgalerie. ✉ *Zeil 112–114, City Center* ☎ *069/9139–7621* ⊕ *www.journal-ticketshop.de* ⊗ *Mon.–Sat. 10–8.*

Frankfurt Ticket. Theater, concert, and sports event tickets are all available. ✉ *Hauptwache Passage, City Center* ☎ *069/134–0400* ⊕ *www. frankfurtticket.de.*

BALLET, CONCERTS, AND OPERA

Alte Oper. The most glamorous venue for classical-music concerts is the Alte Oper, one of the most beatuful buildings in Frankfurt. Tickets to performances can range from €20 to nearly €150. ✉ *Opernpl., City Center* ⊕ *www.alteoper.de* ⊗ *Weekdays 10–2.*

Bockenheimer Depot. Frankfurt's ballet company performs in the Bockenheimer Depot, a former trolley barn also used for other theatrical performances and music events. ✉ *Carlo-Schmidt-Pl. 1, Bockenheim.*

Festhalle. The Festhalle, on the city's fairgrounds, is the scene of many rock concerts, horse shows, ice shows, sporting events, and other large-scale spectaculars. Tickets are available through Frankfurt Ticket. ✉ *Ludwig-Erhard-Anlage 1, Messe* ☎ *069/92 00 92–13* ⊕ *festhalle. messenfrankfurt.de.*

Frankfurt Opera. Widely regarded as one of the best in Europe, the Frankfurt Opera is known for its dramatic artistry. Richard Wagner and Richard Strauss both oversaw their own productions for the company. ✉ *Städtische Bühnen, Untermainanlage 11, City Center* ☎ *069/2124– 9494* ⊕ *www.oper-frankfurt.de.*

Kammermusiksaal. The city is the home of the Radio-Sinfonie-Orchester Frankfurt, part of Hessischer Rundfunk. Considered one of Europe's best orchestras, it performs regularly in the 850-seat Kammermusiksaal, part of that broadcasting operation's campuslike facilities. ✉ *Bertramstr. 8, Dornbusch* ☎ *069/155–2000.*

THEATER

Theatrical productions in Frankfurt are usually in German, except for those at the English Theater.

Die Schmiere. For a zany theatrical experience, try Die Schmiere, which offers trenchant cabaret-style satire and also disarmingly calls itself "the worst theater in the world." The theater is closed in summer for a "creative break." ✉ *Seckbächerg. 4, City Center* ☎ *069/281–066* ⊕ *www. die-schmiere.de.*

English Theatre. For English-language productions, try the English Theater, continental Europe's largest English-speaking theater, which offers an array of musicals, thrillers, dramas, and comedy with British or American casts. ✉ *Gallusanlage 7, City Center* ☎ *069/2423–1620* ⊕ *www.English-theatre.org.*

Internationales Theater Frankfurt. This theater bills itself as presenting "the art of the world on the Main." It also has regular performances in English, as well as in German, French, Spanish, Italian, Romanian, and Russian. ✉ *Hanauer Landstr. 7, Ostend* ☎ *069/499–0980* ⊕ *www. internationales-theater.de.*

The elegant illumination of the Alte Oper (Old Opera House) and fountain make for magical nighttime viewing.

Künstlerhaus Mousonturm. This cultural center hosts a regular series of concerts of all kinds, as well as plays, dance performances, and exhibits. ✉ *Waldschmidtstr. 4, Nordend* ☎ *069/4058–9520* ⊕ *www. mousonturm.de.*

Schauspielhaus. The municipally owned Schauspielhaus has a repertoire that includes works by Sophocles, Goethe, Shakespeare, Brecht, and Beckett, along with more contemporary plays. ✉ *Willy-Brandt-Pl., Neue Mainzer Straße 17, City Center* ☎ *069/2124–9494* ⊕ *www. schauspielfrankfurt.de.*

NIGHTLIFE

Most bars close between 2 am and 4 am. Nightclubs typically charge entrance fees ranging from €5 to €20. In addition, some trendy places, such as King Kamehameha, enforce dress codes—usually no jeans, sneakers, shorts or khaki pants admitted.

Sachsenhausen (Frankfurt's "Left Bank") is a good place for bars, clubs, and traditional Apfelwein taverns. The fashionable Nordend has an almost equal number of bars and clubs but fewer tourists. Frankfurt was a real pioneer in the German jazz scene, and also has done much for the development of techno music. Jazz musicians make the rounds from smoky backstreet cafés all the way to the Old Opera House, and the local broadcaster Hessischer Rundfunk sponsors the German Jazz Festival in fall. The Frankfurter Jazzkeller has been the most noted venue for German jazz fans for decades.

CITY CENTER

BARS

EuroDeli. Because this bar is near many of the city's major banks, its happy hour is weekdays from 5 to 7. There's a DJ on Tuesday. ⊠ *Neue Mainzerstr. 60–66, City Center* ☎ *069/2980–1950* ⊕ *www.eurodeli.de* ⊗ *Closed weekends and holidays.*

Gibson Club. This nightclub in the heart of the Zeil attracts a mostly young crowd with its live music performances by international musicians. It's open Thursday from 8 pm and Friday and Saturday from 11 pm. ⊠ *Zeil 85–93, City Center* ☎ *069/9494–7770* ⊕ *www.gibson-club.de.*

DANCE AND NIGHTCLUBS

Odeon. The type of crowd at Odeon depends on the night. The large club hosts student nights on Thursday, a "27 Up Club" on Friday (exclusively for guests 27 or older), disco nights on Saturday, as well as "Black Mondays"—a night of soul, hip-hop, and R&B. It's housed in a beautiful white building that looks like a museum. ⊠ *Seilerstr. 34, City Center* ☎ *069/285–055* ⊕ *www.theodeon.de.*

Tigerpalast. There's not much that doesn't take place at Frankfurt's international variety theater, the Tigerpalast. Guests are entertained by international cabaret performers and the Palast's own variety orchestra. There's an excellent French restaurant that has been awarded a Michelin star, and the cozy Palastbar, under the basement arches, looks like an American bar from the 1920s. Despite pricey show tickets, shows often sell out, so book tickets as far in advance as possible. It's closed Monday. ⊠ *Heiligkreuzg. 16–20, City Center* ☎ *069/9200220* ⊕ *www.tigerpalast.de.*

JAZZ

Der Frankfurter Jazzkeller. The oldest jazz cellar in Germany, Der Frankfurter Jazzkeller was founded by legendary trumpeter Carlo Bohländer. The club, which once hosted such luminaries as Louis Armstrong and Ella Fitzgerald, now offers hot, modern jazz, at a cover of €5 to €25. There are jam sessions on Wednesday and "Latin-funky" dances on Friday. It's closed Sunday to Tuesday. ⊠ *Kleine Bockenheimerstr. 18, City Center* ☎ *069/284–927* ⊕ *www.facebook.com/jazzkeller.frankfurt.*

Zoom. Sinkkasten, a Frankfurt musical institution, was renamed Zoom in 2013. By any name it is a class act—a great place for blues, jazz, pop, and rock, with live performances nightly, often up-and-coming ones. It's open from 9 pm to 1 am every day but Monday. ⊠ *Brönnerstr. 5, City Center* ☎ *069/280–385* ⊕ *www.zoomfrankfurt.de.*

OSTEND

Jazzlokal Mampf. With posters of Chairman Mao on the walls, time seems to have stood still at the Jazzlokal Mampf. It looks straight out of the 1970s, but with live music to match, many don't think that's so bad. Since it opens at 6 pm, there's a lively after work crowd on weekdays. Closed Mondays. ⊠ *Sandweg 64, Ostend* ☎ *069/448–674* ⊕ *www.mampf-jazz.de.*

Beer Bitte

The lager style that most of the world has come to know as "beer" originated in Germany. However, Germans don't just produce one beverage called beer; they brew more than 5,000 varieties in about 1,300 breweries. The hallmark of the country's dedication to beer is the Purity Law, *das Reinheitsgebot,* unchanged since Duke Wilhelm IV introduced it in Bavaria in 1516. The law decrees that only malted barley, hops, yeast, and water may be used to make beer, except for the specialty *Weiss* or *Weizenbier* (wheat beers). Although the law has been repealed, many breweries continue to follow its precepts.

The beer preferred in most of Germany is *Pils* (Pilsner), which has a rich yellow hue, hoppy flavor, and an alcohol content of about 5%. Frankfurt's local Pils brands are Binding and Henninger, but Licher, from the village of Lich nearby, is especially well balanced and crisp. The area is also home to Schöfferhofer, which brews Germany's number-two style, *Hefeweizen* (wheat beer), which is cloudy and yeasty. Light, or *helles,* is sweeter than *dunkel,* or dark.

Few German bars offer more than one type of Pils or Weizen on tap, so you'll need to hit a few bars to sample a good variety. Not a bad proposition.

QUAFF IT HERE
Begin a night at **Klosterhof** (✉ *Weissfrauenstr. 3* ☎ *069/9139–9000* ⊕ *www.klosterhof-frankfurt. de* Ⓜ *Willy-Brandt-Platz [U-bahn]*), a traditional restaurant and beer garden in the City Center, where you can try Hessian favorites like *Handkäs mit Musik* (literally, hand cheese with music, a strong soft cheese served with chopped onions, oil, and vinegar), as well as their custom-brewed *Naturtrüb,* an unfiltered (and thus naturally cloudy) lager.

Eckhaus (✉ *Bornheimer Landstr. 45* ☎ *069/491–197* Ⓜ *Merianplatz [U-bahn]*) is the perfect neighborhood bar to down a cold Binding or two. The restaurant, in a great location just off the Berger Strasse strip in leafy Nordend, offers a solidly executed menu of standards like schnitzel and roast chicken, along with a few creative specials.

King Kamehameha Club. One of Frankfurt's biggest clubs occupies several floors in the Japan Tower; there's a concert area and DJs who spin everything from soul to salsa. Get there early if you want the free buffet (6–8 pm), and stay until the wee hours if your ears can last that long. Admission is free Monday through Wednesday; other days it ranges from €3 to €5. ✉ *Hanauer Landstr. 192, Ostend* ☎ *069/4800–9610* ⊕ *www.king-kamehameha.de.*

HAUSEN

Brotfabrik. An important address for jazz, rock, and disco, the "Bread Factory" really is set in a former bakery. The building houses two stages, a concert hall, two restaurants, three not-for-profit projects, an ad agency, and a gallery. ✉ *Bachmannstr. 2–4, Hausen* ☎ *069/2479–0800* ⊕ *www.brotfabrik.info.*

MESSE AND WESTEND

Fox and Hound. Frankfurt is teeming with Irish pubs, but there is an occasional English pub, too. A good example is the Fox and Hound. Its patrons, mainly British, come to watch the latest football (soccer to Americans), rugby, and cricket matches. Enjoy the authentic British pub food; 35 whiskies, bitters and stouts; and the basket of chips. ✉ *Niedenau 2, Westend* ☎ *069/9720–2009* ⏰ *10 am–1 am.*

Jimmy's Bar. Jimmy's Bar, the meeting place of business executives since 1951, is classy and expensive—just like the hotel it's in. There is live piano music, mostly jazz, and the kitchen is open every evening from 10 pm to 3 am. ▪TIP➜ **You must ring the doorbell to get in, although regulars have their own keys.** ✉ *Hessischer Hof, Friedrich-Ebert-Anlage 40, Messe* ☎ *069/7540–2461* ⊕ *www.hessischer-hof.de/en/hotel-bar-frankfurt* ⏰ *Daily 8 pm–4 am.*

SACHSENHAUSEN

Balalaika. The spacious Balalaika has an intimate feel, as candles are just about the only source of light. The proprietor is Anita Honis, an American singer from Harlem, who likes to get out her acoustic guitar and perform on occasion. Everyone is invited to sing or play on the piano, which is set up for impromptu and scheduled performances. ✉ *Schifferstr. 3, Sachsenhausen* ☎ *069/612–226* ⏰ *Closed Sun.*

Stereobar. University students and young professionals frequent this bar in a cellar beneath a narrow Sachsenhausen alleyway. DJs usually spin the music, although there are occasional live acts. There's a tiny dance floor if you feel like showing off your moves. ✉ *Abstgässchen 7, Sachsenhausen* ☎ *069/617–116* ⊕ *www.stereobar.de.*

SPORTS AND THE OUTDOORS

9

Despite an ever-growing number of skyscrapers, Frankfurt is full of parks and other green oases where you can enjoy wide-open spaces.

Stadtwald. South of the city lies Sachsenhausen, the huge, 4,000-acre Stadtwald (city forest) makes Frankfurt one of Germany's greenest metropoles. ▪TIP➜ **The forest has innumerable paths and trails, bird sanctuaries, impressive sports stadiums, and a good restaurant.** The Oberschweinstiege stop on streetcar Line No. 14 is right in the middle of the park. ✉ *Sachsenhausen.*

BICYCLING

There are numerous biking paths within the city limits. The Stadtwald in the southern part of the city is crisscrossed with well-tended paths that are nice and flat. The city's riverbanks are, for the most part, lined with paths open to bikers. These are not only on both sides of the Main but also on the banks of the little Nidda River, which flows through Heddernheim, Eschersheim, Hausen, and Rödelheim before joining the Main at Höchst. Some bikers also like the Taunus Hills, but note that word "Hills."

SHOPPING

Frankfurt, and the rest of Germany, no longer has restrictive laws that kept stores closed evenings and Saturday afternoons, the very times working people might want to shop. Stores now can stay open until 10 pm, but pretty much everything is still closed on Sunday except for restaurants and bakeries.

The tree-shaded pedestrian zone of the **Zeil** is said to be one of the richest shopping strips in Germany. The section between Hauptwache and Konstablerwache famous for its incredible variety of department and specialty stores. But there's much more to downtown shopping. The subway station below the Hauptwache also doubles as a vast underground mall, albeit a rather droll one. West of the Hauptwache are two parallel streets highly regarded by shoppers. One is the luxurious **Goethestrasse,** lined with trendy boutiques, art galleries, jewelry stores, and antiques shops. The other is **Grosse Bockenheimer Strasse,** better known as the Fressgass ("Pig-Out Alley"), an extension of the Zeil that's lined with cafés, restaurants, and pricey food shops.

One gift that's typical of the city is the Apfelwein. You can get a bottle of it at any grocery store, but more enduring souvenirs would be the Bembel pottery pitchers and ribbed glasses that are an equal part of the Apfelwein tradition. Then there is the sausage. You can get the "original hot dog" in cans or vacuum-packed at any grocery store.

CITY CENTER

Café Mozart. Reminiscent of a traditional coffeehouse, this café offers all types of sweets and pastries, along with breakfast, lunch, and dinner. Open daily, it's on a quiet, tucked-away street that's steps from the main shopping area. ✉ *Töngesg. 23, City Center* ☎ *069/291–954* ⊕ *www.cafemozart-frankfurt.de/english.*

Galeria Kaufhof. One of Germany's biggest and most popular department stores, the Galeria Kaufhof carries clothing, jewelry, sports equipment, cosmetics, toys, and more. The Frankfurt branch has a food hall on the bottom floor; the restaurant on the top floor has great city views. ✉ *Zeil 116–126, City Center* ☎ *069/21910.*

Karstadt. One of Germany's biggest department store chains, Karstadt is known for both its brand name designer offerings and its splendid food and drink department, with plenty of opportunity to try the offerings. ✉ *Zeil 90, City Center* ☎ *069/929–050* ⊕ *www.karstadt.de/jsp/ filialen/frankfurt-zeil.jsp.*

Kleinmarkthalle. The Kleinmarkthalle is a treasure trove of stands selling spices, herbs, teas, exotic fruits, cut flowers, and live fish flown in from the Atlantic. Plus, it offers all kinds of snacks in case you need a break while shopping. ✉ *Haseng. 5–7, City Center* ☎ *069/2123–3696* ☉ *Weekdays 8–6, Sat. 8–4.*

Peek & Cloppenburg. At this huge branch of the clothing chain, men and women can find what they need for the office, gym, and nightclub. Prices range from easily affordable to sky-high for certain designer labels. ✉ *Zeil 71–75, City Center* ☎ *069/298–950.*

The Eiserner Steg (Iron Bridge) was Europe's very first suspension bridge, and a walk across promises great photo ops of Frankfurt's skyline.

Pfüller Modehaus. In addition to being a major source for kids' designer clothing, Pfüller Modehaus also carries a wide range of choices on three floors for women, from classic to trendy. You're likely to find items and labels you've never seen before. ✉ *Goethestr. 12, City Center* ☎ *069/1337–8070.*

Schillerpassage. The Schillerpassage shopping area is lined with men's and women's fashion boutiques. ✉ *Rahmhofstr. 2, City Center.*

Weinhandlung Dr. Teufel. Weinhandlung Dr. Teufel is well known for its wide selection of regional wines, including rare vintages costing three figures or more. There are also chocolate and cigars, a complete line of glasses, carafes, corkscrews, and other accessories, and books on all aspects of viticulture. The store also has a location in the Westend. ✉ *Kleiner Hirschgraben 4, City Center* ☎ *069/448989* ⊕ *www. weinteufel.de/aktuelles.htm.*

Zeilgallerie. The moderately priced Zeilgallerie has nearly 60 shops and an outstanding view from the rooftop terrace. ✉ *Zeil 112–114, City Center* ⊙ *Mon.–Sat. 10–8.*

WESTEND

Café Laumer. The pastry shop at Café Laumer has local delicacies such as *Bethmännchen und Brenten* (marzipan cookies) and *Frankfurter Kranz* (a kind of creamy cake). It's open daily. ✉ *Bockenheimer Landstr. 67, Westend* ☎ *069/727–912* ⊕ *www.cafelaumer.de.*

SACHSENHAUSEN

Sachsenhausen's weekend **flea market** is on Saturday from 9 to 2 on the riverbank between Dürerstrasse and the Eiserner Steg. Purveyors of the cheap have taken over, and there's lots of discussion as to whether it is a good use for the elegant, museum-lined riverbank. ▥ TIP→ Get there early for the bargains, as the better-quality stuff gets snapped up quickly. Shopping success or no, the market can be fun for browsing.

SIDE TRIPS FROM FRANKFURT

Destinations reachable by the local transportation system include Höchst and the Taunus Hills, which include Bad Homburg and Kronberg. Just to the northwest and west of Frankfurt, the Taunus Hills are an area of mixed pine and hardwood forest, medieval castles, and photogenic towns many Frankfurters regard as their own backyard. It's home to Frankfurt's wealthy bankers and business executives, and on weekends you can see them enjoying their playground: hiking through the hills, climbing the Grosse Feldberg, taking the waters at Bad Homburg's health-enhancing mineral springs, or just lazing in elegant stretches of parkland.

BAD HOMBURG

12 km (7 miles) north of Frankfurt.

Emperor Wilhelm II, the infamous "Kaiser" of World War I, spent a month each year at Bad Homburg, the principal city of the Taunus Hills. Another frequent visitor to Bad Homburg was Britain's Prince of Wales, later King Edward VII, who made the name *Homburg* world famous by associating it with a hat.

GETTING HERE AND AROUND

Bad Homburg is reached easily by the S-bahn from Hauptwache, the main station, and other points in downtown Frankfurt. The S5 goes to Bad Homburg. There's also a Taunusbahn (from the main station only) that stops in Bad Homburg and then continues into the far Taunus, including the Römerkastell-Saalburg and Wehrheim, with bus connections to Hessenpark. Bad Homburg is about a 30- to 45-minute drive north of Frankfurt on A-5.

The Bad Homburg tourist office is open until 6:30 pm weekdays, 2 pm Saturday, and is closed Sunday.

ESSENTIALS

Visitor Information Kur- und Kongress GmbH Bad Homburg ⊠ *Louisenstr. 58* ☎ *06172/178–110* ⊕ *www.bad-homburg.de.*

EXPLORING

Casino Bad Homburg. This casino boasts with some justice that it is the "Mother of Monte Carlo." The first casino in Bad Homburg, and one of the first in the world, was established in 1841, but closed in 1866 because Prussian law forbade gambling. Proprietor François Blanc then established the famous Monte Carlo casino on the French Riviera, and

For a total shopping blitz, head to the Zeil, where you'll find some of Germany's most upscale shops.

the Bad Homburg casino wasn't reopened until 1949. A bus from south side of Frankfurt's Hauptbahnhof leaves every 60 to 90 minutes between 2 pm and 1 am. Buses back to Frankfurt run every 1–2 hours from 4:30 pm to 4 am. The €6.10 fare will be refunded after the casino's full entry fee has been deducted. You must show a passport or other identification to gain admission. ✉ *Kisseleffstr. 35* ☎ *06172/17010* ✉ *Slot-machine area free, gaming area €2.50* ⊙ *Slot machines noon–4 am, gaming area 2:30 pm–3 am (until 4 am Thurs.–Sat.).*

FAMILY **Freilichtmuseum Hessenpark.** About an hour's walk through the woods along a well-marked path from the Römerkastell-Saalburg is an open-air museum at Hessenpark, near Neu-Anspach. The museum presents a clear picture of the world in which 18th- and 19th-century Hessians lived, using 135 acres of rebuilt villages with houses, schools, and farms typical of the time. The park, 15 km (9 miles) outside Bad Homburg in the direction of Usingen, can also be reached by public transportation. Take the Taunusbahn from the Frankfurt main station to Wehrheim; then transfer to Bus No. 514. ✉ *Laubweg 5, Neu-Anspach* ☎ *06081/5880* ⊕ *www.hessenpark.de* ✉ *€6* ⊙ *Mar.–Oct., daily 9–6; Nov., daily 10–5.*

Kurpark (*Spa*). Bad Homburg's greatest attraction has been the Kurpark, in the heart of the Old Town, with more than 31 fountains. Romans first used the springs, which were rediscovered and made famous in the 19th century. In the park you'll find not only the popular, highly salty Elisabethenbrunnen spring, but also a Thai temple and a Russian chapel, mementos left by royal guests—King Chulalongkorn of Siam and Czar Nicholas II.

FAMILY **Römerkastell-Saalburg** (*Saalburg Roman Fort*). The remains of a Roman fortress built in AD 120, the Römerkastell-Saalburg could accommodate a cohort (500 men) and was part of the fortifications along the Limes Wall, which ran from the Danube to the Rhine and was meant to protect the Roman Empire from barbarian invasion. The fort was restored more than a century ago. The site, which includes a museum of Roman artifacts, is 6½ km (4 miles) north of Bad Homburg on Route 456 in the direction of Usingen. It's accessible by direct bus service. ⊠ *Archäologischer Park, Saalburg 1* 🕿 *06175/93740* ⊕ *www.saalburgmuseum.de* 🎫 *€5* ⊗ *Mar.–Oct., daily 9–6; Nov.–Feb., Tues.–Sun. 9–4.*

Schloss Homburg. The most historically noteworthy sight in Bad Homburg is the 17th-century Schloss, where the Kaiser stayed when he was in town. The state apartments are exquisitely furnished, and the Spiegelkabinett (Hall of Mirrors) is especially worthy of a visit. In the surrounding park look for two cedars from Lebanon, both now about 200 years old. ⊠ *Schloß, Bad Homburg vor der Höhe* 🕿 *06172/926–2148* ⊕ *www.schloss-homburg.de* 🎫 *€5* ⊗ *Tues.–Sun. 10–5.*

WHERE TO EAT AND STAY

$$$ 🛏 **Steigenberger Bad Homburg.** This hotel, which opened in 1883, HOTEL was renowned for catering to Europe's royalty in its pre–World War I heyday, and it's still good at pleasing a well-heeled clientele. **Pros:** old-world class; handy to the Kurpark. **Cons:** expensive; parking is difficult. 💲 *Rooms from: €180* ⊠ *Kaiser-Friedrich-Promenade 69–75* 🕿 *06172/1810* ⊕ *www.bad-homburg.steigenberger.de* ⌁ *152 rooms, 17 suites* ⫟ *No meals.*

THE PFALZ AND RHINE TERRACE

WELCOME TO THE PFALZ AND RHINE TERRACE

TOP REASONS TO GO

★ **Wine:** German Rieslings are some of the most versatile white wines in the world—on their own or with food. If you've only had the sweeter style, then the rest may be a revelation.

★ **Festivals:** Wine is a great excuse for merrymaking, and there are scores of wine festivals throughout the region. The biggest and best is in the town of Bad Dürkheim, which features a wine barrel the size of a building.

★ **Pfälzerwald:** The Palatinate Forest is a paradise for hiking and cycling. Even a brief walk under the beautiful pine and chestnut trees is relaxing and refreshing.

★ **Castles:** Burg Trifels and Schloss Villa Ludwigshöhe are a contrast in style, inside and out. Both are wonderful settings for concerts.

★ **Cathedrals:** The cathedrals in Speyer, Worms, and Mainz are the finest examples of grand-scale Rhenish Romanesque architecture in Germany.

1 The German Wine Road. The picturesque *Deutsche Weinstrasse* (German Wine Road) weaves through the valleys and among the lower slopes of the Haardt Mountains. Along its length is a string of pretty half-timber wine-producing villages, each more inviting than the last.

2 The Rhine Terrace. Rheinhessen, or "Rhine Terrace," is a broad fertile river valley, where grapes are but one of many crops. Here the medieval cities of Mainz, Worms, and Speyer all bear testament to the great power and wealth brought by the important trading route created by the mighty Rhine itself.

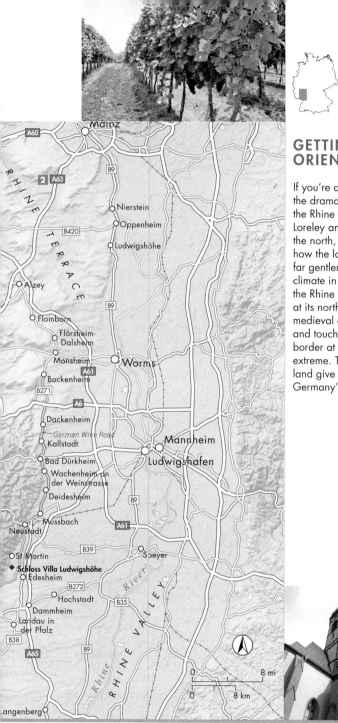

A60
Mainz
2 A63
B9
R H I N E   T E R R A C E
Nierstein
Oppenheim
B420
Ludwigshöhe
B9
Alzey
Flomborn
Flörsheim-Dalsheim
Monsheim
Worms
A61
Bockenheim
B271
A6
Dackenheim
German Wine Road
Kallstadt
Bad Dürkheim
Mannheim
Wachenheim an der Weinstrasse
Ludwigshafen
Deidesheim
B9
Mussbach
Neustadt
A61
St Martin
B39
Speyer
◆ Schloss Villa Ludwigshöhe
Edesheim
B272
Hochstadt
B35
Dammheim
Landau in der Pfalz
B38
A65
B9
Langenberg

Rhine River

R H I N E   V A L L E Y

0   8 mi
0   8 km

10

GETTING ORIENTED

If you're arriving from the dramatic stretch of the Rhine centered on the Loreley and Koblenz to the north, you'll notice how the landscape here is far gentler. So, too, is the climate in this region of the Rhine Valley, guarded at its northern edge by the medieval city of Mainz and touching the French border at its southern extreme. This helps the land give birth to some of Germany's greatest wines.

DRIVING THE GERMAN WINE ROAD

Due to its sunny skies, warm weather, and fertile fields, many Germans consider the Pfalz their version of Tuscany. In addition to vineyards, the mild climate fosters fig, lemon, and chestnut trees.

(above) Autumn is a gorgeous time of year to tour the region. (upper right) Vineyards in Pfalz (lower right) Winery-hopping by bike is a nice alternative to driving.

The best time for a drive is early spring, when the path is awash in pink and white almond blossoms, or early fall, when you can sample sweet young wines. The Deutsche Weinstrasse begins in Schweigen-Rechtenbach and runs alongside the *Bundesstrassen* (highways) B-38 and B-271. Yellow signs depicting a cluster of grapes guide visitors along a picturesque path of villages and vineyards north, to the end of the route at the "House of the German Wine Road" in Bockenheim. The entire road is just a little more than 50 miles and can be driven in a few hours. However, it can easily turn into a two-day drive if you stop to sample the local wines. Get an early start and allow yourself to get lost in the charming villages along the way, leaving ample time for a hike or two (or perhaps a bike ride) among the beautiful vines.

—Updated by Liz Humphreys

DRINKING AND DRIVING

Germany has strict laws against driving (and biking) under the influence, so if you're planning to take advantage of the numerous *Weinprobe* (wine samples) offered along the route, make sure you have a designated driver. Alternatively, just let the vintner know what you like, and he can help you pick a bottle to enjoy when you reach your final destination.

The entire route is scenic, but if you're short on time, the stretch between Gleiszellen and Bad Dürkheim is particularly rich with castles, vineyards, and vistas. If you opt to start at Schweigen-Rechtenbach on the French border, the southern-most point of the route, you can begin by snapping a photo in front of the *Deutsches Weintor* (German Wine Gate). Otherwise, pick up the route in **Gleiszellen,** where you should stop to savor a glass of the hard-to-find Muskateller wine, with its distinctly sweet aroma. **Weinstube Wissing** has a homey atmosphere and offers Muskateller in red, yellow, and rosé varieties.

Depending on the time of year, your trip may coincide with a local wine or produce festival—as you drive, keep your eyes peeled for signs advertising "Weinfest." Summer is the best time for festivals, but there are roadside stands with seasonal produce year-round. When you arrive in Edenko-ben, stretch your legs at the Pompeian-style palace **Schloss Villa Ludwigshöhe,** then continue uphill via the Rietburg-bahn chairlift to the vantage point at the **Rietburg Castle Ruins.** Evening is the perfect time for the journey, when the pathway is lit by Chinese lanterns (the chairlift is open until midnight in summer). If you plan to split the drive into two days, the neighboring village of **St. Martin** is an ideal place to overnight because it's about halfway through the drive. Spend the next morning exploring the winding streets of this charming village on foot.

Continue north, driving leisurely through the vineyards of **Deidesheim** and **Forst,** and stopping off at the imposing ruins of **Burgruine Hardenburg** (Hardenburg Fortress). End your day with a visit to the world's biggest wine barrel in **Bad Dürkheim.**

QUICK BITES

Alter Kastanienhof. For a delicious rendition of the regional specialty *Saumagen* (meat and potatoes cooked in a sow's stomach), stop here. The restaurant has a charming interior courtyard and sunny south-facing terrace. ⊠ *Theresienstr. 79, Rhodt u. Rietburg* ☎ *06323/81752* ⊟ *No credit cards.*

Consulat des Weines. Oenophiles won't want to miss this Vinothek in the charming village of St. Martin. It offers more than 80 varieties of wine from its vineyards in St. Martin and nearby Edenkoben (cash only). There's also a hotel and restaurant on-site. ⊠ *Maikam-merer Str. 44, St. Martin* ☎ *06323/8040* ⊕ *www. schneider-pfalz.de* ⊟ *No credit cards* ⊘ *Closed Sun. after noon.*

Wochenmarkt. Head to this farmers' market on Saturday for flow-ers, bread, wine, meats, cheeses, and vinegars. ⊠ *Am Obermarkt, Bad Dürkheim* ☎ *06323/8040* ⊕ *www.wochenmarkt-duerkheim.de* ⊘ *Sat. 7 am–1 pm.*

10

Updated by
Liz Humphreys

Pfalz and wine go hand in hand. This region of vineyards and picturesque villages is the home of the German Wine Road and the country's greatest wine festival at Bad Dürkheim. Six of Germany's 13 wine-growing regions are in the area.

The Pfalz has a mild, sunny climate, and that seems to affect the mood here, too. Vines carpet the foothills of the thickly forested Haardt Mountains, an extension of the Alsatian Vosges. The Pfälzerwald (Palatinate Forest) with its pine and chestnut trees is the region's other natural attraction. Hiking and cycling trails lead through the vineyards, the woods, and up to castles on the heights.

The border between the Pfalz and Rheinhessen is invisible, but a few miles after crossing it you begin to get a sense of Rheinhessen's character. It's a region of gentle, rolling hills and expansive farmland, where grapes are but one of many crops; vineyards are often scattered miles apart. The slopes overlooking the Rhine between Worms and Mainz—the so-called Rhine Terrace—are a notable exception, with a nearly uninterrupted ribbon of vines, including the famous vineyards of Oppenheim, Nierstein, and Nackenheim on the outskirts of Mainz.

PLANNING

WHEN TO GO
The wine-festival season begins in March with the *Mandelblüten* (blossoming of the almond trees) along the Wine Road and continues through October. By May the vines' tender shoots and leaves appear. As the wine harvest progresses in September and October, foliage takes on reddish-golden hues.

FESTIVALS
Attending a wine festival is fun and a memorable part of any vacation in wine country. You can sample local food and wine inexpensively, and meet winegrowers without making an appointment. Wine, *Sekt* (sparkling wine), and *Schorle* (wine spritzer) flow freely from March

through October at festivals that include parades, fireworks, and rides. See ⊕ *www.germanwines.de* for an events calendar with an up-to-date overview of the many smaller, local wine festivals that take place in virtually every village.

Brezelfest (*Pretzel Festival*). Beer and pretzels are central to this annual six-day celebration, held the second weekend in July in Speyer. Other highlights include carnival rides and games, and a grand parade. ⊠ *Festpl., Speyer* ⊕ *www.brezelfest-speyer.de.*

Deidesheim Weinkerwe. For 10 days in August, the wine town of Deidesheim fills up with stalls where visitors can sample local wines and hearty cuisine. Deidesheim's wineries also stay open late, offering live entertainment most nights during the festival. ⊠ *Marktpl., Deidesheim.*

Deutsches Weinlesefest (*German Wine Harvest Festival*). In Neustadt, the German Wine Queen is crowned during this 10-day wine festival in early October. The festival includes the largest wine festival parade in Germany and a huge fireworks display on the final night. ⊠ *Near Neustadt train station, Neustadt* ⊕ *www.neustadt.eu/Wein-Tourismus/ Deutsches-Weinlesefest.*

Dürkheimer Wurstmarkt (*Sausage Market*). The Pfalz is home to the world's largest wine festival, held in Bad Dürkheim in mid-September. Some 400,000 pounds of sausage are consumed during eight days of merrymaking. ⊠ *Sankt-Michaels-Allee 1, Bad Dürkheim* ⊕ *www. duerkheimer-wurstmarkt.de.*

Mainzer Johannisnacht (*Mainz Midsummer St. John's Night Festival*). Live performances from local and international bands, as well as theater and cabaret performances, are done on six stages in the city center in late June. Since the festival is at least nominally in honor of Johannes Gutenberg, printers' apprentices are also dunked in water as part of a "printers' baptism" ceremony in front of the Gutenberg Museum. ⊠ *Various locations, Mainz* ⊕ *www.johannisnacht.de.*

Wormser Backfischfest (*Fried Fish Festival*). Carnival rides, traditional folk music and dance, jousting on the Rhine, and fireworks create a jovial atmosphere at this annual festival, starting in late August, which honors the city's fishermen. Don't pass up the chance to taste more than 400 wines at the festival's Wonnegauer Wine Cellar. ⊠ *Festpl., Worms* ⊕ *www.backfischfest.de* ⊗ *Late Aug.–early Sept.*

PLANNING YOUR TIME

Central hubs such as Bad Dürkheim or Neustadt make good bases for exploring the region; smaller towns such as St. Martin and Gleiszellen are worth an overnight stay because of their charm. Driving the Wine Road takes longer than you might expect, and will probably involve spur-of-the-moment stops, so you may want to consider a stopover in one of the many country inns en route.

GETTING HERE AND AROUND

AIR TRAVEL

Frankfurt is the closest major international airport for the entire Rhineland. International airports in Stuttgart and France's Strasbourg are closer to the southern end of the German Wine Road. If you're traveling from within Europe, the frequently disliked Ryanair hub in the remote Frankfurt suburb of Hahn is actually a convenient jumping-off point for a tour of the region, with bus service to Koblenz, Heidelberg, and Karlsruhe.

BIKE TRAVEL

There's no charge for transporting bicycles on local trains throughout Rheinland-Pfalz weekdays after 9 am and anytime weekends and holidays. For maps, suggested routes, bike-rental locations, and details on *Pauschalangebote* (package deals) or *Gepäcktransport* (luggage-forwarding service), contact Pfalz.Touristik or Rheinhessen-Touristik.

CAR TRAVEL

It's 162 km (100 miles) between Schweigen-Rechtenbach and Mainz, the southernmost and northernmost points of this region. The main route is the Deutsche Weinstrasse, which is a Bundesstrasse, abbreviated "B," as in B-38, B-48, and B-271. The route from Worms to Mainz is B-9.

TRAIN TRAVEL

Mainz is on the high-speed ICE (InterCity Express) train route linking Wiesbaden, Frankfurt, and Dresden, and so forms a convenient gateway to the region. An excellent network of public transportation called **Rheinland-Pfalz-Takt** operates throughout the region with well-coordinated **RegioLinie** (buses) and **Nahverkehrszüge** (local trains). Regional trains link Mainz with other towns along the Rhine Terrace, including Worms and Speyer, while local branch lines serve key hubs along the Wine Road such as Neustadt and Bad Dürkheim. (Even more direct express trains are on schedule to be added by 2015 as part of a large-scale expansion project.) Smaller towns and villages connect with these hubs by an excellent network of local buses.

▨ TIP➔ The Rheinland-Pfalz Ticket is a great value if you plan to travel on the train. The ticket costs €22 for the first person and €4 for each additional person, up to five people. It's valid for a whole day, beginning at 9 am on weekdays and midnight on weekends and holidays. It can be used on all regional trains and buses, but not the high-speed ICE trains.

RESTAURANTS

Lunch in this region is generally served from noon until 2 or 2:30, dinner from 6 until 9:30 or 10. Credit cards have gained a foothold, but many restaurants will accept only cash or debit cards issued by a German bank. Casual attire is typically acceptable at restaurants here, and reservations are generally not needed.

Prices in the reviews are the average cost of a main course at dinner, or if dinner is not served, at lunch.

HOTELS

Book in advance if your visit coincides with a large festival. Bed-and-breakfasts abound. Look for signs reading "Fremdenzimmer" or "Zimmer frei" (rooms available). A *Ferienwohnung* (holiday apartment),

CLOSE UP

The Wines of Rheinland-Pfalz

The Romans planted the first Rhineland vineyards 2,000 years ago, finding the mild, wet climate hospitable to grape growing. By the Middle Ages viticulture was flourishing and a bustling wine trade had developed. Wine making and splendid Romanesque cathedrals are the legacies of the bishops and emperors of Speyer, Worms, and Mainz. This region, now the state of Rheinland-Pfalz (Rhineland Palatinate), remains a major wine center, with two of the largest wine districts in the country, Rheinhessen and the Pfalz.

In the Pfalz, you can follow the Deutsche Weinstrasse as it winds its way north from the French border. Idyllic wine villages beckon with flower-draped facades and courtyards full of palms, oleanders, and fig trees. "Weinverkauf" (wine for sale) and "Weinprobe" (wine-tasting) signs are posted everywhere—an invitation to stop in to sample the wines.

Most of the wines from both Pfalz and Rheinhessen are white, and the ones from Rheinhessen are often fragrant and sweeter than their counterparts from the Pfalz. Many are sold as *offene Weine* (wines by the glass). The classic white varieties are Riesling, Silvaner, Müller-Thurgau (also called Rivaner), Grauburgunder (pinot gris), and Weissburgunder (pinot blanc). Spätburgunder (pinot noir), Dornfelder, and Portugieser are the most popular red wines. The word *Weissherbst*, after the grape variety, indicates a rosé wine.

Riesling is the king of German grapes. It produces wines that range widely in quality and character; Rieslings are noted for their strong acidity, sometimes-flowery aroma, and often mineral-tasting notes—all reflections of the soil in which they're grown. Riesling made its name throughout the world as a sweet (*lieblich*) wine, but many Germans (and, increasingly, others) prefer dry (*trocken*) versions. Importers, especially in the United States, have tended not to bring over many dry Rieslings, so take the opportunity to sample some while in Germany.

---

abbreviated FeWo in tourist brochures, is an economical option if you plan to stay in one location for several nights.

Prices in the reviews are the lowest cost of a standard double room in high season. For expanded reviews, facilities, and current deals, visit Fodors.com.

DISCOUNTS AND DEALS

The **Freizeit Card** (€14 for one day, €41.50 for three days, €66 for six days) offers free or reduced admission to 168 museums, castles, and other sights, as well as city tours and boat trips throughout Rheinland-Pfalz and Saarland. The days you use the three- and six-day cards needn't be consecutive, as long as they're in the same season. The six-day card also includes admission to the Holiday Park in Hassloch. The website ⊕ *www.freizeitcard.info* lists all of the sites you can visit with the card, and also gives you the opportunity to order it online. You can also buy it at all the community tourist offices in the region.

10

VISITOR INFORMATION

Contacts Deutsche Weinstrasse ✉ *Martin-Luther-Str. 69, Neustadt a.d. Weinstrasse* ☎ *06321/912–333* ⊕ *www.deutsche-weinstrasse.de* ☉ *Mon.– Thurs. 8:30–5, Fri. 8:30–1.* **Pfalz.Touristik** ✉ *Martin-Luther-Str. 69, Neustadt a.d. Weinstrasse* ☎ *06321/39160* ⊕ *www.pfalz.de* ☉ *Jan.–Mar., Mon.–Thurs. 8–5, Fri. 8–4; Apr.–Dec., Mon.–Thurs. 8–5, Fri. 8–4, Sat. 10–noon.* **Pfalzwein** ✉ *Martin-Luther-Str. 69, Neustadt a.d. Weinstrasse* ☎ *06321/912–328* ⊕ *www.pfalzwein. de* ☉ *Mon.–Thurs. 8:30–5, Fri. 8:30–1.* **Rheinhessen-Touristik** ✉ *Friedrich-Ebert-Str. 17, Ingelheim* ☎ *06132/44170* ⊕ *www.rheinhessen.de* ☉ *Weekdays 9–5.* **Rheinhessenwein** ✉ *Otto-Lilienthal-Str. 4, Alzey* ☎ *06731/951–0740* ⊕ *www. rheinhessenwein.de.* **Rheinland-Pfalz Tourismus** ☎ *01805/915–200 for info hotline, €.14/min., mobile max €.42/min.* ⊕ *www.rlp-info.de.*

THE GERMAN WINE ROAD

The Wine Road spans the length of the Pfalz wine region. You can travel from north to south or vice versa. Given its central location, the Pfalz is convenient to visit before or after a trip to the Black Forest, Heidelberg, or the northern Rhineland.

SCHWEIGEN-RECHTENBACH

21 km (13 miles) southwest of Landau on B-38.

The southernmost wine village of the Pfalz lies on the French border. During the economically depressed 1930s, local vintners established a route through the vineyards to promote tourism. The German Wine Road was inaugurated in 1935; a year later the massive stone Deutsches Weintor (German Wine Gate) was erected to add visual impact to the marketing concept. Halfway up the gateway is a platform that offers a fine view of the vineyards—to the south, French, to the north, German. Schweigen's 1-km (½-mile) Weinlehrpfad (educational wine path) wanders through the vineyards and, with signs and exhibits, explains the history of viticulture from Roman times to the present.

BAD BERGZABERN

10 km (6 miles) north of Schweigen-Rechtenbach on B-38.

The landmark of this little spa town is the baroque **Schloss** (palace) of the dukes of Zweibrücken. The Gasthaus Zum Engel (✉ *Königstr. 45*) is an impressive Renaissance house with elaborate scrolled gables and decorative oriels. ■ TIP➜ Visit Café Herzog (✉ *Marktstr. 48*) for scrumptious, homemade chocolates, cakes, and ice creams made with unexpected ingredients, such as wine, pepper, cardamom, curry, thyme, or *Feigenessig* (fig vinegar). The café is closed Monday.

GETTING HERE AND AROUND

From Landau, you can take the regional train to Bad Bergzabern, which takes about an hour and requires a change in Winden (Pfalz). Bus No. 543 also connects Bad Bergzabern along the Wine Road to Schweigen, over the French border to Wissembourg. The Rheinland-Pfalz ticket is valid on the train and the bus until the French border.

Some wineries offer seasonal outdoor seating areas where guests can enjoy samples.

GLEISZELLEN

4 km (2½ miles) north of Bad Bergzabern on B-48.

Gleiszellen's **Winzergasse** (Vintners' Lane) is a little vine-canopied street lined with a beautiful ensemble of half-timber houses. Try a glass of the town's specialty: spicy, aromatic Muskateller wine, a rarity seldom found even elsewhere in Germany.

GETTING HERE AND AROUND

Gleiszellen is on the No. 543 bus line that runs from Landau to the French border town of Wissembourg. The bus runs hourly.

OFF THE
BEATEN
PATH

Burg Trifels. Burg Trifels is on the highest of three sandstone bluffs overlooking Annweiler, which is 15 km (9 miles) northwest of Gleiszellen. Celts, Romans, and Salians all had settlements on this site, but it was under the Hohenstaufen emperors (12th and 13th centuries) that Trifels was built on a grand scale. It housed the crown jewels from 1125 to 1274 (replicas are on display today). It was also an imperial prison, perhaps where Richard the Lionheart was held captive in 1193–94.

Although it was never conquered, the fortress was severely damaged by lightning in 1602. Reconstruction began in 1938, shaped by visions of grandeur to create a national shrine of the imperial past. Accordingly, the monumental proportions of some parts of today's castle bear no resemblance to those of the original Romanesque structure. The imperial hall is a grand setting for the *Serenaden* (concerts) held in summer.

Arriving on foot: From the main train station in Annweiler, follow the local signs for Burg Trifels. The hike is about an hour. **Arriving by car:** Follow the A65 direction Karl-Ludwigshafen, take exit Landau-Sued, then B10 to Annweiler West. From there follow the local signs. Parking is at the foot of the fortress, a 20-minute walk from the top. ⊠ *Trifels, Annweiler* ☎ *06346/8470* ⊕ *www.burgen-rlp.de* 🎫 *€3* ☉ *Apr.–Sept., daily 9–6; Oct., Nov., and Jan.–Mar., daily 9–5.*

WHERE TO EAT AND STAY

For expanded hotel reviews, visit Fodors.com.

$ ✕**Weinstube Wissing.** Friendly service and a homey atmosphere awaits
GERMAN   guests this restaurant. Wines, fine spirits, and regional delicacies are offered in the former premises of the family-owned distillery. Don't miss a chance to sample their fruity Muskateller wine, and you might also want to pick up a bottle of their fresh *Pfälzer Traubensaft* (grape juice) for a tasty souvenir. ⑤ *Average main: €15* ⊠ *Winzerg. 34* ☎ *06343/4711* ⊕ *www.weingut-wissing.de* ▭ *No credit cards* ☉ *Closed Mon. and Tues. No lunch Wed.–Sat.*

$ 🏨 **Gasthof Zum Lam.** Flowers cascade from the windowsills of this half-
B&B/INN   timber inn in the heart of town, where the good rates include free
Fodor's Choice   Wi-Fi and an enjoyable breakfast buffet. **Pros:** quiet location; charming
★   courtyard; beautiful old building. **Cons:** no elevator; no a/c. ⑤ *Rooms from: €86* ⊠ *Winzerg. 37* ☎ *06343/939–212* ⊕ *www.zum-lam.de* 🛏 *11 rooms, 1 apartment* ☉ *Restaurant closed Wed. No lunch Nov.–Mar.* †◯┤ *Breakfast.*

SCHLOSS VILLA LUDWIGSHÖHE

24 km (15 miles) north of Annweiler, slightly west of Edenkoben on the Wine Road.

For a cultural break from all that wine tasting, head to this Pompeian-style palace, followed by a chairlift ride with wonderful views to reach the vantage point of the Rietburg Castle Ruins. Or get your heart racing by following the example of the hardy German tourists who can often be seen hiking uphill between the two sights.

Fodor's Choice   **Schloss Villa Ludwigshöhe.** Bavaria's King Ludwig I built a summer resi-
★   dence on the slopes overlooking Edenkoben, in what he called "the most beautiful square mile of my realm." The layout and decor of the palace—Pompeian-style murals, splendid parquet floors, and Biedermeier and Empire furnishings—are quite a contrast to those of medieval castles elsewhere in the Pfalz.

You can reach the neoclassical Schloss Villa Ludwigshöhe by car, bus, or walking. The No. 506 Palatina bus goes directly from Edenkoen on Sunday and holidays. If you opt to walk, the Weinlehrpfad takes about 45 minutes. Historical winepresses and vintners' tools are displayed at intervals along the path, which starts at the corner of Landauer Strasse and Villa Strasse in Edenkoben. ⊠ *Schloss Villa Ludwigshöhe, Villastr. 64, Edenkoben* ☎ *06323/93016* ⊕ *www. schloss-villa-ludwigshoehe.de* 🎫 *€6* ☉ *Apr.–Sept., daily 10–6; Oct., Nov., and Jan.–Mar., daily 10–5.*

The German
Wine Road

WHERE TO STAY

For expanded hotel reviews, visit Fodors.com.

$$$ **Alte Rebschule.** Fireside seating in the lobby lounge and spacious
HOTEL rooms (all with a balcony) make for a pleasant, peaceful stay in this
former *Rebschule* (vine nursery) on the edge of the forest. **Pros:** beauti-
ful vineyard views; quiet; good restaurant. **Cons:** room decor a bit old-
fashioned; no Wi-Fi in rooms, only DSL. $ *Rooms from: €194* ⊠ *3 km
(2 miles) west of Schloss Villa Ludwigshöhe, Theresienstr. 200, Rhodt
u. Rietburg* ☎ *06323/70440* ⊕ *www.alte-rebschule.de* ↝ *34 rooms,
3 suites* ⦿ *Some meals.*

ST. MARTIN

*26 km (16 miles) north of Annweiler, slightly west of the Wine Road.
Turn left at the northern edge of Edenkoben.*

This is one of the most charming wine villages of the Pfalz. Narrow
cobblestone streets go past historic half-timber houses that now hold
appealing inns, restaurants, and wine shops, making the compact, his-
torically preserved *Altstadt* (Old Town) a pleasure to stroll.

EATING WELL IN THE PFALZ

Wine has a big influence on the cuisine here, turning up as an ingredient in dishes as well as an accompaniment to them. The *Weinkraut* is sauerkraut braised in wine; *Dippe-Has* is hare and pork baked in red wine; and *Backes Grumbeere* is scalloped potatoes cooked with bacon, sour cream, white wine, and a layer of pork. During the grape harvest, from September through November, there is *Federweisser*—fermenting grape juice. Among the regional dishes well suited to wine is the *Pfälzer Teller*—a platter of bratwurst, *Leberknödel* (liver dumplings), and slices of *Saumagen* (a spicy meat-and-potato mixture cooked in a sow's stomach), with *Kartoffelpüree* (mashed potatoes) on the side. *Spargel* (asparagus), *Wild* (game), chestnuts, *Zwiebelkuchen* (onion quiche), and mushrooms, particularly *Pfifferlinge* (chanterelles), are seasonal favorites.

GETTING HERE AND AROUND

The easiest way to reach St. Martin is by car. There's no train station, but Bus No. 501 connects St. Martin with Neustadt and Edenkoben. The trip takes about 20 minutes, and the buses run approximately every half hour.

EXPLORING

Kropsburg. Now romantic ruins, this castle was originally constructed in the early 13th century and was used by the bishops of Speyer; from the 15th to the 19th centuries, the Knights of Dalberg resided there. You can see Kropsburg from the hills above St. Martin. Hike up to the castle's outskirts, where you can have a traditional sausage lunch at the charming inn and restaurant Burgschänke an der Kropsburg ($) while admiring the views. ⊠ *Kropsburg 1* ⊗ *Restaurant closed Tues. No dinner.*

Pfarrkirche St. Martin (*Church of St. Martin*). Perched dramatically on the northern edge of St. Martin with a backdrop of vineyards, this late-Gothic church was thought to have been built around 1200 (the interior was renovated in the mid-1980s). Renaissance tombstones and a Madonna sculpture carved from a single piece of oak are among the intriguing artworks found inside. ⊠ *Kirchgasse 6* ☎ *06323/5100.*

WHERE TO STAY

$
B&B/INN
Landhaus Christmann. This bright, modern house in the midst of the vineyards outside of St. Martin has stylish rooms decorated with both antiques and modern furnishings, and is close enough to walk into town. **Pros:** excellent value rooms; quiet location. **Cons:** rooms are very simple; breakfast costs extra (€10) if you're staying in an apartment. ⑤ *Rooms from: €92* ⊠ *Riedweg 1* ☎ *06323/94270* ⊕ *www.landhaus-christmann. de* ⌂ *6 rooms, 3 apartments* ⊟ *No credit cards* ⑪ *Breakfast.*

$$
HOTEL
Fodor'sChoice
★
St. Martiner Castell. The Mücke family transformed a simple vintner's house into a fine hotel and restaurant, retaining many of the original features, such as exposed beams and an old winepress. **Pros:** beautiful old house; central location; free Wi-Fi in rooms. **Cons:** can be noisy; not all rooms are nonsmoking. ⑤ *Rooms from: €104* ⊠ *Maikammerer Str. 2* ☎ *06323/9510* ⊕ *www.hotelcastell.de* ⌂ *24 rooms, 2 suites* ⊗ *Restaurant closed Tues.* ⑪ *Breakfast.*

THE ARTS

Schloss Villa Ludwigshöhe, Kloster Heilsbruck (a former Cistercian convent near Edenkoben), and **Schloss Edesheim** serve as backdrops for concerts and theater in summer. For a calendar of events, contact the Südliche Weinstrasse regional tourist office in Landau (☎ *06341/940–407* ⊕ *www.suedlicheweinstrasse.de*).

SHOPPING

Doktorenhof. Artist Georg Wiedemann is responsible for both the contents and the design of the containers at Germany's premier wine-vinegar estate, Doktorenhof. Make an appointment for a unique vinegar tasting and tour of the cellars or pick up a gift at his shop (cash only). The estate's in Venningen, 2 km (1 mile) east of Edenkoben. ⊠ *Raiffeisenstr. 5, Venningen* ☎ *06323/5505* ⊕ *www.doktorenhof.de* ⊘ *Weekdays 8–4, Wed. 8–6, and Sat. 9–2.*

EN ROUTE

Leave St. Martin via the Totenkopf-Höhenstrasse, a scenic road through the forest. Turn right at the intersection with Kalmitstrasse and proceed to the vantage point atop the **Kalmit,** the region's highest peak (2,200 feet). The view's amazing.

Hambacher Schloss. On the Wine Road, it's a brief drive to the Neustadt suburb of Hambach. The sturdy block of Hambacher Schloss is considered the cradle of German democracy. It was here, on May 27, 1832, that 30,000 patriots demonstrated for German unity, raising the German colors for the first time. Inside there are exhibits about the uprising and the history of the castle. The French destroyed the 11th-century imperial fortress in 1688. Reconstruction finally began after World War II, in neo-Gothic style, and the castle is now an impressive setting for theater and concerts. On a clear day you can see the spire of Strasbourg Cathedral and the northern fringe of the Black Forest from the terrace restaurant.

Tours take about 45 minutes and begin at 11, noon, 2, 3, and 4 from April to October, and at 11, noon, and 2 from November to March. ⊠ *Hambach, Neustadt* ☎ *06321/926–290* ⊕ *www.hambacher-schloss.de* ☑ *€8* ⊘ *Mar.–Nov., daily 10–6; Dec.–Feb., daily 11–5.*

10

NEUSTADT

8 km (5 miles) north of St. Martin, 5 km (3 miles) north of Hambach on the Wine Road.

Neustadt and its nine wine suburbs are at the midpoint of the Wine Road and the edge of the district known as Deutsche Weinstrasse–Mittelhaardt. With around 5,000 acres of vines, they jointly make up Germany's largest wine-making community.

GETTING HERE AND AROUND

Regular trains connect Neustadt with Ludwigshafen (connecting to Worms and Mainz). Coming from Speyer, change in Schifferstadt. Local buses connect Neustadt to other towns along the Wine Road. Once you're in Neustadt, the best way to get around is on foot. Neustadt tours cost €5 and take place April through October, Wednesday and Saturday at 10:30.

ESSENTIALS

Visitor Information Neustadt-an-der-Weinstrasse ✉ *Tourist-Information, Hetzelpl. 1* ☎ *06321/926–892* ⊕ *www.neustadt.pfalz.com* ⊗ *Apr.–Oct., weekdays 9:30–6, Sat. 9:30–2; Nov.–Mar., weekdays 9:30–5.*

EXPLORING

FAMILY **Eisenbahn Museum.** Thirty historic train engines and railway cars are on display at the Eisenbahn Museum, behind the main train station. Take a ride through the Palatinate Forest on one of the museum's historic steam trains, the *Kuckucksbähnel* (€14 round-trip), which departs from Track 5 around 10:45 am some Sundays and Wednesdays between Easter and mid-October (check the website for the latest schedule). It takes a little over an hour to cover the 13-km (8-mile) stretch from Neustadt to Elmstein. ✉ *Neustadt train station, Schillerstr. entrance* ☎ *06321/30390* ⊕ *www.eisenbahnmuseum-neustadt.de* ⍣ *€5 for adults, €2 for children 4–14* ⊗ *Tues.–Fri. 10–1, weekends 10–4.*

Haus des Weines (*House of Wine*). At the Haus des Weines, opposite the town hall, you can sample some 30 of the 100 Neustadt wines sold. The Gothic house from 1276 is bordered by a splendid Renaissance court-yard, the Kuby'scher Hof. ✉ *Rathausstr. 6* ☎ *06321/355–871* ⊕ *www. haus-des-weines.com* ⊗ *Tues.–Fri. 10–6, Sat. 10–2.*

Marktplatz (*market square*). The Marktplatz is the focal point of the Old Town and a beehive of activity on Tuesday, Thursday, and Saturday, when farmers come to sell their wares. The square itself is ringed by baroque and Renaissance buildings (Nos. 1, 4, 8, and 11) and the Gothic **Stiftskirche** (Collegiate Church), built as a burial church for the Palatinate counts. In summer, concerts take place in the church (Saturday 11:30–noon). Afterward, you can ascend the southern tower (187 feet) for a bird's-eye view of the town. The world's largest cast-iron bell—weighing more than 17 tons—hangs in the northern tower. Indoors, see the elaborate tombstones near the choir and the fanciful grotesque figures carved into the baldachins and corbels. ✉ *Marktplatz* ⊕ *www.stiftskirche-nw.de.*

Otto Dill Museum. The impressionist painter Otto Dill (1884–1957), a native of Neustadt, is known for powerful animal portraits (especially lions, tigers, and horses) and vivid landscapes. The Otto Dill Museum displays some 100 oil paintings and 50 drawings and watercolors from the Manfred Vetter collection. ✉ *Rathausstr. 12, at Bachgängel 8* ☎ *06321/398–321* ⊕ *www.otto-dill-museum.de* ⍣ *€2.50* ⊗ *Wed. and Fri. 2–5, weekends 11–5.*

WHERE TO EAT

$$ ✕ **Altstadtkeller bei Jürgen.** Tucked behind a wooden portal on a cobble-
GERMAN stone street, this vaulted sandstone "cellar" (it's actually on the ground floor) feels very cozy. Equally inviting is the terrace, with its citrus, olive, palm, and fig trees. The regular menu includes a number of salads and a good selection of fish and steaks. Owner Jürgen Reis is a wine enthusiast, and his well-chosen list shows it. $ *Average main: €18* ✉ *Kunigundenstr. 2* ☎ *06321/32320* ⊕ *www.altstadtkeller-neustadt.de* ⊗ *Closed Mon. No dinner Sun.*

Pink and white almond blossoms line the roads of the region in spring.

$$ \times $$ **Nett's Restaurant-Weinbar.** Susanne and Daniel Nett operate a chic wine
GERMAN restaurant-bar filled with modern art within a 16th-century vaulted
Fodor's Choice stone cellar at Weingut A. Christmann, a top wine estate. The short,
★ seasonal menu has Spanish and Italian influences, with such dishes as
gnocchi and pot au feu with crayfish, which is served with asparagus,
morels, peas, and tomatoes. The thoughtful wine list includes lots of
Pfälzer wines by the glass, including those from the Christmann winery.
Dining in the intimate courtyard overlooking the vineyards is a romantic option in summer. The Netts also offer seven rooms ($) for overnight
guests, each with hardwood floors and Wi-Fi. $ *Average main: €20*
✉ *Meerspinnstr. 46, Neustadt-Gimmeldingen* ☎ *06321/60175* ⊕ *www.*
nettsrestaurant.de ☾ *Closed Mon. and Tues. No lunch except summer*
Sun. and some holidays.

$$$ $$ \times $$ **Urgestein.** Dine inside the cozy brick-lined former horse stables or
GERMAN outside on the lovely patio at this restaurant inside the historic stone
Fodor's Choice houses of the Steinhauser Hof hotel (its name, *Urgestein,* translates as
★ "stone"). The ambitious tasting menus highlight local products and are
best when paired with one of the 350 wines from the massive wine list,
all from the Pfalz region. Splurge on the six-course surprise menu for
€130 (including wine pairings), or try the €95 six-course or €70 four-
course menus (wine is extra); you can also order such à la carte dishes as
pigeon marinated for a week with carrots that have been roasted for an
hour, chanterelle cream, and sunflower seeds; or sea turbot with a prune
cream and baby cabbage. Leave room for the tasty desserts, includ-
ing brioche with caramel sauce and honey ice cream. $ *Average main:*
€25 ✉ *Rathausstr. 6* ☎ *06321/489–060* ⊕ *www.restaurant-urgestein.de*
☾ *Closed Mon. No dinner Sun.*

BIKING, HIKING, AND WALKING

Country roads and traffic-free vineyard paths make the area perfect for cyclists. There are also well-marked cycling trails, such as the **Radwanderweg Deutsche Weinstrasse**, which runs parallel to its namesake from the French border to Bockenheim, and the **Radweg** (cycling trail) along the Rhine between Worms and Mainz. The Palatinate Forest, Germany's largest single tract of woods, has more than 10,000 km (6,200 miles) of paths.

The **Wanderweg Deutsche Weinstrasse**, a walking route that traverses vineyards, woods, and wine villages, covers the length of the Pfalz. It connects with many trails in the Palatinate Forest that lead to Celtic and Roman landmarks and dozens of castles dating primarily from the 11th to 13th century. In Rheinhessen you can hike along two marked trails parallel to the Rhine: the **Rheinterrassenwanderweg** and the **Rheinhöhenweg** along the heights.

WHERE TO STAY

$
B&B/INN

Gästehaus Rebstöckel. This 17th-century stone guesthouse has its beautiful cobblestone courtyard and magnificent fig tree; all the rooms have blond-wood furnishings, and some have kitchenettes. **Pros:** quiet; friendly; rustic location. **Cons:** no Internet; light from street lamp may bother light sleepers. ⑤ *Rooms from: €79* ✉ *Kreuzstr. 11, Neustadt-Diedesfeld* ☎ *06321/484–060* ⊕ *www.gaestehaus-rebstoeckel-pfalz.de/en* ⤺ *5 rooms* ▬ *No credit cards* ⑩ *Breakfast.*

$
RENTAL

Mithras-Stuben/Weinstube Kommerzienrat. In the picturesque village of Gimmeldingen, the convivial proprietor and wine devotee Bernd Hagedorn rents four spacious apartments with contemporary furnishings, Oriental rugs, and modern baths. **Pros:** spacious; perfect for longer stays. **Cons:** no elevator; no a/c. ⑤ *Rooms from: €65* ✉ *Loblocherstr. 34, Neustadt-Gimmeldingen* ☎ *06321/679–0335, 06321/68200 after 6 pm* ⊕ *www.weinstube-kommerzienrat.de* ⤺ *4 apartments* ▬ *No credit cards* ⊗ *Closed 2 wks in late Apr. Restaurant closed Thurs.; no lunch* ⑩ *No meals.*

$
HOTEL

Steinhäuser Hof. This architectural gem dates back to 1276 and is one of the oldest preserved stone mansions in Rhineland-Palatinate. **Pros:** beautiful old building; central location; friendly staff; renowned restaurant. **Cons:** basic rooms; some street noise; no elevator. ⑤ *Rooms from: €82* ✉ *Rathausstr. 6* ☎ *06321/489–060* ⊕ *www.steinhaeuserhof.de* ⤺ *6 rooms* ⊗ *Restaurant closed Mon. No dinner Sun.* ⑩ *No meals.*

SPEYER

25 km (15 miles) east of Neustadt via B-39, 22 km (14 miles) south of Mannheim via B-9 and B-44.

Speyer was one of the great cities of the Holy Roman Empire, founded in pre-Celtic times, taken over by the Romans, and expanded in the 11th century by the Salian emperors. Between 1294, when it was declared a Free Imperial City, and 1570, no fewer than 50 imperial diets were convened here. The term "Protestant" derives from the Diet of 1529, referring to those who protested when the religious freedom granted to evangelicals at the Diet of 1526 was revoked and a return to Catholicism was decreed. The neo-Gothic **Gedächtniskirche** on Bartolomäus-Weltz-Platz commemorates those 16th-century Protestants.

GETTING HERE AND AROUND

Speyer is a little ways off the German Wine Road. It is served by regular trains from Mannheim and Mainz. Buses go down the main street, but the center is compact enough that getting around on foot is not a problem. Tours (€5) are Saturday at 11 and 2, and Sunday at 11 year-round.

ESSENTIALS

Visitor Information Speyer ⊠ *Tourist-Information, Maximilianstr. 13* ☏ *06232/142–392* ⊕ *www.speyer.de* ⊗ *Apr.–Oct., weekdays 9–5, Sat. 10–3, Sun. 10–2; Nov.–Mar., weekdays 9–5, Sat. 10–noon.*

EXPLORING

Altpörtel. Ascend the Altpörtel, the impressive town gate, for a grand view of Maximilianstrasse, the street that once led kings and emperors straight to the cathedral. ⊠ *Rossmarktstr. 1* ☐*€1.50* ⊗ *Apr.–Oct., weekdays 10–noon and 2–4, weekends 10–5.*

Historisches Museum der Pfalz (*Palatinate Historical Museum*). Opposite the cathedral, the museum houses the **Domschatz** (Cathedral Treasury). Other collections chronicle the art and cultural history of Speyer and the Pfalz from the Stone Age to modern times. Don't miss the "Golden Hat of Schifferstadt," a Bronze Age headdress used in religious ceremonies dating back to approximately 1300 BC. The **Wine Museum** houses the world's oldest bottle of wine, which is still liquid and dates to circa AD 300. The giant 35-foot-long wooden wine-press from 1727 is also worth a look. ⊠ *Dompl. 4* ☏ *06232/620–222, 06232/13250* ⊕ *www.museum.speyer.de* ☐*€7, special exhibitions €12* ⊗ *Tues.–Sun. 10–6.*

Fodor's Choice ★ **Jewish quarter.** Speyer was an important medieval Jewish cultural center. In the Jewish quarter, behind the Palatinate Historical Museum, are synagogue remains from 1104; Germany's oldest (circa 1126) *Mikwe*, the 33-foot-deep ritual baths; and the Museum SchPIRA, which displays objects such as grave stones and coins from the Middle Ages. ⊠ *Kleine Pfaffeng. 21, near Judeng.* ☏ *06232/291–971* ☐*€3* ⊗ *Apr.–Oct., daily 10–5; Nov.–Mar., Tues.–Sun. 10–4.*

Fodor's Choice ★ **Kaiserdom** (*Imperial Cathedral*). The Kaiserdom, one of the finest Romanesque cathedrals in the world and a UNESCO World Heritage site, conveys the pomp and majesty of the early Holy Roman Emperors. It was built between 1030 and 1061 by the emperors Konrad II, Henry III, and Henry IV. ■TIP→ There's a fine view of the east end of the structure from the park by the Rhine. Much of the architectural detail,

10

including the dwarf galleries and ornamental capitals, was inspired and executed by stonemasons from Lombardy, which belonged to the German Empire at the time. The four towers symbolize the four seasons and the idea that the power of the empire extends in all four directions. Look up as you enter the nearly 100-foot-high portal. It's richly carved with mythical creatures. In contrast to Gothic cathedrals, whose walls are supported externally by flying buttresses, allowing for a minimum of masonry and a maximum of light, at Speyer the columns supporting the roof are massive. The *Krypta* (crypt) lies beneath the chancel. It's the largest crypt in Germany and is strikingly beautiful in its simplicity. Four emperors, four kings, and three empresses are buried here. ⊠ *Edith-Stein-Pl.* ☎ *06232/102–118* 🖅 *Donation requested* ☉ *Apr.– Oct., Mon.–Sat. 9–7, Sun. noon–5; Nov.–Mar., Mon.–Sat. 9–5, Sun. noon–5; closed during services.*

FAMILY **Sea Life.** If you're traveling with kids or just need some indoor entertainment on a rainy day, Sea Life, in Speyer's old harbor, has aquariums that offer a look at marine life in the Rhine as well as the world's oceans. ■TIP→ **Save money on the entrance fee by booking your tickets online in advance.** ⊠ *Im Hafenbecken 5, 15-min walk from large parking lot on Festpl.* ☎ *06232/69780* ⊕ *www.sealife.de* 🖅 *€15.50* ☉ *Daily 10–5 or 10–6, depending on dates (check website).*

WHERE TO EAT AND STAY

$ ✕ **Kutscherhaus.** Charming rustic decor and a profusion of flowers have
GERMAN   replaced the *Kutschen* (coaches) in this turn-of-the-20th-century coachman's house. The menu offers *Flammkuchen* (similar to pizza but with a wafer-thin crust) as well as creative fish, vegetarian, and pasta dishes. *Ochsenbrust mit Meerrettichsauce* (beef brisket with horseradish sauce) is a favorite. In summer you can sit beneath the old plane trees in the beer garden for a sumptuous buffet. $ *Average main: €12* ⊠ *Fischmarkt 5a* ☎ *06232/70592* ⊕ *www.kutscherhaus-speyer.de* ☉ *Closed Wed. No lunch Thurs. Beer garden closed Oct.–Apr.*

$ ✕ **Rabennest.** It's small and often packed with local families, but the
GERMAN   rustic cooking in this cozy restaurant is worth the wait. Hearty portions of regional specialties will delight both your mouth and your wallet. The *Leberknoedel* (liver dumplings) and *Rumpsteak* (round steak) are both excellent, and there's also a nice the selection of fresh salads. In the summer months, the patio seating is great for people-watching. $ *Average main: €7* ⊠ *Korngasse 5* ☎ *06232/623–857* ▭ *No credit cards* ☉ *Closed Sun.*

$ ✕ **Ratskeller.** Friendly service and fresh seasonal dishes make for an
GERMAN   enjoyable dining experience in the town hall's vaulted cellar (1578). The frequently changing menu offers creative soups and other starters (pretzel soup, Tuscan bread soup) and entrées, such as *Sauerbraten nach Grossmutters Art* (grandmother's marinated pot roast) or *Bachsaibling* (brook trout in a red wine–butter sauce). Wines from the Pfalz predominate, with 18 available by the glass. Small plates and drinks are served in the courtyard May through September. $ *Average main: €15* ⊠ *Maximilianstr. 12* ☎ *06232/78612* ⊕ *www.ratskeller-speyer.de* ☉ *Closed Mon. and 2–3 wks in Feb. No dinner Sun.*

The Marktplatz in Neustadt is your best bet for a meal alfresco.

$$
GERMAN
✕**Wirtschaft Zum Alten Engel.** This 200-year-old vaulted brick cellar has rustic wood furnishings and cozy niches. Seasonal dishes made from local ingredients supplement the large selection of Pfälzer and Alsatian specialties, such as *Ochsenfetzen* (slices of beef in garlic sauce), *Fleeschknepp* (spicy meatball in horseradish sauce), or a hearty *Pfälzer Platte* (a platter of bratwurst, Saumagen, and Leberknödel with sauerkraut and home-fried potatoes). The wine list features about 180 Pfälzer, European, and New World wines. $ *Average main: €17* ⊠ *Mühlturmstr. 7* ☎ *06232/70914* ⊕ *www.zumaltenengel.de* ⊗ *No lunch.*

$$
HOTEL
🏨 **Hotel Goldener Engel.** A scant two blocks west of the Altpörtel is the "Golden Angel," a friendly, family-run hotel furnished with antiques and innovative metal-and-wood designer furniture. **Pros:** friendly; good location. **Cons:** some rooms are a little small; air conditioned rooms cost €10 extra; charge for Wi-Fi. $ *Rooms from: €110* ⊠ *Mühlturmstr. 5–7* ☎ *06232/13260* ⊕ *www.goldener-engel-speyer.de* ⟿ *44 rooms, 2 suites* ❙⃝❙ *Breakfast.*

NIGHTLIFE AND THE ARTS

City highlights for music lovers are **Orgelfrühling,** the organ concerts in the Gedächtniskirche (Memorial Church) in spring, the jazz festival in mid-August, and the concerts in the cathedral during September's **Internationale Musiktage.** Contact the Speyer tourist office for program details and tickets.

Kulturhof Flachsgasse. Walk into the town-hall courtyard to enter the Kulturhof Flachsgasse, home of the city's art collection and special exhibitions. ⊠ *Flachsg. 3* ☎ *06232/142–399* ▱ *Free* ⊗ *Tues.–Sun. 11–6.*

10

THE ALTRHEIN

From April to October, you can take a brief river cruise to the north or south of Speyer to discover the idyllic landscape of the ancient, forested islands along the *Altrhein*, the original course of the Rhine. The islands are home to rare flora, fauna, and many birds. There are grand views of the cathedral from the boat.

Fahrgastschifffahrt Speyer. In the summer months, boat tours depart from just outside the Sea Life Aquarium at noon, 2, and 4. The trip lasts about 1½ hours and offers a unique look at Speyer's old harbor. ⊠ *Hafenstr. 22* ☎ *06232/291–150* ⊕ *www.ms-sealife.de* 🎫 *€9.*

Pfälzerland Fahrgastschiff. Enjoy a peaceful tour of the Speyer harbor on a ship built for 200 passengers. Homemade cakes and drinks are available on board. On Tuesday through Friday, 1½-hour tours depart at 1 and 3, and on Saturday at 3. The pick-up and drop-off point is on the Leinpfad. ⊠ *Dock: Leinpfad (via Rheinallee), on the Rhine riverbank, Rheinalle 2* ☎ *06232/71366* ⊕ *www.personenschifffahrt-streib. de* 🎫 *€9.50.*

DEIDESHEIM

8 km (5 miles) north of Neustadt via the Wine Road, B-271.

The half-timber houses and historical facades on Deidesheim's Marktplatz make a handsome group. Sites of interest include the Gothic Church of St. Ulrich, the Rathaus, and the elegant Hotel Deidesheimer Hof. In August, the Deidesheim Weinkerwe (wine festival) begins at the Markplatz, and in December, it's the site of a lively Christmas market.

Deidesheim is the first of three Wine Road villages that are renowned for their vineyards and the wine estates in the area, known as the Three Bs of the Pfalz—Bassermann, Buhl, and Bürklin-Wolf. As for Deidesheim itself, it's got some romantic restaurants tucked into hidden courtyards and some of the most upscale hotels in the region—though the main reason to visit remains the chance to taste some of the best wines the Pfalz has to offer at the numerous *Weingüter* (wineries) lining the streets. Most are open to visitors daily year-round.

TOURS

The Deidesheim visitor center conducts tours May through October on Saturday at 10 (€3).

ESSENTIALS

Visitor Information Deidesheim ⊠ *Tourist-Information, Bahnhofstr. 5* ☎ *06326/96770* ⊕ *www.deidesheim.de* 🕙 *Apr.–Oct., weekdays 9–noon and 2–5, Sat. 9–12:30; Nov.–Mar., weekdays 9–noon and 2–5.*

EXPLORING

Church of St. Ulrich. A Gothic gem inside and out, this is the only 15th-century church in the Palatinate region whose walls have been entirely preserved, though the interior has changed according to the style of the times. Though looted during the French Revolution and turned into a wine warehouse and later a military prison, the basic exterior structure of the church hasn't been altered. The interior includes stained glass that dates from the Middle Ages and wooden figures from around 1500. ⊠ *Pfarrgasse 3* ☎ *06326/345* ⊕ *www.st-ulrich-deidesheim.de.*

Rathaus und Museum für Weinkultur (*Town Hall and Museum of Wine Culture*). The old Rathaus, whose doorway is crowned by a baldachin and baroque dome, is on the Marktplatz. The attractive open staircase leading up to the entrance is the site of the festive *Geissbock-Versteigerung* (billy-goat auction) every Pentecost Tuesday, followed by a parade and folk dancing. The goat is the tribute neighboring Lambrecht has paid Deidesheim since 1404 for grazing rights. Inside, in addition to a richly appointed Ratssaal (council chamber), is a museum of wine culture, which examines the importance of wine throughout history. There's also a wine bar where you can taste and buy wines from the area. ⊠ *Marktpl. 9* ☎ *06326/981–561* ⊕ *www.weinkultur-deidesheim. de* ⊠ *Donation requested* ⊙ *Mar.–Dec., Wed.–Sun. 4–6.*

Schloss Deidesheim. Vines, flowers, and *Feigenbäume* (fig trees) cloak the houses behind St. Ulrich on Heumarktstrasse and its extension, Deichelgasse (nicknamed Feigengasse). To see the workshops and ateliers of about a dozen local artists and goldsmiths, follow the Künstler-Rundweg, a signposted trail (black on yellow signs). The tourist office has a brochure with a map and opening hours. Cross the Wine Road to reach the grounds of Schloss Deidesheim, now a wine estate and pub. The bishops of Speyer built a moated castle on the site in the 13th century. Twice destroyed and rebuilt, the present castle dates from 1817, and the moats have been converted into gardens. ⊠ *Schlossstr. 4* ☎ *06326/96690* ⊕ *www.schloss-deidesheim.de* ⊙ *Pub: Apr.–Oct., closed Tues., no lunch Mon.–Thurs.; Nov.–Mar., dinner only Fri.–Sun., lunch weekends only.*

SWEET SOUVENIRS

Josef Biffar & Co. The Biffar family not only runs a first-class wine estate but also manufactures candied fruits and ginger that make for delicious souvenirs. ⊠ *Niederkircher Str. 15, Deidesheim* ☎ *06326/96760* ⊕ *www.biffar.com* ⊙ *Weekdays 9–5, Sat. 10–1:30.*

WHERE TO EAT AND STAY

$$$
GERMAN

✕ **Gasthaus Zur Kanne.** This friendly family-run restaurant, with an outdoor stone-walled patio hidden inside a lovely courtyard, has been a guesthouse of some sort since 1160. The short but smart menu focuses on the local and seasonal, listing the producers of every product; the Pfalz-focused wine list is organized by the towns where the bottles were produced. The set menu of three courses for €27 (€37 with wine pairings) is a good deal. If they're available, the red-deer meatballs and chanterelles with dumplings are both delicious regional options. As a bonus, this is one of the only dining options in the region with an English menu. ⑤ *Average main: €21* ⊠ *Weinstr. 31* ☎ *06326/96600* ⊕ *www. gasthauszurkanne.de* ⊙ *Closed Mon. and Tues.*

$$$$
GERMAN
Fodor's Choice
★

✕ **Restaurant Freundstück im Ketschauer Hof.** An 18th-century complex in a beautiful park is the home to the Bassermann-Jordan wine estate and an elegant restaurant, which has one Michelin star. Inside the restaurant and the bistrolike wine bar, elements of the original structures harmonize with modern, minimalist decor. The chef prepares elaborate dishes in the restaurant and upscale regional dishes in the wine bar. To truly take in the range of dishes, try one of the tasting menus, priced from €89 to €109, though you can also order à la carte. $ *Average main: €55 ⊠ Ketschauerhofstr. 1 ☎ 06326/70000 ⊕ www.ketschauer-hof.com ⊗ Closed 3 wks in Jan. Restaurant closed Sun. and Mon. No lunch Sat. and Tues.*

$$$
GERMAN
✕ **Restaurant St. Urban.** Named after the patron saint of the wine industry, this upscale wine restaurant offers traditional Palatinate cuisine and wines from more than 50 local wineries. If the weather is nice, have a ginger fizz (an aperitif of lemon, gin, and ginger) on the terrace before sampling one of the hearty regional dishes. $ *Average main: €22 ⊠ Hotel Deidesheimer Hof, Am Marktpl. 1 ☎ 06326/96870 ⊕ www.deidesheimerhof.de ⊗ Closed 2 wks in Jan.*

$$
HOTEL
Fodor'sChoice
★
Hotel Deidesheimer Hof. Despite the glamour of some of its clientele—the heads of state, entertainers, and sports stars line the guest book—this hotel retains its country charm and friendly service. **Pros:** some rooms have whirlpool baths; friendly staff; central location on the Marktplatz. **Cons:** breakfast costs an impressive €21. $ *Rooms from: €125 ⊠ Am Marktpl. 1 ☎ 06326/96870 ⊕ www.deidesheimerhof.de ⤳ 24 rooms, 4 suites ⊗ Hotel closed 2 wks in Jan. Restaurant closed Sun. and Mon., Jan. to mid-Feb., and early July to late Aug. No lunch.* ⷮ⊘ *No meals.*

$$$$
HOTEL
Fodor'sChoice
★
Hotel Ketschauer Hof. This sleek, sophisticated former manor-house, one of the only modern design hotels in the region attracts a discerning crowd. **Pros:** beautiful design; close to the center of town; friendly service. **Cons:** expensive, and breakfast costs €25 extra; few public spaces in the hotel. $ *Rooms from: €230 ⊠ Ketschauerhofstr. 1 ☎ 06326/70000 ⊕ www.ketschauer-hof.com ⤳ 5 rooms, 13 suites* ⷮ⊘ *No meals.*

EN
ROUTE
Forst and **Wachenheim**, both a few minutes' drive north of Deidesheim, complete the trio of famous wine villages. As you approach Forst, depart briefly from B-271 (take the left fork in the road) to see the Old Town and its vine- and ivy-clad sandstone and half-timber vintners' mansions. Peek through the large portals to see the lush courtyards. Many estates on this lane have pubs, as does the town's *Winzerverein* (cooperative winery). Wachenheim is another 2 km (1 mile) down the road. Its cooperative, Wachtenburg Winzer (with a good restaurant), is on the left at the entrance to town. Head for the Wachtenburg (castle) ruins up on the hill for a glass of wine. The *Burgschänke* (castle pub) is open if the flag is flying.

BAD DÜRKHEIM

6 km (4 miles) north of Deidesheim on B-271.

This pretty spa-town is nestled into the hills at the edge of the Palatinate Forest and ringed by vineyards. The saline springs discovered here in 1338 are the source of today's drinking and bathing cures, and at harvest time there's a detoxifying *Traubenkur* (grape-juice cure). The town is the site of the Dürkheimer Wurstmarkt, the world's largest wine festival, held in mid-September. Legendary quantities of *Weck, Worscht, un Woi* (dialect for rolls, sausage, and wine) are consumed at the fair, including enough wine to fill half a million *Schoppen*, the

A splendid example of Romanesque architecture, the Kaiserdom (Imperial Cathedral) has the largest crypt in Germany.

region's traditional glasses, which hold a half-liter (about a pint). The festival grounds are also the site of the world's largest wine cask, the **Dürkheimer Riesenfass,** with a capacity of 450,000 gallons. Built in 1934 by an ambitious cooper, the cask is now a restaurant that can seat more than 450 people.

GETTING HERE AND AROUND

Regional trains link Bad Dürkheim with Freinsheim and Neustadt. Once in town, all the hotels and restaurants are within easy walking distance. Bad Dürkheim has tours (€4–€5.50, including a glass of champagne) May through October. The departing on Monday at 11 and on Thursday and Saturday at 10:30 in front of the Tourist-Information office. You can check with Tourist-Information for a number of other interesting programs, including a Wine Road tour, wine tastings, and visits to the cure facilities.

ESSENTIALS

Visitor Information Bad Dürkheim ⊠ *Tourist-Information, Kurbrunnenstr. 14* ☎ *06322/956–6250* ⊕ *www.bad-duerkheim.com* ⊙ *Mar.–early Nov., weekdays 9–6; early Nov.–Feb., weekdays 9–5.*

EXPLORING

Burgruine Hardenburg (*Hardenburg Fortress*). The massive ruins of 13th-century Hardenburg Castle lie 3 km (2 miles) west (via B-37) of Kloster Limburg. In its heyday, it was inhabited by more than 200 people. It burned down in 1794. ⊠ *B-37* ☎ *06322/7530* ⊕ *www.schloss-hardenburg.de* 🎟 *€3* ⊙ *Apr.–Sept., Tues.–Sun. 9–6; Jan.–Mar., Oct., and Nov., Tues.–Sun. 9–4:30.*

Heidenmauer (*literally, "heathen wall"*). One kilometer northwest of town lies the Heidenmauer, the remains of an ancient Celtic ring wall more than 2 km (1 mile) in circumference and up to 20 feet thick in parts. The remnants are on the Kastanienberg, above the quarry. Nearby are the rock drawings at **Kriemhildenstuhl,** an old Roman quarry where the legionnaires of Mainz excavated sandstone.

Kloster Limburg (*Limburg Monastery*). Overlooking the suburb of Grethen are the ruins of Kloster Limburg. Emperor Konrad II laid the cornerstone in 1030, supposedly on the same day that he laid the cornerstone of the Kaiserdom in Speyer. The monastery was never completely rebuilt after a fire in 1504, but it's a majestic backdrop for open-air performances in summer. From the tree-shaded terrace of the adjacent restaurant Spötzl's Klosterschänke Limburg ($–$$), you can combine good food and wine with a great view. ⊠ *Luitpoldweg 1* ☎ *06322/935–140* ⊕ *www.klosterschaenkelimburg.de* ⌷ *€1 for tower visit* ⊙ *Apr.–Oct., daily 9–8; Nov.–Mar., daily 9–5:30. Restaurant closed Mon. mid-Apr.–Nov., and closed Mon. and Tues. Nov.–mid-Apr.*

WHERE TO EAT

$
GERMAN
✕ **Dürkheimer Riesenfass.** Sure, it's a bit of a tourist trap, but then again, how often do you get the chance to eat in the world's biggest wine barrel? The two-story "giant cask" is divided into various rooms and niches with rustic wood furnishings. Venture upstairs to see the impressive *Festsaal mit Empore* (banquet hall with gallery). There's also extensive outdoor seating if the weather's nice. Regional wines, Pfälzer specialties, and international dishes are served year-round. ⑤ *Average main: €14* ⊠ *St. Michael Allee 1* ☎ *06322/2143* ⊕ *www. duerkheimer-fass.de.*

$
GERMAN
✕ **Petersilie.** Behind a group of lush, potted plants and a sign on a pink-and-white house reading "bier- und weinstube tenne" stands this gem, which stands out from the many other cafés and eateries on Römerplatz. Patio seating is great for people-watching; indoors is warm and cozy, with rustic wooden tables, beamed ceilings, and pillow-lined benches. The three-course Sunday menu ($) is a great value and a good way to experience the homey Pfälzer cuisine here. ⑤ *Average main: €15* ⊠ *Römerpl. 12* ☎ *06322/4394* ⊕ *www.weinstube-petersilie.de.*

WHERE TO STAY

$$
HOTEL
▦ **Mercure Hotel Bad Dürkheim an den Salinen.** Within walking distance to the center of town, this well-maintained chain hotel offers free admission to the Salinarium water park and spa next door, where there are indoor and outdoor pools and wellness treatments. **Pros:** free Wi-Fi; plenty of free parking; three restaurants and two bars in the hotel. **Cons:** not a lot of character. ⑤ *Rooms from: €135* ⊠ *Kurbrunnenstr. 30–32* ☎ *06322/6010* ⊕ *www.mercure.com* ⌷ *100 rooms* ⑂*⊙I Breakfast.*

$
B&B/INN
▦ **Weingut Fitz-Ritter.** At the Fitz-Ritter wine estate there are two different places to stay: a centuries-old stone cottage that sleeps up to four people and has its own pool on the parklike grounds, and four more rooms in a courtyard full of oleanders, palms, fig trees, and nesting swallows.

The Rhine Terrace

Pros: quiet location amid the vines; friendly staff; short walk to the town center. **Cons:** minimum stay in the cottage is seven nights; on weekends Apr.–Oct. all four rooms need to be rented together. ⑤ *Rooms from: €100 ⊠ Weinstr. Nord 51 ☎ 06322/5389 ⊕ www.fitz-ritter.de ☞ 1 cottage, 4 rooms* ⓘ *No meals.*

10

\$
B&B/INN 🏠 **Weingut und Gästehaus Ernst Karst und Sohn.** Rooms at this cheerful guesthouse in the middle of the vineyards are airy and furnished mostly in pine; all of them have splendid views of the countryside, which you are invited to explore on bikes that you can borrow. **Pros:** quiet vineyard location; friendly staff. **Cons:** rooms include breakfast, but apartments don't; far from the sights. ⑤ *Rooms from: €75 ⊠ In den Almen 15 ☎ 06322/2862 ⊕ www.weingut-karst.de ☞ 3 rooms, 6 apartments* ▭ *No credit cards* ⓧ *Closed Nov.–Feb.* ⓘ *Breakfast.*

NIGHTLIFE AND THE ARTS

Spielbank (*Casino*). This casino is open daily at 11 am for the slot machines, 2 pm for roulette and poker, and 6 pm for blackjack. Jacket and tie are no longer required, but tennis shoes, T-shirts, and shorts are not allowed. Be certain to bring your passport for identification; the minimum age is 18. ⊠ *Kurparkhotel, Schlosspl. 6* ⊕ *www.casino-bad-duerkheim.de* ▭ *€3.50.*

SHOPPING

Weindom. Several hundred wines from Bad Dürkheim and vicinity can be sampled and purchased at this shop, next to the Dürkheimer Riesenfass (giant cask). The shop also sells other grape products and accessories. ⊠ *St.-Michaels-Allee 10* ⊕ *www.weindom.de* ⊗ *Daily 10–6.*

SPORTS AND THE OUTDOORS

Kurhaus Staatsbad. The Kurhaus Staatsbad houses all kinds of bathing facilities, including thermal baths, herbal steam baths, a sauna, and a *hammam* (Turkish bath). ⊠ *Kurbrunnenstr. 14* ☎ *06322/9640* ⊕ *www. kurzentrum-bad-duerkheim.de* ⊗ *Mon., Tues., Thurs., and Fri. 9–8, Wed. 9–8, Sat. 9–5, Sun. 9–2:30.*

THE RHINE TERRACE

Like Speyer, the cities of Worms and Mainz were Free Imperial Cities and major centers of Christian and Jewish culture in the Middle Ages. Germany's first synagogue and Europe's oldest surviving Jewish cemetery, both from the 11th century, are in Worms. The imperial diets of Worms and Speyer in 1521 and 1529 stormed around Martin Luther (1483–1546) and the rise of Protestantism. In 1455 Johannes Gutenberg (1400–68), the inventor of the printing press and of movable type in Europe, printed the first Gutenberg Bible in Mainz.

WORMS

15 km (9 miles) east of Bockenheim via B-47 from Monsheim, 45 km (28 miles) south of Mainz on B-9.

In addition to having a great Romanesque cathedral, Worms is a center of the wine trade, as well as one of the most storied and cities in Germany, with a history going back some 6,000 years. Settled by the Romans, Worms (pronounced *vawrms*) later became one of the imperial cities of the Holy Roman Empire. More than 100 imperial diets (assemblies) were held here, including the 1521 meeting where Martin Luther pleaded his cause.

Worms developed into an important garrison town under the Romans, but it's better known for its greatest legend, the *Nibelungenlied,* derived from the short-lived kingdom established by Gunther and his Burgundian tribe in the early 5th century. The complex and sprawling story was given its final shape in the 12th century and tells of love, betrayal, greed, war, and death. It ends when Attila the Hun defeats the Nibelungen (Burgundians), who find their court destroyed, their treasure lost, and their heroes dead. One of the most famous incidents tells how Hagen, treacherous and scheming, hurls the court riches into the Rhine. Near the Nibelungen Bridge there's a bronze statue of him caught in the act. The Nibelungenlied may be legend, but the story is based on fact. A Queen Brunhilda, for example, is said to have lived here. It's also known that a Burgundian tribe was defeated in 436 by Attila the Hun in what is present-day Hungary.

Not until Charlemagne resettled Worms almost 400 years later, making it one of the major cities of his empire, did the city prosper again. Worms was more than an administrative and commercial center—it was a great ecclesiastical city as well. The first expression of this religious importance was the original cathedral, consecrated in 1018. Between 1130 and 1181 it was rebuilt in three phases into the church you see today.

GETTING HERE AND AROUND

Worms can be reached by direct trains from both Mannheim and Mainz (approximately 30 minutes from each). The city center is quite compact and negotiable on foot. Worms begins its tours at the southern portal (main entrance) of the cathedral on Saturday at 10:30 and Sunday at 2 March through October. The cost is €6.

ESSENTIALS

Visitor Information Worms ⊠ *Tourist-Information, Neumarkt 14* ☎ *06241/853–7306* ⊕ *www.worms.de* ☉ *Late Mar.–Oct., weekdays 9–6, weekends 10–2; Nov.–late Mar., weekdays 9–5.*

EXPLORING

TOP ATTRACTIONS

Heylshofgarten. An imperial palace once stood in this park just north of the cathedral. It was the site of the fateful 1521 meeting between Luther and Emperor Charles V that ultimately led to the Reformation. Luther refused to recant his theses demanding Church reforms and went into exile in Eisenach, where he translated the New Testament in 1521-22. ⊠ *Stephansg. 9.*

Judenfriedhof Heiliger Sand (*Holy Sand Cemetery*). This is the oldest Jewish cemetery in Europe and also one of the most atmospheric and picturesque. The oldest of some 2,000 tombstones date from 1076. Entry is via the gate on Willy-Brandt-Ring. ⊠ *Andreasstr. and Willy-Brandt-Ring* ☉ *Daily 8–8 in summer and 8–sunset in winter.*

Fodor's Choice ★ **Kunsthaus Heylshof** (*Heylshof Art Gallery*). Located in the Heylshofgarten, this is one of the leading art museums of the region. It has an exquisite collection of German, Dutch, and French paintings as well as stained glass, glassware, porcelain, and ceramics dating from the 15th to the 19th century. ⊠ *Stephansg. 9* ☎ *06241/22000* ⊕ *www.museumheylshof.de* ⊡ *€3.50* ☉ *May–Sept., Tues.–Sun. 11–5; Oct.–Dec. and mid-Feb.–Apr., Tues.–Sat. 2–5, Sun. 11–5.*

Liebfrauenkirche (*Church of Our Lady*). This twin-towered Gothic church is set amid vineyards on the northern outskirts of Worms. It's the namesake of the popular, sweet white wine Liebfraumilch, literally, the "Milk

---

TOURING TIPS

Information: The tourist office is near the cathedral. Pick up "Two Thousand Years of History," a handy map with suggested walking tours and descriptions of the main sights.

Scenic spot: The Old Town wall between the two towers of the Nibelungen Museum affords a great view of the town.

Scenic spot: From the Holy Sand Jewish Cemetery there's a good view of a portion of the massive Old Town wall, and the cemetery itself is worth exploring.

10

of Our Lady." The wine (Blue Nun is one brand) was originally made from the grapes of the small vineyard surrounding the church, but today it's produced throughout Rheinhessen, the Pfalz, the Nahe, and the Rheingau wine regions. ⊠ *Liebfrauenring 21* ⊕ *www.liebfrauen-worms.de.*

Nibelungen Museum. This stunning sight-and-sound exhibition is dedicated to *Das Nibelungenlied (Song of the Nieblungs),* the epic German poem dating to around 1200. Cleverly installed in two medieval towers and the portion of the Old Town wall between them, the exhibition brings to life the saga of the dragon slayer Siegfried. The architecture of the structure itself is also fascinating, and the rampart provides a wonderful view of the town. The tour script (via headphones and printed matter) is offered in English. ▧ TIP➜ Allow 1½ hours for a thorough visit. ⊠ *Fischerpförtchen 10* ☎ *06241/202–120* ⊕ *www.nibelungen-museum.de* ⊡ *€5.50* ⊙ *Tues.–Fri. 10–5, weekends 10–6.*

Synagogue. This first synagogue in Worms was built in 1034, rebuilt in 1175, and expanded in 1213 with a building for women. Destroyed in 1938, it was rebuilt in 1961 using as much of the original masonry as had survived. It is located in the Jewish quarter, which is along the town wall between Martinspforte and Friesenspitze and between Judengasse and Hintere Judengasse. ⊠ *Hintere Judeng.* ⊙ *Apr.–Oct., daily 10–12:30 and 1:30–5; Nov.–Mar., daily 10–noon and 2–4; closed during services.*

Fodor'sChoice **Wormser Dom St. Peter.** In contrast to Speyer's Romanesque cathedral,
★ the Worms Cathedral of St. Peter is much more Gothic. In part this is
simply a matter of chronology, since Speyer Cathedral was finished in
1061, nearly 70 years before the one in Worms was even begun—and
long before the lighter, more vertical lines of the Gothic style evolved. In
addition, Speyer Cathedral was left largely untouched, but the Worms
Cathedral underwent frequent remodeling. The Gothic influence here
can be seen both inside and out, from the elaborate tympanum with
biblical scenes over the southern portal (today's entrance) to the great
rose window in the west choir to the five sculptures in the north aisle
recounting the life of Christ. The cathedral was gutted by fire in 1689
in the War of the Palatinate Succession. For this reason many of the
furnishings are baroque, including the magnificent gilt high altar from
1742, designed by the master architect Balthasar Neumann (1687–
1753). The choir stalls are no less decorative. They were built between
1755 and 1759 in rococo style. Walk around the building to see the
artistic detail of the exterior. ⊠ *Lutherring 9* ☎ *06241/6115* ⊕ *www.*
wormser-dom.de ✉ *Donation requested* ☉ *Apr.–Oct., daily 9–6; Nov.–*
Mar., daily 10–5; closed during services.

WORTH NOTING

Museum der Stadt Worms (*Municipal Museum*). To find out more about
the history of Worms, visit this museum, housed in the cloisters of a
Romanesque church in the Andreasstift. The collection includes artifacts from the Roman period, including one of the largest collections
of Roman glass in Germany, all the way up to local art from the 20th
century. ⊠ *Weckerlingpl. 7* ☎ *06241/946–390* ✉ *€2* ☉ *Tues.–Sun. 10–5.*

WHERE TO EAT

$ ✕ **Gasthaus Hagenbräu.** Located a little to the west of the center, by the
GERMAN banks of the Rhine, this house brewery serves a good range of classic
German dishes and regional specialties such as Saumagen. Service and
decor are bright and cheery, and you will be surrounded by copper
vats and oak barrels as you dine. The summer terrace by the river is a
chance to enjoy a brew with a view. ⓢ *Average main: €11* ⊠ *Am Rhein*
3 ☎ *06241/921–100* ⊕ *www.hagenbraeu.de.*

10

WHERE TO STAY

$ ⚟ **Dom-Hotel.** The appeal of this hotel, with comfortable if somewhat
HOTEL bland rooms, lies in its friendly staff and its terrific location in the heart
of the pedestrian zone (a parking garage is available for free). **Pros:**
central location; breakfast included. **Cons:** building design doesn't have
much charm; hotel in need of a refresh; Wi-Fi only free for first hour,
then €6 per day. ⓢ *Rooms from: €72* ⊠ *Obermarkt 10* ☎ *06241/9070*
⊕ *www.dom-hotel.de* ⤳ *55 rooms, 2 apartments* ⦿ *Breakfast.*

$ ⚟ **Land- und Winzerhotel Bechtel.** The friendly Bechtel family, winegrow-
HOTEL ers and proud parents of a former German Wine Queen, offer very
pleasant accommodations on the grounds of their wine estate in the
suburb of Heppenheim, about 10 km (6 miles) west of Worms. **Pros:**
quiet location; excellent value; rooms have balconies. **Cons:** far from the
sights; extra charge for breakfast; check out is on the early side, at 10
am. ⓢ *Rooms from: €65* ⊠ *Pfälzer Waldstr. 100, Worms-Heppenheim*

☎ *06241/36536* ⊕ *www.landhotel-bechtel.de* ⤴ *11 rooms* ⊙ *Restaurant closed Tues. No lunch Mon.–Sat.* ⦿ *No meals.*

$ ⦿ **Landhotel Zum Schwanen.** Bärbel Berkes runs this lovingly restored
HOTEL country inn in Osthofen, 10 km (6 miles) northwest of Worms. **Pros:**
quiet location; friendly staff; free Wi-Fi in rooms. **Cons:** far from the
sights; no elevator. ⑤ *Rooms from: €98* ⊠ *Friedrich-Ebert-Str. 40, west
of B-9, Osthofen* ☎ *06242/9140* ⊕ *www.zum-schwanen-osthofen.de*
⤴ *30 rooms, 3 suites* ⦿ *Breakfast.*

SHOPPING

Der Weinladen. For wine accessories and other grape-related products,
drop by this shop near the Municipal Museum, opposite the cathedral.
⊠ *Weckerlingpl. 1* ☎ *06241/911–180* ⊕ *www.derweinladenworms.de*
⊟ *No credit cards* ⊙ *Closed Sun. and Mon.*

Star Region. This store and restaurant specializes in culinary items from
Rheinhessen, Odenwald, and Pfalz. There's also an excellent lunch buffet
($) featuring local specialties like creamed sauerkraut and *Spätburgun-
dergulasch* (red wine goulash). ⊠ *Kammererstr. 60* ☎ *06241/269–796*
⊕ *www.starregion.de* ⊙ *Closed Sun.*

OPPENHEIM

*26 km (16 miles) north of Worms, 23 km (14 miles) south of Mainz
on B-9.*

Oppenheim is slightly off the beaten path, making it an ideal destination
if you're looking to avoid the hordes of tourists that often descend on
the Wine Road in mid-summer.

The Katharinenkirche is the obvious crown of Oppenheim, but the picturesque Altstadt also hides a mysterious gem: the **Oppenheimer Kellerlab-
yrinth**, a 40-km, five-level-deep, underground passageway system. Tours
cost €7.50; contact the **Oppenheim Tourist Office** in advance for tickets.

GETTING HERE AND AROUND

An excellent network of regional trains connect Oppenheim with
Mainz and Worms. Either journey takes about 15–20 minutes, and
trains depart about every half hour. Nierstein is just one stop away on
the same regional train.

ESSENTIALS

Oppenheim Tourist Office ⊠ *Merianstr. 2* ☎ *06133/490–919, 06133/490–914*
⊕ *www.stadt-oppenheim.de/index.php?id=10* ⊙ *Apr. 15–Oct. 15, weekdays 10–5,
weekends 11–5; Oct. 16–Apr. 14, Sat. 11–2 and Sun. 11-4.*

EXPLORING

Deutsches Weinbaumuseum (*German Viticultural Museum*). Oppenheim and its neighbors to the north, Nierstein and Nackenheim, are
home to some of Rheinhessen's best-known vineyards. The Deutsches
Weinbaumuseum has wine-related artifacts that chronicle the region's
2,000-year-old wine-making tradition, not to mention the world's largest collection of mousetraps and more than 2,000 corkscrews. ⊠ *Wormser Str. 49* ☎ *06133/2544* ⊕ *www.dwb-museum.de* ⤴ *€4* ⊙ *Apr.–Oct.,
Tues.–Fri. 2–5, weekends 10–5.*

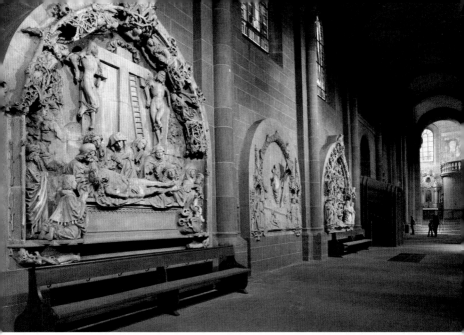
One of the focal points of the Gothic Wormser Dom St. Peter (Worms Cathedral of St. Peter) is the gilded altar.

Katharinenkirche (*St. Katharine's Church*). On the way to Oppenheim, the vine-covered hills parallel to the Rhine gradually steepen. Then, unexpectedly, the spires of Oppenheim's Gothic Katharinenkirche come into view. The contrast of its pink sandstone facade against a bright blue sky is striking. Built between 1220 and 1439, it's the most important Gothic church between Strasbourg and Köln. The interior affords a rare opportunity to admire original 14th-century stained-glass windows and two magnificent rose windows, the Lily Window and the Rose of Oppenheim. The church houses masterfully carved tombstones, and the chapel behind it has a *Beinhaus* (charnel house) that contains the bones of 20,000 citizens and soldiers from the 15th to 18th century. ✉ *Merianstr. 6, just north of Marktpl.* ☎ *06133/2381* ⊕ *www.katharinen-kirche.de* ☉ *Apr.–Oct., daily 8–6; Nov.–Mar., daily 9–5.*

NIGHTLIFE AND THE ARTS

Burgruine Landskrone. Concerts are held in St. Katharine's, and open-air theater takes place in the Burgruine Landskrone, the 12th-century imperial fortress ruins. ■ **TIP→** From here there's a wonderful view of the town and the vineyards, extending all the way to Worms on a clear day. The castle ruins are northwest of the church. Follow the Dalbergerstrasse north; from there it's a short walk up to the ruins. For tickets to the open-air theater performances contact the Oppenheim tourist office.

NIERSTEIN

3 km (2 miles) north of Oppenheim on B-9.

Surrounded by 2,700 acres of vines, Nierstein is the largest wine-growing community on the Rhine. It also has Glöck, Germany's **oldest documented vineyard** (AD 742), which surrounds St. Kilian's Church.

GETTING HERE AND AROUND

Regional trains leave roughly every hours between Neirstein and both Mainz and Worms. The trips take about 30 minutes.

Winzergenossenschaft (*Cooperative winery*). The Winzergenossenschaft can be the starting point of an easy hike or drive to the vineyard heights and the vantage point at the Wartturm (watchtower). In mid-June, wine tasting stands are set up along the route, which is called *roten Hang*, or "red slope"—the soil here has a lot of red clay in it. ✉ *Karolingerstr. 6* ☎ *06133/971–720* ⊕ *www.roter-hang.de.*

WHERE TO STAY

$
HOTEL
📺 **Best Western Wein & Parkhotel.** Spacious, light rooms decorated in warm shades of ocher, chic bathrooms, and an inviting lounge and terrace make for comfortable, relaxing quarters here. **Pros:** friendly; quiet location; free Wi-Fi throughout hotel. **Cons:** a chain hotel with few surprises. $ *Rooms from: €95* ✉ *An der Kaiserlinde 1* ☎ *06133/5080* ⊕ *www.weinhotel.bestwestern.de* ⤴ *55 rooms* ⑩ *Breakfast.*

$
B&B/INN
Fodor's Choice
★
📺 **Jordan's Untermühle.** The spacious grounds of an old mill are home to a country inn, a restaurant, and a *Vinothek* (wine store). **Pros:** beautiful buildings; great value; very quiet. **Cons:** a long way from anywhere; difficult to reach without a car. $ *Rooms from: €95* ✉ *Ausserhalb 1, Köngernheim ⊹ West of B-9, at Nierstein turn left on B-420 (toward Wörrstadt), drive through Köngernheim and turn right toward Selzen* ☎ *06737/71000* ⊕ *www.jordans-untermuehle.de* ⤴ *25 rooms, 1 suite, 4 studios* ☉ *Restaurant: No lunch except Sun.* ⑩ *Breakfast.*

MAINZ

14 km (9 miles) north of Nackenheim, 45 km (28 miles) north of Worms on B-9, and 42 km (26 miles) west of Frankfurt on A-3.

Mainz is the capital of the state of Rheinland-Pfalz. Today's city was built on the site of a Roman citadel dating to 38 BC. Given its central location at the confluence of the Main and Rhine rivers, it's not surprising that Mainz has always been an important trading center, rebuilt time and again in the wake of wars.

GETTING HERE AND AROUND

As the regional hub, Mainz is well served by trains, with fast connections to Frankfurt (40 minutes) and Köln (1 hour, 40 minutes). The station is a short walk west of the center. A comprehensive network of local buses makes getting around the city a breeze (route maps and timetables are posted at bus stops), while the upper areas of town are also served by trams. Although the sights are fairly spread out, they're manageable on foot if you're in reasonably good shape.

TOURS

Mainz has year-round tours departing Saturday at 11 and 2 (€7) from the Touristik Centrale. The office is one story above street level on the footbridge over Rheinstrasse. There are additional tours from May through October, on Sunday, Monday, Wednesday, and Friday at 2.

DISCOUNTS AND DEALS

■ TIP➜ To see the sights, head for the Touristik Centrale (tourist office) to pick up a MainzCard, a two-day pass, for about €10. It covers a basic walking tour, unlimited use of public transportation (including travel to and from Frankfurt Airport), and free entry to museums and the casino, as well as a reduction in price on some KD cruises and theater tickets. The card can also be bought from the station, some hotel receptions, and participating museums.

ESSENTIALS

Visitor Information Mainz ⊠ *Touristik Centrale, Brückenturm am Rathaus* ☎ *06131/286–210* ⊕ *www.touristik-mainz.de* ⊗ *Weekdays 9–6, Sat. 10–4, Sun. 11–3.*

EXPLORING

TOP ATTRACTIONS

Fodor'sChoice ★ **Dom** (*Cathedral of St. Martin and St. Stephan*). This cathedral's interior is a virtual sculpture gallery of elaborate monuments and tombstones of archbishops, bishops, and canons, many of which are significant artworks in their own right. Emperor Otto II began building the oldest of the Rhineland's trio of grand Romanesque cathedrals in 975, the year in which he named Willigis archbishop and chancellor of the empire. Henry II, the last Saxon emperor of the Holy Roman Empire, was crowned here in 1002, as was his successor, Konrad II, the first Salian emperor, in 1024. In 1009, on the very day of its consecration, the cathedral burned to the ground. It was the first of seven fires the Dom has endured. Today's cathedral dates mostly from the 11th to 13th century. During the Gothic period, remodeling diluted the Romanesque identity of the original; an imposing baroque spire was added in the 18th century. Nevertheless, the building remains essentially Romanesque, and its floor plan demonstrates a clear link to the cathedrals in Speyer and Worms. ⊠ *Domstr. 3* ☎ *06131/253–412* ⊕ *www.mainz-dom.de* ⊴ *Donations requested* ⊗ *Mar.–Oct., weekdays 9–6:30, Sat. 9–4, Sun. 12:45–3 and 4–6:30; Nov.–Feb., weekdays 9–5, Sat. 9–4, Sun. 12:45–3 and 4–5; closed during services.*

Dom und Diözesanmuseum. From the Middle Ages until secularization in the early 19th century, the archbishops of Mainz, who numbered among the imperial electors, were extremely influential politicians and property owners. The wealth of religious art treasures they left behind can be viewed in the cathedral cloisters. ⊠ *Domstr. 3* ☎ *06131/253–344* ⊕ *www.dommuseum-mainz.de* ⊴ *€5* ⊗ *Tues.–Fri. 10–5, weekends 11–6.*

Gutenberg Museum. Opposite the east end of the cathedral (and closest to the Rhine) stands this fascinating museum, which is devoted to the history of writing and printing. Exhibits include historical printing presses, incunabula (books printed in Europe before 1501), and medieval manuscripts with illuminated letters, as well as three precious

10

In addition to Bibles printed circa 1455, the Gutenberg Museum has artifacts that tell the story of the printed word, including ancient manuscripts and presses.

42-line Gutenberg bibles printed circa 1455. A replica workshop demonstrates how Gutenberg implemented his invention of movable type. ⊠ *Liebfrauenpl. 5* ☎ *06131/122–640* ⊕ *www.gutenberg-museum.de* 🎫 *€5* ⊙ *Tues.–Sat. 9–5, Sun. 11–3.*

Kupferberg Terrasse (*sparkling wine cellars*). These hillside cellars were built in 1850 on a site where the Romans had cultivated vines and cellared wine. The Kupferberg family expanded, creating 60 seven-story-deep vaulted cellars—the deepest in the world. The winery has a splendid collection of glassware; posters from the belle-époque period (1898–1914); richly carved casks from the 18th and 19th centuries; and the **Traubensaal** (Grape Hall), a tremendous example of the art-nouveau style. Tours lasting from 1½ to 2 hours are offered most Saturdays and some Wednesdays and Fridays in summer and fall, and include several glasses of sparkling wines and champagne. Online reservations are required. The Kupferberg Terrassen restaurant ($$$) here is a lovely place to dine before or after your tour. ⊠ *Kupferbergterrasse 17–19* ☎ *06131/9230* ⊕ *www.kupferbergterrasse.com* 🎫 *€16 1½-hr tour, €21–€28.50 2-hr tour.*

Landesmuseum. The various collections of the Museum of the State of Rheinland-Pfalz are in the former electors' stables, easily recognized by the statue of a golden stallion over the entrance. Exhibits range from the Middle Ages to the 20th century. Among the highlights are paintings by Dutch masters, artworks from the baroque to art-nouveau period, and collections of porcelain and faience. ⊠ *Grosse Bleiche 49–51* ☎ *06131/28570* ⊕ *www.landesmuseum-mainz.de* 🎫 *€6* ⊙ *Tues. 10–8, Wed.–Sun. 10–5.*

Römisch-Germanisches Zentralmuseum. The wonderful collection here chronicles cultural developments in the area up to the early Middle Ages. One of the highlights is a tiny Celtic glass dog from the 1st or 2nd century BC. The entrance for the museum, which is in the Kurfürstliches Schloss (Electoral Palace), is around the back, on the river (east) side of the building. ⊠ *Ernst-Ludwig-Pl. 2* ☏ *06131/91240* ⊕ *web.rgzm.de/ rgzmmuseum.html* ⊡ *Free* ⊙ *Tues.–Sun. 10–6.*

Fodor's Choice **St. Stephanskirche** (*St. Stephen's Church*). It's just a short walk up Gaus-
★ trasse from Schillerplatz to the church, which affords a hilltop view of the city. Nearly 200,000 people make the trip each year to see the nine magnificent blue stained-glass windows designed by the Russian-born artist Marc Chagall. ⊠ *Kleine Weissg. 12, via Gaustr.* ☏ *06131/231– 640* ⊕ *www.st-stephan-mainz.de* ⊙ *Mar.–Oct., Mon.–Sat. 10–5, Sun. noon–5; Nov.–Feb., Mon.–Sat. 10–4:30, Sun. noon–4:30.*

WORTH NOTING

Marktplatz. The area around the cathedral and the *Höfchen* (little court-yard) are the focal points of the town. ▉ TIP➜ Both are especially color-ful on Tuesday, Friday, and Saturday, when farmers set up their stands to sell produce and flowers.

FAMILY **Schillerplatz.** This square, ringed by beautiful baroque palaces, is the site of the ebullient **Fastnachtsbrunnen** (Carnival Fountain), with 200 figures related to Mainz's "fifth season" of the year. ⊠ *Schillerpl.*

WHERE TO EAT

$ ✕ **Eisgrub-Bräu.** It's loud, it's busy, and the beer is brewed in the vaulted
GERMAN cellars on-site. An Eisgrub brew is just the ticket to wash down a hearty plate of *Schweinehaxen* (pork knuckle) or *Meterwurst* (yard-long, rolled bratwurst), *Bratkartoffeln* (home fries), and sauerkraut. During the week, there's a lunch special for €5.90. Brewery tours are free, but make reservations in advance. It's open most days from 11:30 am–mid-night, and on Friday and Saturday until 1 am. ⑤ *Average main: €12* ⊠ *Weisslilieng. 1a* ☏ *06131/221–104* ⊕ *www.eisgrub.de.*

$$$ ✕ **Gebert's Weinstuben.** Gebert's traditional wine restaurant serves
GERMAN refined versions of regional favorites. In summer, the fresh asparagus dishes are popular. The *geeister Kaffee* (coffee ice cream and chocolate praline in a cup of coffee) uses delicious, homemade chocolate pralines. German wines, especially Rheinhessen, dominate the excellent wine list. You can also dine outside in the appealing courtyard. ⑤ *Aver-age main: €22* ⊠ *Frauenlobstr. 94, near the Rhine* ☏ *06131/611–619* ⊕ *www.geberts-weinstuben.de* ⊙ *Closed Mon. and 3 wks in July or Aug. No lunch Sat.*

$ ✕ **Haus des Deutschen Weines.** Late hours and luncheon specials are
GERMAN among the crowd-pleasers here, and the menu is broad enough to encompass both snacks and full-course meals, with huge salads and game year-round. Mainz specialties include *Spundekäs* (cheese whipped with cream and onions) or *Handkäse mit Musik* (pungent, semihard cheese served with diced onions in vinaigrette). As the name suggests, there's also a great selection of German wines. ⑤ *Average main: €14* ⊠ *Gutenbergpl. 3–5* ☏ *06131/221–300* ⊕ *www.hdw-gaststaetten.de.*

10

CLOSE UP

Gutenberg: The Father of Modern Printing

His invention—printing with movable type—transformed the art of communication, yet much about the life and work of Johannes Gutenberg is undocumented, starting with his year of birth. It's estimated that he was born in Mainz circa 1400 into a patrician family that supplied the city mint with metal to be coined. Gutenberg's later accomplishments attest to his own skill in working with metals. Details about his education are unclear, but he probably helped finance his studies by copying manuscripts in a monastic scriptorium. He moved to Strasbourg circa 1434, where he was a goldsmith by day and an inventor by night. It was here that he worked—in great secrecy—to create movable type and develop a press suitable for printing by adapting the conventional screw press used for wine making. By 1448

Gutenberg had returned to Mainz. Loans from a wealthy businessman enabled him to set up a printer's workshop and print the famous 42-line Bible. The lines of text are in black ink, yet each of the original 180 Bibles printed from 1452 to 1455 is unique, thanks to the artistry of the hand-painted illuminated letters.

Despite its significance, Gutenberg's invention was not a financial success. His quest for perfection rather than profit led to a legal battle during which his creditor was awarded the workshop and the Bible type. Gutenberg's attempts to set up another print shop in Mainz failed, but from 1465 until his death in 1468 he received an allowance for service to the archbishop of Mainz, which spared the "father of modern printing" from dying in poverty.

$$ × **Heiliggeist.** This lively café-bistro-bar serves breakfast, lunch, and

MEDITERRANEAN dinner on weekends and dinner until midnight during the week. The compact menu includes elaborate salad platters as well as creatively spiced and sauced fish and meat dishes. In summer the beer garden is always packed, and there's an extensive drink list. One house specialty worth trying is the *Croustarte*, an upscale version of pizza. Heiliggeist's modern, minimal decor is an interesting contrast to the historic vaulted ceilings in this former almshouse and hospital church, which was built in 1236. $ *Average main: €16* ⊠ *Mailandsg. 11* ☎ *06131/225–757* ⊕ *www.heiliggeist-mainz.de* ⌫ *Reservations not accepted* ⚌ *No credit cards* ⊘ *No lunch weekdays.*

WHERE TO STAY

$$ ⊡ **FAVORITE parkhotel.** Mainz's city park is a lush setting for this amenity-

HOTEL filled hotel; it's a 10-minute downhill walk through the park to the Old Town. **Pros:** quiet location; friendly staff; good views. **Cons:** a bit far from the sights; you can hear the train from some rooms; daily charge for Wi-Fi; not all rooms have air-conditioning. $ *Rooms from: €167* ⊠ *Karl-Weiser-Str. 1* ☎ *06131/80150* ⊕ *www.favorite-mainz.de* ⌷ *115 rooms, 7 suites* ⊘ *Favorite restaurant closed Mon. and Tues.* ⎪⊙⎪ *Breakfast.*

$ ⊡ **Ibis Mainz City.** Here you'll find modern and functional rooms and

HOTEL a great location on the edge of the Old Town. **Pros:** central location; good rates and deals; a/c in all rooms. **Cons:** chain hotel lacking in character; buffet breakfast costs €10 extra; fee for garage parking. $ *Rooms from: €59* ✉ *Holzhofstr. 2, at Rheinstr.* ☎ *06131/2470* ⊕ *www.ibishotel.com* ⤴ *144 rooms* ❘◯❘ *Breakfast.*

$$$$ ☎ **Hyatt Regency Mainz.** From the
HOTEL spacious atrium lobby to the luxurious rooms, everything is sleek, modern, and comfortable at this hotel. **Pros:** grand public spaces; friendly staff; riverside location. **Cons:** expensive; breakfast costs extra; Wi-Fi charges are €18 a day. $ *Rooms from: €229* ✉ *Malakoff-Terrasse 1* ☎ *06131/731–234* ⊕ *www.mainz.regency.hyatt.com* ⤴ *265 rooms, 3 suites.*

CARNIVAL IN MAINZ

Carnival season runs from November 11 at 11:11 am to Ash Wednesday. There are dozens of costume balls, parties, and political cabaret sessions, but most of the heavy celebrating doesn't start until *Weiberfastnacht*, the Thursday preceding Ash Wednesday. The season culminates in a huge parade of colorful floats and marching bands through downtown on the Monday before Lent.

NIGHTLIFE AND THE ARTS

Mainz supports a broad spectrum of cultural events—classical as well as avant-garde music, dance, opera, and theater performances—at many venues throughout the city. Music lovers can attend concerts in venues ranging from the cathedral and the Rathaus to the market square and historic churches.

Nightlife centers on its numerous wine pubs. Rustic and cozy, they're packed with locals who come to enjoy a meal or snack with a glass (or more) of local wine. Most are on the Old Town's main street, Augustinerstrasse, and its side streets (Grebenstrasse, Kirschgarten, Kartäuserstrasse, Jakobsbergstrasse), or around the Gutenberg Museum, on Liebfrauenplatz.

Weinhaus Schreiner. An old Mainz favorite, Schreiner attracts a mixed, jovial clientele who come to enjoy local wine and beer paired with German cuisine. During periods of warm weather, the outdoor "vineyard" stays open till 9:45, Tuesday through Thursday, and till 10:45, Friday and Saturday. ✉ *Rheinstr. 38* ☎ *06131/225–720* ⊕ *www. weinhausschreiner.de* ⊗ *Closed Sun. and Mon.*

Weinhaus Wilhelmi. This wood-panel pub is a favorite with postcollegiates, who come to enjoy glasses of local wine while nibbling on traditional sausage and cheeses or heartier fare such as fried pork steak and meatballs with pepper sauce. ✉ *Rheinstr. 53* ☎ *06131/224–949* ⊕ *www.weinhaus-wilhelmi.de* ⊗ *No lunch.*

SHOPPING

The Old Town is full of boutiques, and the major department stores (Karstadt and Kaufhof-Galeria) typically have food halls in their lower levels. The shopping district lies basically between the Grosse Bleiche and the Old Town and includes the **Am Brand Zentrum,** an ancient marketplace that is now a pedestrian zone full of shops.

Fodor's Choice **Gutenberg-Shop.** Located in the building of the local newspaper, *Allge-*
★ *meine Zeitung Mainz,* the Gutenberg-Shop has splendid souvenirs and gifts—including pages from the Bible, books, posters, pens, and

10

stationery. The friendly staff will also arrange to ship your purchases outside the country. There's a similar selection at the shop in the Gutenberg Museum. ✉ *Marktpl. 17* ☎ *06131/143–666* ⊕ *www.gutenberg-shop.de* ⊘ *Closed Sun.*

Krempelmarkt. Antiques and perhaps a few hidden treasures await the patient shopper at Krempelmarkt. The flea market is on the banks of the Rhine (Rheinufer) between the Hilton hotel and Kaiserstrasse. At the Theodor Heuss Bridge is the the children's flea market, where the youngest sellers offer clothes, toys, and books. ✉ *Rheinufer* ⊘ *Apr.–Oct., 1st and 3rd Sat. of month 7–4; Nov.–Mar., 3rd Sat. 7–3.*

Römerpassage. This city-center shopping mall offers 100,000 square feet of stores and restaurants. It also houses the remains of a Roman temple (AD 1) discovered in 1999 during construction of the mall. The temple, which is dedicated to the goddess Isis and Magna Mater, is in the basement. ✉ *Adolf-Kolping-Str. 4* ☎ *06131/600–7100* ⊕ *www.roemerpassage.com* ⊘ *Closed Sun.*

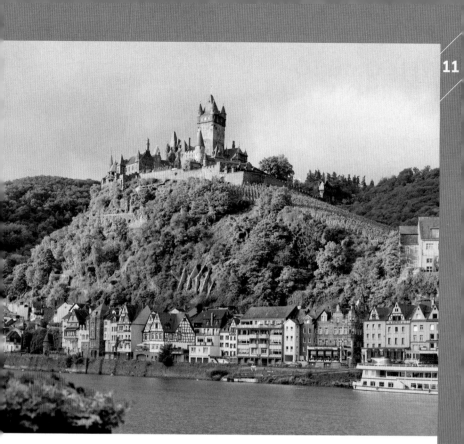

THE RHINELAND

WELCOME TO THE RHINELAND

TOP REASONS TO GO

★ **Drachenfels:**
This dramatic castle in Königswinter crowns a high hill overlooking the Rhine.

★ **Fastnacht:** Germany's Carnival season culminates with huge parades, round-the-clock music, and dancing in Düsseldorf, Köln, and Mainz the week before Ash Wednesday.

★ **Rhine in Flames:**
These massive displays of fireworks take place the first Saturday in May in Linz-Bonn; the first Saturday in July in Bingen-Rüdesheim; the second Saturday in August in Koblenz; the second Saturday in September in Oberwesel; and the third Saturday in September in St. Goar.

★ **The romance of the Rhine:** From cruises to Rhine-view rooms, castles to terraced vineyards, the Rhine does not disappoint.

★ **Spectacular wine:**
A whole culinary tradition has grown up around the distinctive light white wines of the Rhine and Mosel.

1 The Rheingau. Though the course of the Rhine is generally south to north, it bends sharply at Wiesbaden and flows east to west for 31 km (19 miles) to Rüdesheim. This means that the steep hills on its right bank have a southern exposure, and that vineyards there produce superb wines.

2 The Mittelrhein. The romance of the Rhine is most apparent in the Middle Rhine, from Bingen to Koblenz. The 65-km (40-mile) stretch of the Upper Middle Rhine Valley was designated a UNESCO World Heritage Site in 2002 with its concentration of awesome castles, medieval towns, and the vineyards of the Rhine Gorge.

3 The Mosel Valley. Koblenz and Trier aren't very far apart as the crow flies, but the driving distance along the incredible twists and turns of the Mosel River is 201 km (125 miles). The journey is worth it, though. The region is unspoiled, the towns gemlike, the scenery a medley of vineyards and forests, and there's a wealth of Roman artifacts, medieval churches, and castle ruins to admire.

4 Bonn and the Köln (Cologne) lowlands. North of Koblenz, the Rhine is less picturesque, but it does shoulder the cosmopolitan cities Köln and Düsseldorf, as well as the former capital city of Bonn.

GETTING ORIENTED

The most spectacular stretch of the Rhineland is along the Middle Rhine, between Mainz and Koblenz, which takes in the awesome castles and vineyards of the Rhine Gorge. Highways hug the river on each bank (B-42 on the north and eastern sides, and B-9 on the south and western sides), and car ferries crisscross the Rhine at many points. Cruises depart from many cities and towns, including as far south as Frankfurt. Trains service all the towns, and the Mainz–Bonn route provides river views all the way.

CRUISING THE RHINE AND MOSEL RIVERS

Lined by some of Europe's oldest, steepest vineyards, the Rhine and Mosel rivers boast breathtaking scenery marked by storybook castles and half-timber villages. A river cruise is a must.

(above) Bernkastel-Kues is one of the beautiful towns that line the Mosel. (upper right) Medieval Burg Eltz broods above the Mosel. (lower right) Cruising by Cochem

Today, the Rhine and Mosel rivers are best known for their Riesling wines and the formidable medieval castles once used by robber barons to extort tolls from passing ships. But the rivers' history goes back even further to the Romans, who first established the region's viniculture.

Although the fastest way to get around the rivers is by car or train (and there are some gorgeous train routes directly on the Rhine), the rivers have been navigated by ship for thousands of years, and this option remains the most scenic, and the safest for visitors looking to drink a little wine as well as a little history. The Rhine is the more popular of the two rivers, but many find its little sister, the Mosel, even more beautiful with its narrow, twisting landscapes.

—David Levitz

WHEN TO GO

Day cruises on the Rhine and Mosel generally start around Easter and run through October. In summer, the hills are at their greenest and crowds gather to celebrate the Rhein in Flammen fireworks festivals. However, most wine festivals don't take place until August or September. Some multi-day cruises also make extra trips in November and December to stop at Christmas markets.

A DAY ON THE RHINE AND MOSEL RIVERS

Day-trippers don't generally need advance reservations and the tourist offices in any major Rhine or Mosel town can give you information about short round-trip cruises (*Rundfahrten*) or waterbuses (*Linienfahrten*), which allow you to hop on or off the boat, and generally run on the Rhine daily from Easter to late October and on the Mosel from June through September. Although there are many boat trips available from Köln and Düsseldorf, the Rhine doesn't truly turn scenic until south of Bonn. The most popular starting point is Koblenz, where the two rivers converge. The area between Koblenz and Bingen, the Rhine Gorge, offers the shortest cruises with the highest concentration of castles.

From **Koblenz,** you can take a water taxi run by one of the biggest operators on the Rhine, **Köln-Düsseldorfer Deutsche Rheinschiffahrt** (*KD Rhine Line* ☎ *0221/208–8318* ⊕ *www.k-d.com*), which has many special offers, such as half-price travel on your birthday; 30% off for seniors; and free travel for up to three children for every adult on Wednesday. One good place to disembark and stretch your legs is **Boppard.** Take some time to sample the local wine, Bopparder Hamm. This route provides not only fantastic white wines, but also views of the legendary **Loreley** cliff and the **Marksburg,** the only Rhine castle never laid to ruin.

Personenschiffahrt Merkelbach (☎ *0261/76810* ⊕ *www.merkelbach-personenschiffe.de*) also does round-trip castle cruises on the Rhine from **Koblenz** to **Schloss Stolzenfels** (one hour) or the **Marksburg** (two hours).

Meanwhile, the Mosel's stunning, medieval **Burg Eltz** castle, and the towns of **Cochem** and **Bernkastel-Kues** between Koblenz and Trier, rival any sights along the Rhine. **Mosel-Schiffstouristic Hans Michels** of Bernkastel-Kues (☎ *06531/8222* ⊕ *www.mosel-personenschifffahrt.de*), goes from Bernkastel to Traben-Trarbach. **Personenschiffahrt Kolb** of Briedern (☎ *02673/1515* ⊕ *www.moselfahrplan.de*) runs a fleet of boats that cruise shorter stretches between Koblenz and Trier.

MULTIDAY CRUISES

Viking River Cruises (☎ *0800/188–710–033,* 800/304–9616 *in U.S.* ⊕ *www.vikingrivers.com*) offers various multiday cruises on cabin ships between Amsterdam and Basel. The luxury **Uniworld** cruise line (☎ 800/555–8333 *in U.S.* ⊕ *www.uniworld.com*) offers a two-week cruise of both rivers.

Updated by
Dan Allen

The banks of the Rhine are crowned by magnificent castle after castle and by breathtaking, vine-terraced hills that provide the livelihood for many of the villages hugging the shores. In the words of French poet Victor Hugo, "The Rhine combines everything. The Rhine is swift as the Rhône, wide as the Loire, winding as the Seine . . . royal as the Danube and covered with fables and phantoms like a river in Asia."

The importance of the Rhine can hardly be overestimated. Although not the longest river in Europe (the Danube is more than twice as long), the Rhine has been the main river-trade artery between the heart of the continent and the North Sea (and Atlantic Ocean) throughout recorded history. The Rhine runs 1,230 km (765 miles) from the Bodensee (Lake Constance) west to Basel, then north through Germany, and, finally, west through the Netherlands to Rotterdam.

Vineyards, a legacy of the Romans, are an inherent part of the Rhine landscape from Wiesbaden to Bonn. The Rhine tempers the climate sufficiently for grapes to ripen this far north, and the world's finest Rieslings come from the Rheingau and from the Rhine's most important tributary, the Mosel. Thanks to the river, these wines were shipped far beyond the borders of Germany, giving rise to the wine trade that shaped the fortune of many riverside towns. Rüdesheim, Bingen, Koblenz, and Köln (Cologne) remain important commercial wine centers to this day.

The river is steeped in legend and myth. The Loreley, a jutting sheer slate cliff, was once believed to be the home of a beautiful and bewitching maiden who lured boatmen to a watery end in the swift currents. Heinrich Heine's poem *Song of Loreley* (1827), inspired by Clemens Brentano's *Legend of Loreley* (1812) and set to music in 1837 by Friedrich Silcher, has been the theme song of the landmark ever since. The Nibelungen, a legendary Burgundian people said to have lived on the banks of the Rhine, serve as subjects for Wagner's epic opera cycle *Der Ring des Nibelungen* (1852–72).

William Turner captured misty Rhine sunsets on canvas. Famous literary works, such as Goethe's *Sankt-Rochus-Fest zu Bingen* (*The Feast of St. Roch*; 1814), Lord Byron's *Childe Harold's Pilgrimage* (1816), and Mark Twain's *A Tramp Abroad* (1880), captured the spirit of Rhine Romanticism on paper, encouraging others to follow in their footsteps.

PLANNING

WHEN TO GO

The peak season for cultural, food, and wine festivals is March–mid-November, followed by colorful Christmas markets in December. The season for many hotels, restaurants, riverboats, cable cars, and sights is from Easter through October, particularly in smaller towns. Opening hours at many castles, churches, and small museums are shorter in winter. Orchards blossom in March, and the vineyards are verdant from May until late September, when the vines turn a shimmering gold.

GETTING HERE AND AROUND

AIR TRAVEL

The Rhineland is served by three international airports: Frankfurt, Düsseldorf, and Köln-Bonn. Bus and rail lines connect each airport with its respective downtown area and provide rapid access to the rest of the region. There are direct trains from the Frankfurt airport to downtown Köln and Düsseldorf.

No-frills carriers that fly within Europe are based at smaller Frankfurt-Hahn Airport in Lautzenhausen, between the Rhine and Mosel valleys (a 1-hour drive from Wiesbaden or Trier; a 1½-hour bus ride from Frankfurt Airport). The Luxembourg Findel International Airport (a 30-minute drive from Trier) is close to the upper Mosel River valley.

Airport Contacts Flughafen Düsseldorf ☎ *0211/4210* ⊕ *www.dus.com.* **Flughafen Frankfurt** ☎ *01805/372–4636* ⊕ *www.frankfurt-airport.de.* **Flughafen Frankfurt-Hahn** ☎ *06543/509–200* ⊕ *www.hahn-airport.de.* **Flughafen Köln/Bonn** ☎ *02203/404–001* ⊕ *www.koeln-bonn-airport.de.* **Luxembourg Findel International Airport** ☎ *00352/24640* ⊕ *www.luxairport.lu.*

TRAIN TRAVEL

InterCity and EuroCity expresses connect all the cities and towns of the area. Hourly InterCity routes run between Düsseldorf, Köln, Bonn, and Mainz, with most services extending as far south as Munich and as far north as Hamburg. The city transportation networks of Bonn, Köln, and Düsseldorf are linked by S-bahn, regional and local trains (for information contact the KVB).

Train Contacts Deutsche Bahn ☎ *0180/599–6633* ⊕ *www.bahn.de.* **Kölner Verkehrs-Betriebe** (*KVB*). ☎ *01803/504–030* ⊕ *www.kvb-koeln.de.*

RESTAURANTS

Although Düsseldorf, Köln, and Wiesbaden are home to many talented chefs, some of Germany's most creative classic and contemporary cooking is found in smaller towns or country inns.

Prices in the reviews are the average cost of a main course at dinner, or if dinner is not served, at lunch.

HOTELS

The most romantic places to lay your head are the old riverside inns and castle hotels. Ask for a *Rheinblick* (Rhine-view) room. Hotels are often booked well in advance, especially for festivals and when there are trade fairs in Köln, Düsseldorf, or Frankfurt, making rooms even in Wiesbaden and the Rheingau scarce and expensive. Many hotels close for winter.

Prices in the reviews are the lowest cost of a standard double room in high season. For expanded reviews, facilities, and current deals, visit Fodors.com.

PLANNING YOUR TIME

Those seeking "Rhine romance" should probably concentrate on its southern part, particularly the Rhine Gorge, with its castles, vineyards, and the Loreley. If nightlife and culture are your preferences, you'll like the cathedral city of Köln and cosmopolitan Düsseldorf; you can still take a day cruise along the Rhine from Köln.

DISCOUNTS AND DEALS

The **FreizeitCARD** (€14 for one day, €41.50 for three days, €66 for six days) gives you free or reduced admission to museums, castles, and other sights, plus city tours and boat trips throughout the Rhineland, as well as scores of attractions across nearby Saarland, Lorraine, Luxembourg, Wallonia and East Belgium. It's available at tourist offices throughout the region.

VISITOR INFORMATION

Rheingau–Taunus Kultur & Tourismus ⊠ *Pfortenhaus-Kloster Eberbach, Eltville* ☎ *06723/99550* ⊕ *www.rheingau-taunus-info.de.***Rheinland-Pfalz Tourismus** ⊠ *Löhrstr. 103–105, Koblenz* ☎ *01805/915–200* ⊕ *www.romantic-germany.info.*

THE RHEINGAU

The heart of the region begins in Wiesbaden, where the Rhine makes a sharp bend and flows east to west for some 30 km (19 miles) before resuming its south to north course at Rüdesheim. Wiesbaden is a good starting point for touring any of the well-marked cycling, hiking, and driving routes through the Rheingau's villages and vineyards. ■ TIP➔ Nearly every Rheingau village has an outdoor Weinprobierstand (wine-tasting stand), usually near the riverbank. It is staffed and stocked by a different wine estate every weekend in summer.

WIESBADEN

40 km (25 miles) west of Frankfurt via A-66.

Wiesbaden, the capital of the state of Hesse, is a small city of tree-lined avenues with elegant shops and handsome facades. Its hot mineral springs have been a drawing card since the days when it was known as Aquis Mattiacis ("the waters of the Mattiaci")—the words boldly inscribed on the portal of the Kurhaus—and Wisibada ("the bath in the meadow").

EATING WELL IN THE RHINELAND

11

The Rhineland's regional cuisine features fresh fish and *Wild* (game), as well as sauces and soups based on the local Riesling and Spätburgunder (pinot noir) wines. Boiled beef, once known in the region as *Tellerfleisch* ("dish meat") or *Ochsenbrust* (brisket), is nowadays called by the more familiar Austrian name *Tafelspitz*. *Rheinischer Sauerbraten* (Rhenish marinated pot roast in a sweet-and-sour raisin gravy) is another traditional favorite. The *Kartoffel* (potato) is prominent in soups, *Reibekuchen* and *Rösti* (potato pancakes), and *Dibbe-* or *Dippekuchen* (dialect: *Döppekoche*), a casserole baked in a cast-iron pot and served with apple compote. *Himmel und Erde,* literally "heaven and earth," is a mixture of mashed potatoes and chunky applesauce, topped with panfried slices of blood sausage and onions.

The region is known for its wines: Riesling is the predominant white grape, and Spätburgunder the most important red variety in the Rheingau, Mittelrhein, and Mosel wine regions, all covered in this chapter. Three abutting wine regions—Rheinhessen and the Nahe, near Bingen, and the Ahr, southwest of Bonn—add to the variety of wines available along the route.

Wines of Germany and the German Wine Institute provide background information and brochures about all German wine-producing regions. Tips on wine-related events and package offers are available from regional wine-information offices and any visitor information center along the Rhine and Mosel will put you in touch with local winegrowers.

Wine Information German Wine Institute ⊕ *www.germanwines.de.* **Wines of Germany** ☎ *212/994–7523* ⊕ *www.germanwineusa.com.*

In the 1st century AD the Romans built thermal baths here, a site then inhabited by a Germanic tribe, the Mattiaci. Modern Wiesbaden dates from the 19th century, when the dukes of Nassau and, later, the Prussian aristocracy commissioned the grand public buildings and parks that shape the city's profile today. Wiesbaden developed into a fashionable spa that attracted the rich and the famous. Their ornate villas on the Neroberg and turn-of-the-20th-century town houses are part of the city's flair.

GETTING HERE AND AROUND

English-language walking tours of Wiesbaden depart from the tourist information office every Saturday from April through October at 11. For a one-hour ride through the city, board the little train **THermine** (⊕ *www.thermine.de*). The one-day ticket (€7) enables you to get on and off as often as you'd like to explore the sights. From Easter to October it departs seven times daily (10–4:30) from Café Lumen (behind the Marktkirche) and stops at the Bowling Green, Greek Chapel, and Neroberg railway station. In winter, it operates only on weekends.

ESSENTIALS

Visitor Information Wiesbaden Tourist-Information ✉ *Marktpl. 1* ☎ *0611/172–9930* ⊕ *www.wiesbaden.eu.*

EXPLORING

Altstadt. Wiesbaden's Old Town is just behind the Stadtschloss (a former duke's palace, now the seat of state parliament, the Hessischer Landtag) on Grabenstrasse, Wagemannstrasse, and Goldgasse.

Kaiser-Friedrich-Therme. You can "take the waters" in an ambience reminiscent of Roman times in the **Kaiser-Friedrich-Therme**, a superb art-nouveau bathhouse from 1913. ⊠ *Langg. 38–40* ☏ *0611/317–060.*

Kochbrunnen Fountain. Fifteen of Wiesbaden's 26 springs converge at the steaming Kochbrunnen Fountain, where the sulfurous but at least theoretically healthful waters are there for the tasting. ⊠ *Kochbrunnenpl.*

Fodor's Choice ★ **Kurhaus.** Built in 1907, the neoclassical Kurhaus is the cultural center of town. It houses the casino and the Thiersch-Saal, a splendid setting for concerts. The Staatstheater (1894), opulently appointed in baroque and rococo revival styles, and two beautifully landscaped parks flank the Kurhaus. ⊠ *Kurhauspl. 1* ⊕ *www.wiesbaden.de/kurhaus.*

Marktplatz (*Market Square*). Historic buildings ring the Schlossplatz (Palace Square) and the adjoining Marktplatz, site of the annual wine festival (mid-August) and Christmas market (December). The farmers' market (Wednesday and Saturday) takes place behind the neo-Gothic brick Marktkirche (Market Church).

Museum Wiesbaden. Nature and culture come together under one roof at the Museum Wiesbaden, where two long-closed wings reopened after renovation in 2013. The museum's natural history section exhibits a wealth of geological finds and preserved animals; the art collection ranges from 12th-century polychromes to present-day installations. The museum is best-known for its expressionist paintings, particularly the works of Russian artist Alexej Jawlensky. ⊠ *Friedrich-Ebert-Allee 2* ☏ *0611/335–2250* ⊕ *www.museum-wiesbaden.de* 🎫 *€6* ⊗ *Tues. and Thurs. 10–8, Wed. and Fri.–Sun. 10–5.*

WHERE TO EAT

$$$$
ECLECTIC
✕ **Käfer's Bistro.** This popular bistro with striking art-nouveau decor, a grand piano (live music nightly), and a good-size bar attracts an upscale clientele. Book a table for two in one of the window alcoves (Nos. 7, 12, 25, and 29) at least four weeks in advance for some privacy among the otherwise close-set tables. *Lachstatar* (salmon tartare) and *Bauernente* (farmer's duck) are standard favorites. A few champagnes are available by the glass and bottle. Käfer's also caters the beer garden behind the Kurhaus and the Bowling Green's terrace with concerts in summer. $ *Average main: €26* ⊠ *Kurhauspl. 1* ☏ *0611/536–200* ⊕ *www. kurhaus-gastronomie.de* ⌦ *Reservations essential.*

$
ECLECTIC
✕ **Sherry & Port.** Austrian expat Gerd Royko's friendly neighborhood bistro hosts live music on Friday and Saturday from October through March. During warm months, you can dine at outdoor tables surrounding a fountain on tree-lined Adolfsallee. In addition to the fantastic number of sherries and ports (60), there are more than 20 malt whiskies served by the glass. There is also a good selection of beers and wines to accompany the menu's tapas, salads, steaks, and well-priced daily specials. $ *Average main: €17* ⊠ *Adolfsallee 11* ☏ *0611/373–632* ⊕ *www. sherry-und-port.de* ⊟ *No credit cards.*

WHERE TO STAY

$$ **HOTEL** 🏨 **Hotel de France.** Behind this 1880 facade is a lovingly restored hotel and a restaurant that serves good upscale food; both have sleek, modern furnishings and lots of fresh flowers. **Pros:** centrally located. **Cons:** on a busy street; small rooms. *$ Rooms from: €130 ✉ Taunusstr. 49 ☎ 0611/959–730 ⊕ www.hoteldefrance.de ⤳ 34 rooms, 3 suites* ⦿*Breakfast.*

$$$ **HOTEL** 🏨 **Hotel Nassauer Hof.** Wiesbaden's premier address for well over a century boasts luxuriously appointed rooms, top-flight service, and three restaurants—and a guest list ranging from Dostoyevsky to the Dalai Lama. **Pros:** nice location opposite the Kurhaus; warm spring-fed pool. **Cons:** expensive. *$ Rooms from: €225 ✉ Kaiser-Friedrich-Pl. 3–4 ☎ 0611/1330 ⊕ www.nassauer-hof.de ⤳ 136 rooms, 23 suites* ⦿*No meals.*

$ **HOTEL** 🏨 **ibis Wiesbaden City.** This modern hotel opposite the Kochbrunnen on Kranzplatz is an excellent value and has a location within walking distance of the shop-filled pedestrian zone, the Old Town, and all sights. **Pros:** bar stays open 24 hours; four wheelchair-accessible rooms. **Cons:** small rooms; breakfast not included. *$ Rooms from: €89 ✉ Georg-August-Zinn-Str. 2 ☎ 0611/36140 ⊕ www.ibishotel.com ⤳ 131 rooms* ⦿*No meals.*

SAUNA KNOW-HOW

Visiting one of Germany's fabulous saunas and bathhouses can be the perfect way to unwind from a busy travel itinerary, and it generally costs no more than a decent meal (between 10 and 20 euros). But be aware: These day spas are enjoyed in the buff, but as you might expect, Germany has many rules when it comes to the bathhouses. Although bathing suits are required at German swimming pools, you can expect a stern talking to for wearing one in a sauna or steam room that's classified as *textilfrei* (textile-free, meaning no clothing allowed). Hygiene is also a big concern: in steam rooms, find the hose to rinse off your seat before sitting down. In a dry sauna, bring a large towel and make sure to place it underneath you, especially under your feet, to avoid sweat getting on the wood. Those who like it really hot should check for an *Aufguss* schedule in front of dry saunas. The event, which literally means "on-pouring," gets visitors packed elbow to elbow for a good sweat as the *Saunameister* pours scented water over the sauna's coals. He or she might also distribute melted honey to rub into your skin, or even give you some sort of healthy snack at the end. After each time in the sauna, Germans take a cold shower to cool down. Note that saunas are generally mixed-sex, except on special women's days.

$ **Town Hotel.** The Gerbers' modern hotel is a five-minute walk from the Kurhaus, Old Town, and the shopping district. **Pros:** a good deal; free
HOTEL telephone calls to North America and most of Europe. **Cons:** often full
Fodor's Choice during the week. $ *Rooms from: €119 ⊠ Spiegelg. 5 ☎ 0611/360–160*
★ *⊕ www.townhotel.de ⟿ 24 rooms ❑ No meals.*

NIGHTLIFE AND THE ARTS
In addition to the casino, restaurants, bars, and beer garden at the Kurhaus, nightlife is centered on the many bistros and pubs on Taunusstrasse and in the Old Town. The tourist office provides schedules and sells tickets for most venues listed here.

Hessisches Staatstheater. Classical and contemporary opera, theater, ballet, and musicals are presented on the Hessisches Staatstheater's four stages: Grosses Haus, Kleines Haus, Studio, and Wartburg. ⊠ *Chr.-Zais-Str. 3 ☎ 0611/132–325 ⊕ www.staatstheater-wiesbaden.de.*

Kurhaus. The Hessian State Orchestra performs several programs a year at the Kurhaus. ⊠ *Kurhauspl. 1 ☎ 0611/17290.*

Marktkirche. Many churches offer concerts, including the free organ concerts that are held Saturday at 11:30 am in the Marktkirche. ⊠ *Schlosspl. 4 ☎ 0611/900–1611 ⊕ www.marktkirche-wiesbaden.de.*

Spielbank (*casino*). The *Klassische Spiel* (roulette, blackjack) in the Kurhaus is busy from 2:45 pm to 4 am, while the *Automatenspiel* (slots and poker) in the neighboring Kolonnade is hopping from noon to 4 am. The former is one of Europe's grand casinos, where a jacket is required and tie recommended. You can be less formal at the Automatenspiel. To enter either, you must be 18 or over (bring your passport). ⊠ *Kurhauspl. 1 ☎ 0611/536–100 ⊕ www.spielbank-wiesbaden.de.*

Thalhaus. In addition to having an art gallery and theater, this lively multiarts venue has featured music performances, cabaret revues (sometimes performed in drag), and the occasional dance party. ⊠ *Nerotal 18* ☎ *0611/185–1267* ⊕ *www.thalhaus.de.*

THERMAL SPRINGS, SPAS, AND POOLS

Kaiser-Friedrich-Therme. Pamper yourself with the thermal spring and cold-water pools, various steam baths and saunas, two solaria, and a score of health- and wellness treatments in elegant art-nouveau surroundings. Towels and robes can be rented on-site, but come prepared for bathing nude. Children under 16 are not admitted. On Tuesday the facility is for women only. ⊠ *Langg. 38–40* ☎ *0611/317–060* ⊠ *May–Aug. €4.50 per hr, Sept.–Apr. €6 per hr* ☉ *Sept.–Apr., Mon.–Thurs. 10–10, Fri. and Sat. 10 am–midnight; May–Aug., daily 10–10.*

Thermalbad Aukammtal. There's year-round swimming indoors and out thanks to the thermal springs (32°C [90°F]) that feed the pools here. The facility includes seven saunas, a whirlpool, massage, and various other treatments. ⊠ *Leibnizstr. 7, Bus No. 18 from Wilhelmstr. to Aukamm Valley* ☎ *0611/317–080* ⊠ *Pools €10, saunas €18, combined ticket €23* ☉ *Sun., Mon., Wed. and Thurs. 8 am–10 pm, Tues. 6 am– 1 am, Fri. and Sat. 8 am–midnight.*

SHOPPING

Broad, tree-lined Wilhelmstrasse, with designer boutiques housed in its fin de siècle buildings, is one of Germany's most elegant shopping streets. Wiesbaden is also known as one of the best places in the country to find antiques; Taunusstrasse and Nerostrasse have excellent antiques shops. The Altstadt is full of upscale boutiques; Kirchgasse and its extension, Langgasse, are the heart of the shops-filled pedestrian zone.

ELTVILLE

14 km (9 miles) west of Wiesbaden via A-66 and B-42.

The largest town in the Rheingau, Eltville rose to prominence in the Middle Ages as the residence of the Archbishops of Mainz. Today it's cherished for its wine and roses, which are celebrated most colorfully during its *Rosentage* (Rose Days), held the first weekend of June.

Burg Crass (Crass Castle), located on the riverbank, is well worth a look, as are the half-timber houses and aristocratic manors on the lanes between the river and Rheingauer Strasse (B-42), notably the Bechtermünzer Hof (Kirchgasse 6), Stockheimer Hof (Ellenbogengasse 6), and Eltzer Hof (at the Martinstor gateway).

GETTING HERE AND AROUND

Just 9 miles from Wiesbaden and 12 from Mainz, Eltville is easily accessible by road, rail, or bus service via RTV.

ESSENTIALS

Visitor Information Eltville Tourist-Information ⊠ *Burgstr. 1 (in Kurfürstliche Burg)* ☎ *06123/90980* ⊕ *www.eltville.de.*

EXPLORING

Kiedrich. For a good look at the central Rheingau, make a brief circular tour from Eltville. Drive 3 km (2 miles) north via the Kiedricher Strasse to the Gothic village of Kiedrich. In the distance you can see the tower of Scharfenstein Castle (built in 1215) and the spires of St. Valentine's Basilica and St. Michael's Chapel, both from the 15th century. The latter, once a charnel house (a building near a cemetery used for storing dug-up bones), has a unique chandelier sculpted around a nearly life-size, two-sided Madonna. These Gothic gems have survived intact thanks to 19th-century restorations sponsored by the English baronet John Sutton.

> **HESSIAN STATE WINE DOMAINS**
>
> *Sekt* (sparkling wine) production in the Rheingau is concentrated in Eltville, Wiesbaden, and Rüdesheim. The tree-lined Rhine promenade in Eltville hosts the annual Sekt festival during the first weekend of July. The administrative headquarters and main cellars of the Hessian State Wine Domains, Germany's largest wine estate, are in town. The estate owns nearly 500 acres of vineyards throughout the Rheingau and in the Hessische Bergstrasse wine region south of Frankfurt. Its shops in the early Gothic hospital at Kloster Eberbach stock a comprehensive regional selection.

Weingut Robert Weil. Built by the English aristocrat John Sutton, this beautiful villa south of St. Valentine's Church is home to one of Germany's leading wine estates, Weingut Robert Weil. Its famed Kiedricher Gräfenberg Riesling wines can be sampled in the tasting room. ⊠ *Mühlberg 5, Kiedrich* 🕾 *06123/2308* ⊕ *www.weingut-robert-weil.com* ☉ *Weekdays 8–5:30, Sat. 10–5, Sun. 11–5*

Fodor's Choice ★ **Kloster Eberbach.** The former Cistercian monastery Kloster Eberbach is idyllically set in a secluded forest clearing 3 km (2 miles) west of Kiedrich. ▥ TIP→ Its Romanesque and Gothic buildings (12th–14th century) look untouched by time—one reason why the 1986 film of Umberto Eco's medieval murder mystery *The Name of the Rose* was filmed here. The monastery's impressive collection of old winepresses bears witness to a viticultural tradition that spans nearly nine centuries. The wines can be sampled year-round in the *Vinothek* (wine shop) or restaurant on the grounds. The church, with its excellent acoustics, and the large medieval dormitories are the settings for concerts, wine auctions, and festive wine events. ⊠ *Stiftung Kloster Eberbach* 🕾 *06723/917–8115* ⊕ *www.klostereberbach.de* 🎫 *€6.50* ☉ *Apr.–Oct., daily 10–6; Nov.–Mar., daily 11–5.*

Kurfürstliche Burg (*Electors' Castle*). Eltville flourished as a favorite residence of the archbishops of Mainz in the 14th and 15th centuries, and it was during this time that the castle—which now houses Eltville's tourist information center—was built. More than 300 varieties of roses grow in the castle's courtyard garden, on the wall, and along the Rhine promenade. During "Rose Days" (the first weekend in June) the flower is celebrated in shops and restaurants (as an ingredient in recipes) throughout town. ⊠ *Burgstr. 1* 🕾 *06123/909–840* ⊕ *www.eltville.de* 🎫 *Tower €2.50, rose garden free* ☉ *Tower: Apr.–mid-Oct.,*

Kloster Eberbach, a former Cistercian monastery, is worth a stop for its well-preserved architecture and its winery.

Fri. 2–6, weekends 11–6. Garden: Apr.–mid-Oct., daily 9:30–7; mid-Oct.–March, daily 10:30–4:30.

Sts. Peter und Paul. The parish church of Saints Peter and Paul has late-Gothic frescoes, Renaissance tombstones, and a carved baptismal likely created by the Rhenish sculptor Hans Backoffen. ✉ *Roseng.*

Steinberg. Kloster Eberbach's premier vineyard, Steinberg, is surrounded by a 3-km-long (2-mile-long) stone wall (13th–18th century). In warmer months you can enjoy its vintages outdoors, overlooking the vines. To visit from Eberbach, take the road toward Hattenheim, stopping at the first right-hand turnoff. Other prominent wineries in the area, Nussbrunnen, Wisselbrunnen, and Marcobrunn, get their name from the *Brunnen* (wells) that are beneath the vineyards. ✉ *Domäne Steinberg* ⊕ *www.kloster-eberbach.de/en/wine-estate/das-weingut-seine-domaenen/domaene-steinberg.html* 🎫 *Wine cellar tour €10 with tasting* ⊙ *Guided cellar tour: Apr.–Oct., weekends at 1 and 3; Nov.–Mar., Sun. at 2. Group tours available at other times via Eltville tourist center.*

WHERE TO EAT

$$
GERMAN

✕ **Gutsausschank im Baiken.** This restaurant is on a hilltop amid the Rauenthaler Baiken vineyard. The panorama from the vine-canopied terrace, the regional cooking, and local wines make for a complete "Rheingau Riesling" experience. 💲 *Average main: €18* ✉ *Wiesweg 86, via Eltville* ☎ *06123/900–345* ⊕ *www.baiken.de* ⊙ *Closed Feb. Closed Mon. Apr.–Oct., Mon.–Wed. Nov.–Mar. No lunch Mon.–Sat.*

$$ ×**Klosterschänke und Gästehaus Kloster Eberbach.** Beneath the vaulted
GERMAN ceiling of the Klosterschänke you can pair local wines with regional
cuisine. Try the *Weinfleisch* (pork goulash in Riesling sauce) or *Zister-*
zienser Brot, which translates to "Cistercian bread" (minced meat in a
plum-and-bacon dressing with boiled potatoes). $ *Average main: €16*
⊠ *Kloster Eberbach, via Kiedrich or Hattenheim* ☎ *06723/993–299*
⊕ *www.klostereberbach.de* ▭ *No credit cards.*

$$$$ ×**Kronenschlösschen.** The young chef Sebastian Lühr, who took over in
FRENCH 2013, carries on the acclaimed culinary traditions that made this stylish
Fodor's Choice and intimate art nouveau house one of the Rheingau's top restaurants. The
★ wine list focuses on the finest local estates for whites, and old- and new-
world estates for reds. In warmer months, you can also enjoy sensational
fish creations in the parklike garden. $ *Average main: €44* ⊠ *Rheinallee,*
Eltville-Hattenheim ☎ *06723/640* ⊕ *www.kronenschloesschen.de.*

$$$$ ×**Schloss Reinhartshausen.** A palace in every sense of the word, this hotel
GERMAN and wine estate overlooks the Rhine and beautifully landscaped gar-
dens. Antiques and artwork fill the house. You can enjoy breakfast,
lunch, and afternoon tea with *Rieslingtorte* in the airy, glass-lined Win-
tergarten. Upscale dinners are served in the elegant Prinzess von Erbach.
The less pricey Schloss Schänke, located in the old press house, serves
light fare and hearty snacks. The estate's wines are also sold daily in
the Vinothek. $ *Average main: €30* ⊠ *Hauptstr. 41, Eltville-Erbach*
☎ *06123/6760* ⊕ *www.kempinski.com/en/eltville.*

$$$ ×**Zum Krug.** Winegrower Josef Laufer more than lives up to the hos-
GERMAN pitality promised by the wreath and *Krug* (an earthenware pitcher)
hanging above the front door. The wood-panel restaurant, with its old
tiled stove is cozy. The German fare includes wild duck, goose, game,
or sauerbraten served in rich, flavorful sauces and gravies. The wine list
is legendary for its scope (600 Rheingau wines) and selection of older
vintages. In 2011, the former Hattenheim City Hall became part of Zum
Krug's Rheingau-themed inn, nearly doubling its rooms to 15. $ *Aver-*
age main: €23 ⊠ *Hauptstr. 34, Eltville-Hattenheim* ☎ *06723/99680*
⊕ *www.hotel-zum-krug.de* ☯ *Closed 4 wks in Dec. and Jan., and 2*
wks in July and Aug.

WHERE TO STAY

$$ ☲ **Weinhotel Hof Bechtermünz.** Set within a 15th-century structure on Elt-
HOTEL ville's Weingut Koegler complex, Weinhotel Hof Bechtermünz brings mod-
ern style to its historic setting (Johannes Gutenberg printed the world's first
dictionary here in 1467). **Pros:** historic and central setting; delicious wine
selection. **Cons:** no a/c. $ *Rooms from: €140* ⊠ *Kirchg. 5* ☎ *06123/2437*
⊕ *www.weingut-koegler.de/weinhotel* ⟿ *10 rooms* ⦿ *Breakfast.*

OESTRICH-WINKEL

21 km (13 miles) west of Wiesbaden, 7 km (4½ miles) west of Eltville
on B-42.

Oestrich's vineyard area is the largest in the Rheingau. Lenchen and
Doosberg are the most important vineyards. You can sample the wines
at the outdoor wine-tasting stand, opposite the 18th-century wine-load-
ing crane on the riverbank of Oestrich (nearly opposite Hotel Schwan).

EXPLORING

Fodor's Choice ★ **Schloss Johannisberg.** The origins of this grand wine estate date from 1100, when Benedictine monks built a monastery and planted vines on the slopes below. The palace and remarkable cellars (tours by appointment) were built in the early 18th century. There are tastings at the estate's restaurant. To get here, first head to Winkel, to the west of Oestrich. From its main street, drive north on Schillerstrasse and proceed all the way uphill. After the road curves to the left, watch for the left turn to the castle. ⊠ *Weinbaudomäne Schloss Johannisberg, Geisenheim-Johannisberg* ☏ *06722/70090* ⊕ *www. schloss-johannisberg.de* ⊗ *Wine shop: Mar., Apr., and Oct., weekdays 10–6, weekends 11–6; May–Sept., weekdays 10–6, weekends 11–7; Nov.–Feb., weekdays 10–6, weekends 11–5.*

> **BETTER LATE**
>
> Schloss Johannisberg was once owned by the prince-abbots of Fulda, and every autumn a courier was sent from Johannisberg to Fulda to obtain permission to harvest the grapes. In 1775 the courier returned after considerable delay. The harvest was late and the grapes were far riper than usual; the resulting wines were exceptionally rich and fruity. *Spätlese* (literally, "late harvest," pronounced *shpate-layzeh*) wines have been highly esteemed ever since. A statue in the courtyard commemorates the "late rider."

Fodor's Choice ★ **Schloss Vollrads.** Built in 1211, Schloss Vollrads is the oldest of Germany's major wine estates. The tower, built in 1330 and surrounded by a moat, was the Greiffenclau residence for 350 years until the present palace was built in the 17th century. There is a wineshop, and the period rooms are open during concerts, festivals, and wine tastings. It's 3 km (2 miles) north of town. ⊠ *Vollradser Allee* ✛ *North on Kirchstr., continue on Vollradser Allee* ☏ *06723/6626* ⊕ *www.schlossvollrads. com* ⊗ *Apr.–Oct., weekdays 9–6, weekends 11–7; Nov.–Mar., weekdays 9–5, weekends 11–4.*

WHERE TO EAT

$$$
GERMAN

✗ **Die Wirtschaft.** Beate and Florian Kreller provide you with a warm welcome to their historic building on Winkel's Hauptstrasse (main street). Fresh flowers and candles top the tables set in a labyrinth of cozy niches with exposed beams and old stone walls. No less inviting is the pretty courtyard. Special emphasis is placed on fresh, local ingredients in season. Their lunch (€9.50 for two courses and €11 for three) is a good deal. $ *Average main: €21* ⊠ *Hauptstr. 70, Winkel* ☏ *06723/7426* ⊕ *www.die-wirtschaft.net* ⊟ *No credit cards* ⊗ *Closed Mon., and 2 wks in July and Aug. No dinner Sun.*

$$
MEDITERRANEAN
Fodor's Choice ★

✗ **Gutsrestaurant Schloss Vollrads.** Chef Alexander Ehrgott's seasonal German and light Mediterranean dishes are served with the estate's wines in the cavalier house (1650) or on the flower-lined terrace facing the garden. $ *Average main: €19* ⊠ *Schloss Vollrads, Vollradser Allee, north of Winkel* ☏ *06723/660* ⊕ *www.schlossvollrads.com/restaurant. html* ⊗ *Closed late Dec.–Apr.; closed Mon. and Tues. Nov.–mid-Dec.; closed Wed. May–Oct.*

$$　✕**Gutschänke Schloss Johannisberg.** The glassed-in terrace affords a spec-
GERMAN　tacular view of the Rhine and the vineyards where the wine you're
drinking originated. Rheingau Riesling soup and *Bauernente* (farmer's
duck) are among the house specialties. **$** *Average main: €20* ⊠ *Schloss
Johannisberg, Geisenheim-Johannisberg* ☎*06722/96090* ⊕ *www.
schloss-johannisberg.de* ⌕ *Reservations essential.*

WHERE TO STAY

$　🏨 **Hotel Schwan.** Owned by the Wenckstern family since it was built in
B&B/INN　1628, this green-and-white half-timber inn offers considerable comfort,
Fodor's Choice　though the rooms in the guesthouse are simpler than in the historic
★　main building. **Pros:** nice location right at the 18th-century crane on
the river; outdoor wine stands. **Cons:** rooms in the guesthouse are plain.
$ *Rooms from: €98* ⊠ *Rheinallee 5, Oestrich* ☎*06723/8090* ⊕ *www.
hotel-schwan.de* ⌁ *52 rooms, 3 suites* ⋈*Breakfast.*

RÜDESHEIM

*30 km (19 miles) west of Wiesbaden, 9 km (5½ miles) west of Oestrich-
Winkel on B-42.*

Tourism and wine are the heart and soul of Rüdesheim. With south-
facing slopes reaching down to the riverbanks, wine growing has thrived
here for 1,000 years. Since being discovered by English and German
romanticists in the early 19th century for its picturesque solitude,
Rüdesheim has long lost its quiet innocence, as the narrow, medieval
alleys fill with boatloads of cheerful visitors from all over the world.

ESSENTIALS

Visitor Information Rüdesheim Tourist-Information ⊠ *Rheinstr. 29a*
☎ *06722/906–150* ⊕ *www.ruedesheim.de.*

EXPLORING

Drosselgasse (*Thrush Alley*). Less than 500 feet long, Drosselgasse is a
narrow, pub-lined lane that buzzes with music and merrymaking from
noon until well past midnight every day from Easter through October.
⊠ *between Rheinstr. and Oberstr.*

Luftsport-Club Rheingau. With the wings of a glider you can silently soar
over the Rhine Valley. At the Luftsport-Club Rheingau you can catch
a 30- to 60-minute *Segelflug* (glider flight) on a glider plane between
Rüdesheim and the Loreley; allow 1½ hours for pre- and postflight
preparations. ⊠ *Flugplatz Eibinger Forstwiesen, Kammerforsterstr., 3
km (2 miles) north of Niederwald-Denkmal and Landgut Ebenthal*
☎ *06722/2979* ⊕ *www.lsc-rheingau.de* ⌁ *First 5 mins €15, each addi-
tional min €0.50; first 15 mins in glider with motor €30, each additional
min €2* ⊗ *Apr.–Oct., weekends 10–7.*

Niederwalddenkmal. High above Rüdesheim and visible for miles stands
Germania, a colossal female statue crowning the Niederwald Monu-
ment. This tribute to German nationalism, all spruced up following
a renovation in 2012, was built between 1877 and 1883 to com-
memorate the rebirth of the German Empire after the Franco-Prussian
War (1870–71). Germania faces across the Rhine toward its eternal

Take the Seilbahn over picturesque vineyards to the Niederwald-Denkmal monument above Rüdesheim.

enemy, France. At her base are the words to a stirring patriotic song: "Dear Fatherland, rest peacefully! Fast and true stands the watch, the watch on the Rhine!" There are splendid panoramic views from the monument and from other vantage points on the edge of the forested plateau. You can reach the monument on foot, by car (via Graben-strasse), or over the vineyards in the *Seilbahn* (cable car). There's also a *Sessellift* (chairlift) to and from Assmannshausen, a red-wine enclave, on the other side of the hill; for €13, a "Ringticket" will take you from the Old Town to Niederwald by Seilbahn, from Nie-derwald to Assmannshausen by Sessellift, and back to Rüdesheim by boat. ⊠ *Oberstr. 37* ☎ *06722/2402* ⊕ *www.seilbahn-ruedesheim. de* ☞ *One-way €5, round-trip €7, combined ticket for cable car and chairlift €7.50* ⊗ *Mar., Apr., and Oct., weekdays 9:30–5, weekends 9:30–6; May, daily 9:30–6; June and Sept., weekdays 9:30–6, week-ends 9:30–7; July and Aug., daily 9:30–7; Nov., daily 9:30–4; early and mid-Dec., weekdays 11–6, weekends 11–7.*

Weinmuseum Brömserburg (*Brömserburg Wine Museum*). Housed in one of the oldest castles on the Rhine (it was built around the year 1000), the museum displays wine-related artifacts and drinking vessels dating from Roman times. ▓TIP➜ There are great views from the roof and the terrace, where there are occasionally wine tastings (ask at the desk). ⊠ *Rheinstr. 2* ☎ *06722/2348* ⊕ *www.rheingauer-weinmuseum.de* ☞ *€5* ⊗ *Mar.–Oct., daily 10–6.*

WHERE TO STAY

$$ ☷ **Breuer's Rüdesheimer Schloss.** Vineyard views grace most of the rooms
HOTEL at this stylish, historic hotel where guests are welcomed with a drink
from the family's Rheingau wine estate. **Pros:** right off the Drossel-
gasse; if you stay a week you only pay for six days. **Cons:** noisy tour-
ist area. ⑤ *Rooms from: €155* ⊠ *Steing. 10* ☏ *06722/90500* ⊕ *www.
ruedesheimer-schloss.com* ⤵ *23 rooms, 3 suites* ⊙ *Closed late Dec.–
early Jan.* ⦿\ *Breakfast.*

$$ ☷ **Hotel Krone Assmannshausen.** From its humble beginnings in 1541
HOTEL as an inn for sailors and ferrymen, the Krone evolved into an elegant,
Fodor'sChoice antique-filled hotel with a fine restaurant ($$$$). **Pros:** restaurant has
★ a terrace overlooking the Rhine; lovely views of vineyards as well as
river. **Cons:** right on a main rail line; rooms at the back have a less than
spectacular view. ⑤ *Rooms from: €139* ⊠ *Rheinuferstr. 10, Rüdesheim-
Assmannshausen* ☏ *06722/4030* ⊕ *www.hotel-krone.com* ⤵ *53 rooms,
12 suites, 1 penthouse* ⦿\ *Breakfast.*

THE MITTELRHEIN

Bingen, like Rüdesheim, is a gateway to the Mittelrhein. From here to
Koblenz lies the greatest concentration of Rhine castles. Most date from
the 12th and 13th centuries, but were destroyed after the invention of
gunpowder, mainly during invasions by the French. It's primarily thanks
to the Prussian royal family and its penchant for historical preservation
that numerous Rhine castles were rebuilt or restored in the 19th and
early 20th centuries.

Two roads run parallel to the Rhine: B-42 (east side) and B-9 (west
side). The spectacular views from the heights can best be enjoyed via
the routes known as the Loreley-Burgenstrasse (east side), from Kaub
to the Loreley to Kamp-Bornhofen; or the Rheingoldstrasse (west side),
from Rheindiebach to Rhens.

BINGEN

*35 km (22 miles) west of Wiesbaden via Mainz and A-60; ferry from
wharf opposite Rüdesheim's train station.*

Bingen overlooks the Nahe-Rhine conflux near a treacherous stretch
of shallows and rapids known as the Binger Loch (Bingen Hole). Early
on, Bingen developed into an important commercial center, for it was
here—as in Rüdesheim on the opposite shore—that goods were moved
from ship to shore to circumvent the impassable waters. Bingen was
also the crossroads of Roman trade routes between Mainz, Koblenz,
and Trier. Thanks to this central location, it grew into a major center
of the wine trade and remains so today. Wine is celebrated during
11 days of merrymaking in late August and early September at the
annual **Winzerfest.**

ESSENTIALS

Visitor Information Bingen Tourist-Information ⊠ *Rheinkai 21*
☏ *06721/184–205* ⊕ *www.bingen.de.*

EXPLORING

Basilika St. Martin. The late-Gothic Basilika St. Martin was built on the site of a Roman temple and first mentioned in 793. The 11th-century crypt and Gothic and baroque furnishings make it worth a visit. Not far away is the thousand-year-old Drususbrücke, a stone bridge that runs over the Nahe. ⊠ *Basilikastr. 1* ⊗ *Mon. and Wed.–Fri. 8–5; Tues. and weekends 8–8.*

Burg Klopp. Bingen was destroyed repeatedly by wars and fires; thus there are many ancient foundations but few visible architectural remains of the past. Since Celtic times the Kloppberg (Klopp Hill), in the center of town, has been the site of a succession of citadels, all named Burg Klopp, since 1282.

> ### TAKE A HIKE!
>
> The Rheinhöhenweg (Rhine Heights Path) gives its hikers splendid views and descents into the villages en route. These marked trails run between Oppenheim on the Rhine Terrace and Bonn for 240 km (149 miles) and between Wiesbaden and Bonn-Beuel for 272 km (169 miles). The most extensive hiking trail is the Rheinsteig, from Wiesbaden to Bonn on the right side of the Rhine. It comprises 320 km (199 miles) of well-marked paths that offer everything from easy walks to challenging stretches on a par with Alpine routes.

Here you'll find a terrace with good views of the Rhine, the Nahe, and the surrounding hills. From April to October, the castle's tower can be climbed from 8 to 6 daily. ⊠ *Kloppg. 1.*

Fodor's Choice ★ **Historisches Museum am Strom** (*History Museum*). Here you can see the most intact set of Roman surgical tools ever discovered (2nd century), period rooms from the Rhine Romantic era, and displays about Abbess St. Hildegard von Bingen (1098–1179), one of the most remarkable women of the Middle Ages. An outspoken critic of papal and imperial machinations, she was a highly respected scholar, naturopath, and artist whose mystic writings and (especially) music became very popular from the 1990s onward. An excellent illustrated booklet in English on Rhine Romanticism, *The Romantic Rhine,* is sold at the museum shop. The museum is housed in a former power station (1898) on the riverbank. ⊠ *Museumsstr. 3* ☎ *06721/184–350, 06721/184–353* ⊕ *www.bingen.de* 🎟 *€3* ⊗ *Tues.–Sun. 10–5.*

Rochuskapelle (*St. Roch Chapel*). The forested plateau of the Rochusberg (St. Roch Hill) is the pretty setting of the Rochuskapelle. Originally built in 1666 to celebrate the end of the plague, it has been rebuilt twice. On August 16, 1814, Goethe attended the consecration festivities, the forerunner of today's Rochusfest, a weeklong folk festival in mid-August. The chapel (open during Sunday services at 8 and 10) contains an altar dedicated to St. Hildegard and relics and furnishings from the convents she founded on the Ruppertsberg (in the suburb of Bingerbrück) and in Eibingen (east of Rüdesheim). ⊠ *Rochusberg 3* ☎ *06721/14225.*

Hildegard Forum. Located near the St. Roch Chapel, the Hildegard Forum has exhibits related to St. Hildegard, a medieval herb garden, and a restaurant serving tasty, wholesome foods—many based on Hildegard's theories of nutrition. The lunch buffets are a good value. ⊠ *Rochusberg 1* ☎ *06721/181–000* ⊕ *www.hildegard-forum.de* ⊗ *Tues.–Sun. 11–6.*

WHERE TO EAT

$$$$
EUROPEAN
Fodor's Choice
★

✕ **Johann Lafer's Stromburg.** It's a pretty 15-minute drive through the Binger Wald (Bingen Forest) to this luxurious castle hotel and restaurant overlooking Stromberg. Johann Lafer is a prolific chef who pioneered cooking shows in Germany. In the elegant Val d'Or the *Variationen* (medley) of foie gras and the *Hirschrücken mit Rosenkohl* (venison with Brussels sprouts) are classics. The less formal Bistro d'Or serves tasty regional dishes. The wine list features some 200 top Nahe wines and several hundred Old and New World wines, with a particularly fine collection from Bordeaux and Burgundy. ⑤ *Average main: €46* ✉ *Am Schlossberg 1, 12 km (7½ miles) west of Bingerbrück via Weiler and Waldalgesheim, Stromberg* ☎ *06724/93100* ⊕ *www.johannlafer. de/stromburg* ⌔ *Reservations essential* ⊙ *Le Val d'Or closed Mon. and Tues. No lunch weekdays.*

$$
GERMAN

✕ **Weinstube Kruger-Rumpf.** It's well worth the 10-minute drive from Bingen (just across the Nahe River) to enjoy Cornelia Rumpf's refined country cooking with Stefan Rumpf's exquisite Nahe wines. Seasonal house specialties include *geschmorte Schweinebacken* (braised pork jowls) with kohlrabi, boiled beef with green herb sauce, and *Winzerschmaus* (a casserole of potatoes, sauerkraut, bacon, cheese, and herbs). The house dates from 1790; the wisteria-draped garden beckons in summer. ⑤ *Average main: €17* ✉ *Rheinstr. 47, 4 km (2½ miles) southwest of Bingen, Münster-Sarmsheim* ☎ *06721/43859* ⊕ *www.kruger-rumpf.com* ⌔ *Reservations essential* ⊙ *Closed Mon. and 2 wks in Jan. No lunch weekdays.*

EN
ROUTE

Mäuseturm (*Mouse Tower*). On the 5-km (3-mile) drive on B-9 to Trechtingshausen you will pass by Bingen's landmark, the Mäuseturm, perched on a rocky island near the Binger Loch. The name derives from a gruesome legend. One version tells that during a famine in 969 the miserly Archbishop Hatto hoarded grain and sought refuge in the tower to escape the peasants' pleas for food. The stockpile attracted scads of mice to the tower, where they devoured everything in sight, including Hatto. In fact, the tower was built by the archbishops of Mainz in the 13th and 14th centuries as a *Mautturm* (watch tower and toll station) for their fortress, Ehrenfels, on the opposite shore (now a ruin). It was restored in neo-Gothic style by the king of Prussia in 1855, who also rebuilt Burg Sooneck. ✉ *Mäuseturminsel.*

The three castles open for visits near Trechtingshausen (turnoffs are signposted on B-9) will especially appeal to lovers of history and art. As you enter each castle's gateway, consider what a feat of engineering it was to have built such a massive Burg (fortress or castle) on the stony cliffs overlooking the Rhine. They have all lain in ruin once or more during their turbulent histories. Their outer walls and period rooms still evoke memories of Germany's medieval past as well as the 19th-century era of Rhine Romanticism.

Burg Rheinstein. This castle was the home of Rudolf von Habsburg from 1282 to 1286. To establish law and order on the Rhine, he destroyed the neighboring castles of Burg Reichenstein and Burg Sooneck and hanged their notorious robber barons from the oak trees around the Clemens Church, a late-Romanesque basilica near Trechtingshausen. The Gobelin tapestries, 15th-century stained glass, wall and ceiling frescoes, a floor of royal apartments, and antique furniture—including a rare "giraffe spinet," which Kaiser Wilhelm I is said to have played—are the highlights here. All of this is illuminated by candlelight on some summer Fridays. Rheinstein was the first of many a Rhine ruin to be rebuilt by a royal Prussian family in the 19th century. ✉ *From the A-61, take exit AS Bingen center. Continue on the B-9 heading toward Bingerbrück, driving through Bingerbrück; the castle is between Bingerbrück and Trechtingshausen; parking is below the castle, at B-9, Trechtingshausen* ☎ *06721/6348* ⊕ *www.burg-rheinstein.de* ✆ *€5* ☉ *Mid-Mar.–mid-Nov., daily 9:30–6; mid-Nov.–late Dec. and early to mid-Mar., weekends only 10–5 (weather permitting—call ahead).*

Burg Reichenstein. This castle has collections of decorative cast-iron slabs (from ovens and historical room-heating devices), hunting weapons and armor, period rooms, and paintings. It's the only one of the area's three castles directly accessible by car. ✉ *Burgweg 7, Trechtingshausen* ☎ *06721/6117* ⊕ *www.burg-reichenstein.de* ✆ *€4.50* ☉ *Mar.–mid-Nov., Tues.–Sun. 10–6; mid-Nov.–Feb., Tues.–Sun. 11–5 (weather permitting—call ahead).*

Burg Sooneck. On the edge of the Soon (pronounced *zone*) Forest, this castle houses a valuable collection of Empire, Biedermeier, and neo-Gothic furnishings, medieval weapons, and paintings from the Rhine Romantic era. ✉ *Sooneckstr. 1, Niederheimbach* ☎ *06743/6064* ⊕ *www.burgen-rlp.de* ✆ *€4* ☉ *Apr.–Sept., Tues.–Sun. 9–6; Oct., Nov., and Jan.–Mar., Tues.–Sun. 9–5.*

BACHARACH

16 km (10 miles) north of Bingen, ferry 3 km (2 miles) north of town, to Kaub.

Bacharach, whose name may derive from the Latin *Bacchi ara* (altar of Bacchus), has long been associated with wine. Like Rüdesheim, Bingen, and Kaub, it was a shipping station where barrels would interrupt their Rhine journey for land transport. Riesling wine from the town's most famous vineyard, the Bacharacher Hahn, is served on the KD Rhine steamers, and Riesling is used in local cooking for marinades and sauces; you can even find Riesling ice cream. In June you can sample wines at the Weinblütenfest (Vine Blossom Festival) in the side-valley suburb of Steeg, and, in late August, at Kulinarische Sommernacht in Bacharach proper (⊕ *www.kulinarische-sommernacht.de*).

Park on the riverbank and enter the town through one of its medieval gateways. You can ascend the 14th-century town wall for a walk along the ramparts around the town, then stroll along the main street (one street but three names: Koblenzer Strasse, Oberstrasse, and Mainzer Strasse) for a look at patrician manors, typically built around a *Hof* (courtyard), and half-timber houses. Haus Sickingen, Posthof, Zollhof, Rathaus (Town Hall), and Altes Haus are fine examples.

ESSENTIALS

Visitor Information Bacharach Tourist-Information ✉ *Oberstr. 10* ☎ *06743/919–303* ⊕ *www.rhein-nahe-touristik.de.*

EXPLORING

St. Peter. The massive tower in the center of town belongs to the parish church of St. Peter. A good example of the transition from Romanesque to Gothic styles, it has an impressive four-story nave. ⊠ *Blücherstr. 1.*

Wernerkapelle. From the parish church a set of stone steps (signposted) leads to Bacharach's landmark, the sandstone ruins of the Gothic Wernerkapelle, highly admired for its filigree tracery. The chapel's roof succumbed to falling rocks in 1689, when the French blew up Burg Stahleck. Originally a Staufen fortress (11th century), the castle lay dormant until 1925, when a youth hostel was built on the foundations. The sweeping views from there are worth the 10-minute walk. ⊠ *Obertstr.*

> ### BIKE THE MIDDLE RHINE
>
> There is a 132-km (82-mile) cycle path (Rheinradweg) through the Middle Rhine Valley running parallel to the road and the railway tracks from Bingen to Bonn. It's an ideal way of combining sightseeing with some not-so-strenuous exercise, unless you attempt to reach the castles on the hills. Watch out for pedestrians and other bicyclists.

WHERE TO EAT AND STAY

$
GERMAN
Fodor'sChoice
★

✕**Altes Haus.** This charming medieval half-timber house (1368) is a favorite setting for films and photos. The restaurant uses the freshest ingredients possible and buys meat and game from local butchers and hunters. *Rieslingrahmsuppe* (Riesling cream soup), *Reibekuchen* (potato pancakes), and a refined version of boiled beef with horseradish sauce, *Tafelspitz mit Wasabi*, are favorites, in addition to the seasonal specialties. There is also a good selection of local wines. $ *Average main: €10* ⊠ *Oberstr. 61* ☎ *06743/1209* ☾ *Closed Wed. and Dec.–Easter; closed weekdays in Apr. and Nov.*

$
GERMAN

✕**Gutsausschank Zum Grünen Baum.** The Bastian family (also owners of the vineyard Insel Heyles'en Werth, on the island opposite Bacharach) runs this cozy tavern in a half-timber house dating from 1421. The "wine carousel" is a great way to sample a full range of wine flavors and styles (15 wines). Snacks are served (from 1 pm), including delicious *Wildsülze* (game in aspic), with potato salad, sausages, and cheese. Reservations are a good idea on summer weekends. $ *Average main: €12* ⊠ *Oberstr. 63* ☎ *06743/1208* ⊕ *www.weingut-bastian-bacharach. de* ☾ *Closed Thurs. and Jan.–mid-Mar.*

$
HOTEL

⌂**Altkölnischer Hof.** Flowers line the windows of country-style rooms in this pretty half-timber hotel near the market square. **Pros:** half-timber romance. **Cons:** noisy tourist area; 10-minute walk from the station. $ *Rooms from: €60* ⊠ *Blücherstr. 2* ☎ *06743/1339* ⊕ *www. altkoelnischer-hof.de* ⇌ *18 rooms, 2 suites, 4 apartments* ☾ *Closed Nov.–Mar.* ☉ *Breakfast.*

$
HOTEL

⌂**Rhein-Hotel Bacharach.** The modern rooms in this friendly, family-run operation, each of them named after a vineyard, come with Rhine and castle views. **Pros:** Rhine and castle views; free bike and laptop loans for hotel guests. **Cons:** no elevator; next to railway. $ *Rooms from: €90* ⊠ *Langstr. 50* ☎ *06743/1243* ⊕ *www.rhein-hotel-bacharach.de* ⇌ *13 rooms, 1 apartment* ☾ *Closed late Dec.–Feb.* ☉ *Breakfast.*

OBERWESEL

8 km (5 miles) north of Bacharach.

Oberwesel retains its medieval silhouette. Sixteen of the original 21 towers and much of the town wall still stand in the shadow of Schönburg Castle. The "town of towers" is also renowned for its Riesling wines, which are celebrated during a festival held the first half of September. Both Gothic churches, on opposite ends of town, are worth visiting.

ESSENTIALS

Visitor Information Oberwesel Tourist-Information ⊠ *Rathausstr. 3* ☎ *06744/710–624* ⊕ *www.oberwesel.de.*

EXPLORING

Liebfrauenkirche (*Church of Our Lady*). Popularly known as the "red church" because of its brightly colored exterior, Liebfrauenkirche has superb sculptures, tombstones and paintings, and one of Germany's oldest altars (1331). ⊠ *Kirchstr. 1.*

St. Martin. Set on a hill and with a fortresslike tower, the so-called "white church" has beautifully painted vaulting and a magnificent baroque altar. ⊠ *Martinsberg 1.*

Stadtmuseum Oberwesel. Oberwesel's city museum offers a virtual tour of the town, as well as a multimedia "journey through time" showing the area from the Stone Age to present day. It also houses a fine collection of old etchings and drawings of the Rhine Valley, including one by John Gardnor, an English clergyman and painter, who published a book of sketches upon his return to England and kicked off a wave of Romantic tourism in the late 18th century. ⊠ *Rathausstr. 23* ☎ *06744/714–726* ⊕ *www.kulturhaus-oberwesel.de* ⊡ *€3* ☉ *Apr.–Oct., Tues.–Fri. 10–5, weekends 2–5; Nov.–Mar., Tues.–Fri. 10–2.*

WHERE TO EAT AND STAY

$
GERMAN

✗ **Historische Weinwirtschaft.** Tables in the flower-laden garden in front of this lovingly restored half-timber house are at a premium in summer, thought the seats in the nooks and crannies indoors are just as inviting. Dark beams, exposed stone walls, and antique furniture set the mood on the ground and first floors, and the vaulted cellar houses contemporary-art exhibitions. Ask Iris Marx, the ebullient proprietor, for an English menu if you're stumbling over the words in local dialect. She offers country cooking at its best. The wine list has 32 wines by the glass. ⑤ *Average main: €13* ⊠ *Liebfrauenstr. 17* ☎ *06744/8186* ⊕ *www.historische-weinwirtschaft.de* ☉ *Closed Tues. and Jan. No lunch Mon.–Sat.*

$$
GERMAN

✗ **Hotel Römerkrug.** Rooms with exposed beams, pretty floral prints, and historic furnishings are tucked behind the half-timber facade (1458) of Elke Matzner's small inn on the market square. Fish (such as fresh trout from the Wisper Valley) and game are house specialties, but Marc Matzner also prepares local favorites, such as *Himmel und Erde* (mashed apples and potatoes with bacon and onions). There's a well-chosen selection of Mittelrhein wines that can be bought to take home. ⑤ *Average main: €19* ⊠ *Marktpl. 1* ☎ *06744/7091* ⊕ *www.hotel-roemerkrug. rhinecastles.com* ☉ *Closed Wed. and 3 wks in Nov. and Feb.*

$$$
B&B/INN
Fodor's Choice
★ ▦ **Burghotel "Auf Schönburg."** Antique furnishings and historic rooms (a library, chapel, and prison tower) make for an unforgettable stay at this lovingly restored hotel and restaurant in the 12th-century Schönburg Castle complex. **Pros:** castle right out of a storybook. **Cons:** lots of climbing; parking lot 100 yards downhill; train tracks nearby; very expensive. ⑤ *Rooms from: €220* ⊠ *Oberwesel* ☎ *06744/93930* ⊕ *www.hotel-schoenburg.com* ⇲ *20 rooms, 5 suites* ⊘ *Closed early Jan.–mid-Mar.* ⦿| *Breakfast.*

ST. GOAR

7 km (4½ miles) north of Oberwesel, ferry to St. Goarshausen.

St. Goar and St. Goarshausen, its counterpoint on the opposite shore, are named after a Celtic missionary who settled here in the 6th century. He became the patron saint of innkeepers—an auspicious sign for both towns, which now live off tourism and wine. September is especially busy, with Weinforum Mittelrhein (a major wine-and-food presentation in Burg Rheinfels) on the first weekend, and the annual wine festivals and the splendid fireworks display "Rhine in Flames" on the third weekend.

GETTING HERE AND AROUND
Highway B-9 and rail service link St. Goar to other towns on the Mittelrhein's west side; ferries to St. Goarshausen connect it to the east.

ESSENTIALS
St. Goar Tourist-Information ⊠ *Heerstr. 86* ☎ *06741/383* ⊕ *www.st-goar.de.*

EXPLORING
FAMILY **Burg Rheinfels.** The castle ruins overlooking the town bear witness to the fact that St. Goar was once the best-fortified town in the Mittelrhein. From its beginnings in 1245, it was repeatedly enlarged by the counts of Katzenelnbogen, a powerful local dynasty, and their successors, the Landgraviate of Hesse. Rheinfels was finally blasted by the French in 1797. Take time for a walk through the impressive ruins and the museum, which has a detailed model of how the fortress looked in its heyday. To avoid the steep ascent on foot, buy a round-trip ticket (€4) for the Burgexpress, which departs from the bus stop on Heerstrasse, opposite the riverside parking lot for tour buses. ⊠ *Off Schlossberg Str.* ☎ *06741/7753* ⊕ *www.burg-rheinfels.com* ⚏ *€4* ⊘ *Mid-Mar.–Oct., daily 9–6; early Nov., daily 9–5; mid-Nov.–mid-Mar., weekends 11–5.*

Stiftskirche. This 15th-century collegiate church was built atop the tomb of St. Goar, despite the fact that the tomb itself (an ancient pilgrimage site) was discovered to be empty during the church's construction. The 11th-century crypt has been called the most beautiful to be found on the Rhine, between Köln and Speyer. ⊠ *Marktpl.* ⊘ *Apr.–Oct., daily 10–6; Nov.–Mar., daily 11–6.*

WHERE TO EAT AND STAY

$$
GERMAN

✕ **Weinhotel Landsknecht.** Members of the Nickenig family make everyone feel at home in their riverside restaurant and hotel north of St. Goar. Daughter Martina and her winemaker husband, Joachim Lorenz, operate the Vinothek, where you can sample his delicious Bopparder Hamm wines. These go well with the hearty local dishes, such as Rhine-style Sauerbraten or seasonal specialties (asparagus, game), at the Ausblick restaurant. ▥ TIP➡ The hotel is an official Rheinsteig and Rhein-Burgen trail partner—perfect for hikers. Ⓢ *Average main: €16 ✉ Rheinuferstr. B-9, St. Goar–Fellen ☎ 06741/2011 ⊕ www. hotel-landsknecht.de.*

$$
HOTEL
Fodor's Choice
★

🏨 **Romantik Hotel Schloss Rheinfels.** Directly opposite Burg Rheinfels, this hotel offers modern comfort and expansive views from rooms furnished in country-manor style. **Pros:** marvelous views of the Rhine and the town. **Cons:** villa section, with one of the suites and all three of the apartments, is well removed from the hotel and lacking charm. Ⓢ *Rooms from: €170 ✉ Schlossberg 47 ☎ 06741/8020 ⊕ www.schloss-rheinfels.de ⇆ 55 rooms, 4 apartments, 4 suites ⏁ Breakfast.*

ST. GOARSHAUSEN

29 km (18 miles) north of Rüdesheim, ferry from St. Goar.

The town closest to the famous Loreley rock, the pretty St. Goarshausen even calls itself *Die Loreleystadt* (Loreley City). It's a popular destination for Rhineland travelers, especially during the Weinwoche (Wine Week festival), which leads up to the third weekend in September.

GETTING HERE AND AROUND

Roads (B-42 and B-274) and rail service connect St. Goarshausen to neighboring towns on the east side of the Mittelrhein. Ferries to St. Goar link it to the west.

EXPLORING

Katz and Maus Castles. St. Goarshausen lies at the foot of two 14th-century castles whose names, Katz (Cat) and Maus (Mouse), reflect but one of the many power plays on the Rhine in the Middle Ages. Territorial supremacy and the privilege of collecting tolls fueled the fires of rivalry. In response to the construction of Burg Rheinfels, the archbishop of Trier erected a small castle north of St. Goarshausen to protect his interests. In turn, the masters of Rheinfels, the counts of Katzenelnbogen, built a bigger castle directly above the town. Its name was shortened to Katz, and its smaller neighbor was scornfully referred to as Maus. Both castles are closed to the public.

Liebenstein and Sterrenberg. Some 10 km (6 miles) north of the Maus castle, near Kamp-Bornhofen, is a castle duo separated by a "quarrel wall": Liebenstein and Sterrenberg, known as the *Feindliche Brüder* (rival brothers). Both impressive ruins have terrace cafés with good views. ✉ *Zu den Burgen 1, Kamp-Bornhofen.*

Loreley. One of the Rhineland's main attractions lies 4 km (2½ miles) south of St. Goarshausen: the steep (430-foot-high) slate cliff named after the beautiful blond nymph Loreley. Here she supposedly sat, singing songs so lovely that sailors and fishermen were lured to the treacherous rapids—and their demise. The rapids really were treacherous: the Rhine is at its narrowest here and the current the swiftest. The Loreley nymph was invented in 1801 by author Clemens Brentano, who drew his inspiration from the sirens of Greek legend. Her tale was retold as a ballad by Heinrich Heine and set to music by Friedrich Silcher at the height of Rhine Romanticism in the 19th century. The haunting melody is played on the PA systems of the Rhine boats whenever the Loreley is approached. ⊠ *Lorely Visitor Center, Auf der Loreley 7.*

BOPPARD

17 km (11 miles) north of St. Goar, ferry to Filsen.

Boppard is a pleasant little resort that evolved from a Celtic settlement into a Roman fortress, Frankish royal court, and Free Imperial City. Boppard's tourism board conducts walking tours (in German, €3) mid-April to mid-October, Saturday at 11, starting at its office on the market square. Special tours in English are also bookable for groups.

ESSENTIALS

Visitor Information Boppard Tourist-Information ⊠ *Am Marktplatz, Altes Rathaus* ☎ *06742/3888* 🖷 *06742/81402* ⊕ *www.boppard-tourismus.de.*

EXPLORING

Bodobrica. The Roman garrison Bodobrica, established here in the 4th century, was enclosed by a 26-foot-high rectangular wall (1,010 by 505 feet) with 28 defense towers. You can see portions of these in a fascinating open-air archaeological park. ⊠ *Angertstr., near B-9 and the railroad tracks.*

Karmeliterkirche (*Carmelite Church*). Two baroque altars dominate the interior of the Gothic Karmeliterkirche on Karmeliterstrasse, near the Rhine. It houses intricately carved choir stalls and tombstones and several beautiful Madonnas. Growers still observe the old custom of laying the first-picked *Trauben* (grapes) at the foot of the Traubenmadonna (1330) to ensure a good harvest. The annual wine festival takes place in late September or early October, just before the Riesling harvest. ⊠ *Rheinallee 44.*

Severuskirche (*Church of St. Severus*). Excavations in the 1960s revealed ancient Roman baths beneath the twin-tower, Romanesque Severuskirche on the market square. The large triumphal crucifix over the main altar and a lovely statue of a smiling Madonna date from the 13th century. ⊠ *Marktpl.*

Vierseenblick. From the Mühltal station, let the *Sesselbahn* (chairlift) whisk you a half-mile uphill to the Vierseenblick, where the Rhine looks like a chain of lakes. ⊠ *Mühltal 12* ☎ *06742/2510* ⊕ *www.sesselbahn-boppard.de* 🚡 *Round-trip €7* ⊗ *Mid-Apr.–Sept., daily 10–6; 1st half of Apr. and last half of Oct., daily 10–5; 1st half of Oct., daily 10–5:30.*

WHERE TO EAT AND STAY

$ ✕ **Weinhaus Heilig Grab.** This wine estate's tavern, Boppard's oldest, is
GERMAN   full of smiling faces: the wines are excellent, the food is simple and
hearty, and the welcome is warm. Old chestnut trees shade tables
in the courtyard. If you'd like to visit the cellars or vineyards, ask
the friendly hosts. $ *Average main: €8* ⊠ *Zelkesg. 12* ☏ *06742/2371*
⊕ *www.heiliggrab.de* ☉ *Closed Tues. and 3 wks late Dec.–early Jan.
No lunch.*

$$ ⊞ **Best Western Bellevue Rheinhotel.** You can enjoy a Rhine view from
HOTEL   many of the rooms in this traditional hotel or from the terrace next
to the waterfront promenade. **Pros:** marvelous view. **Cons:** parking is
a problem; breakfast costs €11 extra. $ *Rooms from: €170* ⊠ *Rhein-
allee 41* ☏ *06742/1020* ⊕ *www.bellevue-boppard.de* ⤳ *93 rooms, 1
suite* ⦿ *No meals.*

SPORTS AND THE OUTDOORS

Mittelrhein Klettersteig. For those with Alpine hiking ambitions, there
is this climbing path, a "via ferrata" complete with cables, steps, and
ladders to help reach heights more quickly. It's an alternate route of the
Rhein-Burgen-Wanderweg (hiking trail from Koblenz to Bingen). The
trail starts at St.-Remigius-Platz, about 1 km (½ mile) from Boppard
Hauptbahnhof. Allow two to three hours for the climb, though there are
several possibilities to return to the "normal" path in-between climbs.
Rent the necessary gear at the Aral gas station on Koblenzer Strasse in
Boppard. ⊠ *St.-Remigius-Pl.* ☏ *06742/2447 for Aral gas station.*

Weinwanderweg (*Wine Hiking Trail*). The 10-km (6-mile) hiking trail
from Boppard to Spay begins north of town on Peternacher Weg. Many
other marked trails in the vicinity are outlined on maps and in brochures
available from the tourist office.

KOBLENZ

20 km (12 miles) north of Boppard.

The ancient city of Koblenz is at a geographic nexus known as the
Deutsches Eck (German Corner) in the heart of the Mittelrhein region.
Rivers and mountains converge here: the Mosel flows into the Rhine
on one side; the Lahn flows in on the other a few miles south; and three
mountain ridges intersect.

Founded by the Romans in AD 9, the city was first called Castrum
ad Confluentes (Fort at the Confluence). It became a powerful city
in the Middle Ages, when it controlled trade on both the Rhine and
the Mosel. Air raids during World War II destroyed 85% of the city,
but extensive restoration has done much to re-create its former atmo-
sphere. As the host of Germany's Federal Horticultural Show in 2011,
the city saw widespread urban development, including the new Seil-
bahn that transports visitors across the river and up to the Ehrenb-
reitstein fortress.

GETTING HERE AND AROUND

You can get here speedily by autobahn or train, or via a leisurely scenic drive along the Rhine (or even more mellow, by cruise boat). The Koblenz tourist office has guided English-language tours on Saturday at 3 from May to October. Tours are €3 and depart from the Historisches Rathaus on Jesuitenplatz.

ESSENTIALS

Visitor Information Koblenz Tourist-Information ✉ *Jesuitenpl. 2–4, in Forum Confluentes* ☎ *0261/130–920* ⊕ *www.koblenz-touristik.de.*

EXPLORING

TOP ATTRACTIONS

Deutsches Eck (*German Corner*). This pointed bit of land, jutting into the river like the prow of an early ironclad warship, is at the sharp intersection of the Rhine and Mosel rivers. One of the more effusive manifestations of German nationalism—an 1897 equestrian statue of Kaiser Wilhelm I, first emperor of the newly united Germany—was erected here. It was destroyed at the end of World War II and replaced in 1953 with a ponderous monument to Germany's unity. After German reunification a new statue of Wilhelm was placed atop this monument in 1993. Pieces of the Berlin Wall stand on the Mosel side—a memorial to those who died as a result of the partitioning of the country.

Festung Ehrenbreitstein. Europe's largest fortress, towering 400 feet above the left bank of the Rhine, offers a magnificent view over Koblenz and where the Mosel and the Rhine rivers meet. The earliest buildings date from about 1100, but the bulk of the fortress was constructed in the 16th century. In 1801 it was partially destroyed by Napoléon, and the French occupied Koblenz for the next 18 years. For an introduction to the fortress and its history, head for the *Besucherdienst* (visitor center). English-language tours are for groups only, but you can often join a group that is registered for a tour.

A Seilbahn carries you from the street Konrad-Adenauer-Ufer over the river to Ehrenbreitstein, with spectacular views of the Deutsches Eck below. The half-mile trip can accommodate 7,000 passengers in an hour. Lifts run continually throughout the day starting at 10 am. From late March to late October they run until 6 pm, from late April to early September till 7 pm, and from November to late March they run on weekdays only until 5 pm. ☎ *0261/6675–4000* ⊕ *www.diefestungehrenbreitstein.de* ✉ *Fortress entrance €6, Seilbahn €8 round-trip, combined ticket €11.80* ☽ *Mid-Apr.–Oct., daily 10–6; Nov.–mid-Apr., daily 10–5; year-round, free access to grounds and dining usually till midnight.*

Landesmuseum Koblenz (*State Museum*). The Festung Ehrenbreitstein's museum has exhibits on the history of local technologies, from wine growing to technology. Pride of place is given over to the fortress's 16th-century Vogel Greif cannon, which has done a lot of traveling over the years. The French absconded with it in 1794, the Germans took it back in 1940, and the French commandeered it again in 1945. The 15-ton cannon was peaceably returned by French president François Mitterrand in 1984. ✉ *Festung Ehrenbreitstein* ☎ *0261/66750* ⊕ *www.landesmuseum-koblenz.de* ✉ *€4* ☽ *Apr.–Oct., daily 10–6; Nov.–Mar., daily 10–5.*

Ludwig Museum. Just behind the Deutsches Eck, housed in the spic-and-span Deutschherrenhaus, is this restored 13th-century building. Industrialist Peter Ludwig, one of Germany's leading contemporary-art collectors, has filled this museum with part of his huge collection. ✉ *Danziger Freiheit 1* ☎ *0261/304–040* ⊕ *www.ludwigmuseum.org* 💶 *€5* ☽ *Tues.–Sat. 10:30–5, Sun. 11–6.*

Mittelrhein Museum. Relocated in 2013 to the new Forum Confluentes, this museum houses the city's art collection, including extensive holdings of landscapes focusing on the Rhine. It also has a notable collection of secular medieval art and works by regional artists. ✉ *Zentralpl. 1* ☎ *0261/129–2520* ⊕ *www.mittelrhein-museum.de* 💶 *€6, €6–8 for special exhibition, €10 for both* ☽ *Tues.–Sun. 10–6.*

St. Kastor Basilika (*St. Castor Basilica*). It was in this sturdy Romanesque basilica, consecrated in 836, that plans were drawn for the Treaty of Verdun a few years later, formalizing the division of Charlemagne's great empire and leading to the creation of Germany and France as separate states. Inside, compare the squat Romanesque columns in the nave with the intricate fan vaulting of the Gothic sections. The **St. Kastor Fountain** outside the church is an intriguing piece of historical one-upmanship. It was built by the occupying French to mark the beginning of Napoléon's ultimately disastrous Russian campaign of 1812. ✉ *Kastorhof* ⊕ *www.sankt-kastor-koblenz.de* ☽ *Daily 9–6.*

WORTH NOTING

Kurfürstliches Schloss. Strolling along the promenade toward town, you'll pass this gracious castle. It was built in the late 18th century by Prince-Elector Clemens Wenzeslaus as an elegant escape from the grim Ehrenbreitstein fortress. Though the palace is primarily used these days as a congress and event center, its Grand Café is open to the public.

Liebfrauenkirche (*Church of Our Lady*). War damage is evidenced by the blend of old buildings and modern store blocks on and around Am Plan. This church stands on Roman foundations at the Old Town's highest point. The bulk of the church is of Romanesque design, but its choir is one of the Rhineland's finest examples of 15th-century Gothic architecture, and the west front is graced with two 17th-century baroque towers. ✉ *Am Plan* ☽ *Mon.–Sat. 8–6, Sun. 9–8.*

Rheinkran (*Rhine Crane*). The squat form of this crane, built in 1611, is one of Koblenz's landmarks. Marks on the side of the building indicate the heights reached by floodwaters of bygone years. In the mid-19th century a pontoon bridge consisting of a row of barges spanned the Rhine here; when ships approached, two or three barges were simply towed out of the way to let them through.

Weindorf. Just off the Pfaffendorf Bridge, which marks the beginning of the Old Town, and between the modern blocks of the Rhein-Mosel-Halle and the Hotel Mercure, is the Weindorf, a wine "village" constructed for a mammoth exhibition of German wines in 1925. It's now a restaurant. Running along the riverbank past the Weindorf is a 10-km (6-mile) promenade, the Rheinanlagen (Rhine Gardens). ⊕ *www.weindorf-koblenz.de.*

WHERE TO EAT

$ ✕ **Café Einstein.** Portraits of Einstein line the walls of this busy restau-
ECLECTIC rant, where locals gather to watch live soccer matches. The friendly
Tayhus family serves tasty fare daily, from a hearty breakfast buffet
(there's brunch on Sunday—reservations recommended) to late-night
finger food. Fish specials are served year-round. **$** *Average main: €15*
✉ *Firmungstr. 30* ☎ *0261/914–4999* ⊕ *www.einstein-koblenz.de.*

$$$ ✕ **Da Vinci.** At this smart restaurant in the heart of the Old Town, Da
GERMAN Vinci reproductions, including an original-size rendition of *The Last
Supper,* adorn the walls. Leather upholstery, an elegant bar, and soft
lighting round out the ambience. Celebrity chef Thomas Jaumann,
who came aboard in 2013, presents a seasonally changing local menu
with a European slant, with classic dishes like sirloin steak, rack of
lamb, and loup de mer (European sea bass). The wine list includes
more than 200 bottles, with a focus on German, Italian, and French
wines. **$** *Average main: €23* ✉ *Firmungstr. 32b* ☎ *0261/921–5444*
⊕ *www.davinci-koblenz.de.*

$ ✕ **Weindorf-Koblenz.** This reconstructed "wine village" of half-timber
GERMAN houses is grouped around a tree-shaded courtyard with an adjacent
vineyard. The fresh renditions of traditional Rhine and Mosel special-
ties, a good selection of local wines, and a fabulous Sunday brunch (res-
ervation recommended) where wine, beer, and nonalcoholic beverages

are included in the price (€26.40) all make this a popular spot. ⑤ *Average main: €11* ⊠ *Julius-Wegeler-Str. 2* ☎ *0261/133-7190* ⊕ *www. weindorf-koblenz.de* ☉ *No lunch Nov.–Mar.*

$ ✕ **Weinhaus Hubertus.** Hunting scenes and trophies line the wood-panel
GERMAN walls of this cozy wine restaurant named after the patron saint of hunters. The decorations also include 100-year-old murals. Hearty portions of fresh, traditional fare are what you'll find on offer. ⑤ *Average main: €14* ⊠ *Florinsmarkt 6* ☎ *0261/31177* ⊕ *weinhaus-hubertus.de* ☉ *Closed Tues. No lunch Mon.–Sat.*

$$ ✕ **Zum Weissen Schwanen.** Guests have found a warm welcome in this
GERMAN half-timber inn and mill since 1693, a tradition carried on by the Kunz family. This is a charming place to overnight or enjoy a dinner of well-prepared, contemporary German cuisine with regional specialties. Brasserie Brentano ($) serves lighter dishes as well as lunch and Sunday brunch. It's located next to the 13th-century town gateway of Braubach, just below the Marksburg. The hotel is an official Rheinsteig trail partner. ⑤ *Average main: €20* ⊠ *Brunnenstr. 4, 12 km (7½ miles) south of Koblenz via B-42, Braubach* ☎ *02627/9820* ⊕ *www. zum-weissen-schwanen.de.*

WHERE TO STAY

$ ⌂ **Hotel Kleiner Riesen.** You can literally watch the Rhine flowing by from
HOTEL the four front rooms of this friendly, family-operated hotel about a 10-minute walk from the station. **Pros:** quiet; on the river; close to piers. **Cons:** 20-minute walk from city center. ⑤ *Rooms from: €95* ⊠ *Januarius-Zick Str. 11, on the Rhine promenade* ☎ *0261/303–460* ⊕ *www. hotel-kleinerriesen.de* ⇥ *19 rooms, 3 Suites* ⏹ *Breakfast.*

NIGHTLIFE AND THE ARTS

Café Hahn. Located in the suburb of Güls, this place features cabaret, stand-up comedians, popular musicians and bands. and other shows. ⊠ *Neustr. 15* ☎ *0261/42302* ⊕ *www.cafehahn.de.*

Circus Maximus. You'll find dancing, live music, and theme parties practically every evening here. On a balmy night, visit Circus Maximus's Statt Strand beach bar, on Universitätsstrasse on the banks of the Mosel near the university. ⊠ *Stegemannstr. 30, at Viktoriastr* ☎ *0261/300–2357* ⊕ *www.circus-maximus.org.*

Staatsorchester Rheinische Philharmonie (*Rhenish Philharmonic Orchestra*). The Philharmonic plays regularly at different concert venues around town. ⊠ *Eltzerhofstr. 6a* ☎ *0261/301–2272* ⊕ *www.rheinische-philharmonie.de.*

Theater Koblenz. Built in 1787, this gracious neoclassic theater is still in regular use. ⊠ *Clemensstr. 1–5* ☎ *0261/129–2870* ⊕ *www.theater-koblenz.de.*

SHOPPING

Koblenz's most pleasant shopping is in the Old Town streets around the market square Am Plan.

Löhr Center. This modern, American-style mall has some 130 shops and restaurants. ⊠ *Hohenfelder Str. 22* ⊕ *www.loehr-center.de.*

Stroll through Koblenz's Old Town, stopping for a bite at a sidewalk café along one of the squares, such as Jesuitenplatz.

THE MOSEL VALLEY

The Mosel is one of the most hauntingly beautiful river valleys on Earth—with the added draw of countless ancient vineyards on the banks, creating abundant opportunities for sampling some of Germany's best wines. Here, as in the Rhine Valley, forests and vines carpet steep hillsides; castles and church spires dot the landscape; and medieval wine hamlets line the riverbanks. The Mosel landscape is no less majestic, but narrower and more peaceful than that of the Rhine Gorge; the river's countless bends and loops slow its pace and lend the region a leisurely charm.

WINNINGEN

11 km (7 miles) southwest of Koblenz on B-416.

Winningen is a gateway to the Terrassenmosel (Terraced Mosel), the portion of the river characterized by steep, terraced vineyards. Winches help haul miniature monorails with the winegrowers and their tools aboard up the steep incline, but tending and harvesting the vines are all done by hand. ■TIP➜ For a bird's-eye view of the valley, drive up Fährstrasse to Am Rosenhang, the start of a pleasant walk along the Weinlehrpfad (Educational Wine Path).

As you head upstream toward Kobern-Gondorf, you'll pass the renowned vineyard site Uhlen. In Kobern the Oberburg (upper castle) and the St. Matthias Kapelle, a 12th-century chapel, are good vantage points. Half-timber houses reflecting the architectural styles of three centuries ring the town's pretty market square.

WHERE TO EAT AND STAY

$$$
GERMAN

✕ **Alte Mühle Thomas Höreth.** Thomas and Gudrun Höreth's enchanting country inn is a labyrinth of little rooms and cellars grouped around ole-ander-lined courtyards. They have restored this former mill, originally dating to 1026, and furnished it with thoughtful details and authentic materials. Highlights of the menu include homemade cheeses, terrines, pâtés, and *Entensülze* (goose in aspic), served with the Höreths' own wines. For those who want to get away from the river, the Höreths have a pleasing hotel in the forest, Höreth im Wald ($$$). ⑤ *Average main: €23* ✉ *Mühlental 17, via B-416, Kobern-Gondorf* ☎ *02607/6474* ⊕ *www.thomas-hoereth.de* ⊗ *No lunch weekdays.*

$
B&B/INN

⛿ **Hotel Simonis.** Two of the suites in this traditional hotel on Kobern-Gondorf's market square are across the courtyard, in what might be Germany's oldest half-timber house (1321). **Pros:** half-timber setting. **Cons:** no elevator. ⑤ *Rooms from: €89* ✉ *Marktpl. 4, Kobern-Gondorf* ☎ *02607/203* ⊕ *www.hotelsimonis.com* ⤳ *13 rooms, 2 suites* ⊗ *Closed Jan. and Feb.* ❖ *Breakfast.*

ALKEN

22 km (13½ miles) southwest of Koblenz.

One of the Mosel's oldest towns (the Celts were here by 450 BC), today Alken is best known for its 12th-century castle, Burg Thurant. With a pretty seaside setting backdropped by rolling vineyards and the castle above, Alken's among the lovelier wine village stops along the Untermosel (Lower Mosel) between Koblenz and Pünderich.

GETTING HERE AND AROUND

The B-49 connects Alken to Koblenz, about 14 miles away. The nearest train stop (Regionalbahn from Koblenz) is at Löf across the river, linked to Alken by a bridge and a mile and a half walk.

EXPLORING

Burg Thurant. This 12th-century castle towers over the village and the Burgberg (castle hill) vineyard. Wine and snacks are served in the courtyard; castle tours include the chapel, cellar, tower, and a weapons display. Allow a good half hour for the climb from the riverbank. Call ahead in winter to make sure it's open. ☎ *02605/2004* ⊕ *www.thurant.de* ⤳ *€3.50* ⊗ *Mar. and Apr., daily 10–5; May–Oct., daily 10–6; Nov.–Feb. (weather permitting), daily 10–4.*

EN
ROUTE

Burg Eltz (*Eltz Castle*). Genuinely medieval (12th–16th century) and genuinely stunning, Burg Eltz deserves as much attention as King Ludwig's trio of castles in Bavaria. For the 40-minute English-language tour, given when enough English speakers gather, ask at the souvenir shop. It guides you through the period rooms and massive kitchen. There's also a popular treasure vault filled with gold and silver. To get here, exit B-416 at Hatzenport (opposite and southwest of Alken), proceed to Münstermaifeld, and follow signs to the parking lot near the Antoniuskapelle. From here it's a 15-minute walk, or take the shuttle bus (€2). Hikers can reach the castle from Moselkern in about an hour. ✉ *Burg Eltz, Münstermaifeld* ☎ *02672/950–500* ⊕ *www.burg-eltz.de* ⤳ *Tour and treasure vault €9* ⊗ *Apr.–Oct., daily 9:30–5:30.*

The Mosel Valley

COCHEM

51 km (31½ miles) southwest of Koblenz on B-49, approximately 93 km (58 miles) from Trier.

Cochem is one of the most attractive towns of the Mosel Valley, with a riverside promenade to rival any along the Rhine. It's especially lively during the wine festivals in June and late August. If time permits, savor the landscape from the deck of a boat—many excursions are available, lasting from one hour to an entire day. From the **Enderttor** (Endert Town Gate) you can see the entrance to one of Germany's longest railway tunnels, the Kaiser-Wilhelm, an astonishing example of 19th-century engineering. The 4-km-long (2½-mile-long) tunnel saves travelers a 21-km (13-mile) detour along one of the Mosel's great loops.

ESSENTIALS

Visitor Information Cochem Tourist-Information. The tourist office has an excellent English-language outline for a walking tour of the town. ✉ *Endertpl. 1* ☎ *02671/60040* ⊕ *www.cochem.de.*

EXPLORING

Cochemer Sesselbahn (*Cochem Chairlift*). A ride on the chairlift to the Pinner Kreuz provides great vistas. ✉ *Endertstr. 44* ☎ *02671/989–063* ⊕ *www.cochemer-sesselbahn.de* 🎫 *Round-trip €6.30* ☉ *Late*

Mar.–June, Sept., and Oct., daily 10–6; early July–Aug., daily 9:30–7; Sept., daily 10–6:30; early–mid-Nov., daily 11–4.

Historische Senfmühle. Wolfgang Steffens conducts daily tours at 11, 2, 3, and 4, showing how he produces the gourmet mustard at his 200-year-old mill. Garlic, cayenne, honey, curry, and Riesling wine are among the flavors you can sample and buy in the shop. From the Old Town, walk across the bridge toward Cond. The mill is to the left of the bridgehead. ⊠ *Stadionstr. 1* ☎ *02671/607–665* ⊕ *www.senfmuehle.net* ☜ *Tours €2.50* ⊙ *Daily 10–6.*

Reichsburg (*Imperial Fortress*). The 15-minute walk to this 1,000-year-old castle overlooking the town will reward you with great views of the area. In a tie-in with the fortress's past, falconry demonstrations are put on from Good Friday through October, Tuesday to Sunday at 11, 1, 2:30, and 4. With advance reservations, you can also get a taste of the Middle Ages at a medieval banquet, complete with costumes, music, and entertainment. Banquets take place on Friday (7 pm) and Saturday (6 pm) and last four hours; the price (€45) includes a castle tour. During the *Burgfest* (castle festival) the first weekend of August, there's a medieval market and colorful tournaments. ⊠ *Schlossstr. 36* ☎ *02671/255* ⊕ *www.reichsburg-cochem.de* ☜ *€5, including 40-min tour; falconry €4* ⊙ *Mid-Mar.–early Nov., daily 9–5.*

WHERE TO EAT

$
GERMAN

✕ **Alte Gutsschänke.** Locals and tourists mingle naturally here, near the open fireplace and antique wine-making equipment. The food is local and fortifying: sausages, cheeses, ham, and homemade soups served with the wines from host Arthur Schmitz's own estate. As the night progresses, locals might unpack their musical instruments and start playing. Note that this place doesn't serve beer. $ *Average main: €8* ⊠ *Schlossstr. 6, on the way up to the castle* ☎ *02671/8950* ▬ *No credit cards* ⊙ *No lunch weekdays.*

$$$$
FRENCH

✕ **Lohspeicher–l'Auberge du Vin.** In times past, oak bark for leather tanners was dried and stored in this building, built in 1834. Now it's a charming inn; the French-German delicacies on the menu are a pleasure for the palate and the eye. Don't miss the dessert *Variation* (medley). Some 20 French and Italian wines supplement the restaurant's own estate-bottled wines. Of the nine rooms available, four have a view of the castle. $ *Average main: €29* ⊠ *Oberg. 1, at Marktpl.* ☎ *02671/3976* ⊕ *www.lohspeicher.de* ⊙ *Closed Wed. and Feb.*

$$$
GERMAN
FAMILY

✕ **Moselromantik Hotel Weissmühle.** This rustic family inn is set amid the forested hills of the Enderttal (Endert Valley) on the site of a historic mill that belonged to the current proprietor's great-great-grandfather. Lined with photos and memorabilia from the original mill, it's an oasis from traffic and crowds yet only 2½ km (1½ miles) from Cochem. Beneath the exposed beams and painted ceiling of the restaurant, trout from the hotel's own fish farm will grace your table. German and French wines are served. ▮▮▮ TIP➔ **The inn's underground bar, originally built to become a swimming pool, opens around 9 pm and is a bit of a time capsule with lots of 1970s German kitsch.** $ *Average main: €25* ⊠ *Wilde Endert 2* ☎ *02671/8955* ⊕ *www.hotel-weissmuehle.de.*

EDIGER-ELLER

61 km (38 miles) southwest of Koblenz on B-49.

Ediger-Eller, once two separate hamlets, is another photogenic wine village with well-preserved houses and remnants of a medieval town wall. It's particularly romantic at night, when the narrow alleys and half-timber buildings are illuminated by historic streetlights.

Martinskirche (*St. Martin's Church*). The church is a remarkable amalgamation of art and architectural styles, inside and out. Take a moment to admire the 117 carved bosses in the star-vaulted ceiling of the nave. Among the many fine sculptures throughout the church and the chapel is the town's treasure: a Renaissance stone relief, *Christ in the Winepress.* ⊠ *Kirchstr.*

WHERE TO STAY

$ � **Zum Löwen.** This simply furnished hotel comes with friendly ser-
HOTEL   vice and a splendid terrace overlooking the Mosel. **Pros:** fine view of the Mosel. **Cons:** on a busy street; no elevator. ⑤ *Rooms from: €95* ⊠ *Moselweinstr. 23* ☎ *02675/208* ⊕ *www.mosel-hotel-loewen.de* ⤶ *20 rooms* ☾ *Hotel and restaurant closed late Dec.–Mar.* ⑩ *Breakfast.*

EN
ROUTE   **Calmont.** As you continue along the winding course of the Mosel, you'll pass Europe's steepest vineyard site, Calmont, just before the loop at Bremm. Opposite Calmont are the romantic ruins of a 12th-century Augustinian convent.

Zell. This popular village is full of pubs and wineshops that ply the crowds with Zeller Schwarze Katz, "Black Cat" wine, a commercially successful product and the focal point of a large wine festival in late June. Some 6 million vines hug the slopes around Zell, making it one of Germany's largest wine-producing communities. The area between Zell and Schweich (near Trier), known as the Middle Mosel, is home to some of the world's finest Riesling.

TRABEN-TRARBACH

30 km (19 miles) south of Cochem.

The Mosel divides Traben-Trarbach, which has pleasant promenades on both sides of the river. Its wine festivals are held the second and last weekends in July. Traben's art nouveau buildings are worth seeing (Hotel Bellevue, the gateway on the Mosel bridge, the post office, the train station, and town hall).

EXPLORING

Mittelmosel Museum. For a look at fine period rooms and exhibits on the historical development of the area, visit the Mittelmosel Museum, in the Haus Böcking (1750). ⊠ *Casino Str. 2* ☎ *06541/9480* ⤳ *€2.50* ☾ *Easter–Oct., Tues.–Sun. 10–5.*

Weingut Martin Müllen. Established in 1991, this winery is very new compared to many others here. Its success has its roots in modern and traditional winemaking principles, and it has one of the best Grand Cru vineyards in the region. Try the light but complex Trarbacher Hühnerberg Riesling Spätlese. ⊠ *Alte Marktstr. 2* ☎ *06541/9470* ⊕ *www.muellen.de.*

Continued on page 500

In the heart of the Mosel Valley lies the Mittelmosel (Middle Mosel), where vineyards tumble down steep slate slopes to riverside villages full of half-timbered, baroque, and belle époque architecture. Famed for its warm climate and 2,000-year-old wine-making tradition, it produces some of the best Rieslings in the world. The Middle Mosel's many wineries and tasting rooms are concentrated along a meandering 75-mile stretch of lush river valley, picturesque towns, and rural estates between the ancient town of Trier and the village of Zell, allowing for multiple sips in a short amount of time.

By Jeff Kavanagh

Above, Dr Pauly-Bergweiler bottle.
Left, Vineyards in the Mosel Valley.

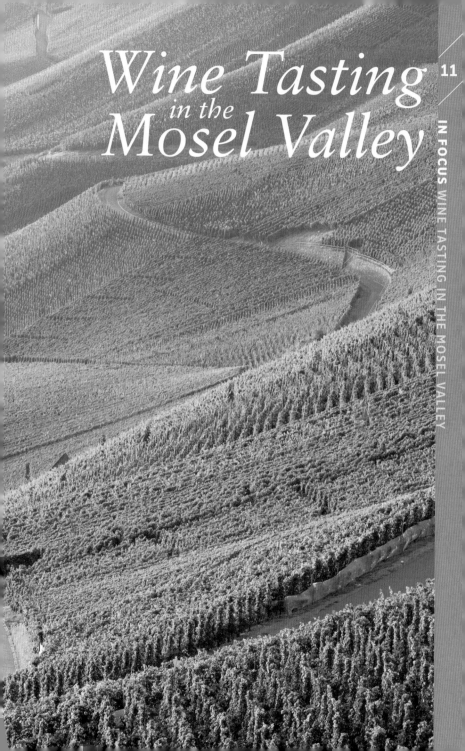

Wine Tasting
in the
Mosel Valley

TWO DAYS IN THE MIDDLE MOSEL

DAY 1

Traben-Trarbach

Small, family-run wineries that have been producing high-quality wines for generations dominate the Middle Mosel. Starting in Trier, just across the border from Luxembourg, the tour follows the B-53 and the Mosel River as it flows northwest through a succession of pretty wine villages and steep-sloped estates.

Episcopal Wine Estates
Drop down into a labyrinth of cellars beneath Trier's streets or visit the estate's elegant *vinothek* (wine store) to sample fine Rieslings built upon almost two millennia of priestly tradition. **Try:** fruity and elegant Scharzhofberger Riesling.
✉ Gervasiusstrasse 1, Trier
☎ 0651/145760
🌐 www.bwgtrier.de

Mosel grape harvest

Sektgut St. Laurentius
Whether in the spacious tasting room, on the outdoor terrace, or in the modern little wine bar near the river, there are plenty of places to taste this winery's *sekt* (sparkling wine), considered some of the best in the region. **Try:** fruity, creamy, and yeasty Cremant.
✉ Laurentiusstrasse 4, Leiwen
☎ 06507/3836
🌐 www.st-laurentius-sekt.de

Weingut Lehnert-Veit
In addition to Riesling, visitors can sample Merlot, Pinot Noir, and Chardonnay in this winery's Mediterranean-style garden on the banks of the Mosel. **Try:** delicately flinty, well-balanced Falkenberg Riesling Mineral Kabinett Feinherb.
✉ In der Dur 6–10, Piesport
☎ 06507/2123
🌐 www.weingut-lv.net

Weingut Karp-Schreiber
This welcoming winery's varietals include Riesling, Weissburgunder, and Regent; and it also produces a nice Rotling, a *cuvée* (blend) of all three. When the sun's shining, the best place to taste them is on the winery's little trellised veranda. **Try:** fresh, elegant "my karp" Riesling.
✉ Moselweinstrasse 186, Brauneberg
☎ 06534/236
🌐 www.karp-schreiber.de

Weingut Bauer
An extension of the family home, where four generations reside beneath the same roof, the Bauer's simple, modern tasting room is a good place to sample award-winning still and sparkling white wines presented with old-fashioned hospitality. **Try:** fruity, refreshing Winzersekt Riesling Brut.
✉ Moselstrasse 3, Mülheim
☎ 06534/571
🌐 www.weingut-bauer.de

Wine barrels at Kerpen

Weingut Karp-Schreiber

Vineyards in the Mosel Valley

DAY 2

From the quiet village of Mülheim, the Mosel makes a couple of sweeping loops up the valley, passing through the towns of Bernkastel-Kues and Traben-Trarbach as it winds along.

Dr. Pauly-Bergweiler

This winery's presence in the Mosel includes vineyards in seven different villages and a grand villa in the center of Bernkastel, where its cozy vinothek finds space within the mansion's vaulted cellars. **Try:** racy, flinty Alte Badstube am Doktorberg Riesling.

✉ Gestade 15, Bernkastel
☎ 06531/3002
🌐 www.pauly-bergweiler.com

Kerpen

A friendly husband-and-wife-run winery, Kerpen has eight generations of winemaking tradition, a special collection of Rieslings with labels designed by visiting artists, and an unpretentious tasting room within a stone's throw of the river. **Try:** dry Graacher Himmelreich Riesling Kabinett Feinherb.

✉ Uferallee 6, Bernkastel-Wehlen
☎ 06531/6868
🌐 www.weingut-kerpen.de

Rebenhof

You'll find only Rieslings in Rebenhof's stylish, contemporary tasting room, which shares space with stainless-steel fermentation tanks. **Try:** flinty, old-vine Ürziger Würtgarten Riesling Spätlese.

✉ Hüwel 2-3, Ürzig
☎ 06532/4546
🌐 www.rebenhof.de

Schmitges

Located on an unassuming village lane, Schmitges specializes in the production of high-quality dry whites that, along with the modern, wine-bar style of their vinothek, distinguishes them from many other local establishments. **Try:** light, summery Rivaner.

✉ Hauptstrasse 4, Erden
☎ 06532/2743
🌐 www.schmitges-weine.de

Weingut Martin Müllen

Established in 1991, this winery is a mere infant compared to many others here, but its success has its roots in modern and traditional winemaking principles, and one of the best *Grand Cru* (great growth) vineyards in the region. **Try:** light but complex Trarbacher Hühnerberg Riesling Spätlese.

✉ Alte Marktstrasse 2, Traben-Trarbach
☎ 06541/9470
🌐 www.muellen.de

STOP FOR A BITE

✗ Weinstube Kesselstatt

Sitting beneath vines in the shadow of the Liebfrauenkirche and the Trier Dom you can sip Kesselstatt estate wines and snack on wild boar and locally produced cheese.

✉ Liebfrauenstrasse 10, Trier
☎ 0651/41178
🌐 weinstube-kesselstatt.de

✗ Weinromantik Richtershof Hotel

An ideal place for lovers of the grape, this stately hotel has a bistro that serves seasonal dishes such as white asparagus and ham, a gourmet restaurant offering contemporary cuisine, and a wine list that runs to 350 bottles, 150 of which are from the Mosel.

✉ Hauptstrasse 81-83, Mülheim
☎ 06534/9480
🌐 www.weinromantikhotel.de

✗ Der Ratskeller

Just off Bernkastel's main square, Der Ratskeller's uncomplicated regional fare can be enjoyed at an outside table with a view of the action or inside cozily surrounded by dark wood and leadlight windows.

✉ Markt 30, Bernkastel-Kues
☎ 06531/973/000

✗ Jugendstilhotel Bellevue

Traben-Trarbach's premier hotel has a first-class reputation that derives from its belle époque architecture, fine cuisine, professional, knowledgeable staff, and superb wine list.

✉ An der Mosel 11, Traben-Trarbach
☎ 06541/7030
🌐 www.bellevue-hotel.de

WINE TOURING AND TASTING

WHEN TO GO

The best time to visit the region is between May and September, when a lightly chilled glass or two of wine is the perfect complement to a sunny spring day or a warm summer evening. This coincides with high season in the valley, when roads and cycle paths swell with tourists, particularly in the warmer months, and in September during the wine harvest. Fortunately, the next wine village is never far along the Mosel River. If you arrive and find a tasting room that's too busy, there's invariably another just around the corner.

IN THE TASTING ROOM

While varietals such as Müller-Thurgau, Weissburgunder, and Pinot Noir are produced in the Middle Mosel, the staple of most estates is Riesling. Given that the wineries are predominantly small, family-owned operations, there tends to be an emphasis on the production of high-quality, low-quantity wines. Their tasting rooms, when not part of the winery itself, are frequently extensions of family homes, affording visitors intimate contact with the winemakers. Naturally, German is the dominant language spoken by local tourists and many of the Dutch, Belgians, and Luxembourgers who pop across the border for a visit, but most winemakers speak English at least well enough to describe their wines. Opening hours vary, and although you can drop into most tasting rooms outside of these times, there may not always be someone around to serve you. To avoid disappointment it's worth checking websites for opening times first.

BOTTLE PRICES AND TASTING FEES

Once the most expensive wines in the world, Mosel Valley Rieslings have come down significantly in price since their heyday in the early 20th century, yet they remain world class. The average price for a quality bottle of Riesling is about €7–€10; each winery's price list is generally detailed in brochures found in its tasting room. Most wineries won't charge to taste a couple of their wines, but will expect you to purchase a bottle or two if you try more. Those that do have tasting fees, which are commonly between €5 and €15, will often waive them if you purchase a bottle.

Left, Romantic wine village on the Mosel River. Right, Bottle display from Mosel-Weinmuseum in Bernkastel-Kues

WINE TASTING PRIMER

Ordering and tasting wine—whether at a winery, bar, or restaurant—is easy once you master a few simple steps.

LOOK AND NOTE

Hold your glass by the stem and look at the wine in the glass. Note its color, depth, and clarity.

For whites, is it greenish, yellow, or gold? For reds, is it purplish, ruby, or garnet? Is the wine's color pale or deep? Is the liquid clear or cloudy?

SWIRL AND SNIFF

Swirl the wine gently in the glass to intensify the scents, then sniff over the rim of the glass. What do you smell? Try to identify aromas like:

- **Fruits**—citrus, peaches, berries, figs, melon
- **Minerals**—earth, steely notes, wet stones
- **Flowers**—orange blossoms, honey, perfume
- **Dairy**—butter, cream, cheese, yogurt
- **Spices**—baking spices, pungent, herbal notes
- **Oak**—toast, vanilla, coconut, tobacco
- **Vegetables**—fresh or cooked, herbal notes
- **Animal**—leathery, meaty notes

Are there any unpleasant notes, like mildew or wet dog, that might indicate that the wine is "off?"

SIP AND SAVOR

Prime your palate with a sip, swishing the wine in your mouth. Then spit in a bucket or swallow.

Take another sip and think about the wine's attributes. Sweetness is detected on the tip of the tongue, acidity on the sides of the tongue, and tannins (a mouth-drying sensation) on the gums. Consider the body—does the wine feel light in the mouth, or is there a rich sensation? Are the flavors consistent with the aromas? If you like the wine, try to pinpoint what you like about it, and vice versa if you don't like it.

Take time to savor the wine as you're sipping it—the tasting experience may seem a bit scientific, but the end goal is your enjoyment.

EN
ROUTE During the next 24 km (15 miles) of your drive down the Mosel you'll pass by world-famous vineyards, such as Erdener Treppchen, Ürziger Würzgarten, the *Sonnenuhr* (sundial) sites of Zeltingen and Wehlen, and Graacher Himmelreich, before reaching Bernkastel-Kues.

BERNKASTEL-KUES

22 km (14 miles) southwest of Traben-Trarbach, 100 km (62 miles) southwest of Koblenz on B-53.

Bernkastel and Kues straddle the Mosel, on the east and west banks, respectively. Bernkastel is home to famed Bernkasteler Doctor, a small, especially steep vineyard that's also one of Europe's most expensive. Early German humanist Nikolaus Cusanus (1401–64) was from Kues: Today his birthplace and St.-Nikolaus-Hospital are popular attractions.

GETTING HERE AND AROUND
By car, Bernkastel-Kues is about 45 minutes northeast of Trier and 90 minutes southwest of Koblenz. The closest train station (Regionalbahn) is in Wittlich, about a 20-minute taxi ride away.

ESSENTIALS
Visitor Information Bernkastel-Kues Tourist-Information ⊠ *Gestade 6* ☎ *06531/500–190* ⊕ *www.bernkastel.de.*

EXPLORING
Burg Landshut. From the hilltop ruins of the 13th-century castle, Burg Landshut, there are splendid views. It was here that Trier's Archbishop Boemund II is said to have recovered from an illness by drinking the local wine. This legendary vineyard, still known as "the Doctor," soars up from Hinterm Graben street near the town gate, Graacher Tor. You can purchase these well-regarded wines at some of the shops around town.

Jewish cemetery. Bernkastel's former Jewish population was well assimilated into town society until the Nazis took power. You can ask the tourist center to borrow a key to the town's Jewish cemetery, reachable by a scenic half-hour hike through the vineyards in the direction of Traben-Trarbach. Opened in the mid-19th century, it contains a few headstones from a destroyed 17th-century graveyard. ⊠ *About 1 km from Graacher Tor, Old Town.*

Kerpen. A friendly husband-and-wife team run this winery, which has eight generations of winemaking tradition behind it. They make a special collection of Rieslings with labels designed by visiting artists, and have an unpretentious tasting room close to the river. Try the dry Graacher Himmelreich Riesling Kabinett Feinherb. ⊠ *Uferallee 6, Bernkastel-Wehlen* ☎ *06531/6868* ⊕ *www.weingut-kerpen.de.*

Market square. Elaborately carved half-timber houses (16th–17th centuries) and a Renaissance town hall (1608) frame St. Michael's Fountain (1606) on Bernkastel's photogenic market square. In early September the square and riverbank are lined with wine stands for one of the region's largest wine festivals, the Weinfest der Mittelmosel.

St.-Nikolaus-Hospital. The Renaissance philosopher and theologian Nikolaus Cusanus (1401–64) was born in Kues. The St.-Nikolaus-Hospital
is a charitable *Stiftung* (foundation) he established in 1458, and it still
operates a home for the elderly and a wine estate. ⊠ *Cusanusstr. 2*
☎ *06531/2260* ⊕ *www.cusanus.de* ⊠ *Tours €5* ☉ *Tours Tues. at 10:30
and Fri. at 3.*

Mosel-Weinmuseum (*Wine museum*). Within St.-Nikolaus-Hospital
is a wine museum as well as a bistro. There's also a Vinothek in the
vaulted cellar, where you can sample more than 150 wines from the
entire Mosel-Saar-Ruwer region. ⊠ *St.-Nikolaus-Hospital, Cusanusstr. 2*
⊕ *www.moselweinmuseum.de* ⊠ *Museum €5, Vinothek €15 for admission and wine tasting* ☉ *Apr.–Oct., daily 10–6; Nov.–Mar., daily 11–5.*

WHERE TO EAT

$$
FRENCH
✕ **Rotisserie Royale.** The fish menu, vegetarian selection, and fancy twists
on traditional and regional dishes are what set this initially unassuming
restaurant apart from the crowd. It's in one of Burgstrasse's charming
half-timber houses. 💲 *Average main: €16* ⊠ *Burgstr. 19* ☎ *06531/6572*
⊕ *www.rotisserie-royale.de* ☉ *Closed Wed.*

$$$$
FRENCH
Fodor'sChoice
★
✕ **Waldhotel Sonnora.** At their elegant country inn in the forested Eifel
Hills, Helmut and Ulrike Thieltges offer guests one of Germany's abso-
lute finest dining experiences. Helmut is an extraordinary chef, renowned
for transforming truffles, foie gras, and Persian caviar into masterful
dishes. Challans duck in an orange-ginger sauce is his specialty. The
wine list is equally superb. The dining room, with gilded and white-
wood furnishings and plush red carpets, has a Parisian look, and the
pretty gardens add to a memorable visit. ▬ **TIP→ Sonnora can prepare a
vegetarian menu, but call ahead.** 💲 *Average main: €50* ⊠ *Auf'm Eichelf-
eld, 8 km (5 miles) southwest of Wittlich, which is 18 km (11 miles) west
of Kues via B-50; from A-1, exit Salmtal, Dreis* ☎ *06578/98220* ⊕ *www.
hotel-sonnora.de* ⌒ *Reservations essential* ☉ *Restaurant and hotel closed
Mon. and Tues., Jan., and 1st 2 wks in July.*

$$
EUROPEAN
✕ **Weinhotel St. Stephanus.** Rita and Hermann Saxler operate a comfortable, modern hotel and upscale restaurant in a 19th-century manor
house on the *Ufer* (riverbank) at Zeltingen. Whether you opt for the
handsome dining room or the terrace overlooking the Mosel, Saxler's
Restaurant is a good destination refined regional cooking with a Mediterranean touch. The spa offers vinotherapy—treatments using grape-
based products, such as grapeseed oil. 💲 *Average main: €18* ⊠ *Uferallee
9, Zeltingen-Rachtig* ☎ *06532/680* ⊕ *www.hotel-stephanus.de* ☉ *No
lunch Mon.–Thurs. Jan.–Mar.*

WHERE TO STAY

$
B&B/INN
🛏 **Wein- & Landhaus S. A. Prüm.** The traditional wine estate S. A. Prüm
has state-of-the-art cellars and an attractive Vinothek for cellar tours
and tastings, as well as a stunning dining room and an idyllic patio
facing the Mosel and the vineyards. **Pros:** good rooms, some of which
have vineyard and Mosel views. **Cons:** no elevator. 💲 *Rooms from:
€95* ⊠ *Uferallee 25, north of Kues, Bernkastel-Wehlen* ☎ *06531/3110*
⊕ *www.sapruem.com* ⤳ *8 rooms, 2 self-catering apartments* ☉ *Rooms
closed mid-Dec.–Feb.* ⊚ *Breakfast.*

⊞ **Weinromantikhotel Richtershof.** This renovated 17th-century manor in a shady park offers comfortable rooms and first-class friendly service. **Pros:** garden terrace; wheelchair-accessible rooms; 24-hour room service. **Cons:** thin walls. ⑤ *Rooms from: €156* ⊠ *Hauptstr. 81–83, 5 km (3 miles) south of Bernkastel via B-53, Mülheim* ☎ *06534/9480* ⊕ *www.weinromantikhotel.de* ⤳ *38 rooms, 5 suites* ⦿ *Breakfast.*

TRIER

55 km (34 miles) southwest of Bernkastel-Kues via B-53, 150 km (93 miles) southwest of Koblenz; 30 mins by car from Luxemburg airport.

Thanks to its deep history, the Trier of today holds a wealth of ancient sites. It's also an important university town, and accordingly boasts a surprisingly rich modern cultural landscape for a city of its size (just over 100,000 residents).

Its roots reach back to at least 400 BC, by which time a Celtic tribe, the Treveri, had settled the Trier Valley. Eventually Julius Caesar's legions arrived at this strategic point on the river, and Augusta Treverorum ("the town of [Emperor] Augustus in the land of the Treveri") was founded in 16 BC. It was described as an opulent city, as beautiful as any outside Rome.

Around AD 275 an Alemannic tribe stormed Augusta Treverorum and reduced it to rubble. But it was rebuilt in even grander style and renamed Treveris. Eventually it evolved into one of the leading cities of the empire, and was promoted to "Roma secunda" (a second Rome) north of the Alps. As a powerful administrative capital it was adorned with all the noble civic buildings of a major Roman settlement, as well as public baths, palaces, barracks, an amphitheater, and temples. The Roman emperors Diocletian (who made it one of the four joint capitals of the empire) and Constantine both lived in Trier for years at a time.

Trier survived the collapse of Rome and became an important center of Christianity and, ultimately, one of the most powerful archbishoprics in the Holy Roman Empire. The city thrived throughout the Renaissance and baroque periods, taking full advantage of its location at the meeting point of major east–west and north–south trade routes and growing fat on the commerce that passed through.

GETTING HERE AND AROUND

The area is excellent for biking. The train station in Trier rents bikes; call the Deutsche Bahn bicycle hotline to reserve. Cyclists can follow the marked route of the *Radroute Nahe-Hunsrück-Mosel* from Trier to Bingen.

FESTIVALS

Europa-Volksfest. Held in May or in early June, this festival features wine and food specialties from several European countries, in addition to rides and entertainment. ⊕ *trier.volksfest-trier.de.*

Altstadtfest. In late June, more than 100,000 people come out for this musical festival in the Old Town, which also features a citywide run. ⊕ *www.altstadtfest-trier.de.*

Moselfest Zurlauben. Wine, sparkling wine, beer, and fireworks fill this annual July celebration along the riverbank in Zurlauben district. ⊕ *www.zurlaubener-heimatfest.de.*

Weinfest (*Wine Festival*). This popular wine-focused event happens over a four-day weekend in early August in the Olewig district.

Weihnachtsmarkt. This Christmas market and festival features nearly a hundred booths, and takes place on the market square and in front of the cathedral. ⊕ *www.trierer-weihnachtsmarkt.de.*

TOURS

You can circumnavigate the town with the narrated tours of the Römer-Express trolley (€9) or a tourist office bus (€8.50). Both depart from Porta Nigra, near the tourist office. There is also a hop-on, hop-off bus. A 24-hour ticket on it costs €11.

There are also toga tours every Saturday at 12:30 May through October, in which actors dressed in Roman costume bring the history of the amphitheater, the Kaiserthermen (Imperial Baths), and the old town gate to life. A tour lasts two hours and costs €9.50. Reservations are essential. If you don't speak German, speak up. The tour guide or someone else in the group probably speaks some English and will translate the basic points. The tourist office sells tickets for all tours and also leads various walks. A tour in English (€8.50) departs Saturday, May through October, at 1:30.

TIMING

To do justice to Trier, consider staying for at least two full days. A walk around Trier will take a good two hours, and you will need extra time to climb the tower of the Porta Nigra, walk through the vast interior of the Dom and its treasury, visit the underground passageways of the Kaiserthermen, and examine the cellars of the Amphitheater. Allow at least another half hour each for the Bischöfliches Museum and Viehmarktthermen, as well as an additional hour for the Rheinisches Landesmuseum.

DISCOUNTS AND DEALS

The **Trier Card,** available from the visitor center's website or at the center in Porta Nigra, entitles the holder to free public transportation and discounts on tours and admission fees to Roman sights, museums, and sports and cultural venues. It costs €9.90 and is valid for three successive days.

ESSENTIALS

Tour Information Deutsche Bahn ☎ *01805/151–415 for bicycle hotline.*

Visitor Information Trier Tourist-Information ✉ *An der Porta Nigra* ☎ *0651/978–080* ⊕ *www.trier.de.*

EXPLORING
TOP ATTRACTIONS

Fodor'sChoice
★

Amphitheater. The sheer size of Trier's oldest Roman structure (circa AD 100) is impressive; in its heyday it seated 20,000 spectators. You can climb down to the cellars beneath the arena—animals were kept in cells here before being unleashed to do battle with gladiators. ✉ *Olewiger Str.* ▱ *€3* ☉ *Apr.–Sept., daily 9–6; Oct. and Mar., daily 9–5; Nov.–Feb., daily 9–4.*

Museum am Dom Trier (*Museum at the Trier Cathedral*). This collection, just behind the Dom, focuses on medieval sacred art, and there are also fascinating models of the cathedral as it looked in Roman times. Look for 15 Roman frescoes, discovered in 1946, that may have adorned the Emperor Constantine's palace. ⊠ *Bischof-Stein-Pl. 1* 🕾 *0651/710–5255* ⊕ *www.bistum-trier.de/museum* 🖃 *€3.50, combined ticket with Domschatzkammer €4* ☉ *Tues.–Sat. 9–5, Sun. 1–5.*

Fodor'sChoice **Dom** (*Cathedral*). The oldest Christian church north of the Alps, the
★ Dom stands on the site of the Palace of Helen. Constantine tore the palace down in AD 330 and put up a large church in its place. The church burned down in 336, and a second, even larger one was built. Parts of the foundations of this third building can be seen in the east end of the present structure (begun in about 1035). The cathedral you see today is a weighty and sturdy edifice with small round-head windows, rough stonework, and asymmetrical towers, as much a fortress as a church. Inside, Gothic styles predominate—the result of remodeling in the 13th century—although there are also many baroque tombs, altars, and confessionals. ⊠ *Domfreihof* 🕾 *0651/979–0790* ⊕ *www.dominformation.de* 🖃 *Tours €3.50* ☉ *Apr.–Oct., daily 6:30–6; Nov.–Mar., daily 6:30–5:30.*

Domschatzkammer (*Cathedral Treasure Chamber*). The highlight of the cathedral's museum is the 10th-century Andreas Tragaltar (St. Andrew's Portable Altar), constructed of oak and covered with gold leaf, enamel, and ivory by local craftsmen. It's a reliquary for the soles of St. Andrew's sandals, as signaled by the gilded, life-size foot on the top of the altar. ⊠ *Dom, Domfreihof* 🖃 *€1.50, combined ticket with Bischöfliches Museum €4* ☉ *Mid-Mar.–Oct. and Dec., Mon.–Sat. 10–5, Sun. 12:30–5; Nov. and Jan.–mid-Mar., Tues.–Sat. 11–4, Sun. 12:30–4.*

Fodor'sChoice **Kaiserthermen** (*Imperial Baths*). This enormous 4th-century bathing
★ palace once housed cold- and hot-water baths and a sports field. Although only the masonry of the Calderium (hot baths) and the vast basements remain, they are enough to give a fair idea of the original splendor and size of the complex. Originally 98 feet high, the walls you see today are just 62 feet high. ⊠ *Weimarer-Allee and Kaiserstr.* 🕾 *0651/436–2550* 🖃 *€3* ☉ *Apr.–Sept., daily 9–6; Oct. and Mar., daily 9–5; Nov.–Feb., daily 9–4.*

Fodor'sChoice **Porta Nigra** (*Black Gate*). The best-preserved Roman structure in Trier
★ was originally a city gate, built in the 2nd century (look for holes left by the iron clamps that held the structure together). The gate served as part of Trier's defenses and was proof of the sophistication of Roman military might and its ruthlessness. Attackers were often lured into the two innocent-looking arches of the Porta Nigra, only to find themselves enclosed in a courtyard. In the 11th century the upper stories were converted into two churches, in use until the 18th century. The tourist office is next door. ⊠ *Porta-Nigra-Pl.* 🕾 *0651/718–2451* 🖃 *€3* ☉ *Apr.–Sept., daily 9–6; Oct. and Mar., daily 9–5; Nov.–Feb., daily 9–4.*

Fodor'sChoice **Rheinisches Landesmuseum** (*Rhenish State Museum*). The largest collec-
★ tion of Roman antiquities in Germany is housed here. The highlight is the 4th-century stone relief of a Roman ship transporting barrels

of wine up the river. This tombstone of a Roman wine merchant was discovered in 1874, when Constantine's citadel in Neumagen was excavated. Have a look at the 108-square-foot model of the city as it looked in the 4th century—it provides a sense of perspective to many of the sights you can still visit today. ⊠ *Weimarer-Allee 1* ☎ *0651/97740* ⊕ *www.landesmuseum-trier.de* ⊡ *€6* ⊙ *Tues.–Sun. 10–5.*

Konstantin Basilika (*Constantine Basilica*). An impressive reminder of Trier's Roman past, this edifice is now the city's major Protestant church. This structure was built by the emperor Constantine around AD 310 as the imperial throne room of the palace. At 239 feet long, 93 feet wide, and 108 feet high, it demonstrates the astounding ambition of its Roman builders and the sophistication of their building techniques. ■ TIP➔ The basilica is one of the two largest Roman interiors in existence (the other is the Pantheon in Rome). Look up at the deeply coffered ceiling; more than any other part of the building, it conveys the opulence of the original structure. An ornate rococo garden now separates the basilica from the Landesmuseum. ⊠ *Konstantinpl.* ☎ *0651/42570* ⊙ *Apr.–Oct., Mon.–Sat. 10–6, Sun. noon–6; Nov.–Mar., Tues.–Sat. 11–noon and 3–4, Sun. noon–1.*

WORTH NOTING

Hauptmarkt. The main market square of Old Trier—lined with gabled houses from several ages—is easily reached via Simeonstrasse. The market cross (958) and richly ornate St. Peter's Fountain (1595), dedicated to the town's patron saint, stand in the square. ■ TIP➡ There is a flower and vegetable market held here every weekday, while a farmers' market can be found at Viehmarktplatz on Tuesday and Friday 8–2.

Karl-Marx-Haus. Marx was born on May 5, 1818, in this bourgeois house built in 1727. Visitors with a serious interest in social history will be fascinated by its small museum. Some of Marx's personal effects, as well as first-edition manifestos are on display. Audio guides are available in English, and English-language tours can be arranged on request. ⊠ *Brückenstr. 10* ☎ *0651/970–680* ⊕ *www.fes.de/karl-marx-haus* ⊠ *€4* ⊘ *Apr.–Oct., daily 10–6; Nov.–Mar., Mon. 2–5, Tues.–Sun. 11–5.*

OFF THE BEATEN PATH

Roscheider Hof. For a look at 19th- and 20th-century rural life in the Mosel-Saar area, visit this hilltop *Freilichtmuseum* (open-air museum) near Konz-Saar, 10 km (6 miles) southwest of Trier via B-51. Numerous farmhouses and typical village buildings in the region were saved from the wrecking ball by being dismantled and brought to the Roscheider Hof, where they were rebuilt and refurnished as they appeared decades ago. Old schoolrooms, a barbershop and beauty salon, a tavern, a shoemaker's workshop, a pharmacy, a grocery, and a dentist's office have been set up in the rooms of the museum proper, along with period rooms and exhibitions on local trades and household work, such as the history of laundry. A large collection of tin figures is here too, and there's also a Biedermeier rose garden, museum shop, and restaurant with beer garden (closed Monday, cash only) on the grounds. ⊠ *Roscheiderhof 1, Konz* ☎ *06501/92710* ⊕ *www.roscheiderhof.de* ⊠ *€5* ⊘ *Apr.–Oct., Tues.–Fri. 9–6, weekends 10–6; Nov.–Mar. (indoor facilities only), Tues.–Fri. 9–5, weekends 10–5.*

Stadtmuseum Simeonstift Trier (*Simeon Foundation City Museum*). Built around the remains of the Romanesque Simeonskirche, this church is now a museum. It was constructed in the 11th century by Archbishop Poppo in honor of the early medieval hermit Simeon, who for seven years shut himself up in the east tower of the Porta Nigra. Collections include art and artifacts produced in Trier from the Middle Ages to the 19th century. ⊠ *Simeonstr. 60* ☎ *0651/718–1459* ⊕ *www.museum-trier. de* ⊠ *€5.50, €1 on 1st Sun. of month* ⊘ *Tues.–Sun. 10–5.*

Viehmarktthermen. Trier's third Roman bath (early 1st century) was discovered when ground was broken for a parking garage. Finds of the excavations from 1987 to 1994 are now beneath a protective glass structure. You can visit the baths and see the cellar of a baroque Capuchin monastery. ⊠ *Viehmarktpl.* ☎ *0651/994–1057* ⊠ *€3* ⊘ *Tues.–Sun. 9–5.*

WHERE TO EAT

$$$$

GERMAN

✕ **Becker's Hotel.** This wine estate in the peaceful suburb of Olewig features a gourmet restaurant with prix-fixe menus, a second restaurant serving regional cuisine, and a casual Weinstube. Dining alfresco is a nice option in summer. Bordeaux and Burgundy wines are available in addition to the estate's own wines, and wine tastings, cellar visits, and guided tours on the wine path can be arranged. $ *Average main: €27*

Trier's Porta Nigra (Black Gate), a city gate dating from the 2nd century, is the largest Roman structure north of the Alps.

⊠ *Olewiger Str. 206, Trier-Olewig* ☎ *0651/938–080* ⊕ *www.beckers-trier.de* ☾ *Gourmet restaurant closed Sun. and Mon.*

$$$$
GERMAN

✕ **Schlemmereule.** The name means "gourmet owl," and, indeed, chef Peter Schmalen caters to gourmets in the 19th-century Palais Walderdorff complex opposite the cathedral. Truffles are a specialty, and the fish is always excellent. Wines from top German estates, particularly from the Mosel, and an extensive selection of red wines are available. Lots of windows lend a light, airy look to the restaurant, and a replica of one of Michelangelo's Sistine Chapel paintings is on the ceiling. There's courtyard seating in summer. ⑤ *Average main: €27* ⊠ *Palais Walderdorff, Domfreihof 1B* ☎ *0651/73616* ⊕ *www.schlemmereule. de* ⌂ *Reservations essential* ☾ *Closed Sun.*

$
GERMAN

✕ **Weinstube Kesselstatt.** The interior has exposed beams and polished wood tables; the shady terrace is popular in summer. Two soups daily, hearty fare, and fresh, regional cuisine are served with wines from the Reichsgraf von Kesselstatt estate. The *Tagesgericht* (daily special) and *Aktionsmenü* (prix-fixe menu) are a good bet. Das Beste der Region (the region's best) is an ample selection of local hams, cheeses, fish, and breads, served on a wooden board for two. ⑤ *Average main: €15* ⊠ *Liebfrauenstr. 10* ☎ *0651/41178* ⊕ *www.weinstube-kesselstatt.de.*

$
GERMAN

✕ **Zum Domstein.** Whether you dine inside or out, don't miss the collection of Roman artifacts displayed in the cellar. In addition to the German dishes on the regular menu, you can order à la carte or prix-fixe menus based on recipes attributed to the Roman gourmet Marcus Gavius Apicius in the evening. ⑤ *Average main: €13* ⊠ *Hauptmarkt 5* ☎ *0651/74490* ⊕ *www.domstein.de.*

WHERE TO STAY

$$ 🔲 **Hotel Ambiente.** Markus and Monika Stemper—a passionate cook
B&B/INN and a gracious hostess—bring modern style to their country inn near
the Luxembourg border. **Pros:** country atmosphere; legendary gar-
den. **Cons:** removed from city center. 💲 *Rooms from: €109* ✉ *In der
Acht 1–2, 7 km (4½ miles) southwest of Trier via B-49, Trier-Zewen*
☎ *0651/827–280* ⊕ *www.ambiente-trier.de* ⤳ *12 rooms* ☉ *Restaurant
closed Sun. and Thurs.* ⏺ *Breakfast.*

$$ 🔲 **Hotel Petrisberg.** The Pantenburgs' friendly, family-run hotel is high
HOTEL on Petrisberg hill overlooking Trier, not far from the amphitheater and
a 20-minute walk to the Old Town. **Pros:** fine view of Trier. **Cons:**
somewhat removed from the city center. 💲 *Rooms from: €105* ✉ *Sick-
ingenstr. 11–13* ☎ *0651/4640* ⊕ *www.hotelpetrisberg.de* ⤳ *24 rooms,
2 apartments* ⏺ *Breakfast.*

$$ 🔲 **Römischer Kaiser.** Centrally located near the Porta Nigra, this handsome
HOTEL patrician manor from 1885 offers well-appointed rooms with handsome
baths. **Pros:** near the Porta Nigra; free Wi-Fi. **Cons:** some rooms are dark
due to a neighboring building. 💲 *Rooms from: €116* ✉ *Porta-Nigra-Pl. 6*
☎ *0651/977–0100* ⊕ *www.friedrich-hotels.de* ⤳ *43 rooms* ⏺ *Breakfast.*

NIGHTLIFE AND THE ARTS

Most of the town's pubs and cafés are on Viehmarktplatz and Stockplatz
in the Old Town. ▮**TIP**➔ For up-to-the-minute information on perfor-
mances, concerts, and events all over town, visit ⊕ *www.trier-today.de.*

Metropolis. International DJs, theme parties, and live music are all
featured here. ✉ *Hindenburgstr. 4* ☎ *0651/710–378–000* ⊕ *www.
metropolis-trier.de.*

Theater Trier. The theater puts on opera, theater, and ballet performances
as well as concerts. ✉ *Am Augustinerhof* ☎ *0651/718–1818* ⊕ *www.
theater-trier.de.*

TUFA–Tuchfabrik. Concerts, theater, and cultural events are all staged here.
✉ *Wechselstr. 4, at Weberstr.* ☎ *0651/718–2412* ⊕ *www.tufa-trier.de.*

BONN AND THE KÖLN (COLOGNE) LOWLANDS

Bonn, the former capital of West Germany, and of reunified Germany
until 1999, is the next major stop after Koblenz on the Rhine. It's close
to the legendary Siebengebirge (Seven Hills), a national park and site
of western Germany's northernmost vineyards. According to German
mythology, Siegfried (hero of the Nibelungen saga) killed a dragon
here and bathed in its blood to make himself invincible. The lowland,
a region of gently rolling hills north of Bonn, lacks the drama of the
Rhine Gorge upstream but offers the urban pleasures of Köln (Cologne),
an ancient cathedral town, and Düsseldorf, an elegant city of art and
fashion. Although not geographically in the Rhineland proper, Aachen
is an important side trip for anyone visiting the region. Its stunning
cathedral and treasury are the greatest storehouses of Carolingian art
and architecture in Europe.

Bonn and the
Köln Lowlands

BONN

61 km (38 miles) north of Koblenz, 28 km (17 miles) south of Köln.

Bonn was the postwar seat of the federal government and parliament until Berlin became its capital again in 1999. Aptly described by the title of John le Carré's spy novel *A Small Town in Germany,* the quiet university town was chosen as a stopgap measure to prevent such weightier contenders as Frankfurt from becoming the capital, a move that would have lessened Berlin's chances of regaining its former status. With the exodus of the government from Bonn, the city has become a bit less cosmopolitan. Still, Bonn thrives as the headquarters of two of Germany's largest multinational corporations (Deutsche Telekom and Deutsche Post/DHL), and the UN has expanded its presence in the city as well. The fine museums and other cultural institutions that once served the diplomatic elite are still here to be enjoyed.

GETTING HERE AND AROUND

The town center is a car-free zone; an inner ring road circles it with parking garages on the perimeter. A convenient parking lot is just across from the railway station and within 50 yards of the tourist office, which is on Windeckstrasse near the Hauptbahnhof. Bonn has extensive bike paths downtown; these are designated paths (often demarcated with blue-and-white bicycle symbols) on the edges of roads or sidewalks.

▉ **TIP➜** Pedestrians, beware: anyone walking on a bike path risks getting mowed down. Bicyclists are expected to follow the same traffic rules as cars. In Bonn the Radstation, at the main train station, will not only rent you a bike and provide maps, but will also fill your water bottle and check the pressure in your tires for free.

Bilingual bus tours of Bonn cost €16 and start from the tourist office. They're conducted daily at 2 from Easter to October, and Saturday only November to March. A variety of walking tours are also available, including the "Bonn zu Fuss" city tour (€9), offered Saturday at 11 am from late April to October.

FESTIVALS

Beethoven-Festival. Concerts are held at numerous indoor and outdoor venues during September's month-long Beethoven-Festival. ☎ *0228/201–0345* ⊕ *www.beethovenfest.de.*

Bonner Sommer. From May through September, the Bonner Sommer festival offers folklore, music, and street theater, much of it outdoors and most of it free. Information is available at the tourist office. ☎ *0228/775–000.*

DISCOUNTS AND DEALS

Bonn's tourism office sells the **Bonn Regio Welcome Card**, which offers an array of reductions, plus free entry into most museums, in combination with low- or no-cost transportation; the card costs €9 per 24-hour period.

ESSENTIALS

Bicycle Contact Radstation ⊠ *Quantiusstr. 26* ☎ *0228/981–4636.*

Visitor Information Bonn Information ⊠ *Windeckstr. 1, on Cathedral Square* ☎ *0228/775–000* ⊕ *www.bonn.de.*

EXPLORING
TOP ATTRACTIONS

Beethoven-Haus (*Beethoven House*). Beethoven was born in Bonn in 1770 and, except for a short stay in Vienna, lived here until the age of 22. You'll find scores, paintings, a grand piano (his last, in fact), and an ear trumpet or two. Thanks to the modern age, there's now a "Stage for Music Visualization," an interactive exhibit involving 3-D glasses that shows Beethoven's best-loved works. The attached museum shop carries everything from kitsch to elegant Beethoven memorabilia. ⊠ *Bonng. 20* ☎ *0228/981–7525* ⊕ *www.beethoven-haus-bonn.de* ☜ *€6* ⊙ *Apr.–Oct., daily 10–6; Nov.–Mar., Mon.–Sat. 10–5, Sun. 11–5.*

Bundesviertel (*Federal Government District*). Walking through the pleasant area that was once the government district is like taking a trip back in time, to an era when Bonn was still the sleepy capital of West Germany. Bordered by Adenauerallee, Kaiser-Friedrich-Strasse, Franz-Josef-Strasse, and the Rhine, the quarter boasts sights such as the **Bundeshaus**, which includes the Plenarsaal (plenary hall). Designed to serve as the new Federal Parliament, the Bundeshaus was completed only seven years before the capital was relocated to Berlin in 1999. A few steps away, you'll find the historic **Villa Hammerschmidt,** the German equivalent of the White House. This stylish neoclassical mansion began serving as the Federal president's permanent residence in 1950,

Bonn is the city of Beethoven: he was born here, you can tour his home, there is a concert hall named after him, and a monument to him on Münsterplatz.

and is still his home when he stays in Bonn. Equally impressive is the **Palais Schaumburg,** another fine example of the Rhein Riveria estates that once housed the Federal Chancellery (1949–76). It became the center of Cold War politics during the Adenauer administration. Tours of the quarter, including a visit to the Villa Hammerschmidt, are offered by the Bonn Tourist Office. ⊠ *Heussallee (U-bahn)*.

Kunstmuseum Bonn (*Art Museum*). Changing exhibits are generally excellent at this large museum that focuses on Rhenish expressionists and German art since 1945 (Beuys, Baselitz, and Kiefer, for example). The museum's airy and inexpensive café is better than the stuffier version across the plaza at the Kunst- und Ausstellungshalle. ⊠ *Friedrich-Ebert-Allee 2* ☎ *0228/776–260* ⊕ *www.kunstmuseum-bonn.de* ⊠ *€7* ⊗ *Tues., Thurs.–Sun. 11–6, Wed. 11–9*.

Kurfürstliches Schloss (*Prince-Electors' Palace*). Built in the 18th century by the prince-electors of Köln, this grand palace now houses Bonn's university. If the weather is good, stroll through Hofgarten park in front of it. When Bonn was a capital, this patch of grass drew tens of thousands to antinuclear demonstrations. Today it's mostly used for games of pickup soccer and ultimate Frisbee. ⊠ *Am Hofgarten*.

Münster (*Minster*). The 900-year-old church is vintage late Romanesque, with a massive octagonal main tower and a soaring spire. It stands on a site where two Roman soldiers were executed in the 3rd century for being Christian. It saw the coronations of two Holy Roman Emperors (in 1314 and 1346) and was one of the Rhineland's most important ecclesiastical centers in the Middle Ages. The 17th-century bronze figure of St. Helen and the ornate rococo pulpit are highlights of the interior; outside you'll find two giant stone heads: those of Cassius and Florentius, the martyred soldiers. ✉ *Münsterpl.* ☎ *0228/985–880* ⊕ *www.bonner-muenster.de* ✆ *Free* ⊙ *Mon.–Sat. 8–7, Sun. 9–8.*

WORTH NOTING

Altes Rathaus (*Old Town Hall*). This 18th-century rococo town hall looks somewhat like a pink dollhouse. Its elegant steps and stair entry have seen a great many historic figures, including French president Charles de Gaulle and U.S. president John F. Kennedy. For information about possible tours, contact the visitor center. ✉ *Am Markt* ☎ *774–288.*

Haus der Geschichte (*House of History*). German history since World War II is the subject of this museum, which begins with "hour zero," as the Germans call the unconditional surrender of 1945. The museum displays an overwhelming amount of documentary material organized on five levels and engages various types of media. It's not all heavy either—temporary exhibits have featured political cartoonists, Cold War–era sporting contests pitting East Germany versus West Germany, and an in-depth examination of the song "Lili Marleen," sung by troops of every nation during World War II. ✉ *Willy-Brandt-Allee 14* ☎ *0228/91650* ⊕ *www.hdg.de* ✆ *Free (with audio guide in English)* ⊙ *Tues.–Fri. 9–7, weekends 10–6.*

Kunst- und Ausstellungshalle der Bundesrepublik Deutschland (*Art and Exhibition Hall of the German Federal Republic*). This is one of the Rhineland's most important venues for major temporary exhibitions about art, culture, andarchaeology. Its modern design, by Viennese architect Gustave Peichl, is as interesting as anything on exhibit in the museum. It employs three enormous blue cones situated on a lawn-like rooftop garden. ✉ *Friedrich-Ebert-Allee 4* ☎ *0228/91710* ⊕ *www.bundeskunsthalle.de* ✆ *€10 for one exhibition, €15 for all exhibitions (€6 2 hrs before closing)* ⊙ *Tues. and Wed. 10–9, Thurs.–Sun. 10–7.*

Poppelsdorfer Schloss (*Poppelsdorf Palace*). This former electors' palace, built in the baroque style between 1715 and 1753, now houses the university's mineralogical collection. Its botanical gardens are home to 12,000 species, among the largest variety in Germany. ✉ *Meckenheimer Allee 171* ☎ *0228/732–764* ⊕ *www.steinmann.uni-bonn.de/museen; www.botgart.uni-bonn.de* ✆ *Mineralogical collection €2.50; botanical garden free weekdays, Sun. €2* ⊙ *Mineralogical collection: Wed. and Fri. 3–6, Sun. 10–5. Botanical garden: Apr.–Oct., Sun.–Wed. and Fri. 10–6, Thurs. 10–8; Nov.–Mar., weekdays 10–4.*

CLASSICAL MUSIC

Few regions in Europe rival the quality of classical music performances and venues on the Rhine. Beethoven was born in Bonn, and the city hosts a Beethoven festival every year in mid- to late September. Düsseldorf, once home to Mendelssohn, Schumann, and Brahms, has the finest concert hall in Germany after Berlin's Philharmonie: the Tonhalle, in a former planetarium. Köln also has one of Germany's best concert halls, and its opera company is known for exciting classical and contemporary productions. The cathedrals of Aachen, Köln, and Trier are magnificent settings for concerts and organ recitals.

WHERE TO EAT

$
GERMAN
✕ **Em Höttche.** Beethoven was a regular at this tavern, which has been around since the late 14th century. Today it offers one of the best-value lunches in town, and the kitchen stays open until 1 am. The interior is rustic, the food hearty and non-fussy. $ *Average main: €15* ⊠ *Markt 4* ☎ *0228/690–009* ⊕ *www.em-hoettche.de.*

$$$
ITALIAN
✕ **Ristorante Sassella.** When the Bundestag was still in town, this Bonn institution used to be cited in the press as frequently for its backroom political dealings as for its Lombardy-influenced food. Locals, prominent and otherwise, still flock to the restaurant, in an 18th-century house in the suburb of Kessenich. The style is pure Italian farmhouse, with stone walls and exposed beams, but the handmade pastas often stray from the typical, as in the salmon-filled black-and-white pasta pockets in shrimp sauce. $ *Average main: €25* ⊠ *Karthäuserpl. 21* ☎ *0228/530–815* ⊕ *www.ristorante-sassella.de* ⌂ *Reservations essential* ☉ *Closed Mon. No lunch Sat., no dinner Sun.*

$$$$
EUROPEAN
Fodor's Choice
★
✕ **Strandhaus.** On a quiet residential street, and hidden from view in summer by an ivy-covered patio, this restaurant feels like a true escape—befitting its laid-back name ("beach house"). Chef Astrid Kuth insists on local produce, and presents her delicate, innovatively spiced food with elegance, but no fuss. A carefully compiled wine list long on Geman bottles, along with a frequently changing menu, means locals

come here often. $ *Average main: €27* ✉ *Georgstr. 28* ☏ *0228/369–4949* ⊕ *www.strandhaus-bonn.de* ☾ *Closed Sun. and Mon. No lunch.*

WHERE TO STAY

$$$ 🏨 **Best Western Domicil.** A group of
HOTEL   buildings around a quiet, central
courtyard has been converted into
a charming and comfortable hotel,
with rooms individually furnished
and decorated in styles ranging
from fin de siècle romantic to Italian modern. **Pros:** quiet courtyard;
handy to the train station. **Cons:**
plain exterior. $ *Rooms from: €185* ✉ *Thomas-Mann-Str. 24–26* ☏ *0228/729–090* ⊕ *domicil-bonn. bestwestern.de* ⮐ *43 rooms, 1 apartment* ⦿ *Breakfast.*

$ 🏨 **Hotel Mozart.** Elegant on the outside and simple on the inside, this small,
HOTEL   attractive hotel is often recommended to friends by locals. **Pros:** quiet
tree-lined street; close to the train station. **Cons:** thin walls. $ *Rooms from: €99* ✉ *Mozartstr. 1* ☏ *0228/659–071* ⊕ *www.hotel-mozart-bonn. com* ⮐ *38 rooms* ⦿ *Breakfast.*

$$$ 🏨 **Sternhotel.** For solid comfort and a picturesque, central location, the
HOTEL   Sternhotel is tops—and their weekend rates are a bargain. **Pros:** in the
center of town; partnership with gym across the square, allowing guests
free entry. **Cons:** market square location can be noisy in the morning;
expensive for the area. $ *Rooms from: €185* ✉ *Markt 8* ☏ *0228/72670* ⊕ *www.sternhotel-bonn.de* ⮐ *80 rooms* ⦿ *Breakfast.*

THE ARTS

Beethovenhalle. The Bonn Symphony Orchestra opens its season in grand
style every year in late summer with a concert on the market square, in
front of town hall. Many of its other concerts are held in the Beethovenhalle. ✉ *Wachsbleiche 16* ☏ *0228/722–20* ⊕ *www.beethovenhalle.de.*

Beethoven-Haus. In the Beethoven-Haus, recitals are sometimes given on
a 19th-century grand piano, and concerts take place regularly in the
chamber music hall. ✉ *Bonng. 20* ☏ *0228/981–750.*

Pantheon Theater. This is a major venue for comedy and cabaret.
✉ *Bundeskanzlerpl. 2–10* ☏ *0228/212–521* ⊕ *www.pantheon.de.*

Schumannhaus. Chamber-music concerts are given regularly at the
Schumannhaus, where composer Robert Schumann spent his final years.
✉ *Sebastianstr. 182* ☏ *0228/773–656* ⊕ *www.schumannhaus-bonn.de.*

Theater Bonn. Operas are staged regularly at the Theater Bonn, which
also hosts musicals and performances by world-renowned dance companies, including ballet. ✉ *Am Boeselagerhof 1* ☏ *0228/778–000* ⊕ *www.theater-bonn.de.*

BIER AM RHEIN

When it's warm out, most Germans like nothing better than to sit outside with a beer in hand. In Bonn, the best beer gardens are right on the River Rhine, which runs through the city. On the Bonn city center side, there's the **Alter Zoll** (✉ *Brassertufer 1*) and **Schänzchen** (✉ *Rosental 105*). Across the Kennedy Bridge in Beuel, however, is where the late afternoon sun shines best. On either side of the bridge are **Rheinlust** (✉ *Rheinaustr. 134*) and **Bahnhöfchen** (✉ *Rheinaustr. 116*).

SHOPPING

There are plenty of department stores and boutiques in the pedestrian shopping zone around the Markt and the Münster.

Flohmarkt (*Flea Market*). Bargain hunters search for secondhand goods and knickknacks at the city's renowned—and huge—flea market. It's held in Rheinaue south of the Konrad-Adenauer-Brücke on the third Saturday of each month from April through October. ⊠ *Rheinaue.*

Wochenmarkt (*Weekly Market*). Bonn's Wochenmarkt is open every day but Sunday, filling the Markt with vendors of produce and various edibles. Things get really busy in springtime, when the locals flock to find the best asparagus and strawberries. ⊠ *Markt.*

KÖNIGSWINTER

12 km (7 miles) southeast of Bonn.

Home to one of Germany's most popular castles, Drachenfels, Königswinter is also the gateway to the 30 large and small hills that makes up the Siebengebirge, the country's oldest nature reserve. In early May, festivities and fireworks light up the town as part of the "Rhine in Flames" fireworks display.

GETTING HERE AND AROUND

Königswinter is 15 minutes south of Bonn by car. It can also be reached by a 40-minute train ride (via Regionalbahn) from Köln.

Fodor's Choice ★ **Drachenfels.** The town of Königswinter has one of the most-visited castles on the Rhine, the **Drachenfels.** Its ruins crown one of the highest hills in the Siebengebirge, with a spectacular view of the Rhine. It's also part of Germany's oldest nature reserve, with more than 100 km (62 miles) of hiking trails. The castle was built in the 12th century by the archbishop of Köln, and takes its name from a dragon said to have lived in a nearby cave. (The dragon was slain by Siegfried, hero of the epic *Nibelungenlied.*)

The castle ruins can be reached via two different hikes, each of about 45 minutes. One route begins at the Drachenfelsbahn station, and passes the Nibelungenhalle reptile zoo along the way. The other route starts at Rhöndorf on the other side of the hill. The Siebengebirge Tourist Office at Drachenfelstrasse 51 in Königswinter can provide a map that includes these and other local hiking trails.

Drachenfelsbahn. If hiking to Drachenfels isn't for you, you can also reach the castle ruins by taking the Drachenfelsbahn, a steep, narrow-gauge train that makes trips to the summit every half hour March through October, and hourly in winter (except late November and December). ⊠ *Drachenfelsstr. 53* ☎ *02223/92090* ⊕ *www. drachenfelsbahn-koenigswinter.de* 🖃 *€10 round-trip* ⊙ *Mar. and Oct., daily 10–6; Apr., daily 10–7; May–Sept., daily 9–7; early Nov. and Jan.–Feb., weekdays noon–5, weekends 11–6*

FAMILY **Sea Life.** Königswinter's huge aquarium features 2,000 creatures from the sea. The biggest pool has a glass tunnel that enables you to walk on the "bottom of the sea." ⊠ *Rheinallee 8* ☎ *0180/5666–90101 for tickets (€0.20–€0.60 per call)* ⊕ *www.visitsealife.com* 🖃 *€14.95* ⊙ *Easter–Oct., daily 10–6; Nov.–Easter, weekdays 10–5, weekends 10–6.*

BRÜHL

20 km (12 miles) northwest of Bonn.

In the center of Brühl stands the Rhineland's most important baroque palace, the Augustusburg. Brühl is also home to one of Germany's most popular theme parks, Phantasialand.

EXPLORING

Schloss Augustusburg. This castle and the magnificent pleasure park that surrounds it were created in the time of Prince Clemens August, between 1725 and 1768. The palace contains one of the most famous achievements of rococo architecture, a staircase by Balthasar Neumann. The castle can be visited only on guided tours, which leave the reception area every hour or so. An English-language recorded tour is available. ⊠ *Max-Ernst-Allee* ☎ *02232/44000* ⊕ *www.schlossbruehl.de* 💰 *€6* 🕙 *Feb.–Nov., Tues.–Fri. 9–noon and 1:30–4, weekends 10–5.*

Jagdschloss Falkenlust. This small castle, at the end of an avenue leading under the tracks across from Schloss Augustusburg's grounds, was built as a getaway where the prince could indulge his passion for falconry. ⊠ *Otto-Wels-Str.* ☎ *02232/44000* ⊕ *www.schlossbruehl.de* 💰 *€4.50* 🕙 *Feb.–Nov., Tues.–Fri. 9–noon and 1:30–4, weekends 10–5.*

KÖLN (COLOGNE)

28 km (17 miles) north of Bonn, 47 km (29 miles) south of Düsseldorf, 70 km (43 miles) southeast of Aachen.

Köln (Cologne in English) is the largest city on the Rhine (the fourth largest in Germany) and one of the most interesting. The city is vibrant and bustling, with a lightness and cheerfulness that's typical of the Rhineland. At its heart is tradition, manifested in the abundance of bars and brew houses serving the local Kölsch beer and old Rhine cuisine. These are good meeting places to start a night on the town. Tradition, however, is mixed with the contemporary, found in a host of elegant shops, sophisticated restaurants, modern bars and dance clubs, and a contemporary-art scene that's now just hanging on against unstoppable competition from Berlin.

Although not as old as Trier, Köln has been a dominant power in the Rhineland since Roman times, and it remains a major commercial, intellectual, and ecclesiastical center. Köln was first settled in 38 BC. For nearly a century it grew slowly, in the shadow of imperial Trier, until a locally born noblewoman, Julia Agrippina, daughter of the Roman general Germanicus, married the Roman emperor Claudius. Her hometown was elevated to the rank of a Roman city and given the name Colonia Claudia Ara Agrippinensium (Claudius Colony at the Altar of Agrippina). For the next 300 years Colonia (hence Cologne, or Köln) flourished. Evidence of the Roman city's wealth resides in the Römisch-Germanisches Museum. In the 9th century Charlemagne, the towering figure who united the sprawling German lands (and ruled much of present-day France) as the first Holy Roman Emperor, restored Köln's fortunes and elevated it to its preeminent role in the Rhineland by appointing the first archbishop of Köln. The city's ecclesiastical heritage is one of its most striking features; it has a full dozen Romanesque churches and one of the world's largest and finest Gothic cathedrals. In the Middle Ages it was a member of the powerful Hanseatic League, occupying a position of greater importance in European commerce than either London or Paris.

Köln was a thriving modern city until World War II, when bombings destroyed 90% of it. Only the cathedral remained relatively unscathed. But like many other German cities that rebounded during the "Economic Miracle" of the 1950s, Köln is a mishmash of old and new, sometimes awkwardly juxtaposed. A good part of the former Old Town along the Hohe Strasse (old Roman High Road) was turned into a remarkably charmless pedestrian shopping mall. It's all framed by six-lane expressways winding along the rim of the city center—barely yards from the cathedral—illustrating the problems of postwar reconstruction. However, much of the Altstadt, ringed by streets that follow the line of the medieval city walls, is closed to traffic. Most major sights are within this area and are easily reached on foot. Here, too, you'll find the best shops.

KÖLN, GERMANY'S GAY CAPITAL

Köln is widely considered to be Germany's gay capital (despite what Berliners may say). Every summer, up to 1 million visitors come for two weeks to attend **Cologne Pride** (⊕ www.colognepride.de), transforming Köln into an international LGBT hospot. Beginning in mid-June, the festivities culminate in early July in the citywide **Christopher Street Day Parade**. The city's gay nightlife centers on what locals call the "Bermuda Triangle"—the city's biggest concentration of gay bars, on Schaafenstrasse.

GETTING HERE AND AROUND
As one of Germany's most important rail hubs, Köln is connected by fast trains to cities throughout northwestern Europe, including Paris, Brussels, and Frankfurt. German rail lines link Köln to the entire nation. You can reach Köln from Bonn in about 20 minutes, and Brühl in about 15.

FESTIVALS
Weihnachtsmarkt am Kölner Dom. Of Cologne's four main Christmas markets the Weihnachtsmarkt am Kölner Dom, in the shadow of the city's famed cathedral, is the most impressive. Set against the backdrop of the church's magnificent twin spires, a giant Christmas tree stands proudly in the middle of the market's 160 festively adorned stalls, which sell mulled wine, roasted chestnuts, and many other German yuletide treats. ⊕ *www.koelnerweihnachtsmarkt.com* ☉ *Late Nov.–Dec. 23, Sun.–Wed. 11–9, Thurs. and Fri. 11–10, Sat. 10–10.*

TOURS
City bus tours leave from the tourist office and from Trankgasse, beside the cathedral, once per hour from 10 am, year-round. The 90-minute tours cost €12–€15, leave every hour, from 10 am, year-round, and are conducted in English and German. Walking tours in English are often available by arrangement with the tourist office. Bus trips into the countryside (to the Eifel Hills, the Ahr Valley, and the Westerwald) are organized by several city travel agencies.

Radstation Köln offers bike rental by the day (€10) from April through October as well as three-hour guided bike tours of the city (€15), departing daily at 1:30.

DISCOUNTS AND DEALS

Most central hotels sell the **Köln Tourismus Card** (€9 for one day, €14 for two days), which entitles you to discounts on sightseeing tours, admissions to all the city's museums, free city bus and tram travel, and other reductions.

ESSENTIALS

Bicycle Contacts Radstation Köln ⊠ *Markmannsg. next to Deutzer Brücke (bridge)* ☎ *0221/629–8796* ⊕ *www.radstationkoeln.de.*

Visitor Information Köln Tourismus Office ⊠ *Kardinal-Höffner-Pl. 1, opposite cathedral* ☎ *0221/2213–0400* ⊕ *www.cologne-tourism.com.*

EXPLORING

TOP ATTRACTIONS

Fodor's Choice ★ **Dom** (*Cathedral*). Köln's landmark embodies one of the purest expressions of the Gothic spirit in Europe. The cathedral, meant to be a tangible expression of God's kingdom on Earth, was conceived with such immense dimensions that construction, begun in 1248, was not completed until 1880, after the original plan was rediscovered. At 515 feet high, the two west towers of the cathedral were briefly the tallest structures in the world when they were finished (before being eclipsed by the Washington Monument). The cathedral was built to house what are believed to be the relics of the Magi, the three kings who paid homage to the infant Jesus (the trade in holy mementos was big business in the Middle Ages—and not always scrupulous). The size of the building was not simply an example of self-aggrandizement on the part of the people of Köln, however; it was a response to the vast numbers of pilgrims who arrived to see the relics. The ambulatory, the passage that curves around the back of the altar, is unusually large, allowing cathedral authorities to funnel large numbers of visitors up to the crossing (where the nave and transepts meet and where the relics were originally displayed), around the back of the altar, and out again.

Today the relics are kept just behind the altar, in the original, enormous gold-and-silver **reliquary.** The other great treasure of the cathedral, in the last chapel on the left as you face the altar, is the **Gero Cross,** a monumental oak crucifix dating from 971. The Altar of the City Patrons (1440), a triptych by Stephan Lochner, Köln's most famous medieval painter, is to the right. Other highlights are the stained-glass windows, some dating from the 13th century and another, designed by Gerhard Richter with help from a computer program, from the 21st; the 15th-century altarpiece; and the early-14th-century high altar, with its glistening white figures and intricate choir screens. If you're up to it, climb to the top of the bell tower to get the complete vertical experience (but be aware that viewing Köln from the Dom itself removes the skyline's most interesting feature). The treasury includes the silver shrine of Archbishop Engelbert, who was stabbed to death in 1225. Allow at least an hour for the whole tour of the interior, treasury, and tower climb. ⊠ *Dompl., Altstadt* ☎ *0221/9258–4730* ⊕ *www.koelner-dom.de* 🎫 *Tower €3, cathedral treasury €5, guided tours €7.*

Köln (Cologne)

Hauptbahnhof

Gereonstr.

Unter Sachsenhausen

Zeughausstr. Komödienstrasse

Burgmauerstr.

Dom

Domplatz

Wallraf-
platz

Am Hof

Hohenzollern
Brücke

Breitestrasse Minoritenstr. Grosse Budengasse

Glockengasse

Brücken strasse

Kleine
Budengasse

Rhine

Alter
Markt

Ling.

Schildergasse

Neumarkt Kroneng.

Gürzenichstr. Gürzenichstr.

Heumarkt

Deutzer
Brücke

Cäcilienstrasse

Augustinerstr.

Pipinstr.

KEY

Tourist information

0   200 yards

0   200 meters

Museum Ludwig. This museum is dedicated to art from the beginning of the 20th century to the present day. Its American pop-art collection (including Andy Warhol, Jasper Johns, Robert Rauschenberg, Claes Oldenburg, and Roy Lichtenstein) rivals that of most American museums. ⊠ *Heinrich-Böll-Pl., Innenstadt* ☎ *0221/2212–6165* ⊕ *www.museum-ludwig.de* ⊠ *€10* ⊗ *Tues.–Sun. 10–6, 1st Thurs. of every month 10–10. Closed 1 wk during Karneval, mid-Feb.–early Mar.*

Fodor's Choice **Römisch-Germanisches Museum** (*Roman-Germanic Museum*). This cul-
★   tural landmark was built in the early 1970s around the famous Diony-
sius mosaic discovered here during the construction of an air-raid shelter in 1941. The huge mosaic, more than 800 square feet, once formed the dining-room floor of a wealthy Roman trader's villa. Its millions of tiny earthenware and glass tiles depict some of the adventures of Dionysius, the Greek god of wine. The pillared 1st-century tomb of Lucius Publicius (a prominent Roman officer), some stone Roman coffins, and everyday objects of Roman life are among the museum's other exhibits. Bordering the museum on the south is a restored 90-yard stretch of the old Roman harbor road. ⊠ *Roncallipl. 4, Altstadt* ☎ *0221/2212–4438* ⊕ *www.museenkoeln.de* ⊠ *€6 (sometimes higher during special exhibitions)* ⊗ *Tues.–Sun. 10–5, 1st Thurs. of every month 10–10.*

Wallraf-Richartz-Museum. This museum contains paintings spanning the years 1300 to 1900. The Dutch and Flemish schools are particularly well represented, as is the 15th- to 16th-century Köln school of German painting. Its two most famous artists are the Master of the St. Veronica (whose actual name is unknown) and Stefan Lochner, represented by two luminous works, *The Last Judgment* and *The Madonna in the Rose Bower.* Large canvases by Rubens, who spent his youth in Köln, hang prominently on the second floor. There are also outstanding works by Rembrandt, Van Dyck, and Frans Hals, and the largest collection of French Impressionism in Germany. ⊠ *Obenmarspforten, Altstadt* ☎ *0221/2212–1119* ⊕ *www.wallraf. museum* ⊠ *€8* ☉ *Tues. and Wed. 10–6, Thurs. 10–9, Fri.–Sun. 10–6.*

WORTH NOTING

Altes Rathaus (*Old Town Hall*). The Rathaus is worth a look, even from the outside. (Tours of the interior, for groups only, must be booked at the tourist office.) It's the oldest town hall in Germany, with elements remaining from the 14th century. The famous bell tower rings its bells daily at 9, noon, 3, and 6. Standing on pedestals at one end of the town hall are figures of prophets made in the early 15th century. Ranging along the south wall are nine additional statues, the so-called *Nine Good Heroes,* carved in 1360. Charlemagne, Alexander the Great, and King David are among them. Sculptures of 124 later Cologne heroes, up through the 20th-century, have been added outside at the Town Hall Tower. Beneath a small glass pyramid near the south corner of the Rathaus is the **Mikwe,** a 12th-century ritual bath from the medieval Jewish quarter that surrounded it at that time. ⊠ *Rathauspl. 2, Altstadt* ☎ *0221/2212–3332.*

Gross St. Martin (*Great St. Martin*). This remarkable Romanesque parish church was rebuilt after being flattened in World War II. Its massive 13th-century tower, with distinctive corner turrets and an imposing central spire, is another Köln landmark. The church was built on the site of a Roman granary. ⊠ *Martinspförtchen 8, Altstadt* ☎ *1642–5650* ☉ *Sept.–July, Tues.–Sat. 9–7:30, Sun. 1–7:15; Aug., Tues.–Sat. noon– 7:30, Sun. 1–7:15.*

Gürzenich. This Gothic structure, located at the south end of Martinsviertel, was all but demolished in World War II, but carefully reconstructed afterward. It's named after a medieval knight from whom the city acquired valuable real estate in 1437. The official reception and festival hall here has played a central role in civic life through the centuries. At one end of the complex are the remains of the 10th-century Gothic church of **St. Alban,** which were left ruined after the war as a memorial. On what's left of the church floor you can see a sculpture of a couple kneeling in prayer, *Mourning Parents,* by Käthe Kollwitz, a memorial to the ravages of war. ⊠ *Martinstr. 29–37, Altstadt* ⊕ *www.koelnkongress.de.*

Käthe Kollwitz Museum. The works of Käthe Kollwitz (1867–1945), the most important German female artist of the 20th century, focus on social themes like the plight of the poor and the atrocities of war. This is the larger of the country's two Kollwitz collections and comprises all of her woodcuts, as well as paintings, etchings, lithographs, and sculptures. There are also changing exhibits of other modern artists. ⊠ *Neumarkt 18–24, in Neumarkt Passage, Innenstadt* ☎ *0221/227– 2899* ⊕ *www.kollwitz.de* ⊠ *€4* ☉ *Tues.–Fri. 10–6, weekends 11–6.*

KARNEVAL IN KÖLN

As the biggest city in the traditionally Catholic Rhineland, Köln puts on Germany's most exciting and rowdy carnival. The Kölsch starts flowing on November 11 at 11:11 am with screams of the famous motto *Kölle alaaf!* ("Köln is alive!"). Karneval then calms down for a few months, only to reach a fever pitch in February for the last five days before Lent. On Fat Thursday, known as *Weiberfastnacht,* women roam the streets with scissors and exercise merciless precision in cutting off the ties of any men foolish enough to wear them. Starting then, bands, parades, and parties go all night, and people of all ages don silly costumes, including the customary red clown nose. It's a good time to meet new people; in fact, it is practically impossible not to, as kissing strangers is considered par for the course. ■ TIP→ During this time, visitors who are claustrophobic or who don't want to risk having beer spilled on them should avoid the Heumarkt area in the Old Town, and possibly the whole city. The festivities come to an end Tuesday at midnight with the ritual burning of the "Nubbel"— a dummy that acts as the scapegoat for everyone's drunken, embarrassing behavior. Note: Many museums are closed during Karneval.

Kölnisches Stadtmuseum (*Cologne City Museum*). The triumphs and tragedies of Köln's rich past are packed into this museum at the historic *Zeughaus,* the city's former arsenal. Here you'll find an in-depth chronicle of Köln's history—including information about the lives of ordinary people and high-profile politicians, the industrial revolution (car manufacturer Henry Ford headquartered his European operations here), and the destruction incurred during World War II. For those who've always wanted to be privy to the inside stories surrounding local words such as *Klüngel, Kölsch,* and *Karneval,* the answers are waiting to be discovered within the museum's walls. ⊠ *Zeughausstr. 1–3, Altstadt* ☎ *0221/2212–5789* ⊕ *www.museenkoeln.de* 🎫 *€5* ⊙ *Wed.–Sun. 10–5, Tues. 10–8, 1st Thurs. of every month 10–10.*

Kolumba. The origins of the official art museum of the Archdiocese of Cologne stretch back to 1853, but the institution received a big boost in 2007, with the opening of a unique new home atop—and masterfully incorporating— the ruins of the Gothic parish church of St. Kolumba. Designed by the Swiss architect Peter Zumthor, the new building pays homage to the site's Roman, Gothic, and medieval heritage, while unstuffily presenting a collection of art spanning from late antiquity to the present. ⊠ *Kolumbastr. 4, Innenstadt* ☎ *0221/933– 1930* ⊕ *www.kolumba.de* 🎫 *€5* ⊙ *Wed.–Mon. noon–5.*

Museum Schnütgen. A treasure house of medieval art from the Rhine region, the museum has an ideal setting in a 12th-century basilica. Don't miss the crucifix from the St. Georg Kirche or the original stained-glass windows and carved figures from the Dom. Other exhibits include intricately carved ivory book covers, rock-crystal reliquaries, and illuminated manuscripts. ⊠ *Cäcilienstr. 29, Innenstadt* ☎ *0221/2212–2310* ⊕ *www. museenkoeln.de* 🎫 *€6* ⊙ *Tues., Wed., and Fri.–Sun. 10–6, Thurs. 10–8, 1st Thurs. of every month 10–10.*

St. Gereon. This exquisite Romanesque basilica stands on the site of an old Roman burial ground six blocks west of the train station. An enormous dome rests on walls that were once clad in gold mosaics. Roman masonry forms part of the medieval structure, which is believed to have been built over the grave of its namesake, the 4th-century martyr and Köln's patron. ⌧ *Gereonskloster   2–4* ☎ *0221/134–922* ⊕ *www.stgereon. de* ☚ *Free* ☉ *Weekdays 10–6, Sat. 10–5:30, Sun. 12:30–6.*

St. Kunibert. The most lavish of the churches from the late-Romanesque period is by the Rhine, three blocks north of the train station. The apse's precious stained-glass windows have filtered light for more than 750 years (they were put in protective storage during World War II). Consecrated in 1247, the church contains an unusual room, concealed under the altar, which gives access to a pre-Christian well once believed to promote fertility in women. ⌧ *Kunibertsklosterg. 2, Altstadt-Nord* ☎ *0221/121–214* ⊕ *www.basilika-st-kunibert.de* ☚ *Free* ☉ *Mon.–Sat. 10–1 and 3–6, Sun. 3–6.*

FAMILY **Schokoladenmuseum** (*Chocolate Museum*). This riverside museum south of the cathedral is a real hit, and so crowded on weekends that it can be unpleasant. It recounts 3,000 years of civilization's production and enjoyment of chocolate, from the Central American Maya to the colonizing and industrializing Europeans. It's also a real factory, with lava flows of chocolate and a conveyer belt jostling thousands of truffles. The museum shop, with a huge variety of chocolate items, does a brisk business, and the riverside panorama café serves some of the best cake in town. ⌧ *Am Schockoladenmuseum 1a, Rheinufer* ☎ *0221/931–8880* ⊕ *www.schokoladenmuseum.de* ☚ *€8.50* ☉ *Tues.– Fri. 10–6, weekends 11–7; Mon. 10–6 (Dec. only).*

WHERE TO EAT

$ ✕ **Café Elefant.** For three decades, writers and artists from Köln's ele-
EUROPEAN gant Agnesviertel neighborhood have been meeting at this cosy locale on a quiet, tree-lined street. Inside, the ambience—like a little corner of Montmartre—is just right for thinking deep thoughts, or simply chatting over a slice of chocolate cake. Even when the cake's all gone, night owls can enjoy the café's delicious camembert and lingonberry blintzes. $ *Average main: €7* ⌧ *Weissenburgstr. 50* ☎ *0221/734–520* ⊟ *No credit cards.*

EAU DE COLOGNE

The original "eau de Cologne" was first produced here in the early 18th century from an Italian formula. It's made from a secret formula and aged in oak barrels. The most famous cologne is 4711, which derives its name from the firm's address at 4711 Glockengasse. The building itself is equipped with a carillon, a museum, and (naturally) a gift shop. The light scent, primarily derived from citrus, rosemary, and lavender, may seem a little old-fashionted to some, but it comes in an elegant bottle with a turquoise-and-gilt label, and makes a nice souvenir.

$$$
FRENCH
Fodor's Choice
★

✕ **Capricorn i Aries.** This corner brasserie—part neighborhood bistro, part upscale restaurant—serves the staples of French rural cuisine with a Rhineland twist, whether it's a simple soup or a five-course dinner. The owners' award-winning, four-table restaurant across the street is also available for special events. Those aiming to improve their own skills can participate in a Sunday cooking class, in which students prepare and then eat four courses. $ *Average main: €22* ✉ *Alteburger Str. 31, Neustadt Süd* ☎ *0221/397–5710* ⊕ *www.capricorniaries.com* ⏣ *Reservations essential* ▭ *No credit cards* ◷ *Closed Sun. No lunch Sat.*

$$$
ITALIAN
Fodor's Choice
★

✕ **Casa di Biase.** The sophisticated Italian cuisine is served here in a warm, elegant setting. The seasonally changing menu focuses on fish and game, and the wine list is interesting and extensive—although sometimes pricey. Next door is Casa di Biase's smaller and more casual sister, the Teca di Biasi. This cozy, wood-panel wine bar serves antipasti, salads, and main dishes for under €15. $ *Average main: €22* ✉ *Eifelpl. 4, Südstadt* ☎ *0221/322–433* ⊕ *www.casadibiase.de* ◷ *Closed Sun. No lunch Sat.*

$
GERMAN

✕ **Früh am Dom.** For real down-home cooking, there are few places that compare with this time-honored former brewery in the shadow of the Dom. It's often crowded, but the mood's fantastic. Bold frescoes on the vaulted ceilings establish the mood, and the authentically Teutonic experience is completed by such dishes as *Hämmchen* (pork knuckle). The beer garden is perfect for summer dining. $ *Average main: €12* ✉ *Am Hof 12–18, Altstadt* ☎ *0221/261–3211* ⊕ *www.frueh.de* ▭ *No credit cards.*

$$
ECLECTIC

✕ **Heising & Adelmann.** A young crowd gathers here to do what people along the Rhine have done for centuries—talk, drink, and enjoy good company. There's a party every Friday and Saturday with a DJ. Consistently voted one of the best deals in town, this restaurant offers good German beer, tangy cocktails, and a creative mixture of German and French food. $ *Average main: €19* ✉ *Friesenstr. 58–60, Neustadt-Nord* ☎ *0221/130–9424* ⊕ *www.heising-und-adelmann.de* ◷ *Closed Sun. and Mon. No lunch.*

$
GERMAN

✕ **Päffgen.** There's no better Bräuhaus in Köln for drinking Kölsch, the city's home brew. You won't sit long in front of an empty glass before a blue-aproned waiter sweeps by and places another one before you. With its worn wooden decor, colorful clientele, and typical Rhenish fare (Sauerbraten, pork knuckle, and potato pancakes), Päffgen sums up local tradition. The brewery is the family business of the late singer-actress Nico, née Christa Päffgen, who became famous in the '60s through her collaborations with Andy Warhol and the Velvet Underground. $ *Average main: €11* ✉ *Friesenstr. 64–66, Friesenviertel* ☎ *0221/135–461* ⊕ *www.paeffgen-koelsch.de* ▭ *No credit cards.*

WHERE TO STAY

The tourist office, across from the cathedral, can make hotel bookings for you for the same night, at a cost of €3 per booking. If you plan to be in town for Karneval, be sure to reserve a room well in advance.

$$$$
HOTEL

🛏 **Excelsior Hotel Ernst.** Old-master paintings, including a Van Dyck, grace this 1863 hotel's sumptuous Empire-style lobby, while Gobelin tapestries hang in the ballroom; the rooms are spacious, with upscale linens on the beds. **Pros:** Van Dyck paintings and Gobelins. **Cons:** expensive. $ *Rooms* *from: €270* ⊠ *Dompl., Trankg. 1, Altstadt* ☎ *0221/2701* ⊕ *www. excelsiorhotelernst.de* ⤵ *108 rooms, 34 suites* ❶❶ *No meals.*

$$ **Hopper Hotel et cetera.** The rooms
HOTEL in this former monastery in the Belgian Quarter are spare but not spartan, though a startlingly realistic sculpture of a bishop, sitting in the reception area, serves as a constant reminder of the building's ecclesiastic origins. **Pros:** chicly renovated; attractive neighborhood. **Cons:** not centrally located, showers tricky for older guests. $ *Rooms from: €125* ⊠ *Brüsselerstr. 26, Belgisches Viertel* ☎ *0221/924–400* ⊕ *www. hopper.de* ⤵ *48 rooms, 1 suite, 1 apartment* ❶❶ *Breakfast.*

$$ **Hotel Chelsea.** This designer hotel
HOTEL with classic modern furnishings has a strong following among artists and art dealers, as well as with the musicians who come to play at the nearby Stadtgarten jazz club. **Pros:** an artsy clientele and neighborhood. **Cons:** some rooms need freshening up and not all have their own bathroom. $ *Rooms from: €165* ⊠ *Jülicherstr. 1, Belgisches Viertel* ☎ *0221/207–150* ⊕ *www.hotel-chelsea.de* ⤵ *35 rooms (3 without bath), 3 suites, 1 apartment* ❶❶ *No meals.*

$$ **Hotel im Kupferkessel.** The best things about this small, unassuming,
HOTEL family-run hotel are its immaculate housekeeping—the very model of German fastidiousness—and the price (small single rooms with shared bath can be had for as low as €40). **Pros:** inexpensive, with breakfast included. **Cons:** no elevator. $ *Rooms from: €135* ⊠ *Probsteig. 6, Alstadt-Nord* ☎ *0221/270–7960* ⊕ *www.im-kupferkessel.de* ⤵ *12 rooms (5 without bath)* ❶❶ *Breakfast.*

$$$ **Hotel im Wasserturm.** What used to be Europe's tallest water tower is
HOTEL now an independent, 11-story luxury hotel that's welcomed guests like Brad Pitt and fashion mogul Wolfgang Joop. **Pros:** modern luxury at its finest. **Cons:** expensive. $ *Rooms from: €210* ⊠ *Kayg. 2, Altstadt* ☎ *0221/20080* ⊕ *www.hotel-im-wasserturm.de* ⤵ *45 rooms, 33 suites* ❶❶ *No meals.*

NIGHTLIFE AND THE ARTS

Kölnticket. Tickets to most arts events can be purchased through Kölnticket. ☎ *0221/2801* ⊕ *www.koelnticket.de.*

THE ARTS

Antoniterkirche. Organ recitals and chamber concerts are presented in many of the Romanesque churches around town, and in the Antoniterkirche. ⊠ *Schilderg. 57, Innenstadt* ☎ *0221/925–8460* ⊕ *www. antonitercitykirche.de.*

KÖLSCH, BITTE!

It is said that the city's beloved beer can only be called Kölsch if it's brewed within sight of the cathedral. The beverage is served in traditional *Kölschkneipen.* Your waiter, called a *Köbes,* is likely to tease you (that's the Rhenish humor) and will replace your empty glass with a full one whether you order it or not. (If you want to avoid this, leave a swallow in the nearly empty glass or cover it with a coaster.) This automatic replacement is justified by the fact that the glass, called a *stange* (pole), is quite small due to the belief that Kölsch doesn't stay fresh for long after it has been poured.

Oper der Stadt Köln. Köln's opera company is known for exciting classical and contemporary productions, including collaborative efforts with the French fashion designer Christian Lacroix. The opera house on Offenbachplatz is under major renovation until late 2015, so the primary performance space is currently the striking Oper am Dom, between the main train station and the Rhine. ⊠ *Oper am Dom, Goldg. 1, Innenstadt* ☎ *0221/2212–8400* ⊕ *www.operkoeln.com.*

Philharmonie. Köln's Westdeutsche Rundfunk (WDR) Orchestra performs regularly in the city's excellent concert hall. ⊠ *Bischofsgartenstr. 1, Altstadt* ☎ *0221/204–080* ⊕ *www.koelner-philharmonie.de.*

Schauspielhaus. Köln's principal theater is the Schauspielhaus, home to the 20 or so private theater companies in the city. While its main space on Offenbachplatz is being renovated (it's due to reopen in late 2015), Schauspielhaus productions have been moved to an industrial space in the Mülheim neighborhood. ⊠ *Carlswerk, Depots 1 and 2, Schanzenstr. 6–20, Mülheim* ☎ *0221/2212–8400* ⊕ *www.schauspielkoeln.de.*

NIGHTLIFE

Köln's nightlife is centered on three distinct areas: along the river in the Old Town, which seems to be one big party on weekends; on Zulpicherstrasse near the university; and around the Friesenplatz U-bahn station. Many streets off the Hohenzollernring and Hohenstaufenring, particularly Roonstrasse and Aachenerstrasse, also provide a broad range of nightlife. In summer the Martinsviertel, a part of the Altstadt around the Gross St. Martin church, which is full of restaurants, brew houses, and *Kneipen* (pubs), is a good place to go around sunset.

Alter Wartesaal. For a true disco experience, make for the Alter Wartesaal in the Hauptbahnhof on Friday or Saturday night. The old train-station waiting room has been turned into a concert hall and dance club, where groovers swivel on ancient polished parquet and check their style in mirrors with mahogany frames. ⊠ *Am Hauptbahnhof, Johannisstr. 11, Altstadt* ☎ *0221/912–8850* ⊕ *www.wartesaal.de.*

Papa Joe's Biersalon. This classic, kitschy Altstadt bar plays oldies from Piaf to Porter. ⊠ *Alter Markt 50–52, Altstadt* ☎ *0221/258–2132* ⊕ *www.papajoes.de.*

Papa Joe's Jazzlokale. For live jazz, head to the tiny Papa Joe's Jazzlokale, where there's never a cover charge. ⊠ *Buttermarkt 37, Altstadt* ☎ *0221/257–7931* ⊕ *www.papajoes.de.*

Stadtgarten. In summer, head straight for the Stadtgarten and sit in the Biergarten for some good outdoor *Gemütlichkeit* (coziness). At other times of the year it's still worth a visit for its excellent jazz club. ■TIP➔ Stadtgarten also runs a beer garden with cheap, tasty eats in the shaded Rathenauplatz park, by Köln's synagogue. ⊠ *Venloerstr. 40* ☎ *0221/952–9940* ⊕ *www.stadtgarten.de.*

SHOPPING

A good shopping loop begins at the **Neumarkt Galerie**. From there, head down the charmless but practical pedestrian shopping zone of the Schildergasse. From Schildergasse, go north on Herzogstrasse to arrive at **Glockengasse**. A block north is Breite Strasse, another pedestrian shopping street. At the end of Breite Strasse is Ehrenstrasse, where the young and young-at-heart can shop for hip fashions and trendy housewares. After a poke around here, explore the small boutiques on Benesisstrasse, which will lead you to Mittelstrasse, best known for high-tone German fashions and luxury goods. Follow Mittelstrasse to the end to return to the Neumarkt.

Glockengasse. Köln's most celebrated product, Eau de Cologne No. 4711, was first concocted here by the 18th-century Italian chemist Johann Maria Farina. At the company's flagship store there's a small exhibition of historical 4711 bottles, as well as a perfume fountain you can dip your fingers in. ⊠ *House of 4711, Glockeng. 4, Innenstadt* ☎ *0221/2709–9910* ⊕ *www.4711.com.*

Neumarkt Galerie. This bright, modern indoor shopping arcade has a web of shops and cafés surrounding an airy atrium. Just look for the huge sculpture of an upside-down ice cream cone above the entrance. ⊠ *Richmodstr. 8* ⊕ *www.neumarktgalerie.com.*

Peek & Cloppenburg. This big clothing store is a highlight of Shildergasse. The 2005 building, designed by the architect Renzo Piano, looks like a spaceship, and its selection of fashions—for men and women, from budget to couture—is out of this world. ⊠ *Schilderg. 65–67, Innenstadt* ☎ *0221/453–900* ⊕ *www.peek-cloppenburg.com.*

> **GO BELGIAN**
>
> Among Köln's most enticing areas for a drink or light meal is the leafy and attractive Belgian quarter. German soap stars and media power brokers flock to eateries like **Pepe** (⊠ *Antwerpenerstr. 63*). There's a hipper crowd at cafés like **Hallmackenreuther** (⊠ *Brüsselerpl. 9*) and **Salon Schmitz** (⊠ *Aachenerstr. 30*)—a place to see and be seen.

AACHEN

70 km (43 miles) west of Köln.

At the center of Aachen, the characteristic three-window-wide facades, give way to buildings dating from the days when Charlemagne made Aix-la-Chapelle (as it was then called) the great center of the Holy Roman Empire. Thirty-two German emperors were crowned here, gracing Aachen with the proud nickname "Kaiserstadt" (Emperors' City). Roman legions had been drawn here for the healing properties of the sulfur springs emanating from the nearby Eifel Mountains. (The name "Aachen," based on an old Frankish word for "water," alludes to this.) Charlemagne's father, Pepin the Short, also settled here to enjoy the waters, and to this day the city is also known as Bad Aachen and still drawing visitors in search of a cure. One-and-a-half-hour walking tours depart from the tourist office throughout the year at 11 on weekends, as well as at 2 on weekdays from April to December. The Saturday tours are conducted in English as well as German.

ESSENTIALS

Visitor Information Aachen Tourist-Information ⊠ *Friedrich-Wilhelm-Pl.* ☎ *0241/180–2960* ⊕ *www.aachen.de* ☉ *Weekdays 9–6, Sat. 9–2.*

EXPLORING

TOP ATTRACTIONS

Dom (*Cathedral*). Aachen's stunning cathedral, the "Chapelle" of the town's earlier name of Aix-la-Chapelle, remains the single greatest storehouse of Carolingian architecture in Europe, and it was the first place in Germany to be named a UNESCO World Heritage Site. Though it was built over the course of 1,000 years and reflects architectural styles from the Middle Ages to the 19th century, its commanding image remains the magnificent octagonal royal chapel, rising up two arched stories to end in the cap of the dome. It was this section, the heart of the church, that Charlemagne saw completed in AD 800. His bones now lie in the Gothic choir, in a golden shrine surrounded by wonderful carvings of saints. Another treasure is his marble throne. Charlemagne had to journey all the way to Rome for his coronation, but the next 32 Holy Roman emperors were crowned here in Aachen, and each marked the occasion by presenting a lavish gift to the cathedral. In the 12th century Emperor Friederich I (aka Barbarossa) donated the great chandelier now hanging in the center of the Palatine chapel; his grandson, Frederick II, donated Charlemagne's shrine. English-language guided tours of the cathedral (€4) are offered daily at 2. ⊠ *Münsterpl., Domhof 1* ☎ *0241/477–090* ⊕ *www.aachendom.de* ⊠ *Free* ☾ *Apr.–Dec., daily 7–7; Jan.–Mar., daily 7–6.*

Domschatzkammer (*The Cathedral Treasury*). The cathedral houses sacred art from late antiquity and the Carolingian, Ottonian, and Hohenstaufen eras. A bust of Charlemagne on view here was commissioned by Emperor Karl IV in the late 14th century, who traveled here from Prague for the sole reason of having it made. The bust incorporates a piece of Charlemagne's skull. Other highlights include the Cross of Lothair and the Persephone Sarcophagus. ⊠ *Klosterpl. 2* ☎ *0241/4770–9127* ⊕ *www.aachendom.de/schatzkammer.html* ⊠ *€5* ☾ *Jan.–Mar., Mon. 10–1, Tues.–Sun. 10–5; Apr.–Dec., Mon. 10–1, Tues.–Sun. 10–6.*

Elisenbrunnen (*Elisa Fountain*). Southeast of the cathedral and the site of the city's tourist-information center is an arcaded, neoclassical structure built in 1822. The central pavilion contains two fountains with thermal water—the hottest north of the Alps—that is reputed to help cure a wide range of ailments in those who drink it. If you can brave a gulp of the sulfurous water, you'll be emulating the likes of Dürer, Frederick the Great, and Charlemagne, who drank it before you. ⊠ *Friedrich-Wilhelm-Pl.*

Rathaus (*Town Hall*). Aachen's town hall sits behind the Dom, across Katschhof Square. It was built in the early 14th century on the site of the *Aula Regia*, or "great hall," of Charlemagne's palace. Its first major official function was the coronation banquet of Emperor Karl IV in 1349, held in the great Gothic hall you can still see today (though this was largely rebuilt after World War II). On the north wall of the building are statues of 50 emperors of the Holy Roman Empire. The greatest of them all, Charlemagne, stands in bronze atop the Karlsbrunnen in the center of the market square. ⊠ *Marktpl.* ☎ *0241/432–7310* ⊠ *€5* ☾ *Daily 10–6.*

WORTH NOTING

Ludwig Forum für Internationale Kunst. One of the world's most important art collectors, chocolate magnate Peter Ludwig, who died in 1996, endowed two museums in the town he called home. The Forum, the larger of the two, holds a portion of Ludwig's enormous collection of contemporary art and hosts traveling exhibits. ✉ *Jülicher Str. 97–109* ☎ *0241/180–7104* ⊕ *www.ludwigforum.de* 💶 *€5* 🕙 *Tues., Wed., and Fri. noon–6, Thurs. noon–10, weekends 11–6.*

Suermondt-Ludwig Museum. The smaller of the two Ludwig art institutions in town (the Ludwig Forum is the larger one) has a collection that concentrates paintings from the 12th to the early 20th century. ✉ *Wilhelmstr. 18* ☎ *0241/479–80* ⊕ *www.suermondt-ludwig-museum.de* 💶 *€5* 🕙 *Tues., Thurs., and Fri. noon–6, Wed. noon–8, weekends 11–6.*

WHERE TO EAT

$
GERMAN

✕ **Am Knipp.** At this Bierstube dating from 1698, guests dig into their regional dishes at low wooden tables next to the tile stove. Pewter plates and beer mugs line the walls. 💲 *Average main: €15* ✉ *Bergdriesch 3* ☎ *0241/33168* ⊕ *www.amknipp.de* 🕙 *Closed Tues., Dec. 24–Jan. 2, and 2 wks in Apr. and Oct. No lunch.*

$
GERMAN
Fodor's Choice
★

✕ **Der Postwagen.** This annex of the more upscale Ratskeller is worth a stop for the building alone, a half-timber medieval edifice at one corner of the old Rathaus. You'll be impressed by the food as well, which also comes from the kitchen of Ratskeller chef Maurice de Boer. Sitting at one of the low wooden tables, surveying the marketplace through the wavy old glass, you can dine well on solid German fare. If you really want to go local, try *Himmel und Erde* (mashed potatoes and applesauce topped by panfried slices of blood sausage and onions). 💲 *Average main: €15* ✉ *Markt 40* ☎ *0241/35001* ⊕ *www.ratskeller-aachen.de.*

$$$$
FRENCH

✕ **La Becasse.** Chef Christof Lang's sophisticated French nouvelle cuisine and attentive staff are a hit with upscale locals. The restaurant, which is named for the woodcock, has been in operation just outside the Old Town by the Westpark for three decades. Try the distinctively light veal kidney or the Wagyu beef salad. The five-course lunch menu (around €35) changes daily. 💲 *Average main: €37* ✉ *Hanbrucherstr. 1* ☎ *0241/74444* ⊕ *www.labecasse.de* ⌨ *Reservations essential* 🕙 *Closed Sun. No lunch Sat. or Mon.*

WHERE TO STAY

$
HOTEL

🛏 **ibis Styles Aachen City.** A 15-minute walk from the Dom, this colorfully furnished modern budget hotel (formerly the All Seasons) is a good value, especially for families with children. **Pros:** kids under 16 get their own room at half price. **Cons:** on a busy street somewhat removed from the center. 💲 *Rooms from: €88* ✉ *Jülicherstr. 10–12* ☎ *0241/51060* ⊕ *www.ibis.com* ⤳ *102 rooms* ⧠ *Breakfast.*

$$$
HOTEL

🛏 **Pullmann Aachen Quellenhof.** This old-fashioned and grand hotel has rooms with high ceilings, a Roman-style spa area, and an inviting pool. **Pros:** spacious; elegant; formal. **Cons:** on a busy street; expensive. 💲 *Rooms from: €185* ✉ *Monheimsallee 52* ☎ *0241/91320* ⊕ *www.accorhotels.com* ⤳ *183 rooms, 2 suites* ⧠ *Breakfast.*

NIGHTLIFE AND THE ARTS

Most activity in town is concentrated around the market square and Pontstrasse, a pedestrian street that radiates off the square.

Domkeller. Aachen's most popular bar is a good place to mingle with locals of all ages at old wooden tables, enjoying an impressive selection of Belgian beers in a historic building from 1658. There are free concerts every Monday, apart from a short break in summer. ⊠ *Hof 1* ☎ *0241/34265* ⊕ *www.domkeller.de.*

Wild Rover. This Irish pub has Murphy's Stout on tap. On most nights, there's live music starting at 8:30. It's closed Sunday and Monday, except for special occasions. ⊠ *Hirschgraben 13* ☎ *0241/35453.*

Eurogress Aachen. The Aachen Symphony, along with touring bands and orchestras from across Europe, give regular concerts in Aachen's Eurogress convention center. ⊠ *Monheimsallee 48* ☎ *0241/91310* ⊕ *www.eurogress-aachen.de.*

SHOPPING

Don't leave Aachen without stocking up on the traditional local gingerbread, *Aachener Printen.* Each bakery in town offers its own varieties (topped with whole or crushed nuts, milk or dark chocolate, etc.), and guards its recipe like a state secret.

Café Van den Daele. One of Aachen's most beloved cafés, Van den Daele (also known as Alt Aachener Kaffeestuben) is worth a visit if for nothing more than its atmosphere and tempting aromas. Some of the best *Aachener Printen* (gingerbread) can be found here, as can another tasty Aachen specialty, *Reisfladen* (a sort of tart filled with milk rice and often topped with fruit—often pears, apricots, or cherries). The café can also mail its goods to you (or others) back home. ⊠ *Büchel 18* ☎ *0241/35724* ⊕ *www.van-den-daele.de.*

DÜSSELDORF

47 km (29 miles) north of Köln.

Düsseldorf, the state capital of North Rhine–Westphalia, may suffer by comparison to Köln's remarkable skyline, but the elegant city has more than enough charm—and money—to keeps its own self-esteem high. By contrast to Cologne's boisterous, working-class charm, Düsseldorf is known as one of the country's richest cities, with an extravagant lifestyle that epitomizes the economic success of postwar Germany. Because 80% of Düsseldorf was destroyed in World War II, the city has since been more or less rebuilt from the ground up—and that includes re-creating landmarks of long ago and restoring a medieval riverside quarter.

At the confluence of the Rhine and Düssel rivers, this dynamic city started as a small fishing town. The name means "village on the Düssel," but obviously this Dorf is a village no more. Raised expressways speed traffic past towering glass-and-steel structures; within them, glass-enclosed shopping malls showcase the finest clothes, furs, jewelry, and other goods that money can buy.

Düsseldorf's elegant high-end malls are great for window-shopping.

GETTING HERE AND AROUND

Trains connect Düsseldorf to the Rheinland region's main cities; a trip from Köln takes under 25 minutes. The impressive Flughafen Düsseldorf, Germany's third largest airport, serves more than 180 destinations.

TOURS

Hop-on, hop-off bus tours of Düsseldorf depart from the main train station at 10 and every half hour from 11 to 5 from mid-March to early November; hourly 10 to 6 from early November to late December; and at 11, 1 and 3 from late December to mid-March. Tickets (€15, or €13 with no intermediate stops) can be purchased on the bus or at the information center. A walking tour of the Old Town (April to October, daily at 3, plus 4 on Friday, and 1 and 4 on Saturday; November to March, Friday and Saturday at 3, Sunday at 11) is offered for €10. The tour leaves from the Altstadt tourist-info center (Marktstrasse/Rheinstrasse corner).

DISCOUNTS AND DEALS

The **Düsseldorf WelcomeCard** costs €9 for 24 hours, €14 for 48 hours, and €19 for 72 hours, and allows free public transportation and reduced admission to museums, theaters, and even boat tours on the Rhine.

ESSENTIALS

Visitor Information Düsseldorf Tourist-Information ✉ *Marktstr. 6* ☎ *0211/172–020* ⊕ *www.duesseldorf-tourismus.de.*

EXPLORING
TOP ATTRACTIONS

Altstadt (*Old Town*). This party-hearty district has been dubbed "the longest bar in the word" by locals. Narrow alleys thread their way to some 300 restaurants and taverns. All crowd into the 1-square-km (½-square-mile) area between the Rhine and Heinrich-Heine-Allee. When the weather cooperates, the area really does seem like one big sidewalk café.

Königsallee. Düsseldorf's main shopping avenue epitomizes the city's affluence, lined as it is with designer boutiques and stores. Known as the Kö, this wide, double boulevard is divided by an ornamental waterway fed by the River Düssel. Rows of chestnut trees line the Kö, shading a string of sidewalk cafés. Beyond the Triton Fountain, at the street's north end, begins a series of parks and gardens. In these patches of green you can sense a joie de vivre that might be surprising in a city devoted to big business.

Kunstsammlung Nordrhein-Westfalen (*Art Collection of North Rhine–Westphalia*). This important fixture on Düsseldorf's art scene is split into two parts, plus an installation space. Behind the sleek, polished black stone facade of **K20** is a treasure trove of art (kunst, hence the K) of the 20th century, including works from masters like Picasso, Klee, and Richter. Within the more conservative 19th-century architecture of **K21** is edgier fare—international art since about 1980, including the works of Thomas Ruff and Nam June Paik. Rounding things off is the quirky, modern **Schmela Haus** (1967), a former commercial gallery, which the museum uses as a space for experimental art. ⊠ *K20, Grabbepl. 5* ☎ *0211/838–1130* ⊕ *www.kunstsammlung.de* ⊠ *€12 K20, €12 K21, €21 for both (prices vary), free 1st Wed. of month, 6–10. Schmela Haus free of charge.* ☉ *Tues.–Fri. 10–6, weekends 11–6; 1st Wed. of each month 10–10.* ⊠ *K21, Ständehausstr. 1*

Neanderthal Museum. Just outside Düsseldorf, the Düssel River forms a valley, called the Neanderthal, where the bones of a Stone Age relative of modern man were found. The impressive museum, built at the site of discovery in the suburb of Mettmann, includes models of the original discovery, replicas of cave drawings, and life-size models of Neanderthal Man. Many scientists think he was a different species of human; short, stocky, and with a sloping forehead. The bones were found in 1856 by workers quarrying the limestone cliffs to get flux for blast furnaces. ⊠ *Talstr. 300, Mettmann* ☎ *02104/97970* ⊕ *www.neanderthal. de* ⊠ *€10* ☉ *Tues.–Sun. 10–6.*

Rhine Promenade. Traffic is routed away from the river and underneath this pedestrian strip, which is lined by chic shopping arcades and cafés. Joggers, rollerbladers, and folks out for a stroll make much use of the promenade as well.

WORTH NOTING

Museum Kunst Palast. This impressive art museum lies at the northern extremity of the Hofgarten, close to the Rhine. Its excellent German expressionist collection (Beckmann, Kirchner, Nolde, Macke, etc.) makes it worth a trip, as does its collection of glass art—among the largest in Europe. ✉ *Ehrenhof 4–5* ☏ *0211/899–2460* ⊕ *www.smkp.de* 🎫 *€5 for permanent collection, special exhibition prices vary* ☉ *Tues., Wed., and Fri.–Sun. 11–6, Thurs. 11–9.*

St. Lambertus. This Gothic church is near the palace tower on Burgplatz. Its spire became distorted because unseasoned wood was used in its construction. The Vatican elevated the 14th-century brick church to a basilica minor (small cathedral) in 1974 in recognition of its role in church history. Built in the 13th century, with additions from 1394, St. Lambertus contains the tomb of William the Rich and a graceful late-Gothic tabernacle. ✉ *Stiftspl. 7* ⊕ *www.lambertuspfarre.de.*

Schloss Jägerhof. At the far-east edge of the Hofgarten, this baroque structure is more a combination town house and country lodge than a palace. It houses the **Goethe-Museum,** featuring original manuscripts, first editions, personal correspondence, and other memorabilia of Germany's greatest writer. There's also a museum housing a collection of Meissen porcelain. ✉ *Jacobistr. 2* ☏ *0211/899–6262* ⊕ *www.goethe-museum.com* 🎫 *€4* ☉ *Tues.–Fri. and Sun. 11–5, Sat. 1–5.*

Schlossturm (*Palace Tower*). A squat tower is all that remains of the palace built by the Berg family, which ruled Düsseldorf for more than five centuries. The tower also houses the **SchifffahrtMuseum,** which charts 2,000 years of Rhine boatbuilding and navigation. ✉ *Burgpl. 30* ☏ *0211/899–4195* ⊕ *www.freunde-schifffahrtmuseum.de* 🎫 *€3* ☉ *Tues.–Sun. 11–6.*

WHERE TO EAT

$$$$ ✕ **Berens am Kai.** Set in the redeveloped Düsseldorf harbor, this glass-
FRENCH   and-steel building with ceiling-to-floor windows looks more like a modern office complex than the sleek restaurant it is. Head here for creative French recipes, a wine list with vintages from around the world, and tempting desserts—it's a good option if you're hankering for a change from old-style German cooking. The steep, expense-account-ready prices are warranted by chef Holger Berens' exquisite cuisine, the refined service, and the great setting with magnificent views of the harbor and the city, which are particularly stunning at night. $ *Average main: €40* ✉ *Kaistr. 16* ☏ *0211/300–6750* ⊕ *www.berensamkai.de* 🍽 *Reservations essential* ☉ *Closed Sun. No lunch Sat.*

$ ✕ **Bistro Zicke.** Weekend brunch (served until 4 pm) can get busy at
FRENCH   this French-inspired artists' café on a quiet square one block from the riverfront. Otherwise, the bistro—with its big windows and walls plastered with old movie and museum posters—is an oasis from the hustle and bustle of the busy Altstadt. The word *Zicke* ("nanny goat") is a common insult for a moody woman, but whatever your feelings, this is a friendly place to stop in for a drink or to try the simple French-Italian cooking. $ *Average main: €13* ✉ *Bäckerstr. 5a* ☏ *0211/327–800* ⊕ *www.bistro-zicke.de* 🚫 *No credit cards.*

$
GERMAN

✕ **Brauerei Zur Uel.** A nontraditional brew house, the Uel is the popular hangout for Düsseldorf's students. The basic menu consists of soups, salads, and pastas; the ingredients are fresh and the portions are generous. What seems like every cultural and political event in the city is advertised in the entry hall. $ *Average main: €12* ✉ *Ratingerstr. 16* ☎ *0211/325–369* ⊕ *www.zuruel.de* ▭ *No credit cards.*

$$$$
FRENCH
Fodor'sChoice
★

✕ **Im Schiffchen.** Although Im Schiffchen is out of the way, it's also one of Germany's best restaurants and more than worth the trip. This is grande luxe, with cooking turned into fine art through the skills of chef Jean-Claude Bourgueil and his staff. The restaurant Enzo im Schiffchen (formerly Jean-Claude's) on the ground floor features lighter Continental created by the same chef but at lower prices. There are more than 1,100 wines in the cellar, many available by the glass. $ *Average main: €42* ✉ *Kaiserswerther Markt 9* ☎ *0211/401– 050* ⊕ *www.im-schiffchen.de* ⌦ *Reservations essential* ☉ *Closed Sun. and Mon. No lunch.*

$$
GERMAN

✕ **Weinhaus Tante Anna.** This charming restaurant, six generations in the same family, is furnished with antiques. The cuisine (courtesy of the chef, Murat Avcioglu) presents modern versions of German classics, demonstrating that there's a lot more to the country's cooking than wurst and sauerkraut—a specialty is a hearty rump steak baked with mustard and onions. The restaurant also offers a full vegetarian prix-fixe menu. $ *Average main: €22* ✉ *Andreasstr. 2* ☎ *0211/131–163* ⊕ *www.tanteanna.de* ☉ *Closed Sun. No lunch.*

$
GERMAN

✕ **Zum Uerige.** Düsseldorf is famous for its *Altbier,* so called because of the old-fashioned brewing method. This tavern, which brews its own beer, provides the perfect atmosphere for drinking it. The beer is poured straight out of polished oak barrels and served with hearty local food by busy waiters in long blue aprons. The food offered is mainly snacks, with a few entrées. After dinner, try the bar's tasty house liquor, called "Stickum"—a sort of beer brandy. $ *Average main: €8* ✉ *Bergerstr. 1* ☎ *0211/866–990* ⊕ *www.uerige.de* ▭ *No credit cards.*

WHERE TO STAY

$$$$
HOTEL

⛯ **Breidenbacher Hof.** The owners razed the original, two-centuries-old hotel of the same name to the ground to open this opulent, high-tech establishment in 2008. **Pros:** luxury; fun gadgets; great location on the Kö. **Cons:** expensive; somewhat charmless. $ *Rooms from: €290* ✉ *Königsallee 11* ☎ *0211/1609–0909* ⊕ *www.capellahotels.com/ dusseldorf* ⇗ *79 rooms, 16 suites* ⊚ *Breakfast.*

FLINGERN DISTRICT: ON THE RISE

Even straitlaced Düsseldorf knows how to get funky when it comes to the Flingern district. Cool indie cafés, galleries, and local designer shops line Ackerstrasse between Hermannstrasse and Birkenstrasse. At night, youngsters flock to **Trinkhalle** (✉ *Ackerstr. 144*), a popular watering hole offering live music and DJ sets. But the neighborhood's not all hipster yet; there's still a neat mix of people and businesses, as evidenced by places like **Okra** (✉ *Ackerstr. 119*), a simple Ethiopian restaurant with a retired bowling alley in its basement.

$$ ⊞ **carathotel Düsseldorf.** Besides bright, good-size rooms, the true
HOTEL strength of this modern hotel is its location, near the market in the
Altstadt. **Pros:** right in the Altstadt; free Wi-Fi. **Cons:** modern exterior
may be a little jarring to some. $\boxed{\$}$ *Rooms from: €155* ⊠ *Benratherstr.
7a* ☎ *0211/13050* ⊕ *www.carat-hotel-duesseldorf.de* ⇴ *72 rooms, 1
suite* ⏴⦿⏵ *Breakfast.*

$$ ⊞ **Hotel Orangerie.** Steps away from Altstadt action and the Rhine, this
HOTEL small hotel on a cobblestone road offers simple comfort and a surpris-
Fodor's Choice ing amount of quiet. **Pros:** unbeatable location; free Wi-Fi. **Cons:** small
★ rooms; no parking at the hotel; caters to business travelers. $\boxed{\$}$ *Rooms
from: €130* ⊠ *Bäckerg. 1* ☎ *0211/866–800* ⊕ *www.hotel-orangerie-
mcs.de* ⇴ *27 rooms* ⏴⦿⏵ *Breakfast.*

NIGHTLIFE AND THE ARTS

The **Altstadt** is a landscape of pubs, dance clubs, ancient brewery houses,
and jazz clubs in the vicinity of the Marktplatz and along cobblestone
streets named Bolker, Kurze, Flinger, and Mühlen. These places may be
crowded, but some are very atmospheric. The local favorite for nightlife
is the **Hafen** neighborhood. Its restaurants and bars cater to the youngish
professionals who work and party there.

Deutsche Oper am Rhein. The city's highly regarded opera company
and ballet troupe are showcased here. ⊠ *Heinrich-Heine-Allee 16a*
☎ *0211/892–5210* ⊕ *www.rheinoper.de.*

Robert-Schumann-Saal. Classical and pop concerts, symposia, film, and
international theater are presented at the Robert-Schumann-Saal. ⊠ *Ehrenhof 4–5* ☎ *0211/899–2450* ⊕ *www.smkp.de.*

Tonhalle. The finest concert hall in Germany after Berlin's Philharmonie
is a former planetarium on the edge of the Hofgarten. It's the home of
the Düsseldorfer Symphoniker, which plays from September to June.
⊠ *Ehrenhof 1* ☎ *0211/899–6123* ⊕ *www.tonhalle-duesseldorf.de.*

SHOPPING

For antiques, go to the area around Hohe Strasse. The east side of the
Königsallee is lined with some of Germany's trendiest boutiques, grandest jewelers, and most extravagant furriers.

Kö Center. This shopping arcade houses clothing stores like Eickhoff,
a Düsseldorf institution with more than 10,000 square feet of very
high-end goods, many straight from the runways of Paris and Milan.
⊠ *Königsallee 28–30.*

Kö Galerie. High-end boutiques and half a dozen restaurants line this
luxurious two-story mall. ⊠ *Königsallee 60* ⊕ *www.koe-galerie.com.*

THE FAIRY-TALE ROAD

WELCOME TO
THE FAIRY-TALE ROAD

TOP REASONS TO GO

★ **Valley Road:** Drive or bike the scenic highway between Hannoversch-Münden and Hameln—it's a landscape of green hills, Weser Renaissance towns, and inviting riverside taverns.

★ **Marburg:** Staircase streets cover the steep hillsides of this half-timber university town; sit outdoors and soak up the atmosphere.

★ **Bremen:** Browse the shops and galleries lining the picturesque Böttcherstrasse and Schnoorviertel, then savor the city's rich coffee tradition.

★ **Dornröschenschloss Sababurg:** The supposed inspiration for Sleeping Beauty's castle. Its spiral staircases, imposing turrets, and fairy-tale setting will delight lovers of the tale.

★ **Schlosspark Wilhelmshöhe:** Home to a stunning, crescent-moon palace and a fairy-tale castle, the park's trees, ponds, and wide-open spaces offer a dramatic contrast to the urbanity below.

12

1 Hesse. Eighth in area among Germany's 16 states and fifth in population, Hesse has most of its major cities to the south. Its northern part, a place of forests and castles, inspired the tales recorded by the Grimm brothers.

2 Lower Saxony. Germany's second-largest state after Bavaria and fourth most populous, Lower Saxony (Niedersachsen) has a diverse landscape, including the Weser River, which forms a picturesque part of the Fairy-Tale Road, and the Lüneburg Heath. Its capital and largest city is Hannover.

GETTING ORIENTED

The Fairy-Tale Road begins 20 minutes east of Frankfurt in the city of Hanau, and from there heads north 700 km (about 430 miles) to the North Sea port of Bremerhaven, through the states of Hesse and Lower Saxony, following the Fulda and Weser rivers and traversing countryside as beguiling as any other in northern Europe. It may not have the glamour of the Romantic Road or the cosmopolitan flair of Germany's great cities, but it doesn't have the crowds and commercialism either.

DRIVING THE FAIRY-TALE ROAD

Weaving its way through rolling hills and a gentle river valley, between whispering woods and past stone castles, this drive along the Fairy-Tale Road connects Göttingen, a vibrant university town, with tranquil riverside villages and the modern state capital of Hannover along the way.

Beginning in the south of Lower Saxony and ending in the heart of the state, with a brief excursion into Hesse, this two-day drive is best enjoyed in early spring, when cherry and apple blossoms dot the countryside. Late summer is another good time to go—the weather is at its best and the roads are no longer cluttered with peak-season traffic. Avoiding the high-speed stress of the autobahns, the drive keeps mainly to country roads, which allow time to take in the surroundings between stops. Gazing out at the landscape, it's not difficult to conjure images of wicked witches lurking among the trees, kind woodsmen, and fair maidens trapped in distant towers.

—Jeff Kavanagh

(above) Hannover's impressive Altes Rathaus illuminates a foggy night. (upper right) A kayaker paddles the flat Weser River.

PADDLE THE WESER

Flowing placidly between Hannoversch Münden and Hameln, and on to the North Sea, the Weser passes through many towns offering canoe and boating equipment for rent. If time and weather permit, swap the car for a canoe and paddle the river's glassy waters. Check out ⊕ *www.weserbergland-tourismus.de* for details on canoe operators.

A hearty German breakfast at **Bullerjahn** in the lively town square in front of **Göttingen's Altes Rathaus** is a great way to start your trip. Once sated, jump in the car and drive 29 km (18 miles) west through the **Hannoversch-Münden** nature reserve to the town itself. Here, you can stroll among its delightful Renaissance architecture and watch the Fulda and Werra rivers converge to form the Weser River. Half an hour up the road is the town of **Sababurg**, and perhaps the Fairy-Tale Road's most famous landmark, the **Dornröschenschloss**, Sleeping Beauty's castle. Spend some time wandering the castle's rose gardens and contemplating the princess's enchanted 100-year slumber. From the castle it's an easy 20-minute drive across the border to Hesse and the baroque spa town of **Bad Karlshafen**, where you can soothe whatever ails you with a long soak in a thermal, saltwater spring at **Weser-Therme**. Suitably relaxed, head to the peaceful riverside town of **Bodenweder**, which lies just more than 50 km (31 miles) to the north along winding country roads. Stay overnight here, and visit the small but fun **Münchhausen Museum** in the morning and enjoy the gentle murmur of the Weser as it flows its way past. Before lunch, travel 25 minutes north to **Hameln** and the home of the *Rattenfänger*, the Pied Piper, where you can experience rat-themed dining at the **Rattenfängerhaus**. Afterward, drive the 47 km (29 miles) up to **Hannover** for an afternoon of culture in one of the city's impressive museums and a predinner drink on the terrace of the stunning **Neues Rathaus**.

12

QUICK BITES

✕ **Back und Naschwerk.** Delicious breads are baked in the back of this little bakery, using only natural ingredients and real butter. Their maple syrup and walnut or poppy seed and nougat muffins are worth a visit alone. $ *Average main: €5* ✉ *Kramerstr. 14, Hannover* ☎ *0511/7003–5221* ⊕ *www.back-und-naschwerk.de* ▭ *No credit cards.*

✕ **Bullerjahn.** For a hearty breakfast at this cellar-level restaurant, order the enormous "Ratsfrühstück," which consists of bread rolls, jams, honey, Gouda, cold cuts, salmon, yogurt and fruit, orange juice, coffee, sparkling wine, and a boiled egg. $ *Average main: €10* ✉ *Markt 9, Göttingen* ☎ *0551/307–0100* ⊕ *www.bullerjahn.info.*

✕ **Museums Café.** Afternoon coffee and cake is as a strong a culinary tradition in Germany as tea and scones are in England. This elegant cafe in Hameln has cakes and tortes that'll have you embracing the custom like a local in no time. $ *Average main: €5* ✉ *Osterstr. 8, Hameln* ☎ *05151/21553* ⊕ *www.museumscafe.de.*

Updated by
Jeff Kavanagh

With a name evocative of magic and adventure, the Fairy-Tale Road (Märchenstrasse) takes its travelers on a path through the land of the Brothers Grimm and a rolling countryside of farmland and forests that inspired tales of sleeping princesses, hungry wolves, and gingerbread houses. Flowing through the heart of western Germany to its North Sea coast, the Märchenstrasse stops along the way at towns and villages where the brothers spent much of their lives two centuries ago.

It was here among medieval castles and witch towers that the brothers, first as young boys, and then later as students and academics, listened to legends told by local storytellers, and adapted them into the fairy tales that continue to be read around the world today; enchanted and frequently dark tales that include "Sleeping Beauty," "Little Red Riding Hood," and "Hansel and Gretel."

Following the Grimms' footsteps through a landscape of river valleys and wide-open skies, or down cobblestone streets flanked by half-timber houses and baroque palaces, it's possible to imagine things haven't changed that much since the brothers' time. Traditional taverns serving strong German beers and thick slabs of beef and pork dot the way, and storytelling continues to be a major attraction along the Fairy-Tale Road, though nowadays more commonly in the form of guided tours and interactive museum displays.

The Fairy-Tale Road, of course, is also a modern route, and its wide, smooth roads pass through larger urban areas, such as Kassel and Bremen, full of contemporary hotels, eateries, and stores. Like large parts of the rest of the country, many of these towns and cities were greatly damaged during World War II, and their hurried reconstruction often favored functionality over form, so that many buildings are much more stark than those they replaced. This contrast, however, often only serves to emphasize the beauty of what remained.

Not every town on the road can lay claim to a connection to the Brothers Grimm or the inspiration for a specific tale, but many continue to celebrate the region's fairy-tale heritage with theme museums, summer festivals, and outdoor plays.

It's this heritage, the natural appeal of the countryside, and the tradition and culture found in its towns and cities that attract travelers along the Märchenstrasse; that, mixed with the promise of adventure and the opportunity to create some tales of their own.

12

PLANNING

WHEN TO GO

Summer is the ideal time to travel through this varied landscape, although in spring you'll find the river valleys carpeted in the season's first flowers, and in fall the sleepy Weser is often blanketed in mist. Keep in mind that retail stores and shops in the smaller towns in this area often close for two to three hours at lunchtime.

GETTING HERE AND AROUND

AIR TRAVEL

The closest international airports to this region are in Frankfurt, Hannover, and Hamburg. Frankfurt is less than a half hour from Hanau, and Hamburg is less than an hour from Bremen.

Airport Information City Airport Bremen ✉ *Flughafenallee 20, Bremen* ☎ *0421/55950* ⊕ *www.airport-bremen.de.* **Hannover-Langenhagen Airport** ✉ *Petzelstr. 84, Hannover* ☎ *0511/9770* ⊕ *www.hannover-airport.de.*

BIKE TRAVEL

The Fulda and Werra rivers have 190 km (118 miles) of bike paths, and you can cycle the whole length of the Weser River from Hannoversch-Münden to the outskirts of Bremen without making too many detours from the river valley. Five- and seven-day cycle tours of the Fulda and Werra river valleys are available. These typically include bike rentals, overnight accommodations, and luggage transport between stops.

Bike Tours SRJ GästeService ✉ *Herrmannstr. 46, Minden* ☎ *0571/889–1900* ⊕ *www.srj.de.*

BOAT TRAVEL

The eight boats of Flotte Weser operate short summer excursions along a considerable stretch of the Weser River between Bremen and Bad Karlshafen. The trip between Corvey and Bad Karlshafen, for example, takes slightly less than three hours and costs €15.

Rehbein-Linie Kassel operates a service from Kassel to Bad Karlshafen. It also prides itself on the only "three-river tour" in the area. In a single trip you travel on the Fulda and Werra rivers and also on the river formed when these two meet at the tour's starting point of Hannoversch-Münden, the Weser. Personenschifffahrt K. & K. Söllner's excursion boat that go between Kassel and Hannoversch-Münden.

Boat Tours **Flotte Weser** ✉ *Am Stockhof 2, Hameln* ☎ *05151/939–999*
⊕ *www.flotte-weser.de.* **Personenschiffahrt K. & K. Söllner** ✉ *Die Schlagd,*
Kassel ☎ *0561/774–670* ⊕ *www.personenschiffahrt.com/kassel/route.html.*
Rehbein-Linie Kassel ✉ *Ostpreussenstr. 8, Fuldatal* ☎ *0561/18505*
⊕ *www.fahrgastschiffahrt.com.*

BUS TRAVEL

Bremen, Kassel, Göttingen, Fulda, and Hanau are all reachable via
Deutsche Touring's Europabus. A local bus serves the scenic Weser
Valley Road stretch (B-80 and B-83), between Hannoversch-Münden
and Hameln.

Year-round tours of the region are offered by Herter-Reisen.

Bus Tours **Eurolines Germany** ☎ *069/7903–501* ⊕ *www.eurolines.de.*
Herter-Reisen ✉ *Hildesheimer Str. 6, Hameln/Afferde* ☎ *05159/969–244*
⊕ *www.herter-reisen.de.*

CAR TRAVEL

The best way to travel is by car. The autobahn network serves Hanau,
Fulda, Kassel, Göttingen, and Bremen directly, but you can't savor the
fairy-tale country from this high-speed superhighway. Bremen is 60 km
(35 miles) northwest of Hannover.

The Fairy-Tale Road incorporates one of Germany's loveliest scenic
drives, the Wesertalstrasse, or Weser Valley Road (B-80 and B-83),
between Hannoversch-Münden and Hameln; the total distance is
approximately 103 km (64 miles).

TRAIN TRAVEL

Hanau, Fulda, Kassel, Göttingen, Hannover, and Bremen are reach-
able via InterCity Express (ICE) trains from Frankfurt and Hamburg.
Rail service, but not ICE service, is available to Hannoversch-Münden,
Marburg, and Hameln.

Train Information **Deutsche Bahn** ☎ *0800/150–7090* ⊕ *www.bahn.de.*

RESTAURANTS

In this largely rural area many restaurants serve hot meals only between
11:30 am and 2 pm, and 6 pm and 9 pm. You rarely need a reservation
here, and casual clothing is generally acceptable.

Prices in the reviews are the average cost of a main course at dinner, or
if dinner is not served, at lunch.

HOTELS

Make hotel reservations in advance if you plan to visit in summer.
Though it's one of the less-traveled tourist routes in Germany, the main
destinations on the Fairy-Tale Road are popular. Hannover is particularly busy during trade-fair times.

Prices in the reviews are the lowest cost of a standard double room in
high season. For expanded reviews, facilities, and current deals, visit
Fodors.com.

PLANNING YOUR TIME

The Fairy-Tale Road isn't really for the traveler in a hurry. If you only have a day or two to savor it, concentrate on a short stretch. A good suggestion is the Weser River route between Hannoversch-Münden and Hameln. The landscape is lovely, and the towns are romantic. If you have more time, but not enough to travel the whole route, focus on the southern half of the road. It's more in character with the fairy tales.

12

DISCOUNTS AND DEALS

Free summer weekend performances along the Fairy-Tale Road include Münchhausen plays in Bodenwerder, the Dr. Eisenbart reenactments in Hannoversch-Münden, the Town Musicians shows in Bremen, and especially the Pied Piper spectacle at Hameln. Kassel, Hannover, and Bremen also sell visitor cards that let you ride free on public transportation, grant reduced admissions at museums, and give other perks.

VISITOR INFORMATION

Deutsche Märchenstrasse ⊠ *Kurfürstenstr. 9, Kassel* ☎ *0561/9204–7911* ⊕ *www.deutsche-maerchenstrasse.de.*

HESSE

The first portion of the Fairy-Tale Road, from Hanau to Bad Karlshafen, lies within the state of Hesse. Much of its population is concentrated in the south, in such cities as Frankfurt, Darmstadt, and Wiesbaden; the northern part is quite rural, hilly, forested, and very pretty. Here you'll find Steinau, the almost vertical city of Marburg, and Kassel, all of which have associations with the Grimm brothers.

HANAU

16 km (10 miles) east of Frankfurt.

The Fairy-Tale Road begins in Hanau, the town where the Brothers Grimm were born. Although Grimm fans will want to start their pilgrimage here, Hanau is now a traffic-congested suburb of Frankfurt, with post–World War II buildings that are not particularly attractive.

ESSENTIALS

Visitor Information Tourist-Information Hanau ⊠ *Am Markt 14–18* ☎ *06181/295–950* ⊕ *www.hanau.de.*

GETTING HERE AND AROUND

Less than a 50-minute S-bahn (Line No. 9) journey from Frankfurt Airport, Hanau is also reachable by high-speed ICE trains from Berlin and Munich, or a combination of ICE and regional trains from Hannover, Bremen, and Hamburg.

EXPLORING

Nationaldenkmal Brüder Grimm (*Brothers Grimm Memorial*). Hanau's main attraction can be reached only on foot. The bronze memorial, erected in 1898, is a larger-than-life-size statue of the brothers, one seated, the other leaning on his chair, the two of them pondering an open book. ⊠ *Marktpl.*

Schloss Philippsruhe. This palace museum has a small Grimm exhibit that includes clothing, artifacts, and writings. It's on the bank of the Main in the suburb of Kesselstadt (Bus No. 5 will take you there in 10 minutes). ▥TIP➔ Historical Hanau treasures, including a priceless collection of faience, are also on display here. ⊠ *Philippsruher Allee 45* ☎ *06181/295–564* ⊕ *www.museen-hanau.de* ✉ *€2.50* ◷ *Tues.–Sun. 11–6.*

Rathaus. Hanau's bulky, 18th-century town hall stands behind the Grimm brothers statue. Every day at noon its bells play tribute to another of the city's famous sons, the composer Paul Hindemith (1895–1963), by chiming out one of his canons. ⊠ *Marktpl. 14.*

GELNHAUSEN

20 km (12 miles) northeast of Hanau, 35 km (21 miles) northeast of Frankfurt.

Perched elegantly on the side of a hill above the Kinzig River, Gelnhausen's picturesque Altstadt (Old Town) offers the first taste of the half-timber houses and cobblestone streets that lie in abundance farther north. In spring and summer tours of school children dressed in traditional garb are guided down its winding streets and through lively little squares flanked by ice cream parlors and outdoor cafés, and listen to tales of Red Beard, and the fate of those poor townswomen suspected of being witches.

GETTING HERE AND AROUND

If you're flying into Frankfurt, Gelnhausen is an ideal spot for your first night on the Fairy-Tale Road. It's smaller and more charming than Hanau, and is still less than an hour's drive from Frankfurt's main airport. Trains to Gelnhausen leave from Frankfurt's main station every half hour and take approximately 35 minutes, and there are frequent connections from Hanau. Once here, the historic Old Town is hilly, but small enough to walk around. April through October, a walking tour leaves from the town hall at 2 on Sunday.

ESSENTIALS

Visitor Information Gelnhausen Tourist-Information ⊠ *Obermarkt 7* ☎ *06051/830–300* ⊕ *www.gelnhausen.de.*

EXPLORING

Hexenturm (*Witches' Tower*). The Hexenturm, once a grim prison, remains from the time when Gelnhausen was the center of a witch hunt in the late 16th century. Dozens of women were either burned at the stake or bound hand and foot and then thrown into the Kinzig River. Suspects were held in the Hexenturm of the town battlements. Today it houses a bloodcurdling collection of medieval torture instruments. The tower is being renovated until sometime in 2014, so until then visitors who wish to venture inside are required to join a tour, which are offered in German on Sunday afternoon from May through October. English-language tours for groups of up to 30 people can be booked in advance for €52. ⊠ *Am Fratzenstein* ☎ *06051/830–300* ◷ *May–Oct., tour Sun. at 2.*

Kaiserpfalz. On an island in the gentle little Kinzig River you'll find the remains of the Kaiserpfalz. Emperor Friedrich I—known as Barbarossa, or Red Beard—built the castle in this idyllic spot in the 12th century; in 1180 it was the scene of the first all-German Imperial Diet, a gathering of princes and ecclesiastical leaders. Today only parts of the russet walls and colonnaded entrance remain. Still, you can stroll beneath the castle's ruined ramparts on its water site and you'll get a tangible impression of the medieval importance of the court of Barbarossa. ⌧ *Burgstr. 14* ☎ *06051/3805* ⌧*€3* ☼ *Mar.–Oct., Tues.–Sun. 10–5; Nov. and Dec., Tues.–Sun. 10–4.*

WHERE TO STAY

$ 🏨 **Romantisches Hotel Burg Mühle.** This peaceful hotel, a few steps from
HOTEL the Kaiserpfalz and within an easy walk of the Altstadt, was once the castle's mill ("Mühle") and sawmill. **Pros:** large rooms (many with balconies). **Cons:** showing a little wear. ⑤ *Rooms from: €77* ⌧ *Burgstr. 2* ☎ *06051/82050* ⊕ *www.burgmuehle.de* ⤳ *40 rooms* ⦿ *Breakfast.*

STEINAU AN DER STRASSE

30 km (18 miles) northeast of Gelnhausen, 65 km (40 miles) northeast of Frankfurt.

The little town of Steinau—full name Steinau an der Strasse (Steinau "on the road," referring to an old trade route between Frankfurt and Leipzig)—had a formative influence on the Brothers Grimm. They were preschoolers on arrival and under age 12 when they left after their father's death.

Steinau dates from the 13th century, and is typical of villages in the region. Marvelously preserved half-timber houses are set along cobblestone streets; an imposing castle bristles with towers and turrets. In its woodsy surroundings you can well imagine encountering Little Red Riding Hood, Snow White, or Hansel and Gretel. A major street is named after the brothers; the building where they lived is now named after them.

GETTING HERE AND AROUND

Regional trains leave hourly from Gelnhausen and take about 15 minutes to reach Steinau an der Strasse. The train station is just more than a kilometer from the Old Town's center and, should the walk be too far, the MKK90 bus goes into the town, albeit at irregular and sometimes lengthy intervals (get off at Ringstrasse). Or you can take a taxi. A city walking tour takes place April to October, the first Sunday of the month, leaving at 2 from the Märchenbrunnen (fountain).

ESSENTIALS

Visitor Information Steinau an der Strasse Verkehrsbüro ⊠ *Brüder-Grimm-Str. 70* ☎ *06663/96310* ⊕ *www.steinau.eu.*

EXPLORING

FAMILY **Brüder Grimm Haus and Museum Steinau.** Occupying both the house where the Brothers Grimm lived for much of their childhoods as well as the house's old barn, the Brüder Grimm Haus and Museum Steinau are fun and engaging museums. Featuring a reconstruction of the family's old kitchen, the brothers' former house also displays old personal posessions such as letters and reading glasses, and has an upper floor divided into nine rooms with interactive displays that celebrate the Grimms' stories and other fairy tales from around Europe. Across a small courtyard, the town's museum documents what life was like on the old trade route that ran through Steinau, incorporating into its exhibits a coach, inn signs, milestones, and the type of pistols travelers used to defend themselves from bandits. ⊠ *Brüder-Grimm-Str. 80* ☎ *06663/7605* ⊕ *www.museum-steinau.de* 🎫 *€5* ⊙ *Daily 10–5; closed 2 wks in late Dec.*

Schloss Steinau (*Steinau Castle*). Schloss Steinau is straight out of a Grimm fairy tale. It stands at the top of the town, with a "Fairy-tale Fountain" in front of it. Originally an early-medieval fortress, it was rebuilt in Renaissance style between 1525 and 1558 and first used by the counts of Hanau as their summer residence. Later it was used to guard the increasingly important trade route between Frankfurt and Leipzig. It's not difficult to imagine the young Grimm boys playing in the shadow of its great gray walls or venturing into the encircling dry moat.

To begin your tour of the Grimm Brothers' fairy-tale landscape, head to the Nationaldenkmal Brüder Grimm (Brothers' Grimm Memorial) in Hanau.

The castle houses a **Grimm Museum,** one of two in Steinau, as well as an exhibition of marionettes from the marionette theater. The Grimm Museum exhibits the family's personal effects, including portraits of the Grimm relatives, the family Bible, an original copy of the Grimms' dictionary (the German equivalent of the *Oxford English Dictionary*), and all sorts of mundane things such as spoons and drinking glasses. Climb the tower for a breathtaking view of Steinau and the countryside. ☎ 06663/6843 ⊠ *Museum €2.50, tower €1, tour of castle and museum €6* ⊘ *Mar.–Oct., Tues.–Sun. 10–5; Nov.–mid-Dec., Tues.–Sun. 10–4.*

FAMILY **Steinauer Marionettentheater.** Located in what was once the stables at Schloss Steinau, this marionette theater portrays Grimm fairy tales and other children's classics. Performances are held most weekends at 3. ⊠ *Schloss Steinau, Am Kumpen 2* ☎ 06663/245 ⊕ *www.die-holzkoeppe.de* ⊠ *€7.50.*

WHERE TO EAT AND STAY

$ ✕ **Brathähnchenfarm.** This cheery hotel-restaurant is a long, long way GERMAN from the center of Steinau, uphill all the way. But it's worth it. As your nose will tell you immediately, just about everything on the menu is charcoal-grilled. The name ("Roast Chicken Farm') sets the theme, though other grilled meats are available. It's also good for peace and quiet. ⑤ *Average main: €14* ⊠ *Im Ohl 1* ☎ 06663/228 ⊕ *www. brathaehnchenfarm.de* ⊘ *Closed Mon. and late Dec.–mid-Feb.*

$ ⬚ **Burgmannenhaus.** Previously a 16th-century customs house, sitting on B&B/INN 1,000-year old foundations and a secret tunnel that runs to the nearby Schloss and church, this friendly travelers' inn is the type of place made for history buffs. **Pros:** in the middle of Steinau; tasty regional beer on tap. Cons: restaurant ($) serves solid, if unspectacular German food; Wi-Fi sometimes hard to pick up in guest rooms. $ *Rooms from: €78* ⊠ *Brüder Grimm Str. 49* ☎ *06663/911–2902* ⊕ *www.burgmannenhaus-steinau.de* ⟿ *5 rooms* ❄ *No meals.*

FULDA

32 km (20 miles) northeast of Steinau an der Strasse, 100 km (62 miles) northeast of Frankfurt.

The cathedral city of Fulda is well worth a detour off the Fairy-Tale Road. There are two distinct parts to its downtown area. One is a stunning display of baroque architecture, with the cathedral, orangery, and formal garden, which grew up around the palace. The other is the Old Town, where the incredibly narrow and twisty streets are lined with boutiques, bistros, and a medieval tower. ■ TIP➔ **You'll find Kanalstrasse and Karlstrasse in the Old Town lined with good, inexpensive cafés and restaurants, serving German, Mediterranean, and other dishes.**

GETTING HERE AND AROUND

InterCity Express trains connect Fulda with Frankfurt, Hannover and Hamburg, while regional trains link the city with many other Fairy-Tale Road destinations. Within Fulda itself, the Old Town and the city's other main attractions are all in walking distance of each other. Fulda's walking tours include a recording with earphones, enabling you to follow the German tours in English. These start at the tourist office on Bonifatiusplatz, daily at 11:30 and 3.

ESSENTIALS

Visitor Information Fulda Tourismus- und Kongressmanagement ⊠ *Bonifatiuspl. 1* ☎ *0661/102–1813* ⊕ *www.tourismus-fulda.de.*

EXPLORING

Dom. Fulda's 18th-century cathedral, which has two tall spires, stands on the other side of the broad boulevard that borders the palace park. The basilica accommodated the ever-growing number of pilgrims who converged on Fulda to pray at the grave of the martyred St. Boniface, the "Apostle of the Germans." A black alabaster bas-relief depicting his death marks the martyr's grave in the crypt. ⊠ *Eduard Schick Pl. 1–3* ☉ *Apr.–Oct., daily 10–6; Nov.–Mar., daily 10–5.*

Cathedral Museum. The Cathedral Museum contains a document bearing St. Boniface's writing, along with several other treasures, including Lucas Cranach the Elder's fine 16th-century painting *Christ and the Adulteress.* ☎ *0661/87207* ⊠ *€2.10* ☉ *Apr.–Oct., Tues.–Sat. 10–5:30, Sun. 12:30–5:30; Nov., Dec., and mid-Feb.–Mar., Tues.–Sat. 10–12:30 and 1:30–4, Sun. 12:30–4.*

Fodor's Choice ★ **Stadtschloss** (*City Palace*). The city's grandest example of baroque design is the immense Stadtschloss, formerly the residence of the prince-bishops. The **Fürstensaal** (Princes' Hall), on the second floor, provides a breathtaking display of baroque decorative artistry, with ceiling paintings by the 18th-century Bavarian artist Melchior Steidl, and fabric-clad

The Brothers Grimm

CLOSE UP

The Grimm fairy tales originated in the southern part of the Märchenstrasse. This area, mainly in the state of Hesse, was the home region of the brothers Jacob (1785–1863) and Wilhelm (1786–1859) Grimm. They didn't create the stories they are famous for. Their feat was to mine the great folklore tradition that was already deeply ingrained in local culture.

For generations, eager children had been gathering at dusk around the village storyteller to hear wondrous tales of fairies, witches, and gnomes, tales passed down from storytellers who had gone before. The Grimms sought out these storytellers and recorded their tales.

The result was the two volumes of their work *Kinder- und Hausmärchen* (*Children's and Household Tales*), published in 1812 and 1814 and revised and expanded six times during their lifetimes. The last edition, published in 1857, is the basis for the stories we know today. Earlier versions contained more violence and cruelty than was deemed suitable for children.

That is how the world got the stories of Cinderella, Sleeping Beauty, Hansel and Gretel, Little Red Riding Hood, Snow White and the Seven Dwarfs,

Rumpelstiltskin, Puss-in-Boots, Mother Holle, Rapunzel, and some 200 others, many of which remain unfamiliar.

Both Jacob and Wilhelm Grimm had distinguished careers as librarians and scholars, and probably would be unhappy to know that they are best remembered for the fairy tales. Among other things, they began what would become the most comprehensive dictionary of the German language and produced an analysis of German grammar.

The brothers were born in Hanau, near Frankfurt, which has a statue memorializing them as well as a Grimm exhibit at Schloss Philippsruhe. They spent their childhood in Steinau, 30 km (18 miles) to the north, where their father was magistrate. There are two Grimm museums there, one in their home. On their father's untimely death they moved to their mother's home city of Kassel. It, too, has an important Grimm museum. They attended the university at Marburg from 1802 to 1805, then worked as librarians in Kassel. It was in the Kassel area that they found the best of their stories. They later worked as librarians and professors in the university town of Göttingen, and spent their last years as academics in Berlin.

walls. The palace also has permanent displays of the Fulda was once known for, as well as some fine Fulda porcelain.

Also worth seeing is the **Spiegelsaal,** with its many tastefully arranged mirrors. Pause at the windows of the Grünes Zimmer (Green Chamber) to take in the view across the palace park to the **Orangery,** a large garden with summer-flowering shrubs and plants. ⊠ *Schlossstr. 1* ☎ *0661/102–1813* ⌧ *€3.50* ☉ *Sat.–Thurs. 10–5, Fri. 2–5.*

FAMILY **Vonderau Museum.** The Vonderau Museum is housed in a former Jesuit seminary. Its exhibits chart the cultural and natural history of Fulda and eastern Hesse. A popular section of the museum is its **planetarium,** which has a variety of shows, including one for children. Since it has only 35 seats, an early reservation is advisable. Shows take place Friday at 7, and on weekends at 2:30 and 3:30. ⊠ *Jesuitenpl. 2* ☎ *0661/928–350* ⊕ *www.kultur-fulda.de/vonderau-museum* 🖃 *Museum €3.50, planetarium €4.00* ☉ *Tues.–Sun. 10–5.*

WHERE TO EAT AND STAY

$ ✕ **La Gondola.** The faded interior of this popular Italian restaurant in
PIZZA   the Altstadt pedestrian zone may be at odds with the gold lettering and elegant window frames adorning its facade, but it's cozy and welcoming nonetheless. A local favorite for more than a quarter century, La Gondola serves homemade pasta, pizza (also family size), and salad. Note that it's closed from 2:30 to 5. ⑤ *Average main: €9* ⊠ *Karlstr. 29* ☎ *0661/71711.*

$$ 🛏 **Maritim Hotel am Schlossgarten.** At the luxurious showpiece of the
HOTEL   Maritim chain, guests can breakfast beneath frescoed ceilings and enormous chandeliers in a stunning 18th-century orangery overlooking Fulda Palace Park. **Pros:** large, comfortable rooms; lovely terrace with views of park and nearby cathedral. **Cons:** no a/c; expensive for the area. ⑤ *Rooms from: €175* ⊠ *Pauluspromenade 2* ☎ *0661/2820* ⊕ *www.maritim.de* ⤙ *111 rooms, 1 suite* ⑩ *No meals.*

$$ 🛏 **Romantik Hotel Goldener Karpfen.** An institution in Fulda for more than
HOTEL   a hundred years, the Goldener Karpfen has remained family-owned and
Fodor's Choice   -run, with an elegant disposition and engaging hosts that have brought
★   singers, actors, and archbishops through its doors. **Pros:** luxury lodging; a short stroll to the town's major attractions; excellent breakfast buffet. **Cons:** expensive; public spaces can feel cluttered with knickknacks. ⑤ *Rooms from: €165* ⊠ *Simpliziusbrunnen 1* ☎ *0661/86800* ⊕ *www.hotel-goldener-karpfen.de* ⤙ *46 rooms, 4 suites* ⑩ *Breakfast.*

▊▊▊▊▊
▊ EN
ROUTE
Marburg is the next major stop on the road. Take B-254 to **Alsfeld** (34 km [21 miles] northwest of Fulda), where you can make a short stop to admire its half-timber houses and narrow streets; then take B-62 into Marburg.

MARBURG

Fodor's Choice   *60 km (35 miles) northwest of Fulda.*
★
"I think there are more steps in the streets than in the houses." That is how Jacob Grimm described the half-timber hillside town of Marburg, which rises steeply from the Lahn River to the spectacular castle that crowns the hill. Many of the winding, crooked "streets" are indeed stone staircases, and several of the hillside houses have back doors five stories above the front doors. The town's famous university and its students are the main influence on its social life, which pulses through the many cafés, restaurants, and hangouts around the marketplace. The Grimms themselves studied here from 1802 to 1805.

Many of the streets are closed to traffic, and are filled with outdoor tables when the weather cooperates. There is a free elevator near the tourist-information office on Pilgrimstein that can transport you from the level of the river to the Old Town.

12

EATING WELL ON THE FAIRY-TALE ROAD

A specialty of northern Hesse is sausages with *Beulches,* made from potato balls, leeks, and black pudding. *Weck,* which is local dialect for "heavily spiced pork," appears either as *Musterweck,* served on a roll, or as *Weckewerk,* a frying-pan concoction with white bread. Heading north into Lower Saxony, you'll encounter the ever-popular *Speckkuchen,* a heavy and filling onion tart. Another favorite main course is *Pfefferpothast,* a sort of heavily browned goulash with lots of pepper. Trout and eels are common in the rivers and streams around Hameln, and by the time you reach Bremen, North German cuisine has taken over the menu. *Aalsuppe grün,* eel soup seasoned with dozens of herbs, is a must in summer, and the hearty *Grünkohl mit Pinkel,* a cabbage dish with sausage, bacon, and cured pork, appears in winter. Be sure to try the coffee. Fifty percent of the coffee served in Germany comes from beans roasted in Bremen. The city has been producing the stuff since 1673, and knows just how to serve it in pleasantly cozy or, as locals say, *gemütlich* surroundings.

GETTING HERE AND AROUND

Two hours away from Fulda by train, the cheapest way to get here is by taking a regional train to the town of Giessen, and changing there; and every two hours a regional train runs between Marburg and Kassel. By car, take the B-254 and then B-62 from Fulda.

ESSENTIALS

Visitor Information Marburg Tourismus und Marketing ⊠ *Pilgrimstein 26* ☎ *06421/99120* ⊕ *www.marburg.de.*

EXPLORING

Elisabethkirche (*St. Elizabeth Church*). Marburg's most important building is the Elisabethkirche, which marks the burial site of St. Elizabeth (1207–31), the town's favorite daughter. She was a Hungarian princess, betrothed at age 4 and married at 14 to a member of the nobility, Ludwig IV of Thuringia. In 1228, when her husband died in the Sixth Crusade, she gave up all worldly pursuits. She moved to Marburg, founded a hospital, gave her wealth to the poor, and spent the rest of her very short life (she died at the age of 24) in poverty, caring for the sick and the aged. She is largely responsible for what Marburg became. Because of her selflessness she was made a saint four years after her death. The Teutonic Knights built the Elisabethkirche, which quickly became the goal of pilgrimages, enabling the city to prosper. You can visit the shrine in the sacristy that once contained her bones, a masterpiece of the goldsmith's art. The church is a veritable museum of religious art, full of statues and frescoes. Walking tours of Marburg begin at the church on Saturday at 3, year-round. ⊠ *Elisabethstr. 1.*

WHERE TO EAT AND STAY

$ ✕ **Cafe Vetter.** This café has the most spectacular view in town—and
CAFÉ Marburg is famous for its panoramas. Both an outdoor terrace and a glassed-in terrace take full advantage of the site. It's all very "Viennese coffeehouse traditional" here, and the homemade cakes and chocolate

creams are hard to resist. This institution, four generations in the same family, has piano music on weekend afternoons. ⑤ *Average main: €7* ✉ *Reitg. 4* ☏ *06421/25888* ⊕ *www.cafe-vetter-marburg.de* ⊟ *No credit cards* ⊘ *No dinner.*

$ ✕ **Weinlädele.** If you've tired of the big glasses of beer and plates of enor-
GERMAN mous schnitzel on offer in many of Marburg's traditional eating establish-
ments, this half-timbered wine bar's fine selection of German wines, and light, crispy *Flammkuchen* (a flambéed tart) is a welcome break. Just up the street from the Old Town's main marketplace, it's a busy spot, popular with patrons of all ages. When the weather is good, get there early, grab a table on its little terrace for a view down the hill, order a cheese plat-ter and glass of white, and watch the world idle by. ⑤ *Average main: €9* ✉ *Schlosstreppe 1* ☏ *06421/14244* ⊕ *www.weinlaedele.com.*

$$ ☒ **Welcome Hotel Marburg.** While the plain facade of this large, modern
HOTEL   hotel may suffer in comparison with much of Marburg's traditional architecture, its generous rooms, comfy beds, and excellent breakfast buffet draw guests back. **Pros:** across from the elevator to the Altstadt. **Cons:** no real views from many of the rooms. ⑤ *Rooms from: €131* ✉ *Pilgrimstein 29* ☏ *06421/9180* ⊕ *www.welcome-hotels.com* ⇝ *147 rooms, 3 suites* ❍ *Breakfast.*

KASSEL

100 km (62 miles) northeast of Marburg.

The Brothers Grimm lived in Kassel, their mother's hometown, as teen-agers, and also worked there as librarians at the court of the king of Westphalia, Jerome Bonaparte (Napoléon's youngest brother), and for the elector of Kassel. In their researching of stories and legends, their best source was not books but storyteller Dorothea Viehmann, who was born in the Knallhütte tavern, which is still in business in nearby Baunatal.

Much of Kassel was destroyed in World War II, and the city was rebuilt with little regard for its architectural past. The city's museums and the beautiful Schloss Wilhelmshöhe and Schlosspark, however, are well worth a day or two of exploration.

GETTING HERE AND AROUND

On a main InterCity Express line between Munich and Hamburg, you can also travel to Kassel-Wilhelmshöhe from Hannover and Bremen by high-speed train. By car, travel northeast from Marburg on the B-3 to Borken, then take autobahn A-49 into Kassel.

TOURS

Guided bus tours of Kassel set off from the Stadttheater on Saturday at 11.

DISCOUNTS AND DEALS

When you arrive, you may want to buy a **Kassel Card,** which gives you a reduced rate for the city bus tour, free travel on the local transportation system, and reduced admission to the museums and the local casino. It's available at the tourist office for €9 for 24 hours and €12 for 72 hours.

ESSENTIALS

Visitor Information Kassel Marketing GmbH ✉ *Obere Königstr. 15* ☏ *0561/707–707* ⊕ *www.kassel.de.*

Many of Marburg's cobblestone streets are pedestrian-only zones, perfect for strolling and people-watching.

EXPLORING

Fodor's Choice ★ **Brüder Grimm Museum** (*Brothers Grimm Museum*). Despite the widespread destruction suffered by Kassel during World War II, some architectural gems remain. One of them, the 18th-century, baroque Palais Bellevue, is home to the city's Brothers Grimm Museum. Eschewing modern technology in its exhibits in favor of relics from the Grimm's family home and original illustrations of their stories, the museum seeks to create an authentic experience of what life was like in the brothers' time. Pride of place among the memorabilia is taken up by first and second editions of the brothers' collection of tales. There's plenty to excite younger visitors to the museum, too, and every three months it has a new interactive children's exhibition based on a different fairy tale originally recorded in German, English, Russian or Turkish. ⊠ *Schöne Aussicht 2* ☎ *0561/103–235* ⊕ *www.grimms.de* ⊠ *€3* ☉ *Tues. and Thurs.–Sun. 10–5, Wed. 10–8.*

Fodor's Choice ★ **Schloss und Bergpark Wilhelmshöhe** (*Wilhelmshöhe Palace and Palace Park*). The magnificent grounds of the 18th-century Schloss and the Bergpark Wilhelmshöhe, at the western edge of Kassel, are said to be Europe's largest hill park. If you have time, plan to spend an entire day at this UNESCO World Heritage Site, exploring its wonderful gardens, water features, museums, and castle. Wear good walking shoes and bring some water if you want to hike all the way up to the giant statue of Hercules that crowns the hilltop.

The Wilhelmshöher Park was laid out as a baroque park in the early 18th century, its elegant lawns separating the city from the thick woods of the Habichtswald (Hawk Forest). Schloss Wilhelmshöhe was added between 1786 and 1798. The great palace stands at the end of the 5-km-long (3-mile-long) Wilhelmshöher Allee, an avenue that runs straight as an arrow from one side of the city to the other.

Kassel's leading art gallery and the state art collection lie within Schloss Wilhelmshöhe as part of the **Museumslandschaft Hessen Kassel**. Its collection includes 11 Rembrandts, as well as outstanding works by Rubens, Hals, Jordaens, Van Dyck, Dürer, Altdorfer, Cranach, and Baldung Grien. ⊠ *Schloss Wilhelmshöhe, Schlosspark 1* ☎ *0561/316–800* ⊕ *www.wilhelmshoehe.de* ⊠ *Museum Schloss Wilhelmshöhe €6* ⊘ *Tues., Thurs.–Sun. 10–5, Wed. 10–8. Closed Mon.*

Löwenburg (*Lion Fortress*). Amid the thick trees of the Wilhelmshöher Park, it comes as something of a surprise to see the turrets of a medieval castle breaking the harmony. There are more surprises at the Löwenburg, for this is not true medieval castle but a fanciful, stylized copy of a Scottish castle, built in 1793 (70 years after the Hercules statue that towers above it). The Löwenburg contains a collection of medieval armor and weapons, tapestries, and furniture. ⊠ *Schlosspark 9* ☎ *0561/3168–0244* ⊕ *www.museum-kassel.de* ⊠ *€4 including tour* ⊘ *Mar.–Oct., Tues.–Sun. 10–5; Nov.–Feb., Fri.–Sun. 10–4.*

Statue of Hercules. The giant 18th-century statue of Hercules that crowns the Wilhelmshöhe heights is an astonishing sight. You can climb the stairs of the statue's castlelike base—and the statue itself—for a rewarding look over the entire city. At 2:30 pm on Sunday and Wednesday from mid-May through September, water gushes from a fountain beneath the statue, rushes down a series of cascades to the foot of the hill, and ends its precipitous journey in a 175-foot-high jet of water. A café lies a short walk from the statue. ⊠ *Schlosspark 3* ☎ *0561/312–456* ⊠ *Hercules Octagon €3* ⊘ *Mar.–Oct., Tues.–Sun. 10–5.*

WHERE TO EAT AND STAY

$ | GERMAN | ✕ **Brauhaus Knallhütte.** This brewery and inn, established in 1752, was the home of the village storyteller Dorothea Viehmann, who supplied The Grimms with some of the best of their stories, including "Little Red Riding Hood," "Hansel and Gretel," and "Rumpelstiltskin." To this day "Dorothea" tells her stories here (in German only) every first and third Saturday of the month at 5:30. Once a wayside inn on the road to Frankfurt, the Knallhütte now sits alongside a busy highway. However, this hasn't diminished its popularity, and if you're planning on visiting on the weekend, it's best to book ahead. Those that arrive hungry can tour the brewery and then eat and drink as much as they want for €24.90. ⑤ *Average main: €14* ⊠ *Knallhütte. 1, Baunatal-Rengershausen* ☎ *0561/492–076* ⊕ *www.knallhuette.de.*

$$ | HOTEL | Fodor's Choice | ★ | ⛳ **Hotel Gude.** It may be 10 minutes by tram away from the city center, but this modern, friendly hotel and its spacious rooms, sauna, and excellent restaurant ($$$) justify the journey. **Pros:** close to the autobahn; easy parking; comfortable beds. **Cons:** removed from the city center; on a busy street. ⑤ *Rooms from: €119* ⊠ *Frankfurter Str. 299* ☎ *0561/48050* ⊕ *www.hotel-gude.de* ⇔ *84 rooms, 1 suite* ⎮⊘⎮ *Breakfast.*

Climb to the top of the Schloss und Bergpark Wilhelmshöhe, where a giant statue of Hercules and a fantastic view of Kassel await.

$$ 🏨 **Schlosshotel Wilhelmshöhe.** Positioned beside the lovely baroque gardens and woodland paths of the hilltop Wilhelmshöhe Park, this comfortable, modern hotel and its rooms take in views on the park grounds on one side and stunning vistas over Kassel on the other. **Pros:** tranquil atmosphere; historic setting; views. **Cons:** no minifridge minibar in "classic" rooms; a modern-looking hotel, despite its romantic name. $ *Rooms from: €129* ⊠ *Am Schlosspark 8* ☎ *0561/30880* ⊕ *www.schlosshotel-kassel.de* ↗ *120 rooms, 2 suites* ❚◎❚ *Breakfast.*

BAD KARLSHAFEN

50 km (31 miles) north of Kassel.

Popular with holidaymakers in mobile homes and trailers, who park up on the banks of the Weser directly across from its historic center, Bad Karlshafen's a pretty little spa town whose baroque architecture, while impressive, is showing some signs of wear and tear. Best viewed from the campsite side of the river, the town is surrounded by hills covered in dense forest and has for some time also found favor as a health resort. Its elevation and rural location provide fresh air, and there are salt springs that the locals believe can cure just about whatever ails you.

GETTING HERE AND AROUND
Regional trains run here from Göttingen, but only infrequently, so check train timetables well ahead of any visit.

ESSENTIALS
Visitor Information Bad Karlshafen Kur- und Touristik-Information
⊠ *Hafenpl. 8* ☎ *05672/999–922* ⊕ *www.bad-karlshafen.de.*

EXPLORING

Rathaus. Bad Karlshafen's baroque beauty stands in surprising contrast to the abundance of half-timber architecture found along the rest of the Weser. Its stately Rathaus is the town's best baroque example. A walking tour leaves from there on Sunday at 3, May through October. ⊠ *Hafenpl. 8.*

FAMILY **Weser-Therme.** This huge spa facility sitting on the banks of the Weser River has whirlpools, sauna and steam baths, thermal saltwater pools, and an outdoor pool that supposedly is as salty as the Dead Sea. The spa's waters are famed for their therapeutic benefits, and a couple of hours bathing in them often helps relieve aches and stress. Massages are available to further aid the relaxation process. ⊠ *Kurpromenade 1* ☎ *05672/92110* ⊕ *www.wesertherme.de* ☞ *€10.50 pools, €14 pools and sauna (3 hrs)* ⊗ *Sun.–Thurs. 9 am–10 pm, Fri. and Sat. 9 am–11 pm.*

WHERE TO STAY

$ 📺 **Hotel zum Weserdampfschiff.** From the snug riverside rooms of this pop-
HOTEL ular hotel-tavern, guests can watch passengers step directly off Weser pleasure boats and into the hotel's welcoming beer garden below. **Pros:** river view; low rates; near spa facilities. **Cons:** on a busy street; rooms a bit small. ⑤ *Rooms from: €88* ⊠ *Weserstr. 25* ☎ *05672/2425* ⊕ *www. weserdampfschiff.de* ⤴ *14 rooms* ⊟ *No credit cards* ❑ *Breakfast.*

SABABURG

50 km (31 miles) west of Göttingen, 100 km (62 miles) south of Hannover.

Sababurg's not really a village as such, but it is the location of an enchanting, 700-year-old Renaissance castle, an impressive animal park, and Germany's oldest forest nature reserve, all of which lie within the peaceful, wooded surrounds of the Reinhardswald. The castle, which sits proudly on the crest of a hill in the forest, is also known as Dornröschenschloss, and is widely believed to be the source of inspiration for the tale of "Sleeping Beauty."

GETTING HERE AND AROUND

Given that Sababurg is removed from the main highway and has no rail connection, visits to Dornröschenschloss and the nearby Sababurg Tierpark are best made by car.

EXPLORING

Fodor's Choice **Dornröschenschloss** (*Sleeping Beauty's Castle*). The story goes that after
★ Sleeping Beauty had slumbered for a hundred years, the thick thorn hedge surrounding her castle suddenly burst into blossom, thereby enabling a daring prince a way in to lay a kiss upon her lips and reawaken her. Nowadays home to a handsome hotel, the stony exterior of Dornröschenschloss continues to be clad in colorful roses, and its walled garden is home to an impressive collection of the flowers. Even if you don't stay the night, a drive here is scenic, and there are ruins as well as the garden to explore, and a pleasant outdoor terrace with views over forest-covered hills to enjoy afterward.

12

FAMILY **Tierpark Sababurg.** The Tierpark Sababurg is one of Europe's oldest wildlife refuges. Bison, red deer, wild horses, and all sorts of waterfowl populate the park. There's also a petting zoo for children. ⊠ *Sababurg 1* 🕾 *05671/766-4990* ⊕ *www.tierpark-sababurg.de* ⊡ *€7* ⊙ *Apr.–Sept., daily 8–7; Oct., daily 9–6; Nov.–Feb., daily 10–4; Mar., daily 9–5.*

WHERE TO STAY

$$ **Dornröschenschloss Sababurg.** The medieval fortress thought to have
HOTEL inspired the tale of "Sleeping Beauty" is today a small luxury hotel, complete with domed turrets, spiral staircases,and tower rooms with four-poster beds and spa baths. **Pros:** sylvan setting; incredibly romantic. **Cons:** some dated rooms; takes some effort to find the place. $ *Rooms from: €165* ⊠ *Im Reinhardswald, Hofgeismar* 🕾 *05671/8080* ⊕ *www. sababurg.de* ↩ *17 rooms* †⊙† *Breakfast.*

$$ **Hotel Burg Trendelburg.** Ivy-bedecked towers, a shadowy foyer deco-
HOTEL rated with suits of armor and swords, and guest rooms with four-poster beds and little bathrooms hidden behind cupboard doors endow this fine establishment with an atmosphere of fairy-tale adventure. **Pros:** great views; authentic castle experience. **Cons:** some rooms small; in a otherwise uninspiring village. $ *Rooms from: €155* ⊠ *Steinweg 1, Trendelburg* 🕾 *05675/9090* ⊕ *www.burg-hotel-trendelburg.com* ↩ *22 rooms, 2 suites* †⊙† *Breakfast.*

LOWER SAXONY

Lower Saxony (Niedersachsen) was formed from an amalgamation of smaller states in 1946. Its picturesque landscape includes one of Germany's most haunting river roads, along the Weser River between Hannoversch-Münden and Hameln. This road, part of the Fairy-Tale Road, follows green banks where it's hard to see where the water ends and the land begins. Standing sentinel are superb little towns whose half-timber architecture gave rise to the term "Weser Renaissance." The Lower Saxon landscape also includes the juniper bushes and flowering heather of the Lüneburg Heath.

HANNOVERSCH-MÜNDEN

24 km (15 miles) north of Kassel, 150 km (93 miles) south of Hannover.

You'll have to travel a long way through Germany to find a grouping of half-timber houses as harmonious as those in this delightful town, seemingly untouched by the modern age—there are some 700 of them. Hannoversch-Münden is surrounded by forests and the Fulda and Werra rivers, which join here and flow northward as the Weser River.

GETTING HERE AND AROUND

Regional trains linking Hannoversch Münden to both Kassel and Göttingen run every hour. A walking tour of town takes place May to October, leaving daily at 10:30 and 2:30 from the town hall.

ESSENTIALS

Visitor Information Hannoversch-Münden ⊠ *Touristik Naturpark Münden, Lotzestr. 2* 🕾 *05541/75313* ⊕ *www.hann.muenden.de.*

EXPLORING

Johann Andreas Eisenbart. Much is made of the fact that the quack doctor to end all quacks died in Hannoversch-Münden. Dr. Johann Andreas Eisenbart (1663–1727) would be forgotten today if a ribald 19th-century drinking song ("Ich bin der Doktor Eisenbart, widda, widda, wit, boom! boom!") hadn't had him shooting out aching teeth with a pistol, anesthetizing with a sledgehammer, and removing boulders from the kidneys. He was, as the song has it, a man who could make "the blind walk and the lame see." This is terribly exaggerated, of course, but the town takes advantage of it.

The good Dr. Eisenbart has "office hours" in the town hall at 1:30 on Saturday, May through December; and a glockenspiel on the town hall depicts Eisenbart's feats, to the tune of the Eisenbart song, daily throughout the year at noon, 3, and 5. There's a statue of the doctor in front of his home at Langestrasse 79, and his grave is outside the St. Ägidien Church. ☎ *05541/75313* ⊕ *www.hann.muenden.de.*

GÖTTINGEN

30 km (19 miles) northeast of Hannoversch-Münden, 110 km (68 miles) south of Hannover.

Distinguished by its famous university, where the Brothers Grimm served as professors and librarians between 1830 and 1837, the fetching town of Göttingen buzzes with student life. Young people on bikes zip past bookshops and secondhand boutiques; when night falls, the town's cozy bars and cafés swell with students making the most of the drinks specials and free Wi-Fi on offer.

Full of elegant, gable-roofed architecture, it's also a large and modern place and boasts the shiny stores, chain coffee shops, and other trappings you'd expect of a 21st-century German town. Though not strictly on the Fairy-Tale Road, despite its association with the Grimms, Göttingen is still well worth visiting.

GETTING HERE AND AROUND

Göttingen is a stop on the same InterCity Express line between Munich and Hamburg as Kassel-Wilhelmshöhe, and is also easily reached from Bremen.

TOURS

Göttingen offers walking tours in English on the first and third Saturday of the month, April to October at 11 from the Old Town Hall.

ESSENTIALS

Visitor Information Göttingen Tourist-Information ✉ *Altes Rathaus, Markt 9* ☎ *0551/499–800* ⊕ *www.goettingen-tourismus.de.*

EXPLORING

Altes Rathaus. The Old Town Hall was begun in the 13th century but is basically a part-medieval, part-Renaissance building. The tourist-information office is on the first floor. ✉ *Markt 9* ☎ *0551/499–800* ⊕ *www. goettingen.de* 🎟 *Free* ☉ *Weekdays 9:30–6, Sat. 10–6, Sun. 10–4.*

Gänseliesel. The statue of Gänseliesel, the little Goose Girl of German folklore, stands in Göttingen's central market square, symbolizing the strong link between the students and their university city. The girl, according to the story, was a princess who was forced to trade places with a peasant, and the statue shows her carrying her geese and smiling shyly into the waters of a fountain. The students of Göttingen gave her a ceremonial role: Traditionally, graduates who earn a doctorate bestow a kiss of thanks upon Gänseliesel. Göttingen's citizens say she's the most kissed girl in the world.

WHERE TO EAT AND STAY

$$$
MEDITERRANEAN

✕ **Gaudi.** In a town rich with cozy taverns and hearty local food, the appearance of this Mediterranean restaurant, with its terra-cotta and blue color scheme, arty chandeliers, and light, airy spaces, stands out as much as its cuisine. Right in the middle of Göttingen's historic Börner Viertel, the restaurant is a favorite with staff from the university, who feast on its fine consommés, tapas, pasta, and fish and meat dishes. The food and excellent service are worth the extra cost here. $ *Average main: €24* ⊠ *Rote Str. 16* ☎ *0551/531–3001* ⊕ *www.restaurant-gaudi. de* ⊗ *Closed Sun. No lunch Mon.*

$$ ✕ **Landgasthaus Lockemann.** If you

GERMAN like to walk and hike, consider this half-timber lodge at the edge of the Stadtwald (city forest). Locals descend on the friendly, country-style restaurant for hearty German cooking ($), particularly on weekends, when it's also open for lunch. Take Bus No. 10 from the Busbahnhof, direction Herbershausen, to the last stop; then walk left on Im Beeke. The trip will take 20 minutes. $ *Average main: €16* ✉ *Im Beeke 1* ☎ *0551/209–020* ⊕ *www. landgasthaus-lockemann.de* 🚫 *No credit cards* 🕙 *Closed Mon. No lunch weekdays.*

$$$ 🏨 **Romantik Hotel Gebhards.** This

HOTEL family-run hotel stands aloof and unflurried on its own grounds, a modernized 18th-century building that's something of a local landmark. **Pros:** across from the train station. **Cons:** on a busy street; expensive. $ *Rooms from: €208* ✉ *Goethe-Allee 22–23* ☎ *0551/49680* ⊕ *www. gebhardshotel.de* 🛏 *45 rooms, 5 suites* 🍴 *Breakfast.*

HIKING AND WALKING

Two protected nature parks—the Weserbergland and the Lüneburg Heath—are in or near the Fairy-Tale Road. You can hike the banks of the Weser, stopping at ancient waterside inns, from Hannoversch-Münden, in the south, to Porta-Westfalica, where the Weser River breaks through the last range of North German hills and into the plain of Lower Saxony. The Lüneburg Heath is flat, and hiking is particularly pleasant in late summer, when the heather is in bloom. The tourist offices can tell you where to find nearby trails.

NIGHTLIFE

Among the delights of Göttingen are the ancient taverns where generations of students have lifted their steins. Among the best known are the Kleiner Ratskeller and Trou. Don't be shy about stepping into either of these taverns or any of the others that catch your eye; the food and drink are inexpensive, and the welcome is invariably warm and friendly.

HÖXTER

24 km (14 miles) north of Bad Karlshafen, 100 km (62 miles) south of Hannover.

Höxter is not actually in Lower Saxony, but just over the border in North Rhine-Westphalia. The town appeal lies in its Rathaus, a perfect example of the Weser Renaissance style, and its proximity to the impressive Reichsabtei Corvey, an abbey that's a short drive away. There's not much Grimm here; overshadowed by Sababurg's claim to Sleeping Beauty's castle and Bodenwerder's Baron von Münchhausen, Höxter's connection to a fairy tale is limited to a small Hansel and Gretel fountain in the middle of town.

GETTING HERE AND AROUND

Every couple of hours buses and regional trains run from Bad Karlshafen to Höxter Rathaus and take about 45 minutes, or you can take a combination of regional trains from Göttingen that take from 90 minutes to 2½ hours.

Between April and October, a town walking tour leaves from the Rathaus at 3 on Wednesday and 11 on Saturday.

The virgin forests of Sababurg, where Sleeping Beauty slept for 100 years, are still wild and dense.

ESSENTIALS

Visitor Information Höxter Tourist-Info ✉ *Weserstr. 11* ☎ *05271/963–431* ⊕ *www.hoexter-tourismus.de.*

EXPLORING

Fodor's Choice ★ **Reichsabtei Corvey** (*Imperial Abbey of Corvey*). The impressive Reichsabtei Corvey, or Schloss Corvey, is idyllically set between the wooded heights of the Solling region and the Weser River. During its 1,200-year history it has provided lodging for several Holy Roman emperors. Heinrich Hoffmann von Fallersleben (1798–1874), author of the poem "Deutschland, Deutschland über Alles," worked as librarian here in the 1820s. The poem, set to music by Joseph Haydn, became the German national anthem in 1922. A music festival is held in the church and great hall, the Kaisersaal, in May and June. Corvey is reached on an unnumbered road heading east from Höxter (3 km [2 miles]) toward the Weser. There are signposts to "Schloss Corvey." ✉ *Schloss Corvey* ☎ *05271/68120* ⊕ *www.schloss-corvey.de* 🎫 *€6, abbey church €0.80* ⊗ *Apr.–Oct., Tues.–Sun. 10–6.*

WHERE TO EAT

$ GERMAN ✕ **Schlossrestaurant.** In summer you can dine on flambéed tart and salad under centuries-old trees. When it's cooler, slip inside the Reichsabtei Corvey's excellent and elegant restaurant for a hot coffee and a piece of one its delicious cakes. ▓TIP➔ With advance notice, a *Fürstenbankett*, or princely banquet, can be arranged for groups in the vaulted cellars. ⑤ *Average main: €12* ✉ *Schloss Corvey* ☎ *05271/8323* ⊗ *Closed Mon. and Nov.–Mar. Closed Tues. in May and Oct.*

BODENWERDER

34 km (21 miles) north of Höxter, 70 km (43 miles) south of Hannover.

The charming Weser town of Bodenwerder is the home of the Lügen-baron (Lying Baron) von Münchhausen (1720–97), who was known as a teller of whoppers and whose fantastical tales included a story about riding a cannonball toward an enemy fortress but then, having second thoughts, returning to where he started by leaping onto a cannonball heading the other way. Stretched out along a peaceful valley, the nicest part of the town is around the Baron's old home, now the town hall, its half-timber architecture set against a backdrop of the river and surrounding hills. A regular stop for cyclists on the Wesertal route, the town also attracts canoeists, and anglers who can tell their own whoppers about the one that got away.

ESSENTIALS

Visitor Information Bodenwerder Tourist-Information ⊠ *Münchausenpl. 3* ☎ *05533/40542* ⊕ *www.muenchhausenland.de.*

GETTING HERE AND AROUND

Reachable from Höxter by a combination of bus and regional train, or by bus from Hameln, changes are required along the way and any visits requiring public transport should be planned in advance.

EXPLORING

Münchhausen Museum. Housed in an old, renovated farm building right next to the imposing family home in which Baron von Münchhausen grew up (it's now the Rathaus), the Münchhausen Museum is crammed with mementos of his adventurous life, including his cannonball. A fountain in front of the house represents another story. The baron, it seems, was puzzled when his horse kept drinking insatiably at a trough. Investigating, he discovered that the horse had been cut in two by a closing castle gate and that the water ran out as fast as the horse drank. The water in the fountain, of course, flows from the rear of a half-horse. At 3 on the first, second, and fourth Sundays of the month from May through October, townspeople retell von Münchhausen's life story with performances in front of the Rathaus. ⊠ *Münchhausenpl. 1* ☎ *05533/409–147* 🎫 *Museum €2.50* ☉ *Apr.–Oct., daily 10–5.*

WHERE TO STAY

$
HOTEL

🏨 **Hotel Goldener Anker.** The riverside rooms of this friendly, family-owned and run hotel on the banks of the Weser river come with the best view in town. **Pros:** directly beside the river; friendly staff. **Cons:** standard rooms are very simple; close to the town's main bridge. ▮**TIP**➜ **Pay the extra few euros and upgrade to a deluxe room with a river view, it's well worth the money spent.** ⑤ *Rooms from: €79* ⊠ *Brücken-str. 5* ☎ *05533/400–730* ⊕ *www.bodenwerder-hotel.de* ⇘ *19 rooms* ⑩ *Breakfast.*

HAMELN

24 km (15 miles) north of Bodenwerder, 47 km (29 miles) southwest of Hannover.

Given their relationship with one of the most famous fairy-tale characters of all time, it's unsurprising that Hameln's townsfolk continue to take advantage of the Pied Piper. Known locally as the *Rattenfänger,* or "rat-catcher," these days he tends to be celebrated more than exploited (even if his name does adorn everything from coffee mugs to restaurants), and regular costumed tours through the town relive his deeds, while a bronze statue of him stands proudly in the town's lovely pedestrian zone. Not as exciting as Hannover to the north or as relaxing as Bodenwerder to the south, Hameln's fairy-tale legacy, elegantly painted and inscribed half-timber buildings, and laid-back atmosphere will, nonetheless, please plenty of its visitors.

WORD OF MOUTH

"Opposite to the Romantic Road, the Fairy-Tale Road goes thru very nice and diverse landscapes, mostly hill country and river valleys. The northernmost section between Minden and Bremen is less scenic, as it's all just flat terrain. From London, you can either go to Hannover or Frankfurt to drive the most scenic part, which is Hameln/Hamelin to Marburg or Hanau. If you go in late November or early December you will find Christmas Markets in all those quaint towns already open. But the days will be short already, and the weather not always good."
—Cowboy1968

GETTING HERE AND AROUND

45 minutes away from Hannover by S-bahn (Line No. 5), Hameln is within easy reach of the Lower Saxon capital.

TOURS

Walking tours of Hameln are held year-round, leaving from the tourist office (April to October, daily at 10:30 and 2:30; November to March, Saturday at 2:30, Sunday at 10:30; December, daily at 10:30).

ESSENTIALS

Visitor Information Hameln Marketing und Tourismus ✉ *Deisterallee 1* ☎ *05151/957–823* ⊕ *www.hameln.de.*

EXPLORING

Hochzeitshaus (*Wedding House*). On central Osterstrasse you'll see several examples of Weser Renaissance architecture, including the Rattenfängerhaus (Rat-Catcher's House) and the Hochzeitshaus, a beautiful 17th-century building now used for city offices. From mid-May to mid-September the Hochzeitshaus terrace is the scene of two free open-air events commemorating the legend. From May to September, local actors and children present a half-hour reenactment each Sunday at noon, and there is also a 40-minute musical, *Rats,* each Wednesday at 4:30 during the same months. The carillon of the Hochzeitshaus plays tunes every day at 9:35 and 11:35, and mechanical figures enact the piper story on the west gable of the building at 1:05, 3:35, and 5:35.

WHERE TO EAT AND STAY

$ ✕ **Rattenfängerhaus.** This brilliant example of Weser Renaissance archi-
GERMAN tecture is Hameln's most famous building, where the Pied Piper supposedly stayed during his rat-extermination assignment (it wasn't
actually built until centuries after his supposed exploits). A plaque
in front of it fixes the date of the incident at June 26, 1284. "Rats"
are all over the menu, from the "rat-killer liqueur" to a "rat-tail
flambé." But don't be put off by the names: the traditional dishes are
excellent. $ *Average main: €13 ⊠ Osterstr. 28 ☎ 05151/3888 ⊕ www.
rattenfaengerhaus.de.*

$ ⛉ **Hotel zur Börse.** A few paces off Hameln's picturesque pedestrian and
HOTEL shopping zone, this pleasant, modern hotel is also within easy walking
distance of the rest of the town's main attractions. **Pros:** in the pedestrian zone; flat-screen TVs. **Cons:** modern look seems out of place;
bathrooms on the small side. $ *Rooms from: €93 ⊠ Osterstr. 41a,
entrance on Kopmanshof ☎ 05151/7080 ⊕ www.hotel-zur-boerse.de
⤹ 31 rooms ⦿ Breakfast.*

$ ⛉ **Hotel zur Krone.** On the Old Town's pedestrian zone, Hotel zur Krone
HOTEL has a terrace that lets you watch locals coming and going, and afternoon coffee here is a summer delight. **Pros:** a half-timber marvel; lovely
terrace. **Cons:** modern annex lacks charm; new guest rooms a little
small. $ *Rooms from: €99 ⊠ Osterstr. 30 ☎ 05151/9070 ⊕ www.
hotelzurkrone.de ⤹ 32 rooms ⦿ Breakfast.*

HANNOVER

47 km (29 miles) northeast of Hameln.

A little off the Fairy-Tale Road, and better known internationally as
a trade-fair center than a tourist destination, the Lower Saxon capital holds an attractive mix of culture, arts, and nature that justifies a
visit here all the same. With several leading museums, an opera house
of international repute, and the finest baroque park in the country,
it's a place that packs a surprising amount into a city of only half a
million people. Conveniently centered between the city's main train
station and its pleasant inner city lake, most of Hannover's major
attractions, including its fine New and Old Town Halls, are within
an easy walk of one another. In spring and summer the city's parks
fill with picnicking families, while fall and winter are celebrated first
with the second biggest Oktoberfest in the world and then cheery
Christmas markets.

GETTING HERE AND AROUND

Travel northeast from Hameln on autobahn A-33 to Hannover. There is
also frequent direct rail service from Hameln. Hannover has an airport,
and is served by the InterCity Express (ICE) trains and the Europabus.
From mid-April through the end of October, hop-on, hop-off city bus
tours of Hannover leave from the tourist office daily at 10:30, 12:30,
and 2:30 (and 4:30 on Saturday).

DISCOUNTS AND DEALS

A **Hannover Card** entitles you to free travel on local transportation, reduced admission to seven museums, and discounts on certain sightseeing events and performances at the theater and opera. It's available through the tourist office for €9.50 per day (€17.50 for three days).

ESSENTIALS

Visitor Information Hannover Tourismus ⊠ *Ernst-August-Pl. 8* ☎ *0511/1684–9700* ⊕ *www.hannover.de.*

TOURING TIPS

Scenic spot: The formal park and gardens at Herrenhausen, complete with moat and fountains, are a great photo op.

Red thread: Hannover's points of interest lie along a tourist trail marked by a red line on the sidewalk. It starts at the tourist office.

EXPLORING

TOP ATTRACTIONS

Altes Rathaus (*Old Town Hall*). It took nearly 100 years, starting in 1410, to build this gabled brick edifice that once contained a merchants' hall and an apothecary. In 1844 it was restored to the style of about 1500. The facade's fired-clay frieze depicts coats of arms and representations of princes, and a medieval game similar to arm wrestling. Inside is a modern interior with boutiques and a restaurant. ⊠ *Köbelingerstr. 2.*

Fodor's Choice ★   **Herrenhausen.** The gardens of the former Hannoverian royal summer residence are the city's showpiece (the 17th-century palace was never rebuilt after wartime bombing). The baroque park is unmatched in Germany for its formal precision, with patterned walks, gardens, hedges, and chestnut trees framed by a placid moat. There is a fig garden with a collapsible shelter to protect it in winter and dining facilities behind a grotto. From Easter until October there are fireworks displays and fountains play for a few hours daily (weekdays 10–noon and 3–5, weekends 10–noon and 2–5). Herrenhausen is outside the city, a short ride on Tram No. 4 or 5. ⊠ *Herrenhauserstr. 5* ☎ *0511/1684–4543* ⊕ *www.hannover.de/herrenhausen* ⊠ *€8* ⊗ *Mar., Apr., and Sept., daily 9–7; May–Aug., daily 9–8; Oct., daily 9–6; Nov.–Feb., daily 9–4:30.*

Landesmuseum Hannover. The priceless art collection of this regional museum includes works by Tilman Riemenschneider, Veit Stoss, Hans Holbein the Younger, Claude Monet, and Lucas Cranach. There are also historical and natural history sections. ⊠ *Willy-Brandt-Allee 5* ☎ *0511/980–7686* ⊕ *www.landesmuseum-hannover.niedersachsen.de* ⊠ *€4* ⊗ *Tues., Wed., and Fri.–Sun. 10–5, Thurs. 10–7.*

Leineschloss. The former royal palace of the Hanovers—whose members sat on the British throne from 1714 to 1837 as kings George I–IV—stands grandly beside the River Leine, and is now home to the Lower Saxony State Parliament. Although the interior of the palace is largely closed to the public, its imposing Corinthian columns and river setting provide some excellent photo ops. ⊠ *Hinrich-Wilhelm-Kopf-Pl. 1.*

Sprengel Museum. An important museum of modern art, the Sprengel holds major works by Max Beckmann, Max Ernst, Paul Klee, Emil Nolde, Oscar Schlemmer, Hans Arp, and Pablo Picasso. The street where it's located is named after Kurt Schwitters, a native son and

12

prominent dadaist, whose works are also exhibited. ⊠ *Kurt-Schwitters-Pl. 1* ☎ *0511/1684–3875* ⊕ *www.sprengel-museum.de* €7 ⊙ *Tues. 10–8, Wed.–Sun. 10–6.*

WORTH NOTING

Neues Rathaus. The massive New Town Hall was built at the start of the 20th century in Wilhelmine style (named for Kaiser Wilhelm). The pomp and circumstance were important ingredients of the heavy German bureaucracy of the time. Four scale models on the ground floor depict Hannover in various stages of development and destruction: as a medieval walled city, in the years before World War II, immediately following World War II, and in its present-day form. An elevator rises diagonally to the dome for a splendid view. ⊠ *Trammpl. 2* ☎ *0511/1684–5333* Dome €3 ⊙ *Mar.–Oct., weekdays 9:30–6:00, weekends 10–6:00.*

Opernhaus. Hannover's neoclassical opera house, completed in 1852, has two large wings and a covered, colonnaded portico adorned with statues of great composers and poets. The building originally served as the court theater, but now is used almost exclusively for opera. It was gutted by fire in a 1943 air raid and restored in 1948. ■ TIP➜ Unless you have tickets to a performance, the only part of the interior you can visit is the foyer. ⊠ *Opernpl. 1* ☎ *0511/9999–1111* ⊕ *www. staatstheater-hannover.de/oper.*

WHERE TO EAT

$$$
ECLECTIC
× **Basil.** Constructed in 1867 as a riding hall for the Royal Prussian military, this upmarket restaurant's home is as striking as the menu. Cast-iron pillars support the vaulted brick ceiling, and two-story drapes hang in the huge windows. The menu, which changes every few weeks, includes dishes from the Mediterranean to Asia. Game and white *Spargel* (asparagus) are served in season. $ *Average main: €22 ⊠ Dragonerstr. 30 ☎ 0511/622–636 ⊕ www.basil.de ☾ Closed Sun. No lunch.*

$
GERMAN
× **Brauhaus Ernst August.** This brewery has so much artificial greenery that you could imagine yourself in a beer garden. Hannoverian pilsner is brewed on the premises, and regional specialties are the menu's focus. Besides beer paraphernalia such as mugs and coasters, you can also buy, empty or full, a huge old-fashioned beer bottle with a wired porcelain stopper. There's also live music and DJs on Friday nights and weekends. $ *Average main: €13 ⊠ Schmiedstr. 13 ☎ 0511/365–950 ⊕ www.brauhaus.net.*

$$
GERMAN
× **Broyhan Haus.** The claim of "Hannoverian hospitality over three floors" written on the exterior of this half-timber tavern in the middle of town isn't made frivolously. Convivial waitstaff ferry plates loaded with sauerkraut and pork, and large glasses of the local, crisp-tasting Einbecker beer to diners in the tavern's upstairs room, and to tables outside on the pedestrian zone in summer. On the ground floor there's a well-stocked bar to pull up a seat at, and downstairs the cellar can be booked for private parties and events. $ *Average main: €16 ⊠ Kramerstr. 24 ☎ 0511/323–919 ⊕ www.broyhanhaus.de.*

WHERE TO STAY

$$
HOTEL
⊞ **Concorde Hotel am Leineschloss.** Near the elegant Altes Rathaus and the stately Leineschloss, and only a leisurely stroll from the Neues Rathaus, Opernhaus, and the city's main museums, this simple, modern hotel has easily one of the best locations in the city. **Pros:** in the middle of the shopping district; close to the U-bahn (Line Nos. 3, 7, and 9); every double room has a bath. **Cons:** no restaurant; not much character. $ *Rooms from: €136 ⊠ Am Markte 12 ☎ 0511/357–910 ⊕ www.concordehotel-am-leineschloss.de ⤳ 81 rooms ⦵ Breakfast.*

$$
HOTEL
Fodor's Choice
★
⊞ **Kastens Hotel Luisenhof.** Antiques are everywhere in this elegant hotel, which is traditional both in appearance and service; tapestries adorn the lobby walls, oil paintings hang in the foyer, and copper engravings enliven the bar. **Pros:** near the train station; helpful staff; elegant. **Cons:** expensive; on a narrow, ordinary street. $ *Rooms from: €169 ⊠ Luisenstr.1–3 ☎ 0511/30440 ⊕ www.kastens-luisenhof.de ⤳ 131 rooms, 11 suites, 4 apartments ⦵ No meals.*

NIGHTLIFE AND THE ARTS

Hannover's nightlife is centered on the Bahnhof and the Steintor redlight district.

Casino. The town's elegant casino is open daily from 10 am to 3 am. ⊠ *Osterstr. 40 ☎ 0511/980–660.*

Opera company. The opera company of Hannover is internationally known, with productions staged in one of Germany's finest

19th-century classical opera houses. Call or visit the website for program details and tickets. ✉ *Opernpl. 1* ☎ *0511/9999–1111* ⊕ *www. staatstheater-hannover.de/oper.*

SHOPPING

Hannover is one of northern Germany's most fashionable cities, and its central pedestrian zone has international shops and boutiques, as well as the very best of German-made articles, including stylish clothes and handmade jewelry.

Galerie Luise. In the glassed-over Galerie Luise, accessible from an underground garage, you can spend a couple of hours browsing, with a leisurely lunch or afternoon tea at one of the restaurants and cafés. ✉ *Luisenstr. 5* ⊕ *www.galerie-luise.de* ⊘ *Weekdays 10–7, Sat. 10–6.*

EN ROUTE The Fairy-Tale Road continues north of Hannover as far as Bremen, though any connection to the Grimm brothers is faint here. You can reach Bremen in less than an hour by taking autobahn A-7 to the Walsrode interchange and then continuing on autobahn A-27. An alternative is to return to Hameln and follow the Weser as it breaks free of the Wesergebirge upland at Porta Westfalica. The meandering route runs through the German plains to the sea and Bremen. You can also take a quick side trip to the northeast, to the Lüneburg Heath and Bergen-Belsen.

OFF THE BEATEN PATH

Gedenkstätte Bergen-Belsen (*Bergen-Belsen Memorial*). The site of the infamous POW and concentration camp is now a memorial to the victims of World War II and the Holocaust. Anne Frank was among the more than 70,000 Jews, prisoners of war, homosexuals, Roma, and others who died here.

A place of immense cruelty and suffering, the camp was burned to the ground by British soldiers, who liberated the camp in April 1945, arriving to find thousands of unburied corpses and typhus, typhoid fever, tuberculosis, and other diseases spreading rapidly among the survivors. All that physically remains of the camp today, which is inside a nature preserve, are the foundations of some of its prisoner barracks and a number of burial mounds overgrown with heather and grass and bearing stark inscriptions such as "Here lie 1,000 dead."

The history of the camp and its victims is explained further through a series of moving video, audio, photo, and text exhibits within the slender, minimalist structure of the 200-meter-long, 18-meter-wide Documentation Center. Built almost entirely of plain concrete panels, the center is softly lit and peaceful inside, its floor sloping gently upward from the entrance and beyond the exhibits to windows that let in light and views of the trees outside.

Visitors to the Memorial should plan to stay at least two or three hours. Free 90-minute tours of the site in German and English leave the Documentation Center information desk at 2:30 on Thursday and Fridays and at 11:30 and 2:30 on weekends, from March to September. ▐ TIP→ **Don't try to see everything when visiting the memorial, but do take some time to walk around outside, visiting the site of the barracks to gain a better understanding of the atrocious living conditions inmates of the camp were forced to suffer.**

Bergen-Belsen is 58 km (36 miles) northeast of Hannover. Although it's possible to get here on public transport, it requires traveling first to the town of Celle by train, and then taking an hour-long bus journey. Buses run every two hours and require multiple changes. By car, take autobahn exits Mellendorf or Solltau Süd and follow the signposts to the memorial. ⊠ *Anne-Frank-Pl., Lohheide* ☎ *05051/47590* ⊕ *www.bergenbelsen.de* 🎫 *Free* ⊗ *Apr.–Sept., daily 10–6; Oct.–Mar., daily 10–5.*

BREMEN

110 km (68 miles) northwest of Hannover.

Germany's smallest city-state, Bremen, is also Germany's oldest and second-largest port (only Hamburg is larger). Together with Hamburg and Lübeck, Bremen was an early member of the merchant-run Hanseatic League, and its rivalry with the larger port on the Elbe River is still tangible. Though Hamburg may still claim its title as Germany's "gateway to the world," Bremen likes to boast, "But we have the key." Bremen's symbol is, in fact, a golden key, which you will see displayed on flags and signs throughout the city.

GETTING HERE AND AROUND

Bremen's international airport is a gate to many European destinations, and Intercity (IC) trains connect the city with much of the rest of Germany.

TOURS

Bremen offers both bus and walking tours in English. The bus tours depart Tuesday through Sunday at 10:30 from the central bus station on Breiteweg, the walking tours daily at 2 from the Tourist-Information Center on Oberstrasse.

ESSENTIALS

Visitor Information Bremen Tourist-Information ⊠ *Obernstr. 1* ☎ *0421/101–030* ⊕ *www.bremen-tourism.de.*

DISCOUNTS AND DEALS

Bremen has an **ErlebnisCARD,** which lets you ride free on the public transportation, gets you into museums and other cultural facilities at half price, and gets you a reduction on tours. It costs €9.50 for one day and €11.50 for two days. You can buy it at tourist information centers.

EXPLORING

TOP ATTRACTIONS

Böttcherstrasse (*Barrel Maker's Street*). Don't leave Bremen's Altstadt without strolling down this street, at one time inhabited by coopers. Between 1924 and 1931 the houses were torn down and reconstructed, in a style at once historically sensitive and modern, by the Bremen coffee millionaire Ludwig Roselius. (He was the inventor of decaffeinated coffee, and held the patent for decades.) Many of the restored houses are used as galleries for local artists.

Marktplatz. Bremen's impressive market square sits in the charming Altstadt. It's bordered by the St. Petri Dom, an imposing 900-year-old Gothic cathedral; an ancient Rathaus; a 16th-century guildhall; and a modern glass-and-steel state parliament building, with gabled town houses finishing the panorama. Alongside the northwest corner of the Rathaus is the famous bronze statue of the four **Bremen Town Musicians,** one atop the other in a sort of pyramid. Their feats are reenacted in a free, open-air play at the Neptune Fountain near the cathedral, at noon each Sunday, from May to September. Another well-known figure on the square is the stone statue of **Roland,** a knight in service to Charlemagne, erected in 1404. Three times larger than life, the statue serves as Bremen's good-luck piece and a symbol of freedom and independence. It is said that as long as Roland stands, Bremen will remain a free and independent state.

THE BREMEN TOWN

In this folktale adapted by the Brothers Grimm, a donkey, dog, cat, and rooster ran away because they had become old and their masters were going to dispose of them. In order to support themselves they headed toward Bremen. After some adventures, they came upon a cottage occupied by robbers. The menagerie managed to scare the miscreants away by standing on each other's backs and singing. The robbers fled, and the animals lived in their new house happily ever after. Although in most versions of the stories the animals never actually make it to Bremen, their statues are now found throughout the city.

Fodor's Choice ★ **Schnoorviertel.** Stroll through the narrow streets of this idyllic district, a jumble of houses, taverns, and shops. This is Bremen's oldest district, dating back to the 15th and 16th centuries. The neighborhood is fashionable among artists and craftspeople, who have restored the tiny cottages to serve as galleries and workshops. Other buildings have been converted into popular antiques shops, cafés, and pubs. The area's definitely a great source for souvenirs, with incredibly specialized stores selling porcelain dolls, teddy bears, African jewelry, and smoking pipes, among many other things. There's even an all-year-round Christmas store.

WORTH NOTING

Rathaus. A 15th-century statue of Charlemagne, together with seven princes, adorns the Gothic town hall. It was he who established a diocese here in the 9th century. The Rathaus acquired a Weser Renaissance facade during the early 17th century. Tours, given when no official functions are taking place, are in German and English. ⊠ *Am Markt 21* ☞ *Tour €5* ☉ *Tours Mon.–Sat. at 11, noon, 3, and 4; Sun. at 11 and noon.*

Roselius-Haus. This 14th-century building, now a museum, stands at one end of Böttcherstrasse. It showcases German and Dutch art, notably the paintings of Paula Modersohn-Becker, a noted early expressionist of the Worpswede art colony. Notice also the arch of Meissen bells at the rooftop. ▣ TIP➔ Except when freezing weather makes them dangerously brittle, the bells chime daily on the hour from noon to 6 from May to December (and only at noon, 3, and 6 January– April). ⊠ *Böttcherstr. 6–10* ☎ *0421/336–5077* ⊕ *www.pmbm.de* ☞ *€6* ☉ *Tues.–Sun. 11–6.*

St. Petri Dom (*St. Peter's Cathedral*). Construction of the cathedral began in the mid-11th century. Its two prominent towers, one of which can be climbed, are Gothic, but in the late 1800s the cathedral was restored in the Romanesque style. It served as the seat of an archbishop until the Reformation turned the cathedral Protestant. It has a small museum and five functioning organs. ⊠ *Sandstr. 10–12* 🖼 *Free* 🕙 *June–Sept., weekdays 10–8, Sat. 10–2, Sun. 2–6; Oct.–May, weekdays 10–5, Sat. 10–2, Sun. 2–5.*

WHERE TO EAT AND STAY

$$$$
FRENCH
Fodor's Choice
★

✕ **Grashoffs Bistro.** An enthusiastic crowd, willing to put up with cramped conditions, descends at lunchtime on this restaurant and deli. The room is so small that there's little room between the square tables; a table has to be pulled out for anyone who has a seat next to the wall. The menu has a French touch, with an emphasis on fresh fish from the Bremerhaven market. The deli has a whole wall of teas, another of cheeses, and a huge assortment of wines. 💲 *Average main: €27* ⊠ *Contrescarpe 80* 🕾 *0421/178–8952* ⊕ *www.grashoff.de* ⌛ *Reservations essential* 🕙 *Closed Sun. No dinner.*

$
GERMAN

✕ **Ratskeller.** This cavernous cellar with vaulted ceilings is said to be Germany's oldest and most renowned town-hall restaurant—it's been here for 600 years. Is walls are lined with wine casks, and there are small alcoves with sliding wooden doors, once shut tight by merchants as they closed their deals. The food's solid traditionally North German fare. ◼ TIP➔ **By long tradition only German wines are served here, and the only beer you can get is Beck's and Franziskaner from the barrel.** 💲 *Average main: €15* ⊠ *Am Markt 1* 🕾 *0421/321–676* ⊕ *www. ratskeller-bremen.de.*

$
HOTEL

🏨 **Hotel Pension Weidmann.** There are only five rooms in this small and friendly family-run pension in one of the brick buildings so characteristic of Bremen. **Pros:** English-speaking staff; welcomes dogs (even large ones). **Cons:** no restaurant; shared bathroom. 💲 *Rooms from: €50* ⊠ *Am Schwarzen Meer 35* 🕾 *0421/498–4455* ⊕ *www.pension-weidmann.de* ⌇ *5 rooms* ⊟ *No credit cards* 🍽 *No meals.*

$$$$
HOTEL
Fodor's Choice
★

🏨 **Dorint Park Hotel Bremen.** This palatial hotel comes with an enviable location between a small lake and an extensive area of park and forest not far from the main train station. **Pros:** traditional luxury; on a lake. **Cons:** expensive; outside the city. 💲 *Rooms from: €239* ⊠ *Im Bürgerpark* 🕾 *0421/340–800* ⊕ *www.parkhotel-bremen.de* ⌇ *160 rooms, 15 suites* 🍽 *No meals.*

NIGHTLIFE AND THE ARTS

Bremen may be Germany's oldest seaport, but it can't match Hamburg for racy nightlife. Nevertheless, the streets around the central Marktplatz and in the historic Schnoor District are filled with all sorts of taverns and cafés. The Bremen coffee tradition will be evident when you have your coffee and cake at a café in a charming old building with plush sofas, huge mirrors, and chandeliers.

Bremen casino. Try your luck at American roulette, poker, slot machines, and blackjack at the Bremen casino, open daily noon–3 am. ⊠ *An der Schlachte 26* 🕾 *0421/329–000* 🖼 *€3.*

BREMERHAVEN

66 km (41 miles) north of Bremen.

This busy port city, where the Weser empties into the North Sea, is part of Bremen, which is an hour to the south. You can take in the enormity of the port from a promenade, which runs its length. In addition to being a major port for merchant ships, it is the biggest fishery pier in Europe, and its promenade is lined with excellent seafood restaurants.

GETTING HERE AND AROUND

Regional trains run every two hours from Bremen to this North Sea port, and take 35 minutes to get here. Reederei HaRuFa offers a one-hour trip around the Bremerhaven harbor for €10. If you'd like to go farther afield and view Schnoorviertel and the stark, red cliff island of Helgoland from the sky, OFD has a daily round-trip flight for €175 per person.

ESSENTIALS

Visitor Information Bremerhaven Touristik ⊠ *H.-H.-Meierstr. 6* ☎ *0471/946–4610* ⊕ *www.bremerhaven-touristik.de.* **OFD Airlines** ⊠ *Flughafen, Am Luneort 15* ☎ *0471/77188* ⊕ *www.fliegofd.de.* **Reederei HaRuFa** ⊠ *H.-H.-Meierstr. 4* ☎ *0471/415–850* ⊕ *www.hafenrundfahrt-bremerhaven.de.*

EXPLORING

Fodor'sChoice ★ **Deutsches Auswandererhaus** (*German Emigration Center*). Located at the point where seven million Europeans set sail for the New World, the Deutsches Auswandererhaus is made to order for history buffs and those wanting to trace their German ancestry. "Passengers" get boarding passes; wait on dimly lit docks with costumed mannequins and piles of luggage; and once on board navigate their way through cramped and creaky sleeping and dining cabins. After being processed at Ellis Island, visitors can then research their genealogy using the museum's emigration database and its extensive collection of passenger lists. Further on, there is a section of the museum dedicated to immigrants to Germany, complete with an impressive 1970s-era shopping mall, and a retro movie theater screens short films about German emigrants and their families. ⊠ *Columbusstr. 65* ☎ *0471/902–200* ⊕ *www.dah-bremerhaven.de* ⊠ *€12.50* ⊙ *Mar.–Oct., daily 10–6; Nov.–Feb., daily 10–5.*

Deutsches Schifffahrtsmuseum (*German Maritime Museum*). The country's largest and most fascinating maritime museum, the Deutsches Schifffahrtsmuseum, includes a harbor, open from April through October, that shelters seven old trading ships. ⊠ *Hans-Scharoun-Pl. 1, from Bremen take A–27 to exit for Bremerhaven-Mitte* ☎ *0471/482–070* ⊕ *www.dsm.national.museum* ⊠ *€6* ⊙ *Nov.–Mar., Tues.–Sun. 10–6; Apr.–Oct., daily 10–6.*

WHERE TO STAY

$$
HOTEL
Hotel Haverkamp. Not far from Bremerhaven's harbor and world-class museums, this modern hotel may not look much from the outside, but its enviable reputation is built on excellent service, a fine restaurant, and quiet, tidy guest rooms. **Pros:** convenient location; quiet area; good restaurant. **Cons:** plain exterior; pool is very small; no views. $ *Rooms from: €129* ⊠ *Pragerstr. 34* ☎ *0471/48330* ⊕ *www.hotel-haverkamp.de* ⇆ *85 rooms* ⊙| *Breakfast.*

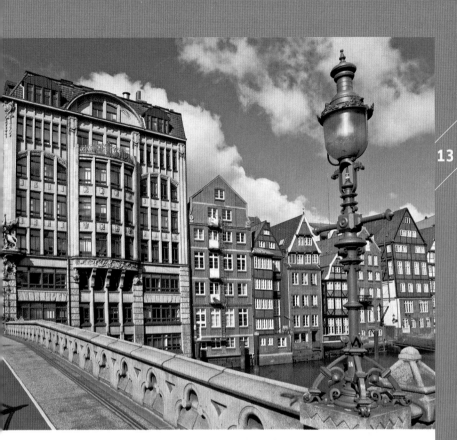

HAMBURG

WELCOME TO HAMBURG

TOP REASONS TO GO

★ **Alster cruises:** Marvel at the luxurious villas gracing the shores of the Alster lakes and its canals, relax and sip *Glühwein* (mulled wine) or a cool beer while listening to the major and minor details about the city.

★ **Historic harbor district:** Travel back in time and walk the quaint cobblestone alleys around Deichstrasse and the Speicherstadt.

★ **Hamburger Kunsthalle and the Deichtorhallen:** Spend an afternoon browsing through the fantastic art collections at two of Germany's leading galleries of modern art.

★ **Retail therapy:** Indulge your inner shopper as you weave your way through the streets behind the elegant Jungfernstieg, move up and down Mönckebergstrasse, stroll through Altona and the Schanzenviertel and end the afternoon at one of the funky cafés nearby.

★ **Sin City:** Stroll down Reeperbahn, browse in the quirky sex shops, and dive into the nightlife of Europe's biggest party district.

1 Altstadt and Neustadt. Together, "Old Town" and the "New Town" make up the *Innenstadt*, or inner city. Humming with locals and tourists on weekends and public holidays, the center of town is the place to come for shopping and culture.

2 St. Pauli and Schanzenviertel. An entertainment district since the 17th century, St. Pauli continues to draw fun seekers to its massive red light and party district. Down the road, the Schanzenviertel is filled with little shops and cafés.

3 St. Georg. The center of Hamburg's gay and lesbian scene and also home to a large Turkish community, St. Georg is an intriguing mix of

GETTING ORIENTED

The second-largest city in Germany after Berlin, Hamburg sits on northern Germany's fertile lowlands, within easy reach of the North and Baltic seas. A city-state of 1.8 million inhabitants, Hamburg covers an area of 755 square km (291 square miles), making it one of the least densely populated cities to have more than a million people. Taking up some of that space are its many parks and trees; it's centered on two major bodies of water. The Elbe River is the site of the city's busy port, and it's near some of its most colorful quarters. The inner and outer Alster lakes, meanwhile, are encircled by Hamburg's downtown, and a cluster of upscale neighborhoods. It's here, somewhere between the commerce of the river and the tranquility of the lakes, that visitors to the city tend to spend most of their time.

KEY

S	S-Bahn
ℹ	Tourist information
U	U-Bahn

affluence, relaxed attitudes, and cultures.

4 Speicherstadt and HafenCity. The old and the new are both part of Hamburg's inner city port, with 19th-century warehouses at the Speicherstadt and state-of-the-art riverside apartment and office complexes at HafenCity.

5 Altona and Ottensen. These former working-class areas are now desirable places to live and visit. Many of the old buildings and factories have been refurbished to accommodate fancy restaurants, art-house cinemas, and design hotels.

6 Blankenese and Beyond. Many of Hamburg's suburbs have their own distinct feel—none more so than the riverside neighborhood of Blankenese, which locals compare to the French and Italian Rivieras.

COFFEE AND CAKE

When the afternoon rolls around, it's time for *Kaffee und Kuchen*, one of Germany's most beloved traditions. In villages and cities alike, patrons still stroll into their favorite *Konditorei* (pastry shop) for a leisurely cup of coffee and slice of cake.

(above) Cake is serious business in Germany, and you'll have your pick of many at any Konditorei worth its salt. (upper right) Mohnkuchen (lower right) Gugelhupf

The tradition stretches back hundreds of years, when coffee beans were first imported to Germany in the 17th century. Coffee quickly became the preferred hot drink of the aristocracy, who paired it with cake, their other favorite indulgence. Within time, the afternoon practice trickled down to the bourgeoisie, and was heartily embraced. Now everyone can partake in the tradition.

There are hundreds of German cakes, many of which are regional and seasonal with an emphasis on fresh fruits in summer, and spiced cakes in winter. Due to modern work schedules, not as many Germans take a daily coffee and cake break anymore. Families will have theirs at home on the weekend, and it's often an occasion for a starched tablecloth, the best china, and candles.

—Tania Ralli

VISITING THE KONDITOREI

Seek out the most old-fashioned shops, as these tend to have the best cakes. Check out what's in the glass case, since most Konditorein don't have printed menus. Don't worry about a language barrier, when it comes time to order just point to the cake of your choice.

BEST CAKES TO TRY

FRANKFURTER KRANZ

The *Frankfurter Kranz,* or Frankfurt wreath, is a butter cake flavored with lemon zest and a touch of rum. It's then split into three layers and spread with fillings of buttercream and red preserves. The cake's exterior is generously coated with crunchy cookie crumbs or toasted nuts, and each slice is graced with a swirl of buttercream frosting and a bright red cherry.

GUGELHUPF

Of all cakes, the *Gugelhupf* has the most distinctive shape, one that you'll likely recognize as a bundt cake. It tends to be more popular in southern Germany. Gugelhupf had its start as a bready yeast cake, studded with raisins and citrus peel, but today you're just as likely to have it as a marble cake. During the Biedermeier period, in the early 19th century, the wealthy middle class regarded the Gugelhupf as a status symbol.

HERRENTORTE

A layer cake of dark chocolate, *Herrentorte* means "gentleman's cake." It's not as sweet or creamy as most layer cakes, and thus meant to appeal to a man's palate. A *Torte* refers to a fancier layered cake, as opposed to the more humble *Kuchen,* which is more rustic. The Herrentorte has a rich and refined taste—in

Germany, all chocolate is required to have a high cocoa content, improving its overall taste and texture.

MOHNKUCHEN

Mohnkuchen is a poppy seed cake—in fact, this is a cake so completely brimming with poppy seeds you could mistake it for a piece of chocolate cake. You'll come across it as a tall wedge, sprinkled with powdered sugar, or a fat square glazed with a lick of icing. The poppy seeds are mixed with sugar, butter, and sometimes milk. Lightly crushed they make for a very moist filling.

STREUSELKUCHEN

This cake became especially popular in the 19th century, in Prussia. Owing to its versatility, you'll find it today all over Germany. The simple, buttery yeast cake's selling point is its sugary, crunchy topping of pebbled *Streusel,* which can stand on its own or be combined with rhubarb, apricots, cherries, apples, or other fruit. *Streuselkuchen* is baked on large sheet pans and cut into generous squares.

13

Updated by
Jeff Kavanagh

Frequently described as "the gateway to the world" by its proud citizens, the handsome port city of Hamburg has for centuries welcomed merchants, traders, and sailors to a rich assortment of grand hotels, fine restaurants, and, yes, seedy bars and brothels.

This vibrant, affluent city's success began with its role as a founding member of the Hanseatic League, a medieval alliance of northern European cities that once dominated the shipping trade in the North and Baltic Seas. To this day, the city is known as "the Free and Hanseatic City of Hamburg," reflecting both its association with the league and its status as an independent city-state.

Shipping continues to be a major industry. Straddling the mighty Elbe River, over 100 km (62 miles) inland from the North Sea, Hamburg's inner city harbor is the third biggest port in Europe. The city is now also one of Germany's major media hubs, serving as headquarters for the publishing giants Axel Springer, Grüner + Jahr, and Bau Verlag; and for such influential publications as *Die Zeit, Der Spiegel,* and *Stern.*

The profits of these endeavors are apparent throughout Hamburg, from its imposing neo-Renaissance town hall, to the multitude of luxury boutiques studding the adjacent Neuerwall, to the Elbchausee, a long, leafy stretch of road lined with Hollywood-like mansions and overlooking the Elbe. Hamburg has more millionaires per capita than any other German city.

Like many other of the country's urban centers, however, the city has suffered a tumultuous history. Since its founding as "Hammaburg" in 811, Hamburg has been destroyed by Vikings, burned down by Poles, and occupied by Danish and French armies. The Great Fire of 1842 devastated much of its commercial center, and in 1943 the Allied Forces' Operation Gomorrah bombing raids and the resulting firestorms left 40,000 people dead and large swathes of Hamburg in ruins.

Scars from World War II still remain, and you need only walk down a residential street to see the plain, functional apartment buildings that were built to replace those destroyed by bombs. There are also frequent reminders of the terrible fate suffered by Hamburg's Jews, and others considered enemies of the state during this time. Memorials in Hafen-City and near Dammtor train station mark where those persecuted by Nazis were deported to concentration camps. As part of a Germany-wide project, small brass plaques set into sidewalks outside apartment buildings commemorate former residents executed by the regime.

Modern-day Hamburg is a progressive city endowed with attractive architecture, cultural diversity, and liberal attitudes. It's notable for its parks and trees and a pair of beautiful inner city lakes, but it's famous for its enormous red-light party district, which fans off from the seamy, neon-lit Reeperbahn. Shabby but chic quarters such as St. Pauli and the Schanzenviertel are as beloved by locals as the affluent Blankenese and Eppendorf, and the city's annual schedule of spring and summer festivals has enough room for a huge gay-pride parade in the middle of town, as well as a celebration of *Hafengeburtstag*—the harbor's birthday.

As you'd expect in such a wealthy city, Hamburg has more than its share of world-class museums and art galleries, as well as an assortment of grand theaters and music venues, an opera company, and an internationally renowned ballet company. Not content to rest on its laurels, the city is also steaming ahead with the ambitious HafenCity, an urban-renewal project that has transformed a significant section of the city's port front. The Elbphilharmonie—a futuristic concert hall that the city hopes will become as iconic as the Sydney Opera House—is to be its centerpiece.

PLANNING

WHEN TO GO

Known for its long, gray winters, Hamburg is frequently treated to a pleasant spring come late March or early April. Once the weather warms, the city's mood visibly improves. One of the highlights of the season is Hafengeburtstag, in early May, when the Elbe comes alive with a long parade of ships and riverside festivities.

Summer may be the best time of the year to visit. Temperatures rarely exceed the mid-80s, and the days are long, with the sun rising at around 5 am and light still in the sky till after 10 pm. Tables outside cafés and bars fill up with alfresco diners and drinkers; plumes of smoke rise from grills in parks and beaches along the Elbe. From mid-June to August, the *Schlemmersommer* (Gourmet Summer) comes to tempt food lovers. During this time, more than 100 restaurants throughout the city, including a number of award-winners, offer four-course dinners for two for €59.

September and October are usually good months to visit, despite the fact that October can often be quite cold and wet. September's Reeperbahn Festival is great for music fans hoping to see the next big thing, and Hamburg's small but popular film festival (held the same month) usually attracts one or two of the leading lights of European and world cinema.

The mercury drops quickly once the clocks go back an hour at the end of October. Happily, Christmas markets selling Glühwein begin to spring up on street corners and in public squares around the last week of November, and many continue on to *Silvester* (New Year's Eve). December, despite temperatures frequently dropping below zero, is a fun time to visit the city. January and February, however, are quiet and fairly uneventful.

EVENTS

Historischer Weihnachtsmarkt. Hamburg's Historischer Weihnachtsmarkt enjoys a spectacular backdrop—the city's Gothic town hall. The market's stalls are filled with rows of candy apples, chocolates, and doughnuts. Woodcarvers from Tyrol, bakers from Aachen, and gingerbread makers from Nuremburg come to sell their wares. And in an appearance arranged by the circus company Roncalli, Santa Claus ho-ho-hos his way along a tightrope high above the market every evening at 4, 6, and 8. ✉ *Rathausmarkt 1* ⊕ *www.hamburger-weihnachtsmarkt.com* ⊗ *Nov. 25–Dec. 23, Sun.–Thurs. 10–9, Fri. and Sat. 10–10.*

GETTING HERE AND AROUND

AIR TRAVEL

Hamburg Airport is 5 miles northwest of the city. S-bahn Line No. 1 runs about every 10 minutes from the airport to Hamburg's main station (*Hauptbahnhof*) on its way to Altona. The trip takes 25 minutes, and tickets are €2.90. A taxi to the center of the city (Alstadt and Neustadt) will cost about €20. If you're driving a rental car from the airport, follow the signs to Zentrum (Center). ■ TIP→ There is an Edeka supermarket on the arrivals level between Terminal 1 and 2. It's a bit smaller than a full-size German supermarket and the prices are a bit higher than they would be in town. However, it is a great place to pick up some snacks or drinks for your hotel room or some food for an extended journey.

Airport Information Hamburg Airport ✉ *Flughafenstr. 1–3* ☎ *040/50750* ⊕ *www.airport.de.*

BUS AND SUBWAY TRAVEL

The HVV, Hamburg's public transportation system, includes the U-bahn (subway), the S-bahn (commuter train), ferries, buses, and express buses (which cost an additional €1.80). Distance determines fares; a single trip costs €2.95 for longer journeys (such as the airport into Hamburg's main station); €1.90 for shorter distances (for instance, from St. Pauli or Altona into the center of town); and €1.40 if you're only traveling a couple of stops. If you're planning to make multiple trips about the city, then you may want to get the Tageskarte, or day pass, which for an adult and three children under 15 costs €7.10 when purchased before 9 am and €5.80 after that. A €10.40 Gruppenkarte is the best option for those traveling in a group. A group of five adults can use this card after 9 am on weekdays and all day on weekends.

Tickets and passes are available on all buses and from vending machines in every U- or S-bahn station. HVV is partially based on the honor system. You only need to show a ticket to the bus driver after 9 pm and all day on Sunday to bus drivers, but not on trains or ferries unless asked by a ticket inspector during random checks. Those caught without a ticket are fined €40 on the spot. Subway and commuter trains run throughout the night on weekends, but stop running around 12:30 am during the week. After that, night buses (Nos. 600–640) take over.

Information is available in English at ⊕ *www.hvv.de/en*. The trip planner function gives the times, prices, walking directions, and maps for each journey. If you don't know the address of a site, you can simply type in the name of the popular destination, such as "Hamburg airport." Prepared commuters can buy tickets (even the €1.30 ticket) and passes from the website and print them out, or use HVV's smart phone app.

Don't be afraid to take the bus. Buses have dedicated traffic lanes, and most of their stops aren't too close together, so travel tends to be fast. It's a good way to see more of this beautiful city.

Hamburg's intercity bus station, the Zentral-Omnibus-Bahnhof (ZOB), is located diagonally across from the south exit of the main train station.

Contacts HVV (*Hamburg Transportation Association*). ⊠ *Johanniswall 2, Altstadt* ☏ *040/19449* ⊕ *www.hvv.de.* **Zentral-Omnibus-Bahnhof** (*ZOB*). ⊠ *Adenauerallee 78, St. Georg* ☏ *040/247–576* ⊕ *www.zob-hamburg.de.*

CAR TRAVEL
With its popular public transportation system, Hamburg is easier to negotiate by car than many other German cities, and traffic here is relatively free flowing outside of rush hours. Several autobahns (A-1, A-7, A-23, A-24, and A-250) connect with Hamburg's three beltways, which then lead to the Downtown area. Follow the "Zentrum" signs.

TAXI TRAVEL
Taxi meters start at €2.90, then add €2.00 for the first 4 km; €1.90 for the next 6 km; and €1.40 after that. You can hail taxis on the street, outside subway and train stations, and at popular locations (like along Mönckebergstrasse). You can also order one by phone or online.

Taxi Information Taxi ☏ *040/211–211* ⊕ *www.taxi211211.de.*

TRAIN TRAVEL
Hamburg Hauptbahnhof (Hamburg Main Station) is the city's central hub for local, regional, long-distance, and international trains. InterCity Express (ICE) trains going to and from Basel, Stuttgart, and Munich all start and terminate in Hamburg-Altona, and pass through Hauptbahnhof and Dammtor stations on the way.

Train Information Deutsche Bahn ☏ *0180/699–6633* ⊕ *www.bahn.de.*

VISITOR INFORMATION
Hamburg Tourismus (Hamburg Tourism Office) has several outlets around the city. The main office is in the Hauptbahnhof and is open Monday to Saturday 9–7, Sunday 10–6. The airport branch is open from 6 am to 11 pm daily and sits on the departure level between Terminals 1 and 2. At the harbor there's an office at the St. Pauli Landungsbrücken, between Piers 4 and 5, open 9–6 Sunday to Wednesday and 9–7, Thursday to Saturday. All tourist offices can help with accommodations, and there's a central call-in booking office for hotel and ticket reservations and general information, the Hamburg-Hotline.

Visitor Information Hamburg Tourismus ⊠ *Steinstr. 7, Altstadt* ☏ *040/3005–1300 for hotline* ⊕ *www.hamburg-travel.com.*

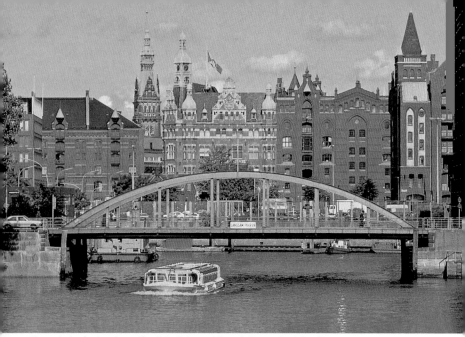

Take a relaxing boat cruise on the Alster Lakes and through the canals of the city.

TOURS
BOAT TOURS
There are few better ways to get to know the city than by taking a trip on its waters. Alster Touristik operates a variety of picturesque boat trips around the Alster lakes and through the canals. Alster and canal tours leave from a small dock at the Jungfernstieg. The round-trip Alster cruise lasts one hour, costs €14.50, and leaves every half hour, daily 10–6 from the end of March to the end of September. From the end of September until the end of October, it leaves at 10 and 5, and every half hour from 11 to 4. The Winter Warmer Trip offers trips with hot chocolate and *glühwein* (for an additional charge) several times a day from the end of October through to the end of March. Alster Touristik also offers twilight tours through the canals from Jungfernstieg to the bucolic Harvestehude neighborhood May through August and the waters around the historic warehouse district in September. Both tours start at 8 and run May through October, and cost €20. A one-hour Speicherstadt canal tour costs €20 and runs April through October daily at 10:45, 1:45, and 4:45, and November through December at 1:45 Friday through Sunday. All tours offer commentary in English.

Rainer Abicht offers one-hour tours of the harbor in English aboard one of its small fleet of boats, which include its famous *Louisiana Star* riverboat. The tours leave every day at midday from April until October from Landungsbrücken Pier 4. They cost €18.

Every day of the year, Kapitän Prüsse offers cruises around the Elbe harbor that last 60–90 minutes. These include a night cruise that costs €20 and leaves between 6 and 9 at night (depending on the time of the year) from Pier 3.

The Maritime Circle Line tours major attractions on the Elbe; passengers embark at St Pauli Landungsbrücken Pier 10 and can hop on and hop off at a number of stops including BallinStadt, Hamburg Harbor Museum, HafenCity, and the historic ship MV *Cap San Diego*. The tours run every two hours daily from 10 to 4, April through October, and every two hours from noon to 4 on weekends, November to March. Tickets, which can be bought at the pier or online, are € 14.50 and include discounts at all the venues.

■**TIP**➜ An HVV public transport day pass is valid for trips on the number 62 HADAG ferry between Landungsbrücken Pier 1 and Finkenwerder, a suburb on the south side of the Elbe river. There's no commentary on the ferry, but on a fine day the top deck's a great spot to watch ships sailing in and out of the harbor, and for superb views of the city from the river.

Boat Contacts Alster Touristik ☎ *040/357-4240* ⊕ *www.alstertouristik.de*. **HADAG** ☎ *040/311-7070* ⊕ *www.hadag.de*. **Kapitän Prüsse** ☎ *040/357-4240* ⊕ *www.kapitaen-pruesse.de*. **Maritime Circle Line** ✉ *Landungsbrücken 10, St. Pauli* ☎ *040/2849-3963* ⊕ *www.maritime-circle-line.de*. **Rainer Abicht** ☎ *040/317-8220* ⊕ *www.abicht.de*.

ORIENTATION TOURS

Sightseeing bus tours of the city, all with guides, who rapidly narrate in both English and German, leave from Kirchenallee by the main train station. A 90-minute bus tour sets off at varying times daily and costs € 17.50. For € 30, one of the bus tours can be combined with a one-hour boat trip on the harbor. Departure times for tours vary according to season.

Contacts Hamburger Stadtrundfahrt ☎ *040/792-8979* ⊕ *www.die-roten-doppeldecker.de*.

WALKING TOURS

A great way to learn more about the city while also getting some exercise is on a walking tour. There are plenty of tours to choose from, although many only run from April through November. In addition to guided walks of the Altstadt and Neustadt, the harbor district, HafenCity, and St. Pauli, there are also themed excursions, such as Beatles tours and a red-light walking tour of the Reeperbahn. To find a guided walk in English, contact Hamburg Tourismus, the tourist office.

PLANNING YOUR TIME

Hamburg's almost custom-made for a long weekend visit. Its airport is less than half an hour by train or taxi from the city center; it has an efficient and extensive public transport system; taxis are reasonably priced and plentiful; and the city's flat terrain is perfectly suited to walking and cycling. Exploring the Altstadt and Neustadt areas, where Hamburg's Rathaus (Town Hall), the Alster lakes, the Kunsthalle and Deichtorhallen galleries, and a number of the city's churches are all within a short stroll of one another, can easily fill a day and night—particularly if you throw in some shopping, and then dinner in nearby St. Georg. Another day can be spent wandering the harbor, taking a cruise and perhaps bicycling around the Speicherstadt and HafenCity, followed by a night out in St. Pauli or the Schanzenviertel. A less vigorous day's activities might include brunch in a café in Altona, lunch and a riverside walk in Blankenese, and some dinner back in Ottensen.

13

DISCOUNTS AND DEALS

Hamburg is one of Germany's most expensive cities, but the several citywide deals can make attractions more affordable.

The **Hamburg Card** allows unlimited travel on all public transportation (including express buses) within Hamburg and discounts on more than 130 museums, cruises, restaurants, and stores. A one-day card, which is valid until 6 am the following morning, costs €8.90 for one adult and up to three children under 15. The three-day card will set you back €21.90. A *Gruppenkarte* costs €14.90 for one day, €38.90 for three days, and covers five people. The Hamburg Card is available from HVV buses, vending machines, and service centers; tourist offices; and many hotels and hostels; as well as online at ⊕ *www.hvv.de* and ⊕ *www.hamburg-travel.com.*

TOURING TIPS

Information: Before you start your walk, stock up on maps and brochures at the tourist office inside the Hauptbahnhof.

Scenic spot: Wander around the Binnenalster to the Lombardsbrücke for lovely views of the lake and the grand office buildings, department stores, and hotels that frame it.

Snacks: There are many inexpensive restaurants in and around the Hauptbahnhof, as well as on Mönckebergstrasse. You can easily get a filling snack and soft drink for under €6.

EXPLORING HAMBURG

Despite being a large, sprawling city that covers about as much ground as Berlin, Hamburg feels a lot more compact. The bulk of its major attractions and sights are between the Alster lakes to the north and the city's harbor and the Elbe River to the south. At the center of the city are the Altstadt and Neustadt—the city's historical core. East of the Altstadt is St. Georg, a major gay neighborhood. To the west of the Neutstadt lie the nightlife district of St. Pauli and its neighbor the Schanzenviertel, while farther down the river are the more multicultural areas of Altona and Ottensen, and the quaint settlement of Blankenese. Just south of the Altstadt are the portside districts of the Speicherstadt and the HafenCity.

ALTSTADT AND NEUSTADT

Divided by the *Binnenalster* (inner Alster lake) and the Kleine Alster canal, the Altstadt (Old Town) and Neustadt (New Town) form the heart of Hamburg's *Innenstadt* (inner city). Stretching from Hauptbahnhof to Hamburg's town hall and down to the canals of the Speicherstadt and the Elbe, the Altstadt was heavily bombed during World War II (as was the Neustadt). Much of its splendor was restored during the postwar reconstruction of the city. Sprinkled between its office blocks and modern department stores are a number of majestic churches, handsome museums, and stately government buildings.

To the west of the Altstadt, and bordered by the *Aussenalster* (outer Alster) to the north and the Elbe to the south, lies the Neustadt. The area dates back to the 17th century, when a second wall was built to protect the city during the Thirty Years' War. The Neustadt these days is more or less indistinguishable from its older neighbor. Similarly blessed with a number of stunning buildings, including those that line the pretty lakeside promenade of Jungfernsteig, the Neustadt is also famed many great stores.

GETTING HERE AND AROUND

The best way to get to the center of the city is to take the U-bahn or S-bahn to the Hauptbahnhof or the U-bahn stations of Mönckeberg-strasse, Jungfernstieg, Rathaus or Gänsemarkt. Once here, most of the sights and attractions are within an easy walk of each other.

TIMING

If you plan four hours for visits to the museums and the Rathaus and two more hours for a boat tour on the Alster lakes, you'll comfortably end up spending a full day here.

TOP ATTRACTIONS

Fodor'sChoice
★
Alster Lakes. The twin lakes of the Binnenalster (Inner Alster) and Aussenalster (Outer Alster) provide Hamburg with some of its most celebrated vistas. The two lakes meet at the Lombardsbrücke and Kennedybrücke (Lombard and Kennedy bridges). The boat landing at the Jungfernstieg, below the Alsterpavillon, is the starting point for lake and canal cruises. Small sailboats and rowboats, hired from yards on the shores of the Alster, are very much a part of the summer scene.

Every Hamburger dreams of living within sight of the Alster, but only the wealthiest can afford it. Those that can't still have plenty of opportunities to enjoy the waterfront, however, and the outer Alster is ringed by 7 km (4.3 miles) of tree-lined public pathways. ■ TIP➔ Popular among joggers, these paths are also a lovely place for a stroll. ⊠ *Altstadt* Ⓜ *Jungfernstieg (U-bahn).*

Fodor'sChoice
★
Deichstrasse. The oldest residential area in the Old Town of Hamburg now consists of lavishly restored houses from the 17th through the 19th century. Many of the original, 14th-century houses on Deichstrasse were destroyed in the Great Fire of 1842, which broke out in No. 38 and left approximately 20,000 people homeless; only a few of the early dwellings escaped its ravages. Today Deichstrasse and nearby streets, which are steps away from the site of former city wall, are of great historical interest. At No. 35–39 Peterstrasse, for example, is the replica of baroque facade of the Beylingstift complex, built in 1751. Today, the Johannes Brahms Museum sits in No. 39, the composer's former home. All the buildings in the area have been painstakingly designed to look like the original buildings, thanks largely to nonprofit foundations. ⊠ *Altstadt* Ⓜ *Rödingsmarkt (U-bahn)* ⊠ *Neustadt* Ⓜ *St. Pauli (U-bahn).*

Hamburger Kunsthalle (*Art Gallery*). One of the most important art museums in Germany, the Kunsthalle has 3,500 paintings, 650 sculptures, and a coin and medal collection that dates from the ancient Roman era. In the postmodern, cube-shaped building designed by Berlin architect O. M. Ungers, the **Galerie der Gegenwart** has housed a collection of

The Beatles in Hamburg

It was on the mean streets of St. Pauli, and specifically Grosse Freiheit, that four young lads from Liverpool cut their teeth playing to frequently hostile crowds of sailors, prostitutes, and thugs before going on to become the biggest band in the world. Signed by Bruno Koschmider, a nightclub owner and entrepreneur of dubious character, the Beatles first arrived in Hamburg in August 1960. Their first gig was at Koschmider's Indra Club, a seedy joint that doubled as a strip club, and their first lodgings consisted of a couple of windowless rooms in the back of a cinema, the Bambi Kino. Over the next two and a half years, the young Beatles would visit Hamburg five times and play almost 300 concerts in the city. During one stint in 1961, they performed 98 nights in a row, often starting at 8:30 at night and playing their last song around the same time the next morning.

Perhaps surprisingly, some of the venues where the Beatles strutted their stuff remain. The Star Club, the site of their last Hamburg concert, on New Year's Eve 1962, may be gone, but the **Indra Club** is still at Grosse Freiheit 64. Down the road, at No. 36, is the **Kaiserkeller**, where the boys moved after the Indra was closed down for being too rowdy. In addition to hitting the clubs, fans of the Fab Four can pose beside the life-size, metal sculptures of the five original Beatles on the **Beatles-Platz**, and also retrace the band's steps on a number of walking tours, which take in the **Bambi Kino** and other venues they played at, along with the **Gretel und Alfons** pub, a favorite haunt.

international modern art since 1960, including works by Andy Warhol, Joseph Beuys, Georg Baselitz, and David Hockney. With 1,200 drawings and other works, graphic art is well represented, including works by Pablo Picasso and Horst Janssen, a Hamburg artist famous for his satirical worldview. In the other areas of the museum, you can view works by local artists dating from the 16th century. The outstanding collection of German Romantic paintings includes pieces by Caspar David Friedrich. Paintings by Holbein, Rembrandt, Van Dyck, Tiepolo, and Canaletto are also on view, while late-19th-century Impressionism is represented by works by Leibl, Liebermann, Manet, Monet, and Renoir. ⊠ *Glockengiesserwall, Altstadt* ☎ *040/4281–31200* ⊕ *www. hamburger-kunsthalle.de* 🖾 *€12* ⊘ *Tues., Wed., and Fri.–Sun. 10–6, Thurs. 10–9.* Ⓜ *Hauptbahnhof (U-bahn and S-bahn).*

Jungfernstieg. This wide promenade looking out over the Alster lakes is the beginning of the city's premier shopping district. Laid out in 1665, it used to be part of a muddy millrace that channeled water into the Elbe. Hidden from view behind the sedate facade of Jungfernstieg is a network of several small shopping centers that together account for almost a mile of shops selling everything from souvenirs to haute couture. Many of these passages have sprung up in the past two decades, but some have been here since the 19th century; the first glass-covered arcade, called Sillem's Bazaar, was built in 1845. ⊠ *Neustadt* Ⓜ *Jungfernstieg (U-bahn).*

NEED A BREAK?

Alex im Alsterpavillon. Perhaps Hamburg's best-known café, the Alex im Alsterpavillon is sleek yet comfortable, and an ideal spot for observing the constant activity on the Binnenalster. ⊠ *Jungfernstieg 54, Neustadt* ☎ *040/350–1870.*

DID YOU KNOW?

Although Germans love to compare Hamburg to Venice, it's a bit of a stretch. Still, Hamburg is threaded with countless canals and waterways spanned by about 2,500 bridges, even more than you'll find in Venice, Amsterdam, and London combined. Swans glide on the canals and arcaded passageways run along the waterways. In front of the Rathaus is a grand square that some say resembles the Piazza San Marco in Venice.

13

Mönckebergstrasse. This broad street of shops—Hamburg's major thoroughfare—cuts through the city's Altstadt. Built between 1908 and 1911 to connect the main train station to the town hall, but only open to taxis and buses, the street is perfect for a stroll. Home to the Karstadt and Galeria Kaufhof department stores, electronics mega-store Saturn, as well as a host of global brand stores from Adidas to Zara, it swells with local and out-of-town shoppers on Saturday and public holidays. ▓ **TIP→ The best cafés and restaurants tend to be found on side streets off Mönckebergstrasse, where the rents for shop space are generally not as high.** ⊠ *Altstadt* Ⓜ *Mönckebergstrasse (U-bahn), Hauptbahnhof (U-bahn and S-bahn), Jungfernstieg (U-bahn).*

Fodor's Choice ★ **Rathaus** (*Town Hall*). To most Hamburgers this impressive neo-Renaissance building is the symbolic heart of the city. The seat of the city's *Senate* (State Government) and *Bürgerschaft* (Parliament), it was constructed between 1886 and 1897, with 647 rooms and an imposing clock tower. Along with much of the city center, the Rathaus was heavily damaged during World War II, but was faithfully restored to its original beauty in the postwar years, and it's now one of the most photographed sights in Hamburg. The forty-minute tours of the building begin in the ground floor Rathausdiele, a vast pillared hall. Although visitors are only shown the state rooms, their tapestries, glittering chandeliers, coffered ceilings, and grand portraits give you a sense of the city's great wealth in the 19th century and the Town Hall's status as an object of civic pride. Outside, the Rathausmarkt (Town Hall Square) is the site of regular festivals and events, including the annual Stuttgarter Wine Festival and the city's biggest Christmas market. ⊠ *Rathausmarkt, Altstadt* ☎ *040/42831–2064* ⊕ *www.hamburgische-buergerschaft.de* 💰 *€4* ⊙ *Daily tours in English hourly from 10:15 on* Ⓜ *Rathaus (U-bahn), Jungfernstieg (U-bahn and S-bahn).*

St. Jacobi Kirche (*St. James's Church*). This 15th-century church was almost completely destroyed during World War II. Only the interiors survived, and reconstruction was completed in 1963. The interior is not to be missed—it houses such treasures as a massive baroque organ and three Gothic altars from the 15th and 16th centuries. ⊠ *Jacobikirchhof 22, at Steinstr., Altstadt* ☎ *040/303–7370* ⊕ *www.jacobus.de* ⊙ *Apr.–Sept., Mon.–Sat. 10–5, Sun. after service;*

Hamburg

Moorweidenstr.

E.-Siemers Allee

Marseillerstr.

11

11

Theodor Heuss-pl.

Dammtor Ⓢ

U Dammtor Damm

Stephans-Platz

Esplanade

Aussenalster

Mittelweg

Warbugstr.

Alsterufer

Alsterglacis

Kennedybrücke

An der Alster

Koppel

Lombardsbrücke

ST. GEORG

Lange Reihe

Holzdamm

Callmacherreihe

U Gänsemarkt

Gänse-markt

Fuhlenwiete

Hohebleichen

Poststr.

Dammtor Str.

Colonnaden

Neuer Jungfernstieg

Binnenalster

Ballindamm

Ferdinandstr.

Brandsende

Glockengiesser wall

Ernst-Merck-Str.

2

i **U** Ⓢ Hbf.-Nord

Grosse Bleichen

Jungfernstieg

10

U Jungfern-Stieg Ⓢ

Hermannstr.

Raboisen

Kurze Mühren

3

Hbf.-süd

Ⓢ**U**

Adenauer allee

NEUSTADT

Bleichenbr.

Neuer Wall

Adolfstr.

Alter Wall

Bergstr.

Gerh Hauptm Pl.

Mönckebergstr.

Lange Mühren

4

Kurt-Schumacher-Allee

Steintor-wall

Klosterwall

Düsternstr.

Stadthausbr.

Neuer Wall

9

8

U Rathaus

Gr. Johannisstr.

Petzerstr.

7

5

6

Steinstr.

Johannis Wall

Ⓢ Stadthaus-Brücke

Mönkedamm

Gr. Burstah

Speer sort

Burchardstr.

Burchard-pl.

Steinstr. **U**

Deichtor Pl.

Admiralitat Str.

U Rödingsmarkt

Gr. Burstah

Domstrasse

ALTSTADT

Kl. Reichenenstr.

27 **28**

Rödings-Markt

Deichstr.

16

Willy-Brandt-Strasse

Messberg **U**

Obertbaumbrücke

Deichtorstr.

Banksstr.

21

15

Kornhausbrücke

Dovenfleet

Zippelhaus

Alter Wandrahm

Kajen

U Baumwall

Binnenhafen

Neuen Krahn

B.D. Mühten

Zollkanal

Kehrwieder Brook

Neuer Wandrahm

SPEICHERSTADT

Brooktorkai

18

20

19

HAFENCITY

Am Sandtorkai

KEY	
Ⓢ	*S-Bahn*
i	*Tourist information*
U	*U-Bahn*

Oct.–Mar., Mon.–Sat. 11–5, Sun. after service. German guided tours: 1st Sat. at 2 and 3; 3rd Fri. at 12:30. English guided tours available on request by emailing ahead of time. Ⓜ *Rathaus (U-bahn), Jungfernstieg (U-bahn and S-bahn).*

Fodor's Choice ★ **St. Michaelis Kirche** (*St. Michael's Church*). The Michel, as it's called locally, is Hamburg's principal church and northern Germany's finest baroque-style ecclesiastical building. Its first incarnation, built between 1649 and 1661 (the tower followed in 1669), was razed after lightning struck almost a century later. It was rebuilt between 1750 and 1786 in the decorative Nordic baroque style, but was gutted by a terrible fire in 1906. The replica, completed in 1912, was demolished during World War II. The present church is a reconstruction.

The distinctive 436-foot brick-and-iron tower bears the largest tower clock in Germany, 26 feet in diameter. Just above the clock is a viewing platform (accessible by elevator or stairs) that affords a magnificent panorama of the city, the Elbe River, and the Alster lakes. ▇ TIP➜ Twice a day, at 10 am and 9 pm (Sunday at noon), a watchman plays a trumpet solo from the tower platform. In the crypt a 30-minute movie about the 1,000-year history of Hamburg and its churches is shown.

For a great view of Hamburg's skyline, head to the clock tower at night. In the evenings you can sip a complimentary soft drink while listening to classical music in a room just below the tower. This is usually held from 5:30 to 11:00: check ⊕ *www.nachtmichel.de* to confirm times. ✉ *Englische Planke 1, Neustadt* ☎ *040/376–780* ⊕ *www. st-michaelis.de* 🎫 *Tower €5; crypt and movie €4; show, tower, and crypt €7* ⊙ *May–Oct., daily 9–7:30; Nov.–Apr., daily 10–5:30* Ⓜ *Rödingsmarkt (U-bahn), Stadthausbrücke (S-bahn).*

St. Petri Kirche (*St. Peter's Church*). This church was created in 1195 and has been in continuous use since then. St. Petri is the only one of the five main churches in Hamburg that came out of World War II relatively undamaged. The current building was built in 1849, after the previous building burned down in the Great Fire of 1842. ▇ TIP➜ Every Wednesday at 5:15 pm brings the Stunde der Kirchenmusik, an hour of liturgical organ music. ✉ *Bei der Petrikirche 2, Altstadt* ☎ *040/325–7400* ⊕ *www.sankt-petri.de* ⊙ *Mon., Tues., Thurs., Fri. 10–6:30, Wed. 10–7, Sat. 10–5, Sun. 9–8. Tower: Mon.–Sat. 11–5, Sun. 11:30–4. Tours: Thurs. at 3 and 1st Sun. of month at 11:30* Ⓜ *Rathaus (U-bahn), Jungfernstieg (U-bahn and S-bahn).*

▇ QUICK BITES

Old Commercial Room. Just opposite the St. Michaelis Kirche is one of Hamburg's most traditional and best loved restaurants, the Old Commercial Room. Book a table in one of its cozy booths for one of the local specialties, such as *Labskaus* (a curious mixture of potato, corned beef, beet, and herring). If you don't make it to the restaurant, you can buy cans of the stuff in Hamburg supermarkets and department stores. ✉ *Englische Planke 10, Neustadt* ☎ *040/366–319* ⊕ *www.oldcommercialroom.de.*

Hamburg's neo-Renaissance Rathaus is worth a peek inside for its opulent interiors.

WORTH NOTING

Bucerius Kunst Forum. This independent art gallery, considered one of the leading exhibition houses in northern Germany, has staged four major exhibitions a year since opening in 2002 inside a historic Reichsbank building next door to the Rathaus. The museum commissions guest curators from around the world to create shows that cover every art period and style. ⊠ *Rathausmarkt 2, Neustadt* ☎ *040/360–9960* ⊕ *www.buceriuskunstforum.de* 🎟 *€8, €5 on Mon.* ⊙ *Fri.–Wed. 11–7, Thurs. 11–9* Ⓜ *Rathaus (U-bahn).*

Deichtorhallen. A pair of large markets built in 1911–12, not far from the main train station, now house two of Germany's largest exhibition halls for contemporary art and photography. One of the Deichtorhallen's modern, airy interiors resembles an oversized loft space, and its changing exhibits have presented the works of such artists as Andy Warhol, Roy Lichtenstein, and Miró. ⊠ *Deichtorstr. 1–2, Altstadt* ☎ *040/321–030* ⊕ *www.deichtorhallen.de* 🎟 *€9* ⊙ *Tues.–Sun. 11–6* Ⓜ *Steinstrasse (U-bahn).*

Hamburg Hauptbahnhof (*Main Train Station*). This central train station's cast-iron-and-glass architecture evokes the grandiose self-confidence of imperial Germany. The chief feature of the enormous 680-foot-long structure is its 446-foot-wide glazed roof. One of the largest structures of its kind in Europe, it's remarkably spacious and bright inside. Though completed in 1906 and having gone through many modernizations, it continues to have tremendous architectural impact. Today it sees a heavy volume of international, national, and suburban rail traffic. ⊠ *Steintorpl., St. Georg* Ⓜ *Hauptbahnhof (U-bahn).*

FAMILY **Hamburg Museum** (*Museum of Hamburg History*). The museum's vast and comprehensive collection of artifacts gives you an excellent overview of Hamburg's development, from its origins in the 9th century to the present. Pictures and models portray the history of the port and shipping here, from 1650 onward. ✉ *Holstenwall 24, Neustadt* ☎ *040/42813–22380* ⊕ *www.hamburgmuseum.de* ✆ *€7.50* ⊙ *Tues.– Sat. 10–5, Sun. 10–6* Ⓜ *St. Pauli (U-bahn), Hamburger Museum (Bus No. 112)*.

Krameramtswohnungen (*Shopkeepers' Houses*). The shopkeepers' guild built this tightly packed group of courtyard houses between 1620 and 1626 for members' widows. The houses became homes for the elderly after 1866. The half-timber, two-story dwellings, with unusual twisted chimneys and decorative brick facades, were restored in the 1970s. A visit inside gives you a sense of what life was like in these 17th-century dwellings. ✉ *Historic House C, Krayenkamp 10, Neustadt* ☎ *040/3750–1988* ✆ *€2* ⊙ *Tues.–Sun. 10–5* Ⓜ *Rödingsmarkt (U-bahn), Stadtbahnstrasse (S-bahn)*.

Mahnmal St. Nikolai (*St. Nicholas Memorial*). Originally erected in 1195 and destroyed by fire in 1842, the church was rebuilt in neo-Gothic style, before it burned down again during the air raids of World War II. Today, the remains of the church serve as a memorial for the victims of war and persecution from 1933 to 1945. The memorial features an exhibition on the air raids and the destruction of Hamburg and other European cities. A glass elevator on the outside of the building takes visitors 250 feet up to the steeple, which offers magnificent views of the surrounding historic streets. Lectures, film screenings, panel discussions, and concerts also take place at the memorial. ✉ *Willy-Brandt-Str. 60, at Hopfenmarkt, Altstadt* ☎ *040/371–125* ⊕ *www. mahnmal-st-nikolai.de* ✆ *€5* ⊙ *Oct.–Mar., daily 10–5; Apr.–Sept., daily 10–8* Ⓜ *Rödingsmarkt (U-bahn)*.

Museum für Kunst und Gewerbe Hamburg (*Arts and Crafts Museum*). The museum houses a wide range of exhibits, from 15th- to 18th-century scientific instruments to an art-nouveau interior complete with ornaments and furnishings. It was built in 1876 as a combination museum and school. Its founder, Justus Brinckmann, intended it to be a bastion of the applied arts that would counter what he saw as a decline in taste owing to industrial mass production. A keen collector, Brinckmann amassed a wealth of unusual objects, including ceramics from around the world. ✉ *Steintorpl., Altstadt* ☎ *040/4281–34880* ⊕ *www.mkg-hamburg.de* ✆ *€10, €7 Thurs. after 5* ⊙ *Tues., Wed., and Fri.–Sun. 11–6, Thurs. 11–9* Ⓜ *Hauptbahnhof (U-bahn and S-bahn)*.

FAMILY **Planten un Blomen** (*Plants and Flowers Park*). In 1821, a botanist planted a sycamore tree in a park near Dammtor train station. From this tree, a sanctuary for birds and plants evolved and a botanical garden that resembles the current park opened in 1930. This 116-acre oasis features a grand Japanese garden, a mini-golf course, an outdoor roller-skating rink, trampolines, pony rides, and water features. The original sycamore tree still stands near an entrance. If you visit on a summer evening, you'll see the *Wasserlichtkonzerte,* the play of an illuminated fountain set to organ music. ■TIP➔ Make sure you get to the lake in plenty of time for the nightly show, which begins at 10 May through August and at 9 in September. ✉ *Stephanspl., Neustadt* ☎ *040/4285–44723* ⊕ *www.plantenunblomen.hamburg. de* ✄ *Free* ☉ *Apr., daily 7 am–10 pm; May–Sept., daily 7 am–11 pm; Oct.–Mar., daily 7 am–8 pm* Ⓜ *Dammtor-Bahnhof (S-bahn), Messehallen (U-bahn), St. Pauli (S-bahn), Handwerkskammer (Bus No. 112).*

Portugiesenviertel (*Portuguese Quarter*). On the edge of the harbor, tucked in between Landungsbrücken and Baumwall, lies a small slice of Iberia in Hamburg. Famed for its cluster of tapas restaurants and little cafés on and around Ditmar-Koel-Strasse, the Portugiesenviertel is a great place to go to feast on a plate of grilled sardines or have a creamy *galão* (espresso with foamed milk). Head here in summer, when the streets are flooded with tables and diners making the most of the good weather. ✉ *Ditmar-Koel-Str., Neustadt* Ⓜ *Landungsbrücken (U-bahn and S-bahn), Baumwall (U-bahn).*

> **TOURING TIPS**
>
> **Scenic spot:** A great way to experience harbor life is to visit St. Pauli Landungsbrücken, where cruise boats and ferries chug in and out and a couple of handsome museum ships are permanently moored. The best cluster of souvenir shops in Hamburg call these piers home, and a tourist office sits among them.
>
> **Snacks:** If you are an early riser stop by the Fischmarkt Sunday morning for a Fischbrötchen (a bread roll filled with fried, smoked, or pickled fish), or grab a similar seafood treat from one of the many stands along St. Pauli Landungsbrücken later in the day.

ST. PAULI AND SCHANZENVIERTEL

The harborside quarter of St. Pauli is perhaps the city's best-known neighborhood, its web of narrow streets branching off the bright neon vein of the Reeperbahn. Named after the rope makers that once worked here, the long street runs the length St Pauli's extensive red-light district—one of the largest in Europe. The broad sidewalks here are lined with strip joints, sex shops, and bars. In the early 1960s, the Beatles famously cut their teeth in clubs just off the street, playing 12-hour-long gigs in front of drunken revelers. These days St. Pauli's all-night bars, nightclubs, and pubs continue to be a big draw. Despite the seediness of its sex industry, however, the area has undergone some serious gentrification over the years, and those dive bars and flophouses now rub shoulders with trendy eateries and design hotels.

The neighboring Schanzenviertel has also experienced a significant makeover in the last decade. Once filled with artists, punks, and students, and infused with an antiestablishment culture, the "Schanze" remains a neighborhood whose most recognizable building is the Rote Flora, an old theater occupied by squatters who use it for concerts and cultural events. Now, however, it's also a place where cool young Hamburgers go to browse through clothes boutiques and then drink and dine in laid-back, reasonably priced bars and restaurants. Germany's answer to Jamie Oliver, Tim Mälzer has a hugely popular café and restaurant here, and global labels such as Adidas and American Apparel have also set up shop in recent years. Ten minutes from the center of town by S-bahn, Schanzenviertel has elegant old apartment buildings that have found favor with Hamburg's media and finance professionals. This has driven the rents up, and forced out many of the same tenants who once imbued the Schanzenviertel with its original edginess.

GETTING HERE AND AROUND

The harbor can be reached by taking a U-bahn or S-bahn train to Landungsbrücken. The mile-long Reeperbahn is bookended by the Reeperbahn S-bahn and St. Pauli U-bahn stations. The Schanzenviertel is served by the Sternschanze U-bahn and S-bahn station.

TIMING

You can easily spend a full day and a long night here, starting with breakfast and shopping in the Schanzenviertel, then lunch and a river cruise at the harbor and a night on the Reeperbahn afterwards.

TOP ATTRACTIONS

Fischmarkt (*Fish Market*). A trip to the Altona Fischmarkt is definitely worth getting out of bed early—or staying up all night—for. The Sunday markets hark back to the 18th century, when fishermen sold their catch before church services. Today, freshly caught fish sold by salty auctioneers to the locals from little stalls is only a part of the scene. You can find almost anything here: live parrots and palm trees, armloads of flowers and bananas, valuable antiques, and fourth-hand junk. Those keen to continue partying from the night before can get down to live bands rocking the historic Fischauktionshalle. ⊠ *Grosse Elbestr. 9, St. Pauli* ☉ *Apr.–Oct., Sun. 5 am–9:30 am; Nov.–Mar., Sun. 7 am–9:30 am* Ⓜ *Landungsbrücken (U-bahn and S-bahn), Fischmarkt (Bus No. 112).*

FAMILY   **Landungsbrücken** (*Piers*). Hamburgers and tourists flock to the city's impressive port (Germany's largest) to marvel at the huge container and cruise ships gliding past, pick up maritime-themed gifts from souvenir stores, and treat themselves to something from the many snack- and ice-cream stands. It's best to take a tour to get a complete idea of the massive scale of the place, which is one of the most modern and efficient harbors in the world. Barge tours leave from the main passenger terminal, along with a whole range of ferries and boats heading to other destinations on the Elbe and in the North Sea. ▥ **TIP➜ There's frequently a breeze here, so it's worth packing something warm, particularly if you're planning on taking an open-top harbor tour.** ⊠ *Bei den St. Pauli Landungsbrücken, St. Pauli* ☎ *040/3005–1300* Ⓜ *Landungsbrücken (U-bahn and S-bahn).*

Rickmer Rickmers. This majestic 19th-century sailing ship once traveled as far as Cape Town. Now it's permanently docked at Hamburg's piers, where it serves as a museum and site for exhibitons and readings. ⊠ *St. Pauli Landungsbrücken Ponton 1a, St. Pauli* ☎ *040/319–5959* ⊕ *www.rickmer-rickmers.de* ☒ *€4* ☉ *Sun.–Thurs. 10–6, Fri. and Sat. 10–8* Ⓜ *Landungsbrücken (U-bahn).*

Grosse Freiheit, a side street off the Reeperbahn, comes alive at night with crowds looking for a good time.

Cap San Diego. Close to the *Rickmer Rickmers* ship at Hamburg's piers sits the *Cap San Diego,* a seaworthy museum and hotel. Before it docked at Hamburg permanently, it regularly sailed between Germany and South America. ⊠ *Überseebrücke, Landungsbrücken, St. Pauli* ☎ *040/364–209* ⊕ *www.capsandiego.de* ⊡ *Cap San Diego €7* ⊗ *Daily 10–6* Ⓜ *Landungsbrücken (U-bahn).*

Reeperbahn. The hottest nightspots in town are concentrated on and around St. Pauli's pulsating thoroughfare, the Reeperbahn, and a buzzing little side street known as Grosse Freiheit ("Great Freedom"). It was there, in the early 1960s, that a then-obscure band called the Beatles polished their live act. The Kiez, as the area is known colloquially, is a part of town that never sleeps—literally, in the case of at least a couple of bars that claim to never close their doors. It has long been famed for its music halls and drinking holes, but also for its strip clubs, sex shops, and brothels. The first brothel was registered here in the 15th century, and although the love-hungry sailors that the area became famous for no longer roam the streets, street walkers still line Davidstrasse; around the corner, on Herbertstrasse, skimpily dressed women sit in windows and offer their services to passersby.

The Kiez is about more than just its red-light activities, however, and the Reeperbahn swells on evenings and weekends with bar hoppers and nightclubbers, concert- and theatergoers, and locals and out-of-towners out for dinner and a few drinks. And maybe a walk on or at least through the wild side afterward. ⊠ *Reeperbahn, St. Pauli* Ⓜ *St. Pauli (U-bahn), Reeperbahn (S-bahn).*

WORTH NOTING

Beatles-Platz. At the entrance to Grosse Freiheit stand life-size steel silhouettes commemorating the five original Beatles—John Lennon, Paul McCartney, George Harrison, Pete Best and Stuart Sutcliffe. In the summer of 1960, they played in the area while seeking fame and fortune. Although the statues are rather ordinary looking during the day, they make for a good photo op when they're lit up at night. ⊠ *Reeperbahn end of Grosse Freiheit, St. Pauli* Ⓜ *Reeperbahn (S-bahn).*

HARBOR TOURS

A cruise of Germany's "gateway to the world" is a must. The energy from the continuous ebb and flow of huge cargo vessels and container ships, the harbor's prosperity, and its international flavor best symbolize the city's spirit. The surrounding older parts of town, with their narrow cobblestone streets and late-medieval warehouses, testify to Hamburg's powerful Hanseatic past.

ST. GEORG

First-time visitors to Hamburg may have some trouble, at least initially, getting their heads around this vibrant quarter. Fanning out to the northeast of the Altstadt, St. Georg is a place whose rich diversity is best understood by trips down its three main streets: Steindamm, Lange Reihe, and An der Alster. Just across the main station, Steindamm begins as a one-way street full of sex shops and prostitutes lurking in doorways and turns into a busy road lined with Middle Eastern restaurants and minimarkets and a large mosque. A few blocks over, in the middle of the three, is Lange Reihe, a long, narrow thoroughfare brimming with gay and lesbian bars and cafés and some of the best places to drink and eat in town. Lastly, a short walk from Lange Reihe to the outer Alster lake's edge, sits An der Alster and a row of luxury hotels and penthouse apartments that come with million-euro views.

GETTING HERE AND AROUND

The closest station for U-bahn and S-bahn trains is Hauptbahnhof, and the No. 6 bus runs the length of Lange Reihe. St. Georg is compact, making it easy enough to stroll around.

TIMING

With all its cafés and little restaurants, St. Georg is an ideal spot for a lazy breakfast or an afternoon coffee or two. Factor in a stroll along the lake, and a few hours here can soon slip by.

SPEICHERSTADT AND HAFENCITY

No two places in Hamburg embody the changing commerce of the city and its love affair with the Elbe as vividly as the harbor districts of the Speicherstadt and the HafenCity. Built around a series of narrow canals, the stunning redbrick, Gothic architecture of the former's warehouses (which make up the largest complex of integrated warehouses in the world) sits next to the gleaming glass and steel of Europe's largest urban renewal development project. The Speicherstadt's 100-year-old warehouses continue to store and trade in everything from coffee to oriental carpets, but now count restaurants, museums and the world's largest model railway amongst their tenants. The HafenCity, meanwhile, has become a popular site for the headquarters of many of the city's largest firms, as well as home to a number of new apartment blocks, hotels and restaurants, a university, and the jewel in its crown, the hugely ambitious Elbphilharmonie concert hall, which is scheduled to open in 2015.

GETTING HERE AND AROUND

To get to the Speicherstadt, take the U-bahn to Messberg or Baumwall stations, or walk or bike over from the Altstadt. The HafenCity is now served by the city's new U4 train line, which stops at the U-bahn stations of Überseequartier and HafenCity Universität. Both areas are close enough to each other to walk between.

TIMING

This part of town is a popular spot for Sunday strollers, and ambling along its canals, taking snaps of the area's impressive riverside edifices, combined with a visit to a museum or the Miniatur Wunderland can happily fill half a day.

QUICK BITES

There are two good basement restaurants in this area.

Alt-Hamburger Aalspeicher. The Alt-Hamburger Aalspeicher specializes in fish dishes, including Hamburg's famous *Aalsuppe* (a clear broth with a variety of vegetables, seafood, and meat—everything that is leftover). Over time the German word for everything—*alle*—became mistaken for the word for eel (*aal*), so some restaurants make eel the focus, while others stick with creating their own light soup. ⊠ *Deichstr. 43, Altstadt* ☎ *040/362–990.*

Das Kontor. Seasonal dishes such as plaice in spring and game in winter are served at this upscale Hamburg tavern. You could also head here for some of the city's best fried potatoes and traditional desserts. ⊠ *Deichstr. 32, Altstadt* ☎ *040/371–471* ⊕ *www.das-kontor-hamburg.de.*

HafenCity Infocenter Kesselhaus (*HafenCity Information Center*). In an old 19th-century boiler house, this popular information center documents the HafenCity urban development project. In addition to changing photographic and architectural exhibitions, the center also has an impressive 1:500 scale-model of the HafenCity. Free walking and cycling tours in English of the HafenCity are also available. They last approximately two hours and can be booked ahead of time on the center's website. ⊠ *Am Sandtorkai 30, HafenCity* ☎ *040/3690–1799* ⊕ *www.hafencity.com* ✆ *Free* ☉ *May–Sept., Tues., Wed., and Fri.–Sun. 10–6, Thurs. 10–8; Oct.–Apr., Tues.–Sun. 10–6* Ⓜ *Baumwall (U-bahn), Überseequartier (U-bahn).*

FAMILY
Fodor's Choice
★

Miniatur Wunderland. You don't need to be a model railway enthusiast or a 10-year-old to be blown away by the sheer scale and attention to detail of the Miniatur Wunderland. The largest model railway in the world features more than 14,000 square feet of little trains click-clacking their way through wonderfully faithful miniature replicas of

Hamburg itself as well as foreign towns in Switzerland, Austria, the United States, and elsewhere. Planes land at a little airport; every 15 minutes, day turns into night and hundreds of thousands of LED lights illuminate the trains, buildings and streets. Unsurprisingly, it's one of Hamburg's most popular attractions, so it's best to book ahead, particularly on weekends and school holidays, when waiting times for entry can stretch to a couple of hours. ⊠ *Kehrwieder 2–4, Block D, Speicherstadt* ☎ *040/300-6800* ⊕ *www.miniatur-wunderland.com* ✉ *€12* ☉ *Mon., Wed., and Thurs. 9:30–6, Tues. 9:30–9, Fri. 9:30–7, Sat. 8 am–9 pm, Sun. 8:30–8* Ⓜ *Baumwall (U-bahn), Messberg (U-bahn).*

Speicherstadtmuseum. The Speicherstadt's old warehouses are still used to store many products, and although you won't be able to tour them, the nonstop comings and goings of the merchants that still trade carpets and spices in the area will give you a good sense of a port at work. If you want to learn more about the area's history and architecture, detour to the small but informative Speicherstadtmuseum. ⊠ *Am Sandtorkai 36, Speicherstadt* ☎ *040/321–191* ⊕ *www.speicherstadtmuseum. de* ✉ *€3.60* ☉ *Apr.–Oct., weekdays 10–5, weekends 10–6; Nov.–Mar., Tues.–Sun. 10–5* Ⓜ *Baumwall (U-bahn).*

ALTONA AND OTTENSEN

Generally the closer an area is to water in Hamburg, the more desirable a place it is to live. This is particularly true of the borough of Altona and Ottensen, an upscale neighborhood. Bordered by the Elbe, where Altona forms part of the port, and centered on a large domestic and international train station, the area has an allure heightened by a lively shopping boulevard and narrow side streets with bakeries, boutiques, and bars.

Much of this predominantly working-class area has been transformed over the last few decades. Nineteenth-century factories and industrial plants now accommodate cultural centers, movie theaters, offices, and hotels. Despite its increasingly middle-class makeup the quarter remains multicultural, and a large Turkish population continues to live and run all sorts of businesses here. It's a part of Hamburg that in many ways feels separate from the city surrounding it, which is unsurprising given its history. Part of Denmark until 1864, Altona was an independent city as late as 1937, and its stately town hall above the river is a reminder of its distinguished past.

GETTING HERE AND AROUND

The Altona train station, 15 minutes from Hauptbahnhof, is the starting and finishing point for all domestic and international InterCity Express trains that pass through the main station. It's also a stop on a number of local S-bahn lines. The main shopping area surrounds the station.

TIMING

The area is a good place to while away an afternoon people-watching and browsing through shops, perhaps followed by a drink or two in one the area's many fine cafés.

Check out HafenCity for a look at the Hamburg of the future, a planned development with offices, apartments, restaurants, museums, and entertainment spaces all in one neighborhood.

QUICK
BITES

Elbe beach. No Hanseatic summer would be complete without a visit to the Elbe beach, which is alive with activity then. Chic bars, volleyball games, pulsating dance clubs, barbecue grills, and sunbathers appear on sand trucked onto the banks of the Elbe. ⊠ *Am Schulberg, Altona* Ⓜ *Neumühlen/ Övelgönne (Bus No. 112), Neumühlen (Ferry No. 62).*

BLANKENESE AND ELSEWHERE

Twenty or so minutes along the Elbe by car or by S-bahn from the middle of the city lies the lovely riverside suburb of Blankenese. It's nicely situated on the side of a hill, with steep flights of narrow steeps that snake between its handsome villas. It makes a popular destination for weekend walks and coffee and cake afterward.

Other parts of town within easy reach of the main station, and worth a visit, include the upmarket neighborhood of Eppendorf, its more modest, less self-conscious neighbor Eimsbüttel, and the lakeside suburbs of Harvestehude, Winterhude, and Uhlenhorst.

Farther afield are the BallinStadt emigration museum in Veddel and the Neuengamme Concentration Camp.

GETTING HERE AND AROUND

Other than driving, the best way to get to Blankenese and Veddel is to take the S-bahn to their respective stations. Neuengamme is reachable by a combination of S-bahn and bus. The other suburbs are no more than 15 minutes away from the center of town by U-bahn.

TIMING

Given that a major selling point of Blankenese is that's a place far from the hustle and bustle of the city, and the fact that you'll need an hour to get there and back, it's best to give yourself half a day to visit. Excursions to Ballinstadt and Neuengamme shouldn't be rushed either.

BallinStadt. This museum and family-research center tells the story of European emigration to the United States and elsewhere. The complex on the peninsula here, completed in 1901, was built by the HAPAG shipping line for its passengers, which came from all across Europe to sail across the Atlantic.

> ## THE SPICE TRADE
>
> **Spicy's Gewürzmuseum.** Hamburg's proud past as Europe's gateway to the world comes to life at the tiny but fascinating Spicy's Gewürzmuseum, where you can smell and touch more than 50 spices. Nearly 1,000 objects chronicle five centuries of the once-prosperous spice trade in Hamburg. ⊠ *Am Sandtorkai 34, Speicherstadt* ☎ *040/367–989* ⊕ *www.spicys.de* 🎫 *€4* ⊙ *Nov.– June, Tues.–Sun. 10–5; July–Oct., daily 10–5.*

When the immigrants landed in the United States, there were subjected to thorough physical examinations. Those who were deemed sick were quarantined for weeks or returned to their home country. To reduce the likelihood of trouble, HAPAG began examining passengers before they left Hamburg for new shores. During the first 34 years of the 20th century, about 1.7 million people passed through emigration halls. Processing this many people took a long time, and Hamburg officials did not want foreigners roaming the city. To accommodate visitors for several days or months, the shipping company built a town, complete with a hospital, church, music hall, housing, and hotels. The emigrant experience comes to life with artifacts; interactive displays; detailed reproductions of the buildings (all but one was demolished); and first-hand accounts of oppression in Europe, life in the "city," conditions during the 60-day ocean crossing, and life in their new home.

As compelling as the exhibits are, the main draw is the research booths, where you can search the complete passenger lists of all ships that left the harbor. ■TIP➜ Research assistants are available to help locate and track your ancestors. From St. Pauli, the museum can be reached by S-bahn or Maritime Circle Line at St. Pauli Landungsbrücken No. 10. ⊠ *Veddeler Bogen 2, Veddel* ☎ *040/3197–9160* ⊕ *www.ballinstadt.de* 🎫 *€12.50* ⊙ *Apr.–Oct., daily 10–6; Nov.–Mar., daily 10–4:30* Ⓜ *Veddel (S-bahn).*

Konzentrationslager Neuengamme (*Neuengamme Concentration Camp*). Hamburg is a city of great beauty but also tragedy. On the southeastern edge of the city, between 104,000 and 106,000 people, including children, were held at Neuengamme concentration camp in its years of operation from 1938 to 1945. It was primarily a slave-labor camp, not an area focused on extermination, where bricks and weapons were the main products. German political prisoners and Europeans pushed into servitude composed most of the population. Neuengamme held gays, Roma (gypsies), and Jews. Jewish children were the subjects of cruel medical experiments; others worked with their parents or simply grew up in prison. To keep people in line, there were random acts of violence, including executions, and atrocious living conditions. Officials estimate that as many as 50,000 people died at Neuengamme before it ceased operation in May 1945.

A memorial opened on the site in 2005. Where the dormitories, dining hall, and hospital once sat, there are low pens filled with large rocks. With so much open space, the camp has an eerie silence. There is still a gate at the entrance. The camp has several regions. The main area has exhibits describing working conditions in an actual factory as well as a museum. The museum has interactive displays describing the prisoner experience. Firsthand accounts, photographs from prisoners, furniture, clothing, and possessions make the experience even more affecting. ⊠ *Jean-Dolidier-Weg 75, Neuengamme* ☎ *040/4281–31500* ⊕ *www.kz-gedenkstaette-neuengamme.de* ☞ *Free* ☉ *Grounds 24 hrs. Exhibits: Apr.–Sept., weekdays 9:30–4, weekends noon–7; Oct.–Mar., weekdays 9:30–4, weekends noon–5* Ⓜ *Bergedorf (S-bahn), then Bus No. 227 or 327.*

FAMILY **Tierpark Hagenbeck** (*Hagenbeck Zoo*). One of the country's oldest and most popular zoos, the Tierpark Hagenbeck was founded in 1907 and is family owned. It was the world's first zoo to let wild animals such as lions, elephants, chimpanzees, and others roam freely in vast, open-air corrals. In summer, you can ride a pony.

The Tropen-Aquarium, on the same property as the zoo, is like a trip around the world. Sealife, insects, curious reptiles, marvelous birds, and exotic mammals live in replicas of their natural habitat. Detailed re-creations of deserts, oceans, rain forests, and jungles are home to birds, fish, mammals, insects, and reptiles from almost every continent, including black-tailed lemurs living in a "Madagascar" village. ⊠ *Lokstedter Grenzstr. 2, Stellingen* ☎ *040/530–0330* ⊕ *www.hagenbeck.de* ☞ *€20 for zoo, €14 for aquarium, €30 for combination ticket* ☉ *Zoo: Mar.–June, Sept., and Oct., daily 9–6; July and Aug., daily 9–7; Nov.–Feb., daily 9–4:30. Aquarium daily 9–6* Ⓜ *Hagenbecks Tierpark (U-bahn).*

WHERE TO EAT

Hamburg has plenty of chic restaurants to satisfy the fashion-conscious local professionals, as well as the authentically salty taverns typical of a harbor town. There may not be a huge range of restaurants, but what's available is delicious.

Prices in the reviews are the average cost of a main course at dinner, or if dinner is not served, at lunch. Use the coordinate (✛ B2) at the end of each listing to locate a site on the corresponding map.

ALTSTADT AND NEUSTADT

$$ ✕ **Café Paris.** This busy restaurant is across from the Rathaus. The excel-
FRENCH lent traditional French fare includes steak frites, beef tartare, croque-monsieur, and other classics. Breakfast here is a treat and a far cry from the traditional German bread-and-meat options. The main dining room

is crowded with tables. For a more intimate experience, reserve a table in the salon. Café Paris also has an excellent French wine list. $ *Average main: €20 ⊠ Rathausstr. 4, Altstadt ☎ 040/3252–7777 ⊕ www. cafeparis.net Ⓜ Rathaus (U-bahn) ✛ F5.*

$$$ ✕ **Deichgraf.** This small and elegant fish restaurant in the heart of the
SEAFOOD   historic district is a Hamburg classic. It's one of the best places to get traditional dishes such as *Hamburger Pannfisch* (fried pieces of the day's catch in a wine-and-mustard sauce) at a very reasonable price. The restaurant is in an old merchant house, and oil paintings in the dining room feature ships from the 19th century. Reservations are essential on weekends. $ *Average main: €22 ⊠ Deichstr. 23, Altstadt ☎ 040/364–208 ⊕ www.deichgraf-hamburg.de ⊗ Closed Sun. Sept.–June. No lunch Sat. Ⓜ Rödingsmarkt (U-bahn) ✛ E6.*

$$$$ ✕ **Die Bank.** Venture beyond the grand exterior of this 19th-century
FRENCH   bank building and you'll find yourself in an elegant bar and brasserie where opulent chandeliers droop from a ceiling supported by handsome black columns. Diners can feast on steaks, lobster, and sashimi at white-clothed tables or out on the restaurant's spacious, sunny terrace. $ *Average main: €27 ⊠ Hohe Bleichen 17, Neustadt ☎ 040/238–0030 ⊕ www. diebank-brasserie.de ⊗ Closed Sun. Ⓜ Gänsemarkt (U-bahn) ✛ E5.*

$$$ ✕ **Fillet of Soul.** The art of fine dining is celebrated in the open show
GERMAN   kitchen of this hip, fairly casual restaurant set among the modern art
Fodor's Choice   exhibits of the Deichtorhallen. The chefs prepare straightforward, light
★   German dishes with an emphasis on fresh fish. The minimalist dining room, highlighted only by an orange wall, might not be to everyone's liking, but the buzzing atmosphere, artsy clientele, fragrant food, and great personal attention from the waitstaff make this a top choice. ▮▮TIP➜ **Although it's not as sophisticated as the evening's offerings, the lunch menu here is still very good. And with most dishes hovering around €10, it's also a good deal.** $ *Average main: €21 ⊠ Deichtorstr. 2, Altstadt ☎ 040/7070–5800 ⊕ www.fillet-of-soul.de ⊗ No dinner Sun. and Mon. Ⓜ Steinstrasse (U-bahn) ✛ H6.*

$$ ✕ **Manee Thai.** After a move to a location near the Speicherstadt, this
THAI   long-running restaurant continues to deliver authentic and delicious Thai food to hungry locals and visiting businesspeople. Hamburg isn't known for its love of spicy, aromatic food, but pad thai sits happily on the menu here beside fiery red curries. The predominantly white décor, decorated with lithographs of a Buddhist temple, won't distract you from the food, but the extensive wine list is worth a look, particularly for Rieslings, which go so well with Thai dishes. $ *Average main: €18 ⊠ Brandstwiete 46, Altstadt ☎ 040/3339–5005 ⊕ www.manee-thai. com ⊗ Closed Sun. Ⓜ Messberg ✛ F6.*

$$ ✕ **Parlament.** Set in what was once the Ratsweinkeller, the town hall's
GERMAN   traditional pub, this restaurant is an almost ironic tribute to the basement's former occupant, with an eclectic mix of historic and modern styles. On the menu are no-nonsense meat and fish meals with a light touch of German nouvelle cuisine. This grand restaurant also creates amazing *Flammkuchen,* Alsace's take on pizza. $ *Average main: €18 ⊠ Rathausmarkt 1, Altstadt ☎ 040/7038–3399 ⊕ www.parlament-hamburg.de ⊗ Closed Sun. Apr.–Oct. Ⓜ Rathaus (U-Bahn) ✛ F5.*

BEST BETS FOR HAMBURG DINING

Fodor's Choice ★	Vienna, p. 614	By Experience
Doria, $$, p. 611	**$$$**	BRUNCH
Fillet of Soul, $$$, p. 606	**Nil**, p. 610	**Café Gnosa**, $, p. 611
Landhaus Scherrer, $$$$, p. 614	**$$$$**	**Café Paris**, $$, p. 605
Mess, $$$, p. 610	**Landhaus Scherrer**, p. 614	GREAT VIEW
By Price	By Cuisine	**Carl's an Der Elbphilhar-monie**, $$$, p. 613
		Rive, $$$, p. 614
$	AUSTRIAN	HOT SPOTS
Café Gnosa, p. 611	**Vienna**, $$$, p. 614	**Bullerei**, $$$, p. 610
Restaurant Eisenstein, p. 614	GERMAN	**Mess**, $$$, p. 610
$$	**Landhaus Scherrer**, $$$$, p. 614	LUNCH
Cox, p. 611	**Vlet**, $$$, p. 613	**Fillet of Soul**, $$$, p. 606
Doria, p. 611	ITALIAN	**Zipang**, $$, p. 614
Saliba Alsterarkaden, p. 607	**Il Buco**, $$, p. 611	

13

$$
MIDDLE EASTERN

✕ **Saliba Alsterarkaden.** Underneath the arches of an elegant arcade, this popular café has superb views of the Town Hall. If the sun peeks out, the inside is empty, because everyone is perched at a canalside table. There they can sip on some excellent German wine and watch swans glide across the water. The menu includes may Syrian and other Middle Eastern dishes. $ *Average main: €20* ⊠ *Neuer Wall 13, Neustadt* ☎ *040/345–021* ⊕ *www.saliba.de* ✛ *F5.*

$$$$
ECLECTIC

✕ **Se7en Oceans.** It may not have the best location, being as it's inside a busy shopping mall, but this intriguing combination of a Michelin-starred restaurant, sushi bar, bistro, and cigar lounge, is worth a visit nonetheless. Located on the upper floor (OG2) of the large Europa Passage, Se7ven Oceans has a wall of windows to provide amazing views of the inner Alster lake and Jungfernstieg, its promenade. Promoting itself as a "multidimensional" culinary experience, the restaurant aims to cater to every size of wallet and appetite, with scallop and Persian caviar starters in the high-end restaurant, sashimi and sake, or cocktails and chicken wings at the Oceans Bar. ■TIP→ The sushi bar is a great option for lunch. It's reasonably priced and rarely crowded. $ *Average main: €35* ⊠ *Europa Passage, Ballindamm 40, Altstadt* ☎ *40/3250–7944* ⊕ *www.se7en-oceans.de* ⊛ *Reservations essential* Ⓜ *Jungfernstieg (U-bahn and S-bahn)* ✛ *F5.*

Where to Eat and Stay in Hamburg

A   **B**   **C**   **D**

Zipang

Hoheluftchaussee

Bismarckstrasse

Bogenstrasse

Gartnerstr.

Grindelallee

1

Lindner
Park-Hotel
Hagenbeck

Weg

Eppendorfer

EIMSBÜTTEL

Fruchtallee

YoHo

Bundesstrasse

2

Doormansweg

Juwelier

Vienna

Schäferkamp

Schröderstiftstrasse

Renzelstr.

Amandastrasse

Langenfelderstr.

Altonaerstr.

fritzhotel

U STERNSCHANZE

Verbindungsb.
Tiergartenstr.

The Boston

Schulterblatt

Bullerei

Mövenpick
Hotel Hamburg

Lagerstr.

Junggiusstrasse

Stresemannstrasse

SCHANZENVIERTEL

3

Kielerstrasse

Gastwerk Hotel
Hamburg

25hours Hotel
Number One

B.D.
Kirchhöfen

Bernstorffstrasse

Lerchenstr.

Schanzenstrasse

Karolinenstrasse

Holstenglacis

Gorch

Max-Brauer-Allee

Thadenstr.

Wohlwillstr.

Neuer
Kamp

U

Feldstrasse

Mess

Chemnitzstr.

Budapesterstr.

Nil

FELDSTR.

Karl-Muck-
Platz

4

Holstenstrasse

Paulinen-
pl.

Heiligengeistfeld

Biltrothstr.

Kl. Freiheit

Clemens

Wohlwill-
str.

Glacischaussee

Grosse
Wallanlagen

Holstenwall

Hütten Plutusbool

Schombergstr.

Restaurant
Eisenstein

Simon von Utrechtstr.

Schultzstr.

ST. PAULI

Neander-
str.

Adina
Apartment
Hotel

Louise-Schroederstr.

east
Hotel

Holstenwall

Hütten

5

Königstrasse

REEPERBAHN

S

Detlev Bremerstr.

Millerntorpl.

Motel One
am Michel

Ludwig-Erhard-Str.

Neuer Steinweg

ALTONA

Hamburger-
Hocht-str.

Reeperbahn

ST. PAULI

Hein-Hoyer-
Str.

Davidstr.

Spielbudenpl.

Elb
Park

Gerstäckerstr.

ST. MICHAELIS KIRCHE

Pepermöhlenbek

Langest.

Hopfenstr.

Talstr.weg

 R. steinweg

Böhmkenstr.

Abendmahl

Seewartenstr.

Hotel Louis C. Jacob

Bernhard-Nacht-Str.

Empire
Riverside
Hotel

Rothesoodstr.

Au Quai

River
Kasematten

St.-Pauli-Hafenstr.

Hotel Hafen
Hamburg

Venusberg

Schaar
steinweg

Martin-Luther-str.

Fischereihafen Restaurant
Hamburg

Gerhardstr.

S

U

Ditmar Koelstr.

Werkstr.

Neuweg

Neust.

Strübbenhuk

Landhaus Scherrer

6

i

LANDUNGS-
BRÜCKEN

Johannis Bollwerk

Rive

Seven Seas

Vorsetzen Baumwall

Elbe

0   1/2 mile

0   1/2 kilometer

Das Feuerschiff

ST. PAULI AND SCHANZENVIERTEL

$$ ⚔ **Abendmahl.** On a quiet square off the Reeperbahn, Abendmahl is a
ECLECTIC great launching point for a night out on the town. Candlelight, wooden
tables, and deep red decor set the tone. Relaxed yet romantic, it's the
type of place where you can show up in everything from jeans and a
T-shirt to a suit, and still get the same attentive service. In addition to
a small selection of primarily Mediterranean and northern German
dishes on the à la carte menu, there's also a four-course menu that
changes daily. ⑤ *Average main: €19* ✉ *Hein-Köllisch-Pl. 6, St. Pauli*
☎ *040/312–758* ⊕ *www.restaurantabendmahl.de* ▭ *No credit cards*
☾ *No lunch* Ⓜ *Reeperbahn (S-bahn)* ✛ *B6.*

$$$ ⚔ **Bullerei.** The success of this extremely popular café and restaurant
STEAKHOUSE derives from being owned and run by celebrity chef Tim Mälzer (an old
colleague and friend of Jamie Oliver) and its menu's heavy emphasis
on meat. The stripped-down interior with exposed brick and pipes is
inside a former livestock hall in the heart of the Schanze. Every night,
the busy but friendly waitstaff ferries large plates of steak and pork to
tables, while diners dig into bowls of lamb bolognese in the white-tiled
"deli" next door. ▮**TIP**➜ If you can't get a table, grab a place at the
busy bar and eat there instead. ⑤ *Average main: €24* ✉ *Lagerstr. 34
B, Schanzenviertel* ☎ *040/3344–2100* ⊕ *www.bullerei.com* ⚖ *Reservations essential* ☾ *No lunch* Ⓜ *Sternschanze (U-bahn and S-bahn).*

$$$ ⚔ **Juwelier.** Despite its luxurious name ("Jeweler"), this excellent little
MODERN restaurant not far from Schanzenpark is simply laid out. Its wood tables
EUROPEAN are covered in white tablecloths, and the cream-color walls are gently
lit by art deco lampshades. The food, however, is anything but plain.
Diners can order enticing dishes that include chicken with asparagus,
strawberries, and wild herbs, or turbot with mashed peas and bacon.
There are also three- or four-course prix-fixe menus. ⑤ *Average main:
€21* ✉ *Weidenallee 27, Schanzenviertel* ☎ *040/2548–1678* ⊕ *www.
juwelier-restaurant.de* ▭ *No credit cards* ☾ *No lunch* Ⓜ *Christuskirche
(U-bahn), Sternschanze (U-bahn and S-bahn).*

$$$ ⚔ **Mess.** This is one of the most popular restaurants in the hip Karolinen-
GERMAN viertel (called "Karo-Viertel" by Hamburgers). It serves wild flavors like
Fodor's Choice *Thunfisch-Mangostapel mit Grüne Tomatenmarmelade, Pak Choi und*
★ *Jasminreis* (a tower of tuna and mango with green-tomato chutney served
with bok choi and jasmine rice) along with more traditional German
fare such as Wiener schnitzel and *Bratkartoffeln* (fried potatoes). For
lunch, order the two-course lunch menu (€20) or the pasta special for €9.
▮**TIP**➜ In summer, try to get a table in the small garden under the per-
gola and sample vintages from the restaurant's own wine store. ⑤ *Average main: €25* ✉ *Turnerstr. 9, Schanzenviertel* ☎ *040/4325–0152* ⊕ *www.
mess.de* ☾ *Closed Sun. No lunch Sat.* Ⓜ *Feldstrasse (U-bahn)* ✛ *C4.*

$$$ ⚔ **Nil.** The simple but cool style, excellent service, and high-quality food
GERMAN at this busy bistro keep the locals coming back. The focus is on seafood
and modern German dishes, with seasonal variations using local pro-
duce. Inventive four-course menus merge typical German cuisine with
international flavors. ⑤ *Average main: €21* ✉ *Neuer Pferdemarkt 5, St.
Pauli* ☎ *040/439–7823* ⊕ *www.restaurant-nil.de* ⚖ *Reservations essential*
▭ *No credit cards* ☾ *Closed Tues. No lunch* Ⓜ *Feldstrasse (U-bahn)* ✛ *C4.*

ST. GEORG

$
GERMAN

✕ **Café Gnosa.** Very much a part of Hamburg's gay and lesbian neighborhood, this local favorite has produced delicious desserts and the perfect breakfasts since 1987. It also serves delicious comfort foods like pasta and schnitzel as well as salads. The friendly service and occasional drag performances both add to its popularity. Ⓢ *Average main: €9* ✉ *Lange Reihe 93, St. Georg* ☎ *040/243–034* ⊕ *www. gnosa.de* ✛ *H4.*

$$
GERMAN

✕ **Cox.** Cox has delighted guests with its nouvelle German cuisine for years. It remains one of the hippest places around, but the waitstaff (and the patrons, for that matter) won't give you any attitude. The dishes feature the careful use of fresh produce and spices from around the globe. The simple and cool interior with red-leather banquettes is reminiscent of a French brasserie. Ⓢ *Average main: €19* ✉ *Lange Reihe 68, at Greifswalder Str. 43, St. Georg* ☎ *040/249–422* ⊕ *www.restaurant-cox.de* ◷ *No lunch weekends.* Ⓜ *Gurlittstrasse (Bus No. 6), Hauptbahnhof (U-bahn and S-Bahn)* ✛ *H4.*

$$
MODERN
EUROPEAN
Fodor's Choice
★

✕ **Doria.** At the end of 2010, Doria started drawing adventurous foodlovers to the seedy Hansaplatz. Ignoring the prostitutes and junkies outside, they came for the modern European cuisine that the convivial owner Hasko Sadrina expertly prepared—and for Doria's softly lit, rustic ambience. These days the square isn't quite as sketchy, but the food and service is just as good. You still might have to sidestep the occasional streetwalker, but you'll be rewarded with expertly prepared dishes that include poached salmon with asparagus and wild venison with cranberry sorbet. Ⓢ *Average main: €20* ✉ *Hansapl. 14, St. Georg* ☎ *040/3867–2848* ⊕ *www.doria14.de* ◷ *Closed Mon.* Ⓜ *Hauptbahnhof (U-bahn)* ✛ *H4.*

$$
ITALIAN

✕ **Il Buco.** This neighborhood favorite is easily missed, sitting as it does on a street off Hansaplatz. Intrepid diners must then descend five steps and open a door to the warm and cozy dining room. The atmosphere is definitely more grandmother's living room than downtown trattoria. There's even a sofa-size painting of a cliff perched over water. In place of a menu, a server asks what you are in the mood for, describes the evening's options, and makes recommendations. In a typical evening, a hearty saltimbocca may follow a colorful antipasti plate. Even if you're dining alone, meals are comforting—and they're always quite filling. Ⓢ *Average main: €18* ✉ *Zimmerpforte 5, St. Georg* ☎ *040/247–310* ◷ *Closed Sun. No lunch* Ⓜ *Hauptbahnhof (U-bahn and S-bahn)* ✛ *H4.*

CAFÉ CULTURE

The area around the Alster lakes and the canals is dotted with small restaurants with outside dining and an excellent selection of wine. They make good places to discover a refreshing *Grauburgunder* (pinot gris) while watching swans glide on the canal waters, sample classic French fare, or sip a perfect cup of coffee at one of the cafés sprinkled throughout central Hamburg.

13

SPEICHERSTADT AND HAFENCITY

$$$ ✕ **Carl's an der Elbphilharmonie.** This extension of the Hotel Louis C.
FRENCH Jacob, at the edge of the Elbe and next to the site of the Elbphilharmonie, is a pleasure on many levels. The relaxed Bistro restaurant serves quiche, tartines, and other small dishes. The more formal Brasserie looks like typically Parisian brasserie and features a large bay window with excellent views of ships gliding up the Elbe. The French menu has touches of German flavors and local fish dishes, and service here is warm and knowledgeable. Below the two restaurants sits an elegant bar and the Kultur Salon, with live classical music concerts and jazz performances. Ⓢ *Average main: €25* ✉ *Am Kaiserkai 69, HafenCity* ☎ *40/3003–22400* ⊕ *www.carls-brasserie.de* 🍴 *Reservations essential* ✛ *G6.*

$$$ ✕ **Das Feuerschiff.** This bright-red lightship served in the English Channel before it retired to the city harbor in 1989 and became a landmark restaurant, guesthouse, and pub. Local favorites such as *Hamburger Pannfisch* (panfried fish with mustard sauce) and *Labskaus* (a mixture of corned beef, potato, onion, beet, and, if you're brave, herring) are on the ship's extensive menu, along with Argentinian steaks and Iberian pork. ▦ **TIP➔ Jazz musicians take the stage on Monday, and a variety of bands play a few times a month.** Ⓢ *Average main: €22* ✉ *Vorsetzen, City Sporthafen, Speicherstadt* ☎ *040/362–553* ⊕ *www.das-feuerschiff. de* Ⓜ *Baumwall (U-bahn)* ✛ *D6.*

$$$ ✕ **Vlet.** Inspired by its location inside a Speicherstadt warehouse, this
GERMAN modern restaurant has exposed brick and beams that add a rustic charm to the large dining room and its sleek furniture and lighting. Like the architecture, Vlet's menu combines traditional German methods with new techniques. The restaurant's Labskaus, in a twist on the old Hamburg favorite of beef, potato and beet, is made as a clear soup instead of a stew. The kitchen also offers diverse à la carte menus, including a tasting menu that can be accompanied by corresponding glasses of wine, and the permanent "Durable" menu, which includes beef tartare prepared at the table. Although service is formal, the dining room is relaxed. Ⓢ *Average main: €24* ✉ *Am Sandtorkai 23/24, entrance at Kibbelstegbrücke, Speicherstadt* ☎ *040/3347–53750* ⊕ *www.vlet.de* ◷ *Closed Sun. No lunch Sat.* ✛ *F6*

ALTONA AND OTTENSEN

$$$$ ✕ **Fischereihafen Restaurant Hamburg.** For some of the best fish in Ham-
SEAFOOD burg, book a table at this splendid portside restaurant. Plain from the outside, the restaurant feels like a dining room aboard a luxury liner inside, with oil paintings of nautical scenes hanging on the walls and white linen on the tables. The menu changes daily according to what's available in the fish market that morning; the elegant oyster bar here is a favorite with the city's beau monde. ▦ **TIP➔ In summer, try to get a table on the sun terrace for a great view of the Elbe.** Ⓢ *Average main: €29* ✉ *Grosse Elbstr. 143, Altona* ☎ *040/381–816* ⊕ *www.fischereihafenrestaurant.de* 🍴 *Reservations essential* Ⓜ *Altona (S-bahn)* ✛ *A6.*

13

$$$$ ✕ **Landhaus Scherrer.** Though this establishment is just a 10-minute drive
GERMAN from the center of town, its parklike setting seems worlds away from
Fodor's Choice the high-rise clamor of the city. A proud owner of a Michelin star since
★ it opened its doors in 1978, Landhaus Scherrer continues to be one of
the city's best-known and most celebrated restaurants. The restaurant's
focus is on the use of organic, sustainable ingredients to produce classic
and modern German cuisine with international touches. Wood-panel
walls and soft lighting create a low-key mood in the main building,
which was once a brewery. Unsurprisingly, the accompanying wine list
is exceptional. There's also a small bistro here, where diners can feast
on similar fare at lower prices. For delicious German comfort food
(currywurst and potato salad), try the sister property, Ö1. $ *Average
main: €32* ✉ *Elbchaussee 130, Ottensen* ☎ *040/880–1325* ⊕ *www.
landhausscherrer.de* ⊗ *Closed Sun.* Ⓜ *Hohenzollernring (Bus Nos. 15
and 36), Königstrasse (S-bahn)* ✛ *A6.*

$ ✕ **Restaurant Eisenstein.** A longtime neighborhood favorite, Eisenstein
ITALIAN serves fantastic food at affordable prices. The bubbly and mostly stylish
crowd enjoys the Italian and Mediterranean dishes. The Pizza Helsinki
(made with crème fraîche, onions, and salmon) is truly delicious. The
setting, a 19th-century industrial complex with high ceilings and dark
brick walls, feels very rustic. $ *Average main: €14* ✉ *Friedensallee 9,
Ottensen* ☎ *040/390–4606* ⊕ *www.restaurant-eisenstein.de* ⚥ *Reservations essential* ▭ *No credit cards* Ⓜ *Altona (S-bahn)* ✛ *A5.*

$$$ ✕ **Rive.** This handsome harborside oyster bar is known for both its
SEAFOOD German nouvelle cuisine and its classic local dishes. Media types come
to this shiplike building for the fresh oysters and clams, as well as its
spectacular views. Choose between such dishes as hearty *Matjes mit
dreierlei Saucen* (herring with three sauces) or *Loup de Mer in der
Salzkruste* (European sea bass in a salt crust). $ *Average main: €23*
✉ *Van-der-Smissen-Str. 1, Kreuzfahrt-Center, Altona* ☎ *040/380–5919*
⊕ *www.rive.de* ⚥ *Reservations essential* Ⓜ *Königstrasse (S-bahn)* ✛ *A6.*

BLANKENESE AND ELSEWHERE

$$ ✕ **Vienna.** The trick to getting a table at this much-loved little bistro in
AUSTRIAN Eimsbüttel is to get there early. The kitchen officially opens for busi-
ness at 7, but Vienna opens its doors midafternoon for those wanting
an espresso or aperitif from their tiny bar. Early arrivers might still be
asked to share a table in the dining room or outside in the courtyard
but, given the delicious schnitzels, fresh fish dishes, and hearty deserts
coming out of the kitchen, it will matter little to most. $ *Average main:
€17* ✉ *Fettstr. 2, Eimsbüttel* ☎ *040/439–9182* ⊕ *www.vienna-hamburg.
de* ⚥ *Reservations not accepted* ▭ *No credit cards* ⊗ *Closed Mon. No
lunch* Ⓜ *Christuskirche (U-bahn).*

$$ ✕ **Zipang.** Hamburg may not have that many good Japanese restau-
JAPANESE rants, but this modern bistro-style restaurant is undoubtedly a gem.
It's in the middle of Eppendorfer Weg, a long artery of little eateries
and clothes and jewelry shops between Eppendorf and Eimsbüttel.
Zipang has developed a loyal clientele of locals and Japanese expats
through its warm service and modern interpretation of Japanese
haute cuisine. As well as the typical offerings of sushi and tempura

udon, the menu here features such treats as Wagyu beef with dipping sauces and duck and eggplant in red miso sauce. ■ TIP→ The restaurant has a daily lunch special with a small miso soup and a dessert for around €10. $ *Average main: €18* ✉ *Eppendorfer Weg 171, Eppendorf* ☎ *040/4328–0032* ⊕ *www.zipang.de* ⊗ *Closed Tues. No lunch Sun.* Ⓜ *Hoheluftbrücke (U-bahn).*

$$ ╳ **Genno's.** Genno's is far from the downtown district, in Hamburg-Hamm—a rundown residential area where you would hardly expect to find such a gem of high-quality dining. Chef Eugen Albrecht makes you feel at home with warm service and tasty dishes. The cuisine is a mixture of his personal preferences, including dishes such as *Lammfilet mit Rotweinsauce* (filet of lamb with red-wine sauce). $ *Average main: €16* ✉ *Hammer Steindamm 123, Hamm* ☎ *040/202–567* ⊕ *www.gennos.de* ⊕ *Reservations essential* ▭ *No credit cards* ⊗ *Closed Sun. No lunch* Ⓜ *Hasselbrook (S-bahn)* ✛ *H5.*

ITALIAN

$$$$ ╳ **Seven Seas.** The location of this sophisticated hotel and restaurant complex, a small hill in the countryside along the Elbe, comes with one of the greatest views of the river you'll find anywhere. The Seven Seas' award-winning French kitchen is run by one of Europe's premier chefs, Karlheinz Hauser, and features fish specialties served in three- to five-course dinners. $ *Average main: €36* ✉ *Süllbergsterrasse 12, Blankenese* ☎ *040/8662–5212* ⊕ *www.suellberg-hamburg.de* ⊕ *Reservations essential* ⊗ *Closed Mon. and Tues. No lunch Wed.–Sat.* Ⓜ *Blankenese (S-bahn), Kahlkamp (Bus No. 48)* ✛ *A6.*

FRENCH

WHERE TO STAY

Hamburg has simple pensions as well as five-star luxury enterprises. Nearly year-round conference and convention business keeps most rooms booked well in advance, and the rates are high. But many of the more expensive hotels lower their rates on weekends, when business-people have gone home. The tourist office can help with reservations if you arrive with nowhere to stay. In Hamburg, independent hotels may not have coffeemakers or an information book in the guest rooms, but, in general, you will find generously sized rooms and staffs willing to answer questions about the hotel. Hotels without business centers will fax and copy for you. At hotels without concierges, front-desk staff will whip out a map and give recommendations.

All accommodations offer no-smoking rooms. Although breakfast is not usually included, those who opt for the meal are usually greeted with an all-you-can-eat masterpiece with hot food options that sometimes includes an omelet station.

Keep in mind that you'll probably encounter nudity in coed saunas at most hotels. Also, most double beds are made of two single beds on a large platform and an individual blanket for each mattress.

Prices in the reviews are the lowest cost of a standard double room in high season. For expanded reviews, facilities, and current deals, visit Fodors.com. Use the coordinate (✛ B3) at the end of each listing to locate a site on the corresponding map.

BEST BETS FOR HAMBURG LODGING

Fodor'sChoice★

east Hotel, $$$, p. 618

Fairmont Vier Jahreszeiten, $$$$, p. 616

Hotel Louis C. Jacob, $$$$, p. 621

Le Royal Méridien Hamburg, $$$, p. 620

Park Hyatt Hamburg, $$$$, p. 617

By Price

$

fritzhotel, p. 618

Hotel Village, p. 619

YoHo, p. 621

$$

Empire Riverside Hotel, P. 618

Henri Hotel, p. 617

SIDE, p. 618

$$$

east Hotel, p. 618

Le Royal Méridien Hamburg, p. 620

$$$$

Fairmont Vier Jahreszeiten, p. 616

Hotel Louis C. Jacob, p. 621

Park Hyatt Hamburg, p. 617

By Experience

BEST BEDS

Le Royal Méridien Hamburg, $$$, p. 620

Sofitel Hamburg Alter Wall, $$$, p. 618

BEST GRANDE DAMES

Fairmont Vier Jahreszeiten, $$$$, p. 616

Hotel Atlantic Kempinski Hamburg, $$$$, p. 619

BEST FOR KIDS

Lindner Park-Hotel Hagenbeck, $$, p. 621

Park Hyatt Hamburg, $$$$, p. 617

BEST VIEW

Empire Riverside Hotel, $$, p. 618

Radisson Blu Hotel, Hamburg, $$ p. 617

ALTSTADT AND NEUSTADT

$$ ⊡ **Adina Apartment Hotel Hamburg Michel.** The Adina is less like a hotel
HOTEL and more like an apartment swap involving some really cool friends.
Pros: excellent location; huge guest rooms with many amenities; free
Wi-Fi in public spaces. **Cons:** indoor pool area is small and can be
rowdy; Wi-Fi fee in guest rooms. $ *Rooms from: €129 ⊠ Neuer Stein-
weg 26, Altstadt* ☎ *040/226–3500* ⊕ *www.adina.eu* ⤶ *128 apartments*
⎮◯⎮*No meals* Ⓜ *Stadhausbrücke (S-bahn)* ✛ *D5.*

$$$$ ⊡ **Fairmont Vier Jahreszeiten.** Some claim that this beautiful 19th-cen-
HOTEL tury town house on the edge of the Binnenalster is the best hotel in
Fodor'sChoice Germany. **Pros:** luxury hotel with great view of Alster lakes; close
★ to shopping on Jungfernstieg; large, charming rooms. **Cons:** high
prices even in off-season; not much in way of nightlife outside of the
hotel. $ *Rooms from: €395 ⊠ Neuer Jungfernstieg 9–14, Neustadt*
☎ *040/34940* ⊕ *www.fairmont-hvj.de* ⤶ *123 rooms, 33 suites* ⎮◯⎮*No
meals* Ⓜ *Jungfernstieg (U-bahn)* ✛ *F4.*

$$$ ⊡ **Grand Elysée Hamburg.** The "grand" at the Grand Elysée Hamburg
HOTEL refers to its size, from the near 11,000-square-foot wellness area
and five restaurants to the 511 guest rooms and extra-wide beds.
Pros: large guest rooms; close to tourist sites; diverse art throughout
hotel; free Wi-Fi. **Cons:** rooms are rather plain; busy public spaces.

$ Rooms from: €200 ⌧ Rothenbaumchaussee 10, Altstadt ☎ 040/414–120 ⊕ www.grand-elysee.com ⤴ 494 rooms, 17 suites ⁌ No meals Ⓜ Dammtor (S-bahn) ⊹ F3.

$$ ⌕ **Henri Hotel.** Concealed down a side street not far from the main sta-
HOTEL tion, this small boutique hotel, with its retro-styled rooms, furniture, and phones, will undoubtedly please fans of film noir and *Mad Men*. **Pros:** inti-mate, friendly service; very quiet; excellent house cocktail; stylish black-and white-tiled bathrooms. **Cons:** may seem a little masculine for some tastes; on an otherwise uninspiring side street; limited nightlife in the area. $ Rooms from: €118 ⌧ Bugenhagenstr. 21, Altstadt ☎ 040/554–3570 ⊕ www.henri-hotel.com ⤴ 65 rooms ⁌ No meals Ⓜ Hauptbahnhof (U-bahn and S-bahn), Mönckebergstrasse (U-bahn) ⊹ C5.

$$ ⌕ **Hotel Baseler Hof.** It's hard to find fault with this handsome central
HOTEL hotel near the Binnenalster and the opera house; the service is friendly and efficient, the rooms are neatly albeit plainly furnished, and the prices are reasonable for such an expensive city. **Pros:** directly across from the casino; walking distance from Dammtor train station. **Cons:** small rooms; rooms at the front of the hotel face onto a busy street. $ Rooms from: €154 ⌧ Esplanade 11, Neustadt ☎ 040/359–060 ⊕ www.baselerhof.de ⤴ 176 rooms, 8 suites ⁌ No meals Ⓜ Stepha-nsplatz (U-bahn) ⊹ F4.

$$ ⌕ **Hotel Fürst Bismarck.** Despite its slightly sketchy location on a busy
HOTEL street opposite the Hauptbahnhof, the Fürst Bismarck is a surpris-ingly attractive hotel that feels homey yet contemporary. **Pros:** cen-trally located; competitive prices; free pass for public transportation. **Cons:** basic bathrooms; small rooms; small additional fee for Wi-Fi. $ Rooms from: €129 ⌧ Kirchenallee 49, Altstadt ☎ 040/280–1091 ⊕ www.fuerstbismarck.de ⤴ 102 rooms ⁌ No meals Ⓜ Hauptbahn-hof (U-bahn and S-bahn) ⊹ H5.

$ ⌕ **Motel One Am Michel.** This branch of the Motel One chain is ideal for
HOTEL those looking for a trendy, design-minded, central yet inexpensive base. **Pros:** close to the best nightlife in town; bar open 24 hours; free Wi-Fi. **Cons:** no amenities; no restaurant; small rooms. $ Rooms from: €84 ⌧ Ludwig-Erhard-Str. 26, Altstadt ☎ 040/3571–8900 ⊕ www.motel-one.com ⤴ 437 rooms ⁌ No meals ⊹ D5.

$$$$ ⌕ **Park Hyatt Hamburg.** Housed within the historic Levantehaus, a luxury
HOTEL mall on the city's main shopping drag, the Park Hyatt delivers the hospi-
Fodor's Choice tality and comfort expected of one of Germany's best hotels, with plush
★ beds, marble bathrooms, and peace and quiet. **Pros:** close to museums; warm interior design; large, quiet rooms with all modern amenities; friendly and helpful service. **Cons:** area can feel dead on Sunday, when all the stores are closed; far from most nightlife. $ Rooms from: €235 ⌧ Bugenhagenstr. 8, Neustadt ☎ 040/3332–1234 ⊕ www.hamburg.park.hyatt.com ⤴ 176 rooms, 21 suites, 31 apartments ⁌ No meals Ⓜ Mönckebergstrasse (U-bahn) ⊹ G5.

$$ ⌕ **Radisson Blu Hotel, Hamburg.** There's no missing the black glass and
HOTEL gray concrete form of the Radisson Blu, which towers 100 meters above Dammtor train station, with sweeping views of Planten un Blomen and the city. **Pros:** some of the best views in town; very stylish; next to a major train station; ladies-only sauna. **Cons:** small gym; sleeping area

13

has a window into bathroom, and the blinds are controlled from outside the bathroom; few good restaurants in immediate area. ⑤ *Rooms from: €175* ⌧ *Marseiller Str. 2, Neustadt* ☎ *040/35020* ⊕ *www.radissonblu. de* ↩ *556 rooms, 9 suites* ⑩ *No meals* Ⓜ *Dammtor (S-bahn)* ✛ *E3.*

$$
HOTEL

🏨 **SIDE.** Futuristic, minimalistic—call it what you like, but this hip five-star hotel has been a byword for inner city cool since its opening in 2001. **Pros:** Nespresso pod coffeemakers in rooms; convenient but quiet location. **Cons:** some might find decor sterile; most guest rooms lack views. ⑤ *Rooms from: €160* ⌧ *Drehbahn 49, Neustadt* ☎ *040/309–990* ⊕ *www.side-hamburg.de* ↩ *168 rooms, 10 suites* ⑩ *No meals* Ⓜ *Gänsemarkt (U-bahn)* ✛ *E4.*

$$$
HOTEL

🏨 **Sofitel Hamburg Alter Wall.** Behind the facade of a centrally located, former Deutsche Post building hides the sleek décor and famously comfortable beds of one of the city's finest business hotels. **Pros:** in the historic downtown area; close to luxury shops; large rooms. **Cons:** somewhat cold design; no real nightlife within walking distance. ⑤ *Rooms from: €215* ⌧ *Alter Wall 40, Altstadt* ☎ *040/369–500* ⊕ *www.sofitel.com* ↩ *223 rooms, 18 suites* ⑩ *No meals* Ⓜ *Rödingsmarkt (U-bahn)* ✛ *F6.*

ST. PAULI AND SCHANZENVIERTEL

$$
HOTEL

🏨 **The Boston.** Taking its cue from the funky Sternschanze neighborhood where it's located, The Boston is ultramodern and sleek, and its small staff works hard for its mostly business clientele. **Pros:** the design is chic and comfortable; staff is very helpful; close to great bars and restaurants. **Cons:** no a/c (the hotel has some fans for guests); windows open but noise from street traffic can be a problem. ⑤ *Rooms from: €160* ⌧ *Missundestr. 2, Schanzenviertel* ☎ *040/5896–66700* ⊕ *www.boston-hamburg.de* ↩ *34 rooms, 12 suites* ⑩ *No meals* Ⓜ *Holstenstrasse (S-bahn)* ✛ *B3.*

$$
HOTEL

🏨 **Empire Riverside Hotel.** The location near the Reeperbahn and the harbor, the clever use of space and light, and a cool bar that attracts thousands every weekend make the Empire a favorite. **Pros:** close to nightlife; excellent view of the city and river; bright rooms; free Wi-Fi. **Cons:** a steep hill separates the hotel from the harbor; top-floor bar gets crowded after 9 pm on weekends. ⑤ *Rooms from: €159* ⌧ *Bernhard-Nocht-Stra. 97, St. Pauli* ☎ *040/311–190* ⊕ *www.empire-riverside.de* ↩ *315 rooms, 12 suites* ⑩ *No meals* Ⓜ *Reeperbahn (S-bahn)* ✛ *B6.*

$$$
HOTEL
Fodor's Choice
★

🏨 **east Hotel.** Not content to limit itself to merely being a place to sleep, this chic landmark hotel combines a buzzing cocktail bar with a similarly trendy sushi and steak restaurant to create one of the hottest spots in town. **Pros:** unique; popular nightclub on third floor (Friday and Saturday only); excellent service. **Cons:** a small fee for the gym after 6 pm; parking garage is removed from main building; area around the hotel can be frenetic on weekends. ⑤ *Rooms from: €190* ⌧ *Simon-von-Utrecht-Str. 31, St. Pauli* ☎ *040/309-930* ⊕ *www.east-hamburg.de* ↩ *122 rooms, 6 suites* ⑩ *No meals* Ⓜ *St Pauli (U-bahn)* ✛ *C5.*

$
HOTEL

🏨 **fritzhotel.** Squeezed into an old apartment building in the center of the Schanzenviertel, the hotel has small but modern and comfortable rooms that are best for those who just want somewhere good to lay their head for a night or two. **Pros:** tidy, clean rooms for reasonable prices; the S- and U-bahn are across the street. **Cons:** noisy due to the S-bahn tracks; area crowded on weekend nights; can be difficult to find a parking place near the hotel. ⑤ *Rooms from: €97* ✉ *Schanzenstr. 101–103, Schanzenviertel* ☎ *040/8222–2830* ⊕ *www.fritzhotel.com* ⥱ *15 rooms* ⍟ *No meals* Ⓜ *Sternschanze (U-bahn and S-bahn)* ✛ *C3.*

$$ 🛏 **Hotel Hafen Hamburg.** This harbor landmark, just across from the
HOTEL famous St. Pauli Landungsbrücken, is a good value considering its four-star status. **Pros:** top location for harbor and St. Pauli sightseeing; great views; comfortable, fairly large rooms; free Wi-Fi. **Cons:** smoking allowed in Tower Bar; poor restaurant selection in immediate neighborhood; a bit of a climb to reach hotel from the pier. ⑤ *Rooms from: €120* ✉ *Seewartenstr. 7–9, St. Pauli* ☎ *040/311–130* ⊕ *www.hotel-hafen-hamburg.de* ⥱ *380 rooms* ⍟ *No meals* Ⓜ *Landungsbrücken (U-bahn)* ✛ *C6.*

$$ 🛏 **Mövenpick Hotel Hamburg.** For its Hamburg outpost, the Mövenpick
HOTEL chain transformed a 19th-century water tower on a hill in the middle of the leafy Schanzenpark into a state-of-the-art business hotel. **Pros:** in the middle of a quiet park; unique building; amazing views from upper floors; English-language newspaper available in restaurant. **Cons:** paid Wi-Fi in some guest rooms; some lower level rooms have ordinary views. ⑤ *Rooms from: €139* ✉ *Sternschanze 6, Schanzenviertel* ☎ *040/334–4110* ⊕ *www.moevenpick-hamburg.com* ⥱ *226 rooms, 10 suites* ⍟ *No meals* Ⓜ *Sternschanze (U-bahn and S-bahn)* ✛ *C3.*

ST. GEORG

$$$ 🛏 **The George Hotel.** At the end of a strip of funky cafés and bars, the
HOTEL George, with its groovy New British styling, fits right in; despite the sleek look and the hip guests, the staff is eager to please. **Pros:** free Wi-Fi; DJs play in the hotel on weekends; a stone's throw from the Alster. **Cons:** can be noisy, particularly for guests on the first floor; some may find the design unwelcoming. ⑤ *Rooms from: €185* ✉ *Barcastr. 3, St. Georg* ☎ *040/280–0300* ⊕ *www.thegeorge-hotel.de* ⥱ *118 rooms, 7 suites* ⍟ *No meals* Ⓜ *Hauptbahnhof (U-bahn and S-bahn), AK St. Georg (Bus No. 6)* ✛ *H3.*

$ 🛏 **Hotel Village.** Near the central train station and once a thriving
HOTEL brothel, this hotel and its red-and-black carpets, glossy wallpaper, and dinky chandeliers still exudes lasciviousness. **Pros:** in the heart of downtown; individually designed rooms; fun decor; free coffee at reception. **Cons:** sometimes casual service; although it's slowly being gentrified, the neighborhood remains a little seedy. ⑤ *Rooms from: €85* ✉ *Steindamm 4, St. Georg* ☎ *040/480–6490* ⊕ *www.hotel-village.de* ⥱ *20 rooms, 3 suites, 4 apartments* ⍟ *No meals* Ⓜ *Hauptbahnhof (U-bahn and S-bahn)* ✛ *H5.*

$$$$ 🛏 **Hotel Atlantic Kempinski Hamburg.** There are few hotels in Germany
HOTEL more sumptuous than this gracious Edwardian palace facing the Aussenalster, which draws both celebrities and the not-so-famous searching for a luxe retreat. **Pros:** large rooms; great views of lakeside skyline; impeccable service; historic flair; free Wi-Fi throughout the hotel. **Cons:** public areas can be crowded; faces onto a busy thoroughfare. ⑤ *Rooms from: €229* ✉ *An der Alster 72–79, St. Georg* ☎ *040/28880* ⊕ *www.kempinski.com* ⥱ *215 rooms, 30 suites* ⍟ *No meals* Ⓜ *Hauptbahnhof (U-bahn and S-bahn)* ✛ *G4.*

$$$ ⬚ **Le Royal Méridien Hamburg.** This luxury hotel along the Alster offers
HOTEL you beauty inside and outside its walls. **Pros:** great location with views
Fodor'sChoice of the Alster; smartly designed, large rooms; outstanding pool area;
★ Wi-Fi free in lobby. **Cons:** pricey Wi-Fi; top-floor bar and restaurant can
get crowded. $ *Rooms from: €189* ✉ *An der Alster 52–56, St. Georg*
☎ *040/21000* ⊕ *www.leroyalmeridienhamburg.com* ⤳ *265 rooms, 19*
suites ⦿ *No meals* Ⓜ *Hauptbahnhof (U-bahn and S-bahn)* ✛ *H4.*

$ ⬚ **Steen's Hotel.** This small, family-run hotel in a four-story town house
HOTEL near the central train station provides modest but congenial service.
Pros: highly competitive prices; good breakfast; friendly service. **Cons:**
rooms fairly plain; few amenities and hotel services; no elevator; fee for
Wi-Fi. $ *Rooms from: €85* ✉ *Holzdamm 43, St. Georg* ☎ *040/244–642*
⊕ *www.steens-hotel.com* ⤳ *15 rooms* ⦿ *Breakfast* Ⓜ *Hauptbahnhof*
(U-bahn and S-bahn) ✛ *H4.*

$$ ⬚ **Wedina.** A laid-back oasis in the bustling neighborhood of St. Georg,
HOTEL this unique small hotel is spread over four different buildings a short
amble from the outer Alster. **Pros:** cozy, comfortable, and quiet rooms;
very accommodating; knowledgeable staff; free Wi-Fi throughout hotel;
great breakfast. **Cons:** hotel spread over several buildings; smallish
rooms. $ *Rooms from: €145* ✉ *Gurlittstr. 23, St. Georg* ☎ *040/280–*
8900 ⊕ *www.wedina.de* ⤳ *46 rooms, 13 apartments* ⦿ *Breakfast*
Ⓜ *Hauptbahnhof (U-bahn and S-bahn), Gurlittstrasse (Bus No. 6)* ✛ *H4.*

SPEICHERSTADT AND HAFENCITY

$$ ⬚ **25Hours Hotel HafenCity.** Although the trendy 25hours Hotel HafenCity
HOTEL is a little more kitsch than absolutely necessary, it does take guests on a fun
trip back to Hamburg's maritime past. **Pros:** cool design; up-and-coming
part of town; free Wi-Fi. **Cons:** trendy decor might be too trendy for some;
not a lot of other nightlife options within walking distance. $ *Rooms from:*
€125 ✉ *Überseeallee 5, Speicherstadt* ☎ *040/257–7770* ⊕ *www.25hours-*
hotels.com ⤳ *170 rooms* Ⓜ *Überseequartier (U-bahn)* ✛ *G6.*

ALTONA AND OTTENSEN

$$ ⬚ **25hours Hotel Number One.** Packing fun and retro design into a relaxed
HOTEL package that includes beanbag chairs, shag carpets, and bold wall-
papers, this is the type of place for travelers seeking something a bit
different. **Pros:** free Wi-Fi; shopping center and supermarket nearby.
Cons: removed from the city center; a 10-minute walk to the nearest train station. $ *Rooms from: €135* ✉ *2 Paul-Dessau-Str., Altona*
☎ *040/855–070* ⊕ *www.25hours-hotels.com* ⤳ *128 rooms* ⦿ *No*
meals Ⓜ *Bahrenfeld (S-bahn)* ✛ *A3.*

$$ ⬚ **Gastwerk Hotel Hamburg.** Proudly dubbing itself Hamburg's first
HOTEL design hotel, the Gastwerk, named after the 100-year-old gasworks
housed inside, is certainly one of the most stylish places to stay in town.
Pros: large and well-equipped health club; free use of a MINI car. **Cons:**
removed from downtown area and most sightseeing spots; breakfast
room, bar and other public spaces can get crowded. $ *Rooms from: €160*
✉ *Beim Alten Gaswerk 3, Altona* ☎ *040/890–620* ⊕ *www.gastwerk.com*
⤳ *127 rooms, 14 suites* ⦿ *No meals* Ⓜ *Bahrenfeld (S-bahn)* ✛ *A3.*

BLANKENESE AND ELSEWHERE

$$$$
HOTEL
Fodor's Choice
★

🏨 **Hotel Louis C. Jacob.** Those who make the effort to travel 20 minutes from the center of town to this small yet luxurious hotel perched above Elbe will gain a mixture of sophistication, Michelin-starred dining, and fine Hanseatic hospitality. **Pros:** outstanding service with attention to personal requests; quiet, serene setting; historic building; extremely comfortable beds. **Cons:** lounge is a little stuffy; away from downtown area and most nightlife, restaurants, and shopping; expensive. $ *Rooms from: €275* ✉ *Elbchausee 401–403, Blankenese* ☎ *040/822–550* ⊕ *www.hotel-jacob.de* 🛏 *66 rooms, 19 suites* ⦿ *No meals* Ⓜ *Hochkamp (S-bahn)* ✛ *A6.*

$$
HOTEL
FAMILY

🏨 **Lindner Park-Hotel Hagenbeck.** Everything at this hotel is aimed at transporting you from metropolitan Hamburg to the wilds of Asia and Africa. **Pros:** smartly designed Africa and Asia theme carried throughout hotel; a/c in guest rooms; good restaurants. **Cons:** removed from the city center; not much else going on in the immediate area; fee for Wi-Fi. $ *Rooms from: €149* ✉ *Hagenbeckstr. 150* ☎ *040/8008–08100* ⊕ *www.lindner.de* 🛏 *151 rooms, 7 suites* ⦿ *No meals* Ⓜ *Hagenbecks Tierpark (U-bahn)* ✛ *A1.*

$$
HOTEL

🏨 **Nippon Hotel.** You'll be asked to remove your shoes before entering your room at this small but welcoming Japanese-style hotel, where tatami mats line the floor and shoji blinds cover the windows. **Pros:** quiet, residential neighborhood; a/c in guest rooms; free Wi-Fi throughout hotel. **Cons:** location removed from major sightseeing sights; limited parking. $ *Rooms from: €126* ✉ *Hofweg 75, Uhlenhorst* ☎ *040/227–1140* ⊕ *www.nipponhotel.de* 🛏 *41 rooms, 1 suite* ⦿ *No meals* Ⓜ *Mundsburg (U-bahn), Zimmerstrasse (Bus No. 6)* ✛ *H4.*

$
HOTEL

🏨 **YoHo.** Housed in a historic villa that's an easy walk from the Schanzenviertel, this friendly, modern little hotel was originally designed and priced to attract a young, cosmopolitan crowd, but lots of others head here, too. **Pros:** quiet neighborhood; free Wi-Fi throughout hotel; free parking. **Cons:** sometimes noisy due to young travelers; removed from all major sightseeing sights. $ *Rooms from: €99* ✉ *Moorkamp 5, Eimsbüttel* ☎ *040/284–1910* ⊕ *www.yoho-hamburg.de* 🛏 *30 rooms* ⦿ *No meals* Ⓜ *Christuskirche (U-bahn), Schlump (U-bahn)* ✛ *C2.*

NIGHTLIFE AND THE ARTS

THE ARTS

The arts flourish in this cosmopolitan city. Hamburg's ballet company is one of the finest in Europe, and the Hamburger Ballett-Tage, its annual festival, brings the best from around the world to Hamburg.

At the end of September, the city comes alive with movie showings. The Hamburg Film Festival features the best feature films, documentary, short films, and children's movies. About 80% of the films are in English or have English subtitles. For two weeks, thousands of people watch mainstream and quirky films in various theaters around town.

13

Information on all major events are available on the Hamburg Tourism Office website. ▮TIP➜ The best way to order tickets for all major Hamburg theaters, musicals, and most cultural events is through the Hamburg-Hotline (☎ 040/3005–1300).

Funke Konzertkassen. Hamburg's largest ticket seller has box offices throughout Hamburg, including one at Dammtor train station with English-speaking agents. The website is only in German, but a ticket hotline will connect you with English-speaking representatives. ✉ *Dammtorbahnhof, Dag-Hammarskjöldpl., Neustadt* ☎ *040/663–661* ⊕ *www.funke-ticket.de.*

Hamburg.de. The city's official website is a good source for information about cultural and arts events going on in the city. Just click the "What's on" tab. ⊕ *www.english.hamburg.de.*

Landungsbrücken. A number of agencies, including the Hamburg tourist office at Landungsbrücken, sell tickets for plays, concerts, and the ballet. ✉ *Between Piers 4 and 5, between Brücke 4 and 5, St. Pauli* ☎ *040/3005–1300* ⊕ *www.hamburg-travel.com.*

BALLET AND OPERA

Hamburgische Staatsoper. One of the most beautiful theaters in the country, the Hamburgische Staatsoper is the leading northern German venue for opera and ballet. The Hamburg Ballet is directed by the American John Neumeier. ✉ *Grosse Theaterstr. 25, Neustadt* ☎ *040/356–868* ⊕ *www.hamburgische-staatsoper.de.*

TUI Operettenhaus. The TUI Operettenhaus stages productions of top musicals. A musical adaptation of *Rocky* has called the theater home since November 2011. Tour of the theater are also available. ✉ *Spielbudenpl. 1, St. Pauli* ☎ *01805/4444 for tickets* ⊕ *www.stage-entertainment.de.*

CONCERTS

Laeiszhalle. Both the Philharmoniker Hamburg (Hamburg Philharmonic) and the Hamburger Symphoniker (Hamburg Symphony) appear regularly in the magnificent neo-baroque interior of the Laeiszhalle, which also hosts international orchestras and some of the biggest names in contemporary music. ✉ *Johannes-Brahms-Pl., Neustadt* ☎ *040/3576–6666* ⊕ *www.elbphilharmonie.de.*

FILM

Abaton. Mainstream, art-house, and independent films are shown at this comfy, three-screen movie theater next to the University of Hamburg. ✉ *Allendepl. 3, Neustadt* ☎ *040/320–320* ⊕ *www.abaton.de.*

Savoy Filmtheater. The Savoy's a fantastic, old-school movie theater with impressive modern features that include high-quality sound and enormous, reclinable leather seats. It shows mainstream and independent movies in English. ✉ *Steindamm 54, St. Georg* ☎ *040/2840–93628* ⊕ *www.savoy-filmtheater.de.*

THEATER

Ticket and theater information is available at ⊕ *www.stage-entertainment. de* or by calling ☎ *01805/4444.*

Deutsches Schauspielhaus. One of Germany's leading drama stages, Deutsches Schauspielhaus has been lavishly restored to its full 19th-century opulence. It's the most important venue in town for classical and modern theater. ✉ *Kirchenallee 39, St. Georg* ☎ *040/248–710* ⊕ *www.schauspielhaus.de.*

English Theatre of Hamburg. The name says it all: the English Theatre, first opened in 1976, is the city's premier theater for works in English. Actors from near and far bring contemporary and classic drama to life on the small stage of this historic building. ✉ *Lerchenfeld 14, Uhlenhorst* ☎ *040/227–7089* ⊕ *www.englishtheatre.de.*

Neue Flora Theater. Handily located just across the street from the Holstenstrasse S-bahn, the 2,000-seat Neuer Flora attracts big crowds, who come for popular, long-running musicals such as *Tarzan* and *The Phantom of the Opera.* ✉ *Stresemannstr. 159a, at Alsenstr., Schanzenviertel* ☎ *01805/4444 for tickets, 040/4316–5133 for theater* ⊕ *www. stage-entertainment.de.*

NIGHTLIFE

ALTSTADT AND NEUSTADT
JAZZ AND LIVE MUSIC

Cotton Club. A visit to the Cotton Club, Hamburg's oldest jazz club, is worth it for the house beer alone. Throw in the club's relaxed vibe and nights devoted to jazz, blues, soul and Dixieland, and it's not difficult to find a reason to drop in. ✉ *Alter Steinweg 10, Neustadt* ☎ *040/343–878* ⊕ *www.cotton-club.de.*

ST. PAULI AND SCHANZENVIERTEL

Whether you think it sexy or gross, the Reeperbahn, in the St. Pauli District, is as important to the Hamburg scene as the classy shops along Jungfernstieg. On nearby Grosse Freiheit you'll find a number of the better-known dance clubs. Hans-Elber-Platz has a cluster of bars, some with live music.

BARS

Hamburg has many buzzy and upscale bars, with many spots that feature live music or DJs and dancing.

20 Up at the Empire Riverside Hotel. For a smooth cocktail, cool lounge music, and amazingly good views over the city and harbor, try this bar, which is one of the most popular nightspots in town. It's best to book ahead. ✉ *Bernhard-Nocht-Str. 97, St. Pauli* ☎ *040/31119–70470* ⊕ *www.empire-riverside.de.*

Christiansen's. The cozy Christiansen's Fine Drinks & Cocktails, a short distance from the Fischmarkt, mixes some of the best cocktails in town. ✉ *Pinnasberg 60, St. Pauli* ☎ *040/317–2863* ⊕ *www.christiansens.de.*

HIP AND HAPPENING NIGHTLIFE

People flock to Hamburg for shopping, but there's much more to experience come nightfall. The city has plenty of places where you can hop from bar to bar or lounge to lounge. Here are some of the most fun streets in Hamburg:

Grindelallee and side streets in the Univiertel: Home to the Universität der Hamburg, the quarter, with its mix of affordable cafés and Asian and Middle Eastern restaurants, is popular with students and townies alike.

Grosse Elbstrasse in Altona: This is the home of the Altona Fischmarkt and a variety of popular riverside restaurants and bars.

Grossneumarkt: This square is packed with comfortable, relaxing pubs and German restaurants. In summer it's a popular meeting point for Hamburgers who want to sit outside and eat and drink in relaxed surroundings.

Reeperbahn, Grosse Freiheit, and the streets around Spielbudenplatz in St. Pauli: This sinful mile has everything—strip clubs, pubs, live music, dive bars, and nightclubs. It's loud and crazy and fun just to walk up and down the streets.

Schanzenstrasse in Sternschanze: Hipsters flock to this compact row of buzzing bars and laid-back lounges that pour onto the sidewalk when the weather is warm.

Mandalay. This is one of several upscale, sleek bars catering to thirty-somethings that are in and around St. Pauli and Sternschanze. ⊠ *Neuer Pferdemarkt 13, Schanzenviertel* ☎ *040/4321–4922* ⊕ *www.mandalay.tv.*

Tower Bar at Hotel Hafen Hamburg. The view from this bar that's almost 200 feet up, on top of a riverside hotel, makes it an ideal spot to sip cocktails and watch the sun go down—particularly if you're a smoker. ⊠ *Seewartenstr. 9, St. Pauli* ☎ *040/31113–70450* ⊕ *www.hotel-hafen-hamburg.de.*

Yakshi's Bar at the East Hotel. With its combination of exposed brickwork, soft lighting, and soothing, curvy shapes—not to mention a drink list that runs to over 250 drinks—it's little wonder that this popular cocktail bar draws fashionable people of all ages. ⊠ *Simon-von-Utrecht-Str. 31, St. Pauli* ☎ *040/309–930* ⊕ *www.east-hamburg.de.*

CABARET THEATER
Schmidts Theater and Schmidts Tivoli. The quirky Schmidt Theater and Schmidts Tivoli has become Germany's most popular variety theater, presenting a classy repertoire of live music, vaudeville, and cabaret. ⊠ *Spielbudenpl. 24–28, St. Pauli* ☎ *040/3177–8899* ⊕ *www.tivoli.de.*

DANCE CLUBS
China Lounge. The China Lounge, in a former Chinese restaurant, remains one of Hamburg's coolest lounges, attracting many hip and beautiful thirtysomethings. ⊠ *Nobistor 14, St. Pauli* ☎ *040/3197–6622* ⊕ *www.china-hamburg.de.*

Mojo Club. After changing locations, the storied Mojo Club has been reborn and is now located beneath a spaceship-like hatch, which rises out of the sidewalk to allow in revelers who come to dance to its live DJs and their eclectic mix of jazz, funk, soul, and electronic beats. ⊠ *Reeperbahn 1, St. Pauli* ☎ *040/430–4616* ⊕ *www.mojo.de.*

JAZZ AND LIVE MUSIC

Docks. There's a stylish bar here, as well as one of Hamburg's largest venues for live music acts from around the world. When the concert stage is empty, a hip-hop club takes over. ⊠ *Spielbudenpl. 19, St. Pauli* ☎ *040/317–8830* ⊕ *www.docks.de.*

Grosse Freiheit 36. One of the best-known nightspots in town, Grosse Freiheit 36 has made its name as both a popular venue for big names from around the world and as the location of the Kaiserkeller, a night-club where the Beatles once played that's still going strong. ⊠ *Grosse Freiheit 36, St. Pauli* ☎ *040/317–7780* ⊕ *www.grossefreiheit36.de.*

Indra Club. The Beatles' first stop on the road to fame was the Indra Club. The club's owner, Bruno Koschmider, asked for one thing, and that was a wild show. These days, the Indra is still a nightclub, with live music acts nearly every night. ⊠ *Grosse Freiheit 64, St. Pauli* ⊕ *www.hotel-jacob.de.*

PUBS

Altes Mädchen. Beer fans will be hard pressed to find a better spot in town to sample that amber nectar. With a number of local beers on tap and more than 60 craft beers to order from, plus a decent selection of German pub food, it's unsurprising that this gastropub quickly developed a glowing reputation after opening in early 2013. ⊠ *Lagerstr. 28b, Schanzenviertel* ☎ *040/8000–77750* ⊕ *www.altes-maedchen.com.*

Gretel und Alfons. Germans are not known for mingling, but at this small pub in the middle of Grosse Freiheit, you can strike up a conversation with the person sitting next to you. Perhaps that's why it was a firm favorite with the Beatles, who could often be found here when not per-forming at a number of clubs on the street. ⊠ *Grosse Freiheit 29, St. Pauli* ☎ *040/313–491* ⊕ *www.gretelundalfons.de.*

ST. GEORG

BARS

Bar DaCaio at the George Hotel. This bar has a black-on-black design, good looks all over, great service, and endless drink options. It's also located in one of the hottest hotels in town. ⊠ *Barcastr. 3, St. Georg* ☎ *040/280–0300* ⊕ *www.thegeorge-hotel.de.*

DANCE CLUBS

Golden Cut. At Golden Cut, just across from the main train station, DJs spin house, hip-hop, and electronic music. ⊠ *Holzdamm 61, St. Georg* ☎ *040/8510–3532* ⊕ *www.goldencut.org.*

13

SPORTS AND THE OUTDOORS

BICYCLING

More or less flat as a pancake, and with dedicated cycle paths running parallel to sidewalks throughout the city, Hamburg's an incredibly bike-friendly place. A number of hotels let their guests borrow bikes, but perhaps the most convenient option is to hire a "Stadtrad"—a city bike. Chunky and red-framed, and outfitted with locks and lights, they can be picked up and dropped off at a multitude of locations around the city, including at the Hauptbahnhof, at larger U-bahn and S-bahn stations, and near popular tourist spots. Bikes are free for the first 30 minutes, and then cost 8¢ per minute up to a maximum daily rate of €12. For more information and to register, visit ⊕ *www.stadtradhamburg.de.*

Hamburg City Cycles. From a central location, this friendly little outfit rents bikes and also offers guided tours and day trips to destinations that are farther afield. ⊠ *Bernhard-Nocht-Str. 89–91, St. Pauli* ☏ *040/7421–4420* ⊕ *www.hhcitycycles.de.*

JOGGING

The best places for going for a run are the Planten un Blomen and Alter Botanischer Garten parks and along the leafy promenade around the Alster. The latter route is about 7 km (4.3 miles) long.

SAILING

You can rent rowboats and sailboats on the Alster in summer between 10 am and 9 pm. Rowboats cost around €10 to €12 an hour, sailboats around €16 an hour (and they usually accommodate two adults). The largest selection of boats is at the Gurlitt-Insel pier off An der Alster (on the east bank of the Aussenalster). Another rental outlet is at the very tip of the Alster, at the street Fernsicht.

SHOPPING

Although not appearing as rich or sumptuous as Düsseldorf or Munich, Hamburg is nevertheless expensive, and ranks first among Germany's shopping experiences. Some of the country's premier designers, such as Karl Lagerfeld, Jil Sander, and Wolfgang Joop, are native Hamburgers, or at least worked here for quite some time. Hamburg has the greatest number of shopping malls in the country—they're mostly small, elegant Downtown arcades offering entertainment, fashion, and fine food.

All the big luxury names—Chanel, Versace, Armani, Prada, Louis Vuitton, Cartier, Tiffany—are found in the warren of streets bounded by Jungferstieg, the Rathaus, and Neue ABC-Strasse. International chain stores, like Fossil, Adidas and MAC, and European chains, such as Görtz shoe stores, Zara clothing stores, and Christ jewelry stores, and German department stores mingle on Mönckebergstrasse. Independent boutiques sell primarily distinguished and somewhat conservative fashion; understatement is the style here. Eppendorf offers miles of unique shops for shoes, clothes, home design, and housewares with quaint cafés sprinkled among them. Sternschanze offers a funky mix of stores selling cool home accessories and fashion, with dive bars and small restaurants for pit stops.

The ImtechArena is home to the Hamburger SV football team.

SHOPPING DISTRICTS

Hamburg's shopping districts are among the most elegant on the continent, and the city has Europe's largest expanse of covered shopping arcades, most of them packed with small, exclusive boutiques. The streets **Grosse Bleichen** and **Neuer Wall**, which lead off Jungfernstieg, are a big-ticket zone. The Grosse Bleichen holds four malls with the most sought-after labels, and several of these shopping centers are connected. The marble-clad **Galleria** is reminiscent of London's Burlington Arcade. Daylight streams through the immense glass ceilings of the **Hanse-Viertel,** an otherwise ordinary reddish-brown brick building. At 101, **Kaufmannshaus** is one of the oldest malls in Hamburg. Steps away from these retail giants are the fashionable **Hamburger Hof,** the historic Alte Post with a beautiful, waterfront promenade, the posh Bleichenhof, and the stunningly designed, larger Europa Passage.

In the fashionable Rotherbaum district, take a look at Milchstrasse and Mittelweg. Both are filled with small boutiques, restaurants, and cafés.

Walk down Susannenstrasse and Schanzestrasse in Sternschanze to find unique clothes, things for the home, and even LPs. Eppendorfer Landstrasse and Eppendorfer Weg are brimming with stores that sell clothing in every flavor—high-end labels, casual wear, sportswear, German designers—and elegant and fun home decor.

Running from the main train station to Gerhard-Hauptmann-Platz, the boulevard Spitalerstrasse is a pedestrians-only street lined with stores. ▥TIP→ Prices here are noticeably lower than those on Jungfernstieg.

ALTSTADT AND NEUSTADT

ANTIQUES

Neustadt and St.Georg. ABC-Strasse in the Neustadt is a happy hunting ground for antiques lovers, as are the shops in the St. Georg district behind the train station, especially those along Lange Reihe and Koppel. You'll find a mixture of genuine antiques (*Antiquitäten*) and junk (*Trödel*) there. You'll also be lucky if you find many bargains, however.

DEPARTMENT STORES

Alsterhaus. Hamburg's large and high-end department store is a favorite with locals, as well as an elegant landmark. A food hall and a champagne bar on the top level are both worth a stop. ⊠ *Jungfernstieg 16–20, Neustadt* ☎ *040/3590–1218* ⊕ *www.alsterhaus.de.*

Karstadt. Germany's leading department-store chain isn't as posh as the Alsterhaus, but it still has a good and varied selection of clothing, perfume, watches, household goods, and food. ■TIP➡ **Hamburg's downtown Karstadt Sports, which is up the street from the main store at Lange Mührn 14, is the city's best place to shop for sports clothing and gear.** ⊠ *Mönckebergstr. 16, Altstadt* ☎ *040/30940* ⊕ *www.karstadt.de.*

JEWELRY

Wempe. Germany's largest seller of fine jewelery has two locations in Hamburg, and this is its flagship. The selection of watches here is particularly outstanding. ⊠ *Jungfernstieg 8, Neustadt* ☎ *040/3344–8824* ⊕ *www.wempe.com.*

MEN'S CLOTHING

Thomas I-Punkt. The five-story Thomas I-Punkt, a Hamburg tradition, sells fashion-conscious clothes and its own private-label suits and shirts. ⊠ *Mönckebergstr. 21, Altstadt* ☎ *040/327–172* ⊕ *www.thomas-i-punkt.de.*

Wormland. The Hamburg outlet of the chain store is the city's largest store for men's clothes. Wormland offers both affordable no-name yet very fashionable clothes, as well as (much more expensive) top designer wear. ⊠ *Europa Passage, Ballindamm 40, Altstadt* ☎ *040/4689–92700* ⊕ *www.wormland.de.*

WOMEN'S CLOTHING

Hamburger Hof. The historic Hamburger Hof is one of the most beautiful, upscale shopping complexes, with a wide variety of designer clothing, jewelry, and gift stores that are primarily for women. ⊠ *Jungfernstieg 26–30/Grosse Bleichen, Neustadt* ☎ *040/350–1680* ⊕ *www.hhof-passage.de.*

Linette. A small but elegant store, Linette stocks only top designers. ⊠ *Hohe Bleichen 17, Neustadt* ☎ *040/346–411* ⊕ *www.linette-hamburg.de.*

ST. PAULI AND SCHANZENVIERTEL

ANTIQUES

Flohschanze. Germans in search of a great deal love a good *Flohmarkt* (flea market). These markets unfold every weekend throughout Hamburg, and the best of the lot may be the one at Flohschanze. With acres of clothes, furniture, books, CDs, records, home accessories, jewelry, and art, the market attracts both collectors and bargain hunters every Saturday from 8 until 4. ⊠ *Neuer Kamp 30, Schanzenviertel* ☎ *040/270–2766* ⊕ *www.marktkultur-hamburg.de.*

GIFTS

Baqu. The two storefronts of this store are filled with wacky knickknacks, useful home appliances, and modern decor. ⊠ *Susannenstr. 39, Schanzenviertel* ☎ *040/433–814.*

Captain's Cabin. Don't miss this Hamburg institution, which is the best place for all of the city's specialty maritime goods, including elaborate model ships and brass telescopes. This souvenir emporium is open daily. ⊠ *Landungsbrücken 3, St. Pauli* ☎ *040/316–373* ⊕ *www.captains-cabin.de.*

Lille/Stor. Head here for a mix of casual clothes, shoes, colorful items for the home, and small jewelry. ⊠ *Schanzenstr. 97, Schanzenviertel* ☎ *040/343–741* ⊕ *www.lille-stor.de.*

Mimulus Naturkosmetik. The all-natural cosmetics and toiletries here, as well as the facial and body treatments, are available at surprisingly reasonable prices. ⊠ *Schanzenstr. 39a, Schanzenviertel* ☎ *040/430–8037* ⊕ *www.mimulus-kosmetik.de.*

Yokozuna. At this funky little shop, the quirky notebooks, earrings, handbags and postcards are all made by local designers, who rent shelves in the shop to sell their products. It's a great place for creative gift ideas. ⊠ *Weidenallee 17, Schanzenviertel* ☎ *040/3199–3729* ⊕ *www.yokozuna.de.*

MEN'S CLOTHING

Herr von Eden. Fine suits and everything else you need to become a true gentleman are sold at this elegant store on the vintage-clothing-filled Marktstrasse. ⊠ *Marktstr. 33, Schanzenviertel* ☎ *040/439–0057* ⊕ *www.herrvoneden.com.*

WOMEN'S CLOTHING

Anna Fuchs. One of Hamburg's most famous fashion designers is widely known for her modern and elegant but still-affordable dresses. ⊠ *Karolinenstr. 27, Schanzenviertel* ☎ *040/4018–5408* ⊕ *annafuchs.de.*

Fräuleinwunder. This small emporium sells trendy sportswear, shoes, accessories, and jewelry for women. There's also a small selection of casual clothing for men. ⊠ *Susannenstr. 13, Schanzenviertel* ☎ *40/3619–3329.*

Kauf dich glücklich. With a name that translates to "Shop yourself happy," this inviting store selling clothes and shoes for men and women, as well as sunglasses, jewelry, scarves, hats, and other accessories. ⊠ *Susannenstr. 4, Schanzenviertel* ☎ *040/8000–6155* ⊕ *www.kaufdichgluecklich-shop.de.*

La Paloma. This small store features a well-edited collection of trendy clothes from casual labels from around the world. There's a focus on Danish designers. ✉ *Susannenstr. 5, Schanzenviertel* ☎ *040/4321–5333.*

Purple Pink. A tiny shop that sells a good selection of cool Scandinavian labels, such as Stine Goya, Carin Wester, and Minimarket. It's also great for jewelery and bags. ✉ *Weidenallee 21, Schanzenviertel* ☎ *040/4321–5379* ⊕ *www.purple-pink.de.*

ALTONA AND OTTENSEN

ANTIQUES

Kleidermarkt. This massive secondhand clothes shop is a few blocks down the road from the Altona train station. If the normal thrift-store prices for these duds from the 1960s through '80s aren't enough of an enticement, keep in mind that the store offers shoppers a 30% discount from 11 to 4 each Wednesday. ✉ *Max-Brauer-Allee 174, Altona* ☎ *040/433–717* ⊕ *www.kleidermarkt.de.*

BLANKENESE AND ELSEWHERE

FOOD MARKETS

Wochenmarkt Blankenese. This small but top-class food market in the heart of Blankenese manages to preserve the charm of a small village. It sells only fresh produce from what it considers environmentally friendly farms. ✉ *Blankeneser Bahnhofstr., Blankenese* ⊙ *Tues. 8–2, Fri. 8–6, Sat. 8–1* Ⓜ *Blankenese (S-bahn).*

GIFTS

WohnDesign Così. The most interesting pieces of contemporary design from around the world are on view at this home-furnishings store. ✉ *Eppendorfer Landstr. 48, Eppendorf* ☎ *040/470–670* ⊕ *www. wohndesign-cosi.de.*

WOMEN'S CLOTHING

Anita Hass. This impressive store covers several storefronts and carries the newest apparel, shoes, jewelry, handbags, and accessories, such as iPhone covers. It's a Hamburg classic that carries both international brands and several German designers. ✉ *Eppendorfer Landstr. 60, Eppendorf* ☎ *040/465–909* ⊕ *www.anitahass.de.*

Kaufrausch. The upscale shop Kaufrausch carries mostly clothing and accessories stores for women. ✉ *Isestr. 74, Harvestehude* ☎ *040/477–154* ⊕ *www.kaufrausch-hamburg.de.*

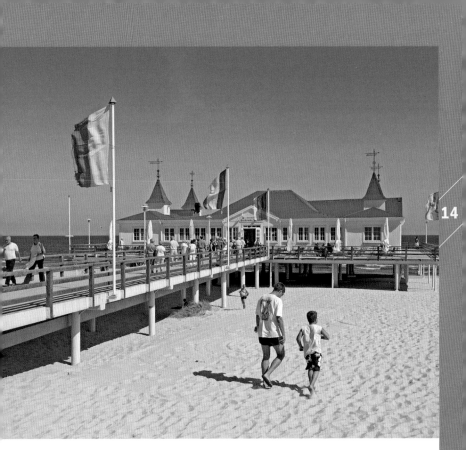

SCHLESWIG-HOLSTEIN
AND THE BALTIC COAST

WELCOME TO SCHLESWIG-HOLSTEIN AND THE BALTIC COAST

TOP REASONS TO GO

★ **Gothic architecture:** The historic towns of Lübeck, Wismar, and Stralsund have some of the finest redbrick Gothic architecture in northern Europe. A walk through medieval Stralsund, in particular, is like a trip into the proud past of the powerful Hansetic League.

★ **Rügen:** One of the most secluded islands of northern Europe, Rügen is a dreamy Baltic oasis whose endless beaches, soaring chalk cliffs, and quiet pace of life have charmed painters, writers, and artists for centuries.

★ **Schwerin:** Nestled in a romantic landscape of lakes, rivers, forests, and marshland, the Mecklenburg state capital and its grand water palace make a great place to relax.

★ **Sylt:** A windswept outpost in the rough North Sea, Sylt is home to Germany's jet set, who come here for the tranquility, the white beaches, the gourmet dining, and the superb hotels throughout the year.

1 Schleswig-Holstein. Rural Schleswig-Holstein is accented by laid-back, medieval towns and villages famed for their fresh seafood and great local beers (such as Asgaard in Schleswig), and the bustling island of Sylt, a summer playground for wealthy Hamburgers.

2 Western Mecklenburg. Lakes, rivers, and seemingly endless fields of wheat, sunflowers, and yellow rape characterize this rural landscape. Although the area is extremely popular with Germans, only a few western tourists or day-trippers from nearby Berlin venture here to visit beautiful Schwerin or enjoy the serenity. The area is famous for its many wellness and spa hotels, making it a year-round destination.

14

GETTING ORIENTED

The three major areas of interest are the western coastline of Schleswig-Holstein, the lakes inland in Western Mecklenburg, and Vorpommern's secluded, tundralike landscape of sandy heath and dunes. If you only have three days, slow down to the area's pace and focus on one area. In five days you could easily cross the region. Berlin is the natural approach from the east; Hamburg is a launching point from the west.

3 Vorpommern.
Remote and sparsely populated, Vorpommern is one of Europe's quietest corners. Compared to the coast and islands in the West, sleepy Vorpommern sea resorts like Putbus, Baabe, and the Darss area have preserved a distinct, old-fashioned charm worth exploring. Bismarck popularized the area by saying that it was like going back 20 years in time.

BALTIC COAST BEACHES

Although Germany may not be the first place on your list of beach destinations, a shore vacation on the Baltic never disappoints. The coast here ranges from the remote bucolic shores of Usedom to the chic beaches of Sylt.

(above) You can rent one of the colorful Strandkorb on Usedom Island's beaches. (upper right) Stroll along Ahlbeck's beach and pier. (lower right) The "it" crowd hangs out on Sylt.

Be sure to rent a *Strandkorb*, a kind of beach chair in a wicker basket, which gives you all of the sun, but protects you from the wind and flying sand. You can rent these chairs by the hour, half day, or day. There is usually an office near the chairs; look for the kiosk that sells sundries and beach toys nearest the chair you want.

Look for the blue flag on the beach that indicates that the water is safe for swimming. But, be aware that water temperatures even in August rarely exceed 20°C (65°F). There's a *Kurtaxe* (a tax that goes to the upkeep of the beaches) of €1.50–€5 for most resort areas; the fees on Sylt average €3 per day. Fees are usually covered by your hotel; you should get a card indicating that you've paid the tax. You can use the card for discounted services, but don't need to present it to visit the beach.

BALTIC AMBER

It is believed that a pine forest once grew in the area that is now the Baltic Sea about 40 million years ago. Fossilized resin from these trees, aka amber, lies beneath the surface. In fact, this area has the largest known amber deposit, at about 80% of the world's known accessible deposits. The best time for amber "fishing," dipping a net into the surf, is at low tide after a storm when pieces of amber dislodge from the sea floor.

BALTIC COAST BEST BEACHES

HIDDENSEE ISLAND

If you're looking for bucolic and tranquil, head to the car-free island of **Hiddensee,** Rügen's neighbor to the west. With a mere 1,300 inhabitants, Hiddensee is the perfect place to look for washed-up amber.

RÜGEN ISLAND

Germany's largest island, Rügen is dotted with picture-perfect beaches, chalk cliffs, and pristine nature. It also served as the stomping ground for the likes of Albert Einstein, Christopher Isherwood, and Caspar David Friedrich. An easy day trip from Berlin, the town of **Binz** is the perfect Rügen getaway. Binz has a nice boardwalk, a pretty beach dotted with Strandkörbe, and fine mansions.

You'll find a wonderful white sand beach at **Prora** and a smattering of artist studios; the hulking abandoned resort here was designed by the Nazis to house 20,000 vacationers in the *Kraft durch Freude* (Strength Through Joy) program.

SYLT

Germany's northernmost island is the granddaddy of all beach resorts and by far the most popular seaside destination in Germany. Sylt is chic and trendy, but, despite being overrun by tourists, it is still possible to find your own romantic abandoned stretch of beach. **Westerland** is the most popular beach, with its long

promenade and sun-drenched sand. The "Fun-Beach Brandenburg" bursts at the seams with family-friendly activities, volleyball, and other sporting contests. Farther afield, the red cliffs of **Kampen** are the perfect backdrop for a little mellow sun and schmoozing with the locals. It's a lovely place for a walk along the shore and up the cliffs, where the view can't be beat. The best beach for families is at **Hörnum**, where a picture-perfect red-and-white lighthouse protects the entrance to the bay.

USEDOM ISLAND

The towns of **Ahlbeck** and **Herringsdorf** are the most popular on Usedom Island, with pristine 19th-century villas and mansions paired with long boardwalks extending into the sea. For the true and unspoiled experience, head west to **Ückeritz,** where the beach feels abandoned.

WARNEMÜNDE

A resort town popular with German tourists and local day-trippers from Rostock, the 20 km (12.4 miles) of wind-swept white-sand beach can't be beat. A fun beach promenade stretches the length of the beach and features daily music performances and restaurants ranging from fine dining to fish shacks where you can get a paper bag filled with fried mussels.

Updated by
Lee A. Evans

Germany's true north is a quiet and peaceful region that belies, but takes a great deal of pride in, its past status as one of the most powerful trading centers in Europe. The salty air and lush, green landscape of marshlands, endless beaches, fishing villages, and lakes are the main pleasures here, not sightseeing. The Baltic coast is one of the most visited parts of Germany, but because most visitors are German, you'll feel like you have discovered Germany's best-kept secret. On foggy November evenings, or during the hard winter storms that sometimes strand islanders from the mainland, you can well imagine the fairy tales spun by the Vikings who lived here.

In Schleswig-Holstein, Germany's most northern state, the Danish-German heritage is the result of centuries of land disputes, flexible borders, and intermarriage between the two nations—you could call this area southern Scandinavia. Since the early 20th century its shores and islands have become popular weekend and summer retreats for the well-to-do from Hamburg. The island of Sylt, in particular, is known throughout Germany for its rich and beautiful sunbathers.

The rest of Schleswig-Holstein, though equally appealing in its green and mostly serene landscape, is far from rich and worldly. Most people farm or fish, and often speak Plattdütsch, or Low German, which is difficult for outsiders to understand. Cities such as Flensburg, Husum, Schleswig, Kiel (the state capital), and even Lübeck all exude a laid-back, small-town charm.

The neighboring state of Mecklenburg-Vorpommern includes the Baltic Coast and is even more rural. On the resort islands of Hiddensee and Usedom, the clock appears to have stopped before World War II. Though it has long been a popular summer destination for families and city-weary Berliners, few foreign tourists venture here.

PLANNING

WHEN TO GO

The region's climate is at its best when the two states are most crowded with vacationers—in July and August. Winter can be harsh in this area, and even spring and fall are rather windy, chilly, and rainy. ■ TIP→ To avoid the crowds, schedule your trip for June or September. But don't expect tolerable water temperatures or hot days on the beach.

GETTING HERE AND AROUND

AIR TRAVEL

The international airport closest to Schleswig-Holstein is in Hamburg. For an eastern approach to the Baltic Coast tour, use Berlin's Tegel or Schönefeld Airports.

BOAT AND FERRY TRAVEL

The Weisse Flotte (White Fleet) line operates ferries linking the Baltic ports, as well as short harbor and coastal cruises. Boats depart from Warnemünde, Zingst (to Hiddensee), Sassnitz, and Stralsund. In addition, Scandlines ferries run from Stralsund and Sassnitz to destinations in Sweden, Denmark, Poland, and Finland.

Scandlines also operates ferries between Rostock/Warnemünde and the Danish island of Bornholm, as well as Sweden.

Contacts Scandlines ☎ 01805/116–688 ⊕ www.scandlines.de. **Weisse Flotte** ☎ 0180/321–2120 for Warnemünde and Stralsund, 0385/557–770 for Schwerin ⊕ www.weisseflotte.de.

BUS TRAVEL

Local buses link the main train stations with outlying towns and villages, especially the coastal resorts. Buses operate throughout Sylt, Rügen, and Usedom islands.

CAR TRAVEL

The two-lane roads (*Bundesstrassen*) along the coast can be full of traffic in summer. The ones leading to Usedom Island can be extremely log-jammed, as the causeway bridges have scheduled closings to let ships pass. Using the Bundesstrassen takes more time, but these often tree-lined roads are by far more scenic than the autobahn.

Sylt island is 196 km (122 miles) from Hamburg via Autobahn A-7 and Bundesstrasse B-199 and is ultimately reached via train. B-199 cuts through some nice countryside, and instead of A-7 or B-76 between Schleswig and Kiel you could take the slow route through the coastal hinterland (B-199, B-203, or B-503). Lübeck, the gateway to Mecklenburg-Vorpommern, is 56 km (35 miles) from Hamburg via A-1. B-105 leads to all sightseeing spots in Mecklenburg-Vorpommern. A faster route is the A-20, connecting Lübeck and Rostock. From Stralsund, B-96 cuts straight across Rügen Island, a distance of 51 km (32 miles). From Berlin, take A-11 and head toward Prenzlau for B-109 all the way to Usedom Island, a distance of 162 km (100 miles). A causeway connects the mainland town of Anklam to the town of Peenemünde, on Usedom Island; coming from the west, use the causeway at Wolgast.

TRAIN TRAVEL

Trains connect almost every notable city in the area and it's much more convenient than bus travel. Sylt, Kiel, Lübeck, Schwerin, and Rostock have InterCity train connections to either Hamburg or Berlin, or both.

A north–south train line links Schwerin and Rostock. An east–west route connects Kiel, Hamburg, Lübeck, and Rostock, and some trains continue through to Stralsund and Sassnitz, on Rügen Island.

TOURS

Although tourist offices and museums have worked to improve the English-language literature about this area, English-speaking tours are infrequent and must be requested ahead of time through the local tourist office. Because most tours are designed for groups, there's usually a flat fee of €20–€30. Towns currently offering tours are Lübeck, Stralsund, and Rostock. Schwerin has two-hour boat tours of its lakes. Many of the former fishermen in these towns give sunset tours of the harbors, shuttle visitors between neighboring towns, or take visitors fishing in the Baltic Sea, which is a unique opportunity to ride on an authentic fishing boat. In Kiel, Rostock, and on Sylt, cruise lines make short trips through the respective bays and/ or islands off the coast, sailing even as far as Denmark and Sweden. Inquire at the local tourist office about companies and times, as well as about fishing-boat tours.

RESTAURANTS

Don't count on eating a meal at odd hours or after 10 pm in this largely rural area. Many restaurants serve hot meals only between 11:30 am and 2 pm, and 6 pm and 9 pm. You rarely need a reservation here, and casual clothing is generally acceptable.

Prices in the reviews are the average cost of a main course at dinner, or if dinner is not served, at lunch.

HOTELS

In northern Germany you'll find both small *Hotelpensionen* and fully equipped large hotels; along the eastern Baltic Coast, some hotels are renovated high-rises dating from GDR (German Democratic Republic, or East Germany) times. Many of the small hotels and pensions in towns such as Kühlungsborn and Binz have been restored to the romantic, quaint splendor of German *Bäderarchitektur* (spa architecture) from the early 20th century. In high season all accommodations, especially on the islands, are in great demand. ■TIP➔ **If you can't book well in advance, inquire at the local tourist office, which will also have information on the 150 campsites along the Baltic Coast and on the islands.**

Prices in the reviews are the lowest cost of a standard double room in high season. For expanded reviews, facilities, and current deals, visit Fodors.com.

PLANNING YOUR TIME

The bigger coastal Hanse cities make for a good start before exploring smaller towns. Lübeck is a natural base for exploring Schleswig-Holstein, particularly if you arrive from Hamburg. From here it's easy to venture out into the countryside or explore the coastline and towns such as Schleswig, Flensburg, or Husum. The island of Sylt is a one- or two-day trip from Lübeck, though.

If you have more time, you can also travel east from Lübeck into Mecklenburg-Vorpommern: Some of the must-see destinations on an itinerary include Schwerin and the surrounding lakes, the island of Rügen, and the cities Wismar and Rostock.

DISCOUNTS AND DEALS

Larger cities such as Kiel, Lübeck, Wismar, Schwerin, and Rostock offer tourism "welcome" cards, which include sometimes-considerable discounts and special deals for attractions and tours as well as local public transport. Ask about these at the visitor information bureaus.

VISITOR INFORMATION

Tourismusverband Mecklenburg-Vorpommern ⊠ *Pl. der Freundschaft 1, Rostock* ☎ *0381/403–0500* ⊕ *www.tmv.de.*

SCHLESWIG-HOLSTEIN

This region once thrived, thanks to the Hanseatic League and the Salzstrasse (Salt Route), a merchant route connecting northern Germany's cities. The kings of Denmark warred with the dukes of Schleswig and, later, the German Empire over the prized northern territory of Schleswig-Holstein. The northernmost strip of land surrounding Flensburg became German in 1864. The quiet, contemplative spirit of the region's people, the marshland's special light, and the ever-changing face of the sea are inspiring. Today the world-famous Schleswig-Holstein-Musikfestival ushers in classical concerts to farmhouses, palaces, and churches.

HUSUM

158 km (98 miles) northwest of Hamburg.

The town of Husum is the epitome of northern German lifestyle and culture. Immortalized in a poem as the "gray city upon the sea" by its famous son, Theodor Storm, Husum is actually a popular vacation spot in summer.

The central **Marktplatz** (Market Square) is bordered by 17th- and 18th-century buildings, including the historic Rathaus (Town Hall), which houses the tourist-information office. The best impression of Husum's beginnings in the mid-13th century is found south of the Marktplatz, along **Krämerstrasse**; the **Wasserreihe,** a narrow and tortuous alley; and **Hafenstrasse,** right next to the narrow **Binnenhafen** (city harbor).

ESSENTIALS

Visitor Information Husum ⊠ *Grossstr. 27* ☎ *04841/89870* ⊕ *www.husum.de.*

EXPLORING

Schloss vor Husum (*Husum Castle*). Despite Husum's remoteness, surrounded by the stormy sea, wide marshes, and dunes, the city used to be a major seaport and administrative center. The Husum Castle, which was originally built as a Renaissance castle in the late 16th century, was transformed in 1752 by the dukes of Gottorf into a red-brick baroque country palace. ⊠ *Professor-Ferdinand-Tönnies-Allee, König-Friedrich V-Allee* ☎ *04841/897–3130* ✇ *€5* ☉ *Mar.–Oct., Tues.–Sun. 11–5.*

Theodor-Storm-Haus. This is the most famous house on Wasserreihe, where writer Theodor Storm (1817–88) lived between 1866 and 1880. It's a must if you're interested in German literature or if you want to gain insight into the life of the few well-to-do people in this region during the 19th century. The small museum includes the poet's living room and a small *Poetenstübchen* (poets' parlor), where he wrote many of his novels. ⊠ *Wasserreihe 31* ☎ *04841/803–8630* ✇ *€3* ☉ *Apr.–Oct., Tues.–Fri. 10–5, Mon. and Sun. 2–5, Sat. 11–5; Nov.–Mar., Tues., Thurs., and Sat. 2–5.*

WHERE TO STAY

$$

HOTEL

Fodor's Choice

★

🏨 **Geniesser Hotel Altes Gymnasium.** In a former redbrick high school behind a pear orchard, you'll find a surprisingly elegant country-style hotel. **Pros:** stylish and quiet setting; a perfect overnight stop on the way to Sylt. **Cons:** far from any other sights. ⑤ *Rooms from: €179* ⊠ *Süderstr. 2–10* ☎ *04841/8330* ⊕ *www.altes-gymnasium.de* ⤳ *66 rooms, 6 suites* ❖ *Breakfast.*

SYLT

44 km (27 miles) northwest of Husum, 196 km (122 miles) northwest of Hamburg.

Sylt (pronounced ts-oo-LT) is a long, narrow island (38 km [24 miles] by as little as 220 yards) of unspoiled beaches and marshland off the western coast of Schleswig-Holstein and Denmark. Famous for its clean air and white beaches, Sylt is the hideaway for Germany's rich and famous.

A popular activity here is *Wattwanderungen* (walking in the Watt, the shoreline tidelands), whether on self-guided or guided tours. The small villages with their thatch-roof houses, the beaches, and the nature conservation areas make Sylt one of the most enchanting German islands.

GETTING HERE AND AROUND

Trains are the *only* way to access Sylt (other than flying from Hamburg or Berlin). The island is connected to the mainland via the train causeway Hindenburgdamm. Deutsche Bahn will transport you and your car from central train stations at Dortmund, Düsseldorf, Hamburg, Stuttgart, and Frankfurt directly to the station Westerland on the island. In addition, a daily shuttle car train leaves Niebüll roughly every 30 minutes from 5:10 am to 10:10 pm (Friday and Sunday from 5:10 am to 9:40 pm). There are no reservations on this train.

ESSENTIALS

Visitor Information Tourismus-Service Kampen ⊠ *Hauptstr. 12, Kampen* ☎ *04651/46980* ⊕ *www.kampen.de.* **Sylt Marketing GmbH** ⊠ *Stephanstr. 6, Sylt / OT Rantum* ☎ *04651/82020* ⊕ *www.sylt.de.* **Westerland.** There's also a location at Stephanstr. 6. ⊠ *Strandstr. 35, Westerland* ☎ *04651/9988* ⊕ *www.westerland.de.*

EXPLORING

TOP ATTRACTIONS

Kampen. The Sylt island's unofficial capital is the main destination for the wealthier crowd and lies 9 km (6 miles) northeast of Westerland. Redbrick buildings and shining white thatch-roof houses spread along the coastline. The real draw—apart from the fancy restaurants and chic nightclubs—is the beaches.

Rotes Kliff (*Red Cliff*). One of the island's best-known features is this dune cliff on the northern end of the Kampen beaches, which turns an eerie dark red when the sun sets. ⊠ *Kampen.*

WORTH NOTING

Altfriesisches Haus (*Old Frisian House*). For a glimpse of the rugged lives of 19th-century fishermen, visit the small village of **Keitum** to the south, and drop in on the Old Frisian House, which preserves an Old World peacefulness in a lush garden setting. The house also documents a time when most seamen thrived on extensive whale hunting. ⊠ *Am Kliff 13, Keitum* ☎ *04651/31101* ⊠ *€3.50* ⊙ *Easter–Oct., weekdays 10–5, weekends 11–5; Nov.–Easter, Tues.–Fri. 1–4.*

FAMILY   **The Naturschutzgebiet Kampener Vogelkoje** (*Birds' Nest Nature Conservation Area*). Built in the mid-17th century, this conservation area once served as a mass trap for wild geese. Today it serves as a nature preserve for wild birds. ✉ *Lister Str., Kampen* ☎ *04651/871–077* 🎫*€3* ☉ *Apr.–Oct., weekdays 10–5, weekends 11–5.*

> **AWAY FROM THE CROWDS**
>
> If you're looking for privacy on Sylt, detour to the village of **List**, on the northern tip of the island, or to **Archsum** or **Hörnum**. The last is on the southernmost point of the island and, like List, has a little harbor and lighthouse.

St. Severin Church. The 800-year-old church was built on the highest elevation in the region. Its tower once served the island's fishermen as a beacon. Strangely enough, the tower also served as a prison until 1806. Today the church is a popular site for weddings. ✉ *Pröstwai 20, Keitum* ☎ *04651/31713* ⊕ *www.st-severin.de* 🎫 *Free* ☉ *Church daily 9–6. Tours: Apr.–Oct., Sun. at 10; Nov.–Mar., Sun. at 4.*

Sylter Heimatmuseum (*Sylt Island Museum*). This small museum tells the centuries-long history of the island's seafaring people. It presents traditional costumes, tools, and other gear from fishing boats and tells the stories of islanders who fought for Sylt's independence. ✉ *Am Kliff 19, Keitum* ☎ *04651/31669* 🎫*€3.50* ☉ *Easter–Oct., weekdays 10–5, weekends 11–5; Nov.–Easter, Tues.–Fri. 1–4.*

FAMILY   **Westerland.** The island's major town is not quite as expensive as Kampen, but it's more crowded. An ugly assortment of modern hotels lines an undeniably clean and broad beach. Each September windsurfers meet for the Surf Cup competition off the **Brandenburger Strand,** the best surfing spot.

WHERE TO EAT

$$ **✗ Dorfkrug Rotes Kliff.** The Dorfkrug has fed the island's seafaring inhab-
GERMAN   itants since 1876. Enjoy meals such as *Steinbuttfilet* (turbot filet) or *Gebratener Zander* (fried perch filet) in a homey setting where the walls are covered in traditional blue-and-white Frisian tiles. The same owners run the Wiinkööv wine bar next door. Visitors to both venues can take advantage of their impressive wine knowledge and cellar 💲 *Average main: €16* ✉ *Braderuper Weg 3, Kampen* ☎ *04651/43500* ☉ *Closed Mon. in Jan.*

$$$$ **✗ Hotelrestaurant Jörg Müller.** Set in an old thatch-roof farmhouse, which
SEAFOOD   doubles as a small hotel, chef and owner Jörg Müller is considered by
Fodor's Choice   many to be the island's leading chef, delivering haute cuisine served in a
★   gracious and friendly setting. Müller even makes his own salt from the North Sea water. Of the two restaurants, the Pesel serves local fish dishes, whereas the formal Jörg Müller offers a high-quality blend of international cuisines, where any of the four- to six-course menus are a nice option. 💲 *Average main: €46* ✉ *Süderstr. 8, Westerland* ☎ *04651/27788* ⊕ *www.hotel-joerg-mueller.de* 🍽 *Reservations essential.*

$$$$ **✗ Sansibar.** A longtime favorite, Sansibar is *the* island's most popu-
ECLECTIC   lar restaurant—more a way of life than a place to eat. A diverse clientele often make it a rambunctious night out by imbibing loads of

The beach at Westerland on Sylt is clean and wide.

drinks under the bar's maverick logo, crossed pirates' sabers. The cuisine includes seafood and fondue; more than 800 wines are on offer. The Sunday brunch is incredible. ■TIP→ To get a table even in the afternoon, you must reserve at least six weeks in advance. ⑤ *Average main: €28* ✉ *Strand, Rantum-Süd, Hörnumer Str. 80* ☎ *04651/964–546* ⊕ *www.sansibar.de* 🍴 *Reservations essential.*

WHERE TO STAY

$$$$ 🏨 **Dorint Söl'ring Hof.** This luxurious resort is set *on* the dunes in a
RESORT white, thatch-roof country house: the view from most of the rooms
Fodor's Choice is magnificent—with some luck you may even spot frolicking harbor
★ porpoises. **Pros:** one of the few luxury hotels on the island with perfect service and a top-notch restaurant; right on the beach. **Cons:** remote location; often fully booked; rooms tend to be small. ⑤ *Rooms from: €395* ✉ *Am Sandwall 1* ☎ *04651/836–200* ⊕ *www.soelring-hof.de* 🛏 *11 rooms, 4 suites* 🍴 *Breakfast.*

$$ 🏨 **Ulenhof Wenningstedt.** The Ulenhof, one of Sylt's loveliest old thatch-
B&B/INN roof apartment houses, is a quiet alternative to the busier main resorts in Kampen and Westerland. **Pros:** a great, but small, spa. **Cons:** off the beaten track and away from the main action in Kampen and Westerland. ⑤ *Rooms from: €150* ✉ *Friesenring 14, Wenningstedt* ☎ *04651/94540* ⊕ *www.ulenhof.de* 🛏 *35 apartments* 🍴 *Breakfast.*

NIGHTLIFE AND THE ARTS

Club Rotes Kliff. The nightspots in Kampen are generally more upscale and more expensive than the pubs and clubs of Westerland. One of the most classic clubs on Sylt is the Club Rotes Kliff, a bar and dance club that attracts a hip crowd of all ages. ✉ *Braderuper Weg 3, Kampen* ☎ *04651/43400.*

Compass. The Compass is not as trendy as the typical Sylt nightclub. The mostly young patrons, however, create a cheerful party atmosphere on weekend nights. ⊠ *Friedrichstr. 40, Westerland* ☎ *04651/23513.*

SPORTS AND THE OUTDOORS

BEACHES

Buhne 16 and Roter Kliff. Kampen's beach—divided into the **Buhne 16** and the **Roter Kliff**—is the place where the rich and famous meet average joes. Bunhe 16 is Germany's most popular nudist beach and Germans call this section the great equalizer, as managers, stars, bus drivers, and carpenters are all equal without clothing. The Red Cliff section is less crowded than Buhne 16 and clothing is required. The beach access point offers one of the best views of the Cliffs and North Sea; the viewing platform is wheelchair accessible. The beaches are surrounded by a ring of dunes that beg for exploration. **Amenities:** food and drink; lifeguards; parking; showers; toilets; water sports. **Best for:** partiers; nudists; snorkeling; sunrise; sunset; surfing; swimming; walking; windsurfing. ⊠ *Kurstr. 33, Kampen.*

Fun-Beach Brandenburg. Westerland's Fun-Beach Brandenburg bursts at the seams in the summer months. More than 4 miles of pristine white sand is filled with more than 4,000 *Strandkorbs,* a kind of beach chair in a wicker basket, which are all for rent. There's also volleyball, soccer, darts, and other beach sports, and everyone is invited to participate in the Beach Olympics, which are held every Friday at 2 in the summer months. Despite its popularity, it is easy to find some privacy on the many secluded bike and foot paths. **Amenities:** food and drink; lifeguards; parking; showers; toilets; water sports. **Best for:** partiers; swimming; walking. ⊠ *Kurpromenade, Westerland.*

Hornum Beach. The town of Hornum is surrounded on three sides by a rock-free, fine-white-sand beach that is perfect for paddling, quick dips in the sea, or simply lounging in one of the ever-present Strandkorben. The main beach is one of the most family-friendly on the island and it's easily accessible from the promenade. A magnificent red-and-white lighthouse looms over the beach. Hornum is the best place to take long walks along the Wattenmeer. **Amenities:** food and drink; lifeguards; parking; showers; toilets; water sports. **Best for:** snorkeling; sunrise; sunset; surfing; swimming; walking; windsurfing. ⊠ *An Der Dune, Hornum.*

SCHLESWIG

82 km (51 miles) southeast of Sylt, 114 km (71 miles) north of Hamburg.

Schleswig-Holstein's oldest city is also one of its best-preserved examples of a typical north German town. Once the seat of the dukes of Schleswig-Holstein, it has not only their palace but also ruins left by the area's first rulers, the Vikings. The Norse conquerors, legendary and fierce warriors from Scandinavia, ruled northern Germany between 800 and 1100. Although they brought terror and domination to the region, they also contributed commerce and a highly developed social structure. Under a wide sky, Schleswig lies on the Schlei River in a landscape of freshwater marshland and lakes, making it a good departure point for bike or canoe tours.

EATING WELL IN SCHLESWIG-HOLSTEIN

The German coastline is known for fresh and superb seafood, particularly in summer. A few of the region's top restaurants are on Sylt and in Lübeck. Eating choices along the Baltic Coast tend to be more down-to-earth. However, restaurants in both coastal states serve mostly seafood such as *Scholle* (flounder) or North Sea *Krabben* (shrimp), often with fried potatoes, eggs, and bacon. Mecklenburg specialties to look for are *Mecklenburger Griebenroller*, a custardy casserole of grated potatoes, eggs, herbs, and chopped bacon; *Mecklenburger Fischsuppe*, a hearty fish soup with vegetables, tomatoes, and sour cream; *Gefüllte Ente* (duck with bread stuffing); and *Pannfisch* (fish patty). A favorite local nightcap since the 17th century is *Grog*, a strong blend of rum, hot water, and local fruits.

14

GETTING HERE AND AROUND

Schleswig's train station is 3 km (2 miles) from the city center. It's easiest to take Bus No. 1501, 1505, or 1506 into town. The buses leave from across the street from the front of the train station, and all stop at Schloss Gottorf.

EXPLORING

The Holm. The fishing village comes alive along the Holm, an old settlement with tiny and colorful houses. The windblown buildings give a good impression of what villages in northern Germany looked like 150 years ago. ⊠ *Süderholmstr., Holm.*

Schloss Gottorf. The impressive baroque Schloss Gottorf, dating from 1703, once housed the ruling family. It has been transformed into the **Schleswig-Holsteinisches Landesmuseum** (State Museum of Schleswig-Holstein) and holds a collection of art and handicrafts of northern Germany from the Middle Ages to the present, including paintings by Lucas Cranach the Elder. ⊠ *Schlossinsel 1* ☎ *04621/8130* ⊕ *www.schloss-gottorf.de* 🎫 *€9* ⊙ *Apr.–Oct., daily 10–6; Nov.–Mar., Tues.–Fri. 10–4, weekends 10–5.*

FAMILY **Wikinger-Museum Haithabu** (*Haithabu Viking Museum*). The most thrilling museum in Schleswig is at the site of an ancient Viking settlement. This was the Vikings' most important German port, and the boats, gold jewelry, and graves they left behind are displayed in the museum. Be sure to walk along the trail to the Viking village, to see how the Vikings really lived. The best way to get there is to take the ferry across the Schlei from the Schleswigs main fishing port. ⊠ *Haddeby, Am Haddebyer Noor 2, Busdorf* ☎ *04621/813–222* ⊕ *www.schloss-gottorf.de* 🎫 *€7* ⊙ *Apr.–Oct., daily 9–5; Nov.–Mar., Tues.–Sun. 10–4.*

WHERE TO EAT AND STAY

$ ✕ **Asgaard Brauerei.** Taste the "Divine beer of the Vikings" at Schleswig's
GERMAN only brewery. While the restaurant offers typical brewpub fare, it is the small Viking twists, like roast meat served only with a knife and horned glasses that make this place worth a visit. The Divine beer is a malty cold-fermented amber lager that can be highly addictive. $ *Average main: €12* ⊠ *Königstr. 27* ☎ *04621/29206* ⊕ *www.asgaard.de.*

$ ✕ **Stadt Flensburg.** This small restaurant in a city mansion dating back
GERMAN to 1699 serves mostly fish from the Schlei River. The food is solid
regional fare such as *Zanderfilet* (pike-perch filets) or *Gebratene Ente*
(roast duck). The familial, warm atmosphere and the local dark tap
beers more than make up for the simplicity of the setting. Reservations
are advised. Ⓢ *Average main: €13* ✉ *Lollfuss 102* ☏ *04621/23984*
🕓 *Closed Wed.*

$ 🏠 **Ringhotel Strandhalle Schleswig.** A modern hotel overlooking the
HOTEL small yacht harbor, this establishment has surprisingly low rates.
Pros: hotel occupies central spot in the heart of Schleswig with great
views. **Cons:** lack of flair; rather bland rooms. Ⓢ *Rooms from: €90*
✉ *Strandweg 2* ☏ *04621/9090* ⊕ *www.hotel-strandhalle.de* ⤳ *25
rooms* 🍽 *Breakfast.*

SHOPPING

Keramik-Stube. The tiny Keramik-Stube offers craft work and beautiful
traditional handmade pottery. ✉ *Rathausmarkt 14* ☏ *04621/24757.*

Teekontor Hansen. Northern Germans are devout tea-drinkers, and the
best place to buy tea is Teekontor Hansen. Try the *Schliekieker,* a strong
blend of different types, or the *Ostfriesenmischung,* the traditional daily
tea. ✉ *Kornmarkt 3* ☏ *04621/23385.*

KIEL

*53 km (33 miles) southeast of Schleswig, 130 km (81 miles) north
of Hamburg.*

The state capital of Schleswig-Holstein, Kiel, is known throughout
Europe for the annual Kieler Woche, a regatta that attracts hundreds
of boats from around the world. Despite the many wharves and industries concentrated in Kiel, the **Kieler Föhrde** (Bay of Kiel) has remained
mostly unspoiled. Unfortunately, this cannot be said about the city
itself. Because of Kiel's strategic significance during World War II—it
served as the main German submarine base—the historic city, founded
more than 750 years ago, was completely destroyed. Sadly, due to the
modern reconstruction of the city, there is no real reason to spend more
than half a day in Kiel.

ESSENTIALS

Visitor Information Kiel ✉ *Andreas-Gayk-Str. 31* ☏ *0431/679–100*
⊕ *www.kiel.de.*

EXPLORING

FAMILY **Kieler Hafen** (*Kiel Harbor*). At Germany's largest passenger-shipping harbor, you can always catch a glimpse of one of the many ferries leaving
for Scandinavia from the **Oslokai** (Oslo Quay). ✉ *Oslokai.*

Kunsthalle zu Kiel (*Kiel Art Gallery*). One of northern Germany's best collections of modern art can be found here. Russian art of the 19th and early
20th centuries, German expressionism, and contemporary international
art are on display. ✉ *Düsternbrooker Weg 1* ☏ *0431/880–5756* ⊕ *www.
kunsthalle-kiel.de* 💶 *€7* 🕓 *Tues. and Thurs.–Sun. 10–6, Wed. 10–8.*

U-Boot-Museum (*Submarine Museum*). A grim reminder of a different marine past is exhibited at this museum in Kiel-Laboe. The vessels of the much-feared German submarine fleet in both World Wars were mostly built and stationed in Kiel, before leaving for the Atlantic, where they attacked American and British supply convoys. Today the submarine U995, built in 1943, serves as a public-viewing model of a typical World War II German submarine. The 280-foot-high **Marineehrenmal** (Marine Honor Memorial), in Laboe, was built in 1927–36. You can reach Laboe via ferry from the Kiel harbor or take B–502 north. ⊠ *Strandstr. 92, Kiel-Laboe* ☎ *04343/42700* ⊠ *Memorial €5.50, museum €4, combination €8.50* ⊙ *Apr.–Oct., daily 9:30–6; Nov.–Mar., daily 9:30–4.*

> ### WHAT'S NEARBY
>
> Two attractive beach towns close to Kiel, **Laboe** and **Strande**, are crowded with sun-loving Kielers on summer weekends. Both retain their fishing-village appeal, and you can buy fresh fish directly from the boats in the harbor, such as famous *Kieler Sprotten*, a small, salty fish somewhat like a sardine. Though you can get to Laboe and Strande by car, it's more fun to catch a ferry leaving from Kiel.

14

WHERE TO EAT AND STAY

$ ✕ **Kieler Brauerei.** The only historic brewery in town has produced beer

GERMAN   since the Middle Ages. You can try the *Naturtrübes Kieler* and other north German beers in pitchers. ■ TIP→ You can also order a small barrel for your table and tap it yourself (other patrons will cheer you). The hearty food—mostly fish, pork, and potato dishes—does not earn awards, but it certainly helps get down just one more beer. $ *Average main: €10* ⊠ *Alter Markt 9* ☎ *0431/906–290.*

$ ✕ **Quam.** Locals aren't looking for old-fashioned fish dishes—that's why

ECLECTIC   there isn't a traditional fish restaurant in town. They prefer preparations of fish from all over the world. The stylish Quam, its yellow walls and dimmed lights paying homage to Tuscany, serves specialties from Germany, Italy, France, and Japan to a mostly young, very chic crowd. $ *Average main: €15* ⊠ *Düppelstr. 60* ☎ *0431/85195* ⚠ *Reservations essential* ⊙ *Closed Sun. No lunch.*

$$$ ⊡ **Hotel Kieler Yachtclub.** This traditional hotel provides standard yet

HOTEL   elegant, newly refurbished rooms in the main building and completely new, bright accommodations in the Villentrakt. **Pros:** central location in the heart of Kiel; nice views. **Cons:** service and attitude can feel a bit too formal at times. $ *Rooms from: €197* ⊠ *Hindenburgufer 70* ☎ *0431/88130* ⊕ *www.hotel-kyc.de* ⤴ *57 rooms, 4 suites* ⦿ *Breakfast.*

NIGHTLIFE AND THE ARTS

Hemingway. This is one of the many chic and hip bars in Kiel. ⊠ *Alter Markt 19* ☎ *0431/96812.*

Traumfabrik. A college crowd goes to Traumfabrik to eat pizza, watch a movie, or dance (Friday is best for dancing). ⊠ *Grasweg 19* ☎ *0431/544–450.*

LÜBECK

60 km (37 miles) southeast of Kiel, 56 km (35 miles) northeast of Hamburg.

Fodor's Choice   The ancient core of Lübeck, dating from the 12th century, was a chief
★   stronghold of the Hanseatic merchant princes. But it was the roving
Heinrich der Löwe (King Henry the Lion) who established the town
and, in 1173, laid the foundation stone of the redbrick Gothic cathedral.
The town's famous landmark gate, the **Holstentor,** built between 1464
and 1478, is flanked by two round squat towers and serves as a solid
symbol of Lübeck's prosperity as a trading center.

GETTING HERE AND AROUND

Lübeck is accessible from Hamburg in 45 minutes either by InterCity
trains or by car via the A-24 and A-1, which almost takes you from one
city center to the other. Lübeck is also well connected by autobahns and
train service to Kiel, Flensburg, and the neighboring eastern coastline.
The city, however, should be explored on foot or by bike, as the many
tiny, medieval alleys in the center cannot be accessed by car. Tours of
Old Lübeck depart daily from the tourist Welcome Center on Holsten-
torplatz (🖃 €7 ☉ *June–Aug., Sat. at 11:30*).

ESSENTIALS

Visitor Information Lübeck ✉ *Holstentorpl. 1* ☎ *00451/889–9700*
⊕ *www.luebeck.de.*

EXPLORING

TOP ATTRACTIONS

Altstadt (*Old Town*). In the egg-shaped Altstadt, proof of Lübeck's former position as the golden queen of the Hanseatic League is found
at every step. ▐ TIP➡ **More 13th- to 15th-century buildings stand in
Lübeck than in all other large northern German cities combined. This
fact has earned the Altstadt a place on UNESCO's register of the world's
greatest cultural and natural treasures.**

Lübecker Dom (*Lübeck Cathedral*). Construction of this, the city's oldest
building, began in 1173. ✉ *Domkirchhof* ☎ *0451/74704* ☉ *Apr.–Oct.,
daily 10–6; Nov.–Mar., daily 10–4.*

Rathaus. Dating from 1240, the Rathaus is among the buildings lining
the arcaded Marktplatz, one of Europe's most striking medieval market
squares. ✉ *Breitestr. 64* ☎ *0451/122–1005* 🖃 *Guided tour in German
€4* ☉ *Tour weekdays at 11, noon, and 3, Sat. at 1:30.*

WORTH NOTING

Buddenbrookhaus. Two highly respectable-looking mansions are devoted
to two of Germany's most prominent writers, Thomas Mann (1875–
1955) and Günter Grass (born 1927). The older mansion is named
after Mann's saga *Buddenbrooks.* Mann's family once lived here, and
it's now home to the **Heinrich und Thomas Mann Zentrum,** a museum
documenting the brothers' lives. A tour and video in English are offered.
✉ *Mengstr. 4* ☎ *0451/122–4240* ⊕ *www.buddenbrookhaus.de* 🖃 *€6*
☉ *Jan.–Mar., Tues.–Sun. 11–5; Apr.–Dec., daily 10–5.*

Günter Grass-Haus. Near the museum is the second mansion, which is devoted to Germany's most famous living writer and winner of the Nobel Prize for Literature (1999), Günter Grass. ✉ *Glockengiesserstr. 21* ☎ *0451/122–4230* ⊕ *grass-haus.de* 🎫 *€6* ⊘ *Jan.–Mar., Tues.–Sun. 11–5; Apr.–Dec., daily 10–5.*

Heilig-Geist-Hospital (*Hospital of the Holy Ghost*). Take a look inside the entrance hall of this Gothic building. It was built in the 14th century by the town's rich merchants and was one of the country's first hospitals. It still cares for the sick and infirm. ✉ *Am Koberg 11* ☎ *0451/790–7841* 🎫 *Free* ⊘ *Apr.–Sept., Tues.–Sun. 10–5; Oct.–Mar., Tues.–Sun. 10–4.*

Marienkirche (*St. Mary's Church*). The impressive redbrick Gothic structure, which has the highest brick nave in the world, looms behind the Rathaus. ▥**TIP→** Look for the old bells, as they are still in the spot where they fell during the bombing of Lübeck. ✉ *Marienkirchhof* ☎ *0451/397–700* ⊕ *www.st-marien-luebeck.de* ⊘ *Nov.–Feb., daily 10–4; Mar. and Oct., daily 10–5; Apr.–Sept., daily 10–6.*

WHERE TO EAT

$$
GERMAN
Fodor'sChoice
★

✕**Schiffergesellschaft.** This dark, wood-paneled restaurant dating back to 1535 is the city's old Mariners' Society house, which was off-limits to women until 1870. Today locals and visitors alike enjoy freshly brewed beer and great seafood in church-style pews at long 400-year-old oak tables. Above are a bizarre collection of low-hanging old ship models. A good meal here is the *Ostseescholle* (plaice), fried with bacon and served with potatoes and cucumber salad. ⑤*Average main: €18* ✉*Breitestr. 2* ☎*0451/76776* ⊕ *schiffergesellschaft.com* ⌕ *Reservations essential.*

$$$$
GERMAN

✕**Wullenwever.** This restaurant has set a new standard of dining sophistication for Lübeck. Committed to the city's maritime heritage, Wullenwever serves fish such as bass, halibut, plaice, pike, and trout, which is fried or sautéed according to local country cooking. It's certainly one of the most attractive establishments in town, with dark furniture, chandeliers, and oil paintings on pale pastel walls. In summer, tables fill a quiet flower-strewn courtyard. Don't order à la carte here; instead choose one of the three- to seven-course menus, paired with wine. ⑤*Average main: €40* ✉ *Beckergrube 71* ☎ *0451/704–333* ⊕ *www.wullenwever.de* ⌕ *Reservations essential* ⊘ *Closed Sun. and Mon. No lunch.*

WHERE TO STAY

$
B&B/INN

▦**Hotel zur Alten Stadtmauer.** This historic town house in the heart of the city is Lübeck's most charming hotel with small, modest, well-kept guest rooms on two floors. **Pros:** cozy hotel with personal, friendly service; great location. **Cons:** rather simply furnished rooms; if fully booked, the hotel feels cramped. ⑤*Rooms from: €93* ✉*An der Mauer 57* ☎*0451/73702* ⊕ *www.hotelstadtmauer.de* ⇲*22 rooms* ⭐*Breakfast.*

$$
HOTEL

▦**Ringhotel Friederikenhof.** A lovely country hotel set in 19th-century, redbrick farmhouses 10 minutes outside Lübeck, the family-run Friederikenhof is a perfect hideaway with a soothing garden and great view of the city's skyline. **Pros:** charming, old-style farmhouse typical of the region; personal and very friendly service. **Cons:** distant location outside Lübeck. ⑤*Rooms from: €110* ✉ *Langjohrd 15–19* ☎ *0451/800–880* ⊕ *www.friederikenhof.de* ⇲*30 rooms* ⭐*Breakfast.*

14

$ **Ringhotel Jensen.** Only a stone's
HOTEL   throw from the Holstentor, this
hotel is close to all the main attractions and faces the moat surrounding the Old Town. **Pros:** perfect
location in the heart of Lübeck's
downtown area; major sights are
all within walking distance. **Cons:**
small pensionlike hotel without
many of the amenities of larger hotels; blandly decorated rooms.
⑤ *Rooms from: €93* ✉ *An der Obertrave 4–5* ☎ *0451/702–490* ⊕ *www.
hotel-jensen.de* ⤴ *41 rooms, 1 suite* ⊧⊙⊧ *Breakfast.*

DID YOU KNOW?

In 1922 filmmaker Friedrich Wilhelm Murnau used the tortuous
streets of Wismar's Old Town in
his expressionist horror-film classic, *Nosferatu.*

$$ **SAS Radisson Senator Hotel Lübeck.** Close to the famous Holstentor, this
HOTEL   ultramodern hotel, with its daring architecture, still reveals a north Ger-
man heritage: the redbrick building, with its oversize windows and gen-
erous, open lobby, mimics an old Lübeck warehouse. **Pros:** luxury hotel
in a central location. **Cons:** lacks the historic charm typical of medieval
Lübeck. ⑤ *Rooms from: €137* ✉ *Willy-Brandt-Allee 6* ☎ *0451/1420*
⊕ *www.senatorhotel.de* ⤴ *217 rooms, 7 suites* ⊧⊙⊧ *Multiple meal plans.*

THE ARTS

Musik und Kongresshallen Lübeck. Contact the Musik und Kongresshal-
len Lübeck for schedules of the myriad concerts, operas, and theater
performances in Lübeck. ✉ *Willy-Brandt-Allee 10* ☎ *0451/79040*
⊕ *www.muk.de.*

Schleswig-Holstein Music Festival. In summer, try to catch a few perfor-
mances at this annual music festival (mid-July–late August), which
features orchestras composed of young musicians from more than 25
countries. Some concerts are held in the Dom or the Marienkirche;
some are staged in barns in small towns and villages. For exact
dates and tickets, contact Schleswig-Holstein Konzertorganisation.
☎ *0431/570–470* ⊕ *www.shmf.de.*

SHOPPING

Local legend has it that marzipan was invented in Lübeck during the
great medieval famine. According to the story, a local baker ran out of
grain for bread and, in his desperation, began experimenting with the
only four ingredients he had: almonds, sugar, rosewater, and eggs. The
result was a sweet almond paste known today as marzipan. The story
is more fiction than fact; it is generally agreed that marzipan's true ori-
gins lie in the Middle East. ■TIP➜ **Lübecker Marzipan, an appellation
that has been trademarked, is now considered among the best in the
world. Any Marzipan that uses the appellation Lübecker, must be made
within the city limits.**

Holstentor-Passage. The city's largest downtown shopping mall is next to
the Holstentor and is filled with stores selling clothing or home acces-
sories. ✉ *An der Untertrave 111* ☎ *0451/75292.*

Konditorei-Café Niederegger. Lübeck's most famous marzipan maker,
Konditorei-Café Niederegger, sells the delicacy molded into a mul-
titude of imaginative forms at its flagship store. ✉ *Breitestr. 89*
☎ *0451/530–1127.*

14

WESTERN MECKLENBURG

This long-forgotten Baltic Coast region, pinned between two sprawling urban areas—the state capital of Schwerin, in the west, and Rostock, in the east—is thriving with trade, industry, and tourism. Though the region is close to the sea, it's made up largely of seemingly endless fields of wheat and yellow rape and a hundred or so wonderful lakes. "When the Lord made the Earth, He started with Mecklenburg," wrote native novelist Fritz Reuter.

WISMAR

60 km (37 miles) east of Lübeck on Route 105.

The old city of Wismar was one of the original three sea-trading towns, along with Lübeck and Rostock, which banded together in 1259 to combat Baltic pirates. From this mutual defense pact grew the great and powerful private-trading bloc, the Hanseatic League (the *Hanse* in German), which dominated the Baltic for centuries. The wealth generated by the Hanseatic merchants can still be seen in Wismar's ornate architecture.

ESSENTIALS

Visitor Information Wismar Stadthaus ⊠ *Am Markt 11* ☎ *03841/19433* ⊕ *www.wismar.de.*

EXPLORING

TOP ATTRACTIONS

Marktplatz (*Market Square*). One of the largest and best-preserved squares in Germany is framed by patrician gabled houses. Their style ranges from redbrick late Gothic through Dutch Renaissance to 19th-century neoclassical. The square's **Wasserkunst,** the ornate pumping station built in Dutch Renaissance style, was constructed between 1580 and 1602 by the Dutch master Philipp Brandin.

St. Georgen zu Wismar. This church, another victim of the war, stands next to the Fürstenhof. One of northern Germany's biggest Gothic churches, built between 1315 and 1404, it has been almost completely restored. ⊠ *St.-Georgen-Kirchhof 6.*

To'n Zägenkrog. If you have an hour to spare, wander among the jetties and quays of the port, a mix of the medieval and the modern. To'n Zägenkrog, a seamen's haven decorated with sharks' teeth, stuffed seagulls, and maritime gear, is a good pit stop along the harbor. ⊠ *Ziegenmarkt 10* ☎ *03841/282–716.*

WORTH NOTING

Fürstenhof (*Princes' Court*). The home of the former dukes of Mecklenburg stands next to the Marienkirche. It's an early-16th-century Italian Renaissance palace with touches of late Gothic. The facade is a series of fussy friezes depicting scenes from the Trojan War. ⊠ *Fürstenhof 1.*

Marienkirche (*St. Mary's Church*). The ruins of this church with its 250-foot tower, bombed in World War II, lie just behind the Marktplatz; the church is still undergoing restoration. ■**TIP→** At noon, 3, and 5, listen for one of 14 hymns played on its carillon. ⊠ *St.-Marien-Kirchhof.*

St. Nikolaikirche (*St. Nicholas's Church*). The late-Gothic church, with a 120-foot-high nave, was built between 1381 and 1487. A remnant of the town's long domination by Sweden is the additional altar built for Swedish sailors. ⊠ *St.-Nikolai-Kirchhof 15* ☏ *03841/210–143* ⊙ *May–Sept., daily 8–8; Apr. and Oct., daily 10–6; Nov.–Mar., daily 11–4.*

WHERE TO EAT

$
GERMAN
✕ **Alter Schwede.** Regarded as one of the most attractive, authentic taverns on the Baltic—and correspondingly busy—this eatery focuses on Mecklenburg's game and poultry dishes, such as the traditional *Mecklenburger Ente* (Mecklenburg duck). This filling dish is filled with baked plums, apples, raisins, and served with red cabbage and potatoes. ⑤ *Average main: €14* ⊠ *Am Markt 19* ☏ *03841/283–552.*

$
GERMAN
✕ **Brauhaus am Lohberg.** Wismar's first brewery (1452) is the only place that still brews *Wismarer Mumme*, a dark beer with enough alcohol to keep it fresh for export as far away as St. Petersburg. The restaurant serves up good-value typical pub food in an old half-timber house near the harbor. ⑤ *Average main: €13* ⊠ *Kleine Hohe Str. 15* ☏ *03841/250–238.*

WHERE TO STAY

$$
B&B/INN

⬚ **Citypartner Hotel Alter Speicher.** This small and very personal family-owned hotel is behind the facade of an old merchant house in the downtown area. **Pros:** good location, as medieval parts of Wismar are within easy walking-distance. **Cons:** rooms have outdated furnishings and ambience. ⑤ *Rooms from: €110* ⊠ *Bohrstr. 12–12a* ☎ *03841/211–746* ⊕ *www.hotel-alter-speicher.de* ↪ *70 rooms, 3 suites, 2 apartments* ⑪ *Breakfast.*

$$
B&B/INN

⬚ **Seehotel Neuklostersee.** Set at the dreamy Naun Lake, this country hotel is a hidden gem 15 km (9 miles) east of Wismar. **Pros:** great rural setting in quaint surroundings. **Cons:** outside Wismar; many day-trip visitors. ⑤ *Rooms from: €135* ⊠ *Seestr. 1, Nakenstorf* ☎ *038422/4570* ⊕ *www. seehotel-neuklostersee.de* ↪ *10 suites, 3 apartments* ⑪ *Breakfast.*

$
HOTEL

⬚ **Steigenberger–Hotel Stadt Hamburg.** This first-class hotel hides behind a rigid gray facade dating back to the early 19th century. **Pros:** the only upscale hotel in town, with an appealing interior design; great package deals available. **Cons:** lacks atmosphere and personal touches. ⑤ *Rooms from: €96* ⊠ *Am Markt 24* ☎ *03841/2390* ⊕ *www.wismar. steigenberger.de* ↪ *102 rooms, 2 suites* ⑪ *Breakfast.*

SCHWERIN

32 km (20 miles) south of Wismar on Route 106.

Schwerin, the second-largest town in the region after Rostock and the capital of the state of Mecklenburg-Vorpommern, is worth a trip just to visit its giant island castle.

ESSENTIALS

Visitor Information Schwerin ⊠ *Am Markt 14* ☎ *0385/592–5212* ⊕ *www.schwerin.de.*

EXPLORING

FAMILY   **Alter Garten** (*Old Garden*). The town's showpiece square was the setting of military parades during the years of Communist rule. It's dominated by two buildings: the ornate neo-Renaissance state theater, constructed in 1883–86; and the **Kunstsammlungen Schwerin** (Schwerin Art Collection), which houses an interesting collection of paintings by Max Liebermann and Lovis Corinth. ⊠ *Alter Garten 3* ☎ *0385/595–8119* ⊕ *www.museum-schwerin.de* ⬚ *€8* ⊙ *Mid-Apr.–mid-Oct., Tues.–Sun. 10–6; mid-Oct.–mid-Apr., Tues.–Sun. 10–5.*

Schweriner Dom (*Schwerin Cathedral*). This Gothic cathedral is the oldest building (built 1222–48) in the city. The bronze baptismal font is from the 14th century; the altar was built in 1440. Religious scenes painted on its walls date from the late Middle Ages. Sweeping views of the Old Town and lake await those with the energy to climb the 219 steps to the top of the 320-foot-high cathedral tower. ⊠ *Am Dom 4* ☎ *0385/565–014* ⊙ *Tower and nave: May–Oct., Mon.–Sat. 10–5, Sun. noon–5; Nov.–Apr., weekdays 11–4, Sat. 11–4, Sun. noon–4.*

Schlossmuseum. North of the main tower is the **Neue Lange Haus** (New Long House), built between 1553 and 1555 and now used as the Schlossmuseum. The Communist government restored and maintained

If the weather is fine, take a stroll along Wismar's historic harbor.

the fantastic opulence of this rambling, 80-room reminder of an absolutist monarchy—and then used it to board kindergarten teachers in training. Antique furniture, objets d'art, silk tapestries, and paintings are sprinkled throughout the salons (the throne room is particularly extravagant), but of special interest are the ornately patterned and highly burnished inlaid wooden floors and wall panels. ⊠ *Lennéstr. 1* ☎ *0385/525–2920* ⊕ *www.museum-schwerin.de* 🖾 *€6* ⊗ *Mid-Apr.–mid-Oct., daily 10–6; mid-Oct.–mid-Apr., Tues.–Sun. 10–5.*

Schweriner Schloss. On island near the edge of Lake Schwerin, the meticulously restored palace once housed the Mecklenburg royal family. The original palace dates from 1018, but was enlarged by Henry the Lion when he founded Schwerin in 1160. Portions of it were later modeled on Chambord, in the Loire Valley. As it stands now, the palace is surmounted by 15 turrets, large and small, and is reminiscent of a French château. The portions that are neo-Renaissance in style are its many ducal staterooms, which date from between 1845 and 1857. ⊠ *Lennéstr. 1.*

FAMILY **Weisse Flotte.** The quintessential experience in Schwerin is one of the Weiss Flotte boat tours of the lakes—there are seven in the area. A trip to the island of Kaninchenwerder, a small sanctuary for more than 100 species of waterbirds, is an unforgettable experience. Boats for this 1½-hour standard tour depart from the pier adjacent to the Schweriner Schloss. ⊠ *Anlegestelle Schlosspier* ☎ *0385/557–770* ⊕ *www. weisseflotteschwerin.de* 🖾 *€12.50* ⊗ *Apr.–Oct., daily 10–5:30.*

WHERE TO EAT

$
GERMAN

✕ **Alt-Schweriner Schankstuben.** A small family-owned restaurant and hotel with 16 guest rooms, the Schankstuben emphasizes Mecklenburg tradition. Its inviting restaurant is perfect for sampling local recipes such as *Rullbraten von Spanferkel* (roast suckling pig) or *Maisscholle* (corn-fed plaice). ⑤ *Average main: €12* ✉ *Schlachtermarkt 9–13* ☎ *0385/592–530* ⊕ *www.alt-schweriner-schankstuben.de.*

$
GERMAN

✕ **Weinhaus Krömer.** One of the most traditional and popular eateries in Schwerin, this restaurant has a long history of serving good wines that date from 1740. The *Weinbistro* offers primarily German wine and a small menu (mostly cheese plates or soups such as lobster cream soup). Regional and international specialties are served in the modern restaurant, while in summer the Weingarten courtyard is one of the city's most secluded spots to enjoy a good glass of wine. ⑤ *Average main: €13* ✉ *Grosser Moor 56* ☎ *0385/562–956.*

$
GERMAN

✕ **Zum Stadtkrug-Altstadtbrauhaus.** Don't be fooled by the prefab exterior, Schwerin's only brewery is an oasis of great beer and down-to-earth regional and Brauhaus specialties like the Malzsack (a cordon bleu breaded with brewing malt) or Mecklenburger lamb. Wash it down with the house-brewed unfiltered light or dark beer. ⑤ *Average main: €10* ✉ *Wismarsche Str. 126* ☎ *0385/593–6693* ⊕ *www.altstadtbrauhaus.de* ▭ *No credit cards.*

WHERE TO STAY

$$
HOTEL

🏨 **Hotel Niederländischer Hof.** The city's most elegant hotel has a 4½-star rating in view of its luxurious interior, decorated in a classic style; its romantic, airy rooms; the impeccable service; and, of course, the fine nouvelle cuisine à la Mecklenburg (mostly seafood dishes). **Pros:** interesting packages include tours, dinner, and more; great location right off a lake and within walking distance of the Schloss, boat docks, and downtown museums. **Cons:** formal atmosphere. ⑤ *Rooms from: €150* ✉ *Alexandrinenstr. 12–13* ☎ *0385/591–100* ⊕ *www.niederlaendischer-hof.de* ⤳ *27 rooms, 6 suites* ⑪ *Breakfast.*

$$
HOTEL

🏨 **Sorat-Hotel Speicher am Ziegelsee.** Towering seven stories above the old harbor, the Speicher am Ziegelsee was once a wheat warehouse. **Pros:** unbeatable location on a lovely lake and lakeside dining; very friendly and professional service. **Cons:** old-style warehouse building, whose rooms may seem cramped for some travelers; a bit far from the action. ⑤ *Rooms from: €105* ✉ *Speicherstr. 11* ☎ *0385/50030* ⊕ *www.speicher-hotel.com* ⤳ *59 rooms, 20 apartments* ⑪ *Breakfast.*

NIGHTLIFE AND THE ARTS

Mecklenburgisches Staatstheater. The Mecklenburgisches Staatstheater stages German drama and opera. ✉ *Am Alten Garten* ☎ *0385/53000* ⊕ *www.theater-schwerin.de.*

Mexxclub. This is the city's hottest dance club. It features house and soul DJs who attract a stylish young crowd every Saturday night. ✉ *Klöresgang 2.*

Schlossfestspiele. Started in 1993, this annual summertime festival features open-air drama or comedy performances, which are held at various venues around Schwerin including the Mecklenburg State Theatre, the castle garden, the National Theatre, and the National Museum. ✉ *Schlossstr. 1, Schwein.*

SHOPPING

Antiques and bric-a-brac that have languished in cellars and attics since World War II are still surfacing throughout eastern Germany, and the occasional bargain can be found. The best places to look in Schwerin are on and around Schmiedestrasse, Schlossstrasse, and Mecklenburgstrasse.

BAD DOBERAN

60 km (37 miles) east of Wismar on Route 105, 90 km (56 miles) northeast of Schwerin.

14

Bad Doberan, mostly famous for its cathedral, is a quaint town that also has Germany's oldest sea resort, Heiligendamm. The city is a popular weekend and summer getaway for people from Rostock and Berlin, but it's managed to maintain its laid-back charm.

ESSENTIALS

Visitor Information Bad Doberan ✉ *Severinstr. 6* ☎ *038203/62154* ⊕ *www.bad-doberan.de.*

EXPLORING

Doberaner Münster (*Monastery church*). Bad Doberan is home to the meticulously restored redbrick church, one of the finest of its kind in Germany. It was built by Cistercian monks between 1294 and 1368 in the northern German brick Gothic style, with a central nave and transept. The main altar dates from the early 14th century. ✉ *Klosterstr. 2* ☎ *038203/62716* ⊕ *www.doberanermuenster.de* 🎫 *€2* 🕐 *May–Sept., Mon.–Sat. 9–6, Sun. 11–6; Mar., Apr., and Oct., Mon.–Sat. 10–5, Sun. 11–5; Nov.–Feb., Mon.–Sat. 10–4, Sun. 11–4. Tours: May–Oct., Mon.–Sat. at noon and 3; Nov.–Apr., Mon.–Sat. at 11 and 1.*

FAMILY **Molli.** No visit to this part of the country would be complete without a ride on this narrow-gauge steam train that has been chugging the 16 km (10 miles) through the streets of Bad Doberan to the nearby beach resorts of **Heiligendamm** and **Kühlungsborn** since 1886. The train was nicknamed after a little local dog that barked its approval every time the smoking iron horse passed by. In summer *Molli* runs 13 times daily between Bad Doberan and Kühlungsborn. ✉ *Mecklenburgische Bäderbahn Molli, Küstenbus GmbH, Am Bahnhof* ☎ *038203/4150* ⊕ *www.molli-bahn.de* 🎫 *Same-day round-trip €8–€12* 🕐 *From Bad Doberan: May–Sept., daily 8:35–6:45; Oct.–Apr., daily 8:35–4:40.*

WHERE TO EAT AND STAY

$ ✕ **Weisser Pavillon.** Here's a mixed setting for you: a 19th-century Chinese-pagoda-type structure in an English-style park. Come for lunch or high tea; regional specialties are featured. In summer the café stays open until 10 pm. ⑤ *Average main: €9* ✉ *Auf dem Kamp* ☎ *038203/62326* 🚫 *No credit cards.*

GERMAN

$$$$
HOTEL
Fodor'sChoice
★

📺 **Grand Hotel Heiligendamm.** The small beach resort of Heiligendamm has regained its prewar reputation as a getaway for Berlin's up-and-coming crowd. **Pros:** the only real first-class hotel on the Baltic Coast, with a wide range of sports and activities. **Cons:** very large hotel spread out in somewhat long distances; service is formal and stiff at times; books up quickly in high season. ⑤ *Rooms from: €220* ✉ *Grand Hotel at Heiligendamm, Prof.-Dr.-Vogel-Str. 16–18, Heiligendamm* 📞 *038203/7400* ⊕ *www.grandhotel-heiligendamm.de* 🛏 *118 rooms, 107 suites* 🍽*Breakfast.*

ROSTOCK

14 km (9 miles) east of Bad Doberan on Route 105.

Rostock, the biggest port and shipbuilding center of the former East Germany, was founded around 1200. Of all the Hanseatic cities, the once-thriving Rostock suffered the most from the dissolution of the League in 1669. The GDR reestablished Rostock as a major port, but shipbuilding work has been cut in half since unification. Ferries from Gedser (Denmark) and Trelleborg (Sweden) come here. The population of Rostock doubles in the summer due to Baltic cruise ships that dock in Warnemünde. ▮**TIP→** The biggest local annual attraction is Hanse Sail, a week of yacht racing held in August.

ESSENTIALS

Visitor Information Rostock ✉ *Universitätspl. 6* 📞 *0381/32222* ⊕ *www.rostock.de.*

EXPLORING

TOP ATTRACTIONS

Kröpelinerstrasse. This pedestrian-only shopping street stretches from the old the Kröpeliner Tor (the old western gate) to the Neuer Markt. Here you'll find the finest examples of late-Gothic and Renaissance houses of rich Hanse merchants.

St. Marienkirche (*St. Mary's Church*). This four-century-old church, the Gothic architectural prize of Rostock, boasts a bronze baptismal font from 1290 and some interesting baroque features, notably the oak altar (1720) and organ (1770). The huge astronomical clock, dating from 1472, has a calendar extending to 2017. ✉ *Am Ziegenmarkt 4* 📞 *0381/492–3396* ⊘ *Oct.–Apr., Mon.–Sat. 10–12:15 and 2–4, Sun. 11–12:15; May–Sept., Mon.–Sat. 10–6, Sun. 11:15–5.*

Universitätsplatz (*University Square*). The triangular University Square, commemorating the founding of northern Europe's first university here in 1419, is home to Rostock University's Italian Renaissance–style main building, finished in 1867.

WORTH NOTING

Neuer Markt (*Town Square*). Here, you'll immediately notice the architectural potpourri of the **Rathaus.** The pink baroque facade from the 18th century hides a wonderful 13th-century Gothic building underneath. The town hall spouts seven slender, decorative towers that look like candles on a peculiar birthday cake. Walk around back to see more of the Gothic elements. Historic gabled houses surround the rest of the square.

FAMILY **Schifffahrtsmuseum** (*Maritime Museum*). Tracing the history of shipping on the Baltic, this museum displays models of ships, which especially intrigue children. It's just beyond the city wall, at the old city gateway, Steintor. ✉ *August-Bebel-Str. 1* ☎ *0381/492–2697* ⊕ *www. schifffahrtsmuseum-rostock.de* 💰 *€4* ☾ *Tues.–Sun. 11–6.*

FAMILY **Zoologischer Garten** (*Zoological Garden*). Here you'll find one of the largest collections of exotic animals and birds in northern Germany. This zoo is particularly noted for its polar bears, some of which were bred in Rostock. If you're traveling with children, a visit is a must. ✉ *Rennbahnallee 21* ☎ *0381/20820* ⊕ *www.zoo-rostock.de* 💰 *€16* ☾ *Nov.–Mar., daily 9–5; Apr.–Oct., daily 9–7.*

WHERE TO EAT

$ ✕ **Petrikeller.** Once you've crossed the threshold of the Petrikeller, you'll
GERMAN find yourself in the medieval world of Hanseatic merchants, seamen, and wild pirates such as Klaus Störtebecker. The restaurant's motto, "Wer nicht liebt Wein, Weib und Gesang bleibt ein Narr sein Leben lang" ("He who doth not love wine, woman and song will be a fool his whole life long"), a quote from reformer Martin Luther no less, sets the right tone. Ⓢ *Average main: €13* ✉ *Harte Str. 27* ☎ *0381/455–855* ⊕ *www.petrikeller.de* ▭ *No credit cards* ☾ *Closed Mon. No lunch.*

$$$ ✕ **Restaurant & Bar Silo 4.** Rostock's latest culinary venture is proof that
ASIAN eastern Germany can do sleek and modern. At the top of a waterfront office tower, this innovative restaurant offers spectacular views of the river and a fun and interesting approach to Asian-fusion cuisine. The buffet consists of a list of ingredients and seasonings. Guests choose what they like and then leave it to the experts in the show kitchen to work their magic. Ⓢ *Average main: €23* ✉ *Am Strande 3d* ☎ *0381/458–5800* ⊕ *www.silo4.de* ☾ *Closed Mon. No lunch.*

$ ✕ **Zur Kogge.** Looking like the cabin of a Kogge, a Hanseatic sailing ves-
SEAFOOD sel, the oldest sailors' beer tavern in town serves mostly fish. Order the *Mecklenburger Fischsuppe* (fish soup) if it's on the menu. The *Grosser Fischteller,* consisting of three kinds of fish—depending on the day's catch—served with vegetables, lobster and shrimp sauce, and potatoes, is also a popular choice. Ⓢ *Average main: €12* ✉ *Wokrenterstr. 27* ☎ *0381/493–4493* ✎ *Reservations essential.*

WHERE TO STAY

$ 🏨 **Pental Hotel.** A 19th-century mansion, this hotel is a genuine part
HOTEL of Rostock's historic Old Town. **Pros:** good location; very quiet backstreet. **Cons:** restaurant isn't very good; bland room design. Ⓢ *Rooms from: €76* ✉ *Schwaansche Str. 6* ☎ *0381/49700* ⊕ *www.pentahotels. com* ⤳ *150 rooms, 2 suites* ⦿ *Breakfast.*

$$ 🏨 **Steigenberger–Hotel zur Sonne Rostock.** With more than 200 years of
HOTEL history behind it, the "Sun," located within the Old Town, is one of the nicest hotels in Rostock. **Pros:** nice view and near many sights; good restaurants, cafés, and bars nearby. **Cons:** rooms get direct sunlight in summer, and therefore are very warm; open setting of bed in the middle of the room may be unsettling for some. Ⓢ *Rooms from: €159* ✉ *Neuer Markt 2* ☎ *0381/49730* ⊕ *www.rostock.steigenberger.de* ⤳ *90 rooms, 21 suites* ⦿ *Breakfast.*

14

NIGHTLIFE AND THE ARTS

The summer season brings with it a plethora of special concerts, sailing regattas, and parties on the beach.

Volkstheater. The Volkstheater presents plays and concerts, from the classics to more contemporary works. ✉ *Patriotischer Weg 33* ☎ *0381/4600.*

SHOPPING

Echter Rostocker Doppel-Kümmel und -Korn, a kind of schnapps made from various grains and flavored with cumin, is a traditional liquor of the area around Rostock. Fishermen have numbed themselves to the cold for centuries with this 80-proof beverage. A bottle costs €8–€11; Lehmmet is the best brand of this local moonshine.

WARNEMÜNDE

14 km (9 miles) north of Rostock on Route 103.

Warnemünde is a quaint seaside resort town with the best hotels and restaurants in the area, as well as 20 km (12 miles) of beautiful white-sand beach. It's been a popular summer getaway for families in eastern Germany for years.

There is little to do in Warnemünde except relax, and the town excels brilliantly at that. However, Warnemünde is a major cruise ship terminal. Whenever there is more than one ship at dock, the town explodes with a county fair–like atmosphere, where shops and restaurants stay open until the ships leave at midnight. The city celebrates the *dreifache Anlauf,* when three ships dock simultaneously, with fireworks.

GETTING HERE AND AROUND

Thanks to its close location to Rostock and the A-20, Warnemünde is easily accessible from any major city in the region. Traffic between the seaside district of Rostock and the downtown area can be heavy on summer weekends. The best way to explore the city is by riding a bike or walking.

EXPLORING

Alter Strom (*Old Stream*). Inland from the lighthouse is this yacht marina. Once the entry into the port of Warnemünde, it now has bars, plenty of good restaurants, and touristy shops. The fishing boats lining the Strom sell the day's catch, smoked fish, and bags of fried mussels. ✉ *Alter Strom 1.*

FAMILY **Leuchtturm.** Children enjoy climbing to the top of the town landmark, a 115-foot-high lighthouse, dating from 1898; on clear days it offers views of the coast and Rostock Harbor. ✉ *Seepromenade.*

WHERE TO EAT AND STAY

$ ✕ **Fischerklause.** Sailors have stopped in at this restaurant's bar since
SEAFOOD the turn of the 20th century. The smoked fish sampler, served on a lazy Susan, is delicious, and the house specialty of fish soup is best washed down with some Rostocker Doppel-Kümmel schnapps. An accordionist entertains the crowd on weekends. $ *Average main: €11* ✉ *Am Strom 123* ☎ *0381/52516* ✍ *Reservations essential.*

$ **⊞ Landhotel Ostseetraum.** This family-owned hotel, in a thatch-roof
RESORT farmhouse outside Warnemünde, blends contemporary style with
rural architecture. **Pros:** quiet; green setting not far away from the sea;
friendly and personalized service; very private apartments. **Cons:** old-
fashioned interior design in need of updating in some rooms and public areas; located outside Warnemünde proper. **⑤** *Rooms from: €89*
✉ *Stolteraerweg 34b, Warnemünde-Diedrichshagen* ☎ *0381/519–1848*
⊕ *www.ostseetraum.de* ⤴ *18 rooms* ⦅◎⦆ *Breakfast.*

$$$ **⊞ Yachthafenresidenz Hohe Düne.** The star on the Baltic Coast is this
RESORT huge, modern resort comfortably residing on a peninsula between the
yacht harbor, a sandy beach, and the port entrance. **Pros:** very well run;
stylish hotel with a great ambience and all the amenities; impressive
wellness and spa area. **Cons:** outside Warnemünde; accessible only by
ferry from the town center and not along the central promenade; only
a few attractions and restaurants in walking distance, pretentious staff.
⑤ *Rooms from: €205* ✉ *Hohe Düne, Am Yachthafen 1–8* ☎ *0381/5040*
⊕ *www.yhd.de* ⤴ *345 rooms, 23 suites* ⦅◎⦆ *Breakfast.*

NIGHTLIFE
The pubs in the marina **Alter Strom** are fun gathering places.

Skybar. The Skybar is open Friday and Saturday until 3 am. ▇ **TIP➔ Roof
access gives you the chance to sit under the stars and watch ship lights
twinkle on the sea.** ✉ *Neptun Hotel, Seestr. 19, 19th fl., Rostock-War-
nemünde* ☎ *0381/7770.*

SPORTS AND THE OUTDOORS
BEACHES
Warnemünde. The beach fronting the resort town of Warnemünde is one
of Germany's most popular beaches and it can get fairly crowded in
summer. The expansive beach, with its soft, clean sand, is fabulous for
sunbathing, relaxing, or walking. The pleasant sea breeze invites kite-
flyers and you can purchase different kinds of kites from the open-air
market along the promenade. Food and drink are available from many
vendors and at several supermarkets in the town itself. **Amenities:** food
and drink; parking; showers; toilets; water sports.

Best for: partiers; sunrise; sunset; surfing; swimming; walking. ✉ *See
promende 1.*

EN
ROUTE
Ribnitz-Damgarten. This town, 30 km (19 miles) northeast of Warne-
münde, is the center of the amber (in German, Bernstein) business,
unique to the Baltic Coast. Amber is a yellow-brown fossil formed from
the sap of ancient conifers. Head for a beach and join the locals seeking
the amber stones washed up among the seaweed.

Deutsches Bernsteinmuseum (*German Amber Museum*). At this museum,
which adjoins the main amber factory, you can see a fascinating exhibit
of how "Baltic gold" is collected from the sea and refined to make
jewelry. Some of the amber here is between 35 and 50 million years
old. ✉ *Im Kloster 1–3, Ribnitz-Damgarten* ☎ *03821/2931* ⊕ *www.
deutsches-bernsteinmuseum.de* ⦅⦆ *€8.50* ⊘ *Mar.–Oct., daily 9:30–6;
Nov.–Feb., Tues.–Sun. 9:30–5; last entry 30 mins before closing.*

14

VORPOMMERN

The best description of this region is found in its name, which simply means "before Pomerania." This area, indeed, seems trapped between Mecklenburg and the authentic, old Pomerania farther east, now part of Poland. Its remoteness ensures an unforgettable view of unspoiled nature, primarily attracting families and younger travelers.

STRALSUND

68 km (42 miles) east of Rostock on Route 105.

This jewel of the Baltic has retained its historic city center and parts of its 13th-century defensive wall. The wall was built following an attack by the Lübeck fleet in 1249. In 1815 the Congress of Vienna awarded the city, which had been under Swedish control, to the Prussians.

GETTING HERE AND AROUND

Stralsund is well linked to both Rostock and Berlin by A-20 and A-19. The city is an ideal base for exploring the coast via the well-developed network of Bundesstrassen around it. Inside the city, walking or biking are better options, though, as the dense, historic downtown area makes it difficult to drive.

ESSENTIALS

Visitor Information Stralsund ⊠ *Alter Markt 9* ☎ *03831/24690* ⊕ *www.stralsund.de.*

EXPLORING
TOP ATTRACTIONS

Alter Markt (*Old Market Square*). The Alter Markt has the best local architecture, ranging from Gothic to Renaissance to baroque. Most homes belonged to rich merchants, notably the late-Gothic **Wulflamhaus,** with 17 ornate, steeply stepped gables. Stralsund's architectural masterpiece, however, is the 14th-century **Rathaus,** considered by many to be the finest secular example of redbrick Gothic. The Rathaus is a mirror image of the a similar building in Lübeck, Stralsund's main rival in the Hanseatic League ⊠ *Alter Markt 1.*

FAMILY **Deutsches Meeresmuseum** (*German Sea Museum*). The Stralsund aquarium of Baltic Sea life is part of this three-floor museum, which also displays the skeletons of a giant whale and a hammerhead shark, and a 25-foot-high chunk of coral. ⊠ *Katharinenberg 14–20, entrance on Mönchstr.* ☎ *03831/265–021* ⊕ *www.meeresmuseum.de* ☜ *€9* ⊙ *Oct.– May, daily 10–5; June–Sept., daily 10–6.*

St. Marienkirche (*St. Mary's Church*). This enormous church is the largest of Stralsund's three redbrick Gothic churches. With 4,000 pipes and intricate decorative figures, the magnificent 17th-century Stellwagen organ (played only during Sunday services) is a delight to see and hear. The view from the church tower of Stralsund's old city center is well worth climbing 349 steps. ⊠ *Neuer Markt, entrance at Bleistr., Marienstr.* ☎ *03831/293–529* ☜ *Tour of church tower €4* ⊙ *May–Oct., weekdays 9–6, weekends 10–noon; Nov.–Apr., weekdays 10–noon and 2–6, weekends 10–noon.*

WORTH NOTING

Katherinenkloster (*St. Catherine's Monastery*). A former cloister, 40 of its rooms now house two museums: the famed Deutsches Meeresmuseum, and the Kulturhistorisches Museum. ✉ *Bielkenhagen.*

Kulturhistorisches Museum (*Cultural History Museum*). This museum exhibits diverse artifacts from more than 10,000 years of this coastal region's history. Highlights include a toy collection and 10th-century Viking gold jewelry found on Hiddensee. You reach the museums by walking along Ossenreyerstrasse through the Apollonienmarkt on Mönchstrasse. ✉ *Kulturhistorisches Museum, Mönchstr. 25–27* ☎ *03831/28790* 💲 *€6* ⊗ *Tues.–Sun.10–5.*

St. Nikolaikirche (*St. Nicholas's Church*). The treasures of the 13th-century Gothic church include a 15-foot-high crucifix from the 14th century, an astronomical clock from 1394, and a famous baroque altar. ✉ *Alter Markt* ☎ *03831/297–199* ⊗ *Apr.–Sept., Mon.–Sat. 10–6, Sun. 11–noon and 2–4; Oct.–Mar., Mon.–Sat. 10–noon and 2–4, Sun. 11–noon and 2–4.*

WHERE TO EAT AND STAY

$
SEAFOOD
✕ **Wulflamstuben.** This restaurant is on the ground floor of the Wulflamhaus, a 14th-century gabled house on the old market square. Steaks and fish are the specialties; in late spring or early summer, get the light and tasty *Ostseescholle* (grilled plaice), fresh from the Baltic Sea. In winter the hearty *Stralsunder Aalsuppe* (Stralsund eel soup) is a must. 💲 *Average main: €14* ✉ *Alter Markt 5* ☎ *03831/291–533* ⊕ *www.wulflamstuben.de* ⌂ *Reservations essential.*

$
GERMAN
✕ **Zum Alten Fritz.** It's worth the trip here just to see the rustic interior and copper brewing equipment. Since the restaurant is owned by the Stralsunder Brewery, all Stralsunder and several Störtebecker beers are on tap, including the rare Störtebecker Roggen-Weizen, a wheat beer made with rye, and Germany's first India Pale Ale. In summer the beer garden gets somewhat rambunctious. 💲 *Average main: €11* ✉ *Greifswalder Chaussee 84–85, at B–96a* ☎ *03831/25550.*

$$
HOTEL
⛉ **Hotel zur Post.** This redbrick hotel is a great deal for travelers looking for a homey yet first-class ambience. **Pros:** very good location in the heart of the historic downtown area; good deals offered on hotel website. **Cons:** very small rooms with too much furniture; some rooms in need of updating. 💲 *Rooms from: €122* ✉ *Am Neuen Markt, Tribseerstr. 22* ☎ *03831/200–500* ⊕ *www.hotel-zur-post-stralsund.de* ⌁ *104 rooms, 2 suites, 8 apartments* ⦿ *Breakfast.*

$$
HOTEL
⛉ **Radisson Blu Hotel Stralsund.** This hotel, part of the Radisson brand, is a modern property with winning amenities and great hospitality at an unbeatable price. **Pros:** top spa; solid and reliable services and amenities; long breakfast service (until 11 am). **Cons:** for Stralsund, this is a large, busy hotel; far away from city center (15 minutes). 💲 *Rooms from: €129* ✉ *Grünhofer Bogen 18–20* ☎ *03831/37730* ⊕ *www.radissonblu.com/hotel-stralsund* ⌁ *109 rooms, 5 suites* ⦿ *Breakfast.*

NIGHTLIFE

Bar Hemingway. This bar lures a thirtysomething clientele with the best cocktails in town. ✉ *Tribseerstr. 22* ☎ *03831/200–500.*

DID YOU KNOW?

Sellin's pier on Rügen Island is a delightful place for a stroll at night, when the pier building is illuminated.

Fun und Lollipop. A young crowd dances at Fun und Lollipop. ⊠ *Grünhofer Bogen 11* ☎ *03834/399–039.*

Störtebeker-Keller. For a genuine old harbor *Kneipe* (tavern), head to the Störtebeker-Keller, named for an infamous pirate. ⊠ *Ossenreyerstr. 49* ☎ *03831/292–758.*

SHOPPING

Buddelschiffe (ships in a bottle) are a symbol of the magnificent sailing history of this region. They look easy to build, but they aren't, and they're quite delicate. Expect to pay more than €70 for a 1-liter bottle. Also look for *Fischerteppiche* (fishermen's carpets). Eleven square feet of these traditional carpets take 150 hours to create, which explains why they're meant only to be hung on the wall—and why they cost from €260 to €1,200. They're decorated with traditional symbols of the region, such as the mythical griffin.

14

RÜGEN ISLAND

4 km (2½ miles) northeast of Stralsund on B-96.

Fodor's Choice ★ Rügen's diverse and breathtaking landscapes have inspired poets and painters for more than a century. Railways in the mid-19th century brought the first vacationers from Berlin and many of the grand mansions and villas on the island date from this period. The island's main route runs between the **Grosser Jasmunder Bodden** (Big Jasmund Inlet), a giant sea inlet, and a smaller expanse of water, the **Kleiner Jasmunder Bodden** (Little Jasmund Inlet Lake), to the port of Sassnitz. You're best off staying at any of the island's four main vacation centers—Sassnitz, Binz, Sellin, and Göhren.

GETTING HERE AND AROUND

Rügen is an easy two-hour drive from Rostock and a 15-minute drive from Stralsund via the B-96. As there is only one bridge connecting the island to the mainland, the road can get clogged occasionally in summer. On the island, a car is highly recommended to reach the more-remote beaches, but watch out for island teenagers and their infatuation with muscle cars; give them a wide berth.

ESSENTIALS

Visitor Information Rügen Island ⊠ *Tourismusverband Rügen, Bahnhofstr. 15, Bergen* ☎ *03838/807–780* ⊕ *www.ruegen.de.* **Sassnitz** ⊠ *Bahnhofstr. 19a, Sassnitz* ☎ *038392/6490* ⊕ *www.insassnitz.de.*

EXPLORING
TOP ATTRACTIONS

Binz. The largest resort town on Rügen's east coast, it has white villas and a beach promenade. Four kilometers (2½ miles) north of Binz are five concrete quarters of **Bad Prora**, where the Nazis once planned to provide vacation quarters for up to 20,000 German workers. The complex was never used, except by the East German army. Museums and galleries here today include one that documents the history of the site. ⊠ *Strandpromenade 1, Binz.*

Jagdschloss Granitz. Standing on the highest point of East Rügen is the Jagdschloss Granitz, a hunting lodge built in 1836. It offers a splendid view in all directions from its lookout tower and has an excellent hunting exhibit. ⊠ *2 km (1 mile) south of Binz* ☎ *038393/663–814* ⊕ *www.jagdschloss-granitz. de* ⊡ *€3* ☉ *May–Sept., daily 9–6; Oct.–Apr., Tues.–Sun. 10–4*

Kap Arkona. Marking the northernmost point in eastern Germany is the lighthouse at Kap Arkona, a nature lover's paradise filled with blustery sand dunes. The redbrick lighthouse was designed by Karl Friedrich Schinkel, the architect responsible for so many of today's landmarks in Berlin. ⊠ *Kap Arkona, Putgarten.*

Sassnitz. This small fishing town is the island's harbor for ferries to Sweden. Sassnitz is surrounded by some of the most pristine nature to be found along the Baltic Coast. Ten kilometers (6 miles) north of Sassnitz are the twin chalk cliffs of Rügen's main attraction, the **Stubbenkammer** headland. From here you can best see the much-photographed white-chalk cliffs called the **Königstuhl,** rising 350 feet from the sea. A steep trail leads down to a beach. ⊠ *Merkelstr., Sassnitz.*

Jasmund Nationalpark. From Sassnitz, walk to Jasmund Nationalpark to explore the marshes, lush pine forests, and towering chalk cliffs. ⊠ *Johanniskirchstr., Sassnitz* ⊕ *www.nationalpark-jasmund.de*

WORTH NOTING

Bergen. This small town is the island's administrative capital, founded as a Slavic settlement some 900 years ago. The **Marienkirche** (St. Mary's Church) has geometric murals dating back to the late 1100s and painted brick octagonal pillars. The pulpit and altar are baroque. Outside the front door and built into the church facade is a gravestone from the 1200s. ⊠ *Bergen.*

Putbus. The heart of this town, 28 km (17 miles) southwest of Binz, is the Circus, a round central plaza dating back to the early 19th century. The immaculate white buildings surrounding the Circus give the city its nickname, "Weisse Stadt" (White City). In summer the blooming roses in front of the houses (once a requirement by the ruling noble family of Putbus) are truly spectacular. ⊠ *Alleestr., Putbus.*

Rasender Roland (*Racing Roland*). From Putbus you can take a ride on the 90-year-old narrow-gauge steam train, which runs 24 km (16 miles) to Göhren, at the southeast corner of Rügen. Trains leave hourly from Göhren to Binz and every two hours from Binz to Putbus; the ride takes 70 minutes one way. ⊠ *Binzer Str. 12, Putbus* ☎ *038301/8010* ⊕ *www.rasender-roland.de* ⊡ *€20 day ticket* ☉ *Apr.–Oct., daily 7:48 am–7:46 pm; Nov.–Mar., daily 7:48 am–5:44 pm.*

SHOPPING

At the end of the 19th century, 16 pieces of 10th-century Viking jewelry were discovered on the Baltic coastline (presently housed in the Kulturhistorisches Museum in Stralsund). Gold and silver replicas of the **Hiddensee Golden Jewelry** are a great souvenir, and their distinctive patterns are found in shops on Rügen Island and on Hiddensee Island.

Vacationers sunbathe in Strandkorb, or on a towel on Ahlbeck's beach.

**OFF THE
BEATEN
PATH**

Hiddensee. Off the northwest corner of Rügen is a smaller island called Hiddensee. The undisturbed solitude of this sticklike island has attracted such visitors as Albert Einstein, Thomas Mann, Rainer Maria Rilke, and Sigmund Freud. As Hiddensee is an auto-free zone, leave your car in Schaprode, 21 km (13 miles) west of Bergen, and take a ferry. Vacation cottages and restaurants are on the island. ✉ *Insel Hiddensee.*

WHERE TO EAT

$

GERMAN

✗**Panoramahotel Lohme.** Dinner at this restaurant dubbed "Rügen's balcony" offers some of the most beautiful views on the island. While enjoying fresh fish from local waters, prepared with a light Italian touch, you can watch the sunset over the cliffs of Kap Arkona. Chef Marcus Uhlich uses fresh produce from local farmers, and the superb vintages are from small private wineries. ▮**TIP➔ Make a reservation, and insist on a table in the** *Fontane-Veranda* **(in winter) or the** *Arkonablick-Terrasse* **(in summer).** $ *Average main: €15* ✉ *An der Steilküste 8, Lohme* ☎ *038302/9110.*

WHERE TO STAY

$

B&B/INN

🏨**Hotel Godewind.** This small hotel offers food and lodging at very reasonable prices. **Pros:** quiet setting; very cozy rooms with nice furniture. **Cons:** almost no amenities and services offered. $ *Rooms from: €98* ✉ *Süderende 53, Vitte-Hiddensee* ☎ *038300/6600* ⊕ *www.hotelgodewind.de* ⤳*23 rooms, 19 cottages* ❏*Breakfast.*

$

RENTAL

🏨**Hotel Villa Granitz.** This mostly wooden mansion is a small and quiet retreat for those who want to avoid the masses. **Pros:** cozy hotel in the traditional architectural style of the area; very competitive prices for the size and comfort of rooms. **Cons:** off the beaten track at the outskirts of the city; a distance from the beach. **$** *Rooms from: €78* ⊠ *Birkenallee 17, Baabe* ☎ *038303/1410* ⊕ *www.villa-granitz.de* ⤳ *44 rooms, 6 suites, 8 apartments* ⦿| *Breakfast.*

$$$ ⛭ **Travel Charme Hotel Kurhaus Binz.** The grand old lady of the Baltic Sea,
HOTEL   the neoclassical 19th-century Kurhaus Binz is reviving the splendor of times past, when Binz was called the Nice of the North. **Pros:** great breakfast buffet; extremely clean rooms and public areas; highly trained and friendly personnel; all the amenities. **Cons:** lacks the feel of a typical Rügen hotel; not very personal or intimate. **$** *Rooms from: €206* ⊠ *Strandpromenade 27, Binz* ☎ *038393/6650* ⊕ *www.travelcharme. com* ⤳ *106 rooms, 20 suites* ⦿| *Breakfast.*

$$ ⛭ **Vier Jahreszeiten.** This first-class beach resort in Binz is a sophisticated
HOTEL   blend of historic seaside architecture and modern elegance. **Pros:** one of the area's few four-star hotels; varied cultural and entertainment programs; stylish spa with great massages. **Cons:** small rooms and bathrooms; many rooms with worn-out mattresses. **$** *Rooms from: €130* ⊠ *Zeppelinstr. 8, Binz* ☎ *038393/500* ⊕ *www.vier-jahreszeiten.de* ⤳ *69 rooms, 7 suites, 50 apartments* ⦿| *Breakfast.*

SPORTS AND THE OUTDOORS
BEACHES

Vitte. Tucked away on the west coast of Hiddedsee near Vitte, is a 5-km-long (3-mile-long) beach with shimmering turquoise waters and sand so fine that you might mistake it for the Caribbean. The 50-meter-wide beach is ideal for families with children, but is only accessible by bicycle. The water is quite shallow and it's easy to walk out to the sandbanks. Vitte is divided between a nudist section to the south and a textile section to the north. Locals decorate the beach with baskets of flowers in summer. **Amenities:** showers; toilets; water sports. **Best for:** solitude; nudists; snorkeling; sunrise; sunset; swimming; walking. ⊠ *Süderende, Insel Hiddensee.*

Binz. The rule of the Baltics most exclusive beach is "see and be seen." The 5-km-long (3-mile-long) and 54-yard-wide beach is the perfect place to sunbathe and swim, as well as stroll—there's a 150-year-old beach path promenade. The somewhat rocky beach is punctuated by the *Seebrücke,* a boardwalk that extends into the sea, and the nearby Smart Beach Tour Stadium, which regularly hosts parties, beach volleyball tournaments, and other events. **Amenities:** food and drink; lifeguards; parking; showers; toilets; water sports. **Best for:** partiers; snorkeling; sunrise; sunset; swimming; walking. ⊠ *Strandpromenade, Binz.*

Prora. This is one of the finest beaches on Rügen, and there's probably not another place like it in the world—think fine white beach bordered by a dense pine forest sitting in the shadows of the ruins of a monstrous Nazi beach resort. Prora actually sits in the *Prorer Wiek,* a pleasant cove with shallow water and plentiful sandbanks. **Amenities:** food and drink; lifeguards; parking; showers; toilets; water sports. **Best for:** solitude, partiers; nudists; snorkeling; sunrise; sunset; surfing; swimming; walking; windsurfing. ⊠ *Binz.*

USEDOM ISLAND

67 km (42 miles) to Wolgast bridge from Stralsund.

Fodor's Choice Usedom Island has almost 32 km (20 miles) of sandy shoreline and a
★ string of resorts. Much of the island's untouched landscape is a nature
preserve that provides refuge for a number of rare birds, including the
giant sea eagle, which has a wingspan of up to 8 feet. Even in summer this island is more or less deserted, and is ready to be explored
by bicycle.

GETTING HERE AND AROUND

From the west, Usedom is accessed via the causeway at **Wolgast.** The
bridge closes to traffic at times to allow boats to pass through. From the
south, the B-110 leads from Anklam to Usedom. In summer, particularly
before and after weekends, traffic can be very heavy on both roads.

ESSENTIALS

Visitor Information Usedom Island Tourismus GmbH. ⊠ *Waldstr. 1, Seebad
Bansin* ☎ *038378/47710* ⊕ *www.usedom.de.*

EXPLORING

Ahlbeck. The island's main town is also one of its best resorts. The tidy
and elegant resort is one of the three *Kaiserbäder* (imperial baths)—the
two others are Heringsdorf and Bansin—where the Emperor Wilhelm
II liked to spend his summers in the early 20th century. Noble families
and rich citizens followed the emperor, turning Ahlbeck into one of
the prettiest villas on the Baltic Coast. Ahlbeck's landmark is the 19th-
century wooden pier with four towers. Stroll the beach to the right of
the pier and you'll arrive at the Polish border. ⊠ *1 Kurstr., Ahlbeck.*

Peenemünde. At the northwest tip of Usedom, 16 km (10 miles) from
landside Wolgast, is the launch site of the world's first jet rockets, the
V1 and V2, developed by Germany during World War II. You can
view these rockets as well as models of early airplanes and ships at the
extensive ⊠ *Fährstr. 10, Peenemünde.*

Das Historisch-Technische Museum Peenemünde (*Historical-Techni-
cal Museum Peenemünde*). At this museum housed in the former factory
power plant, one exhibit in particular covers the moral responsibility of
scientists who develop new technology, by focusing on the secret plants
where most of the rocket parts were assembled and where thousands of
slave laborers died. Explanations of the exhibits in English are available.
⊠ *Im Kraftwerk, Peenemünde* ☎ *038371/5050* ⊕ *www.peenemuende.
de* ☒ *€8* ☉ *Apr.–Sept., daily 10–6; Oct.–Mar., daily 10–4; Nov.–Feb.,
Tues.–Sun. 10–4*

WHERE TO STAY

$$$ 🖭 **Romantik Seehotel Ahlbecker Hof.** The first lady of Ahlbeck, this four-
HOTEL star hotel calls to mind the island's past as a getaway for Prussian
nobility in the 19th century. **Pros:** has one of the area's best spas; two
gourmet restaurants; near beach. **Cons:** no elevator. ⑤ *Rooms from:
€207* ⊠ *Dünenstr. 47, Ahlbeck* ☎ *038378/620* ⊕ *www.seetel.de* ☞ *70
rooms* �‖ *Breakfast.*

14

SPORTS AND THE OUTDOORS

BEACHES

Úckeritz. One of the best-kept secrets on Usedom, this 7½-mile-long beach is quite busy in the north but almost abandoned further south. The area is quite rustic and the perfect beach to feel like you have the place to yourself. **Amenities:** food and drink; parking **Best for:** solitude; nudists; sunrise; sunset; walking. ⊠ *Uferpromenade, Úckeritz.*

Kaiserbäder. The Kaiserbäder Strand stretches for more than 12 km (7 miles) along Usedom Island's northeast coast from Bansin to Herringsdorf to Ahlbeck. A promenade connects the three towns and the Imperial Bathing Beaches are a mix of 19th-century beach architecture on one side and beach chair relaxation on the other. A stroll through the windy sea air is said to have magical recuperative powers and the beach is so pure and pristine that the locals claim that when the conditions are right, the sand actually sings when the grains rub together. The wide beach bustles with weekend Berliners and long-term visitors in summer. **Amenities:** food and drink; lifeguards; parking; showers; toilets; water sports. **Best for:** partiers; sunrise; sunset; swimming; walking. ⊠ *Strandpromenade, Herringsdorf.*

BERLIN

WELCOME TO BERLIN

TOP REASONS TO GO

★ **Affordability:** Of the European capitals, Berlin is the best bargain. It's a city of high culture and low prices—tickets for the opera, theater, and museums tend to hover around €10.

★ **Long, creative nights:** The only European city without official closing hours, Berlin's young artists put on installations, performance events, and parties to keep you up all night.

★ **Museum Island (Museuminsel):** The architectural monuments and art treasures here will take you from an ancient Greek altar to Egyptian busts and a Roman market town to 18th-century Berlin and back.

★ **The Reichstag's cupola:** Reserve a coveted spot on a tour of Berlin's seat of parliament to admire the spectacular glass cupola, and to enjoy great views of Berlin.

★ **Trace history's path:** The division of Berlin was a major historical event and an anomaly in urban history. Follow the cobblestone markers of the Wall's path.

1 Mitte. Once home to the city's Jewish quarter, after the war Mitte was part of East Berlin. Today, it's packed with monuments, museums, galleries, and shops.

2 Tiergarten. This neighborhood extends around the Tiergarten ("animal garden"), which is Berlin's version of New York's Central Park.

3 Potsdamer Platz. One of the busiest squares in prewar Europe, Potsdamer Platz is still the center of commercial action.

4 Friedrichshain. This area's offbeat bars, restaurants, clubs, and parks draw creative types from around the world.

5 Kreuzberg. When Berlin was divided, West Berlin's Kreuzberg was alongside

GETTING ORIENTED

In eastern Germany, almost halfway between Paris and Moscow, Berlin is Germany's largest city. When the city-state of Berlin was incorporated in 1920, it swallowed towns and villages far beyond what had been the downtown area around the two main rivers, the Spree and the Havel. After World War II, Berlin was divided among the conquering powers, and in 1961 the East German government built a wall through the middle of the city, more or less overnight. For the next decades, the city was divided. In November 1989, the wall fell, and a peaceful revolution put an end to the Communist East German regime. In 1999, Berlin became the capital of a reunified Germany, once again.

15

the wall. The neighborhood drew punks, artists, and anarchists. Today, it's still edgy and artsy.

6 Prenzlauer Berg. Once a working-class neighborhood, Prenzlauer Berg is now one of the city's most gentrified areas.

7 Wedding. This working-class neighborhood is where Berlin's artists are heading, as rents rise elsewhere.

Whether you're looking for an underground art gallery or authentic Turkish coffee, Wedding is the place to go.

8 Neukölln. Here, abandoned storefronts have turned into DIY art galleries, homemade fashion shops, secondhand shops, and funky wine bars.

9 Charlottenburg. This beautifully sedate West Berlin neighborhood hasn't

changed as much as much of the rest of the city.

10, 11 Wannsee and Oranienburg. The concentration camp in Oranienburg is a somber excursion; Wannsee also has a dark past but there are also parks and lakes to explore.

BERLIN WALL WALK

The Berlin Wall (*Berliner Mauer*) came down more than 20 years ago, but it's still a major tourist draw. How does a structure no longer standing affect the city even in its absence?

(above) Checkpoint Charlie
(upper right) Ampelmann
crosswalk signs (lower left)
Mauer Park flea market

When the Wall fell on November 9, 1989, it followed massive protests, an astonishing amount of community organizing, and the prayers of thousands in both west and east, all of whom couldn't quite believe such a momentous event was happening in their lifetimes. Many had felt the same way 28 years earlier, when the East German government, in an attempt to keep their beleaguered citizens from leaving, built the wall practically overnight. Now, except for a few sections left standing, all that remains of one of history's most notorious symbols of postwar oppression and imprisonment is a line of cobblestones wending its way through the streets of Berlin.

FOLLOW THE COBBLESTONES

When the wall fell, Berliners couldn't wait to get rid of it and there are few places where it remains intact. One is the **East Side Gallery**; another is the **Gedenkstätte Berliner Mauer** (the Berlin Wall Memorial Site) at the former Checkpoint Charlie. Or just look down: where the wall used to stand, a cobblestone path bifurcates the city, with plaques stating "Berliner Mauer 1961–1989."

TWO BERLIN WALL WALKS

FRIEDRICHSHAIN TO TREPTOW VIA THE OBERBAUM-BRÜCKE AND THE FLUTGRABEN

Starting at the **East Side Gallery**, cross the **Oberbaumbrücke**, a former border checkpoint, and turn left at **Schlesische Strasse**. There's no sign of the Wall here, but ubiquitous graffiti and crumbling buildings make it easy to imagine isolated Kreuzberg when it stood. At **Am Flutgraben**, you'll pick up the trail again, and up ahead is the **Grenzwachturm** (border watchtower). Stop at the nonprofit art collective **Flutgraben e.V.**, which hosts infrequent exhibitions. Turn right to follow the **Flutgraben** (small canal) south until you reach an overpass, part of an elevated railway that used to lead to the prewar train station Görlitzer Bahnhof. Now, the railway is a park connecting **Treptow** with **Görlitzer Park**, the site of the old station and a meeting point for anarchist groups, punks, and revolutionaries before the Wall fell.

BERNAUER STRASSE TO BORNHOLMER BRÜCKE VIA MAUER PARK

Behind **Nordbahnhof** (S-bahn), follow Bernauer Strasse to the **Gedenkstätte Berliner Mauer**, located in the former "death strip," where a church was blown up by the East because it was an obstruction to guards and an alleged hiding place for those trying to flee. Follow **Bernauer Strasse** until you reach the corner of Schwedter Strasse, then take the path that cuts through **Mauer Park**. Also in the former death strip, the park has one of the best flea markets in town (and, in summer, massive karaoke shows). At the park's northern end, Schwedter Strasse turns into the **Schwedter Steg**, a footbridge over an impressive chasm of connecting train tracks and S-bahn lines. Turn around for a spectacular view of the TV tower. Head down steps on your left and continue along Norwegerstrasse. After going under the famous **Bornholmer Brücke**, take the flight of steps up to it. This is where East Berliners, having heard an official announcement that the wall was open, first pushed through to West Berlin.

ICONIC EAST BERLIN

Many East Berlin designs have crept into daily life in Berlin, including the stocky East Berlin *Ampelmann* ("streetlight man") that appears on the crosswalk traffic lights. He wears a wide-brim hat and walks with an animated gait. After the wall fell, this icon found himself at the center of heated controversy, as the city decided to replace him with the more dour West Berlin traffic men. Easterners felt like this was a symbol of the ways in which the West was acting like a colonizing power, rather than an equal partner in reunification, and mounted a protest. The Ampelmann was saved. And he's now a mini-franchise: adorning coffee cups and T-shirts, and there's even candy made in his image. Entire gift shops are dedicated to selling items imprinted with his likeness.

15

Updated
by Sally
McGrane and
Giulia Pines

Since the fall of the Iron Curtain, no other city in Europe has seen more change than Berlin, the German capital. The two Berlins that had been physically separated for almost 30 years have become one, and the reunited city has become a cutting-edge destination for architecture, culture, entertainment, nightlife, and shopping.

After successfully uniting its own East and West, Berlin now plays a pivotal role in the European Union. But even as the capital thinks and moves forward, history is always tugging at its sleeve. Between the wealth of neoclassical and 21st-century buildings there are constant reminders, both subtle and stark, of the events of the 20th century.

Berlin is quite young by European standards, beginning as two separate entities in 1237 on two islands in the Spree River: Cölln and Berlin. By the 1300s, Berlin was prospering, thanks to its location at the intersection of important trade routes, and rose to power as the seat of the Hohenzollern dynasty. The Great Elector Friedrich Wilhelm, in the nearly 50 years of his reign (1640–88), touched off a cultural renaissance. Later, Frederick the Great (1712–86) made Berlin and Potsdam glorious centers of his enlightened yet autocratic Prussian monarchy.

In 1871, Prussia, ruled by the "Iron Chancellor" Count Otto von Bismarck, unified the many independent German states into the German Empire. Berlin maintained its status as capital for the duration of that Second Reich (1871–1918), through the post–World War I Weimar Republic (1919–33), and also through Hitler's so-called Third Reich (1933–45). The city's golden years were the Roaring '20s, when Berlin evolved as the energetic center for the era's cultural avant-garde. World-famous writers, painters, and artists met here while the impoverished bulk of its 4 million inhabitants lived in heavily overpopulated quarters. This "dance on the volcano," as those years of political and economic upheaval have been called, came to a grisly and bloody end after January 1933, when Adolf Hitler became chancellor. The Nazis made Berlin their capital but ultimately failed to remake the city into a monument to their power, as they had planned. By World War II's end, 70% of the city lay in ruins, with more rubble than in all other German cities combined.

Along with the division of Germany after World War II, Berlin was partitioned into American, British, and French zones in the West and a Soviet zone in the East. The three western-occupied zones became West Berlin, while the Soviets, who controlled not only Berlin's eastern zone but also all of the east German land surrounding it tried to blockade West Berlin out of existence. (They failed thanks to the year-long Berlin Airlift [1948–49], during which American airplanes known in German as "raisin bombers," dropped supplies until the blockade lifted.) In 1949 the Soviet Union established East Berlin as the capital of its new satellite state, the German Democratic Republic (GDR). The division of the city was cruelly finalized in concrete in August 1961, when the GDR erected the Berlin Wall, the only border fortification in history built to keep people from leaving rather than to protect them.

For nearly 30 years, the two Berlins served as competing visions of the new world order: Capitalist on one side, Communist on the other. West Berlin, an island of democracy in the Eastern bloc, was surrounded by guards and checkpoints. Nonetheless, thanks in part to being heavily subsidized by Western powers, the city became a haven for artists and freethinkers. Today, with the Wall long relegated to history (most of it was recycled as street gravel), visitors can appreciate the whole city and the anything-goes atmosphere that still pervades.

15

PLANNING

WHEN TO GO
Berlin tends to be gray and cold; it can be warm and beautiful in summer but there's no guarantee, so it's best to always pack a jacket. The best time to visit is from May to early September, though late July and early August can get hot—in which case, everyone heads to one of the city's many lakes. Many open-air events are staged in summer, when the exceedingly green city is at its most beautiful. October and November can be overcast and rainy, though the city occasionally sees crisp blue autumn skies. If you want to get a real feel for Berlin, come during the long winter months, when a host of indoor cultural events combat perpetually gray skies, but bring a heavy winter coat to combat the sleet, icy rain, strong winds, and freezing temperatures.

DISCOUNTS AND DEALS
The **Berlin WelcomeCard** (sold by EurAid, Berliner Verkehrsbetriebe offices, the tourist office, and some hotels) entitles one adult and three children up to age 6 to two, three, or five days of unlimited travel in the ABC zones for €20.50, €26.50, or €36.50, respectively, and includes admission and tour discounts detailed in a booklet. The **CityTourCard**, good for two, three, or five days of unlimited travel in the ABC zones, costs €18.90, €24.90, and €34.90, respectively, and details 50 discounts on a leaflet; up to three children under age 6 can accompany an adult.

Many of the 17 Staatliche Museen zu Berlin (state museums of Berlin) offer several ticket options (children up to 18 are welcomed free of charge). A single ticket ranges €8–€12. A three-day pass (*Tageskarte* or *SchauLust Museen Ticket*) to all state museums costs €24. This ticket allows entrance to all state museums plus many others for three consecutive days. State museums tend to cluster near one another, and usually a single entrance ticket grants admission to all museums in that area. These areas include Charlottenburg (€12), Dahlem (€8), the Kulturforum in Tiergarten (€12), Hamburger Bahnhof in Moabit (€14), and all museums on Museum Island (€18) in Mitte. Except for the Hamburger Bahnhof ticket, which includes all temporary exhibits, all these entrance tickets are for the permanent exhibitions only, and include an audio guide.

GETTING HERE AND AROUND

AIRPORT TRANSFERS

Tegel Airport is 6 km (4 miles) from the downtown area. The express X9 airport bus runs at 10-minute intervals between Tegel and Bahnhof Zoologischer Garten (Zoo Station), the center of west Berlin. From here you can connect to bus, train, or subway. The trip takes 19 minutes; the fare is €2.60. The express bus TXL runs at 10-minute intervals between Tegel and Alexanderplatz via Hauptbahnhof and takes about 30 minutes. Alternatively, you can take Bus No. 128 to Kurt Schumacher Platz or Bus No. 109 to Jakob-Kaiser-Platz and change to the U-bahn, where your bus ticket is also valid. Expect to pay about €20 for a taxi from the airport to most destinations in central Berlin. If you rent a car at the airport, follow the signs for the Stadtautobahn into Berlin. The exit to Kurfürstendamm is clearly marked.

At Schönefeld, which is quite a bit farther out, buy an Einzelfahrschein or single ride ticket (€3.20) for the ABC zone from the DB (Deutsche Bahn) office or from an S-bahn platform vending machine (no credit cards) to get you into town. This ticket is good for both the S-bahn and the Airport Express train, which runs about every half hour from a track that has no vending machine. To take the Airport Express, look for a small dark-blue sign at the foot of the stairs leading to its platform. Bus 171 also leaves Schönefeld every 20 minutes for the Rudow U-bahn station. A taxi ride from Schönefeld Airport takes about 40 minutes and will cost around €35. By car, follow the signs for Stadtzentrum Berlin.

Airport Information Central airport service ☎ *030/500–0186* ⊕ *www.berlin-airport.de.*

AIR TRAVEL

Major airlines will continue to serve western Berlin's Tegel Airport (TXL) after a first stop at a major European hub (such as Frankfurt or London) until eastern Berlin's Schönefeld Airport, about 24 km (15 miles) outside the center, has been expanded into BBI "Berlin-Brandenburg International," otherwise known as "Willy Brandt"— the international airport of the capital region. Until then, Schönefeld is mostly used by charter and low-budget airlines. The two working Berlin airports share a central phone number.

BICYCLE TRAVEL

Berlin is a great city for biking. Particularly in summer, you can get just about anywhere you want by bike. An extensive network of bike paths are generally marked by red pavement or white markings on the sidewalks (when you're walking, try to avoid walking on bike paths if you don't want to have cyclists ring their bells at you). Many stores that rent or sell bikes carry the Berlin biker's atlas, and several places offer terrific bike tours of the city.

Bicycle Information Fahrradstation. This company rents bikes for €15 per day (12 hours) or €35 for three days. Bring ID and call for its other locations. ⊠ *Dorotheenstr. 30, Mitte* ☎ *0180/510–8000* ⊕ *www.fahrradstation.de.*

BUS TRAVEL

BerlinLinien Bus is the only intra-Germany company serving Berlin. Make reservations through ZOB-Reisebüro, or buy your ticket at its office at the central bus terminal, the Omnibusbahnhof. Public buses are the best way to reach the bus terminal, served by line nos. X34, X49, 104, 139, 218, and 349. A more central place to buy bus tickets is Mitfahrzentrale, a tiny, busy office that also arranges car-ride shares. Only EC bank cards and cash are accepted.

Bus Information Mitfahrzentrale ☎ *01805/194–444* ⊕ *www.mf24.de* ⊙ *Weekdays 9–6, weekends 10–2.* **ZOB-Reisebüro** ⊠ *Zentrale Omnibusbahn-hof, Masurenallee 4–6, at Messedamm, Charlottenburg* ☎ *030/301–0380 for reservations* ⊕ *www.zob-reisebuero.de* ⊙ *Weekdays 6 am–9 pm, weekends 6 am–8 pm.*

CAR TRAVEL

Rush hour is relatively mild in Berlin, but the public transit system is so efficient here that it's best to leave your car at the hotel altogether (or refrain from renting one in the first place). All cars entering downtown Berlin inside the S-bahn ring need to have an environmental certificate. All major rental cars will have these—if in doubt, ask the rental-car agent, as without one you can be fined €40. Daily parking fees at hotels can run up to €18 per day. Vending machines in the city center dispense timed tickets to display on your dashboard. Thirty minutes costs €0.50.

PUBLIC TRANSIT

The city has an efficient public-transportation system, a smoothly integrated network of subway (U-bahn) and suburban (S-bahn) train lines, buses, and trams (almost exclusively in eastern Berlin). Get a map from any information booth. ■**TIP→ Don't be afraid to try buses and trams—in addition to being well marked, they often cut the most direct path to your destination.**

From Sunday through Thursday, U-bahn trains stop around 12:45 am and S-bahn trains stop by 1:30 am. All-night bus and tram service operates seven nights a week (indicated by the letter N next to bus route numbers). On Friday and Saturday nights some S-bahn and all U-bahn lines except U4 run all night. Buses and trams marked with an M for Metro mostly serve destinations without an S-bahn or U-bahn link.

Most visitor destinations are in the broad reach of the fare zones A and B. The €2.60 ticket (fare zones A and B) and the €3.20 ticket (fare zones A, B, and C) allow you to make a one-way trip with an unlimited number of changes between trains, buses, and trams. There are reduced rates for children ages 6–13. Buy a Kurzstreckentarif ticket (€1.50) for short rides of up to six bus or tram stops or three U-bahn or S-bahn stops. The best deal if you plan to travel around the city extensively

15

is the Tageskarte (day card for zones A and B), for €6.70, good on all transportation until 3 am (€7.20 for A, B, and C zones). A 7-*Tage-Karte* (seven-day ticket) costs €28.80, and allows unlimited travel for fare zones A and B; €35.60 buys all three fare zones.

Tickets are available from vending machines at U-bahn and S-bahn stations. After you purchase a ticket, you are responsible for validating it when you board the train or bus. Both Einzelfahrt and Kurzstreckentarif tickets are good for 120 minutes after validation. If you're caught without a ticket or with an unvalidated one, the fine is €40.

■ TIP➔ The BVG website (⊕ *www.bvg.de*) makes planning any trip on public transportation easier. Enter your origin and destination point into their "Journey Planner" to see a list of your best routes, and a schedule of the next three departure times. If you're not sure which station is your closest, simply type in your current address and the system will tell you (along with the time it takes to walk there).

Most major S-bahn and U-bahn stations have elevators, and most buses have hydraulic lifts. Check the public transportation maps or call the Berliner Verkehrsbetriebe. The Deutscher Service-Ring-Berlin e.V. runs a special bus service for travelers with physical disabilities, and is a good information source on all travel necessities, that is, wheelchair rental and other issues.

Public Transit Information Berliner Verkehrsbetriebe (*BVG*). ☎ *030/19449* ⊕ *www.bvg.de*. **S-Bahn Berlin GmbH** ☎ *030/2974–3333* ⊕ *www.s-bahn-berlin. de*. **VBB** ☎ *030/2541–4141 for info* ⊕ *www.vbbonline.de* ⊗ *Weekdays 8–8, weekends 9–6.*

TAXI TRAVEL
The base rate is €3.20, after which prices vary according to a complex tariff system. Figure on paying around €8–€10 for a ride the length of the Ku'damm. ■ TIP➔ If you've hailed a cab on the street and are taking a short ride of up to 2 km (1 mile), ask the driver as soon as you start off for a special fare (€4) called "Kurzstreckentarif." You can also get cabs at taxi stands or order one by calling; there's no additional fee if you call a cab by phone. U-bahn employees will call a taxi for passengers after 8 pm.

BikeTaxi, rickshawlike bicycle taxis, pedal along Kurfürstendamm, Friedrichstrasse, Unter den Linden, and in Tiergarten. Just hail a cab on the street along the boulevards mentioned. The fare is €5 for up to 1 km (½ mile) and €3 for each additional kilometer, and €22.50 to €30 for longer tours. Velotaxis operate April–October, daily noon–7. ■ TIP➔ Despite these fixed prices, make sure to negotiate the fare before starting the tour.

Taxi Information Taxis ☎ *030/210–101, 030/443–322, 030/261–026.*

TRAIN TRAVEL
All long-distance trains stop at the huge and modern central station, Hauptbahnhof, which lies at the northern edge of the government district in central Berlin. Regional trains also stop at the two former "main" stations of the past years: Bahnhof Zoo (in the West) and Ostbahnhof (in the East), as well as at the central eastern stations Friedrichstrasse and Alexanderplatz.

A boat tour along the Spree River is a lovely way to take in the sights.

VISITOR INFORMATION

The main information office of Berlin Tourismus Marketing is in the Neues Kranzler Eck, a short walk from Zoo Station. There are branches in the south wing of the Brandenburg Gate, at Hauptbahnhof (Level 0), and in a pavilion opposite the Reichstag that are open daily 10–6. The tourist-information centers have longer hours April–October. The tourist office publishes the Berlin Kalender (€1.60) six times a year and Berlin Buchbar (free) two times a year; both are written in German and English. The tourist office and Berlin's larger transportation offices (BVG) sell the Berlin WelcomeCard (€18.50 to €36.50), which pays for between three and five days of transportation depending on which one you get, along with 25%–50% discounts at museums and theaters (it does not include the state museums). Some *Staatliche* (state) museums are closed Monday. A free audio guide is included at all state museums. The MD Infoline provides comprehensive information about all of Berlin's museums, exhibits, and themed tours.

Visitor Information Visit Berlin (*Berlin Tourist Info*). ⊠ *Kurfürstendamm 22, in the Neues Kranzler Eck, Charlottenburg* ☎ *030/250–025* ⊕ *www.visitberlin.de* ☉ *Mon.–Sat. 9:30–8, Sun. 10–6.* **Museumsinformation Berlin** ☎ *030/2474–9888* ☉ *Weekdays 9–4, weekends 9–1.* **Staatliche Museen zu Berlin** ☎ *030/2664–24242 operator* ⊕ *www.smb.museum* ☉ *Weekdays 9–4.* **Tourist-Information Center in Prenzlauer Berg** ⊠ *Kuturbrauerei closest entrance Schönhauser Allee 36, Schönhauser Allee 36, in the Kulturbrauerei, entrances on Knaackstr. or Sredzkistr., Prenzlauer Berg* ☎ *030/4435–2170* ⊕ *www.tic-berlin.de* ☉ *Daily, 11-7.*

TOURS
BOAT TOURS

Tours of central Berlin's Spree and the canals give you up-close views of sights such as Museum Island, Charlottenburg Palace, the Reichstag, and the Berliner Dom. Tours usually depart twice a day from several bridges and piers in Berlin, such as Schlossbrücke in Charlottenburg; Hansabrücke and Haus der Kulturen der Welt in Tiergarten; Friedrichstrasse, Museum Island, and Nikolaiviertel in Mitte; and near the Jannowitzbrücke S-bahn and U-bahn station. Drinks, snacks, and *wurst* are available during the narrated trips. Reederei Riedel offers multiple inner-city trips that range from €11.50 to €20 depending on theme and distance.

A tour of the Havel Lakes (which include Tegeler See and Wannsee) begins at the Wannsee, where you can sail on either the whale-shape vessel *Moby Dick* or the *Havel Queen*, a Mississippi-style boat, and cruise 28 km (17 miles) through the lakes and past forests (Stern- und Kreisschiffahrt). Tours can last from one to seven hours, and cost between €10.50 and €20. There are 20 operators.

Boat Tour Information Reederei Bruno Winkler ☎ *030/349–9595* ⊕ *www.reedereiwinkler.de.* **Reederei Riedel** ☎ *030/6796–1470* ⊕ *www.reederei-riedel.de.* **Stern und Kreisschiffahrt** ☎ *030/536–3600* ⊕ *www.sternundkreis.de.*

BUS TOURS

Four companies (Berliner Bären Stadtrundfahrten, Berolina Berlin-Service, Bus Verkehr Berlin, and BEX Sightseeing) jointly offer city tours on yellow, double-decker City Circle buses, which run every 15 or 30 minutes, depending on the season. The full circuit takes two hours, as does the recorded narration listened to through headphones. For €20 you can jump on and off at between 13 and 20 stops depending on the company. The bus driver sells tickets. During the warmer months, the last circuit leaves at 6 pm from the corner of Fasanenstrasse and Kurfürstendamm. Most companies have tours to Potsdam.

The Stadtrundfahrtbüro Berlin offers a 2¼-hour (€15) or 2¾-hour (€20) tour at 10:15, 10:45, 11, 11:30, 1, and 1:30, 2, 3:30, and 4. A guide narrates in both German and English. The bus departs from Tauentzienstrasse 16, at the corner of Marbuger Strasse.

Bus Tour Information BBS Berliner Bären Stadtrundfahrt (*BBS*). ☎ *030/3519–5270* ⊕ *www.bbsberlin.de.* **Berolina Berlin-Service** ☎ *030/8856–8030* ⊕ *www.berolina-berlin.com.* **BEX Sightseeing** ✉ *Mannheimer Str. 33–34, Wilmersdorf* ☎ *030/880–4190* ⊕ *www.bex.de.* **Stadtrundfahrtbüro Berlin** ✉ *Kurfürstendamm 236, Western Downtown* ☎ *030/261–2001* ⊕ *www.stadtrundfahrtbuero-berlin.de.*

WALKING AND BIKE TOURS

Getting oriented through a walking tour is a great way to start a Berlin visit. In addition to daily city highlight tours, companies have themed tours such as Third Reich Berlin, Potsdam, and pub crawls. Berlin Walks offers a Monday "Jewish Life" tour, a Potsdam tour on Thursday and Sunday, and visits to the Sachsenhausen concentration camp. Insider Tours has a "Cold War" Berlin tour about the Soviet era and a

Berlin Public Transit System

bike tour as well as a Cruise'n'Walk tour, a combination of boating and walking. Brit Terry Brewer's firsthand accounts of divided and reunified Berlin are a highlight of the all-day "Brewer's Best of Berlin" tour. Tours cost €15. Printable discount coupons may be available on the tour operators' websites; some companies grant discounts to WelcomeCard and CityCard holders. Fat Tire Bike Tours rides through Berlin daily early March–November and has a Berlin Wall tour; the 4½-hour city tour costs €24, bike rental included. For a truly memorable experience, check out Berliner Unterwelten, which translates as "Berlin Underworlds." The company offers access to several of Berlin's best-preserved WWII bunkers that are normally closed to the public on intriguing yet eerie tours that take you literally underground.

Walking and Bike Tour Information Berliner Unterwelten e. V.
✉ *Brunnenstr. 105, at the U Gesundbrunnen exit, Wedding* ☎ *030/499–1517*
⊕ *www.berliner-unterwelten.de.* **Brewer's Berlin Tours** ☎ *0177/388–1537*
⊕ *www.brewersberlintours.com.* **Fat Tire Bike Tours** ✉ *Panoramastr. 1a, base of TV tower, Mitte* ☎ *030/2404–7991* ⊕ *www.fattirebiketoursberlin.com.* **Insider Tour** ✉ *Bahnhof Zoologischer Garten, outside McDonalds, Charlottenburg* ☎ *030/692–3149* ⊕ *www.insidertour.com.* **Original Berlin Walks** ☎ *030/301–9194* ⊕ *www.berlinwalks.com.*

MAKING THE MOST OF YOUR TIME

With so much to see, a good place to start your visit is in Mitte. You can walk around the Scheunenviertel, which used to be the city's Jewish quarter and is now a center for art galleries and upscale shops, punctuated by memorials to the Holocaust.

For culture buffs, great antique, medieval, Renaissance, and modern art can be found at the Kulturforum in the Tiergarten, and on Museum Island in Mitte—both cultural centers are a must, and either will occupy at least a half day. On your way to the Tiergarten, visit the emotionally moving Memorial to the Murdered Jews of Europe (referred to by many as simply the Holocaust Memorial), the Brandenburg Gate, and the Reichstag with its astonishing cupola. Most of the historic sights of German and Prussian history line the city's other grand boulevard, Unter den Linden, in Mitte. Unter den Linden, which can be strolled in a leisurely two hours, with stops. Other spots not to miss are Potsdamer Platz and the Kulturforum in Tiergarten, and the hip and edgy neighborhoods of Wedding and Neukölln. Walk along the East Side Gallery in Friedrichshain, then head to Simon-DachStrasse or cross the bridge over the Spree to Kreuzberg for something to eat. Head over to Charlottenburg for an elegant, old-fashioned afternoon of coffee and cake.

If you need to spiff up your wardrobe with major labels, Kurfürstendamm is the city's premier shopping boulevard. Note that most shops are closed on Sunday, with the exception of those located in major train stations.

The city's outlying areas offer palaces, lakes, and museums set in lush greenery. In Zehlendorf, just a short ride on the S-Bahn from the center, you can swim in the lovely Schlachtensee Lake. The nearby town of Potsdam has the fabulous palace, Schloss Sanssouci, as well as extensive parks and lakes. To the north, in Oranienburg, is the Gedenkstätte und Museum Sachsenhausen concentration camp.

EXPLORING BERLIN

MITTE

After the fall of the wall, Mitte, which had been in East Germany, became the geographic center of Berlin, once again. The area has several minidistricts, each of which has its own distinctive history and flair. Alexanderplatz, home of the TV Tower, was the center of East Berlin. With its communist architecture, you can still get a feel for the GDR aesthetic here. The Nikolaiviertel nearby, was part of the medieval heart of Berlin. Left largely intact by the war, it was destroyed for ideological reasons, then rebuilt decades later by the Communist regime. The Scheunenviertel, part of the Spandauer Vorstadt, was home to many of the city's Jewish citizens. Today, the narrow streets that saw so much tragedy house art galleries and upscale shops. Treasures once split between East and West Berlin museums are reunited on Museuminsel, the stunning Museum Island, a UNESCO World Heritage Site. Bordering Tiergarten and the government district is the meticulously restored Brandenburger Tor (Brandenburg Gate), the unofficial symbol of the city, and the Memorial to the Murdered Jews of Europe, whose design and scope engendered many debates.

The historic boulevard Unter den Linden proudly rolls out Prussian architecture and world-class museums. Its major cross street is Friedrichstrasse, which was revitalized in the mid-1990s with car showrooms (including Bentley, Bugatti, and Volkswagen) and upscale malls.

The Scheunenviertel (Barn Quarter) is the hip part of Mitte and the historic core of Berlin. It's made up of narrow streets and courtyard mazes in the old Spandauer Vorstadt (the old Jewish neighborhood), and the area around Oranienburger Strasse. There are upscale shops, tony bars, and increasingly excellent restaurants, as well as successful art galleries. During the second half of the 17th century, artisans, small-businessmen, and Jews moved into this area at the encouragement of the Great Elector, who sought to improve his financial situation through their skills. As industrialization intensified, the quarter became poorer, and in the 1880s many East European Jews escaping pogroms settled here.

TIMING

You must reserve a spot on a tour in advance in order to visit the Reichstag, but don't let that stop you: the new rules have done a lot to dissipate the lines that used to snake around the building. The Hamburger Bahnhof, Museum für Gegenwart–Berlin is just down the street from Hauptbahnhof. A quick ride on Berlin's newest—and with only three stops, shortest—underground line, the U55, will get you there from the Brandenburg Gate or the Reichstag.

To speed your way down Unter den Linden, there are three bus lines that make stops between Wilhelmstrasse and Alexanderplatz and act as unofficial tourist buses. Note that a few state museums in this area are closed Monday.

15

The modern sculpture on Breitscheidplatz frames the Kaiser-Wilhelm-Gedächtnis-Kirche in the background.

TOP ATTRACTIONS

Bebelplatz. After he became ruler in 1740, Frederick the Great personally planned the buildings surrounding this square (which has a huge parking garage cleverly hidden beneath the pavement). The area received the nickname "Forum Fridericianum," or Frederick's Forum. On May 10, 1933, Joseph Goebbels, the Nazi minister for propaganda and "public enlightenment," organized one of the nationwide book-burnings here. The books, thrown on a pyre by Nazi officials and students, included works by Jews, pacifists, and Communists. In the center of Bebelplatz, a modern and subtle memorial (built underground but viewable through a window in the cobblestone) marks where 20,000 books went up in flames. The **Staatsoper Unter den Linden** (State Opera) is on the east side of the square. **St. Hedwigskathedrale** is on the south side. The **Humboldt-Universität** is to the west. Ⓜ *Französische Strasse (U-bahn)*.

Berliner Dom (*Berlin Cathedral*). A church has stood here since 1536, but this enormous version dates from 1905, making it the largest 20th-century Protestant church in Germany. The royal Hohenzollerns worshiped here until 1918, when Kaiser Wilhelm II abdicated and left Berlin for Holland. The massive dome wasn't restored from World War II damage until 1982; the interior was completed in 1993. The climb to the dome's outer balcony is made easier by a wide stairwell, plenty of landings with historic photos and models, and even a couple of chairs. The 94 sarcophagi of Prussian royals in the crypt are significant, but to less trained eyes can seem uniformly dull. Sunday services include communion. ✉ *Am Lustgarten 1, Mitte* ☎ *030/2026–9136* ⊕ *www.berlinerdom.de* 🎫 *€8 with audio guide, €5 without* ☉ *Mon.–Sat. 9–8, Sun. noon–8* Ⓜ *Hackescher Markt (S-bahn)*.

FAMILY **Berliner Fernsehturm** (*TV Tower*). Finding Alexanderplatz is no problem: just head toward the 1,207-foot-high tower piercing the sky. Built in 1969 as a signal to the west—clearly visible over the Wall, no less— that the East German economy was thriving, it is deliberately higher than both western Berlin's broadcasting tower and the Eiffel Tower in Paris. You can get the best view of Berlin from within the tower's disco ball–like observation level; on a clear day you can see for 40 km (25 miles). One floor above, the city's highest restaurant rotates for your panoramic pleasure. ■**TIP**➜ During the summer season, order VIP tickets online to avoid a long wait. ✉ *Panoramastr. 1a, Mitte* ☎ *030/247– 5750* ☜ *€12.50* ☉ *Nov.–Feb., daily 10 am–midnight; Mar.–Oct., daily 9 am–midnight; last admission ½ hr before closing* Ⓜ *Alexanderplatz (U-bahn and S-bahn).*

Fodor's Choice ★ **Brandenburger Tor** (*Brandenburg Gate*). Once the pride of Prussian Berlin and the city's premier landmark, the Brandenburger Tor was left in a desolate no-man's-land when the Wall was built. Since the Wall's dismantling, the sandstone gateway has become the scene of the city's Unification Day and New Year's Eve parties. This is the sole remaining gate of 14 built by Carl Langhans in 1788–91, designed as a triumphal arch for King Frederick Wilhelm II. Its virile classical style pays tribute to Athens's Acropolis. The *quadriga,* a chariot drawn by four horses and driven by the Goddess of Victory, was added in 1794. Troops paraded through the gate after successful campaigns—the last time in 1945, when victorious Red Army troops took Berlin. The upper part of the gate, together with its chariot and Goddess of Victory, was destroyed in the war. In 1957 the original molds were discovered in West Berlin, and a new quadriga was cast in copper and presented as a gift to the people of East Berlin. A tourist-information center is in the south part of the gate.

The gate faces one of Europe's most famous historic squares, **Pariser Platz,** with bank headquarters, the ultramodern French embassy, and the offices of the federal parliament. On the southern side, Berlin's sleek Academy of Arts, integrating the ruins of its historic predecessor, and the DZ Bank, designed by star architect Frank Gehry, stand next to the new American embassy, rebuilt on its prewar location and reopened on July 4, 2008. The legendary Hotel Adlon (now the Adlon Kempinski) looks on from its historic home at the southeast edge of the square. ✉ *Pariser Pl., Mitte* Ⓜ *Unter den Linden (S-bahn).*

Fodor's Choice ★ **DDR Museum.** Half museum, half theme park, the DDR Museum is an interactive and highly entertaining exhibit about life during socialism. It's difficult to say just how much the museum benefits from its prime location beside the Spree, right across from the Berliner Dom, but it's always packed, filled with tourists, families, and student groups trying to get a hands-on feel for what the East German experience was really like. Exhibitions include a re-creation of an East German kitchen, all mustard yellows and bilious greens; a simulated drive in a Trabi, the only car the average East German was allowed to own; and a walk inside a very narrow, very claustrophobic interrogation cell. For an added glimpse into the life of an "Ossi" (an "easterner"), stop at the DDR Restaurat Domklause, where traditional East German dishes

15

KEY

- Ⓢ   *S-Bahn*
- 🛈   *Tourist information*
- Ⓤ   *U-Bahn*

provide sustenance with a side of history. ⊠ *Karl-Liebknecht-Str. 1, at the Spree opposite the Berliner Dom, Mitte* 🕾 *030/8471-23731* ⊕ *www. ddr-museum.de* 🖾€6 ⊙ *Sun.-Fri. 10-8, Sat. 10-10* Ⓜ *Alexanderplatz (U-bahn and S-bahn), Hackescher Markt (S-bahn).*

Fodor's Choice   **Denkmal für die Ermordeten Juden Europas** (*Memorial to the Murdered*
★   *Jews of Europe*). An expansive and unusual memorial dedicated to the 6 million Jews who were killed in the Holocaust, the monument was designed by American architect Peter Eisenman. The stunning place of remembrance consists of a grid of more than 2,700 concrete stelae, planted into undulating ground. The abstract memorial can be entered from all sides and offers no prescribed path. ■TIP➙ An information center that goes into specifics about the Holocaust lies underground at the southeast corner. ⊠ *Cora-Berliner-Str. 1, Mitte* 🕾 *030/2639–4336* ⊕ *www.stiftung-denkmal.de* 🖾 *Free* ⊙ *Daily 24 hrs. Information center: Oct.–Mar., Tues.–Sun. 10–7; Apr.–Sept., Tues.–Sun. 10–8 (last admission 45 mins before closing)* Ⓜ *Unter den Linden (S-bahn).*

Deutsches Historisches Museum (*German History Museum*). The museum is composed of two buildings. The magnificent pink, baroque Prussian arsenal (Zeughaus) was constructed between 1695 and 1730, and is the oldest building on Unter den Linden. It also houses a theater, the Zeughaus Kino, which regularly presents a variety of films, both German and international, historic and modern. The new permanent exhibits, reopened after much debate in mid-2006, offer a modern and fascinating view of German history since the early Middle Ages. Behind the arsenal, the granite-and-glass Pei-Bau building by I. M. Pei holds often stunning and politically controversial changing exhibits, such as 2010's unprecedented blockbuster "Hitler und die Deutschen" ("Hitler and the Germans"), which explored the methods of propaganda used by Hitler and the Nazis to gain power, and 2013's "Zerstörte Vielfalt" or "Destroyed Diversity," which documents the multi-faceted societal, ethnic, and political ruination of Berlin in the years leading up to WWII. The museum's Café im Zueghaus is a great place to stop and restore your energy. ⊠ *Unter den Linden 2, Mitte* 🕾 *030/203–040* ⊕ *www.dhm.de* 🖾€8 ⊙ *Daily 10–6.*

Ehemalige Jüdische Mädchenschule. This boxy brick building in central Berlin, which formerly served as a Jewish girls' school and then a military hospital during WWII, sat neglected until recently. Now it is one of the city's newest star attractions: a renovated multiplex with art galleries, restaurants, and a bar. The former gymnasium is now the restaurant Pauly Saal; upstairs, three art galleries share space with the newly relocated Kennedys museum. Berlin's now-thriving Jewish community still owns the building and leases it out to the current management. Both Jewish and non-Jewish visitors will rejoice at the inclusion of Mogg & Melzer, a deli dedicated to Jewish delicacies like matzoh ball soup, pastrami, and shakshuka. ⊠ *Auguststr. 11–13, Mitte* ⊕ *www.maedchenschule.org* ⊙ *Varies according to business* Ⓜ *Oranienburger Strasse (S-bahn).*

Friedrichstrasse. The once-bustling street of cafés and theaters of prewar Berlin has risen from the rubble of war and Communist neglect to reclaim the crowds with shopping emporiums. Heading south from the Friedrichstrasse train station, you'll pass hotels and various stores

Berliner Dom (Berlin's Cathedral) is one of the city's landmark buildings, and the vast lawn across from it is a popular gathering spot in nice weather.

(including the sprawling, comprehensive bookstore **Dussmann** and its large but cozy new English-language bookshop around the corner). After crossing Unter den Linden, you'll come upon the Berlin outpost of the Parisian department store **Galeries Lafayette** on your left. North of the train station you will see the rejuvenated heart of the entertainment center of Berlin's Roaring Twenties, including the **Admiralspalast** and the somewhat kitschy **Friedrichstadt Palast**.

Admiralspalast. The meticulously restored Admiralspalast is the successful rebirth of a glittering Jazz Age entertainment temple. Reopened with a hotly debated production of Brecht's *Threepenny Opera*, it now houses two stages, a club, and an upscale but generic Italian restaurant. ⊠ *Friedrichstr. 101, Mitte* ☎ *030/4799–7499*.

Gendarmenmarkt. This is without a doubt the most elegant square in former East Berlin. Anchored by the beautifully reconstructed 1818 **Konzerthaus** and the **Deutscher Dom** and **Französischer Dom** (German and French cathedrals) and lined with some of the city's best restaurants, it also hosts one of Berlin's classiest annual Christmas markets.

Hugenottenmuseum. Inside the Französischer Dom (French Cathedral), built by Kaiser Friedrich II for the Protestant Huguenots who fled France and settled in Berlin, is the Hugenottenmuseum, with exhibits charting their history and art. The Huguenots were expelled from France at the end of the 17th century by King Louis XIV. Their energy and commercial expertise contributed much to Berlin. ⊠ *Französischer Dom, Gendarmenmarkt 5, Mitte* ☎ *030/229–1760* ⊠ *€2* ☺ *Tues.–Sun. noon–5.*

Hackesche Höfe (*Hacke Courtyards*). Built in 1905–07, this series of eight connected courtyards is the finest example of art-nouveau industrial architecture in Berlin. Most buildings are covered with glazed white tiles, and additional Moorish mosaic designs decorate the main courtyard off Rosenthaler Strasse. Shops (including one dedicated to Berlin's beloved street-crossing signal, the "Ampelmann"), restaurants, the variety theater Chamäleon Varieté, and a movie theater populate the spaces once occupied by ballrooms, a poets' society, and a Jewish girls' club. ✉ *Rosenthaler Str. 40–41, and Sophienstr. 6, Mitte* ☎ *030/2809–8010* ⊕ *www.hackesche-hoefe.com* Ⓜ *Hackescher Markt (S-bahn).*

Fodor's Choice ★ **Museumsinsel** (*Museum Island*). On the site of one of Berlin's two original settlements, this unique complex of five state museums—a UNESCO World Heritage Site—is an absolute must.

The **Alte Nationalgalerie** (Old National Gallery, entrance on Bodestrasse) houses an outstanding collection of 18th-, 19th-, and early 20th-century paintings and sculptures. Works by Cézanne, Rodin, Degas, and one of Germany's most famous portrait artists, Max Liebermann, are part of the permanent exhibition. Its Galerie der Romantik (Gallery of Romanticism) collection has masterpieces from such 19th-century German painters as Karl Friedrich Schinkel and Caspar David Friedrich, the leading members of the German Romantic school. The **Altes Museum** (Old Museum), a red-marble, neoclassical building abutting the green Lustgarten, was Prussia's first structure purpose-built to serve as a museum. Designed by Karl Friedrich Schinkel, it was completed in 1830. The permanent collection of the Altes Museum consists of everyday utensils from ancient Greece as well as vases and sculptures from the 6th to 4th century BC. Etruscan art is its highlight, and there are a few examples of Roman art. Antique sculptures, clay figurines, and bronze art of the Antikensammlung (Antiquities Collection) are also housed here; the other part of the collection is in the Pergamonmuseum. At the northern tip of Museum Island is the **Bode-Museum,** a somber-looking gray edifice graced with elegant columns. The museum presents the state museums' stunning collection of German and Italian sculptures since the Middle Ages, the Museum of Byzantine Art, and a huge coin collection. Even if you think you aren't interested in the ancient world, make an exception for the **Pergamonmuseum** (entrance Am Kupfergraben), one of the world's greatest museums. The museum's name is derived from its principal display, the Pergamon Altar, a monumental Greek temple discovered in what is now Turkey and dating from 180 BC. The altar was shipped to Berlin in the late 19th century. Equally impressive are the gateway to the Roman town of Miletus and the Babylonian processional way. Museum Island's new shining star, however, is the **Neues Museum** (New Museum), which reopened in 2009. Originally designed by Friedrich August Stüler in 1843–55, the building was badly damaged in World War II and has only now been elaborately redeveloped by British star architect David Chipperfield, who has been overseeing the complete restoration of Museum Island. Instead of completely restoring the Neues Museum, the architect decided to integrate modern elements into the historic landmark, while leaving many of its heavily bombed and dilapidated areas untouched. The result is a stunning experience, considered by many to be one of the world's greatest museums. Home to the Egyptian

Part of Museumsinsel (Museum Island), the Pergamonmuseum is where you'll find a wealth of artifacts from the ancient world.

Museum, including the famous bust of Nefertiti (who, after some 70 years, has returned to her first museum location in Berlin), it also features the Papyrus Collection and the Museum of Prehistory and Early History. If you get tired of antiques and paintings, drop by any of the museums' cafés. ⊠ *Museumsinsel, Mitte* ☎ *030/2664–24242* ⊕ *www.smb.museum* ✉ *All Museum Island museums: €18* ⊙ *Pergamonmuseum: Fri.–Wed. 10–6, Thurs. 10–8. Alte Nationalgalerie: Tues., Wed., and Fri.–Sun. 10–6, Thurs. 10–8. Altes Museum: Tues., Wed., and Fri.–Sun. 10–6, Thurs. 10–8. Neues Museum: Fri.–Wed. 10–6, Thurs. 10–8. Bode-Museum: Tues., Wed., and Fri.–Sun. 10–6, Thurs. 10–8* Ⓜ *Hackescher Markt (S-bahn).*

Neue Synagoge (*New Synagogue*). This meticulously restored landmark, built between 1859 and 1866, is an exotic amalgam of styles, the whole faintly Middle Eastern. Its bulbous, gilded cupola stands out in the skyline. When its doors opened, it was the largest synagogue in Europe, with 3,200 seats. The synagogue was damaged on November 9, 1938 (*Kristallnacht*—Night of the Broken Glass), when Nazi looters rampaged across Germany, burning synagogues and smashing the few Jewish shops and homes left in the country. It was destroyed by Allied bombing in 1943, and it wasn't until the mid-1980s that the East German government restored it. The effective exhibit on the history of the building and its congregants includes fragments of the original architecture and furnishings. ▰ **TIP→** Sabbath services are held in a modern addition. ⊠ *Oranienburger Str. 28–30, Mitte* ☎ *030/8802–8300* ⊕ *www.zentrumjudaicum. de* ✉ *€3.50* ⊙ *Apr.–Sept., Sun. and Mon. 10–8, Tues.–Thurs. 10–6, Fri. 10–5; Nov.–Feb., Sun.–Thurs. 10–6, Fri. 10–2; Mar. and Oct., Sun. and Mon. 10–8, Tues.–Thurs. 10–6, Fri. 10–2. English/Hebrew audio guides €3* Ⓜ *Oranienburger Tor (U-bahn), Oranienburger Strasse (S-bahn).*

Nikolaiviertel (*Nicholas Quarter*). Renovated in the 1980s and a tad concrete-heavy as a result, this tiny quarter grew up around Berlin's oldest parish church, the medieval, twin-spire **St. Nikolaikirche** (St. Nicholas's Church), now a museum, dating from 1230. The adjacent Fischerinsel (Fisherman's Island) area was the heart of Berlin 765 years ago, and retains a bit of its medieval character. At Breite Strasse you'll find two of Berlin's oldest buildings: No. 35 is the **Ribbeckhaus,** the city's only surviving Renaissance structure, dating from 1624, and No. 36 is the early baroque **Marstall,** built by Michael Matthais between 1666 and 1669. The area feels rather artificial, but draws tourists to its gift stores, cafés, and restaurants. ✉ *Nikolaikirchpl., Mitte* ☎ *030/2400–2162* ⊕ *www.stadtmuseum.de* Ⓜ *Alexanderplatz (U-bahn and S-bahn).*

Fodor's Choice   **Reichstag** (*Parliament Building*). After last meeting here in 1933, the
★   Bundestag, Germany's federal parliament, returned to its traditional seat in the spring of 1999. British architect Sir Norman Foster lightened up the gray monolith with a glass dome, which quickly became one of the city's main attractions: you can circle up a gently rising ramp while taking in the rooftops of Berlin and the parliamentary chamber below. At the base of the dome is an exhibit on the Reichstag's history, in German and English. Completed in 1894, the Reichstag housed the imperial German parliament and later served a similar function during the ill-fated Weimar Republic. On the night of February 27, 1933, the Reichstag burned down in an act of arson, a pivotal event in Third Reich history. The fire led to state protection laws that gave the Nazis a pretext to arrest their political opponents. The Reichstag was rebuilt but again badly damaged in 1945. The graffiti of the victorious Russian soldiers can still be seen on some of the walls in the hallways. After terrorism warnings at the end of 2010, the Reichstag tightened its door policy, asking all visitors to register their names and birthdates in advance and reserve a place on a guided tour. Since then, the crowds that used to snake around the outside of the building have subsided, and a visit is worth the planning. ■ **TIP➔ As always, a reservation at the pricey rooftop Käfer restaurant (**☎**030/2262–9933) will also get you in.** Those with reservations can use the doorway to the right of the Reichstag's main staircase. The building is surrounded by ultramodern federal government offices, such as the boxy, concrete **Bundeskanzleramt** (Federal Chancellery), which also has a nickname of course: the "Washing Machine." Built by Axel Schultes, it's one of the few new buildings in the government district by a Berlin architect. Participating in a guided tour of the Chancellery is possible if you apply in writing several weeks prior to a visit. A riverwalk with great views of the government buildings begins behind the Reichstag. ✉ *Pl. der Republik 1, Mitte* ☎ *030/2273–2152 for Reichstag Bundeskanzleramt* ⊕ *www.bundestag.de* ✉ *Free with prior registration* ☉ *Daily 8 am–11 pm* Ⓜ *Unter den Linden (S-bahn), Bundestag (U-bahn).*

Unter den Linden. The name of this historic Berlin thoroughfare, between the Brandenburg Gate and Schlossplatz, means "under the linden trees," and it was indeed lined with fragrant and beloved lindens until the 1930's. Imagine Berliners' shock when Hitler decided to fell the trees in order to make the street more parade-friendly. The grand boulevard began as a riding path that the royals used to get from their palace to their hunting grounds (now the central Berlin park called Tiergarten). It is once again lined with linden trees planted after World War II.

WORTH NOTING

Alexanderplatz (*Alexander Square*). This bleak square, bordered by the train station, the Galeria Kaufhof department store, and the 37-story Park Inn Berlin-Alexanderplatz hotel, once formed the hub of East Berlin and was originally named in 1805 for Czar Alexander I. German writer Alfred Döblin dubbed it the "heart of a world metropolis"—text from his 1929 novel *Berlin Alexanderplatz* is written on a building across the northeastern side of the square. Today it's a basic center of commerce and the occasional demonstration. The unattractive modern buildings are a reminder not just of the results of Allied bombing but also of the ruthlessness practiced by East Germans when they demolished what remained. A famous meeting point in the south corner is the World Time Clock (1969), which even keeps tabs on Tijuana.

FAMILY **AquaDom & Sea Life Berlin.** These commercially run, giant indoor tanks showcase local marine life, beginning with the Spree River, moving on to Berlin's lakes, and then taking you from fresh- to saltwater. Waterfront city scenes are part of the decor, which gradually give way to starfish-petting beds, overhead tanks, and a submarine-like room. Don't come looking for sharks or colorful tropical fish: the most exotic creatures here are perhaps the tiny sea horses and spotted rays. The aquarium's finale is the Aquadom, a state-of-the-art glass elevator that brings you through a silo-shaped fish tank to the exit. Young children love this place, but the timed wait for the elevator can be frustrating for all ages. Be prepared for a line at the entrance, too. ⊠ *Spandauer Str. 3, Mitte* ☎ *030/992–800* ⊕ *www.sealife.de* ☜ *€17.50, €11.35 in advance* ⊙ *Daily 10–7 (last admission at 6)* Ⓜ *Hackescher Markt (S-bahn).*

Berliner Rathaus (*Berlin Town Hall*). Nicknamed the "*Rotes Rathaus*" (Red Town Hall) for its redbrick design, the town hall was completed in 1869. Its most distinguishing features are its neo-Renaissance clock tower and frieze that depicts Berlin's history up to 1879 in 36 terra-cotta plaques, each 20 feet long. Climb the grand stairwell to view the coat-of-arms hall and a few exhibits. ▧TIP➔ **The Rathaus has a very inexpensive, cafeteria-style canteen offering budget lunches. The entrance is inside the inner courtyard.** ⊠ *Rathausstr. 15, Mitte* ☎ *030/90260* ☜ *Free* ⊙ *Weekdays 9–6* Ⓜ *Alexanderplatz (U-bahn and S-bahn).*

Deutscher Dom. The Deutscher Dom holds an extensive exhibition on the emergence of the democratic parliamentary system in Germany since the late 1800's. The free museum is sponsored by the German parliament. Leadership and opposition in East Germany are also documented. ▧TIP➔ **An English-language audio guide covers a portion of the exhibits on the first three floors. Floors four and five have temporary exhibitions with no English text or audio.** ⊠ *Gendarmenmarkt 1, Mitte* ☎ *030/2273–0431* ☜ *Free* ⊙ *Oct.–Apr., Tues.–Sun. 10–6; May–Sept., Tues.–Sun. 10–7.*

15

Hamburger Bahnhof - Museum für Gegenwart (*Museum of Contemporary Art*). This light-filled, remodeled train station is home to a rich survey of post-1960 Western art. The permanent collection includes installations by German artists Joseph Beuys and Anselm Kiefer, as well as paintings by Andy Warhol, Cy Twombly, Robert Rauschenberg, and Robert Morris. An annex presents the hotly debated Friedrich Christian Flick Collection, the largest and most valuable collection of the latest in the world's contemporary art. The 2,000 works rotate, but you're bound to see some by Bruce Naumann, Rodney Graham, and Pipilotti Rist. ⊠ *Invalidenstr. 50–51, Mitte* ☎ *030/3978–3411* ⊕ *www.smb.museum* ⊠ *€12* ⊙ *Tues., Wed., Fri. 10–6, Thurs. 10–8, weekends 11–6* Ⓜ *Naturkundemuseum (U-bahn), Hauptbahnhof (S-bahn)*.

Märkisches Museum (*Brandenburg Museum*). This redbrick attic includes exhibits on the city's theatrical past, its guilds, its newspapers, and the March 1848 revolution. Paintings capture the look of the city before it crumbled in World War II. ▮**TIP➔** On Sunday at 3 pm, fascinating mechanical musical instruments from the collection are played. ⊠ *Am Köllnischen Park 5, Mitte* ☎ *030/2400–2162* ⊕ *www.stadtmuseum.de* ⊠ *€5* ⊙ *Tues.–Sun. 10–6* Ⓜ *Märkisches Museum (U-bahn)*.

Neue Wache (*New Guardhouse*). One of many Berlin projects by the early-19th-century architect Karl Friedrich Schinkel, this building served as both the Royal Prussian War Memorial (honoring the dead of the Napoleonic Wars) and the royal guardhouse until the kaiser abdicated in 1918. In 1931 it became a memorial to those who fell in World War I. Badly damaged in World War II, it was restored in 1960 by the East German state and rededicated as a memorial for the victims of militarism and fascism. After unification it regained its Weimar Republic appearance and was inaugurated as Germany's central war memorial. Inside is a copy of Berlin sculptor Käthe Kollwitz's *Pietà*, showing a mother mourning over her dead son. The inscription in front of it reads, "To the victims of war and tyranny." ⊠ *Unter den Linden, Mitte* ⊙ *Daily 10–6*.

Staatsoper Unter den Linden (*State Opera*). Frederick the Great was a music lover and he made the Staatsoper Unter den Linden, on the east side of Bebelplatz, his first priority. The lavish opera house was completed in 1743 by the same architect who built Sanssouci in Potsdam, Georg Wenzeslaus von Knobelsdorff. The house is currently undergoing a complete makeover, set to be completed in 2015, when the historic interior will be replaced with a modern design. The show goes on at the Schiller Theater across town, where maestro Daniel Barenboim continues to oversee a diverse repertoire. ⊠ *Unter den Linden 7, Mitte* ⊕ *www.staatsoper-berlin.de* ⊙ *Box office: Mon.–Sat. 10–8, Sun. 12–8* Ⓜ *Französische Strasse (U-bahn)*.

Siegessäule (*Victory Column*). The 227-foot granite, sandstone, and bronze column is topped by a winged, golden goddess and has a splendid view of Berlin. It was erected in front of the Reichstag in 1873 to commemorate Prussia's military successes and then moved to the Tiergarten in 1938–39. You have to climb 270 steps up through the column to reach the observation platform, but the view is rewarding. The gold-tipped cannons surrounding the column are those the Prussians captured from the French in the Franco-Prussian War. ⊠ *Str. des 17. Juni, am Grossen Stern, Mitte* ☎ *030/391–2961* ☜ *€2.20* ⊙ *Nov.–Mar., weekdays 10–5, weekends 10–5:30; Apr.–Oct., weekdays 9:30–6:30, weekends 9:30–7; last admission ½ hr before closing.* Ⓜ *Tiergarten (S-bahn), Bellevue (S-bahn).*

Sowjetisches Ehrenmal Tiergarten (*Soviet Memorial*). Built immediately after World War II, this monument stands as a reminder of the Soviet victory over the shattered German army in Berlin in May 1945. The Battle of Berlin was one of the deadliest on the European front. A hulking bronze statue of a soldier stands atop a marble plinth taken from Hitler's former Reichkanzlei (headquarters). The memorial is flanked by what are said to be the first two T-34 tanks to have fought their way into the city. ⊠ *Str. des 17. Juni, Mitte* Ⓜ *Unter den Linden (S-bahn).*

TIERGARTEN

15

The Tiergarten, a bucolic 630-acre park with lakes, meadows, and wide paths, is the "green heart" of Berlin. In the 17th century it served as the hunting grounds of the Great Elector (its name translates into "animal garden"). Now it's the Berliners' backyard for sunbathing and barbecuing.

The government district, Potsdamer Platz, and the embassy district ring the park from its eastern to southern edges.

TIMING
A leisurely walk from Zoo Station through the Tiergarten to the Brandenburger Tor and the Reichstag will take at least 90 minutes.

TOP ATTRACTIONS
Tiergarten (*Animal Garden*). The quiet greenery of the 630-acre Tiergarten is a beloved oasis, with some 23 km (14 miles) of footpaths, meadows, and two beer gardens. The inner park's 6½ acres of lakes and ponds were landscaped by garden architect Joseph Peter Lenné in the mid-1800s. ⊠ *Tiergarten.*

Café am Neuen See. On the shore of the lake in the southwest corner of the park, you can relax at the Café am Neuen See, a café and beer garden. ▆ **TIP→ For a particularly nice walk here from the S-bahn stop at Zoologischer Garten, take the path into the Tiergarten, then turn right at Schleusenkrug to follow the Landwehrkanal around the back of the zoo. Sneak a peek at the owls, flamingoes, and ostriches for free.** ⊠ *Lichtensteinallee 2, Tiergarten* ☎ *030/254–4930* ⊕ *www.cafe-am-neuen-see.de* ⊙ *Daily 9–late.*

Haus der Kulturen der Welt. Off the Spree River and bordering the Kanzleramt (Chancellery) is the former congress hall, now serving as the Haus der Kulturen der Welt. It is fondly referred to as the "pregnant oyster" because the sweeping, 1950's design of its roof resembles a shellfish opening. Thematic exhibits, festivals, and concerts take place here, and it's also a boarding point for Spree River cruises. ⊠ *House of World Cultures, John-Foster-Dulles Allee 10, Tiergarten* ☎ *030/397–870* ⊕ *www.hkw.de* ⊙ *Daily 10–7.*

Schleusenkrug. Forget the fast-food options at Zoo Station. Instead, follow the train tracks to the back of the taxi and bus queues, where you'll enter Tiergarten and within 100 yards come upon the best hideaway in the area: Schleusenkrug. In warmer weather you can order at the window and sit in the beer garden or on the back patio, watching pleasure ships go through the lock. Inside is a casual restaurant with a changing daily menu. Between November and mid-March the Krug closes at 7 pm. ⊠ *Müller-Breslau-Str., Tiergarten* ☎ *030/313–9909* ⊕ *www. schleusenkrug.de/* ⊙ *Daily 10 am–midnight.*

POTSDAMER PLATZ

The once-divided Berlin is rejoined at Potsdamer Platz, which now links Kreuzberg with the former East once again. Potsdamer Platz was Berlin's inner-city center and Europe's busiest plaza before World War II. Bombings and the Wall left this area a sprawling, desolate lot, where tourists in West Berlin could climb a wooden platform to peek into East Berlin's death strip. After the Wall fell, various international companies made a rush to build their German headquarters on this prime real estate. In the mid-1990s, Potsdamer Platz became Europe's largest construction site. Today's modern complexes of red sandstone, terracotta tiles, steel, and glass have made it a city within a city.

A few narrow streets cut between the hulking modern architecture, which includes two high-rise office towers owned by Daimler, one of which was designed by star architect Renzo Piano. The round atrium of the Sony Center comes closest to a traditional square used as a public meeting point. Farther down Potsdamer Strasse are the state museums and cultural institutes of the Kulturforum.

TOP ATTRACTIONS

Fodor'sChoice ★ **Kulturforum** (*Cultural Forum*). This unique ensemble of museums, galleries, and the Philharmonic Hall was long in the making. The first designs were submitted in the 1960s and the last building completed in 1998. Now it forms a welcome modern counterpoint to the thoroughly restored Prussian splendor of Museum Island, although Berliners and tourists alike hold drastically differing opinions on the area's architectural aesthetics. Whatever your opinion, Kulturforum's artistic holdings are unparalleled and worth at least a day of your time, if not more. The Kulturforum includes the **Gemäldegalerie** (Picture Gallery), the **Kunstbibliothek** (Art Library), the **Kupferstichkabinett** (Print Cabinet), the **Kunstgewerbemuseum** (Museum of Decorative Arts), which is closed until at least 2014 for renovations, the **Philharmonie**, the **Musikinstrumenten-Museum** (Musical Instruments Museum), and the **Staatsbibliothek** (National Library). ⊠ *Potsdamer Platz.*

Gemäldegalerie (*Picture Gallery*). The Kulturforum's Gemäldegalerie reunites formerly separated collections from East and West Berlin. It's one of Germany's finest art galleries, and has an extensive selection of European paintings from the 13th to 18th century. Seven rooms are reserved for paintings by German masters, among them Dürer, Cranach the Elder, and

Holbein. A special collection has works of the Italian masters—Botticelli, Titian, Giotto, Lippi, and Raphael—as well as paintings by Dutch and Flemish masters of the 15th and 16th centuries: Van Eyck, Bosch, Brueghel the Elder, and van der Weyden. The museum also holds the world's second-largest Rembrandt collection. ✉ *Kulturforum, Matthäikirchpl., Potsdamer Platz* ☎ *030/2664–24242* ⊕ *www.smb.museum* ☎ *€10* ⊗ *Tues., Wed., and Fri.–Sun. 10–6, Thurs. 10–8* Ⓜ *Potsdamer Platz (U-bahn and S-bahn).*

Kunstbibliothek (*Art Library*). With more than 400,000 volumes on the history of European art, the Kunstbibliothek, in the Kulturforum, is one of Germany's most important institutions on the subject. It contains art posters and advertisements, examples of graphic design and book design, ornamental engravings, prints and drawings, and a costume library. Visitors can view items in the reading rooms, but many samples from the collections are also shown in rotating special exhibitions. ✉ *Kulturforum, Matthäikirchpl., Potsdamer Platz* ☎ *030/2664–24242* ⊕ *www.smb.museum* ☎ *Varies according to exhibition* ⊗ *Tues.–Fri. 10–6, weekends 11-6. Reading room weekdays 9–8.*

Kupferstichkabinett (*Drawings and Prints Collection*). One of the Kulturforum's smaller museums, Kupferstichkabinett has occasional exhibits, which include European woodcuts, engravings, and illustrated books from the 15th century to the present (highlights of its holdings are pen-and-ink drawings by Dürer and drawings by Rembrandt). You can request to see one or two drawings in the study room. Another building displays paintings dating from the late Middle Ages to 1800. ✉ *Kulturforum, Matthäikirchpl. 4, Potsdamer Platz* ☎ *030/2664–24242* ⊕ *www.smb.museum* ☎ *€6* ⊗ *Tues.–Fri. 10–6, weekends 11–6.*

Musikinstrumenten-Museum (*Musical Instruments Museum*). Across the parking lot from the Philharmonie, the Kulturforum's Musikinstrumenten-Museum has a fascinating collection of keyboard, string, wind, and percussion instruments. ■ **TIP→** These are demonstrated during an 11 am tour on Saturday, which closes with a 20-minute Wurlitzer organ concert for an extra €2. ✉ *Kulturforum, Ben-Gurion-Str. 1, Potsdamer Platz* ☎ *030/2548–1178* ⊕ *www.sim.spk-berlin.de* ☎ *€6* ⊗ *Tues., Wed., and Fri. 9–5, Thurs. 9–8, weekends 10–5.*

Staatsbibliothek (*National Library*). The Kulturforum's Staatsbibliothek is one of the largest libraries in Europe, and was one of the Berlin settings in Wim Wenders's 1987 film *Wings of Desire.* ✉ *Kulturforum, Potsdamer Str. 33, Potsdamer Platz* ☎ *030/2664-32333* ⊕ *staatsbibliothek-berlin.de* ⊗ *Weekdays 9–9, Sat. 10–7.*

Neue Nationalgalerie (*New National Gallery*). Bauhaus member Mies van der Rohe originally designed this glass-box structure for Bacardi Rum in Cuba, but Berlin became the site of its realization in 1968. The main exhibits are below ground. Highlights of the collection of 20th-century paintings, sculptures, and drawings include works by expressionists Otto Dix, Ernst Ludwig Kirchner, and Georg Grosz. Special exhibits often take precedence over the permanent collection. ✉ *Potsdamer Str. 50, Potsdamer Platz* ☎ *030/2664–24242* ⊕ *www.smb.museum* ☎ *Varies according to exhibition* ⊗ *Tues., Wed., and Fri. 10–6, Thurs. 10–8, weekends 11–6* Ⓜ *Potsdamer Platz (U-bahn and S-bahn).*

15

Panoramapunkt. Located 300 feet above Potsdamer Platz at the top of one of its tallest towers, the new Panoramapunkt (Panoramic Viewing Point) not only features the world's highest-standing original piece of the Berlin wall, but also a fascinating, multimedia exhibit about the dramatic history of Berlin's former urban center. A café and a sun terrace facing west make this open-air viewing platform one of the city's most romantic. ⊠ *Potsdamer Pl. 1, Potsdamer Platz* ☎ *030/2593–7080* ⊕ *www.panoramapunkt.de* ✉ *€5.50* ⊙ *Summer, daily 10–8; winter, daily 10–5 (last entrance 30 mins before closing).*

Sony Center. This glass-and-steel construction wraps around a spectacular circular forum. Topping it off is a tentlike structure meant to emulate Mount Fuji. The architectural jewel, designed by German-American architect Helmut Jahn, is one of the most stunning public spaces of Berlin's new center, filled with restaurants, cafés, movie theaters, and apartments. A faint reminder of glorious days gone by is the old **Kaisersaal** (Emperor's Hall), held within a very modern glass enclosure, and today a pricey restaurant. The hall originally stood 75 yards away in the Grand Hotel Esplanade (built in 1907) but was moved here lock, stock, and barrel. Red-carpet glamour returns every February with the Berlinale Film Festival, which has screenings at the commercial cinema within the center. ⊠ *Potsdamer Platz.*

Deutsche Kinemathek Museum für Film und Fernsehen. Within the Sony Center is the small but fun Museum für Film und Fernsehen, which presents the groundbreaking history of German moviemaking with eye-catching displays. Descriptions are in English, and there's an audio guide as well. Memorabilia includes personal belongings of Marlene Dietrich and other German stars, while special exhibitions go into depth about outstanding directors, movements, and studios. A good selection of films, from the best classics to the virtually unknown art house finds, are shown in the theater on the lower level. During the Berlinale film festival in February, this place becomes one of the centers of the action. ⊠ *Sony Building, Potsdamer Str. 2, Potsdamer Platz* ☎ *030/300–9030* ⊕ *www.deutsche-kinemathek.de* ✉ *€7* ⊙ *Tues., Wed., and Fri.–Sun. 10–6, Thurs. 10–8.*

FRIEDRICHSHAIN

There's plenty to see in Friedrichshain, including Karl-Marx-Allee, a long, monumental boulevard lined by grand Stalinist apartment buildings (conceived of as "palaces for the people" that would show the superiority of Communist system over the Capitalist one); the area's funky parks; the East Side Gallery; and lively Simon-Dach-Strasse. It's cool, it's hip, it's historical. If you're into street art, this is a good place to wander.

TOP ATTRACTIONS

Fodor's Choice ★ **East Side Gallery.** This 1-km (½-mile) stretch of concrete went from guarded border to open-air gallery within three months. East Berliners breached the Wall on November 9, 1989, and between February and June of 1990, 118 artists from around the globe created unique works of art on its longest-remaining section. Restoration in 2010 renewed the old images with a fresh coat of paint, but while the colors of the artworks now look like new, the gallery has lost a bit of its charm. One of the best-known works, by Russian artist Dmitri Vrubel, depicts Brezhnev and Honnecker (the former East German leader) kissing, with the caption "My God. Help me survive this deadly love." The stretch along the Spree Canal runs between the Warschauer Strasse S- and U-bahn station and Ostbahnhof. The redbrick Oberbaumbrücke (an 1896 bridge) at Warschauer Strasse makes that end more scenic. Just past the bridge there's also a man-made beach with a bar, restaurant, and club popular with the after-work crowd, called Strandgut (⊕ *www.strandgut-berlin. com*). ✉ *Mühlenstr., Friedrichshain* Ⓜ *Warschauer Strasse (U-bahn and S-bahn), Ostbahnhof (S-bahn).*

KREUZBERG

Kreuzberg, stretching from the West Berlin side of the border crossing at Checkpoint Charlie all the way to the banks of the Spree next to Friedrichshain, was and is a lively Berlin district. A large Turkish population shares the residential streets with a variegated assortment of political radicals and bohemians of all nationalities. In the minds of most Berliners, it is split into two even smaller sections: Kreuzberg 61 is a little more upscale, and contains a variety of small and elegant shops and restaurants, while Kreuzberg 36 has stayed grittier, as exemplified by the garbage-strewn, drug-infested, but much-beloved Görlitzer Park. Oranienstrasse, the spine of life in the Kreuzberg 36 district, has mellowed from hardcore to funky since reunification. When Kreuzberg literally had its back against the Wall, West German social outcasts, punks, and the radical left made this old working-class street their territory. Since the 1970s the population has also been largely Turkish, and many of yesterday's outsiders have turned into successful owners of shops and cafés. The most vibrant stretch is between Skalitzer Strasse and Oranienplatz. Use Bus No. M29 or the Görlitzer Bahnhof or Kottbusser Tor U-bahn stations to reach it.

TIMING

Owing to its small size and popularity, you may experience a wait or slow line at the Checkpoint Charlie Museum. Monday is a popular day for this museum—and for the nearby, must-see Jüdisches Museum—since the state museums are closed that day.

TOP ATTRACTIONS

Fodor'sChoice **Mauermuseum-Museum Haus am Checkpoint Charlie.** Just steps from the
★ famous crossing point between the two Berlins, the Wall Museum–House at Checkpoint Charlie presents visitors with the story of the Wall and, even more riveting, the stories of those who escaped through, under, and over it. An infamous hot spot during the Cold War, this border crossing for non-Germans was manned by the Soviet military in East Berlin's Mitte district and, several yards south, by the U.S. military in West Berlin's Kreuzberg district. Tension between the superpowers in October 1961 led to an uneasy standoff between Soviet and American tanks. Today the touristy intersection consists of a replica of an American guardhouse and signage, plus cobblestones that mark the old border.

This homespun museum reviews the events leading up to the Wall's construction and, with original tools and devices, plus recordings and photographs, shows how East Germans escaped to the West (one of the most ingenious contraptions was a miniature submarine). Exhibits about human rights and paintings interpreting the Wall round out the experience. ■■ TIP➜ Come early or late in the day to avoid the multitudes dropped off by tour buses. Monday can be particularly crowded because the state museums are closed on Mondays. ⊠ *Friedrichstr. 43–45, Kreuzberg* ☎ *030/253–7250* ⊕ *www.mauermuseum.com* ⬚ *€12.50* ⊘ *Daily 9 am–10 pm* Ⓜ *Kochstrasse (U-bahn).*

Fodor'sChoice
★
Topographie des Terrors (*Topography of Terror*). Before 2010, Topographie des Terrors was an open-air exhibit, fully exposed to the elements. Now, in a stunning new indoor exhibition center at the same location, you can view photos and documents explaining the secret state police and intelligence organizations that planned and executed Nazi crimes against humanity. The fates of both victims and perpatrators are given equal attention here. The cellar remains of the Nazis' Reich Security Main Office (composed of the SS, SD, and Gestapo) where the main exhibit used to be, are still open to the public and now contain other exhibitions, which typically run from April to October as the remains are open air. ⊠ *Niederkirchnerstr. 8, Mitte* ☎ *030/2545–0950* ⊕ *www. topographie.de* ⬚ *Free* ⊘ *Daily 10–8.*

WORTH NOTING

Berlinische Galerie. Talk about site-specific art: all the modern art, photography, and architecture models and plans here, created between 1870 and the present, were made in Berlin (or in the case of architecture competition models, intended for the city). Russians, secessionists, Dadaists, and expressionists all had their day in Berlin, and individual works by Otto Dix, George Grosz, and Georg Baselitz, as well as artists' archives such as the Dadaist Hannah Höch's, are highlights. There's a set price for the permanent collection, but rates vary for special exhibitions, which are usually well-attended and quite worthwhile. ■■ TIP➜ Bus No. M29 to Waldeckpark/Oranienstrasse is the closest transportation stop. ⊠ *Alte Jakobstr. 124–128, Kreuzberg* ☎ *030/7890–2600* ⊕ *www.berlinischegalerie.de* ⬚ *€8* ⊘ *Wed.–Mon. 10–6* Ⓜ *Kochstrasse (U-bahn).*

Deutsches Technikmuseum (*German Museum of Technology*). A must if you're traveling with children, this museum will enchant anyone who's interested in technology or fascinated with trains, planes, and automobiles. Set in the remains of Anhalter Bahnhof's industrial yard and enhanced with a newer, glass-enclosed wing, the museum has several floors of machinery, including two airplane rooms on the upper floors crowned with a "Rosinenbomber," one of the beloved airplanes that delivered supplies to Tempelhof Airport during the Berlin Airlift of 1948. Don't miss the train sheds, which are like three-dimensional, walkable timelines of trains throughout history, and the historical brewery, which has a great rooftop view of today's trains, U-bahn line nos. 1 and 2, converging at the neighboring Gleisdreieck station. ⊠ *Trebbiner Str. 9, Kreuzberg* ☎ *030/902–540* ⬚ *€6* ⊘ *Tues.–Fri. 9–5:30, weekends 10–6* Ⓜ *Gleisdreieck (U-bahn), Anhalter Bahnhof (S-bahn).*

15

Golgatha. This beloved local watering hole has taken up space in Viktoriapark since 1928. Open all day long and late into the night, it's the perfect place to while away the hours with a cup of coffee during the day, or sip a cocktail or beer during the evening, when a DJ is spinning. It's also a reliable lunch spot, with salads, grilled meats, and the "German pizzas" known as *Flammkuchen* on the menu. ⊠ *Dudenstr. 40–64, in Viktoriapark, closest entrance at Katzbachstr., Kreuzberg* ☎ *030/785–2453* ⊕ *www.golgatha-berlin.de* ⊘ *Apr.–Oct., 9 am–late* ⊘ *Closed Nov.–Mar.* Ⓜ *Yorckstrasse (S-bahn and U-bahn).*

Jüdisches Museum Berlin (*Jewish Museum*). The history of Germany's Jews from the Middle Ages through today is chronicled here, from prominent historical figures to the evolution of laws regarding Jews' participation in civil society. A few of the exhibits document the Holocaust itself, but this museum celebrates Jewish life and history far more than it focuses on the atrocities committed during WWII. An attraction in itself is the highly conceptual building, designed by Daniel Libeskind, where various physical "voids" in the oddly constructed and intensely personal modern wing of the building represent the idea that some things can and should never be exhibited when it comes to the Holocaust. Libeskind also directed the construction of the recently opened "Akademie" of the museum just across the street, which offers a library and temporary exhibitions, as well as space for workshops and lectures. ▥ TIP➜ Reserve at least three hours for the museum and devote more time to the second floor if you're already familiar with basic aspects of Judaica, which are the focus of the third floor. ⊠ *Lindenstr. 9–14, Kreuzberg* ☎ *030/2599–3300* ⊕ *www.jmberlin.de* ▦ *€7* ⊘ *Mon. 10–10, Tues.–Sun. 10–8* Ⓜ *Hallesches Tor (U-bahn).*

Käthe-Kollwitz-Museum. Right next door to the Literaturhaus, this small but lovingly curated museum in a formerly private home pays homage to one of Berlin's favorite artists, the female sculptor, print-maker, and painter Käthe Kollwitz. Perhaps best known for her harrowing sculpture of a mother mourning a dead child inside the Neue Wache on Unter den Linden, she also lent her name to one of the city's most beautiful squares, the posh, leafy Kollwitzplatz, which contains a sculpture of her. ⊠ *Fasanenstr. 24, Charlottenburg* ☎ *030/882–5210* ⊕ *www.kaethe-kollwitz.de* ▦ *€6* ⊘ *Daily 10–6* Ⓜ *Uhlandstrasse (U-bahn).*

Martin-Gropius-Bau. This magnificent palazzo-like exhibition hall first opened in 1881, and once housed Berlin's Arts and Crafts Museum. Its architect, Martin Gropius, was the great-uncle of Walter Gropius, the Bauhaus architect who also worked in Berlin. The international, changing exhibits on art and culture have recently included Aztec sculptures, Henri Cartier-Bresson's photographs, an expansive Frida Kahlo retrospective, and works from Anish Kapoor and Meret Oppenheim. ⊠ *Niederkirchnerstr. 7, Kreuzberg* ☎ *030/254–860* ⊕ *www.gropiusbau. de* ▦ *Varies with exhibit* ⊘ *Wed.–Mon. 10–7* Ⓜ *Kochstrasse (U-bahn), Potsdamer Platz (U-bahn and S-bahn).*

PRENZLAUER BERG

Once a spot for edgy art spaces, squats, and all manner of alternative lifestyles, Prenzlauer Berg has morphed into an oasis of artisanal bakeries, cute kids clothes stores (where the prices could knock your socks off) and genteel couples with baby strollers. That said, it's a beautiful area, with gorgeous, perfectly renovated buildings shaded by giant plantain and chestnut trees. If you're in the mood for an upscale, locally made snack and a nice stroll, this is the place to be. You'll find a denser concentration of locals and long-settled expats in Prenzlauer Berg than in other parts of the city like the Scheunenviertel.

WORTH NOTING

Jüdischer Friedhof Weissensee (*Jewish Cemetery*). More than 150,000 graves make up this peaceful retreat in Berlin's Weissensee district, Europe's largest Jewish cemetery. The grounds and tombstones are in excellent condition—a seeming impossibility, given its location in the heart of the Third Reich—and wandering through them is like taking an extremely moving trip back in time through the history of Jewish Berlin. To reach the cemetery, take Tram No. M4 from Hackescher Markt to Albertinenstrasse and head south on Herbert-Baum-Strasse. At the gate you can get a map from the attendant. The guidebook is in German only. ⊠ *Herbert-Baum-Str. 45, Weissensee* ☎ *030/925–3330* ⊙ *Summer, Mon.–Thurs. 7:30–5, Fri. 7:30–2:30, Sun. 8–5; Winter., Mon.–Thurs. 7:30–4, Fri. 7:30–2:30, Sun 8–4.*

Kollwitzplatz (*Kollwitz Square*). Named for the painter, sculptor, and political activist Käthe Kollwitz (1867–1945), who lived nearby, the square is the center of the old working-class district of Prenzlauer Berg. Kollwitz, who portrayed the hard times of area residents, is immortalized here in a sculpture based on a self-portrait. Ironically, this image of the artist now has a view of the upwardly mobile young families who have transformed the neighborhood since reunification. Bars and restaurants peal off from the square, and one of the best organic markets in town takes over on weekends. ⊠ *Prenzlauer Berg.*

Kulturbrauerei (*Culture Brewery*). The redbrick buildings of the old Schultheiss brewery are typical of late-19th-century industrial architecture. Parts of the brewery were built in 1842, and at the turn of the 20th century the complex expanded to include the main brewery of Berlin's famous Schultheiss beer, then the world's largest brewery. Today, the multiplex cinema, pubs, clubs, and a concert venue that occupy it make up an arts and entertainment nexus (sadly, without a brewery). Pick up information at the Prenzlauer Berg tourist office here, and come Christmastime, visit the Scandinavian-themed market, which includes children's rides. ⊠ *Schönhauser Allee 36, entry at Sredzkistr. 1 and Knaackstr. 97, Prenzlauer Berg* ☎ *030/4431–5152* ⊕ *www. kulturbrauerei-berlin.de* Ⓜ *Eberswalder Strasse (U-bahn).*

15

Continued on page 712

Art Berlin Contemporary 2010 Opening

Paste-up street art

East Side Gallery, Berlin Wall

Capitain Petzel

Stencil by XOOOOX

Molecule Men in the River Spree

Neue Nationalgalerie

Alexandre da Cunha, "Mono-lith," Sommer & Kohl Gallery

BERLIN'S EVOLVING ART SCENE

Berlin's contemporary art world is a perpetual work in progress. Hip galleries appear and then move on to bigger or trendier spaces almost before the paint is dry. The hottest players rotate with the seasons. But a few things always stay the same, like edgy ideas and constantly expanding frontiers in a city with a seemingly endless supply of spaces to reclaim. The art world here is unpretentious and easy to access—you might just meet Berlin's next art star along the way.

By Kimberly Bradley

Gallery Weeekend Opening

The art scene has exploded in the past decade, evolving from a local community of dealers and artists to an international urban art center. Emerging artists of the 1990s, like Olafur Eliasson and Tacita Dean, remain in Berlin, despite having become international stars. And while a true "Berlin School" doesn't exist, the admittedly fragmented scene shows a strong tendency toward conceptual and performance art. Artist collectives also tap into the city's collaborative spirit.

EXPANDING FROM THE CENTER

In recent years the scene has evolved in ways no one could have predicted. What used to be two centralized art hubs—the edgy, experimental Mitte in the east and established, blue-chip Charlottenburg in the west—have multiplied throughout the city. Galleries have opened, often in clusters, far beyond Mitte's original main drag of Auguststrasse, to Heidestrasse behind the Hamburger Bahnhof museum, Lindenstrasse and the area around the Jewish Museum on Mitte's southern edge, and most recently Potsdamer Strasse near the New National Gallery.

ART FAIRS

Two recently founded events now bring in the well-heeled international crowd: **Gallery Weekend Berlin** (⊕ *www.gallery-weekend-berlin.de*) in early May and **Art Berlin Contemporary** (⊕ *www.artberlincontemporary.com*), which began as a rogue sculpture exhibition in 2008 and is now the city's only large-scale fall art fair.

RECESSION AND REBOUND

Berlin's art scene has not been immune to global issues. There were about 500 galleries in Berlin before 2008's financial crash, and the number has gone down to a bit more than 400 since then as galleries are forced to close. Still, a few truly top-notch venues have since settled into architecturally interesting spaces: **Sprüth Magers** (⊕ *www.spruethmagers.com*) shows art stars in a vast gallery, **Capitain Petzel** (⊕ *www.capitainpetzel.de*) exhibits large-scale work in a modernist East German building that resembles a glass cube, and **Koch Oberhuber Wolff** (⊕ *www.kow-berlin.info*) takes up three floors of a striking new concrete building by local architect Arno Brandlhuber.

LOOKING FORWARD

Berlin being Berlin, the underground is never far away. Curators here throw innovative party-shows in garages and nightclubs around town, like **Stattbad Wedding** (⊕ *stattbad.net*) and **Autocenter** (⊕ *www.autocenterart.de*). Young artists are settling into the city's newest art neighborhood, Neukölln, in the southeast, and project spaces and new galleries can't be far behind.

ART OUTSIDE THE BOX

Museums and galleries are merely the tip of Berlin's art-world iceberg.

STREET ART

Street art abounds in the German capital. Tags (symbols identifying individual graffiti artists) adorn walls everywhere, but the areas around Köpernicker Strasse or Schlesiches Tor in Kreuzberg are especially thick with expertly executed paste-ups (posters) and stenciled art. Building-size murals can be seen around the Schlesiche Strasse area on the border between the Kreuzberg and Treptow districts, and in 2011, a sanctioned art project invited major international bombers (graffiti artists) to paint murals on blank firewalls in Berlin's Wedding district.

Take note of the **yellow bananas** marking gallery spaces; they are artist Thomas Baumgärtel's seal of approval, which he has been bestowing on worthy locations since 1986.

For curated exhibitions featuring works by artists with street-art backgrounds, head to **Circle Culture Gallery** (✉ *Gipsstrasse 11* ☎ *27581/7886* ⊕ *circleculture-gallery. de*) in Mitte. For online insight into the scene, see ⊕ *urbanartcore.eu.*

PRIVATE COLLECTIONS

Following in the footsteps of the **Sammlung Hoffmann** (✉ *Sophie-Gips-Höfe, Aufgang C, Sophienstr. 21* ☎ *2849/*
9120 ⊕ *www.sammlung-hoffmann.de* ✉ *€8*), several private collectors have opened their own mini-museums. Inside an ominous war bunker in Mitte is the **Boros Collection** (✉ *Reinhardtstrasse 20* ☎ *27594/065* ⊕ *sammlung-boros.de* ✉ *€10*), which highlights early work by some of Berlin's finest artists, like Olafur Eliasson. Now in a huge, new location, **Sammlung Haubrok** (✉ *Herzbergstrasse 40-43* ☎ *172210/9525* ⊕ *sammlung-haubrok.de*) mounts exhibitions using the collection of Barbara and Axel Haubrok, who own more than 500 works by mostly European artists. And Thomas Olbricht's **me Collector's Room** (✉ *Auguststrasse 68* ☎ *86008/510* ⊕ *www.me-berlin.com* ✉ *€6*) displays his admittedly kitschy art and his collection of curiosities, like shrunken heads and ivory carvings.

TOURS

AlternativeBerlin (☎ *16281/98264 walternativeberlin.com*) offers workshops and tours of street art. For a customized art tour of the city, no one beats **Go Art!'s** (✉ *Potsdamer Str. 81B* ☎ *3087/3626* ⊕ *goart-berlin.de*) Miriam Bers, a Berlin art-world veteran.

GALLERY WALK: POTSDAMER STRASSE

Aurel Scheibler.

Berlin's galleries are notorious for playing musical chairs, and since 2009, a critical mass of excellent art venues have convened in—surprise!—former West Berlin, which represents a shift away from the hipper eastern district. The somewhat nondescript area on and around Potsdamer Strasse, not far from Potsdamer Platz, is now home to both Berlin stalwarts and highbrow newcomers. But you wouldn't necessarily see them from the street; most galleries here are in second-floor apartment-like spaces or tucked away in courtyards.

PLANNING

Two to three hours is plenty of time for a gallery overview, but you may want to spend more time looking at the art. If you only have an hour, limit your tour to these blue-chip best bets: Esther Schipper, Isabella Bortolozzi, Blain|Southern, Klosterfelde, and Helga Maria Klosterfelde Edition. Galleries are generally open Tuesday to Saturday, noon to 6.

POTSDAMER STRASSE TO SCHÖNEBERGER UFER

Start at the **Neue Nationalgalerie** at Potsdamer Strasse 50. Architect Mies van der Rohe's impressive glass box—his only museum project—has been up for more than 50 years, and it often mounts blockbuster shows by artists like Thomas Demand or Jenny Holzer.

Cross the canal, turn right, and walk along Schöneberger Ufer

to see the **Galerie Verein Berliner Künstler** in a lovely townhouse at No. 55. Founded in 1841, this is Germany's oldest artist-run association, and the exhibition halls are dedicated to showing members' work.

At No. 61, **Galerie Isabella Bortolozzi** exhibits some of the city's edgiest artists, including brilliant Vietnamese artist Danh Vo, whose conceptual work explores the overlap between public and private life.

One of Berlin's top dealers, **Esther Schipper**, moved to her second-floor gallery and sleek courtyard at No. 65 in 2011. Her star-studded roster includes multitalented Young British Artists star Liam Gillick, Belgian artist Carsten Höller, and Thomas Demand, whose still photographs subtly criticize modern society. New in the district since summer 2012 is **Aurel Scheibler** (✉ *Schoeneberger Ufer 71*), which occupies the ground floor of a building constructed in 1911 as the Berlin Association of Female Artists (and held several galleries in the interwar years). The top-lit

exhibition spaces showcase Scheibler's intriguing artwork.

BISS TO KURFÜRSTENSTRASSE

Backtrack along the canal to Potsdamer Strasse and turn right. On the far side of the street, at Nos. 77-87, pass through a drive into a courtyard. The first gallery on the right is the impressive **Blain|Southern**, which opened in a vast space that was once the printing room of the *Tagesspiegel* daily newspaper, in spring 2011. Created by the original founders of international power-gallery Haunch of Venison, Blain|Southern brings a formidable artist roster from its base in London. Other galleries have crept into spaces in the same courtyard, like the excellent **Galerie Judin Berlin** next door, which favors artists who are master draftspeople, like Danica Phelps. In the historical townhouses in the same courtyard are a number of other new exhibition spaces, like **401 Contemporary**, which shows a mix of younger and older artists, and **Galerie Thomas Fischer**, a young dealer who has already established a reputation by mounting challenging shows in a beautiful space. And there's more: Past Galerie Judin in the second courtyard is the new location of **Galeria Plan B**, an edgy Romanian import that shows

Neue Nationalgalerie

Art Opening at Sprüth Magers

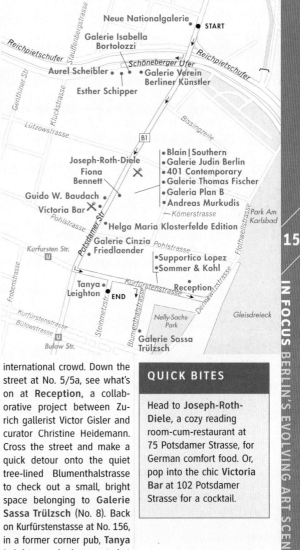

evocative eastern European art. Berlin fashion pioneer **Andreas Murkudis** also moved his exclusive stores, with carefully curated women's and menswear, here in July 2011.

Back out on Potsdamer Strasse, take a look into the windows of veteran Berlin hatmaker **Fiona Bennett**, (✉ *Potsdamer Strasse 81-83*) who recently moved here from Mitte, before heading upstairs to hot Berlin dealer **Guido W. Baudach's** new space (No. 85). A bit further is **Helga Maria Klosterfelde Edition** (No. 97), a former stationery store that is the Berlin branch of a longstanding Hamburg gallery, and features works on paper and prints by art stars like Matt Mullican or Rirkrit Tiravanija. Continuing past bakeries and second-hand clothing shops is **Galerie Cinzia Friedlaender** (No. 105), which shows funky, sometimes lighthearted work by artists like Sunah Choi.

KURFÜRSTENSTRASSE TO BLUMENTHALSTRASSE

Continue to Kurfürstenstrasse and turn left. In a courtyard at No 13 is **Sommer + Kohl** gallery, which represents some of the international art scene's most promising young talent in a former featherbed factory. In the same courtyard is **Supportico Lopez** (No. 14/b), a curatorial project originally from Naples that attracts an international crowd. Down the street at No. 5/5a, see what's on at **Reception**, a collaborative project between Zurich gallerist Victor Gisler and curator Christine Heidemann. Cross the street and make a quick detour onto the quiet tree-lined Blumenthalstrasse to check out a small, bright space belonging to **Galerie Sassa Trülzsch** (No. 8). Back on Kurfürstenstrasse at No. 156, in a former corner pub, **Tanya Leighton**—who has curated at the Whitney Museum in New York—not only mounts fascinating conceptual exhibitions but also hosts lectures and events that explore art's wider meaning.

QUICK BITES

Head to **Joseph-Roth-Diele**, a cozy reading room-cum-restaurant at 75 Potsdamer Strasse, for German comfort food. Or, pop into the chic **Victoria Bar** at 102 Potsdamer Strasse for a cocktail.

Gallery Weekend Opening

WEDDING

While much of Berlin has gentrified rapidly in recent years, Wedding, north of Mitte, is still an old-fashioned, working-class district. Because rents are still relatively low, it will probably be the next hot spot for artists and other creative types looking for cheap studios and work places. If you want to be on the cutting edge, ferret out an underground show or two in this ethnically-diverse neighborhood.

For an historical perspective on the years of Berlin's division, head to the excellent Berlin Wall Memorial Site. This illuminating museum (some of which is open-air) is located along one of the few remaining stretches of the wall, and chronicles the sorrows of the era.

Gedenkstätte Berliner Mauer (*Berlin Wall Memorial Site*). This site combines memorials and a museum and research center on the Berlin Wall. The division of Berlin was particularly heart-wrenching on Bernauer Strasse, where neighbors and families on opposite sides of the street were separated overnight. The Reconciliation Chapel, completed in 2000, replaced the community church dynamited by the Communists in 1985. The church had been walled into the "death strip," and was seen as a hindrance to patrolling it. A portion of the Wall remains on Bernauer Strasse, along with an installation meant to serve as a memorial, which can be viewed 24/7. The documentation center will be closed until late 2014 for renovation and the addition of a new permanent exhibition. ⊠ *Bernauer Str. 111, Wedding* ☎ *030/4679–86666* ⊕ *www.berliner-mauer-gedenkstaette.de* 🚇 *Free, tours €3* ⊘ *Memorial 24 hrs. Visitor center: Apr.–Oct., Tues.–Sun. 9:30–7; Nov.–Mar., Tues.–Sun. 9:30–6* Ⓜ *Bernauer Strasse (U-bahn), Nordbahnhof (S-bahn).*

NEUKÖLLN

If you missed Prenzlauer Berg's heyday, you can still get a good feel for its raw charm and creative flair if you head to ultrahip Neukölln. Just southeast of Kreuzberg below the Landwehrkanal, Neukölln was an impoverished, gritty West Berlin neighborhood until the hip crowd discovered it a few years ago. It's since been almost completely transformed. Makeshift bars/galleries brighten up semi-abandoned storefronts, and vintage café or breakfast spots put a new twist on old concepts. Everything has a salvaged feel, and the crowds are young and savvy. If you're looking for nightlife, there are bars galore.

CHARLOTTENBURG

An important part of former West Berlin but now a western district of the united city, Charlottenburg has retained its old-world charm. Elegance is the keyword here. Whether you're strolling and shopping around Savignyplatz or pausing for a refreshment at the LiteraturHaus, you'll be impressed with the dignity of both the neighborhood's architecture and its inhabitants. Kurfürstendamm (or Ku'damm, as the locals call it) is the central shopping mile, where you'll find an international clientele browsing brand-name designers, or drinking coffee at sidewalk cafés.

CLOSE UP 15

Jewish Berlin Today

As Berlin continues to grapple with the past, important steps toward celebrating Jewish history and welcoming a new generation of Jews to Berlin are in the making.

Somber monuments have been built in memory of victims of the Holocaust and National Socialism. An especially poignant but soft-spoken tribute is the collection of **Stolpersteine** (stumbling blocks) found all over Berlin, imbedded into sidewalks in front of the pre-Holocaust homes of Berlin Jews, commemorating former residents simply with names and dates. German artist Gunter Demnig has personally installed these tiny memorials in big cities and small towns across Germany and Austria, and continues to do so as requests come in from communities across Europe.

The **Ronald S. Lauder Foundation** has gone a step further. Along with **Lauder Yeshurun**, Berlin's Jewish communities have been further strengthened by building housing for Jews in the city center, founding a *Yeshiva*, a rabbinical school, and offering special services for returning Jews.

It's difficult to say how many Jews live in Berlin today, but an official estimate puts the number at 22,000–27,000.

About 12,000 members of the Jewish community are practicing Jews, mostly from the former Soviet Union, who belong to one of several synagogues. Berlin is also gaining in popularity among young Israelis, and today, some estimates say there may be as many as 20,000 Israelis who call Berlin home. These numbers don't include the secular and religious Jews who wish to remain anonymous in the German capital.

The government supports Jewish businesses and organizations with funding, keeps close ties with important members of the community, and, perhaps most visibly, provides 24-hour police protection in front of any Jewish establishment that requests it. Two recent events proved that Jewish Berlin is thriving once again. On November 4, 2010, three young rabbis were ordained at the Pestalozzi Strasse synagogue, the first ceremony of its kind to occur in Berlin since before the Holocaust. Also in 2010, Charlotte Knobloch, a Holocaust survivor and the president of the German Jewish Council at the time, showed the ultimate faith in Germany's recovery and reparation efforts by declaring the country "once again a homeland for Jews."

TOP ATTRACTIONS

Kaiser-Wilhelm-Gedächtnis-Kirche (*Kaiser Wilhelm Memorial Church*). A dramatic reminder of World War II's destruction, the ruined bell tower is all that remains of this once massive church, which was completed in 1895 and dedicated to the emperor, Kaiser Wilhelm I. The Hohenzollern dynasty is depicted inside in a gilded mosaic, whose damage, like that of the building, will not be repaired. The exhibition revisits World War II's devastation throughout Europe. On the hour, the tower chimes out a melody composed by the last emperor's great-grandson, the late Prince Louis Ferdinand von Hohenzollern. In stark contrast to the old bell tower (dubbed the "Hollow Tooth"), which is in sore need of restoration now, are the adjoining Memorial Church and Tower, designed by the noted German architect

Egon Eiermann and finished in 1961. These ultramodern octagonal structures, with their myriad honeycomb windows, have nicknames as well: the "Lipstick" and the "Powder Box." Brilliant, blue stained glass designed by Gabriel Loire of Chartres, France dominates the interiors. Church music and organ concerts are presented in the church regularly, which is slated for restoration in the near future. ⊠ *Breitscheidpl., Charlottenburg* ☎ *030/218–5023* ⊕ *www.gedaechtniskirche-berlin.de* ⊠ *Free* ⊙ *Memorial church daily 9–7* Ⓜ *Zoologischer Garten (U-bahn and S-bahn).*

Fodor'sChoice **Kurfürstendamm.** This busy thoroughfare began as a riding path in the
   ★   16th century. The elector Joachim II of Brandenburg used it to travel between his palace on the Spree River and his hunting lodge in the Grunewald. The Kurfürstendamm (Elector's Causeway) was transformed into a major route in the late 19th century, thanks to the initiative of Bismarck, Prussia's Iron Chancellor.

Even in the 1920s, the Ku'damm was still relatively new and by no means elegant; it was fairly far removed from the old heart of the city, Unter den Linden in Mitte. The Ku'damm's prewar fame was due mainly to its rowdy bars and dance halls, as well as the cafés where the cultural avant-garde of Europe gathered. Almost half of its 245 late-19th-century buildings were completely destroyed in the 1940s, and the remaining buildings were damaged to varying degrees. As in most of western Berlin, what you see today is either restored or newly constructed. Many of the 1950s buildings have been replaced by high-rises, in particular at the corner of Joachimstaler Strasse. Although Ku'damm is still known as the best shopping street in Berlin, its establishments have declined in elegance and prestige over the years. Nowadays you'll want to visit just to check it off your list, but few of the mostly downmarket chain stores will impress you with their luxury.

Museum Berggruen. This small modern-art museum just reopened in 2013 after extensive renovations. It holds works by Matisse, Klee, Giacometti, and Picasso, who is particularly well represented with more than 100 works. Heinz Berggruen (1914–2007), a businessman who left Berlin in the 1930s, collected the excellent paintings. He narrates portions of the free audio guide, sharing anecdotes about how he came to acquire pieces directly from the artists, as well as his opinions of the women portrayed in Picasso's portraits. ⊠ *Schlossstr. 1, Charlottenburg* ☎ *030/2664-24242* ⊕ *www.smb.museum* ⊠ *€10* ⊙ *Tues.–Sun. 10–6* Ⓜ *Sophie-Charlotte-Platz (U-bahn), Richard-Wagner-Platz (U-bahn).*

Fodor'sChoice **Schloss Charlottenburg** (*Charlottenburg Palace*). A grand reminder of
   ★   imperial days, this showplace served as a city residence for the Prussian rulers. The gorgeous palace started as a modest royal summer residence in 1695, built on the orders of King Friedrich I for his wife, Sophie-Charlotte. In the 18th century Frederick the Great made a number of additions, such as the dome and several wings designed in the rococo style. By 1790 the complex had evolved into a massive royal domain that could take a whole day to explore. Behind heavy iron gates, the Court of Honor—the front courtyard—is dominated by a baroque statue of the Great Elector on horseback. ■TIP➔ **Buildings can be visited separately for different admission prices, or altogether as part of a €19 Tageskarte.**

Charlottenburg

KEY

Ⓢ S-Bahn
🛈 Tourist information
Ⓤ U-Bahn

0	200m	
0		1,000ft

The **Altes Schloss** is the main building of the Schloss Charlottenburg complex, with the ground-floor suites of Friedrich I and Sophie-Charlotte. Paintings include royal portraits by Antoine Pesne, a noted court painter of the 18th century. A guided tour visits the Oak Gallery, the early-18th-century palace chapel, and the suites of Friedrich Wilhelm II and Friedrich Wilhelm III, furnished in the Biedermeier style. Tours leave hourly from 9 to 5. The upper floor has the apartments of Friedrich Wilhelm IV, a silver treasury, and Berlin and Meissen porcelain and can be seen on its own.

The **Neuer Flügel** (New Building), where Frederick the Great once lived, was designed by Knobbelsdorff, who also built Sanssouci. It is closed for restoration until 2015. ⊠ *Spandauer Damm 20–24, Charlottenburg* ☎ *030/331–9694–200* ⊕ *www.spsg.de* ⊠ *Tageskarte €19, covers admission for all buildings, excluding tour of Altes Schloss baroque apartments* Ⓜ *Richard-Wagner-Platz (U-bahn).*

Schlosspark Charlottenburg. The park behind the Charlottenburg Palace was laid out in the French baroque style beginning in 1697, and was transformed into an English garden in the early 19th century. In it stand the Neuer Pavillon by Karl Friedrich Schinkel and Carl Langhan's Belvedere Pavillon, which overlooks the lake and the Spree River and holds a collection of Berlin porcelain. ⊕ *www.spsg.de* ⊠ *€3* ⊙ *Park daily. Belvedere: Apr.–Oct., Tues.–Sun. 10–6; Nov.–Mar., weekends 10–5.*

FAMILY **Zoologischer Garten** (*Zoological Gardens*). Even though Knut, the polar bear cub who captured the heart of the city, is sadly no longer with us, there are 14,000 other animals to see here, many of whom may be happy to have their time in the spotlight once again. There are 1,500 different species (more than any other zoo in Europe), including those rare and endangered, which the zoo has been successful at breeding. New arrivals in the past years include a baby rhinoceros. The animals' enclosures are designed to resemble their natural habitats, though some structures are ornate, such as the 1910 Arabian-style Zebra House. Pythons, frogs, turtles, invertebrates, Komodo dragons, and an amazing array of strange and colorful fish are part of the three-floor aquarium. ▮▮TIP→ Check the feeding times posted to watch creatures such as seals, apes, hippos, crocodiles, and pelicans during their favorite time of day. ⊠ *Hardenbergpl. 8 and Budapester Str. 32, Charlottenburg* ☎ *030/254–010* ⊕ *www.zoo-berlin.de* ⊠ *Zoo or aquarium €13, combined ticket €20* ⊙ *Zoo: Oct.–mid-Mar., daily 9–5; mid-Mar.–Aug., daily 9–7; Sept.–Oct., daily 9–6:30. Aquarium: daily 9–6* Ⓜ *Zoologischer Garten (U-bahn and S-bahn).*

WORTH NOTING

Käthe-Kollwitz-Museum. Right next door to the Literaturhaus, this small but lovingly curated museum in a formerly private home pays homage to one of Berlin's favorite artists, the female sculptor, print-maker, and painter Käthe Kollwitz. Perhaps best known for her harrowing sculpture of a mother mourning a dead child inside the Neue Wache on Unter den Linden, she also lent her name to one of the city's most beautiful squares, the posh, leafy Kollwitzplatz, which contains a sculpture of her. ⊠ *Fasanenstr. 24, Charlottenburg* ☎ *030/882–5210* ⊕ *www.kaethe-kollwitz.de* ⊠ *€6* ⊙ *Daily 10–6* Ⓜ *Uhlandstrasse (U-bahn).*

Literaturhaus Berlin. This grand, 19th-century villa on one of West Berlin's prettiest streets, is best known for its café, which approximates a Viennese coffeehouse in both food and atmosphere. It also serves as an intellectual meeting place for high-minded and well-to-do Berliners. The house hosts readings, literary symposia, exhibitions and writing workshops year-round, and has a cozy and comprehensive bookstore (one of the city's best) on the lower level. ⊠ *Fasanenstr. 23, Charlottenburg* ☎ *030/887–2860* ⊕ *www.literaturhaus-berlin.de* ⊙ *Bookshop weekdays 10:30–7:30, Sat. 10:30–6. Café daily 9–midnight* Ⓜ *Uhlandstrasse (U-bahn).*

Museum für Fotografie–Helmut Newton Stiftung. Native son Helmut Newton (1920–2004) pledged this collection of 1,000 photographs to Berlin months before his unexpected death. The man who defined fashion photography in the 1960s through the 1980s was an apprentice to Yva, a Jewish fashion photographer in Berlin in the 1930s. Newton fled Berlin with his family in 1938, and his mentor was killed in a concentration camp. The photographs, now part of the state museum collection, are shown on a rotating basis in the huge Wilhelmine building behind the train station Zoologischer Garten. You'll see anything from racy portraits of models to serene landscapes. ⊠ *Jebensstr. 2, Charlottenburg* ☎ *030/2664–24242* ⊕ *www.helmutnewton.com* ☞ *€10* ⊙ *Tues., Wed., Fri.–Sun. 10–6, Thurs. 10–8* Ⓜ *Zoologischer Garten (U-bahn and S-bahn).*

FAMILY **The Story of Berlin.** You can't miss this multimedia museum for the airplane wing exhibited outside. It was once part of a "Raisin bomber," a U.S. Air Force DC-3 that supplied Berlin during the Berlin Airlift in 1948 and 1949. Eight hundred years of the city's history, from the first settlers casting their fishing lines to Berliners heaving sledgehammers at the Wall, are conveyed through hands-on exhibits, film footage, and multimedia devices in this unusual venue. The sound of footsteps over broken glass follows your path through the exhibit on the Kristallnacht pogrom, and to pass through the section on the Nazis' bookburning on Bebelplatz, you must walk over book bindings. Many original artifacts are on display, such as the stretch Volvo that served as Erich Honnecker's state carriage in East Germany. ▓ TIP➔ The eeriest relic is the 1974 nuclear shelter, which you can visit by guided tour on the hour. Museum placards are also in English. ⊠ *Ku'damm Karree, Kurfürstendamm 207–208, Charlottenburg* ☎ *030/8872–0100* ⊕ *www.story-of-berlin.de* ☞ *€12* ⊙ *Daily 10–8 (last entry at 6)* Ⓜ *Uhlandstrasse (U-bahn).*

WANNSEE

Most tourists come to leafy, upscale Wannsee to see the House of the Wannsee Conference, where the Third Reich's top officials met to plan the "Final Solution." Beyond this dark historical site, however, there are parks, lakes, and islands to explore. Leave a day for a trip here, especially in warm weather: the Wannsee lake is a favorite spot for a summer dip.

TOP ATTRACTIONS

Gedenkstätte Haus der Wannsee-Konferenz (*Wannsee Conference Memorial Site*). The lovely lakeside setting of this Berlin villa belies the unimaginable Holocaust atrocities planned here. This elegant edifice hosted the fateful conference held on January 20, 1942, at which Nazi leaders and German bureaucrats, under SS leader Reinhard Heydrich, planned the systematic deportation and mass extinction of Europe's Jewish population. Today this so-called *Endlösung der Judenfrage* ("Final Solution of the Jewish Question") is illustrated with a chilling exhibition that documents the conference and, more extensively, the escalation of persecution against Jews and the Holocaust itself. A reference library offers source materials in English. ⊠ *Am Grossen Wannsee 56–58, from the Wannsee S-bahn station, take Bus No. 114, Zehlendorf* ☎ *030/805–0010* ⊕ *www.ghwk.de* 🖼 *Free, tour €2* ☉ *Daily 10–6; library weekdays 10–6* Ⓜ *Wannsee (S-bahn).*

ORANIENBURG

In this little village a short drive north of Berlin, the Nazis built one of the first concentration camps (neighbors claimed not to notice what was happening there). After the war, the Soviets continued to use it. Only later did the GDR regime turn it into a memorial site. If you feel like you've covered all the main sites in Berlin, this is worth a day trip.

EXPLORING

Fodor'sChoice ★ **Gedenkstätte und Museum Sachsenhausen** (*Sachsenhausen Memorial and Museum*). This concentration camp was established in 1936 and held 200,000 prisoners from every nation in Europe, including British officers and Joseph Stalin's son. It is estimated that tens of thousands died here, among them more than 12,000 Soviet prisoners of war.

Between 1945 and 1950 the Soviets used the site as a prison, and malnutrition and disease claimed the lives of 20% of the inmates. The East German government made the site a concentration camp memorial in April 1961. Many original facilities remain; the barracks and other buildings now hold exhibits.

To reach Sachsenhausen, take the S-bahn Line No. 1 to Oranienburg, the last stop. The ride from the Friedrichstrasse Station will take 50 minutes. Alternatively, take the Regional Train No. 5, direction north, from one of Berlin's main stations. From the Oranienburg Station it's a 25-minute walk (follow signs), or you can take a taxi or Bus No. 804 (a 7-minute ride, but with infrequent service) in the direction of Malz. ▮▮▮ TIP→ **An ABC zone ticket will suffice for any type of train travel and bus transfer. Allow three hours at the memorial, whose exhibits and sites are spread apart.** Oranienburg is 35 km (22 miles) north of Berlin's center. ⊠ *Str. der Nationen 22, Oranienburg* ☎ *03301/200–200* ⊕ *www.stiftung-bg.de* 🖼 *Free, audio guide €3* ☉ *Visitors center and grounds: Mid-Mar.–mid-Oct., daily 8:30–6; mid-Oct.–mid-Mar., daily 8:30–4:30; last admission ½ hr before closing. Museum closed Mon.* Ⓜ *Oranienburg (S-bahn).*

WHERE TO EAT

Updated by
Giulia Pines

Berlin has plenty of unassuming neighborhood restaurants serving old-fashioned German food; but happily, the dining scene in this thriving city has expanded to incorporate all sorts of international cuisine. Italian food is abundant, from relatively mundane "red sauce" pizza and pasta establishments to restaurants offering specific regional Italian delicacies. Asian food, in particular, has made a big entrance, with Charlottenburg's Kantstrasse leading the way as Berlin's unofficial "Asiatown." Turkish food continues to be popular, too, especially *döner kebab* shops that sell pressed lamb or chicken in flat-bread pockets with a variety of sauces and salads, which are great for a quick meal. Wurst, especially *Currywurst*—pork sausage served with a mildly curried ketchup—is also popular if you're looking for a quick meal on the go.

And as in other big cities around the world, eating local is more and more the rage in Berlin. Restaurants are beginning to understand that although they could import ingredients from other European countries, fresh farm resources are closer to home. Surrounding the city is the rural state of Brandenburg, whose name often comes before *Ente* (duck) on a menu. In spring, *Spargel,* white asparagus from Beelitz, is all the rage, showing up in soups and side dishes.

It's worth noting that Berlin is known for curt or slow service, except at high-end restaurants. And keep in mind that many of the top restaurants are closed Sunday.

If you want to experience that old-fashioned German cuisine, Berlin's most traditional four-part meal is *Eisbein* (pork knuckle), always served with sauerkraut, pureed peas, and boiled potatoes. Other old-fashioned Berlin dishes include *Rouladen* (rolled stuffed beef), *Spanferkel* (suckling pig), *Berliner Schüsselsülze* (potted meat in aspic), and *Hackepeter* (ground beef).

Use the coordinates (✢ 1:B3) at the end of each listing to locate a site on the corresponding map.

MITTE

$
GERMAN

✕ **Altes Europa.** By day, this is a quiet café reminiscent of a classic Viennese coffeehouse, shabby but trendy, with fashionable Mitte-ites chatting in while middle-aged intellectuals page through newspapers and magazines. At night, it turns into a comfortable but bustling neighborhood pub, just crowded enough to look like a scene, but never too packed. And throughout it all, Altes Europa ("Old Europe") manages to construct a daily menu of six or seven tasty dishes like classic German *Knödel* (dumplings) baked with mushrooms and spinach or *Tafelspitz* (boiled beef) with potatoes. The food is inventively prepared and served in record time. ⑤ *Average main: €8* ✉ *Gipsstr. 11, Mitte* ☎ *303/2809–3840* ▭ *No credit cards* Ⓜ *Weinmeisterstrasse (U-bahn)* ✢ *1:A6.*

$ ✕ **Bandol sur Mer.** This tiny, 20-seat eatery serves French classics. The foie

FRENCH   gras, tartar, and entrecôte are standouts, and desserts like crème brûlée round out the menu. The wine selection is good and the atmosphere is comfortable, though ever since Brad Pitt paid Bandol a visit, getting a table has gotten much more difficult. Its location, right in the middle of bustling Torstrasse, makes it a magnet for the hip and fashionable. ▦ **TIP➔ If you can't get a reservation here, try their sister restaurant next door: the larger and slightly more casual 3 Minutes Sur Mer is also open for lunch.** ⑤ *Average main: €15* ⊠ *Torstr. 167, Mitte* ☎ *030/6730–2051* ⌂ *Reservations essential* ▭ *No credit cards* ⊘ *Closed Sun. No lunch weekdays* Ⓜ *Rosenthaler Platz (U-bahn)* ✛ *1:F1.*

$ ✕ **Chén Chè.** Tucked into a courtyard behind the bflat jazz club, this

ASIAN   elegant restaurant benefits from fresh ingredients, expert cooking, and an enticing exotic tea list. It has a lovely location; the outdoor space is adorned with paper lamps and canopies. You'll find the usual suspects, like fresh summer rolls and skewered meats with peanut sauce, but there are also some excellent original dishes, like the pickled Vietnamese eggplant and the rice "burger" with smoked tofu and lotus root. Brunch is served on the weekends. ⑤ *Average main: €8* ⊠ *Rosenthalerstr. 13, Mitte* ☎ *030/2888–4282* ⊕ *www.chenche-berlin.de* ▭ *No credit cards* Ⓜ *Weinmeisterstrasse (U-bahn)* ✛ *1:A6.*

$$ ✕ **Cookies Cream.** With three restaurants, a club, and a bar to his name,

VEGETARIAN   Berlin nightlife "mogul" Cookie is a fixture on the Mitte scene and

Fodor's Choice   Cookies Cream, the vegetarian fine-dining establishment above the club

★   Cookies, is his crowning achievement. The restaurant is accessible only via a dingy alleyway between the Westin Grand Hotel and the Komische Oper next door, and its entrance seems designed to deter would-be visitors but once you're through the door the service is friendly and casual, and the vibe not at all intimidating. Chef Stephan Hentschel makes a point of never serving pasta or rice dishes, saying that would be too easy in a vegetarian restaurant. Instead, he focuses on innovative preparations like kohlrabi turned into ravioli-esque pockets filled with lentils, or celery that's wrapped cannelloni-style around potato puree and chanterelle mushrooms. ⑤ *Average main: €18* ⊠ *Behrenstr. 55, Mitte* ☎ *030/2749–2940* ⌂ *Reservations essential* ⊘ *Closed Sun. and Mon. No lunch* Ⓜ *Französische Strasse (U-bahn)* ✛ *1:E3.*

$$$ ✕ **Habel Weinkultur.** Under the arches of the S-bahn tracks connecting

GERMAN   Friedrichstrasse with Hauptbahnhof, Habel Weinkultur seems unassuming from outside, but inside you'll find a typical old Berlin ambience melding elegance with industrial chic: leather banquettes, crystal chandeliers dangling from the arched brick ceilings, and rumbling trains overhead. The no-nonsense waiters serve local classics, like lamb, Wiener schnitzel, *weisser Spargel* (white asparagus), and Knödel with mushrooms and ham. There's a huge wine selection. ⑤ *Average main: €24* ⊠ *Luisenstr. 19, Mitte* ☎ *030/2809–8484* ⊕ *www.wein-habel.de* ⊘ *No dinner Sun.* Ⓜ *Brandenburger Tor (U-bahn and S-bahn)* ✛ *1:E3.*

$$ ✕ **Hackescher Hof.** This huge-yet-cozy German restaurant is in the

GERMAN   middle of the action at bustling Hackesche Höfe, and one of the best places to munch on internationally flavored German food while doing some excellent people-watching. The Hackescher Hof—which sports

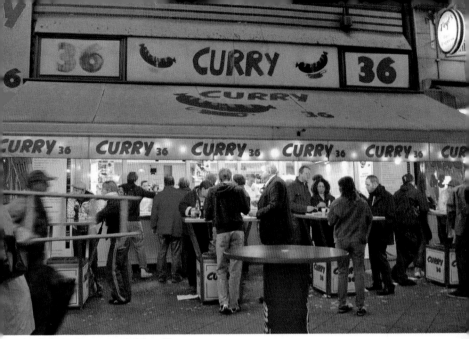

Locals line up for currywurst at Curry 36.

the walking green man symbol from East Berlin's stoplights—is a mix of *Ostalgie* (nostalgia for the East), solid cooking (if available, go for the regional country dishes like Brandenburg wild boar), and an intriguing clientele made up of tourists, intellectuals, artists, and writers, in a beautiful, wood-paneled but always smoky dining hall—there are also some outside tables in the courtyard, too. It's usually packed in the evening, so reservations are strongly recommended. $\boxed{\$}$ *Average main: €16* ✉ *Rosenthalerstr. 40–41, inside Hackesche Höfe, Mitte* ☎ *030/283–5293* ⊕ *www.hackescher-hof.de* Ⓜ *Hackescher Markt (S-bahn)* ✛ *1:A6.*

$$$
AUSTRIAN
✕ **Lutter & Wegner.** One of the city's oldest vintners (*Sekt*, German champagne, was first conceived here in 1811 by actor Ludwig Devrient), Lutter & Wegner has returned to its historic location across from Gendarmenmarkt. The dark-wood-panel walls, parquet floor, and multiple rooms take diners back to 19th-century Vienna, and the food, too, is mostly Austrian, with superb game dishes in winter and, of course, the classic Wiener schnitzel with potato salad. The sauerbraten with red cabbage is a national prizewinner. ▥**TIP➜** In the Weinstube, a cozy room lined with wine shelves meat and cheese plates are served until 3 am. There are several other locations around Berlin but this one is widely considered the best. $\boxed{\$}$ *Average main: €23* ✉ *Charlottenstr. 56, Mitte* ☎ *030/2029–5417* ⊕ *www.l-w-berlin.de* Ⓜ *Französische Strasse (U-bahn), Stadtmitte (U-bahn)* ✛ *1:F4.*

$
MODERN ITALIAN
✕ **Mädchenitaliener.** This cozy Mitte spot has two different spaces: the bustling and sometimes drafty front room with high tables where they put walk-ins, and a darker, more romantic back room for those who remember to reserve ahead—so you should, too. The short but well-thought-out

BEST BETS FOR BERLIN DINING

With hundreds of restaurants to choose from, how will you decide where to eat? Fodor's writers and editors have selected their favorite restaurants by price, cuisine, and experience in the Best Bets lists below. In the first column, Fodor's Choice properties represent the "best of the best" in every price category. You can also search by neighborhood for excellent eats—just peruse our reviews on the following pages.

Fodor's Choice ★

Café Einstein Stammhaus, $$, p. 736

Cookies Cream, $$, p. 720

Die Henne, $, p. 728

Facil, $$$$, p. 727

Hartmanns, $$$$, p. 729

Paris-Moskau, $$$, p. 727

Pauly Saal, $$$$, p. 723

Restaurant Reinstoff, $$$$, p. 723

Weinbar Rutz, $$$$, p. 727

Best by Price

$

Cookies Cream, p. 720

Die Henne, p. 728

Hot Spot, p. 734

Lubitsch, p. 734

Maria Bonita, p. 730

Monsieur Vuong, p. 723

Sasaya, p. 731

$$

Café Einstein Stammhaus, p. 736

Engelbecken, p. 732

$$$

Francucci's, p. 735

Lutter & Wegner, p. 721

$$$$

Facil, p. 727

Best by Cuisine

ASIAN

Hot Spot, $, p. 734

AUSTRIAN

Lutter & Wegner, $$$, p. 721

Ottenthal, $$, p. 734

FRENCH

Bandol sur Mer, $, p. 720

GERMAN

Die Henne, $, p. 728

Florian, $$, p. 732

Renger-Patzsch, $$, p. 736

Restaurant Reinstoff, $$$$, p. 723

ITALIAN

Da Baffi, $, p. 731

Francucci's, $$$, p. 735

Best By Experience

BUSINESS DINING

Café Einstein Stammhaus, $$, p. 736

Lubitsch, $, p. 734

Sra Bua, $$$ p. 726

CHILD-FRIENDLY

Engelbecken, $$, p. 732

HIDDEN HISTORY

Lavanderia Vecchia, $$$$, p. 732

Paris-Moskau, $$$, p. 727

Zur Letzten Instanz, $, p. 727

LATE-NIGHT DINING

Habel Weinkultur, $$$, p. 720

Lubitsch, $, p. 734

Lutter & Wegner, $$$, p. 721

MOST ROMANTIC

Facil, $$$$, p. 727

Hartmanns, $$$$, p. 729

QUIET MEAL

Defne, $, p. 728

Ottenthal, $$, p. 734

menu includes small and large antipasti plates with grilled vegetables, olives, cheeses, and meats, and unusual pastas like tagliatelle with crawfish in a lemon-mint sauce, or with pine nuts and balsamic-roasted figs. Chestnut-filled ravioli with pears is a favorite in winter. The lunch menu, with an appetizer and a pasta dish for only €8.50, is a great deal, especially for the area. ⑤ *Average main: €11* ✉ *Alte Schönhauserstr. 12, Mitte* ☎ *030/4004–1787* ➦ *No credit cards* ☺ *Lunch served Mon.–Sat.* Ⓜ *Rosa-Luxemburg-Platz (U-bahn)* ✚ *1:B6.*

$ ╳ **Monsieur Vuong.** This hip Vietnamese eatery is a convenient place to meet before hitting Mitte's galleries
VIETNAMESE
or clubs, or for a light lunch after browsing the area's popular boutiques. The atmosphere is always lively, and the clientele is an entertaining mix of tech geeks on their lunch breaks from the area's many start-ups, fashionistas with multiple shopping bags, tourists lured in by the crowd, or students from the nearby Goethe Institut, Germany's most prestigious language school. There are only five items and two specials to choose from, but the delicious *goi bo* (spicy beef salad) and *pho ga* (chicken noodle soup) keep the regulars coming back. The teas and shakes are also excellent. ⑤ *Average main: €7* ✉ *Alte Schönhauserstr. 46, Mitte* ☎ *030/9929–6924* ⊕ *www.monsieurvuong.de* ⊱ *Reservations not accepted* Ⓜ *Weinmeister Strasse (U-bahn), Rosa-Luxemburg-Platz (U-bahn)* ✚ *1:B6.*

$$$$ ╳ **Pauly Saal.** A new meeting point for the hip Mitte set, Pauly Saal is
GERMAN
Fodor's Choice in the newly renovated and converted Ehemalige Jüdische Mädchenschule (Old Jewish Girls' School), a worthy destination in its own right
★ due to its beautifully restored interior and several noteworthy galleries. With indoor seating in what used to be the school gym, and outdoor tables taking over the building's expansive courtyard, the setting alone is a draw, but the food is also some of the most exquisite in this part of Mitte. The focus is on artful presentation and local ingredients, like meat sourced directly from Brandenburg. ■**TIP**➙ **The lunch prix fixe (€28) is a great way to sample the restaurant's best dishes.** ⑤ *Average main: €34* ✉ *Auguststr. 11–13, Ehemalige Jüdische Mädchenschule, Mitte* ☎ *030/3300–6070* ⊕ *www.paulysaal.com* ☺ *Closed Sun.* Ⓜ *Tucholskystrasse (S-bahn)* ✚ *1:F2.*

$$$$ ╳ **Restaurant Reinstoff.** One of the top newcomers of the past few years,
CONTEMPORARY the Michelin-starred Reinstoff is a delight. The perfectly crafted and
Fodor's Choice creative haute cuisine, prepared by renowned chef Daniel Achilles,
★ focuses on traditional German ingredients but gives them an avant-garde twist and often playful presentations. The competent yet relaxed service and great atmosphere make this one of the most enjoyable dining destinations. Guests choose from five-, six-, or eight-course

BERLIN MARKETS

On Saturday, visit the sprawling **Winterfeldplatz market** in Schöneberg and try a *Bismarck Herring Brötchen,* a crusty roll with pickled herring or Russian *pelmeni* dumplings doused with sour cream and dill. At Prenzlauer Berg's **Kollwitzplatz market,** also Saturday, try a falafel sandwich. Berlin's largest Turkish market is held on Tuesday and Friday on the **Maybachufer.** Snack on *gözleme,* a savory, flat Turkish pastry filled with meat, cheese, spinach, or potato.

15

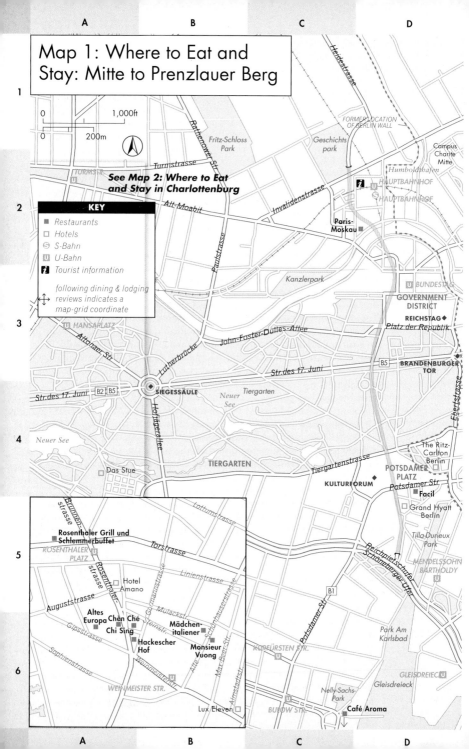

Map 1: Where to Eat and Stay: Mitte to Prenzlauer Berg

A **B** **C** **D**

1

0   1,000ft

0   200m

Fritz-Schloss Park

FORMER LOCATION OF BERLIN WALL

Geschichts park

Campus Charité Mitte

Heidestrasse

Turmstrasse

TURMSTR.

See Map 2: Where to Eat and Stay in Charlottenburg

Humboldthafen

HAUPTBAHNHOF

🛈 HAUPTBAHNHOF

Alt-Moabit

Invalidenstrasse

Paris-Moskau ■

2

KEY

■ Restaurants
□ Hotels
Ⓢ S-Bahn
Ⓤ U-Bahn
🛈 Tourist information

following dining & lodging reviews indicates a map-grid coordinate

Paulstrasse

Rathenower Str.

Kanzlerpark

Ⓤ BUNDESTAG

GOVERNMENT DISTRICT

REICHSTAG ◆

3

Ⓜ HANSAPLATZ

Altonaer Str.

Lutherbrücke

John-Foster-Dulles-Allee

Platz der Republik

B5 BRANDENBURGER TOR

Str. des 17. Juni

Str. des 17. Juni B2 B5

◉ SIEGESSÄULE

Neuer See

Tiergarten

Hofjägerallee

Ebertstrasse

4

Neuer See

□ Das Stue

TIERGARTEN

Tiergartenstrasse

KULTURFORUM ◆

Potsdamer Str.

The Ritz-Carlton Berlin

POTSDAMER PLATZ □

■ Facil

□ Grand Hyatt Berlin

Tilla-Durieux Park

MENDELSSOHN BARTHOLDY

Ⓤ

5

Brunnenstrasse

Lottumstrasse

Torstrasse

■ Rosenthaler Grill und Schlemmerbuffet

ROSENTHALER PLATZ

Rosenthaler strasse

Linienstrasse

Reichpietschufer

Schöneberger Ufer

B1

Potsdamer Str.

Park Am Karlsbad

Augustrasse

□ Hotel Amano

Gormannstr.

Mulackstr.

Schendelgasse

Altes Europa ■ Chen Ché
Chi Sing ■

Hirtenstr.

Gipsstrasse

■ Mädchen-italiener

Schönhauser Str.

KURFÜRSTEN STR.

Ⓤ

■ Hackescher Hof

Monsieur Vuong ■

Sophienstrasse

Weinmeisterstr.

Alte Schönhauser Str.

Max-Beer-Str.

Almstadtstr.

GLEISDREIECK Ⓤ

Gleisdreieck

6

WEINMEISTER STR.

Ⓤ

Lux Eleven □

BÜLOW STR.

Nelly-Sachs-Park

Ⓤ

Café Aroma ■

A **B** **C** **D**

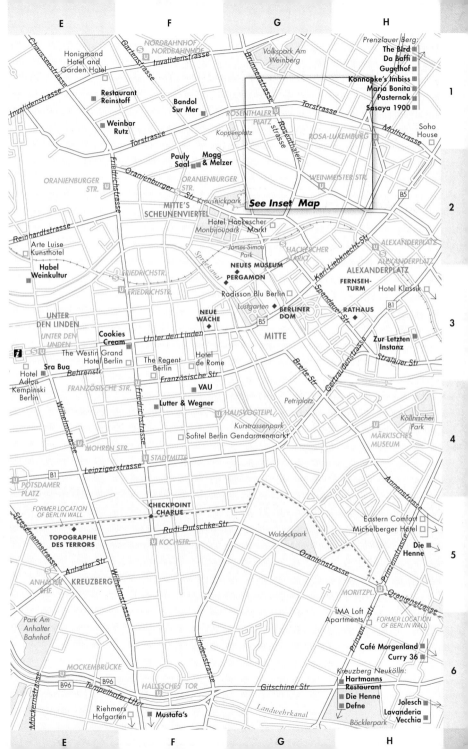

Prenzlauer Berg:
The Bird
Da Baffi
Gugelhof
Konnopke's Imbiss
Maria Bonita
Pasternak
Sasaya 1900

Soho House

E   **F**   **G**   **H**

1

2

3

4

5

6

NORDBAHNHOF
NORDBAHNHOF

Honigmond
Hotel and Garden Hotel

Volkspark Am
Weinberg

Invalidenstrasse

Restaurant
Reinstoff

Bandol
Sur Mer

ROSENTHALER
PLATZ

Torstrasse

Weinbar
Rutz

Torstrasse

Koppenplatz

ROSA-LUXEMBURG

Pauly
Saal

Mogg
& Melzer

Oranienburger

ORANIENBURGER
STR.

ORANIENBURGER
STR.

Kraunickpark

WEINMEISTER STR.

B5

ORANIENBURGER
STR.

MITTE'S
SCHEUNENVIERTEL

See Inset Map

Reinhardtstrasse

Hotel Hackescher
Markt

Monbijoupark

Arte Luise
Kunsthotel

James-Simon
Park

HACKESCHER
MRKT.

ALEXANDERPLATZ

Habel
Weinkultur

FRIEDRICHSTR.

NEUES MUSEUM

PERGAMON

ALEXANDERPLATZ
ALEXANDERPLATZ

FRIEDRICHSTR.

Radisson Blu Berlin

FERNSEH-
TURM

Hotel Klassik

UNTER
DEN LINDEN

NEUE
WACHE

Lustgarten

BERLINER
DOM

RATHAUS

UNTER DEN
LINDEN

Cookies
Cream

Unter den Linden

B5

MITTE

Zur Letzten
Instanz

The Westin Grand
Hotel Berlin

The Regent
Berlin

Hotel
de Rome

Behrenstr.

Strauer Str

Sra Bua

Französische Str.

VAU

Breite Str.

Hotel
Adlon
Kempinski
Berlin

FRANZÖSISCHE STR.

Lutter & Wegner

HAUSVOGTEIPL.

Petriplatz

Köllnischer
Park

Kurstrassenpark

MÄRKISCHES
MUSEUM

MOHREN STR.

Sofitel Berlin Gendarmenmarkt

STADTMITTE

B1

Leipzigerstrasse

POTSDAMER
PLATZ

FORMER LOCATION
OF BERLIN WALL

CHECKPOINT
CHARLIE

Eastern Comfort

KOCHSTR.

Rudi-Dutschke-Str.

Waldeckpark

Michelberger Hotel

TOPOGRAPHIE
DES TERRORS

Oranienstrasse

Die
Henne

ANHALTER
BHF.

Anhalter Str.

KREUZBERG

MORITZPL.

Oranienstrasse

Park Am
Anhalter
Bahnhof

IMA Loft
Apartments

FORMER LOCATION
OF BERLIN WALL

Café Morgenland

Curry 36

MOCKERNBRÜCKE

B96

B96

Tempelhofer Ufer

HALLESCHES
TOR

Gitschiner Str

Kreuzberg Neukölln:
Hartmanns
Restaurant

Riehmers
Hofgarten

Mustafa's

Landwehrkanal

Die Henne
Defne

Jolesch
Lavanderia
Vecchia

Böcklerpark

E   **F**   **G**   **H**

menus (there is no à la carte) that are carefully orchestrated to create an unforgettable dining experience. The wine selection is heavy on German and Spanish wines. $ *Average main: €50* ⊠ *Schlegelstr. 26c, in Edison Höfe, Mitte* ☎ *030/3088–1214* ⊕ *www.reinstoff.eu* ⚭ *Reservations essential* ⊗ *Closed Sun. and Mon.* Ⓜ *Nordbahnhof (S-bahn)* ✛ *1:E1.*

$
CAFÉ
✕ **Mogg & Melzer.** In the renovated Ehemalige Jüdische Mädchenschule (Old Jewish Girls' School), this deli-style café pays homage to the building's roots in the best way possible: with delectable Jewish delicacies that are hard to find elsewhere in Berlin—think matzoh-ball soup or pastrami on rye. At breakfast there is a delicious *shakshuka* (tomato stew with eggs) and the classic New York bagel with cream cheese and lox. More standard fare like a beet and goat cheese salad and French onion soup round out the menu. The space is comfortable, too, with a simple interior featuring wooden floors and tables, light blue walls, and low, deep purple banquettes. $ *Average main: €10* ⊠ *Auguststr. 11–13, Ehemalige Jüdische Mädchenschule, Mitte* ☎ *030/3300–60770* ⊕ *www.moggandmelzer.com* ⊟ *No credit cards* Ⓜ *Tucholskystrasse (S-bahn)* ✛ *1:F2.*

$
GERMAN
✕ **Rosenthaler Grill und Schlemmerbuffet.** Döner kebab aficionados love this restaurant for the delicious food; the fact that it's in the middle of the city and open 24 hours a day is an added bonus. The friendly staff expertly carve paper-thin slices of perfectly cooked meat from the enormous, revolving spit. If you like things spicy, ask for the red sauce. $ *Average main: €6* ⊠ *Torstr. 125, Mitte* ☎ *030/283–2153* Ⓜ *Rosenthaler Platz (U-bahn)* ✛ *1:A5.*

$$$
THAI
✕ **Sra Bua.** There aren't many Thai restaurants in Berlin but even if the competition was fierce, this exciting addition to the city's high-end dining scene would stand out. The service is attentive and the setting is lavish at this fourth Sra Bua location (after Bangkok, Switzerland, and St. Moritz). Spicy, flavorful curries are front and center on the menu, excellently complemented by salads and raw fish starters that play with some of the freshest ingredients around. Save room for the "deconstructed" yuzu cheesecake dessert, and make sure to sample the cocktails, which also pay homage to Southeast Asia with ingredients like chili, ginger, mango, and sesame oil. $ *Average main: €24* ⊠ *Adlon Kempinski Hotel, Behrenstr. 72, Mitte* ☎ *030/2261–1590* ⊕ *www.srabua-adlon.de* ⚭ *Reservations essential* Ⓜ *Brandenburger Tor (U-bahn and S-bahn)* ✛ *1:E4.*

$$$$
GERMAN
✕ **VAU.** Trendsetter VAU defined hip in the Mitte district years ago and remains a favorite even as it ages. The excellent German fish and game dishes prepared by chef Kolja Kleeberg have earned him endless praise and awards. Menu options might include duck with red cabbage, quince, and sweet chestnuts, or turbot with veal sweetbread with shallots in red wine. The six-course dinner menu is €120, but dishes you can also order á la carte. The best bargain is a lunch entrée at €18. The cool interior was designed by Meinhard von Gerkan, one of Germany's leading industrial architects. $ *Average main: €40* ⊠ *Jägerstr. 54–55, Mitte* ☎ *030/202–9730* ⊕ *www.vau-berlin.de* ⚭ *Reservations essential* ⊗ *Closed Sun.* Ⓜ *Französische Strasse (U-bahn), Stadtmitte (U-bahn)* ✛ *1:F4.*

$$$$
GERMAN
Fodor's Choice
★

× **Weinbar Rutz.** Rutz might be the most unassuming Michelin-starred restaurant in the world. Its narrow facade is tucked away on a sleepy stretch of Chausseestrasse, but the elegant and enjoyable interior matches the quality of the food, with surprising combinations like roe deer with stinging nettle puree, or monkfish with a ginger and radish ragout. The restaurant's "Inspiration" tasting menus of 6, 8, or 10 courses (starting at €115s) offer dual interpretations (labeled "experiences") of luxury ingredients like goose liver or Wagyu beef, though there are à la carte options as well. For those wishing for just a taste of the magic rather than a multicourse affair, the separate Weinbar (downstairs) has a more reasonably priced à la carte menu. Sommelier and owner, Billy Wagner, is usually in-house to recommend wines from a list of more than 1,000 vintages. ⑤ *Average main: €60 ⊠ Chausseestr. 8, Mitte ☎ 030/2462–8760 ⊕ www.weinbar-rutz.de ☉ Closed Sun. and Mon. Ⓜ Oranienburger Tor (S-bahn) ✛ 1:E1.*

$
GERMAN

× **Zur Letzten Instanz.** Berlin's oldest restaurant (established in 1621) lies half hidden in a nest of medieval streets, though it's welcomed some illustrious diners: Napoléon is said to have sat alongside the tile stove, Mikhail Gorbachev sipped a beer here in 1989, and Chancellor Gerhard Schröder treated French president Jacques Chirac to a meal here in 2003. The small menu focuses on some of Berlin's most traditional specialties, including *Eisbein* (pork knuckle), and takes its whimsical dish titles from classic legal jargon—the national courthouse is around the corner, and the restaurant's name is a rough equivalent of the term "at the 11th hour." Inside, the restaurant is cozy, and while the service is always friendly it can sometimes feel a bit erratic. ⑤ *Average main: €11 ⊠ Waisenstr. 14–16, Mitte ☎ 030/242–5528 ⊕ www.zurletzteninstanz.de ⌂ Reservations essential ☉ Closed Sun. Ⓜ Klosterstrasse (U-bahn) ✛ 1:H3.*

15

TIERGARTEN

$$$$
ECLECTIC
Fodor's Choice
★

× **Facil.** One of Germany's top restaurants, Facil is also one of the more relaxed of its class. The elegant, minimalist setting—it's in the fifth-floor courtyard of the Mandala Hotel, with exquisite wall panels and a glass roof that opens in summer—and impeccable service give the place an oasislike feel. Diners can count on a careful combination of German classics and Asian inspiration; the options are to choose from the four- to eight-course set meals, or order à la carte. Seasonal dishes include goose liver with celery and hazelnuts, char with an elderflower emulsion sauce, or roasted regional squab. The wine list is extensive but the staff can provide helpful advice. ⑤ *Average main: €40 ⊠ Mandala Hotel, Potsdamerstr. 3, Tiergarten ☎ 030/5900–51234 ⊕ www.facil.de ☉ Closed weekends Ⓜ Potsdamer Platz (U-bahn and S-bahn) ✛ 1:D4.*

$$$
ECLECTIC
Fodor's Choice
★

× **Paris-Moskau.** If you're looking for a one-of-a-kind dining experience, head to the rather barren stretch of land between Hauptbahnhof and the government quarter, where a single half-timbered house stands, now dwarfed by a government complex going up around it: The restaurant Paris-Moskau was built more than 100 years ago as a pub and guesthouse along the Paris-Moscow railway. Today, it serves dishes so intricately prepared they look like works of art, with refreshing flavor combinations such as smoked eel with pork belly ray, or guinea hen with beetroots and dates. In addition to the à la carte menu, there are a variety of set menus in the evening menu—you can choose four, five, six, or eight courses. The well-edited wine list and attentive service help make this restaurant a standout. ⑤ *Average main: €25 ⊠ Alt-Moabit 141, Tiergarten ☎ 030/394–2081 ⊕ www. paris-moskau.de ⌲ Reservations essential ☉ Closed Wed., no lunch weekends ⓂBerlin Hof (S-bahn) ✛ 1:D2.*

KREUZBERG

$

MIDDLE EASTERN

✕ **Café Morgenland.** Within view (and earshot) of the elevated U-bahn Line No. 1, Café Morgenland is a relatively unremarkable neighborhood haunt on weekdays but on Sunday it devotes an entire room to its extremely popular brunch buffet, which means table space can be scarce. The Turkish-inspired dishes (an ode to the home country of many a Kreuzberg native) are the perfect alternative to more traditional brunches in town. ⑤ *Average main: €10 ⊠ Skalitzerstr. 35, Kreuzberg ☎ 030/611–3291 ⊕ www.morgenland-berlin.de ▭ No credit cards* Ⓜ *Görlitzer Bahnhof (U-bahn) ✛ 1:H6.*

$

GERMAN

Fodor's Choice

★

✕ **Curry 36.** This currywurst stand in Kreuzberg has a cult following and anytime of day or night you'll find yourself amid a crowd of cab drivers, students, and lawyers while you have your currywurst *mit Darm* (with skin) or *ohne Darm* (without skin). Most people order their sausage with a big pile of crispy fries served *rot-weiss* (red and white)—with ketchup and mayonnaise. Curry 36 stays open until 5 in the morning. ⑤ *Average main: €6 ⊠ Mehringdamm 36, Kreuzberg ☎ 030/251–7368* Ⓜ *Mehringdamm (U-bahn) ✛ 1:H6.*

$

TURKISH

✕ **Defne.** In a city full of Turkish restaurants, Defne stands out for its exquisitely prepared food, friendly service, and pleasant setting. Beyond simple kebabs, the fresh and healthy menu here includes a great selection of hard-to-find fish dishes from the Bosphorus, such as *acili ahtapot* (spicy octopus served with mushrooms and olives in a white-wine-and-tomato sauce), as well as a selection of delicious *meze* (small plates) and typical Turkish dishes like "the Imam Fainted," one of many eggplant preparations. The vegetable dishes are especially popular. Defne is near the Maybachufer, on the bank of the Landwehrkanal that runs through Berlin, and its beloved Turkish market. ⑤ *Average main: €11 ⊠ Planufer 92c, Kreuzberg ☎ 030/8179–7111 ⊕ www.defne-restaurant.de ▭ No credit cards ☉ No lunch* Ⓜ *Kottbusser Tor (U-bahn) ✛ 1:H6.*

$

GERMAN

Fodor's Choice

★

✕ **Die Henne.** This 100-year-old Kreuzberg stalwart has survived a lot. After two world wars, it found itself quite literally with its back against the wall: the Berlin Wall was built right next to the front door, forcing it to close its front-yard beer garden. But Die Henne (which means "the hen") has managed to stick around thanks in part to its most famous dish, which is still just about all they serve: crispy, buttermilk fried chicken. The rest of the menu is short: coleslaw, potato salad, a few *boulette* (meat patty) options, and several beers on tap. For "dessert," look to their impressive selection of locally sourced brandies and fruit schnapps. The small front yard beer garden, reopened after 1989, is once again a lovely and lively place to sit in summer. Die Henne is full nearly every night it's

Hackesche Höfe's eight connected courtyards are an always-buzzing, hip place to hang out in the city.

open so make reservations a few of days in advance to secure a table. $ *Average main: €8* ⊠ *Leuschnerdamm 25, Kreuzberg* ☎ *030/614–7730* ▬ *No credit cards* ⊗ *Closed Mon.* Ⓜ *Moritzplatz (U-bahn)* ✛ *1:H5.*

$

ECLECTIC

✕ **Gugelhof.** Although far from Alsatian France and the Mosel and Saar regions of Germany's southwest that inspire the hearty fare here, a visit to this busy but homey Kollwitzplatz restaurant will leave you pleasantly surprised—and thoroughly stuffed. The raclette for two and the *pâté de canard* (Alsatian duck pâté) are the best you're likely to get this side of the Rhine, and classic choucroute comes with *Blutwurst* (blood sausage) provided by an award-winning Berlin butcher. The vegetarian Tarte Flambée, a crispy crust topped with creamy cheese and grilled vegetables, holds its own on the meat-centric menu. Breakfast and lunch are served only on the weekends; it's dinner only during the week. $ *Average main: €14* ⊠ *Knaackstr. 37, Kreuzberg* ☎ *030/442–9229* ⊕ *www.gugelhof.de* ⚏ *Reservations essential* Ⓜ *Senefelderplatz (U-bahn)* ✛ *1:H1.*

$$$$

GERMAN

Fodor's Choice

★

✕ **Hartmanns Restaurant.** Named for the acclaimed chef Stefan Hartmann, Hartmanns Restaurant is in the heart of Kreuzberg, on a residential street that manages to be both elegant and jarringly historical (a 19th-century gasometer used as a bunker in WWII sits directly opposite). The restaurant's sublevel interior, however, is all warm lighting and white-painted walls. The changing menu uses market-fresh ingredients to revive classic German dishes, though there are also some Mediterranean influences here and there. You can order à la carte, but the real treat is the chef's three- to seven-course tasting menu, which cost between €65 and €110, and can be served with or without wine pairings. Each plate is like a work of art, and the service is impeccable and friendly.

$ *Average main: €30* ✉ *Fichtestr. 31, Kreuzberg* ☎ *030/6120–1003* ⊕ *www.hartmanns-restaurant.de* ⚒ *Reservations essential* ☾ *Closed Sun. and Mon.* Ⓜ *Südstern (U-bahn)* ✛ *1:H6.*

$ ╳ **Jolesch.** With a front bar area and a cozy, sage-color dining room,
AUSTRIAN Jolesch is usually filled with chattering locals and the occasional dog peeking out from under the table (pets are allowed in unexpected places in Berlin, including many restaurants). The house specialties include Viennese classics like Wiener schnitzel and apple strudel, but there are surprises on the seasonal daily menu, which is full of inspiring ingredients and unusual combinations like grilled octopus with saffron sorbet in spring, or a trio of duck, including silky foie gras, in fall. ▇ **TIP➔ Look for a special menu if you're here in late April and May, during "Spargelzeit," the white asparagus season.** $ *Average main: €15* ✉ *Muskauerstr. 1, Kreuzberg* ☎ *030/612–3581* ⊕ *www.jolesch. de* Ⓜ *Görlitzer Bahnhof (U-bahn)* ✛ *1:H6.*

$ ╳ **Mustafa's.** For a twist on the traditional *döner kebab,* head to to Mus-
MEDITERRANEAN tafa's for mouthwateringly delicious vegetable kebabs. The specialty is toasted pita bread stuffed full of roasted veggies—carrots, potatoes, zucchini—along with fresh tomato, lettuce, cucumber, and cabbage. The sandwich is topped with sauce, a generous squeeze of fresh lemon juice, and sprinkling of the creamy feta cheese. You'll lick your fingers and contemplate getting in line for another. $ *Average main: €7* ✉ *Mehringdamm 32, Kreuzberg* ☎ *283/2153* Ⓜ *Mehringdamm (U-bahn)* ✛ *1:F6.*

PRENZLAUER BERG

$ ╳ **The Bird.** Yes it serves burgers, and yes it's run by Americans, but the
AMERICAN Bird, overlooking a corner of Mauerpark in Prenzlauer Berg, is more than just an expat burger joint. Burger spots have recenly been popping up everywhere, but the Bird remains one of the best, and is practically the only place in town where the word "rare" actually means pink and juicy on the inside. Besides cheekily named burgers like the "Bronx Jon" (mushrooms and swiss cheese) and "Da Woiks" (everything, including guacamole if you ask for it), the Bird also serves up a mean steak frites suitable for two. Your best bet is to grab a seat at the bar, yell out the order, chow down, and be on your way unless you're with a large group, as the place can get pretty packed. $ *Average main: €12* ✉ *Am Falkpl. 5, Prenzlauer Berg* ☎ *030/5105–3283* ⊕ *www.thebirdinberlin.com* ⚒ *Reservations essential* ▭ *No credit cards* ☾ *Lunch on weekends* ✛ *1:H1.*

$ ╳ **Konnopke's Imbiss.** Under the tracks of the elevated U-bahn Line No.
GERMAN 2 is Berlin's most beloved sausage stand. Konnopke's is a family business that's been around for more than 70 years and it's famous for currywurst, which is served on a paper tray with a plastic prong that can be used to spear the sauce-covered sausage slices. The location, in the center of one of Berlin's trendiest neighborhoods, makes it super convenient. $ *Average main: €18* ✉ *Schönhauser Allee 44b, Prenzlauer Berg* ☎ *030/442–7765* Ⓜ *Eberswalderstrasse (U-bahn)* ✛ *1:H1.*

$ ╳ **Maria Bonita.** This Mexican restaurant is an unassuming space on
MEXICAN Prenzlauer Berg's Danziger Strasse. The young owners (hailing from Mexico and Australia) had different ideas of what Mexican food could be, but shared one dream: to bring the authentic cuisine to Berlin. The

food is authentic, as fans will attest, and the hot sauce is satisfyingly hot in a country known for sensitive taste buds and blandly spiced dishes. But diners also keep coming back is the sense of camaraderie: the restaurants host frequent parties (Cinco de Mayo is the most raucous, of course) and have done a lot to invite the neighborhood in. ■**TIP**➔ **If you get a craving for Mexican food in Kreuzberg, visit the sister restaurant Santa Maria at** ⊠ *Oranienstrasse 170.* ⑤ *Average main: €6* ⊠ *Danzigerstr. 33, Prenzlauer Berg* ☎ *030/2025–5338* ⊕ *www. mariabonitaberlin.wordpress.com* ⌀ *Reservations not accepted* ▭ *No credit cards* ۞ *Closed Mon.* Ⓜ *Eberswalderstr. (U-bahn)* ✛ *1:H1.*

$ ✕**Pasternak.** Russian-inspired treats such as deviled eggs topped with
RUSSIAN salmon roe, blini with sour cream and dill, and pierogi, are the draw at Pasternak. Lunch and dinner are popular, but brunch is the major reason to come here, and it gets quite crowded. At €12 per person, it's not the cheapest brunch in town, but it's far from the most expensive and the food is tasty and inventive. If you nab an outside table, you'll be eating within view of a Berlin oddity: a historic brick water tower that is now an apartment complex. ⑤ *Average main: €13* ⊠ *Knaackstr. 22–24, Prenzlauer Berg* ☎ *030/441–3399* ⊕ *www.restaurant-pasternak. de* ▭ *No credit cards* Ⓜ *Senefelder Platz (U-bahn)* ✛ *1:H1.*

$ ✕**Sasaya.** In a city that still sometimes struggles to get sushi right, Sasa-
JAPANESE ya's concept can seem groundbreaking: simple, authentic Japanese food in an equally comfortable, no-fuss atmosphere. Don't expect sushi rolls to be the center of the menu, though—the focus is on reasonably priced small plates made for sharing. Pickled vegetables, seaweed salad, crispy pork belly, raw octopus, and a number of soups served with the traditional Japanese dashi (fish and seaweed) broth are highlights. Dessert favorites include green tea ice cream and satisfyingly chewy balls of mochi. ■**TIP**➔ **Reservations are essential; call early enough and you might score one of the low tables by the windows, where long, low couches mean you can recline languidly during your meal.** ⑤ *Average main: €12* ⊠ *Lychenerstr. 50, Prenzlauer Berg* ☎ *030/4471–7721* ⊕ *www. sasaya-berlin-en.tumblr.com* ⌀ *Reservations essential* ▭ *No credit cards* ۞ *Closed Tues.–Wed.* Ⓜ *Eberswalder Strasse (U-bahn)* ✛ *1:H1.*

WEDDING

$ ✕**Da Baffi.** At the quieter end of bustling Leopoldplatz, Da Baffi is a
ITALIAN bright Italian light in Berlin. The interior is charming and casual, with white-painted wood, community tables, fresh wildflowers, and dishtowel placemats—all of which complement the fresh, seasonal menu, which is presented in a notebook and changes weekly. Favorites tend to stick around though, and that means the paper-thin octopus carpaccio and the aromatic tagliatelle with shaved black truffles are almost always available, along with cannelloni with wild boar ragù, or whole grilled fish stuffed with herbs and lemon. ■**TIP**➔ **Hungry for Italian in Kreuzberg? Da Baffi's sister café Salumeria Lamuri (**⊠ *Köpenickerstr. 183)* **is open weekdays for breakfast and lunch.** ⑤ *Average main: €15* ⊠ *Nazarethkirchstr. 41, Wedding* ☎ *0175/692–6545* ⊕ *www.dabaffi. com* ⌀ *Reservations essential* ▭ *No credit cards* ۞ *Closed Sun. and Mon.* Ⓜ *Leopoldplatz (U-bahn)* ✛ *1:H1.*

15

NEUKÖLLN

$$$$ ✕ **Lavanderia Vecchia.** Hidden away in a courtyard off a busy Neu-
ITALIAN kölln street, Lavanderia Vecchia is no longer the secret it was when
it opened, in 2010, in a space that used to contain an old laundrette
(hence the name, which means "old laundrette" in Italian) but it's still
very much a destination spot, and one of the best meals in the city.
Come hungry, though, as the prix-fixe-only menu includes at least 10
appetizers, a pasta "primi," a meat or fish "secondi," and a dessert,
followed by coffee and a digestif. The open kitchen allows diners to
watch as the chef makes classics like Insalata di Polpo (octopus and
potato salad) or homemade tagliatelle with eggplant, and the contrast
of the industrial space strewn with wash lines hung with vintage ker-
chiefs and aprons is oh-so-Berlin. ⑤ *Average main: €45* ✉ *Flughafenstr. 46, Neukölln* ☎ *030/6272–2152* ⊕ *www.lavanderiavecchia.de*
⌕ *Reservations essential* ⊘ *Closed Sun. and Mon.* Ⓜ *Boddinstrasse
(U-bahn) and Rathaus Neukölln (U-bahn)* ✛ *1:H6.*

CHARLOTTENBURG

$$ ✕ **Engelbecken.** The beer coasters are trading cards of the Wittelsbach
GERMAN dynasty in this relaxed restaurant that focuses on food from Bavaria
and the Alps. Excellent renditions of classics like Wiener schnitzel and
grilled saddle steak are made of "bio" meat and vegetable products,
meaning that even the veal, lamb, and beef are the tasty results of
organic and humane upbringing. The corner location facing a park on
Lake Lietzensee makes this a lovely spot for open-air dining. Lunch is
only served on Sunday and holidays. ⑤ *Average main: €17* ✉ *Witzleben-
str. 31, Charlottenburg* ☎ *030/615–2810* ⊕ *www.engelbecken.de* ⊘ *No
lunch Mon.–Sat.* Ⓜ *Sophie-Charlotte-Platz (U-bahn)* ✛ *2:B1.*

$$ ✕ **Florian.** The handwritten menu is just one page, but everything on
GERMAN the menu is fresh and delicious at this well-established restaurant in
the heart of the buzzing nightlife scene around Savignyplatz. *Stein-
beisser*, a white, flaky fish, might be served with a salsa of rhubarb,
chili, coriander, and ginger, or you can opt for some Franconian comfort cuisine such as *Kirchweihbraten* (marinated pork with baked
apples and plums) or their legendary *Nürnberger Rostbratwurst*
(small pork sausages) served as late-night snacks. ■ TIP➜ The kitchen
is open until 1 am, and smaller dishes are available until 2 am. ⑤ *Average main: €18* ✉ *Grolmanstr. 52, Charlottenburg* ☎ *030/313–9184*
⊕ *www.restaurant-florian.de* ⌕ *Reservations essential* ⊘ *No lunch*
Ⓜ *Savignyplatz (S-bahn)* ✛ *2:B3.*

$$$$ ✕ **Glass.** One of the only Berlin restaurants tackling the world of
ECLECTIC molecular gastronomy, Glass is also one of the newest dining establishments in Charlottenburg. Diners choose the six- or eight-course
option from the regular or the vegan menu and then enjoy surprises
that emerge from the kitchen burning, smoking, enveloped by a whiff
of dry ice, or arranged in cubes and dustings on UFO-like dishware.
Israeli chef Gal Ben Moshe has worked in top restaurants around
the world, including Chicago's Alinea, and his culinary expertise
is tempered by playfulness. One dish, with fruits, vegetables, and

Map 2: Where to Eat and Stay in Charlottenburg

KEY

- ■ Restaurants
- □ Hotels
- Ⓢ S-Bahn
- Ⓤ U-Bahn
- 🛈 Tourist information
- ↔ following dining & lodging reviews indicates a map-grid coordinate

edible breadcrumb "earth" is an homage to Berlin's parks and gardens. A highlight is the wacky dessert made up of childhood sweets including marshmallows, fruit gummies, and exploding chocolate pop rocks, served directly on the tabletop. $ *Average main: €50* ⊠ *Uhlandstr. 195, Charlottenburg* ☎ *030/5471–0861* ⊕ *www.glassberlin. de* ⌂ *Reservations essential* ⊗ *Closed Sun. and Mon.* Ⓜ *Savignyplatz (S-bahn)* ✛ *2:B3.*

$ ✕ **Hot Spot.** In a city that's unfortunately full of mediocre pseudo-Asian
CHINESE   restaurants that serve bland, tasteless versions of curries, noodles, and rice dishes, Hot Spot stands out for its daring and authenticity. The menu features recipes from the provinces of Sichuan, Jiangsu, and Shanghai, and the freshest ingredients are guaranteed—with no MSG. *Mala* (spicy) dishes are a specialty, and the mostly cold appetizers, like the beef in chili sauce, can't be found anywhere else in Berlin. Mr. Wu and his wife, who own the restaurant, have a love for German wines and offer a large selection. In summer, make a reservation for a table on the sidewalk for the added bonus of people-watching. $ *Average main: €14* ⊠ *Eisenzahnstr. 66, Charlottenburg* ☎ *030/8900–6878* ⊕ *www.restaurant-hotspot.de* Ⓜ *Adenauerplatz (U-bahn)* ✛ *2:C1.*

$ ✕ **Lubitsch.** One of the few traditional, artsy restaurants left in bohe-
GERMAN   mian Charlottenburg, the Lubitsch—named after the famous Berlin film director Ernst Lubitsch—exudes an air of faded elegance and serves hearty local fare (and lighter international options) that's hard to find these days. Dishes like *Königsberger Klopse* (cooked dumplings in a creamy caper sauce) and *Kassler Nacken mit Sauerkraut* (salted, boiled pork knuckle) are examples of home-style German cooking. The local clientele don't mind the dingy seating or good-humored, but sometimes cheeky service. In summer the outdoor tables are perfect for people-watching on one of Berlin's most beautiful streets. The three-course lunch is a great bargain at €10. $ *Average main: €13* ⊠ *Bleibtreustr. 47, Charlottenburg* ☎ *030/882–3756* ⊕ *www.restaurant-lubitsch.de* ⊗ *No lunch Sun.* Ⓜ *Savignyplatz (S-bahn)* ✛ *2:B3.*

$$ ✕ **Ottenthal.** This intimate restaurant with white tablecloths is owned
AUSTRIAN   by Austrians from the small village of Ottenthal, and serves as an homage to their hometown—the wines, pumpkinseed oil, and organic ingredients on the menu all come from there. Interesting and delicious combinations might include pike-perch with lobster sauce and pepper-pine-nut risotto, or venison medallions with vegetable-potato strudel, red cabbage, and rowanberry sauce. The huge Wiener schnitzel extends past the plate's rim, and the pastas and strudel are homemade. ■TIP→ **Ottenthal opens at 5 pm, which makes it a good option for a leisurely meal before catching a show at Theater des Westens around the corner. This is also a good choice on Sunday evening, when many of Berlin's fine restaurants are closed.** $ *Average main: €16* ⊠ *Kantstr. 153, Charlottenburg* ☎ *030/313–3162* ⊕ *www.ottenthal.com* ⊗ *No lunch* Ⓜ *Zoologischer Garten (U-bahn and S-bahn)* ✛ *2:B4.*

Berliners anxiously await the first warm day of the year to sunbathe in deck chairs on the banks of the Spree River.

WILMERSDORF

$$$ ✕ **Francucci's.** This upscale restaurant on the far western end of
ITALIAN Kurfürstendamm is one of the best-kept Italian secrets in Berlin. You
won't find many tourists here but the posh neighborhood's residents
pack the cheerful, rustic dining room. The high-quality, straightforward
cooking means incredibly fresh salads and appetizers (the bruschetta
is excellent), as well as homemade breads and exquisite pasta dishes.
More refined Tuscan and Umbrian creations might include meat options
like wild boar but there might also be Mediterranean fish classics such
as grilled loup de mer or dorade. In warm weather there are tables on
the sidewalk. ⑤ *Average main: €24* ✉ *Kurfürstendamm 90, at Lehniner
Pl., Charlottenburg* ☎ *030/323–3318* ⊕ *www.francucci.de* Ⓜ *Adenau-
erplatz (U-bahn)* ✛ *2:C1.*

SCHÖNEBERG

$ ✕ **Café Aroma.** A neighborhood institution, Café Aroma sits in the curve
ITALIAN of a small winding street in an area between Kreuzberg and Schöneberg
known as *Rote Insel* or "red island" because of its location between
two S-bahn tracks and its socialist, working-class history. An early
advocate of the Slow Food movement, Aroma serves some of the most
eclectic Italian food in town, made from locally sourced ingredients.
Brunch here is on the pricier side, but well worth it: pile your plate
high with Italian delicacies like stuffed mushrooms, meatballs in home-
made tomato sauce, and bean salads, but leave room for the fluffy
tiramisu, which, of course, they'll bring out the moment you declare

yourself stuffed. $ *Average main: €13* ✉ *Hochkirchstr. 6, Schöneberg* ☎ *030/782–5821* ⊕ *www.cafe-aroma.de* ▬ *No credit cards* ⊘ *No lunch weekdays* Ⓜ *Yorkstrasse (S-bahn)* ✛ *1:C6.*

$$ ✕ **Café Einstein Stammhaus.** The Einstein is a Berlin landmark and one of the leading coffeehouses in town. In the historic grand villa of silent movie star Henny Porten, it charmingly recalls the elegant days of the Austrian-Hungarian empire, complete with slightly snobbish waiters gliding across squeaking parquet floors. The Einstein's very own coffee roasting facility produces some of Germany's best java, and the cakes are fabulous, especially the fresh strawberry cake—probably best enjoyed in summer, in the shady garden behind the villa. The café also excels in preparing solid Austrian fare such as schnitzel or goulash for an artsy, high-brow clientele. ■TIP➡ Up one flight of stairs is the cocktail bar Lebensstern, which matches the restaurant in sumptuous, old-world feel. $ *Average main: €18* ✉ *Kurfürstenstr. 58, Schöneberg* ☎ *030/2639–1918* ⊕ *www.cafeeinstein.com* Ⓜ *Kurfürstenstrasse (U-bahn)* ✛ *2:C6.*

AUSTRIAN
Fodor'sChoice
★

$$ ✕ **Hisar.** The lines here are often long, but they move fast and the combination of seasoned, salty meat, with crunchy salad and warm bread is unbeatable. If you're just stopping for a quick döner kebab, line up outside on the sidewalk and order from the window. If you prefer a more leisurely sit-down meal, head into the adjoining Turkish restaurant for the *Dönerteller* (*döner* plate), heaped with succulent meat, rice, potatoes, and salad. $ *Average main: €18* ✉ *Yorckstr. 49, Schöneberg* ☎ *030/216–5125* Ⓜ *Yorckstrasse (U-bahn and S-bahn).*

TURKISH

$$ ✕ **Renger-Patzsch.** Black-and-white photographs from German landscape photographer Albert Renger-Patzsch, the restaurant's namesake, decorate the darkwood-paneled dining room at this beloved local gathering place. With a changing daily menu, chef Hannes Behrmann focuses on top-notch ingredients, respecting the classics while also reinventing them. Juicy bits of quail sit atop a bed of celery puree, and lamb is braised in red wine and oranges with crisp polenta dumplings. Lighter bites like selection of *Flammküchen* (Alsatian flatbread pizzas) are great to share. The attentive and good-humored service makes this an excellent place to relax, even on the busiest nights. $ *Average main: €16* ✉ *Wartburgstr. 54, Schöneberg* ☎ *030/784–2059* Ⓜ *Eisenacherstr. (U-bahn)* ✛ *2:D5.*

GERMAN

WHERE TO STAY

Updated by
Katherine
Sacks

For expanded hotel reviews, visit Fodors.com.

Use the coordinate (✛ 1:B3) at the end of each listing to locate a site on the corresponding map.

Tourism is on the upswing in Berlin. Though prices in midrange to luxury hotels have increased, Berlin's first-class hotels still tend to be cheaper than their counterparts in Paris, London, or Rome. Many are housed in beautiful historic buildings and, compared to other European cities, most hotel rooms in Berlin are large, though many are part of chains that allow for less individual character.

Hotels listed here as $$$$ often come down to a $$ level on weekdays or when there is low demand. You often have the option to decline the inclusion of breakfast, which can save you anywhere from €8 to €30 per person per day.

▦ TIP → The least expensive accommodations are in pensions, which are similar to bed-and-breakfasts. They providing basic lodgings with limited services and amenities, but with breakfast included. These are mostly found in western districts such as Charlottenburg, Schöneberg, and Wilmersdorf.

German and European travelers often use apartment rental agencies for longer stays, and Americans on a budget should consider this as well (apartments start at €350 per month). In Berlin, double rooms with shared bathrooms in private apartments begin around €33 per day.

$ **☷ Wohn-Agentur Freiraum.** This English-speaking agency has its own
RENTAL guesthouse with rooms and apartments, as well as private room listings all over Berlin. $ *Rooms from: €36* ⊠ *Wiener Str. 14, Kreuzberg* ☎ *030/618–2008* ⊕ *www.frei-raum.com* ⫶○⫶ *No meals.*

15

MITTE

$$ **☷ Arte Luise Kunsthotel.** The Luise is one of Berlin's most original bou-
HOTEL tique hotels, with each fantastically creative room in the 1825 building
Fodor'sChoice or 2003 built-on wing—facing the Reichstag—styled by a different
★ artist. **Pros:** central location; historic flair; individually designed rooms. **Cons:** simple rooms with limited amenities and hotel facilities; can be noisy because of the nearby rail station. $ *Rooms from: €110* ⊠ *Luisenstr. 19, Mitte* ☎ *030/284–480* ⊕ *www.luise-berlin.com* ↙ *54 rooms, 36 with bath* ⫶○⫶ *No meals* Ⓜ *Friedrichstrasse (U-bahn and S-bahn)* ✛ *1:E2.*

$$$ **☷ Grand Hyatt Berlin.** Stylish guests feel at home at Europe's first Grand
HOTEL Hyatt, which has a feng shui–approved design that combines inspi-
Fodor'sChoice rations from tropical decor, thought-provoking modern art, and the
★ city's history with Bauhaus photographs. **Pros:** large rooms; excellent service; stylish spa; large pool area. **Cons:** location can be very busy; ongoing construction may be a nuisance for some travelers; in-room Wi-Fi is only free for the first 30 minutes. $ *Rooms from: €210* ⊠ *Marlene-Dietrich-Pl. 2, Mitte* ☎ *030/2553–1234* ⊕ *www.berlin. grand.hyatt.de* ↙ *326 rooms, 16 suites* ⫶○⫶ *Breakfast* Ⓜ *Potsdamer Platz (U-bahn and S-bahn)* ✛ *1:D5.*

$$ **☷ Honigmond Hotel and Garden Hotel.** These two hotels are charming,
HOTEL quaint oases only a few steps away from the buzzing neighborhoods of Mitte. **Pros:** individually designed rooms; warm, welcoming service; quiet courtyard rooms. **Cons:** front rooms can be noisy due to busy street; restaurant is expensive relative to the area's budget choices. $ *Rooms from: €125* ⊠ *Tieckstr. 12 and Invalidenstr. 122, Mitte* ☎ *030/284–4550* ⊕ *www.honigmond.de* ↙ *50 rooms* ⫶○⫶ *Breakfast* Ⓜ *Nordbahnhof (S-bahn)* ✛ *1:E1.*

$$$$ **Hotel Adlon Kempinski Berlin.** The first Adlon was considered Europe's
HOTEL   ultimate luxury resort until it was destroyed in the war and the new
Fodor's Choice   version, built in 1997, has a nostalgic aesthetic, and the elegant rooms
★   are furnished with turn-of-the-century photos of the original hotel,
along with cherrywood trim, mahogany furnishings, and brocade silk
bedspreads. **Pros:** top-notch luxury hotel; surprisingly large rooms;
excellent in-house restaurants. **Cons:** sometimes stiff service with an
attitude; rooms off Linden are noisy with the windows open; inviting
lobby often crowded. $⑤ Rooms from: €260 ⊠ Unter den Linden 77,
Mitte ☎ 030/22610 ⊕ www.kempinski.com/adlon ⤳ 304 rooms, 78
suites ⦿❙No meals Ⓜ Brandenburger Tor (U-bahn and S-bahn) ✛ 1:E3._

$ **Hotel Amano.** Built as a "budget design hotel," the basic rooms of
HOTEL   the Amano are faily small, and there is no real restaurant or room
service, but stay here and you'll be in the center of the action. **Pros:**
excellent location; happening bar scene; roof deck and garden. **Cons:**
no room service; too trendy for some. $⑤ Rooms from: €85 ⊠ Auguststr.
43, Mitte ☎ 030/809–4150 ⊕ www.hotel-amano.com ⤳ 71 rooms, 46
apartments ⦿❙No meals Ⓜ Rosenthaler Platz (U-bahn) ✛ 1:A5._

$$$$ **Hotel de Rome.** Discreet service and a subdued but boutiquey atmo-
HOTEL   sphere make the Hotel de Rome a major draw for the Hollywood jet set.
Fodor's Choice   **Pros:** great location; large rooms. **Cons:** design may be over the top for
★   some guests; expensive even for five-star hotel; can be dark during the
day due to low lighting. $⑤ Rooms from: €270 ⊠ Behrenstr. 37, Mitte
☎ 030/460–6090 ⊕ www.hotelderome.com ⤳ 109 rooms, 37 suites
⦿❙No meals Ⓜ Französische Strasse (U-bahn) ✛ 1:F3._

$$ **Hotel Hackescher Markt.** Amid the nightlife around Hackescher Markt,
HOTEL   this hotel provides discreet and inexpensive top services. **Pros:** great
location for shops, restaurants, and nightlife; large rooms. **Cons:** some
rooms may be noisy due to tram stop; rooms in need of an update.
$⑤ Rooms from: €119 ⊠ Grosse Präsidentenstr. 8, Mitte ☎ 030/280–030
⊕ www.hotel-hackescher-markt.com ⤳ 27 rooms, 5 suites ⦿❙No meals
Ⓜ Hackescher Markt (S-bahn) ✛ 1:G2._

$$$ **Regent Berlin.** One of Germany's most esteemed hotels, the Regent
HOTEL   pairs the opulence of gilt furniture, thick carpets, marble floors, tas-
seled settees, and crystal chandeliers with such modern conveniences as
flat-screen TVs. **Pros:** Berlin's most hushed five-star hotel; unobtrusive
service; very large rooms and top location off Gendarmenmarkt. **Cons:**
some public areas in need of update; the primary hotel restaurant specializes in fish only. $⑤ Rooms from: €225 ⊠ Charlottenstr. 49, Mitte
☎ 030/20338 ⊕ www.regenthotels.com ⤳ 156 rooms, 39 suites ⦿❙No
meals Ⓜ Französischestr. (U-bahn) ✛ 1:F3._

$$$ **The Ritz-Carlton Berlin.** Judging from the outside of this gray, high-
HOTEL   rise hotel that soars above Potsdamer Platz, you may never guess that
inside it's all luxurious, 19th-century grandeur. **Pros:** stylish and luxu-
rious interior design; great views; elegant setting yet informal service.
Cons: rooms surprisingly small for a luxury hotel; not family-friendly
(business-oriented atmosphere). $⑤ Rooms from: €215 ⊠ Potsdamer
Pl. 3, Mitte ☎ 030/337–777 ⊕ www.ritzcarlton.com ⤳ 264 rooms, 39
suites ⦿❙No meals Ⓜ Potsdamer Platz (U-bahn and S-bahn) ✛ 1:D4._

BEST BETS FOR BERLIN LODGING

Fodor's offers a selective listing of quality lodging in every price range, from the city's best budget beds to its most sophisticated luxury hotels. Here, we've compiled our top recommendations by price and experience.

Fodor's Choice★

Arte Luise Kunsthotel, $$, p. 737

Das Stue, $$, p. 740

Ellington Hotel Berlin, $$, p. 742

Grand Hyatt Berlin, $$$, p. 737

Hotel Adlon Kempinski Berlin, $$$$, p. 738

Hotel de Rome, $$$$, p. 738

Soho House, $$$, p. 741

Best by Price

$

Bleibtreu Berlin, p. 741

Eastern Comfort, p. 740

Hotel Bogota, p. 742

$$

Arte Luise Kunsthotel, p. 737

Ellington Hotel Berlin, p. 742

Honigmond Hotel and Garden Hotel, p. 737

$$$

Das Stue, p. 740

Grand Hyatt Berlin, p. 737

The Ritz-Carlton Berlin, p. 738

Soho House, p. 741

$$$$

Hotel Adlon Kempinski Berlin, p. 738

Hotel de Rome, p. 738

Best by Experience

BEST CONCIERGE

Eastern Comfort, $, p. 740

Hotel Adlon Kempinski Berlin, $$$$, p. 738

Regent Berlin, $$$, p. 738

BEST GRANDE DAME HOTELS

Hotel Adlon Kempinski Berlin, $$$$, p. 738

Regent Berlin, $$$, p. 738

Schlosshotel im Grunewald, $$$$, p. 744

BEST INTERIOR DESIGN

Das Stue, $$$, p. 740

Grand Hyatt Berlin, $$$, p. 737

Hotel Q!, $$, p. 743

Hotel de Rome, $$$$, p. 738

Michelberger Hotel, $, p. 741

Propeller Island City Lodge, $$, p. 743

BEST-KEPT SECRET

Arte Luise Kunsthotel, $$, p. 737

Bleibtreu Berlin, $, p. 741

Das Stue, $$, p. 740

Honigmond Hotel and Garden Hotel, $$, p 737

Hotel Bogota, $, p. 742

ÏMA Loft Apartments, $, p. 740

BEST LOCATION

Ellington Hotel Berlin, $$, p. 742

Grand Hyatt Berlin, $$$, p. 737

Hotel Adlon Kempinski Berlin, $$$$, p. 738

Hotel Amano, $, p. 738

Hotel Hackescher Markt, $$, p. 738

Swissôtel Berlin, $$, p. 743

Waldorf Astoria Berlin, $$$$, p. 743

BEST SERVICE

Bleibtreu Berlin, $, p. 741

Grand Hyatt Berlin, $$$, p. 737

Hotel de Rome, $$$$, p. 738

Regent Berlin, $$$, p. 738

Schlosshotel im Grunewald, $$$$, p. 744

BUSINESS TRAVEL

Brandenburger Hof, $$$, p. 741

Hotel Amano, $, p. 738

Sofitel Berlin Gendarmenmarkt, $$$, p. 740

Swissôtel Berlin, $$, p. 743

HIPSTER HOTELS

Hotel Q!, $$, p. 743

Michelberger Hotel, $, p. 741

Soho House, $$$, p. 741

15

$$$
HOTEL
Sofitel Berlin Gendarmenmarkt. This luxurious place to stay has maximized the minimalist look of East Berlin architecture. **Pros:** great location off one of the city's most beautiful squares; sumptuous breakfast buffet; great Austrian restaurant, Aigner. **Cons:** limited facilities for a luxury hotel; smallish rooms. $ *Rooms from: €200* ✉ *Charlottenstr. 50–52, Mitte* ☎ *030/203–750* ⊕ *www.sofitel.com* ↝ *70 rooms, 22 suites* ⊺⊖⧵ *No meals* Ⓜ *Französische Strasse (U-bahn)* ✛ *1:F4.*

$$$$
HOTEL
The Westin Grand Hotel Berlin. This large hotel in a renovated East German building has a great location at the corner of Friedrichstrasse and Unter den Linden. **Pros:** impressive lobby; recently updated rooms; perfect location for historic sights and shopping. **Cons:** service often not on five-star level; no great views; may feel street vibrations in lower rooms off Friedrichstrasse, as well as noise due to street construction. $ *Rooms from: €250* ✉ *Friedrichstr. 158–164, Mitte* ☎ *030/20270* ⊕ *www.westingrandberlin.com* ↝ *350 rooms, 50 suites* ⊺⊖⧵ *No meals* Ⓜ *Französische Strasse (U-bahn)* ✛ *1:F3.*

TIERGARTEN

$$
HOTEL
Fodor's Choice
★
Das Stue. History meets contemporary style in the heart of Berlin, in a building that once housed the Royal Danish Embassy and still retains governmental grandeur—from the classical facade to the dramatic entry staircase—now mixed with warming touches like cozy nooks designed by Patricia Uriquola. **Pros:** central location; popular restaurants and bar; Berlin Zoo views. **Cons:** small spa can book up fast. $ *Rooms from: €153* ✉ *Drakestr. 1, Tiergarten* ☎ *49/3031–17220* ⊕ *www.dasstue.com/en* ↝ *80 rooms and suites* ⊺⊖⧵ *No meals* ✛ *1:A4.*

KREUZBERG

$
Eastern Comfort. The Spree River is one of Berlin's best assets, and at Eastern Comfort you'll wake up on it in this moored, three-level ship with simple cabins. **Pros:** unique accommodation on a boat; friendly staff; perfect location for nightclubbing in Kreuzberg and Friedrichshain. **Cons:** insects may be a bother in summer; smallish rooms not pleasant in rainy or stormy weather; lack of privacy. $ *Rooms from: €62* ✉ *Mühlenstr. 73–77, Kreuzberg* ☎ *030/6676–3806* ⊕ *www.easterncomfort.com* ↝ *26 cabins* ⊺⊖⧵ *No meals* Ⓜ *Warschauer Strasse (U-bahn and S-bahn)* ✛ *1:H5.*

$
RENTAL
ÍMA Loft Apartments. A comfortable cross between apartment rental and hotel, ÍMA's aim is to throw its guests into the fray of Kreuzberg's hectic, artistic, multicultural scene. **Pros:** maximum privacy (a separate entrance means you never have to interact with hotel staff and other guests unless you want to). **Cons:** minimal amenities and services. $ *Rooms from: €79* ✉ *Ritterstr. 12–14, Kreuzberg* ☎ *030/6162–8913* ⊕ *www.imalofts.com* ↝ *20 apartments* ⊺⊖⧵ *No meals* Ⓜ *Moritzplatz (U-bahn)* ✛ *1:H6.*

FRIEDRICHSHAIN

$ ⊞ **Hotel Klassik.** One of the best things about the Hotel Klassik is its
HOTEL central location, walking distance to Friedrichshain's countless eating,
drinking, and shopping hot spots. **Pros:** excellent location for neighborhood vibe and access to transportation; plentiful, fresh breakfast buffet; friendly and helpful staff. **Cons:** Located on a loud and
busy corner. $ *Rooms from: €89* ⊠ *Revaler Str. 6* ☏ *30/319–8860*
⊕ *www.hotelklassik-berlin.com* ↩ *57 rooms, 2 suites* ⋔ *Breakfast*
Ⓜ *Warschauer Strasse (U-bahn and S-bahn)* ✢ *1:H3.*

$ ⊞ **Michelberger Hotel.** Started by a group of young Berliners who dreamed
HOTEL of a uniquely designed, artsy space, the Michelberger Hotel is part budget hotel, part clubhouse, and part bar and restaurant. **Pros:** located
at the epicenter of eastern Berlin nightlife; great design and fun atmosphere; affordable prices. **Cons:** busy thoroughfare and transit hub, so
front rooms can be noisy; casual service without luxury amenities; no
phone in rooms. $ *Rooms from: €60* ⊠ *Warschauer Str. 39–40, Fried-
richshain* ☏ *030/2977–8590* ⊕ *www.michelbergerhotel.com* ↩ *113
rooms* ⋔ *No meals* Ⓜ *Warschauer Strasse (S-bahn)* ✢ *1:H5.*

15

PRENZLAUER BERG

$$ ⊞ **Radisson Blu Berlin.** This hotel has an ideal location in the heart of
HOTEL Berlin near the Berlin Cathedral, Nikolai Church, and Unter den Lin-
den, but you may prefer a view into the courtyard, where the world's
largest cylindrical aquarium is located. **Pros:** central location; dis-
counted entry to the adjacent Sea Life Berlin. **Cons:** location can be very
busy. $ *Rooms from: €159* ⊠ *Karl-Liebknecht-Str. 3, Prenzlauer Berg*
☏ *030/238–280* ⊕ *www.radissonblu.com/hotel-berlin* ↩ *403 rooms, 24
suites* ⋔ *No meals* Ⓜ *Hackescher Markt (S-bahn)* ✢ *1:G3.*

$$$ ⊞ **Soho House.** The Berlin branch of this luxury hotel–club brings
HOTEL the chic atmosphere of London and New York's Soho to the Ger-
Fodor's Choice man capital. **Pros:** great staff; perfect location for club- and bar-
★ hopping; rooftop pool. **Cons:** may seem too clubby. $ *Rooms from:
€180* ⊠ *Torstr. 1, Mitte: Scheunenviertel* ☏ *030/405–0440* ⊕ *www.
sohohouseberlin.com* ↩ *65 rooms* ⋔ *No meals* Ⓜ *Rosa-Luxemburg-
Platz (U-bahn)* ✢ *1:H1.*

CHARLOTTENBURG

$ ⊞ **Bleibtreu Berlin.** Opened in 1995, Berlin's first design hotel is relatively
HOTEL unassuming, with simple and serene rooms decorated with untreated
oak, polished stone, and neutral shades. **Pros:** warm, welcoming service;
top location on one of Ku'damm's most beautiful side streets; international clientele. **Cons:** design somewhat dated; rooms not overly comfortable for price; few amenities. $ *Rooms from: €92* ⊠ *Bleibtreustr.
31, Charlottenburg* ☏ *030/884–740* ⊕ *www.bleibtreu.com* ↩ *60 rooms*
⋔ *No meals* Ⓜ *Uhlandstrasse (U-bahn)* ✢ *2:C3.*

$$$ ⊞ **Brandenburger Hof.** On a quiet residential street this turn-of-the-
HOTEL 20th-century mansion feels like a hideaway even though Ku'damm
is a short walk away. **Pros:** great mansion; quiet location only steps

away from the Ku'damm; large rooms. **Cons:** stuffy atmosphere; extras are expensive; no pool or fitness club on site. $ *Rooms from: €215* ✉ *Eislebenerstr. 14, Tiergarten* ☎ *030/214–050* ⊕ *www. brandenburger-hof.com* 🔍 *58 rooms, 14 suites* ⦿ *No meals* Ⓜ *Augsburger Strasse (U-bahn)* ⊕ *2:C4.*

$$ 🏨 **Ellington Hotel Berlin.** Tucked away behind the beautiful, historic
HOTEL facade of a grand Bauhaus-style office building, this sleek, modern
Fodor's Choice hotel has small but stylish rooms, accentuated with modern art. **Pros:**
★ stylish interior design with alluring 1920s touches; perfect location off Tauentzienstrasse and great for shopping sprees; nice bar; great, green courtyard. **Cons:** small rooms; no spa. $ *Rooms from: €128* ✉ *Nürnbergerstr. 50–55, Tiergarten* ☎ *030/683–150* ⊕ *www.ellington-hotel. com* 🔍 *285 rooms* ⦿ *No meals* Ⓜ *Wittenbergplatz (U-bahn)* ⊕ *2:C5.*

$$ 🏨 **Hotel Art Nouveau.** The English-speaking owners' discerning taste in
B&B/INN antiques, color combinations, and even televisions (a few designed by Philippe Starck) makes this B&B-like pension a great place to stay. **Pros:** stylish ambience; friendly and personal service; great B&B feeling; despite being a hotel. **Cons:** front rooms can be noisy due to heavy traffic on Leibnizstrasse; few amenities for a hotel of this price category; downtown location, yet longer walks to all major sights in the area. $ *Rooms from: €126* ✉ *Leibnizstr. 59, Charlottenburg* ☎ *030/327– 7440* ⊕ *www.hotelartnouveau.de* 🔍 *16 rooms, 6 suites* ⦿ *Breakfast* Ⓜ *Adenauerplatz (U-bahn)* ⊕ *2:C2.*

$ 🏨 **Hotel Astoria at Kurfürstendamm.** Each simple room in this small build-
HOTEL ing, which dates back to 1898, is different, and the service is standout. **Pros:** some rooms are individually designed with old-world style; warm and personal service; quiet location on central Ku'damm side street. **Cons:** furniture and rooms need update; many rooms on the smaller side; many rooms without a/c. $ *Rooms from: €94* ✉ *Fasanenstr. 2, Tiergarten* ☎ *030/312–4067* ⊕ *www.hotelastoria.de* 🔍 *32 rooms* ⦿ *No meals* Ⓜ *Uhlandstrasse (U-bahn), Zoologsicher Garten (U-bahn and S-bahn)* ⊕ *2:B4.*

$ 🏨 **Hotel Bogota.** Fashion photography and colorful artwork remind
B&B/INN guests of the artists and designers who lived in this circa 1900 apartment house on an elegant Ku'damm side street. **Pros:** historic ambience; on one of Ku'damm's most beautiful side streets; large, comfortable rooms. **Cons:** thin walls; some rooms with 1950s feeling; breakfast is included, but nothing special. $ *Rooms from: €85* ✉ *Schlüterstr. 45, Charlottenburg* ☎ *030/881–5001* ⊕ *www.bogota.de* 🔍 *114 rooms, 70 with bath* ⦿ *Breakfast* Ⓜ *Uhlandstrasse (U-bahn)* ⊕ *2:C3.*

$$ 🏨 **Hotel Palace.** This is one of the only privately owned first-class hotels
HOTEL in the heart of western downtown, and although it may not look like much from the outside, inside, the friendly staff and spacious rooms make it a popular choice. **Pros:** large rooms; quiet, central location; impeccable service. **Cons:** interior design outdated in some areas; nearby area of Europa-Center and Breitscheidplatz not the most interesting. $ *Rooms from: €128* ✉ *Europa-Center, Budapesterstr. 45, Tiergarten* ☎ *030/25020* ⊕ *www.palace.de* 🔍 *238 rooms, 40 suites* ⦿ *No meals* Ⓜ *Zoologsicher Garten (U-bahn and S-bahn)* ⊕ *2:B5.*

$$ 🔲 **Hotel Q!.** The Q! is the recipient of several international design awards,
HOTEL and it's easy to see how the gently sloping, sweeping interior of the hotel
could charm any judge. **Pros:** beautiful design; affordable rates; great
location for exploring western downtown. **Cons:** not for families; night-
life makes hotel noisy at times. $ *Rooms from: €120* ✉ *Knesebeckstr.*
67, Charlottenburg ☎ *030/810–0660* ⊕ *www.loock-hotels.com* ⤳ *73*
rooms, 4 suites ❖ *No meals* Ⓜ *Uhlandstrasse (U-bahn), Savignyplatz*
(S-bahn) ✛ *2:C3.*

$$ 🔲 **Propeller Island City Lodge.** At this wildly eccentric accommodation,
B&B/INN you can choose from 27 Wonderlands, each with one-of-a-kind design
by multitalented artist Lars Stroschen. **Pros:** individually designed
rooms; personal and friendly atmosphere; quiet location on Ku'damm
side street. **Cons:** designer art rooms can be overwhelming; few amenities; slow service. $ *Rooms from: €130* ✉ *Albrecht-Achilles-Str. 58,*
Charlottenburg ☎ *030/891–9016 8 am–noon, 0163/256–5909 noon–8*
pm ⊕ *www.propeller-island.de* ⤳ *25 rooms, 20 with bath, 2 suites*
Ⓜ *Adenauerplatz (U-bahn)* ✛ *2:D1.*

$$ 🔲 **Swissôtel Berlin.** At the bustling corner of Ku'damm and Joachimstha-
HOTEL ler Strasse, this hotel excels with its reputable Swiss hospitality—from
accompanying guests to their floor after check-in to equipping each
room with an iron, an umbrella, and a Nespresso espresso machine
that preheats the cups. **Pros:** large rooms; unobtrusive service; great
location. **Cons:** the lobby is on the third floor, with shops on the low-
ers levels; mostly for business travelers. $ *Rooms from: €130* ✉ *Augs-*
burger Str. 44, Charlottenburg ☎ *030/220–100* ⊕ *www.swissotel.com*
⤳ *296 rooms, 20 suites* ❖ *No meals* Ⓜ *Kurfürstendamm (U-bahn)*
✛ *2:C4.*

$$$$ 🔲 **Waldorf Astoria Berlin.** This impressive skyscraper, a nod to the Wal-
HOTEL dorf's original New York location, has a chic art deco look and unparal-
leled service. **Pros:** ideal location near Ku'damm; large, luxurious rooms
and bathrooms; several eateries and bars. **Cons:** limited amenities for
the price; nearby construction may bother some travelers. $ *Rooms*
from: €230 ✉ *Hardenbergst. 28, Charlottenburg* ☎ *030/814–0000*
⊕ *www.waldorfastoriaberlin.com* ⤳ *152 rooms, 50 suites* ❖ *No meals*
Ⓜ *Zoologsicher Garten (U-bahn and S-bahn)* ✛ *2:B4.*

FRIEDENAU

$ 🔲 **Hotel Klee.** Located on a quiet residential street, this new basic hotel
HOTEL is a great option if you're looking for a reasonable price with some
extras. **Pros:** large rooms and good amenities for the price; pretty, quiet
street; near transportation with quick access to city center. **Cons:** very
residential neighborhood is not within walking distance to landmarks;
smallish beds; furniture a bit dated. $ *Rooms from: €99* ✉ *Bundesallee*
75, Friedenau ☎ *030/4050–8630* ⊕ *www.hotelklee.com* ⤳ *79 rooms, 3*
suites ❖ *No meals* Ⓜ *Friedrich-Wilhelm-Platz (U-bahn)* ✛ *2:D4.*

15

GRUNEWALD

$$ ⛩ **InterContinental Berlin.** From the heavily trafficked street, the huge
HOTEL   "InterConti," the epitome of old West Berlin, evokes the Louvre with
its glass pyramid entrance. **Pros:** large rooms with great views; friendly
and impeccable service; one of Berlin's best spa areas. **Cons:** street is
not inviting; huge hotel lacks atmosphere and can feel businesslike;
room design somewhat bland. ⑤ *Rooms from: €104* ⌂ *Budapester
Str. 2, Charlottenburg* ☎ *030/26020* ⊕ *www.berlin.intercontinental.
com* ↗ *498 rooms, 60 suites* Ⓜ *Zoologsicher Garten (U-bahn and
S-bahn)* ✛ *2:B5.*

$$$$ ⛩ **Schlosshotel im Grunewald.** In the beautiful, verdant setting of
HOTEL   residential Grunewald, the small but palatial hotel is full of clas-
sic style and lavish decor. **Pros:** quiet and green setting with lovely
garden; large rooms in classic style; impeccable service. **Cons:** far
away from any sights; sometimes stiff atmosphere; not for families.
⑤ *Rooms from: €239* ⌂ *Brahmsstr. 10, Grunewald* ☎ *030/895–840*
⊕ *www.schlosshotelberlin.com* ↗ *43 rooms, 10 suites* ⊙ *No meals*
Ⓜ *Grunewald (S-bahn)* ✛ *2:D1.*

NIGHTLIFE AND THE ARTS

NIGHTLIFE

Updated by
Giulia Pines

Clubs often switch the music they play from night to night, so crowds
and popularity can vary widely. Although club nights are driven by the
DJ name, the music genres are written in English in listing magazines.

Clubs and bars in Charlottenburg and in Mitte tend to be dressier
and more conservative; the scene in Kreuzberg, Prenzlauer Berg, the
Scheunenviertel, and Friedrichshain is laid-back and alternative. For the
latest information on Berlin's house, electro, and hip-hop club scene,
pick up *(030)*, a free weekly. Dance clubs don't get going until about
12:30 am, but parties labeled "after-work" start as early as 8 pm for
professionals looking to socialize during the week.

Note that Berlin's nightspots are open to the wee hours of the morn-
ing, but if you stay out after 12:45 Sunday–Thursday, you'll have to
find a night bus (designated by "N" before the number, which often
corresponds to the subway line it is replacing) or catch the last S-bahn
home. On Friday and Saturday nights all subway lines (except U-bahn
Line No. 4) run every 15 to 20 minutes throughout the night.

BARS AND LOUNGES

In Germany the term *Kneipen* is used for down-to-earth bars that are
comparable to English pubs. These places are pretty simple and laid-
back; you probably shouldn't try to order a three-ingredient cocktail
at one unless you spot a lengthy drink menu.

Elegant bars and lounges can be found in Mitte's Scheunenviertel, in
Charlottenburg, and in Berlin's five-star hotels, and new cocktail bars
are cropping up in Kreuzberg and Schöneberg, too.

CLOSE UP

Berlin's Hot Spots

Here's a quick list of the city's best streets and squares.

■ Savignyplatz in Charlottenburg: great restaurants and shopping.

■ Ludwigkirchplatz in Wilmersdorf: charming cafés surrounding a beautiful church.

■ Nollendorfplatz and Winterfeldplatz in Schöneberg: the cultural centers of Schöneberg; the latter hosts a fabulous weekly market.

■ Oranienstrasse and Wiener Strasse as well as both riverbanks of the Spree in Kreuzberg and Friedrichshain to Treptow: the former is the lively center of Turkish Kreuzberg; the banks of the Spree have a number of large clubs in industrial spaces.

■ Hackescher Markt and Oranienburgerstrasse as well as the surrounding side streets in Mitte-Scheunenviertel: the center of historical and cultural Berlin, with the most mainstream and popular nightlife.

■ Kastanienallee and Helmholzplatz in Prenzlauer Berg: a widely trafficked street and square in Berlin, full of both young expats and local families.

■ Boxhagenerplatz and Boxhagener Strasse in Friedrichshain: home to a weekly flea market, this is a busy area, day and night, with cafés, bars, and restaurants.

■ Hermannplatz in Neukölln: the jumping off point for a night out in one of Berlin's hip districts.

15

MITTE

Newton Bar. This posh bar in Mitte has been around for ages. Helmut Newton's larger-than-life photos of nude women decorate the walls. ✉ *Charlottenstr. 57, Mitte* ☎ *030/2029–5421* ⊕ *www.newton-bar.de* Ⓜ *Stadtmitte U2 (U-bahn).*

Redwood. Run by a California native, this simple, solid cocktail bar serves near-perfect concoctions that belie the bare wood surroundings. If loud crowds and smoky rooms aren't your thing, this is the place for you—the cocktails are excellent and you'll be able to carry on a conversation in a normal voice. The menu is helpfully arranged according to "dry" or "sweet and sour" but if you're still unsure whether to go for a Dark and Stormy or a Blood and Sand, ask the friendly young bartenders—everyone speaks English here. ✉ *Bergstr. 25, Mitte* ☎ *030/7024–8813* ⊕ *www.redwoodbar.de* ☉ *Closed Sun.– Mon.* Ⓜ *Nordbahnhof (S-bahn).*

TIERGARTEN

Victoria Bar. The elegant Victoria Bar is a stylish homage to 1960s and '70s jet-setters, and the cocktails are mixed with care. It usually attracts a middle-age, affluent, and artsy crowd. ✉ *Potsdamerstr. 102, Tiergarten* ☎ *030/2575–9977* ⊕ *www.victoriabar.de* Ⓜ *Kurfürstenstr. (U-bahn).*

KREUZBERG

Bellmann Bar. The candle-lit, rough wood tables, water-stained walls, and frequent appearances by local musicians just dropping by for a few tunes gives this cozy cocktail bar an artsy old-world feel. Lovingly nicknamed "the gramophone bar" for the old gramophone that sits in its window, Bellmann is a place to linger and chat over a glass of wine or a whiskey from the outstanding collection. ✉ *Reichenbergerstr. 103, Kreuzberg* ☎ *030/3117–3162* Ⓜ *Görlitzer Bahnhof (U-bahn).*

Freischwimmer. When it's warm out, the canalside deck chairs at Freischwimmer are the perfect place to be, though heat lamps and an enclosed area make this a cozy setting for cool nights, too. To get here, walk five minutes east of the elevated Schlesisches Tor U-bahn station and turn left down a path after the 1920s Aral gas station, the oldest in Berlin. ✉ *Vor dem Schlesischen Tor 2a, Kreuzberg* ☎ *030/6107–4309* ⊕ *www.freischwimmer-berlin.com* Ⓜ *Schlesisches Tor (U-bahn).*

Würgeengel. Named after a 1962 surrealist film by Luis Buñuel (it's "The Exterminating Angel" in English), this classy joint has offered an elaborate cocktail menu in a well-designed space off Kottbusser Tor since 1992—long before this part of Kreuzberg was hip, or even safe. Today, the bar's loyal fans spill out onto the streets on busy nights, and an evening tapas menu comes from the neighboring restaurant **Gorgonzola Club.** The team behind the restaurant **Renger-Patzsch** run Würgeengel and the Gorgonzola Club. ✉ *Dresdenerstr. 122, Kreuzberg* ✥ *Dresdenerstr. is reachable through passageway under buildings at Kottbusser Tor, next to Adalbertstr.* ☎ *030/615–5560* ⊕ *www. wuergeengel.de* ◷ *Daily 7–late* Ⓜ *Moritzplatz (U-bahn).*

SCHÖNEBERG

Green Door. A grown-up crowd focused on conversation and appreciating outstanding cocktails heads to Green Door, a Schöneberg classic. The decor is 1960s retro style, with gingham walls and stand-alone lamps. ▉**TIP➜ Although the expertly crafted drinks are not cheap by Berlin standards, happy hour (6–8) means you can order them at nearly half price.** ✉ *Winterfeldstr. 50, Schöneberg* ☎ *030/215–2515* ⊕ *www. greendoor.de* Ⓜ *Nollendorfplatz (U-bahn).*

CLUBS

MITTE

Fodor's Choice ★ **Clärchen's Ballhaus.** A night out at Clärchen's Ballhaus (Little Clara's Ballroom) is like a trip back in time. Opened in 1913, the club is an impressive sight on Mitte's now-upscale Auguststrasse. On summer nights, lines often stretch out the door, while the front courtyard comes alive with patrons dining alfresco on brick-oven pizzas. The main ballroom features a different style of music every night and there are often dance lessons before the party starts. One of the best things about this place, though, is the variety of people of different ages, nationalities, and social backgrounds mix. The upstairs Spiegelsaal ("mirror hall") has intimate, salon-type concerts on Sunday. ✉ *Auguststr. 24, Mitte* ☎ *030/282–9295* ⊕ *www.ballhaus.de* ◷ *Lunch and dinner daily* Ⓜ *Rodenthaler Platz (U-bahn).*

Felix. The over-the-top Felix greatly benefits from its location behind the famous Adlon Kempinski Hotel—Hollywood stars drop by when they're in town, or during the frenzied weeks of the Berlinale. The door policy can be tough, but dress in your finest and hope for the best. ✉ *Behrenstr. 72, Mitte* ☎ *030/3011–17152* ⊕ *www.felix-clubrestaurant. de* Ⓜ *Brandenburger Tor (U-bahn and S-bahn).*

Havanna Club heats up on salsa and merengue nights.

Kaffee Burger. More of a neighborhood clubhouse than a bar, there's always something going on at Kaffee Burger. The original home of writer Wladimir Kaminer's popular Russendisko ("Russian disco") nights, this spot has a cozy dance floor and a separate smoking room. On any given night, you might encounter electro, rock, funk, swing, or Balkan beats; live bands play frequently. ✉ *Torstr. 58–60, Mitte* ☎ *030/2804–6495* ⊕ *www.kaffeeburger.de* Ⓜ *Rosa-Luxembourgstr. (U-bahn).*

Sage Club. House and techno music make this a popular venue for a younger crowd. On some nights it can be tough getting past the man with the "by invitation only" list. Expect a line out the door, and very different partiers depending on the night of the week (check the program on the website). ✉ *Köpenicker Str. 76, Mitte* ☎ *030/278–9830* ⊕ *www.sage-club.de* Ⓜ *Heinrich-Heimestr. (U-bahn).*

KREUZBERG

Watergate. The elegant Watergate is a club for people who usually don't like clubbing. It sits languidly at the base of the Oberbaumbrücke, on the Kreuzberg side, and has two dance floors with bars. The terrace extending over the River Spree is one of the city's best chill-out spaces. In addition to hosting internationally renowned DJs, the club is beautiful and intimate setting for infrequent but popular classical music nights. ✉ *Falckenstein-str. 49, Kreuzberg* ☎ *030/6128–0396* ⊕ *www.water-gate.de* Ⓜ *Schle-sisches Tor (U-bahn), Warschauer Strasse (U-bahn and S-bahn).*

SCHÖNEBERG

Havanna Club. Berlin's multiculti crowd frequents the Havanna Club, where you can dance to soul, R&B, or hip-hop on four different dance floors. The week's highlights are the wild salsa and merengue nights

(Wednesday at 9, Friday and Saturday at 10). If your Latin steps are weak, come an hour early for a lesson. ■ TIP➔ Friday and Saturday are "ladies free" nights until 11. ⊠ *Hauptstr. 30, Schöneberg* ☏ *030/784–8565* ⊕ *www.havanna-berlin.de* Ⓜ *Julius-Leber-Brücke (S-bahn).*

TREPTOW

Fodor's Choice **Club der Visionaere.** It may not be much more than a series of wooden
★ rafts and a few shoddily constructed shacks, but this club is one of the most beloved outdoor venues in town. The place is packed at all hours, either with clubbers on their last stop of the evening, or with students soaking up the sunshine on a Sunday morning. Since it shares a narrow canal with Freischwimmer, which hosts a massive brunch on Sunday, an easy hop across the water (by bridge, of course) will get you coffee and breakfast at dawn. ⊠ *Am Flutgraben 1, Treptow* ✛ *Follow Schlesische Str. east from the U-bahn station until you cross two small canals. After the second bridge, look left.* ☏ *030/6951–8942* ⊘ *Weekdays 2 pm–late, weekends noon–late* Ⓜ *Schlesisches Tor (U-bahn).*

GAY AND LESBIAN BARS

Berlin is unmistakably Germany's gay capital, and many Europeans come to partake in the diverse scene, which is concentrated in Schöneberg (around Nollendorfplatz) and Kreuzberg. Check out the magazines *Siegessäule, (030),* and *blu.*

KREUZBERG

Roses. If you don't find any eye candy at tiny Roses there are always the furry red walls and kitschy paraphernalia to admire. It opens at 10 pm. ⊠ *Oranienstr. 187, Kreuzberg* ☏ *030/615–6570* Ⓜ *Kottbusser Tor (U-bahn).*

SchwuZ. This spot moved to the newly hip Neukölln neighborhood from its original location on Mehringdamm, in Kreuzberg, and the new digs in the old Kindl brewery should serve it well: in addition to 1980s music and house dance nights, expect more varied offerings like exhibitions, as well as a new stage and lounge room. ⊠ *Rollbergstr. 26, Neukölln* ☏ *030/629–0880* ⊕ *www.schwuz.de* Ⓜ *Rathaus Neukölln (U-bahn).*

FRIEDRICHSHAIN

Fodor's Choice **Berghain.** In an imposing power station in a barren stretch of land
★ between Kreuzberg and Friedrichshain (the name borrows from both neighborhoods), Berghain has achieved international fame as the hedonistic heart of techno music—it was originally a '90s techno club called Ostgut. Although it's also a well-respected center of gay nightlife in Berlin, the club welcomes both genders. It's only open on weekends (for 48 hours straight, from midnight on Friday to midnight on Sunday), and it has become something of a local tradition to arrive on Sunday morning and dance until closing. Upstairs, the slightly smaller (but by no means intimate) Panorama Bar offers different beats and a place to go on Friday before the main club opens at midnight. ⊠ *Am Wriezener Bahnhof, Friedrichshain* ✛ *Exit north from Ostbahnhof and follow Str. der Pariser Kommune, then make a right on badly marked Am Wriezener Bahnhof and look for a line* ☏ *030/2936–0210* Ⓜ *Ostbahnhof (S-bahn).*

Gay Berlin

The area around Nollendorfplatz is the heart and soul of gay Berlin, even though areas like Schönhauser Allee in Prenzlauer Berg, Schlesische Strasse in Kreuzberg, and various clubs in the Mitte-Scheunenviertel area are more popular with the younger crowd. However, in a city that historically has been a center of gay culture and one that has an openly gay mayor, Klaus Wowereit, the gay scene is not limited to these areas. Typical for Berlin is the integration of homosexuals of all walks of life throughout the city—from the politician and manager to the bus driver and waiter. The general attitude of most Berliners toward gays is tolerant and open-minded; however, openly gay couples should avoid outer areas such as Lichtenberg and Marzahn or towns in Brandenburg, the region surrounding Berlin. These areas are exceptions in a city that has an estimated 300,000 gays and lesbians in residence.

Large festivals such as the annual Christopher Street Day bring together hundreds of thousands of gays and lesbians each summer. Gay travelers are embraced by the city's tourist office: up-to-date information is provided in special brochures, such as "Out in Berlin" at tourist info-stores.

Mann-o-Meter. Detailed information on gay-friendly hotels and the clubbing and bar scene are provided by the city's largest gay community center, the Mann-o-Meter. Talks are sometimes held in the café, which has a variety of books and magazines. It's open Tues.–Fri. 5–10, and Sat.–Sun. 4–8. ⊠ *Bülowstr. 106, Schöneberg* ☎ *030/216–8008* ⊕ *www.mann-o-meter.de.*

15

SCHÖNEBERG
Connection Club. Just south of Wittenbergplatz, the dance club Connection is known for heavy house music and lots of dark corners. ⊠ *Fuggerstr. 33, Schöneberg* ☎ *030/218–1432* ⊕ *www.connection-berlin.de* Ⓜ *Augsburgerstr. (U-bahn).*

Hafen. The decor and the energetic crowd at Hafen make it a popular singles hangout. ⊠ *Motzstr. 19, Schöneberg* ☎ *030/211–4118* ⊕ *www. hafen-berlin.de* Ⓜ *Nullendorf Platz (U-bahn).*

JAZZ CLUBS
MITTE
b-flat. Young German artists perform most nights at b-flat. The club has some of the best sight lines in town, as well as a magnificent floor-to-ceiling front window that captures the attention of passersby. The well-known and well-attended Wednesday jam sessions focus on free and experimental jazz, and once a month on Thursday the Berlin Big Band takes over the small stage with up to 17 players. Snacks are available. ⊠ *Rosenthalerstr. 13, Mitte* ☎ *030/283–3123* ⊕ *www.b-flat-berlin. de* Ⓜ *Rosenthaler Platz (U-bahn).*

Kunstfabrik Schlot. Schlot hosts Berlin jazz scenesters, aspiring musicians playing Monday night free jazz sessions, and local heavy-hitters. It's a bit hard to find—it's in the cellar of the Edison Höfe—but enter the courtyard via Schlegelstrasse and follow the music. ⊠ *Invalidenstr.*

117, *entrance at Schlegelstr. 26, Mitte* ☏ *030/448–2160* Ⓜ *Nordbahnhof (S-bahn), Naturkundemuseum (U-bahn).*

CHARLOTTENBURG

A-Trane. A-Trane in West Berlin has hosted countless greats throughout the years, including Herbie Hancock and Wynton Marsalis. Weekly free jam nights on Saturday and numerous other free events make it a good place to see jazz on a budget. ✉ *Bleibtreustr. 1, Charlottenburg* ☏ *030/313–2550* ⊕ *www.a-trane.de* Ⓜ *Savignyplatz (S-bahn).*

Quasimodo. To get to Quasimodo, the most established and popular jazz venue in the city, you'll need to descend a small staircase to the basement of the Theater des Westens. Despite its college-town pub feel, the club has hosted many Berlin and international greats. Seats are few, but there's plenty of standing room in the front. ✉ *Kantstr. 12a, Charlottenburg* ☏ *030/312–8086* ⊕ *www.quasimodo.de* Ⓜ *Zoologischer Garten Bahnhof (U-bahn and S-bahn).*

THE ARTS

Detailed information about events is covered in the *Berlin Programm,* a monthly tourist guide to Berlin arts, museums, and theaters. The magazines *Tip* and *Zitty,* which appear every two weeks, provide full arts listings (in German), although the free weekly *(030)* is the best source for club and music events. For listings in English, consult the monthly *Ex-Berliner,* or their website (⊕ *www.exberliner.com*), which is updated regularly.

Hekticket offices. The Hekticket offices offers discounted and last-minute tickets, including half-price, same-day tickets daily at 2pm. ✉ *Karl-Liebknecht-Str. 13, off Alexanderpl., Mitte* Ⓜ *Alexanderplatz Bahnhof (S-bahn).*

Showtime Konzert und Theaterkassen. If your hotel can't book a seat for you or you can't make it to a box office directly, go to a ticket agency. Surcharges are 18%–23% of the ticket price. Showtime Konzert und Theaterkassen has offices within the major department stores, including KaDeWe and Karstadt. ✉ *KaDeWe, Tauentzienstr. 21, Charlottenburg* ☏ *030/8060–2929* ⊕ *www.showtimetickets.de.*

CONCERTS

Konzerthaus Berlin. The beautifully restored hall at Konzerthaus Berlin is a prime venue for classical music concerts. The box office is open from noon to curtain time. ✉ *Gendarmenmarkt, Mitte: Unter den Linden* ☏ *030/2030–92101* ⊕ *www.konzerthaus.de.*

Berliner Philharmonie. The Berlin Philharmonic Orchestra is one of the world's best and their resident venue is the Philharmonie, comprising the Grosser Saal or large main hall, and the smaller Kammermusiksaal, dedicated to chamber music. Tickets sell out in advance for the nights when Sir Simon Rattle or other star maestros conduct, but other orchestras and artists appear here as well. ■TIP➔ Tuesday's free Lunchtime Concerts fill the foyer with eager listeners of all ages at 1 pm. Daily guided tours (€3) also take place at 1 pm. ✉ *Herbert-von-Karajan-Str. 1, Tiergarten* ☏ *030/254–880* ⊕ *www.berliner-philharmoniker.de.*

DANCE, MUSICALS, AND OPERA

Berlin's three opera houses also host guest productions and companies from around the world. Vladimir Malakhov, a principal guest dancer with New York's American Ballet Theatre, is a principal in the Staatsballett Berlin as well as its director. The company performs its classic and modern productions at the Deutsche Oper and the Schiller Theater while the famed Staatsoper on Unter den Linden undergoes renovations (⇨ See the Staatsoper listing in Exploring for more about the building).

Deutsche Oper Berlin. Of the 17 composers represented in the repertoire of Deutsche Oper Berlin, Verdi and Wagner are the most frequently presented. ⊠ Bismarckstr. 35, Charlottenburg ☎ 030/343–8401 ⊕ www. deutscheoperberlin.de.

Hebbel am Ufer Theater (HAU). This theater consists of three houses (HAU 1, 2, 3) within a five-minute walk of one another. Fringe theater, international modern dance, and solo performers share the stages. ⊠ Stresemannstr. 29, Kreuzberg ☎ 030/2590–0427 ⊕ www.hebbel-am-ufer.de.

Komische Oper. Most of the operas performed here are sung in German but the lavish and at times over-the-top and kitschy staging and costumes make for a fun night even if you don't speak the language. ⊠ Behrenstr. 55–57, Mitte ☎ 030/4799–7400 ⊕ www.komische-oper-berlin.de.

Neuköllner Oper. The small and alternative Neuköllner Oper puts on fun, showy performances of long-forgotten operas as well as humorous musical productions. It also is more likely than other Berlin opera houses to stage productions offering modern social commentary and individual takes on the immigrant experience—which is fitting for this international neighborhood. ⊠ Karl-Marx-Str. 131–133, Neukölln ☎ 030/6889–0777.

Schiller Theater. Currently serving as interim stage for the Staatsoper, until renovations are finished in 2015, the Schiller Theater is also known for light musical and theater fare. ⊠ Bismarckstr. 110, Charlottenburg ☎ 030/2035–4555.

Tanzfabrik. The Tanzfabrik is Berlin's best venue to see young dance talent and the latest from Europe's avant-garde. ⊠ Möckernstr. 68, Kreuzberg ☎ 030/786–5861 ⊕ www.tanzfabrik-berlin.de.

Tempodrom. The white, tentlike Tempodrom, beyond the ruined facade of Anhalter Bahnhof, showcases international music and rock stars. ⊠ Möckernstr. 10, behind Askanischer Pl., Kreuzberg ☎ 01806/554–111 ⊕ www.tempodrom.de.

Theater des Westens. The late-19th-century Theater des Westens, one of Germany's oldest musical theaters, features musicals such as Dance of the Vampires; We Will Rock You, the over-the-top musical about the rock band Queen; and recently, the German-language version of the international sensation War Horse. ⊠ Kantstr. 12, Western Downtown ☎ 030/01805–4444 ⊕ www.stage-entertainment.de.

15

FESTIVALS

Berliner Festspiele. This annual Berlin festival, held from late August through September or early October, unites all the major performance halls as well as some smaller venues for concerts, opera, ballet, theater, and art exhibitions. It also sponsors some smaller-scale events throughout the year. ⊠ *Ticket office, Schaperstr. 24* ☎ *030/2548–9100* ⊕ *www.berlinerfestspiele.de.*

FILM

International and German movies are shown in the big theaters on Potsdamer Platz and around the Ku'damm. If a film isn't marked "OF" or "OV" (*Originalfassung*, or "original version") or "OmU" ("original with subtitles"), it's dubbed. Many Berlin theaters let customers reserve seats in advance when purchasing tickets, so buy them early to nab those coveted center spots. ■TIP➜ Previews and commercials often run for 25 minutes, so don't worry if you walk in late.

Babylon. Partially hidden behind Kottbusser Tor, Babylon shows English-language films with German subtitles. Ticket prices vary according to the day of the week, with Monday being the cheapest at €6. ⊠ *Dresdener Str. 126, Kreuzberg* ☎ *030/6160–9693* ⊕ *www.yorck.de.*

CineStar im Sony Center. Mainstream U.S. and British movies are screened in their original versions at the CineStar im Sony Center. Tuesday is a discount evening. ⊠ *Potsdamer Str. 4, Tiergarten* ☎ *030/2606–6400.*

Freiluftkinos. When warm weather hits the city and Berliners come out of hibernation, they often head to the Freiluftkinos (open-air cinemas). These outdoor viewing areas are in just about every park in town, offer food and drinks, and screen a good balance of German and international films, many of them new releases. Check the website for schedules from three of the city's best, in Volkspark Friedrichshain, Mariannenplatz Kreuzberg, and Volkspark Rehberge in Wedding. ⊕ *www.freiluftkino-berlin.de* ☜*€6.50.*

Hackesche Höfe Kino. Documentary films, international films in their original language, and German art-house films are shown at the Hackesche Höfe Kino, or cinema. There's no elevator to this top-floor movie house, but you can recover on the wide banquettes in the lounge. Monday and Tuesday are discount evenings. ⊠ *Rosenthaler Str. 40–41, Mitte* ☎ *030/283–4603* ⊕ *www.hoefekino.de.*

Berlinale: Internationale Filmfestspiele (*Internationale Filmfestspiele*). In February, numerous cinemas band together to host the prestigious Internationale Filmfestspiele, or Berlinale, a 10-day international festival at which the Golden Bear award is bestowed on the best films, directors, and actors. Ticket counters open three days before the party begins, but individual tickets are also sold on each day of the festival, if you're willing to wait in line for what can be hours. ■TIP➜ Film buffs should purchase the season pass, or act quickly when tickets are sold online. ⊕ *www.berlinale.de* ☯ *10 days in Feb.*

In hip Kreuzberg, you can sip drinks canalside at Freischwimmer.

THEATER

Theater in Berlin is outstanding, but performances are usually in German. The exceptions are operettas and the (nonliterary) cabarets. Keep in mind that tourist high season is always theater low season: most theaters take a one- to two-month break in July and August.

Berliner Ensemble. The excellent Berliner Ensemble is dedicated to Brecht and works of other international playwrights. The company might be losing its lease in 2013 so check the website for updates about a new location. ✉ *Bertolt Brecht-Pl. 1, off Friedrichstr., Mitte* ☎ *030/2840–8155* ⊕ *www.berliner-ensemble.de.*

Deutsches Theater. The theater most renowned for both its modern and classical productions is the Deutsches Theater. ✉ *Schumannstr. 13a, Mitte* ☎ *030/2844–1225* ⊕ *www.deutschestheater.de.*

English Theatre Berlin. The English Theatre presents dramas and comedies in English. ✉ *Fidicinstr. 40, Kreuzberg* ☎ *030/691–1211* ⊕ *www.etberlin.de.*

Grips Theater. For children's theater, head to the world-famous Grips Theater, whose musical hit *Linie 1*, about life in Berlin viewed through the subway, is just as appealing for adults. ✉ *Altonaer Str. 22, Tiergarten* ☎ *030/3974–740* ⊕ *www.grips-theater.de.*

Schaubühne am Lehniner Platz. The rebellious actors at the Schaubühne am Lehniner Platz, once the city's most experimental stage, have mellowed somewhat but still put on great performances. Their frequent, avant-garde stagings of well-known Shakespeare plays are a wonderful opportunity to enjoy German theater, even if you don't know a word of German. (You can always brush up on the story beforehand

and follow along with your own English text.) ✉ *Kurfürstendamm 153, Wilmersdorf* ☎ *030/890–023* ⊕ *www.schaubuehne.de.*

Volksbühne am Rosa-Luxemburg-Platz. The Volksbühne am Rosa-Luxemburg-Platz is unsurpassed for its aggressively experimental style, and the 750 seats are often sold out. The unusual building was reconstructed in the 1950s using the original 1914 plans. It also houses two smaller performance spaces—the Roter Salon and the Grüner Salon—which host everything from retro motown nights and salsa classes for all levels to touring pop and rock acts. ✉ *Linienstr. 227, Mitte* ☎ *030/2406–5777* ⊕ *www.volksbuehne-berlin.de.*

VARIETY SHOWS, COMEDY, AND CABARET
Berlin's variety shows can include magicians, circus performers, musicians, and classic cabaret stand-ups. Be aware that in order to understand and enjoy traditional cabaret, which involves a lot of political humor, your German has to be up to snuff.

Admiralspalast. The completely restored 1920s entertainment emporium Admiralspalast draws on its glitzy Jazz Age glamour, and houses several stages and a restaurant. The main theater features everything from large-scale shows to theater, comedy, and concerts. ✉ *Friedrichstr. 101, Mitte* ☎ *030/4799–7499* ⊕ *www.admiralspalast.de.*

Bar Jeder Vernunft. The intimate Bar Jeder Vernunft is inside a glamorous tent and usually showcases intriguing solo entertainers. Note that the venue is set back from the street and is hard to find. Just to the left of Haus der Berliner Festspiele, look for a lighted path next to a parking lot and follow it until you reach the tent. ✉ *Schaperstr. 24, Wilmersdorf* ☎ *030/883–1582* ⊕ *www.bar-jeder-vernunft.de.*

BKA–Berliner Kabarett Anstalt. Social and political satire has a long tradition in cabaret theaters and the BKA–Berliner Kabarett Anstalt is known for performances by Germany's leading young comedy talents as well as chanson vocalists. ✉ *Mehringdamm 34, Kreuzberg* ☎ *030/202–2007* ⊕ *www.bka-theater.de.*

Chamäleon Varieté. Within the Hackesche Höfe, the Chamäleon Varieté is the most affordable and offbeat variety venue in town. German isn't required to enjoy most of the productions. ✉ *Rosenthaler Str. 40–41, Mitte* ☎ *030/4000–590* ⊕ *www.chamaeleonberlin.com.*

Grüner Salon. This is one of Berlin's hippest venues for live music, cabaret, dancing, and drinks. The programs change almost daily. ✉ *Freie Volksbühne, Rosa-Luxemburg-Pl., Mitte* ☎ *030/2859–8936* ⊕ *www.gruener-salon.de.*

Tipi am Kanzleramt (*Tipi am Kanzleramt*). Tipi is a tent venue between the Kanzleramt (Chancellor's Office) and Haus der Kulturen der Welt. Artists featured are well suited for an international audience, and you can opt to dine here before the show. Even the back-row seats are good. ✉ *Grosse Querallee, Tiergarten* ☎ *030/3906–6550* ⊕ *www.tipi-am-kanzleramt.de.*

Wintergarten Varieté. The Wintergarten Varieté pays romantic homage to the old days of Berlin's original variety theater in the 1920s. ✉ *Potsdamer Str. 96, Tiergarten* ☎ *030/588–433* ⊕ *www.wintergarten-variete.de.*

SHOPPING

What's fashionable in Berlin is creative, bohemian style, so designer labels have less appeal here than in Hamburg, Düsseldorf, or Munich. For the young and trendy, it is bad form to be seen wearing clothes that appear to have cost much more than a *Brötchen* (bread roll), so most step out in vintage and secondhand threads.

MITTE

The finest shops in historic Berlin are along Friedrichstrasse, including the French department store Galeries Lafayette and the international luxury department store Departmentstore Quartier 206. Nearby, Unter den Linden offers a few souvenir shops and a Meissen ceramic showroom, while the area surrounding the picturesque Gendarmenmarkt is home to top fashion designers and many international brands.

Tthe charming side streets of Mitte's Scheunenviertel area have turned into a true destination for serious fashion aficionados. The area between Hackescher Markt, Weinmeister Strasse, and Rosa-Luxemburg-Platz alternate pricey independent designers with groovy secondhand shops, and a string of ultrahip flagship stores by the big sports and fashion designer brands. Neue Schönhauser Strasse meets up with Rosenthaler Strasse on one end and curves into Alte Schönhauser Strasse on the other. All three streets are full of stylish and original casual wear. Galleries along Gipsstrasse and Sophienstrasse round out the mix.

BOOK STORES

Fodor's Choice ★ **Do You Read Me?.** Whether you're looking for something to read on the plane or a special present, this charming bookstore is guaranteed to have something to pique your literary interests. The wide selection of magazines and literature—many of the titles are in English—comes from around the world and spans fashion, photography, architecture, interior design, and cultural topics. ⊠ *Auguststr. 28, Mitte: Scheunenviertel* ☏ *030/6954–9695* ⊕ *www.doyoureadme.de* ⊗ *Closed Sun.*

CLOTHING

14 oz. Inside a beautiful old building in the heart of Mitte's Hackescher Markt shopping district, 14 oz. sells high-end denim (Citizens of Humanity, Dondup, 3x1 Denim), along with sneakers, accessories, knitwear, and outerwear. For true VIP treatment, a private shopping area is available on the second floor. ⊠ *Neue Schönhauserstr. 13, Mitte: Scheunenviertel* ⊕ *www.14oz-berlin.com/berlin* ⊗ *Closed Sun.*

Apartment. Don't be deterred when you arrive at this seemingly empty storefront: the real treasure lies at the bottom of the black spiral staircase. On the basement level you'll find one of Berlin's favorite shops for local designs and wardrobe staples for both men and women. Think distressed tops, shoes, leather jackets, and skinny jeans. ⊠ *Memhardstr. 8, Mitte: Scheunenviertel* ☏ *030/2804–2251* ⊕ *www.apartmentberlin. de* ⊗ *Closed Sun.*

Baerck. This shop artfully displays its mix of European and Berlin men's and women's wear on wheeled structures, allowing them to be rearranged in the store whenever necessary. Along with designers like Stine Goya, Henrik Vibskov, and Hope, you'll find the store's own labels

NIA and llot llov. Lifestyle and interior decor items are on the basement level. ✉ *Mulackstr. 12, Mitte: Scheunenviertel* ☏ *030/2404–8994* ⊕ *www.baerck.net* ⊗ *Closed Sun.*

Claudia Skoda. One of Berlin's top avant-garde designers, Claudia Skoda's creations are mostly for women, but there's also a selection of men's knitwear. ✉ *Mulackstr. 8, Mitte: Scheunenviertel* ☏ *030/4004–1884* ⊕ *www.claudiaskoda.com* ⊗ *Closed Sun.*

The Corner Berlin. In the heart of the stunning Gendarmarkt, this luxury concept store sells a contemporary collection of new and vintage clothing from high-end designers like Yves Saint Laurent and Chloé, as well as cosmetics, home furnishings, and art books. The shop is also a popular venue for exclusive fashion events and is home to a gallery and café. ✉ *Franzoesischestr. 40, Mitte: Unter den Linden* ☏ *030/2067–0940* ⊕ *www.thecornerberlin.de* ⊗ *Closed Sun.*

CLOTHING: MEN'S

Fodor'sChoice
★ **Atelier Akeef.** This Mitte store combines men's luxury style with a holistic, eco-conscious shopping approach. The upcycled wood-paneled store was constructed using nontoxic colorants, sustainable clay, and energy-saving lightening, and each garment comes with a tag outlining the specifics of its eco-production. ✉ *Max-Beer-Str. 31, Mitte: Scheunenviertel* ☏ *030/2198–2645* ⊕ *www.atelierakeef.com.*

Fodor'sChoice
★ **SOTO.** The name of the hip, fashion-forward area of Mitte stands for 'SOuth of TOrstrasse. The shop is filled with charming side streets and numerous fashion boutiques. At the SOTO boutique you'll find a mix of timeless and trendsetting menswear including the house label, Le Berlinois, along with brands like Band of Outsiders, Norse Projects, and Our Legacy, grooming products, and accessories ranging from cameras to lanyards. ✉ *Torstr. 72, Mitte: Scheunenviertel* ☏ *030/257–62070* ⊕ *www.sotostore.com* ⊗ *Closed Sun.*

Made in Berlin. One of the more established second hand shops in Berlin, this outpost has popular two locations that crowd with trend-setting locals and discerning visitors looking for hidden gems. The selection is more curated thrift looks than high-end designs, and includes an extensive range of 1980s wear as well broad selection of shoes. ■ **TIP→ Make sure to pop in for the shops' happy hours, where you'll get 20 percent off on purchases (Tues. 12–3 at Neue Schönhauser Str.; Wed 10–3 at Friedrichstr.).** ✉ *Neue Schönhauser Str. 19, Mitte: Scheunenviertel* ☏ *030/2404–8900* ⊕ *www.facebook.com/MadeinBerlinVintage* ⊗ *Mon.–Sat. 12–8.*

CLOTHING: WOMEN'S

Annette Görtz. This Gendarmenmarkt showroom is German fashion icon Annette Görtz's Berlin flagship. Her collection of women's clothing is known for the clean lines, dark colors, and a combination of comfort and refined tailoring and elegance. ✉ *Markgrafenstr. 42, Mitte: Unter den Linden* ☏ *030/20074–613* ⊕ *www.annettegoertz.de.*

Fodor'sChoice
★ **C'est Tout.** Formerly the head of style for MTV networks, Katja Will opened this boutique in 2007 to share her love of French style and bring a Parisian look to the German capital. Layering the neutral pieces here with a touch of sparkle creates a defininte *ooh-la-la* effect. ✉ *Mulackstr. 26, Mitte: Scheunenviertel* ☏ *030/2759–5530* ⊕ *www.cesttout.de* ⊗ *Closed Sun.*

The dome atop Reichstag is one of the city's top attractions, and a walk inside it offers superb views.

Fodor's Choice ★ **Das Neue Schwarz.** Whether you want a new little black dress or a cool vintage bag to carry around this season, a peek into the lovely Das Neue Schwarz (The New Black) is guaranteed to result in some special finds. In the midst of Mitte's fashionista neighborhood of avant-garde designers and exclusive boutiques, this shop holds its own with a collection secondhand items, many never worn, from big name designers including Vivienne Westwood, Helmet Lang, and Yves Saint Laurent. ✉ *Mulackstr. 38, Mitte: Scheunenviertel* ☎ *030/2787–4467* ⊕ *www. dasneueschwarz.de* ⊘ *Closed Sun.*

Fodor's Choice ★ **Lala Berlin.** Former MTV editor Lelya Piedayesh is one of Berlin's top young design talents and she has a contemporary boutique on Mulackstrasse. It's pricey, but the scarves are to die for; clothes have bold prints on high-quality fabric. ✉ *Mulackstr. 7, Mitte: Scheunenviertel* ☎ *030/2576–2924* ⊕ *www.lalaberlin.com* ⊘ *Closed Sun.*

Oukan. This demure boutique originally began as a fundraising project during Berlin's Fashion Week in response to the 2011 Japanese tsunami. Along with two floors of avant garde Japanese designs, lifestyle products, and interior décor, the space is also home to Avan, an in-house tea house serving a variety of Asian-fusion dishes like banh mi sandwiches, dumplings, and curries. ✉ *Kronenstr. 71, Mitte: Unter den Linden* ☎ *030/2062–6700* ⊕ *www.oukan.de* ⊘ *Mon.–Sat. 12–7.*

DEPARTMENT STORES

Fodor's Choice ★ **DepartmentStore Quartier 206.** The smallest, and often considered the most luxurious, department store in town, DepartmentStore Quartier 206 has a wide range of women's and men's international designers from the likes of Prada, Givenchy, and Tom Ford. Much of the store's inventory is handpicked by founder Anne Maria Jagdfeld on travels around the world, and the store also carries a variety of cosmetics, perfumes, home accessories, art, and books. ⊠ *Friedrichstr. 71, Mitte: Unter den Linden* ☎ *030/2094–6500* ⊕ *www.dsq206.com* ⊙ *Closed Sun.*

Fodor'sChoice   **Galeries Lafayette.** At the corner of Französische Strasse (it means
★   "French Street" and is named for the nearby French Huguenot cathedral) is the French department store Galeries Lafayette. French architect Jean Nouvel included an impressive steel-and-glass funnel at the center of the building, and it's surrounded by four floors of expensive clothing and luxuries as well as an excellent food department with counters offering French cuisine, and a market with some of the best produce in the area. Intimate and elegant, Galeries Lafayette carries almost exclusively French products. ⊠ *Friedrichstr. 76–78, Mitte: Unter den Linden* ☎ *030/209–480* ⊕ *www.galerieslafayette.de* ⊙ *Closed Sun.*

Hackesche Höfe. Tucked behind the tourist heavy streets of Hackesche Markt, this labyrinth of small galleries, boutiques, and shops offers a wide range of fashion. The outdoor shopping mall links Rosenthaler- and Sophienstrassen with big brands like H&M and Mac Cosmetics, as well as independent boutiques and small gift shops. ⊠ *Rosenthalerstr. 40–41, Mitte: Scheunenviertel* ☎ *030/280–98010* ⊕ *www.hackesche-hoefe.com.*

GIFTS

Ampelmann. This gallery shop opened in the mall-like Hackesche Höfe shopping area in 2001, promoting the red and green Ampelmännnchen, the charming symbol used on the former East traffic lights. The brand now operates six shops in Berlin, and you can find the logo on everything from T-shirts and umbrellas to ice cube trays and candy. Perfect for souvenirs. ⊠ *Hackesche Höfe, Hof 5, Rosenthalerstr. 40–41, Mitte: Scheunenviertel* ☎ *030/4472–6515* ⊕ *ampelmann.de* ⊙ *Mon.–Sat. 9:30–10, Sun. 10–7.*

ausberlin. This small shop near Alexanderplatz provides a wide range of Berlin memories, all designed and manufactured in the city. There is everything from Berlin-themed emergency candy bars and tote bags with city landmark designs to Berlin produced liquors. ⊠ *Karl-Liebknechtstr. 17, Mitte: Alexanderplatz* ☎ *030/4199–7896* ⊕ *www.ausberlin.de* ⊙ *Closed Sun.*

Berlin Story. More than 5,000 different books, maps, and souvenirs about the city of Berlin can be found at this shop, which is, unlike many, open on Sunday. The company also runs a translation and publishing house and a small museum, as well as a webshop for those still looking for souvenirs after the trip is over. ⊠ *Unter den Linden 40, Mitte: Unter den Linden* ☎ *030/2045–3842* ⊕ *www.berlinstory.de.*

Fodor'sChoice   **Bonbonmacherei.** Tucked into a small courtyard near the New Syna-
★   gogue, this charming candy store has been making and selling handmade sweets for the past 100 years. The brightly colored sugar bonbons are pressed on vintage molds into leaf, raspberry, and diamond shapes, and more than 30 different varieties are available. For a real insider's peek at candy production, join one of the store's daily tours, which walk customers step-by-step through the candy production. Note that the store is only open Wednesday and Thursday. ⊠ *Oranienburgerstr. 32, Mitte: Scheunenviertel* ☎ *030/4405–5243* ⊕ *www.bonbonmacherei. de* ⊙ *Closed Sun.–Tues., and July and Aug.*

JEWELRY

Fodor's Choice
★ **Hecking.** Designer Luisa Hecking opened this accessories boutique in 2007 as a showcase for her timeless collection of HeckingHandermann bags and sunglasses. It's one of the best place for scarves in the city, with a wide selection of designs, at a variety of price points. ✉ *Gormannstr. 8–9, entrance on Mulackstr., Mitte: Scheunenviertel* ☏ *030/2804–7528* ⊕ *www.hecking-shop.com* ⊘ *Closed Tues. and Sun.*

Fodor's Choice
★ **Sabrina Dehoff.** The flagship store of German jewelry designer Sabrina Dehoff balances bling and minimalism—bright crystals are paired with chunky metals. ✉ *Torstr. 175, Mitte: Scheunenviertel* ☏ *030/9362–4680* ⊕ *www.sabrinadehoff.com* ⊘ *Closed Sun.*

PRENZLAUER BERG

Stretching east of Mitte's Rosenthaler Platz, the fashionable boutiques continue into Prenzlauer Berg. This area is well known for its own collection of designer boutiques, secondhand shops, and original designs. The busy Kastanienallee is packed with shops and boutiques, as is the more quiet area around Hemholzpatz.

15

CLOTHING

Fodor's Choice
★ **Garments.** This chic store offers Prenzlauer Berg's fashion lovers an excellent selection of vintage and secondhand clothing, costume jewelry, and accessories. There is also a branch in Mitte, at Linienstrasse 204–205. ✉ *Stargarderstr. 12 A, Prenzlauer Berg* ☏ *030/7477–9919* ⊕ *www.garments-vintage.de* ⊘ *Closed Sun.*

Kauf Dich Glücklich. With an odd assortment of retro furnishings, this ice cream café and waffle shop takes over the entire corner of a Prenzlauer Berg sidewalk, especially on sunny days. Head to the second story and you'll find a shop the captures young Berliner style, with vintage pieces, bold prints, and skinny fits, as well as shoes and jewelry. The collection focuses on womenswear although there is also a small offering of men's clothing. ✉ *Kastanien Allee 54, Prenzlauer Berg* ☏ *030/4172–5651* ⊕ *www.kaufdichgluecklich-shop.de* ⊘ *Mon.–Sat. 10–8.*

Temporary Showroom. This small boutique showcases a revolving collection of select European and international designers, spanning high fashions, streetwear, and accessories. The store is rearranged every six months in collaboration with a new designer's collection. ✉ *Kastanienallee 36a, Prenzlauer Berg* ☏ *030/6220–4563* ⊕ *www. temporaryshowroom.com* ⊘ *Mon.–Sat. 11–7.*

Workaholic Fashion. This showroom puts Berlin's music culture front and center, with fashion inspired by the DJ and club scene. Along with a collection of shoes, bags, accessories, the store also carries records and CDs and has a separate music room with a DJ stand. ✉ *Kastanienallee 60, Prenzlauer Berg* ☏ *030/8411–8358* ⊕ *www.workaholicfashion.net* ⊘ *Mon.–Fri. 11–8, Sat. 12–8.*

GIFT IDEAS

Fodor's Choice
★ **Dr. Kochan Schapskultur.** This small shop embodies traditional German liquor culture; there are schnapps and fruit brandies from family farms and independent distilleries for sale, among other items to pique a tippler's interest. ✉ *Immanuelkirchstr. 4, Prenzlauer Berg* ☏ *030/3462– 4076* ⊕ *www.schnapskultur.de* ⊘ *Closed Sun.*

MARKETS

Markt am Kollwitzplatz. One of the city's best farmer's markets sits on the pretty Kollwitplatz Square in Prenzlauer Berg. During its smaller Thursday and bustling Saturday markets, you'll not only find a suburb selection of organic produce, meats, cheeses, and pantry items, but also an array of prepared foods and sellers offering handmade home goods and gifts. ⊠ *Kollwitzpl., Prenzlauer Berg* ⊘ *Thurs. 12–7, Sat. 9–4.*

POTSDAMER PLATZ

On the border between the city's former east and west regions, this touristy area is popular thanks to the towering Sony Center, which offers an English-language movie theater as well as restaurants and bars. The main shopping arcade here, also named Potsdamer Platz, offers a wide selection of chain shops, but you'll find a few original shops tucked on the side streets.

CLOTHING

Andreas Murkudis. Andreas Murkudis moved his successful concept shop from Mitte to the former Taggespiegel newspaper office space near Potsdamer Platz in 2011. Inside the stark white room you'll find hand-picked mens, women's, and children's clothing, including designs by brother Kostas Murkudis, Dries van Noten, and Christian Haas, as well as accessories, and contemporary homeware. ⊠ *Potsdamer Str. 81e, Potsdamer Platz* ☎ *030/6807–98306* ⊕ *www.andreasmurkudis. com* ⊘ *Closed Sun.*

F95. This designer showroom is the permanent space for the biannual international fashion trade fair Premium. The rest of the time, the space showcases established brands like T by Alexander Wang and Diane von Furstenberg, alongside up-and-coming designers. Expect a combination of offbeat looks, trendsetting pieces, and classic wardrobe staples. ⊠ *Luckenwalderstr. 4–6, Potsdamer Platz* ☎ *030/4208–3358* ⊕ *www. f95store.com* ⊘ *Closed Sun.*

GIFT IDEAS

Fodor's Choice ★ **Frau Tonis Parfum.** This elegant perfumery will help you create a completely personal scent; choose from vials filled with perfumes like acacia, linden tree blossoms, cedar wood, or pink peppercorns. All the perfumes are produced locally in Berlin, creating a really one-of-a kind gift. ⊠ *Zimmerstr. 13, Potsdamer Platz* ☎ *030/2021–5310* ⊕ *www.frau-tonis-parfum.com* ⊘ *Closed Sun.*

FRIEDRICHSHAIN

The cobblestone streets and densely packed neighborhoods of cafés, shops, and boutiques make the area between Frankfurter Allee and Warschauer Strasse an ideal shopping stretch. Both Boxhagener Platz and Simon-Dach Strasse are home to fashionable shops, and the neighborhood holds shopping nights on select Saturdays.

CLOTHING

Prachtmädchen. Nearby Boxhagener Platz, this is great shop to find a piece of Berlin's young, hip style. Prachtmädchen specializes in trendy T-shirts, fashion forward coats, sustainable pieces from Scandinavian and Japanese brands, and accessories from their own line. There is also a small inventory of menswear. ✉ *Wühlischst. 28, Friedrichshain* ☎*030/97002780* ⊕ *www.prachtmaedchen.de* ☯ *Weekdays 11–8, Sat. 11–4.*

Latte Wie Hose. This shop understands the importance of keeping energized during shopping sprees, and dishes out illy coffee specialties alongside their high ends jeans. Denim labels include Dr. Denim, Patrick Mohr, and Friis & Company, and the store also stocks shoes, bags, and other accessories. ✉ *Kopernikusstr. 13, Friedrichshain* ☎*030/61740817* ⊕ *www.lattewiehose.com* ☯ *Mon.–Sat. 11–8.*

CLOTHING: WOMEN'S
Something Coloured. This Friedrichshain boutique looks like a trendy concept shop at first glance, but inside you'll find a selection of stylish second hand pieces. Among their advertised "1,000 pieces paired with rationality," expect to find jeans from Paige and J brand, bags from Chanel, and pieces from COS, Comptoir des Cotonniers, and Zoe Karssen. ✉ *Grünberger Str. 90, Friedrichshain* ☎*030/29352075* ⊕ *www.facebook.com/sometimescoloured* ☯ *Tue.–Fri. 12–8, Sat. 11–7.*

KREUZBERG
Locals love Kreuzberg for its grittier, gratified landscape, and the fashion style here is more urban as well. The lively Bergmannstrasse is home to several worthy destinations, as is Mehringdamm. This, along with neighboring Neukölln, is the place to score a unique Berlin find.

CLOTHING
Fodor'sChoice ★ **Voo.** This "super boutique" in former locksmith's workship is a Berlin favorite for women's and men's separates, shoes, accessories, and outwear, often from rare collections around the world. It's also home to Companion Coffee, for when you need a shopping pick-me-up. ✉ *Oranienstr. 24, Kreuzberg* ☎*030/6165–1119* ⊕ *www.vooberlin.com* ☯ *Closed Sun.*

GIFT IDEAS
Hardwax. This iconic record store is run by music veteran Mark Ernestus, who handpicks all the vinyl and CDs with a heavy focus on techno, electronic, and dubstep. On the third floor of a heavily graffitied building, it's the true essence of Berlin grunge and totally worth a visit for music lovers. ✉ *Paul-Lincke-Ufer 44a, Kreuzberg* ☎*030/6113–0111* ⊕ *www.hardwax.com* ☯ *Closed Sun.*

Süper Store. Located in the charming neighborhood of Kreuzberg known as the Graefekiez, this cute little shop supplies a variety of lovely odds and ends, sourced from all over the world, including Turkey, Italy, and Switzerland, as well as locally produced items. Inside you'll find items linens, housewares, pantry items, and jewelry. ✉ *Dieffenbachstr. 12, Kreuzberg* ☎*030/98327944* ⊕ *www.sueper-store.de* ☯ *Tue.–Fri. 11–7, Sat. 11–4.*

NEUKÖLLN
Just over the canal from Kreuzberg, the neighborhood of Neukölln is home to a large Turkish population, and brims with Turkish shops, cafés, and restaurants, as well as a lovely weekly market. More and more of the city's young creatives are moving into this area, and it caters to their bohemian lifestyle with a number of second-hand and vintage shops.

15

CLOTHING

Let Them Eat Cake. A favorite of the vintage shoppers in Nuekölln, this delightful shop offers a mixture of handmade pieces and high-quality second-hand. ☒ *Weserstr. 164, Neukölln* ☏ *030/6096–5095* ⊕ *letthemeatcake-berlin.tumblr.com* ☽ *Tue.–Sat. 1–7.*

Shio. This shop not only stocks a variety of redesigned second hand and vintage wear, as well as new-label sustainable lines, but also offers dressmaking and alteration services, and encourages customers to bring in their own pieces for trendy modifications. ☒ *Weichselstr. 59, Neukölln* ⊕ *www.shiostore.com* ☽ *Mon.–Sat. 12–8.*

Sing Blackbird. This Kreuzkölln shop, located on the border between Kreuzberg and Neukölln, has become popular for its carefully edited collection of vintage finds, dating back to the 1960s and 70s. The shop also holds a monthly flea market, as well as occasional movies nights, and is also home to a popular café, where a menu of homemade cakes and weekend vegan brunch is served on mismatched vintage china. ☒ *Sanderstr. 11, Neukölln* ☏ *030/5484–5051* ⊕ *www.facebook.com/singblackbir* ☽ *Daily 12–7.*

Vintage Galore. Imagine bringing the midcentury European look home with a walk through this shop, which features a collection of Scandinavian furniture and lamps. The shop also has a limited selection of clothing, bags and accessories, as well as small housewares like teapots and ceramics, which should all fit more comfortably inside a suitcase. ☒ *Sanderstr. 12, Neukölln* ☏ *030/6396–3338* ⊕ *www.vintagegalore.de* ☽ *Tues.–Fri. 2–8, Sat. 12–6.*

MARKETS

Türkischer Markt. On the edge of the Kreuzberg-Neukölln border, this weekly market is a gathering spot for the local Turkish community, and offers many traditional products, including delicious delicacies (olives, cheese, dried fruits, hummus, and fresh breads) and a bazaar of house goods. ☒ *Maybachufer, Kreuzberg* ☏ *030/9170–0700* ⊕ *www.tuerkenmarkt.de.*

CHARLOTTENBURG

Although Ku'damm is still touted as the shopping mile of Berlin, many shops are ho-hum retailers. The best stretch for exclusive fashions, such as Louis Vuitton, Hermès, and Jil Sander, are the three blocks between Leibnizstrasse and Bleibtreustrasse. For home furnishings, gift items, and unusual clothing boutiques, follow this route off Ku'damm: Leibnizstrasse to Mommsenstrasse to Bleibtreustrasse, then on to the ring around Savignyplatz. Fasanenstrasse, Knesebeckstrasse, Schlüterstrasse, and Uhlandstrasse are also fun places to browse.

Ku'damm ends at Breitscheidplatz, but the door-to-door shopping continues along Tauentzienstrasse, which, in addition to international retail stores, offers continental Europe's largest department store, the upscale Kaufhaus des Westens, or KaDeWe.

BOOKSTORES

Fodor's Choice **Bucherbogen.** Peek under the rails of Charlottenburg's Savignyplatz and
★ you'll find this much-loved bookstore. The large selection of books, many special-edition or out-of-print, include numerous titles on art, design, and architecture, and the international offerings are extensive.

✉ *Stadtbahnbogen 593, Charlottenburg* ☎ *303/186–9511* ⊕ *www. buecherbogen.com* ⊙ *Closed Sun.*

CLOTHING: MEN'S

Fodors Choice **Chelsea Farmer's Club.** This living-room-like space is the go-to for sophis-
★ ticated menswear with a British posh edge; you'll find everything from tuxedoes to hunting jackets on their shelves. The owner's manufacture their own line of quality British-style smoking jackets, and the inventory also includes top brands and small fashion accessories. There's a small bar in the back, where you can toast your latest purchase in style. ✉ *Schlüterstr. 50, Charlottenburg* ☎ *030/8872–7474* ⊕ *www. chelseafarmersclub.de* ⊙ *Closed Sun.*

CLOTHING: WOMEN'S

Jil Sander. The flagship store of German designer Jil Sander carries the newest collections from this iconic, understated brand, including fashions for men. ✉ *Kurfürstendamm 185, Charlottenburg* ☎ *030/886–7020* ⊕ *www.jilsander.com.*

DEPARTMENT STORES

Fodors Choice **Kaufhaus des Westens** (*KaDeWe*). The largest department store in con-
★ tinental Europe, classy Kaufhaus des Westens (KaDeWe) has a grand selection of goods, spread over seven floors, as well as food and deli counters, champagne bars, beer bars, and a beautiful art deco–style atrium café on the top floor. The wealth of services offered here includes luxury gift basket arrangements, exclusive travel guides, and an international box office. ✉ *Tauentzienstr. 21–24, Charlottenburg* ☎ *030/21210* ⊕ *www.kadewe.de* ⊙ *Closed Sun.*

GIFTS AND SOUVENIRS

Harry Lehmann. If you want a taste—or rather, a smell—of old Berlin, head to Harry Lehmann on Kantstrasse in Charlottenburg. The shopkeeper will greet you in a white lab coat, helpfully explaining the origin and inspiration of the expertly mixed perfumes, which fill large apothecary jars along a mirrored wall. This is definitely old school—the shop has been opened in 1926. Scents are fresh, simple, and clean, and a 30-ml bottle (€15.50) makes for a reasonably priced gift or souvenir. ✉ *Kantstr. 106, Charlottenburg* ☎ *030/324–3582* ⊕ *www.parfum-individual.de* ⊙ *Closed Sun.*

Königliche Porzellan Manufaktur. Fine porcelain is still produced by Königliche Porzellan Manufaktur, the former Royal Porcelain Manufactory for the Prussians, also called KPM. You can buy this delicate handmade, hand-painted china at KPM's two stores, but it may be more fun to visit the factory salesroom, which also sells seconds at reduced prices. ✉ *Wegelystr. 1, Tiergarten* ☎ *030/390–09215* ⊕ *de-de.kpm-berlin.com* ✉ *Kurfürstendamm 27, Charlottenburg* ☎ *030/8862–7961.*

Fodors Choice **Paper & Tea.** Enter this serene shop just off Kantstrasse and you'll be
★ stepping into a world of high-quality, looseleaf teas. Rather than bulk up on inventory, the store has a restrained selection of 70 teas, all displayed in museumlike cases, where you can smell the wares. There are two tasting areas, where expert attendants brew and explain the teas. ✉ *Bleibtreust. 4, Charlottenburg* ☎ *030/9561–5468* ⊕ *www. paperandtea.com* ⊙ *Closed Sun.*

15

Fodor's Choice **Wald Konesberg Marzipan.** This third-generation artisan shop offers a
★ taste of the old-world treat marzipan, using a family recipe that dates
back to the turn of the 20th century. The vintage-style shop features
candy-striped wallpaper, vintage tools, and rows of handmade marzipan, all wrapped in delicate packaging. ⊠ *Pestalozzistr. 54 a, Charlottenburg* ☎ *030/323–8254* ⊕ *www.wald-koenigsberger-marzipan.de*
☽ *Closed Sun.*

SIDE TRIP TO POTSDAM

Updated by
Katherine
Sacks

A trip to Berlin wouldn't be complete without paying a visit to Potsdam
and its park, which surrounds the important Prussian palaces Neues
Palais and Sanssouci. This separate city, the state capital of Brandenburg
(the state surrounding Berlin), can be reached within a half hour from
Berlin's Zoo Station and most major Berlin S-bahn stations.

Potsdam still retains the imperial character it earned during the many
years it served as a royal residence and garrison quarters. The Alter
Markt and Neuer Markt show off stately Prussian architecture, and
both are easily reached from the main train station by any tram heading into the town center.

GETTING HERE AND AROUND

Potsdam is 20 km (12 miles) southwest of Berlin's center and a half-
hour journey by car or bus. From Zoo Station to Potsdam's main train
station, the regional train RE-1 takes 17 minutes, and the S-bahn Line
No. 7 takes about 30 minutes; use an ABC zone ticket for either service.
City traffic is heavy, so a train journey is recommended. Several Berlin
tour operators have Potsdam trips.

There are several tours that include Potsdam (most are two or six
hours). They leave from the landing across from Berlin's Wannsee
S-bahn station between late March and early October. Depending on
the various tours on offer, a round-trip ticket costs €7.50–€23.

ESSENTIALS

Visitor Information Potsdam Tourist Office. Two-hour walking tours (9€)
are led around Potsdam's historical center from this tourist information center.
⊠ *Touristenzentrum Potsdam, Brandenburgerstr. 3, at Brandenburger Tor, Potsdam* ☎ *0331/275–580* ⊕ *www.potsdamtourismus.de.*

EXPLORING

Alter Markt. This "Old Market" Square is the hub of Potsdam's historical
center and was, for three centuries, home to the city's baroque palace.
The area was heavily damaged by Allied bombing in World War II
and then destroyed by the East German regime in 1960. After reunification, Potsdam decided to rebuild its palace, and the reconstructed
structure will house the state parliament. Thanks to private donors, the
first element, a magnificent replica of the **Fortunaportal,** now stands
proudly on the square, while the palace's main sections are currently
being built with a combination of modern and historic elements. ⊠ *Am
Alten Markt 1.*

Haus der Brandenburg-Preussischen Geschichte (*House of Brandenburg-Prussian History*). The region's history museum, the Haus der Brandenburg-Preussischen Geschichte, is in the royal stables in the square opposite the Nikolaikirche. ⊠ *Am Neuen Markt 9* ☎ *0331/620–8550* ⊕ *www.hbpg.de* 🎟 *€4.50* ⊙ *Tues.–Thurs. 10–5, Fri.–Sun. 10–6.*

Holländisches Viertel. The center of the small Holländisches Viertel—the Dutch Quarter—is an easy walk north along Friedrich-Ebert-Strasse to Mittelstrasse. Friedrich Wilhelm I built the settlement in the 1730s to entice Dutch artisans who could support the city's rapid growth. The 134 gabled, mansard-roof brick houses make up the largest Dutch housing development outside of the Netherlands today. Antique shops, boutiques, and restaurants fill the buildings now, and the area is one of Potsdam's most visited.

Neues Palais (*New Palace*). The Neues Palais, a much larger and grander palace than Sanssouci, stands at the end of the long avenue that runs through Sanssouci Park. It was built after the Seven Years' War (1756–63), when Frederick loosened the purse strings. It's said he wanted to demonstrate that the state coffers hadn't been depleted too severely by the long conflict. Interiors that impress include the Grotto Hall with walls and columns set with shells, coral, and other aquatic decor. The royals' upper apartments have paintings by 17th-century Italian masters. You can opt to tour the palace yourself only on weekends between late April and mid-May. ✉ *Str. am Neuen Palais, Sanssouci* ☎ *0331/969–4200* ⊕ *www.spsg.de* 🎫 *€8* ⊘ *Apr.–Oct., Wed.–Mon. 10–6; Nov.–Mar., Wed.–Mon. 10–5.*

Nikolaikirche. Karl Friedrich Schinkel designed the Alter Markt's domed Nikolaikirche. In front of it stands an Egyptian obelisk erected by Schloss Sanssouci architect von Knobelsdorff. ✉ *Am Alten Markt.*

Altes Rathaus. A gilded figure of Atlas tops the tower of the old Rathaus, built in 1755. ✉ *Am Alten Markt 9.*

QUICK
BITES

Wiener Restaurant. Fine coffee blends and rich cakes are available at the Wiener Restaurant, an old-style European coffeehouse not far from the Grünes Gitter entrance to Sanssouci. ✉ *Luisenpl. 4* ☎ *0331/6014–9904* ⊕ *www.wiener-potsdam.de.*

Schloss Cecilienhof (*Cecilienhof Palace*). Resembling a rambling, Tudor manor house, Schloss Cecilienhof was built for Crown Prince Wilhelm in 1913, on a newly laid-out stretch of park called the Neuer Garten (New Garden), which borders the Heiliger See. It was in this, the last palace to be built by the Hohenzollerns, that the Allied leaders Stalin, Truman, and Churchill (later Attlee) hammered out the fate of postwar Germany at the 1945 Potsdam Conference. ■**TIP**➔ From Potsdam's main train station, take a tram to Reiterweg/Alleestrasse, and then transfer to Bus No. 603 to Schloss Cecilienhof. ☎ *0331/969–4200* ⊕ *www.spsg.de* 🎫 *€6 with tour (mandatory Nov.–Mar.), €4 tour of royal couple's private apartments* ⊘ *Apr.–Oct., Tues.–Sun. 10–6.; Nov.–Mar., Tues.–Sun. 10–5. Tours of royal couple's private apartments at 10, 12, 2, 4.*

Schloss Charlottenhof. Schloss Charlottenhof is in the southern part of Sanssouci Park, an expansive, landscaped promenade with fountains, streams, manicured gardens, and wide walkways as well as some hidden paths. After Frederick the Great died in 1786, the ambitious Sanssouci building program ground to a halt, and the park fell into neglect. It was 50 years before another Prussian king, Friedrich Wilhelm IV, restored Sanssouci's earlier glory. He engaged the great Berlin architect Karl Friedrich Schinkel to build this small palace for the crown prince. Schinkel's demure interiors are preserved, and the most fanciful room is the bedroom, decorated like a Roman tent, with its walls and ceiling draped in striped canvas. Between the Sanssouci palaces are later additions to the park. ☎ *0331/969–4228* 🎫 *€4 with tour* ⊘ *May–Oct., Tues.–Sun. 10–6.*

Chinesisches Teehaus (*Chinese Teahouse*). The Chinesisches Teehaus was erected in 1754 in the Chinese style that was all the rage at the time. It houses porcelain from Meissen and Asia. 🎫 *€2* ⊘ *May–Oct., Tues.–Sun. 10–6.*

Friedenskirche (*Peace Church*). Completed in 1854, the Italianate Friedenskirche houses a 13th-century Byzantine mosaic taken from an island near Venice. ☎ *0331/974–009* 🎫 *Free* ⊘ *Apr. 24–30, Mon.–Sat. 11–5, Sun. 12–5; May–Sept., Mon.–Sat. 10–6, Sun. 12–6; Oct. 2–16, Mon.–Sat. 11–5, Sun. 12–5; Oct. 17–Apr. 23, Sat. 11–4, Sun. 11:30–4.*

Orangerieschloss und Turm. The Orangerieschloss und Turm was completed in 1864; its two massive towers linked by a colonnade evoke an Italian Renaissance palace. Today it houses more than 50 copies of paintings by Raphael. ⬛ *Guided tour €4, tower only €2* ◔ *Apr., weekends and holidays 10–6; May–Oct., Tues.–Sun. 10–6.*

Römische Bäder (*Roman Baths*). Friedrich Wilhelm IV built the Römische Bäder (Roman Baths), also designed by Schinkel, from 1829 to 1840. Like many of the other structures in Potsdam, this one is more romantic than authentic. Half Italian villa, half Greek temple, the structure is nevertheless a charming addition to the park. ⬛ *€3 with exhibit* ◔ *May–Oct., Tues.–Sun. 10–5.*

Schloss Sanssouci. Prussia's most famous king, Frederick the Great, spent more time at his summer residence, Schloss Sanssouci, than in the capital of Berlin. Its name means "without a care" in French, the language Frederick cultivated in his own private circle and within the court. Some experts believe that Frederick actually named the palace "Sans, Souci," which they translate as "with and without a care," a more apt name, since its construction caused him a lot of trouble and expense, and sparked furious rows with his master builder, Georg Wenzeslaus von Knobelsdorff. His creation nevertheless became one of Germany's greatest tourist attractions. The palace lies on the edge of Park Sanssouci, which includes various buildings and palaces with separate admissions and hours. ■TIP➜ Be advised that during peak tourism times, timed tickets for Schloss Sanssouci tours can sell out before noon.

Executed according to Frederick's impeccable French-influenced taste, the palace, built between 1745 and 1747, is extravagantly rococo, with scarcely a patch of wall left unadorned. Leading up to the building is an unusual formal terrace where wine grapes were once cultivated. ✉ *Park Sanssouci* ☎ *0331/969–4200* ⊕ *www.spsg.de* ⬛ *€12* ◔ *Apr.–Oct., Tues.–Sun. 10–6; Nov.–Mar., Tues.–Sun. 10–5.*

Bildergalerie (*Picture Gallery*). Just east of Sanssouci Palace sits the picture gallery, which displays Frederick II's collection of 17th-century Italian and Dutch paintings, including works by Caravaggio, Rubens, and Van Dyck. The main cupola contains expensive marble from Siena. ☎ *0331/969–4181* ⬛ *€6* ◔ *May–Oct., Tues.–Sun. 10–6.*

Neue Kammern (*New Chambers*). To the west of the palace are the Neue Kammern, which housed guests of the king's family after its beginnings as a greenhouse. ☎ *0331/969–4206* ⬛ *€4 guided tour only* ◔ *Apr.–Oct, Tues.–Sun. 10–6.*

QUICK
BITES

Drachenhaus (*Dragon House*). Halfway up the hill leading to the Belvedere, past the Orangerie, stands the curious Drachenhaus, modeled in 1770 after the Pagoda at London's Kew Gardens and named for the gargoyles ornamenting the roof corners. It now houses a popular restaurant and café. ✉ *Maulbeerallee 4* ⊕ *www.drachenhaus.de.*

15

WHERE TO EAT

$$ ✗ **Restaurant Juliette.** In a city proud of its past French influences, the
FRENCH   highly praised French cuisine here is often delivered to your table by
French waiters, no less. The intimate restaurant at the edge of the Dutch
Quarter has old-fashioned brick walls and a fireplace. The menu offers
small portions of dishes such as rack of lamb, quail with roasted chan-
terelles, and a starter plate of seasonal foie-gras preparations. Its wine
list of 120 French vintages is unique in the Berlin area. ■ **TIP➔ Company
chief Ralph Junick has really cornered the market in Potsdam, with
four other French restaurants, including a tasty crêperie and a coffee
shop. If you'll be in Potsdam for more than one meal, check Juliette's
website to see what else is in town.** $ *Average main: €20* ✉ *Jägerstr.
39* ☎ *0331/270–1791* ⊕ *www.restaurant-juliette.de.*

SAXONY,
SAXONY-ANHALT,
AND THURINGIA

WELCOME TO SAXONY, SAXONY-ANHALT, AND THURINGIA

TOP REASONS TO GO

★ **Following Martin Luther:** Trace the path of the ultimate medieval rebel in Wittenberg, Erfurt, Eisenach, and the Wartburg, and gain valuable insight into the mind and culture of a person whose ideas helped change the world.

★ **Frauenkirche in Dresden:** Rising like a majestic baroque phoenix, the church is a worthy symbol of a city destroyed and rebuilt from its ashes.

★ **Görlitz:** Balanced on the border between Germany and Poland, this architectural gem is relatively undiscovered; you'll feel as if you have the whole town to yourself.

★ **Weimar:** The history of Germany seems to revolve around this small town, whose past residents are a veritable who's who of the last 400 years, including Goethe, Schiller, Bach, Liszt, and Gropius.

★ **Wine tasting in the Salle-Unstrut:** The castle-topped, rolling hills covered in terraced vineyards are perfect for biking, hiking, and horseback riding.

1 Saxony. The pearl of eastern Germany, Saxony's countryside is dotted with beautifully renovated castles and fortresses, and the people are charming and full of energy. (They also speak in an almost incomprehensible local dialect.) Dresden and Leipzig are cosmopolitan centers that combine the energy of the avant-garde with a distinct respect for tradition.

2 Saxony-Anhalt. Although long ignored by travelers, Saxony-Anhalt has more UNESCO World Heritage sites than any other region in Europe. The city of Naumburg is famed for its cathedral and for the wines produced in the surrounding vineyards.

GETTING ORIENTED

These three states cover the southeastern part of the former East Germany, and the area holds Germany's most historical and beautiful cities. You'll still see old, dirty, and depressing industrial towns that recall the Communist past, but 25 years of reconstruction programs have slowly turned them into things of the past. Dresden revels in its reputation as "the Florence on the Elbe," and just downstream Meissen has undergone an impressive face-lift. Weimar, one of the continent's old cultural centers, and Leipzig, in particular, have washed off their grime and almost completely restored their historic city centers. Görlitz, Germany's easternmost city, benefited from an infusion of cash and is consistently lauded as one of the country's 10 most beautiful cities.

3 Thuringia. Of all the eastern German states, Thuringia has the best tourist infrastructure. Visitors to the classical jewel of Weimar and those interested in outdoor sports in the lush Thuringian Forest flock to the area, much as they have for centuries. Thuringia offers unparalleled natural sights as well as classical culture at reasonable prices.

16

FOLLOWING MARTIN LUTHER

Saxony-Anhalt and Thuringia are currently celebrating the "Luther decade," preparing to mark the Protestant Reformation's 500th anniversary in 2017. A drive between the *Lutherstädte* (Luther Cities) allows for a deeper understanding of Martin Luther and the Reformation.

(above) Lutherhaus in Eisenach, where he lived as a student (upper right) Martin Luther (lower right) Memorial for Martin Luther in Eisleben

Dissatisfaction was already brewing, but Martin Luther (1483–1546) was the first German to speak out against the Catholic Church. He took issue with the sale of indulgences—letters from the Pope purchased by wealthy Christians to absolve them of sins. His 95 Theses, which he brashly nailed to a church door, called for a return to faith in the Bible's teachings over the Pope's decrees, and an end to the sale of indulgences. Despite such so-called heretical beginnings, Luther overcame condemnation by the Pope and several other governing bodies. He continued to preach, building a family with Katharina von Bora, a former nun he married after "rescuing" her from a convent. After his death, Lutheranism spread across Europe as an accepted branch of Christianity.

—Giulia Pines

LUTHER QUOTES

"I am more afraid of my own heart than of the pope and all his cardinals. I have within me the great pope, Self."

"When the Devil...sees men use violence to propagate the gospel, he... says with malignant looks and frightful grin: 'Ah, how wise these madmen are to play my game! Let them go on; I shall reap the benefit...'"

ON THE TRAIL OF MARTIN LUTHER

Start in the town of Wittenberg, the unofficial capital of the Reformation. The comprehensive **Lutherhaus** museum is in the Augustinian monastery where Luther lived twice, first as a monk and later with his family. This multilevel, bilingual museum will convince the skeptics that Luther is worth remembering. From the museum, it's a short walk down the main thoroughfare Collegienstrasse to two churches that felt the influence of his teachings. The first is **Stadtkirche St. Marien** (Parish Church of St. Mary), where Luther often preached. The second, **Schlosskirche** (Castle Church), is where Luther changed history by posting his 95 Theses. The original wooden doors were destroyed in a 1760 fire, now replaced by bronze doors with the Latin text of the 95 Theses. On the way from one church to the other, stop to admire the statues of Luther and his friend and collaborator Philipp Melanchthon—they are buried next to each other in Schlosskirche.

In the nearby town of Eisleben, the houses where Luther was born, the **Luthers Geburtshaus** (⊠ *Lutherstr. 15* ☎ *03475/714–7814*), and died, **Luthers Sterbehaus** (⊠ *Sangerhäuser Str. 46* ☎ *03475/67680*) lie 10 minutes from each other. From there, it's easy to spot the steeples of two churches: **St. Petri-Pauli-Kirche** (*Church of Sts. Peter and Paul* ⊠ *Petristr.* ☎ *03475/602–229*) and **St. Andreaskirche** (*St. Andrew's Church* ⊠ *Andreaskirchpl.* ☎ *03475/602–229*). The first was Luther's place of baptism, while the second houses the pulpit where Luther gave his last four sermons. His funeral was also held here before his body was taken back to Wittenberg.

Continuing southwest the stunning medieval castle **Wartburg** is in the hills high above the town of Eisenach. Luther took refuge here after he was excommunicated by the Pope and outlawed by a general assembly called the Diet of Worms, famously translating the New Testament from the original Greek into German.

REFORMATION TIMELINE

1517: Luther nails his 95 Theses to Wittenberg's Schlosskirche.

1521: Refusing to recant, Luther is excommunicated.

1537: Denmark's Christian III declares Lutheranism the state religion, leading to its spread in Scandinavia.

1555: Charles V signs Peace of Augsburg, ending open hostilities between Catholicism and Lutheranism and granting the latter official status. Due to the rise of Calvinism, conflict bubbles under the surface.

1558: Queen Elizabeth I of England supports the establishment of the English Protestant Church.

1577: The Formula of Concord ends disputes between sects, strengthening and preserving Lutheranism.

1618: Religious tensions explode in Bohemia, thrusting Europe into the Thirty Years' War. At war's end, much of Central Europe is in ruins, with 40% of people dead.

1650s and beyond: Lutheran explorers and settlers bring their beliefs to the New World.

16

BAUHAUS IN WEIMAR

(above) Bauhaus Museum in Weimar (upper right) Bauhaus Building in Dessau

Begun in Weimar, the Bauhaus movement's futuristic design, "form from function" mentality, and revolutionary spirit have inspired artists worldwide.

Founded in 1919 by architect Walter Gropius, the Bauhaus movement had roots in the past but was also unabashedly modern. Based on the principles of William Morris and the Arts and Crafts movement, Bauhaus promoted the idea of creation as a service to society, holding practical objects such as a chair, teapot, or lamp to the same high standards as true works of art. Its style was art deco but less ornate, machine-age but not industrial, its goal to put both spaces and materials to their most natural and economical uses. Although the Bauhaus school was shut down by the Nazis in the early 1930s, many former Bauhaus students left Germany and went to work in other parts of the world. Today, their influence can even be seen as far away as Tel Aviv, where Jewish architects fleeing Europe came to build their vision of a modern city.

—Giulia Pines

BAUHAUS IN DESSAU

If you have an extra day, take the train to Dessau, Bauhaus's second city, to see the iconic **Bauhaus Building**, adorned on one side with vertical block lettering spelling out "Bauhaus." Still an architecture school, it now houses the Bauhaus Dessau Foundation, and a multilevel Bauhaus Museum. You can even stay in the monastic Bauhaus studio flats here.

A BAUHAUS WALK IN WEIMAR

Start with the **Bauhaus Museum** in Weimar's central Theaterplatz, which offers a film about the history of Bauhaus and rotating exhibitions covering much of what there is to see in Weimar. Head south along Schützengasse and continue down Amalienstrasse to catch a glimpse of the Henry van de Velde–designed main building of **Bauhaus University** (✉ *Geschwister-Scholl-Str. 8* ☎ *03643/580* ⊕ *www.uni-weimar.de*), formerly the Grand Ducal School of Arts and Crafts. A faithful reconstruction of Gropius's office can be found here as well. The **Bauhaus Atelier** (✉ *Geschwister-Scholl-Str. 6a* ☎ *03643/583–000*) at the university is a central meeting place for students. It contains a café and shop offering books about the movement as well as Bauhaus-designed souvenirs, and also marks the starting point for university-run Bauhaus walks. Head just south for the Gropius-designed **Monument to the March Dead** in Weimar's **Historischer Friedhof** (Historical Cemetery). This jagged expressionist structure, built in 1921, commemorates those who died in the Kapp Putsch, an attempt to overthrow the Weimar Republic a year earlier. Follow the signs for **Goethes Gartenhaus** (perhaps the most visited historical structure in Weimar) through the Park on the Ilm, and look just beyond it for the **Haus am Horn** (✉ *Am Horn 61* ☎ *03643/904–056*). This modest, cubical structure designed by Georg Muche for the 1923 Bauhaus exhibition was meant to be a model of Bauhaus's functional philosophy. It was fully restored in 1999 to mark the 80 anniversary of the founding of Bauhaus.

STYLE ELEMENTS

According to the standards of Bauhaus, good design should be accompanied by good engineering. That's why so many Bauhaus buildings still look strikingly modern, even industrial, even though they may have been designed as early as the 1920s. Bauhaus's timelessness results from its use of three basic shapes—square, circle, and triangle—and three basic colors—red, blue, and yellow. To spot its influence, look for unadorned, **boxlike structures** with repeating parallel lines, **flat roofs,** and rectangular windowpanes. Furniture and household objects feature strong lines, retro-futuristic shapes, and the abundant use of **metals.** Bauhaus designers also revolutionized typography: the sign on the Bauhaus Building in Dessau is a prime example: look for **clear, boxy typefaces,** often combined collage-like with photographs and **colorful graphics** and shapes to create bold messages. The Swedish furniture chain IKEA owes a lot to Bauhaus.

16

Updated by
Lee A. Evans

Germany's traditional charm is most evident in the eastern states of Saxony, Saxony-Anhalt, and Thuringia. The area formed the core of the former communist German Democratic Republic (referred to by its German acronym, DDR, or its English equivalent, GDR), but there is hardly any left today. Instead an unspoiled German state of mind predominates.

Eastern Germans resolutely cling to their German heritage. They proudly preserve their connections with such national heroes as Luther, Goethe, Schiller, Bach, Handel, Wagner, and the Hungarian-born Liszt. Towns in the regions of the Thüringer Wald (Thuringian Forest) or the Harz Mountains—long considered the haunt of witches—are drenched in history and medieval legend. The area hides a fantastic collection of rural villages and castles unparalleled in other parts of the country.

Many cities, such as Erfurt, escaped World War II relatively unscathed, and the East Germans extensively rebuilt towns damaged by bombing. Although historical city centers were faithfully restored to their past glory, there are also plenty of eyesores of industrialization and stupendously bland housing projects, which the Germans refer to as *Bausünden* (architectural sins). Famous palaces and cultural wonders— the rebuilt historical center of Dresden, the Wartburg at Eisenach, the Schiller and Goethe houses in Weimar, Luther's Wittenberg, as well as the wonderfully preserved city of Görlitz—are waiting for to have their subtle and extravagant charms discovered.

PLANNING

WHEN TO GO
Winters in this part of Germany can be cold, wet, and dismal, so unless you plan to ski in the Harz Mountains or the Thüringer Wald, visit in late spring, summer, or early autumn. Avoid Leipzig at trade-fair times, particularly in March and April. In summer every city, town, and village has a festival, with streets blocked and local culture spilling out into every open space.

GETTING HERE AND AROUND
AIR TRAVEL

It's easiest, and usually cheapest, to fly into Berlin or Frankfurt and rent a car from there. Dresden and Leipzig both have international airports that are primarily operated by budget carriers serving European destinations. Dresden Flughafen is about 10 km (6 miles) north of Dresden, and Leipzig's Flughafen Leipzig-Halle is 12 km (8 miles) northwest of the city.

Airport Contacts Dresden Flughafen ⊠ *Flughafenstr., Dresden* ☎ *0351/881–3360* ⊕ *www.dresden-airport.de.* **Flughafen Leipzig-Halle** ⊠ *Termanalring 11, Schkeuditz* ☎ *0341/224–1155* ⊕ *www.leipzig-halle-airport.de.*

BUS TRAVEL

Long-distance buses travel to Dresden and Leipzig. Bus service within the area is infrequent and mainly connects with rail lines. Check schedules carefully at central train stations or call the service phone number of Deutsche Bahn (German Railway) at local railway stations.

CAR TRAVEL

Expressways connect Berlin with Dresden (A-13) and Leipzig (A-9). Both journeys take about two hours. The A-4 stretches east–west across the southern portion of Thuringia and Saxony.

A road-construction program in eastern Germany is ongoing, and you should expect traffic delays on any journey of more than 300 km (186 miles). The Bundesstrassen throughout eastern Germany are narrow, tree-lined country roads, often jammed with traffic. Roads in the western part of the Harz Mountains are better and wider.

Cars can be rented at the Dresden and Leipzig airports, at train stations, and through all major hotels. Be aware that you are not allowed to take rentals into Poland or the Czech Republic.

TRAIN TRAVEL

The fastest and least expensive way to explore the region is by train. East Germany's rail infrastructure is exceptional; trains serve even the most remote destinations with astonishing frequency. Slower S, RB, and RE trains link smaller towns, while Leipzig, Dresden, Weimar, Erfurt, Naumburg, and Wittenberg are all on major InterCity Express (ICE) lines. Some cities—Dresden and Meissen, for example—are linked by commuter trains.

From Dresden a round-trip ticket to Leipzig costs about €43 (a 1½-hour journey one-way); to Görlitz it's about €38 (a 1½-hour ride). Trains connect Leipzig with Halle (a 30-minute ride, €10), Erfurt (a 1-hour ride, €28), and Eisenach (a 1½-hour journey, €28). The train ride between Dresden and Eisenach (2½ hours) costs €56 one-way.

■ TIP➜ Consider using a Länder-Ticket: a €22 (plus €3 per person up to five people) regional day ticket from the German Railroad that covers local train travel in the respective state (for example, within Saxony, Saxony-Anhalt, or Thuringia).

16

TOURS

With two luxury ships, Viking K–D operates a full program of cruises on the Elbe River, from Hamburg as far as Prague. They run up to eight days from mid-April until late October. All the historic cities of Saxony and Thuringia are ports of call—including Dresden, Meissen, Wittenberg, and Dessau. ⇨ *For details see Cruise Travel in Travel Smart Germany.*

Weisse Flotte's historic paddle-steam tours depart from and stop in Dresden, Meissen, Pirna, Pillnitz, Königsstein, and Bad Schandau. Besides tours in the Dresden area, boats also go into the Czech Republic. For more information contact the Sächsische Dampfschiffahrt.

In Saxony two historic narrow-gauge trains still operate on a regular schedule. Both the *Lössnitzgrundbahn,* which connects Ost-Radebeul-Ost and Radeburg, as well as the *Weisseritzelbahn,* which operates between Freital-Hainsberg and Kurort Kipsdorf, are perfect for taking in some of Saxony's romantic countryside and the Fichtelberg Mountains. A round-trip ticket is between about €7 and €11, depending on the length of the ride. For schedule and information, contact Deutsche Bahn's regional Dresden office.

The famous steam locomotive *Harzquerbahn* connects Nordhausen-Nord with Wernigerode and Gernerode in the Harz Mountains. The most popular track of this line is the *Brockenbahn,* a special narrow-gauge train transporting tourists to the top of northern Germany's highest mountain. For schedule and further information, contact the Harzer Schmalspurbahnen GmbH.

Tour Contacts German Railroad (Deutsche Bahn) ☎ *0180/599–6633* ⊕ *www.bahn.de.* **Harzer Schmalspurbahnen GmbH** ⊠ *Friedrichstr. 151, Wernigerode* ☎ *03943/5580* ⊕ *www.hsb-wr.de.* **Lössnitzgrundbahn** ⊠ *Geyersdorfer Str. 32, Annaberg-Buchholz* ☎ *0351/46165–63684.* **Sächsische Dampfschiffahrt** ⊠ *Hertha-Lindner-Str. 10, Dresden* ☎ *0351/866–090* ⊕ *www.saechsische-dampfschiffahrt.de.* **Weisseritztalbahn** ⊠ *Dresdner Str. 280, Freital* ☎ *0351/641–2701* ⊕ *www.weisseritztalbahn.de.*

RESTAURANTS

Enterprising young managers and chefs have established themselves in the East, so look for new, usually small, restaurants. People in the region are extremely particular about their traditional food (rumor has it that one can be deported for roasting Mützbraten over anything other than birch), but some new chefs have successfully blended contemporary German with international influences. Medieval-theme restaurants and "experience dining," complete with entertainment, are all the rage in the East, and warrant at least one try. Brewpubs have sprouted up everywhere, and are a good bet for meeting locals.

Prices in the reviews are the average cost of a main course at dinner, or if dinner is not served, at lunch.

HOTELS

Hotels in eastern Germany are up to international standards and, due to economic subsidies in the 1990s, often far outshine their West German counterparts. In the East it's quite normal to have a major international hotel in a 1,000-year-old house or restored mansion. Smaller and family-run hotels are more charming local options, and often include a good restaurant. Most big hotels offer special weekend or activity-oriented packages that aren't found in the western part of the country. All hotels include breakfast, unless indicated otherwise.

During the trade fairs and shows of the **Leipziger Messe,** particularly in March and April, most Leipzig hotels increase their prices.

Prices in the reviews are the lowest cost of a standard double room in high season. For expanded reviews, facilities, and current deals, visit Fodors.com.

PLANNING YOUR TIME

Eastern Germany is a small, well-connected region that's well suited for day trips. Dresden and Leipzig are the largest cities with the most facilities, making them good bases from which to explore the surrounding countryside, either by car or train. Both are well connected with Berlin, Munich, and Frankfurt. Leipzig, Dresden, Lutherstadt-Wittenberg, and Dessau can be explored as day trips from Berlin. Any of the smaller towns offer a quieter, possibly more authentic look at the area. A trip into the Salle-Unstrut wine region is well worth the time, using Naumburg as a base.

DISCOUNTS AND DEALS

Most of the region's larger cities offer special tourist exploring cards, such as the **Dresdencard**, **Hallecard**, **Leipzigcard**, and **Weimarcard**, which include discounts at museums, concerts, hotels, and restaurants or special sightseeing packages for up to three days. For details, check with the local visitor information office.

THE FIVE KS

A long-standing joke is that the priorities of the people of Saxony, Saxony-Anhalt, and Thuringia can be summed up in five Ks: Kaffee, Kuchen, Klösse, Kartoffeln, and Kirche (coffee, cake, dumplings, potatoes, and church)—in that order.

SAXONY

The people of Saxony identify themselves more as Saxon than German. Their hardworking and rustic attitudes, their somewhat peripheral location on the border with the Czech Republic and Poland, and their almost incomprehensible dialect are the targets of endless jokes and puns. However, Saxon pride rebuilt three cities magnificently: Dresden and Leipzig—the showcase cities of eastern Germany—and the smaller town of Görlitz, on the Neisse River.

LEIPZIG

184 km (114 miles) southwest of Berlin.

Leipzig is, in a word, cool—but not so cool as to be pretentious. With its world-renowned links to Bach, Schubert, Mendelssohn, Martin Luther, Goethe, Schiller, and the fantastic Neue-Leipziger-Schule art movement, Leipzig is one of the great German cultural centers. It has impressive art-nouveau architecture, an incredibly clean city center, meandering narrow streets, and the temptations of coffee and cake on every corner. In *Faust*, Goethe describes Leipzig as "a little Paris"; in reality it's more reminiscent of Vienna, while remaining a distinctly energetic Saxon town.

Leipzig's musical past includes Johann Sebastian Bach (1685–1750), who was organist and choir director at Leipzig's Thomaskirche, and the 19th-century composer Richard Wagner, who was born in the city in 1813. Today's Leipzig continues the cultural focus with extraordinary offerings of music, theater, and opera, not to mention fantastic nightlife.

Wartime bombs destroyed much of Leipzig's city center, but reconstruction efforts have uncovered one of Europe's most vibrant cities. Leipzig's art-nouveau flair is best discovered by exploring the countless alleys, covered courtyards, and passageways. Some unattractive buildings from the postwar period remain, but only reinforce Leipzig's position on the line between modernity and antiquity.

With a population of about 535,000, Leipzig is the third-largest city in eastern Germany (after Berlin and Dresden) and has long been a center of printing and bookselling. Astride major trade routes, it was an important market town in the Middle Ages, and it continues to be a trading center, thanks to the *Leipziger Messe* (trade and fair shows) throughout the year that bring together buyers from East and West.

Unfortunately, Leipzig has a tendency to underwhelm first-time visitors. If you take Leipzig slow and have some cake, its subtle, hidden charms may surprise you.

GETTING HERE AND AROUND

Leipzig is an hour from Berlin by train. Leipzig-Halle airport serves many European destinations, but no North American ones.

FESTIVALS

Music Days. Leipzig's annual music festival is in June. ✉ *Augustuspl.*

TIMING

Leipzig can easily be explored in one day; it's possible to walk around the downtown area in just about three hours. The churches can be inspected in less than 20 minutes each. But if you're interested in German history and art, plan for two full days, so you can spend one day just visiting the museums and go to the symphony. The Völkerschlachtdenkmal is perfect for a three-hour side trip.

ESSENTIALS

Visitor Information Leipzig Tourismus und Marketing ✉ *Augustuspl. 9* ☎ *0341/710–4260* ⊕ *www.leipzig.de.*

EXPLORING

TOP ATTRACTIONS

Grassimuseum. British star architect David Chipperfield restored and modernized this fine example of German art deco in 2003–05. The building, dating to 1925–29, houses three important museums. ⊠ *Johannispl. 5–11* ⊕ *www.grassimuseum.de* ⊙ *Tues.–Sun. 10–6.*

Museum für Angewandte Kunst (*Museum of Applied Art*). This museum showcases 2,000 years of works from Leipzig's and eastern Germany's proud tradition of handicrafts, such as exquisite porcelain, fine tapestry art, and modern Bauhaus design. ⊠ *Johannispl. 5–11* 🕾 *0341/222–9100* ⊕ *www.grassimuseum.de* 🔖 *€5* ⊙ *Tues.–Sun. 10–6.*

Museum für Völkerkunde (*Ethnological Museum*). Presenting arts and crafts from all continents and various eras, this museum includes a thrilling collection of Southeast Asian antique art and the world's only Kurile Ainu feather costume, in the Northeast Asia collection. ⊠ *Johannispl. 5–11* 🕾 *0341/973–1300* ⊕ *www.grassimuseum.de* 🔖 *€6* ⊙ *Tues.–Sun. 10–6.*

Museum für Musikinstrumente (*Musical Instruments Museum*). Historical musical instruments, mostly from the Renaissance, include the world's oldest clavichord, constructed in 1543 in Italy. There are also spinets, flutes, and lutes. Recordings of the instruments can be heard at the exhibits. ⊠ *Johannispl. 5–11* 🕾 *0341/973–0750* 🔖 *€5* ⊙ *Tues.–Sun. 10–6.*

Mädlerpassage (*Mädler Mall*). The ghost of Goethe's Faust lurks in every marble corner of Leipzig's finest shopping arcade. One of the scenes in *Faust* is set in the famous Auerbachs Keller restaurant, at No. 2. A bronze group of characters from the play, sculpted in 1913, beckons you down the stone staircase to the restaurant. ■TIP➡ Touching the statues' feet is said to bring good luck. A few yards away is a delightful art-nouveau bar called Mephisto. ⊠ *Grimmaische Str.*

Markt. Leipzig's showpiece is its huge, old market square. One side is completely occupied by the Renaissance town hall, the **Altes Rathaus.**

Stadtgeschichtliches Museum. Inside the Altes Rathaus, this museum documents Leipzig's past. The entrance is behind the Rathaus. The museum is expanding its exhibition space behind the Museum for Applied Arts. ⊠ *Böttchergässchen 3* 🕾 *0341/965–130* ⊕ *www.stadtgeschichtliches-museum-leipzig.de* 🔖 *€6* ⊙ *Tues.–Sun. 10–6.*

Museum der Bildenden Künste (*Museum of Fine Arts*). The city's leading art gallery is minimalism incarnate, set in a huge concrete cube encased in green glass in the middle of Sachsenplatz Square. The museum's collection of more than 2,700 paintings and sculptures represents everything from the German Middle Ages to the modern Neue Leipziger Schule. Especially notable are the collections focusing on Lucas Cranach the Elder and Caspar David Friedrich. ■TIP➡ Be sure to start at the top and work your way down. Don't miss Max Klinger's Beethoven as Zeus statue. ⊠ *Katharinenstr. 10* 🕾 *0341/216–990* ⊕ *www.mdbk.de* 🔖 *€5, €6–€8 for special exhibits* ⊙ *Tues. and Thurs.–Sun. 10–6, Wed. noon–8.*

Nikolaikirche (*St. Nicholas Church*). This church with its undistinguished facade was center stage during the demonstrations that helped bring down the Communist regime. Every Monday for months before the government collapsed, thousands of citizens gathered in front of the church chanting "Wir sind das Volk" ("We are the people"). Inside are a soaring Gothic choir and nave. Note the unusual patterned ceiling supported by classical pillars that end in palm-tree-like flourishes. Martin Luther is said to have preached from the ornate 16th-century pulpit. ■ TIP→ The prayers for peace that began the revolution in 1989 are still held on Monday at 5 pm. ⊠ *Nikolaikirchhof* ☎ *0341/960–5270* ⊠ *Free* ⊗ *Mon.–Sat. 10–6; Sun. services at 9:30, 11:15, and 5.*

TOURING TIPS

Information: The friendly tourist-information office is at Augustusplatz 1. If you plan to visit any museums, consider the Leipzigcard.

People-watching: Take a seat upstairs—above the elephant heads—at the coffeehouse Riquet and watch the world go by.

Typically Leipzig: Drink a Gose and try the "Meadowlark" pastry.

16

Fodor'sChoice ★ **Thomaskirche** (*St. Thomas's Church*). Bach was choirmaster at this Gothic church for 27 years, and Martin Luther preached here on Whitsunday 1539, signaling the arrival of Protestantism in Leipzig. Originally the center of a 13th-century monastery, the tall church (rebuilt in the 15th century) now stands by itself. Bach wrote most of his cantatas for the church's famous boys' choir, the Thomanerchor, which was founded in the 13th century; the church continues as the choir's home as well as a center of Bach tradition.

The great music Bach wrote during his Leipzig years commanded little attention in his lifetime, and when he died he was given a simple grave, without a headstone, in the city's Johannisfriedhof (St. John Cemetery). It wasn't until 1894 that an effort was made to find where the great composer lay buried, and after a thorough, macabre search, his coffin was removed to the Johanniskirche. That church was destroyed by Allied bombs in December 1943, and Bach subsequently found his final resting place in the church he would have selected: the Thomaskirche. You can listen to the famous boys' choir during the *Motette*, a service with a special emphasis on choral music.

Bach's 12 children and the infant Richard Wagner were baptized in the early-17th-century font; Karl Marx and Friedrich Engels also stood before this same font, godfathers to Karl Liebknecht, who grew up to be a revolutionary as well.

In front of the church is a memorial to Felix Mendelssohn, rebuilt with funds collected by the Leipzig Citizens Initiative. The Nazis destroyed the original in front of the Gewandhaus. ⊠ *Thomaskirchhof* ☎ *0341/222–240* ⊕ *www.thomaskirche.org* ⊠ *Free, Motette €2* ⊗ *Daily 9–6; Motette Fri. at 6 pm, Sat. at 3; no Motette during Saxony summer vacation (usually mid-July–Aug.).*

Bach was choirmaster at the Thomaskirche and is buried here. Bach wrote cantatas for the boys' choir, which you can still hear performed.

WORTH NOTING

Bach-Museum im Bach-Archiv Leipzig (*Bach Museum at the Bach Archives Leipzig*). The Bach family home, the old Bosehaus, stands opposite the Thomaskirche, and is now a museum devoted to the composer's life and work. The newly renovated museum offers several interactive displays; arranging the instrumental parts of Bach's hymns is by far the most entertaining. ✉ *Thomaskirchhof 16* ☎ *0341/913–7200* ⊕ *www. bach-leipzig.de (German only)* 💳 *€6* ⊘ *Tues.–Sun. 10–6.*

Hauptbahnhof. With 26 platforms, Leipzig's main train station is Europe's largest railhead. It was built in 1915 and is now a protected monument, but modern commerce rules in its bilevel shopping mall (the Promenaden). The only thing the complex is missing is a pub. Many of the shops and restaurants stay open until 10 pm and are open on Sunday. Thanks to the historic backdrop, this is one of the most beautiful shopping experiences in East Germany. ✉ *Willy-Brandt-Pl.* ☎ *0341/141–270 for mall, 0341/9968–3275 for train station.*

Leipziger Universitätsturm (*Leipzig University Tower*). Towering over Leipzig's city center is this 470-foot-high structure, which houses administrative offices and lecture rooms. Dubbed the "jagged tooth" or "wisdom tooth" by some University of Leipzig students, it supposedly represents an open book. Students were also largely responsible for changing the university's name, replacing its postwar title, Karl Marx University, with the original one. The **Augustusplatz** spreads out below the university tower like a space-age campus. ✉ *Augustuspl. 9.*

Mendelssohn Haus (*Mendelssohn House*). The only surviving residence of the composer Felix Mendelssohn-Bartholdy is now Germany's only museum dedicated to him. Mendelssohn's last residence and the place of his death has been preserved in its original 19th-century state. Concerts are held every Sunday at 11. ✉ *Goldschmidtstr. 12* ☎ *0341/127-0294* ⊕ *www.mendelssohn-haus.de* 🎫 *€4.50, concert €15* ☉ *Daily 10–6.*

Museum in der Runden Ecke (*Museum in the Round Corner*). This building once served as the headquarters of the city's detachment of the Communist secret police, the dreaded *Staatssicherheitsdienst.* The exhibition *Stasi—Macht und Banalität* (Stasi—Power and Banality) presents not only the Stasi's offices and surveillance work, but also hundreds of documents revealing the magnitude of its interests in citizens' private lives. Though the material is in German, the items and atmosphere convey an impression of what life under the regime might have been like. The exhibit about the death penalty in the GDR is particularly chilling. ✉ *Dittrichring 24* ☎ *0341/961–2443* ⊕ *www. runde-ecke-leipzig.de* 🎫 *Free; €4 with tour in English, by appointment* ☉ *Daily 10–6.*

Museum zum Arabischen Kaffeebaum (*Arabic Coffee Tree Museum*). This museum and café-restaurant tells the fascinating history of coffee culture in Europe, particularly in Saxony. The café is one of the oldest on the continent, and once proudly served coffee to such luminaries as Gotthold Lessing, Schumann, Goethe, and Liszt. The museum features many paintings, Arabian coffee vessels, and coffeehouse games. It also explains the basic principles of roasting coffee. The café is divided into traditional Viennese, French, and Arabian coffeehouses, but no coffee is served in the Arabian section, which is only a display. ▥ TIP➜ The cake is better and the seating more comfortable in the Viennese part. ✉ *Kleine Fleischerg. 4* ☎ *0341/960–2632* ⊕ *www. coffe-baum.de* 🎫 *Free* ☉ *Tues.–Sun. 11–5.*

WHERE TO EAT

$
GERMAN
Fodor's Choice
★

✕ **Auerbachs Keller.** The most famous of Leipzig's restaurants is actually two restaurants: one that's upscale, international, and gourmet (down the stairs to the right), and a rowdy beer cellar (to the left) specializing in hearty Saxon fare, mostly roasted meat dishes. The fine-dining section's five-course menus (€110) are worth a splurge, and it also has a good wine list. The beer cellar has been around since 1530, making it one of the oldest continually running restaurants on the continent. Goethe immortalized one of the vaulted historic rooms

---

GOSE

Bismark once remarked that "Gose isn't a beer, it is a way of viewing the world." *Gose,* which originated in Goslar, is an obscure, top-fermented wheat beer flavored by adding coriander and salt to the wort. Gose came to Leipzig in 1738, and was so popular that by the end of the 1800s it was considered the local brewing style. It's extremely difficult to make, and after beer production stopped during the war (due to grain shortages), the tradition seemed lost. Today, through the efforts of Lothar Goldhahn at the Bayrischer Bahnhof, Gose production is steaming ahead in Leipzig.

in his *Faust*, and Bach was a regular here because of the location halfway between the Thomaskirche and the Nikolaikirche. $ *Average main: €15 ⊠ Mädlerpassage, Grimmaische Str. 2–4 ☎0341/216–100 ⌂ Reservations essential ⊘ Closed Mon.*

$ ✕**Barthels Hof.** The English-language menu at this restaurant explains
GERMAN   not only the cuisine but also the history of Leipzig. Waitresses wear traditional *Trachten*, but the rooms are quite modern. With a prominent location on the Markt, the restaurant is popular with locals, especially for the incredible breakfast buffet. Barthels has managed to elevate the local *Leipziger Allerlei* (vegetables and crayfish in beef bouillon) to an art form. Enjoy a meal here with a fresh Bauer Gose. $ *Average main: €12 ⊠ Hainstr. 1 ☎0341/141–310.*

$ ✕**Gasthaus & Gosebrauerei Bayrischer Bahnhof.** Hidden on the far south-
GERMAN   east edge of the city center, the Bayrischer Bahnhof was the terminus of the first rail link between Saxony and Bavaria. The brewery here is the heart of a cultural renaissance, and is the only place currently brewing Gose in Leipzig. The restaurant is well worth a visit for its solid Saxon and German cuisine. Brewery accents surface in dishes such as rump steak with black-beer sauce, and the onion rings can't be beat. If the Gose is too sour for your tastes, order it with one of the sweet syrups—raspberry is the best. Groups of four or more can try dinner prepared in a *Römertopf* (a terra-cotta baking dish; the first was brought to Germany by the Romans, centuries ago). ▮TIP➜ **In summer the beer garden is a pleasant place to get away from the bustle of the city center.** $ *Average main: €11 ⊠ Bayrischer Pl. 1 ☎0341/124–5760 ⊕ www.bayrischer-bahnhof.de ▭ No credit cards.*

$ ✕**Kaffeehaus Riquet.** The restored art nouveau house dates from 1908.
CAFÉ   Riquet is a company that has had dealings in the coffee trade in Africa and East Asia since 1745, as is indicated by the large elephant heads adorning the facade of the building. The upstairs section houses a pleasant Viennese-style coffeehouse—the best views are had from up here—while downstairs is noisier and more active. ▮TIP➜ **Afternoon coffee and cake are one of Leipzig's special pleasures (in a country with an obsession for coffee and cake), and Riquet is the best place in the city to satisfy the urge.** $ *Average main: €4 ⊠ Schulmachergässchen 1 ☎0341/961–0000 ▭ No credit cards ⊘ No dinner.*

$ ✕**Thüringer Hof.** One of Germany's oldest restaurants and pubs (dating
GERMAN   back to 1454) served its hearty Thuringian and Saxon fare to Martin Luther and the like—who certainly had more than a mere pint of the beers on tap. The menu in the reconstructed, cavernous, and always buzzing dining hall doesn't exactly offer gourmet cuisine, but rather an impressively enormous variety of game, fish, and bratwurst dishes. The Thuringian sausages (served with either sauerkraut and boiled potatoes or onions and mashed potatoes) and the famous Thuringian *Sauerbraten* (beef marinated in a sour essence) are musts. $ *Average main: €12 ⊠ Burgstr. 19 ☎0341/994–4999.*

$ ✕**Zill's Tunnel.** The "tunnel" refers to the barrel-ceiling ground-floor
GERMAN   restaurant, where foaming glasses of excellent local beer are served with a smile. The friendly staff will also help you decipher the Old Saxon descriptions of the menu's traditional dishes. Upstairs there's

EATING WELL IN SAXONY

The cuisine of the region is hearty and seasonal, and almost every town has a unique specialty unavailable outside the immediate area. Look for *Sächsische Sauerbraten* (marinated sour beef roast), spicy *Thüringer Bratwurst* (sausage), *Schlesische Himmelreich* (ham and pork roast smothered in baked fruit and white sauce, served with dumplings), *Teichlmauke* (mashed potato in broth), *Blauer Karpfe* (blue carp, marinated in vinegar), and *Raacher Maad* (grated and boiled potatoes fried in butter and served with blueberries). Venison and wild boar are standards in forest and mountainous areas, and lamb from Saxony-Anhalt is particularly good. In Thuringia, *Klösse* (potato dumplings) are virtually a religion.

Eastern Germany is experiencing a renaissance in the art of northern German brewing. The first stop for any beer lover should be the Bayrische Bahnhof in Leipzig, to give Gose a try. Dresden's Brauhaus Watzke, Quedlinburg's Lüddebräu, and even the Landskron Brauerei in Görlitz are bringing craft brewing back to a region inundated with mass-produced brew.

Saxony has cultivated vineyards for more than 800 years, and is known for its dry red and white wines, among them Müller-Thurgau, Weissburgunder, Ruländer, and the spicy Traminer. The Sächsische Weinstrasse (Saxon Wine Route) follows the course of the Elbe River from Diesbar-Seusslitz (north of Meissen) to Pirna (southeast of Dresden). Meissen, Radebeul, and Dresden have upscale wine restaurants, and wherever you see a green seal with the letter *S* and grapes depicted, good local wine is being served. One of the best-kept secrets in German wine making is the Salle-Unstrut region, which produces spicy Silvaner and Rieslings.

a larger wine restaurant with an open fireplace. Try the pan-seared *Maischolle*, a type of flatfish. ⑤ *Average main: €13 ⊠ Barfussgässchen 9 ☎ 0341/960–2078.*

WHERE TO STAY

$$
HOTEL
Fodor's Choice
★
🏨 **Hotel Fürstenhof Leipzig.** The city's grandest hotel—part of Starwood's Luxury Collection—is inside the renowned Löhr-Haus, a revered old mansion 500 meters from the main train station on the ring road surrounding the city center. **Pros:** an elegant full-service hotel with stunning rooms; safes big enough for a laptop are a nice touch. **Cons:** the ring road can be noisy at night, especially on Friday and Saturday. ⑤ *Rooms from: €149 ⊠ Tröndlinring 8 ☎ 0341/140–370 ⊕ www.luxurycollection.com ⤵ 80 rooms, 12 suites.*

$
HOTEL
🏨 **Ringhotel Adagio Leipzig.** The quiet Adagio, tucked away behind the facade of a 19th-century city mansion, is centrally located between the Grassimuseum and the Neues Gewandhaus. **Pros:** large rooms with luxurious bathrooms; breakfast available all day. **Cons:** room decor is slightly bland; hotel not built to accommodate disabled guests. ⑤ *Rooms from: €75 ⊠ Seeburgstr. 96 ☎ 0341/216–690 ⊕ www.hotel-adagio.de ⤵ 30 rooms, 2 suites, 1 apartment ⑩ Breakfast.*

NIGHTLIFE AND THE ARTS
THE ARTS

Krystallpalast. This variety theater features a blend of circus, vaudeville, and comedy that is fairly accessible for non-German speakers. ✉ *Magazing. 4* ☎ *0341/140–660* ⊕ *www.krystallpalast.de.*

Leipziger Pfeffermühle. One of Germany's most famous cabarets has a lively bar off a courtyard opposite the Thomaskirche. On pleasant evenings the courtyard fills with benches and tables, and the scene rivals the indoor performance for entertainment. ✉ *Katharinenstr. 17* ☎ *0341/960–3196* ⊕ *www. kabarett-leipziger-pfeffermuehle.de.*

LEIPZIGER LERCHE

As far back as the 18th century, Leipzig was known for a bizarre culinary specialty: roast meadowlark in crust. The dish was so popular that Leipzig consumed more than 400,000 meadowlarks every month. When the king of Saxony banned lark hunting in 1876, Leipzig's industrious bakers came up with a substitute: a baked shortcrust pastry filled with almonds, nuts, and strawberries. Today, the substitute Meadowlark, when prepared correctly, is a delicious treat—found only in Leipzig.

Neues Gewandhaus. This controversial piece of architecture is home to an undeniably splendid orchestra. Tickets to concerts are difficult to obtain unless you reserve well in advance. Sometimes spare tickets are available at the box office a half hour before the evening performance. ✉ *Augustuspl. 8* ☎ *0341/127–0280* ⊕ *www.gewandhaus.de.*

NIGHTLIFE

With a vast assortment of restaurants, cafés, and clubs to match the city's exceptional musical and literary offerings, Leipzig is a fun city at night. The *Kneipenszene* (pub scene) is centered on the **Drallewatsch** (a Saxon slang word for "going out"), the small streets and alleys around Grosse and Kleine Fleischergasse and the Barfussgässchen.

Moritzbastei. A magnet for young people, this is reputedly Europe's largest student club, with bars, a disco, a café, a theater, and a cinema. Nonstudents are welcome—if you're cool enough. ✉ *Universitätsstr. 9* ☎ *0341/702–590.*

Schauhaus. A favorite hangout among the city's business elite, this stylish bar serves great cocktails. ✉ *Bosestr. 1* ☎ *0341/960–0596.*

Spizz Keller. This hip place is one of the city's top dance clubs. ✉ *Markt 9* ☎ *0341/960–8043.*

Tanzpalast. In the august setting of the *Schauspielhaus* (city theater), the Tanzpalast attracts a thirtysomething crowd. This was *the* place to be seen in GDR Leipzig. ✉ *Bosestr. 1* ☎ *0341/960–0596.*

Weinstock. This upscale bar, pub, and restaurant in a Renaissance building offers a huge selection of good wines. ✉ *Markt 7* ☎ *0341/1406–0606.*

SHOPPING

Small streets leading off the Markt attest to Leipzig's rich trading past. Tucked in among them are glass-roof arcades of surprising beauty and elegance, including the wonderfully restored **Specks Hof, Barthels Hof, Jägerhof,** and the **Passage zum Sachsenplatz.** Invent a headache and step into the *Apotheke* (pharmacy) at Hainstrasse 9—it is spectacularly art nouveau, with finely etched and stained glass and rich mahogany. For more glimpses into the past, check out the antiquarian bookstores of the nearby **Neumarkt Passage.**

Hauptbahnhof. Leipzig's main train station has more than 150 shops, restaurants, and cafés, all open Monday through Saturday 9:30 am–10 pm; many are also open on Sunday, with the same hours. ⊠ *Willy-Brandt-Pl.*

DRESDEN

25 km (16 miles) southeast of Meissen, 140 km (87 miles) southeast of Leipzig, 193 km (120 miles) south of Berlin.

Sitting in baroque splendor on a wide sweep of the Elbe River, Dresden has been the capital of Saxony since the 15th century, although most of its architectural masterpieces date from the 18th century and the reigns of Augustus the Strong and his son, Frederick Augustus II. Today the city's yellow and pale-green facades are enormously appealing, and their mere presence is even more overwhelming when you compare what you see with photographs of Dresden from February 1945. That's when Allied bombing destroyed the Altstadt (Old City) overnight. But Dresden has risen from these ashes, regaining its reputation as "the Florence on the Elbe."

16

Although parts of the city center still look stuck between demolition and construction, the city's rebuilding is an enormous tribute to Dresdeners' skill, dedication, and thoroughness. The resemblance of today's riverside to Dresden cityscapes painted by Canaletto in the mid-1700s is remarkable. Unfortunately, war-inflicted gaps in other parts of the city are too big to be closed anytime soon. Main sights are contained within the Altstadt. On the other side of the river, the Neustadt (New City), which escaped wartime destruction, is the place to go out at night.

GETTING HERE AND AROUND

Dresden is two hours from Berlin on the Hamburg-Berlin-Prague-Vienna train line. The city's international airport serves mostly European destinations with budget airlines. The newly completed Norman Foster train station is a short walk along the Prager Strasse from the city center. Streetcars are cheap and efficient.

Dresden bus tours (in German and English, run by the Dresdner Verkehrsbetriebe) leave from Postplatz daily at 10, 11:30, and 3; the Stadtrundfahrt Dresden bus tours (also in German and English) leave from Theaterplatz/Augustusbrücke (April–October, daily 9:30–5, every 30 minutes; November–March, daily 10–3, every hour) and stop at most sights.

FESTIVALS

Filmnächte am Elbufer (*Elbe Riverside Film Nights*). In addition to the annual film festival in April, open-air Filmnächte am Elbufer take place on the bank of the Elbe from late June to late August. ⊠ *Am Königsufer, next to State Ministry of Finance* ☎ *0351/899–320.*

Jazz. May brings an annual international festival of Dixieland jazz, and the Jazz Autumn festival follows in October. ⊠ *Altmarkt.*

TIMING

A long full day is sufficient for a quick tour of historic Dresden with a brief visit to one of the museums. The focus of your day should be a visit to the Grünes Gewölbe. If you plan to explore any of the museums at length, such as the Zwinger, or take a guided tour of the Semperoper, you'll need more time. One of the best ways to see Dresden is as a stop between Berlin and Prague.

ESSENTIALS

Tour Information Dresdner Verkehrsbetriebe AG ⊠ *Service Center, Postpl. 1* ☎ *0351/857–2201.* **Stadtrundfahrt Dresden** ⊠ *Theaterpl.* ☎ *0351/899–5650.*

Visitor Information Dresden Tourist ⊠ *Schlossstr. 1, inside the Kulturpalast* ☎ *0351/491–920* ⊕ *www.dresden.de.*

EXPLORING
TOP ATTRACTIONS

Fodor's Choice ★ **Frauenkirche** (*Church of Our Lady*). This masterpiece of baroque church architecture was completed in 1743. The huge dome set on a smaller square base, known as the Stone Bell, was the inspiration of George Bähr, who designed the church to be built "as if it was a single stone from the base to the top." On February 15, 1945, two days after the bombing of Dresden, the burned-out shell of the magnificent Stone Bell collapsed. For the following five decades the remains of the church, a pile of rubble, remained a gripping memorial to the horrors of war. In a move shocking to the East German authorities, who organized all public demonstrations, a group of young people spontaneously met here on February 13, 1982, for a candlelight vigil for peace.

Although the will to rebuild the church was strong, the political and economic situation in the GDR prevented it. It wasn't until the reunification of Germany that Dresden began to seriously consider reconstruction. In the early 1990s a citizens' initiative, joined by the Lutheran Church of Saxony and the city of Dresden, decided to rebuild the church using the original stones. The goal of completing the church by 2006, Dresden's 800th anniversary, seemed insurmountable. Money soon started pouring in from around the globe, however, and work began. The rubble was cleared away, and the size and shape of each stone were cataloged. Computer-imaging technology helped place each recovered stone in its original location. On Sunday, October 30, 2005 (almost a year ahead of schedule), Dresden's skyline became a little more complete with the consecration of the Frauenkirche. Leading the service was the Bishop of Coventry. Although the church is usually open to all, it closes frequently for concerts and other events. Check the English-language schedule next to Entrance D. ⊠ *An der Frauenkirche* ☎ *0351/498–1131* ⊕ *www.frauenkirche-dresden.org* ✉ *Free, cupola and tower €8, audio guides in English €2.50* ☉ *Weekdays 10–noon and 1–6, cupola and tower daily 10–6.*

Residenzschloss (*Royal Palace*). Restoration work is still under way behind the Renaissance facade of this former royal palace, much of which was built between 1709 and 1722. Some of the finished rooms in the **Georgenbau** (Count George Wing) hold historical exhibits, among them an excellent one on the reconstruction of the palace itself. The

16

palace's main gateway, the Georgentor, has an enormous statue of the fully armed Saxon count George. ▪TIP➔ From April through October, the palace's old Hausmannsturm (Hausmann Tower) offers a wonderful view of the city and the Elbe River. The main attraction in the Royal Palace, though, is the world-famous **Grünes Gewölbe** (Green Vault). Named after a green room in the palace of Augustus the Strong, the collection is divided into two sections.

The palace also houses the **Münzkabinett** (Coin Museum) and the **Kupferstichkabinett** (Museum of Prints and Drawings), with more than 500,000 pieces of art spanning several centuries. Changing exhibits at the Kupferstichkabinett have presented masterworks by Albrecht Dürer, Peter Paul Rubens, and Jan van Eyck; 20th-century art by Otto Dix, Edvard Munch, and Ernst Ludwig Kirchner; East European art; and some Southeast Asian prints. The **Türckische Cammer** (Turkish Chamber) comprises a huge number of Ottoman artifacts collected by Saxon dukes over centuries. It's worth going just to see the six carved Arabian horses, bedecked with jeweled armor. ⊠ *Schlosspl.* ☎ *0351/491–4619* ⊕ *www.skd.museum* 🎫 *All museums and collections except Historic Green Vault €10; Historic Green Vault €14* ⊗ *Wed.–Mon. 10–6; Historic Green Vault by appointment.*

Historisches Grünes Gewölbe (*Historic Green Vault*). This section of the castle most reflects Augustus the Strong's obsession with art as a symbol of power. The intricately restored baroque interior is an integral part of the presentation, highlighting the objects in the collection. The last section of the museum houses the Jewel Room, which displays the ceremonial crown jewels of Augustus the Strong and his son. Access to the Historic Green Vault is limited to 100 visitors per hour and is by appointment only, reserved by phone or online. ⊠ *Taschenberg 2* ☎ *0351/4919–2285 for tours* ⊕ *www.skd.museum* 🎫 *€14* ☉ *By appointment.*

Neues Grünes Gewölbe (*New Green Vault*). The exquisite collection here consists of objets d'art fashioned from gold, silver, ivory, amber, and other precious and semiprecious materials. Among the crown jewels are the world's largest "green" diamond, 41 carats in weight, and a dazzling group of tiny gem-studded figures called *Hofstaat zu Delhi am Geburtstag des Grossmoguls Aureng-Zeb* (the Court at Delhi during the Birthday of the Great Mogul Aureng-Zeb). The unwieldy name gives a false idea of the size of the work, dating from 1708; some parts of the tableau are so small they can be admired only through a magnifying glass. Somewhat larger and less delicate is the drinking bowl of Ivan the Terrible, perhaps the most sensational artifact in this extraordinary museum. ⊠ *Taschenberg 2* ⊕ *www.skd.museum.*

Semperoper (*Semper Opera House*). One of Germany's best-known and most popular theaters, this magnificent opera house saw the premieres of Richard Wagner's *Rienzi, Der Fliegende Holländer,* and *Tannhäuser* and Richard Strauss's *Salome, Elektra,* and *Der Rosenkavalier.* The Dresden architect Gottfried Semper built the house in 1838–41 in Italian Renaissance style, then saw his work destroyed in a fire caused by a careless lamplighter. Semper had to flee Dresden after participating in a democratic uprising, but his son Manfred rebuilt the theater in the neo-Renaissance style you see today, though even Manfred Semper's version had to be rebuilt after the devastating bombing raid of February 1945. On the 40th anniversary of that raid—February 13, 1985—the Semperoper reopened with a performance of *Der Freischütz,* by Carl Maria von Weber, the last opera performed in the building before its destruction. There is a statue of Weber, another artist who did much to make Dresden a leading center of German music and culture, outside the opera house in the shadow of the Zwinger. Even if you're no opera buff, the Semper's lavish interior can't fail to impress. Velvet, brocade, and well-crafted imitation marble create an atmosphere of intimate luxury (it seats 1,323). Guided tours (must be reserved in advance) of the building are offered throughout the day, depending on the opera's rehearsal schedule. Check the website for schedules. Tours begin at the entrance to your right as you face the Elbe River. ⊠ *Theaterpl. 2* ☎ *0351/491–1496* ⊕ *www.semperoper-erleben.de* 🎫 *Tour €9.*

Fodor's Choice ★ **Zwinger** (*Bailey*). Dresden's magnificent baroque showpiece is entered by way of the mighty Kronentor (Crown Gate), off Ostra-Allee. Augustus the Strong hired a small army of artists and artisans to create a "pleasure ground" worthy of the Saxon court on the site of the former bailey, part of the city fortifications. The artisans worked under the direction

The Frauenkirche was painstakingly rebuilt after it was reduced to rubble in the bombing of Dresden.

of the architect Matthäus Daniel Pöppelmann, who came reluctantly out of retirement to design what would be his greatest work, begun in 1707 and completed in 1728. Completely enclosing a central courtyard filled with lawns, pools, and fountains, the complex is made up of six linked pavilions, one of which boasts a carillon of Meissen bells, hence its name: Glockenspielpavillon.

The Zwinger is quite a scene—a riot of garlands, nymphs, and other baroque ornamentation and sculpture. Wide staircases beckon to galleried walks and to the romantic Nymphenbad, a coyly hidden courtyard where statues of nude women perch in alcoves to protect themselves from a fountain that spits unexpectedly. The Zwinger once had an open view of the riverbank, but the Semper Opera House now occupies that side. Stand in the center of this quiet oasis, where the city's roar is kept at bay by the outer wings of the structure, and imagine the court festivities once held here. ⊠ *Ostra–Allee* ⊕ *www. skd.museum* ☉ *Tues.–Sun. 10–6.*

Gemäldegalerie Alte Meister (*Gallery of Old Masters*). This museum, in the northwestern corner of the complex, was built to house portions of the royal art collections. Among the priceless paintings are works by Dürer, Holbein, Jan van Eyck, Rembrandt, Rubens, Van Dyck, Hals, Vermeer, Raphael, Titian, Giorgione, Veronese, Velázquez, Murillo, Canaletto, and Watteau. On the wall of the entrance archway you'll see an inscription in Russian, one of the few amusing reminders of World War II in Dresden. It rhymes in Russian: "Museum checked. No mines. Chanutin did the checking." Chanutin, presumably, was the Russian soldier responsible for checking one of Germany's greatest art galleries for anything more explosive than a Rubens nude. The highlight of the collection is Raphael's *Sistine Madonna,* whose mournful look is slightly less famous than the two cherubs who were added by Raphael after the painting was completed, in order to fill an empty space at the bottom. ☏ *0351/491–4679* ✉ *€12* ☉ *Tues.–Sun. 10–6.*

Porzellansammlung (*Porcelain Collection*). Stretching from the curved gallery that adjoins the Glockenspielpavillon to the long gallery on the east side, this collection is considered one of the best of its kind in the world. The focus, naturally, is on Dresden and Meissen china, but there are also outstanding examples of Japanese, Chinese, and Korean porcelain. ☏ *0351/491–4619* ✉ *€6* ☉ *Tues.–Sun. 10–6.*

Rüstkammer (*Armory*). Holding medieval and Renaissance suits of armor and weapons, the Rüstkammer is in two parts: the main exhibit in the Semperbau and the Türckische Cammer in the Residenzschloss. ☏ *0351/491–4619* ✉ *€10* ☉ *Tues.–Sun. 10–6.*

WORTH NOTING

Albertinum. Named after Saxony's King Albert, who between 1884 and 1887 converted a royal arsenal into a suitable setting for the treasures he and his forebears had collected, this massive, imperial-style building houses one of the world's great galleries featuring works from the romantic period to the modern. The Galerie Neue Meister (New Masters Gallery) has an extensive collection ranging from Caspar David Friedrich and Gauguin to Ernst Kirchner and Georg Baselitz. ✉ *Am Neumarkt, Brühlsche Terrasse* ☏ *0351/49849–14973* ⊕ *www.skd. museum* ✉ *€10* ☉ *Wed.–Mon. 10–6.*

Altmarkt (*Old Market Square*). Although dominated by the nearby, unappealing, Kulturpalast (Palace of Culture), the Altmarkt is a fascinating concrete leftover from the 1970s (check out the workers and peasants GDR mosaic); the broad square and its surrounding streets are the true center of Dresden. The colonnaded beauty (from the Stalinist-era architecture of the early 1950s) survived the efforts of city planners to turn it into a huge outdoor parking lot. The rebuilt **Rathaus** (Town Hall) is here (go around the front to see bullet holes in the statuary), as is the yellow-stucco, 18th-century Landhaus, which contains the Stadtmuseum Dresden im Landhaus. ⚠ Dresdners joke that you should never park your car here because the square is under almost constant construction and you might never find it again.

Augustusbrücke (*Augustus Bridge*). This bridge, which spans the river in front of the Katholische Hofkirche, is the reconstruction of a 17th-century baroque bridge blown up by the SS shortly before the end of World War II. It was restored and renamed for Georgi Dimitroff, one of the Bulgarian Communists accused by the Nazis of instigating the Reichstag fire; after the fall of Communism the original name, honoring Augustus the Strong, was reinstated.

Johanneum. At one time the royal stables, this 16th-century building now houses the **Verkehrsmuseum** (Transportation Museum), a collection of historic conveyances, including vintage automobiles and engines. The former **stable exercise yard,** behind the Johanneum and enclosed by elegant Renaissance arcades, was used during the 16th century as an open-air festival ground. A ramp leading up from the courtyard made it possible for royalty to reach the upper story to view the jousting below without having to dismount. More popular even than jousting in those days was *Ringelstechen*, a risky pursuit in which riders at full gallop had to catch small rings on their lances. Horses and riders often came to grief in the narrow confines of the stable yard.

■ TIP➔ On the outside wall of the Johanneum is a remarkable example of porcelain art: a 336-foot-long Meissen tile mural of a royal procession. More than 100 members of the royal Saxon house of Wettin, half of them on horseback, are represented on the giant mosaic, known as the "Procession of Princes," which is made of 25,000 porcelain tiles, painted in 1904–07 after a design by Wilhelm Walther. The representations are in chronological order: at 1694, Augustus the Strong's horse is trampling a rose, the symbol of Martin Luther and the Protestant Reformation. The Johanneum is reached by steps leading down from the Brühlsche Terrasse. ⊠ *Am Neumarkt at Augustusstr. 1* ☎ *0351/86440* ⊕ *www.verkehrsmuseum-dresden.de* ⌑ *€7* ☾ *Tues.–Sun. 10–5.*

Katholische Hofkirche (*Catholic Court Church*). The largest Catholic church in Saxony is also known as the Cathedral of St. Trinitatis. Frederick Augustus II (who reigned 1733–63) brought architects and builders from Italy to construct a Catholic church in a city that had been the first large center of Lutheran Protestantism (like his father, Frederick Augustus II had to convert to Catholicism to be eligible to wear the Polish crown). Inside, the treasures include a beautiful stone pulpit by the royal sculptor Balthasar Permoser and a painstakingly restored 250-year-old organ, said to be one of the finest ever to come from the mountain workshops of the famous Silbermann family. In the cathedral's crypt are the tombs of 49 Saxon rulers and a reliquary containing the heart of Augustus the Strong, which is rumored to start beating if a beautiful woman comes near. ⊠ *Schlosspl.* ☎ *0351/484–4712* ⌑ *Free* ☾ *Mon.–Thurs. 9–5, Fri. 1–5, Sat. 10–5, Sun. noon–4:30.*

Kreuzkirche (*Cross Church*). Soaring high above the Altmarkt, the richly decorated tower of the baroque Kreuzkirche dates back to 1792. The city's main Protestant church is still undergoing postwar restoration, but the tower and church hall are open to the public. A famous boys' choir, the Kreuzchor, performs here regularly (check website or call for times). ⊠ *Altmarkt* ☎ *0351/439–390* ⌑ *Tower €1.50* ☾ *Nov.–Mar., weekdays 10–4, Sun. 11–4; Apr.–Oct., daily 10–6.*

Pfund's Molkerei (*Pfund's Dairy Shop*). This decorative 19th-century shop has been a Dresden institution since 1880, and offers a wide assortment of cheese and other goods. The shop is renowned for its intricate tile mosaics on the floor and walls. Pfund's is also famous for introducing pasteurized milk to the industry; it invented milk soap and specially treated milk for infants as early as 1900. ⊠ *Bautzener Str. 79* ☎ *0351/808–080* ⊕ *www.pfunds.de* ☾ *Mon.–Sat. 10–6, Sun. 10–3.*

16

Panometer Dresden. You can step back in time and get a sense of how Dresden looked in 1756 by viewing this 360-degree panorama portrait of the city. Artist Yadegar Asisi's monumental 105-by-27-meter painting locates the viewer on the tower of the Stadtschloss, with extremely detailed vistas in all directions. The painting is located in an old natural-gas store. To get here from Dresden Main Station, take S1 or S2 to the station Dresden-Reick/Asisi Panometer (five minutes). From the Altmarkt take Tram No. 1 or 2 to the Liebstädterstrasse stop (15 minutes). ⊠ *Gasanstaltstr. 8b* ☎ *0351/860–3940* ⊕ *www.asisi.de* ✆*€10* ☽ *Tues.–Fri. 9–7, weekends 10–8.*

Stadtmuseum Dresden im Landhaus (*Dresden City Museum at the Landhaus*). The city's small but fascinating municipal museum tells the ups and downs of Dresden's turbulent past—from the dark Middle Ages to the bombing of Dresden in February 1945. There are many peculiar exhibits on display, such as an American 250-kilogram bomb and a stove made from an Allied bomb casing. The building has the most interesting fire escape in the city. ⊠ *Wilsdruffer Str. 2* ☎ *0351/656–480* ⊕ *www.stmd.de* ✆*€5* ☽ *Tues.–Sun. 10–6 (Fri. until 8).*

WHERE TO EAT

$$ ✕ **Alte Meister.** Set in the historic mansion of the architect who rebuilt the
GERMAN Zwinger, and named after the school of medieval painters that includes Dürer, Holbein, and Rembrandt, the Alte Meister has a sophisticated Old World flair that charms locals and tourists alike. The food is very current, despite the decor, and the light German nouvelle cuisine with careful touches of Asian spices and ingredients has earned chef Dirk Wende critical praise. In summer this is one of the city's premier dining spots, offering a grand view of the Semperoper from a shaded terrace. ⑤ *Average main: €18* ⊠ *Theaterpl. 1a* ☎ *0351/481–0426.*

$ ✕ **Ball und Brauhaus Watzke.** One of the city's oldest microbreweries, the
GERMAN Watzke offers a great reprieve from Dresden's mass-produced Radeberger. Several different homemade beers are on tap—you can even help brew one. Tours of the brewery cost €5 with a tasting, or €12.50 with a meal, and you can get your beer to go in a 1- or 2-liter jug called a *Siphon.* The food is hearty, contemporary Saxon. When the weather is nice, enjoy the fantastic panoramic view of Dresden from the beer garden. ⑤ *Average main: €12* ⊠ *Koetzschenbroderstr. 1* ☎ *0351/852–920.*

$ ✕ **Sophienkeller.** One of the liveliest restaurants in town re-creates an
GERMAN 18th-century beer cellar in the basement of the Taschenberg Palace. The furniture and porcelain are as rustic as the food is traditional, including the typically Saxon *Gesindeessen* (rye bread, panfried with mustard, slices of pork, and mushrooms, baked with cheese). The Sophienkeller is popular with larger groups; you might have to wait if you're a party of three or fewer. During the wait, check out the bread baker near the entrance. ⑤ *Average main: €12* ⊠ *Taschenbergpalais, Taschenberg 3* ☎ *0351/497–260.*

$ ✕ **Watzke Brauereiausschank am Goldenen Reiter.** Watzke microbrewery
GERMAN operates this smaller restaurant with the same beer and hearty menu, directly across from the Goldene Reiter statue of Augustus the Strong. ⑤ *Average main: €12* ⊠ *Hauptstr. 11* ☎ *0351/810–6820.*

16

WHERE TO STAY

$ ▦ **art'otel Dresden.** This hotel keeps the promise of its name: it's all mod-
HOTEL   ern, designed by Italian interior architect Denis Santachiara, and decorated with more than 600 works of art by Dresden-born painter and
sculptor A R. Penck. **Pros:** art elements make the hotel fun. **Cons:** bathrooms have an opaque window into the room; decor is not for everyone.
⑨ *Rooms from: €99* ✉ *Ostra-Allee 33* ☎ *0351/49220* ⊕ *www.artotels.
com* ⤳ *155 rooms, 19 suites* ⑩ *Breakfast.*

$$ ▦ **Hotel Bülow-Residenz.** One of the most intimate first-class hotels in
HOTEL   eastern Germany, the Bülow-Residenz is in a baroque palace built in
1730 by a wealthy Dresden city official. **Pros:** extremely helpful staff.
Cons: a/c can be noisy; hotel is located in Neustadt, a 10-minute walk
across the river to the city center. ⑨ *Rooms from: €159* ✉ *Rähnitzg.
19* ☎ *0351/80030* ⊕ *www.buelow-residenz.de* ⤳ *25 rooms, 5 suites.*

$ ▦ **Hotel Elbflorenz.** This centrally located hotel with Dresden's some-
HOTEL   what presumptuous nickname ("Florence on the Elbe") contains Ital-
ian-designed rooms bathed in red and yellow and arranged alongside
a garden courtyard. **Pros:** extraordinary breakfast buffet. **Cons:** in
need of renovation; located at edge of city center. ⑨ *Rooms from:
€86* ✉ *Rosenstr. 36* ☎ *0351/86400* ⊕ *www.hotel-elbflorenz.de* ⤳ *212
rooms, 15 suites* ⑩ *Breakfast.*

$$$ ▦ **Kempinski Hotel Taschenbergpalais Dresden.** Rebuilt after wartime
HOTEL   bombing, the historic Taschenberg Palace—the work of Zwinger
architect Matthäus Daniel Pöppelmann—is Dresden's premier address
and the last word in luxury, as befits the former residence of the Saxon
crown princes. **Pros:** ice-skating in the courtyard in winter; concierge
knows absolutely everything about Dresden. **Cons:** expensive extra
charges for breakfast and Internet. ⑨ *Rooms from: €199* ✉ *Taschenberg 3* ☎ *0351/49120* ⊕ *www.kempinski-dresden.de* ⤳ *188 rooms,
25 suites.*

$ ▦ **Rothenburger Hof.** One of Dresden's smallest and oldest luxury hotels,
HOTEL   the historic Rothenburger Hof opened in 1865, and is only a few steps
away from the city's sightseeing spots. **Pros:** nice garden and indoor
pool. **Cons:** across the river in Neustadt, about 20 minutes from the city
center; street can be noisy in summer. ⑨ *Rooms from: €99* ✉ *Rothenburger Str. 15–17* ☎ *0351/81260* ⊕ *www.dresden-hotel.de* ⤳ *26 rooms,
13 apartments* ⑩ *Breakfast.*

NIGHTLIFE AND THE ARTS

THE ARTS

Philharmonie Dresden (*Philharmonic Orchestra Dresden*). Dresden's fine
orchestra takes center stage in the city's annual music festival, from
mid-May to early June. ✉ *Kulturpalast am Altmarkt* ☎ *0351/486–6286*
⊕ *en.dresdnerphilharmonie.de.*

Semperoper Dresden (*Semper Opera House*). The opera in Dresden holds
an international reputation largely due to its opera house. Destroyed
during the war, the building has been meticulously rebuilt and renovated. Tickets are reasonably priced but also hard to come by; they're
often included in package tours. ▬TIP➔ Try reserving tickets on the
website, or stop by the box office about a half hour before the performance. If that doesn't work, take one of the opera-house tours, a

The Semperoper (Semper Opera House) saw the openings of several of Richard Wagner's and Richard Strauss's best-loved operas. Its plush interiors are rich with velvet and brocade.

nice consolation that gets you into the building. ⊠ *Theaterpl.* ⊕ *www. semperoper.de* ⊠ *Evening box office (Abendkasse), left of main entrance* ☎ *0351/491–1705.*

NIGHTLIFE

Dresdeners are known for their industriousness and efficient way of doing business, but they also know how to spend a night out. Most of Dresden's pubs and *Kneipen* (bars) are in the **Neustadt** district, across the river from most sights, and along the buzzing **Münzgasse** (between the Frauenkirche and the Brühlsche Terrasse).

Aqualounge. This groovy and hip place is one of the best bars in town. ⊠ *Louisenstr. 56* ☎ *0351/810–6116* ⊕ *www.aqualounge.de.*

Bärenzwinger. Folk and rock music are regularly featured here. ⊠ *Brühl- lscher Garten* ☎ *0351/495–1409* ⊕ *www.baerenzwinger.de.*

Motown Club. Hot African rhythms attract a young and stylish crowd. ⊠ *St. Petersburger Str. 9* ☎ *0351/487–4150.*

Planwirtschaft. The name ironically refers to the planned socialist economic system; it attracts an alternative crowd. ⊠ *Louisenstr. 20* ☎ *0351/801–3187.*

Tonne Jazz Club. Jazz musicians perform most nights of the week at this friendly, laid-back club. ⊠ *Waldschlösschen, Am Brauhaus 3* ☎ *0351/802–6017.*

SHOPPING

Dresden's Striezelmarkt. Dating to 1434, this market was named after the city's famous Stollen, a buttery Christmas fruitcake often made with marzipan and sprinkled with powdered sugar. The market hosts a festival in its honor, complete with a 9,000-pound cake, on the Saturday of the second weekend of Advent. Traditional wooden toys produced in the nearby Erzgebirge mountains are the other major draw. ⊠ *Altmarkt* ⊕ *www.dresden-striezelmarkt.de* ⊘ *Nov. 24–Dec. 23, daily 10–9; Dec. 24, 10–2.*

MEISSEN

25 km (15 miles) northwest of Dresden.

This romantic city with its imposing castle looming over the Elbe River is known the world over for Europe's finest porcelain, emblazoned with its trademarked crossed blue swords. The first European porcelain was made in this area in 1708, and in 1710 the Royal Porcelain Workshop was established in Meissen, close to the local raw materials.

The story of how porcelain came to be produced here reads like a German fairy tale: the Saxon elector Augustus the Strong, who ruled from 1694 to 1733, urged his court alchemists to find the secret of making gold, something he badly needed to refill a state treasury depleted by his extravagant lifestyle. The alchemists failed to produce gold, but one of them, Johann Friedrich Böttger, discovered a method for making something almost as precious: fine hard-paste porcelain. Already a rapacious collector of Oriental porcelains, the prince put Böttger and a team of craftsmen up in a hilltop castle—Albrechtsburg—and set them to work.

GETTING HERE AND AROUND

Meissen is an easy 45-minute train ride from Dresden. On arrival, exit the station and walk to the left; as you turn the corner there is a beautiful view of Meissen across the river. Trains run about every 30 minutes.

ESSENTIALS

Visitor Information Tourist-Information Meissen ⊠ *Markt 3* ☎ *03521/41940* ⊕ *www.touristinfo-meissen.de.*

EXPLORING

Albrechtsburg. The story of Meissen porcelain actually began high above Old Meissen. Towering over the Elbe River, this 15th-century castle is Germany's first truly residential one, a complete break with the earlier style of fortified bastions. In the central *Schutzhof*, a typical Gothic courtyard protected on three sides by high rough-stone walls, is an exterior spiral staircase, the **Wendelstein,** a masterpiece of early masonry hewn in 1525 from a single massive stone block. The ceilings of the castle halls are richly decorated, although many date only from a restoration in 1870. Adjacent to the castle is an early Gothic cathedral. It's a bit of a climb up Burgstrasse and Amtsstrasse to the castle, but a bus runs regularly up the hill from the Marktplatz. ☎ *03521/47070* ⊕ *www.albrechtsburg-meissen. de* ⊟*€8* ⊘ *Mar.–Oct., daily 10–6; Nov.–Feb., daily 10–5.*

Altes Brauhaus (*Old Brewery*). Near the Frauenkirche, the Altes Brauhaus dates to 1460 and is graced by a Renaissance gable. It now houses city offices. ⊠ *An der Frauenkirche 3.*

Franziskanerkirche (*St. Francis Church*). The city's medieval past is recounted in the museum of this former monastery. ⊠ *Heinrichspl. 3* ☎ *03521/458–857* ⊟*€3* ⊘ *Daily 11–5.*

Frauenkirche (*Church of Our Lady*). A set of porcelain bells at the late-Gothic Frauenkirche, on the central Marktplatz, was the first of its kind anywhere when installed in 1929. ✉ *An der Frauenkirche.*

Nikolaikirche (*St. Nicholas Church*). Near the porcelain works, this church holds the largest set of porcelain figures ever crafted (8¼ feet tall) as well as the remains of early Gothic frescoes. ✉ *Neumarkt 29.*

Staatliche Porzellan–Manufaktur Meissen (*Meissen Porcelain Works*). Outgrowing its castle workshop in the mid-19th century, today's porcelain factory is on the southern outskirts of town. One of its buildings has a demonstration workshop and a museum whose Meissen collection rivals that of Dresden's Porzellansammlung. ✉ *Talstr. 9* ☎ *03521/468–208* ⊕ *www.meissen. de* 🎟 *€9 including workshop and museum* ⊘ *May–Oct., daily 9–6; Nov.–Apr., daily 9–5.*

THE ORIGINS OF THE MEISSEN FUMMEL

At the beginning of the 18th century, the Great Elector of Saxony routinely sent proclamations by messenger to his subjects in Meissen. The messengers were known to chase women and behave poorly, often drinking so much of the famous Meissen wine that their horses were the only ones who remembered the way back to Dresden. To curb this behavior, the elector charged the bakers of Meissen with creating an extremely fragile cake, which the messengers would have to remain sober enough to deliver to the elector intact. Today, the Meissner Fummel remains a local specialty.

WHERE TO EAT AND STAY

$
GERMAN
✕ Domkeller. Part of the centuries-old complex of buildings ringing the town castle, this ancient and popular hostelry is a great place to enjoy fine wines and hearty German dishes. It's also worth a visit for the sensational view of the Elbe River valley from the large dining room and tree-shaded terrace. ⑤ *Average main: €12* ✉ *Dompl. 9* ☎ *03521/457–676.*

$
GERMAN
✕ Restaurant Vincenz Richter. Tucked away in a yellow wooden-beam house, this historic restaurant has been painstakingly maintained by the Richter family since 1873. The dining room is adorned with rare antiques, documents, and medieval weapons, as well as copper and tin tableware. Guests can savor the exquisite dishes on the Saxon-German menu while sampling the restaurant's own personally produced white wines; a bottle of the Riesling is a real pleasure. Try the delicious wild rabbit with bacon-wrapped plums, paired with a glass of Kerner *Meissener Kapitelberg.* ⑤ *Average main: €13* ✉ *An der Frauenkirche 12* ☎ *03521/453–285* ⊘ *Closed Mon. No dinner Sun.*

$$
HOTEL
🛏 Welcome Parkhotel Meissen. Most of the luxuriously furnished and appointed rooms are in newly built annexes, but for turn-of-the-century charm, opt for a room in the art-nouveau villa, which sits on the bank of the Elbe across from the hilltop castle. **Pros:** gorgeous views; elegant rooms; fine dining. **Cons:** villa rooms are not as newly furnished; international chain hotel. ⑤ *Rooms from: €110* ✉ *Hafenstr. 27–31* ☎ *03521/72250* ⊕ *www.welcome-hotel-meissen.de* ⟳ *92 rooms, 5 suites* ⑪ *Breakfast.*

16

THE ARTS

Concerts. Regular concerts are held at the Albrechtsburg castle, and in early September the *Burgfestspiele*—open-air evening performances—are staged in the castle's romantic courtyard. ☎ *03521/47070.*

Dom. Meissen's cathedral, the Dom, has a yearlong music program, with organ and choral concerts every Saturday in summer. ⊠ *Dompl. 7* ☎ *03521/452–490.*

SHOPPING

Sächsische Winzergenossenschaft Meissen. To wine connoisseurs, the name "Meissen" is associated with vineyards producing top-quality white wines much in demand throughout Germany. Müller-Thurgau, Weissburgunder, and Goldriesling are worth choices and can be bought directly from the producer, Sächsische Winzergenossenschaft Meissen. ⊠ *Bennoweg 9* ☎ *03521/780–970.*

Staatliche Porzellan–Manufaktur Meissen. Meissen porcelain is available directly from the porcelain works as well as in every china and gift shop in town. ⊠ *Talstr. 9* ☎ *03521/468–700.*

BAUTZEN/BUDYŠIN

53 km (33 miles) east of Dresden.

Bautzen has perched high above a deep granite valley formed by the River Spree for more than 1,000 years. Its almost-intact city walls hide a remarkably well-preserved city with wandering back alleyways and fountain-graced squares. Bautzen is definitely a German city, but it is also the administrative center of Germany's only indigenous ethnic minority, the Sorbs.

In the area, the Sorb language enjoys equal standing with German in government and education, and Sorbs are known for their colorful folk traditions. As in all Slavic cultures, Easter Sunday is the highlight of the calendar, when ornately decorated eggs are hung from trees and when the traditional *Osterreiten,* a procession of Catholic men on horseback who carry religious symbols and sing Sorbian hymns, takes place.

GETTING HERE AND AROUND

Bautzen is halfway between Dresden and Görlitz. Trains leave both cities once every hour; travel time is about an hour.

ESSENTIALS

Visitor Information Tourist-Information Bautzen-Budyšin ⊠ *Hauptmarkt 1* ☎ *03591/42016* ⊕ *www.bautzen.de.*

EXPLORING

Alte Wasserkunst (*Old Waterworks*). Erected in 1558, the Alte Wasserkunst served as part of the town's defensive fortifications, but its true purpose was to pump water from the Spree into 86 cisterns spread throughout the city. It proved so efficient that it provided the city's water supply until 1965. It is now a technical museum. ⊠ *Wendischer Kirchhof 7* ☎ *03591/41588* ᠁*€3* ⊙ *Daily 10–5.*

Dom St. Petri (*St. Peter's Cathedral*). Behind the Rathaus is one of Bautzen's most interesting sights: Dom St. Petri is Germany's only *Simultankirche*, or "simultaneous" church. In order to avoid the violence that often occurred during the Reformation, St. Peter's has a Protestant side and a Roman-Catholic side in the same church. A short fence, which once reached a height of 13 feet, separates the two congregations. The church was built in 1213 on the sight of a Milzener (the forerunners of the Sorbs) parish church. ⊠ *An der Petrikirche 6* ☎ *03591/31180* ⊕ *www.dompfarrei-bautzen.de* ▣ *Free* ⊙ *May–Oct., Mon.–Sat. 10–3, Sun. 1–4; Nov.–Apr., daily 11–noon.*

Hexenhäuser (*Witches' Houses*). Below the waterworks and outside the walls, these three reddish houses were the only structures to survive all the city's fires—leading Bautzeners to conclude that they could only be occupied by witches. ⊠ *Fischerg.*

Rathaus. Bautzen's main market square is actually two squares, the **Hauptmarkt** (Main Market) and the **Fleischmarkt** (Meat Market), separated by the yellow, baroque Rathaus. The current town hall dates from 1705, but there has been a town hall in this location since 1213. Bautzen's friendly tourist-information center, next door, has a great Bautzen-in-two-hours walking-tour map and an MP3 guide to the city. ⊠ *Fleischmarkt 1.*

Reichenturm (*Rich Tower*). Bautzen's city walls have a number of gates and towers. This one, at the end of Reichenstrasse, is the most impressive. Although the tower base dates from 1490, it was damaged in four city fires (in 1620, 1639, 1686, and 1747) and rebuilt, hence its baroque cupola. The reconstruction caused the tower to lean, however, and its foundation was further damaged in 1837. The "Leaning Tower of Bautzen" currently sits about 5 feet off center. ■TIP➜ **The view from the top is a spectacular vista of Bautzen and the surrounding countryside.** ⊠ *Reichenstr. 1* ☎ *03591/460–431* ▣ *€1.40* ⊙ *Daily 10–5.*

WHERE TO EAT AND STAY

$ ✕ **Wjelbik.** The name of Bautzen's best Sorbian restaurant means "pantry." Very popular on Sorb holidays, Wjelbik uses exclusively regional produce in such offerings as the *Sorbisches Hochzeitsmenu* (Sorb wedding feast)—a vegetable and meatball soup followed by beef in creamed horseradish. The restaurant is in a 600-year-old building near the cathedral. ⑤ *Average main: €14* ⊠ *Kornstr. 7* ☎ *03591/42060.*

EASTERN
EUROPEAN

> **BAUTZEN CUTS THE MUSTARD**
>
> Bautzen is famous for mustard, which has been ground here since 1866. Mustard is Germany's favorite condiment, and East Germans consume an average of 5 pounds of the stuff annually. It's so deeply ingrained that here one "gives his mustard" in the same way English speakers would their "two cents." The most popular Bautzen mustard, Bautz'ner Senf, is one of the rare East German products that sells well in the West. Available at almost every supermarket, a 200-milliliter tub costs approximately €0.30, making it a great present for those at home.

16

$ 🖵 **Hotel Goldener Adler.** This pleasant hotel occupies a 450-year-old
HOTEL   building on the main market square, and great effort has been made
to incorporate traditional building elements into the modern and spacious rooms. **Pros:** a complete package: comfortable historical hotel,
good restaurant, and yummy fondue. **Cons:** a little too modern for a
historical town. ⑤ *Rooms from: €90* ✉ *Hauptmarkt 4* ☎ *03591/48660*
⊕ *www.goldeneradler.de* ↩ *30 rooms.*

GÖRLITZ

48 km (30 miles) east of Bautzen, 60 km (38 miles) northeast of Dresden.

Tucked away in the country's easternmost corner (bordering Poland),
Görlitz's quiet, narrow cobblestone alleys and exquisite architecture
make it one of Germany's most beautiful cities. It emerged from the
destruction of World War II relatively unscathed. As a result it has
more than 4,000 historic houses in styles including Gothic, Renaissance, baroque, rococo, Wilhelminian, and art nouveau. Although the
city has impressive museums, theater, and music, it's the ambience created by the casual dignity of these buildings, in their jumble of styles,
that makes Görlitz so attractive. Notably absent are the typical socialist eyesores and the glass-and-steel modernism found in many eastern
German towns.

The Gothic Dicker Turm (Fat Tower) guards the entrance to the city; it's
the oldest tower in Görlitz, and its walls are 5 meters thick.

GETTING HERE AND AROUND

Görlitz can be reached by hourly trains from Dresden (1½ hours) and
from Berlin (3 hours, with a change in Cottbus). Görlitz's train station
(a wonderful neoclassical building with an art nouveau interior) is a
short tram ride outside town.

ESSENTIALS

Visitor Information Görlitz-Information und Tourist-Service ✉ *Bruderstr. 1*
☎ *03581/47570* ⊕ *www.goerlitz.de.*

EXPLORING

Biblical House. This house is interesting for its Renaissance facade decorated with sandstone reliefs depicting biblical stories. The Catholic
Church banned religious depictions on secular buildings, but by the
time the house was rebuilt after a fire in 1526, the Reformation had
Görlitz firmly in its grip. ✉ *Neissestr. 29.*

Dreifaltigkeitskirche (*Church of the Holy Trinity*). On the southeast side
of the market lies this pleasant Romanesque church with a Gothic interior, built in 1245. The interior houses an impressive Gothic triptych
altarpiece. The clock on the thin tower is set seven minutes fast in
remembrance of a trick played by the city guards on the leaders of a
rebellion. In 1527 the city's disenfranchised cloth makers secretly met
to plan a rebellion against the city council and the powerful guilds.
Their plans were uncovered, and by setting the clock ahead the guards
fooled the rebels into thinking it was safe to sneak into the city. As a
result they were caught and hanged. ✉ *Obermarkt* 🖵 *€3.*

Görlitz's Untermarkt contains the Rathaus and also building No. 14, where all goods coming into the city were weighed and taxed.

Karstadt. Dating from 1912–13, Germany's only original art-nouveau department store has a main hall with a colorful glass cupola and several stunning freestanding staircases. The store dominates the Marienplatz, a small square outside the city center that serves as Görlitz's transportation hub. It's next to the 15th-century Frauenkirche, the parish church for the nearby hospital and the poor condemned to live outside the city walls. ⚠ Though the department store is closed (the city is trying to open it to the public), you can peek inside through the perfume shop. ✉ *An der Frauenkirche 5–7* ☎ *03581/4600.*

Kirche St. Peter und Paul (*St. Peter and Paul Church*). Perched high above the river is one of Saxony's largest late-Gothic churches, dating to 1423. The real draw is the church's famous one-of-a-kind organ, built in 1703 by Eugenio Casparini. The Sun Organ gets its name from the circularly arranged pipes and not from the golden sun at the center. Its full and deep sound, as well as its birdcalls, can be heard on Sunday and Wednesday afternoons. ✉ *Bei der Peterkirche 5* ☎ *03581/409–590* 🎫 *Free* ⊙ *Mon.– Sat. 10:30–4, Sun. 11:30–4; guided tours Thurs. and Sun. at noon.*

OFF THE BEATEN PATH

Landskron Brauerei (*Landskron Brewery*). Germany's easternmost Brauhaus is one of the few breweries left that gives tours. Founded in 1869, Landskron isn't very old by German standards, but it's unique in that it hasn't been gobbled up by a huge brewing conglomerate. *Görlitzer* are understandably proud of their own Premium Pilsner, but the brewery also produces good dark, Silesian, and winter beers. Landskron Hefeweizen is one of the best in the country. ✉ *An der Landskronbrauerei* ☎ *03581/465–121* ⊕ *www.landskron.de* 🎫 *Tours €7–€18* ⊙ *Tours Sun.–Thurs., by appointment.*

Obermarkt (*Upper Market*). The richly decorated Renaissance homes and warehouses on the Obermarkt are a vivid legacy of the city's wealthy past. During the late Middle Ages the most common merchandise here was cloth, which was bought and sold from covered wagons and on the ground floors of many buildings. Napoléon addressed his troops from the balcony of the house at No. 29.

Schlesisches Museum (*Silesian Museum*). Exploring 900 years of Silesian culture, this is a meeting place for Silesians from Germany, Poland, and the Czech Republic. The museum is housed in the magnificent Schönhof building, one of Germany's oldest Renaissance *Patrizierhäuser* (grand mansions of the city's ruling business and political elite). ☒ *Brüderstr. 8* ☎ *03581/87910* ⊕ *www.schlesisches-museum.de* ☒ *€5* ☉ *Tues.–Sun. 10–5.*

> ## GÖRLITZ'S SECRET ADMIRER
>
> After German unification, Görlitz was a run-down border town, but renovations costing upward of €400 million returned the city to much of its former splendor. In 1995 it got an additional boost when an anonymous philanthropist pledged to the city a yearly sum of 1 million marks. Every March, Görlitz celebrates the arrival in its coffers of the mysterious Altstadt-Million (albeit, with the change in currency, now €511,000).

Untermarkt (*Lower Market*). One of Europe's most impressive squares, this market is a testament to the prosperity brought by the cloth trade. It's built up in the middle, and the most important building is No. 14, which formerly housed the city scales. The duty of the city scale masters, whose busts adorn the Renaissance facade of the Gothic building, was to weigh every ounce of merchandise entering the city and to determine the taxes due.

The square's most prominent building is the Rathaus. Its winding staircase is as peculiar as its statue of the goddess of justice, whose eyes—contrary to European tradition—are not covered. The corner house on the square, the Alte Ratsapotheke (Old Council Pharmacy), has two intricate sundials on the facade, painted in 1550.

Verrätergasse (*Traitors' Alley*). On Verrätergasse, across the Obermarkt square from the church, is the **Peter-Liebig-Haus,** where the initials of the first four words of the rebels' meeting place, *Der verräterischen Rotte Tor* (the treacherous gang's gate), are inscribed above the door. The Obermarkt is dominated by the **Reichenbach Turm,** a tower built in the 13th century, with additions in 1485 and 1782. Until 1904 the tower housed the city watchmen and their families. The apartments and armory are now a museum. There are great views of the city from the tiny windows at the top. The massive **Kaisertrutz** (Emperor's Fortress) once protected the western city gates, and now houses late-Gothic and Renaissance art from the area around Görlitz, as well as some impressive historical models of the city. Both buildings are part of the Kulturhistorisches Museum. ☎ *03581/671–355* ⊕ *www.museum-goerlitz.de* ☒ *€10, tickets valid on day of purchase and following day* ☉ *Tues.– Thurs. and weekends 10–5.*

WHERE TO EAT AND STAY

$ ✕ **Die Destille.** This small family-run establishment overlooks the Niko-
GERMAN laiturm, one of the towers from the city's wall. The restaurant offers
good solid Silesian fare and absolutely the best *Schlesische Himmelreich*
(ham and pork roast smothered in baked fruit and white sauce, served
with dumplings) in town. There are also eight inexpensive, spartan guest
rooms where you can spend the night. $ *Average main: €10* ⊠ *Nikolaistr.
6* ☎ *03581/405–302* ▭ *No credit cards* ☾ *Sometimes closed in Sept.*

$ ⊡ **Hotel Bon-Apart.** The name says it all: this hotel is an homage to
HOTEL Napoléon, whose troops occupied Görlitz, and it's a splendid departure
from a "normal" hotel. **Pros:** large rooms with kitchens and artistically
decorated bathrooms; huge breakfast buffet. **Cons:** eclectic design may
not appeal to everyone; neighboring market can be noisy in the morning; no elevator. $ *Rooms from: €95* ⊠ *Elisabethstr. 41* ☎ *03581/48080*
⊕ *www.bon-apart.de* ⤺ *20 rooms.*

SAXONY-ANHALT

The central state of Saxony-Anhalt is a region rich in history and natural beauty, almost completely untouched by modern visitors. In the
Altmark, on the edge of the Harz Mountains, fields of grain and sugar
beets stretch to the horizon. In the mountains themselves are the deep
gorge of the Bode River and the stalactite-filled caves of Rubeland. The
songbirds of the Harz are renowned, and though pollution has taken
its toll, both the flora and the fauna of the Harz National Park (which
encompasses much of the region) are coming back. Atop the Brocken,
the Harz's highest point, legend has it that witches convene on Walpur-
gis Night (the night between April 30 and May 1).

16

LUTHERSTADT-WITTENBERG

107 km (62 miles) southwest of Berlin, 67 km (40 miles) north of Leipzig.

Protestantism was born in the little town of Wittenberg (officially called
Lutherstadt-Wittenberg). In 1508 the fervently idealistic young Martin
Luther, who had become a priest only a year earlier, arrived to study
and teach at the new university founded by Elector Frederick the Wise.
Nine years later, enraged that the Roman Catholic Church was pardon-
ing sins through the sale of indulgences, Luther attacked the policy by
posting his 95 Theses on the door of the Schlosskirche (Castle Church).

Martin Luther is still the center of attention in Wittenberg, and sites
associated with him are marked with plaques and signs. You can see
virtually all of historic Wittenberg on a 2-km (1-mile) stretch of Collegienstrasse and Schlossstrasse that begins at the railroad tracks and
ends at the Schlosskirche.

GETTING HERE AND AROUND

Lutherstadt-Wittenberg is approximately halfway between Berlin and
Leipzig, and is served by regional and ICE trains. The station is slightly
outside the city center, a pleasant walking distance away.

ESSENTIALS

Visitor Information Tourist-Information Lutherstadt Wittenberg
⊠ Schlosspl. 2 ☎ 03491/498–610 ⊕ www.wittenberg.de. Wittenberg District
Rural Information Office ⊠ Neustr. 13 ☎ 03491/402–610.

FESTIVALS

Luthers Hochzeit (*Luther's Wedding*). The best time to visit Wittenberg is during this city festival that commemorates (and reenacts) Martin Luther's marriage to Katharina von Bora. On the second weekend in June the city center goes back in time to 1525, with period costumes and entertainment. ⊕ *www.lutherhochzeit.de*.

EXPLORING

Cranachhaus (*Cranach House*). Lucas Cranach the Elder—court painter, printer, mayor, pharmacist, friend of Luther's, and probably the wealthiest man in Wittenberg—lived in two houses during his years in town. This Cranachhaus is believed to have been the first one. His son, the painter Lucas Cranach the Younger, was born here. Some of the interior has been restored to its 17th-century condition. It's now a gallery with exhibits about Cranach's life and work. Check out the goldsmith and potter that are occasionally on hand demonstrating their crafts in the courtyard. ⊠ *Markt 4* ☎ *03491/420–190* 🖾 *€3* ⊗ *Mon.–Sat. 10–5, Sun. 1–5.*

Cranachhaus (*Cranach House*). In the second Wittenberg home of Cranach the Elder, the Renaissance man not only lived and painted but also operated a print shop, which has been restored, and an apothecary. The courtyard, where it's thought he did much of his painting, remains much as it was in his day. Children attend the *Malschule* (painting school) here. ⊠ *Schlossstr. 1* ☎ *03491/410–912* 🖾 *Free* ⊗ *Mon.–Thurs. 8–4, Fri. 8–3.*

Haus der Geschichte (*House of History*). This museum makes a valiant attempt to evaluate the history of the GDR. It provides fascinating insight into the day-to-day culture of East Germans through the display of more than 20,000 objects, including detergent packaging and kitchen appliances. A special section deals with Germans and Russians in the Wittenberg region. ⊠ *Schlossstr. 6* ☎ *03491/409–004* ⊕ *www.pflug-ev. de* 🖾 *€6* ⊗ *Weekdays 10–5, weekends 11–6.*

Luther Melanchthon Gymnasium (*Luther Melanchthon High School*). In 1975 the city erected a typical East German prefab building to house the Luther Melanchthon Gymnasium, but in the early 1990s, art students contacted Friedensreich Hundertwasser, the famous Austrian architect and avant-garde artist who designed the Hundertwasserhaus in Vienna. Hundertwasser, who argued that there are no universal straight lines or completely flat surfaces in nature, agreed to transform the school, and renovations were completed in 1998. The school is one of only three Hundertwasser buildings in eastern Germany and an interesting contrast to the medieval architecture in the rest of the city. Although the building is a school, the students operate a small office that distributes information about the school and Hundertwasser's art. ⊠ *Str. der Völkerfreundschaft 130* ☎ *03491/881–131* ⊕ *www.hundertwasserschule.de* 🖾 *€2* ⊗ *Tues.–Fri. 2:30–4, weekends 10–4.*

Luthereiche (*Luther Oak*). In a small park, the Luthereiche marks the spot where, in 1520, Luther burned the papal bull excommunicating him for his criticism of the Church. The present oak was planted in the 19th century. ⊠ *Weserstr. and Collegienstr.*

Fodor's Choice ★ **Lutherhaus** (*Luther's House*). Within Lutherhhaus is the Augustinian monastery where Martin Luther lived both as a teacher-monk and later, after the monastery was dissolved, as a married man. Today it's a museum dedicated to Luther and the Reformation. Visitors enter through a garden and an elegant door with a carved stone frame; it was a gift to Luther from his wife, Katharina von Bora. Be sure to visit the monks' refectory, where works by the painter Lucas Cranach the Elder, Luther's contemporary, are displayed. The room that remains closest to the original is the dark, wood-panel Lutherstube. The Luthers and their six children used it as a living room, study, and meeting place for friends and students. Prints, engravings, paintings, manuscripts, coins, and medals relating to the Reformation and Luther's translation of the Bible into the German vernacular are displayed throughout the house. ⊠ *Collegienstr. 54* ☎ *03491/42030* ⊕ *www.martinluther.de* ⊡ *€6* ☉ *Apr.–Oct., daily 9–6; Nov.–Mar., Tues.–Sun. 10–5.*

Marktplatz (*Market Square*). Two statues are the centerpiece here: an 1821 statue of Luther by Johann Gottfried Schadow, designer of the quadriga and Victory atop Berlin's Brandenburg Gate, and an 1866 statue of Melanchthon by Frederick Drake. Gabled Renaissance houses containing shops line part of the square.

Rathaus. The handsome, white High Renaissance town hall forms the backdrop for the Marktplatz's two statues. ⊠ *Markt 26* ☏ *03491/421–720* ☉ *Daily 10–5.*

Melanchthonhaus (*Melanchthon House*). In this elegantly gabled Renaissance home, the humanist teacher and scholar Philipp Melanchthon corrected Luther's translation of the New Testament from Greek into German. Luther was hiding in the Wartburg in Eisenach at the time, and as each section of his manuscript was completed it was sent to Melanchthon for approval. (Melanchthon is a Greek translation of the man's real name, *Schwarzerdt*, which means "black earth"; humanists routinely adopted such classical pseudonyms.) The second-floor furnishings have been painstakingly re-created after period etchings. ⊠ *Collegienstr. 60* ☏ *03491/403–279* ⊕ *www.martinluther.de* ⊠ *€4* ☉ *Apr.–Oct., daily 10–6; Nov.–Mar., Tues.–Sun. 10–5.*

Fodor's Choice ★   **Schlosskirche** (*Castle Church*). In 1517 an indignant Martin Luther nailed his 95 Theses, which attacked the Roman Catholic Church's policy of selling indulgences, to this church's doors. Written in Latin, the theses might have gone unnoticed had not someone—without Luther's knowledge—translated them into German and distributed them. In 1521 the Holy Roman Emperor Charles V summoned Luther to Worms when Luther refused to retract his position. On the way home from his confrontation with the emperor, Luther was "captured" by his protector, Elector Frederick the Wise, and hidden from papal authorities in Eisenach for the better part of a year. Today the theses hang in bronze on the door, while inside, simple bronze plaques mark the burial places of Luther and his contemporary, Philipp Melanchthon. ⊠ *Schlosspl. 1* ☏ *03491/402–585* ⊠ *Free, tower €2* ☉ *May–Oct., Mon.–Sat. 10–5, Sun. 11:30–5; Nov.–Apr., Mon.–Sat. 10–4, Sun. 11:30–4.*

Stadtkirche St. Marien (*Parish Church of St. Mary*). From 1514 until his death in 1546, Martin Luther preached two sermons a week in the twin-tower Stadtkirche St. Marien. He and Katharina von Bora were married here (Luther broke with monasticism in 1525 and married the former nun). The altar triptych by Lucas Cranach the Elder includes a self-portrait, as well as portraits of Luther wearing the knight's disguise he adopted when hidden at the Wartburg; Luther preaching; Luther's wife and one of his sons; Melanchthon; and Lucas Cranach the Younger. Also notable is the 1457 bronze baptismal font by Herman Vischer the Elder. On the church's southeast corner is a discomforting juxtaposition of two Jewish-related **monuments**: a 1304 mocking caricature called the Jewish Pig, erected at the time of the expulsion of the town's Jews, and, on the cobblestone pavement, a contemporary memorial to the Jews who died at Auschwitz. ⊠ *Kirchpl.* ☏ *03491/404–415* ⊠ *€1.50, including tour* ☉ *May–Oct., daily 10–5; Nov.–Apr., daily 10–4.*

Martin Luther taught in the Lecture Hall within Lutherhaus, which is now a museum dedicated to Martin Luther and the Reformation.

Wittenberg English Ministry. English-speaking visitors can worship in the churches where Martin Luther conducted his ministry thanks to *this* ministry. During the summer months it brings English-speaking pastors from the United States to provide Lutheran worship services in the Schlosskirche and Stadtkirche St. Marien. Services follow German Protestant tradition (albeit in English) and conclude with singing Luther's "A Mighty Fortress Is Our God," accompanied on the organ. Tours of Wittenberg and other Luther sites are also offered. ⊠ *Schlosspl. 2* ☎ *03491/498–610* ⊕ *www.wittenberg-english-ministry.com* ☉ *May–Oct., Sat. at 5, other times by appointment.*

WHERE TO EAT

$

GERMAN

✕ **Brauhaus Wittenberg.** This historic brewery and restaurant is the perfect stop for a cold beer after a long day of sightseeing. ▉TIP➔ Set in the Old Town's magnificent Beyerhof courtyard, the Brauhaus still produces local beer such as Wittenberger Kuckucksbier. In the medieval restaurant with its huge beer kettles, you can sample local and south German cuisine; a specialty is the smoked fish—such as eel, trout, and halibut—from the Brauhaus smokery. In summer, try to get a table in the courtyard. ⑤ *Average main: €10* ⊠ *Markt 6* ☎ *03491/433–130.*

$

GERMAN

✕ **Schlosskeller.** At the back of the Schlosskirche, this restaurant's four dining rooms are tucked away in a basement with 16th-century stone walls and barrel-vaulted ceilings. The kitchen specializes in German dishes, such as *Kümmelfleisch mit Senfgurken* (caraway beef with mustard-seed pickles). ⑤ *Average main: €12* ⊠ *Schlosspl. 1* ☎ *03491/480–805.*

DESSAU

35 km (22 miles) southwest of Wittenberg.

The name "Dessau" is known to students of modern architecture as the epicenter of architect Walter Gropius's highly influential Bauhaus school of design. During the 1920s, Gropius hoped to replace the dark and inhumane tenement architecture of the 1800s with standardized yet spacious and bright apartments. His ideas and methods were used in building 316 villas in the city's Törten neighborhood in the 1920s.

GETTING HERE AND AROUND
Dessau makes an excellent day trip from Berlin. The direct Regional Express train leaves Berlin every hour, and the trip takes 90 minutes.

ESSENTIALS
Visitor Information Tourist-Information Dessau ⊠ *Zerbster Str. 2c* ☎ *0340/204–1442* ⊕ *www.dessau.de.*

EXPLORING
Bauhaus Building. The architecture school is still operating in this building, where artists conceived styles that influenced the appearance of such cities as New York, Chicago, and San Francisco. Other structures designed by Gropius and the Bauhaus architects, among them the Meisterhäuser, are also open for inspection off Ebertallee and Elballee. ⊠ *Gropiusallee 38* ☎ *0340/650–8251* ⊕ *www.bauhaus-dessau.de* ⊠ *€17, includes all Bauhaus sites* ⊗ *Daily 10–6; Meisterhäuser: mid-Feb.–Oct., Tues.–Sun. 10–6; Nov.–mid-Feb., Tues.–Sun. 10–5.*

Georgkirche (*St. George's Church*). Like other older buildings in downtown Dessau, this Dutch-baroque church, built in 1712, is quite a contrast to the no-nonsense Bauhaus architecture. ⊠ *Georgenstr. 15.*

Technikmuseum Hugo Junkers (*Hugo Junkers Technical Museum*). The Bauhaus isn't the only show in town. Professor Hugo Junkers, one of the most famous engineers-cum-inventors of the 20th century, was at the forefront of innovation in aircraft and industrial design until his inventions were expropriated by the Nazis in 1933. The star of the museum is a completely restored JU-52/3—the ubiquitous German passenger airplane transformed into military transport. The museum also houses a fascinating collection of industrial equipment, machinery, engines, and the original Junkers wind tunnel. ⊠ *Kühnauerstr. 161a* ☎ *0340/661–1982* ⊕ *www.technikmuseum-dessau.de* ⊠ *€4* ⊗ *Daily 10–5.*

HALLE

52 km (32 miles) south of Dessau.

This city deserves a second look. The first impression of ever-under-construction train station and dismal tram ride into town hides a pretty 1,000-year-old city built on the salt trade. The name Halle comes from the Celtic word for salt, while the Saale, the name of the river the city straddles, is derived from the German word for salt. Halle has suffered from the shortfalls of Communist urban planning, yet the Old Town has an unusual beauty, particularly in its spacious central marketplace, the **Markt**, with its five distinctive sharp-steeple towers.

GETTING HERE AND AROUND

Frequent S-bahn trains connect Halle with Leipzig (30 minutes) and with Naumburg (20 minutes).

FESTIVALS

Handel Festival. This annual festival takes place in the first half of June, and two youth-choir festivals occur in May and October. ☎ *0345/5009–0222.*

ESSENTIALS

Visitor Information Stadtmarketing Halle ✉ *Marktpl. 1360* ☎ *0345/122–9984* ⊕ *www.halle.de.*

EXPLORING

Dom (*Cathedral*). Halle's only early-Gothic church, the Dom stands about 200 yards southeast of the Moritzburg. Its nave and side aisles are of equal height, a common characteristic of Gothic church design in this part of Germany. ✉ *Dompl. 3* ☎ *0345/202–1379* 🕮 *Free* ⊗ *June–Oct., Mon.–Sat. 2–4.*

SALT AND CHOCOLATE

In Halle the salt trade was controlled by the *Halloren* (members of the brotherhood of salt workers), who cooked brine into salt on the banks of the Saale River. All that remains of the once incredibly powerful Halloren are the tasty *Halloren-Kügel*, a praline made by the Halloren Schokoladenfabrik, Germany's oldest chocolate factory. The candy is modeled after the silver buttons worn by the Halloren. Very popular in eastern Germany, the chocolates can be purchased just about anywhere in town—there is an outlet store in the train station.

16

OFF THE BEATEN PATH

Halloren Schokoladenfabrik. Germany's oldest chocolate factory was founded in 1804 and has changed hands several times (including a brief period when it was used to manufacture airplane wings during the war). Its Schokoladenmuseum explores 200 years of chocolate production and contains a 27-square-meter room made entirely from chocolate. Entrance to the museum also allows entrance to the glass-enclosed production line, where you can watch almost all aspects of chocolate making. ■**TIP**➜ The factory is on the other side of the train station from the main town. To get here, take Tram No. 7 to Fiete-Schultze-Strasse and walk back 200 meters. ✉ *Delitzscherstr. 70* ☎ *0345/5642–192* ⊕ *www.halloren.de* 🕮 *€4, includes samples* ⊗ *Mon.–Sat. 9–4.*

Händelhaus (*Handel House*). Handel's birthplace is now a museum devoted to the composer. The entrance hall displays glass harmonicas and curious musical instruments perfected by Benjamin Franklin in the 1760s. ■**TIP**➜ Be sure to look for the small courtyard where Handel played as a child. ✉ *Grosse Nikolaistr. 5* ☎ *0345/500–900* 🕮 *Free* ⊗ *Tues.–Wed. and Fri.–Sun. 9:30–5:30, Thurs. 9:30–7.*

Marienkirche (*St. Mary's Church*). Of the four towers belonging to the late-Gothic Marienkirche, two are connected by a vertiginous catwalk bridge. Martin Luther preached in the church, and George Friedrich Handel (Händel in German), born in Halle in 1685, was baptized at its font. He went on to learn to play the organ beneath its high, vaulted ceiling. ✉ *An der Marienkirche 2.*

Marktschlösschen (*Market Palace*). This late-Renaissance building just off the market square houses an interesting collection of historical musical instruments, some of which could have been played by Handel and his contemporaries. ⊠ *Marktpl. 13* ☎ *0345/202–9141* 🎫 *Free* ☉ *Tues.–Fri. 10–7, weekends 10–6.*

Moritzburg (*Moritz Castle*). The Archbishop of Magdeburg built the Moritzburg in the late 15th century, after he claimed the city for his archdiocese. The typical late-Gothic fortress, with a dry moat and a sturdy round tower at each of its four corners, is a testament to Halle's early might, which vanished with the Thirty Years' War. Prior to World War II the castle contained a leading gallery of German expressionist paintings, which were ripped from the walls by the Nazis and condemned as "degenerate." Some of the works are back in place at the **Staatliche Galerie Moritzburg,** together with some outstanding late-19th- and early-20th-century art. ▥**TIP**➜ You'll find Rodin's famous sculpture *The Kiss* here. ⊠ *Friedemann-Bach-Pl. 5* ☎ *0345/212–590* ⊕ *stiftung-moritzburg.de* 🎫 *€7* ☉ *Tues. 11–8:30, Wed.–Sun. 10–6.*

Neue Residenz (*New Residence*). This 16th-century, former archbishop's home houses the **Geiseltalmuseum** and its world-famous collection of fossils dug from brown coal deposits in the Geisel Valley, near Halle. ⊠ *Dornstr. 5* ☎ *0345/552–6135* 🎫 *Free* ☉ *Weekdays 9–noon and 1–5; every 2nd and 4th weekend 9–1.*

Roter Turm (*Red Tower*). The Markt's fifth tower is Halle's celebrated Roter Turm, built between 1418 and 1506 as an expression of the city's power and wealth. The carillon inside is played on special occasions. ⊠ *Markt.*

FAMILY **Technisches Halloren- und Salinemuseum** (*Technical Saline Extraction Museum*). The salt trade on which Halle built its prosperity is documented in this museum. A replica brine mill shows the salt-extraction process, and the exquisite silver-goblet collection of the Salt Workers' Guild (the Halloren) is on display. The old method of evaporating brine from local springs is sometimes demonstrated. The museum is on the south side of the Saale River (across the Schiefer Bridge). ⊠ *Mansfelderstr. 52* ☎ *0345/202–5034* ⊕ *www.salinemuseum.de* 🎫 *€5.20* ☉ *Tues.–Sun. 10–5.*

WHERE TO EAT AND STAY

Halle's café scene spreads out along the Kleine Ullrichstrasse. It's a good area for searching out an affordable meal and lively conversation.

$ ✕ **Hallesches Brauhaus Kühler Brunnen.** Halle's first and best brewpub
GERMAN serves traditional brewery fare in huge portions at reasonable prices. The Brauhaus is most famous for its large selection of *Flammkuchen,* a kind of thin-crust pizza originated in the Alsace region of France. The best beer is the brewery's own *Hallsch,* an amber top-fermented ale served in funky glasses. 🛇 *Average main: €9* ⊠ *Grosse Nikolaistr. 2* ☎ *0345/212–570* 🗩 *No credit cards.*

$ ✕ **Restaurant Mönchshof.** Hearty German fare in heartier portions is
GERMAN served in high-ceiling, dark-wood surroundings. Lamb from Saxony-
FAMILY Anhalt's Wettin region and venison are specialties in season, but there are always fish and crisp roast pork on the menu. The wine list is extensive, with international vintages. The restaurant is popular with locals,

and the staff are particularly accommodating with children. [$] *Average main: €12* ⊠ *Talamtstr. 6* ☎ *0345/202–1726.*

$$
HOTEL
⊞ **Ankerhof Hotel.** In an old warehouse, this reflection on Halle's salt-strewn past contains individually decorated rooms, most with wooden ceiling beams, bare stone walls, and heavy furniture made from exquisite wood. **Pros:** casual elegance worked into a traditional setting. **Cons:** building creaks and groans when it is windy; can be cold in winter. [$] *Rooms from: €105* ⊠ *Ankerstr. 2a* ☎ *0345/232–3200* ⊕ *www.ankerhofhotel.de* ⤳ *49 rooms, 1 suite* ⦿ *Breakfast.*

THE ARTS

The city of Handel's birth is, not surprisingly, an important music center. Halle is famous for its opera productions, its orchestral concerts, and particularly its choirs.

Opernhaus (*Opera House*). Both Halle's opera and its venue are renowned. ⊠ *Universitätsring 24* ☎ *0345/5110–0355.*

Philharmonisches Staatsorchester Halle (*State Philharmonic Orchestra*). The city's main orchestra performs at the Konzerthalle. ⊠ *Grosse Gosenstr. 12* ☎ *0345/523–3141* ⊕ *www.staatskapelle.halle.de.*

16

NAUMBURG

60 km (65 miles) south of Halle.

Once a powerful trading and ecclesiastical city, 1,000-year-old Naumburg is the cultural center of the Salle-Unstrut. Although the city is most famous for its Romanesque/Gothic cathedral, it hides a well-preserved collection of patrician houses, winding back alleys, and a marketplace so distinctive that it warrants the appellation "Naumburger Renaissance."

GETTING HERE AND AROUND

From the train station the fun way to get into the city is to take the Naumburger Historical Tram, which runs every 30 minutes. A single ride on Europe's smallest tramway, in antique streetcars, costs €1.50.

ESSENTIALS

Visitor Information Tourist und Tagungsservice Naumburg ⊠ *Markt 12* ☎ *03445/273–125* ⊕ *www.naumburg-tourismus.de.*

EXPLORING

Dom St. Peter und Paul (*St. Peter and Paul Cathedral*). Perched high above the city and dominating the skyline, this cathedral is the symbol of Naumburg. For the most part constructed during the latter half of the 13th century, it's considered one of the masterpieces of the late Romanesque period. What makes the cathedral unique, however, is the addition of a second choir in the Gothic style less than 100 years later. The Gothic choir is decorated with statues of the cathedral's benefactors from the workshop of the Naumburger Meister. The most famous statues are of Uta and Ekkehard, the city's most powerful patrons. Uta's tranquil face is everywhere, from postcards to city maps. ⊠ *Dompl. 16* ☎ *03445/23010* ▣ *€4* ⊙ *Mon.–Sat. 10–4, Sun. noon–4; guided tours by appointment.*

Marientor. Naumburg was once ringed by a defensive city wall with five gates. The only remaining one, the Marientor, is a rare surviving example of a dual-portal gate from the 14th century. The museum inside the gate provides a brief history of the city's defenses. ▮**TIP→** A pleasant walk along the remaining city walls from Marienplatz to the Weingarten is the easiest way to explore the last intact section of Naumburg's wall, moat, and defensive battlements. ✉ *Marienpl.* 🎫*€0.50* ⏲ *Daily 10–4:30.*

Marktplatz. Naumburg's historic market square lies strategically at the intersection of two medieval trade routes. Although the market burned in 1517, it was painstakingly rebuilt in Renaissance and baroque styles.

16

Kaysersches Haus (*Imperial House*). Supported by seven Gothic gables, the Kaysersches Haus has a carved oak doorway from the Renaissance. ✉ *Markt 10.*

Rathaus. Naumburg's town hall, rebuilt in 1523, incorporates the remnants of the original building destroyed by fire. ✉ *Markt 1.*

Schlösschen (*Little Castle*). The Schlösschen houses the offices of Naumburg's first and only Protestant bishop, Nikolaus von Amsdorf, who was consecrated by Martin Luther in 1542. ✉ *Markt 2.*

Naumburger Wein und Sekt Manufaktur (*Naumburg Wine and Sparkling Wine*). Producing fine still and sparkling wines on the bank of the Salle River, this winery in a 200-year-old monastery is a pleasant 2-km (1-mile) walk or bike ride from Naumburg's city center. Tours of the production rooms and the vaulted cellar, with wine tastings, take place whenever a group forms and last about an hour. The wine garden is a pleasant place to relax on the bank of the river and the restaurant serves small snacks. Larger appetites find relief across the street at the Gasthaus Henne. ✉ *Blütengrund 35* ☎ *03445/202–042* ⊕ *www.naumburger. com* 🎫 *Tours €5* ⏲ *Daily 11–6; tours Apr.–Oct.*

Nietzsche Haus Museum. The philosopher Friedrich Nietzsche's family lived in Naumburg from 1858 to 1897, in a small classical house in the Weingarten. The Nietzsche Haus Museum documents the life and times of one of Naumburg's most controversial residents. The exhibition does not delve too deeply into Nietzsche's philosophy, but focuses a great deal on his bizarre relationship with his sister and her manipulation of his manuscripts. ✉ *Weingarten 18* ☎ *03445/703–503* ⊕ *www. mv-naumburg.de* 🎫 *€3* ⏲ *Tues.–Fri. 2–5, weekends 10–4.*

St. Wenceslas. The parish church of St. Wenceslas dominates the southern end of the Markt. A church has stood on this spot since 1218, but the current incarnation dates from 1426, with interior renovations in 1726. The church is most famous for its huge Hildebrandt Organ, which was tested and tuned by J. S. Bach in 1746. Fans of Lucas Cranach the Elder get their due with two of his paintings, *Suffer the Little Children Come Unto Me* and the *Adoration of the Three Magi*. The 73-meter-tall tower belongs to the city, *not* the church, and was used as a watchtower for the city guards, who lived there until 1994. ⊠ *Topfmarkt* ☎ *03445/208–401* ⌦ *Free, tower €2* ⊗ *Mon.–Sat. 10–noon and 2–5; tower daily 10–5.*

WHERE TO EAT AND STAY

$ ╳ **Alt-Naumburg.** Enjoy simple but tasty regional specialties directly
GERMAN in front of the Marientor. The beer garden is a good place to relax away from the action of the city center. The three-room pension is often booked far in advance. ⑤ *Average main: €11* ⊠ *Marienpl. 13* ☎ *03445/234–425* ⊟ *No credit cards.*

$ ⌂ **Hotel Stadt Aachen.** Many of the simply decorated rooms overlook the
HOTEL central market at this pleasant hotel in a medieval house. **Pros:** comfortable hotel in the middle of the action; helpful staff. **Cons:** location by the market is sometimes noisy. ⑤ *Rooms from: €83* ⊠ *Markt 11* ☎ *03445/2470* ⊕ *www.hotel-stadt-aachen.de* ⇗ *38 rooms.*

FREYBURG

10 km (6 miles) north of Naumburg.

Stepping off the train in the sleepy town of Freyburg, it is not difficult to see why locals call the area "the Tuscany of the North." With clean, wandering streets, whitewashed buildings, and a huge castle perched on a vine-terraced hill, Freyburg is a little out of place. The town owes its existence to Schloss Neuenburg, which was built by the same Thuringian count who built the Wartburg. Although most visitors head straight for the wine, the historic Old Town and castle certainly warrant a visit.

Freyburg is surrounded by a 1,200-meter-long, almost completely intact city wall. The **Ekstädter Tor** was the most important gate into the city and dates from the 14th century. The gate is dominated by one of the few remaining barbicans in central Germany.

ESSENTIALS

Visitor Information Freyburger Fremdenverkehrsverein ⊠ *Markt 2* ☎ *034464/27260* ⊕ *www.freyburg-info.de.*

EXPLORING

Rotkäppchen Sektkellerei (*Little Red Riding Hood Sparkling Wine*). Freyburg is the home of one of Europe's largest producers of sparkling wine, a rare eastern German product with a significant market share in the West. Hour-long tours of the production facility include the world's largest wooden wine barrel. ⊠ *Sektkellereistr. 5* ☎ *034464/340* ⊕ *www.rotkaeppchen.de* ⌦*€5* ⊗ *Daily 10–6; tours weekdays at 11 and 2, weekends at 11, 12:30, 2, and 3:30.*

St. Marien Kirche (*St. Mary's Church*). In 1225 the Thuringian count Ludwig IV erected the St. Marien Kirche as a triple-nave basilica and the only church within the city walls. The coquina limestone building, which resembles the cathedral in Naumburg, was renovated in the 15th century into its current form as a single-hall structure. The great carved altarpiece also dates from the 15th century and the baptistery from 1592. ⊠ *Markt 2.*

Schloss Neuenburg (*Neuenburg Castle*). Since its foundation was laid in 1090 by the Thuringian Ludwig I, this castle has loomed protectively over Freyburg. The spacious residential area and huge towers date from the 13th century, when Neuenburg was a part of Thuringia's eastern defenses. The spartan, Gothic double-vaulted chapel from 1190 is one of the few rooms that evokes an early medieval past, since most of the castle was renovated in the 15th century. ⊠ *Schloss 1* ☎ *34464/35530* 🖃 *€7* ⏱ *Tues.–Sun. 10–5.*

Winzervereinigung-Freyburg (*Freyburg Vintner's Association*). The best way to try Salle-Unstrut wine is with this trade group. Its 500 members produce some of Germany's finest wines, both white and red, mostly varietals, with some limited blends. (A wonderful light red from a hybrid of the Blauer Zweigelt and St. James grape, called Andre, may change how you think about German red wine.) Tastings and tours must be arranged in advance—with options ranging from a simple tour of one of Germany's largest barrel cellars to the grand tasting (€15)—or you can simply show up on Fridays at 1 (€10). The association goes out of its way to cater to the tastes of its guests, and bread, cheese, and water are always in plentiful supply. ⊠ *Querfurter Str. 10* ☎ *034464/30623* ⊕ *www.winzervereinigung-freyburg.de* ⏱ *Mon.–Sat. 10–6, Sun. 10–4.*

WHERE TO EAT

$ ✕ **Burgwirtschaft.** Where better than a castle serenely overlooking the **GERMAN** village of Freyburg for a medieval restaurant? Everything is prepared according to historical recipes with ingredients from the region. Try the roast chicken with honey or any of the grilled meats. Most menu items are available in the spacious beer garden. ⑤ *Average main: €9* ⊠ *Schloss 1* ☎ *034464/66200.*

QUEDLINBURG

79 km (49 miles) northwest of Halle.

This medieval Harz town has more half-timber houses than any other town in Germany: more than 1,600 of them line the narrow cobblestone streets and squares. The town escaped destruction during World War II and was treasured in GDR days, though not very well preserved. Today the nicely restored town is a UNESCO World Heritage Site.

For nearly 200 years Quedlinburg was a favorite imperial residence and site of imperial diets, beginning with the election in 919 of Henry the Fowler (Henry I) as the first Saxon king of Germany. It became a major trading city and a member of the Hanseatic League, equal in stature to Köln.

ESSENTIALS

Visitor Information Quedlinburg Tourismus-Marketing GmbH ⊠ *Markt 2* ☎ *03946/905–624* ⊕ *www.quedlinburg.de.*

EXPLORING

Lyonel Feininger Gallery. This sophisticated, modern gallery is placed behind half-timber houses so as not to affect the town's medieval feel. When the art of American-born painter Lyonel Feininger, a Bauhaus teacher in both Weimar and Dessau, was declared "decadent" by the Hitler regime in 1938, the artist returned to America. Left behind with a friend were engravings, lithographs, etchings, and paintings. The most comprehensive Feininger print collection in the world is displayed here. ⊠ *Finkenherd 5a* ☎ *03946/2238* ⊕ *www.feininger-galerie.de* 💷 *€6* ☉ *Apr.–Oct., Tues.–Sun. 10–6; Nov.–Mar., Tues.–Sun. 10–5.*

Marktplatz. The Altstadt (Old Town) is full of richly decorated half-timber houses, particularly along Mühlgraben, Schuhof, the Hölle, Breitestrasse, and Schmalstrasse. Notable on the Marktplatz are the Renaissance **Rathaus**, with a 14th-century statue of Roland signifying the town's independence, and the baroque 1701 Haus Grünhagen. Street and hiking maps and guidebooks (almost all in German) are available in the information office at the Rathaus. ⊠ *Markt 2* ☎ *03946/90550* 💷 *Free* ☉ *Mon.–Sat. 9–3.*

Schlossmuseum (*Castle Museum*). Quedlinburg's largely Renaissance castle buildings perch on top of the Schlossberg (Castle Hill), with a terrace overlooking woods and valley. The grounds include the Schloss-museum, which has exhibits on the history of the town and castle, artifacts of the Bronze Age, and the wooden cage in which a captured 14th-century robber baron was put on public view. Restored 17th- and 18th-century rooms give an impression of castle life at that time. ⊠ *Schlossberg 1* ☎ *03946/2730* 💷 *€4* ☉ *Mar.–Oct., daily 10–6; Nov.–Feb., Sat.–Thurs. 10–4.*

Ständerbau Fachwerkmuseum (*Half-Timber House*). The oldest half-timber house in Quedlinburg, built about 1310, is now a museum. ⊠ *Wordg. 3* ☎ *03946/3828* 💷 *€3* ☉ *Apr.–Oct., Fri.–Wed. 10–5; Nov.–Mar., Fri.–Wed. 10–4.*

Stiftskirche St. Servatius (*Collegiate Church of St. Servatius*). This simple, graceful church is one of the most important and best-preserved 12th-century Romanesque structures in Germany. Henry I and his wife Mathilde are buried in its crypt. The renowned Quedlinburg Treasure of 10th-, 11th-, and 12th-century gold and silver and bejeweled manuscripts is also kept here (what's left of it). Nazi SS leader Heinrich Himmler made the church into a shrine dedicated to the SS, insisting that it was only appropriate, since Henry I was the founder of the First German Reich. ⊠ *Schlossberg 1* ☎ *03946/709–900* 💷 *€4* ☉ *May–Oct., Tues.–Fri. 10–6, Sat. 10–5, Sun. noon–6; Nov.–Apr., Tues.–Sat. 10–4, Sun. noon–4.*

WHERE TO EAT AND STAY

$ ✕ **Lüdde Bräu.** Brewing *Braunbier* (a hoppy, top-fermented beer) has
GERMAN been a Quedlinburg tradition for several centuries. The Lüdde brewery traces its history to 1807, when Braunbier breweries dotted the

Adorable Quedlinburg has 1,600 half-timber houses: that's more than any other town in Germany.

Harz Mountains, and it was the last surviving brewery when it closed its doors in 1966. After German reunification, Georg Lüdde's niece reopened the business, and it remains the only Braunbier brewery in Quedlinburg. Sampling the reemergence of an almost lost German tradition as well as some incredible beer-based game dishes, makes the restaurant well worth a visit—the top-fermented Braunbier is called *Pubarschknall.* ⑤ *Average main: €11* ⊠ *Carl-Ritter-Str. 1* ☎ *03946/901–481* ⊕ *www.hotel-brauhaus-luedde.de.*

\$ ⚏ **Hotel Zum Brauhaus.** In a beautifully restored half-timber house, **HOTEL** many of the rooms incorporate the bare load-bearing timbers and have pleasant views of the castle. **Pros:** friendly staff; location next to Lüdde brewery. **Cons:** a little rough around the edges; upper rooms get hot in summer. ⑤ *Rooms from: €77* ⊠ *Carl-Ritter-Str. 1* ☎ *03946/901–481* ⊕ *www.hotel-brauhaus-luedde.de* ↪ *50 rooms, 1 suite* ⏺⏺ *Breakfast.*

\$ ⚏ **Hotel Zur Goldenen Sonne.** Rooms in this baroque half-timber inn **HOTEL** are furnished in a pleasing, rustic fashion. **Pros:** beautiful half-timber house with modern conveniences; reasonable rates. **Cons:** the clock on the square strikes every 15 minutes; rooms in the renovated section not quite as nice as the ones in the half-timber house. ⑤ *Rooms from: €69* ⊠ *Steinweg 11* ☎ *03946/96250* ⊕ *www.hotelzurgoldenensonne.de* ↪ *27 rooms* ⏺⏺ *Breakfast.*

THURINGIA

Unlike other eastern states, unassuming Thuringia was not taken from the Slavs by wandering Germanic tribes but has been German since before the Middle Ages. The hilly countryside is mostly rural and forested, and it preserves a rich cultural past in countless small villages, medieval cities, and country palaces. In the 14th century traders used the 168-km (104-mile) Rennsteig ("fast trail") through the dark depths of the Thuringian Forest, and cities such as Erfurt and Eisenach evolved as major commercial hubs. Today the forests and the Erzgebirge Mountains are a remote paradise for hiking and fishing. The city of Weimar is one of Europe's old cultural centers, where Germany attempted its first go at a true democracy in 1918. Thuringia is the land of Goethe and Schiller, but it is also tempered by the ominous presence of one of the Third Reich's most notorious concentration camps: Buchenwald.

EISENACH

140 km (90 miles) southwest of Quedlinburg, 95 km (59 miles) northeast of Fulda.

When you stand in Eisenach's ancient market square it's difficult to imagine this half-timber town as an important center of the East German automobile industry. Yet this is where Wartburgs (very tiny, noisy, and cheaply produced cars, which are now collector's items) were made. The cars were named after the Wartburg, the famous castle that broods over Eisenach from atop one of the foothills of the Thuringian Forest. Today West German automaker Opel continues the tradition by building one of Europe's most modern car-assembly lines on the outskirts of town.

GETTING HERE AND AROUND

Hourly trains connect Eisenach with Leipzig (two hours) and Dresden (three hours). There are frequent connections to Weimar and Erfurt.

ESSENTIALS

Visitor Information Eisenach-Information ⊠ *Markt 24* ☎ *03691/79230* ⊕ *www.eisenach.de.*

EXPLORING

Bachhaus. Johann Sebastian Bach was born in Eisenach in 1685. The Bachhaus has exhibits devoted to the entire lineage of the musical Bach family and includes a collection of historical musical instruments. It is the largest collection of Bach memorabilia in the world, and includes a bust of the composer built using forensic science from a cast of his skull. ⊠ *Frauenplan 21* ☎ *03691/79340* ⊕ *www.bachhaus.de* 🎫 *€8.50* ☉ *Daily 10–6.*

Lutherhaus. This downtown house has many fascinating exhibits illustrating the life of Martin Luther, who lived here as a student. ⊠ *Lutherpl. 8* ☎ *03691/29830* ⊕ *www.lutherhaus-eisenach.de* 🎫 *€4.50* ☉ *Daily 10–5.*

Narrowest house. Built in 1890, this is said to be the narrowest house in eastern Germany. Its width is just over 6 feet, 8 inches; its height, 24½ feet; and its depth, 34 feet. ⊠ *Johannespl. 9.*

Reuter-Wagner-Museum. Composer Richard Wagner gets his due at this museum, which has the most comprehensive exhibition on Wagner's life and work outside Bayreuth. Monthly concerts take place in the old **Teezimmer** (tearoom), a hall with wonderfully restored French wallpaper. The Erard piano, dating from the late 19th century, is occasionally rolled out. ⊠ *Reuterweg 2* ☎ *03691/743–293* ✉ *€4* ☉ *Tues.–Wed. and Fri.–Sun. 11–5, Thurs. 3–8.*

Fodor's Choice

★

Wartburg Castle. Begun in 1067 (and expanded through the centuries), this mighty castle has hosted a parade of German celebrities. Hermann I (1156–1217), count of Thuringia and count palatine of Saxony, was a patron of the poets Walther von der Vogelweide (1170–1230) and Wolfram von Eschenbach (1170–1220). Legend has it that this is where Walther von der Vogelweide, the greatest lyric poet of medieval Germany, prevailed in the celebrated *Minnesängerstreit* (minnesinger contest), which is featured in Richard Wagner's *Tannhäuser.*

Within the castle's stout walls, Frederick the Wise (1463–1525) shielded Martin Luther from papal proscription from May 1521 until March 1522, even though Frederick did not share the reformer's beliefs. Luther completed the first translation of the New Testament from Greek into German while in hiding, an act that paved the way for the Protestant Reformation. You can peek into the simple study in which Luther worked. ▇TIP→ Be sure to check out the place where Luther saw the devil and threw an inkwell at him. Pilgrims have picked away at the spot for centuries, forcing the curators to "reapply" the ink.

Frederick was also a patron of the arts. Lucas Cranach the Elder's portraits of Luther and his wife are on view in the castle, as is a very moving sculpture, the *Leuchterengelpaar* (Candlestick Angel Group), by the great 15th-century artist Tilman Riemenschneider. The 13th-century great hall is breathtaking; it's here that the minstrels sang for courtly favors. ▇TIP→ Don't leave without climbing the belvedere for a panoramic view of the Harz Mountains and the Thuringian Forest. ⊠ *Auf der Wartburg 1* ☎ *03691/2500* ⊕ *www.wartburg-eisenach.de* ✉ *€9, including guided tour* ☉ *Mar.–Oct., daily 8:30–5; Nov.–Feb., daily 9–3:30.*

16

WHERE TO STAY

$$$$

HOTEL

⬚ **Hotel auf der Wartburg.** In this castle hotel, where Martin Luther, Johann Sebastian Bach, and Richard Wagner were guests, you'll get a splendid view over the town and the countryside. **Pros:** medieval music and fireplaces in the lobby. **Cons:** it's a hike to and from the city center. ⑤ *Rooms from: €235* ⊠ *Wartburg* ☎ *03691/7970* ⊕ *www.wartburghotel.de* ↩ *35 rooms* ⦿⎮ *Breakfast.*

$

HOTEL

⬚ **Hotel Glockenhof.** At the base of Wartburg Castle, this former church-run hostel has blossomed into a handsome hotel, cleverly incorporating the original half-timber city mansion into a modern extension. **Pros:** out of the hustle and bustle of the downtown; plenty of parking; an incredible breakfast buffet. **Cons:** uphill walk from the station is strenuous; location is a bit far from the city center. ⑤ *Rooms from: €89* ⊠ *Grimmelg. 4* ☎ *03691/2340* ⊕ *www.glockenhof.de* ↩ *38 rooms, 2 suites* ⦿⎮ *Breakfast.*

ERFURT

55 km (34 miles) east of Eisenach.

The city of Erfurt emerged from World War II relatively unscathed, with most of its innumerable towers intact. Of all the cities in the region, Erfurt is the most evocative of its prewar self, and it's easy to imagine that many of the towns in northern Germany would look like this had they not been destroyed. The city's highly decorative and colorful facades are easy to admire on a walking tour. ∎TIP➔ Downtown Erfurt is a photographer's delight, with narrow, busy, ancient streets dominated by a magnificent 14th-century Gothic cathedral, the Mariendom.

ESSENTIALS

Visitor Information Erfurt Tourist-Information ✉ *Benediktspl. 1* ☎ *0361/66400* ⊕ *www.erfurt-tourist-info.de.*

EXPLORING

The Anger. Erfurt's main transportation hub and pedestrian zone, the Anger developed as a result of urban expansion due to the growth of the railroad in Thuringia in the early 19th century. With some exceptions, the houses are all architecturally historicized, making them look much older than they really are. The **Hauptpostgebäude** was erected in 1892 in a mock-Gothic style.

Domplatz (*Cathedral Square*). This square is bordered by houses dating from the 16th century.

Klein Venedig (*Little Venice*). The area around the bridge, crisscrossed with old streets lined with picturesque and often crumbling homes, is known as Little Venice because of the recurrent flooding it endures.

Fodor'sChoice ★ **Krämerbrücke** (*Merchant's Bridge*). Behind the predominantly neo-Gothic Rathaus, Erfurt's most outstanding attraction spans the Gera River. This Renaissance bridge, similar to the Ponte Vecchio in Florence, is the longest of its kind in Europe and the only one north of the Alps. Built in 1325 and restored in 1967–73, the bridge served for centuries as an important trading center. Today antiques shops fill the majority of the timber-frame houses built into the bridge, some dating from the 16th century. The bridge comes alive on the third weekend of June for the Krämerbrückenfest.

Mariendom (*St. Mary's Cathedral*). This catthedral's Romanesque origins (foundations can be seen in the crypt) are best preserved in the choir's glorious stained-glass windows and beautifully carved stalls, and its biggest bell, the Gloriosa, is the largest free-swinging bell in the world. Cast in 1497, it took three years to install in the tallest of the three sharply pointed towers, painstakingly lifted inch by inch with wooden wedges. No chances are taken with this 2-ton treasure; its deep boom resonates only on special occasions, such as Christmas and New Year's. The Mariendom is reached by way of a broad staircase from the expansive Cathedral Square. ✉ *Dompl.* ☎ *0361/646–1265* 🕭 *Tour €2.50* ⊙ *May–Oct., Mon.–Sat. 9–5, Sun. 1–4; Nov.–Apr., Mon.–Sat. 10–11:30 and 12:30–4, Sun. 1–4.*

St. Augustin Kloster (*St. Augustine Monastery*). The young Martin Luther studied the liberal arts as well as law and theology at Erfurt University from 1501 to 1505. After a personal revelation, Luther asked to become a monk in the St. Augustin Kloster on July 17, 1505. He became an ordained priest here in 1507, and remained at the Kloster until 1511. Today the Kloster is a seminary and retreat hotel. ✉ *Augustinerstr. 10* ☎ *0361/576–600* ⊕ *www.augustinerkloster.de* ⊙ *Mon.–Sat. 10–noon and 2–4, Sun. hrs vary.*

St. Severus. This Gothic church has an extraordinary font, a masterpiece of intricately carved sandstone that reaches practically to the ceiling. It's linked to the cathedral by a 70-step open staircase. ✉ *Dompl.*

Zum Stockfisch. Erfurt's interesting local-history museum is in a late-Renaissance house. ✉ *Johannesstr. 169* ☎ *0361/655–5644* 🖭 *Museum €4* ⊙ *Tues.–Sun. 10–6.*

WHERE TO EAT

$$$$
GERMAN

✕ **Clara.** This restaurant in the historic, elegant Kaisersaal edifice is the jewel in Erfurt's small gourmet crown. Thuringia native chef Maria Gross has worked in top restaurants around Germany and developed her own minimalist style. Here she is pursuing her vision of a gourmet restaurant: a cozy, service-oriented oasis in which to enjoy delicious international dishes with a Thuringian accent. Using local producers, Clara serves delicious four- and five-course menus from a list of 10 dishes. The wine list is one of the best in eastern Germany, offering more than 300 wines from around the world. ⑤ *Average main: €59* ✉ *Futterstr. 1, 15–16* ☎ *0361/568–8207* ⊕ *www.restaurant-clara.de* ⊙ *Closed Sun. and Mon. No lunch.*

$
GERMAN

✕ **Faustus Restaurant.** In the heart of historic Erfurt the stylish Faustus defines fine Thuringian dining. This restaurant is in an old mansion, with both an inviting summer terrace and a bright, airy dining room. An after-dinner drink at the superb bar is a must. ⑤ *Average main: €13* ✉ *Wenigermarkt 5* ☎ *0361/540–0954* 🖃 *No credit cards.*

$
GERMAN

✕ **Luther Keller.** Head down the straw-covered stairs in front of Clara restaurant, and you'll find yourself transported to the Middle Ages. The Luther Keller offers simple but tasty medieval cuisine in a candlelit vaulted cellar. Magicians, minnesingers, jugglers, and other players round out the enjoyable experience. Sure, it's pure kitsch, but it is entertaining, and the roast wild boar is delicious. ⑤ *Average main: €12* ✉ *Futterstr. 15* ☎ *0361/568–8205* ⊙ *Closed Mon. and Sun. No lunch.*

$
GERMAN

✕ **Zum Goldenen Schwan.** Beer lovers rejoice: in addition to the Braugold brewery, Erfurt has six brewpubs, among which the Golden Swan is by far the best. The house beer is a pleasant unfiltered *Kellerbier*, and other beers are brewed according to the season. The constantly changing seasonal menu is a step above normal brewpub fare, and the sauerbraten defines how the dish should be made. ⑤ *Average main: €10* ✉ *Michaelisstr. 9* ☎ *0361/262–3742.*

16

WHERE TO STAY

$$ **Radisson Blu Hotel Erfurt.** Since the SAS group gave the ugly high-
HOTEL rise Kosmos a face-lift, the socialist-realist look of the GDR years no
longer intrudes on Hotel Erfurt. **Pros:** a safe, clean option in the city
center; good restaurant. **Cons:** rather characterless business hotel.
$ *Rooms from: €105* ⌧ *Juri-Gagarin-Ring 127* ☎ *0361/55100* ⊕ *www.
radissonblu.com* ↪ *282 rooms, 3 suites* ⊚ *Breakfast.*

WEIMAR

21 km (13 miles) east of Erfurt.

Sitting prettily in the geographical center of Thuringia, Weimar occupies
a place in German political and cultural history completely dispropor-
tionate to its size (population 63,000). It's not even particularly old by
German standards, with a civic history that started as late as 1410. Yet
by the early 19th century the city had become one of Europe's most
important cultural centers, where poets Goethe and Schiller wrote,
Johann Sebastian Bach played the organ for his Saxon patrons, Carl
Maria von Weber composed some of his best music, and Franz Liszt
was director of music, presenting the first performance of *Lohengrin*
here. In 1919 Walter Gropius founded his Staatliches Bauhaus here,
and behind the classical pillars of the National Theater the German
National Assembly drew up the constitution of the Weimar Republic,
the first German democracy. As the Weimar Republic began to collapse
in 1926, Hitler chose the little city as the site for the second national
congress of his Nazi party, where he founded the Hitler Youth. On the
outskirts of Weimar the Nazis built—or forced prisoners to build for
them—the infamous Buchenwald concentration camp.

GETTING HERE AND AROUND

Weimar is on the ICE line between Dresden/Leipzig and Frankfurt.
IC trains link the city with Berlin. Weimar has an efficient bus system,
but most sights are within walking distance in the compact city center.

ESSENTIALS

Visitor Information Tourist-Information Weimar ⌧ *Markt 10* ☎ *03643/7450*
⊕ *www.weimar.de.*

EXPLORING

Bauhaus Museum. Walter Gropius founded the Staatliches Bauhaus (Bau-
haus design school) in Weimar in 1919. It was Germany's most influen-
tial and avant-garde design school, and it ushered in the era of modern
architecture and design just before the start of World War II. Although the
school moved to Dessau in 1925, Weimar's Bauhaus Museum is a modest,
yet superb collection of the works of Gropius, Johannes Itten, and Henry
van de Velde. ⌧ *Theaterpl.* ☎ *03643/545–961* ⊕ *www.klassik-stiftung.
de* ⊠ *€5* ☉ *Apr.–Oct., Tues.–Sun. 10–6; Nov.–Mar., Tues.–Sun. 10–4.*

OFF THE **Gedenkstätte Buchenwald** (*Buchenwald Memorial*). Just north of Wei-
BEATEN mar, amid the natural beauty of the Ettersberg hills that once served
PATH as Goethe's inspiration, sits the blight of Buchenwald, one of the most
infamous Nazi concentration camps. Sixty-five thousand men, women,
and children from 35 countries met their deaths here through forced

labor, starvation, disease, and gruesome medical experiments. Each is commemorated by a small stone placed on the outlines of the barracks, which have long since disappeared from the site, and by a massive memorial tower. In an especially cruel twist of fate, many liberated inmates returned to the camp as political prisoners of the Soviet occupation; they are remembered in the exhibit Soviet Special Camp #2. Besides exhibits, tours are available. To reach Buchenwald by public transportation, take Bus No. 6 (in the direction of Buchenwald, not Ettersburg), which leaves every 10 minutes from Goetheplatz in downtown Weimar. The one-way fare is €1.90. ☎ *03643/4300* ⊕ *www. buchenwald.de* ✉ *Free* ☉ *May–Sept., Tues.–Sun. 10–5:30; Oct.–Apr., Tues.–Sun. 9–4:30.*

Fodor'sChoice **Goethe Nationalmuseum** (*Goethe National Museum*). Goethe spent 57
★ years in Weimar, 47 of them in a house two blocks south of Theaterplatz that has since become a shrine attracting millions of visitors. The Goethe Nationalmuseum consists of several houses, including the **Goethehaus,** where Goethe lived. It shows an exhibit about life in Weimar around 1750 and contains writings that illustrate not only the great man's literary might but also his interest in the sciences, particularly medicine, and his administrative skills (and frustrations) as minister of state and Weimar's exchequer. You'll see the desk at which Goethe stood to write (he liked to work standing up) and the modest bed in which he died. The rooms are dark and often cramped, but an almost palpable intellectual intensity seems to illuminate them. ✉ *Frauenplan 1* ☎ *03643/545–320* ⊕ *www.weimar-klassik.de/english* ✉ *€10.50* ☉ *Apr.–Oct., Tues.–Sun. 9–6; Nov.–Mar., Tues.–Fri., and Sun. 9–4, Sat. 9–7.*

Goethes Gartenhaus (*Garden House*). Goethe's beloved Gartenhaus is a modest country cottage where he spent many happy hours, wrote much poetry, and began his masterly classical drama *Iphigenie*. The house is set amid meadowlike parkland on the bank of the River Ilm. Goethe is said to have felt very close to nature here, and you can soak up the same rural atmosphere on footpaths along the peaceful little river. ✉ *Im Park an der Ilm, Hans-Wahl-Str. 4* ☎ *03643/545–375* ⊕ *www.weimar-klassik.de/english* ✉ *Cottage €6* ☉ *Apr.–Oct., Wed.–Mon. 9–6; Nov.–Mar., Wed.–Mon. 10–4.*

Herderkirche (*Herder Church*). The Marktplatz's late-Gothic church has a large winged altar started by Lucas Cranach the Elder and finished by his son in 1555. The elder Cranach lived in a nearby house (two blocks east of Theaterplatz) during his last years, 1552–53. Its wide, imposing facade is richly decorated and bears the coat of arms of the Cranach family. It now houses a modern art gallery. ✉ *Herderpl. 8.*

Historischer Friedhof (*Historic Cemetery*). Goethe and Schiller are buried in this leafy cemetery, where virtually every gravestone commemorates a famous citizen of Weimar. Their tombs are in the vault of the classical-style chapel. The cemetery is a short walk past Goethehaus and Wieland Platz. ✉ *Am Poseckschen Garten* ☎ *03643/545–400* ✉ *Goethe-Schiller vault €2.50* ☉ *Apr.–Oct., Wed.–Mon. 9–1 and 2–6; Nov.–Mar., Wed.–Mon. 10–1 and 2–4.*

16

Take a carriage ride through Weimar to absorb the city's impressive history.

Neues Museum Weimar (*New Museum Weimar*). The city is proud of eastern Germany's first museum exclusively devoted to contemporary art. The building, dating from 1869, was carefully restored and converted to hold collections of American minimalist and conceptual art and works by German installation-artist Anselm Kiefer and American painter Keith Haring. In addition, it regularly presents international modern-art exhibitions. ⊠ *Weimarpl. 5* ☏ *03643/545–930* ⊕ *www.kunstsammlungen-weimar.de* ☏ *€5.50* ⏱ *Apr.–Oct., Tues.–Sun. 11–6; Nov.–Mar., Tues.–Sun. 11–4.*

Schillerhaus. This green-shuttered residence, part of the Goethe National Museum, is on a tree-shaded square not far from Goethe's house. Schiller and his family spent a happy, all-too-brief three years here (he died here in 1805). Schiller's study is tucked underneath the mansard roof, a cozy room dominated by his desk, where he probably completed *Wilhelm Tell*. Much of the remaining furniture and the collection of books were added later, although they all date from around Schiller's time. ⊠ *Schillerstr. 17* ☏ *03643/545–350* ⊕ *www.klassik-stiftung.de* ☏ *€7.50* ⏱ *Apr.–Oct., Tues.–Sun. 9–6; Nov.–Mar., Tues.–Sun. 9–4.*

Stadtschloss (*City Castle*). Around the corner from the Herderkirche, this 16th-century castle has a finely restored classical staircase, a festival hall, and a falcon gallery. The tower on the southwest projection dates from the Middle Ages but received its baroque overlay circa 1730. The **Kunstsammlung** (art collection) here includes several works by Cranach the Elder and many early-20th-century pieces by such artists as Böcklin, Liebermann, and Beckmann. ⊠ *Burgpl. 4* ☏ *03643/545–930* ⊕ *www.klassik-stiftung.de* ☏ *€7.50* ⏱ *Apr.–Oct., Tues.–Sun. 10–6; Nov.–Mar., Tues.–Sun. 10–4.*

Theaterplatz. A statue on this square, in front of the National Theater, shows Goethe placing a paternal hand on the shoulder of the younger Schiller.

Wittumspalais (*Wittum Mansion*). Much of Weimar's greatness is owed to its patron, the widowed countess Anna Amalia, whose home, the Wittumspalais, is surprisingly modest. In the late 18th century the countess went talent hunting for cultural figures to decorate the glittering court her Saxon forebears had established. She discovered Goethe, and he served the countess as a counselor, advising her on financial matters and town design. Schiller followed, and he and Goethe became valued visitors to the countess's home. Within this exquisite baroque house you can see the drawing room in which she held soirées, complete with the original cherrywood table at which the company sat. The east wing of the house contains a small museum that's a fascinating memorial to those cultural gatherings. ⊠ *Am Theaterpl.* ☎ *03643/545–377* ⊟ *€6* ⊘ *Apr.–Oct., Tues.–Sun. 9–6; Nov.–Mar., Tues.–Sun. 10–4.*

WHERE TO EAT

$ ✕ **Felsenkeller.** When Ludwig Deinhard purchased the Weimar Stadt-
GERMAN brauerei in 1875, Felsenkeller was already 100 years old. Beer has been brewed here in small batches ever since. Although the brewpub is outside the city center, it's worth a trip to sample the brews and the inventive seasonal selections. The pub serves standard fare at reasonable prices. ⑤ *Average main: €9* ⊠ *Humboldtstr. 37* ☎ *03643/414–741* ⊟ *No credit cards* ⊘ *Closed Mon.*

$ ✕ **Ratskeller.** This is one of the region's most authentic town hall–cel-
GERMAN lar restaurants. Its whitewashed, barrel-vaulted ceiling has witnessed centuries of tradition. At the side is a cozy bar, where you can enjoy a preprandial drink beneath a spectacular art nouveau skylight. The delicious sauerbraten and the famous bratwurst (with sauerkraut and mashed potatoes) are the highlights of the Thuringian menu. If venison is in season, try it—likewise the wild duck or wild boar in red-wine sauce. ⑤ *Average main: €11* ⊠ *Am Markt 10* ☎ *03643/850–573.*

$ ✕ **Scharfe Ecke.** If *Klösse* (dumplings) are a religion, this restaurant is
GERMAN their cathedral. Thuringia's traditional Klösse are at their best here, but
FAMILY be patient—they're made to order and can take up to 20 minutes. The Klösse come with just about every dish, from roast pork to venison stew, and the wait is well worth it. The ideal accompaniment to anything on the menu is one of the three locally brewed beers on tap or the fine selection of Salle-Unstrut wines. ⑤ *Average main: €11* ⊠ *Eisfeld 2* ☎ *03643/202–430* ⊟ *No credit cards* ⊘ *Closed Mon.*

$ ✕ **Sommer's Weinstuben und Restaurant.** The city's oldest pub and restau-
GERMAN rant, a 130-year-old landmark in the center of Weimar, is still going strong. The authentic Thuringian specialties and huge *Kartoffelpfannen* (potato pans), with fried potatoes and various kinds of meat, are prepared by the fifth generation of the Sommer family, and are as tasty as ever. Add to that a romantic courtyard and a superb wine list with some rare vintages from local vineyards. ⑤ *Average main: €10* ⊠ *Humboldtstr. 2* ☎ *03643/400–691* ⊟ *No credit cards* ⊘ *Closed Sun. No lunch.*

16

WHERE TO STAY

$ 🏨 **Amalienhof VCH Hotel.** Book far ahead to secure a room at this friendly
HOTEL   little hotel central to Weimar's attractions. **Pros:** surprisingly good
value; rooms are often upgraded to the highest available category at
check-in. **Cons:** street noise can be bothersome. $ *Rooms from: €97*
⊠ Amalienstr. 2 ☎ *03643/5490* ⊕ *www.amalienhof-weimar.de* ↩ *23
rooms, 9 apartments* ⭤ *Breakfast.*

$$ 🏨 **Grand Hotel Russischer Hof.** This historic, classical hotel, once the haunt
HOTEL   of European nobility and intellectual society, continues to be a luxurious
Fodor'sChoice   gem in the heart of Weimar—it's one of eastern Germany's finest hotels.
★   **Pros:** a quiet hotel in the city center. **Cons:** rooms are on the small side,
with thin walls; some overlook an unsightly back courtyard. $ *Rooms
from: €110* ⊠ *Goethepl. 2* ☎ *03643/7740* ⊕ *www.russischerhof.com*
↩ *119 rooms, 6 suites.*

$$ 🏨 **Hotel Elephant.** The historic Elephant, dating from 1696, has been
HOTEL   famous for its charm—even through the Communist years. **Pros:** a beau-
Fodor'sChoice   tiful historical building right in the city center. **Cons:** no a/c; rooms
★   in the front are sometimes bothered by the town clock if windows
are open. $ *Rooms from: €131* ⊠ *Markt 19* ☎ *03643/8020* ⊕ *www.
hotelelephantweimar.com* ↩ *94 rooms, 5 suites* ⭤ *Breakfast.*

UNDERSTANDING GERMANY

CHRONOLOGY

VOCABULARY

MENU GUIDE

CHRONOLOGY

ca. 5000 BC Indo-Germanic tribes settle in the Rhine and Danube valleys.

ca. 2000–800 BC Distinctive German Bronze Age culture emerges, with settlements ranging from coastal farms to lakeside villages.

ca. 450–50 BC Salzkammergut people, whose prosperity is based on abundant salt deposits (in the area of upper Austria), trade with Greeks and Etruscans; Salzkammerguts spread as far as Belgium and have first contact with the Romans.

9 BC–AD 9 Roman attempts to conquer the "Germans"—the tribes of the Cibri, the Franks, the Goths, and the Vandals—are only partly successful; the Rhine becomes the northeastern border of the Roman Empire (and remains so for 300 years).

212 Roman citizenship is granted to all free inhabitants of the empire.

ca. 400 Pressed forward by Huns from Asia, such German tribes as the Franks, the Vandals, and the Lombards migrate to Gaul (France), Spain, Italy, and North Africa, scattering the empire's populace and eventually leading to the disintegration of central Roman authority.

486 The Frankish kingdom is founded by Clovis; his court is in Paris.

497 The Franks convert to Christianity.

EARLY MIDDLE AGES

776 Charlemagne becomes king of the Franks.

800 Charlemagne is declared Holy Roman Emperor; he makes Aachen capital of his realm, which stretches from the Bay of Biscay to the Adriatic and from the Mediterranean to the Baltic. Under his enlightened patronage there is an upsurge in art and architecture—the Carolingian renaissance.

843 The Treaty of Verdun divides Charlemagne's empire among his three sons: West Francia becomes France; Lotharingia becomes Lorraine (territory to be disputed by France and Germany into the 20th century); and East Francia takes on, roughly, the shape of modern Germany.

911 Five powerful German dukes (of Bavaria, Lorraine, Franconia, Saxony, and Swabia) establish the first German monarchy by electing King Conrad I. Henry I (the Fowler) succeeds Conrad in 919.

962 Otto I is crowned Holy Roman Emperor by the pope; he establishes Austria—the East Mark. The Ottonian renaissance is marked especially by the development of Romanesque architecture.

MIDDLE AGES

1024–1125 The Salian dynasty is characterized by a struggle between emperors and the Church that leaves the empire weak and disorganized; the great Romanesque cathedrals of Speyer, Trier, and Mainz are built.

1138–1254 Frederick Barbarossa leads the Hohenstaufen dynasty; there is temporary recentralization of power, underpinned by strong trade and Church relations.

1158 Munich, capital of Bavaria, is founded by Duke Henry the Lion. He is deposed by Emperor Barbarossa, and Munich is presented to the House of Wittelsbach, which rules it until 1918.

1241 The Hanseatic League is founded to protect trade; Bremen, Hamburg, Köln, and Lübeck are early members. Agencies are soon established in London, Antwerp, Venice, and along the Baltic and North seas; a complex banking and finance system results.

mid-1200s The Gothic style, exemplified by the grand Köln Cathedral, flourishes.

1349 The Black Death plague kills one-quarter of the German population.

RENAISSANCE AND REFORMATION

1456 Johannes Gutenberg (1400–68) prints the first book in Europe.

1471–1553 The Renaissance flowers under influence of painter and engraver Albrecht Dürer (1471–1528); Dutch-born philosopher and scholar Erasmus (1466–1536); Lucas Cranach the Elder (1472–1553), who originates Protestant religious painting; portrait and historical painter Hans Holbein the Younger (1497–1543); and landscape-painting pioneer Albrecht Altdorfer (1480–1538). Increasing wealth among the merchant classes leads to strong patronage of the revived arts.

1517 The Protestant Reformation begins in Germany when Martin Luther (1483–1546) nails his 95 Theses to a church door in Wittenberg, contending that the Roman Church has forfeited divine authority through its corrupt sale of indulgences. Luther is outlawed, and his revolutionary doctrine splits the Church; much of north Germany embraces Protestantism.

1524–30 The (Catholic) Habsburgs rise to power; their empire spreads throughout Europe (and as far as North Africa, the Americas, and the Philippines). Erasmus breaks with Luther and supports reform within the Roman Catholic Church. In 1530 Charles V—a Habsburg—is crowned Holy Roman Emperor; he brutally crushes the Peasants' War, one in a series of populist uprisings in Europe.

1545 The Council of Trent marks the beginning of the Counter-Reformation. Through diplomacy and coercion, most Austrians, Bavarians, and Bohemians are won back to Catholicism, but the majority of Germans remain Lutheran; persecution of religious minorities grows.

THIRTY YEARS' WAR

1618–48 Germany is the main theater for the Thirty Years' War. The powerful Catholic Habsburgs are defeated by Protestant forces, swelled by disgruntled Habsburg subjects and the armies of King Gustav Adolphus of Sweden. The bloody conflict ends with the Peace of Westphalia (1648); Habsburg and papal authority are severely diminished.

ABSOLUTISM AND ENLIGHTENMENT

1689 Louis XIV of France invades the Rhineland Palatinate and sacks Heidelberg. At the end of the 17th century, Germany consolidates its role as a center of scientific thought.

1708 Johann Sebastian Bach (1685–1750) becomes court organist at Weimar and launches his career; he and Georg Friederic Handel (1685–1759) fortify the great tradition of German music. Baroque and, later, rococo art and architecture flourish.

1740–86 Reign of Frederick the Great of Prussia; his rule sees both the expansion of Prussia (it becomes the dominant military force in Germany) and the spread of Enlightenment thought.

ca. 1790 The great age of European orchestral music is raised to new heights with the works of Joseph Haydn (1732–1809), Wolfgang Amadeus Mozart (1756–91), and Ludwig van Beethoven (1770–1827).

early 1800s Johann Wolfgang von Goethe (1749–1832) is part of the Sturm und Drang movement, which leads to Romanticism. Painter Caspar David Friedrich (1774–1840) leads early German Romanticism. Other luminary cultural figures include writers Friedrich Schiller (1759–1805) and Heinrich von Kleist (1777–1811); and composers Robert Schumann (1810–56), Hungarian-born Franz Liszt (1811–86), Richard Wagner (1813–83), and Johannes Brahms (1833–97). In architecture, the severe lines of neoclassicism become popular.

ROAD TO NATIONHOOD

1806 Napoléon's armies invade Prussia; it briefly becomes part of the French Empire.

1807 The Prussian prime minister Baron vom und zum Stein frees the serfs, creating a new spirit of patriotism; the Prussian army is rebuilt.

1813 The Prussians defeat Napoléon at Leipzig.

1815 Britain and Prussia defeat Napoléon at Waterloo. At the Congress of Vienna the German Confederation is created as a loose union of 39 independent states, reduced from more than 300 principalities. The Bundestag (national assembly) is established at Frankfurt. Already powerful Prussia increases its territory, gaining the Rhineland, Westphalia, and most of Saxony.

1848 The "Year of the Revolutions" is marked by uprisings across the fragmented German Confederation; Prussia expands. A national parliament is elected, taking the power of the Bundestag to prepare a constitution for a united Germany.

1862 Otto von Bismarck (1815–98) becomes prime minister of Prussia; he is determined to wrest German-populated provinces from Austro-Hungarian (Habsburg) control.

1866 Austria-Hungary is defeated by the Prussians at Sadowa; Bismarck sets up the Northern German Confederation in 1867. A key figure in Bismarck's plans is Ludwig II of Bavaria. Ludwig—a political simpleton—lacks successors, making it easy for Prussia to seize his lands.

1867 Karl Marx (1818–83) publishes *Das Kapital.*

1870–71 The Franco-Prussian War: Prussia lays siege to Paris. Victorious Prussia seizes Alsace-Lorraine but eventually withdraws from all other occupied French territories.

1871 The four South German states agree to join the Northern Confederation; Wilhelm I is proclaimed first kaiser of the united empire.

MODERNISM

1882 The Triple Alliance is forged between Germany, Austria-Hungary, and Italy. Germany's industrial revolution blossoms, enabling it to catch up with the other great powers of Europe. Germany establishes colonies in Africa and the Pacific.

ca. 1885 Daimler and Benz pioneer the automobile.

1890 Kaiser Wilhelm II (rules 1888–1918) dismisses Bismarck and begins a new, more aggressive course of foreign policy; he oversees the expansion of the navy.

1890s A new school of writers, including Rainer Maria Rilke (1875–1926), emerges. Rilke's *Sonnets to Orpheus* gives German poetry new lyricism.

1905 Albert Einstein (1879–1955) announces his theory of relativity.

1906 Painter Ernst Ludwig Kirchner (1880–1938) helps organize *Die Brücke,* a group of artists who, along with *Der Blaue Reiter,* create the avant-garde art movement expressionism.

1907 Great Britain, Russia, and France form the Triple Entente, which, set against the Triple Alliance, divides Europe into two armed camps.

1914–18 Austrian archduke Franz-Ferdinand is assassinated in Sarajevo. The attempted German invasion of France sparks World War I; Italy and Russia join the Allies, and four years of pitched battle ensue. By 1918 the Central Powers are encircled and must capitulate.

WEIMAR REPUBLIC

1918   Germany is compelled by the Versailles Treaty to give up its overseas colonies and much European territory (including Alsace-Lorraine to France) and to pay huge reparations to the Allies; Kaiser Wilhelm II repudiates the throne and goes into exile in Holland. The tough terms leave the new democracy, called the Weimar Republic, shaky.

1919   The Bauhaus school of art and design, the brainchild of Walter Gropius (1883–1969), is born. Thomas Mann (1875–1955) and Hermann Hesse (1877–1962) forge a new style of visionary intellectual writing.

1923   Germany suffers runaway inflation. Adolf Hitler's Beer Hall Putsch, a rightist revolt, fails; leftist revolts are frequent.

1925   Hitler publishes *Mein Kampf* (*My Struggle*)

1932   The Nazi party gains the majority in the Reichstag (parliament).

1933   Hitler becomes chancellor; the Nazi "revolution" begins. In Berlin, Nazi students stage the burning of more than 25,000 books by Jewish and other politically undesirable authors.

NAZI GERMANY

1934   President Paul von Hindenburg dies; Hitler declares himself Führer (leader) of the Third Reich. Nazification of all German social institutions begins, spreading a policy that is virulently racist and anticommunist. Germany recovers industrial might and re-arms.

1936   Germany signs anticommunist agreements with Italy and Japan, forming the Axis; Hitler reoccupies the Rhineland.

1938   The *Anschluss* (annexation): Hitler occupies Austria. Germany occupies the Sudetenland in Czechoslovakia. *Kristallnacht* (Night of Broken Glass), in November, marks the Nazis' first open and direct terrorism against German Jews. Synagogues and Jewish-owned businesses are burned, looted, and destroyed in a night of violence.

1939–40   In August Hitler signs a pact with the Soviet Union; in September he invades Poland. War is declared by the Allies. Over the next three years there are Nazi invasions of Denmark, Norway, the Low Countries, France, Yugoslavia, and Greece. Alliances form between Germany and the Baltic states.

1941–45   Hitler launches his anticommunist crusade against the Soviet Union, reaching Leningrad in the north and Stalingrad and the Caucasus in the south. In 1944 the Allies land in France; their combined might brings the Axis to its knees. In addition to the millions killed in the fighting, more than 6 million Jews and other victims die in Hitler's concentration camps. Germany is again in ruins. Hitler kills himself in April 1945. East Berlin and what becomes East Germany are occupied by the Soviet Union.

THE COLD WAR

1945 At the Yalta Conference, France, the United States, Britain, and the Soviet Union divide Germany into four zones; each country occupies a sector of Berlin. The Potsdam Agreement expresses the determination to rebuild Germany as a democracy.

1946 East Germany's Social Democratic Party merges with the Communist Party, forming the SED, which would rule East Germany for the next 40 years.

1948 The Soviet Union tears up the Potsdam Agreement and attempts, by blockade, to exclude the three other Allies from their agreed zones in Berlin. Stalin is frustrated by a massive airlift of supplies to West Berlin.

1949 The three western zones are combined to form the Federal Republic of Germany; the new West German parliament elects Konrad Adenauer as chancellor (a post he held until his retirement in 1963). Soviet-held East Germany becomes the Communist German Democratic Republic (GDR).

1950s West Germany, aided by the financial impetus provided by the Marshall Plan, rebuilds its devastated cities and economy—the *Wirtschaftswunder* (economic miracle) gathers speed. The writers Heinrich Böll, Wolfgang Koeppen, and Günter Grass emerge.

1957 The Treaty of Rome heralds the formation of the European Economic Community (EEC); West Germany is a founding member.

1961 Communists build the Berlin Wall to stem the outward tide of refugees.

1969–74 The vigorous chancellorship of Willy Brandt pursues *Ostpolitik,* improving relations with Eastern Europe and the Soviet Union and acknowledging East Germany's sovereignty.

mid-1980s The powerful German Green Party emerges as the leading environmentalist voice in Europe.

REUNIFICATION

1989 Discontent in East Germany leads to a flood of refugees westward and to mass demonstrations. Communist power collapses across Eastern Europe; the Berlin Wall falls.

1990 In March the first free elections in East Germany bring a center-right government to power. The Communists, faced with corruption scandals, suffer a big defeat but are represented (as Democratic Socialists) in the new, democratic parliament. The World War II victors hold talks with the two German governments, and the Soviet Union gives its support for reunification. Economic union takes place on July 1, with full political unity on October 3. In December, in the first democratic national German elections in 58 years, Chancellor Helmut Kohl's three-party coalition is reelected.

1991   Nine months of emotional debate end on June 20, when parliamentary representatives vote to move the capital from Bonn—seat of the West German government since 1949—to Berlin, the capital of Germany until the end of World War II.

1998   Helmut Kohl's record 16-year-long chancellorship of Germany ends with the election of Gerhard Schröder. Schröder's Social Democratic Party (SPD) pursues a coalition with the Greens in order to replace the three-party coalition of the Christian Democratic Union (CDU), Christian Social Union (CSU), and Free Democratic Party (FDP).

1999   The Bundestag, the German parliament, returns to the restored Reichstag in Berlin on April 19. The German federal government also leaves Bonn for Berlin, making Berlin capital of Germany again.

1999–2003   For the first time since 1945, the German army (the *Bundeswehr*) is deployed in combat missions in the former Yugoslavia and Afghanistan.

2000   Hannover hosts Germany's first world's exposition, EXPO 2000, the largest ever staged in the 150-year history of the event.

2005   Chancellor Schröder asks for a vote of confidence in parliament and fails. After a new election in September, Angela Merkel (CDU) becomes the new chancellor with a "grand coalition" of CDU/CSU and SPD.

2006   Germany hosts the 2006 FIFA World Cup, the world's soccer championship.

2007   Angela Merkel as German chancellor and also in her role as the then President of the Council of the European Union hosts the G-8 summit in Heiligendamm, Germany.

2008   Chancellor Merkel (CDU) together with her minister of Finance Steinbrück (SPD) announce at a specially called nationwide TV press conference the safety of all private savings accounts.

2009   In Bundestag elections the alliance of the CDU/CSU and FDP receive an outright majority of seats, ensuring that Angela Merkel continues as chancellor.

GERMAN VOCABULARY

	ENGLISH	GERMAN	PRONUNCIATION
BASICS			
	Yes/no	Ja/nein	yah/nine
	Please	Bitte	**bit**-uh
	Thank you (very much)	Danke (vielen Dank)	**dahn**-kuh (**fee**-lun-dahnk)
	Excuse me	Entschuldigen Sie	ent-**shool**-de-gen zee
	I'm sorry	Es tut mir leid	es toot meer lite
	Good day	Guten Tag	**goo**-ten tahk
	Good-bye	Auf Wiedersehen	auf **vee**-der-zane
	Mr./Mrs.	Herr/Frau	hair/frau
	Miss	Fräulein	**froy**-line
NUMBERS			
	1	Ein(s)	ein(ts)
	2	Zwei	tsvai
	3	Drei	dry
	4	Vier	fear
	5	Fünf	funph
	6	Sechs	zex
	7	Sieben	**zee**-ben
	8	Acht	ahkt
	9	Neun	noyn
	10	Zehn	tsane
DAYS OF THE WEEK			
	Sunday	Sonntag	**zone**-tahk
	Monday	Montag	**moan**-tahk
	Tuesday	Dienstag	**deens**-tahk
	Wednesday	Mittwoch	**mit**-voah
	Thursday	Donnerstag	**doe**-ners-tahk
	Friday	Freitag	**fry**-tahk
	Saturday	Samstag/Sonnabend	**zahm**-stakh/ **zonn**-a-bent

ENGLISH	GERMAN	PRONUNCIATION

USEFUL PHRASES

ENGLISH	GERMAN	PRONUNCIATION
Do you speak	Sprechen Sie	**shprek**-hun zee
English?	Englisch?	**eng**-glish
I don't speak	Ich spreche kein	ich **shprek**-uh kine
German.	Deutsch.	Doych
Please speak	Bitte sprechen Sie	**bit**-uh **shprek**-en-
slowly.	langsam.	zee **lahng**-zahm
I am	Ich bin	ich bin
American/	Amerikaner(in)/	A-mer-i-**kahn**-er(in)/
British	Engländer(in)	**Eng**-glan-der(in)
My name is . . .	Ich heisse . . .	ich **hi**-suh
Where are the	Wo ist die	vo ist dee
restrooms?	Toilette?	twah-**let**-uh
Left/right	links/rechts	links/rekts
Open/closed	offen/geschlossen	**O**-fen/geh-**shloss**-en
Where is . . .	Wo ist . . .	**vo** ist
the train station?	der Bahnhof?	dare **bahn**-hof
the bus stop?	die Bushaltestelle?	dee **booss**-hahlt-uh-**shtel**-uh
the subway	die U-bahn-	dee oo-bahn-**staht**-
station?	Station?	Sion
the airport?	der Flughafen?	dare **floog**-plats
the post office?	die Post?	dee **post**
the bank?	die Bank?	dee **banhk**
the police station?	die Polizeistation?	dee po-lee-tsai-**staht**-sion
the hospital?	das Krankenhaus?	dahs **krahnk**-en-house
the telephone?	das Telefon?	dahs te-le-**fone**
I'd like . . .	Ich hätte gerne . . .	ich **het**-uh gairn-uh
a room	ein Zimmer	ein **tsim**-er
the key	der Schlüssel	den **shlooh**-sul

ENGLISH	GERMAN	PRONUNCIATION
a map	eine Stadtplan	I-nuh **staht**-plahn
a ticket	eine Karte	I-nuh **cart**-uh
How much is it?	Wie viel kostet das?	**vee**-**feel cost**-et dahs
I am ill/sick.	Ich bin krank.	ich bin krahnk
I need . . .	Ich brauche . . .	ich **brow**-khuh
a doctor	einen Arzt	I-nen artst
the police	die Polizei	dee po-li-**tsai**
help	Hilfe	**hilf-uh**
Stop!	Halt!	Hahlt
Fire!	Feuer!	**foy**-er
Look out/Caution!	Achtung!/Vorsicht!	**ahk**-tung/**for**-zicht

DINING OUT

A bottle of . . .	eine Flasche . . .	I-nuh **flash**-uh
A cup of . . .	eine Tasse . . .	I-nuh **tahs**-uh
A glass of . . .	ein Glas . . .	ein glahss
Ashtray	der Aschenbecher	dare **Ahsh**-en-bekh-er
Bill/check	die Rechnung	dee **rekh**-nung
Do you have . . .?	Haben Sie . . .?	**hah**-ben zee
I am a vegetarian.	Ich bin Vegetarier(in)	ich bin ve-guh-**tah**- re-er
I'd like to order . . .	Ich möchte . . . bestellen	ich **mohr**-shtuh . . . buh-**shtel**-en
Menu	die Speisekarte	dee **shpie**-zeh-car-tuh
Napkin	die Serviette	dee zair-vee-**eh**-tuh
Knife	das Messer	das **mess**-ehr
Fork	die Gabel	dee **gah**-bell
Spoon	die Löffel	der **luf**-fell

MENU GUIDE

ENGLISH	GERMAN

GENERAL DINING

Side dishes	Beilagen
Extra charge	Extraaufschlag
When available	Falls verfügbar
Entrées	Hauptspeisen
. . . (not) included	. . . (nicht) inbegriffen
Depending on the season	je nach Saison
Lunch menu	Mittagskarte
Desserts	Nachspeisen
. . . at your choice	. . . nach Wahl
. . . at your request	. . . nach Wunsch
Prices are . . .	Preise sind . . .
Waiter/Waitress	die Bedienung
Service included	inklusive Bedienung
Value added tax included	inklusive Mehrwertsteuer (Mwst.)
Specialty of the house	Spezialität des Hauses
Soup of the day	Tagessuppe
Appetizers	Vorspeisen
Is served from . . . to . . .	Wird von . . . bis . . . serviert

BREAKFAST

Bread	das Brot
Roll(s)	die Brötchen
Egg/Eggs	das Ei/die Eier
Hot	Heiss
Cold	Kalt
Jam	die Konfitüre
Milk	die Milch
Orange juice	der Orangensaft
Scrambled eggs	die Rühreier
Bacon	der Speck
Fried eggs	die Spiegeleier
Lemon	die Zitrone
Sugar	der Zucker

ENGLISH	GERMAN

SOUPS

Stew	der Eintopf
Chicken soup	die Hühnersuppe
Potato soup	die Kartoffelsuppe
Liver dumpling soup	die Leberknödelsuppe
Onion soup	die Zwiebelsuppe

METHODS OF PREPARATION

Blue (boiled in salt and vinegar)	Blau
Baked	Gebacken
Fried	Gebraten
Steamed	Gedämpft
Grilled (broiled)	Gegrillt
Boiled	Gekocht
Sautéed	In Butter geschwenkt
Breaded	Paniert
Raw	Roh

When ordering steak, the English words "rare, medium, (well) done" are used and understood in German.

GAME AND POULTRY

Duck	die Ente
Pheasant	der Fasan
Chicken	das Hähnchen (das Huhn)
Deer	der Hirsch
Rabbit	das Kaninchen
Venison	das Rehfleisch
Pigeon	die Taube
Turkey	die Truthahn
Quail	die Wachtel

FISH AND SEAFOOD

Eel	der Aal
Oysters	die Austern
Trout	die Forelle

ENGLISH	GERMAN
Flounder	die Flunder
Prawns	die Garnelen
Halibut	der Heilbutt
Herring	der Hering
Lobster	der Hummer
Scallops	die Jakobsmuscheln
Cod	der Kabeljau
Crab	die Krabbe
Salmon	der Lachs
Mackerel	die Makrele
Mussels	die Muscheln
Squid	der Tintenfisch
Tuna	der Thunfisch

MEATS

Veal	das Kalb
Lamb	das Lamm
Beef	das Rind
Pork	das Schwein

CUTS OF MEAT

Example: For "Lammkeule" see "Lamm" (above) + ". . . keule" (below)	
Breast	die . . brust
Leg	die . . . keule
Liver	die . . . leber
Tenderloin	die . . . lende
Kidney	die . . . niere
Rib	die . . . rippe
Meat patty	die Frikadelle
Meat loaf	der Hackbraten
Ham	der Schinken

VEGETABLES

Eggplant	die Aubergine
Cauliflower	der Blumenkohl

ENGLISH	GERMAN
Beans	die Bohnen
Green	Grüne
White	Weisse
Peas	die Erbsen
Cucumber	die Gurke
Cabbage	der Kohl
Lettuce	der Kopfsalat
Mix of asparagus, peas, and carrots	die Leipziger Allerlei
Corn	der Mais
Carrots	die Karotte/die Mohrrüben
Peppers	der Paprika
Mushrooms	der Pilze/der Champignon
Celery	der Sellerie
Asparagus (tips)	der Spargel(spitzen)
Tomatoes	die Tomaten
Onions	die Zwiebeln

CONDIMENTS

Vinegar	der Essig
Garlic	der Knoblauch
Horseradish	der Meerettich
Oil	das Öl
Mustard	der Senf
Artificial sweetener	der Süssstoff
Cinnamon	der Zimt
Sugar	der Zucker
Salt	das Salz

FRUITS

Apple	der Apfel
Orange	das Orange/die Apfelsine
Apricot	die Aprikose
Blueberry	die Blaubeere
Strawberry	die Erdbeere

ENGLISH	GERMAN
Raspberry	die Himbeere
Cherry	die Kirsche
Grapefruit	die Pampelmuse
Raisin	die Rosine
Grape	die Weintraube
Banana	die Banane
Pear	die Birne

DRINKS

Water	das Wasser
With/without carbonation	mit/ohne Gas
Juice	der Saft
Beer	das Bier
White Wine/Red Wine	der Weisswein/der Rotwein
Sparkling Wine	der Sekt
Coffee	der Kaffee
Tea	der Tee
Hot Chocolate	die heisse Schokolade
with/without ice	mit/ohne Eis
with/without water	mit/ohne Wasser
straight	pur
mulled claret	der Glühwein
caraway-flavored liquor	der Kümmel
fruit brandy	der Obstler

When ordering a martini, you have to specify "gin (or vodka) and vermouth," otherwise you will be given a vermouth (Martini & Rossi).

You will often see drinks on the menu ending in -*schorle*. Typically sparkling water will be added to either white wine (Weissweinschorle) or many types of fruit juice (for instance Apfelsaftschorle).

TRAVEL SMART
GERMANY

GETTING HERE AND AROUND

Germany's transportation infrastructure is extremely well developed, so all areas of the country are well connected to each other by road, rail, and air. The autobahns are an efficient system of highways, although they can get crowded during holidays. In winter you may have to contend with closed passes in the Alps or difficult driving on smaller roads in the Black Forest and the Saarland region. High-speed trains are perhaps the most comfortable way of traveling. Munich to Hamburg, for example, a trip of around 966 km (600 miles), takes 5½ hours. Many airlines offer extremely cheap last-minute flights, but you have to be fairly flexible.

▌ AIR TRAVEL

The least-expensive airfares on major carriers to Germany are often priced for round-trip travel and usually must be purchased in advance. Budget airline tickets are always priced one way. Airlines generally allow you to change your return date for a fee; most low-fare tickets, however, are nonrefundable. Fares between the British Isles and Germany on "no-frills" airlines such as Air Berlin and EasyJet can range from €15 to €70. ▌TIP→ Although a budget airfare may not be refundable, new EU regulations require that all other supplemental fees and taxes are. That means that when the €1 fare from Berlin to Munich turns out to cost €70 with fuel surcharges and the like, you only lose €1. Refund procedures vary between airlines.

Flying time to Frankfurt is 1½ hours from London, 7½ hours from New York, 10 hours from Chicago, and 12 hours from Los Angeles.

Lufthansa is Germany's leading carrier and has shared mileage plans and flights with Air Canada and United, as well as all members of the Star Alliance.

Germany's internal air network is excellent, with flights linking all major cities in, at most, little more than an hour. Germany's second-largest airline, Air Berlin, is a low-cost, full-service operation flying domestic and international routes from its hubs in Berlin, Stuttgart, Dusseldorf, and Hamburg. It is almost always a cheaper and more comfortable option than a flag carrier. A handful of smaller airlines—Germanwings, EasyJet, and TUIfly—compete with low-fare flights within Germany and to other European cities. These companies are reliable, do business almost exclusively over the Internet, and often beat the German rail fares. The earlier you book, the cheaper the fare.

AIRPORTS

Frankfurt is Germany's air hub. The large airport has the convenience of its own long-distance train station, but if you're transferring between flights, don't dawdle or you could miss your connection.

Munich is Germany's second air hub, with many services to North America and Asia. The airport is like a minicity, with plenty of activities to keep you entertained during a long layover. Experience a true German tradition and have a beer from the world's first airport brewery at the *Hofbräuhaus* here. For a more active layover, play miniature golf, beach volleyball, or soccer, or ice skate in winter. There's also a playground.

United and Air Berlin have nonstop service between New York and Berlin-Tegel. Air Berlin also flies from Berlin-Tegel to Chicago, Miami, and Los Angeles. Major airlines, like Lufthansa, fly in and out of Berlin-Tegel, while most budget airlines use Berlin-Schönefeld. Once the Berlin Brandenburg airport finally opens, both Tegel and Schönefeld will close.

United also has nonstop service between New York and Hamburg. There are a few nonstop services from North America to Düsseldorf. Stuttgart is convenient to the Black Forest. Also convenient to the Black Forest is the EuroAirport Freiburg-Basel-Mulhouse, which is used by many airlines for European destinations and as a stopover.

▍ BOAT TRAVEL

Eurailpasses and German Rail Passes are honored by KD Rhine Line on the Rhine River and on the Mosel River between Trier and Koblenz. (If you use the fast hydrofoil, a supplementary fee is required.) The rail lines follow the Rhine and Mosel rivers most of their length, meaning you can go one way by ship and return by train. Cruises generally operate between April and October. If you are planning to visit Denmark or Sweden after Germany, note that Scandlines ferries offer discounts for Eurailpass owners.

The MS *Duchess of Scandinavia* carries passengers and cars three times a week for the 19½-hour run between Cuxhaven, Germany, and Harwich, England.

Information KD Rhine Line ☎ *0221/208–8318* ⊕ *www.k-d.com.* **MS** *Duchess of Scandinavia* ☎ *08705/333–111 for DFDS Seaways in U.K., 040/389–0371 in Germany* ⊕ *www.dfdsseaways.co.uk.* **Scandlines** ☎ *0381/54350* ⊕ *www.scandlines.de.*

▍ BUS TRAVEL

Germany has good local bus service. Many cities are served by BerlinLinien Bus. Deutsche Touring, a subsidiary of the Deutsche Bahn, has offices and agents countrywide, and travels from Germany to cities elsewhere in Europe. It offers one-day tours along the Castle Road and the Romantic Road. The Romantic Road route is between Würzburg (with connections to and from Frankfurt) and Füssen (with connections to and from Munich, Augsburg, and Garmisch-Partenkirchen). With a Eurailpass or German Rail Pass you get a 10% discount on this route. Buses, with an attendant on board, travel in each direction between April and October.

All towns of any size have local buses, which often link up with trams (streetcars) and electric railway (S-bahn) and subway (U-bahn) services. Fares sometimes vary according to distance, but a ticket usually allows you to transfer freely between the various forms of transportation.

Bus Information BerlinLinien Bus ☎ *030/861–9331* ⊕ *www.berlinlinienbus.de.* **Deutsche Touring** ☎ *069/790–3501* ⊕ *www.touring.de.*

▍ CAR TRAVEL

Entry formalities for motorists are few: all you need is proof of insurance; an international car-registration document; and a U.S., Canadian, Australian, or New Zealand driver's license. If you or your car is from an EU country, Norway, or Switzerland, all you need is your domestic license and proof of insurance. *All* foreign cars must have a country sticker. There are no toll roads in Germany, except for a few Alpine mountain passes. Many large German cities require an environmental sticker on the front windshield. If your rental car doesn't have one, it's likely you'll be required to pay the fine.

CAR RENTAL

It is easy to rent a car in Germany, but not always cheap. You will need an International Driving Permit (IDP); it's available from the American Automobile Association (AAA) and the National Automobile Club. These international permits are universally recognized, and having one in your wallet may save you problems with the local authorities. In Germany you usually must be 21 to rent a car. Nearly all agencies allow you to drive into Germany's neighboring countries. It's frequently possible to return the car in another West European country, but not in Poland or the Czech Republic, for example.

Rates with the major car-rental companies begin at about €55 per day and €300 per week for an economy car with a manual transmission and unlimited mileage. It is invariably cheaper to rent a car in advance from home than to do it on the fly in Germany. Most rentals are manual, so if you want an automatic, be sure to request one in advance. If you're traveling with children, don't forget to ask for a car seat when you reserve. Note that in some major cities, even automobile-producing Stuttgart, rental firms are prohibited from placing signs at major pickup and drop-off locations, such as the main train station. If dropping a car off in an unfamiliar city, you might have to guess your way to the station's underground parking garage; once there, look for a generic sign such as *Mietwagen* (rental cars). The German railway system, Deutsche Bahn, offers discounts on rental cars.

Depending on what you would like to see, you may or may not need a car for all or part of your stay. Most parts of Germany are connected by reliable rail service, so it might be a better plan to take a train to the region you plan to visit and rent a car only for side trips to out-of-the-way destinations.

Major Rental Agencies Avis ☎ *800/331–1212* ⊕ *www.avis.com.* **Budget** ☎ *800/472–3325* ⊕ *www.budget.com.* **Europecar** ⊕ *www.europecar.com.* **Hertz** ☎ *800/654–3001* ⊕ *www.hertz.com.*

Wholesalers Auto Europe ☎ *888/223–5555* ⊕ *www.autoeurope.com.* **Europe by Car** ☎ *212/581–3040 in New York, 800/223–1516* ⊕ *www.europebycar.com.* **Eurovacations** ☎ *877/471–3876* ⊕ *www.eurovacations.com.* **Kemwel** ☎ *877/820–0668* ⊕ *www.kemwel.com.*

GASOLINE

Gasoline costs are around €1.60 per liter—which is higher than in the United States. Some cars use diesel fuel, which is about €0.15 cheaper, so if you're renting a car, find out which fuel the car takes. German filling stations are highly competitive, and bargains are often available if you shop around, but *not* at autobahn filling stations. Self-service, or *SB-Tanken*, stations are cheapest. Pumps marked *Bleifrei* contain unleaded gas.

PARKING

Daytime parking in cities and small, historic towns is difficult to find. Restrictions are not always clearly marked and can be hard to understand even when they are. Rental cars come with a "time wheel," which you can leave on your dashboard when parking signs indicate free, limited-time allowances. Larger parking lots have parking meters (*Parkautomaten*). After depositing enough change in a meter, you will be issued a timed ticket to display on your dashboard. Parking-meter spaces are free at night. In German garages you must pay immediately on returning to retrieve your car, not when driving out. Put the ticket you got on arrival into the machine and pay the amount displayed. Retrieve the ticket, and upon exiting the garage, insert the ticket in a slot to raise the barrier. ■ TIP→ You must lock your car when it is parked. Failure to do so risks a €25 fine and liability for anything that happens if the car is stolen.

ROAD CONDITIONS

Roads are generally excellent. *Bundesstrassen* are two-lane state highways, abbreviated "B," as in B-38. Autobahns are high-speed thruways abbreviated with "A," as in A-7. If the autobahn should be blocked for any reason, you can take an exit and follow little signs bearing a "U" followed by a number. These are official detours.

ROAD MAPS

The best-known road maps of Germany are put out by the automobile club ADAC, by Shell, and by the Falk Verlag. They're available at gas stations and bookstores.

ROADSIDE EMERGENCIES

The German automobile clubs ADAC and AvD operate tow trucks on all autobahns. "Notruf" signs every 2 km (1 mile) on autobahns (and country roads) indicate emergency telephones. By picking up the phone, you'll be connected to an operator who can determine your exact location and get you the services you need. Help is free (with the exception of materials).

Emergency Services Roadside assistance ☎ *01802/222–222.*

RULES OF THE ROAD

In Germany, road signs give distances in kilometers. There *are* posted speed limits on much of the autobahns, and they advise drivers to keep below 130 kph (80 mph) or 110 kph (65 mph). A sign saying *Richtgeschwindigkeit* and the speed indicates this. Slower traffic should stay in the right lane of the autobahn, but speeds under 80 kph (50 mph) are not permitted. Speed limits on country roads vary from 70 kph to 100 kph (43 mph to 62 mph) and are usually 50 kph (30 mph) through small towns.

Don't enter a street with a signpost bearing a red circle with a white horizontal stripe—it's a one-way street. Blue "Einbahnstrasse" signs indicate you're headed the correct way down a one-way street. The blood-alcohol limit for driving in Germany is very low (.05%), and passengers, but not the driver, are allowed to consume alcoholic beverages in the car. Note that seatbelts must be worn at all times by front- *and* back-seat passengers.

German drivers tend to drive fast and aggressively. There is no right turn at a red light in Germany. Though prohibited, tailgating is the national pastime on German roads. Do not react by braking for no reason: this is equally prohibited.

You may not use a handheld mobile phone while driving.

SCENIC ROUTES

Germany has many specially designated tourist roads that serve as promotional tools for towns along their routes. The longest is the Deutsche Ferienstrasse, the German Holiday Road, which runs from the Baltic Sea to the Alps, a distance of around 1,720 km (1,070 miles). The most famous, however, is the Romantische Strasse (⇨ *See Romantic Road Chapter 4)*, which runs from Würzburg to Füssen, in the Alps, covering around 355 km (220 miles).

Among other notable touring routes are the Strasse der Kaiser und Könige (Route of Emperors and Kings), running from Frankfurt to Passau (and on to Vienna and Budapest); the Burgenstrasse (Castle Road), running from Mannheim to Bayreuth; the Deutsche Weinstrasse (⇨ *See German Wine Road Chapter 10)*, running through the Palatinate wine country; and the Deutsche Alpenstrasse, running the length of the country's Alpine southern border from near Berchtesgaden to the Bodensee. Less well-known routes are the Märchenstrasse (⇨ *See Fairy-Tale Road Chapter 12)*, the Weser Renaissance Strasse, and the Deutsche Fachwerkstrasse (German Half-Timber Road).

▌CRUISE SHIP TRAVEL

The American-owned Viking River Cruises company tours the Rhine, Main, Elbe, and Danube rivers, with four- to eight-day itineraries that include walking tours at ports of call. The longer cruises (up to 18 days) on the Danube (Donau, in German), which go to the Black Sea and back, are in great demand, so reserve six months in advance. The company normally books American passengers on ships that cater exclusively to Americans. If you prefer to travel on a European ship, specify so when booking. Köln–Düsseldorfer Deutsche Rheinschiffahrt (KD Rhine Line) offers trips of one day or less on the Rhine and Mosel. Between Easter and October there's Rhine service between Köln and Mainz, and between May and October, Mosel service between Koblenz and Cochem. Check the website for special winter tours. You'll get a free trip on your birthday if you bring a document verifying your date of birth.

Cruise Lines KD Rhine Line ☎ *0221/208–8318* ⊕ *www.k-d.com.* **Viking River Cruises** ☎ *0800/258–4666, 800/1887–10033 in Germany, 800/319–6660 in U.K.* ⊕ *www.vikingrivercruises.com.*

▮ TRAIN TRAVEL

Deutsche Bahn (DB—German Rail) is a very efficient, semi-privatized railway. Its high-speed InterCity Express (ICE), Inter-City (IC), and EuroCity (EC) trains make journeys between the centers of many cities—Munich–Frankfurt, for example—faster by rail than by air. All InterCity and InterCity Express trains have restaurant cars and trolley service. RE, RB, and IRE trains are regional trains. It's also possible to sleep on the train and save a day of your trip. CityNightLine (CNL) trains serving domestic destinations and neighboring countries have sleepers, couches, and recliners.

Once on your platform or *Bahnsteig*—the area between two tracks—you can check the notice boards that give details of the layout of trains (*Wagenstandanzeiger*) arriving on that track (*Gleis*). They show the locations of first- and second-class cars and the restaurant car, as well as where they will stop along the platform. Large railroad stations have English-speaking staff handling information inquiries.

If you would like to work out an itinerary beforehand, Deutsche Bahn has an excellent website in English (⊕ *www.bahn.de*). It will even tell you which type of train you'll be riding on—which could be important if you suffer from motion sickness. The ICE, the French TGV, the Swiss ICN, and the Italian Cisalpino all use "tilt technology" for a less jerky ride. One side effect, however, is that some passengers might feel queasy, especially if the track is curvy. An over-the-counter drug for motion sickness should help.

BAGGAGE

Most major train stations have luggage lockers (in four sizes). By inserting exact change into a storage unit, you release the unit's key. Prices range from €1 for a small locker to €3 for a "jumbo" one. Smaller towns' train stations may not have any storage options.

Throughout Germany, Deutsche Bahn can deliver your baggage from a private residence or hotel to another or even to one of six airports: Berlin, Frankfurt, Leipzig-Halle, Munich, Hamburg, or Hannover. You must have a valid rail ticket. Buy a *Kuriergepäck* ticket at any DB ticket counter, at which time you must schedule a pickup three workdays before your flight. The service costs €13.80 for each of the first two suitcases and €15.80 for each suitcase thereafter.

DISCOUNTS

Deutsche Bahn offers many discount options with specific conditions, so do your homework on its website or ask about options at the counter before paying for a full-price ticket. For round-trip travel you can save 25% if you book at least three days in advance, 50% if you stay over a Saturday night and book at least three to seven days in advance. However, there's a limited number of seats sold at any of these discount prices, so book as early as possible, at least a week in advance, to get the savings. A discounted rate is called a *Sparpreis*. If you change your travel plans after booking, you will have to pay a fee. The surcharge for tickets bought on board is 10% of the ticket cost, or a minimum of €5. Most local, RE, and RB services do not allow for purchasing tickets on board. Not having a ticket is considered *Schwarzfahren* (riding black) and is usually subject to a €40 fine. Tickets booked at a counter always cost more than over the Internet or from an automated ticket machine.

Children under 15 travel free when accompanied by a parent or relative on normal, discounted, and some, but not all, special-fare tickets. However, you must indicate the number of children traveling with you when you purchase the ticket; to ride free, the child (or children) must be listed on the ticket. If you have a ticket with 25% or 50% off, a *Mitfahrer-Rabatt* allows a second person to travel with you for a 50% discount (minimum of €15 for a second-class ticket). The *Schönes Wochenend Ticket* (Happy Weekend Ticket) provides unlimited travel on regional trains on weekends for up to five persons for €37 (€35 if purchased online or at vending machine). Groups of six or more should inquire about *Gruppen & Spar* (group) savings. Each German state, or *Land*, has its own *Länder-Ticket*, which lets up to five people travel from 9 am to 3 am for around €25.

If you plan to travel by train within a day after your flight arrives, purchase a heavily discounted "Rail and Fly" ticket for DB trains at the same time you book your flight. Trains connect with 14 German airports and two airports outside Germany, Basel and Amsterdam.

FARES

A first-class seat is approximately 55% more than a second-class seat. For this premium you get a bit more legroom and the convenience of having meals (not included) delivered directly to your seat. Most people find second class entirely adequate and first class not worth the cost. Many regional trains offer an upgrade to first class for as little as €4. This is especially helpful on weekends when local trains are stuffed with cyclists and day-tripping locals. ICs and the later-generation ICE trains are equipped with electrical outlets for laptops and other gadgets.

Tickets purchased through Deutsche Bahn's website can be retrieved from station vending machines. Always check that your ticket is valid for the type of train you are planning to take, not just for the destination served. If you have the wrong type of ticket, you will have to pay the difference on the train, in cash or by credit card. If you book an online ticket and print it yourself, you must present the credit card used to pay for the ticket to the conductor for the ticket to be valid.

PASSES

If Germany is your only destination in Europe, consider purchasing a German Rail Pass, which allows 4 to 10 days of unlimited first- or second-class travel within a one-month period on any DB train, up to and including the ICE. A Twin Pass saves two people traveling together 50% off one person's fare. A Youth Pass,

sold to those 12–25, is much the same but for second-class travel only. You can also use these passes aboard KD Rhine Line (⇨ *See Cruise Ship Travel*) along certain sections of the Rhine and Mosel rivers. Prices begin at $257 per person in second class. Twin Passes begin at $380 for two people in second class, and Youth Passes begin at $205. Additional days may be added to either pass, but only at the time of purchase and not once the pass has been issued. Extensions of the German Rail Pass to Brussels, Venice, Verona, Prague, and Innsbrück are also available.

Rail 'n' Drive combines train travel and car rental. For instance, two people pay $207 each for two rail-travel days and two car-rental days within a month. You can add up to three more rail days ($66 each), and each additional car-rental day is $63.

Germany is one of 21 countries in which you can use a Eurailpass, which provides unlimited first-class rail travel in all participating countries for the duration of the pass. Two adults traveling together can pay either €482 each for 15 consecutive days of travel or €622 each for 21 consecutive days of travel. The youth fare is €369 for 15 consecutive days and €435 for 10 days within two months. Eurailpasses are available from most travel agents and directly from ⊕ *www.eurail.com.*

Eurailpasses and some of the German Rail Passes should be purchased before you leave for Europe. You can purchase a Eurailpass and 5- or 10-day German Rail Passes at the Frankfurt airport and at some major German train stations, but the cost will be higher (a youth ticket for five days of travel is just under €149). When you buy your pass, consider purchasing rail pass insurance in case you lose it during your travels.

In order to comply with the strict rules about validating tickets before you begin travel, read the instructions carefully. Some tickets require that a train official validate your pass, while others require you to write in the first date of travel.

Many travelers assume that rail passes guarantee them seats on the trains they wish to ride. Not so. You need to book seats ahead even if you are using a rail pass; seat reservations are required on some European trains, particularly high-speed trains, and are a good idea in summer, on national holidays, and on popular routes. If you board the train without a reserved seat, you risk having to stand. You'll also need a reservation if you purchase sleeping accommodations. Seat reservations on InterCity trains cost €6, and a reservation is absolutely necessary for the ICE-Sprinter trains (€12 for second class). There are no reservations on regional trains.

TRAVEL FROM GREAT BRITAIN

There are several ways to reach Germany from London on British Rail. Travelers coming from the United Kingdom should take the Channel Tunnel to save time, the ferry to save money. Fastest and most expensive is the route via the Channel Tunnel on Eurostar trains. They leave at two-hour intervals from St. Pancras International and require a change of trains in Brussels, from which ICE trains reach Köln in 2½ hours and Frankfurt in 3½ hours. Prices for one-way tickets from London to Köln begin at €100–€129. Cheapest and slowest are the 8 to 10 departures daily from Victoria using the Ramsgate–Ostend ferry, jetfoil, or SeaCat catamaran service.

Channel Tunnel Car Transport
Eurotunnel ☎ *0870/535–3535 in U.K., 070/223–210 in Belgium, 0810/630–304 in France* ⊕ *www.eurotunnel.com.* **Rail Europe** ☎ *0870/241–5415* ⊕ *www.raileurope.co.uk.*

Channel Tunnel Passenger Service
Eurostar ☎ *08432/186–186 in the U.K., 1233/617–575 outside the U.K.* ⊕ *www.eurostar.co.uk.* **Rail Europe** ☎ *888/382–7245 in U.S., 0870/584–8848 in U.K., for inquiries and credit-card bookings* ⊕ *www.raileurope.com.*

Train Information Deutsche Bahn (*German Rail*). ☎ *0800/150–7090 for automated schedule information, 11861 for 24-hr hotline (€0.39 per min), 491805/996–633 from outside Germany (€0.12 per min)* ⊕ *www.bahn.de.* **Eurail** ⊕ *www.eurail.com.* **Eurostar** ☎ *0870/518–6186* ⊕ *www.eurostar.com.*

ESSENTIALS

■ ACCOMMODATIONS

The standards of German hotels, down to the humblest inn, are very high. You can nearly always expect courteous and polite service and clean and comfortable rooms. In addition to hotels proper, the country has numerous *Gasthöfe* or *Gasthäuser* (country inns that serve food and also have rooms). At the lowest end of the scale are *Fremdenzimmer,* meaning simply "rooms," normally in private houses. Look for the sign reading "Zimmer frei" (room available) or "zu vermieten" (to rent) on a green background; a red sign reading "besetzt" means there are no vacancies.

If you are looking for a very down-to-earth experience, try an *Urlaub auf dem Bauernhof,* a farm that has rooms for travelers. This can be especially exciting for children. You can also opt to stay at a winery's *Winzerhof.*

Room rates are by no means inflexible and depend very much on supply and demand. You can save money by inquiring about deals: many resort hotels offer substantial discounts in winter, for example. Likewise, many $$$$ and $$$ hotels in cities cut their prices dramatically on weekends and when business is quiet. Major events like Munich's Oktoberfest and the Frankfurt Book Fair will drive prices through the ceiling.

Tourist offices will make bookings for a nominal fee, but they may have difficulty doing so after 4 pm in high season and on weekends, so don't wait until too late in the day to begin looking for your accommodations. If you do get stuck, ask someone—like a mail carrier, police officer, or waiter, for example—for directions to a house renting a Fremdenzimmer or to a Gasthof.

Most hotels and other lodgings require you to give your credit-card details before they will confirm your reservation. If you don't feel comfortable emailing this information, ask if you can fax it (some places even prefer faxes). However you book, get confirmation in writing and have a copy of it handy when you check in.

Be sure you understand the hotel's cancellation policy. Some places allow you to cancel without any kind of penalty—even if you prepaid to secure a discounted rate—if you cancel at least 24 hours in advance. Others require you to cancel a week in advance or penalize you the cost of one night. Small inns and B&Bs are most likely to require you to cancel far in advance. Most hotels allow children under a certain age to stay in their parents' room at no extra charge, but others charge for them as extra adults; find out the cutoff age for discounts.

APARTMENT AND HOUSE RENTALS

If you are staying in one region, renting an apartment is an affordable alternative to a hotel or B&B. *Ferienwohnungen,* or vacation apartments, are especially popular in more rural areas. They range from simple rooms with just the basics to luxury apartments with all the trimmings. Some even include breakfast. The best way to find an apartment is through the local tourist office or the website of the town or village where you would like to stay.

International Agencies
At Home Abroad ☎ *212/421–9165* ⊕ *www.athomeabroadinc.com.* **Barclay International Group** ☎ *516/364–0064, 800/845–6636* ⊕ *www.barclayweb.com.* **Drawbridge to Europe** ☎ *541/482–7778, 888/268–1148* ⊕ *www.drawbridgetoeurope.com.* **Forgetaway** ⊕ *www.forgetaway.com.* **Home Away** ☎ *512/493–0382* ⊕ *www.homeaway.com.* **Interhome** ☎ *954/791–8282, 800/882–6864* ⊕ *www.interhome.us.* **Suzanne B. Cohen & Associates** ☎ *207/622–0743* ⊕ *www.villaeurope.com.* **Vacation Home Rentals Worldwide** ☎ *201/767–9393, 800/633–3284* ⊕ *www.vhrww.com.* **Villanet** ☎ *206/417–3444, 800/964–1891* ⊕ *www.rentavilla.com.*

Villas & Apartments Abroad ☎ 212/213–6435, 800/433–3020 ⊕ www.vaanyc.com. **Villas International** ☎ 415/499–9490, 800/221–2260 ⊕ www.villasintl.com. **Villas of Distinction** ☎ 707/778–1800, 800/289–0900 ⊕ www.villasofdistinction.com. **Wimco** ☎ 800/449–1553 ⊕ www.wimco.com.

BED-AND-BREAKFASTS

B&Bs remain one of the most popular options for traveling in Germany. They are often inexpensive, although the price depends on the amenities. For breakfast, expect some muesli, cheese, cold cuts, jam, butter, and hard-boiled eggs at the very least. Some B&Bs also supply lunch baskets if you intend to go hiking, or arrange an evening meal for a very affordable price.

Reservation Services Bed & Breakfast.com ☎ 512/322–2710, 800/462–2632 ⊕ www.bedandbreakfast.com. **Bed & Breakfast Inns Online** ☎ 615/868–1946, 800/215–7365 ⊕ www.bbonline.com. **BnBFinder.com** ☎ 212/432–7693, 888/469–6663 ⊕ www.bnbfinder.com.

CASTLE-HOTELS

Staying in a historic castle, or *Schloss*, is a great experience. The simpler ones may lack character, but most combine four-star luxury with antique furnishings, four-poster beds, and a baronial atmosphere. Some offer all the facilities of a resort. Euro-Connection can advise you on castle-hotel packages, including four-to six-night tours.

Contacts Euro-Connection ☎ 800/645–3876 ⊕ www.euro-connection.com.

FARM VACATIONS

Almost every regional tourist office has a brochure listing farms that offer bed-and-breakfasts, apartments, and entire farmhouses to rent (*Ferienhöfe*). The German Agricultural Association provides an illustrated brochure, *Urlaub auf dem Bauernhof* (*Vacation Down on the Farm*), that covers more than 2,000 inspected and graded farms, from the Alps to the North Sea. It costs €9.90 and is also sold in bookstores.

German Agricultural Association DLG Reisedienst, Agratour (*German Agricultural Association*). ☎ 069/247–880 ⊕ www.landtourismus.de.

HOME EXCHANGES

With a direct home exchange you stay in someone else's home while they stay in yours. Some outfits also deal with vacation homes, so you're not actually staying in someone's full-time residence, just their vacant weekend place.

Exchange Clubs HomeExchange.com. $120 for a one-year online listing. ☎ 800/877–8723 ⊕ www.homeexchange.com. **HomeLink International.** $119 yearly for Web membership. ☎ 800/638–3841 ⊕ www.homelink.org. **Intervac U.S.** $99 for annual membership. ☎ 800/756–4663 ⊕ www.intervacus.com.

HOTELS

Most hotels in Germany do not have air-conditioning, nor do they need it, given the climate and the German style of building construction that uses thick walls and recessed windows to help keep the heat out. Smaller hotels do not provide much in terms of bathroom amenities. Except in four- and five-star hotels, you won't find a washcloth. Hotels often have nonsmoking rooms or even nonsmoking floors, so it's always worth asking for one when you reserve. Beds in double rooms often consist of two twin mattresses placed side by side within a frame. When you arrive, if you don't like the room you're offered, ask to see another.

Among the most delightful places to stay—and eat—in Germany are the aptly named Romantik Hotels and Restaurants. The Romantik group has 98 members in Germany. All are in atmospheric and historic buildings—a condition for membership—and are run by the owners with the emphasis on excellent amenities and service. Prices vary considerably, but in general they are a good value.

Contacts Romantik Hotels and Restaurants ☎ *800/650–8018, 817/678–0038 from the U.S., 069/661–2340 in Germany* ⊕ *www.romantikhotels.com.*

SPAS

Taking the waters in Germany, whether for curing the body or merely pampering, has been popular since Roman times. More than 300 health resorts, mostly equipped for thermal or mineral-water, mud, or brine treatments, are set within pleasant country areas or historic communities. The word *Bad* before or within the name of a town means it's a spa destination, where many patients reside in health clinics for two to three weeks of doctor-prescribed treatments.

Saunas, steam baths, and other hot-room facilities are often used "without textiles" in Germany—in other words, naked. Wearing a bathing suit is sometimes even prohibited in saunas, but sitting on a towel is always required. (You may need to bring your own towels.) The Deutsche Heilbäderverband has information in German only.

Contacts Deutsche Heilbäderverband (*German Health Resort and Spa Association*). ☎ *0228/201–200* ⊕ *www.deutscher-heilbaederverband.de.*

▌ COMMUNICATIONS

INTERNET

Nearly all hotels have in-room data ports, but you may have to purchase, or borrow from the front desk, a cable with an end that matches German phone jacks. If you're plugging into a phone line, you'll need a local access number for a connection. Wireless Internet (called WLAN in Germany) is more and more common in even the most average hotel. The service is not always free, however. Sometimes you must purchase blocks of time from the front desk or online using a credit card. The cost is fairly high, however, usually around €4 for 30 minutes.

There are alternatives. Some hotels have an Internet room for guests needing to check their email. Otherwise, Internet cafés are common, and many bars and restaurants let you surf the Web. Cybercafes.com lists more than 4,000 Internet cafés worldwide.

Cybercafes ⊕ *www.cybercafes.com.*

PHONES

The good news is that you can make a direct-dial telephone call from Germany to virtually any point on Earth. The bad news? You can't always do so cheaply. Calling from a hotel is almost always the most expensive option; hotels usually add huge surcharges to all calls, particularly international ones. In some countries you can phone from call centers or even the post office. Calling cards usually keep costs to a minimum, but only if you purchase them locally. Because most Germans own mobile phones, finding a telephone booth is becoming increasingly difficult. As expensive as mobile phone calls can be, they are still usually a much cheaper option than calling from your hotel.

The country code for Germany is 49. When dialing a German number from abroad, drop the initial "0" from the local area code.

Many companies have service lines beginning with 0180. The cost of these calls averages €0.12 per minute. Numbers that begin with 0190 can cost €1.85 per minute and more.

CALLING WITHIN GERMANY

The German telephone system is very efficient, so it's unlikely you'll have to use an operator unless you're seeking information. For information in English, dial

☎ *11837* for numbers within Germany and ☎ *11834* for numbers elsewhere. But first look for the number in the phone book or online (⊕ *www.teleauskunft.de*), because directory assistance is costly. Calls to 11837 and 11834 cost at least €0.50, more if the call lasts more than 30 seconds.

A local call from a telephone booth costs €0.10 per minute. Dial the "0" before the area code when making a long-distance call within Germany. When dialing within a local area code, drop the "0" and the area code.

Telephone booths are no longer a common feature on the streets, so be prepared to walk out of your way to find one. Phone booths have instructions in English as well as German. Most telephone booths in Germany are card-operated, so buy a phone card. Coin-operated phones, which take €0.10, €0.20, €0.50, €1, and €2 coins, don't make change.

CALLING OUTSIDE GERMANY

The country code for the United States is 1.

International calls can be made from any telephone booth in Germany. It costs only €0.13 per minute to call the United States, day or night, no matter how long the call lasts. Use a phone card. If you don't have a good deal with a calling card, there are many stores that offer international calls at rates well below what you will pay from a phone booth. At a hotel, rates will be at least double the regular charge.

Access Codes AT&T Direct ☎ *0800/225–5288.* **MCI WorldPhone** ☎ *0800/888–8000.* **Sprint International Access** ☎ *0800/888–0013.*

CALLING CARDS

Post offices, newsstands, and exchange places sell cards with €5, €10, or €20 worth of credit to use at public pay phones. An advantage of a card: it charges only what the call costs. A €5 card with a good rate for calls to the United States, United Kingdom, and Canada is Go Bananas!

MOBILE PHONES

You can buy an inexpensive unlocked mobile phone and a SIM card at almost every corner shop and even at the supermarket. Most shops require identification to purchase a SIM card, but you can avoid this by purchasing a card at any number of phone centers or call shops, usually located near train stations. This is the best option if you just want to make local calls. If you bring a phone from abroad, your provider may have to unlock it for you to use a different SIM card and a prepaid service plan in the destination. You'll then have a local number and can make local calls at local rates. If your trip is extensive, you could also simply buy a new cell phone in your destination, as the initial cost will be offset over time.

Many prepaid plans, like Blau World, offer calling plans to the United States and other countries, starting at €0.03 per minute. Many Germans use these SIM cards to call abroad, as the rates are much cheaper than from land lines.

If you have a multiband phone (some countries use different frequencies from what's used in the United States) and your service provider uses the world-standard GSM network (as do T-Mobile, AT&T, and Verizon), you can probably use your phone abroad. Roaming fees can be steep, however: 99¢ a minute is considered reasonable. And overseas you normally pay the toll charges for incoming calls. It's almost always cheaper to send a text message than to make a call, because text messages have a very low set fee (often less than 5¢).

■ TIP➔ If you travel internationally frequently, save one of your old mobile phones or buy a cheap one on the Internet; ask your cell phone company to unlock it for you, and take it with you as a travel phone, buying a new SIM card with pay-as-you-go service in each destination.

▌ CUSTOMS AND DUTIES

German Customs and Border Control is fairly simple and straightforward. The system works efficiently and professionally, and 99% of all travelers will have no real cause to interact with them.

You're always allowed to bring goods of a certain value back home without having to pay any duty or import tax. But there's a limit on the amount of tobacco and liquor you can bring back duty-free, and some countries have separate limits for perfumes; for exact figures, check with your customs department. The values of so-called duty-free goods are included in these amounts. When you shop abroad, save all your receipts, as customs inspectors may ask to see them as well as the items you purchased. If the total value of your goods is more than the duty-free limit, you'll have to pay a tax (most often a flat percentage) on the value of everything beyond that limit.

For anyone entering Germany from outside the EU, the following limitations apply: (1) 200 cigarettes or 100 cigarillos or 50 cigars or 250 grams of tobacco; (2) 2 liters of still table wine; (3) 1 liter of spirits over 22% alcohol by volume (ABV) or 2 liters of spirits under 22% ABV (fortified and sparkling wines) or 2 more liters of table wine; (4) 50 grams of perfume and 250 milliliters of eau de toilette; (5) 500 grams of roasted coffee or 200 grams of instant coffee; (6) other goods to the value of €175.

If you have questions regarding customs or bringing a pet into the country, contact the Zoll-Infocenter.

Information in Germany Zoll-Infocenter
☎ *0351/4483–4510* ⊕ *www.zoll.de.*

U.S. Information U.S. Customs and Border Protection ⊕ *www.cbp.gov.*

▌ EATING OUT

Almost every street in Germany has its *Gaststätte,* a sort of combination restaurant and pub, and every village its *Gasthof,* or inn. The emphasis in either is on simple food at reasonable prices. A *Bierstube* (pub) or *Weinstube* (wine cellar) may also serve light snacks or meals.

Service can be slow, but you'll never be rushed out of your seat. Something else that may seem jarring at first: people can, and do, join other parties at a table in a casual restaurant if seating is tight. It's common courtesy to ask first, though.

Since Germans don't generally drink from the tap, water always costs extra and comes as still or sparkling mineral water.

BUDGET EATING TIPS

Imbiss (snack) stands can be found in almost every busy shopping street, in parking lots, train stations, and near markets. They serve *Würste* (sausages), grilled, roasted, or boiled, and rolls filled with cheese, cold meat, or fish. Many stands sell Turkish-style wraps called *döner kebab.* Prices range from €1.50 to €2.50 per portion. It's acceptable to bring sandwich fixings to a beer garden so long as you order a beer there; just be sure not to sit at a table with a tablecloth.

Butcher shops, known as *Metzgereien,* often serve warm snacks or very good sandwiches. Try *warmer Leberkäs mit Kartoffelsalat,* a typical Bavarian specialty, which is a sort of baked meat loaf with mustard and potato salad. In northern Germany try *Bouletten,* small meatballs, or *Currywurst,* sausages in a piquant curry sauce. Thuringia has a reputation for its bratwurst, which is usually broken in two and packed into a roll with mustard. Up north, the specialty snack is a herring sandwich with onions.

Restaurants in department stores are especially recommended for appetizing and inexpensive lunches. Kaufhof, Karstadt, Wertheim, and Horton are names to note. Germany's vast numbers of Turkish,

Italian, Greek, Chinese, and Balkan restaurants are often inexpensive.

MEALS AND MEALTIMES

Most hotels serve a buffet-style breakfast (*Frühstück*) of rolls, cheese, cold cuts, eggs, cereals, yogurt, and spreads, which is often included in the price of a room. Cafés, especially the more trendy ones, offer breakfast menus sometimes including pancakes, omelets, muesli, or even Thai rice soup. By American standards, a cup (*Tasse*) of coffee in Germany is very petite, and you don't get free refills. Order a *Pot* or *Kännchen* if you want a larger portion.

For lunch (*Mittagessen*), you can get sandwiches from most cafés and bakeries, and many fine restaurants have special lunch menus that make the gourmet experience much more affordable. Dinner (*Abendessen*) is usually accompanied by a potato or spätzle side dish. A salad sometimes comes with the main dish.

Gaststätten normally serve hot meals from 11:30 am to 9 pm; many places stop serving hot meals between 2 pm and 6 pm, although you can still order cold dishes. If you feel like a hot meal, look for a restaurant advertising *durchgehend geöffnet*, or look for a pizza parlor.

Once most restaurants have closed, your options are limited. Take-out pizza parlors and Turkish eateries often stay open later. Failing that, your best option is a train station or a gas station with a convenience store. Many bars serve snacks.

Unless otherwise noted, the restaurants listed in this guide are open daily for lunch and dinner.

PAYING

Credit cards are generally accepted only in moderate to expensive restaurants, so check before sitting down. You will need to ask for the bill (say "Die Rechnung, bitte.") in order to get it from the waiter, the idea being that the table is yours for the evening. Round up the bill 5% to 10% and pay the waiter directly rather than leaving any money or tip on the table. The waiter will likely wait at the table for you to pay after he has brought the check. He will also wear a money pouch and make change out of it at the table. If you don't need change, say "Stimmt so." ("Keep the change."), otherwise tell the waiter how much change you want back, adding in the tip. Meals are subject to 19% tax (abbreviated as "MwSt" on your bill).

For guidelines on tipping see Tipping, below.

RESERVATIONS AND DRESS

Regardless of where you are, it's a good idea to make a reservation if you can. In most fine dining establishments it's expected. We only mention them specifically when reservations are essential (there's no other way you'll ever get a table) or when they are not accepted. For popular restaurants, book as far ahead as you can (often 30 days), and reconfirm as soon as you arrive. (Parties of more than four should always call ahead to check the reservations policy.) We mention dress only when men are required to wear a jacket or a jacket and tie.

Note that even when Germans dress casually, their look is generally crisp and neat. Jeans are acceptable for most social occasions, unless you're meeting the president.

SMOKING

For such an otherwise health-conscious nation, Germans do smoke. A lot. New anti-smoking laws came into effect in 2008, effectively banning smoking in all restaurants and many pubs, but many Germans, particularly in Berlin and Hamburg, tend to ignore them. Many hotels have nonsmoking rooms and even nonsmoking floors. However, a smoker will find it intrusive if you ask him or her to refrain.

WINES, BEER, AND SPIRITS

Wines of Germany promotes the wines of all 13 German wine regions and can supply you with information on wine festivals and visitor-friendly wineries. It also arranges six-day guided winery tours in spring and fall in conjunction with the German Wine Academy.

It's legal to drink beer from open containers in public (even in the passenger seat of a car), and having a beer at one's midday break is nothing to raise an eyebrow at. Bavaria is not the only place to try beer. While Munich's beers have achieved world fame—Löwenbräu and Paulaner, for example—beer connoisseurs will really want to travel to places farther north like Alpirsbach, Bamberg, Erfurt, Cologne, or Görlitz, where smaller breweries produce top-notch brews.

Wine Information German Wine Academy ☎ 06131/28290 ⊕ www.germanwines.de. **Wines of Germany** ☎ 212/994–7523 ⊕ www.germanwineusa.org.

▌ELECTRICITY

The electrical current in Germany is 220 volts, 50 cycles alternating current (AC); wall outlets take Continental-type plugs, with two round prongs.

Consider making a small investment in a universal adapter, which has several types of plugs in one lightweight, compact unit. Most laptops and mobile phone chargers are dual voltage (i.e., they operate equally well on 110 and 220 volts) so require only an adapter. These days the same is true of small appliances such as hair dryers. Always check labels and manufacturer instructions to be sure. Don't use 110-volt outlets marked "for shavers only" for high-wattage appliances such as hair dryers.

Steve Kropla's Help for World Travelers has information on electrical and telephone plugs around the world. Walkabout Travel Gear has good coverage of electricity under "adapters."

Contacts Steve Kropla's Help for World Travelers ⊕ www.kropla.com. **Walkabout Travel Gear** ⊕ www.walkabouttravelgear.com.

▌EMERGENCIES

Throughout Germany call ☎ 110 for police, ☎ 112 for an ambulance or the fire department.

Foreign Embassies U.S. Embassy ✉ Pariser Platz 2, Berlin ☎ 030/83050, 030/8305–1200 for American citizens (2 pm–4 pm only) ⊕ www.usembassy.de.

▌ETIQUETTE

CUSTOMS OF THE COUNTRY

Being on time for appointments, even casual social ones, is very important. There is no "fashionably late" in Germany. Germans are more formal in addressing each other than Americans. Always address acquaintances as Herr (Mr.) or Frau (Mrs.) plus their last name; do not call them by their first name unless invited to do so. The German language has informal and formal pronouns for "you": formal is *Sie*, and informal is *du*. Even if adults are on a first-name basis with one another, they may still keep to the *Sie* form.

Germans are less formal when it comes to nudity: a sign that reads "freikörper" or "fkk" indicates a park or beach that allows nude sunbathing. At a sauna or steam bath, you will often be asked to remove all clothing.

GREETINGS

The standard "Guten Tag" is the way to greet people throughout the country. When you depart, say "Auf Wiedersehen." "Hallo" is also used frequently, as is Hi among the younger crowd. A less formal leave-taking is "Tschüss" or "ciao." You will also hear regional differences in greetings.

LANGUAGE

English is spoken in most hotels, restaurants, airports, museums, and other places of interest. However, English is not widely spoken in rural areas or by people over 40; this is especially true of the eastern part of Germany. Learning the basics before going is always a good idea, especially *bitte* (please) and *danke* (thank you). Apologizing for your poor German before asking a question in English will make locals feel respected and begins all communication on the right foot.

A phrase book and language-tape set can help get you started.

■TIP→ Under no circumstances use profanity or pejoratives. Germans take these very seriously, and a slip of the tongue can result in expensive criminal and civil penalties. Calling a police officer a "Nazi" or using vulgar finger gestures can cost you up to €10,000 and two years in jail.

▌ HEALTH

Warm winters have recently caused an explosion in the summertime tick population, which often causes outbreaks of Lyme disease. If you intend to do a lot of hiking, especially in the southern half of the country, be aware of the danger of ticks spreading Lyme disease. There is no vaccination against them, so prevention is important. Wear high shoes or boots, long pants, and light-color clothing. Use a good insect repellent, and check yourself for ticks after outdoor activities, especially if you've walked through high grass.

OVER-THE-COUNTER REMEDIES

All over-the-counter medicines, even aspirin, are only available at an *Apotheke* (pharmacy): the German term *Drogerie,* or *Pharmacie,* refers to a shop for sundry items.

Apotheken are open during normal business hours, with those in train stations or airports open later and on weekends. Apotheken are plentiful, and there is invariably one within a few blocks. Every district has an emergency pharmacy that is open after hours. These are listed as *Apotheken Notdienst* or *Apotheken-Bereitschaftsdienst* on the window of every other pharmacy in town, often with directions for how to get there. Pharmacies will have a bell you must ring to enter. Most pharmacists in larger cities speak enough English to help. Some drugs have different names: acetominophen—or Tylenol— is called *paracetomol.*

SHOTS AND MEDICATIONS

Germany is by and large a healthy place. There are occasional outbreaks of measles—including one in North Rhine–Westfalia—so be sure you have been vaccinated.

▌ HOURS OF OPERATION

Business hours are inconsistent throughout the country and vary from state to state and even from city to city. Banks are generally open weekdays from 8:30 or 9 am to 3 or 4 pm (5 or 6 pm on Thursday), sometimes with a lunch break of about an hour at smaller branches. Some banks close by 2:30 on Friday afternoon. Banks at airports and main train stations open as early as 6:30 am and close as late as 10:30 pm.

Most museums are open from Tuesday to Sunday 10–6. Some close for an hour or more at lunch. Many stay open until 8 pm or later one day a week, usually Thursday. In smaller towns or in rural areas, museums may be open only on weekends or just a few hours a day.

All stores are closed Sunday, with the exception of those in or near train stations. Larger stores are generally open from 9:30 or 10 am to 8 or 9 pm on weekdays and close between 6 and 8 pm on Saturday. Smaller shops and some department stores in smaller towns close at 6 or 6:30 on weekdays and as early as 4 on Saturday. German shop owners take their closing times seriously. If you come in five minutes before closing, you may not be treated like royalty. Apologizing profusely and making a speedy purchase will help.

Along the autobahn and major highways, as well as in larger cities, gas stations and their small convenience shops are often open late, if not around the clock.

HOLIDAYS

The following national holidays are observed in Germany: January 1; January 6 (Epiphany—Bavaria, Saxony-Anhalt, and Baden-Württemberg only); Good Friday; Easter Monday; May 1 (Workers' Day); Ascension; Pentecost Monday; Corpus Christi (southern Germany only); Assumption Day (Bavaria and Saarland only); October 3 (German Unity Day); November 1 (All Saints' Day—Baden-Württemberg, Bavaria, North Rhine-Westphalia, Rhineland-Pfalz, and Saarland); December 24–26 (Christmas).

Pre-Lenten celebrations in Cologne and the Rhineland are known as Karneval, and for several days before Ash Wednesday work grinds to a halt as people celebrate with parades, banquets, and general debauchery. Farther south, in the state of Baden-Württenburg, the festivities are called Fasching, and tend to be more traditional. In either area, expect businesses to be closed both before and after "Fat Tuesday."

▌ MAIL

A post office in Germany (*Postamt*) is recognizable by the postal symbol, a black bugle on a yellow background. In some villages you will find one in the local supermarket. Stamps (*Briefmarken*) can also be bought at some news agencies and souvenir shops. Post offices are generally open weekdays 8–6, Saturday 8–noon.

Airmail letters to the United States, Canada, Australia, and New Zealand cost €1.70; postcards, €1. All letters to the United Kingdom and within Europe cost €0.55; postcards, €0.45. These rates apply to standard-size envelopes. Letters take approximately 3–4 days to reach the United Kingdom, 5–7 days to the United States, and 7–10 days to Australia and New Zealand.

You can arrange to have mail (letters only) sent to you in care of any German post office; have the envelope marked "Postlagernd." This service is free, and the mail will be held for seven days. Or you can have mail sent to any American Express office in Germany. There's no charge to cardholders, holders of American Express traveler's checks, or anyone who has booked a vacation with American Express.

SHIPPING PACKAGES

Most major stores that cater to tourists will also ship your purchases home. You should check your insurance for coverage of possible damage.

The Deutsche Post has an express international service that will deliver your letter or package the next day to countries within the EU, within one to two days to the United States, and slightly longer to Australia. A letter or package to the United States weighing less than 200 grams costs €48.57. You can drop off your mail at any post office, or it can be picked up for an extra fee. Deutsche Post works in cooperation with DHL. International carriers tend to be slightly cheaper (€35–€45 for the same letter) and provide more services.

Express Services Deutsche Post
☎ *08105/345–2255* ⊕ *www.deutschepost.de.* **DHL** ☎ *0800/225–5345* ⊕ *www.dhl.de.* **FedEx** ☎ *0800/123–0800* ⊕ *www.fedex.com.* **UPS** ☎ *0800/882–6630* ⊕ *www.ups.com.*

▌ MONEY

Credit cards are welcomed by most businesses, so you probably won't have to use cash for payment in high-end hotels and restaurants. Many businesses on the other end of the spectrum don't accept them, however. It's a good idea to check in advance if you're staying in a budget lodging or eating in a simple country inn.

Prices throughout this guide are given for adults. Substantially reduced fees are almost always available for children, students, and senior citizens.

▥TIP→ Banks almost never have every foreign currency on hand, and it may take as long as a week to order. If you're planning to exchange funds before leaving home, don't wait until the last minute.

ATMS AND BANKS

Twenty-four-hour ATMs (*Geldautomaten*) can be accessed with Plus or Cirrus credit and banking cards. Your own bank will probably charge a fee for using ATMs abroad, and some German banks exact €3–€5 fees for use of their ATMs. Nevertheless, you'll usually get a better rate of exchange via an ATM than you will at a currency-exchange office or even when changing money in a bank. And extracting funds as you need them is a safer option than carrying around a large amount of cash. Since some ATM keypads show no letters, know the numeric equivalent of your password. Always use ATMs inside the bank.

▥TIP→ PINs with more than four digits are not recognized at ATMs in many countries. If yours has five or more, remember to change it before you leave.

CREDIT CARDS

All major U.S. credit cards are accepted in Germany. The most frequently used are MasterCard and Visa. American Express is used less frequently, and Diners Club even less. Since the credit-card companies demand fairly substantial fees, some businesses will not accept credit cards for small purchases. Cheaper restaurants and lodgings often do not accept credit cards.

It's a good idea to inform your credit-card company before you travel, especially if you're going abroad and don't travel internationally very often. Otherwise, the credit-card company might put a hold on your card owing to unusual activity—not a good thing halfway through your trip. Record all your credit-card numbers—as well as the phone numbers to call if your cards are lost or stolen—in a safe place, so you're prepared should something go wrong.

If you plan to use your credit card for cash advances, you'll need to apply for a PIN at least two weeks before your trip. Although it's usually cheaper (and safer) to use a credit card abroad for large purchases (so you can cancel payments or be reimbursed if there's a problem), note that some credit-card companies *and* the banks that issue them add substantial percentages to all foreign transactions, whether they're in a foreign currency or not. Check on these fees before leaving home, so there won't be any surprises when you get the bill.

▥TIP→ Before you charge something, ask the merchant whether he or she plans to do a dynamic currency conversion (DCC). In such a transaction the credit-card processor (shop, restaurant, or hotel, not Visa or MasterCard) converts the currency and charges you in dollars. In most cases you'll pay the merchant a 3% fee for this service in addition to any credit-card company and issuing-bank foreign-transaction surcharges.

Dynamic currency conversion programs are becoming increasingly widespread. Merchants who participate in them are supposed to ask whether you want to be charged in dollars or the local currency, but they don't always do so. And even if they do offer you a choice, they may well avoid mentioning the additional surcharges. The good news is that you *do* have a choice. And if this practice really gets your goat, you can avoid it entirely thanks to American Express; with its cards, DCC simply isn't an option.

Reporting Lost Cards American Express ☎ *800/333–2639 in U.S., 715/343–7977 collect from abroad* ⊕ *www.americanexpress.com.* **Diners Club** ☎ *800/234–6377 in U.S., 303/799–1504 collect from abroad* ⊕ *www.dinersclub.com.* **MasterCard** ☎ *800/622–7747 in U.S., 636/722–7111 collect from abroad* ⊕ *www.mastercard.com.* **Visa** ☎ *800/847–2911 in U.S., 410/581–9994 collect from abroad* ⊕ *www.visa.com.*

CURRENCY AND EXCHANGE

Germany shares a common currency, the euro (€), with 16 other countries: Austria, Belgium, Cyprus, Estonia, Finland, France,

Greece, Ireland, Italy, Luxembourg, Malta, the Netherlands, Portugal, Slovakia, Slovenia, and Spain. The euro is divided into 100 cents. There are bills of 5, 10, 20, 50, 100, and 500 euros and coins of €1 and €2, and 1, 2, 5, 10, 20, and 50 cents. Many businesses and restaurants do not accept €200 and €500 notes. It is virtually impossible to pay for anything in U.S. dollars, but you should have no problem exchanging currency. The large number of banks and exchange services means that you can shop around for the best rate, if you're so inclined. But the cheapest and easiest way to go is using your ATM card.

At this writing time, the exchange rate was €0.75 for a U.S. dollar. But the exchange rate changes daily.

▥ TIP➜ Even if a currency-exchange booth has a sign promising no commission, rest assured that there's some kind of huge, hidden fee. (Oh . . . that's right. The sign didn't say no *fee*.) And as for rates, you're almost always better off getting foreign currency at an ATM or exchanging money at a bank.

▊ PACKING

For visits to German cities, pack as you would for an American city: dressy outfits for formal restaurants and nightclubs, casual clothes elsewhere. Jeans are as popular in Germany as anywhere else, and are perfectly acceptable for sightseeing and informal dining. In the evening, men will probably feel more comfortable wearing a jacket in more expensive restaurants, although it's almost never required. Many German women wear stylish outfits to restaurants and the theater, especially in the larger cities.

Winters can be bitterly cold; summers are warm but with days that suddenly turn cool and rainy. In summer, take a warm jacket or heavy sweater if you are visiting the Bavarian Alps or the Black Forest, where the nights can be chilly even after hot days. In Berlin and on the Baltic, it is windy, which can be quite pleasant in summer but a complete bear in winter. To discourage purse snatchers and pickpockets, carry a handbag with long straps that you can sling across your body bandolier style and with a zippered compartment for money and other valuables.

For stays in budget hotels, pack your own soap. Many provide no soap at all or only a small bar.

▊ PASSPORTS AND VISAS

Visitors from the United States and Canada, including children, are required to have a passport to enter the EU for a period of up to 90 days. There are no official passport controls at any of Germany's land borders, although customs checks are becoming more frequent. Most travelers will only show their documents on entering and leaving the EU. Your passport should be valid for up to six months after your trip ends or this will raise questions at the border. EU citizens can enter Germany with a national identity card or passport. Traveling with children can be problematic. Single parents traveling with their own children rarely face any hassle, but overzealous border guards have been known to ask children about their relationship with the other parent. If you are a parent or grandparent traveling with a child, it helps to have a signed and notarized power of attorney in order to dispel any questions.

▊ RESTROOMS

Public restrooms are found in large cities, although you are not guaranteed to find one in an emergency. If you are in need, there are several options. You can enter the next café or restaurant and ask very politely to use the facilities. You can find a department store and look for the "WC" sign. Museums are also a good place to find facilities.

Train stations are increasingly turning to McClean, a privately run enterprise that demands €0.60 to €1.10 for admission to its restrooms. These facilities, staffed by attendants who clean almost constantly, sparkle. You won't find them in smaller stations, however. Their restrooms are usually adequate.

On the highways, the vast majority of gas stations have public restrooms, though you may have to ask for a key—we won't vouch for their cleanliness. You might want to wait until you see a sign for a restaurant.

Restrooms almost always cost money. It's customary to pay €0.20–€0.70 to the bathroom attendant.

To read up on restrooms in advance of your trip, the Bathroom Diaries is flush with unsanitized info on restrooms the world over—each one located, reviewed, and rated.

Find a Loo The Bathroom Diaries
⊕ *www.thebathroomdiaries.com.*

▌ SAFETY

Germany has one of the lowest crime rates in Europe. There are some areas, such as the neighborhoods around train stations and the streets surrounding red-light districts, where you should keep an eye out for potential dangers. The best advice is to take the usual precautions. Secure your valuables in the hotel safe. Don't wear flashy jewelry, and keep expensive electronics out of sight when you are not using them. Carry shoulder bags or purses so that they can't be easily snatched, and never leave them hanging on the back of a chair at a café or restaurant. Avoid walking alone at night, even in relatively safe neighborhoods. Due to increasing incidents of violence in Berlin, Hamburg, and Munich, use caution late at night in the subway.

When withdrawing cash, don't use an ATM in a deserted area or one that is outside. It is best to avoid freestanding ATMs in subway stations and other locations away from a bank. Make sure that no one is looking over your shoulder when you enter your PIN. And never use a machine that appears to have been tampered with.

FODORS.COM CONNECTION

Before your trip, be sure to check out what other travelers are saying on
⊕ *www.fodors.com.*

▌**TIP→** Distribute your cash, credit cards, IDs, and other valuables between a deep front pocket, an inside jacket or vest pocket, and a hidden money pouch. Don't reach for the money pouch once you're in public.

Contacts Transportation Security Administration (TSA). ⊕ *www.tsa.gov.*

▌ TAXES

Most prices you see on items already include Germany's 19% value-added tax (V.A.T.). Some goods, such as food, books, and antiquities, carry a 7% V.A.T. as a percentage of the purchase price. An item must cost at least €25 to qualify for a V.A.T. refund.

When making a purchase, ask for a V.A.T. refund form and find out whether the merchant gives refunds—not all stores do, nor are they required to. Have the form stamped like any customs form by customs officials when you leave the country or, if you're visiting several European Union countries, when you leave the EU. After you're through passport control, take the form to a refund-service counter for an on-the-spot refund (which is usually the quickest and easiest option), or mail it to the address on the form (or the envelope with it) after you arrive home. You receive the total refund stated on the form, but the processing time can be long, especially if you request a credit-card adjustment.

Global Refund is a Europe-wide service with 225,000 affiliated stores and more than 700 refund counters at major airports and border crossings. Its refund form, called a Tax Free Check, is the most common across the European continent. The service issues refunds in the form of cash, check, or credit-card adjustment.

V.A.T. REFUNDS AT THE AIRPORT

If you're departing from Terminal 1 at Frankfurt Airport, where you bring your purchases to claim your tax back depends on how you've packed the goods. If the items are in your checked luggage, check in as normal, but let the ticket counter know you have to claim your tax still. They will give you your luggage back to bring to the customs office in Departure Hall B, Level 2. For goods you are carrying on the plane with you, go to the customs office on the way to your gate. After you pass through passport control, there is a Global Refund office.

If you're departing from Terminal 2, bring goods in luggage to be checked to the customs office in Hall D, Level 2 (opposite the Delta Airlines check-in counters). For goods you are carrying on the plane with you, see the customs office in Hall E, Level 3 (near security control).

At Munich's airport, the Terminal 2 customs area is on the same level as check-in. If your V.A.T. refund items are in your luggage, check in first, and then bring your bags to the customs office on Level 04. From here your bags will be sent to your flight, and you can go to the Global Refund counter around the corner. If your refund items are in your carry-on, go to the Global Refund office in the customs area on Level 05 south. Terminal 1 has customs areas in modules C and D, Level 04.

V.A.T. Refunds Global Refund ☎ 800/566–9828 ⊕ www.globalblue.com.

▌ TIME

All of Germany is on Central European Time, which is six hours ahead of Eastern Standard Time and nine hours ahead of Pacific Standard Time. Daylight Saving Time begins on the last Sunday in March and ends on the last Sunday in October. Timeanddate.com can help you figure out the correct time anywhere.

Germans use the 24-hour clock, or "military time" (1 pm is indicated as 13:00), and write the date before the month, so October 3 will appear as 03.10.

Time Zones Timeanddate.com
⊕ www.timeanddate.com/worldclock.

▌ TIPPING

Tipping is done at your own discretion. Theater ushers do not necessarily expect a tip, while waiters, tour guides, bartenders, and taxi drivers do. Rounding off bills to the next highest sum is customary for bills under €10. Above that sum you should add a little more.

Service charges are included in all restaurant checks (listed as *Bedienung*), as is tax (listed as *MwSt*). Nonetheless, it is customary to round up the bill to the nearest euro or to leave about 5%–10%. Give it to the waitstaff as you pay the bill; don't leave it on the table, as that's considered rude.

TIPPING GUIDELINES FOR GERMANY	
Bartender	Round up the bill for small purchases. For rounds of drinks, around 10% is appropriate.
Bellhop	€1 per item.
Hotel Concierge	€3–€5 if the concierge performs a special service for you.
Hotel Doorman	€1–€2 if he helps you get a cab.
Hotel Maid	€1 per day.
Hotel Room-Service Waiter	€1 per delivery.
Taxi Driver	Round up the fare if the ride is short. For longer trips, about €1 is appropriate.
Tour Guide	€5–€10 per person, or a bit more if the tour was especially good.
Valet Parking Attendant	€1–€2, but only when you retrieve your car.
Waiter	Round off the bill, giving 5% to 10% for very good service.

▌ TRIP INSURANCE

Comprehensive trip insurance is valuable if you're booking a very expensive or complicated trip (particularly to an isolated region) or if you're booking far in advance. Comprehensive policies typically cover trip-cancellation and interruption, letting you cancel or cut your trip short because of illness, or, in some cases, acts of terrorism in your destination. Such policies might also cover evacuation and medical care. Some cover you for trip delays because of bad weather or mechanical problems as well as for lost or delayed luggage.

Another type of coverage to consider is financial default—that is, when your trip is disrupted because a tour operator, airline, or cruise line goes out of business. Generally you must buy this when you book your trip or shortly thereafter, and it's available to you only if your operator isn't on a list of excluded companies.

Always read the fine print of your policy to make sure that you're covered for the risks that most concern you. Compare several policies to be sure you're getting the best price and range of coverage available.

Comprehensive Insurers AIG Travel Guard ☏ *800/826–4919* ⊕ *www.travelguard.com.* **Allianz Global Assistance** ☏ *866/284–8300* ⊕ *www.allianztravelinsurance.com.* **CSA Travel Protection** ☏ *800/873–9855* ⊕ *www. csatravelprotection.com.* **Travelex Insurance** ☏ *888/228–9792* ⊕ *www.travelexinsurance. com.* **Travel Insured International** ☏ *800/243–3174* ⊕ *www.travelinsured.com.*

Insurance Comparison Information Insure My Trip ☏ *800/487–4722* ⊕ *www.insuremytrip.com.* **Square Mouth** ☏ *800/240–0369* ⊕ *www.squaremouth.com.*

▌ VISITOR INFORMATION

Local tourist offices are listed in the individual chapters. Staff at the smaller offices might not speak English. Many offices keep shorter hours than normal businesses, and you can expect some to close during weekday lunch hours and as early as noon on Friday. Almost all German cities and towns have an Internet presence under ⊕ *www.cityname.de,* for example, ⊕ *www.naumburg.de.* The Internet portal Deutschland.de has lots of information about the country's best-known sights, as well as those that are often overlooked.

Contacts Deutschland.de ⊕ *www.deutschland.de.* **German National Tourist Office** ☏ *212/661–7200* ⊕ *www.germany.travel.*

INDEX